Grasping the World

Frontispiece   The greater Stone Gallery of the Royal Museum, Stockholm, Sweden:
the original display according to the reconstruction of 1992. King Gustavus III
acquired the centrepiece of his collection, the sleeping *Endymion* from Hadrian's
Villa, as a result of his Grand Tour to Italy in 1783–84. The King's sculpture gallery,
personifying the protection of the arts, was delivered, ironically, after the King's
assassination in 1792. Within three months of the King's murder and a failed coup
d'etat, the Royal Art Collections were transformed into a national public museum.
See the further discussion in this volume by Magnus Olausson and Solfrid Söderlind
(in Chapter 5). (Courtesy of the National Museum of Fine Arts, Stockholm.)

Grasping the World

The Idea of the Museum

Edited by Donald Preziosi and Claire Farago

ASHGATE

Published by
Ashgate Publishing Limited
Gower House
Croft Road
Aldershot
Hants GU11 3HR
England

Ashgate Publishing Company
Suite 420
101 Cherry Street
Burlington, VT 05401–4405 USA

Ashgate website: http://www.ashgate.com

British Library Cataloguing-in-Publication Data
Grasping the World: The Idea of the Museum.
 1. Art museums—Philosophy. I. Preziosi, Donald, 1941– . II. Farago, Claire J.
 708'.001

Library of Congress Cataloguing-in-Publication Data
Grasping the World: The Idea of the Museum / edited by Donald Preziosi and Claire Farago.
  p. cm.
 1. Museums—Philosophy. 2. Museums—Social aspects. 3. Museums—Historiography.
 4. Cultural property—Protection. I. Preziosi, Donald, 1941– . II. Farago, Claire J.
 AM7.G58 2003
 069–dc21   2002027773

ISBN 0 7546 0829 8 (hardback)
ISBN 0 7546 0835 2 (paperback)

Typeset by Manton Typesetters, Louth, Lincolnshire, UK and printed in Great Britain by Biddles Limited, King's Lynn.

Contents

Preface

By definition a 'preface' is staged to be read as if it stood outside of or apart from the text it precedes. Normally, it consists – in addition to acknowledgments such as those below – of caveats and apologias. As our book is no exception, we wish to say here that what follows in this volume is an institutional critique of museology at large, investigating the complexities of the relationships of individual practitioners to structures of power. The formation of many modern museum collections and the staging of world fairs in the nineteenth and twentieth centuries were based on educating the public through exemplary objects of human manufacture. It would be naive to infer that this collection of articles and extracts condemns the pleasures that museums elicit or denies that exhibitions can have scholarly value. Instead, we encourage readers to recognize differences between curatorial intentions and the larger effects and stagings of power.

This book is intended to engage its readers with the ethics of academic practice. Our title 'Grasping the World' deserves a note of explanation insofar as the metaphor of touch has a rich but ironic history in Western thought. The ancient Stoic definition of art as the consequence of many 'perceptions of the mind' can serve here as the foundation of an enduring and dynamic heritage. Cicero's praise of the human powers in his *De natura deorum* (2.147f) suggests the close relation between discussions of human judgement and the definition of art in the Western philosophical tradition. The arts, according to Cicero, can be divided into two categories: those invented out of necessity, such as building, agriculture, clothing, and metalwork, and those which are invented for pleasure. Many pleasurable arts have been devised to 'seize' and fulfil the senses. In these cases, the innate sensitivity of the eye to differences in color, shape, beauty, and arrangement is matched by the ability of the fingers to paint, model, and carve.

The Stoic term *katalepsis*, literally meaning to grasp or seize, refers to the mental processes of comprehending the world. Medieval writers continued to discuss art in terms of sense discrimination, commenting on the relationship between sense perception and artistic fabrication and emphasizing the inward process of judgement. In Arabic, Greek, and Latin discussions of mental operations *katalepsis* became a faculty of thought called the *vis cogitationis*, a term derived directly from the classical Latin *cogitare*, meaning to consider thoroughly, to turn over in the mind, picture to oneself, intend, design, or plan. Thomas Aquinas identified the *cogitativa* as the material part of the human mind that compares and distinguishes individual intentions. 'According to the disposition of this power, one man differs from another in talent and in other things belonging to the understanding' (*Summa contra Gentiles* II.60). Art historian David Summers, who in his *Judgment of Sense* (1987) has carefully charted the textual history of aesthetic judgement before Kant, concludes that no other distinction in the literature of the West more clearly reflects and justifies differences in social classes.

We could add that the same cluster of ideas justified differences in what came to be called 'race' and 'culture' by Europeans living in the era of colonial expansion. We hope that our readers will appreciate how the modern idea of the museum is historically in line with the ancient Greek metaphor of touch manifest in the ambivalent notion of 'grasping the world'.

Acknowledgements

Many individuals have contributed to the completion of this volume, and we have benefited from the extensive and generous advice and critical commentary of colleagues, students, and friends at various stages in the book's preparation. The project developed into a collaborative venture during the course of a seminar we jointly taught at UCLA in spring 1998, which led to an international symposium held at the same institution a year later, entitled '"Race", Nation, Aesthetics and the Fabrication of Modernities'. We are especially grateful to the participants in the seminar and to our guest speakers and student presenters at the symposium: Rae Agahari, Debashish Banerji, Homi Bhabha, Joann Byce, Emmanuel Eze, Santhi Kavuri, Barbara Kirshenblatt-Gimblett, Karen Lang, Jennifer Marshall, Mario Ontiveros, David Salomon, Catherine Soussloff, and Damon Willick.

We thank Ruth Iskin and Saloni Mathur for inviting us to participate in their session entitled 'Museums in the Age of Globalization', at the College Art Association annual conference in 2002, where we presented a condensed version of the general introduction in its penultimate draft, to a lively audience. We also presented material in our introductory essays to engaged and engaging audiences in the US, England, Sweden, Hungary, Germany, the Netherlands, and Slovakia. For these opportunities, we are grateful to our hosts at the Nordik Association of Art Historians in Uppsala; the Central European University Institute of the Humanities in Budapest; The Soros Center for Contemporary Art in Bratislava; the Karl Ernst Osthaus-Museum in Hagen, Germany; the British Association of Art Historians in Oxford; the organizers of an international workshop entitled 'Experimenting in the Arts and Sciences' at the University of Maastricht, the Netherlands; and the organizers of a workshop on German art historiography at the Clark Institute in Williamstown, Massachusetts. Donald Preziosi thanks All Souls College, Oxford, the Ashmolean Museum, the Institut de France, and the Department of the History of Art and Centre for Visual Studies at Oxford University for the opportunity to develop some of the ideas incorporated here during his tenure as the Oxford Slade Professor of Fine Art in 2001. During that year, he also had the opportunity to discuss these issues with colleagues and students at the University of Bristol, the Slade School and Goldsmiths College of the University of London; the Central St

Martin's and the Chelsea School of Art and Design, London, as well as the Edinburgh College of Art, Edinburgh.

We are grateful to all the authors for permission to reprint their already-published materials, and we thank Fred Bohrer, Hans-Olof Boström, and Claudia Lazzaro for updating and revising previously published texts especially for this occasion. The essay by Sandra Esslinger and that co-authored by Magnus Olausson and Solfrid Söderlind were especially commissioned for this book. We thank Hans Henrik Brummer, Director of the Nationalmuseum, Stockholm, for generously funding the translation of the latter study. Among students and colleagues in the field and hosts at the institutions named, we are especially grateful for their support and encourage-ment to Dan Adler, Philip Armstrong, Jan Bakos, Mieke Bal, Stephen Bann, Katarina Benova, Viktor Bohm, Norman Bryson, Craig Clunas, Maureen Corey, Rogene Cuerdon, Neil Cummings, Kelly Dennis, Christine Adrian Dyer, Yehudi Elkana, Jas Elsner, Jae Emerling, Michael Fehr, Mitchell Frank, Kay Frost, Allison Furge, Susan Gowen, Lee Greenfield, Dan Jacobs, Amelia Jones, Marcela Juarez, Michael Kaufman, Martin Kemp, Donna Kerwin, Barbara Kirshenblatt-Gimblett, Robert Koons, Marius Kwint, Simon Leung, Marysia Lewandowska, Jason Lujan, Arthur MacGregor, Patricia Mannix, Sally Mansfield, Lyle Massey, Carol Parenteau, Ruth Phillips, Matthew Rampley, Joanna Roche, Irit Rogoff, Jaime Saunders, Marlene Siering, Veronica Valdez, Frauke Von Der Horst, Jenny Wehmeyer, Diana Wilson, Emily Woody, Marcus Young, and Robert Zwijnenberg. The anonymous readers at Ashgate Publishing also provided constructive criticism and insightful commentary.

In addition, we happily acknowledge ongoing support by our home institutions, the University of California, Los Angeles, and the University of Colorado at Boulder. It would be impossible, however, to name all the individuals who have contributed ideas and support over the decade and more during which *Grasping the World* germinated in lectures and seminars on museums, museology, aesthetics, and the historiography of art history and related disciplines, beginning with a seminar on museums that Donald Preziosi taught at UCLA in 1989 under the title 'Framing Memory'. Another highlight of our teaching experience was an exhibition (with catalogue) at the University of Colorado entitled 'Eyes Wide Open: the art of viewing art' (January 20 – March 22, 2000), organized as part of a graduate student seminar on theories of art history. We hope that our presence at various events in the field has stimulated the growth of a more critically self-aware discourse on the role of museums in contemporary society, and we in turn have been inspired by the emergence of a new generation of critical literature on museology during the same years. We warmly thank Pamela Edwardes for her commitment to our idea of the idea of the museum, and her staff at Ashgate Publishing for their extensive efforts in shepherding a complex project through the production stage. Finally, we dedicate this volume to our readers in anticipation of their critical engagement with a provocative subject that, not in our opinion alone, merits an ethical practice.

Copyright acknowledgements

Permission given by the following copyright holders and authors is gratefully acknowledged. In some cases, the form of endnotes has been altered, for consistency. Figure numbers may also have been changed, and not all figures have been reproduced.

Every attempt has been made to contact relevant copyright holders and other appropriate sources of information in order to provide complete references for the articles included in this volume. It is regretted that in a number of instances some of this information could not be established; neither has it been possible to add to the sources already given.

1.   CREATING HISTORICAL EFFECTS

Hayden White, 'The Fictions of Factual Representation', in *Tropics of Discourse* (Baltimore and London: Johns Hopkins University Press, 1978), pp. 121–34. Copyright © Hayden White, 1978. Used by permission of Columbia University Press and the author.

Michel de Certeau, 'Psychoanalysis and its History', originally published as 'Histoire et Psychanalyse', in *La Nouvelle Histoire*, ed. J. Le Goff, R. Chartier and J. Revel (Paris: Retz, 1978), pp. 477–87. Reprinted from *Heterologies: Discourse on the Other*, trans. Brian Massumi; Theory and History of Literature, vol. 17 (Minneapolis and London: University of Minnesota Press, 1986), pp. 3–16. Copyright © Editions Retz. Used by permission of the publisher.

Jean-Louis Déotte, 'Rome, the Archetypal Museum, and the Louvre, the Negation of Division', in *Art in Museums*, ed. Susan Pearce; New Research in Museum Studies: An International Series, 5 (London and New Jersey: Athlone Press, 1995), pp. 215–32. Used by permission of the publisher.

Stephen Bann, 'Poetics of the Museum: Lenoir and Du Sommerard', in *The Clothing of Clio: A Study of the Representation of History in Nineteenth-Century Britain and France* (Cambridge and New York: Cambridge University Press, 1984), pp. 77–92. Copyright © Cambridge University Press. Used by permission of the publisher.

Mieke Bal, 'Telling Objects: A Narrative Perspective on Collecting', in *The Cultures of Collecting*, eds John Elsner and Roger Cardinal (London: Reaktion Books and Cambridge, Mass.: Harvard University Press, 1994), pp. 97–115. Used by permission of the author and publishers.

2. INSTITUTING EVIDENCE

Mary Carruthers, 'Collective Memory and *Memoria Rerum*' ('An Architecture for Thinking'), in her *The Craft of Thought: Meditation, Rhetoric, and the Making of Images, 400–1200* (Cambridge: Cambridge University Press, 1998), pp. 7–21. Copyright © Mary Carruthers. Used by permission of the author and publisher.

Giuseppe Olmi, 'Science-Honor-Metaphor: Italian Cabinets of the Sixteenth and Seventeenth Centuries', in *The Origins of Museums: The Cabinet of Curiosities in Sixteenth- and Seventeenth-Century Europe*, eds Oliver Impey and Arthur MacGregor (Oxford: Clarendon Press, 1985), pp. 1–16. Copyright © Oliver Impey and Arthur MacGregor, 1985. Used by permission of Oxford University Press.

William B. Ashworth Jr, excerpt from 'Natural History and the Emblematic World View', in *Reappraisals of the Scientific Revolution*, eds David C. Lindberg and Robert S. Westman (Cambridge and New York: Cambridge University Press, 1990), pp. 312–25. Copyright © Cambridge University Press. Used by permission of the author and publisher.

Paula Findlen, 'The Museum: Its Classical Etymology and Renaissance Genealogy', in *The Journal of the History of Colllections*, 1/1 (1989), pp. 59–78. Used by permission of Oxford University Press.

Frederick N. Bohrer, 'Inventing Assyria; Exoticism and Reception in Nineteenth-Century England and France', revision of article first published in *The Art Bulletin*, 80/2 (June 1998), pp. 336–56. Used by permission of the author and the College Art Association.

3. BUILDING SHARED IMAGINARIES/EFFACING OTHERNESS

Homi Bhabha, 'Double Visions', in *Artforum*, 30/5 (January 1992), pp. 85–9. Copyright © Artforum, 2002. Used by permission of the author and Artforum International Magazine.

Donna Haraway, excerpt from 'Teddy Bear Patriarchy: Taxidermy in the Garden of Eden, New York City, 1908–1936', in *Social Text*, 11 (Winter 1984/85), pp. 52–8. Copyright © 1985. All rights reserved. Used by permission of Duke University Press.

Carol Duncan, 'From the Princely Gallery to the Public Art Museum: The Louvre Museum and the National Gallery, London' (first published in its initial form in 1980), from her *Civilizing Rituals: Inside Public Art Museums* (London: Routledge, 1995), pp. 21–47, as reproduced in *Representing the Nation: A Reader. Histories, Heritage and Museums*, eds David Boswell and Jessica Evans (London: Routledge, 1999), pp. 304–31. Copyright © Carol Duncan. Used by permission of the author and the publisher.

Annie E. Coombes, 'Museums and the Formation of National and Cultural Identities', in *Oxford Art Journal*, 11/2 (December 1988), pp. 57–68. Used by permission of Oxford University Press.

Beverly K. Grindstaff, 'Creating Identity: Exhibiting the Philippines at the 1904 Louisiana Purchase Exposition', in *National Identities*, 1/3 (1999), pp. 245–63. Used by permission of the author and Taylor and Francis Limited (Website: http://www.tandf.co.uk/journals).

Sandra Esslinger, 'Performing Identity: The Museal Framing of Nazi Ideology'. Copyright © Sandra Esslinger, 2002.

Shelly Errington, 'The Cosmic Theme Park of the Javanese', in her *The Death of Authentic Primitive Art and Other Tales of Progress* (Berkeley and London: University of California Press, 1998), pp. 188–217. Used by permission of the publisher.

4.   OBSERVING SUBJECTS/DISCIPLINING PRACTICE

André Malraux, 'Introduction', in *Museum Without Walls*, trans. Stuart Gilbert and Francis Price (Garden City, N.J.: Doubleday, 1967), pp. 9–12. Originally published as *Le Musée imaginaire*, 1947.

Michel Foucault, 'Texts/Contexts: Of Other Spaces', trans. Jay Miskowiec, in *Diacritics*, 16/1 (Spring 1986), pp. 22–7. Copyright © The Johns Hopkins University Press. Used by permission of the publisher.

Paul Q. Hirst, 'Power/Knowledge – Constructed Space and the Subject', in *Power and Knowledge: Anthropological and Sociological Perspectives*, ed. R. Fardon (Edinburgh: Scottish Academic Press, 1985), pp. 171–89. Copyright © Paul Q. Hirst. Used by permission of the author.

Hans Haacke, 'Museums: Managers of Consciousness', in *Parachute*, 46 (March–May 1987), pp. 84–8. Copyright © Hans Haacke. Used by permission of the author and Parachute Magazine.

Tony Bennett, 'The Exhibitionary Complex', originally published in *New Formations*, 4 (Spring 1988), pp. 73–102. Reprinted from *Thinking about*

Exhibitions, eds Reesa Greenberg, Bruce W. Ferguson, and Sandy Nairne (London and New York: Routledge, 1996), pp. 81–112. Copyright © Tony Bennett. Used by permission of the author and the publisher.

Timothy Mitchell, 'Orientalism and the Exhibitionary Order', originally published in *Comparative Studies in Society and History*, 31 (1989). Reprinted from *The Art of Art History: A Critical Anthology*, ed. Donald Preziosi (Oxford: Oxford University Press, 1998), pp. 455–72. Used by permission.

Craig Clunas, 'China in Britain: The Imperial Collections', originally published in *Belief in China: Art and Politics; Deities and Mortality*, eds Robert Benewick and Stephanie Donald (The Green Centre for Non-Western Art and Culture, Royal Pavilion Arts Gallery and Museums, Brighton, 1996), as a condensed version of the article 'Oriental Antiquities/Far Eastern Art', published in *Positions*, 2/2 (Autumn 1994), pp. 318–57 and later in *Formations of Colonial Modernity in East Asia*, ed. Tani E. Barlow (Durham N.C.: Duke University Press, 1997), pp. 413–46. Reprinted here from *Colonialism and the Object: Empire, Material Culture and the Museum*, ed. Tim Barringer and Tom Flynn (London and New York: Routledge, 1998), pp. 41–51. Used by permission of the author.

5.   SECULARIZING RITUALS

Carol Duncan and Alan Wallach, 'The Museum of Modern Art as Late Capitalist Ritual: An Iconographic Analysis', in *Marxist Perspectives* (Winter 1978), 28–51. Copyright © Carol Duncan and Alan Wallach, 1978 and 2002. Used by permission of the authors.

Claudia Lazzaro, 'Animals as Cultural Signs: Collecting Animals in Sixteenth-Century Medici Florence', condensed revision of article first published in *Reframing the Renaissance: Visual Culture in Europe and Latin America 1450–1650*, ed. Claire Farago (New Haven and London: Yale University Press, 1995), pp. 197–228. Copyright © Claudia Lazzaro. Used by permission of the author.

Thomas DaCosta Kaufmann, 'Remarks on the Collection of Rudolf II: The *Kunstkammer* as a Form of *Representatio*', in *The Art Journal*, 38 (1978), pp. 22–8. Used by permission of the author and the College Art Association.

Hans-Olof Boström, 'Philipp Hainhofer and Gustavus Adolfus's *Kunstschrank* in Uppsala', revision of article first published in *The Origins of Museums*, eds Oliver Impey and Arthur MacGregor (Oxford: Clarendon Press, 1985), pp. 90–101. Copyright © Oliver Impey and Arthur MacGregor, 1985. Used by permission of Oxford University Press.

Francis Haskell and Nicholas Penny, 'Museums in Eighteenth-Century Rome', in their *Taste and the Antique: The Lure of Classical Sculpture 1500–1900* (New Haven and London: Yale University Press, 1981), pp. 62–73. Used by permission of the publisher.

Magnus Olausson and Solfrid Söderlind, 'The Genesis and Early Development of the Royal Museum in Stockholm: A Claim for Authenticity and Legitimacy'. Copyright © Magnus Olausson and Solfrid Söderlind, 2002.

Rosalind Krauss, 'The Cultural Logic of the Late Capitalist Museum', *October*, 54 (Fall 1990), pp. 3–17, reprinted in *October: The Second Decade, 1986–1996*, eds Rosalind Krauss et al. (Cambridge, Mass. and London: MIT Press, 1997), pp. 427–41. Used by permission of the publisher.

Neil Cummings and Marysia Lewandowska, 'Collision', in their *The Value of Things*, preface by Nick Barley and Stephen Coates (Basel, Berlin and Boston: Birkhäuser and London: 2000), pp. 111–17. Text and images © Neil Cummings and Marysia Lewandowska. Used by permission of the authors.

6. INCLUSIONS AND EXCLUSIONS: REPRESENTING ADEQUATELY

Moira Simpson, 'Cultural Reflections', in her *Making Representations: Museums in the Postcolonial Era* (London and New York: Routledge, 1996), pp. 7–13. Used by permission of the publisher.

James Clifford, 'Histories of the Tribal and the Modern', originally published in *Art in America* (April 1985), pp. 164–77. Reprinted from Clifford's *The Predicament of Culture: Twentieth-Century Ethnography, Literature and Art* (Cambridge, Mass.: Harvard University Press, 1988), pp. 189–214. Copyright © the author.

Susan Vogel, 'Always True to the Object, in Our Fashion', in *Exhibiting Cultures: The Poetics and Politics of Museum Display*, eds Ivan Karp and Steven D. Lavine (Washington and London: Smithsonian Institution Press, 1991), pp. 191–204. Copyright © 1991 by the Smithsonian Institution. Used by permission of the publisher and Susan M. Vogel, Independent Film Maker, New York.

Rasheed Araeen, 'From Primitivism to Ethnic Arts', in *The Myth of Primitivism: Perspectives on Art*, ed. Susan Hiller (London and New York: Routledge, 1991), pp. 158–82. Used by permission of the publisher.

Arjun Appadurai and Carol A. Breckenridge, 'Museums are Good to Think: Heritage on View in India', originally published in *Museums and Communities: The Politics of Public Culture*, ed. Ivan Karp (Washington and London:

Suggestions for Further Reading

The literature in museum studies and museology has become so vast and diverse in the past two decades that a comprehensive bibliography would entail a sizeable volume in its own right. What follows is a selection of recent publications to guide interested readers beyond the present volume to current publications in an interdisciplinary field of activity dealing with art, anthropology, and culture museums. This reading list also includes some of the most noteworthy single-authored volumes in a field now dominated by anthologies.

Ames, Michael M., *Cannibal Tours and Glass Boxes: The Anthropology of Museums.* Vancouver: University of British Columbia Press, 1992.

Appadurai, Arjun, ed., *The Social Life of Things: Commodities in Cultural Perspective.* Cambridge: Cambridge University Press, 1988.

Bal, Mieke, *Double Exposures: The Subject of Cultural Analysis, with* Das Gesicht an der Wand *by Edwin Janssen.* New York : Routledge, 1996.

Barringer, Tim, and Tom Flynn, eds, *Colonialism and the Object: Empire, Material Culture and the Museum.* London and New York: Routledge, 1998.

Bennett, Tony, *The Birth of the Museum: History, Theory, Politics.* London and New York: Routledge, 1995.

Boswell, David, and Jessica Evans, eds, *Representing the Nation: A Reader. Histories, Heritage and Museums.* London and New York: Routledge, in association with The Open University, 1999.

Coombes, Annie, *Reinventing Africa: Museums, Material Culture and Popular Imagination in Late Victorian and Edwardian England.* New Haven and London: Yale University Press, 1994.

Crane, Susan, ed., *Museums and Memory.* Stanford: Stanford University Press, 2000.

Crimp, Douglas, *On the Museum's Ruins.* Cambridge, Mass.: MIT Press, 1993.

Déotte, Jean-Louis, *Le Musée, l'origine de l'esthétique.* Paris: L'Harmattan, 1993.

Derrida, Jacques, *Archive Fever: A Freudian Impression*, trans. Eric Prenowitz. Chicago and London: University of Chicago Press, 1995.

Duncan, Carol, *Civilizing Rituals: Inside Public Art Museums*. London and New York: Routledge, 1995.

Elsner, John, and Roger Cardinal, eds, *The Cultures of Collecting*. Cambridge, Mass.: Harvard University Press, 1994.

Fabian, Johannes, *Time and the Other: How Anthropology Makes its Object*. New York: Columbia University Press, 1983.

Farago, Claire, ed., *Reframing the Renaissance: Visual Culture in Europe and Latin American 1450–1650*. London and New Haven: Yale University Press, 1995.

Findlen, Paula, *Possessing Nature: Museums, Collecting, and Scientific Culture in Early Modern Italy*. Berkeley, Los Angeles, and London: University of California Press, 1994.

Geary, Patrick, *Furta Sacra: Thefts of Relics in the Central Middle Ages*. Princeton: Princeton University Press, 1978.

Graburn, Nelson, ed., *Ethnic and Tourist Arts*. Berkeley: University of California Press, 1976.

Greenberg, Reesa, Bruce Ferguson, and Sandy Nairne, eds, *Thinking about Exhibitions*. New York: Routledge, 1995.

Hahn, Cynthia, 'The Voices of the Saints: Speaking Reliquaries', *Gesta*, XXXVI/ II 1997: 20–31.

Heikamp, Detlef, with F. Anders, *Mexico and the Medici*. Exhibition catalogue. Florence: Edam, 1972.

Hodgen, Margaret, *Early Anthropology in the Sixteenth and Seventeenth Centuries*. Philadelphia: University of Pennsylvania Press, 1964.

Hooper-Greenhill, Eilean, *Museums and the Shaping of Knowledge*. London and New York: Routledge, 1992.

Impey, Oliver, and Arthur MacGregor, eds, *The Origins of Museums: The Cabinet of Curiosities in Sixteenth- and Seventeenth-Century Europe*. Oxford: Oxford University Press, 1985.

Jones, Pamela, *Federico Borromeo and the Ambrosiana: Art, Patronage and Reform in Seventeenth-Century Milan*. Cambridge and New York: Cambridge University Press, 1993.

Karp, Ivan, and Steven D. Lavine, eds, *Exhibiting Cultures*. Washington, D.C.: Smithsonian Institution Press, 1991.

Kaufmann, Thomas DaCosta, *The Mastery of Nature: Aspects of Art, Science, and Humanism in the Renaissance*. Princeton; Princeton University Press, 1993.

Kirshenblatt-Gimblett, Barbara, *Destination Culture: Tourism, Museums, and Heritage*. Berkeley, Los Angeles, and London: University of California Press, 1998.

Lach, D., *Asia in the Making of Europe*. Chicago: University of Chicago Press, 1972.

Lugli, Adalgisa, *Naturalia et Mirabilia. Il collezionismo enciclopedico nelle Wunderkammern d'Europa*. Milan: Mondadori, 1983.

MacCannell, Dean, *The Tourist: A New Theory of the Leisure Class*. New York: Schocken Books, 1976.

Macdonald, Sharon, and Gordon Fyfe, eds, *Theorizing Museums: Representing Identity and Diversity in a Changing World*. Oxford: Blackwell Publishers/The Sociological Review, 1996.

Maleuvre, Didier, *Museum Memories: History, Technology, Art*. Stanford: Stanford University Press, 1999.

McClellan, Andrew, *Inventing the Louvre: Art, Politics, and the Origins of the Modern Museum in Eighteenth-Century Paris*. Berkeley, Los Angeles, and London: University of California Press, 1994.

Messenger, Phyllis Mauch, ed., *The Ethics of Collecting Cultural Property: Whose Culture? Whose Property?* foreward by Brian Fagan. Albuquerque, New Mexico: University of New Mexico Press, 2nd edition, 1999.

Mitchell, Timothy, *Colonizing Egypt*. Cambridge and New York: Cambridge University Press, 1988.

Olmi, Giuseppe, *Inventario del Mondo. Catalogazione della natura e luoghi del sapere nella prima età moderna*. Bologna: Società editrice il Mulino, 1992.

Pearce, Susan, ed., *Museum Studies in Material Culture*. Leicester and London: Leicester University Press; Washington, D.C.: Smithsonian Institution Press, 1989.

Phillips, Ruth, *Trading Identities: The Souvenir in Native North American Art from the Northeast, 1700–1900*. Seattle: University of Washington Press; Montreal: MacGill–Queen's University Press, 1998.

Phillips, Ruth B., and Christopher B. Steiner, eds, *Unpacking Culture: Art and Commodity in Colonial and Postcolonial Worlds*. Berkeley, Los Angeles, and London: University of California Press, 1999.

Pointon, Marcia, ed., *Art Apart: Artifacts, Institutions and Ideology in England and America from 1800 to the Present*. Manchester: Manchester University Press, 1994.

Pomian, Krzysztof, *Collectors and Curiosities*. Cambridge, Mass.: Polity Press, 1990.

Preziosi, Donald, *Brain of the Earth's Body: Art, Museums, and the Phantasms of Modernity*. Minneapolis: University of Minnesota Press, 2003.

Rydell, Robert, *All the World's a Fair*. Chicago: University of Chicago Press, 1984.

Shaw, Wendy M. K., *Possessors and Possessed: Museums, Archaeology, and the Visualization of History in the Late Ottoman Empire*. Berkeley and Los Angeles: University of California Press, 2003.

Sheehan, James J., *Museums in the German Art World: From the End of the Old Regime to the Rise of Modernism*. Oxford: Oxford University Press, 2000.

Sherman, Daniel, and Irit Rogoff, eds, *Museum Culture: Histories, Discourses, Spectacles*. Minneapolis: University of Minnesota Press, 1994.

Steiner, Christopher, *African Art in Transit*. Cambridge and New York: Cambridge University Press, 1994.

Stewart, Susan, *On Longing: Narratives of the Miniature, the Gigantic, the Souvenir, the Collection*. Baltimore: Johns Hopkins University Press, 1984.

Stocking, George, ed., *Objects and Others: Essays on Museums and Material Culture*; History of Anthopology, vol. 3. Madison: University of Wisconsin Press, 1985.

Stolzenberg, Daniel, ed., *The Great Art of Knowing: The Baroque Encyclopedia of Athanasius Kircher*. Stanford: Stanford University Press, 2001.

Thomas, Nicholas, *Entangled Objects: Exchange, Material Culture, and Colonialism in the Pacific*. Cambridge, Mass. and London: Harvard University Press, 1991.

Vergo, Peter, ed., *The New Museology*. London: Reaktion Books, 1989.

Wallach, Alan, *Exhibiting Contradiction: Essays on Art Museums in the United States*. Amherst, Mass.: University of Massachusetts Press, 1998.

Walsh, Kevin, *The Representation of the Past: Museums and Heritage in the Postmodern World*. New York: Routledge, 1992.

Weil, Stephen E., *Rethinking the Museum and Other Meditations*. Washington and London: Smithsonian Institution Press, 1990.

General Introduction:
What are Museums *For*?

Art is troublesome not because it is not delightful, but because it is not more delightful: we accustom ourselves to the failure of gardens to make our lives as paradisal as their prospects.　　　　　Robert Harbison, *Eccentric Spaces* (1977)

We begin this book with an observation by Robert Harbison that poignantly articulates not only one of the main aspirations for art, but also one of the main expectations for museums: that it (and they) would satisfactorily ground, establish, and transform our individual and collective lives. To place this hope or expectation on art, or, more generally, human artifice as such – rather than, for example, on religion – may be taken as one of the keystones in an overarching socio-economic system that distinguishes the post-Enlightenment age from the past. The beliefs that have constituted the core of 'modernity' rest upon certain assumptions about the nature of meaningful relationships between subjects and objects, between individuals or communities and the worlds they weave about themselves. It is our contention that the institution of the museum has for some time been essential to the fabrication and sustenance of this system of beliefs.

Grasping the World is a critical investigation of the modern European idea of the museum. But why *yet another* book about museums *now*? More has been written about museums in the past decade, it seems, than in the previous century. It is not easy to characterize this massively diverse body of work in any simple or singular way. A lot of it deals with contemporary museological shortcomings and inadequacies. Much of it in recent years has treated the museum as basically a form of infotainment, and as a 'technical' problem of packaging and dispensing various kinds of cultural information to targeted audiences. Often, questions of technology are imagined to be pre-, post-, or extra-political, with institutional problems commonly framed so that they might appear to be 'solved' by yet more refined imagineering, marketing, or more subtly prefabricated 'interactive' opportunities for audiences – in short, by turning up and fine-tuning the fascination and dramaturgy.

A good deal of other writing, also addressing current problems, has involved museological 'content' and the activities of professional 'content-providers' (art historians, curators, and others) and deals with redressing perceived imbalances in the institutional portrayal of racial, national, ethnic, class, or gender groups. The general concern has been with teaching museums to become better representatives of a wider (multi)cultural world. Yet virtually all of the recent literature treats this concern as if it were a classic map-territory problem of representational adequacy. The most common result has been to call for redress by more refined versions of conventional museum stagecraft, or by the revision, re-staging, or replacement of museum contents by different versions of the same thing, and by more 'accurate' and nuanced representations.

Many solutions to the perceived problems may have perpetuated the same problems but under different guises. They invariably share a fundamental thesis – that a museum is primarily a *representation*, an artifact as 'natural' as the 'specimens' it preserves, rather than an institution for the construction, legitimization, and maintenance of cultural realities. A principal corollary of this assumption is that representational 'adequacy' consists of a *synecdochal* (a part standing in for the whole) relationship between an exhibition's contents and a wider world of cultural objects and social practices. And, conversely, the assumption that an exhibition could represent that wider world in a meaningful way has been the prime justification for taking objects from the settings for which they were initially made and reassembling them for study and contemplation. These assumptions justify the institutional framing of objects as *specimens*.[1] As Nestór García Canclini and other contributors to this volume argue in detail, such assumptions also masquerade the constructedness of the museum frame as 'natural' historical truth or consensus. Most museumgoers are not prepared (educated) to analyze both the framework and its contents, with the result that museums, as informal educational institutions, perpetuate racial/ethnic/national/gender stereotypes. Yet, in the modern museum setting, responsibility for the perpetuation of untenable beliefs and assumptions is distributed across a spectrum of individuals ranging from trustees to curators and educators – with the frequent result that the perpetuation appears to be nobody's 'fault'.

The extraordinary fact is that we live in a world in which virtually anything may be exhibited *in* a museum, and in which virtually anything can be made to function *as* a museum, often through little more than verbal designation. At this juncture, it is often difficult to distinguish museum practices from the entertainment, tourist, and heritage industries; department stores and shopping malls; the art market; and even artistic practices. In such a world, the question of 'representation' (adequate or otherwise) is, to say the least, very complex indeed. The *distinctiveness* of the museum as an institution, and of museology as a practice, has come to be conceived as a mode of representation that deploys and disseminates knowledge. And many museums, aside from their ideological usefulness, are successful because they are good business investments, in every sense of that term.

But this is also a time when critical studies of the museum have begun taking up the arduous and painstaking task of trying to understand and account historically for the evident *indispensability* and universal dissemination of this remarkable and uncanny European invention to so many different cultures, societies, and political regimes around the world. Important critiques of these social practices by a number of writers are included in the present collection of essays. It is not our intention, however, to fetishize museums or to rescue museology from its currently compromised position. The institution of the museum stands at the intersection of a wide variety of social, cultural, scientific, and political developments in every corner of the world. There may be upwards of some 100,000 museums in the world today, of every conceivable form, size, and mission – to the extent that it is fair to claim both that we live in a world in which virtually anything may reasonably be exhibited *in* a museum, and that virtually anything may be made to serve *as* a museum.

It may be more useful, today, to ask not 'What is a museum?', but rather 'When is a museum?' Our principal aim in this anthology is to plot a critical, historical, and ethical understanding of the practices centered on what we commonly understand today about museums as a key force in the fabrication and maintenance of modern identity. More than a genre, and more than simply one institution on a par with others, museums are essential sites for the fabrication and perpetuation of our conception of ourselves as autonomous individuals with unique subjectivities. William Pietz argues persuasively that aesthetics and fetishism are interrelated and complementary Enlightenment inventions.[2] In this case, the origins and development of art history and museology are significantly compounded, rendering even more problematic the professional practices that we normally take for granted, namely the labeling and classifying operations that museum curators routinely perform.

The purpose of this volume, then, is to provide a critical understanding of the origins and history of museums. Inseparable from a critical understanding of museums are the crises of and challenges to European self-knowledge resulting from a half-millennium-long global expansion of experience through conquest and commerce. Consequently, the inseparability of museology, colonialism, and imperialism (and their consequent moral, social, and epistemological effects and affordances) is a central issue for critical historians to investigate. More than simply one among many 'ideological apparatuses' in the institutional arsenal of contemporary society, museums worldwide pervade many of the social practices, both institutionalized and informal, that determine the perception and function of objects and environments, no less than of ourselves as social subjects.

We share with many of our contributors the view that there is much more to museums than the documenting, monumentalizing, or theme-parking of identity, history, and heritage. Though they are commonplace in our cultural landscape, museums are far from 'natural'. Nor does it remedy our perception of museums simply to label them 'cultural', because the terms of such a discussion are tautological. For what does 'culture' signify besides the stuff that museums collect? In general, the power and persuasiveness of the museological construct – its artifice, if you will – is inseparable from that of *art*. And the gradual invention and expansion of the category 'art' to encompass all 'cultures' has been a crucial instrument by which the history of the world's peoples have been retroactively (re)written in the five centuries since European expansion reached global proportions.

The idea of the museum

> If the walls of the museums were to vanish, and with them their labels, what would happen to the works of art that the walls contain, the labels describe? Would these objects of aesthetic contemplation be liberated to a freedom they have lost, or would they become so much meaningless lumber?
>   Jonah Siegel, *Desire and Excess: The Nineteenth-Century Culture of Art* (2000)

Art, in the modern sense that the word acquired in the eighteenth century but not earlier, has been the correlative and indispensible means by which the modern Euro-American subject and its consequent notions of agency have fabricated, sustained, and transformed the rest of the world. The success of museums devoted to history, heritage, and identity is based on a particular kind of object – the artifact – and certain characteristic modes of stagecraft. *Grasping the World* deals with this complex phenomenon. Museum objects are staged or framed to be 'read' in a variety of ways, or in ways that privilege their aesthetic significance (as works of 'art') or their documentary status (as relics or as 'scientific' evidence of a time, place, people, spirit or mentality) or, commonly, some combination of both. In any case, as an *evidentiary* institution, the museum's power and persuasiveness has rested in no small measure upon the deployment of objects of oscillating determinacy. However they are framed, museum objects – whether works of fine art, scientific specimens, mechanical inventions, ethnographic artifacts, fetishes, relics, or what have you – function as diagnostic devices and modular measures for making sense of all possible worlds and their subjects.

Collections of objects are, moreover, framed, opposed, superimposed, and transformed by the discursive practices of aesthetic philosophy, art history, history, psychology, anthropology, and ethnography – all of which are grounded in and follow from the epistemological principles, categories, and assumptions of museology. For the museum is not only a cultural artifact made up of other cultural artifacts; museums serve as theater, encyclopedia, and laboratory for simulating (demonstrating) all manner of causal, historical, and (surreptitiously) teleological relationships. As such, museums are 'performances' – pedagogical and political in nature – whose practitioners are centrally invested in the activity of making the visible legible, thereby personifying objects as the representations of their makers, simultaneously objectifying the people who made them and, in a second order reality that is part of the same historical continuum, objectifying the people who view made objects in their recontextualized museum settings.

How has this state of affairs come about? Museums define (exhibit) relationships by naming agencies and displaying objects. While it is widely accepted that the French Revolution launched the first major state museum, the idea that materialized as the Louvre predated it. Elsewhere, all over Europe and its extensions overseas, public museums were formed on the basis of royal and aristocratic private collections and furnishings in order to fashion citizens in new nation-state formations. The various social practices that accomplished such effects *antedate* the modern museum as we know it and may be seen most readily in earlier European habits of collecting.[3] The birth of the art museum as a modern institution was also enabled, if not precipitated, by the eighteenth-century rise of aesthetics as the philosophical discourse framing the production and reception of art.[4] Crudely stated, aesthetic discourse was a general extension and transformation of activities rooted in sense experience that had long been associated in both theory and practice with the *devotional* function of religious images. In its European context, the transformation of longstanding religious routines into (allegedly) secular set of practices revolved around subjective experiences with art as such.

Any museological collection is, by definition, only made possible by dismembering another context and reassembling a new museological whole. The social practice of publicly viewing art in museums that evolved around the turn of the nineteenth century simultaneously atomized social exchange at the level of individual experience and redefined community in terms of the same practice. The emergence of the modern, state-supported, public museum and the modern categorization of certain cultural artifacts as art coincides exactly with the paradigm shift that engaged Michel Foucault's attention, yet neither he nor others have studied the key role of museums in the 'secularization' of society. Foucault pointed to the birth of a hybrid, 'power/knowledge', that makes use of disciplinary forms of social control rather than of brute force. The European invention of the museum has fundamentally transformed the world itself: this volume foregrounds the ongoing *consequences* of museology as an epistemological technology and its allied practices and institutions. In a very concrete sense then, this book is a critical investigation into the role of museums as staged environments that elicit our selves and locate and orient our desires within the trajectories of an imagined past.

The function of the museum as part of a discursive formation in the Foucauldian sense is as yet insufficiently understood and under-theorized. Carol Duncan and Allan Wallach, in a series of widely influential publications (one of which is included here), have pointed to the 'civilizing rituals' of modern museum experience. Acting on their insights, this volume aims to open up the theoretical discussion of the social transition from a predominantly dynastic and religious to a secular social organization that museums effectively engineered and maintain today. The story of this transformation is complex. As editors who anticipate further studies, we seek and recommend ways out of modernity – not by breaking with the past, because that is an unrealizable and naive desire, but by thinking historically and critically about and beyond such artificially constructed, modern categories as 'art', 'science', and 'religion'.

The organization of this anthology

The subject we want to explore is the extraordinary European *idea* of the museum and its many consequences (on and beyond that continent) in the past and present. This book is about the palpable idea of museums: it is emphatically *not* an architectural or institutional history of museums or museum collections, nor does it deal directly with connoisseurship or the conservation of objects.

It is the tangible result of continuing discussions by two art historians working on either side of the period that customarily establishes the basis for modern discussions about art, namely the Enlightenment. In a very real sense, *Grasping the World* is an ongoing dialogue crystallized here momentarily as a book. In our role as editors of this volume of reprinted and newly commissioned essays, we attempt to provide critical guidance to readers in the form of brief introductions and transitions as well as suggestions for reading certain texts in juxtaposition. It is not an easy task to translate into print the dynamic spirit of the many debates, discussions, conferences, workshops, and pedagogical collaborations that provided the germination of the present volume. What we hope to do here is to clear a space for rumination and to encourage further critical observation and discussion, by providing clues rather than blueprints, and questions and goads rather than pat answers or solutions. Our joint sense of this book was affected by many different experiences, including individual and joint seminars, lectures, debates, conferences jointly organized or attended, the writing of several other books by each of us, and by our continuing to *walk* museums around the world. At times in the past our discussions have led to the pen touching paper or to one or both of us speaking nascent 'pieces' of what this book has now become. Each of us has wrestled with the crucial problem of what *form* an effective and useful critical historiography of museum practices would best take. Our concern here has been with finding ways to responsibly articulate the diversity, richness, and heterogeneity of museological practices over several centuries without succumbing to the temptations of grand historicist schemes. But our aim is not simply to craft a conventional historical genealogy which, in Krzyzstof Pomian's words, avoids 'both the Scylla of empty generalizations and the Charybdis of mountains of unrelated facts'.[5]

The role of museums in modern societies is complex enough, in our view, to require a kind of organization and a mode of writing that weaves together the general and the particular. *Grasping the World* is thus not a consecutive history but an interleaved series of case studies and meta-commentaries, as well as texts that the editors believe can aid the reader in locating the discursive formation that enables museums to perform their agency in contemporary society. This book works with and against the grain of the literature in the fields of museology and art history. It consists of reprinted texts published in the last four decades and several new articles that we commissioned, introduced by jointly authored critical commentaries. The collection addresses readers within many areas of the humanities and social sciences, including museum professionals. Each chapter represents a perspective overlapping with the perspectives on the subject offered by adjacent chapters.

The book's sections proceed roughly (but not exclusively) chronologically, from the early modern period and the beginnings of global commerce in the sixteenth century to the present. Each section contains both theoretical essays and historical studies, interspersing earlier writings with more recent publications. Some directly address issues raised in other essays in the same section. We have often juxtaposed analyses or observations dealing with the same institution or the same issue. The selection and particular grouping of essays is, unavoidably, arbitrary beyond a certain extent. Many more worthy studies have been published than appear here. Our basic intention is to stimulate individual readers and especially readers in professional and classroom settings to examine the active agency that museums have – the societal and epistemological effects that they can be said to 'perform' through their viewing subjects. The arguments themselves were produced within often very highly charged environments of controversy and debate at various times and in specific places around the world. In their present context, these texts are deployed in juxtaposition to a series of *editorial commentaries* that both link and mark differences between texts, and serve as catalysts and workpoints for further discussion. At the same time, each essay is intended to function as an *anamorphic* patch in the overall collection of papers, *reading* the collection of texts (and thereby the narrative histories explicit or covert within) *otherwise*, as a *para*text woven in, through, and against the collection constituting the anthology, to enable our readers to consider the consequences of museums and museology today on their own terms. Taken as a whole, the volume articulates a critical historiography of the institution of the museum and of museology – and inevitably, of art history itself.

One of our central concerns is with exploring alternatives to familiar 'histories' of the institution that are written either in a singular magisterial voice or in a deceptively anonymous 'It happened that ...' mode that masks its own views. In short, the portrayal of the author's subject position 'outside' history is imaginary – a projection (not unlike a slide cast onto a screen) – that actually provides the frame for the narrative itself. That which is staged offstage – the historian or collector (the man and his work) – is in fact never *not* a member of the cast. This real/imaginary dualism is a problem whose timely investigation is one of our chief motivations in publishing this volume. Our framing commentaries can be neither internal nor external to the study: thus they not only frame the work, they also 'square it', as Derrida once aptly put it.[6] The resulting collection is unavoidably museological in its own way. The volume provides a way of critically seeing museums not in isolation from other social productions and effects, but as components in a larger matrix of institutions and professions.

It is often difficult, today, to imagine a truly different world, and to imagine othernesses not already transformed into positively or negatively marked variants of our own identities. What follows is nonetheless an attempt to *foreground* what modernity's visibility routinely veils. But this is to get too far ahead of the story too soon. Let's begin with the multiple historical origins and motivations of museums. The persistence of the museum *idea* can aid us in not reducing the past to a form of the present, and the other to a form of the same. Both strategies, of course, constitute the very fabric of museological, historiographic, and art historical practices' with their virtually irresistible gravity and fascination.

We begin with a look at some of the general ways in which, in museums and collections, memory is given form, and in which objects come to serve roles in the generation of narratives of origins and descent, and of commensurabilities and hierarchies. To what 'idea' have museums responded? Is that idea a retrospective articulation of what museums appear in the present to practice? Is a museum an answer or a question? Fact or fiction? An effect or a proposition mooted?

NOTES

1.   See the work of Hayden White in this regard, and especially his 'The Irrational and the Problem of Historical Knowledge in the Enlightenment', in Hayden White, *Tropics of Discourse* (Baltimore and London, 1978), pp. 135–49.

2. See Pietz, 'Fetishism', in *Critical Terms for Art History*, eds Robert Nelson and Richard Schiff (Chicago, 1996), with further references to his work.

3. Stephen Bann, *Under the Sign: John Bargrave as Collector, Traveler, and Witness* (Ann Arbor, 1994).

4. Donald Preziosi, *The Art of Art History: A Critical Anthology* (Oxford, 1998).

5. Krzysztof Pomian, *Collectors and Curiosities* (Cambridge, Mass., 1990 [first publ. in French 1987), p. 6.

6. Citing Derrida, 'The Parergon', section II of *The Truth in Painting*, reprinted from *October*, 9 (Summer 1979), p. 20.

I.

Creating Historical Effects

Introduction:
Creating Historical Effects

Are the histories staged by museums facts or fictions?

Museum institutions exist above all for the collection, preservation, and conservation of the fragments and relics of the past, and it is commonly assumed that they are dedicated above all to documenting the *facts* of history. Yet, by and large, all museums *stage* their collected and preserved relics in such a way as to enhance the facticity of these surviving objects, documents, and monuments. Indeed, what constitutes 'facticity' is clearly a matter of a certain style of presenting things in what in a given time and place may be *legible as* factual. Facts may be apprehended as such under certain specific conditions of presentation and reception. Museums, then, use theatrical effects to enhance a belief in the historicity of the objects they collect. Thus, they respond to one or another version of the nineteenth-century belief that, as is observed by Hayden White in the first essay in this chapter, 'if one only eschewed ideology and remained true to the facts, history would produce a knowledge as certain as anything offered by the physical sciences and as objective as a mathematical exercise'.

Museology and art history have long remained under the sway of this particular version of scientism. White's 1978 essay, entitled 'The Fictions of Factual Representation', regarded as extremely radical and even counter-intuitive at the time, directly confronted the fiction that history could be written *without* employing any 'fictional' techniques – itself a reflection of the nineteenth-century ideology that a value-neutral description of the facts prior to interpretation or analysis was possible. But what technique is not a 'fiction'? As White succinctly observed, 'What is at issue here is not, What are the facts? but rather, How are the facts to be described in order to sanction one mode of explaining them rather than another?'

What was at stake in the nineteenth century no less than today was the control of 'modes of explaining' – the legitimization of both the 'reality' of history and of a single interpretative truth. This has long been linked to an explicitly political agenda in that it entailed a belief that effective social change could only be built upon a 'scientific' or 'objective' foundation – the true facts of History – thereby appearing to escape the shifting sands of interpretative controversy. The truth (in the guise of the facts of history) is imagined to be sufficient to make us free. Yet, as White argued, the distinction between history and a philosophy of history is one of degree, not of kind, having to do with the explicitness of the philosophical content: every history contains a full-blown if only implicit 'philosophy of history'. History buries its conceptual apparatus in the interior of its narratives, whereas philosophy brings that apparatus to the surface of the text. Factual (re)presentation is grounded in an implicit philosophy which claims that a chain of causes and effects was mere temporal succession and not narration. Chronology is, for these reasons, a powerful and seductive rhetorical apparatus, a fictive construct (a narrative of events) that masks ideology under the guise of 'natural time'.

White's point about the distinctions between history and a philosophy of history being at base a matter of implicit versus explicit philosophical argumentation resonates in a fascinating way with the arguments of Michel de Certeau excerpted below, in 'Psychoanalysis and its History'. He observes that history-writing (what he terms historiography) and psychoanalysis contrast with each other as two *modes* of structuring or distributing the space of memory. They constitute two strategies of time, two methods of formatting the relation between past and present.

History is consequently the product of relations of knowledge and power linking 'two supposedly distinct domains: on one hand, there is the present (scientific, professional, social) place of work, the technical and conceptual apparatus of *inquiry* and interpretation, and the operation of describing and/or explaining; on the other hand, there are places (museums, archives, libraries) where the materials forming the object of this research are kept, and secondarily, set off in time, there are the past systems or *events* to which these materials give analysis access'. Historical representations, de Certeau observes, bring into play past or distant regions from beyond a boundary line separating the present institution from those regions. The differences between the historiographic activity and its object of study are 'established out of principle by a will to objectivity'.

While history juxtaposes past and present, psychoanalysis recognizes the past *in* the present. For history-writing, this relationship is one of succession (one thing after another), cause and effect (one thing following from another), and separation (the past as distinct from the present). But psychoanalysis treats relations between past and present as one of imbrication (one thing in the place of the other) and repetition (one thing reproduces the other but in another form). Both, de Certeau argues, have developed to address analogous problems – 'to understand the differences, or guarantee the continuities, between the organization of the actual and the formations of the past; to give the past explanatory value and/or make the present capable of explaining the past; to relate the representations of the past or present to the conditions which determined their production'.

The argument has important implications for our understanding of museum institutions not only as phenomena that in varying ways incorporate what de Certeau distinguishes as historiographic *and* psychoanalytic 'strategies of time' or ways of 'distributing the space of memory', but as practices that provide the past with 'explanatory value' in the present. In that regard, museums are structured spaces – artifacts – *in* the present which objectify the past in such a way as to simultaneously distinguish past from present and connect it to the here and now. Juxtaposing de Certeau and White may clarify the ways in which the ideologies or philosophies of history fashioned by a particular institution are both implicit and explicit, and the ways in which museums function as mechanisms for explaining the present.

If history and psychoanalysis differ as *modes* of knowledge-production and as different *methods* of shaping the space and time of memory, then what distinguishes museums from other modern institutions and modes of knowledge-production may more cogently concern *how* they work on the relations between the past and the present than *what* they look like or what they may contain. A museum, then, may be less a *what* then a *when*, to paraphrase a remark by the philosopher Nelson Goodman some four decades ago in his attempt to shift the perennial problem of the definition of 'art' from an ontological to an instrumentalist framework. If a museum (like 'art') is more a when than a what, more a *way* of using or working on things than a *kind* of thing in itself, then there will be significant consequences for the ways in which we envision and articulate their origins and historical development.

These issues resonate with many of those currently raised in connection with attempts to understand more critically the ways in which museums work. This is a situation related not only to the exponential growth of museums in recent years but to their extraordinary variety in form and function as well as to the need to delineate what (if anything) links together this diversity. If virtually anything may serve as museum content today, then in a complementary fashion virtually anything may come to serve museological functions, if only by designation.

One of the most important and influential investigations of the ways in which museums format knowledge of the past and relate that past to the present and to the museum visitor is a chapter entitled 'Poetics of the Museum: Lenoir and Du Sommerard' in Stephen Bann's 1984 book on the craft of history, *The Clothing of Clio*. Bann observes that museological modes of organizing data have been polarized for some two centuries between two broad scenographic practices. On the one hand, objects are displayed according to one or another version of chronological and/or stylistic succession, such that they may be viewed along a temporal axis – from the beginning to the end of a historical period, or in gallery spaces corresponding to centuries or political regimes or distinct 'styles' that may be shown to have succeeded each other in a particular place. On the other hand, objects may be assembled from a particular place, historical moment, or school in such a way as to recreate a particularly dramatic effect of 'being there'. Thus, the dining hall or boudoir of a stately home may be reproduced along with all its furniture and accoutrements, creating a powerful 'period' effect, and enveloping the visitor in the illusion of visiting the past.

Bann argues that these two scenographies coexisted as alternative modes of historical presentation, and as coeval but distinct epistemological totalities in early post-Revolutionary Paris: in Lenoir's Musée des Petits-Augustins (organized by centuries) and the Musée de Cluny's 'thematic' rooms, such as the 'Chambre de Francois Ier', organized by Du Sommerard. In the latter, the object from the past becomes the armature around which are grouped both authentic and inauthentic objects, all of which contribute to the production of the experience of historical 'realities'. Regarding the latter, he writes, 'It is [the] assertion of the experiential reality of history which the rhetoric of the museum both produces and annihilates. "History" is made real through the fiction of the transparency of the historical syntagm.'

He thus succinctly and poignantly links the modern institution of the museum to its social mission of crafting and disseminating not only historical knowledge but the 'experiential reality' of such knowledge. And he goes further, suggesting that in asserting history's 'experiential reality', museological practice simultaneously annihilates it. The remark resonates with the thrust of Hayden White's essay, where the point was made that 'the literature of fact' – the writing of history – is precisely a *literature*: an artifact whose forms and techniques of presentation are indistinguishable from those of 'fiction'-writing.

The implication here is that for a museum to be construed as a 'representational' institution, it must use the theatrical techniques of scenography and artifice to *appear* representational in the first place. The polemicism of the institution – in sanctioning a particular political interpretation of the facts of history – is to be masked in the institution's modes of organizing and presenting its facts. Bann notes that these two tropological practices – the alternative and coeval 'poetics' of Lenoir and Du Sommerard – came to merge in an uneasy synthesis with the merger of the two collections by the French state. In a very concrete sense, however, the history of museology since the early nineteenth century has entailed an oscillation between these two semiotic poles – what Bann calls the metonymic and synecdochic – with every possible variation in between. The 'poetics' of the institution, then, as he puts it, 'is not Du Sommerard's system, nor is it that of Lenoir. Instead it lies in the alternation of the two strategies.'

The historiographic implications of this are quite far-reaching with respect to our understanding of the development and evolution of modern disciplines and institutions. It suggests that the principles by which such practices cohere (the 'poetics' of museums) may entail as much a set of relationships between bracketed phenomena (perhaps regardless of media) as the (bracketed or targeted) phenomena themselves. This instrumentalist and functionalist perspective may have much to recommend it in our attempts to understand the genesis, evolution, and fate of the institutions we call museums, as well as their relationships to other modern practices and professions.

Such a perspective is one that also informs the more recent essay by Jean-Louis Déotte, 'Rome, the Archetypal Museum, and the Louvre, the Negation of Division', published in 1995. Déotte discusses the works of Antoine Quatremère de Quincy, one of the most brilliant of Enlightenment and early post-Revolutionary writers on the nature and functions of the museum, on history, art, heritage, and patrimony. Through his consideration of Quatremère's relationships to his late-eighteenth- and early-nineteenth-century critics and contemporaries, Déotte refutes the traditional view that Quatremère saw in museums simply the death of 'living art'. He traces the evolution of Quatremère's thinking from 1787 through 1815, including his critique (in his *Letters to Miranda* of 1796) of Napoleon's 'liberating' (plundering and appropriating) the monuments of Italy and elsewhere, as well as of the burgeoning nationalism promoted by the politics of the French Revolution, seen as contrary to the cultural cosmopolitanism of the Enlightenment.

Quatremère saw the development of museums against the background of what he regarded as the great true Universal Museum of Europe, the city of Rome, which contained within itself and constituted the 'ultimate series of all series' (of works of art of all times and places). The plundering of Rome by Bonaparte left that great Museum in ruined fragments, with the effect that all subsequent museums were fragments of fragments. And since proper aesthetic judgment must be applied not to individual works of art in isolation but to whole series and bodies of work (of an artist or nation), the result of isolating works was an aridity and fragmentation of intelligence fostered by 'modern' (Kantian) aesthetic judgment. Quatremère argued in his *Letters to Miranda* against the various kinds of decontextualizations of works of art that were in effect fostered by the new public museums in France and other parts of Europe – in effect, containing fragments of the fragments of the ruin of Rome.

Déotte argues that Quatremère was not in principle opposed to museums as 'centralized diffusers of knowledge', but rather to the displacement of works from their historical sites and contexts – 'a combination of natural and historical elements' – within which they were created. Everything was measured against the magnificence, antiquity, encyclopedic variety, and unsurpassably rich history of *the city of Rome* which, as Quatremère put it, 'for a truly enquiring mind … is an entire world to be explored, a sort of three-dimensional mappa mundi, which offers a condensed view of Egypt, Asia, Greece, and the Roman Empire, the ancient and modern world'.

The essay suggests that Quatremère's vision of Rome, elaborated during the age of the founding of the new (fragmentary) museums, was the post-hoc projection of a(n imaginary and 'lost') unity and wholeness. Déotte contrasts the views of Quatremère and François de Neufchâteau, the director of the Louvre, on this subject. For the latter, 'the Louvre stands in direct contrast to Rome as the liberator of universal art, a place where one can comprehend that each ancient work of art is a concealed allegory of liberty' – while for the former, the Louvre represents the destruction and dismemberment of European cultures and of the cosmopolitan, pan-European, Enlightenment Republic of Letters.

Although Déotte's essay foregrounds the 'politico-metaphysical discourse' that inspired the new museums of post-Revolutionary France (which he contrasts – incorrectly – with what he calls the 'scant regard for coherence of presentation or critical discourse' of leading museums of great Britain such as the British Museum), the general point made by the essay, that the foundation of the modern civic museum was at the same time a *political and an ethical act*, is an important one. The implications of this for 'art' and for the early-nineteenth-century prospects for the scholarly study of the 'history' and 'theory' of art and of aesthetic judgment are far-reaching. Museums in fact – and not only the 'Museum of the French Revolution' in Paris – 'liberated' art by making it possible for objects to be seen and appreciated by all. Their decontextualization was less a matter of spoliation than of liberation from royal, private, and religious seclusion. But what exactly is it that was thought to be liberated?

'Art,' Déotte suggests, is the 'something that survives and calls out, even though the destination [purpose, function] of the work either no longer exists or, if it does, has become unacceptable. There is a demand,' he says, 'which comes from a long way off, from unknown ages and other lands.' He then asks, 'But is it merely a question of preserving the surviving traces of lost cultures, evidence of past civilizations, historical sites, the deeds of great warriors or politicians, of reinstating or emphasizing a particular meaning?' The temporality at issue here – to recall what was discussed above in connection with de Certeau's essay – is not that of the originating society or religion; it is, as Déotte notes, 'the temporality of suspense, of incompletion, of return, the temporality of a continuity which extends across the ages'. In short, this is the 'temporality' that was in the process of becoming 'the history of art', the trajectory of that *residue* or quality in all cultural artifacts (left over when, for example, one subtracts the religious functions and purposes of an artifact) that 'speaks' to the modern individual of 'timeless' human traits and experience.

This means understanding that 'there can exist, in the most modest of religious objects, in the created work, something that is absent and yet somehow deeply engrained' – something, that is, a meaning that is waiting to be expressed, and whose expression it is the 'destination' of the museum to foreground. The museum exists, in short, to realize the spiritual (aesthetic) potential of all things, and in that respect it liberates the past by fulfilling and foregrounding what by hindsight it takes as *repressed* in what was. In other words, the museum constitutes the fulfillment of the (aesthetic) potential in all made things of all times and places and realizes that fulfilment by reorganizing the history of the world as a history of *art*.

In addition to providing a 'metaphysico-political' backdrop for the aesthetics elaborated by Hegel in his Berlin lectures in the 1820s, this suggests that the modern institution of the museum constituted a synthesis of the 'historiography' and 'psychoanalysis' contrasted by de Certeau. Or rather, it suggests that what were to be defined later in the nineteenth century as history and psychoanalysis may usefully be seen as subsequent abstractions (among others, as we shall see) out of the ethical and political enterprise of the Revolution's museology. The museum, as a house of memory, contained within itself what became distinct practices such as history and psycho-analysis. These and related modes of shaping the spaces of memory still exist, in suspension, simultaneously affording that flexibility and potential for growth and transformation – and surprise – that characterize the institution today. In an analogous manner, the modern discipline of art history keeps in play contrary, contradictory, and opposed modes of explanation, which, like the poles of an alternating current, continue to generate the energy to propel the institution into the future.

Modern aesthetics, museology, and art history are inconceivable apart from, and indeed need to be properly understood as, both a continuation and a metamorphosis of the first modern historical museums, and most particularly that extraordinary Revolutionary institution, the Louvre, whose foundation transformed the way in which earlier institutions came to be understood. The 'temporality of suspense, of incompletion, of return, the temporality of a continuity' noted by Déotte in connection with the formation of a 'history' of art resonates with issues taken up in the last selection in this chapter, Mieke Bal's 'Telling Objects: A Narrative Perspective on Collecting', one of most insightful recent analyses of the interrelations between collecting, narration, fetishism, gender and subject-formation. In this important 1994 essay, Bal discusses collecting itself as a narrative. Underlying most of the motivations commonly attributed to the activity of collecting is another kind of developmental narrative, 'a concept capable of connecting them all: fetishism'. Building upon James Clifford's observations on collecting in the West as a 'strategy for the deployment of a possessive self, culture, and authenticity' (along with an interrogation of Susan Pearce's taxonomy of motivations for collecting),[1] Bal suggests that this attitude is predicated on a view of subject–object relations based on violence and domination.

She argues that the separation between subject and object which this entails makes it impossible for a subject, 'caught up in the individualism characteristic of that separation', to fully engage with a group. This separation between subject and object makes for an 'incurable loneliness' which impels the surrounding of him- or herself with a 'subject-domain that is not-other'. By cutting objects off from their contexts, the 'not-other' objects-to-be must first be made to become 'absolute other' so as to be possessible at all. The desire to extend the limits of the self, to appropriate by 'de-othering', already entwined with a need to dominate, engenders a further 'alterization' of alterity. This paradoxical move, she argues, is precisely the defining feature of fetishism in all senses of the term. The collected artifact is a hybrid (Marxist and psychoanalytic) fetish.

The notion of the collector as a narrative agent engaged in transforming objects into signs resonates with the insights of Quatremère addressed by Déotte, for whom objects were incomprehensible outside the (artistic) contexts in which they were made. Bal sees this as a 'denuding' of their original defining functions so as to make things available for use as signs in new (and continually evolving and mutating) systems of relationship. The new meanings assigned to objects, she suggests, are determined by the syntagmatic relations they enter into with other objects: relations which, while always metaphoric (specimens of a class), may also be either synecdochic (one of a series) or metonymic (related to some other object or idea). As the narrative of collecting develops, the significance of each already-collected object will necessarily change.

Collecting in the Western world, Bal argues, is underlain by 'childhood gendering as well as submission to political history, to memory as well as to lived experience in the present'. But whereas it may be that initially (retrospectively understood) the predominant aspect of the fetishism informing collecting may be 'anchored in anxiety over gender', eventually the relation to the fragility of subjectivity itself may shift. Played against the fictions constituting individual, ethnic, racial, and national identities, and in the light of what we have seen in the essays above on history, museology, and art history, collecting may be seen as occupying the intersection of psychic and capitalist fetishism, for, in Bal's words, 'the narratives such analyses entail turn collecting into something else again: a tale of social struggle'. As subjects, we are engaged with plots 'on both sides of the "logic of narrative possibilities", and on both sides of gender, colonialist and capitalist splits'.

The essay is best understood when juxtaposed to the others in this chapter, for it may be usefully read in the light of something Bal hints at but does not elaborate on, even in her consideration of (some of) the syntagmatic relations entered into by 'collected' objects. This is the perpetual interpretational dilemma in art history: the unresolvable oscillation between 'formalist' and 'contextualist' or historicist approaches to signification. Facets of this oscillation are also addressed by Bann and de Certeau. Despite Bal's insightful articulation of the interplay of modes of fetishism in the collected object, the text can signal a certain nostalgia for the 'lost' meanings and 'original defining functions' of things.

This is a situation addressed in the essay by Timothy Mitchell on orientalism and the exhibitionary order below in Chapter 4, where subject–object relations are again investigated in the context of Western dealings with Egypt (and vice versa) in the nineteenth century, where the staging of 'authenticity' is most patently at stake. A complementary investigation of such phenomena is also to be found in Chapter 2 in the essay by Fred Bohrer on the role of exoticism in the nineteenth-century perception/reception of ancient Assyria in Britain and France. The next chapter brings together several texts on the origins and early histories of museums, and its introduction considers the epistemological status of some of the narrative fictions and the technologies of (re)ordering objects, both familiar and exotic, as material 'evidence' for a wide variety of national and ethnic purposes which, virtually without exception, (re)articulated hierarchically ethnocentric relations between Europe and its Other(s).

NOTE

1.   See James Clifford, 'On Collecting Art and Culture', in his *The Predicament of Culture: Twentieth-Century Ethnography, Literature, and Art* (Cambridge, Mass., 1988), pp. 215–51. Bal's essay begins with an extensive critical commentary of Susan M. Pearce's list of motivations for collecting, recounted in her *Museums, Objects and Collections: A Cultural Study* (Leicester and London, 1992).

1.

The Fictions of Factual Representation

Hayden White

In order to anticipate some of the objections with which historians often meet the argument that follows, I wish to grant at the outset that *historical events* differ from *fictional events* in the ways that it has been conventional to characterize their differences since Aristotle. Historians are concerned with events which can be assigned to specific time-space locations, events which are (or were) in principle observable or perceivable, whereas imaginative writers – poets, novelists, playwrights – are concerned with both these kinds of events and imagined, hypothetical, or invented ones. The nature of the kinds of events with which historians and imaginative writers are concerned is not the issue. What should interest us in the discussion of 'the literature of fact' or, as I have chosen to call it, 'the fictions of factual representation' is the extent to which the discourse of the historian and that of the imaginative writer overlap, resemble, or correspond with each other. Although historians and writers of fiction may be interested in different kinds of events, both the forms of their respective discourses and their aims in writing are often the same. In addition, in my view, the techniques or strategies that they use in the composition of their discourses can be shown to be substantially the same, however different they may appear on a purely surface, or dictional, level of their texts.

Readers of histories and novels can hardly fail to be struck by their similarities. There are many histories that could pass for novels, and many novels that could pass for histories, considered in purely formal (or, I should say, formalist) terms. Viewed simply as verbal artifacts histories and novels are indistinguishable from one another. We cannot easily distinguish between them on formal grounds unless we approach them with specific pre-conceptions about the kinds of truths that each is supposed to deal in. But the aim of the writer of a novel must be the same as that of the writer of a history. Both wish to provide a verbal image of 'reality'. The novelist may present his notion of this reality indirectly, that is to say, by figurative techniques, rather than directly, which is to say, by registering a series of propositions which are supposed to correspond point by point to some extratextual domain of occurrence or happening, as the historian claims to do. But the image of reality which the novelist thus constructs is meant to correspond in its general outline to some domain of human experience which is no less 'real' than that referred to by the historian. It is not, then, a matter of a conflict between two kinds of truth (which the Western prejudice for empiricism as the sole access to reality has foisted upon us), a conflict between the truth of correspondence, on the one side, and the truth of coherence, on the other. Every history must meet standards of coherence no less than those of correspondence if it is to pass as a plausible account of 'the way things *really* were'. For the empiricist prejudice is attended by a conviction that 'reality' is not only perceivable but is also coherent in its structure. A mere list of confirmable singular existential statements does not add up to an account of reality if there is not some coherence, logical or aesthetic, connecting them one to another. So too every fiction must pass a test of correspondence (it must be 'adequate' as an image of something beyond itself) if it is to lay claim to representing an insight into or illumination of the human experience of the world. Whether the events represented in a discourse are construed as atomic parts of a molar whole or as possible occurrences within a perceivable totality, the discourse taken in *its* totality as an image of some reality bears a relationship of correspondence to that *of which* it is an image. It is in these twin senses that all written discourse is cognitive in its aims and mimetic in its means. And this is true even of the most ludic and seemingly expressivist discourse, of poetry no less than of prose, and even of those forms of poetry which seem to wish to illuminate only 'writing' itself. In this respect, history is no less a form of fiction than the novel is a form of historical representation.

This characterization of historiography as a form of fiction-making is not likely to be received sympathetically by either historians or literary critics, who, if they agree on little else, conventionally agree that history and fiction deal with distinct orders of experience and therefore represent distinct, if not opposed, forms of discourse. For this reason it will be well to say a few words about how this notion of the *opposition* of history to fiction arose and why it has remained unchallenged in Western thought for so long.

Prior to the French Revolution, historiography was conventionally regarded as a literary art. More specifically, it was regarded as a branch of rhetoric and its 'fictive' nature generally recognized. Although eighteenth-century theorists distinguished rather rigidly (and not always with adequate philosophical justification) between 'fact' and 'fancy', they did not on the whole view historiography as a representation of the facts unalloyed by elements of fancy. While granting the general desirability of historical accounts that dealt in real, rather than imagined events, theorists from Bayle to Voltaire and De Mably recognized the inevitability of a recourse to fictive techniques in the *representation* of real events in the historical discourse. The eighteenth century abounds in works which distinguish between the study of history on the one side and the writing of history on the other. The writing was a literary, specifically rhetorical exercise, and the product of this exercise was to be assessed as much on literary as on scientific principles.

Here the crucial opposition was between 'truth' and 'error', rather than between fact and fancy, with it being understood that many kinds of truth, even in history, could be presented to the reader only by means of fictional techniques of representation. These techniques were conceived to consist of rhetorical devices, tropes, figures, and schemata of words and thoughts, which, as described by the Classical and Renaissance rhetoricians, were identical with the techniques of poetry in general. Truth was not equated with fact, but with a combination of fact and the conceptual matrix within which it was appropriately located in the discourse. The imagination no less than the reason had to be engaged in any adequate representation of the truth; and this meant that the techniques of fiction-making were as necessary to the composition of a historical discourse as erudition might be.

In the early nineteenth century, however, it became conventional, at least among historians, to identify truth with fact and to regard fiction as the opposite of truth, hence as a hindrance to the understanding of reality rather than as a way of apprehending it. History came to be set over against fiction, and especially the novel, as the representation of the 'actual' to the representation of the 'possible' or only 'imaginable'. And thus was born the dream of a historical discourse that would consist of nothing but factually accurate statements about a realm of events which were (or had been) observable in principle, the arrangement of which in the order of their original occurrence would permit them to figure forth their true meaning or significance. Typically, the nineteenth-century historian's aim was to expunge every hint of the fictive, or merely imaginable, from his discourse, to eschew the techniques of the poet and orator, and to forego what were regarded as the intuitive procedures of the maker of fictions in his apprehension of reality.

In order to understand this development in historical thinking, it must be recognized that historiography took shape as a distinct scholarly discipline in the West in the nineteenth century against a background of a profound hostility to all forms of myth. Both the political Right and the political Left blamed mythic thinking for the excesses and failures of the Revolution. False readings of history, misconceptions of the nature of the historical process, unrealistic expectations about the ways that historical societies could be transformed – all these had led to the outbreak of the Revolution in the first place, the strange course that Revolutionary developments followed, and the effects of Revolutionary activities over the long run. It became imperative to rise above any impulse to interpret the historical record in the light of party prejudices, utopian expectations, or sentimental attachments to traditional institutions. In order to find one's way among the conflicting claims of the parties which took shape during and after the Revolution, it was necessary to locate some standpoint of social perception that was truly 'objective', truly 'realistic'. If social processes and structures seemed 'demonic' in their capacity to resist direction, to take turns unforeseen, and to overturn the highest plans, frustrating the most heartfelt desires, then the study of history had to be demythified. But in the thought of the age, demythification of any domain of inquiry tended to be equated with the defictionalization of that domain as well.

The distinction between myth and fiction which is a commonplace in the thought of our own century was hardly grasped at all by many of the foremost ideologues of the early nineteenth century. Thus it came about that history, the realistic science par excellence, was set over against fiction as the study of the real versus the study of the merely imaginable. Although Ranke had in mind that form of the novel which we have since come to call Romantic when he castigated it as mere fancy, he manifested a prejudice shared by many of his contemporaries when he defined history as the study of the real and the novel as the representation of the imaginary. Only a few theorists, among whom J. G. Droysen was the most prominent, saw that it was impossible to write history without having recourse to the techniques of the orator and the poet. Most of the 'scientific' historians of the age did not see that for every identifiable kind of novel, historians produced an equivalent kind of historical discourse. Romantic historiography produced its genius in Michelet, Realistic historiography its paradigm in Ranke himself, Symbolist historiography produced Burckhardt (who had more in common with Flaubert and Baudelaire than with Ranke), and Modernist historiography its prototype in Spengler. It was no accident that the Realistic novel and Rankean historicism entered their respective crises at roughly the same time.

There were, in short, as many 'styles' of historical representation as there are discernible literary styles in the nineteenth century. This was not perceived by the historians of the nineteenth century because they were captives of the illusion that one could write history without employing any fictional techniques whatsoever. They continued to honor the conception of the opposition of history to fiction throughout the entire period, even while producing forms of historical discourse so different from one another that their grounding in aesthetic preconceptions of the nature of the historical process alone could explain those differences. Historians continued to believe that different interpretations of the same set of events were functions of ideological distortions or of inadequate factual data. They continued to believe that if one only eschewed ideology and remained true to the facts, history would produce a knowledge as certain as anything offered by the physical sciences and as objective as a mathematical exercise.

Most nineteenth-century historians did not realize that, when it is a matter of trying to deal with past facts, the crucial consideration for him who would represent them faithfully are the notions he brings to his representation of the ways parts relate to the whole which they comprise. They did not realize that the facts do not speak for themselves, but that the historian speaks for them, speaks on their behalf, and fashions the fragments of the past into a whole whose integrity is – in its *re*presentation – a purely discursive one. Novelists might be dealing only with imaginary events whereas historians are dealing with real ones, but the process of fusing events, whether imaginary or real, into a comprehensible totality, capable of serving as the *object* of a representation is a poetic process. Here the historians must utilize precisely the same tropological strategies, the same modalities of representing relationships in words, that the poet or novelist uses. In the unprocessed historical record and in the chronicle of events which the historian extracts from the record, the facts exist only as a congeries of contiguously related fragments. These fragments have to be put together to make a whole of a particular, not a general, kind. And they are put together in the same ways that novelists use to put together figments of their imaginations to display an ordered world, a cosmos, where only disorder or chaos might appear.

So much for manifestoes. On what grounds can such a reactionary position be justified? On what grounds can the assertion that historical discourse shares more than it divides with novelistic discourse be sustained? The first ground is to be found in recent developments in literary theory – especially in the insistence by modern Structuralist and text critics on the necessity of dissolving the distinction between prose and poetry in order to identify their shared attributes as forms of linguistic behavior that are as much constitutive of their objects of representation as they are reflective of external reality, on the one side, and projective of internal emotional states, on the other. It appears that Stalin was right when he opined that language belonged neither to the superstructure nor the base of cultural praxis, but was, in some unspecified way, *prior to both*. We do not know the origin of language and never shall, but it is certain today that language is more adequately characterized as being neither a free creation of human consciousness nor merely a product of environmental forces acting on the psyche, but rather the *instrument of mediation* between the consciousness and the world that consciousness inhabits.

This will not be news to literary theorists, but it has not yet reached the historians buried in the archives hoping, by what they call a 'sifting of the facts' or 'the manipulation of the data', to *find* the form of the reality that will serve as the object of representation in the account that they will write when 'all the facts are known' and they have finally 'got the story straight'.

So, too, contemporary critical theory permits us to believe more confidently than ever before that 'poetizing' is not an activity that hovers over, transcends, or otherwise remains alienated from life or reality, but represents a mode of praxis which serves as the immediate base of all cultural activity (this an insight of Vico, Hegel, and Nietzsche, no less than of Freud and Lévi-Strauss), even of science itself. We are no longer compelled, therefore, to believe – as historians in the post-Romantic period had to believe – that fiction is the antithesis of fact (in the way that superstition or magic is the antithesis of science) or that we can relate facts to one another without the aid of some enabling and generically fictional matrix. This too would be news to many historians were they not so fetishistically enamored of the notion of 'facts' and so congenitally hostile to 'theory' in any form that the presence in a historical work of a formal theory used to explicate the relationship between facts and concepts is enough to earn them the charge of having defected to the despised sociology or of having lapsed into the nefarious philosophy of history.

Every discipline, I suppose, is, as Nietzsche saw most clearly, constituted by what it *forbids* its practitioners to do. Every discipline is made up of a set of restrictions on thought and imagination, and none is more hedged about with taboos than professional historiography – so much so that the so-called 'historical method' consists of little more than the injunction to 'get the story straight' (without any notion of what the relation of 'story' to 'fact' might be) and to avoid both conceptual overdetermination and imaginative excess (i.e., 'enthusiasm') at any price.

Yet the price paid is a considerable one. It has resulted in the repression of the *conceptual apparatus* (without which atomic facts cannot be aggregated into complex macrostructures and constituted as objects of discursive representation in a historical narrative) and the remission of the *poetic moment* in historical writing to the interior of the discourse (where it functions as an unacknowledged – and therefore uncriticizable – *content* of the historical narrative).

Those historians who draw a firm line between history and philosophy of history fail to recognize that every historical discourse contains within it a full-blown, if only implicit, philosophy of history. And this is as true of what is conventionally called narrative (or diachronic) historiography as it is of conceptual (or synchronic) historical representation. The principal difference between history and philosophy of history is that the latter brings the conceptual apparatus by which the facts are ordered in the discourse to the surface of the text, while history proper (as it is called) buries it in the interior of the narrative, where it serves as a hidden or implicit shaping device, in precisely the same way that Professor [Northrop] Frye conceives his *archetypes* to do in narrative fictions. History does not, therefore, stand over against myth as its cognitive antithesis, but represents merely another, and more extreme form of that 'displacement' which Professor Frye has analyzed in his *Anatomy* [*of Criticism* (1965)]. Every history has its myth; and if there are different fictional modes based on different identifiable mythical archetypes, so too there are different historiographical modes – different ways of hypotactically ordering the 'facts' contained in the chronicle of events occurring in a specific time-space location, such that events in the same set are capable of functioning differently in order to figure forth different *meanings* – moral, cognitive, or aesthetic – within different fictional matrices.

In fact, I would argue that these mythic modes are more easily identifiable in historiographical than they are in literary texts. For historians usually work with much less *linguistic* (and therefore less *poetic*) self-consciousness than writers of fiction do. They tend to treat language as a transparent vehicle of representation that brings no cognitive baggage of its own into the discourse. Great works of fiction will usually – if Roman Jakobson is right – not only be *about* their putative subject matter, but also *about* language itself and the problematical relation between language, consciousness, and reality – including the writer's own language. Most historians' concern with language extends only to the effort to speak plainly, to avoid florid figures of speech, to assure that the persona of the author appears nowhere identifiable in the text, and to make clear what technical terms mean, when they dare to use any.

This is not, of course, the case with the great philosophers of history – from Augustine, Machiavelli, and Vico to Hegel, Marx, Nietzsche, Croce, and Spengler. The problematical status of language (including their own linguistic protocols) constitutes a crucial element in their own *apparatus criticus*. And it is not the case with the great classic writers of historiography – from Thucydides and Tacitus to Michelet, Carlyle, Ranke, Droysen, Tocqueville, and Burckhardt. These historians at least had a rhetorical self-consciousness that permitted them to recognize that any set of facts was variously, and equally legitimately, describable, that there is no such thing as a single correct original description of anything, on the basis of which an interpretation of that thing can *subsequently* be brought to bear. They recognized, in short, that all original descriptions of any field of phenomena are *already* interpretations of its structure, and that the linguistic mode in which the original description (or taxonomy) of the field is cast will implicitly rule out certain modes of representation and modes of explanation regarding the field's structure and tacitly sanction others. In other words, the favored mode of original description of a field of historical phenomena (and this includes the field of literary texts) already contains implicitly a limited range of modes of emplotment and modes of argument by which to disclose the meaning of the field in a discursive prose representation. If, that is, the description is anything more than a random registering of impressions. The plot structure of a historical narrative (*how* things turned out as they did) and the formal argument or explanation of *why* things happened or turned out as they did are *pre*figured by the original description (of the 'facts' to be explained) in a given dominant modality of language use: metaphor, metonymy, synecdoche, or irony.

Now, I want to make clear that I am myself using these terms as metaphors for the different ways we construe fields or sets of phenomena in order to 'work them up' into *possible objects of narrative representation* and *discursive analysis*. Anyone who originally encodes the world in the mode of metaphor will be inclined to decode it – that is, narratively 'explicate' and discursively analyze it – as a congeries of individualities. To those for whom there is no real resemblance in the world, decodation must take the form of a disclosure, either of the simple *contiguity* of things (the mode of metonymy) or of the *contrast* that lies hidden within every apparent resemblance or unity (the mode of irony). In the first case, the narrative representation of the field, construed as a diachronic process, will favor as a privileged mode of emplotment the archetype of Romance and a mode of explanation that identifies knowledge with the appreciation and delineation of the particularity and individuality of things. In the second case, an original description of the field in the mode of metonymy will favor a tragic plot structure as a privileged mode of emplotment and mechanistic causal connection as the favored mode of explanation, to account for changes topographically outlined in the emplotment. So too an ironic original description of the field will generate a tendency to favor emplotment in the mode of satire and pragmatic or contextual explanation of the structures thus illuminated. Finally, to round out the list, fields originally described in the synecdochic mode will tend to generate comic emplotments and organicist explanations of why these fields change as they do.[1]

Note, for example, that both those great narrative hulks produced by such classic historians as Michelet, Tocqueville, Burckhardt, and Ranke, on the one side, and the elegant synopses produced by philosophers of history such as Herder, Marx, Nietzsche, and Hegel, on the other, become more easily relatable one to the other if we see them as both victims and exploiters of the linguistic mode in which they originally describe a field of historical events *before* they apply their characteristic modalities of narrative representation and explanation, that is, their 'interpretations' of the field's 'meaning'. In addition, each of the linguistic modes, modes of emplotment, and modes of explanation has affinities with a specific ideological position: anarchist, radical, liberal, and conservative, respectively. The issue of ideology points to the fact that there is no value-neutral mode of emplotment, explanation, or even description of any field of events, whether imaginary or real, and suggests that the very use of language itself implies or entails a specific posture before the world which is ethical, ideological, or more generally political: not only all interpretation, but also all language is politically contaminated.

Now, in my view, any historian who simply described a set of facts in, let us say, metonymic terms and then went on to emplot its processes in the mode of tragedy and proceeded to explain those processes mechanistically, and finally drew explicit ideological implications from it – as most vulgar Marxists and materialistic determinists do – would not only not be very interesting but could legitimately be labelled a *doctrinaire* thinker who had 'bent the facts' to fit a preconceived theory. The peculiar dialectic of historical discourse – and of other forms of discursive prose as well, perhaps even the novel – comes from the effort of the author to mediate between alternative modes of emplotment and explanation, which means, finally, *mediating between alternative modes of language use* or *tropological* strategies for originally describing a given field of phenomena and constituting it as a possible object of representation.

It is this sensitivity to alternative linguistic protocols, cast in the modes of metaphor, metonymy, synecdoche, and irony, that distinguishes the great historians and philosophers of history from their less interesting counterparts among the technicians of these two crafts. This is what makes Tocqueville so much more interesting (and a source of so many different later thinkers) than either his contemporary, the doctrinaire Guizot, or most of his modern liberal or conservative followers, whose knowledge is greater than his and whose retrospective vision is more extensive but whose dialectical capacity is so much more weakly developed. Tocqueville writes about the French Revolution, but he writes even more meaningfully about the difficulty of ever attaining to a definitive *objective characterization* of the complex web of facts that comprise the Revolution as a graspable totality or structured whole. The contradiction, the *aporia*, at the heart of Tocqueville's discourse is born of his awareness that alternative, mutually exclusive, original descriptions of what the Revolution *is* are possible. He recognizes that *both* metonymical and synecdochic linguistic protocols can be used, equally legitimately, to describe the field of facts that comprise the 'Revolution' and to constitute it as a *possible object of historical discourse*. He moves feverishly between the two modes of original description testing both, trying to assign them to different mental sets or cultural types (what he means by a 'democratic' consciousness is a metonymic transcription of phenomena; 'aristocratic' consciousness is synecdochic). He himself is satisfied with neither mode, although he recognizes that each gives access to a specific aspect of reality and represents a possible way of apprehending it. His aim, ultimately, is to contrive a language capable of mediating between the two modes of consciousness which these linguistic modes represent. This aim of mediation, in turn, drives him progressively toward the ironic recognition that any given linguistic protocol will obscure as much as it reveals about the reality it seeks to capture in an order of words. This *aporia* or sense of contradiction residing at the heart of language itself is present in *all* of the classic historians. It is this linguistic self-consciousness which distinguishes them from their mundane counterparts and followers, who think that language can serve as a perfectly transparent medium of representation and who think that if one can only find the right language for describing events, the meaning of the events will *display itself* to consciousness.

This movement between alternative linguistic modes conceived as alternative descriptive protocols is, I would argue, a distinguishing feature of all of the great classics of the 'literature of fact'. Consider, for example, Darwin's *Origin of Species*,[2] a work which must rank as a classic in any list of the great monuments of this kind of literature. This work which, more than any other, desires to remain within the ambit of plain fact, is just as much about the problem of classification as it is about its ostensible subject matter, the data of natural history. This means that it deals with two problems: how are events to be described as possible elements of an argument; and what kind of argument do they add up to once they are so described?

Darwin claims to be concerned with a single, crucial question: 'Why are not all organic things linked together in inextricable chaos?' (p. 453). But he wishes to answer this question in particular terms. He does not wish to suggest, as many of his contemporaries held, that all systems of classification are arbitrary, that is, mere products of the minds of the classifiers; he insists that there is a *real* order in nature. On the other hand, he does not wish to regard this order as a product of some spiritual or teleological power. The order which he seeks in the data, then, must be manifest in the facts themselves but not manifested in such a way as to display the operations of any transcendental power. In order to establish this notion of nature's plan, he purports, first, simply to entertain 'objectively' all of the 'facts' of natural history provided by field naturalists, domestic breeders, and students of the geological record – in much the same way that the historian entertains the data provided by the archives. But this entertainment of the record is no simple reception of the facts; it is an entertainment of the facts with a view toward the discrediting of all previous taxonomic systems in which they have previously been encoded.

Like Kant before him, Darwin insists that the source of all error is semblance. Analogy, he says again and again, is always a 'deceitful guide' (see pp. 61, 66, 473). As against analogy, or as I would say merely metaphorical characterizations of the facts, Darwin wishes to make a case for the existence of real 'affinities' genealogically construed. The establishment of these affinities will permit him to postulate the linkage of all living things to all others by the 'laws' or 'principles' of genealogical descent, variation, and natural selection. These laws and principles are the formal elements in his mechanistic explanation of why creatures are arranged in families in a time series. But this explanation could not be offered as long as the data remained encoded in the linguistic modes of either metaphor or synecdoche, the modes of qualitative connection. As long as creatures are classified in terms of either semblance or essential unity, the realm of organic things must remain either a chaos of arbitrarily affirmed connectedness or a hierarchy of higher and lower forms. Science as Darwin understood it, however, cannot deal in the categories of the 'higher' and 'lower' any more than it can deal in the categories of the 'normal' and 'monstrous'. Everything must be entertained as what it manifestly *seems to be*. Nothing can be regarded as 'surprising', any more than anything can be regarded as 'miraculous'.

There are many kinds of facts invoked in *The Origin of Species*: Darwin speaks of 'astonishing' facts (p. 301), 'remarkable' facts (p. 384), 'leading' facts (pp. 444, 447), 'unimportant' facts (p. 58), 'well-established' facts, even 'strange' facts (p. 105); but there are no 'surprising' facts. Everything, for Darwin no less than for Nietzsche, is just what it appears to be – but what things appear to be are data inscribed under the aspect of *mere contiguity in space* (all the facts gathered by naturalists all over the world) *and time* (the records of domestic breeders and the geological record). As the elements of a problem (or rather, of a puzzle, for Darwin is confident that there is a solution to his problem), the facts of natural history are conceived to exist in that mode of relationship which is presupposed in the operation of the linguistic trope of metonymy, which is the favored trope of all *modern* scientific discourse (this is one of the crucial distinctions between modern and premodern sciences). The substitution of the name of a part of a thing for the name of the whole is prelinguistically sanctioned by the importance which the scientific consciousness grants to mere contiguity. Considerations of *semblance* are tacitly retired in the employment of this trope, and so are considerations of *difference* and *contrast*. This is what gives to metonymic consciousness what Kenneth Burke calls its 'reductive' aspect. Things exist in contiguous relationships that are only spatially and temporally definable. This metonymizing of the world, this preliminary encoding of the facts in terms of merely contiguous relationships, is necessary to the removal of metaphor and teleology from phenomena which every *modern* science seeks to effect. And Darwin spends the greater part of his book on the justification of this encodation, or original description, of reality, in order to discharge the errors and confusion which a *merely* metaphorical profile of it has produced.

But this is only a preliminary operation. Darwin then proceeds to restructure the facts – but *only along one axis* of the time-space grid on which he has originally deployed them. Instead of stressing the mere contiguity of the phenomena, he shifts gears, or rather tropological modes, and begins to concentrate on differences – but two kinds of differences: *variations within species*, on the one side, and *contrasts between the species*, on the other. 'Systematists,' he writes, '... have only to decide ... whether any form be sufficiently *constant* and *distinct* from other forms, to be capable of definition; and if definable, whether the differences be sufficiently important to deserve a specific name.' But the distinction between a species and a variety is only a matter of degree.

Hereafter we shall be compelled to acknowledge that the only distinction between species and well-marked varieties is, that the latter are known, or believed, to be connected at the present day by intermediate gradation, whereas *species* were formerly thus connected. Hence, without rejecting the consideration of the *present existence* of intermediate gradations between any two forms, we shall be led to weigh more carefully and to *value higher* the *actual amount of difference between them*. It is quite possible that forms now generally acknowledged to be merely varieties *may hereafter* be thought worthy of *specific names*; and in this case *scientific and common language will come into accordance*. In short, we shall have to treat species in the same manner as those naturalists treat genera, who admit that genera are merely artificial combinations made for convenience. This may not be a cheering prospect; but we shall at least be free from the vain search for the undiscovered and undiscoverable *essence* of the term species. (pp. 474–75; italics added)

And yet Darwin has smuggled in his own conception of the 'essence' of the term *species*. And he has done it by falling back on the geological record, which, following Lyell, he calls 'a history of the world imperfectly kept, ... written in a changing dialect' and of which 'we possess the last volume alone' (p. 331). Using this record, he postulates the descent of all species and varieties from some four or five prototypes governed by what he calls the 'rule' of 'gradual transition' (pp. 180ff.) or 'the great principle of gradation' (p. 251). *Difference* has been dissolved in the *mystery of transition*, such that *continuity-in-variation* is seen as the 'rule' and radical discontinuity or variation as an 'anomaly' (p. 33). But this 'mystery' of transition (see his highly tentative, confused, and truncated discussion of the possible 'modes of transition', pp. 179–82, 310) is nothing but the facts laid out on a time-line, rather than spatially disposed, and treated as a 'series' which is permitted to '*impress* ... the *mind* with the *idea of an actual passage*' (p. 66). All organic beings are then (gratuitously on the basis of both the facts and the theories available to Darwin) treated (metaphorically on the literal level of the text but synecdochically on the allegorical level) as belonging to families linked by genealogical descent (through the operation of variation and natural selection) from the postulated four or five prototypes. It is only his distaste for 'analogy', he tells us, that keeps him from going 'one step further, namely, to the belief that all plants and animals are descended from some one prototype' (p. 473). But he has approached as close to a doctrine of organic unity as his respect for the 'facts', in their original encodation in the mode of contiguity, will permit him to go. He has *transformed* 'the facts' from a structure of merely contiguously related particulars into a sublimated synecdoche. And this in order to put a new and more comforting (as well as, in his view, a more interesting and comprehensible) vision of nature in place of that of his vitalistic opponents.

The image which he finally offers – of an unbroken succession of generations – may have had a disquieting effect on his readers, inasmuch as it dissolved the distinction between both the 'higher' and 'lower' in nature (and by implication, therefore, in society) and the 'normal' and the 'monstrous' in life (and therefore in culture). But in Darwin's view, the new image of organic nature as an essential continuity of beings gave assurance that no 'cataclysm' had ever 'desolated the world' and permitted him to look forward to a 'secure future and progress toward perfection' (p. 477). For 'cataclysm' we can of course read 'revolution' and for 'secure future', 'social status quo'. But all of this is presented, not as image, but as plain fact. Darwin is ironic only with respect to those systems of classification that would ground 'reality' in fictions of which he does not approve. Darwin distinguishes between tropological codes that are 'responsible' to the data and those that are not. But the criterion of responsibility to the data is not extrinsic to the operation by which the 'facts' are ordered in his initial description of them; this criterion is intrinsic to that operation.

As thus envisaged, even the *Origin of Species*, that *summa* of 'the literature of fact' of the nineteenth century, must be read as a kind of allegory – a history of nature meant to be understood literally but appealing ultimately to an image of coherency and orderliness which it constructs by linguistic 'turns' alone. And if this is true of the *Origin*, how much more true must it be of any history of human societies? In point of fact, historians have not agreed upon a terminological system for the description of the events which they wish to treat as facts and embed in their discourses as self-revealing data. Most historiographical disputes – among scholars of roughly equal erudition and intelligence – turn precisely on the matter of which among several linguistic protocols is to be used to *describe* the events under contention, not what explanatory system is to be applied to the events in order to reveal their meaning. Historians remain under the same illusion that had seized Darwin, the illusion that a value-neutral description of the facts, prior to their interpretation or analysis, is possible. It was not the doctrine of natural selection advanced by Darwin that commended him to other students of natural history as the Copernicus of natural history. That doctrine had been known and elaborated long before Darwin advanced it in the *Origin*. What had been required was a redescription of the facts to be explained in a language which would sanction the application to them of the doctrine as the most adequate way of explaining them.

And so too for historians seeking to 'explain' the 'facts' of the French Revolution, the decline and fall of the Roman Empire, the effects of slavery on American society, or the meaning of the Russian Revolution. What is at issue here is not 'What are the facts?' but rather, 'How are the facts to be described in order to sanction one mode of explaining them rather than another?' Some historians will insist that history cannot become a science until it finds the technical terminology adequate to the correct characterization of its objects of study, in the way that physics did in the calculus and chemistry did in the periodic tables. Such is the recommendation of Marxists, Positivists, Cliometricians, and so on. Others will continue to insist that the integrity of historiography depends on its use of ordinary language, its avoidance of jargon. These latter suppose that ordinary language is a safeguard against ideological deformations of the 'facts'. What they fail to recognize is that ordinary language itself has its own forms of terminological determinism, represented by the figures of speech without which discourse itself is impossible.

NOTES

1.   I have tried to exemplify at length each of these webs of relationships in given historians in my book *Metahistory: The Historical Imagination in Nineteenth-Century Europe* (Baltimore and London, 1973).

2.   References in the text to Darwin's *Origin of Species* are to the Dolphin Edition (New York: n.d.).

2.

Psychoanalysis and its History

Michael de Certeau

The process upon which psychoanalysis is based lies at the heart of Freud's discoveries – the return of the repressed. This 'mechanism' is linked to a certain conception of time and memory, according to which consciousness is both the deceptive *mask* and the operative *trace* of events that organize the present. If the past (that which took place during, and took the form of, a decisive moment in the course of a crisis) is *repressed*, it *returns* in the present from which it was excluded, but does so surreptitiously. One of Freud's favorite examples is a figuration of this detour-return, which constitutes the ruse of history: Hamlet's father returns after his murder, but in the form of a phantom, in another scene, and it is only then that he becomes the law his son obeys.

Two strategies of time

There is an 'uncanniness' about this past that a present occupant has expelled (or thinks it has) in an effort to take its place. The dead haunt the living. The past: it 're-bites' [*il re-mord*] (it is a secret and repeated biting).[1] History is 'cannibalistic', and memory becomes the closed arena of conflict between two contradictory operations: forgetting, which is not something passive, a loss, but an action directed against the past; and the mnemic trace, the return of what was forgotten, in other words, an action by a past that is now forced to disguise itself. More generally speaking, any autonomous order is founded upon what it eliminates; it produces a 'residue' condemned to be forgotten. But what was excluded re-infiltrates the place of its origin – now the present's 'clean' [*propre*] place. It resurfaces, it troubles, it turns the present's feeling of being 'at home' into an illusion, it lurks – this 'wild', this 'ob-scene', this 'filth', this 'resistance' of 'superstition' – within the walls of the residence, and, behind the back of the owner (the *ego*), or over its objections, it inscribes there the law of the other.

Historiography, on the other hand, is based on a clean break between the past and the present. It is the product of relations of knowledge and power linking two supposedly distinct domains: on one hand, there is the present (scientific, professional, social) place of work, the technical and conceptual apparatus of *inquiry* and interpretation, and the operation of describing and/or explaining; on the other hand, there are the places (museums, archives, libraries) where the materials forming the object of this research are kept and, secondarily, set off in time, there are the past systems or *events* to which these materials give analysis access. There is a boundary line separating the present institution (which fabricates representations) from past or distant regions (which historiographical representations bring into play).

Even though historiography postulates a continuity (a genealogy), a solidarity (an affiliation), and a complicity (a sympathy) between its agents and its objects, it nevertheless distinguishes a *difference* between them, a difference established out of principle by a will to objectivity. The space it organizes is divided and hierarchical. That space has an 'own' [*un propre*] (the present of this historiography) and an 'other' (the 'past' under study). The dividing line between them affects both the practice (the research apparatus distinguishes itself from the material it treats), and the enactment in writing (the discourse of interpretative knowledge subjugates the known, cited, represented past).

Psychoanalysis and historiography thus have two different ways of distributing the *space of memory*. They conceive of the relation between the past and present differently. Psychoanalysis recognizes the past *in* the present; historiography places them one *beside* the other. Psychoanalysis treats the relation as one of imbrication (one in the place of the other), of repetition (one reproduces the other in another form), of the equivocal and of the *quiproquo* (What 'takes the place' of what? Everywhere, there are games of masking, reversal, and ambiguity). Historiography conceives the relation as one of succession (one after the other), correlation (greater or lesser proximities), cause and effect (one follows from the other), and disjunction (either one or the other, but not both at the same time).

Two strategies of *time* thus confront one another. They do, however, develop in the context of analogous problems: to find principles and criteria to serve as guides to follow in attempting to understand the differences, or guarantee the continuities, between the organization of the actual and the formations of the past; to give the past explanatory value and/or make the present capable of explaining the past; to relate the representations of the past or present to the conditions which determined their production; to elaborate (how? where?) different ways of thinking, and by so doing overcome violence (the conflicts and contingencies of history), including the violence of thought itself; to define and construct a narrative, which is for both disciplines the favored form of elucidating discourse. In order to determine the possibilities and limitations of the renewal of historiography promised by its encounter with psychoanalysis, we will survey the interrelations and debates between these two strategies since the time of Freud (1856–1939).

Freud and history

Freud's method of 'elucidation' (*Aufklärung*) is supported by two pillars he built and considered equally fundamental and founding: *The Interpretation of Dreams* (1900) and *Totem and Taboo* (1912–1913). Of the second, he said in 1914, 'I have made an attempt to deal with problems of social anthropology in the light of analysis; this line of investigation leads directly to the origins of the most important institutions of our civilization, of the structure of the state, of morality and religion, and, moreover, of the prohibition against incest and of conscience.'[2] His method is enacted on two scenes, one individual and the other collective. It takes, in turn, the (biographical) form of 'case histories' (the '*Krankengeschichten*', 1905–1918)[3] and the (global) form of the 'historical novel' (*Moses and Monotheism*, 1939: the original title specifies that the subject is the relation of a single man – 'der Mann Moses' – to the historical configuration of Jewish monotheism).[4]

Freud's forays into historiography are semi-surgical operations which display a certain number of characteristics:

1. He invalidates the break between individual psychology and collective psychology.
2. He thinks of the 'pathological' as a region where the structural modes of functioning of human experience become intensified and display themselves. Accordingly, the distinction between normality and abnormality is only phenomenal; fundamentally, it has no scientific relevance.
3. He identifies the relation of historicity to *crises* which organize and displace it. He reveals, in decisive events (of a relational and conflictual nature, originally genealogical and sexual), the sites where psychic *structures* are constituted. Therapeutic confirmations allow him to orient his analyses in three directions: a) the search for determining factors in the life of the adult which are linked to 'primitive scenes' experienced by the child, and which presuppose that the child (that epigone, until then kept on the sidelines) plays a central role in the story; b) the necessity of postulating a genealogical violence at the origin of peoples (a struggle between the father and the son), the repression of which is the work of tradition (it hides the corpse), but whose repetitive effects are nevertheless identifiable across their successive camouflages (there are traces left behind); c) the assurance of finding in any discourse 'small fragments of truth' ('*Stükchen Wahrheit*')[5] – splinters and debris relative to those decisive moments – the forgetting of which organizes itself into psychosociological systems and the remembrance of which creates possibilities of change for the present state.
4. He alters the historiographical 'genre' of writing by introducing the need for the analyst to *mark his place* (his affective, imaginary, and symbolic place). He makes this explicitness the condition of possibility of a form of lucidity, and thus substitutes for 'objective' discourse (a discourse that aims to express the real) a discourse that adopts the form of a 'fiction' (if by 'fiction' we understand a text that openly declares its relation to the singular place of its production).

Curiously, some of the subsequent avatars of the psychoanalytic tradition and its applications totally reverse these positions. A few instructive examples will suffice. Freudianism, for one thing, was reduced to individual psychology and biography. It was either boxed into the category of the 'pathological' (for example, *economic* and *social* history left an unexplained, abnormal 'residue', in the areas of sorcery and Nazism, which was abandoned to psychoanalysis). Or, to take another example, where Freud found displacements of representations linked to primal conflicts, there was an assumption that all-prevailing and stable 'symbols' or 'archetypes' lurked somewhere beneath the phenomena. In the same way, the subject's division between the pleasure principle (*Eros*) and the law of the other (*Thanatos*) – for Freud an insurmountable division which, from *Beyond the Pleasure Principle* (1920) to *Civilization and its Discontents* (1930), he defined in terms of the alienation of need by society and the constitutive frustration of desires – was 'forgotten' by therapies whose goal was to 'integrate' the ego into society. Perhaps these inheritors 'betrayed' Freud in both senses of the term: they deflected his thought and unveiled it. Their actions conform to the theory of tradition Freud presented in *Moses and Monotheism*, according to which tradition inverts and conceals precisely what it claims to reproduce, and does so in its name. Leaving that aside, it is necessary to review at least two of Freud's positions that are more directly relevant to history. A discussion of two essential texts will be enough for an outline.

1. In *Group Psychology and the Analysis of the Ego* (1921; written on Gustave Le Bon's *The Crowd: A Study of the Popular Mind*), Freud firmly holds that 'the relation of an individual to his parents and to his brothers and sisters, to the object of his love, and to his physician – in fact all the relations which have hitherto been the chief subject of psychoanalytic research – may claim to be considered as social phenomena'.[6] They are only distinguishable from the phenomena treated by collective psychology by a 'numerical consideration' that is irrelevant from the point of view of the psychic structures involved. The constitution of the subject through its relation to other (parents, etc.) and to language postulates from the beginning a social life composed of various formations that are progressively larger in scale, but follow identical laws. Freud thus feels authorized to take his analytical apparatus across the lines dividing the established disciplines, which apportion psychic phenomena among themselves according to a distinction (between 'individual' and 'collective') that Freud challenges and wishes to transform.

2. These already constituted domains are also distinguished from one another by the particular techniques each has adopted. Freud was not equally competent in all of them, which does not, at least theoretically, place in question the object of study that psychoanalysis, like any other science, chose for itself. His first studies were on eels (1877) and crayfish (1882). He was a psychiatric doctor. He effected the psychoanalytic 'conversion' using the materials and methods that specialty provided for him. Afterward, beginning in 1907 (when Freud was 51), he extended it to the study of literary texts;[7] still later, beginning in 1910 (in relation to 'primal words' and Leonardo da Vinci), he further extended it to ethnology and history.[8] But as

the preface to *Totem and Taboo* (1913) – the book marking the second moment in the psychoanalytic *conquista* – makes clear, when it comes to ethnology he no longer has 'a sufficient grasp of the material that awaits ('harrenden') (psychoanalytic) treatment'.[9] Though constructed and verifiable within the bounds of a particular field, his theory was not meant to be anchored there; it was, rather, destined to renew other fields, in relation to which Freud himself nonetheless lacked the necessary elements for first-hand information and technical control. The material (*Materiel*) originating in these foreign realms, culled by their respective explorers, is for Freud both what the analyst 'lacks' and what is 'missed' by a (Freudian) theoretical treatment capable of 'harmonizing' the 'diversity' of facts and throwing 'a ray of light into this obscurity'.[10] Freud calls these domains 'quarries', or 'treasures' to be exploited. He works them, devouring the texts of Smith, Wundt, Crawley, Frazer, and others, as well as documents from the seventeenth century, scholarly studies of the Bible, etc. – but all without the professional 'security' his home territory affords him.

When a theoretical point of view is extended beyond the field within which it was elaborated, where it remains subject to a system of verification, does it not, as Canguilhem said, cross the line between scientific 'theories' and scientific '*ideologies*'? That is frequently the case. Freud himself at times had doubts about the status of his socio-historical research, and toward the end of his life he claimed with irony that he wrote them as a hobby, while smoking his pipe. He was admitting a crack of ambiguity in his analytic edifice. It is up to his posterity to accept the theoretical challenge this admission represents. In history, Freud was a pioneer, but not a practitioner, in spite of his passion for collecting 'antiquities' and the breadth of his readings in the field, begun in adolescence. In addition to a coherent corpus of verifiable, theoretical hypotheses, he injected into historiography the suspense of a detective story ('Who killed Harry?') and the uncanniness of a fantasy novel (there is a ghost in the house). He reintroduced mythic conflicts into a scientific system. He brought back the sorcery in knowledge, taking it even to the offices of the historians, who seem to assume that the past is already neatly ordered, piecemeal, sitting on the archive shelves. A seriousness [*un sérieux*] of history appears, bringing all its dangers with it. A half century after Michelet, Freud observes that the dead are in fact 'beginning to speak'.[11] But they are not speaking through the 'medium' of the historian-wizard, as Michelet believed: *it is speaking* [*ça parle*] in the work and in the silences of the historian, but without his knowledge. These voices – whose disappearance every historian posits, which he replaces with his writing – 're-bite' [*re-mordent*] the space from which they were excluded; they continue to speak in the text/tomb that erudition erects in their place.

Traditions

Freud, in his 1919 preface to Theodor Reik's *Ritual* (Reik believed *Totem and Taboo* to be 'the most important book of its kind ... the standard illustration of what psychoanalysis can perform in the sphere of the [human] sciences'), surveyed psychoanalytic research since the appearance of *Die Bedeutung der Psychoanalyse für die Geisteswissenschaften* (1913), by Otto Rank and Hanns Sachs: 'Mythology and the history of literature and religion appear to furnish the most easily accessible material.' He praises Reik, whose book he says represents the first volume in the 'Psychology of Religions'. 'He keeps steadily in view the relationship between pre-historic man and primitive man of today, as well as the connection between cultural activities and neurotic substitute formations.' This constitutes a declaration of victory in the battle to 'submit the prehistoric and ethnological material ... to psychoanalytic elaboration'.[12] It is the first success scored by the 'attempted invasions by psychoanalysis'.[13]

These three domains ('*mythology* and the history of *literature* and *religion*') were already a preoccupation of the Wednesday night meetings at Freud's office (beginning in 1902), and the discussions continued in the Psychoanalytic Society of Vienna (founded in 1908).[14] In the beginning, Rank (the group's secretary), Adler, Federn, Sachs, Schilder, Steiner, and others (with Reik, Tausk, and Lou Andreas-Salomé joining in later) treated questions concerning incest, symbolism, myth, Wagner, Nietzsche, etc. These 'applications' of psychoanalysis soon became the object of wider discussion involving correspondence with Abraham (Berlin), Ferenczi (Budapest), Groddeck (Baden-Baden), Jung (Zurich), Jones (London), Putnam (Boston), etc. The analyses that were produced diverted psychoanalytic narrative from the 'case study' toward biography, culminating in the 'psychological portrait' of Woodrow Wilson, a joint effort by Freud and William Bullitt.[15]

The creation of the International Psychoanalytic Association (1910), which was endowed with a 'head', means of control, and a charter to 'promote mutual support among its members', did not prevent this line of research (in particular, as Freud said, 'applications of psychoanalysis to the sciences of *language* and history') from diversifying; various currents within it even came into conflict, and with growing frequency.[16] Three (specifically historical) factors seem to have played a more important role in these divergences than any institutional constraint: 1) the personal relation of the authors to Freud (psychoanalytic theory is founded upon the irrationality and particularity of the transference relation with the other, and thus on the singularity of Freud's psychology); 2) the relation of dependence between a theory of history and the elucidation by the analyst of his relation to the psychoanalytic institution (the psychoanalytic association submits its members to the law at the basis of all social organization, a point that is often obscured in the theory); 3) the logic of the sociopolitical and national contexts within which the analyst's position (as the 'subject who is supposed to know' [*sujet supposé savoir*]) functions (social pressure is stronger than the Freudian 'family' or an international association).

The first factor is too complex to summarize, but two facts should be emphasized: the theory is *historicized* by reintroducing into the conceptual debates (on Adler and Jung, for example) the particularity of the author's personal relationship to Freud, which means giving singular, contingent events the role of explaining (or simply designating) the gaps in 'science';[17] and conversely, there is a *mythification* of historiography, since the narration of the past becomes a fictional transposition of present combats between psychoanalytic gods (Freud and his 'sons', in *Totem and Taboo*; Freud against Adler and Jung in 'On the History of the Psychoanalytic Movement', etc.). The theory therefore oscillates between the biographical facts that fragment it and mythic representations that disguise the conditions governing its production. On the one hand, it admits that it is wracked by conflicts (but that means that it is not reducible to a system); on the other hand, the interpretation of distant origins metamorphoses internecine quarrels (but this displacement from a present scene to a past or primitive one also suggests analogous operations between collective representations and histories of the subject).

The second factor is more problematical. In effect, the institution plays the role of mediator between the analyst and history in general. More than that, it links analysis itself to the configuration of powers that make it possible and supports its continued existence (for example, it is necessary to be a member of an association in order to 'practice'; the client's 'free expression' presupposes that the analyst holds a certain social position, and that there is a financial contract, etc.). In short, the institution is a return (mask) of violence within the field of psychoanalysis, but a violence couched in words and repressed on the physical, body-to-body level.[18] Through the workings of the institution – the 'social unconscious of psychoanalysis' (Castel) – history (political, social, economic, even ethnic history) makes a come-back in the insular space of discourse, or of the cure. Thus the successive foundings of psychoanalytic associations over the past sixty years, and their internal disputes and schisms, tell the story of the interactions of the theory with its exteriority – something it often denies. However, it is in these debates that the true beginnings of psychoanalytic history are to be found.

The strategic importance of this site on the border of history and psychoanalysis can be tested for confirmation, if need be. The refusal to accord theoretical validity to institutional problems, the will to keep them outside analysis by treating them as simple 'misfortunes' or as an irrelevant, necessary social evil, in every case leads to the construction of an ideological, doctrinal, or 'mystic' representation of the unconscious. This enables one to postulate the presence in every individual of (unconscious) symbolic, archetypal or imaginary constellations, which the analyst invents like the (for him, conscious) sky above of some universal and immemorial reality. When psychoanalysis 'forgets' its own historicity, that is, its internal relation to conflicts of power and position, it becomes either a mechanism of drives, a dogmatism of discourse, or a gnosis of symbols.

National drifts

We now come to the third factor, the national contexts that bathe the discourse and methods from Vienna in their individual waters. I will discuss three typical cases – leaving aside Nazi Germany, which forced its Jewish analysts into exile. *Reichsführer* Goebbels (the other Goebbels' cousin), who was in charge of national policy on psychiatric therapy, soon gained control over the German Psychoanalytic Association (for a long time – too long – headed by Jung); under Goebbels's tutelage, it went on to elaborate, to take just one example, a typology of dreams according to race.

In the Soviet Union, a Committee of the International Psychoanalytic Association was in contact with Vienna beginning in 1920. In Moscow, Wulff (who was later to move to Jerusalem) argued for the compatibility of Marx and Freud. This position was confirmed in 1923 by Trotsky, who considered Freudianism a variant of Pavlov's 'dialectical materialism', even though 'Pavlov's method is experimentation, and Freud's is conjecture, sometimes farfetched': 'Fundamentally, psychoanalytic method,' he wrote in 1926, 'is based on the fact that the psychological process represents a complex superstructure founded on physiological processes to which it is subordinated.'[19] Luriia developed this point of view. But, beginning in 1930, Soviet criticism made an about-face. Vnukov, in a 1933 article on 'Psychoanalysis' in the Soviet *Medical Encyclopaedia*, attacked psychoanalysis' 'pretentions' of 'having the right to solve problems of vast cultural and historical significance' when it is 'inherent to bourgeois democracy'. Under Stalinism, which by decision of the Communist Party (1936) limited psychology to conscious and practical reason, Freudianism was accused of being ultra-individualist (cf. the article 'Freudianism' in the *Bolshaia Entsiklopediia*, 1935), and was held to be totally false because it could not 'understand psychic processes and needs as the product of social and historical development' (the article 'Psychoanalysis', in the *Bolshaia Entsiklopediia*, 1940, by Luriia, who followed the political tide).[20] The 'pseudo-science' of psychoanalysis, dismissed as 'American' and 'reactionary' (1948), is thus excluded from historiography by Soviet history; only de-Stalinization was to moderate the excommunication.

In the United States, Freud, who (with Jung and Ferenczi) was invited to visit in 1909, felt he was finally seeing psychoanalysis receive the academic consecration that it had been refused in Austria. The 'cause' made rapid progress there. Two psychoanalytic associations were founded in the spring of 1911. Americans such as Kardiner,[21] and even masters like Frink, went to study in Vienna. Aided by the authority of James Jackson Putnam (Harvard), Freudianism set down roots, taking on a new, 'Made in USA' configuration in a country where the experimental positivism of psychiatric neurology existed side by side with the spiritual 'soul healing' of the Emmanuel Movement (organized to combat the 'American nervousness') and the enchanting psychological systems of William James and Bergson.[22] The adoption of Viennese methodology left intact the American confidence in the resourcefulness of the ego, and in society's ability to integrate individuals while guaranteeing their 'self-expression'. This attitude is still evident fifty years later in the work of Norman O. Brown, whose refusal of all repression has the style of a 'revival'.[23]

The privileged position accorded to personal history was not so much a desire to reduce psychoanalysis to individual therapy, as it was a reflection of a certain type of society. Thus, Erik Erikson's subtle biographies present us with the half-political, half-religious, *social* model of the pioneer who, freed from the law of the father, overcomes the tension between rebellion and submission.[24] Psychoanalysis was reflected in the mirrors of a USA mythology; its departures from Freud were due first of all to a restructuring of the psychoanalytic inheritance according to the demands of a particular national experience. The relation of these texts to history cannot be gauged simply by their author's (insufficient) knowledge of the archives, but has to do with the fact that they symbolize an American historicity (even if they were not consciously thought of in those terms). So biography prospered. It has given rise to a series of theoretical examinations,[25] as well as to courses and colloquia.

Gradually, however, the range of investigation extended to include family genealogies and community structures,[26] a result of convergences between the history of kinship systems, an anthropology of the Oedipus complex, and the generalization of the Freudian 'family romance'. This widening of perspective is historically the product of the more anthropologically oriented psychoanalysis of the first associations (in Vienna, Berlin, Frankfort, and Hungary), which was carried into exile in the United States. For example from 1938 on, the extensive investigations of Geza Róheim (whose work began in Hungary near Ferenczi) were completed in the United States; the new direction they were to take for a time, in a departure from the work of the traditional groups, was to confront the Nazi question.

American psychoanalysis was overdetermined in its early stages by the experience of émigrés, particularly Jewish and German, who were fleeing from Nazism. Beginning in 1942, research institutes began to mobilize analysis around the question of popular opinion and the case of Hitler: Erikson, Jahoda, Ackerman, Bettelheim, and others delivered papers on the subject. As Adorno put it: 'the essence of history' was disclosed at Auschwitz.[27] With Reich, Fromm, Adorno, Marcuse (who became interested in Freud only after his arrival in the United States), Horkheimer, etc., all of whom were refugees, similar questions had been under discussion since 1931. For all of them, though admittedly in different modes, to analyze historicity was to analyze the relation between reason and Nazi violence; in particular, in the Marxist context, it was to analyze the failure of the most highly evolved proletariat of Europe – and thus the failure of *revolution* itself – in the face of fascism. Critical reflection looked toward psychoanalysis for aid. Examples are: Reich's 'politico-psychological' analysis, which saw in fascism 'an expression of the irrational character structure of the average man', and, in particular, of religious and/or political forms of the 'need for authority';[28] Fromm's symbolic analysis, which, in its attempt to escape social alienation, took recourse in a kind of pietist anthropology;[29] Marcuse's battle against the technocratic 'over-repression' of the libido in our society, where 'anonymity' makes Freud's 'conflict model' of the struggle between father and son irrelevant, etc.[30] Mourning for a revolution – a tragedy of history – haunted these diagnostics without a therapy. Only Reich (who passed through Marx and Freud and traversed the USA and the USSR, everywhere rejected) chose to attempt an impossible biological mutation of man, and he pursued his dream into insanity.

In France, a triple obstacle closed the door on Freud, especially to the socio-political aspect of his work: the powerful leadership of the Paris School of psychology and psychiatry (Charcot, Clairambault, Janet, Ribot) had nothing to learn from foreigners, since it had already, definitively, outlined the realm of the serious [*le sérieux*] within the individual; a moralizing tradition condemned Freudian 'pansexualism'; linguistic and cultural resistance – nationalist and chauvinist during and after the war – rejected a Germanic influence considered to be too excessive, obscure, and 'Wagnerian'. Moreover, apart from Marie Bonaparte, there was for a long time no disciple of Freud's based in France (Freud himself only spent a few hours in Paris, in 1938); the Psychoanalytic Society of Paris was not founded until 1926. There were no close historical ties between Paris and Vienna. The introduction of psychoanalysis in France was originally the work of men of letters (the first favorable article was written by Albert Thibaudet[31]); André Breton (who was not taken seriously by Freud), Jules Romains, André Gide, Jacques Rivière, Pierre-Jean Jouve, etc., became interested before the psychiatrists did (today the situation is the same in the United States with Lacan). The French scientific establishment became gradually familiar with the Freudian corpus, which finally made it to France (in the form of dispersed and fragmentary translations); but it was removed from its original context (which was long misunderstood). The texts of Freud have been the object of interpretations and disputes, up to (and including) the revolutionary 'return to Freud' undertaken by Jacques Lacan, which precipitated a rupture within the Psychoanalytic Society of Paris and the Paris Institute of Psychoanalysis (Nacht), leading in 1953 to the formation of the French Psychoanalytic Society (Lacan, Lagache), and later the Freudian School of Paris (1964–1980; Lacan). But nothing, or next to nothing, in these traditions was done to explain the strange silence that reigns in France on the subject of the (German) Occupation – those rejected years, that period that is too dangerously close not to be 'forgotten' even by psychoanalysis.

Historiography, which has become intensely professional, was completely under the sway of economic, culturalist methodologies, some of Marxist inspiration. Apart from a few important studies (George Devereux, Alain Besançon)[32] that remained marginal to the discipline, it took the shock of May 1968 for the *ethno-historical* works of Freud – along with Marcuse, Reich, etc. – to be considered relevant and to gain theoretical influence on analyses of psychiatric institutions, law, the 'medical order', history, and the psychoanalytic associations themselves. Filling the vacuum left by the philosophies of consciousness (Sartre, etc.) – and, since 1968, advancing as structuralism receded – psychoanalysis in France, by introducing the question of the subject, has caused fissures to form in all the human sciences, and even in their vulgate. In this all-directional expansionism, the variants can be thought of as falling into two camps, both allied with very old philosophical traditions. One, anthropological in form, is historically the return of a quasi-ontology; its aim is to constitute a domain of knowledge which would link the present ego to symbols which supposedly underlie all human experience. The second, in defining the subject, begins at the point where the institution of language is articulated upon the biological organism; its final form is the one given it by Lacan in his most remarkable (and most historiographical) seminar (1959–1960): an 'Ethics of Psychoanalysis'.

Displacements and perspectives

In 1971, the International Congress of Psychoanalysis was held in Vienna for the first time. A return to origins. Nearly 3,000 analysts gathered at the apartment/museum on Berggassestrasse and filed past the crimson furniture of the lost master, past his couch and his curios. The Western world was assembled there; a Marxist pilgrimage would have gathered the Eastern world together, on that same German soil, the interface of the empires. In Vienna, the silence of the place, analogous to the silence of the Freudian corpus,[33] caused a crowd to speak. But only the ovation given Anna Freud, the daughter of the founder, could drown out the dissonant rumblings, which were simultaneously a testimony to Freud's international success and the dismemberment of his work – as in *Totem and Taboo* – by the horde of its inheritors. Psychoanalysis had become history. It would be a part of it from then on. And its relationship to historiography would be altered by that fact. There are presently, following the displacements that have taken place, three major orientations in psychoanalysis:

A HISTORY OF PSYCHOANALYSIS

The psychoanalysis of the founders treated history as a region to be conquered. Today, history has become the relation of psychoanalysis to itself, of its origin to its subsequent developments, of its theories to its institutions, of transference to filiations, etc. Of course, inscribing personal destinies within a more general genealogy still has some relevance; for example, there is relevance in examining Freud's connections to the Moravian Jewish tradition, which was marked by Sabbateanism,[34] or in recognizing Lacan's links to Surrealism, or to an entire current of Christian thinking which substitutes the *logos* for the lost body. But a psychoanalysis of history must adopt an inward orientation, accepting the necessary work of elucidating the meaning of the gaps in the theory on the following points: a) the relations of transference and the conflictual ones upon which analytic discourse is constructed, b) the functioning of Freudian associations or schools, for example their forms of licensure and the nature of the power inherent in 'holding' the position of analyst, and c) the possibilities of establishing analytic procedures within psychiatric institutions, where psychoanalysis, after emerging from its offices dedicated to a privileged clientele, would come into contact with the administrative alliances of politics and therapy, as well as the popular murmur of madness.

In this respect, the experiences of the La Borde clinic opens a new chapter in psychoanalytic history. It is no longer a question of 'applying' psychoanalysis, but of bringing to light a 'revolutionary subjectivity', of 'grasping the point of *rupture* where political economy and libidinal economy *are finally one and the same*'.[35]

The psychoanalytic interest in biography dates to its very inception: topics of the 'Wednesday meetings' included studies of Lenau, Wedekind, Jean-Paul, K. F. Meyer, Kleist, Leonardo da Vinci. That interest remains central. Biography is the *self-critique* of liberal, bourgeois society, based on the primary unit that society created. The individual – the central epistemological and historical figure of the modern Western world, the foundation of capitalist economy and democratic politics – becomes the stage upon which the certitudes of its creators and beneficiaries (the clientele of cures, or the heroes of historiography) finally come undone. Freud's work, though born of the *Aufklärung*, reverses the act that founded enlightened consciousness – Kant's assertion of the rights and obligations of that consciousness: 'freedom' and full responsibility, autonomous knowledge, and the possibility for a man to progress at a 'steady pace' and escape his 'tutelage'.[36] The response of psychoanalysis to Kant was to send the adult back to its infantile 'tutelage', to send knowledge back to the instinctual mechanisms determining it, freedom back to the law of the unconscious, and progress back to originating events.

Psychoanalytic biography effects a reversal at the place delimited by an ambition, and affirms an erosion of its own postulates. Working from within, it dismantles – like the mysticism of the sixteenth and seventeenth centuries in the context of a *received* religious tradition – the historical and social figure that is the standard unit of the system within which Freudianism developed. Even if social pressures can lead it to encomiums in defense of the individual, psychoanalytic biography is in principle a form of self-critique, and its narrativity is an anti-mythic force, like *Don Quixote* in the Spain of the *hidalgos*. It remains to be seen what new and different form (which will no longer have to be 'biographical') this machinery heralds, or is now preparing for us.

A HISTORY OF NATURE

In taking the individual back to the something other (or unconscious) which determines it without its knowledge, psychoanalysis returned to the symbolic configurations articulated by social practices in traditional civilizations. The dream, fable, myth – these discourses, excluded by enlightened reason, became the site where the critique of bourgeois and technological society developed. Admittedly, the theologians of Freudianism rushed to transform these languages into positivities. But that is not the point. Freudian critique, since it takes the myths and rites repressed by reason and analyzes them as symbolic formations, may now *seem* like an anthropology. But, in fact, it initiated something that could be called a new history of 'nature' which introduced into historicity:

a)   The persistence and lingering action of the *irrational*, the violence at work inside scientificity and theory itself.
b)   A dynamics of *nature* (drives, affects, the libido) conjoined with language – in opposition to the ideologies of history which privilege the relations among people and reduce nature to a passive terrain permanently open to social or scientific conquest.
c)   The relevance of *pleasure* (orgasmic, festive, etc.), which was repressed by the incredibly ascetic ethic of progress; the subversive influence of the pleasure principle has infiltrated our cultural system.

These issues, sown in the field of historiography, are already bearing fruit; they are not necessarily the signs of a psychoanalytic affiliation, but they do signal a Freudian debt and Freudian tasks.

NOTES

1.   *Il re-mord.* A play on words meaning literally, 'it bites again', but also suggesting 'il *remort*' ('it re-deads', repeats death or brings back the dead) and 'le *remords*' ('remorse'). – Tr.

2.   Sigmund Freud, 'On the History of the Psychoanalytic Movement', *Standard Edition*, tr. James Strachey (London: Hogarth, 1953–1974), Vol. 14, p. 37.

3.   'Fragment of an Analysis of a Case of Hysteria' (the case of 'Dora', 1905), *SE*, Vol. 7; 'Analysis of a Phobia in a Five-Year-Old Boy' (the case of 'Little Hans', 1909), 'Notes upon a Case of Obsessional Neurosis' (the 'Rat Man', 1909), *SE*, Vol. 10; 'Case History of Schreber' (1911), *SE*, Vol. 12; 'An Infantile Neurosis', (the 'Wolf Man', 1918), *SE*, Vol. 17.

4.   Freud, *Moses and Monotheism*, *SE*, Vol. 23.

5.   *Moses*, *SE*, Vol. 23, p. 130 (*Gesammelte Werke*, Vol. 16, p. 239 [see note 33, below]).

6.   'Group Psychology and the Analysis of the Ego', *SE*, Vol. 18, p. 69.

7.   *Delusions and Dreams in Jensen's 'Gradiva'*, *SE*, Vol. 9.

8.   'The Antithetical Meaning of Primal Words', *SE*, Vol. 2, pp. 158–62; *Leonardo da Vinci and Memory of Childhood*, *SE*, Vol. 2.

9.   *Totem and Taboo*, *SE*, Vol. 13, p. xiii.

10.   Ibid., p. 126.

11.   Quoted in Roland Barthes, *Michelet* (Paris: Seuil, 1965), p. 92.

12.   Theodor Reik, *Ritual. Psychoanalytic Studies* (New York: Farrar, Strauss, 1946), pp. 10–12, 15.

13.   'On the History', p. 37.

14.   *Papers 1906–1908*, *SE*, Vol. 9.

15.   *Thomas Woodrow Wilson: Twenty-Eighth President of the United States* (Boston: Houghton Mifflin, 1961).

16.   'On the History', pp. 44 and 37.

17.   This gives the *correspondence* between analysts a special importance. It constitutes a transversal narrativity in relation to the modes of scientific discourse.

18.   It has been rightly said that a psychoanalyst is a doctor who is afraid of blood.

19.   Leon Trotsky, *Littérature et révolution* (Paris: 1962), pp. 279–83.

20. Cf. V. Schmidt, *Education psychanalytique en Russie* (1924); M. Wulff, 'Die Stellung der Psychoanalyse in der Sowjet Union', *Psychoanalytische Bewungung* (1930); Joseph Wortis, *Soviet Psychiatry* (Baltimore: Williams and Wilkins, 1950).

21. Cf. Abram Kardiner, *My Analysis with Freud* (New York: Norton, 1977).

22. Nathan G. Hale, Jr., *Freud and the Americans* (Oxford: Oxford University Press, 1971) and *James Jackson Putnam and Psychoanalysis* (Cambridge, Mass.: Harvard University Press, 1971).

23. Norman O. Brown, *Love's Body* (New York: Random House, 1966).

24. Erik Erikson, *Young Man Luther* (New York: Norton, 1958) and *Gandhi's Truth* (New York: Norton, 1969).

25. John A. Garraty, *The Nature of Biography* (New York: Knopf, 1957); Philip Reiff, *Freud, The Mind of a Moralist* (New York: Viking, 1959); C. Strout, 'Ego Psychology and the Historian', in *History and Theory*, Vol. 7 (1969), pp. 281–96, etc.

26. Cf. Lloyd Demause, *The History of Childhood* (New York: Psycho-History Press, 1974); John Demos, *A Little Commonwealth: Family Life in Plymouth Colony* (Oxford: Oxford University Press, 1970).

27. Günter Rohrmoser, *Das Elend der Kristischen Theorie* (Freiburg: Rombach, 1970), p. 20.

28. Wilhelm Reich, *The Mass Psychology of Fascism*, tr. Vincent Carfagno (New York: Farrar, Strauss, 1970).

29. Erich Fromm, *Escape from Freedom* (New York: Farrar and Rinehart, 1941).

30. Herbert Marcuse, *Eros and Civilization* (Boston: Beacon Press, 1966) and 'The Obsolescence of the Freudian Conception of Man' in *Five Lectures* (Boston: Beacon, 1970). Cf. Carl and Sylva Grossman, *The Wild Analysts* (New York: Braziller, 1965) and Paul Robinson, *The Freudian Left* (New York: Harper, 1969).

31. Albert Thibaudet, 'Psychanalyse et critique', *Nouvelle Revue française* (April 1921); he notes the 'curiously nationalist character' of psychology in France (p. 467).

32. George Devereux, *From Anxiety to Method in the Behavioral Sciences* (New York: Humanities Press, 1967); Alain Besaçon, *Le Tsarévitch immolé* (Paris: Plon, 1967).

33. Freud, *Gesammelte Werke* (London: Imago, 1940–1952); *Standard Edition*.

34. There was a Sabbatean saying that 'the law is fulfilled by transgression'.

35. Gilles Deleuze, in his preface to Félix Guattari, *Psychanalyse et Transversalité* (Paris: Maspero, 1974). See also *Recherches*, no. 21 (1976), 'Histoires de la Borde'.

36. Immanuel Kant, 'What Is Enlightenment?, *On History: Immanuel Kant*, ed. Lewis Beck (New York: Library of Liberal Arts, 1963), pp. 3–11.

3.

Rome, the Archetypal Museum, and the Louvre, the Negation of Division

Jean-Louis Déotte

Introduction

Some of the texts written by the architectural historian Antoine Quatremère de Quincy prior to his 'Dissertation' of 1806 (published in 1815 under the title *Les Considérations morales sur la destination des ouvrages de l'art*), contain a critique of museums which, in many respects, invalidates the whole of the traditionally accepted argument of the *Considérations*. In 1787, Quatremère expressed his views on patrimony in the 42nd issue of the *Journal de Paris* with particular reference to the restoration of the Fontaine des Innocents. The argument of the *Considérations* outlined in reports made to the Conseil Général de la Seine on 15 Thermidor in the year VIII (3 August 1800), and to the same Conseil Général on 29 Germinal in the year IX (19 April 1801), forms the basis of a critique of museums as responsible for the death of 'living' art.

The *Lettres à Miranda sur les déplacements des Monuments de l'art de l'Italie* of 1796 (letters discussing the damage that would be done to the arts and sciences by the displacement of artistic monuments from Italy, the dismemberment of its art schools and the spoliation of its art collections, galleries and museums) are particularly worthy of analysis.[1]

Quatremère's idea of Rome as artistic repository

As Napoleon I was carrying out his project for the repatriation of works of art (a project comprehensively defended in an essay by François de Neufchâteau), Quatremère, heir in this respect to the pre-Revolutionary European Republic of arts and sciences, revived the memory of a Europe which would disappear with the age of the nation state. The Europe he described was a community of direct cultural exchanges, an 'electric' Europe: in short, a patrimonial Europe whose capital was Rome.

Against this background of cosmopolitanism, the politics of the French Revolution appeared little more than barbaric, worthy of so many Caesars and Alexanders who, while destroying the nations they conquered, also abolished political freedom. Miranda and Quatremère, both men of the Enlightenment, made early predictions that Bonaparte's 'liberation' enterprise would tend towards imperialism. It is Enlightenment that suffers when national treasures are expropriated. Indeed, is there not a real, if somewhat ambiguous, alliance between works of art and liberty?

As Quatremère's first letter puts it:

The spread of the Enlightenment did Europe the great service of ensuring that no nation would ever be subjected to the humiliation of being described as 'barbaric' by one of its neighbours. There is a noticeable community of learning and knowledge, a concordance of taste, scholarship and industry, among the countries of Europe. In fact, it is true to say that the differences between these countries are often less pronounced than between the provinces of a single empire. And this is because, as a result of a propitious and timely revolution, the arts and sciences belong to the whole of Europe and are not the exclusive property of a single nation. All the thoughts and efforts of right-thinking politics and philosophy should be directed towards maintaining, promoting and developing this community [...] Those who attempt to appropriate a sort of exclusive right and privilege to education and the means to education will soon be punished for this violation of common property by barbarity and ignorance. And there is something actively contagious about ignorance. The nations of Europe are in such close contact with each other that anything that affects one of them cannot but have immediate repercussions for the others.

The seventh letter gives a clearer idea of this reciprocal effect:

Here there is a reciprocal effect. The 'electric' chain which today unites the world of scholarship can only receive and transmit simultaneous impressions. Today, Europe is being carried towards a culture of the arts by a single movement, an impetus which is a direct result of the central power emanating from Italy and Rome. If this power is reduced, then its effect will be diminished.

The European 'republic of letters', which was nothing more than a particular system of communication, presupposed a medium, an 'electric' medium which would be endangered by various national revolutions. Rome, whose works of art the French Revolution intended to liberate, was already an actual historical continuation, i.e. of the Papal cultural policy which consisted of the continuous *reproduction* of Antiquity, Pope Nicholas V having had the idea of 're-establishing the architecture of ancient Rome'. The task, whose vast scope was truly remarkable, still continues today: 'It is as if an ancient world were being discovered and conquered each day.'

But revolutionary actions could only discourage such an undertaking. It would take the whole of Europe to realize the wild dream of Nicholas V. As the second letter puts it:

What will the people of Rome do if these works of art are plundered? Will they continue this task of reproduction? The shamefully venal profit that the city that appropriated them would hope to gain would be profit lost to the arts since, far from benefiting them, it would in fact become the destroyer of this wonderful work of reproduction.

For Quatremère, this implies the promise of a new form of art, a new method which consists of imitating nature, an art born of the spectacle of the reproduction of an entire nation of statues:

Of all the causes that can revolutionise or revitalise the arts, the most powerful and the most capable of producing an entirely new order of impressions is this general resurrection of a nation of statues, of this antique world whose population increases daily. This world, which Leonardo da Vinci, Michelangelo and Raphaël did not live to see, or of which they saw only the very beginnings, should exert great influence on the study of art and the artistic spirit of Europe. (Letter II)

A revolution in the arts caused by the *archaeological* – and therefore the patrimonial – *reproduction* of Antiquity ... One cannot help thinking of the young Brunelleschi, travelling from Florence to Rome, excavating, restoring ruins, measuring, drawing, describing, learning the art of ancient materials, and probably considering the possibility of covering a vast building with a cupola.

But it is not merely art – a new form of art – that is at stake. It is also the human intellect, the history of the human intellect, a history that could not be written without opening the pages of this vast book that is Rome

whose pages have been destroyed or dispersed by time, and in which the spaces and gaps are filled daily by modern research. The power that selected a few of the most interesting monuments with a view to exporting and appropriating them, would be like the illiterate who tears the illustrated pages from a book. (Letter III)

The city of Rome is like a vast, buried library whose 'texts', once excavated and pieced together, will disclose the wealth contained in all these 'repositories of knowledge and instruments of learning, just as it is contained in the repositories' of books, works of art, machines and natural history. Only such centralized 'collections' make it possible to write the complete

history of the human intellect and its discoveries, its errors and its prejudices, the sources of all human knowledge; the discovery of ancient customs, religious beliefs, laws and social institutions; the artistic monuments of Antiquity are an even greater source of inspiration as to the methods of recording history, verifying and interpreting it, resolving its inconsistencies, completing its omissions and throwing light on its obscurities, than they are to the imitative arts. (Letter III)

The history of the human intellect cannot but be monumental, in every sense of the word. And here we see a Quatremère who is not in the least hostile towards museums, to these repositories of information, provided that the collection is as vast as possible. A single museum, a single library – Alexandria for example – would suffice to contain the entire range of knowledge apprehended by the human intellect.

The effects of dispersing the ancient monuments of Rome would therefore be the same as for any source of knowledge whose elements and materials were dispersed and which would be destroyed as a result. So, if we consider the problem from the point of view of the educational value and not the destination of these works of art, then the works as repositories of knowledge are better kept together, like the books in a vast library. The location of the repository itself is of little importance. What is important is that information can be diffused via this repository, information that has been gathered by specialist, 'secondary' agencies.

The development of a synthesis of knowledge, i.e. of the entire history of the human intellect (and here the model of excellence is Winckelmann), does not presuppose any degree of proximity between the scholar and the knowledge. In fact, a certain distance is essential:

The man of genius, wherever and at whatever distance he may be from both the observers and the objects observed, is the point at which they coincide […]

In this way, Pliny and Buffon – without leaving Rome or Paris – were able to embrace the world and see it through the eyes of all travellers when they themselves had only seen a very small part of it. Thus the true synthesis of the knowledge of Antiquity may be achieved by nations who have never possessed, and individuals who have never seen, ancient works of art (Letter III).

In this respect, there is little need to point out that, a century later, ethnology in France (in the works of Mauss in particular) had virtually ceased to be a 'field' science.

The advantage of bringing art treasures together in one repository is that it makes it easier to compare objects and develop parallels: in other words, to develop a chronology. For Quatremère, the judgement of artistic taste was, necessarily, a sequential and informed judgement which presupposed the continuity of the works of a particular artist or school. Aesthetic judgement was not made on an individual work, an isolated example, a solitary masterpiece, but on a complete series. It was based on a comparison of works of varying degrees of quality and, therefore, on the principle of continuity:

The recognition of beauty, so vital to artists, is the result of a sort of sliding scale of comparison which classifies works of art, establishes a system of ranking and a sort of order of merit. These rankings are as numerous as the subtleties and distinctions of the human intellect.

The number of works ascribed to each 'rank' is inversely proportional to its degree of merit. But the more numerous the subsidiary points of comparison, the more apparent and irrefutable the pre-eminence of the minority, and the more striking and instructive their beauty (Letter IV).

We must turn to the Leibnitzian theories of rudimentary perceptions and continuity to legitimize the pyramidal hierarchy of works of art as represented by Rome, the great testing ground of continuity: *Rome the ultimate series of all series*.

Modern – Kantian – aesthetic judgement, as a judgement of an individual work of art and therefore a sequel to the discourse on the presence and consequently the 'aura' of a work of art, is merely the result of a process of dissociation, destructive discontinuity and isolation. Such a result is brought about by the institution of museums which, built on the ruins of the great universal Museum of Rome, can only hope to house fragments of this Museum. Aesthetic judgement and art criticism can therefore only be applied to fragments, and the art invented by museums will be a – modern – art of fragments, as shown by the German Romantics at the same time as Quatremère.

Quatremère, because he fostered the myth of the Museum, still numbers among those who realized that aesthetic judgement in the pre-museum age – because it was concerned with the pyramidal hierarchy of works of art – involved making an infinite number of comparisons: 'Thus the small number of truly beautiful antique statues owes its claim to the beauty we find so striking to the infinite number of statues of a similar style, but not of similar merit, amongst which they stand out'. (Letter IV). This being the case, the admiration of beautiful works of art will – because they are admired in isolation – inevitably be accompanied by a sense of weakening, subsidence and collapse due to the absence of context.

I can confirm that I personally experience this sensation every time I have the opportunity of seeing one of these beautiful antique figures, detached and separated from its family. And yet I am able to say that I have, impressed upon my mind's eye, virtually all the antique figures in Europe, and so carry my points of comparison with me, an advantage which is not shared by the majority of the ordinary viewing public. (Letter IV)

This is an important extract if we take into account that all the European works of art impressed upon his mind's eye must necessarily be *engraved* since, at the time, engravings were the only way of reuniting these fragments and creating a series of images, of which we must assume he was *technically informed*.

And if imagery – like memory and, indeed, knowledge – is always technically informed, then other eras with other reproductive techniques will give rise to other forms of imagery. The difference between the art historian and the ordinary viewing public depends on their ability – or inability – to inform their imagination, avoid the aesthetic contemplation of a work of art in isolation and develop – and (or not) refer to – a background context of *points of comparison*. Judgement for the art historian is therefore a strictly informed judgement, based on the establishment of series.

Quatremère gives some indication of what these points of comparison and series can be. An artist's school or the totality of an artist's work can create a series. This is why it is crucial that the whole of an artist's work is gathered in one place where it can be studied in its entirety. The need is even more pressing for an artist such as Raphaël whose works are widely dispersed and often not on display. Here again, the pyramidal hierarchy must be re-created. This pyramid is a mirror, a prism, a natural system in which nature is automatically analysed. Here we encounter Leibnitz again. Nature (i.e. natural variety) is, as it were, reflected in the many different schools, each school representing a *characteristic*, a reflective system:

Each Italian school [has] its own characteristics. In fact, they can be compared to so many different mirrors, in which nature is reflected in all its various aspects and becomes fixed, as it were, by the imitative and artistic processes. Nature is as varied as the ways of perceiving it are numerous. However, these infinitely varied shades of perception can be reduced to a few main differences or characteristics. And thus the most basic forms of imitation have been, as it were, analysed by the various Italian schools, which have become a sort of pictorial prism, in which students see nature broken down and reduced to a system. (Letter vi)

It is this group of characteristics that forms the substance of museum collections and it is therefore, in the final analysis, natural variety that is impoverished.

The theme of variety in art is, as we all know, a commonplace which was revived, in particular, by Alberti's treatise *Della Pittura*, as a result of which it became an aesthetic standard. But then surely Leibnitz' *Monadologia* could be considered, among other things, as a treatise on art. The treatise of an age – in the strongest sense – of perspective. A school of art could be seen as an extremely complex monad. The true basis of art lies in a certain number of characteristics. And what would Rome have been as a monad: the Museum?

The 'Museum' of Rome in relation to the 'Age of Museums'

If we remain within the sphere of knowledge and therefore, to some extent, of the judgement of beauty and of creation, Quatremère is not radically opposed to museums in so far as they are centralized diffusers of knowledge. This is obviously because the question of the moral (social, but basically *ontological*) destination of the works of art is not raised. The works that he describes no longer have a destination. While being the worst of institutions in that it suspends the destination of works of art, the Museum is at the same time indispensable because it provides the aesthetic – critical in the sense of the Romantics – discourse with a location. And this location is the Museum.

Although Quatremère was a relentless critic of the museums established by the French Revolution, as well as of older collections, when he writes as an art historian and connoisseur he cannot ignore the fact that there has always been a Museum, and that without it there would be no works of art. In his writings on aesthetics, even and especially in his condemnation of the Museum, he always reverts, in spite of himself, to its state of 'potentiality'.

For Quatremère (and herein lies the potential of art and criticism), the age of the Museum was preceded by the universal Museum of Rome. Rome was in fact the archetypal Museum. For Rome, the ultimate series of all series of works of art, was in fact constituted from the spoliation of Greece and Egypt. The works of art that formed the papal collections were as likely to have been confiscated – particularly from ancient royal Italian courts such as Ferrara – as commissioned. In this way, Rome represented a complete voyage which replaced all other voyages:

For a truly enquiring mind, the city of Rome is an entire world to be explored, a sort of three-dimensional mappamundi, which offers a condensed view of Egypt, Asia, Greece and the Roman Empire, the ancient and modern world. To have visited Rome is to have made many voyages in one. Consequently, to disperse the works of art collected together in Rome would be to deprive scholars of both their instruments of learning and the object of their research. (Letter VI)

Factually speaking, just as Rome was the prototype, so the pagan religion provided the aesthetic principle of the Museum. This being so, we consider it important to reinstate a 'white' image – in the sense that Maurice Blanchot uses *la parole blanche* in his *Entretien infini* – of the universal Museum of Rome, an image which already has all the characteristics of the 'black' image of the Revolutionary museum as represented by the Louvre. Quatremère could not avoid discovering this 'original' image of what he was denouncing because this image was, and still is, the precondition of his aesthetic writings.

We are therefore saying that the Museum of Rome already had all the characteristics of the centralized repository of all works of art, of the Louvre for example. With the exception that Rome was also – indivisibly – an historical site, with a particular quality of light, a particular type of sky, and a particular atmosphere. It was a combination of natural and historical elements which, by their very nature, could not be displaced.

But surely the same could be said of any great museum which has become, as it were, the natural site for the works of art it contains, because it has become their setting, their light, in short their permanent resting place. One has only to think of Michelet's despair in the Louvre when the Allies of 1815 repatriated the plundered works of art. Could the *Victory of Samothrace* be moved from the Louvre today? On the contrary, should we not consider that its very landscape, its light, geography and history have become an intrinsic part of the Museum?

By inverting the following text by Quatremère, it becomes clear that everything, from this point on, should be evaluated in relation to the Museum:

The true Museum of Rome, the museum of which I am speaking, consists, it is true, of statues, colossi, temples, obelisks, triumphal columns, baths, arenas, amphitheatres, triumphal arches, tombs, stucco, frescoes, low reliefs, inscriptions, fragments of decorations, building materials, furniture and utensils. But it also consists of places, historical sites, mountains, quarries, ancient roads, the respective sites of ruined cities, relative geographical features, inter-relationships between objects, memories of past local traditions, existing customs, parallels and comparisons that can only be drawn and made in the country itself. (Letter III)

This makes it clear that, from the point at which he introduced the concept of patrimony, everything that Quatremère considered indissociable, indivisible, untransportable – i.e. which constituted the 'natural' site of the vast numbers of antique works of art – either suffered or would suffer the fate of everything for which he fought during his lifetime. His description of the site could have been even more subtle, stressing the importance of a country's language, symbolic systems of proper nouns, and so on.

It was like a collection of items destined to be recorded and preserved for us to enjoy today. Thus it was the Museum which invented the concept of natural patrimony, the need to preserve nature in so far as it was linked to an historic site. All those elements which, according to classical aesthetics, were classified as the conditions under which the works of art were created, today suffer the same fate as those same works of art. Artists, like all those involved in art, and even philosophers, must be preserved in the name of an irreplaceable patrimony. But wasn't this, according to Strabo, the function of the first museum, the Museum of Alexandria, i.e. to enable philosophers to meet and discuss their ideas in a pleasant setting, surrounded by statues?

Quatremère even goes as far as to justify a policy of international patrimonial interventionism, the right to intervene to prevent works of art being neglected:

The great wealth of the arts and sciences is protected by the fact that it belongs to the entire world. As long as it remains public property and is well maintained, it is of little importance which country acts as its custodian. [The country] is merely the curator of my Museum. But it would certainly deserve to be deprived of [its function] if it concealed or abused [this wealth] or allowed it to fall into disrepair. Otherwise, it would have to be paid to take care of it. (Letter v)

The Museum cannot therefore be dissociated from the test of division in the sense that it is used by Machiavelli, whether it is internal – i.e. social and political – division or the division – or rather the difference – of historical time. Both the detractors (Quatremère) and defenders (François de Neufchâteau) of the Museum compare the Louvre with Rome. Quatremère saw the Louvre as contributing to the destruction of an enlightened Europe centred around Rome: a Rome which was at once the great monad, the ultimate collection, the hotbed of (aesthetic) knowledge and the heart of an international society whose links were forged by cultural exchanges. He considered Rome to be a good and sound society because it was the centre of a sound European cultural policy. The Louvre, on the other hand, contributed to the destruction of the concept of 'otherness' and the difference of historical time, without which modernity would cease to exist since the vital point of reference – i.e. Antiquity – had disappeared because it had been plundered. The Louvre therefore introduced a barbaric temporality, which marked the end of imitative art.

But, according to Quatremère's argument, Rome could not be this treasure house and this centre because this was already the age of the Museum. Rome was merely a copy of the Louvre, projected into the past. Rome was the after-event of the establishment of the Louvre. The temporality of the Museum is essentially retroactive; it is a temporality that moves backwards from the point of its establishment. Thus the continual unearthing of statues during excavations is an act of destruction which is an exact parallel of the destruction of European cultures carried out by the Louvre.

The opposite is true for the Directeur, François de Neufchâteau, who saw Rome – i.e. the papal collections – as the paradigm of alienated art. For him, the Louvre stands in direct contrast to Rome as the liberator of universal art, a place where one can comprehend that each ancient work of art is a concealed allegory of liberty. For every work of art, from the very beginning of artistic creation, has been essentially divided.

But this division, and therefore the very essence of art, could only be seen in Paris by the nation which had the privilege of signing the Declaration of Human Rights. The Museum was therefore the precondition of a good and sound society. By inventing art and writing its history, the Museum negated the difference in historical time, since artists have always worked in the same present, and by reconciling beauty and virtue, it necessarily became a veritable temple of negation, the negation of present, internal division.

The Louvre: the negation of division

The leading museums of Great Britain, the British Museum for example, amassed private collections – at least in the early stages of their history – with scant regard for coherence of presentation or critical discourse. Their French counterparts, on the other hand, were inspired by a political or, more precisely, a politico-metaphysical discourse. They were organized in much the same way as the festivals used by the French Revolution to perpetuate its own image.[2] This was the politics of aesthetics and not, as in Germany, an 'aestheticization' of politics.

This political programme was clearly explained in a speech given by François de Neufchâteau, the then Minister for the Interior, during the Festival of Thermidor, held in the year VI to celebrate the return of works of art seized from churches, palaces, Italian collections and, in particular, from the papal collections in Rome. The term *return* is used advisedly, as will become clear.

In his speech, François de Neufchâteau addressed those 'generous and sensitive men, from every clime, [who were] blessed by heaven and tormented by the love of beauty'. These artists and art lovers from other countries and the French provinces were shown around the museums:

> Today, these masterpieces are here for you to admire, steeped in the morality of a free nation. Amidst this cornucopia of good taste which you see before you, and surrounded by these unique treasures, the French nation – which upholds the law of nature and the sacred right of equality – will necessarily be the guardian of your virtues. While its museums enrich your mind, its laws and examples will enrich your soul. It will make you more worthy to practise the arts, because it will have shown you the greatest art of all, the art of betterment. Fine art, in the hands of a free nation, is the main instrument of social happiness and a useful subsidiary of the philosophy which ensures the well-being of the human race.[3]

Fine art and therefore the museums which housed it had a very precise destination, an ethical and political – i.e. a civic – destination. The actual discourse, by combining various types of discourse and their different types of statement (aesthetic, political, ethical and philosophical) and bringing them together under the primacy of the politico-ethical statement, gave this destination a new form, known as modern politics, as defined by the French Revolution. The present article is not so much concerned with analysing this destination as with understanding the implications for art of this politics of the Museum. For museums were indeed the subject of a political theory, of which there does not necessarily appear to be any evidence outside France. This raises the issue of the 'redestination' of the Museum, an institution which, according to Quatremère, in fact suspended destination.

The Museum of the French Revolution *liberated* art. From the time of the Belgian campaign, the Revolutionary armies did not limit themselves to bringing back occasional works of art plundered here and there. On the contrary, there was a positive policy of *liberation* and *annexation* of works of art. Although the two terms are undoubtedly contradictory, they exactly characterize the ambiguity of the Revolution's foreign policy, an ambiguity which lies at the very heart of the Declaration of Human Rights. It is a well-known fact that the Declaration was intended to be universally applied, and yet it was legitimized by a sovereign nation, the French nation. It was an *individual* – nominally identified – political community which answered for the *universal*. From that point on, the Revolutionary wars could only be wars of liberation *and* annexation. Works of art would be liberated but could only be placed on public display in Paris.

The 'liberation' of works of art was not (simply) a matter of their spoliation, as was the opinion of Miranda, Quatremère, Burke, the authors of the

Athenaeum and the artists who objected to their displacement. Prior to the French Revolution, works of art in royal collections and monasteries were not (or rarely) seen by members of the public. The Revolution made it possible for them to be seen without the personal beliefs and values of art lovers being adversely affected:

Royal arrogance can no longer keep you from the object of your studies. You will no longer have to seek the ostentation of royal courts, or endure the aspect of superstition and cloistered ignorance to enjoy the all-too-brief contemplation of the works of art you have travelled so far to see, returning to your countries, possibly a little better informed but certainly more corrupt.[4]

As a product of liberty and equality, French museums were necessarily virtuous and edifying. They were the first institutions to place art on public display. But they primarily housed an art which had developed in the shadow of despotism and superstition. This would appear to be self-evident, but did such an art actually exist? Was there in fact something which resembled authentic art in these places which, as yet, still had a destination?

Towards an aesthetic of art

Was it possible for an authentic art form to develop when commissions were either royal or religious (as were the subjects and the places and people for whom they were destined)? Surely these works of art were *adapted to* and therefore inherently marked by their destination. What was there in these works that was something more than a symbol of religion or despotism? What was there in a religious subject – the painting of an altar for example – that could escape the religious destination and, as it were, demand or express the desire or the vocation to be something more, thereby surviving the collapse of the Ancient World or the world of Christian destination?

The answer is probably *art*. But as yet this is only a name, the name of what remains when the strictly defined element of the work – i.e. the destination – has collapsed and become hated and despised. There is something that survives and calls out, even though the destination of the work either no longer exists or, if it does, has become unacceptable. There is a demand which comes from a long way off, from unknown ages and other lands. And this demand is inextricably bound up with the determination to survive. But is it merely a question of preserving the surviving traces of lost cultures, evidence of past civilizations, historical sites, the deeds of great warriors or politicians, of reinstating or emphasizing a particular meaning? These are the words used to conceal the strangeness of this recurring element, which is transmitted from one collection to another, from one museum to another, from one owner to another. These men and these institutions are merely agents of transmission and the true mystery lies in the need for objects to transmit (the minimal destination) and to serve as obscure staging posts.

Here we encounter a temporality – the temporality of collected objects, works of art – which is not the temporality of religious works which, although the same, are caught up in the stranglehold of a particular age and which, because of this, have to make their mark, to make a statement and have a specific destination. This is the temporality of suspense, of incompletion, of return, the temporality of a continuity which extends across the ages, a cyclic temporality which was excellently described by W. Benjamin and which is analysed in *Le Musée, l'origine de l'esthétique* (1993).

Today, we subscribe to the idea of preserving the patrimony and historical sites which for the Revolutionaries constituted the source of a repressed liberty which had to be allowed to emerge. But the objects themselves had nothing to do with it: they were incidental.

It was therefore necessary to assume that these objects were merely caught up in a system for making historical statements. François de Neufchâteau refers to this distance from the commission's intended destination as an 'awareness of the future' on the part of the creators of the past. This means understanding that there can exist, in the most modest of religious objects, in the created work, something that is absent and yet somehow deeply engrained:

Let it not be thought that the arts wanted to make tyranny agreeable or to embellish the dreams of human credulity. These great men were not labouring for kings and pontiffs, for mistaken beliefs and false doctrines. It could be said that genius is the gold of divinity because it is unsullied by impurity. These great men, thrown into centuries of servitude, gave in to the need to create. They created not so much for their age as in response to an instinct for glory and, if one can so describe it, an awareness of the future.

But this division within the work itself, this *something* in the work that escapes destination as it does utility and function, is nothing other, according to the ultimately reductive interpretation of our ideological Directeur, than a *meaning* seeking – i.e. *waiting* – to be expressed. In this spiritualization of the *quod*, anything that relieves this state of waiting is welcome. The spirit or deeper meaning can always take over from (i.e. relieve) the letter or more literal interpretation, as the Old Testament prepares for and heralds the New. A new form of destination – in this case Revolutionary destination – can always invest this *something*, abandoned by an earlier destination, with new meaning. Thus we can see that it is possible to redefine everything that is in a state of suspense, that the neutrality of the Museum cannot escape the return of metaphysics, that aesthetic judgement in the Kantian sense always risks being subjected to rational Thought as though it were demonstrable, that a subject which emerges as part of a statement of fact can always be reassessed from an empirical and historical point of view.

Theories can always be revised and redefined. But a new destination can only be introduced if we remember that it was to some extent already present throughout the world and has contributed to its sense of direction and meaning. A destination is always introduced after the event: and it is because it already existed that its return can be justified. For example, the works of art of Greece and the Renaissance were already free.

When it does return, it is therefore perfectly legitimate for it to lay claim – if necessary by (Revolutionary) force – to what has (always) introduced it, and – from beyond the time during which it was (temporarily) lost – to re-establish links with itself in the present. And it is in this sense that the liberation of the past, as carried out by the French Revolution, and indeed by every revolution, is also a process of annexation.

In this way, it was possible to interpret historical works both as works of art and as this *something* which could only be truly expressed in a free country – that of the Great Nation – because its very essence was freedom.

This structure of temporality, which is the temporality of the Museum as well as of the history of art and aesthetic criticism, is the temporality of constantly repeated – and extended – creation. In other words, it is the temporality of art. But it is a temporality which necessarily fails in what it creates, since it continually rediscovers what it has contributed. Today, the task of aesthetic criticism consists of identifying the ways in which destination envelops this *something*, which always remains in suspense.

The museums of the French Revolution saw nothing in historical works of art other than images of an alienated liberty crying out to be reinstated. From there, it follows that the seizure of works of art in Italy, Belgium, Holland and subsequently in Spain were not acts of plunder but the fulfilment of a desire expressed by the works themselves. Such a programme could be classified as ideological, but this would be to disregard the temporal structure of all forms of destination, against the ambiguous and paradoxical nature – that intrinsic division – of the work itself, and against the continued belief that art has not been erroneously interpreted as an image of liberty.

To quote François de Neufchâteau:

They [great men, great artists] undoubtedly foresaw the destinies of nations and, through this legacy of sublime paintings, bequeathed to the spirit of liberty the task of granting them their rightful share of glory and the honour of awarding them the acclaim they felt they deserved. Thus, the French nation was not content with enlightening its contemporaries with the flame of reason. It became the avenger of the arts, freeing them from the humiliation they had endured for so long by releasing so many dead artists from the obscurity in which they languished and simultaneously crowning artists from thirty centuries. It is because of the French nation that they have today taken their rightful place in the temple of memory. If it is indeed true that certain perceptions survive beyond the grave, it is reassuring to think that this solemn circumstance has an audience of invisible onlookers, all those grand masters of fine art born of Greece, Egypt and the two Romes. It would seem that past centuries have gathered down the ages to celebrate this wonderful event and to give thanks to this Great Nation for having snatched the superb images honoured by these great artists from the decay in which religious prejudice and monastic ignorance has kept them buried for so long. Famous spirits whose divine genius and admirable works are brought together within these confines! If you are listening, as I believe you are, answer this feeble voice and tell me: as you experienced the torment of glory, did you foresee the century of liberty? Yes, it was for France that you produced these works of art. At last, they have fulfilled their destination. So rejoice, illustrious spirits! You are now enjoying the glory that is rightfully yours. You can see the competition inspired by your works of art, to offer a place of refuge to your spirits and give sanctuary to your works, and to ensure, for the first time, the true immortality of fine art.[5]

Conclusion

The occasion of the Festival of the Return, after the 9 Thermidor (27 July 1798), was obviously seen as marking the end of Jacobin tyranny and the reconciliation of the French nation *vis-à-vis* itself and the power of the Directoire. The suspension of the difference in historical time, embodied by the presentation of works of widely diverse origins, reinforced the suspension of internal political divisions. The destination was still one of a totality which it saw as its ultimate aim and in relation to which it saw itself as *devoir-être*, i.e. as having an obligation to exist. The Museum was therefore a vital instrument in achieving this reconciliatory totality which transcends division. It was a question of constructing a political community using materials which consisted of repatriated works of art and the works which would certainly arise from their unification.

From this point, obscurantism, the despotism of the Ancien Régime and vandalism were driven back upon themselves, like the protagonists in a conflict which formed the very basis of their complicity. It is obvious that the Festival, and therefore the Museum that it commemorated within the same time scale, cannot be regarded as historic landmarks to the memory of a liberated past. This memory, which is created from the suspension of historical time and therefore from the suspension of ages, of the intrinsic destinations of the works of art, and from the suspension of internal conflict within the nation, is in fact based on an act of negation. For it is vital to negate what has caused division within humanity and divided the nation, in spite of the fact that, because of its *raison d'être*, the Museum can only suspend – i.e. not take account of – different destinations, otherwise it would not invent art. That is its system: the need to negate! It must negate the various forms of division and difference!

It will be said that all revolutions make a clean sweep. This may be true, but it is all the more true when a revolution has as its cornerstone an institution which, by definition, denies the difference in historical time. The basis of a political community founded in this way is curious indeed, since art and freedom are generated by an *act of negation*.

Because the Museum constituted a vital part of the new destination, there was an underlying opportunity for that *something* in suspense to emerge. Art would soon triumphantly liberate itself from the Republic. As de Neufchâteau put it:

And when, citizens, will nature and the arts be eager to lavish their favours upon you? In these fortunate times, on the very day that I am addressing you, that transient vandalism has disappeared forever from a land indignant at having borne it! Here is the triumphal procession, the ceremony that will expiate the crimes of the tyranny overthrown on the 9 Thermidor.

Here is a festival, unique among nations, *the festival which undertakes to eradicate all memories*, the triumph of nature, the triumph of the arts, the triumph of liberty [...] Citizens of France! Bestow all your respect on this august tomb of all division ...

The Louvre: the tomb of all division.

NOTES

1. E. Pommier (ed.), *Lettres à Miranda sur les déplacements des monuments de l'art de l'Italie par Quatremère de Quincy* (Paris: Editions Macula, 1989).
2. *Mora Ozouf, La fête révolutionnaire, 1789–1799* (Paris: Gallimard, 1976).
3. Pommier (1989), pp. 61–4.
4. De Neufchâteau, quoted in Pommier (1989), pp. 61–4.
5. Pommier (1989), pp. 61–4.

4.

Poetics of the Museum:
Lenoir and Du Sommerard

Stephen Bann

The story is told by the art historian Lord Clark that, in the days when he used to stay at Berenson's Florentine villa, I Tatti, he would try the experiment of moving a small Renaissance bronze a few inches from its original position each evening on retiring to bed. Each morning, as he came down to breakfast, he was able to note that it had been restored with great precision to its former location. This story illustrates, of course, more than a mere mania for domestic order. To Berenson, no doubt – if not to Lord Clark – the bronze was not simply an object which could be moved here and there without detriment to its aesthetic significance. It was a term in a system, whose exact relationship to other terms had to be maintained as, by imperceptible stages, Berenson's home became the Berenson Museum. Yet when, with Berenson's death, that process had become complete, we may well wonder how much of this original order was in fact preserved for posterity. Given that the original placing of each object within a defined series of contiguities was indeed the result of his intentions, we might ask if these intentions are likely to have been conveyed to the new stewards of his collection in the form of a comprehensible system. If not (and discounting the possibility of an intuitive *rapport* beyond the grave), we would have to envisage the inevitability of the museum collapsing into a form of *anomie*. Borrowing once again the terminology of linguistics, we could say that, the systematic plane being barred by Berenson's absence, the syntagmatic plane (the ordering of objects in real space) would inevitably lose its coherence. If the museum continued to communicate, it would at the same time be afflicted with a speech disorder or *aphasia*. Connections and relationships which were once the visible demonstration of a total view of art and the world, would have been reduced to mere contiguities and juxtapositions.[1]

I choose this contemporary example – which is of course entirely hypothetical – in order to stress the fragility of the type of communication which will be described here. Mention has already been made in my introduction [to his *The Clothing of Clio*, from which this excerpt is taken] of the 'focalising' capacity of rhetoric, which (in line with the theory of Dan Sperber)[2] can establish para-linguistic structures within specific assemblages of objects. It must surely be clear that the objects assembled by a collector, whether perpetuated in a museum or not, form an ideal test case for the proof of such a hypothesis. But it might be argued, on the other hand, that the entropy or loss of order which affects a collection of objects with the passing of time is of so high a degree that we can never in practice recover the integrity of the original system or code. It might even be contended that such a recovery is not desirable, since the objects themselves ought to be emancipated, through the creation of new meanings, from the paranoia of an all-embracing system. We all know the benefits, for any museum collection, of a periodic overhaul.

But what may well be necessary for the well-being of museums does not prevent us from using this line of analysis in trying to understand the relation of museums and collectors to the 'historical-mindedness' of their age. In choosing the title 'Poetics of the museum', I am assuming that it is possible, in certain special circumstances, to reconstruct the formative procedures and principles which determined the type of a particular museum, and to relate these procedures to the epistemological presumptions of our period. Certainly there is no law which states that, in this or any other age, a museum or a collection will exemplify the kind of systematic order which justifies the use of the term 'poetics'. The lengthy pre-history of the British Museum, from the Sloane legacy of 1753 to the opening of the present premises in 1851, would turn out to be somewhat incoherent by this test, because of the makeshift character of the original display in Montagu House. As the Earl of Elgin discovered while humping his inconvenient marbles around London, there is no reason why a collector's objects should reach a point of rest within any existing conceptual, or spatial, scheme. But the stages of the formation of the Musée de Cluny in Paris offer what must surely be regarded as a brilliant counter-example. In the sequence of events which led up to its official adoption by the French state in 1843, we can follow what is both an exemplary pattern of the formation of a museum and, which is more to our purpose, an ideal source for tracing the development of historical discourse and the historical sense in the Romantic epoch.

The argument of the preceding chapters [of *The Clothing of Clio*] is, of course, taken for granted in the analysis which follows. At the close of this chapter, I shall raise some general considerations which emerge from taking the Museum as a special example of the transformation in Romantic attitudes to the past. My starting point must be, however, to question from the basis of contemporary testimony the conventional assumption that historical discourse is essentially (or indeed exclusively) confined to the historical text in the narrow sense of the term. In *Les Arts au Moyen Age* (which began publication in 1838) Alexandre du Sommerard – the founder of the Musée de Cluny – challenged this very assumption as it was implied in Augustin Thierry's much-quoted encomium of Sir Walter Scott, contained in the *Lettres sur l'histoire de France*.[3] Du Sommerard suggests an alternative channel through which an 'ardour' for the medieval period could be stimulated:

Loin de là, l'ardeur pour le moyen âge s'est étendue chez nous du prestige historique aux objects matériels qui contribuèrent tant à l'inspiration du grand peintre écossais zélé collecteur en ce genre. Les mêmes moyens, une collection méthodique des brillants dépouilles de nos aïeux, ajouteraient un vif intérèt à la lecture de nos chroniques.[4]

[Far from that, in our case ardour for the Middle Ages has spread from the prestige of history to the material objects which contributed so greatly to the inspiration of the great Scottish painter, a zealous collector in this genre. The same means, a methodical collection of the brilliant remains of our ancestors, would contribute a lively interest to the reading of our chronicles.]

Du Sommerard thus implies a kind of priority of the historical object over the historical text. A collection of such objects will not simply be parasitic upon the vision of the Middle Ages revealed by Scott and the chroniclers. It will enable a host of antecedent perceptions to enliven the reading of the original texts. And Du Sommerard is surely right to mention Scott's own absorption in the material vestiges of the past – a concern which is evident in Washington Irving's account of his visit to Abbotsford [which Bann discusses in the following chapter].[5] Du Sommerard well understood that it was a gesture of fidelity to Scott to go beyond the written text and demonstrate how the sense of the past could be aroused by the display of historical objects. Always provided, of course, that the objects were the fruit of a 'methodical collection'.

A brief biographical sketch of our protagonist is necessary in the first place. His life was, essentially, the life of a collector, for (as his son Edmond wrote after his death) it was to his collection that he sacrificed everything, 'fortune, health and (his very) existence'.[6] Alexandre du Sommerard was born in 1779, a member of the extensive class of provincial *noblesse de robe* which performed judiciary and financial functions under the crown. He did not emigrate, but in fact served as a volunteer in six campaigns of the revolutionary armies, culminating in Bonaparte's Italian campaign of 1800. The establishment of the Empire allowed him to take up a permanent post in the Cour des Comptes – very much the type of career which he could have expected if there had been no revolution. But even at this early point, much of Du Sommerard's energy was devoted to the patronage of the arts, which he encouraged both by forming a small collection of drawings and by holding a salon largely frequented by artists. With the coming of the Restoration, he became an active member of the reconstituted 'Société des Amis des Arts', and it was in these years (according to his obituary notices) that his collection of medieval and Renaissance objects, as opposed to classical and contemporary French arts, began to be formed.

'A methodical collection' – we can in fact trace in retrospect some of the stages through which method was progressively introduced into Du Sommerard's collector's madness. In the early years of the Restoration, the historical materials appear to have been utilised primarily as a convenience for the artists of his acquaintance, who were invited to examine and draw them. By around 1825, however, this ancillary role – which harmonised well with conventional studio practice and the classicist doctrine of imitation – had given place to something more significant. Du Sommerard was himself the subject of a painting completed in this year by the artist Renoux: he is shown seated beside an interlocutor in his 'Cabinet d'Antiquités', surrounded by items from his collection and identified by a title that could not fail to recall the influence of Scott – 'L'Antiquaire' – The Antiquary. [See Figure

Figure 1.4.1   A chaotic assemblage of objects crammed into a small space: Renoux, *L'Antiquaire* (*The Antiquary* – portrait of A. Du Sommerard), 1825

1.4.1.] Interestingly enough it was in the succeeding year that Du Sommerard divested himself of the earlier part of his collection, which consisted of drawings, mainly of the modern French School. The published auction catalogue describes the anonymous collector as being a 'passionate and insatiable amateur',[7] and recounts how for some time he has had difficulty in reconciling the possession of these drawings with the other items in his collection, notably the proliferating group of 'national antiquities'. The problem is represented in the auction catalogue as one of lack of space, but we may suspect that it was also a question of the need for systematic order. The portrait of 'L'Antiquaire' shows a chaotic assemblage of objects crammed into a small space, with armour and fire-arms invading the carpet. Du Sommerard finally solved the problem of space and of order when, in 1832, he succeeded in becoming tenant of the late Gothic town-house of the Abbots of Cluny, adjacent to the Palais des Thermes at the crossing of the Boulevards St-Germain and St-Michel. The journalist Jules Janin explained the move in the following terms:

Quand il eut bien agrandi sa collection, M. Du Sommerard pensa qu'il était temps de la mettre en ordre, et, comme complément à sa passion dominante, il imagina de la transporter tout simplement dans le plus vieux palais que possède la France, ruine imposante encore ... Comme il n'était pas assez riche pour acheter le palais des Thermes tout entier, ou seulement pour occuper l'hôtel de Cluny, il avait imaginé d'en louer, sa vie durant, la partie la plus pittoresque et la mieux conservée.[8]

[When he had built up his collection, M. Du Sommerard thought that it was time to put it in order, and, to suit his ruling passion, he thought of transporting it quite simply into the most ancient palace which France possesses, still an impressive ruin ... As he was not rich enough to acquire the Palais des Thermes in its entirety, or only to occupy the Hôtel de Cluny, he had had the idea of renting the most picturesque and best preserved part of it for the rest of his life.]

Janin seems to imply that Du Sommerard would ideally have wished to live in the Hôtel de Cluny, while arranging his collection in the vast halls of the Palais des Thermes. But his resources did not allow him this luxury, and this was probably a good thing. Emile Deschamps, writing in 1834, describes the carriages which thronged the small courtyard of the Hôtel de Cluny once it was opened to the public, and he leaves us in little doubt that Du Sommerard himself (as in the portrait of the Antiquary) was a necessary part of the experience of viewing the collection:

Ameublements, tentures, vitraux, vaisselle, armures, ustensiles et joyaux, tout a été miraculeusement retrouvé et conservé; vous marchez au milieu d'une civilisation disparue; vous êtes comme enveloppés de bons vieux temps chevaleresques, et la cordiale hospitalité du maître complète l'illusion.[9]

[Furnishings, hangings, stained glass, dishes, armour, utensils and jewelry – all has been miraculously recovered and preserved; you walk in the midst of a vanished civilisation; you are as if enveloped by the good old chivalric times, and the cordial hospitality of the master rounds off the illusion.]

Obviously, in that initial syntagmatic chain – furnishings, hangings, stained glass, crockery, armour, utensils, jewelry – there is more than a threat of chaos, of meaningless juxtaposition. But the rhetoric of the guide-book triumphantly asserts itself over this threat. The orderliness of the system is celebrated through the alibi of the 'good old chivalric times', and the master himself is on hand to complete the effect of illusion.

In advance of the more detailed analysis which will seek to get beyond the mythic terms of contemporary description, I would stress one crucial point which may not have been made sufficiently clear. Du Sommerard's collection, as displayed in the Hôtel de Cluny from the early 1830s, was not only a striking spectacle. [See Figure 1.4.2.] It was a new experience. Its capacity to 'envelop' Du Sommerard's contemporaries in an illusion of the past was a direct function of this novelty. But since anything new can only be assessed

Figure 1.4.2   Objects have been allotted their respective places: Collection of the Hôtel de Cluny, François Ier room, from Du Sommerard, *Les Arts au moyen âge*

by comparison with what went before, I must now introduce and analyse a previously existing system – one which has in fact a very direct relationship to Du Sommerard's own. The relation which I shall posit between these two types of historical discourse relies implicitly on the principle developed by Michel Foucault in *The Order of Things*: that there is such a thing as an 'épistémè', or epistemological totality, within which the various discourses of an age are structurally related to one another; and that an apparently continuous system of discourse (for example historical discourse) is in effect fractured by the *coupure* or break which signifies the shift from one 'épistémè' to another. What I shall try to demonstrate about Du Sommerard's long, passionate and exhausting progress towards 'a methodical collection of the brilliant remains of our ancestors' is that it reveals in an exemplary way that epistemological break in historical discourse which defines the novelty of the Romantic period. The 'chivalric' space in which Deschamps and the Parisian public of the 1830s are enveloped is no longer the historical space of the eighteenth century, Foucault's classic age.

My example in fact lies near to hand. When the Musée de Cluny was finally accepted as the responsibility of the French state in 1843, it consisted not only of the collection of Du Sommerard, but also of the extensive collection of French antiquities which had been assembled during the revolution by Alexandre Lenoir and installed in the pre-revolutionary Convent of the Petits-Augustins on the Left Bank.[10] It hardly needs to be emphasised that such a collection was put together in quite different circumstances, and in accordance with quite different principles, from those of Du Sommerard. In fact, Lenoir was not so much collecting as salvaging what could be salvaged from the dilapidation and even destruction of French national monuments which followed upon the confiscation of church property by the revolutionary government. The monumental objects which he successfully transported to safety included treasures of considerable value, such as the fountain ascribed to Jean Goujon from Diane de Poitiers' Château of Anet. But they were essentially fragments, often mutilated fragments, which testified eloquently to the drastic reappraisal of French history and institutions during the revolutionary epoch. But Lenoir did not simply salvage. He placed the recuperated objects on exhibition to the public within an overall chronological scheme that appears to have been without precedent. The journal of Lord John Campbell, a visitor to France during the short-lived Peace of Amiens, provides a brief but lucid description:

... we went to see The ci-devant Convent of the Augustins in which are deposited all the tombs and monuments which escaped the fury of the revolutionists, (they are arranged in different cloisters and appartments) each containing the specimens of statuary and sculpture during one century beginning with the earliest periods of the art, and receiving light through windows of coloured glass as nearly of the same antiquity as possible. Some very beautiful and curious specimens ... are among them.[11]

Lord John's testimony gives a slightly over-simplified impression of the organisation of the museum. There was an impressive 'Salle d'Introduction', with original early eighteenth-century ceiling paintings, in which a full historical range of sculptural objects were displayed, from antiquity to the seventeenth century. Nonetheless, it is surely significant that he has singled out as the most striking effect Lenoir's distribution of objects according to centuries, which extended over five separate rooms of the museum. Within this section, at any rate, the history of France was illustrated in clear, paradigmatic form from the thirteenth century until the age of Louis XIV. Lenoir was eventually forced to close the museum in 1816, partly as a result of the inveterate hostility of Quatremère de Quincy, who had been appointed 'Intendant général des arts et monuments publics' by the new Bourbon government. But up to this date, the French and foreign public had the opportunity of witnessing in the Petits-Augustins a form of historical representation which was surely unavailable in any other context. They could experience the notion of the 'century' made concrete by the successive installation of appropriate monumental fragments.

Of course the model which Lenoir had adopted also had its limitations. The unity of the 'century' is a schematic notion, and one may be tempted to conclude that the objects were only weakly bound together by such a link. Indeed Lord John's term 'specimen' seems exactly appropriate. Within each 'century' set, the 'specimen' fragment would represent metonymically the greater whole from which it had been detached, the Abbey or Château of its original location. In relation to the other 'specimens', it could have no assertive link except what arose from the simple fact of contiguity or juxtaposition. Unlike the case of the Musée de Cluny, there would be no effect of illusion, no overall concept of a historically authentic milieu, in the light of which the fragments might achieve overall integration.

Yet we should beware of underlining this contrast as if Lenoir were presenting a rudimentary and imperfect precedent for Du Sommerard's later success. In fact, as my reference to Foucault implies, the question is not one of placing the two collectors at different points in a single evolutionary scheme, but of showing how their differing types of discourse relate to different epistemological totalities. The surviving evidence of the museums themselves is perhaps not enough in itself to establish this point. But there is fascinating additional testimony in the case of Lenoir, which can be found in a remarkable letter which he wrote to the 'Conservateur des monuments publics' at an early stage in the Restoration. It is a published letter which is framed by the righteous indignation of its editor, a M. Guiffrey writing in 1880, who gives every sign of having uncovered an epistemological scandal!

According to Guiffrey, Lenoir determined at an early stage in the life of his museum to supplement his collection of works by great French artists by busts of the same artists, and by busts of a number of great historical figures for whom he had been unable to obtain contemporary effigies. A fascinating point emerges. Lenoir evidently had no scruples about mixing the authentic fragment with the contemporary, archaising bust. But there is an even more surprising detail to underline this point. In order that they might be able to work on the new busts, a number of contemporary sculptors of Lenoir's acquaintance were given 'marble debris' from the historical collection. As Guiffrey remarks:

Combien de fragments précieux ont dû périr, grâce à cette transaction étrange à laquelle d'ailleurs personne ne trouvait alors à redire, et dont Lenoir fait lui-même l'aveu avec une franchise qui prouve la tranquillité de sa conscience.[12]

[How many precious fragments must have perished, as a result of this strange transaction which no one seems to have taken objection to, and which Lenoir himself avows with a frankness which proves that his conscience was clear.]

As Guiffrey implies, Lenoir's 'avowal' strongly suggests that he had no overriding notion of historical authenticity, in accordance with which the 'marble debris' would *automatically* be more important than whatever a modern sculptor might make with the aid of them. Equally, Guiffrey's own horrified reaction to the barbaric behaviour of the classic age shows that he himself implicitly adhered to such a notion. But we have not exhausted the account of Lenoir's revealing lapsus. In the letter published by Guiffrey, Lenoir actually testifies that he supplied the sculptor De Seine with the authentic skull of Heloise (so much useless debris), so that he could refer to it while preparing a bust of that unfortunate lady for the Museum. Lenoir speaks with astounding coolness about De Seine's bust of Heloise, 'which he modelled after the bones of the head of that interesting woman which I supplied him with'.[13] He concludes, with quiet pride: 'This bust is deserving of praise.'

What can we possibly make of a discourse which admits M. De Seine's bust of Heloise to a place of honour, but excludes – indeed dismisses as insignificant except for the purposes of *mimesis* – the mortal remains of 'that interesting woman'? Our own reservations about the authenticity of the remains are, of course, entirely irrelevant. Lenoir evidently believed the remains to be authentic; the significant point is that such authenticity counted for so little in his project of mobilising and displaying the objects of the past. Similarly, we should be warned by this example against supposing that Lenoir's organisation of the museum by centuries *necessarily* betokens an integrated historical milieu, a coherent *system*. That seems unlikely to be the case. Indeed the order which Lenoir established can be viewed as a quite unusually pure example of metonymy, of the reductive rhetorical strategy whereby the part does duty for the whole in a purely mechanistic way, without implying reference to any organic totality. The contemporary bust of Heloise, like every other bust commissioned by Lenoir, enters this metonymic order as a part-object contiguous to other part-objects. And in such a space, the mortal remains have, quite simply, no cognitive status.

My argument up to this stage has relied to a great extent upon the illuminating article by Hayden White, which analyses Foucault's method in tropological terms.[14] White suggests that, in the shift from what might be called the classic to the romantic 'épistème', there is implied a movement from the predominant use of the trope of metonymy to that of synecdoche. Whilst the part–whole relation in metonymy is reductive and mechanistic, that involved in synecdoche is both integrative and organic. The two elements are 'grasped together', as aspects of a whole that is greater than the sum of its parts in isolation (as in the expression 'He is all heart').[15] And if Lenoir's procedure is relentlessly metonymic, the strategy of synechdoche seems to apply exactly to the Musée de Cluny, where the object from the past becomes the basis for an integrative construction of historical totalities. When the historian Prosper de Barante spoke in the Chamber of Peers in favour of the purchase of the collection by the French government he unambiguously stated the principle that each object was to be valued for its synecdochic charge: each object offered access to a historical milieu and to the real historical characters with whom it had once been identified, through a process that derived its imaginative cogency from the myth of the resurrection of the past:

L'épée d'un grand guerrier, les insignes d'un souverain célèbre, les joyaux d'une reine grande ou malheureuse, les livres où un écrivain traça quelques notes, sont autant de reliques qu'on aime à voir, et qui font un autre impression que la lettre morte du volume où nous lisons leur histoire.[16]

[The sword of a great warrior, the insignia of a celebrated sovereign, the jewels of a great or an unhappy queen, the books in which a writer traced a few notes, are so many relics which people like to see and which make a different impression from the dead letter of the volume where we read their history.]

From 'specimen' to 'relic' – the very shift in terms alerts us to a radical change in conceiving the relationship of the historical object to the past. And of course it is not only the relationship, but the class of object which has changed. Where Lenoir assembled monumental fragments, Du Sommerard brought together and displayed (at a stage when this was being done nowhere else) a full range of both precious and utilitarian objects which survived from the late Middle Ages and the Renaissance. He made a special point of distributing these objects into separate rooms. But his principle of differentiation was not the mechanistic division of centuries, as in the Musée des Petits-Augustins: it was a classification which respected the existing distribution of rooms in the Hôtel de Cluny, and the rich associations which they already held:

Dans la chapelle de l'hôtel furent rangés avec ordre tous les objets qui avaient eu jadis une destination religieuse, tels les reliquaires, chasses, livres d'église, etc. Les coupes, les fayences, les poteries trouvèrent leur place dans la salle à manger, les objets d'ameublement tels que lits, sièges, tapis, candélabres, etc. du XVIe siècle servirent à orner une vaste chambre, qui, de l'époque même de ses meubles, prit le nom de François Ier. Enfin le salon et deux galeries formèrent une sorte de terrain neutre, où furent accumulés des objets d'art de toutes les époques.[17]

[In the chapel of the Hôtel, there were arranged in order all the objects which had formerly had a religious destination, such as reliquaries, shrines, church books and so on. The cups, faience and pottery found their place in the dining-room. The objects of furniture like beds, seats, carpets, candelabra and so on from the sixteenth century served to adorn a vast chamber which, from the very period of its furnishings, took the name of the 'Chambre de François Ier'. Finally the salon and two galleries formed a kind of neutral territory, where art objects of all periods were accumulated.]

It is rather refreshing to note the existence of that 'neutral territory', which recalls Foucault's mention of Borges's Chinese encyclopedia with its provision for aberrant taxonomy![18] Clearly Du Sommerard's arrangement of objects eschewed the paranoia of Lenoir's centennial system. This could be seen as relevant to the whole issue of Du Sommerard's passion for collecting, and to the links between such a consuming passion and the much discussed problem of fetishism. Du Sommerard's collecting impulse was, as his son's account testifies, not far short of pathological. Yet, in terms which will gain in relevance when we discuss Scott and Ruskin [later in *The Clothing of Clio*], Du Sommerard can be held to have transcended the overtly fetishistic impulse of his early life as a collector. He can be shown to have successfully integrated the detached fragment within an overall milieu, to have restored the part to the whole.

If we compare the portrait of the 'Antiquary' with a contemporary engraving of the so-called 'Chambre de François Ier', we can immediately see the transformation which has taken place.[19] [See Figures 1.4.1. and 1.4.2.] In the 'Antiquary', the objects are in disorder. Conjunctions seem to be absurd: a miniature nude shares a table-top with household utensils, and the armour clutters up the floor. Perhaps the Antiquary himself has to intervene to sort out this chaos, by picking out an object and telling its story – as appears to be happening in the picture. In the 'Chambre de François Ier', on the other hand, objects have been allotted their respective places. Not only do all of them come from one period, but they are distributed according to a rational and intelligible economy: the central table, though well covered, is covered with objects that belong on tables, like books and gaming dice. The armour has been diligently reassembled, and it even appears that two suits of armour are playing draughts in the window embrasure. We have no need for a learned guide in this new context: the historical portrait, presumably one of François Ier himself, seems to place the whole room under the honorary, mute guardianship of the regal figure who is evoked, synecdochically, by the combined reference of all the objects assembled there.

We can in fact tabulate, in a simple diagram, the differences between the 'century' room of Lenoir and Du Sommerard's 'Chambre de François Ier', or any other of his 'thematic' rooms. [See Figure 1.4.3.] If we take the objects in both examples as units in a syntagmatic chain, then we must allow for two 'systematic' constraints which govern the way in which these syntagmatic units function as discourse: first of all, the organising concept of the 'century' or 'religious' room, and secondly the wider system to which the part-objects relate, to the extent that they evoke a totality outside the walls of the museum. With these features in mind, we can surely establish that Lenoir's museum is marked by the *disjunction* which intervenes after each unit in the chain. Objects are bound together simply

1. Musée des Petits-Augustins: Lenoir

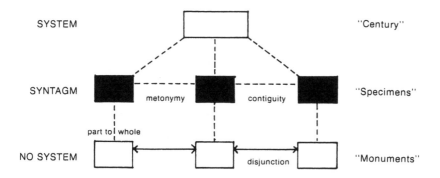

2. Musée de Cluny: Du Sommerard

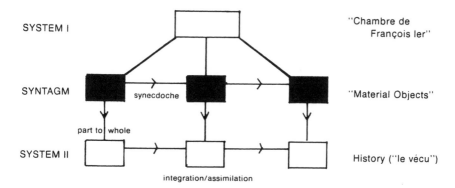

Figure 1.4.3

by the schematic 'century' link, which can find room for the modern bust that merely *replicates* the past. The connection between each tomb, or fountain, and its original context is a reductive one of part to whole, which in no way necessitates an imaginative link between the series of abbeys, châteaux, and other monuments that were Lenoir's sources of material. By contrast, Du Sommerard's museum employs the integrative notions of 'religious life', 'kitchen life' and the 'Chambre de François Ier' to gesture towards a system that is entirely homogeneous. Underlying the operation of the synecdoche, which leads us from the part-object to the revived historical user (whether named or not), there lurks the mythic system of 'lived' history, history as 'le vécu'. It is this assertion of the experiential reality of history which the rhetoric of the museum both produces and annihilates. 'History' is made real through the fiction of the transparency of the historical syntagm.

The two collections which have been reviewed therefore testify to a discernible shift in the character of historical discourse. In their sharp opposition, they suggest the operation of an 'epistemological break' of the type formulated by Foucault, and identified by Hayden White as the substitution of one dominant trope for another. It is clear that Foucault himself does not claim to explain the actual process of 'epistemological break', and White is concerned with answering the claim that Foucault's discontinuity is unsystematic, rather than with resolving the issue on his own terms. In fact, there seems little reason to question Foucault's methodological limitation to an 'archaeology' at this stage of his career even if its necessary consequence is the detachment of discourse from 'le vécu'.[20] After all, the aim of a study such as this is precisely to show that the equation of a certain discourse with 'le vécu' is an effect of rhetoric rather than a natural correspondence which remains inaccessible to critical method. Thus our next task is to broaden the argument by setting Du Sommerard's achievement within a wider context, and relating the Musée de Cluny to the other forms of historical representation which have been discussed [in *The Clothing of Clio*] up to now.

There can be no doubt about the distinctive place which Du Sommerard has here. Two contrasted examples will suffice to recall the spectrum which has been under review. The historian Prosper de Barante, whose stated intention of achieving a kind of stylistic transparency in historical narrative was judged successful by the French critical consensus of 1824, came to be dismissed by later generations, largely because the technical device of writing a substitute chronicle, with no authorial intervention, appeared spurious by comparison with the authentic, newly published medieval sources.[21] By contrast, the historical showman Daguerre, with the novel spectacle of the diorama, harnessed an overwhelming type of technical effect to the project of representing the otherness of the past. And he succeeded in graduating from the diorama to the invention of the daguerreotype, which (in Barthes' terms) annihilates the distance between *dasein* and *dagewessensein* (between 'being there' and 'having-been-there'). In other words, Daguerre achieved through the visual medium of photography what Barante had unsuccessfully striven for in the domain of narrative. But this achievement was a fragile one, as far as historical representation is concerned. No one could deny that the photograph was the imprint of a past event. But that event as recorded was condemned to remain mute – and, as it were, frozen – as long as there was no way of reinserting it within a narrative chain.

As we have seen, Du Sommerard fully appreciated the difficulties which accompanied these two contrasted methods of historical representation. We can follow throughout the course of his published writings an increasing realisation of the technical resource which was necessary to steer between Scylla and Charybdis, and bring his collector's cargo to port. As early as 1822, his modest publication under the title *Vues de Provins* bears traces of his commitment to the new historical mentality; his first task, as he conceives it, is to expel the ironic, or 'satirical', discourse of the previous century:

Nous n'ignorons pas, quoique étranger à Provins, que ses habitants sont divisés depuis plus de trois cent ans, sur la question de l'antiquité plus ou moins reculée de cette ville … La discussion a dès-lors perdu le caractère qu'elle aurait dû conserver; et la polémique, empruntant le langage de la satire, a envenimé la discussion au lieu de l'éclairer.[22]

[We are not unaware, though strangers to Provins, that its inhabitants have been divided for over three hundred years, over the question of the greater or less antiquity of this town … discussion has since lost the character which it ought to have kept; and polemics, borrowing the language of satire, has poisoned the discussion instead of clarifying it.]

Du Sommerard announces the liquidation of these ancestral disputes, and puts forward simply the neutral code: 'a simple description of the monuments and ruins in their present state, presented from their picturesque side'. What might picturesque mean in this context? It means more, one imagines, than the mere selection of the pictorial format for representing the 'monuments and ruins', and the assurance that this convention will be turned to good account. As Prosper Mérimée recalled, the interest of *Vues de Provins* lies particularly in the fact that it was one of the first applications to historical topography of the new technique of lithography, contemporary with the first volumes of Nodier's *Voyages pittoresques*.[23] Du Sommerard himself insisted on stressing in his illuminating introduction 'the effect … which can be expected, in our view, from the invention of lithography, from these local descriptions which are at once picturesque and historical, placed by the modesty of their prices within the range of moderate fortunes'.[24]

That the new printing techniques were not valued by Du Sommerard simply for their cheapness and accessibility is clear from the fact that he continued to work with the most refined modern methods of reproduction available to him, pushing his concern with the perfect 'description' to a stage where it appears almost fanatical. When, in 1838, he finally published the first volume of his crowning documentary achievement, *Les Arts au moyen âge*, he went out of his way to stress the unprecedented combination of techniques which had been used in the reproduction of historical sites and objects: the work had come to fruition 'in spite of the difficulties which we created for ourselves in submitting, *for the first time* [Du Sommerard's italics], the execution of certain plates to four successive operations … (*reduction, engraving, transfer* of the engraving on to stone, colouring and modelling of the line with the lithographic pencil)'.[25] The result, even for the modern eye satiated by photographic reproduction, is quite sensational. In fact, this work, which started to appear only a year before Daguerre announced his discoveries to the world, is a further proof (if any were necessary) of the compelling will to realism which ran parallel to (but was not in any way exhausted by) the technical innovation of photography. Du Sommerard is working in that uneasy space of representation where the classical doctrine of mimesis no longer carries conviction, and truth becomes a function of the ever-increasing virtuosity whereby the gap between the original and the reproduction has to be disavowed and camouflaged in consequence.

Yet, in spite of Du Sommerard's triumphs in pictorial reproduction, it is the grouping of objects in the Musée de Cluny which shows his full originality. This new system is connected with other developments in pictorial represent-ation during the period, but remains essentially distinct from them. A brief comparison with the 'Panstereomachia' of the Battle of Poitiers (a prodigy which was mentioned in passing in the last chapter [of *The Clothing of Clio*]) will clarify this issue. As we learn in the informative pamphlet which accompanied the spectacle, the Panstereomachia could be defined as 'the representation of a Battle, entirely composed of solid figures in their relative proportions'. In other words, the spectators were faced with a coherently organised visual display, divided into 'front ground', 'back ground', 'distance', etc., where groups of related figures enacted different episodes in the course of a particular battle. The figures, or at least those in the front ground, must have been themselves free-standing and complete, since the proprietor of the spectacle was anxious to point out his readiness to meet 'any persons desirous of possessing groups, or single figures'.[26] But they were, at the same time, subordinate to the perspectival ordering of the scene, just as the entire spectacle was subordinate to the narrative of the battle. Indeed the pamphlet is very largely taken up by an 'account', drawn directly from Froissart, of the successive stages in the engagement, and the 'description' of the spectacle itself can only be achieved with the help of frequent injunctions to 'See Historical Account'.[27]

The 'Panstereomachia' is therefore parasitic both on pictorial convention, and on the historical narrative. However carefully Mr Bullock may have studied the 'costume and arms of the period', his 'specimens of the artillery and battering rams' were merely solid models, which cannot have convinced anyone for long. Du Sommerard, on the other hand, found room for the actual objects which survived from the historic past. And not only did he find room for them. He assembled them in groupings which allowed them at one and the same time to retain their individual authenticity, and to participate in an overall, recreative vision of the past. At the Musée de Cluny, there was no need for visualisation according to the laws of perspective, no need for a historical narrative to underpin the presentation, no prodigious technical effect to be striven for: there was simply the inducement to prefigure an order in the synecdochic mode. But we need not, at this late stage, entirely abandon Alexandre Lenoir. For the acceptance of the collection of the Musée de Cluny by the French state foreshadowed the merging of Du Sommerard's legacy with that of Lenoir. Much of what Lenoir had brought together was distributed throughout the imposing remains of the Roman baths which (even today) are connected by a stairway to the medieval apartments of the Abbot. Du Sommerard's own son became the first director of the united collections, while Lenoir's son remained in association as the museum's officially accredited architect.

The 'poetics' of the modern museum is not Du Sommerard's system, nor is it that of Lenoir. Instead it lies in the alternation of the two strategies which have been outlined here. This is a feature which is well illustrated in the arrangement of museums like the Victoria & Albert, in London, or the Philadelphia Museum of Art. Passages and rooms devoted to the metonymic sequence of schools and centuries are interrupted by 'reconstructed' rooms, offering the synecdochic treat of a *salon* transported from the Ile Saint-Louis, or a dining-room from a departed Jacobean manor-house. Perhaps the automatic way in which the ordinary museum-goer shifts between these two modes implies a modern replacement for the synecdochic and the metonymic museums: the ironic museum, in which we oscillate between the different varieties of imaginative projection that are required.

What can hardly be doubted is the extraordinary prestige which still attaches to the notion of reconstructing the historical object or milieu within the museum setting. In the past few years, the Metropolitan Museum of New York has re-erected the Egyptian Temple of Dendur, which rises majestically above a stretch of water in a vast enclosed place set aside exclusively for it; the Metropolitan has also installed, at the expense of Mrs Brooke Russell Astor, a Chinese garden court of the Ming Dynasty which is an outstanding, indeed hyperbolic, demonstration of the search for absolute authenticity in all material details.[28] The scale of these enterprises is, of course, incomparably greater than anything Du Sommerard could have attempted. But more significant, perhaps, is the way in which the reference to history has changed. Du Sommerard worked at a time when his country-men were rediscovering their own history. He devised a unique way of satisfying a social and cultural need which was already being revealed in innumerable different ways by novelists, historians, painters and so on. It can hardly be argued that these new achievements, ingenious and popular though they may be, achieve the same binding relationship to cultural and historical experience. Indeed it could be denied that they have historical significance of any kind, since the historical dimension is almost entirely subsumed in those of the spectacular and the exotic; it is an effect of *transumption*, or far-fetching, rather than of synecdoche, that the Temple of Dendur should stand in mummified isolation a few yards from Fifth Avenue. It is the real thing, and the Getty Museum at Malibu is, by contrast, only a surrogate Roman villa of the first century AD. But the difference between these two monuments of museology is perhaps not so great as might at first sight appear.

The contemporary problem which emerges here cannot be pursued in this chapter. It must be deferred until the concluding section of [*The Clothing of Clio*]. For the moment, it is worth focusing on the intriguing paradox of Du Sommerard's achievement. A passionate collector, he was nonetheless able to transmute his fascination with the objects of the past into an orderly and accessible vision of period and place. No one would claim that the present Musée de Cluny is an exact reflection of his guiding ideas and principles of arrangement. But it could be argued that he managed to devise a formula which would prove resistant to the entropy evoked at the beginning of this chapter. He showed that an original historical setting, amply furnished with authentic objects, would evoke a potent and sustaining image of the past. Even when the 'Antiquary' was no longer there to weave his story around each object, the internal consistency of the milieu would continue its recreative effect.

Of course it is true that such an effect depended (as it still depends) on the museum-goer's historical culture. To this extent, Du Sommerard was being a little disingenuous when he maintained that 'material objects', rather than texts, could have priority in stimulating the sense of the past. But, in audaciously claiming kinship with Scott – the 'great Scottish painter' – in this respect, Du Sommerard raises the fascinating issue of the possibility of a primary, immediated relationship to the objects of the past. What psychological mechanisms could explain this? Du Sommerard's unenlightening biography bars access to any quest for explanation in psychological terms, except by way of the inadequate notion of the collector's fetishism. But Scott himself, the outstanding creative figure in the historical revival of the Romantic period, left many telling signs of the personal, subjective investment which underpinned his poetic reappropriation of the past. In the chapter [of *The Clothing of Clio*] which follows, Clio's allegorical defences are removed, at least for a time. As in Clodion's bas-relief [discussed earlier in the volume], she is disclosed as a sustaining mother, rather than a stern mentor. The trick lies in substituting, for the bust of Napoleon, the figure of Scott.

NOTES

1. Cf. Roland Barthes, *Elements of Semiology*, trans. Annette Lavers and Colin Smith (New York, 1977), p. 21.

2. Cf. p. 4 [of *The Clothing of Cleo*].

3. Cf. Augustin Thierry, *Lettres sur l'histoire de France* (Paris, 1842), p. 81.

4. A. du Sommerard, *Les Arts au moyen âge* ... (Paris, 1838–46), vol. I, p. iii.

5. Cf. 'The Author of the Sketch-Book' (i.e. Washington Irving), *Abbotsford and Newstead Abbey* (London, 1835); this will be cited abundantly in the next chapter [of *The Clothing of Clio*, not printed here].

6. *Les Arts au moyen âge*, vol. II, p. viii. The biographical details which follow are largely taken from the obituary of Du Sommerard which appeared in *Bulletin de la Société de l'Histoire de France* (Année 1841), pp. 294–7.

7. *Catalogue d'une belle collection de tableaux ... provenant du Cabinet de M. Du S.* (March 1826), p. 3.

8. Quoted in *Les Arts au moyen âge*, p. v. Evidently, for Du Sommerard, the attraction of the Hôtel de Cluny lay in its unique condensation of different aspects of French architectural history. It combined, in his words, 'des parties presque intactes des grands travaux des trois belles époques de l'histoire de l'art en France ... Edifice base et étais romains, élevé et décoré en partie par les dernières inspirations de l'architecture gothique ..., et terminé presque immédiatement sous la gracieuse influence de style dit de la renaissance' (Notice sur l'Hôtel de Cluny et sur Palais des Thermes avec des notes sur la culture des Arts ... (Paris, Dec. 1934 p. 6).

9. Ibid., p. 234 (Emile Deschamps, 'Visite à l'hôtel de Cluny', 1834).

10. For early estimates of Lenoir's work, see the biographical article in Michaud's *Biographie universelle* (nouvelle edition), vol. XXIV, p. 133; also the anonymous *Paris à travers les âges* (Paris, 1875–82), vol. II, 53 livre, p. 40. A useful modern summary of his achievement, with many relevant illustrations, is included in the previously cited catalogue, *Le 'Gothique' retrouvé*, Paris, 1979, pp. 75ff (article and notes by Alain Erlande-Brandenburg). This includes a full bibliography. There is a more recent summary of Lenoir's achievement in D. Poulot, 'The birth of the museum of architecture in France during the Revolution', *Lotus International*, (Vol. 33): (1982/II), 32–5.

11. Journal of Lord John Campbell (Inveraray Castle Archives), p. 12 (entry for 24 Feb. 1803).

12. *Nouvelles archives de l'art français*, Deuxième série, vol. II (Paris, 1880–81), p. 378.

13. Ibid., p. 381.

14. Cf. Hayden White, 'Foucault decoded: notes from underground', *History and Theory*, 12 (1973), 23–54.

15. Cf. Hayden White, *Metahistory* (Baltimore, 1973), p. 35.

16. Prosper de Barante, *Etudes littéraires et historiques* (Paris, 1858), vol. II, p. 421.

17. *Bulletin de la Société de l'Histoire de France*, p. 296.

18. Cf. Michel Foucault, *Les Mots et les Choses: une archéologie des sciences humaines* (Paris, 1966), p. 7.

19. Reproduced in *Les Arts au moyen âge, op. cit.*, Album, plates x (Vue de la Chambre dite de François Ier) and XXXIX (L'Antiquaire, réunion d'objets mobiliers de diverses époques, constituant l'ancien cabinet de Mr. D. S. D. en 1825, époque où fut exécuté sur nature le Tableau de l'Antiquaire par M. Renoux).

20. Cf. Michel Foucault, *L'Archéologie du savoir* (Paris, 1969), *passim*.

21. Cf. further discussion of the fortunes of Barante's text at the beginning of Chapter 6 [of *The Clothing of Clio*].

22. *Vues de Provins, dessinées et lithographiées, en 1822, par plusieurs artistes* ... (Paris, 1822), pp. 1–2.

23. E. Du Sommerard, *Musée des Thermes et de l'Hôtel de Cluny: catalogue et description des objets d'art* (Paris, s.d.), p. 681 (Notice on Du Sommerard père by P. Mérimée).

24. *Vues de Provins*, p. 37.

25. *Les Arts au moyen âge*, vol. I, p. i.

26. Cf. *An Historical and Descriptive account of the Battle of Poictiers compiled from the best authorities,*

explanatory of Mr. Charles Bullock's Panstereomachia, or Model of that Memorable Victory ... (London, 1826), p. 6.

27. Cf. ibid., pp. 42ff.

28. Cf. Alfreda Murck and Wen Fong, *A Chinese Garden Court – The Astor Court at the Metropolitan Museum of Art*, reprinted from *The Metropolitan Museum of Art Bulletin* (Winter 1980/81). A special expedition was mounted in the Chinese province of Sichuan to secure supplies of the traditional *nan* wood for the project, and an old imperial kiln in the village of Lumu, outside Suzhou, was reopened in order to obtain the distinctive tiles of local clay, 'fired by burning rice-husks' (ibid., pp. 60–1).

5.

Telling Objects:

A Narrative Perspective on Collecting

Mieke Bal

It is a definite social relation between men, that assumes, in their eyes, the fantastic form of a relation between things.   Karl Marx[1]

In the same process that constructs the world as a view, man is constructed as subject.   Martin Heidegger[2]

When you leave fiction you rediscover fictions.   Jonathan Culler[3]

Narrative introduction

This paper comes from two directions, reflecting two major interests I have been pursuing for some time. The one concerns narrative as a discursive mode; the other, collecting. It seems to me that an integration of these two interests is worth the attempt, and the subject of this collection of essays the best opportunity I can imagine.

To begin with a narrative of my own: I have been working on narrative through the eras of structuralism and poststructuralism. In the beginning, I was interested in analysing literary narratives, and when my search for reliable tools was frustrated, I stepped aside to fix a few, develop some others, and construct one or two more. But I became dissatisfied, for a while, with what I had, or perhaps I lost interest in simply 'applying' those tools. A sense of purpose was lacking. As soon as I understood how narrative was made, I wanted to know how it functioned. Thus I got caught in the question of how narrative functions socially, ideologically, historically; how it changes and what people do to make it change, and to what purpose. All along, the question of what kinds of texts can be called narrative, what makes a narrative special, was part of what I was trying to understand.

Although there are many aspects to narrative, the one I was most fascinated by is the interplay between subjectivity and the cultural basis of under-standing, whether you call it objectivity or intersubjectivity. Not that these two concepts are identical, of course; but they both claim to cover the status of things *outside* the individual subject. This is, of course, the paradoxical status of all art and literature, of all cultural expressions. On the one hand, both in the production and in the reception, subjectivity is the bottom line. Yet, the object produced and interpreted must be accessible, materially (object-ively) and discursively (semiotically, *qua* meaning that is). Cultural objects must signify through common codes, conventions of meaning-making that both producer and reader understand. That is why they have to be inter-subjectively accessible. A culture consists of the people who share enough of these conventions to exchange their views (*inter*-subjectively), so that making cultural artefacts is worth some subject's while.

Here lies my particular fascination with narrative – and, as I will bring up later, with collecting. In narrative, I discovered, this paradoxical situation is doubled up. Objectively, narratives exist as texts, printed and made accessible; at the same time, they are subjectively produced by writer and reader. Analogously, the discursive mode of narrative feeds on this paradox. They are ostentatiously 'objective': in terms of speech-act theory,[4] narratives are *constative* texts: like affirmative sentences, they make a statement – describing situations and events, characters and objects, places and atmospheres. Like newspaper reports – a narrative genre – all narratives sustain the claim that 'facts' are being put on the table. Yet all narratives are not only told by a narrative agent, the narrator, who is the linguistic subject of utterance; the report given by that narrator is also, inevitably, focused by a subjective point of view, an agent of vision whose view of the events will influence our interpretation of them. In my previous works I have given this subjective presence in narratives the name of *focalisor*, and the activity in question, *focalisation*.[5] In many analyses of narratives I have since been engaged in, this concept turned out to be crucial for insight into the tension between socially accessible objecthood and the characteristic subjectivity of narratives. This makes all narratives by definition more or less fictional; or, conversely, it makes fictionality a matter of degree.[6]

Narratives fascinate me because of this dual ambiguity that makes them almost exasperatingly difficult to understand; a difficulty that is at odds with the widespread use of this mode. Not only are the large majority of verbal texts narrative, it is also obvious that verbal texts are not the only objects capable of conveying a narrative. Language is just one medium, perhaps the most conspicuous one, in which narratives can be constructed. Images, as the tradition of history painting demonstrates, can do so as well, not to speak of mixed media like film, opera and comic strips. I began to wonder if the exclusive focus on language in the study of narrative didn't limit the range of observations in a somewhat arbitrary way. But here as with the subjectivity question, one way of exploring the impact of such doubt is to take an apparently extreme counter-example, and see if that is the exception that *breaks* the rule. While stretching the concept beyond its confining force, one must also ask the question: how far can you go? What if the medium consists of real, hard material objects? Things, called objects for a good reason, appear to be the most 'pure' form of objectivity. So examining the question of the inherent fictionality of all narratives can as well begin here. In other words, can things be, or tell, stories? Objects as subjectivised elements in a narrative: this possibility adds a third level to the duality of narrative's paradox.

From the other direction comes a totally private interest in collecting. Not necessarily in collections, but in what might be called the collector's mindset, or the collecting attitude. Whereas it is virtually impossible to define collecting, and, narratively speaking, to mark where that activity begins, a collecting attitude is unmistakable and distinct. Yet, definitions of collecting tend to be irremediably fuzzy. Thus Susan M. Pearce's useful textbook for museum studies, *Museums, Objects and Collections* (1992), defines collecting through a definition of museum collections, which 'are made up of objects' that 'come to us from the past', and which have been assembled with intention by someone 'who believed that the whole was somehow more than the sum of its parts'.[7] If, we take the 'past' element loosely, as I think we must, as loosely as the existence of museums of contemporary art and of contemporary 'exotica' forces us to take it, this definition appears to hold equally for interior decorating, the composition of a wardrobe, and subscribing to a journal or book series, even for finishing reading a book. Starting an inquiry with a definition of its subject-matter inevitably leads to frustration: either the definition is too narrow and doesn't cover the whole range of its objects; or it is so broad that a lot of other things are covered by it too. But perhaps – and here my private interest joins the academic one – these attempts at a priori definition are themselves contingent on a view of knowledge that is ultimately at stake in the problem of collecting. As enigmatic as this may sound, knowledge that begins with definitions is very much like knowledge based on collections and classifications of objects.

If one begins reflecting on collecting in a narrative mode, it is equally hard to say when collecting begins to be collecting, as opposed to, say, buying a thing or two. If you buy a vase, and you then come upon a similar one, you can buy the second one because it matches the first one so nicely. That doesn't make you a collector, not yet. Even when you buy six vases, in different sizes but in matching colour and similar in material, style and historical provenance, you can still argue that you need six different sizes to accommodate the different lengths flowers come in, and you like the matching for the harmony it provides within the house. As someone who lacks the collecting spirit, that is how far I would go myself. But my friend who has the spirit in him pushed on after vase number six, and now he has 50, all beautiful, undamaged period pieces of roughly the same style, and the flower justification doesn't work any more. He doesn't need any justification, because one day he happily found himself a collector. Since then, I have kept an eye on his buying behaviour in general. I see it happening much earlier now, when he starts to collect some new 'series' of objects – a special kind of moulded plastic box, cheap little things; or baskets, or books in first impressions, or bits of stained-glass windows. Sometimes I can see the attraction, and shyly go for an item for a collector's reason myself, but so far it hasn't really happened to me in any serious way.

If I try to integrate my professional interest in narrative with that private one in collecting, I can imagine seeing collecting as a process consisting of the confrontation between objects and subjective agency informed by an attitude. Objects, subjective agency, confrontations as events: such a working definition makes for a narrative, and enables me to discuss and interpret the meaning of collecting in narrative terms. Perhaps it can bring to light aspects of the topic that tend to be overlooked. This, then, will be my particular focus on the subject in this essay. I will discuss collecting as a narrative; not as a process about which a narrative can be told, but as itself a narrative.

Collecting as a narrative

Briefly put, I need the following concepts to discuss narrative, in the subject-oriented sense in which I choose to consider it. I understand narrative to be an account in any semiotic system in which a subjectively focalised sequence of events is presented and communicated. A few terms need clarification here. The sequence of events, brought about and undergone by agents, is the *fabula*, more commonly called plot; the agents – subjects of action – on this level are called *actors*. As I said earlier, the subjectivisation is called focalisation and its agents, focalisors. The subjectivised plot is called *story*: it is what is being told in signs – words, gestures, images or objects – that others can understand. The semiotic subject producing or uttering that account is called the *narrator*. The distinction between focalisor and narrator is necessary because a narrator is able to subsume and present the subjective view of another, as in 'I felt her quiver at the sight of her nerve-wrecking father', where the first-person narrator renders in the compound *nerve-wrecking* the subjectified vision of the other person. This split between narrator and focalisor can even accumulate in several degrees, as in 'He saw that she realized he had noticed that she was aware of the lipstick on his collar.'

According to Aristotle, Western cultural history's first narratologist, a fabula has a beginning, a middle and an end. The story, precisely, manipulates that order, as when it reverses beginning and middle in the structure called *in medias res*, and the possibility of such manipulations is the very characteristic feature of narrative. More often than not, chronology is mixed up in narrative. To consider collecting as a narrative makes us focus, precisely, on the non-obviousness of chronology. So, our first inquiry might be: where does it all begin?

Beginnings: many

Looking back at the story of my friend's vase collection, it is noticeable that the beginning is exactly what is lacking. One object must have been the first to be acquired, but then, when it *was* first it was not being collected – merely purchased, given or found, and kept because it was especially gratifying. In relation to the plot of collecting, the initial event is arbitrary, contingent, accidental. What makes this beginning a specifically narrative one is precisely that. Only retrospectively, through a narrative manipulation of the sequence of events, can the accidental acquisition of the first object *become* the beginning of a collection. In the plot it is pre-historic, in the story it intervenes *in medias res*. The beginning, instead, is a meaning, not an act. Collecting comes to mean collecting precisely when a series of haphazard purchases or gifts suddenly becomes a meaningful sequence. That is the moment when a selfconscious narrator begins to 'tell' its story, bringing about a semiotics for a narrative of identity, history, and situation. Hence, one can also look at it from the perspective of the collector as agent in this narrative. Would that make it easier to pinpoint the beginning? I think not. Even when a person knows him- or herself to have the collector's mind-set, the category of objects that will fall under the spell of that attitude cannot be foreseen. The individual one day becomes aware of the presence of an eagerness that can only be realised *after* it has developed far enough to become noticeable. Initial blindness is even a precondition for that eagerness to be developed, hidden from any internalized ethical, financial or political censorship. It is of the nature of eagerness to be accumulative, and again, only retrospectively can it be seen. Stories of collecting begin by initial blindness – by visual lack. So this beginning, too, is of a narrative nature.

Between the object and the collector stands the question of motivation, the 'motor' of the narrative. Just as Peter Brooks asked the pertinent question, 'What, in a narrative, makes us read on?'[8] – so we may ask what, in this virtual narrative, makes one pursue the potential collection? Motivation is what makes the collector 'collect on', hence, collect at all. Most museologists have that question at the forefront of their inquiry, and in a moment I will survey some of their answers. From the narratological perspective of this essay, the question of motivation underlies the unclear beginning, the false start. This question is called to replace, or repress, that other beginning, which is that of the object itself *before* it became an object of collecting. Motivation is, then, both another narrative aspect of collecting and its intrinsically ungraspable beginning.

When we look at explanations of motivation, however, articulation of understanding recedes and yields to another narrative. Pearce begins her discussion of motivation with yet another beginning:

> The emotional relationship of projection and internalization which we have with objects seems to belong with our very earliest experience and (probably therefore) remains important to us all our lives. Equally, this line of thought brings us back to the intrinsic link between our understanding of our own bodies and the imaginative construction of the material world …[9]

This view is part and parcel of the story of origins of psychic life as constructed by psychoanalysis, in particular the British branch of object-relations theory.[10] Although I cannot go into this theory and its specifically narrative slant here,[11] the unspoken assumption of this quotation is directly indebted to that theory, and therefore deserves mentioning: the desire to collect is, if not innate, at least inherent in the human subject from childhood on. This type of explanation partakes of a narrative bias that, in its popular uses, both explains and excuses adult behaviour.

From motivation in childhood Pearce moves to phenomenologically defined essential humanness – and storytelling is again an indispensable ingredient:

> The potential inwardness of objects is one of their most powerful characteristics, ambiguous and elusive though it may be. Objects hang before the eyes of the imagination, continuously re-presenting ourselves to ourselves, and telling the stories of our lives in ways which would be impossible otherwise.[12]

According to this statement, collecting is an essential human feature that originates in the need to tell stories, but for which there are neither words nor other conventional narrative modes. Hence, collecting is a story, and everyone needs to tell it. Yet, it is obvious that not every human being is, or can afford to be, a collector. The essentialising gesture obscures the class privilege that is thereby projected on the human species as a whole. From this doubly narrative perspective, Pearce goes on to discuss as many as sixteen possible motivations. It is worth listing these, for the list is significant in itself, and each motivation mentioned implies a story in which it unfolds: leisure, aesthetics, competition, risk, fantasy, a sense of community, prestige, domination, sensual gratification, sexual foreplay, desire to reframe objects, the pleasing rhythm of sameness and difference, ambition to achieve perfection, extending the self, reaffirming the body, producing gender-identity, achieving immortality. Most of these motivations have a sharply political edge to them, and the more difficult they are to define, the less innocent they appear when one tries. Thus the aesthetic impulse, probably the most commonly alleged motivation and the least obviously political one, is defined by the French sociologist Pierre Bourdieu in terms that are both tautological and political-utopian:

> The aesthetic disposition, a generalized capacity to neutralize ordinary urgencies and to bracket off practical ends, a durable inclination and aptitude for practice without a practical function, can only be constituted within an experience of the world freed from urgency and through the practice of activities which are an end in themselves.[13]

In other words, you can only bracket off practical ends if you truly do so, and to have this disposition (or 'capacity'!) you need to be rich – so rich, that the rest of the world hardly matters. The means are projected first as disposition, then as capacity: I recognise again the essentializing move that defines humanness through an extension of a feature of one privileged group.

Pearce's list is both troubling and compelling. What makes the list so compelling is the sense of increasing urgency in the 'collecting drive', from relative luxuries like aesthetics to needs as 'deep' as extending body limits, constructing gender identity, and, climactically in the final position, achieving immortality. The trouble with the list, however, is its character *as* list, the enumeration of what thereby appear to be different motivations, none of them explicitly political. Discussed one by one, each motivation is neutralised by its insertion in this mixed list. But the paradigmatic character of this presentation conflicts with the implicit systematic, which appears when the items are ordered differently. The desire for domination, inconspicuously mentioned somewhere in the middle of the list, might receive more emphasis were the list to be turned into a coherent set of aspects of the same impulse, connected, that is, with the construction of gender identity, the achievement of sexual gratification, and the divine – or childish – desire for immortality, to mention only the most obvious ones. Underlying most of these motivations, I would suggest, is another kind of developmental narrative, that of the many strands, developments and framings of a concept capable of connecting them all: fetishism.

This missing term is the one that has a long tradition of connecting the psychoanalytic narrative explanation to the Marxist-political critique. Yet fetishism conflates and sums up the large majority of the motivations in Pearce's list. To help get this concept and its implications for the beginning of collecting as a narrative into focus, let us turn to James Clifford's seminal essay, 'On Collecting Art and Culture'.[14] In answer to the question 'Why do we collect?', the question that enmeshes explanation and origin, articulating the one through narration of the other, Clifford qualifies a certain form of collecting as typical of the Western world:

> In the West, however, collecting has long been a strategy for the deployment of a possessive self, culture, and authenticity.[15]

And Clifford goes on to explore the relevant aspects of that particular collecting attitude. Such an attitude, then, is predicated on a particular view of subject-object relations as based on domination. The separation between subject and object this entails makes it impossible for a subject, caught in the individualism characteristic of that separation, to be part of, or even fully engage with, a group. To the extent that this is a cultural feature, one cannot simply escape it; the most one can do is 'make it strange', make it lose its self-evident universality.[16]

This merciless separation between subject and object makes for an incurable loneliness that, in turn, impels the subject to gather things, in order to surround him- or herself with a subject-domain that is not-other. Small children do this, collecting gravel, sticks, the odd pieces that grown-ups call junk but which, for the child, has no quality other than constituting an extension of the self, called for to remedy the sense of being cut-off. Adults are likely to disavow the similarity between their own forms of collecting and this childish gathering: they would rather claim that the collection makes their environment more 'interesting'; but 'interesting' is a catch-phrase destined to obscure more specific *interests* in the stronger sense of German critical philosophy.[17] This stronger sense of *interests* becomes painfully obvious when, as tends to be the case, the object of gathering is 'the other'. For then, objects of cultural alterity must be made 'not-other'. Clearly, the act of collecting then becomes a form of subordination, appropriation, de-personification.

This process of meaning-production is paradoxical. The 'not-other' objects-to-be must first be made to become 'absolute other' so as to be possessible to all.[18] This is done by cutting objects off from their context. It is relevant to notice that the desire to extend the limits of the self – to appropriate, through 'de-othering' – is already entwined with a need to dominate, which in turn depends on a further 'alterisation' of alterity. This paradoxical move, I will argue, is precisely the defining feature of fetishism in all senses of the term.

In Clifford's analysis, collecting defines subjectivity in an institutional practice, a definition he qualifies, with Baudrillard, as both essential and imaginary: 'as essential as dreams'.[19] Essential, but not universal; rather, this particular need is for him an essential aspect of being a member of a culture that values possessions, a qualification that might need further qualification according to class and gender. And it is imaginary to the extent that it partakes of the formation of subjectivity in the unconscious, which is itself the product of the collision and the collusion of imaginary and symbolic orders. Deceptively, collections, especially when publicly accessible, appear to 'reach out', but through this complex and half-hidden aspect they in fact 'reach in', helping the collector – and, to a certain extent, the viewer – to develop their sense of self while providing them with an ethical or educational alibi.

Beginnings: one

With this reflection as background it becomes easier to understand the narrative nature of fetishism as a crucial motivation for collecting. The literature on fetishism is immense; I will limit myself here to the common ground between the three most directly relevant domains: psychoanalysis, social theory – say, in the guise of Marxist analysis – and visuality. As for the anthropological concept of fetishism, it will be conceived here as largely a Western projection, and as such integrated in both Freudian and Marxist views. Psychoanalytically speaking, fetishism is a strong, mostly eroticised attachment to a single object or category. As is invariably the case in this discipline, that attachment is explained through a story of origin – the perception, crucially visual, of women's lack – and of semiotic behaviour.

It is a story that has been told and retold.[20] The child 'seeing in a flash' that the mother has no penis, identifies with this shocking sight in a first metaphorical transfer of 'absence of penis' to 'fundamental, existential lack', and acts on it. This negative 'presence' in the mother, because of its negativity, can only be the product of symbolisation; visual as the experience is, there is nothing object-ive about vision. 'Lack' is not the object seen, but the supplement provided by the seeing subject. If this negative vision is as crucial in the formation of subjectivity as it appears to be in Freudian theory, I wish to emphasise the crucial negativity of vision it implies. Vision, then, is both bound up with gender formation and with semiotic behaviour; it is an act of interpretation, of construction out of nothingness. If the penis must have this founding status, so be it. But then, it is not the member that makes members of the ruling class, but its absence that is the foundation of vision as a basically negative, gendered, act of fictionalisation.

The child denies the absence in a second act of symbolisation. This time, he denies the negativity. Superposing fiction upon fiction, the absence becomes presence, and the child is back to square one in more than one sense. Later on, the fixation of this denial results in the displacement of the absent penis onto some other element of the body, which must then be eroticized for the grown-up child to become fetishistic. This constitutes the third act of symbolization. This other element of the body – this object that must become the paradigm of object-ivity: semiotically invested objecthood – is subjected to a complex rhetorical strategy. In this strategy three tropes contribute to the perversion of meaning: *synecdoche*, the figure where a part comes to stand for the whole from which it was taken; *metonymy*, where one thing stands for another adjacent to it in place, time or logic; and *metaphor*, where one thing stands for another on the basis of similarity, that is, something both have in common.

Examples of these tropes in general use are well known. A sail stands for a sailboat as a synecdoche: it is part of what it signifies. Smoke stands for fire as a metonymy: it is contiguous to fire, both in space, since you see the smoke above the fire, and in time, since it develops out of the fire; and even in logic, as is suggested in the expression 'no smoke without fire'. A rose stands for love as a metaphor: both rose and love are transient, beautiful, and have the potential to hurt. These rhetorical strategies work as follows in the structure of fetishism. First, the substitute for the penis is synecdochically taken to stand for the whole body of which it is a part, through synecdoche: a foot can become eroticised in this way, for example, or 'a shine on the nose', as in Freud's case history of the English governess 'Miss Lucy R'. in *Studies in Hysteria* (1895). Or the substitute can be valued as contiguous to the body, through metonymy: for example, a fur coat, stockings, or a golden chain. But second, the whole is defined, in its wholeness, by the presence of a single part that is in turn a synecdoche for wholeness, the penis whose absence is denied. In another world this body-part might not have the meaning of wholeness, and therefore of the lack 'we' assign to it. But, if taken synecdochically, the penis can only represent masculinity, whereas the object of fetishism in this story is the woman's body, essentially the mother's. Hence, metaphor intervenes at this other end of the process, in other words, the representation of one thing through another with which it has something in common. The wholeness of the female body can only be synecdochically represented by the stand-in penis that is the fetish, if that body is simultaneously to be metaphorically represented by the male body.[21]

Note that this entire rhetorical machine, which puts the female subject safely at several removes, is set in motion by a *visual* experience.[22] This multiple removal allows us to get a first glimpse of the violence involved in this story, which might well become a classic horror story. I contend that it is this intrinsic violence that connects this Freudian concept of fetishism with the Marxian one, at least, as the latter has been analysed by W. J. T. Mitchell in his seminal study of discourses on word and image distinctions.[23]

Mitchell compares and confronts Marx's uses of the terms *ideology*, with its visual and semiotic roots, *commodity* and *fetish*, and brings to the fore a number of fascinating tensions in those uses. Fetish, Mitchell reminds us, is the specifically concrete term Marx used in order to refer to commodities, a strikingly forceful choice, especially when one considers it against the background of the developments in anthropology at the time. 'Part of this force is rhetorical,' Mitchell states:

The figure of 'commodity fetishism' (*der Fetischcharacter der Ware*) is a kind of catachresis, a violent yoking of the most primitive, exotic, irrational, degraded objects of human value with the most modern, ordinary, rational, and civilized.[24]

The anthropological notion of the fetish is clearly needed for the rhetorical purpose of this contrast in the well-known process of radical 'othering' of other cultural practices – which is why it seems inappropriate even to bring it in as anything other than this Western projection. Mitchell pursues this rhetorical analysis of the concept in a footnote that is worth quoting in full:

The translation of *Ware* by the term 'commodities' loses some of the connotations of commonness and ordinariness one senses in the German. But the etymology of 'commodities', with its associations of fitness, proportion, and rational convenience (cf. 'commodious') sustains the *violence* of Marx's figure, as does the obvious tension between the sacred and the secular. The origin of the word 'fetish', on the other hand (literally, a 'made object') tends to sustain the propriety of the comparison, insofar as both commodities and fetishes are products of human labor.[25]

The violence, both in the Freudian and in the Marxian conception of fetishism, is brought to light through rhetorical analysis, and consists of multiple degrees of *detachment*.

In both cases, it is also through the *visual* nature of the event (Freud) or object (Marx) respectively that this violence is necessary. Mitchell's analysis of the way the visual metaphor functions in Marx's cluster of concepts – ideology, commodity, fetish – convincingly demonstrates how crucial this visuality is for Marx's rhetoric. For my purposes the insistence on vision of both Marx and Freud in their accounts of the (narrative) emergence of fetishism and of fetishism's essence, respectively, matters primarily because of the paradoxical subjectivation of objects that is the intrinsic other side of the objectification of subjectivity described in these theories. What gives visuality its central relevance is the deceptiveness of its object-ivity. Vision is by no means more reliable, or literal, than perception through the other senses; on the contrary, it is a semiotic activity of an inherently rhetorical kind. The violence Mitchell points out is not due to the rhetoric itself, but to the need to obscure it.

This paradox enables Slavoj Žižek to push this subject-constructing power of objects one step further, and to come up, not with a Marxian Freud, but with a Lacanian Marx. In his discussion of ideology he writes:

CREATING HISTORICAL EFFECTS   95

we have established a new way to read the Marxian formula 'they do not know it, but they are doing it': the illusion is not on the side of knowledge, it is already on the side of reality itself, of what the people are doing. What they do not know is that their social reality itself, their activity, is guided by an illusion, by a fetishistic inversion.[26]

And a little further on he 'translates' this relational social reality onto the objects that are positioned in it. Putting it as strongly as he can, Žižek writes:

The point of Marx's analysis, however, is that *the things (commodities) themselves believe in their place*, instead of the subjects; it is as if all their beliefs, superstitions and metaphysical mystifications, supposedly surmounted by the rational, utilitarian personality, are embodied in the 'social relations between things'. They no longer believe, *but the things themselves believe for them.*[27]

Žižek goes on to argue that this is a Lacanian view to the extent that it is a conception of belief as 'radically exterior, embodied in the practical, effective procedure of people'.[28] The function of ideology – Žižek's concern here – is, then, like the junk accumulated by the child, or the objects collected by our hero the collector: 'not to offer us a point of escape from our reality but to offer us the social reality itself as an escape from some traumatic, real kernel'.[29]

There is no point in pushing the similarity between Marx and Freud too far, however. On the contrary, the concept of fetishism needs to be rigorously reinstated in its full ambiguity as a *hybrid*. True, both appear to be not only fixating on the visual aspect of fetishism, but also in its wake on the twisted relation between subject and object to the extent that, for Lacan, they can change places. They both articulate these aspects in a narrative of origin where vision as both positive knowledge and perverting subjectivity constitutes the core event. Yet, it is in the plot of their respective narratives that their crucial difference lies. Freud's story is that of individual development, of the little boy growing up with the burden of his early negative mis-vision. Marx's story is the grand narrative of History. In both cases, there is a discrepancy between the narrator and the focalisor. The narrator 'tells' his story in a non-verbal way, the Freudian subject by acting out his erotic fetishism, the Marxian subject by living his historical role, including the acquisition of commodities, perhaps in the mode of collecting. For Freud, the narrator is an adult male agent, for Marx, the historical agent. This narrator is by necessity stuck with a double vision, embedding the focalisation of adult and child, of lucid agent and deceived idolator, indistinguishably. Freud's focalisor has fully endorsed the doubly negative vision of the child, including the remedial denial and the fetishistic displacement. Marx's focalisor is a selfconscious agent standing within the historical process and endorsing as well as denouncing false consciousness and the idols of the mind.[30] Far from demystifying commodity fetishism from a transcendental position outside history, Marx turns commodities themselves into figurative, allegorical entities, 'possessed of a mysterious life and aura'.[31] The self-evident acceptance of motivations listed by Pearce is an acknowledgement of the inevitability of this double focalisor.

If this double focalisor can be retained as the most central feature of fetishism in both Freud's and Marx's sense, and, in turn, this double-edged fetishism as a crucial element of motivation, then it becomes easier to see, not the self-evidence but the inevitability of the impulse to collect within a cultural situation that is itself hybridic: a mixture of capitalism and individualism enmeshed with alternative modes of historical and psychological existence. In other words, rather than presenting that impulse through a list of independently possible motivations that sound innocent, collecting must become, through an analysis of its complex of motivations, a true *problematic*. A problematic is a complex epistemological problem that is at the same time a political hybrid; it is neither dismissible as simply ethically objectionable, subject to the moralism that sustains liberalism, nor is it ethically indifferent and politically irrelevant. In contrast, the hybrid notion of fetishism, able to account for the entanglement of agency in a political *and* individual history, should be assigned its rightful – because productive – place as the *beginning* of the beginning of collecting seen as narrative. This is why there is no unambiguous beginning. For its very search is bound up with, as Naomi Schor put it in her interpretation of a broken gold chain in Flaubert's *Salammbô*: the 'original and intimate relationship that links the fetish and the shiny, the undecidable and the ornamental'.[32] Collecting fits this bill more than nicely.

Middle

Aristotle wasn't stating the obvious when he insisted that narratives also have a middle. For whereas the beginning is by definition elusive, it is the development of the plot that is the most recognizable characteristic of a narrative. The retrospective fallacy that alone enabled the speculative beginning is itself the *res* in whose middle the structure of *in medias res* takes shape; the beginning *is* the middle, and it is constituted as beginning only to mark the boundaries of the narrative once the latter is called into being. Conversely, once a beginning is established, it becomes easier to perceive the development of the plot of collecting. Again, one can focus on either the objects or the collector as narrative agents, and again, their stories do not converge. The objects are radically deprived of any function they might possibly have outside of being collected items. According to an early theorist of collecting, this deprivation is so fundamental as to change the nature of the objects:

If the *predominant* value of an object or idea for the person possessing it is intrinsic, i.e., if it is valued primarily for use, or purpose, or aesthetically pleasing quality, or other value inherent in the object or accruing to it by whatever circumstances of custom, training, or habit, it is not a collection. If the predominant value is representative or representational, i.e., if said object or idea is valued chiefly for the relation it bears to some other object or idea, or objects, or ideas, such as being one of a series, part of a whole, a specimen of a class, then it is the subject of a collection.[33]

If this change in the nature of the object is not taken as an articulation of a definition but as an event, it might be illuminating to see this event of deprivation as the core of collecting as itself a narrative, particularly as such a change in nature is a *narrator's* decision. Note the strikingly modern semiotic vocabulary employed: objects are inserted into the narrative perspective when their status is turned from objective to semiotic, from thing to sign, from collapse to separation of thing and meaning, or from presence to absence. The object is turned away, abducted, from itself, its inherent value, and denuded of its defining function so as to be available for use as a sign. I use the words 'abducted' and 'denuded' purposefully; they suggest that the violence done to the objects might have a gendered quality. This will become more explicit below.

The new meaning assigned to the object, Durost suggests, is determined by the syntagmatic relations it enters into with other objects. These relations may be synecdochic ('part of a whole', 'one of a series') or metonymic ('valued chiefly for the relation it bears to some other object or idea'). But this relation is also always metaphoric ('a specimen of a class'): the object can only be *made* to be representative when it is made representational, standing for other objects with which it has this representational capacity in common. This insertion, by means of rhetoric, of objects defined by objecthood into a syntagm of signs is the body of the narrative that emerges when we choose to consider collecting so. Violence is done to the objects in each episode of collecting, each event of insertion that is also an act of deprivation. This is not a one-time act, for meaning changes as the collection as a whole changes. As the narrative develops, each object already inserted is modified anew.

This narrative development can perhaps be made clearer through apparent counter-examples. Aberrant plots like single-object collections, aborted collections, as well as anti-collecting – the accumulation of objects *not* related – demonstrate the plotted nature of collecting conceived through the objects. Another way to emphasise this aspect of collecting is the frequently occurring change in the ordering of an extant collection, or a number of different collections whose intersections are reorganised. A striking example of this re-plotting is provided by Debora J. Meijers's analysis of the new organisation by Christian von Mechel around 1780 of the Habsburg painting collection.[34]

Whereas the objects in the collection remained virtually the same, the collection itself was set up in such a different way, conveying, through this re-plotting, such a different conception – not only of this particular collection but of collecting itself as a mode of knowledge production – that Meijers is able to argue for an epistemic break as the meaning-producing agency. In terms of the present discussion, the objects as things remained the same, but the objects *as signs* became radically different, since they were inserted into a different syntagm. The act of insertion, accompanied by the act of deprivation of objecthood as well as of previous meanings, propels the plot forward as it constitutes the development of the narrative. In spite of the anti-narrative synchronicity of Meijers's Foucaultian perspective, in which the two epistemes, before and after the break, are compared in their static epistemological make-up, the dynamic 'life' of the objects during the process of their insertion into a collection clearly stands out in her analysis.

Considering the collector as a narrative agent, the motivation itself is subjected to the development of plot. Unlike the suggestion emanating from Pearce's listing of motivations, motivation changes according to its place in the narrative. The notion, developed above, that a complex and hybrid kind of fetishism – indebted to childhood gendering as well as to submission to political history, to memory as well as to lived experience in the present – underlies collecting in the Western world, implies a fundamental instability of meaning. If initially – always retrospectively understood – the predominant aspect of the fetishism that informs collecting is anchored in anxiety over gender, this emphasis is likely to shift on the way. It may shift, for example, from obsessive attachment to each one of the objects in itself to investment in collecting as an occupation; or from accumulating to ordering. But more significantly, the relation to the fragility of subjectivity itself may shift. In one episode of this narrative, the extension of subjectivity through investment in the series of objects fit to stand in for the absent attribute of the past may overrule other affects. In another episode, not gender but time – death – can get the upper hand. In accordance with Freud's concept of the death instinct, subjects constantly work their way through the difficulty of constituting themselves by re-enacting a primal scenario of separation, of loss and recovery, in order to defer death. Collecting can be attractive as a gesture of endless deferral of death in this way; this view provides Pearce's 'achieving immortality' with a meaning more intimately related to narrative. As Peter Brooks has argued,[35] this need to repeat events in order to hold off death is the very motor of narrative.

But this elaboration of collecting as a narrative of death can also come to stand in tension with its other side: the desire to reach the ending. What if, to recall another of Pearce's categories, the perfection, or completion, strived for is actually reached? Of course, it is not a question of real, 'objective' perfection – although when the series is finite, completion is quite possible. Perfection, as a subjectively construed standard of idealisation, may come so dangerously close that the collector cannot bear to pursue it. Unlike what one might tend to assume, this is not a happy, but an extremely unhappy, ending of our narrative.

Endings

If completion is possible, perfection is dangerous. Completion may be a simple way of putting an end to a collecting narrative – defining it, so to speak, as a short story – in order to begin a new one. The collection that harbours all items of a given series will have no trouble extending itself laterally, and will start a new one. Perfection, the equivalent of death in the sense that it can only be closely approximated, not achieved 'during the life time' of the subject, is one of those typically elusive objects of desire like happiness, or the satisfaction of any other desire. Perfection can only be defined as the ending; as what brings collecting to a close by default. It is an imaginary ending that owes its meaning to the contrast between it and what can be called the contingent ending. The latter is the product of such contingent happenings as running out of space, disposing of collections, changes in desires, changes in forms of storage, sales, gifts or death – not death as constitutive force in subjectivity but as arbitrary event.

Again, in order to make sense of this random set of notions, a narrative perspective can be helpful. According to the logic of plot, or of theories of fabula, of structuralist genealogy, the particular combinations of beginnings, middles and endings that make up a story of collecting allow illuminating specifications of collectings. Reduced to its bare minimum, the structuralist model designed by Claude Bremond, for example, which is the simplest of its kind, presents 'narrative cycles' as processes of amelioration or deterioration of a situation, according to the wish or desire of a primary agent. The possibilities Claude Bremond lists in his model are not so much 'logical' in the general sense (as he claims), but rather, specifically, ideo-logical and psycho-logical.[36] Thus a fetishistic subject whose gender and historical identity heavily depend on the possession of certain objects supposedly undertakes to acquire these. The episode leading up to the acquisition of each object that so contributes to this subject's sense of self and fulfilment constitutes one step in the process of amelioration for this subject. The accomplishment of acquisition constitutes the closing of the cycle, which opens up the next one: either the renewed desire for a similar object that typically indicates the collector's mind-set, or the desire for a different kind of fulfilment that signals the premature ending of the story of collecting. Rendered in this way, the process of amelioration takes place at the intersection of private and public, psychic and historic existence, and the episode contributes to the shaping of this subject as much as the subject shapes the episode.

This structure can, and indeed must, be complicated in two ways. The position of the initiating subject can be filled in differently. A process that brings amelioration to the collector, for example, can bring deterioration to the object-being as it forfeits its function and, by extension, to the subject who held, used or owned it before. Thus, the same process needs to be assessed twice over, in order to expose the subjective nature of the meaning of the event. The second complication is constituted by a further specification of the amelioration itself – or the deterioration. Bremond distinguishes processes like accomplishment of a task, intervention of an ally, elimination of an opponent, negotiation, attack, retribution. These types are obviously derived from folk tales, and their relevance for collecting seems far-fetched. Yet, their allegiance to a specific type of plot – one in which hostility is a major factor – unexpectedly illuminates a side of collecting that was already present in Pearce's list: competition, domination. Each of these – and others are of course conceivable – turn the event into something other than what it seems in the cheerful light of most of the many isolated motivations.

For at the intersection of psychic and capitalist fetishism, the narratives such analyses entail turn collecting into something else again: a tale of social struggle. This struggle over 'ameliorations' by means of an attack on someone else's property with the help of money; negotiation over prices; elimination of a rival; accomplishment of the task of developing 'taste'; expertise competing with that of others – all these plots engage subjects on both sides of the 'logic of narrative possibilities', and on both sides of gender, colonialist and capitalist splits. If the plot evolves so easily around struggle, then the collector's opponents are bound to be the 'other': the one who loses the object, literally by having to sell or otherwise yield it, or, according to the visual rhetoric of Freud's little boy, by forfeiting that for which the collector's item is a stand-in. Paradoxically, the narratives of collecting enable a clearer vision of this social meaning.

NOTES

1. *Capital*, I, p. 72, cited in W. J. T. Mitchell, *Iconology: Language, Text, Ideology* (Chicago, 1986), p. 189.

2. 'The Age of the World View', *Measure*, 2, pp. 269–84, cited in E. Hooper-Greenhill, *Museums and the Shaping of Knowledge* (London, 1992), p. 82.

3. *Framing the Sign: Criticism and Its Institutions* (London, 1988), p. 203.

4. Speech-act theory considers language from the angle of its effectivity. It was first developed by J. L. Austin, and set out in his posthumously published *How to Do Things With Words* (1962). Austin proposes a distinction between utterances that are constative, informative, and those that

are performative – that have no meaning other than the act they, in fact, *are* (like promising). When you say 'I promise', you *do* it; that is the only meaning the verb has.

5. My theory of narrative can be found in M. Bal, *Narratology: Introduction to the Theory of Narrative* (Toronto, 1992). For discussions with other narrative theories, see M. Bal, *On Story-telling: Essays in Narratology* (Sonoma, Calif., 1991).

6. This conclusion is reached through different routes by historiographers like Hayden White, *Metahistory: The Historical Imagination in Nineteenth-century Europe* (Baltimore, 1973); idem, 'Interpretation in History', *Tropics of Discourse* (Baltimore, 1978), pp. 51–80.

7. S. M. Pearce, *Museums, Objects and Collections: A Cultural Study* (Leicester and London, 1992).

8. P. Brooks, *Reading for the Plot: Design and Intention in Narrative* (New York, 1984).

9. Pearce, op. cit., p. 47.

10. Represented primarily by Melanie Klein, *The Psycho-analysis of Children* (New York, 1975), and by D. W. Winnicott, *Playing and Reality* (London, 1980).

11. But for the persistent carry-over between explicating articulation and explanations of origin in psychoanalysis, see T. Pavel, 'Origin and Articulation: Comments on the Papers by Peter Brooks and Lucienne Frappier-Mazur', *Style*, xviii (1984), pp. 355–68.

12. Pearce, op. cit., p. 47.

13. Bourdieu, *Distinction: A Social Critique of the Judgement of Taste* (Cambridge, Mass., 1984), p. 54, cited in Pearce, op. cit., p. 50.

14. Clifford, 'On Collecting Art and Culture', *The Predicament of Culture: Twentieth-Century Ethnography, Literature and Art* (Cambridge, Mass., 1988), pp. 215–51.

15. Clifford, op. cit., p. 218.

16. This was the purpose of my analysis of a few rooms of the American Museum of Natural History, published as 'Telling, Showing, Showing Off', *Critical Inquiry*, xviii/3 (1992), pp. 556–94.

17. For a good, succinct discussion of this concept of interest, see R. Geuss, *The Idea of a Critical Theory: Habermas and the Frankfurt School* (Cambridge, 1981), pp. 45–54, and, of course, Habermas's own seminal book *Knowledge and Human Interest* (London, 1972).

18. To clarify the issue, I am radicalizing Clifford's argument slightly.

19. Jean Baudrillard, *Le Système des objets* (Paris, 1968), p. 135; Clifford, op. cit., p. 220.

20. Sigmund Freud, 'Some Psychological Consequences of the Anatomical Distinction Between the Sexes' (1925), in J. Strachey, ed., *The Standard Edition of the Complete Psychological Works*, xxi (London, 1963), pp. 149–57; Otto Fenichel, 'Fetishism', in *The Psychoanalytic Theory of Neurosis* (London, 1936), pp. 341–51.

21. For a feminist critique of fetishism, see Naomi Schor, 'Salammbô Bound', in *Breaking the Chain: Women, Theory and French Realist Fiction* (New York, 1985), pp. 111–26; and for a feminist reflection on female fetishism, idem, 'Female Fetishism: The Case of George Sand', in *The Female Body in Western Culture: Contemporary Perspectives*, ed. S. Rubin Suleiman (Cambridge, Mass., 1985), pp. 363–72.

22. For a more extensive analysis of the intimate – and narrative – connections between psychoanalysis and visuality, see 'Blindness or Insight? Psychoanalysis and Visual Art' in M. Bal, *Reading Rembrandt: Beyond the Word-Image Opposition* (New York, 1991), pp. 286–325.

23. Mitchell, op. cit., pp. 160–208, esp. p. 191.

24. Mitchell, op. cit., p. 191.

25. Ibid.

26. Slavoj Žižek, *The Sublime Object of Ideology* (London, 1989), p. 32.

27. Žižek, op. cit., p. 34.

28. Ibid.

29. Ibid., p. 45.

30. Mitchell, op. cit., p. 176.

31. Ibid., p. 188.

32.   Schor, 'Salammbô Bound', p. 119.

33.   W. Durost, *Children's Collecting Activity Related to Social Factors* (New York, 1932), p. 10; cited in Pearce, op. cit., p. 48.

34.   D. J. Meijers, *Kunst als natuur: De Habsburgse schilderijengalerij in Wenen omstreeks 1780* (Amsterdam, 1991).

35.   Brooks, op. cit., *passim.*

36.   C. Bremond, *Logique du récit* (Paris, 1973); idem, 'The Logic of Narrative Possibilities', *New Literary History*, XI (1980), pp. 398–411.

II.

Instituting Evidence

Introduction:
Instituting Evidence

So vital is the part played by the art museum in our approach to works of art today that we find it difficult to realize that no museums exist, none has ever existed, in lands where the civilization of modern Europe is, or was, unknown; and that, even in the Western world, they have existed for barely two hundred years.   André Malraux, *Museum Without Walls* (1967)

The sources of museums are many: they can be traced to social practices, such as a diverse and complex history of collecting objects as exemplary specimens of one kind or another; to classificatory schemes originating in ancient Graeco-Roman science and rhetoric; to cognitive habits such as the training of 'memory' with mental images to serve as an instrument for the extemporaneous composition of stories and learned discourse. In the selection of articles that follow, Mary Carruthers describes the Western tradition of artistic invention in terms of the rhetorical arts of memory as the predecessor to modern ideas of creativity and imagination. Medieval adaptations of ancient Stoic formulations of rhetorical theory bear an uncanny, and still under-studied, resemblance to the material 'theaters of the world' assembled by early modern collectors, and to the virtual counterparts of actual collections described in universal terms by visionaries like Giulio Camillo Delminio and Athanasius Kircher, who tried to circumscribe the burgeoning world of created things within a reasonable (and rational) order – even if the significance of this new world remained, for the moment, beyond human grasp. As Paula Findlen observes in her contribution, the institutional history of preserving and interpreting material evidence involves neither text nor context exclusively, but rather the interplay between them was designed to solve a crisis of knowledge.

Briefly stated, the modern museum has its direct antecedents in earlier modes of collecting – inscriptions, sculptures, drawings, paintings, gems, plants, animals (in the 1530s, in an early demonstration of racial typology, Ippolito de' Medici even collected a human menagerie as a form of courtly entertainment).[1] The *Kunst-* and *Wunderkammer*s of all sizes filled with many curious and exotic 'wonders', assembled by princes, aristocrats, and other learned persons since the fifteenth century, became the actual material bases of many modern museums, and – equally important – their erudite ways of using objects in conversation served as the historical antecedent to the performative nature of knowledge that museums entail to the present day, with which should properly be included the modern discourses of art history, art criticism, and aesthetic philosophy. Recently, the intertwining of social habits and entrepreneurial interests in seventeenth-century art collecting has begun to receive critical attention.[2]

The question remains why museums emerged when they did, first as part of a humanist collecting culture and roughly two centuries later as public institutions that helped to shape a shared historical ancestry for the citizens of newly created nation states. The Ashmolean Museum in Oxford was the first to open its doors officially to the general public, in 1682, but the enormous collections of natural specimens and (what later came to be called ethnographic) artifacts that Ulisse Aldrovandi and his colleagues willed to the city of Bologna functioned in a similarly public fashion by the mid-seventeenth century, as did collections of paintings, sculptures, and other works of art in Florence, Dresden, Vienna, and elsewhere.[3]

Each Western nation has its own museum history: some, like that of revolutionary France, have been narrated with consummate skill; other stories are only beginning to be pieced together, as is the case with Sweden, showcased in Chapter 5 of this volume in two extensively documented studies that draw upon the resources of a place never decimated by war in modern times. Unfortunately, in other cases, the evidence that survives the vicissitudes of human conflict is more fragmentary and accidental. For all their individual differences, museums, as André Malraux was among the first to note, are a consistent type of institutional structure, conceived in Europe. The status of the museum of a social institution in maintaining what Foucault called the *episteme*, or epistemological totality of modern society, remains open to interpretation. The transition from the semi-private spheres of dynastic state formations to the public sphere of the modern state that public museums helped to construct and maintain is one dynamic that urgently deserves further study at this moment.

The most convincing critiques to date portray the museum as if it were always, in essence, more than an actual physical presence, a place or an institution housing a collection. The idea of the museum involves socially conditioned cognitive structures. Stephen Bann's groundbreaking study about the 'poetics' of the Louvre, reprinted in Chapter 1 of this volume, argues that the historical significance of the first truly modern museum is due above all to its order of display, part metaphoric and part synedochal, oscillating between two alternatives for configuring the relationship of the past to the present, one representing the past as temporal succession, the other as an 'experiential reality'. In either case, the museum setting conjures up the 'past' using theatrical techniques.

The epistemological status of the illusion that museums create using objects that, until quite recently, were initially made for other purposes, is a matter for careful consideration. Giuseppe Olmi, whose contribution to an out-standing volume on the early modern history of museums, entitled *The Origins of Museums: The Cabinet of Curiosities in Sixteenth- and Seventeenth-Century Europe* (edited by Oliver Impey and Arthur MacGregor, 1985) is included here, emphasizes the importance to modernity of Aristotelian modes of classification imposed on a vast number of species previously unknown to Europeans. Seventeenth-century collectors, more than their predecessors, specialized in certain kinds of objects, publishing printed catalogues (such as the 1677 catalogue of Cospi's collection, written by Lorenzo Legati) that not only enhanced their owners' social status but also made the erudite practices of collecting available to a much wider and less educated reading public. Margaret Hodgen, in a now-classic study of early anthropological practices in the sixteenth and seventeenth centuries (1964), was one of the first to acknowledge that print technology contributed greatly to the construction of new 'Europocentric' categories of classification by enabling the dissemination of attractive illustrated cultural geographies directed at a burgeoning middle class.[4] This highly commoditized from of literature, as Louise Pratt and others have also studied, was based on the ancient schemes of Aristotle, Herodotus, Pliny, and Solinas, who assigned people to either 'barbarian' or 'civilized' societies depending on a preordained set of normative categories such as their forms of religion, education, social organization, and artistic production.

The Aristotelian juxtaposition of *naturalia* and *artificialia* likewise provided many collections with a form of organization that passes as transparent: such binomial schemes seem to mirror the entire world, whereas they actually provide filtering lenses for sorting data, as Paula Findlen and William B. Ashworth, Jr, both emphasize in their contributions to this chapter. Their arguments corroborate Carruthers's analysis of cognitive habits in an earlier period of European culture: the illusory transparency of objects captured in these historical classificatory schemes depends on ascribing symbolic, ideological value to both the natural world and artistic representation along an open-ended continuum. Ashworth calls the effect of this complex activity of classifying the 'emblematic world view'.

There is today a general consensus that the status of all objects, both natural and artifactual, changed dramatically during the course of the Scientific Revolution. Rather than representing a preexisting intelligible order through visual signs syntagmatically and hierarchically linked in multiple associations, the embodied 'truth' of the artifact came to serve as *primary evidence* for the writing of natural and cultural history. Although the first chapter of *Grasping the World* focused on the creation of the Louvre as the founding moment of the modern museum, the history of modes of collecting and display cannot be narrated in biological terms as if the circumstances surrounding the establishment of a single museum originated the entire phenomenon. The history of the idea of the museum deals, more broadly, with ways in which institutions are *structurally* related to one another – what role do museums play in structuring the *episteme* or epistemological totality?

In the first chapter of *Grasping the World*, we have already learned that, for Quatremère de Quincy, who criticized the Louvre and argued against decontextualizing works of art, the new public museum was a poor substitute for living cities, above all, for Rome, that 'three-dimensional *mapamundi* of the ancient and modern world'. The director of the Louvre, François de Neufchâteau, on the other hand, claimed that creation of the public museum along the lines to which Quatremère objected constituted a political and ethical act making it possible for art objects that were made for the elite to be enjoyed by all. What was at stake for the newly created French state in promoting the politics of a class revolution over the cultural cosmopolitanism of continental Enlightenment philosophy? With its egalitarianism, the new nationalist rhetoric encouraged cultural relativism: the chronology of national 'styles' assigned every cultural formation its own distinct historical trajectory.

Yet the revised model was deeply flawed in another way: the idea that cultures are distinct and separate entities with their own parallel trajectories completely disregards the complexities of imperialist expansionism and colonialism practiced on a larger scale. In this respect, the immediate political gains of a class revolution only substituted one set of ethnocentric ideas for another in which European civilization continued to provide the norm. The consequences, as Spivak writes about Germany in a far-reaching critique of the postcolonial subject position, continue into the present:

> The narrative of 'German' cultural self-representation, within the Western European context, is therefore one of difference. Its very singularity provides a sort of link with that earlier scenario of self-representation that would not allow the name 'German', a lack of unified nationhood that could only find a fuller founding through the rediscovery of a German antiquity; a lack of participation in the European Renaissance that would nonetheless allow a modern and active reenactment of the Renaissance.[5]

As Fred Bohrer recounts in his analysis of Assyrian artifacts displayed in nineteenth-century France and England, included in this chapter, the nationalist model adopted at the Louvre and followed by many other public museums made different cultural formations apparently commensurable with one another and silently subservient to a preexisting hierarchical order. Confirming and extending Edward Said's thesis that Europeans defined themselves through their imaginary construction of the Orient as their reduced and inverted mirror image, Bohrer presents new documentation of Europeans' belittling attitudes towards the Middle East established in the mid-nineteenth century. (Similar circumstances simultaneously developed with respect to Native American antiquities.[6]) The apparent commensurability and masked hierarchy were 'performed' in a variety of nineteenth-century contexts including academic painting, popular literature, scholarly publications, world trade fairs, the actual physical arrangement of collections and gallery spaces, and in competition among archaeologists who played out nationalistic rivalries through the amassing of remains exported from newly 'discovered' ancient worlds (regardless of contemporary objections from host countries over the exploitation and exportation of their material cultural heritage).

Bohrer's essay also introduces what might be called the performative implications of these nineteenth-century forms of popular education and entertainment, which are the focus of Chapter 3 of *Grasping the World*. The present chapter is primarily concerned with the ways in which the material evidence itself was ordered at the institutional level. The main conclusion to be drawn from all the essays is that European audiences imposed their preexistent repertory of cultural and aesthetic assumptions onto newly discovered artifacts, thus hardening existing binary distinctions between East and West while also stretching existing taxonomic schemes beyond their tensile strength. Societies that were heterogeneous in various ways were treated as commensurable and thus homologous – the physical experience of the actual artifacts *seemed* objective, but insiduously reinforced the ethnocentric categories (irrelevant to the cultures under study) that illustrated cultural geographies and travel literature had introduced two centuries earlier.

National models of culture and their historical precedents in Enlightenment ideas of community are equally problematic. As George Mosse has emphasized in his study of Jewish emigration immediately before and during World War II, scholars, professionals, artists, and other producers of European culture overcame the racism they experienced in their European setting with a global vision of humanity.[7] Given the political circumstances in Germany and elsewhere in western Europe in the 1930s, it is not surprising that this generation of liberal intellectuals dealt with racism by denying the historical role of racial theory altogether.[8] Panofsky and other European intellectuals who emigrated to escape Nazism sidestepped the embattled issues of 'racism' and 'nationalism' when they revalidated the Enlightenment concept of self-cultivation, or *Bildung*, and conceived of themselves as members of an international community. When Panofsky developed a method of art historical interpretation that relocated Italian Renaissance humanist values at the center of the discipline, however, he not only gave Renaissance humanism an unprecedented status to govern the interpretation of all forms of art, he glossed over the previous generation's objections to a humanist model of culture that grants priority to Greek antiquity and its modern revival.[9]

The pressing concern of the present generation is that the same problems of ethnocentrism that confronted *both* Quatremère and Neufchâteau still confronted Panofsky and Riegl, and still confront us. Why this repetition? What, in the psychoanalytical terms proposed for writing history by de Certeau, is being repressed?

The contemporary problematic involves the ways in which collective memory is and is not preserved in actual archives. Consider Derrida's project, named but not (yet) pursued, to investigate the mechanisms of the 'patriarchive':

The question of the archive is not, we repeat, a question of the past. It is not the question of a concept dealing with the past that might *already* be at our disposal, an *archivable concept of the archive*. It is a question of the future, the question of the future itself, the question of a response, of a promise and of a responsibility for tomorrow.[10]

A 'spectral messianicity', Derrida continues, is at work in the concept of the archive – and what he says about the archive pertains to all historical enterprise – because the past we construct, whether it justifies the present, undermines it, or relates to it in some other way, is nothing other than a *construction*, an arrangement of evidence, a work of human artifice assembled and displayed for purposes at hand, in the present.

In turning to the following studies on the ways in which material evidence and textual documentation have been preserved in Europe at the institutional level, consider that no objectivization is pure, because in exhibiting the document, the archivist also establishes it.[11] Exhibition, in short, is never *not* invested – every historical representation is always, as James Clifford argues, strategically motivated.[12] Historians acknowledge this situation inadequately if they do not take their own institutional subject positions in a historical continuum into account as part of their study – that is, if they mask the point of disjunction between the present and the past that they posit between them. The question of accounting for the history of archives thus turns out to be a questionable enterprise: Derrida asks, 'does one need a first archive in order to conceive of originary archivability?'[13]

NOTES

1. Detlef Heikamp with Ferdinand Anders, *Mexico and the Medici*, Florence: Editrice Edam, 1972; on early humanist collecting, see Roberto Weiss, *The Renaissance Discovery of Classical Antiquity*, 2nd edn, London: Basil Blackwell, 1969.

2. Notably, see the excellent study by Genevieve Warwick, *The Arts of Collecting: Padre Sebastinao Resta and the Market for Drawings in Early Modern Europe*, Cambridge: Cambridge University Press, 2000, which situates both collecting and financial gains made from the sale of art in a direct historical continuum with the age-old practice within the Catholic Church of making financial donations to religious charity (see p. 62).

3. On Aldrovandi's activities, see further *Bologna e il Mondo Nuovo*, ed. Laura Laurencich Minelli, exh. cat., Bologna: Grafix Edizioni, 1991.

4. Margaret Hodgen, *Early Anthropology in the Sixteenth and Seventeenth Centuries*, Philadelphia: University of Pennsylvania Press, 1964, especially 'Collections of Customs: Modes of Classification and Description', pp. 162–206.

5. Gayatri Chakravorty Spivak, *A Critique of Postcolonial Reason: Toward a History of the Vanishing Present*, Cambridge, Mass.: Harvard University Press, 1999, p. 7.

6. See Claire Farago and Donna Pierce, et al., *Transforming Images: Locating New Mexican Santos in-between Worlds*, University Park: Pennsylvania State University Press, forthcoming 2004.

7. George L. Mosse, *German Jews Beyond Judaism*, Bloomington, Ind.: Indiana University Press, 1985. On the mass emigration of Jewish art historians, see the extensive chronicle in Colin Eisler, '*Kunstgeschichte* American Style: A Study in Migration', in *The Intellectual Migration, 1930–1960*, ed. D. Fleming and B. Bailyn (Cambridge, Mass.: Harvard University Press, 1970), pp. 544–629.

8. The sensitive issues go beyond racial *theory* to personal experience of racism. Compare the attitude expressed by Ernst Gombrich, leading proponent of the effort to expunge all forms of essentialism from art history, reminiscing about his upbringing in Vienna: 'Another thing that is often said is that the Viennese contribution to the modern world was in large part Jewish. That is a considerable oversimplification, and one would have to analyse it at much greater length to establish whether it were true. It is a question, anyway, of no particular interest except to racists …' (E. H. Gombrich and Didier Eribon, *Looking for Answers: Conversations on Art and Science*, New York: Harry N. Abrams, 1993, p. 14).

9. For recent critiques of Panofsky's humanistic bias, see Michael Ann Holly, *Panofsky and the Foundations of Art History*, Ithaca, N.Y.: Cornell University Press, 1984; and Keith Moxey, 'Panofsky's Concept of "Iconology" and the Problem of Interpretation in the History of Art', *New Literary History*, 17 (Winter, 1986), pp. 265–75. Moxey, p. 268, argues that Panofsky's discussion of pictorial perspective as a symbolic form in a 'diachronic system of interpretation serves only to privilege the Renaissance above all other periods under consideration'. Other aspects of Panofsky's 'humanist bias', according to Moxey and Holly, include (1) his choice of subject matter that tends to coincide with the values of the academic 'hierarchy of genres'; (2) his reliance on a [narrowminded] tradition of aesthetic judgments; and (3) neglect of the conditions of reception.

10. Jacques Derrida, *Archive Fever: A Freudian Impression*, trans. Eric Prenowitz, Chicago and London: University of Chicago Press, 1995.

11. Ibid., pp. 54–5.

12. James Clifford, *The Predicament of Culture: Twenthieth-Century Ethnography, Literature and Art*, Cambridge, Mass.: Harvard University Press, 1988, p. 19.

13. Derrida, *Archive Fever*, p. 13.

1.

Collective Memory and *Memoria Rerum*: An Architecture for Thinking

Mary Carruthers

Ut sapiens architectus fundamentum posui: alius autem superaedificat.

St Paul

1.   Machina memorialis

This study could be thought of as an extended meditation on the myth that Mnemosyne, 'memory', is the mother of all the Muses. That story places memory at the beginning, as the matrix of invention for all human arts, of all human making, including the making of ideas; it memorably encapsulates an assumption that memory and invention, or what we now call 'creativity', if not exactly one, are the closest thing to it. In order to create, in order to think at all, human beings require some mental tool or machine, and that 'machine' lives in the intricate networks of their own memory.

In terms of the five-fold 'parts' of rhetoric formulated memorably in antiquity for teaching the subject, *The Book of Memory* [Mary Carruthers, *The Book of Memory: A Study of Memory in Medieval Culture*, Cambridge University Press, 1990] centered on *memoria*; this one centers on *inventio*. The order will seem backwards, since 'everybody knows' that the ancients taught Invention, Disposition, Style, Memory, Delivery, in that order. Medieval scholars took Cicero's early treatise 'On Invention' (*De inventione*) as the First Rhetoric, calling the *Rhetorica ad Herennium*, then attributed to Cicero, the Second or New Rhetoric. This latter is the textbook that describes an art of memory based upon the building plan of a familiar house, in whose rooms and recesses an orator should 'place' images that recall to him the material he intends to talk about. So in medieval textbook tradition too, Invention precedes Memory.

Mnemonics, 'artificial memories', and 'memory tricks' (as they were called in the nineteenth century) have been viewed with skepticism; they were so even in antiquity, and certainly are now. One early seventeenth-century Chinese student, to whom the Jesuit missionary Matteo Ricci taught the art of memory as a help in studying for the onerous examination for the imperial civil service, finally complained to a confidant that the system was itself so cumbersome to learn that it was easier and took less memory just to memorize the original material. And surely, his assumption must have been, the good of an art of memory is to remember things in order to regurgitate them by rote later on.[1]

In this matter, as so often, the presentation of a subject in textbooks is misleading about daily practice: it seems to have been at least as much so to Ricci as to the exasperated student. For the orator's 'art of memory' was not in practice designed to let him reiterate exactly in every detail a composition he had previously fabricated. For one thing, to sound as though he were reciting from memory like a parrot was one of the worst faults a Roman orator could commit. It was also foolish, for if he were to forget his lines or if (very likely in the debates of the Republican Senate) he were flustered by some unexpected event or attack, he would have nothing to say. The goal of Roman oratory was to speak eloquently *ex tempore*; this was the sign of a master.[2]

Thus the orator's 'art of memory' was not an art of recitation and reiteration but an art of invention, an art that made it possible for a person to act competently within the 'arena' of debate (a favorite commonplace), to respond to interruptions and questions, or to dilate upon the ideas that momentarily occurred to him, without becoming hopelessly distracted, or losing his place in the scheme of his basic speech. That was the elementary good of having an 'artificial memory'.

The example given in the *Rhetorica ad Herennium*, of imagining the scene of a sick man in his bedroom, to whom a physician, carrying a ram's testicles on his fourth finger, offers a cup, is intended to recall the chief issues of a case at law, not to enable a word-by-word recitation of a previously made up and memorized speech. Remembering these themes as a readily reconstructable quasi-narrative scene of related figures, each of which cues a particular subject in the case, will help an orator readily to compose his speeches *ex tempore*, in response to the actual flow of the court proceedings.

All scholars who study the subject of rhetorical memory remain much indebted to Frances Yates. But for all its pioneering strengths, her work unfortunately does reinforce some common misconceptions about the possible cognitive uses of 'the art of memory', and thus the nature of its influence on the making of images and 'places' for this purpose. Yates herself believed that the goal of the art of memory was solely to repeat previously stored material: she characterized the medieval versions of the ancient art as 'static', without movement, imprisoning thought.[3] She could not have been more wrong.

She also found what she called 'the Ciceronian art', for all its fascination, preposterous and unworkable.[4] Agreeing, if reluctantly, with people like Matteo Ricci's Chinese student, she presented mnemotechnic as becoming first a pious and then an arcane study after antiquity, valued by Renaissance practitioners precisely because, even while they made extravagant claims for its practical utility, it was secret and difficult. Yates presented the medieval authors (such as the Dominican friars Albertus Magnus and Thomas Aquinas) who linked mnemonic craft to piety as mistaken and misdirected. Preferring the arcane to the mainstream, she ignored the basic pedagogy of memory in the Middle Ages, finding only a few medieval sources for the sixteenth- and seventeenth-century authors with whom she was primarily concerned.[5]

I repeat: the goal of rhetorical mnemotechnical craft was not to give students a prodigious memory for all the information they might be asked to repeat in an examination, but to give an orator the means and wherewithal to invent his material, both beforehand and – crucially – on the spot. *Memoria* is most usefully thought of as a compositional art.[6] The arts of memory are among the arts of thinking, especially involved with fostering the qualities we now revere as 'imagination' and 'creativity'.

This is not a development that one can trace by analysing the textbook tradition of rhetoric. As a 'part' of rhetoric, *memoria* was added to the textbook tradition by the Stoics, and its place in the order was not set for quite some time.[7] When it is discussed, authors pay scant attention to it, repeating a few general precepts. The only elaborated examples of mnemotechnical schemes are in the *Rhetorica ad Herennium*. And yet Cicero also says that the master orator's memory is fundamental to his craft. This opinion is repeated often, and classical pedagogy strove to furnish each student's mind with a solid foundation of memorized material. The technique, though not the content, was similar in the Jewish schools that produced the earliest Christian teachers.[8]

The meditational practice of monasticism is not particularly indebted to the pagan rhetorical practice described in the *Rhetorica ad Herennium*. I will make this point at length and often in this study; I emphasize it now because many scholars have assumed, as Yates did, that there was ever only one art of memory, 'the' art of memory. It is clear, however, that the monks also developed what they called an 'art' or 'discipline' of memory. This is different in many respects from the 'Ciceronian' one, but because those who developed it had the same general rhetorical education, the methods used share certain essentials. There are enough similarities that when the art described in the *Rhetorica ad Herennium* was revived in the thirteenth century, it could be made to seem familiar to late medieval culture. But the medieval revival of this specific art, transmitted and adapted primarily by the orders of canons and friars, took place fully within the context of monastic memory craft. That is why it seems to historians now that the ancient art of the *Rhetorica ad Herennium* suffered a peculiar sea-change, and why its cultural translation seems filled with 'mistakes' when they read descriptions of it from the later Middle Ages.

Monastic *memoria*, like the Roman art, is a locational memory; it also cultivates the making of mental images for the mind to work with as a fundamental procedure of human thinking. Because crafting memories also involved crafting the images in which those memories were carried and conducted, the artifice of memory was also, necessarily, an art of making various sorts of pictures: pictures in the mind, to be sure, but with close, symbiotic relationships to actual images and actual words that someone had seen or read or heard – or smelled or tasted or touched, for all the senses, as we will observe, were cultivated in the monastic craft of remembering.

2.   Invention and 'locational memory'

The relationship of memory to invention and cognition may sound straight-forward; it is not. For the notions of what constitutes 'invention' have changed significantly from the small-group societies of the pre-modern West to the rationalist individualism of the nineteenth century. Most importantly, in antiquity and through the Middle Ages, invention or 'creative thinking' received the most detailed attention in the domain of rhetoric, rather than of psychology or what we would now call the philosophy of mind. We should not forget this critical difference from our own intellectual habits.

We tend now to think of rhetoric primarily as persuasion of others, distinguishing 'rhetoric' from 'self-expression' (a distinction now often built into the syllabi of American college composition courses). But in Western monasticism, the craft of rhetoric became primarily focussed not on tasks of public persuasion but on tasks of what is essentially literary invention. It is not true to say (or imply), as histories of the subject have done, that the monks killed off rhetoric. They redirected it to forming citizens of the City of God, a characterization made long ago by Christopher Dawson:

alike in the East and the West, [the Church Fathers] were essentially *Christian rhetoricians* who shared the culture and traditions of their pagan rivals …
Throughout the Church, rhetoric had recovered [its] vital relation to social life: in place of the old *ecclesia* of the Greek city it had found the new ecclesia of the Christian people.[9]

The writings of those Church Fathers, each with an excellent rhetorical education – Augustine, Jerome, Basil, Cassian, Cassiodorus, and Gregory – formed an essential part of the basic curriculum of monasticism.

The Latin word *inventio* gave rise to two separate words in modern English. One is our word 'invention', meaning the 'creation of something new' (or at least different). These creations can be either ideas or material objects, including of course works of art, music, and literature. We also speak of people having 'inventive minds', by which we mean that they have many 'creative' ideas, and they are generally good at 'making', to use the Middle English synonym of 'composition'.

The other modern English word derived from Latin *inventio* is 'inventory'. This word refers to the storage of many diverse materials, but not to random storage: clothes thrown into the bottom of a closet cannot be said to be 'inventoried'. Inventories must have an order. Inventoried materials are counted and placed in locations within an overall structure which allows any item to be retrieved easily and at once. This last requirement also excludes collections that are too cumbersome or too unparticular to be useful; think about why it is so daunting to locate one's car in a vast parking lot.

Inventio has the meanings of both these English words, and this observation points to a fundamental assumption about the nature of 'creativity' in classical culture. Having 'inventory' is a requirement for 'invention'. Not only does this statement assume that one cannot create ('invent') without a memory store ('inventory') to invent from and with, but it also assumes that one's memory-store is effectively 'inventoried', that its matters are in readily-recovered 'locations'. Some type of locational structure is a prerequisite for any inventive thinking at all.[10]

These structures need not bear a direct relationship to the 'art of memory' described in the Republican Roman *Rhetorica ad Herennium*. To limit the study of 'locational memory' to this one variety has obscured both the generic concept and the medieval and even Renaissance developments of *memoria*. More important than (at least through the mid-thirteenth century), and in addition to, the precepts of the *Rhetorica ad Herennium*, there developed very early on in Christianity a *disciplina* or *via* of inventive meditation based on memorized locational-inventory structures (deriving from Biblical sources, but more of that later), which was called by the monks 'memoria spiritalis' or 'sancta memoria'. This traditional practice of meditation also was deeply implicated in the pedagogy of ancient rhetoric as well as the textual pedagogy of Judaism, making many of the same assumptions about 'invention' and how it is to be done that we find more generally in non-Christian sources. As a consequence, it did not develop in total isolation from the ancient rhetorical practices of invention and composition. The monastic art also employed a 'locational memory' as its foundational schema.

The model of memory as inherently locational, and having a particular cognitive role to play, is quite distinct from another philosophical model, equally influential in the West and equally ancient. This is the idea, known to the Middle Ages primarily through the works of Aristotle (and hence not influential in the monastic practice of *sancta memoria*) that defines memories temporally, as being 'of the past'.[11] Augustine too had emphasized the temporal nature of memories in his meditations, in the *Confessions* and elsewhere, on how we perceive 'time' in our minds. The two traditions are frequently confused, even now, and to help sort out their differences, it might be useful to pause over the analysis of prudential *memoria* by Albertus

Magnus, the first medieval philosopher to try seriously to distinguish and reconcile them. Albertus is an early scholastic figure, and wrote some fifty years after 1200, but his analysis clearly shows the continuing influence of monastic *memoria*.

Albertus retained a conviction that a locational model of memory was essential for purposes of cognition. In his treatise 'On the Good' (ca. 1246), when discussing the nature of prudence, he raises the apparent conflict between describing memory as essentially temporal and describing it as essentially locational. The *Rhetorica ad Herennium* states that 'artificial memory consists of backgrounds and images'.[12] How can memory *consist of* 'places' when Aristotle says that its essence is temporal?

Albertus responds that 'place' is required for the mental task of recollection. While it is true that memory can only be 'of' matters that are past, presented to us in 'images', the *task* of remembering requires that the images so stored be in places. Two very different questions are being inappropriately confused by the erroneous observation of a 'conflict' between Aristotle and Cicero concerning the nature of memory, Albertus implies. The one question, 'What is memory?' (answer: 'Memory is stored-up images of past experiences') is an ontological one, 'What is the content of memories?'[13] But the other question, 'What is memory?' (answer 'Memory consists of backgrounds and images') is a psychological one having to do with cognitive use, 'What is the structure of memories?'

'Place,' Albertus says, is 'something the soul itself makes for storing images.' He cites Boethius' commentary on Porphyry's *Isagoge*, one of the basic logic texts of the medieval school, to the effect that 'Everything which is born or made exists in space and time.' The images which memory stores are such creations. But their temporal quality, that they are of the 'past', does not serve to distinguish them, for 'pastness' is a quality which they all share. So, in order to remember particular matters, one focusses on what distinguishes one memory from another, namely the qualities that constitute 'place'.[14]

Our minds 'know' most readily those things that are both orderly and distinct from one another, for 'such things are more strongly imprinted in it and more strongly affect it'. The two qualities which Albertus emphasizes are *solemnis* and *rarus* – 'orderly' and 'spaced apart' from one another. These are not their actual properties, but are imagined to be so. Albertus understood that mnemonic places are entirely pragmatic; they are cognitive schemata rather than objects. They may entail *likenesses* of existing things (a church, a palace, a garden) but they are not themselves real. They should be thought of as fictive devices that *the mind itself makes* for remembering.

The mental 'places' are associatively related to some content, 'through analogy and transference and metaphor, as for example, for "joy" the most similar "place" is a cloister garth [pratum], and for "feebleness" an infirmary [infirmaria] or hospice [hospitale] and for 'justice' a courtroom [consistorium]'. Thus, what we would call an allegorical connection, and seek to attach to some real content (though that reality is conceptual rather than material), is understood here by Albertus as primarily a convenience, made necessary by the epistemological condition that no human being can have direct knowledge of any 'thing'. All knowledge depends on memory, and so it is all retained in images, fictions gathered into several places and regrouped into new 'places' as the thinking mind draws them together.

3.   Having a place to put things

Before I discuss further how creativity was related to locational memory, however, I need to make some more elementary definitions. These are not peculiar to any one mnemonic technique, but are shared by many because they appear to build upon the natural, biological requirements of human learning and thinking. First of all, human memory operates in 'signs'; these take the form of images that, acting as cues, call up matters with which they have been associated in one's mind. So, in addition to being signs, all memories are also mental images (*phantasiai*).[15]

In rhetoric, the term *phantasiai* is generally reserved for emotionally laden fictions that act powerfully in memory and on the mind.[16] Some traditions in ancient philosophy also recognized an emotional component in all memory. Memory images are composed of two elements: a 'likeness' (*similitudo*) that serves as a cognitive cue or token to the 'matter' or *res* being remembered, and *intentio* or the 'inclination' or 'attitude' we have to the remembered experience, which helps both to classify and to retrieve it. Thus, memories are all images, and they are all and always emotionally 'colored'.

Pre-modern psychologies recognized the emotional basis of remembering, and considered memories to be bodily 'affects'; the term *affectus* included all kinds of emotional reactions.[17] This link of strong memory to emotion is, interestingly enough, also emphasized by at least some contemporary observation. A news article on developments in neuropsychology reported that 'emotional memories involving fear [other emotions seem not to have been part of the test] are permanently ingrained on the brain; they can be suppressed but never erased'.[18]

But more is involved than simply an emotional *state* associated with a memory. Latin *intentio*, derived from the verb *intendo*, refers to the attitudes, aims, and inclinations of the person remembering, as well as to the state of physical and mental concentration required. It involves a kind of judgment, but not one that is simply rational. Memories are not tossed into storage at random, they 'are put in' their 'places' there, 'colored' in ways that are partly personal, partly emotional, partly rational, and mostly cultural. Without this coloration or 'attitude', *intentio*, which we give to the matters we know, we would have no inventory and therefore no place to put the matters we have experienced.

Cicero sometimes used the word *intentio* almost as English uses the word 'tuning', as a musician tightens (the root meaning of *intendo*) the strings of his instrument. In his *Tusculan Disputations* (a work revered by Augustine, as he tells us), while reviewing various Greek theories of the soul's nature, Cicero mentions with favor Aristoxenus of Tarentum, 'musician as well as philosopher, who held the soul to be a special tuning-up [intentionem quandam] of the natural body analogous to that which is called harmony in vocal and instrumental music; answering to the nature and confirmation of the whole body, vibrations of different kinds are produced just as sounds are in vocal music'.[19] The Stoic concept which Cicero is rendering is *tonos*, 'tone' (as of muscles and of strings), a word also used generally for the 'modes' of music.[20] The concept is recognizable in monastic *intentio*, but it was applied spiritually and emotionally.

The monks thought of *intentio* as concentration, 'intensity' of memory, intellect, but also as an emotional attitude, what we now might call a 'creative tension', willingly adopted, that enabled productive memory work to be carried on (or that thwarted it, if one's *intentio* were bad or one's will ineffectual). Reading of the sacred text, both communal and in 'silence', needed to be undertaken with a particular *intentio*, that of 'charity'.

This 'intention' is not a matter of doctrinal or philosophical content, of definitions and classifications. Rather, it bears an analogy to the rhetorical notion of *benevolentia*, the attitude of good will and trust which an orator hoped to evoke in his audience by first approaching them in that spirit. As Augustine famously stated: 'I call charity *a movement of the mind toward* [the goal of] *fruitfully enjoying* God for His own sake, and [my]self and my neighbor for God's sake.'[21] A 'movement of the mind toward' something involves not only *affectus*, or emotion, but also *intentio*.

This conception of *intentio* is certainly related to the one I just discussed; if *intentio* is a part of every memory image, if it is the coloration or attitude we have towards an experience, on the basis of which we have determined where to 'hook' it into the linked chains of our 'places', then rekindling that sort of *intentio* will enable us to start finding those memories again. Notice also that in this cognitive model, emotions are not discrete mental 'entities', but are intricately woven into exactly the same memory networks as are the facts and objects of our experience, what we now call 'data'.[22] And, though our memories are 'intended' in this sense from the start, we constantly restructure and recompose them by means of the different other *intentiones* we bring to our various occasions of remembering.

In such a psychology, there can be no such thing as either a truly objective or a truly unconscious memory, because each remembered thing requires to be intentionally 'marked' and 'hooked in' to our own places. But like the cogs and wheels of a machine, the mnemonic 'places' enable the whole structure to move and work. Mnemonic images are called 'agent images' in rhetoric, for they both are 'in action' and 'act on' other things.

The power of this elementary technique is that it provides immediate access to whatever piece of stored material one may want, and it also provides the means to construct any number of cross-referencing, associational links among the elements in such schemes. In short, it provides a random-access memory, and also sets of patterns or foundations upon which to construct any number of additional collations and concordances of material. This latter goal, the making of mental 'locations' for 'gathering up' (*collocare*) and 'drawing in' (*tractare*), is where *memoria* and invention come together in a single cognitive process.

4. 'Like a wise master-builder'

In ancient mnemotechnic, architecture was considered to provide the best source of familiar memory locations. Architecture also plays an essential role in the art of memory which is basic to my present study, but the monastic version of architectural mnemonic carries non-Roman resonances that make something rich and strange from the forensic orator's set of memory 'rooms'. These resonances, as one might have predicted, are Biblical.

The monastic architectural mnemonic is founded, like a vast superstructure, on a key text from St Paul, who, in 1 Corinthians 3:10–17, compares himself to 'a wise master-builder':

According to the grace of God which is given unto me, as a wise master-builder, I have laid the foundation, and another buildeth thereon. But let every man take heed how he buildeth thereupon. For other foundation can no man lay than that is laid, which is Jesus Christ. Now if any man build upon this foundation gold, silver, precious stones, wood, hay, stubble, every man's work shall be made manifest: for the day of the Lord shall declare it, because it shall be revealed by fire; and fire shall try every man's work of what sort it is. If any man's work abide which he hath built thereupon, he shall receive a reward. If any man's work shall be burned, he shall suffer loss: but he himself shall be saved; yet so as by fire. Know ye not that ye are the temple of God, and that the Spirit of God dwelleth in you? If any man defile the temple of God, him shall God destroy; for the temple of God is holy, which temple ye are.[23]

This passage gave license to a virtual industry of exegetical architectural metaphors. Both as activity and artifact, the trope of building has, as Henri de Lubac noted, 'une place privilégée dans la littérature religieuse, doctrinale ou spirituelle'.[24] The trope was used by Philo, the second-century Jewish exegete, and there are also intriguing connections between early Christian use and the mystical 'work' of Jewish *merkabah* meditation, which uses several of the same basic structures as early Christian exegesis.[25] In medieval Christianity, this Pauline text soon became the authority for a fully developed mnemonic technique, using the *planus* (and sometimes also the *elevatio*) of a building laid out in one's mind as the structure for allegorical and moral meditation, the 'superstructures' (*superaedificationes*) of *sacra pagina*.

Paul uses his architectural metaphor as a trope for invention, not for storage. Likening himself to a builder, he says he has laid a foundation – a foundation which can only be Christ – upon which others are invited to build in their own way.[26] From the beginning of Christianity, the architecture trope is associated with invention in the sense of 'discovery', as well as in the sense of 'inventory'. The foundation which Paul has laid acts as a device that enables the inventions of others. This may seem a minor point in this text, but it acquired major significance later on as exegetical scholars elaborated this 'foundation' for meditational compositions of their own, invited to do so by St Paul himself.

The structures to be built upon were, initially, limited to those measured out and described in the Old Testament. This is an early tradition, probably with Jewish roots. De Lubac quotes Quodvultdeus (an associate of Augustine of Hippo): 'If you have a taste for building, you have the construction of the world [Genesis 1], the measurements of the Ark [Genesis 6], the enclosure of the Tabernacle [Exodus 25–27], the erecting of the temple of Solomon [1 Kings 6], all aspects in earthly terms of the Church itself, which they all figure forth.'[27]

The earliest uses of this trope indicate that the compositional devices which utilized Biblical buildings were never treated solely as having a single content, like a diagram, or one specific task, in the manner of a mathematical theorem, but rather as dispositive heuristics, devices for 'finding' out meanings.[28] The distinction between these two cognitive attitudes resides in whether a book or a church is thought of as an object to be observed and studied for what it is in itself – for example, assuming that it just *is*, all by itself, an encyclopedia in symbol-language, which we thus can describe as it 'really' is – or whether one thinks of a book or a church as a machine, a tool that people use for social purposes such as symbol-making. It's the difference between considering the work you are contemplating as an end or as a means – or, in familiar Augustinian terms, between enjoying something for its own sake and using it for social, that is ethical, purposes (remembering that Christians strive to be 'citizens' of the City of God).

Gregory the Great articulated the 'four senses' of Biblical exegesis in the form of a powerful mnemonic, a composition tool which works on the model of the inventive *circumstantiae* (for example, who, what, where, when, how) of ancient forensic rhetoric:[29]

First we put in place the foundations of literal meaning [historia]; then through typological interpretation we build up the fabric of our mind in the walled city of faith; and at the end, through the grace of our moral understanding, as though with added color, we clothe the building.[30]

This maxim, much quoted later in the Middle Ages, is a recollection *ad res* of Paul; Gregory could expect his audience to recognize it as such. And he also casts the act of Biblical interpretation as an invention process, an act of composing and fabrication.

The literal text is treated as though it presented a set of memorial cues for the reader, a 'foundation' which must then be realized by erecting on it a mental fabric that uses everything which the 'citadel of faith' tosses up, and then coloring over the whole surface. In the context of Scriptural hermeneutics, the 'walled city' (*arx, arcis*) puns both aurally on *arca* ('strongbox' and 'Ark') and visually on the Temple citadel of Ezekiel, the 'city on a hill' in Matthew, and the Johannine 'Heavenly Jerusalem'.[31] It is a useful coincidence too that Gregory uses the word *historia* where later writers speak of *sensus litteralis*: for the Biblical histories, especially of the Old Testament, are treated as though each were a story-outline, one of *One Hundred Great Plots*, whose chief purpose is to be retold.

In the minds of monastic writers, every verse of the Bible thus became a gathering place for other texts, into which even the most remote (in our judgments) and unlikely matters were collected, as the associational memory of a particular author drew them in. Associations depending upon assonance and dissimilarity are just as likely to end up being collated as those of consonance and likeness. A memorative web can be constructed using either principle, and often (as in rememberings of the Last Judgment) using both together.

And the proof of a teller is in the quality and character of his fabrication and coloring – the reconstruction, not the repetition of the 'facts' of foundational plots. There seems to be very little interest in 'the facts' *per se*. Instead, retelling a story is cast as a question of judgment and character. Paul says that 'the fire shall try every man's work'. He emphasizes that this is not a determinant of salvation – a poor workman will be saved even if his work burns up (1 Corinthians 3:15). But the assaying fire will manifest the quality of individual work – whether your walls are built of gold or of stubble. The concern in Paul, as in later writers using this theme, is with ethics, not with reproduction, or – to put the matter in terms of memory – with recollection not with rote. *You* are God's temple, the commonplace went, and the inventive work of building its superstructures is entrusted to your memory. This Pauline theme is realized over and over, in literary works, in monastic architecture, and in the decoration of both.

The inventional nature of the master-builder trope is still clear in its twelfth-century use. That master-teacher, Hugh of St Victor, says that since sacred scripture is like a building, those studying it should be like masons, *architecti*.

Take a look at what the mason does. When the foundation has been laid, he stretches out his string in a straight line, he drops his perpendicular, and then, one by one, he lays the diligently polished stones in a row. Then he asks for other stones, and still others ... See now, you have come to your [reading], you are about to construct the spiritual building. Already the foundations of the story have been laid in you: it remains now that you found the bases of the superstructure. You stretch out your cord, you line it up precisely, you place the square stones into the course, and, moving around the course, you lay the track, so to say, of the future walls.[32]

Notice how this passage recalls the Pauline text, without ever directly mentioning it (a very common device for intertextual *memoria*).[33] A student is to use the mental building he has laid out on the foundation of his 'historical' knowledge of the Bible – that is, of its 'story' – as a structure in which to gather all the bits of his subsequent learning. Such mnemotechnically constructed 'superstructures' (a Pauline word) are useful not as devices for reproduction alone (rote), but as collecting and re-collecting mechanisms with which to compose the designs of one's own learning, and 'be able to build [i]nto [t]his structure whatever [one] afterwards finds' in the 'great sea of books and ... the manifold intricacies of opinions' that one will encounter throughout one's own life.[34] It is as important to get this foundation right as it is for any builder to make his foundations 'true'.

But the foundation is not to be confused with the completed structure. It is the *ground*, but not the key: it 'authorizes', in the medieval sense, by initiating and originating further construction. The 'key' – the 'character' and 'finish' of the master-mason's craft – will lie in the relatively beneficial use which one makes of this common grounding. This is, as St Paul stressed, a matter not just of salvation but of beauty and benefit, of *ornamentum* conceived of in the classical sense in which 'usefulness' is merged with 'delight'. Medieval reading habits are based upon a model of craft mastery, the 'courses' of stone or brick or other materials which a master mason may make in building a wall, with concomitant emphasis upon preparation (the ground), routines of exercise (discipline), and stages in a *way* towards making a finished artifact, a mastery that affords pleasure.[35]

When the foundation plan has been laid out with one's internal builder's measuring line, one's *lineus* or *linea*, and picked out with stones, then the walls may be raised:

and if [the mason] by chance finds some [stones] that do not fit with the fixed course he has laid, he takes his file, smoothes off the protruding parts, files down the rough spots and the places that do not fit, reduces to form, and so at last joins them to the rest of the stones set into the row ... The foundation is in the earth, and it does not always have smoothly fitted stones. The superstructure rises above the earth, and it demands a smoothly proportioned construction. The divine page is just the same ... The foundation which is under the earth we have said stands for history, and the superstructure which is built upon it we have said suggests allegory.[36]

The shape or foundation of a composition must be thought of as a place-where-one-invents. Everything is fitted onto it. And as the composer, acting like a master builder or *architectus*, fits his tropes onto the foundation stones of a text, he must smooth, scrape, chip off, and in other ways adapt and 'translate' the *dicta et facta memorabilia* he is using as his materials.[37] So the edifice of one's life (so to speak), although created from stories available to all citizens, is also a fully personal creation, an expression (and creation) of one's character.[38] This is plain in St Paul's injunction to be like a wise master-builder: the fire will try the quality of your work.

Thus, because it builds entirely through the associations made in some individual's mind, memory work has an irreducibly personal and private or 'secret' dimension to it. That is also why it is a moral activity, an activity of character and what was called 'temperament'.[39]

At the same time, because most of its building materials are common to all – are in fact common places – memory work is also fully social and political, a truly civic activity. The constant balance of individual and communal, *ethos* and *pathos*, is adjusted and engineered with the tools of rhetoric: images and figures, topics and schemes. Essential among these tools are the memorial *res*, the building blocks of new composition.

NOTES

1. The anecdote is recounted in J. D. Spence, *The Memory Palace of Matteo Ricci* (New York: Viking Penguin, 1984), p. 4; see also the example of applied mnemotechnic which Spence constructs (pp. 6–8) to illustrate how it works; it is addressed to the task of recalling detailed anatomical information for a medical examination.

2. See M. Carruthers, *The Book of Memory* (Cambridge: Cambridge University Press, 1990), pp. 206–8; cf. Quintilian, *Inst. orat.* XI.2.47.

3. F. A. Yates, *The Art of Memory* (London: Routledge and Kegan Paul, 1966), p. 178; see also her comments about Albertus Magnus, pp. 79–80, and Thomas Aquinas, pp. 86–7. Her opinion of medieval mnemotechnic was repeated in 'Architecture and the Art of Memory': 'The necessity to remember everything in this static way, in the built-up memory, naturally impeded [*sic!*] the free movement of the mind. One of the immensely important things that the advent of printing did, was to liberate the mind and memory from the built-up memory systems' (*Architectural Association Quarterly*, 12, 1980, p. 7).

4. See, for example, *The Art of Memory*, pp. 18–20, 41. It is significant that Yates admits (p. 19) that she never herself tried out the classical precepts. She also assumed that even the classical art was supposed to 'enable [an orator] to deliver long speeches from memory *with unfailing accuracy*' (p. 18; my emphasis). 'Unfailing accuracy' (in relation to what?) is not a quality which rhetoric ever

considered important, let alone commended. We should remember, of course, that truth and accuracy are not synonymous qualities.

5. For expressions of these opinions, see especially the chapters in *The Art of Memory* on 'The Art of Memory in the Middle Ages' and 'The Memory Theatre of Giulio Camillo'. Of Camillo Yates writes that he turned the art of memory into 'an occult art, a Hermetic secret' (p. 161). The chief medieval sources she considers for the occult turn she thinks to be characteristic of sixteenth-century mnemonics are Raimond Llull, and before him, Scotus Eriugena and twelfth-century medieval 'Platonism'. In *The Art of Memory*, she thus manages to divert *memoria* from the main currents of medieval and Renaissance rhetoric altogether. A more recent study of Camillo is L. Bolzoni, *Il teatro della memoria: studi su Giulio Camillo* (Padua: Liviana, 1984); see also her edition of Camillo's work, *L'idea del teatro di Giulio Camillo* (Palermo: Sellerio, 1991).

6. A recent effort to redevelop a pedagogy of rhetorical invention as memory-dependent is S. Crowley, *The Methodical Memory: Invention in Current-Traditional Rhetoric* (Carbondale, IL: Southern Illinois University Press, 1990).

7. G. A. Kennedy, *Classical Rhetoric and its Christian and Secular Tradition from Ancient to Modern Times* (Chapel Hill: University of North Carolina Press, 1980), p. 87. Aristotle does not discuss Memory separately as a part of rhetoric; it was added in the third century BC, under Stoic influence. In the *Rhetorica ad Herennium* (c. 85 BC), though the author defines the parts of rhetoric as 'Invention, Order, Style, Memory, Delivery' in Book I, he actually discusses Memory in Book III and then describes the figures of Style in Book IV. The later textbooks follow the more common order articulated (though with jovial contempt as mere 'textbook precepts') in Cicero's *De oratore*, and discuss Memory with Delivery, after Style.

8. See the description of rabbinical pedagogy in B. Gerhardsson, *Memory and Manuscript*, trans. E. J. Sharpe (Uppsala: Almquist & Wiksells, 1961), esp. pp. 93–189, and the studies of Mishnah teaching by J. Neusner, perhaps especially *Oral Tradition in Judaism: The Case of the Mishnah* (New York: Garland Press, 1987). On earliest Christian pedagogy, see also L. Alexander, 'The Living Voice: Scepticism towards the Written Word in Early Christian and in Graeco-Roman Texts', in *The Bible in Three Dimensions*, eds D. Chines, S. Fowl, and S. Porter (Sheffield: Sheffield Academic Press, 1990).

9. C. Dawson, *The Making of Europe* ([1932] rpt. New York: Meridian Books, 1958), p. 63 (italics in the original). Gehl argues ('Competens Silentium') that monasticism produced 'a genuine rhetoric of silence' (p. 126), impossible as this pairing seems to us now.

10. Though there are a vast number of studies of the term 'invention', for my purposes the most instructive are R. Copeland, *Rhetoric, Hermeneutics and Translation in the Middle Ages* (Cambridge: Cambridge University Press, 1991); K. Eden, 'The Rhetorical Tradition and Augustinian Hermeneutics in *De doctrina christiana*', *Rhetorica*, 8 (1990), and 'Hermeneutics and the Ancient Rhetorical Tradition', *Rhetorica* 5 (1987), and P. Bagni, 'L'*Inventio* nell'ars poetica Latino-medievale', in B. Vickers, ed., *Rhetoric Revalued: Papers from the International Society for the History of Rhetoric* (Birmingham, NY: MRTS, 1982).

11. Aristotle, *De memoria et reminiscentia* 449b 22–3, and the notes and comments by R. Sorabji, ed. and trans., *Aristotle on Memory* (London: Duckworth, 1972 and Providence: Brown University Press, 1972). Another fine discussion of this passage in relation to Aristotle's views on *mneme* and *anamnesis* ('recollecting'), in this treatise and elsewhere, is J. Annas, 'Aristotle on Memory and the Self', in M. C. Nussbaum and A. O. Rorty, eds, *Essays on Aristotle's* De Anima (Oxford: Clarendon Press, 1992). As Annas points out (p. 298), Greek *mneme* is the more general word, from which Aristotle distinguishes two separate mental activities: storage, which he also calls *mneme* ('memory as "of the past"'), and recollecting – which he usually calls *anamnesis*; but even in this treatise Aristotle uses *mneme* for both. As we will see in the next chapter, the monks' common expression *mneme theou*, 'the memory of God', must be added to the already complex background to the medieval versions of this debate on the relationship of memory and 'past', both as 'the past' and as 'my past'. An overview of the debate among philosophers concerning memory and '*the* past' is J. Coleman, *Ancient and Medieval Memories: The Reconstruction of the Past* (Cambridge: Cambridge University Press, 1992).

12. *Rhetorica ad Herennium* III.xvi.29: 'Constat igitur artificiosa memoria ex locis et imaginibus'. A translation of Albertus' discussion appears in Appendix B of *The Book of Memory*.

13. A further complication in defining memories as 'of the past' is not addressed by Aristotle, though it is a critical one, especially for the philosophy of history. This is the distinction between 'the past' and 'my past'. On this matter see especially Annas, 'Aristotle on Memory and the Self'.

14. Albertus Magnus, *De bono* tr. iv, 'De prudentia' Q. II, art. 2, resp. 7 (*Opera Omnia*, vol. 28, ed. H. Kühle et al., Aschendorff: Monasterii Westfalorum, 1951, p. 250.75–82): 'cum tempus omnis

memorabilis sit praeteritum, tempus non distinguit memorabilia et ita non ducit potius in unum quam in alterum. Locus autem praecipue solemnis distinguit per hoc, quod non omnium memorabilium est locus unus, et movet per hoc, quod est solemnis et rarus. Solemnibus enim et raris fortius inhaeret anima, et ideo fortius ei imprimuntur et fortius movent'. Translation quoted from *The Book of Memory*, p. 277. Some relative degree of 'pastness' can be inferred from a memory image, but only as an accidental feature (to use an Aristotelian category) of the cue: for example, in a memory image of a childhood event I may see myself as a child, whereas in an image of what happened to me yesterday I take the form of an adult. But purely among themselves memory images aren't distinguishable as being more and less 'past'.

15.   These ideas were expounded by Augustine: see Coleman, *Ancient and Medieval Memories*. Two earlier essays that contain much good judgment are R. A. Markus, 'St. Augustine on Signs' (1957, rpt. in R. A. Markus, ed., *Augustine: A Collection of Essays*, New York: Anchor Doubleday, 1972, and G. B. Matthews, 'Augustine on Speaking from Memory', 1965, rpt. in Markus, ed., *Augustine*). The concept of 'image' also has a resonance in rhetorical training: Augustine's conception of these terms has as much to do with their rhetorical usage, of which he was master, as with the various philosophical traditions with which he was familiar. On Augustine and Ciceronian rhetoric see the studies of M. Testard, *St. Augustin et Cicéron* (Paris: Etudes augustiniennes, 1958), H. I. Marrou, *St. Augustin et la fin de la culture antique* (Paris: Boccard, 1938), and P. Brown, *Augustine of Hippo* (Berkeley: University of California Press, 1967).

16.   See C. Imbert, 'Stoic Logic and Alexandrian Poetics' in M. Schofield, M. Burnyeat, and J. Barnes, eds, *Doubt and Dogmatism: Studies in Hellenistic Epistemology* (Oxford: Clarendon Press, 1980), esp. pp. 182–5.

17.   The most careful consideration of the meanings of Latin, Greek, and Arabic terms used to describe these matters remains H. A. Wolfson, 'The Internal Senses', *Harvard Theological Review*, 28 (1935); see also D. L. Black, 'Estimation (*Wahm*) in Avicenna: The Logical and Psycho-logical Dimensions', *Dialogue: Canadian Philosophical Review/Revue canadienne de Philosophie*, 32 (1993). Crucially important in the consideration of the emotional content of 'images' in ancient philosophy are the Stoics: in the Latin tradition, these are represented by the anonymous treatise of 'Longinus', *On the Sublime*; see especially Imbert, 'Stoic Logic and Alexandrian Poetics'. Stoic philosophy has a complicated but fruitful relationship to rhetorical teaching in antiquity, and also to Augustine: on the latter, see especially the second edition of M. Colish, *The Mirror of Language* (2nd edn, Lincoln: University of Nebraska Press, 1983). Cicero used *intentio* to translate the Stoic concept of *tonos*, the 'tension' or harmonic resonance of the mind in apprehending the 'things' of its experience (cf. *Oxford Latin Dictionary*, 1982, s.v. *intentio*, 1b; the citation is of *Tusculan Disputations* I.10. See also the note by J. E. King on Cicero's use of *intentio* in II.23, LCL edition, pp. 208–209). I shall have more to say about this later, in Chapter Two [of *The Craft of Thought*].

18.   Quoted from a report by S. Blakeslee on the research chiefly of Joseph LeDoux of New York University and Hanna and Antonio Damasio of the University of Iowa: *The New York Times*, Dec. 6, 1994, section B, pp. 5, 11. See also A. R. Damasio, *Descartes' Error: Emotion, Reason and the Human Brain* (New York: Grosset/Putnam, 1994), and J. LeDoux, *The Emotional Brain: The Mysterious Underpinnings of Emotional Life* (New York: Simon & Schuster, 1996).

19.   Cicero, *Tusculan Disputations* I.10 (LCL, p. 24): 'musicus idemque philosophus, ipsius corporis intentionem quandam, velut in cantu et fidibus quae harmonia dicitur, sic ex corporis totius natura et figura varios motus cieri tamquam in cantu sonos'; edited and translated by J. E. King (2nd edn, LCL 40, London: Heinemann, 1943) (on *intentio*, see esp. his lexicographical note at pp. 207–8). Cicero also uses the word in II.23, II.65, and IV.3. In *De oratore* III.57 Cicero describes how 'the whole frame of a man, and his whole countenance, and the variations of his voice, resonate like strings in a musical instrument, just as they are moved by the affections of the mind [sonant ut motu animi quoque sunt pulsae] ... the tones of the voice, like musical chords, are so wound up [sunt intensae] as to be responsive to every touch'. Cf. *Tusculan Disputations* II.24, in reference to the emotive 'voices' of the orator Marcus Antonius, one of the chief speakers in *De oratore*. As will become clear, the monastic concept of *intentio* very much involves a notion of mental resonance and 'tone', which, when it is 'tuned' properly for meditation, makes of the mind a kind of inner *organum* or musical instrument; see especially the commentary of Augustine on the *locus tabernaculi*, discussed in Chapter Five [of *The Craft of Thought*] below.

20.   Aristoxenus of Tarentum was a Pythagorean and Peripatetic; see F. Wehrli, *Die Schule des Aristoteles* (Basel: Schwabe, 1944), vol. 2, for witnesses and fragments attributed to him. The concept of *tonos* was invoked by the Stoics (according to Calcidius' commentary on Plato's *Timaeus*) in an account of sense perception, particularly vision, which described the soul as 'stretched' during the process; see also H. F. von Arnim, *Stoicorum veterum fragmenta* (Stuttgart:

Teubner, 1968), vol. 2, par. 10, fragments 439–462. My thanks to Peter Lautner for giving me these references, and for emphasizing to me the Stoic context of Cicero's usage in books I and II. On early Greek accounts of vision, including the Stoic, see also D. C. Lindberg, *Theories of Vision from Al-Kindi to Kepler* (Chicago: University of Chicago Press, 1976), pp. 1–17.

21. Augustine, *De doctrina christiana* III.x.16: 'Caritatem uoco motum animi ad fruendum deo propter ipsum et se atque proximo propter deum'. Recall Cicero's use of the idiom *motus animi* in the quotation from *De oratore* III.57 (note 19, above), in the context of emotive rhetorical *intentio*.

22. M. Nussbaum has insisted upon this connection also in Aristotle's philosophy of ethical judgment in *The Therapy of Desire*, the portion of which most relevant to rhetoric was reprinted in A. O. Rorty, *Essays on Aristotle's Rhetoric* (Berkeley: University of California Press, 1996), pp. 303–23.

23. 1 Cor. 3:10–17: 'Secundum gratiam Dei, quae data est mihi, ut sapiens architectus fundamentum posui: alius autem superaedificat. Unusquisque autem videat quomodo superaedificet. Fundamentum enim alius nemo potest ponere praeter id quod positum est, quod est Christus Iesus. Si quis autem superaedificat super fundamentum hoc, aurum, argentum, lapides pretiosos, ligna, foenum, stipulam, uniuscuiusque opus manifestum erit: dies enim Domini declarabit, quia in igne revelabitur: et uniuscuiusque opus quale sit, ignis probabit. Si cuius opus manserit quod superaedificavit, mercedem accipiet. Si cuius opus arserit, detrimentum patietur: ipse autem salvus erit: sic tamen quasi per ignem. Nescitis quia templum Dei estis, et Spiritus Dei habitat in vobis? Si quis autem templum Dei violaverit, disperdet illum Deus. Templum enim Dei sanctum est, quod estis vos.' I have quoted the Authorized Version by preference when I can do so, but when the Latin is significantly different, I have either used the Douay or translated it myself.

24. H. de Lubac, *Exégèse médiévale* (Paris: Aubier, 1959–1964), vol. 4, p. 44; a compendium of brief quotations from a variety of exegetical writers from the first century (Philo) through the twelfth, demonstrating the pervasiveness of the basic trope, is on pp. 41–60. See also B. Smalley, *The Study of the Bible in the Middle Ages* (3rd edn, Oxford: Blackwell, 1983), pp. 3–7 (on Philo Judaeus). Origen is credited with crafting the method of 'spiritual' or allegorical interpretation of Scripture for the Christians: his indebtedness to Jewish hermeneutical traditions is analyzed in N. R. M. De Lange, *Origen and the Jews* (Cambridge: Cambridge University Press, 1976).

25. The standard study of *merkabah* mysticism is G. Scholem, *Major Trends in Jewish Mysticism* (New York: Schocken Books, 1954). But see the cautions expressed by M. D. Swartz, *Mystical Prayer in Ancient Judaism* (Tübingen: Mohr, 1992), esp. pp. 6–18. A review of the various threads of this tradition with reference particularly to literary cultures is M. Lieb, *The Visionary Mode: Biblical Prophecy, Hemeneutics, and Cultural Change* (Ithaca: Cornell University Press, 1991).

26. On the possibility that Paul was himself knowledgeable in *merkabah* texts and traditions, see A. F. Segal, *Paul the Convert: The Apostolate and Apostasy of Saul the Pharisee* (New Haven: Yale University Press, 1990), esp. pp. 40–52. Segal links Paul's reference to the Temple in this passage to antecedent Jewish traditions (p. 168). See also Lieb, *The Visionary Mode*, pp. 173–90, and the bibliography given there. It should be kept in mind, of course, that an injunction to remember the Temple plan as a meditational act of penance is in the text of Ezekiel (43:10–12). I shall have more to say about this later.

27. Quodvultdeus, *Liber promissionum*, 'De gloria regnoque sanctorum capitula'. 13.17 (CCSL 60 (Turnhout: Brepols, 1976), 221.59–62): 'Aedificandi si est affectio, habes fabricam mundi, mensuras arcae, ambitum tabernaculi, fastigium templi Salamonis, ipsiusque per mundum membra Ecclesiae, quam illa omnia figurabant'. See also de Lubac, *Exégèse médiévale*, vol. 4, p. 41.

28. A point well made by Lieb with respect to the traditions of interpretive 'work' regarding the Throne-Chariot: see esp. *The Visionary Mode*, pp. 83–4. See also Eden, 'Hermeneutics and the Ancient Rhetorical Tradition'.

29. I made this suggestion in *The Book of Memory*, p. 165. That the rhetorical inventional function of *circumstantiae*, related closely to mnemonics, continued to exist in the twelfth century is apparent from the title, 'De tribus maximis circumstantiae gestorum', of Hugh of St Victor's preface to his *Chronicon*, a mnemotechnical art (see Appendix A of *The Book of Memory*).

30. Gregory the Great, *Moralia in Job*, Prologue ('Epistola ad Leandrum') 3 (CCSL 143 (Turnhout: Brepols, 1979–1985), 4.110–114). 'Nam primum quidem fundamenta historiae ponimus; deinde per significationem typicam in arcem fidei fabricam mentis erigimus; ad extremum quoque per moralitatis gratiam quasi superducto aedificium colore vestimus'.

31. *Arx* is one of the family of storage-room metaphors for memory (see *The Book of Memory*, Chapter 1, for a descriptive catalogue of many of these). The word was linked with *arca*, according to

Isidore of Seville, *Etymol.* xv.2: 'ab arcendo hostem arces vocantur. Unde et *arcus et arca*', 'they are called *arces* from the warding-off [*arcendo*] of an enemy. Whence also the words *bow* and *arc* ['storage-chest', with an additional pun in Latin on *arch*]'.

32. Hugh of St Victor, *Didascalicon* vi.4 (ed. C. H. Buttimer (Washington: Catholic University Press, 1939), pp. 118.10–13, 119.27–120.1): '[R]espice opus caementarii. collocato fundamento, lineam extendit in directum, perpendiculum demittit, ac deinde lapides diligenter politos in ordinem ponit, alios deinde atque alios quaerit … ecce ad lectionem venisti, spirituale fabricaturus aedificium. iam historiae fundamenta in te locata sunt: restat nunc tibi ipsius fabricae bases fundare. linum tendis, ponis examussim, quadros in ordinem collocas, et circumgyrans quaedam futurorum murorum vestigia figis' (translated by J. Taylor (New York: Columbia University Press, 1961)). The masonry 'courses' referred to are the parts of the curriculum, likened to the layers of stones laid in building a wall: see Taylor's note 15, p. 223, The trope became realized as a material drawing in the thirteenth century, in the common meditational picture known as the 'Torre Sapientiae' or 'Tower of Wisdom', one of a great many such secularizings of monastic cognitive common-places (chiefly by the orders of friars, as this one was). On the *torre sapientiae* drawing itself see L. F. Sandler, *The Psalter of Robert de Lisle* (London: Harvey Miller, 1983), and her bibliographical references. This fourteenth-century English manuscript contains a rich collection of such cognitive-mnemotechnical drawings.

33. See *The Book of Memory*, pp. 98–9. I. Illich, *In the Vineyard of the Text: A Commentary to* Didascalion (Chicago: University of Chicago Press, 1993), has meditated insightfully on Hugh's reading praxis, though I find his analytical terms somewhat more romantic and less rhetorical than I would choose.

34. Hugh of St Victor, *Didascalicon* vi.4 (ed. Buttimer, p. 120.6–8): 'instructus sit, ut, quaecumque postmodum invenerit, tuto superaedificare possit. vix enim in tanto librorum pelago et multiplicibus sententiarum anfractibus'; translated by J. Taylor. P. Sicard, *Hugues de St-Victor et son école* (Turnhout: Brepols, 1993), argues that for Hugh and his students tropes of 'building' acquired a fundamental value. This is certainly true; I am not convinced, however, that the value placed upon the figure of 'building' is so distinctive as to be considered particularly Victorine.

35. The status of the 'letter' in Hugh of St Victor's exegesis has been, and is still, a matter of debate among intellectual historians. See esp. de Lubac, *Exégèse médiévale*, vol. 3, pp. 332–9, and Smalley, *The Study of the Bible*, pp. 97–106. As Smalley succinctly comments (p. 102): 'Hugh's philosophy teaches him to value the letter. It does not teach him to regard the letter as a good in itself'. In his discussion of the matter, de Lubac emphasizes the construction model, as does Hugh himself; this seems to me a most valuable emphasis. The tendency to conceive of the relationships of literal and spiritual 'levels' in interpretation as static hierarchies is modern, I believe, and reflects a failure of historical imagination at the deepest level – a trait not shared by either de Lubac or Smalley. On Hugh's educational model see J. Châtillon, 'Le titre du "Didascalicon" de Hugues de Saint-Victor et sa signification', in A. Cazenave and J. F. Lyotard, eds, *L'art des confins: Mélanges offerts à Maurice de Gandillac* (Paris: Presses Universitaires de France, 1985), and Sicard, *Hugues de Saint-Victor*, esp. pp. 17–34.

36. Hugh of St Victor, *Didascalicon* vi.4 (ed. Buttimer, pp. 118.13–16, 118.20–22, 119.4–6): 'et si forte aliquos primae dispositioni non respondentes invenerit, accipit limam, praeeminentia praecidit, aspera planat, et informia ad formam reducit, sicque demum reliquis in ordinem dispositis adiungit … fundamentum in terra est, nec semper politos habet lapides. fabrica desuper terram, et aequalem quaerit structuram. sic divina pagina … quod sub terra est fundamentum figurare diximus historiam, fabricam quae superaedificatur allegoriam insinuare'. It should be noted that the word *pagina* (as in 'divina pagina') refers both to the columnar layout of manuscript pages and to the compressed and compositionally incomplete nature of what was conventionally written in this format: see *The Book of Memory*, pp. 92–3.

37. On the rhetorical theory of medieval translation, and its roots in classical poetic, see especially Copeland, *Rhetoric, Hermeneutics, and Translation*, and D. Kelly, '*Translatio Studii*: Translation, Adaptation, and Allegory in Medieval French Literature', *Philological Quarterly*, 57 (1978). The construction trope is a particularly rich image of the translation process, for the building stones are literally borne across from one place to another.

38. The relationship between 'character' and the contents of one's memory images is discussed in *The Book of Memory*, esp. pp. 178–83. The word *character* literally meant 'stamp', as in wax: it was thus related to the master trope that memory was 'stamped' or 'impressed' by one's experiences. One's 'character' was thus, quite literally, an important result of one's memories: but 'temperament', like the varying qualities of the wax, is a crucial factor that ensures that memories of 'things' will never be entirely identical from one person to another. A particularly cogent medieval statement of this principle of 'character' is in Canto 2 (esp. lines 121–48) of Dante's *Paradiso*, in which Beatrice explains the nature of the spots on the moon.

39. I have detailed elsewhere how and why meditative reading as memory work was analyzed as a moral activity, and how *memoria* came to be thought of as basic to *prudentia*, the virtue of ethical judgment, esp. in Chapter Five of *The Book of Memory*.

2.

Science-Honour-Metaphor: Italian Cabinets of the Sixteenth and Seventeenth Centuries

Giuseppe Olmi

In the space of a few pages, it is not easy to construct a complete picture of the nature and evolution of collections of natural objects in sixteenth- and seventeenth-century Italy. A major source of difficulty is the great diversity in both form and function which characterizes the numerous important collections formed during this period. It is my intention to concentrate here on private collections of the late sixteenth and seventeenth centuries, with only the briefest mention of the princely and aristocratic collections which form an essential point of reference and comparison against which to measure the diversity and the aims of many of the museums developed by private individuals during the second half of the sixteenth century.

As a starting point, it should be remembered that the collections of the Italian princes were largely characterized by an absence of specialization and by the juxtaposition of natural and artificial objects. With their marvellous appearance and encyclopaedic arrangement, they constitute an arena of competition between art and nature, and, more generally speaking, represent one of the most ambitious and spectacular responses of Mannerism to the crisis of values resulting from the breakdown of Renaissance certainty.

A *studiolo* such as that of Francesco I de' Medici can be seen as an attempt to reappropriate and reassemble all reality in miniature, to constitute a place from the centre of which the prince could symbolically reclaim dominion over the entire natural and artificial world. Therefore, although it is generally incorrect to speak of a didactic or scientific purpose in these collections, it is also inaccurate to claim that there was no principle of order informing them. The detailed project devised by Vincenzo Borghini for the Medici *studiolo* clearly illustrates how complicated the whole layout was.[1] It can therefore be said that order can be discerned in the princely collections but it is primarily symbolic, and centres on man rather than on the natural world.

In parallel with these aristocratic collections, others, completely differing in purpose, content and organization, developed in Italy in the second half of the sixteenth century. Among the most famous were those of Francesco Calceolari in Verona, Ulisse Aldrovandi in Bologna, Michele Mercati in Rome, and Ferrante Imperato in Naples; all four collections are characterized by some definite area of specialization. Although some *artificialia* are included, almost all the objects are animal, plant or mineral in origin, and so we have here specifically scientific collections, or, more precisely, collections of natural objects.[2]

The shape of these collections was determined by two main factors: the social and economic status of the collectors, and, more importantly, their intellectual and professional interests. None of them belonged to the old aristocracy and none had stable relations with princely courts, except for Mercati who enjoyed papal patronage. They all studied medicine and botany at university and all entered professions which naturally followed from such studies. Calceolari and Imperato owned two of the most famous pharmacies in their respective cities; Mercati was a physician at the papal court and was also in charge of the botanic garden in the Vatican; Aldrovandi was professor of natural philosophy at the University of Bologna and director of the botanic garden there.

Sixteenth-century naturalists, while showing a general respect for the ancient authors, did not fail to perceive the inadequacies of most ancient descriptions of the natural world. It therefore became necessary to embark upon a thorough revision of all existing knowledge, to correct past errors and to take the species of the New World into consideration. This was not only an abstract exercise in classification: the use of plants, animals and minerals in medical therapy gave the whole task of identification a manifestly practical purpose. Throughout his life, Aldrovandi never tired of exhorting 'doctors and students of medicine' to apply themselves 'with all their powers' to the study of 'plants, animals and things discovered in the ground'.[3] For the Bolognese scholar, these studies had a twofold basis: theory and direct observation. The essentially practical purpose behind these scientists' museums and botanic gardens was that of providing opportunities for the first-hand observation of natural objects.[4]

Collecting natural objects therefore became a means of creating a didactic and professional resource. This second aspect is seen most clearly in the structure of Calceolari's museum, to which two separate catalogues were dedicated. The two are very different in character: the first was written by the doctor Giovanni Battista Olivi in 1584, and the second compiled by Benedetto Ceruti and Andrea Chiocco in 1622.[5] The latter appeared after

Calceolari's death when the museum had probably been improved and transformed by his nephew Francesco, and already partly reflected the taste which we shall later see to be typical of seventeenth-century collectors. The earlier catalogue, however, clearly set out the practical aims of the museum, and in itself constituted a practical work of reference for physicians, pharmacists and botanists. The close, organic links between the museum and Calceolari's pharmacy are clearly delineated; it was as a result of the interdependence of the two that the museum took on the appearance and function of an actual laboratory and a well-furnished medical repository.

Another aspect heavily stressed in the 1584 catalogue is Calceolari's willingness to show his collection to his pupils, thus turning the three rooms of his museum into a place for study and comparison. Evidently, the specifically scientific function of museums like Calceolari's or Aldrovandi's and their being open to the public make them quite different in character from contemporary aristocratic collections or the intensely personal *studioli* of the princes. The museum is conceived of not as a symbolic place where all reality is reconstituted, but rather as an instrument for the comprehension and exploration of the natural world.

The criteria for the arrangement of the objects are therefore purely functional rather than symbolic. There is generally no trace in the scientists' private museums of complex systems of arrangement such as that devised by Borghini for Francesco I de' Medici, in which striking analogies with Giulio Camillo Delminio's *Teatro della memoria* have recently been detected.[6] Aldrovandi not only states explicitly that he found books on the art of memory useless, but also considers it quite vain and fruitless to attempt to form a coherent idea of reality by first superimposing artificial, abstract schemes upon it.[7] The cupboards filled with countless little drawers, which are to be found in Aldrovandi's museum – as in those of other naturalists – might at first sight recall those in the Medici *studiolo*, but in reality their function is quite different. In the *studiolo* the cupboards are concealed by panels depicting various subjects symbolically related to their contents, whereas in Aldrovandi's museum the two cupboards with 4,554 little drawers containing *'cose sotteranee, et conchilij et Ostreacei'* are conceived of and used as filing cabinets, with actual samples from the natural world taking the place of index cards. Of equal importance is the illustration showing Mercati's *Metallotheca* in the Vatican.[8] The layout in general is far removed from that of the Medici *studiolo* with its nocturnal and saturnine atmosphere and its arcane arrangement which held meaning only for the Grand Duke and a few initiates. Instead, we have the orderly succession of numbered cupboards, each one bearing an inscription with details of the contents.

The tendency towards specialization and the adoption by many Italian scholars of an order of arrangement shaped by medical and pharmaceutical practice also contributed significantly towards modifying the concept of confrontation between art and nature in their museums. Aldrovandi's reflections on the meaning of the visual arts, and painting in particular, sprang directly from his desire to become more familiar with, and to catalogue, the natural world.[9] He considered pictorial representation primarily as a means of supplying deficiencies in the collection, pictures of exotic and unobtainable animals and plants being regarded as substitutes for the things themselves. In addition, illustrations inserted into a printed text helped to clarify the written description, making it more concrete and thus more comprehensible. It follows from this that there was no place in Aldrovandi's theories for the concept of man perfecting or transforming nature by art. Since art was conceived of simply as a means of accumulating scientific data, its functions were necessarily limited to an absolutely true and accurate portrayal of the natural world. It is not necessary to discuss here the actual level of realism attained by the numerous artists employed by Aldrovandi. It is sufficient to note that the scientist's desire to possess a complete documentation of nature led him not only to collect concrete objects but also to undertake an enormous programme for the systematic illustration of the entire natural world.

By about 1595 Aldrovandi's museum contained approximately 8,000 tempera illustrations and fourteen cupboards containing the wood blocks which were used to illustrate his printed works from 1599 onwards. These were in addition to his 11,000 animals, fruits and minerals and 7,000 plants 'dried and pasted' into fifteen volumes. His programme can be viewed as an attempt to transfer the entire world of nature from the often inaccessible outdoors to the restricted interior of a museum.

Some scholars have been misled by this form of organization into anachronistically attributing functions to Aldrovandi's museum which in fact became typical only in late seventeenth- and eighteenth-century museums. There is no doubt that many new elements were to be found in these collections and it has already been said that these consisted particularly in specialization in the direction of natural history and in the definite rejection of any type of abstract symbolic systematization. But it is also evident that although museums like Aldrovandi's and Calceolari's were concrete expressions of that new scientific spirit which gave impetus to enquiry into the natural world, they also reflected some of the most characteristic and traditional traits of late Renaissance culture. Above all, it must be noted that the naturalists' attitude was not altogether neutral with regard to the objects placed in their museums. Their programme certainly provided an inventory of the natural world in all its manifold forms, and their scholarly research was also directed towards more common animals and plants, as can be seen in Aldrovandi's publication of a book on insects;[10]

yet the love of rarity, the typically Mannerist taste for the bizarre and unusual object, although at odds with the original aims of the naturalists, reasserted itself in the new context of an exclusively natural-history collection.[11] It was the rare, outlandish piece which immediately conferred status on a collection and spread its fame beyond the scientific world. What attracted and astonished visitors was not only the great number of objects on show but also, perhaps above all, the display of objects unique to a particular collection. This was the reason behind the naturalists' marked preference for samples of exotic flora and fauna, animals of monstrous appearance, and plants and minerals endowed with extraordinary powers.

Another factor which lay behind the continuing popularity of exotic objects was the opening to the public of this type of museum, a development which naturally gave it a new dimension in addition to its didactic and scientific function. In the second half of the sixteenth century, a great change came about in the status of collections devoted exclusively to natural objects. With the enormous influx of strange and wonderful natural products resulting from new geographical discoveries, with improved communications and with the concomitant development of public interest in far-off mysterious lands, the natural history collection became for the first time a concrete means of enhancing fame and prestige. The countless visitors were not merely naturalists and students: these museums, and also the botanic gardens – those scientific institutions *par excellence* – were frequented for recreation and pleasure as well as instruction, because of the unusual and wonderful objects on display.[12] This explains the fact that the arrangement of the products of nature within this setting was often determined by the desire for symmetry and a pleasing appearance. When late sixteenth-century naturalists speak proudly of the order in their collections, we should not, for the most part, take this as referring to a system of cataloguing objects based on the succession of complete series; instead we should imagine an arrangement based on aesthetic criteria. The imposed order was not one believed to exist in nature itself, but one calculated to appeal to the eye of the visitor.

Moving on from examining the general distribution of the collection to the individual pieces, and particularly to those from the animal kingdom, the question arises as to what precisely the late sixteenth-century naturalists saw and classified. As is well known, the zoological works of Aristotle, or rather some of them, inaugurated the main stream of Western thought which regarded the acquisition of rational and scientific knowledge of animals as being possible solely by means of dissection. The Greek philosopher thus severed the ancient bond of friendship between man and animal, and founded the classification of the latter on the anatomy of the corpse. However, immediately after Aristotle's death another type of approach was developed which emphasized the animal's affinity with man by concentrating on the study of the living creature, its character and intelligence. This alternative tradition began with Theophrastus, continued through the times of Antigony and Plutarch right up to Pliny and Elian, and there were still signs of it in the seventeenth century.[13] For the sixteenth-century naturalists, as for the authors of the medieval bestiaries, this notion was still very much alive. This can be attributed to the great influence still exerted during the Renaissance by the works of ancient authors such as Theophrastus and Pliny and also by those such as Æsop's *Fables* and Artemidoro's *The Interpretation of Dreams*, which emphasized affinities of conduct between man and animal. Having said this, I certainly do not wish to suggest that the sixteenth-century naturalists rejected all anatomical research, especially since we know, for example, that Aldrovandi carried out many accurate dissections. I simply wish to point out, in relation to the present subject, that some reasons which lay behind the internal organization of the museum also promoted the co-existence of a method of classification based on the living animal and its often amazing behaviour.

The great quantity of natural products from distant lands which increasingly flooded Europe during the sixteenth century has already been mentioned. Given the length of most voyages and the rudimentary methods of preservation, we may ask what actually remained of the specimens by the time they came into the hands of the naturalists? When they describe an animal in their works, they often claim to have it under direct observation in their museum, but if we look more carefully into the catalogues of these collections, we realize that we are dealing with an aspect of that fondness for the fragment and the quotation which historians of art and literature have identified as one of the characteristic traits of Mannerism. In most cases, in fact, they were dealing not with whole animals but with parts of them, often very small and insignificant parts such as teeth, horns, tusks, nails, feathers, pieces of skin, or bones. Not only was the naturalist in no position to carry out anatomical dissection, therefore, but he could not even have had an overall conception of the appearance of the whole animal. Hence, in this context the fragment acted simply as a token of an exotic animal, concerning which wider ideas were extremely vague. In view of this ignorance concerning the physical appearance of the animal, the only possible way of writing about it was to describe its habits in accordance with ancient tradition. This led inevitably to the resuscitation of ancient ideas, to the revival of Pliny's treatise and the tradition which he upheld concerning the marvellous behaviour of animals, their intelligence – which was seen as being qualitatively very similar to man's – and their possible use as symbols. The influence of this tradition is apparent in the method of cataloguing. A surprising detail from the engraving of Imperato's museum indicates clearly that the reference is to the living animal and its symbolic significance rather than to the dead, anatomized one.[14] High on the right, amongst other birds, is a stuffed pelican in the act of opening its breast with its beak in order to resuscitate its dead young with its own blood. Such was the influence of secular tradition that the symbol of man's redemption through Christ's blood, taken straight from the pages of the *Physiologus*, appears in and is even classified within the natural history museum. The retention of such traditional elements, however, should not blind one to the objective signs of renewal in the scientists' collections, which put them on a completely different level from the princely *studioli*.

During the following century, notable changes in interests and style can be observed among the collectors. Signs of such changes were already apparent in the princely collections, particularly those of the Medici, at the end of the sixteenth century. Francesco I, now Grand Duke of Tuscany, began to reorganize all the family collections and embarked on a new cultural policy of which the highlight was the opening of the Uffizi Gallery. The new political demands connected with his succession to the throne led the man who had created a *studiolo* at the beginning of the 1570s, to dismantle it in 1584 and to transfer many objects to the Uffizi. It has often been observed that the motifs and complex symbolism present in the *studiolo* in large part blended together in the *Tribuna della Galleria*, but it is also obvious that in this new architectural setting they took on a new role and satisfied quite different requirements.[15] Indeed the *tribuna* and the whole *galleria* represented visually the polar opposite of the secret, nocturnal *studiolo*. All the rare and precious objects, which had once been destined for the private contemplation of the prince alone, were now on view to all in the *tribuna*. The need to legitimize the Grand Duke and his dynasty meant that the glorification of the prince, the celebration of his deeds and the power of his family had constantly to be exposed to the eyes of all and to be strongly impressed on the mind of every subject.

This transition from private to public also entailed a new arrangement of the collections. Works of art and antiquities gradually came to be seen as status symbols and instruments of propaganda, while grand-ducal policy increasingly brought scientific research under state patronage. The main effect of this was that the Uffizi Gallery took on the characteristics of an art museum, even if not in the strict modern sense of the term. It is true that there were scientific instruments and *naturalia* in the *tribuna*, but they were significantly fewer than those in the *studiolo* and were completely integrated with the works of art.

Specific places came to be devoted to scientific research. The Medici concentrated particularly on Pisa, the seat of the university. Ferdinando I oversaw the restructuring of the city's botanic garden and made it a centre for teaching and research, with the addition of a natural history museum.[16] The continuing regard in which scientific enquiry of all kinds was held by the Grand Dukes of Tuscany is illustrated by Cosimo I's summoning Galileo to Pisa and the later creation of the Accademia del Cimento.[17]

While there was a clear division between the arts and the sciences in collecting in the public sphere, the situation with regard to private collections was much more complex. Although it seems quite natural to assume that physicians and naturalists travelled the same road towards professional utilization of the museum for purposes of research and study, this certainly did not exclude the preference for curiosities which had been typical of the sixteenth-century museums, or the presence of some antiques or *objects d'art*. Nevertheless on the whole it is legitimate to see a distinct move towards natural history in collections of this kind. An example of this trend is the '*Museo di cose naturali*' belonging to the botanist Giacomo Zanoni, which appears to have been the most specialized amongst the Bolognese collections described by Paolo Boccone.[18] During the seventeenth century there was not much discussion of the naturalists' cabinets, or at least they were talked of only amongst the initiated. They certainly did not acquire fame on a scale such as that enjoyed by Aldrovandi's or Imperato's museums in the previous century. The reason for this, I believe, is that the ever-increasing importation of specimens from distant lands had shorn the *naturalia* in many collections of their novelty, rendering them somewhat commonplace and thus detracting from their public appeal.

Faced with this new situation, those collectors who were not professional scientists and who wished rather to use their collections as a means of enhancing their social standing had two alternatives: either they could turn back to antiquities and *objets d'art*, or they could employ every possible means to increase the marvellous, original and bizarre elements in their collections. Passing over the rather special case of Kircher's museum,[19] it seems that collectors in Rome, for example, preferred to take the first course.[20] The favourable state of the antiquities market, the continual presence of countless artists in the city (including numerous foreigners), and the considerable financial resources of the many great families and highly placed prelates, were undoubtedly some of the factors which guided the style and choice of the Roman collectors. Encyclopaedic collections were not completely absent, but they were very much in the minority. Examination of the list of approximately 150 collections in Rome left to us by Bellori reveals that more than 90 per cent of the owners preferred paintings, antiques, medals and cameos, while the products of nature were totally excluded.[21] On the other hand the structure of some celebrated private museums in the north of Italy was quite different, for they did contain natural objects, ethnographical documents, scientific instruments and books, together with antiquities and works of art. I am referring to the museums of Manfredo Settala in Milan, Lodovico Moscardo in Verona and Ferdinando Cospi in Bologna, which owed their great fame partly to the publication of catalogues.[22] None of the three owners of these cabinets had studied science at university and, with the partial exception of Settala, neither had they shown any particular scientific interest of the sort which had stimulated so many private collectors in the second half of the sixteenth century. Personally, I am reluctant to share the opinion of those who have spoken of a distinct modern quality in these museums and who have unhesitatingly seen them as actual centres of research.[23] This seems to be an anachronistic approach, which ignores the social and cultural context of which the collections were an expression. Although the presence of individual objects may suggest new interests, it is dangerous to extrapolate from such evidence conclusions as to the general organization and the overall aims of the museums.[24] There is actually very little of the experimental method of the new science, or Galileo's school of thought, or Malpighi's biological research, underlying these museums.

Even the scientific interests of Settala, encouraged especially by his connections with Tuscany, were far from constituting an analytical survey of reality, for they ran in several different directions before converging on one great focal point: the curiosity. His activities as a constructor of scientific and mechanical instruments also fit well into this picture. Microscopes, telescopes, compasses and intricate clocks were seen not so much as working instruments but as precious objects, to be appreciated more from an aesthetic than a practical point of view. They were greatly sought after by noblemen because of their novel character and because in this age of new science they represented the most fashionable and unusual objects. Undoubtedly Settala's collection and his expertise with the lathe were aimed more at meeting this type of demand than at directly satisfying the requirements of scientific practice.

This type of analysis can be applied with even greater reason to the museums of Cospi and Moscardo, which were more obvious expressions of that new Baroque sensitivity which was also characteristic of the literature of the time. In fact, the interrelationship between eclectic collections and contemporary literature is so evident that one can speak of the former as visualized poetry and of some of the latter as imaginary museums. Through many private collections of the seventeenth century runs the same thread of surprise and wonder, typical of the poetics of Giambattista Marino; at the same time one finds evidence in the works of the latter of a taste for analytical inventory and the listing of all aspects of reality.[25]

Further information on the characteristics of these museums can be found in Emanuele Tesauro's *Cannocchiale aristotelico*, which was acclaimed throughout Italy. Many opinions and judgements of this writer from Turin could easily have been those of contemporary collectors; examples include his rather conservative attitude towards the new science and his regret for that sense of mystery which the discovery of the telescope had helped to eliminate. Of even greater importance is the chapter dedicated to *Argutezze della natura* ('The wit of Nature') in which he maintains that all natural phenomena and products of nature constitute so many 'mysterious hieroglyphics', 'symbolic figures' in nature.[26] In short, Tesauro believed that in all things generated by nature there was an allusion to, and concrete image of, a concept. Such an idea was of the first importance where the museum was concerned. If nature speaks (*'fraseggia'*) through such metaphors, then the encyclopaedic collection, which is the sum of all possible metaphors, logically becomes the great metaphor of the world. Such an interpretation is confirmed by the fact that Tesauro, like Marino, was one of the authors used by compilers of museum catalogues.

Other aspects of seventeenth-century museums also make it difficult to justify the view of them as centres of scientific research. In the first place, one may cite the very reasons which the owners gave for forming their collections; these give the definite impression that the collection of diverse objects constituted more a commendable way of spending the time than a scientific activity. Cospi quite clearly defines his museum as 'a pastime of my youth',[27] and Moscardo similarly admits he became a collector to escape idleness by means of an honest occupation.[28] However, collecting on this scale can not have been a common pastime, open to all. In the preface to his catalogue, Moscardo, who had great ambitions to climb the social ladder, sought to dignify his thirty years of diligent collecting. Bearing in mind that the most important European princes had devoted themselves to creating museums, it seems evident that his real aim was to ennoble his own activity. Not only did the creation and enrichment of a museum constitute an occupation worthy of a nobleman; they were also a means of acquiring renown and prestige and of turning the owner's home into an almost obligatory sight for everyone. Nor was it just a question of attracting 'cavaliers and curious ladies' or countless travellers from England, Germany and France. The popularity of the cabinet of curiosities had for a time the effect of overturning rigid social hierarchies, giving the collector the unique opportunity of attracting important personages of royal blood to his own home and of guiding them through his museum. In his old age, Manfredo Settala was obliged to ask his servants to act as guides to his museum, although he would make exceptions for important visitors,[29] considering the effort of showing them round personally well repaid by the reflected glory.

Moreover, the collectors certainly publicized their museums as extensively as possible, emphasizing in particular the amazing objects on display in them. In the second half of the sixteenth century, when the natural collection had functioned as a professional instrument, most physicians and pharmacists had exchanged lists of their possessions among themselves with a view to close scientific collaboration. The printed catalogue, by contrast, is typical of the seventeenth century, an age in which, by a process of involution, Italian society and customs were taking on a Spanish quality which contributed towards an emphasis on external values. The catalogue combined its basic practical function with effective public propaganda. Cospi must have been well aware of this when he took pains to send complimentary copies of his museum catalogue to 'many Italian princes, cardinals and knights of merit' before putting it on sale.[30] Similarly, the prestige which Moscardo acquired from his museum and its catalogue was not without concrete consequences, if it is indeed true that this Veronese collector received the title of *Conte* between the first and the second edition.[31]

Amongst all the seventeenth-century collections, Moscardo's is definitely the most encyclopaedic and the most confused. It contains antiques, mummies, paintings, clocks, musical instruments and natural products. Amongst the latter we find giants' teeth, shells which produce ducks, and stones endowed with magic powers, and these were displayed not with scepticism but with pride.[32] Moreover, almost all the *naturalia* come from distant lands, supporting the idea that here the Mannerist style is recaptured and amplified by Baroque.

The Cospi museum also reveals characteristics typical of its time, which can be analysed by means of the 1677 catalogue. It is true that this catalogue was not actually written by Cospi himself but by Lorenzo Legati; however, I still believe it helps us to bring into focus the mentality of a certain type of collector in seventeenth-century Italy. The encyclopaedic quality is evident from the early pages of the introduction to the reader: Cospi's collection consists of 'peculiar manufactures of Art' and 'curious works of Nature'.[33] At this point it is not necessary to be reminded of how this juxtaposition of *naturalia* and *artificialia* resolves itself yet again into a continual confrontation between art and nature. It is more interesting to note that the natural-history section in the museum is organized in such a way as to exclude systematically all normality. Not only are the more common animals and plants, which would have been familiar to visitors, completely missing, but European flora and fauna in general are very poorly represented. Evidently, the fundamental aim of Cospi's museum was to provoke astonishment and wonder rather than analytically to reconstruct the whole natural world. This theory is borne out by the presence of only very few ordinary objects. In fact, he did not consider such things worth collecting unless they were either monstrous or had some bizarre peculiarity – the fly enclosed in amber, for example. The descriptions of individual pieces in the catalogue also show how outdated the natural history section of this collection was at this stage. There emerges clearly a feeling of nostalgia for a world full of portentous creatures and phenomena which had not yet been sifted out by scientific rationality. There is absolutely no form of anatomical investigation: animals and plants are described in the terms used by ancient and contemporary poets; their presence is recalled in emblems and medals. Above all, those beliefs in the habits and miraculous properties of animals which scientific research had by then shown to be unfounded, are still stubbornly reiterated. Evidently the results of scientific investigation could not be totally ignored; but the rational explanation (often taken from the works of Francesco Redi) is usually confined to a few grudging lines at the end of each description.[34] The effort to maintain the greatest possible sense of mystery and wonder is quite apparent. In the same town, and at the same time as Malpighi was subjecting the vegetable world to microscopic examination, it did not even occur to Cospi to open up a dried Ethiopian fruit to discover the nature of its interior, although the catalogue notes that the fruit rattled when shaken.[35] He still clung to a method of enquiry based largely on vague supposition rather than dissection and empirical analysis.

I believe we now have sufficient evidence to state that museums such as Cospi's, Moscardo's and Settala's represent in some senses a retrogression when compared with the collections of the sixteenth-century naturalists. Julius von Schlosser was quite right when, almost eighty years ago, he detected some aspects of seventeenth-century Italian collections which were similar to those of the Nordic *Wunderkammer*.[36] Moreover, certain seventeenth-century documents would appear to support this interpretation. In his letters, the traveller Maximilian Misson declines to give a detailed description of the contents of Moscardo's museum in order to avoid repeating what he had already written about the Ambras collection.[37] He simply refers the reader to the description of what was possibly the most typical of the *Kunst- und Wunderkammern*, thus emphasizing the similarity between it and the Italian museum.

In addition to the three collections examined here in some detail, many others in Italy provide evidence of a taste for encyclopaedic arrangement. As late as the beginning of the eighteenth century, a Paduan physician, Alessandro Knips Macoppe, advises young physicians to form museums containing numerous tokens of the past as well as exotic and monstrous natural objects, as a means of enhancing prestige.[38] At the time Knips Macoppe was writing, however, signs of a marked and irreversible change were already beginning to show.

Only a few decades after the publication of the catalogues of the museums of Settala, Moscardo, and Cospi, other private collectors with no specific scientific training were giving a completely new slant to their collections. Luigi Ferdinando Marsili, for example, founded his collection of natural objects along strictly specialist lines.[39] Marsili firmly condemned the mixture of *naturalia* and *artificialia*, claiming that encyclopaedic collections 'serve more to delight young men and provoke the admiration of women and the ignorant, rather than teach scholars about nature'.[40] He saw his cabinet exclusively as an instrument for facilitating work and increasing knowledge in which, however, there had to be a true reflection of the natural order itself. This conception automatically makes Marsili introduce another great novelty into the realm of scientific collections: every product of nature, even the most common, had importance and worth, and therefore had to be represented in the museum. Thus the natural-history collection was no longer valued for its curiosities, bizarre objects, wonderful artefacts, or simply for the abundance of the pieces; now the orderly completeness of the natural series was valued because it was fundamentally useful.

The direction of specialization chosen by Marsili was also followed from the end of the seventeenth century by other collectors whose interests differ from those of the naturalists. Scipione Maffei organized a museum of epigraphy in Verona, with definite conservative and didactic aims.[41] Maffei's *lapidario* marked an important turning point in the history of Italian collections. It was not an encyclopaedic collection, nor did it attempt to incorporate the entire realm of antiquity. The Veronese scholar, concentrating his attention exclusively on inscriptions, which he classified with great precision, created a highly specialized collection. Another fundamental distinguishing feature of Maffei's *lapidario* is that, unlike the seventeenth-century collections which were created as pastimes and then opened to visitors in order to arouse wonder, it was envisaged from the beginning as a public institution.

Collections like those of Marsili and Maffei represent the earliest models which incorporated the new criteria governing the formation and arrangement of museums in the eighteenth century. Two of the most notable examples of the application of these criteria were to be the reorganization of the Uffizi Gallery in Florence by Pelli-Bencivenni and Lanzi, and the foundation of the Gabinetto di Fisica e di Storia Naturale under the direction of Felice Fontana.[42]

NOTES

1. Borghini's project can be seen in K. H. W. Frey, *Der literarische Nachlass Giorgio Vasaris*, Munich, 1930, vol. 2, pp. 61–83; G. Lensi Orlandi, *Cosimo e Francesco de' Medici, Alchimisti*, Florence, 1978, pp. 109–35; F. Gandolfo, *Il 'Dolce Tempo'. Mistica, Ermetismo e Sogno nel Cinquecento*, Rome, 1978, pp. 886–91. For the significance of the *studiolo* see L. Berti, *Il principe dello Studiolo: Francesco I dei Medici e la fine del Rinascimento Fiorentino*, Florence, 1967, pp. 263–311; L. Bolzoni, 'L' "invenzione" dello Stanzino di Francesco I', in *Le Arti del Principato Mediceo*, Florence, 1980.

2. For example in 1597 Ferrante Imperato wrote a letter to Agostini saying explicitly 'my theatre of Nature consists of nothing but natural things, such as minerals, animals and plants' (quoted in A. Neviani, 'Ferrante Imperato speziale e naturalista napoletano con documenti inediti', *Atti e Memorie Accademia di Storia dell'arte sanitaria*, ser. 2, 2 (1936), p. 257.

3. Biblioteca Universitaria, Bologna, MS Aldrovandi 70, c. 14.

4. See G. Oimi, 'Farmacopea antica e medicina moderna. La disputa sulla Teriaca nel Cinquecento bolognese', *Physis*, 19 (1977).

5.   G. B. Olivi, *De reconditis et praecipuis collectanies ab honestissimo et solertissimo Francisco Calceolario Veronensi in Musaeo adservatis*, Venice, 1584 (another edition Verona, 1593); B. Ceruti and A. Chiocco, *Musaeum Francisci Calceolari Veronensis*, Verona, 1622.

6.   Bolzoni, 'L' "invenzione"'.

7.   G. Olmi, *Ulisse Aldrovandi. Scienza e natura nel secondo Cinquecento*, Trento, 1976, pp. 82–5.

8.   M. Mercati, *Metallotheca. Opus Posthumum. Auctoriate et Munificentia Clementis Undecimi P. M. e tenebris in lucem eductum: Opera autem et studio Ioannis Lancisii Archiatri Pontificii illustratum*, Rome, 1719. It should be noted that the engraving represents the ideal museum and that Mercati's *Metallotheca* actually consisted of several separate rooms (see B. Accordi, 'Michele Mercati (1541–1593) e la Mettallotheca', *Geologica Romana*, 19, 1980, p. 4).

9.   G. Olmi, 'Osservazione della natura e raffigurazione in Ulisse Aldrovandi (1522–1605', *Annali dell'Istituto storico italo-gemanico in Trento*, 3, 1777); G. Olmi 'Arte e Natura nel cinquecento Bolognese: Ulisse Aldrovandi e la raffigurazione scientifica', in A. Emiliani (ed.), *Le arti a Bologna e in Emilia dal XVI al CVII secolo*, Bologna, 1982.

10. U. Aldrovandi, *De Animalibus Insectis Libri septem*, Bologna, 1602.

11. For this aspect of collections in late Renaissance Italy, see D. Franchini et al., *La scienza a corte. Collezionismo eclettico, natura e imagine a Mantova fra Rinascimento e Manierismo*, Rome, 1979.

12. An idea of the characteristics and functions of Italian botanic gardens is easily obtained from Biblioteca Nazionale, Florence, Targioni Tozzetti, 562 (*Agricoltura Sperimentale del Padre Agostino del Riccio* I) cc. 74v–75v; G. Porro, *L'Horto de i Semplici di Padova*, Venice, 1591. See also Regione Toscana – Giunta Regionale, *Il giardino storico italiano. Problemi di indagine – Fonti letterarie e storiche*, ed. G. Ragioneri, Florence, 1981, and L. Tongiorgi Tomasi, 'Projects for botanical and other gardens: a 16th-century manual', *Journal of Garden History*, 3 (1983).

13. U. Dierauer, *Tier und Mensch im Denken der Antike. Studien zur Tierpsychologie, Anthropologie und Ethik*, Amsterdam, 1977: M. Vegetti, *Il coltello e lo stilo. Animali, schiavi, barbari e donne alle origini della razionalità scientifica*, Milan, 1979; M. Vegetti, 'Lo spettacolo della natura. Circo, teatro e potere in Plinio', *Aut-Aut*, 184–5 (1981). Some reference may also be found in K. Thomas, *Man and the Natural World. Changing Attitudes in England 1500–1800*, London, 1983.

14. F. Imperato, *Dell'Historia Naturale di Ferrante Imperato Napolitano Libri XXVIII Nella quale ordinatamente si tratta della diversa condition di miniere, e pitre. Con alcune historie di Piante, et Animali; sin' hora non date in luce*, Naples, 1599.

15. D. Heikamp, 'Zur Geschichte der Uffizien-Tribuna und der Kunstschränke in Florenz und Deutschland', *Zeitschrift für Kunstgeschichte*, 26 (1963); D. Heikamp, 'La Tribuna degli Uffizi come era nel Cinquecento', *Antichità Viva*, 3 (1964).

16. L. Tongiorgi Tomasi, 'Il giardino dei semplici dello studio pisano. Collezianismo, scienza e imagine tra cinque e seicento', in *Livorno e Pisa: due città e un territorio nella politica dei Medici*, Pisa, 1980.

17. For the general characteristics of Medici patronage of the sciences, see P. Galluzzi, 'Il mecenatismo mediceo e le scienze', in C. Vasoli (ed.), *Idee, istituzioni, scienza ed arti nella Firenze dei Medici*, Florence, 1980.

18. P. Boccone, *Osservazioni naturali ove si contengono materie medico-fisiche e di botanica*, Bologna, 1684, pp. 215–19.

19. G. de Sepi, *Romani Collegii Societatis Jesu Musaeum Celeberrimum*, Amsterdam, 1678; P. B[u]onani, *Musaeum Kircherianum sive Musaeum a P. Athanasio Kirchero incoeptum nuper restitutum, auctum, descriptum, et iconibus illustratum a P. Philippo Bonanni*, Rome, 1709.

20. The fundamental source of information on seventeenth-century Roman collections remains F. Haskell, *Patrons and Painters. A Study in the Relations between Italian Art and Society in the Age of the Baroque*, London, 1963.

21. [G. P. Bellori], *Nota delli Musei, Librerie, Galerie, et ornamenti di Statue e Pitture Ne' Palazzi, nelle Case, e ne' Giardini di Roma*, Rome, 1664.

22. P. M. Terzago, *Musaeum Septalianum Manfredi Septale Patritii Mediolanensis industrioso labore constructum …*, Tortona, 1664; P. F. Scarabelli, *Museo ò Galeria Adunata dal sapere, e dallo studio del Sig. Canonico Manfredo Settala*, Tortona, 1666; L. Moscardo, *Note overo Memorie del Conte Lodovico Moscardo nobile veronese*, Padua, 1656; L. Moscardo, *Note overo Memorie del Museo del Conte Lodovico Moscardo*, Verona, 1672; L. Legati, *Museo Cospiano annesso a quello del famosos Ulisse Aldrovandi e donato alla sua Patria dall'Illustrissimo Signor Ferdinando Cospi*, Bologna, 1677.

23. See, for example, S. A. Bedini, 'The evolution of Science Museums', *Technology and Culture*, 6 (1965); G. Tavernari, 'Manfredo Settala, collezionista e scienzato Milanese del '600', *Annali dell'Istituto e Museo di Storia della Scienza di Firenze*, 1 (1976).

24. This would also appear to be the opinion of R. W. Lightbown, 'Oriental art and the Orient in Late Renaissance and Baroque Italy', *Journal of the Warburg and Courtauld Institutes*, 32 (1969), p. 265.

25. G. Getto, *Barocco in prosa e in poesia*, Milan, 1969, pp. 13–57.

26. E. Tesauro, *Il Cannocchiale Aristotelico, O sia, Idea dell'arguta, et ingegnosa elocutione, che serve a tutta l'Arte oratoria, lapidaria et simbolica ... Settima impressione. Accresciuta dall'Autore di due nuovi Trattati, cioè, De' Concetti Predicabili, & Degli Emblemi*, Bologna, 1675, pp. 49–53.

27. Archivio di Stato, Bologna, Fondo Ranuzzi-Cospi, *Vita del Sig. March.ᵉ Bali Ferdinando Cospi*, c. 37.

28. Moscardo, *Note overo memorie del Museo di Lodovico Moscardo nobile veronese*, preface.

29. See Settala's letter to Kircher quoted in Tavernari, 'Manfredo Settala', p. 57.

30. Archivio di Stato, Bologna, Fondo Ranuzzi-Cospi, *Vita del Sig. March.ᵉ Bali Ferdinando Cospi*, c. 37.

31. L. Franzoni, 'Il collezionismo dal Cinquecento all'Ottocento', in G. P. Marchi (ed.), *Cultura e vita civile a Verona. Uomini e istituzioni dall'epoca carolingia al Risorgimento*, Verona, 1979, p. 624.

32. Moscardo, *Note overo memorie del Museo di Lodovico Moscardo nobile veronese*, pp. 122–3; 201–2.

33. Legati, *Museo Cospiano*, preface.

34. Ibid., for example pp. 11–12, 16, 25, 31, 135.

35. Ibid., pp. 136–7.

36. J. von Schlosser, *Die Kunst- und Wunderkammern der Spätrenaissance. Ein Beitrag zur Geschichte des Sammelwesens*, Leipzig, 1908, pp. 108–9. The judgement of Schlosser concerns in particular Settala's museum.

37. M. T. Misson, *Voyage d'Italie. Edition augmentée de remarques nouvelles et iteressantes*, Amsterdam, 1743, vol. 1, p. 180.

38. A. Knips Macoppe, *Aforismi medio-politici del celebre Alessandro Knips Macoppe volgarizzati col testo a fronte da Giuseppe Antonio del Chiappa*, Pavia, 1822, p. 93.

39. See M. F. Spallanzani, 'Le "Camere di storia naturale" dell' Istituto delle Scienze di Bologna nel Settecento', in *Scienze e letteratura nella cultura italiana del Settecento*, Bologna, forthcoming, and G. Olmi, 'Dal "Teatro del mondo" ai mondi inventariati. Aspetti e forme del collezionismo nell' età moderna', in P. Barocchi and G. Ragionieri (eds), *Gli Uffizi. Quattro secoli di una galleria*, Florence, 1983.

40. Quoted by Spallanzani, 'Le "Camere"'.

41. G. Mariani Canova, 'Il museo maffeiano nella storia della musicologia', *Atte e memorie dell'Accademia di agricoltura, scienza e lettere di Verona*, ser. 6 (1975–76); L. Franzoni, 'L'opere di Scipione Maffei di Alessandro Pompei per il museo pubblico veronese', *Atti e memorie dell'Accademia di agricoltura, scienza e lettere di Verona*, ser. 6 (1975–76); Comune di Verona – Direzioni del musei, *Il Museo Maffeiano riaperto al pubblico*, Verona, 1982; A. Sandrini, 'Il "Lapidarium veronense" e le origini dell' architectura museale', *Studi Storici Luigi Simeoni*, 32 (1982).

42. Olmi 1983.

3.

Natural History and the Emblematic World View

William B. Ashworth, Jr

The emblematic world view

The emblematic world view is, in my opinion, the single most important factor in determining late Renaissance attitudes towards the natural world, and the contents of their treatises about it. The essence of this view is the belief that every kind of thing in the cosmos has myriad hidden meanings and that knowledge consists of an attempt to comprehend as many of these as possible. To know the peacock, as Gesner wanted to know it [Conrad Gesner, *Historia animalium Libra III: De avium* (Zurich: Froschover, 1555), pp. 630–9], one must know not only what the peacock looks like but what its name means, in every language; what kind of proverbial associations it has; what it symbolizes to both pagans and Christians; what other animals it has sympathies or affinities with; and any other possible connection it might have with stars, plants, minerals, numbers, coins, or whatever. Gesner included all this, not because he was uncritical or obtuse, but because knowledge of the peacock was incomplete without it. The notion that a peacock should be studied in isolation from the rest of the universe, and that inquiry should be limited to anatomy, physiology, and physical description, was a notion completely foreign to Renaissance thought.

Once the modern student becomes comfortable with this complex world of symbols and associations and starts to read Renaissance natural histories with more awareness of the way these different discourses interacted, certain developments appear, in this new light, more understandable. We begin to see, for example, why Pierre Belon (1517–1564) and Guillaume Rondelet (1507–1566) did not have more impact in the late Renaissance, if they were in fact better zoologists than Gesner. Historians have fumbled for explanations, but it now seems evident that Belon and Rondelet attempted to place animals in a context that was much too limited. Anatomy, physiology, and classification may be the heart of modern zoology, but in the sixteenth century they were only several strands of a much more complex web, and contemporaries obviously felt that such a stripped-down world was incomplete; the zoological world depicted by Belon and Rondelet was not the zoological world inhabited by Renaissance man; it had lost too much of its richness and meaning. Gesner's world, on the other hand, was complex and interwoven, and the success enjoyed by his works and that of his successors is evidence that readers shared and cared for this world of resemblances.

We can also realize what a mistake it is to call the outlook of Gesner and his followers 'medieval', as historians have often done.[1] The adjective crops up because medieval bestiaries also incorporated animal symbolism and morals. But we can now understand that Gesner's symbolism is of quite a different kind and a higher order. Gesner's ancient sources were mainly classical, rather than Christian, and in addition he drew on many contemporary traditions that were unknown to the Middle Ages. It is noteworthy that bestiary symbolism was drawn primarily from the *Physiologus*, and Gesner hardly used the *Physiologus* at all (perhaps because it was not printed until 1587). There are many tales included by Gesner that are also in the *Physiologus*, but that is because both have a common source in Pliny. And Gesner rarely includes the medieval Christian morals that were the core of the bestiary tradition. So Gesner's world view may have been rich in animal symbolism, but there was nothing distinctively 'medieval' about it.

Another thing we notice is that the world of associations inhabited by Gesner was something quite different from what is sometimes called the 'magical world view'. Gesner was indeed familiar with magical treatises, most notably the *Kiranides*, and his discussions of sympathies usually come from such sources, if they were not drawn from Pliny.[2] But they form only a small fraction of his sources and his world view. Magic, or hermetism, has come in for a lot of attention in the last decades and has been offered up by some as *the* world view of the Renaissance, the outlook that was to be replaced by the mechanical philosophy. I merely wish to point out here that in fact magic, or hermetism, was only one element of a much larger picture; only one tradition among dozens that fused to form the emblematic world view.[3]

Aldrovandi and emblematic natural history

And finally, we are ready to appreciate the difference between Aldrovandi and Gesner. Ulisse Aldrovandi (1522–1605) must be the most underappreciated naturalist of the early modern era. His thirteen massive folios stand high and dry on library shelves, like so many beached whales, forbidding in their bulk, alien in their contents, and apparently seldom read. The encyclopedic format has led most historians to conclude that he was just another Gesner, except that he did not know when to stop.[4] This opinion is unfortunate, because Aldrovandi was not 'Gesner redivivus'. If one concentrates on the biological parts of his compendiums, there are indeed great similarities. But if one reads on for the associations, one discovers that there has been a great change in fifty years. Suppose we turn to Aldrovandi's article on the peacock.[5] We notice, first of all, that it is thirty-one pages long, compared to Gesner's eight. Gesner divided his article into eight sections; Aldrovandi has thirty-three topics in all, and it is well worth listing the titles of these:

aequivoca	aetas	moralia
synonyma	volatus	hieroglyphica
genus	mores	symbola
differentiae	ingenium	proverbia
descriptio	sympathia	usus in sacris icones
locus	antipathia	usus in externis
coitus	corporis affectus	usus in medicina
partus	cognominata	usus in cibis
incubatus	denominata	apologi
educatio	praesagia	fabulosa
vox	mystica	historica

It is one thing to talk about a 'web of associations'; it is much more impressive to see this web laid out, strand by strand, as Aldrovandi does. Aldrovandi's network is similar in kind to Gesner's but many times more intricate. What has happened to the emblematic world in the intervening fifty years to swell it to such splendor?

Gesner had compiled his encyclopedias in the 1550s. At that time the adages of Erasmus were in wide circulation, as was the mythology of Ovid, and Gesner utilized both freely. But many of the other traditions were just beginning to flower. Horapollo had been available in print for quite some time, but only with the publication of the *Hieroglyphics* (Basel, 1556) of Piero Valeriano (1477–1558) did fascination with hieroglyphics really begin to spread. So we find in Gesner only passing attention given to hieroglyphic meanings. The great numismatic encyclopedias did not appear until the mid-1550s. Ripa's *Iconologia* was unavailable to Gesner, as was the printed *Physiologus*. The fable tradition was just catching hold, and most of the best editions of Aesop did not appear until the 1570s. And most important, the emblematic tradition was barely a bud when the first volume of the *History of Animals* lumbered off the presses. Few animal emblems were in circulation in Gesner's day, and although he utilized the ones available, they do not dominate his descriptive associations.

It is the efflorescence of the emblem tradition that marks the biggest difference between Gesner and Aldrovandi, and I would like to demonstrate the growth of animal emblematics before returning to Aldrovandi. Animals did not play a central role in Alciati's *Emblemata*; they were present, but not omnipresent. But when others began composing emblem books, they turned to Horapollo and Piero Valeriano for inspiration, and there animal symbols are abundant. So from 1560 on we begin to see more and more attention given to the epigrammatic meanings of the natural world. This trend culminated in the publication of the *Collection of Symbols and Emblems* of Joachim Camerarius (1534–1598) from 1593 to 1604. This set of four volumes contains four hundred emblems, and every one involves an animal or plant. In the second volume, on quadrupeds, we find emblems for one hundred animals – not only horses and lions, but hedgehogs, ichneumons, chameleons, weasels, and even the New World *simivulpa*, or opossum.

It is important to understand that Camerarius was as much a student of nature as Gesner, and his emblem book was intended as a contribution to natural history, as well as to emblematics. The commentary to his peacock emblem, for example, refers to Aristotle, Pliny, Ovid, Isidore, as well as earlier emblem books, and Camerarius apparently saw no contradiction between his emblem-book production and his botanical work; both illuminated the emblematic world of nature.[6]

By the beginning of the seventeenth century, there was available a cornucopia of animal allegories and symbolism for anyone interested in adding to the traditional animal similitudes. Aldrovandi was very much interested. Just after Camerarius's first volumes of emblems rolled off the press, Aldrovandi began to issue the first volumes of his natural history. The *Ornithology* was the first to appear, in three volumes published between 1599 and 1603. The volume on insects followed. Aldrovandi died, and the production slowed slightly, but not much, as his assistants and heirs took over responsibility for bringing the Aldrovandi corpus to light. The first volume on quadrupeds came out in 1616, and subsequent huge volumes plopped into view with intermittent regularity, right up until 1648. Why did Aldrovandi need three volumes on birds and three for quadrupeds, where Gesner had one for each? The reason is that Aldrovandi's humanist text had been swollen by incorporating all of the new contributions of the sixteenth-century students of hieroglyphics, emblems, adages, and antiquities. Let us consider another specimen animal, this time from the world of quadrupeds.

The *echinus*, or hedgehog, was well known to classical authorities; should one look up the entry in Gesner, one would find most of the interesting hedgehog stories gathered together.[7] One would learn that the hedgehog carries home grapes and apples on its spines – never in its mouth. When *echinus* walks, it squeaks like a cartwheel; when a male and a female copulate, they do so face to face. Gesner transcribes two proverbs from Erasmus's *Adages*: One we have already discussed; the other, *Echinus partum differt* (The hedgehog delays childbirth), likens a poor man, who puts off payment of debts, to the hedgehog mother, who tries to retard the delivery of her spiny whelps. Gesner also adds a long section on medicinal uses. But there are no examples drawn from hieroglyphics, emblems, or numismatics.

Aldrovandi's discussion is much more extensive.[8] There is now a lengthy paragraph on *antipathia*, or antipathies, informing us that the hedgehog is a bitter enemy of the wolf, detests serpents, and is not fond of those plants that have spines themselves. Under the heading 'Emblemata & Symbola' one can find both of Camerarius's emblems quoted in full, with motto and epigram. Aldrovandi includes a section on *simulacra*, or images, where he reveals his familiarity with Ripa's *Iconology*, pointing out that Ripa's figure of *laesiones*, or oratory, has a hedgehog in one hand.

And in other sections on hieroglyphics, morals, omens, symbols, and so forth, one finds every reference to the hedgehog that is made by Piero Valeriano, Horapollo, the *physiologus*, Erasmus, and most of the important emblem writers. With all these resources Aldrovandi is able to spin a net of associations and similitudes that is far more complex than anything that Gesner was able to achieve. Aldrovandi's world needed thirteen volumes to contain it.

The emblematic view of nature continued to prevail through the first half of the seventeenth century, periodically refreshed by the appearance of additional Aldrovandi zoological volumes. And while Aldrovandi was a major force in its persistence, other zoologists fashioned similar world views, often independently. The *Historie of Four-Footed Beastes* (1607) by Edward Topsell (1572–1638) provides a good example. Topsell has been much maligned as an unimaginative plagiarist of Gesner, and some of the criticism is deserved.[9] But it is of interest that Topsell frequently added new material to that he took from Gesner, and most of it consisted of references drawn from emblematic and hieroglyphic literature. Since Topsell wrote before the appearance of Aldrovandi's volumes on quadrupeds, he must have gleaned this new material on his own, by perusing the works of Camerarius and Piero Valeriano. Moreover, whatever his failings as a zoologist, Topsell knew exactly what he was trying to do in his book. His 'Epistle Dedicatory' is a hymn to animals as symbolic images. He suggests that a history of beasts is preferable to a historical chronicle, because it reveals 'that Chronicle which was made by God himselfe, every living beast being a word, every kind being a sentence, and al of them togither a large history, containing admirable knowledge & learning, which was, which is, which shall continue, (if not for ever) yet to the worlds end'.[10]

Jonston and the demise of emblematic natural history

The dominance of natural history by similitude is so complete in the first half of the seventeenth century that one certainly expects Joannes Jonston's multivolume *Natural History* of 1650 – which looks for all the world like another Renaissance encyclopedia – to conform to the Aldrovandi model.[11] All the Aldrovandi illustrations are there, as well as those of Gesner and assorted other Renaissance naturalists. It is a shock, then, to read the text of Jonston's work and realize that, with its publication, the bottom has suddenly dropped right out of the emblematic cosmos.

Joannes Jonston (1603–1675) is not well appreciated by historians of science. He is usually portrayed – when he is portrayed at all – as a secondhand Aldrovandi, and thus a thirdhand Gesner – the last of the Renaissance encyclopedists. It is hard to understand how this image of Jonston has persisted, for the text of his work reflects a remarkable metamorphosis. The entry on *pavo* can serve again to illustrate these changes.[12] It has been trimmed to a tidy two pages. There is a full description – nothing has been cut here – and a discussion of medical applications and culinary uses. But if one looks for peacock emblems, proverbs, or hieroglyphics, there are none to be found. Not a single reference to Camerarius, or Horapollo, or Erasmus – not in the peacock article, not in any article. Even the medicinal uses have been weeded out: The ones that suggest sympathetic cures are gone; those that allow a physical cause are retained.[13] In fact, Jonston's description of the peacock is virtually identical to that of Francis Willughby twenty-five years later. It is apparent that emblematic natural history began to wane long before the Royal Society took a dislike to it.[14]

It was Michel Foucault who suggested that Jonston's encyclopedia marked a clear break with earlier Renaissance natural history, and he does seem to have pointed his finger in the right direction, if not to the precise spot.[15] Something profound had indeed occurred around midcentury, and historians of other fields have noticed it, although they have placed the date of transition earlier or later. One description of the transformation, by François Jacob, is particularly eloquent:

Living bodies were scraped clean, so to speak. They shook off their crust of analogies, resemblances and signs, to appear in all the nakedness of their true outer shape. ... What was read or related no longer carried the weight of what was seen. ... What counted was not so much the code used by God for creating nature as that sought by man for understanding it.[16]

Historians of linguistics have called this metamorphosis the 'decon-textualization' of the world; historians of magic the 'disenchantment' or 'desymbolization' of nature.[17] Historians of the natural sciences have simply not noticed it. But Foucault is right; Jonston's natural history is indeed a watershed publication. To Foucault, however, the 'event' of Jonston's work is an enigma, one of those transitions that cannot be explained. In truth, there are some explanations for the sudden death of 'animal semantics', to use Foucault's own evocative term. I would like to offer several here.

New World natural histories

Certainly one important factor in this mild revolution was the appearance, in the early decades of the seventeenth century, of the first natural histories of New World animals: Charles L'Ecluse's *Exotica* (1605), Jan de Laet's *New World* (1625), Juan Nieremberg's *History of Nature* (1635), and most important, the *Natural History of Brazil* (1648) by Georg Markgraf (1610–1644).[18] These natural histories are occasionally brought into survey accounts of the Scientific Revolution, but their significance is usually seen to lie in their demonstration of a Baconian explosion of knowledge. This, of course, is true, but New World narratives had a far greater influence than simply enlarging the subject matter of natural history. Their impact derived from one simple fact: The animals of the new world had no known similitudes. Anteaters and sloths do not appear in Erasmus or Alciati or Piero Valeriano; they are missing from all the writings of antiquity. They came to the Old World naked, without emblematic significance. Thus naturalists could not approach this new fauna in the manner of Aldrovandi. Instead, they were forced to limit their descriptions to discussions of appearance, habitat, food, and whatever tales could be assembled from native populations. The tension between Old World and New World natural history is particularly evident in the narrative of Juan Nieremberg (1595–1658). He begins his work with a sixteen-page first chapter that is a masterful – indeed rhapsodic – restatement of the emblematic view of nature.[19] Then he parades by the reader a host of capybaras, marmosets, and pacas, and not a single one has a known similitude or emblematic meaning. All he can provide is a physical description and a picture. The contrast between a page of Nieremberg and a page of Aldrovandi is remarkable.

Jonston compiled his natural history from both kinds of sources: Aldrovandi and Gesner on the one hand, Nieremberg and Markgraf on the other. He was confronted – really the first to be so confronted – with this great incongruity of style: Old World animals, clothed in similitudes; New World animals, bereft of associations. Perhaps for uniformity, perhaps for personal preference, perhaps because he did not feel able to create an emblematic New World out of whole cloth, Jonston adopted the model of the New World description. The Old World animals lay naked to the observer's eye for the first time. And never again would they resume their emblematic garb.

Browne and the quest for truth in natural history

There were other factors involved, however, in the demise of the emblematic world view, for we can also see it under attack in a work radically different from Jonston's *Natural History*, namely the *Pseudodoxia epidemica* (1646) of Thomas Browne (1605–1682) or, as it is sometimes called, the *Vulgar Errors*.[20] The *Pseudodoxia* is a concerted attempt to purge natural history of commonly, but erroneously, perceived truths. Many people believed that the badger has legs that are shorter on one side than the other; that the chameleon subsists on air and the salamander survives in fire; that a dead kingfisher, hung by the bill, will point in the direction of the wind. Such ascriptions, and hundreds more, can readily be found in the tomes of Gesner, Aldrovandi, and Topsell. But in the *Pseudodoxia*, Browne asks the remarkable questions: Are these stories true? Can they be demonstrated? By appealing to a threefold criterion of reason, experiment, and authority, Browne proceeds to evaluate a large number of such Vulgar Truths. Can a dead kingfisher truly function as a weathervane? Browne hangs several birds outside and finds that no two point in the same direction. Do toads and spiders have a mutual, innate antipathy? Browne decides the matter by placing a toad and several spiders in a jar, and he relates that the spiders crawled all over the unperturbed toad, who swallowed them contentedly, one by one, as they came near his mouth.[21]

Interestingly, in view of our specimen bird, Browne even puts the peacock to the test. Two of Aldrovandi's statements attracted Browne's notice: that peacocks are ashamed of their own feet, and that cooked peacock meat does not spoil.[22] Concerning the first, Browne says that the notion probably arose because the peacock must keep its head back to maintain its display of feathers; if the head inclines forward, the train collapses. It is not a matter of shame but of mechanics. Browne also does an experiment to test the purported nonputrefaction of roasted peacock flesh and discovers it to be true. But, as he points out, it is also true of the meat of many fowl – turkey and pheasant, for example – and so it is hardly a special virtue of the peacock.

Browne clearly has a different view of nature from Aldrovandi; he is uninterested in aphorisms or emblems that are not *true*. His skepticism is even more remarkable when we note that Browne was a true romantic (if the term makes sense when applied to the English baroque), a writer whose most famous sentiment was 'I love to lose my self in a mystery, to pursue my Reason to an *O altitudo*.'[23] Where did such a man acquire the idea that natural history involves the separation of the true from the false? He did not arrive at these views by reading New World natural histories. I would like to suggest that the inspiration came from seventeenth-century antiquarianism.

Antiquarianism and the quest for historical truth

Antiquarian studies changed markedly in the early seventeenth century, as part of what has been called, perhaps overenthusiastically, a 'historical revolution'.[24] The antiquarianism of sixteenth-century Italy was not considered a historical discipline. As Arnaldo Momigliano pointed out in a now-classic essay, antiquities in Italy were not used as the tools of history, because the history of ancient Rome and Greece had already been written – by Livy and Caesar and Polybius.[25] Thus the coins and relics unearthed in such abundance were put to other uses; they were mined for their emblematic value, as we have already seen, or they were simply amassed in collections, in the museums of Francesco Calzolari, Ferrante Imperato, Michele Mercati, and Aldrovandi.[26] In very few instances in the sixteenth century do we find a historian treating a coin or burial urn as a piece of historical evidence to be used in reconstructing the past.

But antiquarianism began to take quite a different turn in the northern countries around the end of the sixteenth century. Antiquarians in England and Denmark, in particular, began to see their artifacts as vital historical clues. The reason for the different attitude in the north is straightforward: Northern countries had no classical, canonical histories.[27] Except for brief mentions in Caesar and Tacitus, the ancient history of England was a blank. There were, of course, medieval histories that purported to take England back to its first 'plantation' – the works of Geoffrey of Monmouth, Gildas, and Bede – but as their authenticity came to be challenged in the late sixteenth century, the void began to be filled with reconstructions based on artifactual evidence.

In England we see this quite clearly in the work of William Camden (1551–1623), whose *Britannia* of 1586 was a prodigious attempt to reconstruct the entire face of Roman Britain from such things as coins, inscriptions, and the remains of Roman roads.[28] The artifact was being given a new power, and the antiquaries were consciously aware of it. Camden declares, for example, that you can learn more about medieval dress from monuments, glass windows, and reliefs than from the writers of those times.[29] The artifact does not lie. It is this obsession with truth that really distinguishes post-Camden antiquarians from earlier collectors of antiquities and from literary historians. Camden says in the preface of his history of Queen Elizabeth's reign: 'For the love of truth, as it hath beene the only spurre unto me to undertake this work; so hath it also been my onely scope and aime.'[30] When we bear in mind that truth was not high on the list of the essential qualities of literary history – certainly it ranked below moral education as a virtue – we see what a revolution the artifact has wrought.

Antiquarianism and natural history

Antiquarian history did not have an immediate impact on literary history. Bacon kept 'Antiquarianism' and 'Perfect History' quite separate in the *Novum organum*, and they remained apart until after the middle of the seventeenth century.[31] But the antiquarian spirit did have a considerable effect on natural history, because the two fields overlapped considerably. There was, after all, no firm line between the Saxon urn, the stone axhead, the fossilized shark tooth, the unicorn horn, and the agate. Most of the great museum collections of the first half of the century – those of Basil Besler of Nuremberg, Ole Worm of Copenhagen, or the Habsburg emperors in Prague and Vienna – contained a mixture of natural and antiquarian artifacts.[32] And so natural historians who were exposed to the antiquarian attitude toward evidence came to see the natural world quite differently from Aldrovandi.[33]

Thomas Browne certainly falls into this category. He had a passionate interest in antiquities. One of his finest prosodic rhapsodies, the *Hydrotaphia*, or *Urn-Burial*, was inspired by the discovery of several Saxon burial urns in a Norfolk tomb, and in many of his other writings and letters Browne manifested a great fondness for the artifacts of the past.[34] All his works reflect an intimate familiarity with the antiquarian scholars of his century: Camden, Worm, John Twyne, John Stow, Richard Verstegan, Jan Goropius Becanus, William Dugdale, and many more. He was much impressed by the ability of the antiquarian to wrest a truth from 'the ruins of forgotten time' on the basis of slight, but incontrovertible, evidence.[35] Browne tested Roman artifacts for residual magnetism, attempted to determine the age and sex of exhumed skeletons, and suggested how barrows could be dated by the presence of 'distinguishing substances'.[36] In other words, he made artifactual evidence the standard for determining historical truth, and he tended to ignore or downplay the evidence of literary history, in spite of his own literary inclinations. It is not surprising, then, that when Browne approached the writing of natural history, he subjected the literary tradition there to the test of empirical evidence. And with this new conception of what constitutes natural history, the entire emblematic tradition fell apart – or, more accurately, became irrelevant. For Browne, animal symbolism was no longer a part of the study of nature, because it had no basis in truth.

It would seem, then, that Thomas Browne and Joannes Jonston reformulated natural history for quite different reasons but with rather similar results, and, most interestingly to note, at almost exactly the same time.[37] But this is still not the whole story. There is a third factor that should at least be considered in the decline of the emblematic world view, and that is Baconianism. Several observers have pointed to Bacon as being an instrumental force in the rise of a new natural history in the latter part of the seventeenth century,[38] and it is not unreasonable to suppose that Bacon's views might also have been felt in the earlier age of Browne, Markgraf, and Jonston.

Bacon and the real language of nature

Bacon never wrote a natural history; his posthumous *Sylva sylvarum*, of 1627, which is often called his 'natural history', is in reality a heterogeneous collection of random observations and suggestions for further inquiry. But Bacon did have definite ideas on how a proper natural history should be written, and he thought that the existing natural histories were unsatisfactory, because, as his executor William Rawley put it, they showed the world as men made it, not as God made it; Bacon's natural history, in contrast, would have 'nothing of Imagination' in it. And Rawley elaborated:

> For those Natural Histories which are Extant, being gathered for Delight and Use, are full of pleasant Descriptions and Pictures; and affect and seek after Admiration, Rarities, and Secrets. But contrariwise, the Scope which his Lordship intendeth is to write such a Naturall History, as may be Fundamental to the Erecting and Building of a true Philosophy; For the illumination of the Understanding; the extracting of Axiomes, and the producing of many Noble Workes, and Effects.[39]

What makes Bacon particularly striking, however, is that he not only spurned the use of the emblematic tradition in natural history; he rejected the entire emblematic world view as invalid. There is no web of correspondences for Bacon; similitudes do not lead to understanding; the universe is not written in a code that reveals the attributes of God.[40] Bacon was one of the first natural philosophers to take this stance. As early as the 'Valerius terminus' of around 1603, Bacon had stated: 'For if any man shall think by view and inquiry into these sensible and material things, to attain to any light for the revealing of the nature or will of God, he shall dangerously abuse himself.'[41] And in his later writings Bacon regularly warns against trying to impose patterns on nature that do not really exist in nature. 'There is a great difference,' Bacon says, in aphorism 23 of his *Novum organum*, 'between the Idols of the human mind and the Ideas of the divine. That is to say, between certain empty dogmas, and the true signatures and marks set upon the works of creation as they are found in nature.'[42] And elsewhere, more flatly: 'The world is not the image of God.'[43]

Bacon's rejection of the notion that the natural world is a divine language, encoded by God, is almost certainly related to his views on human language. The prevalent, Platonic tendency of the late Renaissance, as we have seen, was to consider the meanings of words as inherent in the words themselves, just as the meanings of animals lay embedded in their very natures. Words and things were all of a piece, and the entire world of objects, letters, signs, and symbols was part of one language, the meaning of which was built in by God.

Bacon argued for separating words from things. Words are not intrinsically connected to objects but are arbitrary and conventional. Their only meanings are the ones we assign to them.[44] Such a view of language, which ultimately (and ironically, considering Bacon's reputation) is derived from Aristotle, undermines to a considerable extent the emblematic world view. If words have no hidden meanings, why should nature? If the language of man is arbitrary, can there be a language of nature at all? How can the Book of Nature shed light on God's plan, if the language of that book is devoid of meaning? Bacon seems to have realized the implications and to have decided that nature is not a multilayered complex of signs and hieroglyphics and that philosophers need not concern themselves with such matters.

The impact of Baconianism on natural history

Baconianism thus contained the seeds of insurrection against the emblematic world view. But did these seeds bear immediate fruit? Did Baconianism play any role in the demise of that view? It seems that the answer is no. Thomas Browne was indebted to Bacon in various ways, especially in the importance he ascribed to experiment and observation, but Browne's view of nature seems independently arrived at and, in any event, is not especially Baconian. Jonston was not touched by Bacon at all, nor were the New World naturalists on whose work Jonston relied, such as Markgraf. In truth, Bacon's attitude seems to have had little impact on naturalists before the era of the Royal Society. If his presence was felt before then, it was so subtle as to be, shall we say, occult.

Natural history, antiquarianism, and the Scientific Revolution

We must conclude then that the dismantling of the emblematic world view was an event prior to, and independent of, the rise of Baconianism. It was also prior to, and independent of, the spread of Cartesian mechanism. Consequently, we historians might well rethink some of *our* commonly perceived truths about the relationship between the rise of the mechanical philosophy and the decline of the world of magic. We seem to take it for granted that the former caused the latter; that nature was stripped of its correspondences and occult forces by a generation of Cartesians committed to a philosophy that allowed only explanations grounded on matter in motion. In truth, Browne, Jonston, and their generation dispensed with sympathies and correspondences for entirely different reasons, because of developments outside the physical sciences, and even outside science itself.

One final point seems worth stressing. We have squeezed antiquarianism in through the back door here, by demonstrating its impact on natural history. But the influence of antiquarianism, and of seventeenth-century historical

thought in general, is broader than this, and the interplay of science and
history is one of the most neglected facets of seventeenth-century studies.
The Scientific Revolution was, after all, itself a historical revolution. It changed
forever the way we would view Aristotle, Ptolemy, Galen. It altered the very
concept of historical process. It is no simple coincidence that scientists of the
seventeenth century developed keen interests in such matters as the origins
of language, the early geological history of the earth, the settlement of the
New World, the chronology of Egyptian and Chinese history, the collection
of fossils, the early history of Christianity. The union of antiquarianism with
literary history fashioned by historians was very similar to the approach of
natural philosophers who forged a workable alliance between experiment
and authority. Both groups developed, really for the first time, a true historical
sense, which allowed them to place the past in proper perspective and,
consequently, opened up the possibilities of the present and future. I merely
suggest here that the similarities are perhaps not coincidental. It may well be
that the historical revolution played a greater role than we now appreciate in
the reconstruction of world views that we call the Scientific Revolution.

NOTES

1.   Charles E. Raven, 'Gesner and the Age of Transition', in Raven, *English Naturalists from Neckham
      to Ray: A Study of the Making of the Modern World* (New York: Kraus Reprint, 1968; 1st publ. 1948
      by Cambridge University Press), p. 47; Paul Delaunay, *La zoologie au seizième siècle*, Histoire de la
      pensée, no. 7 (Paris: Hermann, 1962), pp. 63–81; Lynn Thorndike, *A History of Magic and
      Experimental Science*, 8 vols (New York: Columbia University Press, 1923–1958), 6:277 (discussing
      Aldrovandi).

2.   Very little attention has been given to the impact of the *Kiranides* – the purported writings of
      Kiranus, king of Persia – on Renaissance thought, perhaps because the work never saw its way
      into print. Lynn Thorndike did devote a short chapter to it in the second volume of his *History of
      Magic and Experimental Science*, 2:229–35, but he never picked up on it again, and neither has
      anyone else. And yet Gesner obviously had a manuscript of the *Kiranides*, which he cited
      regularly for the magical attributes of animals.

3.   Since the prospect of citing the current literature on hermeticism is too daunting, I will seek
      relief in the almost certain fact that the subject is well discussed elsewhere in this volume [i.e.
      Reappraisals of the Scientific Revolution, ed. David C. Lindberg and Robert S. Westman
      (Cambridge: Cambridge University Press, 1990].

4.   Aldrovandi is ignored, or deplored, in virtually every English-language discussion of
      Renaissance natural history, whether survey or specialized. Fortunately Italian scholars have
      launched a rescue effort for their beleaguered countryman; see Sandra Tugnoli Pattaro, *Metodo e
      sistema delle scienze nel pensiero de Ulisse Aldrovandi* (Bologna: CLUEB, 1981); Giuseppe Olmi, *Ulisse
      Aldrovandi: Scienze e natura nel secondo cinquecento*, Quaderni di storia e filosofia delle scienze, no.
      4 (Trent: University of Trent, 1976), and the same author's 'Arte e natura nel cinquecento
      Bolognese: Ulisse Aldrovandi e la raffigurazione scientifica', in *Le arti a Bologna e in Emilia dal
      XVI al XVII secolo*, ed. Andrea Emiliani (Bologna: CLUEB, 1982), pp. 151–71 and Figures 195–201.

5.   Ulisse Aldrovandi, *Ornithologia II* (Bologna, 1600), pp. 1–31.

6.   Joachim Camerarius, *Symbolorum & emblematum ex re herbaria desumtorum centuria una collecta*
      (Nuremberg, 1590 [i.e., 1593]); *Symbolorum & emblematum ex animalibus quadrupedibus desumtorum
      centuria altera collecta* (Nuremberg, 1595); *Symbolorum & emblematum ex volatilibus ex insectis
      desumtorum centuria tertia collecta* (Nuremberg, 1596); *Symbolorum et emblematum ex aquatilibus et
      reptilibus desumptorum centuria quarta* (Nuremberg, 1604). The importance of Camerarius for
      natural history is stressed by Wolfgang Harms, 'On Natural History and Emblematics in the
      Sixteenth Century', in *The Natural Sciences and the Arts*, ed. Allan Ellenius, Acta Universitatis

Upsaliensis, Figura Nova, no. 22 (Uppsala: Almqvist & Wiksell, 1985), pp. 67–83. Harms is one of the very few to argue for the unity of natural history and emblematics in the late Renaissance; he is, interestingly, a historian of emblematics, not science. By contrast, we might note that Agnes Arber, in her still-definitive book on herbals, devoted three pages to Camerarius's botanical work, without once mentioning his emblem books; see *Herbals: Their Origin and Evolution* (1938; reprint edition, Cambridge: Cambridge University Press, 1986), pp. 76–8.

7. Gesner, *Historia animalium Lib. I. de quadripedibus viviparis* (Zurich, 1551), 1:399–409.

8. Ulisse Aldrovandi, *De quadrupedibus digitatis* (Bologna, 1637), pp. 459–70.

9. The harshest criticism of Topsell came from Charles E. Raven, *English Naturalists from Neckham to Ray: A Study of the Making of the Modern World* (New York: Kraus Reprint, 1968), who called Topsell 'unimaginative, commonplace. ... He was not a man of high distinction, intellectual or practical', pp. 219–20.

10. Edward Topsell, *A Historie of Four-Footed Beastes* (London, 1607), sig. A5v.

11. Joannes Jonston, *Historia naturalis*, 6 vols (Frankfurt, 1650–1653). The six volumes are on quadrupeds, birds, serpents, fish, marine invertebrates, and insects; all except the last were published in 1650.

12. Jonston, *Historia naturalis de avibus*, pp. 56–8.

13. Our other specimen animal, the hedgehog, has an entry in the volume *De quadrupetibus*, pp. 170–1. The entry is about one-tenth the size of Aldrovandi's article.

14. Willughby's *Ornithologia* (London, 1676) is often referred to as an example of the 'new' natural history inspired by the Royal Society.

15. Foucault, *Order of Things: An Archaeology of the Human Sciences* (New York: Pantheon Books, 1970), pp. 128–30 (citing Jonston, *Historia naturalis*, 1:1); the page cited might provide ammunition to those who question the depth of Foucault's scholarship. Foucault gives 1657 as the 'date of birth' of this new classical natural history; in fact, that is the date of birth only of the Amsterdam reprint of Jonston's work. Although Foucault then claims that the date is not definitive, but only symbolizes a landmark, it still seems that if we are going to use a date at all, it might as well be the right one, that is, 1650.

16. François Jacob, *The Logic of Life: A History of Heredity*, trans. Betty E. Spillman (New York: Vintage Books, 1976), pp. 28–9. In typical Parisian fashion, Jacob and Foucault do not acknowledge each other's existence, but it is hard to believe they were not peeking at one another's work now and then.

17. M. M. Slaughter, *Universal Languages and Scientific Taxonomy in the Seventeenth Century* (New York: Cambridge University Press, 1982), pp. 56–7; Peter Fingesten, *The Eclipse of Symbolism* (Columbia: University of South Carolina Press, 1970), p. 54. See also Owen Hannaway, *The Chemists and the Word: The Didactic Origins of Chemistry* (Baltimore: Johns Hopkins University Press, 1975), who does not give the transformation a name but describes it beautifully.

18. Charles L'Ecluse, *Exoticorum libri decem* (Leiden, 1605); Jan de Laet, *Novis orbis* (Leiden, 1633); Juan Eusebius Nieremberg, *Historia naturae* (Antwerp, 1635); Georg Markgraf, *Historia naturalis Brasiliensis* (Leiden, 1648). Of these four, only Markgraf has been well studied – perhaps because he was such a 'good' zoologist. See the various excellent publications of P. J. P. Whitehead, especially 'Georg Markgraf and Brazilian Zoology', in *Johan Maurits van Nassau-Siegen, 1604–1679: A Humanist Prince in Europe and Brazil*, ed. E. van den Boogaart (The Hague: Johan Maurits van Nassau Stichting, 1979), pp. 424–71. Markgraf's book is often cataloged under the name of his colleague, Willem Piso.

19. Nieremberg, *Historia naturae*, pp. 1–16.

20. Thomas Browne, *Pseudodoxia epidemica: Or, Enquiries into very many received Tenents, and common presumed truths* (London, 1646).

21. Browne, *Pseudodoxia epidemica*, pp. 175 (toad), 157–63 (chameleon), 138–40 (salamander), 127–9 (kingfisher), 115 (badger). Two of the best studies of the *Pseudodoxia* are by Robert R. Cawley: 'The Timeliness of *Pseudodoxia epidemica*' and 'Sir Thomas Browne and His Reading'. Both are in *Studies in Sir Thomas Browne*, ed. Robert R. Cawley and George Yost (Eugene: University of Oregon Books, 1965), pp. 1–40, 104–66.

22. Browne, *Pseudodoxia epidemica*, pp. 172–3.

23. Thomas Browne, *Religio medici*, in *Works*, 6 vols, ed. Geoffrey Keynes (London: Faber & Gwyer, 1928–1931), 1:13.

24. F. Smith Fussner, *The Historical Revolution: English Historical Writing and Thought, 1580–1640* (New York: Columbia University Press, 1962). For one reaction, see Joseph H. Preston, 'Was There an Historical Revolution?', *Journal of the History of Ideas*, 38 (1977): 353–64.

25. Momigliano, 'Ancient History and the Antiquarian', in A. Momigliano, *Studies in Historiography* (New York: Harper and Row, 1966), pp. 1–36.

26. On the nature of the sixteenth-century museum, see the collection of essays in Oliver Impey and Arthur MacGregor, eds, *The Origins of Museums: The Cabinet of Curiosities in Sixteenth- and Seventeenth-century Europe* (Oxford: Oxford University Press [Clarendon Press], 1985).

27. Momigliano, 'Ancient History and the Antiquarian', p. 7.

28. On William Camden, see Stuart Piggott, 'William Camden and the "Britannia"', in *Ruins in a Landscape: Essays in Antiquarianism* (Edinburgh: Edinburgh University Press, 1976), pp. 33–53; T. D. Kendrick, *British Antiquity* (London: Methuen, 1970), pp. 143–59; Hugh Trevor-Roper, 'Queen Elizabeth's First Historian: William Camden', in *Renaissance Essays* (Chicago: University of Chicago Press, 1985), pp. 121–48; F. J. Levy, *Tudor Historical Thought* (San Marino, Calif.: Huntington Library, 1967), pp. 148–63; Fussner, *Historical Revolution*, pp. 230–52.

29. Camden, quoted in Piggott, 'William Camden and the 'Britannia''', p. 37.

30. William Camden, *The Historie of the Most Renowned and Victorious Princesse Elizabeth* (London, 1630), 'To the Reader', sig. B1v; partially quoted (from a different translation) in Herschel Baker, *The Race of Time: Three Lectures on Renaissance Historiography* (Toronto: University of Toronto Press, 1967), p. 20.

31. J. G. A. Pocock, *The Ancient Constitution and Feudal Law: A Study of English Historical Thought in the Seventeenth Century* (Cambridge: Cambridge University Press, 1957; reprint edition, New York: Norton, 1967), pp. 6–7.

32. On early seventeenth-century museums, see Impey and MacGregor, *Origins of Museums*.

33. There is a good discussion of the interaction between natural history and antiquarianism (as well as other historical disciplines) in Barbara Shapiro, 'History and Natural History in Sixteenth- and Seventeenth-century England: An Essay on the Relationship between Humanism and Science', in her *English Scientific Virtuosi in the Sixteenth and Seventeenth Centuries* (Los Angeles: William Andrews Clark Memorial Library, 1979), pp. 1–55. See also my earlier dissertation, 'The Sense of the Past in English Scientific Thought of the Early Seventeenth Century: The Impact of the Historical Revolution', University of Wisconsin at Madison, 1975, which covers similar ground.

34. Browne's *Hydrotaphia – Urne-Burial, or, A Brief Discourse of the Sepulchrall Urnes lately found in Norfolk* was originally published in 1658; it is found in *Works of Thames Browne*, ed. Geoffrey Keynes, 6 vols (London: Faber and Gwyer, 1928–1931), 4:7–50.

35. A splendid example of an antiquarian deduction was John Stow's claim that the Romans buried at least some of their dead in coffins, a claim buttressed solely, but powerfully, by the discovery of tiny nailheads set in a coffin-shaped array around many graves in a Roman cemetery at Spitalfields. Browne refers to Stow and Spitalfields in the *Hydrotaphia* (*Works*, 4:17). On Spitalfields, see M. C. W. Hunter, 'The Royal Society and the Origins of British Archaeology', *Antiquity*, 65 (1971):113–21, 187–92; p. 118.

36. Browne, *Hydrotaphia*, in *Works*, 4:18, 26; 'Of Artificial Hills, Mounts, or Burrows', *Miscellany Tracts*, in *Works*, 5:99–103, p. 102.

37. This conjunction of 'discontinuities' would no doubt have pleased Foucault, although, were he still with us, he would doubtless reject my attempts to give the transition a causal explanation.

38. See especially Joseph M. Levine, 'Natural History and the History of the Scientific Revolution', *Clio*, 13 (1983):57–73. Levine argues that John Ray and his contemporaries viewed natural history as central to the new science. What was significant to them was the accumulation of new facts, and the ordering of these facts, and they saw Francis Bacon as their founder in this approach. Levine argues that we must not ignore 'this primacy of natural history' if we wish to understand seventeenth-century science (p. 69).

39. William Rawley, 'To the Reader', in Francis Bacon, *Sylva sylvarum* (London, 1627), sig. A3r, A1v; or James Spedding et al., eds, *The Works of Francis Bacon*, 14 vols (London: Longmans, 1857–1874), 2:335–7.

40. Paolo Rossi, 'Hermeticism, Rationality, and the Scientific Revolution', in M. L. Righini Bonelli and William R. Shea, eds, *Reason, Experiment, and Mysticism in the Scientific Revolution* (New York: Science History, 1975), pp. 247–73; citing pp. 258–9.

41. Bacon, *Valerius terminus*, in *Works*, 3:218.

42. Bacon, *Novum organum*, in *Works*, 4:51.

43. Bacon, *De augmentis*, in *Works*, 4:341.

44. Martin Elsky, 'Bacon's Hieroglyphs and the Separation of Words and Things', *Philological Quarterly*, 63 (1984):449–60.

4.

The Museum:
Its Classical Etymology and Renaissance Genealogy

Paula Findlen

This essay investigates the social and linguistic construction of musaeum *in sixteenth- and seventeenth-century culture. As a concept which expressed a pattern of activity transcending the strict confines of museum itself, the idea of* musaeum *was an apt metaphor for the encyclopaedic tendencies of the age. Mediating between public and private space, between the humanistic notion of collecting as a textual strategy and the social demands of prestige and display fulfilled by a collection,* musaeum *was an epistemological structure which encompassed a variety of ideas, images and institutions that were central to late Renaissance culture.*

It is never a waste of time to study the history of a word.   Lucien Febvre

'*Museum*,' wrote the Jesuit Claude Clemens, 'most accurately is the place where the Muses dwell.'[1] To investigate the museums of the late Renaissance, we must first begin with the word itself. *Musaeum.* How did it function in contemporary usage and to what sort of structures – intellectual, institutional and otherwise – did it allude? On a general level, this study explores the ways in which *musaeum* structured significant aspects of sixteenth- and seventeenth-century culture. As a concept which expressed a pattern of activity transcending the strict confines of museum itself, the idea of *musaeum* was an apt metaphor for the encyclopaedic tendencies of the period. Most compelling about the usage of the term *musaeum* was its ability to be inserted into a wide range of discursive practices. Linguistically, *musaeum* was a bridge between social and intellectual life, moving effortlessly between these two realms, and in fact pointing to the fluidity and instability of categories such as 'social' and 'intellectual', and 'public' and 'private', as they were defined during the late Renaissance. From a philological standpoint, its peculiar expansiveness allowed it to cross and confuse the intellectual and philosophical categories of *bibliotheca*, *thesaurus*, and *pandechion* with visual constructs such as *cornucopia* and *gazophylacium*, and spatial constructs such as *studio*, *casino*, *cabinet/gabinetto*, *galleria* and *theatro*, creating a rich and complex terminology that described significant aspects of the intellectual and cultural life of early modern Europe while alluding to its social configuration.[2] Mediating between private and public space, between the monastic notion of study as a contemplative activity, the humanistic notion of collecting as a textual strategy and the social demands of prestige and display fulfilled by a collection, *musaeum* was an epistemological structure which encompassed a variety of ideas, images and institutions that were central to late Renaissance culture.

My purpose here is to consider the social and cultural definitions of *musaeum* and the vocabulary of collecting. In organizing my discussion initially around the language of collecting and then around the conceptual spheres within which such terms circulated, I base my work on the premise that a detailed socio-linguistic analysis of certain key words – in this instance those encompassing the experience of collecting – provides insight into the cultural processes of past societies.

The word *musaeum*, however, is merely a starting point: a means of entering a wide range of philosophical discussions of knowing, perceiving and classifying that emerged in the humanistic and encyclopaedic traditions which collectors embraced and ultimately transformed during the sixteenth and seventeenth centuries. Through this approach, a manifest taxonomy of terms emerges. Although scores of words described collecting, collections and museum-like activities, no *one* term was as comprehensive as *musaeum* itself. While the rich and variegated vocabulary of collecting emerged from a multitude of social practices and intellectual traditions, the use of these terms was regulated by their relationship to *musaeum* – the most expansive model for the activity of collecting. The idea of *musaeum* provided the syntax in which the grammar of collecting could be played out; to borrow Baudrillard's phrase, it was structured as 'an immense combinatorial matrix of types and models' that expanded, as needed, to incorporate the new and diverse paradigms of collecting which arose.[3]

Examining a word as rich and complex as museum – a word very much in transition during this period – we learn much about the society that transformed its definition and the territorial implications of its usage. For the museum was certainly an attempt to make sense of the collector's environment; hence its structure was inherently dependent on contemporary discursive practices. As Robert Harbison argues, the museum was – and still is – an 'eccentric space', a setting peculiarly susceptible to the cultural strategies of its creators.[4] As a repository of past activities, created in the mirror of the present, the museum was above all a dialectical structure which served as a meeting point in which the historical claims of the present were invoked in memory of the past.

Our current use of the term 'museum' places it entirely within the public and institutional domain. Yet the original usage emphasized its private and exclusionary functions. The transition of the museum from private to public, from an exclusive to an inclusive construct, in a period in which the relationship between 'private' and 'public' activity was significantly redefined,[5] suggests that the museum did not evolve in isolation, but was deeply and profoundly formulated by the pattern of sixteenth- and seventeenth-century society.

The humanists rediscover the Muses

'At last my little Museum merits such a name,' wrote Giacomo Scafili to Athanasius Kircher upon receipt of his book, 'now rich and complete with the *Musurgia*, the great work and gift of you, Father; even if there were nothing else in it save for this lone book, it could rightfully be called the room of the Muses [*stanza delle Muse*] because the book contains them all.'[6]

The etymology of museum is itself a fascinating subject for study. While the practice of collecting emerged primarily in the sixteenth and seventeenth centuries, we need to understand its background to appreciate the role of medieval and early Renaissance learning in setting the stage for the widespread appearance of museums in the early modern period. Rejecting the classification of the collection at the Roman College as a *galleria*, a term referring primarily to it physical organization and to collections 'made solely for their magnificence', the Jesuit Filippo Bonanni, who restored Athanasius Kircher's museum to its original splendour at the end of the seventeenth century, explained:

Nor is the collection in question here of this kind, because it is improperly named *Galleria*. One should more properly say *Museo*, a term originating from the Greek according to Pliny, which means the same as *Dominiculum Musis dicatum pro diversorio eruditorum*, which Strabo refers to in his last book, *apud Alexandriam fuisse Museum celebratissimum*. Sparta discusses it in his life of Adrian, saying: *Apud Alexandriam Musio multas questiones Professoribus proposuit ...* or, as *musaeum* alludes, one says a place dedicated to the Muses ...[7]

Originally *musaeum* had two definitions. It was most traditionally the place consecrated to the Muses (locus *musis sacer*), a mythological setting inhabited by the nine goddesses of poetry, music, and the liberal arts. 'They are called *Muses*,' wrote the Chevalier de Jaucourt, 'from a Greek word which signifies 'to explain the mysteries', μύειν, because they have taught men very curious and important things which are from there brought to the attention of the vulgar. And, as the *Encyclopédie* article continued, 'The name of Muses, goddesses and protectresses of the Fine Arts, was uncontestably the source of museum.' More specifically, *musaeum* referred to the famous library at Alexandria, the μουσεῖον described by Strabo, which served as a research centre and congregating point for the scholars of the classical world.[10] Even in its original usage, *musaeum* was transformed into an institutional setting in which the cultural resources of a community were ordered and assembled, implying that the classical writers too had recognized the expansiveness of museum as a category of experience.

The fact that the classical conception of museum did not confine itself either spatially or temporally was important for its later usage. As Pliny and Varro remind us, nature was the primary haunt of the Muses, and therefore a 'museum' in the most literal sense. Pliny's conflation of grotto and museum in to *Natural History* further emphasized the image of museum as a potentially pastoral setting, a contemplative place found in nature.[11] Given the passion for constructing grottoes in the gardens of Renaissance Europe, it is obvious that nature's potential to be perceived as a museum expanded in the intricate interplay between art and nature that unfolded in the famous gardens – Boboli, Bomarzo and Pratolino to cite only a few – of the sixteenth and seventeenth centuries.[12]

In a seminal study of late Renaissance and Baroque culture entitled *L'Anti-Rinascimento*, Eugenio Battisti characterized the garden as a 'conceptual system'.[13] The same might well be said of the museum as it evolved during this period; in its crystallization as a category which incorporated and ultimately unified a variety of – from our own perspective – seemingly disparate activities, the museum was indeed a central organizing principle for cultural activity by the late sixteenth century. It was a conceptual system through which collectors interpreted and explored the world they inhabited. 'Those places in which one venerated the Muses were called Museums,' explained Teodoro Bondini in his preface to the 1677 catalogue of Ferdinando Cospi's museum in Bologna. 'Likewise I know you will have understood that, although a great portion of the Ancients approved of the name Muse only for the guardianship of Song and Poetry, none the less many others wished to incorporate all knowledge under such a name.'[14] Thus the museum, as the nexus of all disciplines, became an attempt to preserve, if not fully to reconstitute, the encyclopaedic programme of the classical and medieval world, translated into the humanist projects of the sixteenth century, and later the pansophic vision of universal wisdom that was a leitmotif of seventeenth- and early eighteenth-century culture.

If *musaeum* was indeed a place consecrated to the Muses, then the Renaissance itself can be described as a 'museum'; more than any other period, the cultural and intellectual programmes of the period from the fourteenth to the seventeenth century manifested an overwhelming concern with the very disciplines patronized by the Muses. Tellingly, *musaeum* was a term little used during the Middle Ages; at best it was related to the idea of *studium*, for it does not seem to have had any independent meaning of its own, save for scattered references to its classical roots, until the late sixteenth century. As Liliane Charles-Lange points out in her study of sculpture affections, as late as the sixteenth century *musée* did not appear in any French dictionary.[15] In reviving the liberal arts, the humanists self-consciously placed themselves in the grove of the Muses, creating 'museums' as they did so, to stress their direct ties with ancient wisdom. 'Almost all other rich men support servants of pleasure,' wrote Marsilio Ficino to Lorenzo de' Medici regarding his patronage of humanists, 'but you support priests of the Muses.'[16] References to the Muses are abundant in the texts of the fourteenth and fifteenth centuries. 'The woodland pleases the Muses,' observed Petrarch; 'the city is hostile to the poets.'[17] The attitude that decreed it necessary to separate oneself from public life in order fully to engage in intellectual activity – a monastic ideal translated into the language of humanism – persisted well into the sixteenth century. As Augustine queried of Petrarch in their imagined dialogue in Petrarch's *Secretum*:

Do you remember with what delight you used to wander in the depth of the country? ... Never idle, in your mind you would ponder over some high meditation, with only the Muses as your companions – you were never less alone than when in their company ...[18]

For Petrarch and his contemporaries, the image of the Muses, and concomitantly of *musaeum*, was directly tied to their personal and collective attempts to enter the world of antiquity, regardless of temporal and physical constraints.

More than the claims of erudition or the revival of classical texts through philology, humanism was structured around the objects that served as a basis for most intellectual and cultural activities. Whether it was the Roman ruins that occupied Ciriaco d'Ancona and Francesco Colonna,[19] which gradually emerged as more that just a clutter of objects to define 'antiquity' from the late fourteenth century onwards, or the jumble of natural objects that served as the basis for a new reading of nature in the works of Renaissance natural philosophers such as Aldrovandi, Cesalpino, Gesner, and Mattioli, the philosophical programmes that constituted Renaissance humanism could not have existed without the proliferation of artefacts that provided food for thought. Humanism was primarily an archaeological enterprise in the sense that it reified scholarship by translating vague antiquarian and philosophical concerns into specific projects, whose existence was predicated upon the possession of objects. From this perspective, the proliferation of museums in the sixteenth and seventeenth centuries can be seen as a logical outcome of the desire to gather materials for a text. The pursuit and revival of classical language, literature, and philosophy that have most commonly been identified as the core of the humanists' programmes could not have arisen without the recognition that the piles of information, scattered throughout the world, might be shown to mean something were they to be brought into the study and compared: collecting was about the confrontation of ideas and objects, as old cosmologies met new ways of perceiving, that fuelled the learned and curious discourses of early modern Europe.

More importantly, the museum fulfilled the new sense of history as sketched by the humanists. 'Antiquity' could only serve as a reference point to 'modernity' once the two had been defined as being inherently more 'advanced' (and therefore compatible) than the intermediary period that Petrarch would call the Middle Ages. Thus the direct link between contemporary museums and the ancient *musaeum* stressed the classical images of erudition and learning to reinforce the image of the Renaissance as a newly constituted version of the etymologically ordained home of the Muses.

Reviewing the classical literature on *musaeum*, it is evident that the idea of collecting was simultaneously an open and a closed concept. While gardens and groves were museums without walls, unlocatable in time or even place, the conflation of study with *musaeum* spatially confined it. The comparative and taxonomic functions of humanist collecting needed a defined space in which to operate, in part to identify the producers of and the audience for the museum, that is, the intellectual elite of the Renaissance who identified themselves as patrons of learning; thus *musaeum* was a locating principle, circumscribing the space in which learned activities could occur.

The growth of humanist circles in the courts, churches, academies and publishing houses of fifteenth- and sixteenth-century Europe signalled the beginnings of a more social and contemporaneous setting for the Muses. Praising the writing of Lorenzo de' Medici inspired by the 'vernacular Muses', the philosopher Giovanni Pico della Mirandola clearly delineated the difference between professional and amateur notions of scholarship within a humanistic framework. 'To them [Dante and Petrarch] the Muses were their ordinary and principle employment,' remarked Pico, 'to you, an amusement and a relaxation from cares.'[20] Developing the Ciceronian theme of intellectual activity as the complement of and ideal preparation for the *vita activa*, Pico lauded Lorenzo's ability to combine *studium* with *otium*.

By the sixteenth century, museums as studies proliferated throughout Europe, claiming direct inheritance from their classical antecedents. Perhaps the most explicit example of the Muse-Museum analogy occurred in the decoration of Paolo Giovio's museum near Como. Built on the supposed ruins of Pliny's fabled villa at Borgo Vico between 1538 and 1543, Giovio's *museo* fulfilled its classical paradigm to the letter and became the prototype for many other museums which followed. Visiting the villa shortly after its completion in 1543, Anton Francesco Doni wrote to Agostino Landi of its wonderous contents. He particularly praised 'a most miraculous Room depicting all of the muses one by one with their instruments ... [which] ... one calls properly the Museum'.[21] Equally we can point to Leonello d'Este's *studio* at Ferrara, decorated with images of the Muses, or Federigo da Montefeltro's *Tempietto delle Muse*, strategically located below his famous *studiolo* at Urbino.[22] In all of these instances, form revealed function; for the images reinforced the contemplative and literally 'museal' purpose of the rooms.

The culmination of this phase of humanism, emphasizing the dialectical relationship between active and contemplative purposes of study, is best illustrated by a famous and often-cited passage from Machiavelli. In a letter of 1513 to the Florentine ambassador to Rome, Francesco Vettori, Machiavelli elegantly suggested the ways in which his personal relationship with the study of antiquity shaped his intellectual and political life. Describing his daily activities in exile, Machiavelli underscored the facility with which he translated his *persona* from one context to another:

In the morning, I get up with the sun and go out into a grove that I am having cut; there I remain a couple of hours to look over the work of the past day and kill some time with the woodsmen, who always have on hand some dispute either among themselves or among their neighbours ... When I leave the grove, I go to a spring, and from there into my aviary. I have a book in my pocket, either Dante or Petrarch or one of the minor poets, as Tibullus, Ovid and the like. I read about their tender passions and their loves, remember mine, and take pleasure for a while in thinking about them. Then I go along the road to the inn, talk with those who pass by, ask the news of their villages, learn various things, and note the varied tastes and different fancies of men ... In the evening, I return to my house and go into my study [*scrittoio*]. At the door I take off the clothes I have worn all day, mud spotted and dirty, and put on regal and courtly garments. Thus appropriately clothed, I enter into the ancient courts of ancient men, where, being lovingly received, I feed on the food which is mine alone and which I was born for; I am not ashamed to speak with them and to ask the reasons for their actions, and they courteously answer me. For four hours I feel no boredom and forget every worry; I do not fear poverty, and death does not terrify me. I give myself completely over to the ancients.[23]

What is particularly interesting to note here is the way in which Machiavelli utilized both the pastoral and monastic ideals of *musaeum*, interspersing his moments of intellectual reprieve with more sociable practices, to develop one of the most politically aware statements of the early sixteenth century, *The Prince* (1514).

Yet at the same time it is obvious that he considered his study an inner sanctum – '*cubiculum secretius, ubi quis studio vel scripturae vacat*', as Du Cange described it.[24] More closely, Machiavelli's *scrittoio* resembled the *cubiculum* in which Poggio Bracciolini conducted his studies of antiquity in the early fifteenth century.[25] Like Tasso's Malpiglio, Machiavelli entered his *studio* to flee the multitude (*fuggir la moltitudine*).[26] We are still far from the institutional ideal of cultural activity as connoted by the current use of museum. None the less it is important to note the specific grounding of intellectual (or rather museum-like) activities in the context of the *studio*. 'I wish to bring together all of my books, writings and materials for study [*cose da studio*],' wrote the prelate and papal nuncio Ludovico Beccadelli in 1555 to his cousin, who was planning a *studio* for Beccadelli's secretary, Antonio Giganti, upon his return to Bologna. Later in the century, the humanist Giganti described his collection as 'my *studio*, more than *studio* one calls it a collection of various foreign and natural trinkets'.[27] For the sixteenth- and seventeenth-century humanists and collectors, more than their predecessors, it was the explicit identification between *musaeum* and *studio*, and a number of other terms discussed below, that shaped the social and ultimately the public function of the museum.

Encyclopaedic strategies

At first instance, the Renaissance notion of museum defined imaginary space. Born of the humanist desire to codify the intellectual experience of the self-proclaimed scholar, it was a methodological premise that translated itself into a wide variety of social and cultural forms.

One of the most important intellectual traditions with which the practice of collecting aligned itself was that of encyclopaedism. While the medieval encyclopaedic tradition emphasized knowledge as a continuum, an unbroken plane of information, the sixteenth- and seventeenth-century encyclopaedic tradition delighted in discontinuities.[28] Nowhere was this more evident than in the structure of the museum. Using the term *musaeum* as a starting point, we can trace the foliation of this structure, as word after word from the encyclopaedic corpus – theatre, treasure, mirror, forest, and microcosm to list only a few – became identified with the language of collecting. My purpose here is to relate the presence of museums to the explosion of encyclopaedic traditions, both old and new, that supported and shaped the activity of collecting through the explicit identification of *musaeum* with encyclopaedic paradigms.

On a more abstract level, the process of widening the horizons of *musaeum* operated in a fashion similar to the premise of the Renaissance encyclopaedia. *Musaeum* became the axis through which all other structures of collecting, categorizing, and knowing intersected; interweaving words, images, and things, it provided a space common to all.[29]

The use of the term *musaeum* was not confined only to the tangible; museum was foremost a mental category and collecting a cognitive activity that could be appropriated for social and cultural ends. As an ironic comment on the construction of collections in the late seventeenth century, Sir Thomas Browne created a guidebook to an imaginary museum entitled the *Museum Clausum, or Bibliotheca Abscondita* ('The Enclosed Museum or Secret Library'). 'I am Bold to present you with a list of a collection, which I may justly say you have not seen before.'[30] Dismissing the encyclopaedic projects of Aldrovandi, Gesner, Kircher, and other subscribers to the Aristotelian and Plinian paradigms, Browne invoked the mental structure of collecting to attack its premise, creating a museum so complete and so closed that no one had ever penetrated it. Filling in the gaps in his hypothetical museum of knowledge with improbable marginalia – a cross made out of a frog's bone, the works of Confucius in Spanish and the like – he criticized the epistemological framework of the museum which gave a macrocosmic gloss to every object it encountered. 'I have heard some with deep sighs lament the lost lines of Cicero; others with as many groans deplore the combustion of the library of Alexandria: for my own part, I think there be too many in the world, and could with patience behold the urn and ashes of the Vatican.'[31]

In asking ourselves to what extent the language of collecting penetrated other activities, we need first to consider the fact that the descriptive models of collecting co-opted the linguistic paradigms of encyclopaedism. Certainly the expansion of categories such as *teatro* and *cornucopia*, words relevant in a much more general context which initially held little or no meaning for collecting, suggests that the collectors of the sixteenth and seventeenth centuries drew on a broad humanistic heritage in developing more precise and differentiated ways to articulate the experience of *musaeum*. A museum was not the only 'theatre of nature'; Kircher described Sicily in exactly the same words due to the natural diversity and fecundity that he observed in his visit to the island during the eruption of Vesuvius in 1660.[32] [Editorial note: Vesuvius is not in Sicily.] From the same perspective, the microscope was 'both receptacle and Theatre of the most miraculous Works of Nature' because the lens created a panoramic effect, reinforcing the relativity between museum as theatre and the *theatrum mundi*.[33]

The language of collecting during this period also supported the conflation of museum and theatre. Francesco Calzolari's natural history collection was a museum because it was gathered 'dum uno in theatro, aut Musaeo'. Or as Giovanni Porro wrote of the museum in the botanical garden at Padua, 'And in this little Theatre, almost a little world, one will orchestrate the spectacle of all of nature's wonders.'[34] Similarly the ideal of a *studio* was a closed space: a room without windows that achieved completeness through closure.[35]

Musaeum was a classificatory structure for a wide variety of texts, whose sorting and organizing processes fulfilled the taxonomic principle of collection. Numerous books – ranging from collections of poetry such as

Lorenzo Legati's *Musei Poetriarum* (1668) to Mabillon and Germain's famous guidebook, the *Museum Italicum* (1687–89) – utilized the image of museum to denote the process of compiling and collating.[36]

Similarly the logic of collecting supported the use of parallel structures to describe the mental process of collecting. In 1549 Ulisse Aldrovandi (1522–1605) was called to Rome on suspicion of heresy. Quickly cleared of the charges, Aldrovandi spent the rest of the year exploring the ancient ruins of the city. The resulting book, *Delle statue romane antiche* (1556), was one of the first guidebooks to antiquarian collections in Rome. Reflecting on the process of writing the treatise, Aldrovandi emphasized the ways in which the creation of the book itself had taken the shape of a 'museum' (*scrivere et raccogliere, come in un Theatro*).[37] Written and collected in the 'theatre' or rather museum of the mind, Aldrovandi's words gave expression to the breadth of the encyclopaedic spirit that guided the collecting projects of the sixteenth and seventeenth centuries.[38]

Emphasizing the diversity, variety, and above all the copiousness of the *Museum Hermeticum* (1678), the anonymous editor assured his readers that they were about to enter a museum of alchemy that reduced the literature on this subject to a manageable entity.[39] Similarly the emerging scientific journals often included words such as 'repository', 'collection', and 'museum' in their titles to underline the reductive nature of the enterprise, for the pages formed intellectual walls in the same way that the perfect shape of the theatre closed and completed a concept. If a dictionary, a collection of words, could be called a *galleria di parole*, as the first Crusca vocabulary was, then it was evident that almost any book which functioned in a similar manner would also fall under the rubric of 'museum'.[40]

The language used to describe museum catalogues best illustrates the flexible relationship between text and context. If nature, for example, was the text from which the Renaissance naturalists chose their materials, then their museums were literally the 'con-texts'; likewise the textuality of the artefacts was borne out by the catalogues which described and represented them. The apothecary Ferrante Imperato was described by contemporaries as the 'author of so rich and celebrated a Museum' – an authorship attested not only by the publication of his *Historia naturale* (1599), but more concretely by the existence of his theatre of nature. Aldrovandi described his fellow collector Calzolari's catalogue as 'his printed Museum', again to distinguish it from the equally tangible one that he visited in Verona in 1571; similarly Kircher's assistant Gaspar Schott asked for the *Galleria descritta* while writing his book on universal magic. The Milanese cleric Manfredo Settala, on the other hand, distinguished between his 'vernacular Museum' and his Latin museum as texts for two different types of audiences.[41] The catalogue as 'a reduced Museum' or 'little Museum' functioned as the museum's own microcosm.[42] The encyclopaedic process was one that needed to unfold from beginning to end; like Russian dolls or Chinese boxes, there was always the anticipation of an even smaller overlapping version of the preceding object.

Beyond museum catalogues, most collectors understood their writings to belong to the larger vision of the encyclopaedic enterprise. Remarking on the richness of Hernandez's descriptions of Mexican flora and fauna, which had recently come into the possession of the Accademia dei Lincei, Marc Welser commented that the manuscript 'merits the name of treasure [*thesoro*] and not of book'. The founder of the same academy, Federico Cesi, described his own research as a 'Theatre of Nature', a term most frequently used for the natural history collections of the period.[43]

Aldrovandi designated his own publication schemes as 'the history of my Museum'. At times his manuscripts were referred to more simply as the *musaeum* itself, and they were certainly remarked upon by visitors as being one of the richest aspects of his legacy.[44] The text, as *storia*, furnished what the collection could not, completing it in the process. 'Besides what I have lately observed in my Museum, I have also written a history entitled the *Thesaurus rerum naturalium* … here one will find all of the things … that are not in our Museum.' Urging his brother Francesco to underwrite the publication of Aldrovandi's texts as early as 1576, Ferdinando de' Medici praised the manuscripts as 'almost a part of that *studio*'.[45] The museum was located neither in the text nor in the context; rather it was the interplay between the two that shaped its function and completed its purpose.

Museums were textual structures both in a literal and figurative sense. Created from the materials available to the Renaissance collector, they served as reference points for the reading that the humanist educational programme required of the educated élite. In understanding why a collector acquired or coveted a particular object, one needed to participate in the textual strategy of encyclopaedism. 'Moreover how much light would we glean from interpreting the passages of writers, principally Pliny, if we had in sight those things which he told only with words,' lamented Federico Borromeo in his *Musaeum* (1625).[46] The existence of the museum testified to the memory of the texts which shaped it, creating copies of 'originals' that had long since disappeared.

In a classical and medieval sense, most compendia were museums because, like Pliny's *Natural History* or the medieval encyclopaedias, they compiled and stored knowledge in a comprehensive fashion. As Pliny outlined in the preface to his monumental work:

[It] is not books but store-houses [*thesauros*] that are needed; consequently by perusing about 2000 volumes, very few of which, owing to the abstruseness of their contents [*secretium materiae*] are ever handled by students, we have collected in 36 volumes 20,000 noteworthy facts obtained from one hundred authors that we have explored, with a great number of other facts in addition that were either ignored by our predecessors or have been discovered by subsequent experience.[47]

Such a literal and quantitative schematization was also evident in the acquisitive nature of Renaissance collecting. Surely Aldrovandi's and Gesner's dreams of an alphabetically organized, perfect universe fulfilled (or at least attempted to fulfil) Pliny's encyclopaedic paradigm. Like Pliny, Aldrovandi was obsessed with the size of his collection; not a week passed without his re-counting the total number of 'facts' he had accumulated. 'If I wanted to describe the variety of fish observed, depicted and dried by me, that can be seen by everyone in our microcosm, truly it would be necessary to consume many pages simply to name them …'[48] The collector's activity was one that absorbed him completely; when Jacopino Bronzino described Aldrovandi as 'consumed in the history of natural things'[49] he aptly summarized the encyclopaedic passion for working within one's material, allowing it to absorb the scholar in the process.

'[I am] hoping to see something beautiful in your care,' wrote Aldrovandi to Alfonso Pancio, physician to the d'Este family in Ferrara, 'not ever being sated by the learning of new things. Not a week passes – I will not say a day – in which I am not sent something special. Nor is it to be wondered at, because this science of nature is as infinite as our knowledge.'[50] Drawing upon Pliny's list of Greek titles in the manner of Giovio, Aldrovandi named his largest project, under which all others were to be subsumed, the *Pandechion Epistemonicon*, which he defined as 'a universal forest of knowledge, by means of which one will find whatever the poets, theologians, lawmakers, philosophers and historians … have written on any natural or artificial thing one wished to know about or compose'.[51] Throughout the half-century in which Aldrovandi was active as a collector he constantly strove to fill the space he had created. Words, images, and texts were all incorporated into the universal encyclopaedia of knowledge that he visualized.

The omnipresence of Aldrovandi's pandechion evidenced itself in his flexible use of the term. Like other encyclopaedic terms, it was a semantic structure organized to include 'not only the notion of abundance itself but also the place where abundance is to be found, or, more strictly, the place and its contents'.[52] On the most general level, Aldrovandi described his collection of objects as a '*cimilarchio* and *pandechio* of the things generated in this inferior world'. Thus the encyclopaedia was tangible, defined by the experiential data which constituted one part of his collection. Although he rarely used this term to refer to any but his own collection, the Tuscan Grand Duke's collection also merited such a name, because it was 'full of an infinite number of experimental secrets'.[53] Not surprisingly, the principle of plenitude was operative in his decision to designate it as an encyclopaedic structure. In similar fashion, the first cataloguer of Francesco Calzolari's natural history museum in sixteenth-century Verona called it, among other things, a cornucopia.[54] If nature was the 'cornucopian text' which held the interest of the naturalist, then the museum itself was the receptacle of *copia*.

Discussing with Matthias Lobel some of his rare dessicated plants, 'which I conserve pasted in fifteen volumes in my Pandechion of nature for the utility of posterity', Aldrovandi reiterated the textual nature of the artefacts, which became 'books' organized according to his taxonomy of nature. 'For a full supply of facts [*copia rerum*] begets a full supply of words,' counselled Cicero.[55]

Most importantly, there was the *Pandechion* proper: eighty-three volumes containing scraps of paper which Aldrovandi and his assistants had meticulously cut and alphabetically organized until 1589.[56] Almost unintelligible to the modern reader, this compendium functioned as a lexicon on almost any known subject. Responding to Lorenzo Giacomini's questions on wine-making in a letter of 1587, Aldrovandi quoted Pliny but could not remember the exact citation. 'But where he [Pliny] teaches it, for now I can't recall, though I have seen it and glossed it from head to foot. And if you were able to run through my *Epistemonicon*, you would have found it and infinite other observations …'[57] For Aldrovandi the encyclopaedia was located neither in the text nor in the object alone; rather it was the dialectic between *res* and *verba* that fully defined the universality of his project.

The Jesuits put their world in order

While Aldrovandi's encyclopaedic schemes confined themselves to the territory that the Aristotelian corpus had previously defined, his commentary serving as a gloss on predefined categories, the speculations of seventeenth-century natural philosophers moved beyond this realm. In contrast to sixteenth-century encyclopaedism, which attempted to fill the paradigms prescribed by the classical canons, the logic of seventeenth-century collecting precluded such an unmitigated acceptance of earlier categories, particularly because the frustrated attempts of predecessors such as Aldrovandi and Gesner to flesh out ancient collecting projects indicated that new methods needed to be found and new questions needed to be asked.

The influx of artefacts from the New World and other parts of the globe now reached by Europeans paved the way for new models of knowledge, as collectors found traditional explanations to be increasingly unsatisfactory for the information that they could now incorporate in their museums.[58] Simultaneously, events such as the Reformation and the ensuing religious and political battles waged across Europe from the early sixteenth century until the Peace of Westphalia in 1648, destabilized the social, political, and religious order that had seemed unshakable only a century before (although its roots had certainly eroded long before 1517 in anticipation of these changes). Thus the seventeenth-century natural philosopher, the creator of the new encyclopaedia, was in search of a new model to explain a perplexing, increasingly illogical and pluralistic world.

'How truly enormous is the field of knowledge,' exclaimed Federico Cesi, founder of the Accademia dei Lincei at the beginning of the century, 'large in the copiousness of speculations as in the copiousness of readings.'[59] While the activities of Cesi and his academicians aligned themselves firmly with the camp of Galileo and the 'new' science of the period, a response that effectively eliminated the significance of the encyclopaedic project by refashioning it into a heuristic category,[60] the speculations of Jesuits such as Athanasius Kircher (1602–80) and Gaspar Schott took a more eclectic turn. As R. J. W. Evans describes in his study of Habsburg intellectual life, the philosophical trajectories of Catholic Reformation culture lent an exoticism to intellectual discourse that was not evident in scholarship of the previous century.[61] The Jesuit response to the relativity of their world was to expand outward, in ever-increasing concentric circles, incorporating both old and new within a traditional yet flexible framework, as attested by their missionary activities in Europe, the New World and Asia. The quest for *pansophia* reached its apex in the eclectic attempts by the Jesuits (and later, in a different context, Leibniz and Wolff) to develop universal structures that synthesized humanist philosophies and non-Western cultures with the more programmatic and dogmatic policies of the post-Tridentine church.

The encyclopaedic impulse was not confined to the Catholic world alone, although it was undoubtedly more pervasive in an atmosphere in which the retention of ancient models of knowledge was linked to the persistence of orthodoxy and tradition. For the purpose of limiting my study, due to the richness of material on Italian collecting and the readily apparent links between the persistence of encyclopaedic models and the role of collecting in the seventeenth-century courts and ecclesiastic circles, I have chosen to focus on Catholic collecting rather than looking at both Protestant and Catholic activities together. While I do not believe that collecting and religious affiliation were inevitably intertwined, in many instances – particularly in the case of Kircher in Rome and his contemporary and fellow cleric Manfredo Settala in Milan – religious conviction *did* play a part in the shape and function of seventeenth-century museums.

Spending most of his life in Rome, clearing-house for the Jesuit missionary activities, Kircher was able to draw on the resources of an entire order to sate his thirst for knowledge of non-Western civilizations; books, artefacts, and reports from all corners of the globe flowed into his museum at the Roman College weekly. From these Kircher derived his theories on universal language and the universality of many other aspects of the natural and supernatural world, all part of the Christianizing mission of the post-Tridentine church.[62]

One of his most interesting (and, in the minds of modern Egyptologists, most infamous) projects concerned the decipherment of hieroglyphs. Happening upon a book on the obelisks of Rome, probably the one written by Michele Mercati (keeper of the Vatican mineralogical collection and sculpture garden) in 1589, Kircher recognized the value of the mysterious emblems for his studies of language and religion. 'Immediately my curiosity was aroused and I began to speculate on the meaning of these hieroglyphs,' he wrote in his autobiography. 'At first I took them for mere decoration, designs contrived by the imagination of the engraver, but then, on reading the text of the book I learned that these were the actual figures carved on ancient Egyptian monuments. From time immemorial these obelisks and their inscriptions have been in Rome and so far no one has been able to decipher them.'[63]

Like so many other things studied by the Jesuit, the hieroglyphs were signs, richly encoded, that promised to unlock the mysteries of past civilizations and, most importantly from his theological perspective, would prove to be a means of demonstrating the inherent compatibility of Christianity with ancient pagan wisdom. A symbol, Kircher posited, 'leads our mind through a kind of similitude to an understanding of something very different from the things which offer themselves to our external senses; whose property is to be hidden under a veil of obscurity'.[64] Thus Kircher's studies of Egyptian symbols, like his investigations of Chinese philosophy, ciphers and musical theories of universal harmony, and his attempts to draw forth a theory of universal magnetism or *panspermia* from the natural world, were shaped to fit a hermetic and metaphoric image of the world which assumed that every object was coded with a larger, more universal significance. Applied to the passion for collecting, hermeticism postulated that the museum would be a visually coded presentation of occult knowledge. The world itself was a tangled web of meanings; it remained only for the collector to penetrate its layers through the comparative, taxonomic, and ultimately encyclopaedic nature of his project.

The social configuration of such grandiose projects could only have been the libraries and museums created to organize and assimilate the explosion of knowledge experienced by the sixteenth and seventeenth centuries. What was a *bibliotheca* but a collection of books, a 'multitudo librorum' as Comenius defined it?[65] Libraries formed an essential part of collections; rarely did a museum not have a library attached to it.[66] Carlo Antonio del Pozzo's library in Rome was described as a 'true hotel of the Muses', reinforcing the idea that the library was indeed a museum; likewise the Medici library in Florence was described by Diderot as so copious that 'only the [term] *musaeum Florentinum* can justly represent this magnificent cabinet'.[67]

While the emergence of public libraries during the seventeenth and eighteenth centuries signalled the creation of a public sphere of reading, as Roger Chartier has argued,[68] truly the most magnificent examples of book collecting remained the private libraries of papal Rome, and in general those within the monastic orders throughout Europe, as evidenced by the Biblioteca Angelica in Rome and the Bibliothèque de Sainte Geneviève in Paris.[69] The papal *nipote* Francesco Barberini, favourite of Urban VIII and an active member of Cesi's Lincean Academy, amassed a collection that was still the wonder of Rome a century later. 'There are other wonderful libraries in Rome,' observed Diderot after surveying the Vatican holdings, 'particularly that of Cardinal Francesco Barberini, which is reputed to contain 25,000 printed volumes and 5000 manuscripts.'[70] Barberini's collection of books, as well as art and natural objects, was so well known that scholars vied with each other to give him their books. Over the course of several years the Paduan Aristotelian Fortunio Liceti presented Barberini with his most recent publications, hoping that the Cardinal would honour him by making place for them in his 'most noble Museum'.[71] As Liceti recognized, Barberini's collection was truly a *musaeum*, his own small offering about to be subsumed within its universal and universalizing structure.

Not surprisingly, collectors who prided themselves on their ability to organize knowledge also turned their attention to the classification of books. Aldrovandi, for example, dissected the subject organization of libraries with the same passion that he catalogued nature and every other part of the human experience. Like the Swiss naturalist Conrad Gesner, Aldrovandi perceived his encyclopaedia of nature to be dependent on his more general encyclopaedia of knowledge itself. Thus bibliographies were hoarded as if the names of the books themselves symbolically conveyed the possession of their contents.[72]

Strategies for collecting were not only designed to fulfil the humanistic desire for *prisca scientia*: museums and libraries of this period also conveyed political and religious messages. Claude Clemens, librarian to Philip III of Spain, described the Escorial as 'this Museum of Christendom'; attuned to the rhetoric of the Catholic Reformation he proposed a library that collected and ordered knowledge in order to control it. Not only were libraries necessary for their public utility for a growing community of scholars; they also protected the Catholic world from false erudition.[73] In an age in which even the Jesuits had been refused their privilege to use prohibited books that had not been corrected by the official censors (though one wonders how Kircher was able to transgress this rule), there was a great fear of information falling into the wrong hands. A number of times during this career, Aldrovandi had to submit his library for Inquisitorial inspection, and found many of his books – those by Cardano, Della Porta and Pomponazzi for example – confiscated as a result.[74]

The encyclopaedic vision of knowledge, born of the humanist desire to recapture the knowledge of the ancient world, was used for a variety of purposes by the seventeenth century. The museum had become not only an instrument of erudition, but a means for proselytizing. While Kircher's brand of intellectual pyrotechnics was undoubtedly too eclectic (and potentially philosophically dangerous) for the mainstream Catholic Church, none the less his work was allowed to coexist alongside more orthodox philosophy in an atmosphere fraught with the tension of the Galileo condemnations.[75] While we cannot pretend to do anything more than speculate on the reasons for such laxity, it is possible that the Church, already overly dependent on the Jesuit educational programme, recognized the social value of a highly public figure such as Kircher, even if they were suspicious of the intellectual premise of his research. Most importantly, Kircher's willingness to submit all of his findings to a strictly hierarchical notion of the universe, was in keeping with the Thomist basis of the Jesuit teachings.

From the universal strategies of the sixteenth-century natural philosophers such as Aldrovandi, Cardano, and Gesner to the Christian strategies of their seventeenth-century counterparts within the Catholic Church, the museum was designed as the most complete response to the crisis of knowledge provoked by the expansion of the natural world through the voyages of discovery and exploration, the concomitant explosion of information about the world in general and, more particularly, the moral and social imbalance created by the religious and political events of the sixteenth and seventeenth centuries. In an age of religious plurality, to 'know' was fraught with tensions; the humanist response of Aldrovandi and his contemporaries was to be open to any available strategy for framing the world, an openness that frequently brought them into trouble with the institutional church, as attested by Aldrovandi's, Cardano's and Della Porta's brushes with the Inquisition and the actual condemnations of Bruno and Campanella.[76] The seventeenth-century response diffused potentially 'black' magic through the purification rituals of the Jesuit scientific work in the case of Kircher and his disciples, subsuming natural philosophy to Christian theology, while still leaving the encyclopaedic framework intact. This was most apparent in the structure of museums which, until the end of the eighteenth century, continued to conjoin art and nature in fulfillment of Pliny's premise that everything in this theatre of the world was worthy of memory. From mental to textual to actual museums; the structure of *musaeum* was designed to intermingle harmoniously the natural and the artificial, the real and the imaginary, and the ordinary and the extraordinary, to underscore not only the fecundity of the universe but the breadth of the human faculties for comprehending and explaining the *theatrum mundi*.

Texts and contexts: defining museal space

Returning to an earlier theme – how did the museum make the transition from private to public? – we need to re-enter the social world of collecting to trace briefly the development of the 'public' museum. While Machiavelli, encamped in his *scrittoio*, conceived his intellectual pursuits to be a means of re-entering public life *in absentia* through the medium of literature, he did not conceive of scholarship *per se* as a socially-grounded enterprise. Despite the imprint of the Alexandrian museum as a paradigm of collective intellectual activity, manifested in the formation of humanist circles around the *musaei* of Pietro Bembo and Guillaume Budé for example, the idea of study outside of the university *studio* was predominantly an isolated and isolating process.[77] In contrast to the notion of the academy, one of the most important centres for extra-university intellectual and cultural activity from the sixteenth century onwards (whose emergence was distinct from the museum though later influential in its institutionalization), the museum was at first defined by the domestic, and therefore private, space which it inhabited.[78]

In his will of 5 March 1604 the apothecary Francesco Calzolari left 'the *studio di antichità* that is in my house in Verona' to his nephew.[79] Certain aspects of collecting reinforced the notion that a museum needed to be circumscribed by domestic activity. 'And he who delights in letters must not keep his books in the public study [*scrittoio comune*], but must have a *studiolo* apart, in the most remote corner of the house. It is best and healthy if it can be near the bedroom, so that one can more easily study.'[80] Surviving plans for late Renaissance museums support such an organization. The *studio* of Antonio Giganti in Bologna, secretary to Ludovico Beccadelli and to Gabriele Paleotti and a friend of Aldrovandi, testifies to the conscious placement of a collection within the interior space of a house; its only entrance was the 'door that opens into the bedroom'.[81] The collector, called by the Muses, retired to his study in the same way that he retired to his bedroom. Similarly *cabinet*, as it evolved in seventeenth-century French, connoted the closet beyond the main bedchamber.[82] As Carlo Dionisotti points out, however, the distinctions between public and private need to be considered with care in order to understand their relevance for the early modern period; a bedroom, theoretically the most intimate of spaces, was not fully private, nor for that matter was a museum.[83]

Advice to construct museums, libraries and studies in proximity to the most 'personal' space in the home drew not only on contemporary experience with the arrangement of such rooms, but also on Alberti's classically inspired designs. Describing the layout of a country house in his *Ten Books on Architecture* (1415), Alberti specified that 'The Wife's Chamber should go into the Wardrobe; the Husband's into the Library.'[84] While Alberti sharply defined the *studio* as exclusively masculine space, an image borne out by the relative absence of women in the sphere of collecting, we can point to several noteworthy exceptions – the *Grotta* and *studiolo* of Isabella d'Este at Mantua being one of the most famous examples.[85] For the most part, however, collecting emerged out of a private and domestic culture that was almost exclusively male: a space reserved within the home for scholarly activity (analogous to the contemplative space of the private family chapel) whose purpose was not entirely divested of public life. A museum was created as much for self-promotion as out of genuine interest in the artefacts assembled in it: in this respect it was at once public and private, masculine space within the domicile, and therefore by nature public in the broadest sense of the term.[86]

The museum, as *orbus in domo*, mediated between public and private because it quite literally attempted to bring the world into the home. The endless flow of goods, information, and visitors that appeared on the doorsteps of the most well-known museums determined that the collections of the sixteenth and seventeenth centuries could no longer be the hidden worlds suggested by medieval and monastic images of *studium*.[87] 'If after the arrival of my scribe, Giovan Corneglio, I have not responded to your letter as quickly as you wished,' wrote Aldrovandi to the humanist Giovan Vincenzo Pinelli from his museum, 'Your Most Illustrious Signor will excuse me for having been continuously occupied in various negotiations, public as well as private.'[88] The antiquary Giovan Vincenzo della Porta, 'a man no less learned than unusual for the vast knowledge which he possesses', was singled out for 'having through his own efforts created a most noble Museum to which scholars come from the furthest corners of Europe, drawn by its fame'.[89] As we know from the inventories of his brother's home in 1615, the Della Porta collections were indeed private yet open spaces, publicized through the informal networks of correspondence that formed the basis of the scientific and intellectual communities of late Renaissance Europe. In asking ourselves how did the 'private' become 'public' we need to dissect the sociological process of collecting that identified collectors to each other as well as for a larger audience.[90]

The constellation of terms used to describe collecting by the late sixteenth century created a unified conceptual sphere that fully demonstrated the museum's roles in the public and private realms. By now 'study' connotes a room for private study with 'museum' as its public counterpart. Yet the polarization of these two categories has evolved only in the nineteenth and twentieth centuries, as the images of 'public' and 'private' have also become fixed opposites. Conversely, as discussed earlier, it was only in the fifteenth and sixteenth centuries that the social and philosophical purposes of museum and *studio* were conjoined; it remained for the seventeenth and eighteenth centuries to begin the process of extraction that ultimately set the two words apart. Aldrovandi's collection of natural rarities in Bologna was called simultaneously *museo, studio, theatro, microcosmo, archivio,* and a host of other related terms, all describing the different ends served by his collection and, more importantly, alluding to the analogies between each structure.[91] In the mid-seventeenth century, Ovidio Montalbani, superintendent of the Studio Aldrovandi, distinguished between the public Aldrovandi collection which he oversaw (*Museum*) and his personal, and therefore private, collection through the use of the diminutive (*privatum Museolum; Museolum meum*).[92]

As Claudio Franzoni suggests in his study of antiquarian collecting, one of the most important linguistic divisions within the vocabulary of collecting concerns the distinction between terms which defined a collection spatially and those which alluded to its philosophical configuration.[93] Words such as *stanza, casa, casino, guardaroba, studiolo, tribuna, galleria,* organized the domestic and civic terrain of the museum. 'One can truly call your *Casino* a house of nature, where so many miraculous experiments are done,' wrote Aldrovandi to Francesco, alluding to the Grand Duke's domestication of nature in his alchemical laboratory at San Marco.[94] The famous collection of Flavio Chigi in seventeenth-century Rome was described as a 'room of curiosities'; again the collection was defined by the space which it inhabited as well as by the nature of its contents.[95] Through a similar process, the idea of *musaeum* became associated increasingly with the physical space of the *studio*. Many letters of the sixteenth and seventeenth centuries, most notably those of Aldrovandi and Cesi, are signed 'ex Musaeo nostro' or 'written from the Cesi museum'.[96]

Equally intriguing is the well-documented confusion over the naming of the famous *studiolo* of Francesco I (1569–87) in Florence. The humanist Vincenzo Borghini, who designed the literary *topoi* of the room, called it a *stanzino*, 'by which I mean that it serves as a wardrobe [*guardaroba*] of things rare and precious both for their value and for their craftsmanship'. As Lina Bolzoni and Scott Schaefer have pointed out, the room was most often identified as *stanzino* or *scrittoio* by contemporaries.[97] *Studiolo,* a microcosm of museum, described a cabinet, the *Kunstschrank* that populated the Renaissance courts of northern Europe. 'The Grand Duke has had an ebony *studiolo* made of his own design, which is composed according to all of the rules of Architecture,' wrote Raffaelo Borghini.[98] Thus the *studiolo* was literally a piece of furniture, not unlike a *cassone* in its function, containing the treasures of its owner in miniature; accordingly it was located within a domestic context, albeit a courtly one, and therefore reinforced the private image of collecting.

The transformation of *studiolo* from a domestic concept to a more public one perfectly illustrates the ways in which the museums of the late Renaissance continued to incorporate both private and public notions of space in their conception and utilization. While the *studiolo* of Federico da Montefeltro at Urbino served largely personal functions and the *Grotta* of Isabelle d'Este, entered only through her *studio*,[99] was secreted within the palace at Mantua, the *studiolo* of Francesco I operated in both contexts. Situated in the Palazzo Vecchio in Florence, the seat of government, off the *Sala Grande* and leading into the private family chambers, it was a striking transition point: a room in which the Grand Duke could seclude himself without entirely leaving the realm of public affairs.[100] Yet, on the whole, Francesco's study was more private than public; very few descriptions exist of it because few people – besides the court humanist Borghini who designed the original iconographic program of its *invenzioni*, Vasari, and the other artists who worked on the room – were ever allowed access to it. Surrounded by the political intrigues of the Tuscan court, the *studiolo* and its contents were for the Grand Duke's eyes alone.

The privatizing tendencies of *musaeum* in a court context created hermetic space. From a social perspective, the princely *studio* was hermetic because its function was exclusionary. Equally, museums were hermetic because they were primarily intellectual rather than social constructs, fabricated out of the eclectic humanistic schemes of the Renaissance *virtuosi*. '*Museum* is a place where the Scholar sits alone, apart from other men, addicted to his Studies, while reading books,' wrote Comenius.[101] Scholarship was a process which absorbed its participants (*studiis deditus*) and the locus of study, the museum, created an impermeable physical barrier between the scholar and the outside world.[102] Even as late as the eighteenth century, an age in which the museum had truly become a public spectacle, illustrations of museums reinforced their image as secretive and engrossing environments.[103] Interestingly enough, the most important and elaborate of the *scrittoii* built by Vasari for Cosimo I between 1559 and 1562 was called, among other things, the *scrittoio segreto* and seems to have been the main precursor to his son Francesco's *studiolo*.[104] From this perspective, the scholar, as frequenter of the museum, was as much alchemist as humanist, enhancing his reputation by the hidden nature of his work.

The conflicting demands of the civic and hermetic notions of a museum, both different strands of the humanistic goals of collecting, allowed the museums of the sixteenth and seventeenth centuries to vacillate between openness and closure, depending on the individual goals of their creators. Explicitly contrasting his own civic designs for a chemical laboratory with Tycho Brahe's aristocratic laboratory and astronomical observatory at Uraniborg, the chemical philosopher Andreas Libavius placed the discourse on secrecy versus openness within its scientific context:

Thus we are not going to devise for him [the ideal natural philosopher] just a *chymeion* or laboratory to use as a private study and hideaway in order that his practice will be more distinguished than anyone else's; but rather, what we shall provide for him is a dwelling suitable for decorous participation in society and living the life of a free man, together with all the appurtenances necessary for such an existence.[105]

Libavius's attack on the private *studio* indicated his participation in, and more importantly awareness of, the debate on secrecy versus openness that entered a wide range of discursive practices in the early modern period.[106] The laboratory, argued Libavius, was a civic and not an aristocratic construct; thus the museum had to answer to the humanistic and later Baconian notions of utility that placed knowledge within the public sphere through its service to society.

The advent of printing and the development of an expanding literate culture outside of the courts, universities and the church signalled the decline of the notion of intellectual privacy presupposed by the medieval and, to a lesser extent, Renaissance notion of collecting. By the seventeenth century the museum had become more of a *galleria* than a *studio*: a space through which one passed, in contrast to the static principle of the spatially closed *studio*. Describing the importance of Aldrovandi's collecting projects to Vincenzo Campeggi, one of the *gonfalonieri* of Bologna, Fra Giovanni Volura praised 'his Theatre of nature, visited continuously by all of the scholars that pass through here ...'.[107] The civic notion of museum placed it in motion; forever opening its doors to visitors, the museum as *galleria* – a term standardized by the public character of the Galleria degli Uffizi and made linguistically normative through the Crusca dictionaries of the seventeenth and eighteenth centuries – was the antithesis of the hermetic and individually defined *studio*, ironically promoted by the same creators of the former category.

The *gallerie* of Kircher and Settala in seventeenth-century Rome and Milan perfectly exemplified this addition to the tropes of collecting, for the two museums were mentioned in most of the major travel journals of the day as 'must-sees' on the serious traveller's itinerary. '[N]o foreign visitor who has not seen the museum of the Roman College can claim that he has truly been in Rome,' boasted Kircher.[108] The *galleria* was set in motion by the constantly changing selection of objects as well as visitors that continuously filled the space it created – public in conception, due to the expanded realm of sociability that the museum promised and to the open-ended nature of the contents that it revealed to the gaze.

Despite frequent avowals of the utilitarian ends of the museum, made particularly by scientific collectors, it is obvious that the emergence of a public strategy of collecting did not fully eclipse the private one. Unlike the Medici, Aldrovandi and Kircher depended on patronage for the survival of their projects, and this patronage most often came from rulers who themselves had a personal interest in collecting. While Aldrovandi proclaimed that his *studio* was 'for the utility of every scholar in all of Christendom', borne out by its accessibility during his lifetime and by the donation of the museum to the Senate of Bologna in 1603, he had nothing but praise for the more self-serving activities of his patron Francesco I.[109]

In defining a collection as 'public' versus 'private', what sort of criteria can we use that would be applicable to an early modern context? Certainly museums such as those of Aldrovandi, Kircher, and Settala were not public in the sense that they were open to people from all walks of life. The first museum to proclaim its fully public status was the Ashmolean Museum at Oxford, which opened its doors in 1683. Given to the university by Elias Ashmole, a dabbler in chemistry, magic, and natural philosophy, the accessibility of the collection was remarked upon with disfavour by certain educated visitors in the seventeenth and eighteenth centuries. 'On 23 August we wished to go to the Ashmolean Museum,' wrote the German traveller Zacharias Conrad von Uffenbach in 1710, 'but it was market day and all sorts of country-folk, men and women, were up there (for the *leges* that hang upon the door *parum honeste & liberaliter* allow everyone to go in). So as we could have seen nothing well for the crowd, we went down-stairs again and saved it for another day.'

Von Uffenbach's displeasure at the literal openness of the Ashmolean translated into pointed comments about the general definition of 'public' institutions in England. Not only did the open admission standards dis-integrate the gender and class barriers that defined the private, hence exclusive, nature of the museum – 'even the women are allowed up here for a sixpence' – but the establishment of the price of admission commodified the experience of scholarship. His experience in the 'world-famed public library of this University', the Bodleian, only confirmed his worst fears about the dangers of the public in a scholarly setting:

But as it costs about eight shillings and some trouble to gain an entrance, most strangers content themselves with a casual inspection. Every moment brings fresh spectators of this description and, surprisingly enough, amongst them peasants and women-folk, who gaze at the library as a cow might gaze at a new gate with such noise and trampling of feet that others are much disturbed.[110]

The pinnacle of his trip to England, a visit to the famed Royal Society, provoked equal disillusion. Finding the Society and its museum to be in complete disarray, Von Uffenbach commented on the inevitability of its state.

But that is the way with all public societies. For a short time they flourish, while the founder and original members are there to set the standard; then come all kinds of setbacks, partly from envy and lack of unanimity and partly because all kinds of people of no account become members; their final state is one of indifference and sloth.[111]

The discomfort of Von Uffenbach and other visitors with the public agenda of Baconian science only reinforced the perception that the relationship between private and public that existed on the continent, as far as education was concerned, was more subtly gradated. 'In Italy one finds hardly any fully public museums,' commented Michael Bernhard Valentini in his *Museum museorum* (1714).[112] Beyond Valentini's distinction between rulers and 'Privat-Personen', museums such as Aldrovandi's *studio* were 'public' because they were open to any scholar with an appropriate introduction or to anyone of exalted rank. '[Everything in my museum] is seen by many different gentlemen passing through this city, who visit my *Pandechio di natura*, like an eighth wonder of the world,' boasted Aldrovandi. In many instances visitors arrived with a letter of introduction. 'This [man] is my dear friend,' explained Alfonso Cataneo, professor of medicine and natural philosophy at the University of Ferrara, to Aldrovandi, 'whom I have directed to Your Excellence upon his arrival in Bologna, since he is a doctor and a gentleman, worthy of seeing certain little things [*cosette*] that interest him. I know that you will not neglect to show him the usual courtesy for love of me.'[113]

The humanist notion of utility also distinguished the public yet inaccessible nature of court collections from the privately owned yet open museums of collectors such as Aldrovandi, whose university affiliation gave his collection a public use through its pedagogical utility, and Kircher, who also conducted experiments and demonstrations in the Roman College museum as part of his teaching duties. The Roman patrician Alfonso Donnino cited his 'desire for public good' as one of the reasons for the gift of his collection to the Roman College in 1651.[114] Equally Filippo Bonanni, Kircher's eventual successor as keeper of the Jesuit science museum, praised the British collector James Petiver for making his private museum public through the publication of his *Centuries*, inexpensive guidebooks to his ever-expanding natural history collection.[115]

Certainly Aldrovandi's desire for the establishment of a *Biblioteca pubblica* was prompted by a sense of civic obligation. 'And therefore, wishing that my many labours be continued after my death, for the honour and utility of the City, and so that they may not have been for nothing, I have elected to conserve this Museum and Library of printed books and my own works, leaving it to the most Illustrious Senate of Bologna ...'.[116] The Senate, responding in kind, transferred Aldrovandi's collection to their most public building to underline its part in the *res publica* of the city. In 1660, when the Bolognese senator Ferdinando Cospi requested that his own collection be added to the civic museum, the decree ratifying this addition described the location as the 'Studio Aldrovando in Pubblico Palatio Bononae'.[117]

The visitors' books that have survived intact provide unique and important documentation on Aldrovandi's museum as a public institution. Upon seeing the museum in 1604, shortly before Aldrovandi's death, Pompeo Viziano marvelled at the number of people who had visited the naturalist's *studio*:

[I]n two large books, that he conserves among the others, an infinite number of Princes, Cardinals, Prelates, *Cavallieri*, and other people of note [*alto affare et di elevato ingegno*] that have passed through Bologna, attest in their own hand to having seen and diligently considered [the museum] with great satisfaction.[118]

To begin with, it was not common practice in this period to have a list of visitors; most collectors did not have such a well-defined sense of their audience, or more importantly, such a public image of their own posterity through their collections, as to record who had visited their museums. 'Cardinal Enrico Gaetano, legate to Bologna, saw the *mirabilia* of nature in the *studio* of doctor Ulisse Aldrovandi,' read one entry for 1587.[119] Besides the book for exalted guests, commemorating their visits, there was also a book which recorded all of the visitors to the museum. Composed mainly of signatures, written on scraps of paper by Aldrovandi, his assistants and the visitors themselves, and later pasted into the sections which organized the names by location and profession, the sheer number of visitors testifies to the Bolognese naturalist's willingness to open up his Theatre of Nature to the world.[120] Aldrovandi, however, not only kept records throughout his lifetime, but specified that the names should continue to be recorded after his death. 'It would also please me,' he specified in his gift of 1603, 'if the Gentlemen and Men of Letters who have visited and will visit the Museum after my death will continue to write their names in my two books designated for this purpose.'[121] The visitors' books, rendering a degree of eternity to the museum through the *memoria* of their lists, testified to the public nature of the scientific collecting enterprise, emerging out of the universities, academies, and professional organizations of the doctors and apothecaries in the sixteenth and seventeenth centuries.

  While the idea of a fully public museum would not emerge in Italy until the early eighteenth century, with the establishment of the museum of the Istituto delle Scienze under Luigi Ferdinando Marsili's sponsorship, subsuming both Aldrovandi's and Cospi's collection in the process, and the formation of Scipione Maffei's 'public Museum of Inscriptions' in Verona,[122] the collections of the sixteenth and seventeenth centuries set the stage for this development. During the late Renaissance the parameters of *musaeum* expanded to include more public connotations. No longer simply hidden worlds, a growing number of collections foreshadowed the utilitarian and didactic tendencies of the late seventeenth- and eighteenth-century ideals of the museum. The most obvious change in this realm was the increased institutionalization of the museum, which became a pervasive social artefact in the courts, academies, and universities of early modern Europe. The success of the social grounding of *musaeum* was due in no small part to its coordination with the long and complex intellectual tradition of collecting outlined above. The museums of the late Renaissance mediated between public and private space, straddling the social world of collecting and the humanistic vocabulary which formed its philosophical base. In its ability to transcend cultural and temporal boundaries the museum stood apart from other institutions, synthesizing new cosmologies with old. The synthetic process that forged the Renaissance notion of *musaeum* reflected not only the syncretic abilities of sixteenth- and seventeenth-century culture, emphasizing the flexibility of humanism as a *modus operandi*, but also its desire to collect and be collected. Drawing on Du Cange's false etymological comparison between museum and mosaic, Bonanni defined the newly reconstituted museum at the Roman College. 'Let us say with Du Cange that, since by the word *Opus Musiuum dicitur illud quod tessellatum est lapillis variorum colorum*, thus in the places designated to the meanderings of the erudite there may be various things, which not only delight the eyes with the Mosaic, but enrich the mind.'[123] The museum, as mosaic, brought together the pieces of a cosmology that had all but fallen apart in the course of several centuries. Organizing all known ideas and artefacts under the rubric of museum, the collectors of the period imagined that they had indeed come to terms with the crisis of knowledge that the fabrication of the museum was designed to solve.

NOTES

Aspects of this essay were presented at the Renaissance Society of America's annual meeting at Harvard University in March 1989. I would like to thank Randolph Starn for his criticism and comments on an earlier draft of this paper.

1.   C. Clemens, *Musei sive bibliothecae tam privatae quam publicae extructio, cura, usus* (Leiden, 1634), sig. *4^v.

2.   Regarding the appearance of these and numerous other terms considered analogous to *musaeum*, see L. Berti, *Il principe dello studiolo* (Florence, 1967), pp. 194–5, and L. Salerno, 'Arte e scienza nelle collezioni del Manierismo', in *Scritti di storia dell'arte in onore di Mario Salmi* (Rome, 1963), ii, pp. 193–214. Other words that should be considered are *arca, cimelarchio, scrittoio, pinacotheca, metallotheca, Kunst- und Wunderkammer*, and *Kunstschrank*.

3.   J. Baudrillard, *Selected Writings* (ed. Mark Poster) (Stanford, 1988), p. 15. Michel Foucault's comments on 'the vast syntax of the world' also suggest that *musaeum*, as a framework of activity, can be placed within a general framework, stressing resemblance and repetition, that was the main organizational tool of late Renaissance discourse; see his *The Order of Things* (English tr., New York, 1970), p. 18.

4.   R. Harbison, *Eccentric Spaces* (New York, 1977). Harbison's notion of an eccentric space implies permeability and fluidity – it is a space specifically designed to hold marginalized information and to be easily reshaped by the particular strategies of its users while still retaining its normative function.

5.   See P. Ariès and G. Duby (eds), *Histoire de la vie privée* (Paris, 1985–7), esp. vols iii–iv; both R. Sennett's *The Fall of Public Man* (New York, 1977) and J. Habermas' *Strukturwandel der Offentlichkeit* (1962) [French edn: *L'espace publique*, tr. M. B. de Launay (Paris, 1978)] see the eighteenth century as a critical turning point in the expansion of the public sphere. Though little work has been done to elucidate directly the relations between public and private (as opposed to looking at simply one or the other), the inference that can be drawn by comparing the work on private life to that on the public sphere is that the two domains are intimately and

necessarily intertwined, something I hope to demonstrate in my discussion of the entrance of museums into the public sphere in the period from the sixteenth to the eighteenth century.

6. Pontificia Università Gregoriana (hereafter PUG), *Kircher*, MS 568 (XIV), f. 143ʳ (Trapani, 15 June 1652).

7. Archivum Romanum Societatis Iesu (hereafter ARSI), *Rom.* 138. Historia (1704–29), XVI, f. 182ʳ (Filippo Bonanni, *Notizie circa la Galleria del Collegio Romano*, 10 January 1716).

8. *Thesaurus Linguae Latinae* (Leipzig, 1936–46), VIII, p. 1702; *Lexicon Totius Latinitatis* (Padua, 1871), III, p. 318.

9. Chevalier de Jaucourt, 'Musée', in *Encyclopédie* x (1765), pp. 893–94.

10. Ibid., *Thes. Ling. Lat.* VIII, p. 1702; C. Neickelius, *Museographia* (Leipzig, 1727), pp. 1–2; J. Alsop, *The Rare Arts Traditions* (New York, 1982), p. 163.

11. *Lex. tot. lat.* II, p. 318; C. T. Lewis and C. Short, *A Latin Dictionary* (Oxford, 1958), p. 1179; Felice Feliciano, in his description of a trip taken by Mantegna and the antiquary Ciriaco of Ancona in 1464 described their arrival at 'greenswards like heavenly gardens in the most delicious dwelling places of the Muses', in C. E. Gilbert, *Italian Art 1400–1500* (Englewood Cliffs, NJ, 1980), p. 180.

12. J. Dixon Hunt, *Garden and Grove: The Italian Renaissance Garden in the English Imagination 1600–1750* (London, 1986); D. Coffin (ed), *The Italian Garden* (Washington, DC, 1972); L. Zangheri, *Pratolino: il Giardino delle meraviglie* (Florence, 1979); M. Fagiolo (ed.), *La città effimera e l'universo artificiale del giardino* (Rome, 1980).

13. Cited in L. Tongiorgi Tomasi, 'Projects for botanical and other gardens: a sixteenth-century manual', *Journal of Garden History* (1983), p. 1.

14. 'Protesta di D. Teodoro Bondini a chi legge', in L. Legati, *Museo Cospiano* (Bologna, 1677), n.p.

15. L. Châtelet-Lange, 'Le "museo di Vanres" (1560). Collections de sculpture et musées au XVIe siècle en France', *Zeitschrift für Kunstgeschichte*, 38 (1975), p. 279; see also Du Cange's definition of museum which, aside from a brief reference to the museum at Alexandria, does not give the term the broad framework alluded to by later definitions.

16. *The Letters of Marsilio Ficino* (New York, 1985), I, p. 28.

17. Petrarch, *Epist.* 2.3–43, in E. Cochrane and J. Kirshner (eds), *The Renaissance, Readings in Western Civilization* (Chicago, 1986), V, p. 66.

18. Ibid., pp. 51–2.

19. C. R. Chiarlo, '"Gli fragmenti dilla sancta antiquitate": studi antiquari e produzione delle imaggini da Ciriaco d'Ancona e Francesco Colonna', in *Memoria dell'antico nell'arte italiana*, ed. Salvatore Settis (Turin, 1984), I, pp. 271–87.

20. Giovanni Pico della Mirandola, 'Praise of Lorenzo', in D. Thompson and A. F. Nagel (eds), *The Three Crowns of Florence: Humanist Assessments of Dante, Petrarch and Boccaccio* (New York, 1972), pp. 148, 152.

21. A. Doni, *Tre libri di lettere* (Venice, 1552), p. 81 (Como, 20 July 1543); see also the conference proceedings of *Paolo Giovio: il Rinascimento e la memoria* (Como, 1985).

22. S. J. Schaefer, *The Studiolo of Francesco I de' Medici in the Palazzo Vecchio in Florence*, unpublished Ph.D. dissertation (Bryn Mawr College, 1976), pp. 116–17; C. Franzoni, '"Rimembranze d'infinite cose": le collezioni rinascimentali di antichita', in *Memoria dell'antico nell'arte italiana* (Torino, 1984), I, p. 309.

23. Letter to Francesco Vettori, 10 December 1513 in Cochrane and Kirshner, op. cit. (note 17), pp. 183–4; for the Italian see N. Machiavelli, *Lettere*, ed. F. Gaeta (Milan, 1961), pp. 301–6.

24. D. Du Cange, 'Scriptorium', in *Glossarium Mediae et Infimae Latinitatis* (Paris, 1846), VI, p. 132. This definition corresponds well with the medieval image of *privatus* as a monastic ideal, as discussed in G. Duby, 'Private power, public power', in P. Ariès and G. Duby (eds), *A History of Private Life*, tr. Arthur Goldhammer (Cambridge, MA, 1988), II, p. 5.

25. *Epist.*, III, ep. xv to Niccolo Niccoli, in Franzoni, op. cit. (note 22), p. 305; see also *Two Renaissance Bookhunters: The Letters of Poggius Bracciolini to Nicolaus de Niccolis*, tr. P. Gordan (New York, 1974).

26. T. Tasso, 'Il Malpiglio Secondo, overo de fuggir la moltitudine', in his *Dialoghi* (ed. E. Raimondi) (Florence, 1958), II, tome 2, esp. pp. 569–70.

27. Parma, Biblioteca Palatina, MS Pal. 1012, fasc. 1, c. 13^v (Beccadelli to Petronio Beccadelli, 20 October 1555); Florence, Riccardiana, Cod. 2438, parte I, lett. 66^r (Giganti to Lorenzo Giacomini, Bologna, 11 December 1584); for details of the history of these collections, see G. Fragnito, 'Il museo di Antonio Giganti', in *Scienze, credenze occulte, livelli di cultura* (Florence, 1982), pp. 507–35; L. Laurencich-Minelli, 'L'indice del Museo Giganti', *Museographia scientifica* 1 (1984), nos. 3–4, pp. 191–242.

28. See L. Thorndike, 'Encyclopedias of the fourteenth century', in his *A History of Magic and Experimental Science* (New York, 1923–41), III, pp. 546–67; R. Popkin, 'Theories of knowledge', in Charles B. Schmitt and Quentin Skinner (eds), *The Cambridge History of Renaissance Philosophy* (Cambridge, 1988), pp. 668–84.

29. Foucault, op. cit. (note 3), p. 38.

30. S. Wilkin (ed.), *Sir Thomas Browne's Works* (London, 1835–6), IV, p. 239.

31. Sir Thomas Browne, 'Religio Medici', II, p. 35. In an earlier passage (p. 31) he attacked such literary curiosities as 'pieces fit only to be placed in Pantagruel's library'.

32. A. Kircher, *The Vulcano's: or Burning and Fire-Vomiting Mountains ... Collected for the most part out of Kircher's Subterraneous World* (London, 1669), p. 34.

33. Legati, op. cit. (note 14), p. 215.

34. G. B. Olivi, *De reconditis et praecipius collectaneis* (Verona, 1584), p. 2; G. Porro, *L'orto dei semplici di Padova* (Venice, 1591), sig. +5^r.

35. This was particularly true of Francesco's *studiolo*, though it is also evident in the design of other studies.

36. Legati, professor of Greek at the University of Bologna, discussed his 'Museo delle Poetesse' in his correspondence with the Tuscan scientist Francesco Redi; Florence, Laurenziana. *Redi*, 222, c. 34^r (22 November 1667) and c. 42 (27 April 1668).

37. Biblioteca Universitaria, Bologna (hereafter BUB), *Aldrovandi*, MS 21, III, c. 428^r. For the details of Aldrovandi's brush with the Inquisition, see G. Olmi, *Ulisse Aldrovandi: Scienza e natura nel secondo Cinquecento* (Trento, 1976), pp. 44–66, *passim*; C. Renato, *Opere, documenti e testamonianze* (ed. A. Rotondo) (Florence, 1968), pp. 224–7 (Frammenti del processo di Ulisse Aldrovandi).

38. C. Vasoli, *L'Enciclopedismo del Seicento* (Naples, 1978), esp. p. 27.

39. *Museum Hermeticum* (Frankfurt, 1678), preface, n.p.; 'De hac vera transmutatione metallorum, quae solo Elixire seu lapide philosophorum perficitur, hic nobis potissimum sermo est, de quo etso multorum authorum libri exstant, ut hic ipse liber Musaeum hermeticum nuncupatum, qui iam aliquot abhinc annis in lucis prodiit, attamen cum haud parva authorum chemicorum sit copia, magnaque scriptorum diversits & varietas, ita ut unus altero clavius & apertius scribat, aliusq'.

40. D. Kronick, *A History of Scientific and Technical Periodicals* 2nd edn. (Metuchen, NJ, 1976), p. 27; G. Nencioni, 'La 'Galleria' della lingua', in Paola Barocchi (ed.), *Gli Uffizi: quattro secoli di una galleria* (Florence, 1983), I, pp. 18, 34.

41. Stelluti, *Persio*, p. 170, quoted in G. Gabrieli, 'L'orizzonte intellettuale e morale di Federico Cesi', *Rendiconti della R. Accademia Nazionale dei Lincei* ser. 6, 14 (1938–9), fasc. 7–12, pp. 678–9; 'La vita d'Ulisse Aldrovandi (1586)', in L. Frati (ed.), *Intorno alla vita e alle opere di Ulisse Aldrovandi* (Imola, 1907), p. 16; PUG, *Kircher*, MS 567 (XIII), f. 45 (Herbipoli, 16 June 1657); Florence, Biblioteca Nazionale, *Magl.* Cl. VIII, 1112, c. 13 (Settala to Magliabecchi, Milan, 11 March 1665).

42. L. Moscardo, *Note overo memorie del Museo del Conte Moscardo* (Verona, 1672), sig. sss3r; Bondoni, 'Protesta', in Legati, op. cit. (note 14), n.p.

43. G. Gabrieli, 'Il Carteggio Linceo, I', *Memorie della R. Accademia Nazionale dei Lincei. Classe di scienze morali, storiche e filologiche* (hereafter *Cart. Linc.*), ser. 6, 7 (1938), fasc. 1, p. 168 (Welser to Faber, 29 July 1611); ibid. II, (1939), p. 778 (Cesi to Faber, 19 November 1622); Calzolari's collection, for example, was called a *rerum ... omnium naturalium Theatrum* by its cataloguers B. Ceruti and A. Chiocco, in *Musaeum Franc. Calceolarii* (Verona, 1622), p. 97.

44. BUB, *Aldrovandi*, MS 21, IV, c. 33^r; MS 92, c. 11^v; see also A. Sorbelli, 'Contributo alla bibliographia di Ulisse Aldrovandi', in Frati, op. cit. (note 41), p. 72, which produces an agreement between Aldrovandi and his printers 'di fare stampare l'historia del Museo d'esso signor Aldrovandi in Bologna'.

45. BUB, *Aldrovandi*, MS 70, c. 66^v; Florence, Archivio di Stato, *Mediceo del Principato*, f. 689, c. 1, in S.

De Rosa, 'Alcuni aspetti della "committenza" scientifica medicea prima di Galileo', in *Firenze e la Toscana dei Medici nell'Europa del '500* (Florence, 1983), II, p. 713.

46. A. Quint, *Cardinal Federico Borromeo as a Patron and Critic of the Arts and his Musaeum of 1625* (New York, 1986), p. 233; I have modified her translation somewhat to make it more readable.

47. Pliny, *Natural History*, tr. H. Rackham (Cambridge, Mass., 1938), I, p. 13 (pref., 17–18).

48. U. Aldrovandi, 'Discorso naturale' (1572–3), c. 511ᵛ, in S. Tugnoli Pattaro, *Metodo e sistema della scienze nel pensiero di Ulisse Aldrovandi* (Bologna, 1981), p. 184.

49. BUB, *Aldrovandi*, MS 136, XXVIII, c. 126ʳ (Viadanae, 29 June 1599).

50. Modena, Archivio di Stato, *Archivio per le materie. Storia naturale*, busta 1. Aldrovandi to Panzio (Bologna, 16 December 1577).

51. O. Mattirolo, 'Le lettere di Ulisse Aldrovandi a Francesco I e Ferdinando I', *Accademia Reale delle Scienze di Torino* (1903–4), p. 381 (Letter to Ferdinando, 1588); regarding the origins and use of the term *Pandechion*, see Pliny, *Natural History*, pref., 28, p. 15, where he discusses the πανδέχται ('Hold-alls'); Lewis and Short, op. cit (note 11), p. 1296. It is important to note that the idea of a forest, a *selva universale*, was a common trope in the language of sixteenth- and seventeenth-century natural philosophy. It was used frequently, for example, by Tommaso Garzoni, as P. Cerchi notes in his *Enciclopedismo e politica della riscrittura: Tommaso Garzoni* (Pisa, 1980), cf. 32–3; equally, Zenobbio Bocchi's botanical garden and museum at the Gonzaga court in Mantua was described by contemporaries as a *naturalium rerum selvam*; Ceruti and Chiocco, op. cit. (note 43), sig. *4ᵛ.

52. T. Cave, *The Cornucopian Text: Problems of Writing in the French Renaissance* (Oxford, 1979), p. 6. I have taken this passage from his discussion of the definition of *copia* which defined not only plenitude but also functioned as *thesaurus*.

53. BUB, *Aldrovandi*, MS 91, c. 522ʳ; Venice, Biblioteca Marciana (hereafter BMV) *Arch. Mor. 103* (= *Marc.* 12609), f. 9.

54. Olivi, op. cit. (note 34), sig. ++4ᵛ, p. 2.

55. Cicero, *De oratore* III xxi. 125, quoted in Cave, op. cit. (note 52), p. 6.

56. BUB, *Aldrovandi*, MS 105; Pattaro, op.cit. (note 48), p. 15.

57. Florence, *Ricc.* Cod. 2438, I, f. 1ʳ (Bologna, 27 June 1587).

58. L. Laurencich-Minelli, 'Museography and ethnographical collections in Bologna during the sixteenth and seventeenth centuries', in O. Impey and A. MacGregor (eds), *The Origins of Museums* (Oxford, 1985), pp. 17–23; M. Hodgen, *Early Anthropology in the Sixteenth and Seventeenth Centuries* (Philadelphia, 1964); D. Lach, *Asia in the Making of Europe* (Chicago, 1972).

59. F. Cesi, 'Del natural desiderio di sapere et institutzione de' Lincei per adempimento di esso', in M. L. Biagi and B. Basile (eds), *Scienzati del Seicento* (Milan, 1980), p. 48.

60. Lynn Joy's comments on Gassendi, as a man between the humanistic and Galilean-Cartesian models of knowledge, are particularly suggestive and convincing; see her *Gassendi the Atomist: Advocate of History in an Age of Science* (Cambridge, 1987).

61. R. J. W. Evans, *The Making of the Habsburg Monarchy: An Interpretation* (Oxford, 1979).

62. Ibid., p. 429; D. Pastine, *La nascita dell'idolatria: l'Oriente religioso di Athanasius Kircher* (Florence, 1978), p. 112.

63. In C. Reilly, *Athanasius Kircher S.J. Master of a Hundred Arts 1602–1680* (Studia Kircheriana, Band I) (Wiesbaden, 1974), p. 38.

64. A. Kircher, *Oedipus Aegyptiacus* (Rome, 1652–4), ii, I, classis I, p. 6, quoted in Evans, op. cit. (note 61), p. 437.

65. J. Comenius, *Orbis sensualium pictus* (London, 1659), p. 193.

66. See, for example, Ceruti and Chiocco, op. cit. (note 43), p. 721; P. Terzago, *Musaeum Septalianum* (Tortona, 1664), p. 151: 'Atque dicendum de bibliotheca non immerito, quod Dei, & scientiarum prorsus omnium recondat mysteria, de Musae, quod artis & naturae contineat arcana ...'.

67. G. P. Bellori, *Nota delli musei, librerie, gallerie, et ornamenti di statue e pitture ne' palazzi, nelle case, e ne' giardini di Roma* (Rome, 1664), p. 45; D. Diderot, 1751, 'Bibliothèque', in *Encyclopédie*, I (Paris, 1751), p. 235.

68. See R. Chartier, 'Urban reading practices 1660–1780', in *The Cultural Uses of Print in Early Modern France* (Princeton, 1987), pp. 183–239.

69. See Diderot's survey of libraries to the eighteenth century in the *Encyclopédie*, and C. du Molinet, *Le cabinet de la bibliothèque de Sainte Geneviève* (Paris, 1692).

70. Diderot, op. cit. (note 67), I, p. 235.

71. Biblioteca Apostolica Vaticana (hereafter BAV), *Barberini Lat.* 6467, f. 64 (Padua, 5 September 1642); see also ff. 64–5 (28 May 1641 and 8 November 1642) and f. 51 (21 May 1635): 'restera servito di honorarmi a farle haver luogo nel suo Museo'.

72. BUB, *Aldrovandi*, MS 97, cc. 440–3ʳ; see also his *Bibliologia* (1580–1), MS 83 and his *Bibliotheca secundum nomina authorum*, MS 147.

73. Clemens, op. cit. (note 1), pp. 2–4, 523; Pietro Redondi observes in his *Galileo Heretic*, tr. R. Rosenthal (Princeton, 1987), pp. 80–1: 'As instruments of intellectual monopoly, the great libraries created at the beginning of the century expressed the strength and prestige of traditional humanist and theological culture, which was forging new instruments of erudition and exegesis: the most modern weapons for sustaining, on all intellectual fronts, the effort of Catholic reform and religious struggle'.

74. The Jesuit privilege to censor their own books was revoked by the College of Cardinals in 1596; Thorndike, op. cit. (note 28), V, p. 151; BUB, *Aldrovandi*, MS 136, XXV, c. 122ʳ (*Index librorum quos concessit Ulyssi Aldrovando SS. Inquisitio romano*, June/July 1596) and cc. 135ᵛ–7ʳ (*Catalogus librorum prohibitorum meorum datus Episcopo et Inquisitori*).

75. William Ashworth's remarks on the problems of defining a 'Catholic' science and also on the church's attack on natural magic and, to a more limited extent, alchemy, represent the most useful overview of science, theology, and the institutional church in the post-Tridentine era, in his 'Catholicism and Early Modern Science', in D. Lindberg and R. Numbers (eds), *God and Nature: Historical Essays on the Encounter between Christianity and Science* (Berkeley and Los Angeles, 1986), pp. 136–66.

76. See note 37; there is an extensive literature on heresy and natural philosophy; Thorndike, op. cit. (note 28), 8 vols; L. Amabile, *Il Santo Officio dell'Inquisitione in Napoli* (Citta di Castello, 1892); Tommaso Garzoni, for example, was accused of discussing authors prohibited by the *Index* in his *Piazza universale* (1585), an example of the sort of indiscriminate curiosity that got many other natural philosophers in trouble; Cerchi, op. cit. (note 51), p. 43.

77. Châtelet-Lange, op. cit (note 15), pp. 279–80; Franzoni, op. cit. (note 22), p. 333.

78. As Duby notes in his 'Private power, public power' (op. cit. (note 24), p. 3), *priver* means to domesticate. There is an extensive literature on academies in Early Modern Europe, so only a few of the most basic works are indicated here: E. Cochrane, 'The Renaissance academies in their Italian and European setting', in *The Fairest Flower* (Florence, 1985), pp. 21–39; ibid., *Tradition and Enlightenment in the Tuscan Academies 1690–1800* (Chicago, 1961); M. Maylender, *Storia delle academie d'Italia*, 5 vols (Bologna, 1926–30); F. Yates, *The French Academies of the Sixteenth Century* (London, 1947).

79. U. Tergolina-Gislanzoni-Brasco, 'Francesco Calzolari speziali veronese', *Bolletino storico italiano dell'arte sanitaria* 33 (1934), fasc. 6, p. 15.

80. B. Cotrugli, *Della mercatura e del mercato perfetto* (1573), p. 86, quoted in Franzoni, op. cit. (note 22), p. 307; Du Cange's definition of *studiolum* – 'Cellula, museum, conclave, ubi studetur. Gall. *Cabinet d'Etude*: museolum, scrinia, *Estudiole* dicimus' – also gives several examples that locate the museum next to the bedroom (Du Cange, op. cit. (note 24), VI, p. 395.

81. Milan, Biblioteca Ambrosiana, MS S. 85, sup., f. 235ʳ (*Forma dello studio*, 1586).

82. C. R. Hill, 'The cabinet of Bonnier de la Mosson (1702–1744)', *Annals of Science* 43 (1986), pp. 148–9. A glance at the *Encyclopédie* article on 'cabinet' confirms its entry into the public sphere a century later.

83. C. Dionisotti, 'La galleria degli uomini illustri', in V. Branca and C. Ossola (eds), *Cultura e societa nel Rinascimento* (Florence, 1984), p. 452.

84. L. B. Alberti, *Ten Books on Architecture*, tr. James Leoni (1715), ed. J. Ryckwert (London, 1956) [v. 17], p. 107; Pliny the Younger's description of his villa at Laurentium [*Epist.* II. 17] places his own library/study near the bedrooms.

85. See C. M. Brown, '"Lo insaciabile desiderio nostro di cose antique": new documents on Isabella d'Este's collection of antiquities', in C. H. Clough (ed.), *Cultural Aspects of the Italian Renaissance* (New York, 1976), pp. 324–53. Saint Catherine of Siena, another exceptional woman, also had a *studio* in which she composed her voluminous correspondence. I would like to thank Karen Scott for this information.

86. J. B. Elshtain, *Public Man, Private Woman: Women in Social and Political Thought* (Princeton, 1981), 3–16, *passim*.

87. The inscription above Pierre Borel's museum in Castres read: 'Siste gradum (curiose) hic enim orbem in domo, imo in Musao, id est microcosmum seurerum omnium rariorum Compendium cernes …'; *Catalogue des choses rares de Maistre Pierre Borel* in his *Les Antiquitez, Raretez, Plantes, Mineraux, & autres choses considerables de la Ville, & Comte de Castres d'Albigeois* (Castres, 1649), p. 132.

88. Forli, Biblioteca Comunale, *Autografi Piancastelli*, 51, c. 486ʳ (15 June 1595).

89. BUB, *Aldrovandi*, MS 143, X, c. 284ʳ.

90. Steven Shapin's perceptive analysis of the location of experiment in seventeenth-century British science deals with the transit from private to public, and vice-versa, by similarly considering the spaces in which Royal Society members such as Boyle and Hooke conducted their experiments. His comments on the self-conscious nature of 'publicity' in post-Baconian science further illuminate the background to the contrasting perceptions of the Ashmolean Museum and Continental collections of the seventeenth century discussed later in this paper; see S. Shapin, 'The House of Experiment in seventeenth-century England', *Isis* 79 (1988), pp. 373–404.

91. References to the interchangeability of terms are voluminous; see, for example, BUB, *Aldrovandi*, MS 38², I, c. 229, c. 259; MS 41, c. 2ʳ; MS 136, XXVI, cc. 38–9; Bologna, Archivio di Stato, *Assunteria di Studio. Diversorum*, tome X, no. 6.

92. O. Montalbani, *Curae analyticae* (Bologna, 1671), pp. 5, 15. The use of the diminutive, a linguistic device that played with the macrocosmic potential of the museum, a world in miniature, appears in other texts as well. G. B. Cavallara, for example, described the Mantuan physician Filippo Costa's collection as *suo Studiolino*; 'Lettera dell'eccell.mo Cavallara', in *Discorsi di M. Filippo Costa* 2nd edn. (Mantua, 1586), sig. Ee.3ᵛ. Galileo's often-cited comparison between *Orlando Furioso* and *Gerusalemme Liberata*, which described the two works in the language of collecting, disparaged the latter as a *studietto* (as opposed to the *galleria regia* of Ariosto); in Nencioni, op. cit. (note 40), pp. 18–19.

93. Franzoni, op. cit. (note 22), p. 358.

94. BMV, *Arch. Mor.* 103 (= *Marciana* 12609), f. 29.

95. G. I. della Rocchetta, 'Il museo di curiosità del Card. Flavio Chigi seniore', *Archivio della societa romana di storia patria*, ser. 3, 20 (1967), a. 89, p. 141. Gardens, it should be noted, as a subset of the category *musaeum*, also evidenced the same transition from private to public space. The Biblical image of the Garden of Eden, a closed and perfect space, and the allegorical image of the *hortus conclusus* were transformed in the sixteenth and seventeenth centuries into the more open image of *selva*, the forest whose contents were limitless.

96. Milan, Biblioteca Ambrosiana, MS D. 332 inf., ff. 68–9 (Aldrovandi to Asciano Persio, 17 November 1597); BUB, *Aldrovandi*, MS 21, IV, c. 347ʳ; *Cart. Linc.*, I, p. 403; 1942, III, pp. 1046, 1076.

97. K. Frey, *Der literarische Nachlass Giorgio Vasaris* (Munich, 1923–40), quoted in Schaefer, op. cit. (note 22), p. 22 [Borghini to Vasari, 20 September 1569]; L. Bolzoni, 'L'"invenzione" dello stanzino di Francesco I', in *Le Arti nel principato Mediceo* (Florence, 1980), p. 264; Schaefer, op. cit. (note 22), p. 9; R. Borghini, *Il riposo* (Florence, 1584), pp. 610, 635.

98. Borghini, op. cit. (note 97), p. 610; H. O. Boström, 'Philipp Hainhofer and Gustavus Adolphus's *Kunstschrank* in Uppsala', in O. Impey and A. MacGregor (eds), *The Origins of Museums* (Oxford, 1985), pp. 90–101.

99. Franzoni, op. cit. (note 22), p. 311.

100. Both Lina Bolzoni and Luciano Berti concur on the ambiguity of the *studiolo*'s position; Bolzoni, op. cit. (note 97), p. 264; Berti, op. cit. (note 2), p. 83.

101. Comenius, op. cit. (note 65), p. 200.

102. For an interesting discussion and definition of 'absorption', see M. Fried, *Absorption and Theatricality: Painting and Beholder in the Age of Diderot* (Berkeley, 1980), pp. 7–70, *passim*.

103. See, for example, the frontispiece of Neickelius' *Museographia* (op. cit., note 10).

104. K. Levin, *A Topological Inversion in the Studiolo of Francesco I* (unpublished MA thesis, University of Colorado, 1982), pp. 9–10.

105. A. Libavius, *Commentarium … pars prima* (1606), I, p. 92, quoted in O. Hannaway, 'Laboratory design and the aim of science: Andreas Libavius and Tycho Brahe', *Isis* 77 (1986), p. 599. As

Hannaway notes (p. 585), citing Du Cange, *laboratorium* is a post-classical term, probably of monastic origin, that developed its more modern connotations from the sixteenth century, paralleling the expansion of museum.

106.   See for example, W. Eamon, 'From the secrets of nature to public knowledge: the origins of the concept of openness in science', *Minerva* 23 (1985), pp. 321–47.

107.   BUB, *Aldrovandi*, MS 25, c. 304^r (8 April 1574); Franzoni, Nencioni, and Dionisotti note how the entry of *galleria* into the language of collecting from French in the late sixteenth century heralded a new spatial framework for the museum, as, according to one contemporary description, 'un luogo da passaggiare'; Franzoni, op. cit. (note 22), p. 335; Cellini describes *galleria* as a *loggia* or *androne* in his autobiography; Dionisotti, op. cit. (note 83), p. 449; the Crusca dictionary did not define *galleria* until 1691; Nencioni, op. cit. (note 40), p. 17; in his work on the fall of public man, Richard Sennett defines 'public' as motion, literally space to be moved through – a definition certainly in keeping with the historical development of *galleria*; Sennett, op. cit. (note 5), p. 14.

108.   PUG, *Kircher*, MS 560 (VI), f. 111 (Kircher to G. B. Olivi, 23 October 1671), quoted in V. Rivosecchi, *Esotismo in Roma barocca: studi sul Padre Kircher* (Rome, 1982), p. 141.

109.   BUB, *Aldrovandi*, MS 34, I, c. 6^r. Aldrovandi's lack of a clear distinction between public and private activities evidences certain similarities with what Jürgen Habermas, from a Marxist perspective, has described as the first stage in the formation of the 'bourgeois' public sphere, that is, the pre-capitalist exchange of goods and information that coexisted with the established public order; Habermas, op. cit. (note 5), p. 26.

110.   W. H. and W. J. C. Quarrell (eds), *Oxford in 1710* (Oxford, 1928), pp. 2–3, 24, 31; see M. Welch, 'The foundation of the Ashmolean Museum' and 'The Ashmolean as described by its earliest visitors', in A. MacGregor (ed.), *Tradescant's Rarities: Essays on the Foundation of the Ashmolean Museum* (Oxford, 1983), pp. 41–69. The image of the Ashmolean as the prototype for the 'public' museum appears in the emphasis on this word in contemporary descriptions of it. Borel singled it out as 'Le Cabinet publique' in his list of museums in 1649, alluding to the earlier Tradescant collection that formed the basis (indeed the bulk) of Ashmole's gift to Oxford in 1683; the Chevalier de Jaucourt described it as the museum 'that the University had had built for the progress and the perfection of the different branches of knowledge': 'Musée', in *Encyclopédie*, x, p. 894. The entry in the *Oxford English Dictionary* under 'museum', like the Crusca reference to Aldrovandi, underlines the normative function of the Ashmolean in shaping the use of museum in English, as does reference to it in seventeenth- and eighteenth-century dictionaries.

111.   W. H. Quarrell and Margaret Mare, *London in 1710* (London, 1934), p. 98.

112.   M. B. Valentini, *Museum museorum, oder der allgemeiner Kunst- und Naturalien Kammer* (Frankfurt, 1714), sig. xx2^r.

113.   BAV, *Vat. lat.* 6192, vol. 2, f. 657^r (Aldrovandi to Cardinal Sirleto, Bologna, 23 July 1577); BUB, *Aldrovandi*, MS 1382, c. 37 (Modena, 12 October 1561).

114.   ARSI, *Fondo Gesuitico*, 1060/5, III, no. 1.

115.   British Library, Sloane MS, 4063, f. 231^r (Bonanni to Petiver, Rome, 26 December 1703); R. Stearns, 'James Petiver, promoter of natural science ca. 1663–1718', *Proceedings of the American Antiquarian Society*, new ser. 62 (1952), pp. 243–365.

116.   G. Fantuzzi, *Memorie della vita di Ulisse Aldrovandi* (Bologna, 1774), pp. 76, 84.

117.   BUB, Cod. 738 (1071), vol. xxIII, no. 14 (*Decreto per la concessione di una sala al marchese Ferdinando Cospi appresso lo Studio Aldrovandi* [28 June 1660]).

118.   Biblioteca Comunale dell'Archiginasio, Bologna, B. 164, f. 301^r (Pompeo Viziano, *Del museo del S.r Dottore Aldrovandi*, 21 April 1604).

119.   BUB, *Aldrovandi*, MS 41, c. 2^r (*Liber in quo viri nobilitate, honore et virtute insignes, viso musaeo quod Excellentissimus Ulyssis Aldrovandus Illustriss. Senatus Bononiensi dono dedit, propria nomina ad perpetuam res memoriam scribunt*). The book, however, was started in Aldrovandi's lifetime, since the entries date from 1566 – significantly the first signature was Gabriele Paleotti's – until March 1644. 'Ego Carolus Gonzaga die 22. Mensii Aprilis, 1619 et particular gratia D. Co. Pompei Aldrovandi [one of the two executors named in Aldrovandi's will] in visi nobiliss.a haec bibliothecu properata grati animi ergo scripsi' (c. 6).

120.   BUB, *Aldrovandi*, MS 110.

121.   Fantuzzi, op. cit. (note 116), p. 84.

122.   M. Spallanzani, 'Le "Camere di storia naturale" dell'Istituto delle Scienze di Bologna nel Settecento', in W. Tega (ed.), *Scienza e letterature nella cultura italiana del settecento* (Bologna, 1984), pp. 149–83; S. Maffei, *Epistolario (1700–1755)*, ed. Celestino Garibotto (Milan, 1955), I, p. 238 (Maffei to Anton Francesco Marmi, Verona, end of March 1717); p. 273 (Maffei to Muratori, Verona, 20 September 1718).

123.   ARSI, *Rom.* 138. *Historia* (1704–1729), XVI, f. 182ʳ.

5.

Inventing Assyria: Exoticism and Reception in Nineteenth-Century England and France

Frederick N. Bohrer

Since the Elgin marbles were brought to England, no similar arrival has occurred so calculated to excite the interests of artists and archaeologists, as these Assyrian-Babylonian remains ...   Sidney Smirke, 1847[1]

Among the interesting questions which have arisen along with the recently discovered [Assyrian] monuments, it is certainly quite surprising to find those concerning art for its own sake ...   'Musée de Ninive', *L'Illustration* 1847[2]

The sudden archaeological discovery, starting in 1843, of a wealth of artifacts of the ancient Neo-Assyrian empire brought to the attention of Europeans a form of artistic production that was unique and unexpectedly striking to many contemporary eyes. Roughly comparable arrays of ancient Assyrian artifacts found by both French and English excavators were put on display almost simultaneously in the Louvre and British Museum, starting in 1847. Yet, even as Assyrian art received a (literal) place in the ranks of ancient art, it was problematic and difficult to assimilate into established artistic and cultural discourse. As we shall see, Assyria presented an unsettling addition to a history of ancient art and cultures whose primary touchstones had been objects from ancient Egypt and the Greco-Roman world.

The interplay of Assyrian archaeology with nineteenth-century Western art and visual culture has never been fully assessed. The study of the Western reception of Assyrian art has focused largely on two portions of the phenomenon: a largely positivist narrative of archaeological progress and a narrowly defined 'influence' on aspects of European art.[3]

My goal here will be, to adopt a term of Walter Benjamin, to brush these histories of continual progress, discovery, and innovation 'against the grain'.[4] As we shall see, the varied and contradictory associations impressed upon Assyria not only pre-date the archaeological discoveries themselves but also were decisively shaped by the particular institutional, ideological, aesthetic, and national arenas within which it circulated. Indeed, tracking the different significations of Assyria provides almost a snapshot of structures of power and knowledge active at the time, as well as some of the conflicts and contradictions involved in Western cross-cultural representation. This is a case-study, then, in a given cultural moment, of the principle stated by Johannes Fabian, that '... our ways of making the Other are ways of making ourselves'. Further, as it represents an overlap between the concerns of art history and postcolonial studies, I will draw on the resources of both fields.[5]

My primary focus, then, is not ancient Assyria itself or its excavation, but rather what was made of it within nineteenth-century Europe. I thus approach nineteenth-century Assyrian exoticism as a phenomenon of reception.[6] I am concerned not with distinguishing 'authentic' versus 'inauthentic' representations of Assyrian culture or its artifacts, but rather of articulating the (Western) processes through which all such representations take place, from Courbet's fanciful 'Assyrian' beard to Ford Madox Brown's more painstaking recreation of the interior of an Assyrian palace.

Parallel to the dynamic of imperialist power involved in Mesopotamian archaeology itself, the European reception of Assyria presents a series of conflictual power relations. As we shall see, the establishment of Assyria in the cultural and artistic discourse of the West consistently illuminated, often precisely as it challenged, established norms of cultural discourse. To be more specific, I want to show here how the Assyrian discoveries were involved in a consistent process of identification by means of binarism and bifurcation. The most obvious binary pairing is that in which the West defined itself against its nebulous 'Other'. At the same time, juxtaposing different works of art and moments of reception ultimately undermines the binary logic which underwrites the Western construct of a timeless 'exotic' East. It instead reveals that the exotic subject takes on a variety of forms and roles in the nineteenth century, encompassing a broad array of artistic production.

As we shall see, France and England asserted themselves directly against each other in their representations of Assyria in a way that paralleled the nations' rivalry to gain Assyrian antiquities. Further, though they can only be briefly touched on here, other sorts of bifurcated oppositions were also involved. The distinction between judging an object a work of art or an antiquarian artifact was clearly invoked to evaluate Assyria, by partisans of both positions. Even the conventional roles of male and female were a bit unsettled by the case of Assyria.

Finally, I must add a note on context. I use the term *exoticism* with a full sense of its complex history.[7] Indeed, I use it for that very reason: to underline the contestable and problematic nature of 'non-Western' representation.[8] There are pressing reasons, both historical and contemporary, to question the putatively objective accounts that circulate in the West of the world beyond it. A critical analysis of Assyrian exoticism is part of that project. Nonetheless, the overwhelming majority of postcolonial studies, both in art history and elsewhere, are devoted to European representations of lands contemporary to the artist. This study moves instead toward the (less often examined) implications for understanding the involvement of historical subjects in the representation of exoticist difference.[9]

Martin and Delacroix: the image of ancient Assyria in the early nineteenth century

What did ancient Assyria represent in France and England during the earlier nineteenth century? Consideration of a key artistic monument from each country will allow us to focus on Assyria's primary associations in the period in which the impetus to excavate first developed. To begin, though, we must locate Assyria, and Mesopotamia, both geographically and temporally.[10]

Mesopotamia refers to the land between the Tigris and Euphrates rivers in what is modern-day Iraq. In antiquity, it was for millenia the site of many and varied cultures, chief among them the Assyrian empire centered in northern Mesopotamia and the Babylonian kingdom of southern Mesopotamia. The best-known capitals of these two ancient kingdoms were Nineveh and Babylon, respectively. The names of both resounded in Western discourse (and also blended to some extent), largely through accounts circulated by Greco-Roman writers as well as biblical sources.[11] The view of Mesopotamia communicated to the West derived from the accounts of peoples central to Western self-definition, the ancient Hebrews and those of classical antiquity. That is, Mesopotamia was seen not on its own terms, but rather via those of its historical antagonists. Through these accounts, largely considered documentary in the earlier nineteenth century, Mesopotamia was taken as a cautionary tale, a site of sloth, sin, violence, and transgression: the West's first great 'Other'.[12]

In the nineteenth century, the area was a province at the far eastern edge of the Ottoman empire, a region of semiautonomous *pashaliks* each governed primarily by a local *pasha*, though officially under the control of the Ottoman ruler in Istanbul. Seen by Western travellers as a remote and unwelcoming locale of largely unrelieved desert, Mesopotamia was not part of the itinerary of the Grand Tour, which preferred the more impressive and accessible monuments of Egypt, Palestine, Greece, and the Turkish lands. In a telling turn of illogic, the relatively few nineteenth-century travelogues of the area that existed often used the seemingly 'wasted' state of the land and its current inhabitants to emphasize the notable evils ascribed to its ancient population. Mesopotamia's current state was seen as a lasting trace of the divine punishments said to have rained upon its ancient rulers Sardanapalus of Assyria and Nebuchadnezzar of Babylon.[13] What was not there was taken to prove what had been. Here, then, is the first and most obvious binarism involved in the constructed image of Assyria, in which Western achievement is contrasted with Eastern ruin, and taken as an index of the morality of the former versus the immorality of the latter.

The Western image of Assyria in the early nineteenth century thus subsumed present to past, consistently invoking ancient events supposed to have led to the reputedly wasted state of the region during the nineteenth century. More than any other work of its kind, John Martin's tremendously popular painting of *The Fall of Nineveh* attempted to document in detail such moments in the inherited narrative of ancient Assyria. Martin had made his name with another work of Mesopotamian imagery, *Belshazzar's Feast* of 1821. Seven years later, in *The Fall of Nineveh*, he returned to the subject, creating a work that exemplifies what Morton Paley has termed 'the apocalyptic sublime'.[14] Though perceptions of Assyria and Babylonia were frequently intermingled, and the similarities may have been seen as greater than the differences, *Belshazzar's Feast* (as Martin seems to have realized) is a subject which took place in Babylon, while *The Fall of Nineveh* allows us to address specifically the conception of Assyria.[15]

A huge painting (measuring 84" by 134"), *The Fall of Nineveh* was a vast spectacle of destruction, a panorama of violent disorder in an elaborately detailed setting. In it, the capital of the Assyrian empire is laid waste by invading armies. Martin detailed, to an explicit internal scale, 100-foot walls and a gateway twice that size. At the far right he created the tomb of Ninus, the legendary founder of Nineveh. In the middle ground, the armies of the siege set upon soldiers and citizens of Nineveh, who are in various stages of capitulation. Further, in the same area are civilian fighters, described by Martin as 'Fathers and husbands defending their children and wives'. By contrast, many of the Ninevite soldiers have broken rank, and flee in terror before the well-ordered invaders. A sea of vast columns connects foreground and background, a hybrid order combining Egyptian and Indian architectural features.

Among the most striking features of *The Fall of Nineveh*, a key to both its legibility and profitability, was Martin's descriptive brochure, which circulated with the work. The brochure describes the architecture as 'invented as the most appropriate for a city situate [sic] betwixt the two countries [Egypt and India] and necessarily in frequent intercourse with them'.[16] As we approach the foreground of the image, looking down omnisciently upon a wing of the royal palace, we can make out the figure the descriptive brochure puts at the heart of the drama. At the edge of the steps, gesturing toward the pyre being built for him at left, is Sardanapalus, the legendary final king of Assyria, said to have 'exceeded all his predecessors in sloth and luxury'. As his leaderless army broke apart, the king, we are told

retired into his palace, in a court in which he caused a vast pile of wood to be raised; and, heaping upon it all his gold and silver, and royal apparel, and at the same time enclosing his eunuchs and concubines in an apartment within the pile, he set fire thereto, and so destroyed himself and the rest.[17]

This quotation in the brochure, from a nineteenth-century reference source, largely distills the facts from ancient accounts. But it does not precisely account for Martin's picture, in which the pyre is not located in an apartment within the palace but rather in open space adjoining the city itself.

This sort of disjuncture abounds between the image and the texts purported to explain it. Thus while one portion of the text acknowledges that there is no biblical description of the scene, a quote from the book of Nahum is nonetheless used specifically to justify the action of the queen (also unmentioned in ancient accounts). In Martin's conception she 'casts a farewell look of love and regret upon the king' before being led off to safety, in the opposite direction from the king, together with her maids and advisers. Similarly, in another sort of disjuncture, some of the architectural decoration of Nineveh is justified by Herodotus's description of a temple located not in Nineveh but in Babylon.[18]

Beyond serving mere factual explanation, Martin's brochure testifies to a certain referential obsession, a need to justify. Assembling a bulwark of authoritative sources comes to be more important than demonstrating any internal consistency among them. The brochure is choked with a variety of heterogeneous texts, including much of the Biblical book of Nahum, contemporary reference works, various classical citations, and a poetic account of the incident. But they too are as much pretexts for Martin's inventions as factual validations of the proffered spectacle.

Martin's image of ancient Nineveh exemplifies both the particular subject and judgemental tone that dominated the popular conception of Assyria in the early nineteenth century. The sheer sublime charge of Martin's huge, animated image holds in check, or at least disguises, the jarring discontinuities of the sources from which it is fashioned. In all, the work testifies to a need both to construct and justify an ancient Assyrian 'other'.

Martin's work was well known in France. Throughout the later 1820s and early 1830s Martin's elaborate prints after his oil paintings circulated widely there, to critical, popular, and even royal acclaim, receiving a gold medal from Charles X in 1829. His painting *The Deluge* made a sensation and won a further gold medal at the Salon of 1834.[19] But while Martin's image was circulated among overlapping French and English audiences, to assess its implications more fully it must be seen in counterpoint to a French work of the same subject, begun the year before Martin's *Fall of Nineveh.*

Eugène Delacroix's *The Death of Sardanapalus* stands today as the most famous representation of Assyria of the nineteenth century.[20] The work caused a sensation at the Salon of 1827–8. As with Martin's image, there is further evidence of the work's continuing popularity. Several engravings of the painting exist, as well as a number of copies both by the artist himself and later followers. A further parallel to the cross-Channel currency of Martin's image is that Delacroix's work in the 1820s embraced a number of English sources, notably Shakespeare and Byron. Byron's play *The Tragedy of Sardanapalus*, first published in 1821, has often been considered an inspiration for Delacroix's painting.[21] Thus, while Delacroix's work, like Martin's, suggests a certain common interest in Assyria in France and England, the considerable difference between the two images testifies also to the remarkable degree of invention and variety allowed by the subject. However paradoxical, this 'mobility' of subject consistently coexists with the referential exactitude of both Martin and Delacroix.[22]

Indeed, the treatment by the classically educated Delacroix of the subject corresponds more precisely to the description quoted above from Martin, as the scene is now set inside, within the king's palace, in a locale controlled by his gaze. The smoke of the conflagration already has begun to fill the chamber, and the room is littered with the concubines, servants, animals, and other treasures being destroyed as the king watches.

But Delacroix's scene cannot be taken as a closer transcription of a textual source. To the contrary, this work also maps itself on a field of overlapping and discontinuous textual referents. First, Byron's soulful conception of Sardanapalus is not compatible with that of the classical historians. Byron's play, in fact, does not even include this scene of brilliant immolation. Beyond the divergence between the classical and Byronic conceptions, a third text further problematizes the precise subject. This text is contemporary with Delacroix, and one to which his work clearly was meant to refer. An unattributed paragraph, in quotation marks, was published in the Salon catalogue accompanying the work's original exhibition. Its description of Sardanapalus and his setting follows approximately the account of Diodorus Siculus (the major classical authority for the incident), but also mentions two other characters, including a Bactrian woman, Aïscheh, who is mentioned nowhere else among the established sources of the legend, and does not seem clearly identifiable within Delacroix's image.

Visually, the same sort of referential calculus is work here as in Martin's image. Delacroix again creates Assyria through citations from a wide and heterogeneous range of sources, always substantiating the most imaginary and sensational by including elements agreed to be authentic and attested. But whereas Martin explicitly claimed to have invented a single period style used more or less consistently in the setting, Delacroix employs a pastiche of visual references from a variety of ancient and contemporary cultures. In Delacroix's attempt to pass off details of architecture, costume, and implements as Assyrian, convincing cases have been made for his painstaking transposition of archaic Greek, Mughal Indian, Etruscan, and Egyptian sources in various aspects of the painting.[23]

Delacroix's work, like Martin's, creates a network of references to authoritative texts and artifacts. But the considerable differences between the two images, renditions of the same subject drawn from common sources of a given historical moment, only serve to further undermine the claim of each to objectivity. Ancient Assyria, then, serves as a mirror which reflects the different preconceptions and desires of the representer as much as it does any objective subject being represented. Western artists and audiences, while partaking of a widely accepted network of established references, also differently construe the imagery of a foreign culture in a way related to their own cultural differences. The subject of the fall of Nineveh thus floats on a sea of references without being precisely tied to any one. It is strikingly open to individual manipulation.

Delacroix's conception of the subject, with its explicit violence, sexuality, and cruelty, contrasts sharply with the mock-heroic and sentimentalized conception of Martin. Martin's placement of the king bestows a certain privilege, as he engages in a grand pointing gesture that elevates him above the height of the crowd. Delacroix's king, by contrast, lies in darkness outside the main focus of the composition. Rather than acting he watches impassively.

Further, there is a remarkable difference between the two images in the treatment of gender relations. Martin presents active, loving, familial relations between the sexes. We have seen this already between king and queen, and the fathers fighting to defend their daughters. Even the king's favorite concubine, who is to follow him to her death, leans her head gently on his bosom. Delacroix's Sardanapalus, of course, who watches calmly as his concubines are abjectly murdered, could not be more different.

The differing gender conceptions of Martin and Delacroix reflect different social norms, but also reflect different imaginations. More than a decade ago, Linda Nochlin described *The Death of Sardanapalus* as 'a fantasy space' into which the artist's own erotic and sadistic desires could be projected. As she wrote, '[It is not] Western's man power over the Near East that is at issue, but rather, I believe, contemporary Frenchmen's power over women ...'.[24] This was a decisive move away from interpreting the work purely in terms of the objective conditions of its visual and textual sources, locating the work as well in the subjectivity of the Western artist. Looking more closely at the dynamics of gender in Delacroix's work from the standpoint of reception aesthetics, however, it hardly seems that admitting one interpretation excludes the other.[25] Rather, these two forms of power – Western man's power over the Near East and that of the contemporary Frenchman over women – are related within the work.

Delacroix's *Sardanapalus* thematizes viewing itself. Drawing on the method of reception aesthetics, we can locate the work's 'implied viewer' and then construct a relationship between this viewer and the figures in the work. Especially when seen, as Nochlin suggests, specifically within its masculine-dominated milieu of reception, the work clearly employs both forms of power-relations. The decentered position of the king gives way to the even more privileged view of the women's bodies, and other objects offered to the (presumed male) viewer.[26] To extend Nochlin's observation, the viewer's relation to the women, like that of Sardanapalus to the women, can stand for the power of the contemporary Frenchman over women. Yet at the same time the relation of this same implied viewer to Sardanapalus, as like genders engaged in the same action of viewing, reflects on just the same level the power of West over East. For even as the viewer is intimately present in the room with Sardanapalus, he is also in a position of superiority to the doomed, effeminate ruler. The viewer is thus in a position to validate the excoriating description of Sardanapalus by an early-nineteenth-century critic as 'a prince whose name has become synonymous with debauchery and passivity of the most degraded and notorious sort'.[27]

Considering Delacroix and Martin together, we can see that while relations of gender in conceptions of Assyria may vary, this power of West over East is common to both images. The viewer's closeness to Delacroix's Sardanapalus, and even participation with him in the same activity of viewing, is countered by the infamy of the king's name, and the fate that awaits him. In Martin's work, while the conception and composition are vastly different from Delacroix's, the relation of viewer to subject is comparable. The high, omniscient viewpoint now insulates the viewer from the threat of the action while providing a panoramic view. Even if Sardanapalus is identifiable among the crowd, he is only slightly larger than the rest of the doomed multitude in the distant, roiling sea of the battle. The closest figures to the viewer are the 'rulers' of the state (unattested by any literary source), gesturing toward the heavens and cursing Sardanapalus for ignoring their counsel. Their rebuke is a metaphor for the Western viewer's own stance toward the scene.

More generally, then, the pattern of commonalities and divergences between the two paintings both confirms and complicates the conventional binarist model of exoticism. Each work clearly reinforces the conception of Assyria as a moralizing and cautionary tale, a counterexample to Western 'progress':

a place picturesque, violent, sensual, and, perhaps most significant, doomed. Each work clearly looks down upon its subject, in the directed, imperialistic power relation between West and East dominant at the time. At the same time, the palpable differences we have noted mitigate against finding this binary situation completely adequate as an explanation. There is neither a single Assyria nor a single, given West. Instead, as we have seen, the subject metamorphoses as it circulates among different cultural nodes within the West. The enormous differences of subject, setting, treatment, and even style between Martin and Delacroix testify to the heterogeneity of the Western audience. This in turn has major importance for theorizing nineteenth-century exoticism.

The features we have examined here in the representation of Assyria seem to confirm a judgment that has only recently emerged in postcolonial studies. Rather than a single dominant monolith, the Western conception of 'the East' was multiple, fragmented, and localized. We have found, instead of a closed and coherent system, something closer to what Ali Behdad has recently called Orientalism's 'principle of discontinuity', its dispersion of authority through intermingled but incomplete networks of reference.[28] The authority of exoticist reference in such a system is deferred from an individual representation and taken up, unevenly and idiosyncratically, by a pre-existent repertory of assumptions.

A similar feature has already been noted specifically in connection with nineteenth-century exoticist painting. In her study of Antoine-Jean Gros's *Plague-Stricken of Jaffa*, Darcy Grimaldo Grigsby has observed that 'Orientalist discourse represents its own incompleteness.'[29] It is through just this incompleteness, this purport to represent what is beyond the validating capability of the Western viewer, that the cultural boundedness of the artistic conception is enunciated. These circumstances are at the heart of the discontinuity of exoticist representation. They are the founding conditions for the exoticist 'mobility' we have noted above.

Images such as those of Martin and Delacroix, then, are clearly evidence of a widespread interest in Assyria. But juxtaposing them uncovers the slippery, subtle working exoticist signifier. It is a process, as we have seen, that begins by appealing to a binary relationship between West and East, even while amending the particular subject matter in different ways to fit different situations.

In short, the representation of Assyria must be investigated with a full sense of its Western context, as much as its individual meaning. In precisely this manner, I want to follow Assyria's representational fortunes in France and England through two successive moments. First, we will consider the response to Assyrian archaeological discoveries in the years around 1850, and second, we will look briefly at some representations of Mesopotamia from the years following the discoveries. As we shall see, these discoveries did nothing to 'correct' the imaginative constructions of the earlier artists. Despite new findings based on actual artifacts, Assyria continued to be explicitly infused with the character and expectations of its audience. Further, the debate inspired by its artifacts brought up a new kind of controversy, which emerged from vexing questions about their aesthetic value.

Crises of discovery: the motivation and circulation of early Assyrian archaeology

Following further the European representation of Mesopotamia necessitates a shift from art to archaeology. This underlines the interdependence of the two activities and specifies the contemporary political and cultural conditions under which such representation took place. Like the works of art we have just considered, in their treatment of the actual Mesopotamia (and Mesopotamians) France and England asserted both unique identities and common assumptions. Just as we have noted the overlap of audiences and sources drawn on by Martin and Delacroix, so too the archaeological rediscovery of the ancient Neo-Assyrian kingdom owes much to the projects for geo-political dominance of the two countries. The rivalry of France and England was played out, in part, through the amassing of remains.[30]

Already in the 1820s word was circulating in Europe that the remains of the great Mesopotamian kingdoms had been located. The first sentence of Martin's brochure states that 'The mighty cities of Nineveh and Babylon have long since passed away, and, till lately, the traveller hath in vain sought for the spot where their dust reposed.'[31] The recent development noted in England was indeed part of a chain that led, ironically, to France's making the premiere discovery.

Three years before Martin's picture, in 1825, a collection of some fifty-odd ancient Babylonian baked clay tablets, bricks, and related objects entered the collection of the British Museum. Assembled by Claudius James Rich, and donated to the museum upon his death at age 34, this modest collection was the first significant assembly of ancient Mesopotamian artifacts. Together with Rich's several popular and detailed publications on the sites of ancient Babylon and Nineveh, they raised the profile of Mesopotamia in European discourse.[32]

Rich's presence in Mesopotamia, and the European public's interest, grew from a distinct, and hardly disinterested, source. Instead, they were a by-product of a strategy to promote colonial interests. Rich had been appointed in 1807 as the British East India Company's first 'resident' in Baghdad, in Southern Mesopotamia. His primary mission was defensive. The success of

Napoleon's Egyptian campaign in the previous years (and Britain's own failed occupation of Alexandria in 1807) raised English fears of further French conquests in the region. Rich was to shore up British interests in Mesopotamia, particularly seeing to the maintenance of overland and river routes to India. Mesopotamia thus had a specific function in the map of English interests. The location of Mesopotamia in Martin's brochure as directly between Egypt and India thus bears particular relevance, situating it directly between these contemporary sites of Western power and contention.

As the immediate political threat passed, Rich's interest in the ancient history of Mesopotamia grew. His memoir on Babylon quickly went through four editions and was followed by a second, while a memoir of his visit to Northern Mesopotamia, with a considerable portion devoted to ancient Nineveh, was published posthumously.[33] Thus even in the two decades following his death in 1821, Rich's work continued to bring to attention both textual and artifactual evidence of ancient Mesopotamia. The last works bearing his name were published in 1839.

The circulation of Rich's findings on ancient history and archaeology do not mark a complete break from the overtly political nature of his earlier work, but rather point to the establishment of archaeology as a new arena of contention for the European powers. Around 1841, a French consulate was opened in Mesopotamia. As Baghdad had been taken by the British, the French placed their toehold nearly 200 miles to the north, in the city of Mosul – which proved to be located as strategically for archaeology as for any other purpose. Beside its importance for trade and manufacture (notably a delicate textile soon dubbed in French *mousseline*), Mosul also boasted a location directly across the Tigris from the enormous mounds that had been (correctly) presumed by Rich to be the remains of ancient Nineveh.

In 1842, Paul-Émile Botta was named to the newly created post at Mosul, largely through the backing of Jules Mohl, the driving force behind the Société Asiatique, then the leading organization in France devoted to the study of Near Eastern and Asian languages and the collection of related artifacts. Botta began excavations almost immediately, without official permission from the Ottoman government even to dig much less remove any remains.[34] When little was turned up at the site of Nineveh, Botta moved his entourage to the village of Khorsabad, about 15 miles to the northeast, and began almost immediately to make spectacular finds. From the start of work on 20 March 1843, as he later put it, 'I had the first revelation of a new world of antiquities.'[35]

Botta's letters to Mohl were published and annotated by the latter in the Société's *Journal Asiatique* the following year. These documents, which constitute Botta's only written work to receive any large public distribution, give the first descriptions of Assyrian art published in the West. They were disseminated widely throughout the French and English press, the first dispatches of a remarkable discovery.[36] In Botta's letters, and Mohl's annotations, we find the demands of antiquarian science tied to those of imperialist accumulation.

First, it is clear that a nationalist motivation was central, and that the recovered artifacts were meant from the start to be sent to France and adorn its national collections. Mohl, for instance, assures the reader in an addendum to Botta's letters that 'everything admitting of removal will be sent to France, and there form an Assyrian museum, unique throughout the world ... [U]ntil the Louvre shall be embellished by a hall of Assyrian Sculptures, Europe cannot profit by the discovery of Khorsabad.'[37] Mohl neatly takes France for all of Europe, the measure of his nationalistic viewpoint. It was also through his efforts that permission from the Ottoman government was ultimately obtained for the French acquisition of the artifacts.

Second, and more pervasive, is the scientific/antiquarian project enunciated in Botta's writings. Botta's letters are primarily dedicated to providing an objective transcription of the carved images and cuneiform texts discovered in the underground chambers of Khorsabad. Botta, trained as a natural scientist by an associate of the naturalist Georges Cuvier, had been previously engaged in the collection of biological and botanical specimens. The positivist, descriptive framework of classificatory science is behind the exhaustive coverage of the letters.

Last, however, one finds in Botta's letters something almost unprecedented from Rich's frame of reference: aesthetic judgement. An Assyrian group is said to be superior to the Achaemenid sculpture of Persepolis with '... more animation in the figures and greater anatomical science in the design ... these bas-reliefs give favorable evidence of the tastes and skill of those by whom they were executed'. Another figurative relief is described as 'extremely well sculptured, and the *tout ensemble* has so Grecian an air, that I [almost] doubted its origin ...'.[38] Once uncovered, the huge, elaborately sculpted stones of Assyrian art posed an unexpected visual interest, bearing comparison even with ancient Greek sculpture, the paradigm of classicism. Yet while the language of aesthetic evaluation is dispersed throughout Botta's report, it always plays a subordinate role in his descriptions.

These three modes of evaluation, then – nationalistic, antiquarian, and aesthetic valuation – attended the introduction of the fruits of Assyrian archaeology to a Western audience. Together, they account for virtually all of the published text of Botta's letters. While they establish discursive norms more generally for the Western evaluation of Assyrian antiquities, just as with Martin and Delacroix, they also present terms used by agents of the different countries to conflict and oppose each other. For the same touchstones will be seen to be of equal relevance, although in different proportions and to very different effect, in the communications of the English discoveries which soon followed those of the French.

The history of English archaeology in Assyria begins not with an official appointment, but rather with the stealthy trip of Austen Henry Layard, then an unofficial aide to the British ambassador at Constantinople, Stratford Canning.[39] In November 1845, with a small grant and strict instructions from Canning, Layard traveled from Constantinople to Mosul, posing as a traveler. Excavating tools were prepared for him in secret, and with a small group he began digging just south of Nineveh in the more remote town of Nimrud, which featured a mound rivaling that of Nineveh. Layard made discoveries as quickly as Botta, finding on the first day of digging major portions of two separate Assyrian palaces. Layard's work was ultimately as productive as Botta's, if not more.

Like Botta's, Layard's actions too were illegal under Ottoman law, and only later were remedied with retroactive permissions obtained by Canning from the Sultanate. He thus attempted to shield his work as much as possible from the pasha of Mosul (whom he described as a cunning adversary). Equally, at least, Layard hid his actions from Botta. However he conceived Ottoman interests in the artifacts, he clearly recognized the power of a French claim to the discoveries and sought to work against it. Layard's later work, *Nineveh and its Remains*, triumphantly detailed the many maneuvers and subterfuges involved in his activities.[40] In its own way, it is comparable to the travel narratives of Mesopotamia mentioned above. Though enlivened by much description of contemporary Mesopotamian customs and cultures, it is driven by an interest in what was literally underneath the place itself, which led to conflict with the indigenous inhabitants.

In the reception of the Assyrian discoveries, precisely the same interpretive touchstones were at work in the English situation as in the French. Canning, for one, provided for Layard the same tone of national chauvinism as did Mohl for Botta. He wrote to the Prime Minister to justify his sponsorship of Layard: 'M. Botta's success at Nineveh [sic] has induced me to venture in the same lottery, and my ticket has turned up a prize … there is much reason to believe that Montague House [the British Museum] will beat the Louvre hollow.'[41] The antiquarian value of the discoveries was vouched for principally by Henry Creswicke Rawlinson, a leading scholar in the decipherment of Mesopotamian cuneiform since the mid-1830s. It was on Rawlinson's recommendation, together with that of Canning, that the British Museum ultimately agreed to sponsor Layard's excavation.[42]

Rawlinson had acquired the position of Baghdad resident originally created for Rich. Heir to Rich's political/antiquarian position, he also made explicit an inherent nationalistic interest, writing to Layard, for instance,

It pains me grievously to see the French monopolize the field, for the fruits of Botta's labors, already achieved and still in progress, are not things to pass away in a day but will constitute a nation's glory in future ages.[43]

Layard's approach to the Assyrian works, and much of the tone of his publicization of them, was based directly on the theme we have seen broached by Botta, but only occasionally expressed in his writing: the aesthetic evaluation of the Assyrian objects. In a letter about his discoveries, for instance, he wrote, '[the Assyrians'] knowledge of the arts is surprising, and greatly superior to that of any contemporary nation'. He went on, describing one of the colossal winged animals that became the very emblem of the Assyrian discoveries:[44]

The [colossal winged] lions lastly discovered, for instance, are admirably drawn, and the muscles, bones, veins quite true to nature, and portrayed with great spirit. There is also a great *mouvement* – as the French well term it – in the attitude of the animal, and 'sa pose est parfaite'; excuse the phrase, we have no equivalent. The human head, too, is really grand.[45]

Whereas Botta relied primarily on the language of the antiquarian, Layard most frequently expressed himself in terms redolent of his youthful training as an art conoisseur. Botta had also noted 'mouvement' in the works, but Layard described the works aesthetically at far greater length, and throughout much of his writing, both public and private.[46]

Notably, only in communication with his sponsors did Layard find reason to suppress this aestheticizing tendency. Writing to Canning, just a month after the letter just cited, Layard averred that the sculptures were 'undoubtedly inferior to the most secondary works of Greece or Rome'.[47] The necessity for leaving unquestioned the inherited hierarchies of the established artistic canon was enunciated directly to Layard by Rawlinson:

I still think the Nineveh marbles are not valuable as works of art … Can a mere admirer of the beautiful view them with pleasure? Certainly not, and in this respect they are in the same category with the paintings and sculptures of Egypt and India … We have specimens of the very highest art – and anything short of that is, as a work of art … valueless, for it can neither instruct nor enrapture us. I hope you understand this distinction and when I criticise design and execution, will understand I do so merely because your winged God is not the Apollo Belvedere.[48]

Throughout both France and England, there was little dispute over the antiquarian value of the Assyrian discoveries or the presumed right of European powers to appropriate these artifacts. But Layard's highlighting of the Assyrian artifact as aesthetic object, his concentration on the mode of aesthetic validation kept strictly subordinate by Botta, conflicted with the values of his sponsors. Aesthetic v. non-aesthetic, work of art v. antiquarian artifact: this becomes a further binary pairing in which the Western image of Assyria oscillates. Attention to the purely visual appearance of the Assyrian objects, in the aestheticizing framework suggested by Layard, is perceived to upset a tenet of conventional artistic taste: the dominance of the works of classical antiquity. This is a crucial moment in the reception of the Assyrian artifacts, the first intimation that transplanting the objects to Europe would not merely confirm historical and nationalist beliefs but also might have the power to interfere with established aesthetic doctrine.

Emphasis on aesthetic evaluation, or even extended attention to the visual features of Assyrian works, thus posed a threat that other forms of evaluation did not. In England, the aesthetic approach had clear social implications, carrying the works beyond the narrow circle that initially sponsored Layard's excavations. In a piece excerpted in the antiquarian *Athenaeum*, for instance, Layard wrote of Botta's discoveries in a way that honors all three touchstones of evaluation, while defiantly highlighting the aesthetic appeal of Assyrian art:

they are immeasurably superior to the stiff and ill-proportioned figures of the monuments of the Pharoahs. They discover a knowledge of the anatomy of the human frame, a remarkable perception of character, and wonderful spirit in the outlines and general execution. In fact, the great gulf which separates barbarian from civilized art has been passed.[49]

Without precisely calling the works equal to Greek art, Layard still clearly sets Assyria above the level of Egypt to which Rawlinson had confined it. A paragraph notice on Botta appeared soon after in the *Penny Magazine*, foremost among the cheap, popular, widely circulated magazines then proliferating in England. Notably, the *Penny Magazine* cites the *Athenaeum* as its source and closely follows Layard's language, but it concentrates almost exclusively on his aesthetic evaluation. It refers to 'exquisite taste', 'remarkable knowledge of anatomy', 'great intelligence and harmony of composition' and similar features of the artifacts.[50] Thus, especially through Layard's frame of aesthetic reification, the news of the Assyrian discoveries broke out of the smaller, more rarefied circle represented by the *Athenaeum* for the much larger, lower-class readership of the *Penny Magazine*.

The aesthetic challenge of Assyria took further shape as the Assyrian objects began to reach London and Paris in 1847. There they coexisted directly with the same kinds of sources and spoke to the same expectations we have seen earlier in the case of the images of Martin and Delacroix. These European images, as we have seen, were conceived within a network of established textual references to Assyria, as well as a basis in material evidence for conceiving an ancient Near Eastern culture. The discoveries of Layard and Botta were well positioned to aid in the material reconstruction of Assyria. Yet while on both nationalistic and antiquarian grounds the discoveries clearly were welcomed, the aesthetic treatment of the artifacts consistently posed challenges. An overview of the aesthetic interpretation of Assyria will illuminate the forms of aesthetic discourse at work in the two countries, as well as their social dynamic.

The Louvre's Assyrian display, the first ever mounted in the West, opened to the public in the presence of King Louis-Philippe on 1 May 1847. In the lengthy notice of the opening in *L'Illustration*, the foremost illustrated magazine of the time in France, the question of the aesthetic valuation of Assyria is deemed 'quite surprising'. This same sentence immediately continues, 'but the most important [questions] concern the details of royal usage, of military and domestic life, in a word, of Assyrian customs'.[51] The aesthetic is taken up, only to be deferred in favor of a more directly antiquarian mode of evaluation. In the same way, the question of whether Assyria stood beyond the achievements of Egyptian art, so vexing an assertion to Rawlinson, is also neatly deferred. The article states that when Assyria is compared to Egyptian, as well as to Greek and Etruscan art, it is apparent that 'they have a common origin'.

Still, all these concerns are affected, and overshadowed, by the presence of the king, and perhaps the particular historical moment of Assyria's entry into the French milieu. Louis-Philippe's government was under severe attack, and was to be overthrown in less than a year in the Revolution of 1848. *L'Illustration* stretched to connect the royalty of contemporary France with what was known of Assyrian kingship. It seized upon the same figures we have seen illustrated above by Martin and Delacroix:

Nebuchadnezzar, Sardanapalus or even Ninus himself, since we do not know his identity, the Assyrian monarch now sets foot on the banks of the Seine. A new, more worthy, home has been destined for him, the palace of our kings.[52]

The focus on kingship reflects not only the reputation of Assyria but also the government's consistent association with the excavation. Yet if the sponsorship provided any brief buttress for the king, the tie was disastrous for Mesopotamian excavation. While excavations had ceased provisionally in 1844, with the revolution the consulate at Mosul itself was suppressed, and the royalist Botta fell into disgrace.[53] He was reassigned to lesser positions, first in Jerusalem and later in Tripoli. He died forgotten in 1870, having returned to Europe only two years previously.

The trajectory of Botta's career is matched by the history of its official documentation. Botta's work, and that of the artist Eugène Flandin who was sent to record his finds, was enshrined lavishly in the huge, magisterial five-volume *Monument de Ninive*.[54] It is arguably the most elaborate publication ever devoted to Mesopotamian archaeology, an ancient Near Eastern successor to the Napoleonic *Description de l'Egypte*. Begun soon after the initial discoveries, it was the product of extraordinary outlays of time and money by Louis-Philippe's government. Botta and Flandin had each received an enormous honorarium of 60,000 francs. In all, the government spent almost three times as much on the publication itself as on the entire course of excavations it was meant to describe.[55]

Botta's grand book was the legacy of a very small circle of privileged authorities, whose power was clearly on the wane. While nearly complete (after four years of production) before the revolution, it ultimately appeared in 1849 and 1850, with a press run of only 300 copies. One of the most telling comments on his book appeared in a publication that had not even existed when Botta began to excavate; *Le Tour du Monde* was one of the new, cheap illustrated magazines of the Second Empire, devoted to the literature and imagery of travel. In 1863, on Botta's work, it opined:

It may be regretted that the results of [Botta's] labors have not been published in a form which promotes awareness of them and spreads his fame. Such volumes in a gigantic format, whose price runs into the thousands of francs, are no doubt monuments worthy of a great nation, but they are hardly accessible and will never break out of a very narrow circle.[56]

Mohl, Botta's initial sponsor, had protested about 'the unwieldy format and exorbitant price' of the book even at the time of its publication, but largely on the grounds of its restricting accessibility to the finds among scholars.[57] Here the writer is speaking instead on behalf of the newer and far larger audience of a non-specialist public. Strikingly, the writer pointed to England as a model of such dissemination: 'The wisely practical spirit of our neighbors across the English channel may serve as an example in this regard'.

Botta, then, was both beneficiary and victim of the extraordinary largesse of the July Monarchy. Such a pattern of support had ramifications for the public currency of Assyria itself. This is exemplified by the folio *Monument de Ninive*, a remarkable 'white elephant', as we have seen. But it continued, indeed accelerated, in the image of Assyria in French art after the excavations, as we will examine in the next section. In addition, as we have already begun to see, the contrast with the English coverage of the discoveries could not have been greater.

Much unlike the limited circulation of Botta's words and work in France, news of the Assyrian discoveries pervaded England in the years after Layard's discoveries and was made available at all social levels. Textual and visual information on Assyria appeared throughout the range of publications from the upper-class *Athenaeum* to the popular *Penny Magazine*.[58] The same palpable interest contributed to making Layard's *Nineveh and Its Remains*, an account of his first archaeological campaign and related matters, one of the greatest English best-sellers of the entire nineteenth century. This difference of circulation reflects in part the different arrangement by which Layard, as opposed to Botta, received compensation. He got very little direct support from the British Museum or any other governmental sponsor, but he profited greatly from the sale of his book, which was privately published.[59]

As news of the Assyrian artifacts was promulgated in England, they were frequently made to carry not only nationalistic and antiquarian value, as in France, but also religious significance, a development unique to the English situation. The discussion in both countries, however, nearly always included the inevitably controversial question of the aesthetic value of the works.

For instance, an exhaustive review of Layard's book in the upper-class *Quarterly Review* which covers all the themes mentioned above, is framed with the aesthetic evaluation of the objects. It begins by singling out 'the huge lion and bull' as 'by far the most remarkable and characteristic specimens of Assyrian art'. These works

impressed us with a strange, gigantic majesty, a daringness of conception, which was in no way debased by the barbaric rudeness of the execution, and on the other hand enhanced by its singular symbolic attributes. It is that kind of statue which it takes away one's breath to gaze on.[60]

Forty-odd pages later the reviewer has regained his breath, and adds that Assyrian works are nonetheless inferior to the 'true beauty' and 'exquisite anthropomorphism' of the Greeks. Nonetheless, he counts the discoveries as a new chapter in the history of art.

The *Quarterly Review* writer, reacting viscerally to an object that nonetheless refuses to obey reigning doctrines of sculpture in such matters as scale, finish, subject, and composition, exemplifies a position of ambivalence toward the Assyrian works. The writer is caught in the binary evaluation of the objects, between a tantalizingly aesthetic and a dutifully antiquarian appraisal of the works. Yet this is already a position of far more aesthetic sympathy to Assyria than that of Rawlinson or of others even more closely associated with the British Museum.

The immense popularity of the Assyrian works (and the insistence of the museum's Parliamentary overseers) kept them on public display, ultimately in new galleries designed especially for them.[61] Even so, a number of the museum's own trustees were downright hostile to the works. One trustee deemed them 'a parcel of rubbish' belonging 'at the bottom of the sea'.[62] The testimony of another, Sir Richard Westmacott Sr, elaborates on the position. A professor of sculpture at the British Royal Academy since 1827, Westmacott had served for decades as the 'sculpture advisor' to the museum's trustees. He was present at official meetings and, as the minutes confirm, held considerable sway in decisions about sculptural display. Asked by a Parliamentary commission in 1853 about the artistic worth of the Assyrian discoveries, Westmacott responded with an opinion even more aesthetically denigrating than Rawlinson. Specifically distinguishing them from the Elgin marbles, which are valuable for 'their excellence as works of art', he stated:

The Nineveh Marbles are very curious, and it is very desirable to possess them, but I look upon it that the value of the Nineveh Marbles will be the history that their inscriptions, if they ever are translated, will produce; because if we had one-tenth part of what we have of Nineveh art it would be quite enough as specimens of the arts of the Chaldeans, for it is very bad art ... The less people as artists, look at objects of that kind, the better.[63]

Westmacott's unbridled disapproval, however, was counterbalanced by an enormous outpouring of unqualified aesthetic approval for the artifacts. This was expressed on the part of the same popular audiences that thronged the British Museum (on the days they were allowed in) and that purchased Layard's book in record number (especially the cheaper 'popular edition'). As we have seen above with the *Penny Magazine*, these are the same audiences to whom the discoveries first penetrated in large part through the very language of aesthetic valuation.

For instance, in the preface to one of the many cheap, anonymous books on the discoveries, the reception of Layard's finds is described thus:

A city buried for more than twenty centuries offered its remains for comparison with the aspects of modern London or Paris; and the sculptured monuments of a bygone race rose up to offer a contrast with the works of modern art.[64]

Acceptance of Assyria as a contrast to modern art ultimately goes beyond the terms of contention above. Whereas the question had been whether it was comparable to the Greeks', Assyrian art could now be put to the same use for which the Greek was invoked in the nineteenth century: as a model for evaluating contemporary work, precisely the kind of looking at Assyria explicitly proscribed by Westmacott.

Similarly, one finds significant acknowledgement of Assyria in the central organ of middle-class artistic discourse in England, the *Art-Journal*. The *Art-Journal* carried a number of pieces on the Assyrian discoveries, such as an elaborately illustrated article in 1850 stating that 'the beauty of execution in each of these sculptures so strongly speak of their [the Assyrians'] acquirements also in the arts of peace'.[65] The accepted aesthetic achievement of the objects now allows for the superimposition of other values onto the Assyrians. For the first time, the process is not defined by external, textual sources. The image of Assyria offered by *Art-Journal* is not that of the barbarism attributed to them by others, but rather one of cultivation and refinement.

The most significant trace of the *Art-Journal*'s approval of Assyrian art came three years later, at about the same time the British Museum opened its Nineveh Gallery. The journal associates its own interest not only with Layard's campaign, but also with a central earlier crusader for a change in aesthetic canons:

it is a singular proof of the increased and increasing interest in all things appertaining to ancient Art, that Mr. Bonomi's *Nineveh and Its Palaces*, has also achieved a second edition, notwithstanding the deserved popularity of 'Layard's Nineveh'. When we remember the fight poor Haydon had for the Elgin Marbles, we cannot but congratulate ourselves on our 'progress'.[66]

The fight for the legitimation of the Elgin marbles, in the early nineteenth century, had lasted nearly two decades. It involved most authoritative figures of English artistic taste, and undermined the dominant sense of classicism embodied, most of all, by Sir Richard Payne Knight.[67] Despite their ultimate acceptance, Benjamin Robert Haydon, the indefatigable promoter of the Elgin works, committed suicide, penniless, in 1846, while Knight's influence rapidly faded after the affair.

The *Art-Journal*'s parallel between the reception of the Elgin marbles and that of the Assyrian artifacts posits an inevitable struggle over the acceptance of a heterodox form of artistic production. In light of the continued aesthetic resistance to the works by figures such as Rawlinson, Westmacott, and the British Museum Trustees, 'our progress' for the *Art-Journal* is not that of society as a whole, but the unique portion of the English art audience occupied by the backers of the aesthetic worth of Assyria, that is, the lower- and middle-class audiences of journals from the *Penny Magazine* to *The Illustrated London News* to the *Art-Journal* itself. Notably, representatives of both groups could invoke the Elgin marbles for their competing ideals.

In short, England's Assyrian archaeology as a whole had a variety of supporters. While some opinions about the objects were widely shared, the particular question of the aesthetic value of the objects split the public into opposing camps. Assyria's backers ultimately won the conflict in almost every particular. But what is crucial here is not merely the outcome of the situation but the way it forced a widespread debate which juxtaposed Assyria and the demands of art. Only by their setting the terms of debate in this way could Assyria win aesthetic validation, as in the extraordinary words of praise for Assyrian art as art we have noted above. Here too, the contrast with France could not be greater. No debate comparable to the one in England took place in France. Contrasting opinions about Assyria appeared rarely to confront each other. The French (middle- and lower-class) social groups who might have supported the idea of Assyrian artifacts as works of art were marginalized from the discoveries, and the circulation of Botta's work was constrained.[68]

By the early 1850s, then, France and England had acquired and placed on display roughly comparable collections of Assyrian artifacts. Yet, as we have seen, the two countries presented considerably different milieus of reception. Moreover, the subsequent archaeological fortunes of the two countries diverged, much to England's advantage. While the French excavation had been halted in the later 1840s, Layard returned to Mesopotamia in 1849 for a remarkable campaign that finally succeeded in unearthing ancient Nineveh itself, within the very mound first examined, and then abandoned, by Botta. In 1853, after the fall of the Second Republic, Mohl finally persuaded the succeeding government, the Second Empire, to reopen excavations. Victor Place was sent by the government to continue the work of Botta at Khorsabad. His tenure is most notable for the disastrous loss, through a transport mishap on the Tigris, of a huge cache of Assyrian antiquities entrusted to his care. In what Mohl lamented as 'an irreparable loss', Place's campaign inadvertently deposited on the river's bottom the contents of more than 120 cases of objects from Khorsabad (excavated both by him and Botta), as well as a large array of objects from Layard's excavation at Nineveh, which Place had been allowed to select for acquisition by the Louvre.[69] Subsequent salvage attempts met with only limited success.

In France, then, Assyrian archaeology was both beneficiary and victim of its close political ties. The reproduction and circulation of Assyrian artifacts was constrained by the dominant structure of archaeological sponsorship, largely directed by the small group of scholarly and political figures authorizing the effort. Thus, the essential French monument to Botta's discovery, *Monument de Ninive*, was both extraordinarily lavish and extraordinarily rare, effectively withheld from audiences beyond those of its narrow patronage group. Further, later excavations were hampered by the turbulent history of government sponsorship, as well as embarrassing mishaps.

The reception of Assyrian archaeology in England was far more diffuse. Information on the discoveries circulated far and wide in England, and in a variety of forms. This was aided particularly by the aestheticization of the objects promoted by Layard. Though appealing to many, they also provoked from some an opposing response. The objects were conceived within a bifurcated opposition as either aesthetically based works of art or as antiquarian artifacts. This aestheticization was crucial for the wide social circulation of the artifacts, for while antiquarian evaluation required a certain level of education and erudition, the aesthetic approach to the artifacts could be more widely shared across the social spectrum. At the same time, the aesthetic offered a framework of evaluation more specific and engaged with individual objects than a purely nationalistic (or religious) approach.

Constructing and controlling Assyrian imagery in the later nineteenth century

As we have seen, many of the same assumptions about ancient Assyria were active in France and England in the period before the excavations, even though they were expressed in different ways. The image of the fall of Nineveh served audiences in both countries as a sort of projection of various cultural identities and fascinations. In the period immediately after the discoveries, the two countries also acted in common, if, again, not in concord. They had clearly rivaled each other in the archaeology of the region (albeit with different degrees of success). Yet, the very different structures for archaeological reception in the two countries – circulating the finds to different audiences, through different media, and differing notably on the aesthetic value of the objects – worked to further uncouple the representation of Assyria in the two countries. As the fortunes of France and England in Mesopotamian archaeology came to diverge, so too did their images of the Assyrian past. Art and archaeology, past and present, conspired to underline a last notable bifurcation that has been at work throughout: France v. England.

To assess this contrast, we turn now to a few key representations of Assyria in France and England in the decades after the discoveries. These were not 'pure' attempts to emulate the formal qualities of Assyrian art. In both countries, such decontextualized emulation dates from the late nineteenth and early twentieth centuries, well after Assyria's initial reception.[70] By contrast, the range of representations of Assyria in the period closer to their initial display reflects the heterogeneous and discontinuous moment in which Assyrian antiquities appeared on the European horizon. Even though London and Paris both displayed considerable collections of relatively similar ancient Assyrian objects, the initial circulation of the discoveries fostered a vast, hybrid, and even contradictory array of representations and references.[71] Rather than focus the image of Assyria on a newly prominent visual repertory, we find instead the very contrary, as the variation of representations among different milieus (which we have called representational 'mobility'), was now considerably greater than before.

First, there is the question of continuity with the images created by Martin and Delacroix before the discoveries. Neither artist produced anything directly related to the newly visible Assyrian art. Martin died in 1854, one year after the British Museum formally completed its Assyrian galleries; Delacroix lived considerably longer, and even remarked on the extraordinary treatment of animals in Assyrian works.[72] Yet he never revised the imagery of *The Death of Sardanapalus* or otherwise directly used the visual evidence of Assyria. Indeed, the most telling evidence of Delacroix's relation to actual Assyrian art is a brief notation in his journal from 1858 making clear that it is not Delacroix himself, but rather a relative who was 'quite struck' with Assyrian art.[73]

Delacroix's stance toward Assyria exemplifies the nature of its artistic reception in mid-century France, and follows the same pattern as the passage from *L'Illustration*. Assyria is tacitly acknowledged, but also withheld from concerted artistic consideration. Indeed, this process, strictly controlling and even manufacturing Assyria to the requirements of the audience, accounts for the best-known and longest-lived visual reference to Assyria in nineteenth-century France, the 'Assyrian' profile.

The pose in profile, with a thick beard jutting directly downward from the chin, was claimed perhaps most famously by Gustave Courbet, as in his description of himself at the center of his 1855 *Atelier of the Painter*, as 'myself painting showing the Assyrian profile of my head'.[74] Many of Courbet's paintings of the 1850s show him from a similar angle. Contemporary caricatures also delighted in exaggerating this feature.[75] Much of Assyrian art consists of profile reliefs, and protruding beards are a common characteristic. These contemporary allusions, however, made no attempt to emulate the specific knotting and shaping of Assyrian beards, and Courbet's facial features are not directly comparable to the stylized Assyrian features.[76]

Courbet's 'Assyrian' profile, that is, does not indicate a deep interest in Assyrian art. It would hardly be identifiable as Assyrian on its own. Rather, Assyria offered an occasion for the artist's self-assertion. Courbet almost flaunted his lack of concern with the specifics of antique art, in a manner consistent with his subsumption of all past art to his contemporary concerns.[77]

Courbet's 'Assyrian' profile was a casual, even whimsical gesture of self-fashioning, barely acknowledging the actuality of Assyrian art. Yet its off-handedness, its actual neutralization of the particularity of Assyrian art, should be taken seriously as a means of popularizing Assyria. Strikingly, the Assyrian beard achieved a currency of its own in French visual culture, covering over much of the inherited image of ancient Assyria.

Thus Célestin Nanteuil's poster for the 1867 opera *Sardanapale* by Henri Becque and Victorin Joncières revisited Delacroix's subject without the slightest use of the repertory of Assyrian objects now available in the Louvre. The world of Sardanapalus was recreated instead with specifically Egyptian features such as curved architraves, swelling 'lotus' capitals, and even hieroglyphics. The cache of pots before the king are, like his costume, of classical form. Most prominent among them is a Greek amphora. This heterogeneous assembly is sanctioned as Assyrian by the king's conspicuously 'Assyrian' beard.

The coining of a certain facial feature as Assyrian stood, then, as a substitute for Assyrian art itself. Thus, in the theoretical terms discussed above, exoticism does not merely convey information but actually constructs its subject, producing an Assyria that is more assimilable to established norms than the actual works. The 'Assyrian' beard is the very emblem of this process of assimilating, denaturing, and ultimately constructing Assyria: a hybrid, second-order visual creation.

Finally, counterbalancing an invented Assyrian feature that had achieved considerable currency, the look of actual Assyrian artifacts was strictly controlled, even erased from the artistic contexts in which they had clearly been noted. For instance, in one of Edgar Degas's notebooks from around 1860 are detailed drawings of a number of Near Eastern antiquities, including a portion of an Assyrian relief.[78] They form part of the context of his painting of *Semiramis Constructing a City*. It has been plausibly suggested that the painting was partly inspired by an 1860 production of Rossini's opera *Semiramide*, one which utilized elaborately researched costumes and decor based on the Assyrian discoveries.[79] While Degas would thus seem to have done painstaking preparatory work comparable to that of Delacroix, little in Degas's painting takes up with any specificity the wealth of Assyrian details in these would-be sources. Semiramis, the legendary builder of Babylon, and her party are dressed in neo-classical belted gowns, while the city surveyed by the queen is designed entirely of Greco-Roman architecture. Only the shaped hair of Semiramis and perhaps a chariot just slightly visible bear even a faint resemblance to features that can be found anywhere on Assyrian reliefs.[80] Like Nanteuil's poster, Degas's work largely (though not quite completely) excluded Mesopotamian sources from a Mesopotamian subject.

The examples of Courbet and Degas testify to a fragmentation and marginalization of Assyria in the realist mode that dominated the French art of the time of the discoveries. But the pattern is only slightly different in the proto-Symbolist work of their contemporary Gustave Moreau. A considerable portion of Moreau's library was devoted to 'exotic' arts, while the majority of his paintings depict subjects derived from biblical and classical themes.[81] This might seem a set of interests more amenable to Assyria than the contemporary ones favored by Courbet and Degas. Further, Moreau's penchant for covering his canvases with sgraffito-like ornamentation is visually comparable to the dense ornamentation and use of cuneiform texts in Assyrian artifacts.

Moreau devoted part of a sketchbook from the 1860s to Assyrian works at the Louvre, and clearly knew of the discoveries through printed sources as well.[82] Yet none of his finished paintings directly employs Assyrian subjects or motifs. Perhaps the closest is a full-scale study for *The Suitors* in which an Assyrian figure in a commonly employed gesture of salute is lightly sketched in among the otherwise classically garbed figures seeking the hand of Penelope.[83]

In Moreau's work too, then, Assyria is a very faint visual trace, a source largely excluded. More generally, the seeming solidarity of such different artists as Courbet, Degas, and Moreau in their eliding of Assyrian references is testimony to the continuing deferral and submersion of Assyria throughout contemporary French art. To look for Assyrian imagery in France is, quite literally, to search for glaring absences as well as almost ghostly presences.

The nature of Assyrian representation is, in part, a legacy of the centralized pattern through which Assyrian artifacts were promulgated in France. As we have seen, Assyria's French publicists were beholden to a small circle, and publications were directed to this privileged group. Furthermore, while the question of the aesthetic value of the artifacts was raised, it was still largely subordinated to historical and antiquarian modes of inquiry. Finally, the complexities and misfortunes of French archaeology contribute also to the low standing of the artifacts. In all, it would seem that the effect of the unprecedented initial discovery and later display and circulation of Assyrian art in France was, paradoxically, virtually to erase its presence from contemporary artistic representation.

The image of ancient Assyria in English art in the decades after the discoveries contrasts enormously with that which we have seen in France. It engages with the visual specificity of ancient Assyrian work, rather than largely withholding it, as in the French examples. Paradoxically, the discoveries seem almost to mark an end to the French interest in Assyria, as Delacroix's reaction to the discoveries might suggest. By contrast, the English treatment of Assyria extends the concerns we have found in the pre-discovery imagery of Assyria in both countries. A perfect example is Ford Madox Brown's *Dream of Sardanapalus*.[84] Although Sardanapalus is presented in an 'Assyrian' profile, it is now, unlike in Nanteuil's conception, among the least of a range of Assyrian signifiers within the image. In fact, most of the details of setting and costume in the work come directly and specifically from Assyrian reliefs. Two Assyrian winged animals stand by the sides of the doorway, while the frieze behind the king is filled with figures derived from Assyrian reliefs, most notably the winged, bird-headed genie to the right of the bull. This figure is an Assyrian *apkallu*, a variant of the same figure utilized by Moreau.[85] But Brown, unlike Moreau, presents the image in its entirety, including wings, drapery, and implements.

The more functional features of the scene are equally beholden to Assyrian imagery. Sardanapalus reclines on a couch similar in shape and detailing to that on which the king lies in a famous entertainment scene among the Assyrian finds. His earring and armlet derive from features shown on the reliefs. Even the crown that tops the armor he has set aside is that specifically reserved for the king.[86]

Brown's conception, in short, uses a plethora of visual details from Assyrian artifacts to realize what seems an authentic Assyrian setting. Yet the image is actually no less composite, no less the result of a discontinuous array of references (both visually and textually), than any from before the archaeological discoveries. The Assyrian discoveries, that is, did not lead to a truer or more exact conception of Assyria. Rather, they worked to transform the range of terms through which ancient Assyria was construed, opening up new fictive possibilities for Assyrian subjects. In Brown's image, along with the greater dependence on the now unimpeachable sources in Assyrian art, we find a tiled, or even parquet floor, a purely nineteenth-century anachronism. Even more, this same shift toward the authority of ancient visual remains sanctioned a turn toward a subject now derived specifically from Byron, dropping the precedent of ancient literary sources on which the earlier works of Martin and Delacroix depended. Brown's image depicts a specific moment (the opening of Act 4, Scene 1) of Byron's *Sardanapalus*. It reflects the quiet, sensitive tone of the play, far from the spectacular, apocalyptic conceptions of Martin and Delacroix. Sardanapalus, in Byron's story, has returned wounded from previously leading his army. His left forearm is bandaged. His Greek slave Myrhha (an invention of the Hellenophile Byron) comforts the king as he lies hallucinating, in a dream that prophesies the end of the Assyrian kingdom.

In Brown's *Sardanapalus*, then, the antiquity of the visual details provides an authoritative anchor in tradition which allows the artist to jettison the (previously indispensible) authority associated with ancient texts. In addition, the considerable attention paid to Assyrian art may well be related to the more positive conception of the king. The *Art-Journal* remarked, as we have seen, that Assyrian art seemed to speak well of the civilized achievement of the Assyrians. In the same way, Brown's work envisions in detail both an Assyrian ambience and a soulful, sensitive leader. Though Sardanapalus is still doomed, it is now an occasion for pathos rather than judgemental condescension. Even the viewpoint has changed from the earlier conceptions of Martin and Delacroix, as the viewer is now on the same level as the king, sharing this tender, vulnerable moment.

Brown's work pays great attention to the material specifics of Assyrian art. It is the culmination of the historicist tendency toward material validation in the mid-nineteenth-century conception of Assyria. It also marks a change in the very image of Assyria, coinciding with the addition of Assyrian artifactual sources, but also allowing a shift from the more ostensibly authoritative classical and biblical sources of Martin and Delacroix to that of Byron.

A final work from slightly later, Edwin Long's then-famous *Babylonian Marriage Market*, situates Assyrian imagery within a more diverse audience, and reflects further on larger themes of exoticist representation. Long's work not only adheres to the general mode of conception of Martin and Delacroix; it also inherits the thematization of vision and the gendered imaginary which we found in the earlier works. Yet even as it sought to take up the previous gender dynamic, the changed nature of both subject and audience unsettled its unquestioned binarism of male versus female roles.

Long's subject derives from Herodotus. The painting was exhibited at the British Royal Academy with a lengthy quotation from a nineteenth-century popularization of the work. The custom ascribed to the Babylonians, which Herodotus deemed their wisest, was that once a year all eligible females were gathered together in their villages for men who wished to marry. The most beautiful among them was presented first, for purchase by the highest bidder, followed by the others, in decreasing order of beauty and selling for decreasing amounts. Finally, the deformed and ugly were presented, and the money of those who purchased the more beautiful women went to subsidize the takers of the uglier women, so that:

the plainest was got rid of to some cynical worthy, who placidly preferred lucre to looks. By transferring to the scale of the ill-favoured the prices paid for the fair, beauty was made to endow ugliness, and the rich man's taste was the poor man's gain.[87]

Long's subject is the transformation of women into currency. The characteristic feature of this system is the hierarchical ranking and measurement of the women/commodities. Long's primary innovation lay in setting the scene in a place devoted solely to such ranking, one without a trace of the setting of the village mentioned by Herodotus. Instead, Long set the work in an auction house. Some of the male viewers hold boxes of coins and other valuable objects, while a balance stands in front of the auctioneer's podium.

The woven beards, bracelets, earrings, wrapped garments, headwear, and similar features that are pictured on Assyrian reliefs are transferred to the crowd of male viewers in the picture. The crowd is, though, leavened with some black Africans, a few Italic figures, and a white-bearded, Rembrandtesque Jew. The women, too, notably in their hairstyles, rounded heads, and similarly wrapped garments, are modeled after Assyrian sources. The setting is just as consciously historicized, as most of the wall and floor decorations, the pattern on the curtain, and even the relief on the auctioneer's podium derive from Assyrian reliefs and other decorations.[88]

The reception of Long's work, painted in 1875, suggests that Assyria by this time had become assimilated by Western viewers. On the details of setting, the *Art-Journal* stated, 'We accept the archaeological details as presented to us, and without any hesitancy, fix our attention on the rare disposition of figures.'[89] Long's archaeological details are completely credible to the *Art-Journal* and also quite unremarkable, merely a prologue for the examination of the painting's figures. Yet just as the look of ancient Assyria became commonplace to the English viewer, it highlights larger themes at work throughout the nineteenth-century representation of Assyria. Notably, unlike Brown, but like John Martin before him, Long conflates Assyria and Babylonia. Even more, the primary subject of the work is the display of women, and of men gazing at them with an eye toward possession. This reiterates the gendered power structure of Delacroix's work. The composition again flatters the viewer at the expense of the male figures in the scene.

At the far right, a man looks over a fence at the private zone of the women waiting to be displayed. His relation to these women mirrors that of the painting's viewer to the woman being displayed on the stage. In both cases, the male viewer sees the woman from behind and must guess at her appearance. The face of the man at right, and even more his gesture of raised hands (derived from Renaissance painting), testify to his being moved by the sight he sees.[90] This man's gesture also flatters the external viewer, who can see from his privileged perspective (and knowledge of the ritual) that this man appears to have fallen in love with one of the least beautiful of the women. Thus while internal and external viewing are related, the external, contemporary, Western viewer is again established as superior to the internal, historical one.

Long's work, then, refers to the same themes of the power of men over women and of the contemporary West over the Middle East that are evident in Delacroix's work. Yet the passage of more than forty years from Delacroix's time to Long's, and from France to England, also brought it to a realm where these assumptions were no longer universal. Two comments on Long's work suggest that the work also invited a critique both of its gender assumptions and of its claim to historical veracity.

A reviewer in *Blackwood's Edinburgh Magazine*, which was among the older and more refined of middle-class periodicals, wrote of the piece:

[The woman on display] is evidently the first and finest piece of goods in the collection, and the expression of the crowd of faces all fixed upon her is wonderfully fine and full of variety. The lips parted with that smile of mingled vanity and admiration with which men (out of marriage markets) so often regard the women exposed to their gaze, the gleam of the sensual eye, appear in most of the gazers; but some are pitiful and half tender, with a touch of compassion in them. And if the spectator gazes around him after he has looked at the picture, he will see another picture scarcely less attractive in the curious glances of the living faces that crowd about.[91]

The woman is a 'piece of goods' who offers the spectator a chance to be amused by the varieties of male reactions. This comment would seem to sustain the superiority of external viewer to internal viewer. Yet the implied unity of actual viewers and painted viewers is sundered by acknowledging the explicit gendering of spectatorship. The *Blackwood's* reviewer continues:

We should not wonder if the young women, flower of English youth, who gather round with a curiosity not unmixed with personal feelings, found something like a revelation in the picture. One sees them glance at each other with a half smile, half blush, sometimes with subdued awe or indignation. 'Is that how they think of us, these men, though they dare not look it?' the girls ask themselves.

The dissimilar composition of audiences, between nineteenth-century England and that attributed to ancient Mesopotamia, presents a confrontation of genders in the work's actual audience that would be inadmissible in the ideal realm of the audience in the picture. The acts of viewing thematized in the work, that is, are thus again illuminated as specifically masculine, voyeuristic activities. Yet such a conception of viewing is distinctly unlike the actual viewing context of the work. The work's ideal male viewer is confronted by a actual female viewer, and thus the perfect binarism within the painting of men viewing and women being viewed is confronted and undermined.

A premise of the *Blackwood's* review is that the painting addresses contemporary England at least as much as ancient Babylonia. But the specific manner in which the structure of gender relations calls into question the painting's claim to historical authenticity was only directly considered by John Ruskin. Ruskin's erudite notice of the work was virtually alone in distinguishing between Assyrian and Babylonian artifacts. Although realizing the work's anachronisms he called it 'A painting of great merit, and well deserving purchase by the Anthropological Society'.[92] But this was not because the work was deemed to represent the ethnographic custom of a pristine past:

> As a piece of anthropology, [Long's work] is the natural and very wonderful product of a century occupied in carnal and mechanical science. In the total paralysis of conception – without attempt to disguise the palsy – as to the existence of any higher element in a woman's mind than vanity and spite, or in a man's than avarice and animal passion, it is also a specific piece of the natural history of our own century; but only a partial one, either of it or of the Assyrian ... [93]

To the contrary, Ruskin saw the work as embodying the prejudices of the contemporary viewer. Far from purely exhibiting an extrinsic viewpoint or unusual custom, then, Long's work (for both writers) was a contemporary statement, as much about the present as about the past. At the same time, through this way of approaching the image of the ancient world, the conventional dominance of the contemporary masculine, Western viewer is again put in doubt. Thus, the image of Assyria clearly brings together past and present concerns, while also presenting an occasion for both Ruskin and the *Blackwood's* reviewer to question conventional gender distinctions.

When looked at over the span of almost fifty years from Delacroix to Long, then, Assyrian archaeology did not simply work to provide more authentic envisioning of preexisting subjects, such as the death of Sardanapalus. To the contrary, art and archaeology functioned as two parts of a larger system of cultural circulation, in a continual process of reinventing ancient Assyria. Although images might have been constructed in accord with archaeological and antiquarian knowledge, they also responded to the varying needs and capabilities of artists and audiences.

The works of Brown and Long continued the sort of exoticist mobility with which Martin and Delacroix worked. But the combination of invented and 'authentic' elements on which mobility depends allowed a widening of the conception of Assyria. Brown's use of Assyrian archaeological details allowed a turn from dependence on authoritative ancient textual sources to the near-contemporary Byron. As much as the sources for the subject widened, so too did audience assumptions as the play of exoticist representation became more familiar. In the reception of Long's work we even find an explicit critique of the assumptions of power and gender which had dominated the conception of Assyria and the larger exoticist imagination throughout the earlier nineteenth century.

While even the traditional conception of Assyria was thus transformed, the juxtaposition of France and England is key to a much more radical and varied range of reception between the two countries. The varying fortunes of Assyria in France and England disrupted the prediscovery situation, in which both countries shared the same mode of conceiving the subject. Rather, the works of Courbet, Degas, and Moreau (and even Delacroix's lack of interest in the discoveries) suggest a distinctly different atmosphere in France from that in England, one which forecloses on, governs, and ultimately subordinates the aesthetic challenge of ancient Assyrian art.

Tracking the archaeological history and aesthetic debate over Assyria, as we have done, illuminates the fundamental differences between the milieus of reception in France and England. Not only their pragmatic archaeological histories, but also their methods of disseminating information differed sharply. The subsequent French submersion of Assyrian imagery we have noted is remarkably concordant with the troubled history of French Mesopotamian archaeology as well as the constrained circulation of the discoveries to the public. By contrast, in England, with its vigorous public debate on Assyria and its art, the lionizing of Layard as discoverer, as well as numerous publications on the works, an audience was fostered that was prepared to respond to the specific, detailed Assyrian images of artists such as Brown and Long.

For all the amassing of textual and visual evidence of Assyria, for all the energy expended in the antiquarian project of fixing the Assyrian past, the image of Assyria that arose was thus localized and hybridized as it circulated among Western audiences. Courbet's 'Assyrian' beard was no less the fruit of this process of circulation than was Brown's painstaking Assyrian decor. Ultimately, then, like many another exoticist subject, Assyria served not only as an object in its own right but also as a distant and distorted mirror in which France and England asserted their respective identities. On these grounds, a most telling observation of the early reception of ancient Assyrian objects is this line from a review of an English production of Byron's *Sardanapalus*, which used elaborate sets and costumes almost directly copied from Layard's reliefs: 'That one performance gave us a better insight into the manners and habits of the Assyrians, than a whole lifetime has enabled us to acquire of the French.'[94]

NOTES

1. London, Royal Institute of British Architects Archives, Sidney Smirke to Joseph Scoles, 28 June 1847.

2. 'Musée de Ninive', *L'Illustration*, 15 May 1847, 167–70, at p. 169.

3. For archaeology, see, e.g. Seton Lloyd, *Foundations in the Dust: The Story of Mesopotamian Exploration*, rev. edn, London, 1980; Glyn Daniel, *A Hundred and Fifty Years of Archaeology*, London, 1978. For some suggestive 'revisionist' treatments which engage the specific concerns of the Near East, see Neil Asher Silberman, 'Promised Lands and Chosen Peoples: the Politics and Poetics of Archaeological Narrative', in *Nationalism, Politics, and the Practice of Archaeology*, eds P. L. Kohl and C. Fawcett, New York, 1995, 249–62; Curtis Hinsley, 'Revising and Revisioning the History of Archaeology: Reflections on Region and Context', in *Tracing Archaeology's Past: The Historiography of Archaeology*, ed. A. L. Christenson, Carbondale, Ill., 1989, 79–96; Bruce G. Trigger, 'Alternative Archaeologies: Nationalist, Colonialist, Imperialist', *Man*, n.s., 19 (1984), 355–70. For studies of Assyrian 'influence', see Alexander (below n. 77), Künzl, Burge, Silber, Jirat-Wasiyutinski, and Amishai-Maisels (all below n. 70).

4. Walter Benjamin, 'Theses on the Philosophy of History', in *Illuminations*, trans. H. Zohn, New York, 1969, 257.

5. Johannes Fabian, 'Presence and Representation: The Other and Anthropological Writing', *Critical Inquiry* 16 (1990), 753–72, at p. 756. While I cannot begin to summarize the varieties of contemporary postcolonial criticism, my own approach has been informed by the following works (in addition to the works cited elsewhere in this study), among others (as well as by the arguments between them): Mary Louise Pratt, *Imperial Eyes: Travel Writing and Transculturation*, New York, 1992; Edward Said, *Culture and Imperialism*, New York, 1993; Michael Taussig, *Mimesis and Alterity: A Particular History of the Senses*, New York, 1993; Homi Bhabha, *The Location of Culture*, New York 1994; Nicholas Thomas, *Colonialism's Culture: Anthropology, Travel, and Government*, Princeton, 1994; Iain Chambers and Lidia Curti, eds, *The Post-Colonial Question: Common Skies, Divided Horizons*, New York, 1996.

6. 'Isn't exoticism primarily a phenomenon of reception?', Jean-Pierre Leduc-Adine, 'Exotisme et discours d'art au XIXe siècle', in *L'Exotisme*, eds A. Buisine, N. Dodille, and C. Duchet, Paris, 1988, 457–65, at p. 461. This suggestive essay deserves wider attention. On the general methodological range of reception theory, see Robert C. Holub, *Reception Theory: A Critical Introduction*, New York, 1984; Susan R. Suleiman, 'Introduction: Varieties of Audience-Oriented Criticism', in *The Reader in the Text*, eds S. R. Suleiman and J. Grossman, Princeton, 1980, 3–45. For some specific ramifications of these approaches to visual material, see Wolfgang Kemp, review of John Shearman, *Only Connect: Art and the Spectator in the Italian Renaissance*, Art *Bulletin*, 76 (1994), 364–67; Michael Ann Holly, *Past Looking: Historical Imagination and the Rhetoric of the Image*, Ithaca, NY, 1996, 195–208: Dario Gamboni, 'Histoire de l'art et "reception": Remarques sur l'état d'une problématique', *Histoire de l'Art*, 35–6 (October 1996), 9–14.

7. For a range of definitions, compare the mocking treatment of the term in Aimé Cesaire, *Discourse on Colonialism*, trans. J. Pinkham, New York, 1972, passim, with the largely expository presentation of Vincenette Maigne, 'Exotisme: évolution en diachronie du mot et de son champ sémantique', in *Exotisme et Création: Actes du Colloque Internationale (Lyons 1983)*, Paris, 1985, 7–16.

8. This is a founding tenet of postcolonial theory, starting with Edward Said, *Orientalism*, New York, 1979. Most recently, see the formulation of exoticism in Roger Célestin, *From Cannibals to Radicals: Figures and Limits of Exoticism*, Minneapolis, Minn., 1996.

9. A pioneering study in this direction is Johannes Fabian, *Time and the Other: How Anthropology Makes Its Object*, New York, 1983. For a range of treatments of time in more recent postcolonial studies, see Paul Carter, *The Road to Botany Bay: An Essay in Spatial History*, London, 1987; Homi Bhabha, 'DissemiNation: time, narrative, and the margins of the modern nation', in *Nation and Narration*, ed. H. Bhabha, New York, 1990, 291–322; Chambers and Curti (as n. 5), 65–120.

10. For a detailed account of these regions in antiquity, see Amélie Kuhrt, *The Ancient Near East c. 3000–330 B.C.*, 2 vols, New York, 1995. Among the extensive bibliography of the region's more recent history, a useful comprehensive source is Albert Hourani, *A History of the Arab Peoples*, Cambridge, Mass., 1991.

11. Cyril John Gadd, *The Cities of Babylonia*, Cambridge, 1960, 2–9; Béatrice André-Salvini, '"Où sont-ils ces remparts de Ninive?" Les sources de connaissance de l'Assyrie avant les fouilles', in Fontan, *De Khorsabad à Paris: la découverte des Assyriens, avec la collaboration de Nicole Chevalier*,

Paris, 1994, 22–43; Stephanie Dalley, 'Nineveh, Babylon, and the Hanging Gardens: Cuneiform and Classical Sources Reconciled', *Iraq*, 66 (1994), 45–58.

12. François Hartog, *The Mirror of Herodotus: The Representation of the Other in the Writing of History*, trans. J. Lloyd, Berkeley, 1988; Wilfried Nippel, 'Facts and Fiction: Greek Ethnography and Its Legacy', *History and Anthropology*, 9 (1996), 125–31.

13. Thus James Fletcher, a missionary who visited Mesopotamia in the 1840s, described the scene: 'Yet what a moral might be derived from the present condition of the capital of Assur. In lieu of lofty palaces and gorgeous temples, the eye surveys only the mounds composed of their dust, or the miserable huts which have arisen on their site. The gardens where Sardanapalus revelled are wasted and desolate, the sounds of soft and luxurious music that once floated on the soft Assyrian breezes have yielded to the silence of devastation or decay' (James Phillips Fletcher, *Notes from Nineveh, and Travels in Mesopotamia, Assyria and Syria*, 2 vols, London, 1850, 1.206). See also Asahel Grant, *The Nestorians, or the Lost Tribes*, London, 2nd ed., 1843, 27; Robert Mignan, *Travels in Chaldea*, London, 1829, passim. Significantly, the topos is repeated by Eugène Flandin in an account of Botta's archaeological activity, 'Voyage Archéologique à Ninive', *Revue des Deux Mondes*, 10 (1845), 1083.
     This 'denial of coevalness', which essentializes the contemporary Mesopotamian land and its inhabitants as moral and historical inheritors of ancient forbears, is a common topos of exoticist description and has received considerable attention in postcolonial analysis. See Fabian (as n. 9), 35; Ali Behdad, *Belated Travellers: Orientalism in the Age of Colonial Dissolution*, Durham, N.C., 1994, 46; Pratt (as n. 5), 64.

14. Morton Paley, *The Apocalyptic Sublime*, New Haven, Conn., 1986. For *Belshazzar's Feast*, see esp. 128–38. On Martin, see also Thomas Balston, *John Martin 1789–1854: His Life and Works*, London, 1947; William Feaver, *The Art of John Martin*, Oxford, 1975; *John Martin 1789–1854*, exh. cat., Hazlitt, Gooden, and Fox, London, 1975. The original oil painting of *The Fall of Nineveh*, of 1828, was formerly in the Royal Collection, Cairo, Egypt (Balston, 276; Feaver, 223–4). The work is known now from the many mezzotints Martin produced of it around 1830.

15. *A Description of the Picture, Belshazzar's Feast, Painted by Mr. J. Martin …*, 42nd edn, London, 1825.

16. *Descriptive Catalog*, 14; Norah Monckton, 'Architectural Backgrounds in the Pictures of John Martin', *Architectural Review*, 104 (1948), 81–4.

17. *Descriptive Catalog*, 8; 10–11.

18. Ibid., 11, 15, 14. Saranapalus is mentioned in numerous ancient sources, but by far the most detailed and influential account is that of Diodorus Siculus, 2.23–7.

19. John Gage, *Goethe on Art*, Berkeley, 1980, xv, calls Martin 'the rage of England and the continent in the 1820s'. Jean Seznec, *John Martin en France*, London, 1964; Paley (as n. 14), 142–3; Balston (as n. 14), 90.

20. The basic sources for this work are Jack J. Spector, *The Death of Sardanapalus*, New York, 1974; Lee Johnson, *The Paintings of Eugène Delacroix: A Critical Catalogue*, 6 vols, Oxford, 1981–9, 1.114–21. See also Eric-Henry Berrebi, 'Sardanapale, ou l'impossible étreinte', *L'Ecrit-Voir, Revue d'Histoire des Arts*, no. 8 (1986), 37–49.

21. The similarities and differences between Delacroix's treatment of the subject and Byron's are summarized by Johnson (as n. 20). On the Byronic affinities of the work, see especially Spector (as n. 20), 59–73; Alain Daguerre de Hureaux and Stéphane Guégan, *L'ABCdaire de Delacroix et l'Orient*, Paris, 1994, 38; Rana Kabbani, *Europe's Myths of Orient*, Bloomington, Ind., 1986, 75. Byron was named as inspiration also in Delacroix's time; see Maurice Tourneux, *Eugène Delacroix devant ses contemporains*, Paris, 1886, 48.

22. On exoticist mobility, see Frederick N. Bohrer, 'Eastern Medi(t)ations: Exoticism and the Mobility of Difference', *History and Anthropology*, 9 (1996), 293–307. See also the discussion of Behdad's 'principle of discontinuity' below.

23. Beatrice Farwell, 'Sources for Delacroix's *Death of Sardanapalus*', *Art Bulletin*, 40 (1958), 66–71; Lee Johnson, 'The Etruscan Sources of Delacroix's *Death of Sardanapalus*', *Art Bulletin*, 42 (1960), 296–300, and 'Toward Delacroix's Oriental Sources', *Burlington Magazine*, 120 (1978), 144–51; Donald Rosenthal, 'A Mughal Portrait copied by Delacroix', *Burlington Magazine*, 119 (1977), 505–6; William Steinke, 'An Archaeological Source for Delacroix's *Death of Sardanapalus*', *Art Bulletin*, 66 (1984), 318–20; Helen Whitehouse, lecture, Association of Art Historians meeting, Brighton, England, April 1986.

24. Linda Nochlin, 'The Imaginary Orient', in *The Politics of Vision*, New York, 1989, 33–59 at p. 42.

25. As suggested in another context in Zeynep Çelik and Lila Kinney, 'Ethnography and Exhibitionism at the Expositions Universelles', *Assemblage*, 13 (1990), 34–59. On gender in exoticist representation and its relation to other forms of difference, see also Reina Lewis, *Gendering Orientalism: Race, Femininity and Representation*, New York, 1996; Anne McClintock, *Imperial Leather: Race, Gender and Sexuality in the Colonial Contest*, New York, 1995.

26. An assumption not only of Nochlin. See Kabbani (as n. 21), 67–85; Joanna de Groot, '"Sex" and "Race": the Construction of Language and Image in the Nineteenth Century', in *Sexuality and Subordination: Interdisciplinary Studies of Gender in the Nineteenth Century*, eds S. Mendus and J. Rendall, London, 1989, 89–128.

27. Tourneux (as n. 21), 48.

28. Behdad (as n. 13), 13. On the relation of Said's initial, and seminal, formulation to more recent studies, see Gyan Prakash, '*Orientalism* Now', *History and Theory*, 34 (1995),199–212.

29. Darcy Grimaldo Grigsby, 'Rumor, Contagion and Colonization in Gros's *Plague-Stricken of Jaffa* (1804)', *Representations*, 51 (1995), 1–46 at p. 2.

30. The acquisition of antiquities is acknowledged by John M. MacKenzie in his *Orientalism: History, Theory, and the Arts*, Manchester, 1995, 53, as 'that ultimate imperial act' even though he is otherwise notably opposed to analysis in the direction inspired by Said and Nochlin.

31. *Descriptive Catalog*, 5.

32. Thus Byron states in *Don Juan* of 1819–24 (5.62) 'Though Claudius Rich, Esquire, some bricks has got / and written lately two memoirs upon't.' On Rich, see Lloyd (as n. 3), 12–42, 57–73; Larsen, 9–12; Julian Reade, 'Les relations anglo-françaises en Assyrie', in Fontan, 116–17.

33. Claudius J. Rich, *Memoir on the Ruins of Babylon*, London, 1815; *Second Memoir on the Ruins of Babylon*, London, 1818; *Narrative of a Residence in Koordistan by the Late Claudius James Rich Esquire, edited by his widow*, 2 vols, London, 1836; and *Narrative of a Journey to the Site of Babylon*, London, 1839.

34. Botta referred to himself as 'only a tool of M. Mohl'. Fontan, 13. On Botta's early activities and Mohl's 'nationalistic dream', see Larsen, 21–33. On Botta, see also Giovanni Bergamini, '"Spoliis Orientis onustus". Paul-Émile Botta et la découverte de la civilisation assyrienne' in Fontan, 68–85; Charles Levavasseur, 'Notice sur Paul-Émile Botta' in *Relation d'un voyage dans l'Yémen*, by Paul-Émile Botta, Paris, 1880, 1–34. On Mohl, see also F. Max Müller, 'Notice sur Jules Mohl', in Jules Mohl, 1.ix–xlvii.

35. Paul-Émile Botta, *Monument: de Ninive ...*, 5 vols, Paris, 1849–50, 5.5.

36. Paul-Émile Botta, *Lettres de M. Botta sur ses découvertes à Khorsabad, près de Ninive*, Paris, 1845, and *M. Botta's Letters on the Discoveries at Nineveh, Translated from the French by C.T.*, London, 1850. First published irregularly in *Le Journal Asiatique* from 1843 to 1845, the letters were also quoted frequently in magazine dispatches about the discoveries.

37. Botta, 1850 (as n. 36), 30, 59.

38. Ibid. , 12, 11.

39. On Layard's activities as archaeologist and publicist, see especially Waterfield, 116–77; Larsen; Frederick Mario Fales and Bernard J. Hickey, eds, *Austen Henry Layard tra l'Oriente e Venezia*, Rome, 1987; John W. Swails, 'Austen Henry Layard and the Near East, 1839–1880', Ph.D. dissertation, University of Georgia, 1983; Austen Henry Layard, *Nineveh and Its Remains*, 2 vols, New York, 1850. (first published London, 1849).

40. Layard, *Nineveh* (as n. 39) , 1. 31–133.

41. Stratford Canning, quoted in Stanley Lane-Poole, *The Life of the Right Honourable Stratford Canning ...* , 2 vols, New York, 1976, 2.149 (first published 1888).

42. London, British Museum Archives, Minutes of Trustee Meetings, Sub. Comm., 22 Jan. 1848, f. 399–402; Comm., 29 Jan. 1848, f. 7443–6.

43. London, British Library, Add. ms. 38976, fol. 234: Rawlinson to Layard, 15 October 1845, quoted in H. W. F. Saggs, introduction to *Nineveh and Its Remains*, by A. H. Layard, rept. edn, New York, 1970, 42.

44. The typological nature of Assyrian art makes it difficult to identify precisely which of the many winged animals Layard may have referred to.

45. Austen Henry Layard, *Autobiography and Letters*, 2 vols, London, 1903, 2.166–7, letter of March 22, 1846. Cf. 2.161, 2.175.

46. Cf. Botta's description of two figures in a chariot with the king: 'les poses du serviteur et du cocher sont dessinnées ... avec une perfection de *mouvement* et une naiveté qu'à mon grand regret mon ignorance du dessin ne m'a permis de bien reproduire' (quoted in *Le Magasin Pittoresque* 12 (1844), 285 (emphasis added)). On Layard as connoisseur see Layard, *Autobiography* (as n. 45), 1.27; Julian E. Reade, 'Reflections on Layard's Archaeological Career', in Fales and Hickey (as n. 39), 47–53. Soon after his return to England, Layard became closely involved in the promotion of art, especially early Renaissance art, in England. See Layard, *Autobiography* (as n. 45), 2.203–212; Robyn Cooper, 'The popularisation of Renaissance art in Victorian England: The Arundel Society', *Art History*, 1 (1978): 263–92.

47. Layard to Canning, 4 Aug. 1847, quoted in Ian Jenkins, *Archaeologists and Aesthetes in the Sculpture Galleries of the British Museum, 1800–1939*, London, 1992, 157.

48. British Library, Add. ms 38977, Rawlinson to Layard, 5 August 1846, quoted in Waterfield, 147–8.

49. 'Our Weekly Gossip', *Athenaeum*, 1 Feb. 1845, 120–1; This dispatch was originally written by Layard for *Malta Times*; see John Murray Archive, London, Layard to Murray, 17 May 1847; Saggs (as n. 43), 40; Waterfield, 114.

50. *Penny Magazine*, 5 July 1845, 264. Circulation of the *Penny Magazine* ran as high as 200,000 copies per issue in the 1830s. In 1845, its last year of existence, its circulation was 40,000. The *Athenaeum*, by contrast, circulated only 500 to 1,000 copies weekly in the 1830s and is recorded as rising no higher than 7,200 copies as late as 1854; see Richard D. Altick, *The English Common Reader*, Chicago, 1957, 393–4.

51. *L'Illustration* (as n. 2), 169.

52. Ibid., 168.

53. Larsen, 138. Larsen (14) remarks that Botta 'seems almost be erased from history'.

54. See Botta (as n. 35) .

55. Maurice Pillet, *Khorsabad: les découvertes de V. Place en l'Assyrie*, Paris, 1918, 103–8; Béatrice André-Salvini, 'Introduction aux publications de P. E. Botta et de V. Place', in Fontan, 166–72.

56. 'Ninive', *Le Tour du Monde*, 7 (1863), 318.

57. Mohl, 1.413

58. Frederick N. Bohrer, 'A New Antiquity: The English Reception of Assyria', unpublished Ph.D. dissertation, University of Chicago, 1989, 57–85, 173–211.

59. Frederick N. Bohrer, 'The Printed Orient: the Production of A. H. Layard's Earliest Works', *Culture and History*, 11 (1992), 85–105.

60. *Quarterly Review*, 84 (1848–9), 106–153 at 107. The *Quarterly Review* was published by John Murray, who also published Layard's books. On the journal, see Roger P. Wallins, 'The Quarterly Review', in *British Literary Magazines*, ed. A. Sullivan, 4 vols, Westport, Conn., 1983, 2.359–67.

61. Jenkins (as n. 47), 158–67; Frederick N. Bohrer, 'The Times and Spaces of History: Representation, Assyria, and the British Museum', in *Museum Culture: Histories, Discourses, Spectacles*, eds D. Sherman and I. Rogoff, Minneapolis, Minn., 1994, 197–222.

62. British Library, Add. ms. 38,984, fol. 374: William Vaux to Austen Henry Layard, partially quoted in Edward Miller, *That Noble Cabinet: A History of the British Museum*, London, 1973, 192.

63. House of Commons, 'Minutes of ... the Select Committee on the National Gallery', *Parliamentary Papers 1852–3*, 1853 vol. 31: 9050 ff. On this exchange, see Francis Haskell, *Rediscoveries in Art: Some Aspects of Taste, Fashion and Collecting in England and France*, Ithaca, N.Y., 1976, 101–2.

64. [James S. Buckingham], *The Buried City of the East: Nineveh*, London, 1851, i.

65. 'Nineveh and Persepolis', *Art-Journal*, 12 (1850), 225.

66. 'Reviews', *Art-Journal*, 15 (1853), 235.

67. On the reception of the Elgin marbles, see Jenkins (as n. 47), 24–9; Jacob Rothenberg, *Descensus Ad Terram: The Acquisition and Reception of the Elgin Marbles*, New York, 1977; Massimiliano Pavan, 'Antonio Canova e la Discussione sugli "Elgin Marbles"' *Rivista dell'Instituto Nazionale d'Archelogia e Storia dell'Arte*, n.s., nos 11–12 (1974–75), 219–344. Haydon's role is detailed in Frederick Cummings, 'Benjamin Robert Haydon and the Critical Reception of the Elgin Marbles', unpublished Ph.D. dissertation, University of Chicago, 1967. For the central opponent of the works, see M. Clarke and N. Penny eds, *The Arrogant Connoisseur: Richard Payne Knight,*

1751–1824, Manchester, 1982; Andrew Ballantyne, 'Knight, Haydon, and the Elgin Marbles', *Apollo* 128 (1988), 155–9.

68. The discoveries were, however, steadfastly covered in the French counterpart to the *Penny Magazine, Le Magasin Pittoresque* (16 [1848], 131–4; 17 [1849], 193–4; 20 [1852], 241–4). Though anomalous among the French popular press, it may also suggest a certain submerged interest in the discoveries among popular constituencies.

69. Mohl, 2.36. Cf. 1. xxxiii; Lloyd, (as n. 3), 140; Pillet (as n. 55), 17–70.

70. This tendency can be found in a still obscured portion of European 'Primitivism', including works by artists such as Paul Gauguin, Pablo Picasso, and Jacob Epstein. For Gauguin, see Vojtech Jirat-Wasiyutinski, 'Gauguin's Self Portraits and the Oviri', *Art Quarterly*, n.s. 2 (1979), 189 n. 48; Ziva Amishai-Maisels, *Gauguin's Religious Themes*, New York, 1985, 276 n. 66. For Picasso, see Hannelore Künzl, *Der Einfluss des alten Orients auf die europäische Kunst besonders im 19. und 20 Jh.*, Cologne, 1973, 135; Robert Burge, 'Pablo Picasso's *Man with a Sheep*', *Source: Notes in the History of Art*, 2 (1982), 21–6; Jaime Sabartés, *Picasso à Antibes*, Paris, 1948, quoted in Dore Ashton ed., *Picasso on Art: A Selection of Views*, New York, 1972, 115. For Epstein, see Evelyn Silber, *The Sculpture of Epstein*, Lewisburg, Penn., 1986, 130–2.

71. On modes and means of hybridity, see especially Bhabha, as well as Pratt, and Taussig (all as n. 5); Annie Coombes, 'The recalcitrant object: culture contact and the question of hybridity', in *Colonial Discourse/Postcolonial Theory*, eds F. Barker, P. Hulme, M. Iversen, Manchester, 1994, 89–114. The range of images in this section might be considered as well to exemplify the 'semiotic play' of reception, as described by Norman Bryson, 'Art in Context', in *Studies in Historical Change*, ed. R. Cohen, Charlottesville, Va., 1992, 18–42. This, in turn, tends to corroborate the structural connection of exoticism and reception suggested by Leduc-Adine (as n. 6).

72. Eugène Delacroix, 'Des Variations du Beau', in *Ecrits sur l'art*, eds F. M. Deyrolle and C, Denissel, Paris, 1988, 34 (first published 1857): 'One is struck above all by the perfection with which animals are rendered'.

73. Eugène Delacroix, *Journal*, 3 vols, ed. A. Joubin, Paris, 1932, 3.197, 20 June 1858: 'We go to the museum with my aimable cousin. He is quite struck with Assyrian antiquities'.

74. Gustave Courbet, *Letters of Gustave Courbet*, ed. and trans. P. Chu, Chicago, 1992, 132.

75. See Nadar (Gaspar Félix Tournachon), 'Les contemporains de Nadar: Courbet', *Journal Amusant*, 11 Dec. 1858, reproduced in Linda Nochlin and Sarah Faunce, *Courbet Rediscovered*, exh. cat., New York, Brooklyn Museum, 1988, 9.

76. '[A]s even a cursory look at the original reliefs shows, Courbet invented the "Assyrian" beard entirely from his imagination – the angle and pointed shape of the French "Assyrian" beard is nothing like the vertical, rectangular true Assyrian examples. Courbet was evidently capitalizing on the reputation of the Assyrian discoveries without ever having looked at them' (John Malcolm Russell, letter to author, 21 Feb. 1997).

77. Robert L. Alexander, 'Courbet and Assyrian Sculpture', *Art Bulletin*, 47 (1965), 447–52.

78. Theodore Reff, *The Notebooks of Edgar Degas*, 2 vols, Oxford, 1976, 1.19.

79. Roy McMullen, *Degas: His Life, Times, and Work*, Boston, 1984, 94–6. A photo album of the production is in the Bibliothèque de l'Opéra in Paris, PH 9 (2).

80. The most extensive list of correspondences and contrasts is in *Degas*, exh. cat., New York, Metropolitan Museum of Art, 1988, 89–92. On the creation of the work, see Geneviève Monnier, 'La genèse d'une oeuvre de Degas: *Sémiramis construisant une ville*', *Revue du Louvre et des Musées de France*, 28 (1978), 407–26.

81. Pierre-Louis Mathieu, 'La Bibliothèque de Gustave Moreau', *Gazette des Beaux-Arts*, ser. 6, 91, (1978), 155–62.

82. The sketchbook, dating from 1850 to 1869, is now in the collection of the Musée Gustave Moreau, Paris. There is also in the museum a notebook recording notable articles in *Le Magasin Pittoresque*, including two described by the artist as 'bas-relief découvert à Ninive – Sculpture assyrienne' (1844) and 'poids assyriennes' (1861). I am grateful to Mmes Geneviève Lacambre for her continued assistance with this material.

83. This gesture can be found in a variety of Assyrian deity figures conserved in London and Paris and elsewhere, such as the series from Room H of the Northwest Palace at Nimrud. See Gadd, 236.

84. On the work and its context, see Ford Madox Hueffer [Ford Madox Ford], *Ford Madox Brown*,

London, 1896, 262, 272, and Rowland Elzea, *The Samuel and Mary Bancroft Jr. & Related Pre-Raphaelite Collections*, Wilmington, Del., 1978, 30–31.

85.　A prototype is London, British Museum, Department of Ancient Near Eastern Antiquities (hereafter BM, ANE) 98060. All of the Assyrian artifacts referred to here were collected by and displayed at the museum by the early 1850s.

86.　See, for instance BM, ANE 124533 or 124557.

87.　George C. Swayne, *The History of Herodotus*, Edinburgh, 1870, 36–7, paraphrasing Herodotus, 1.196. On Long's treatment of the subject, see Richard Jenkyns, *Dignity and Decadence: Victorian Art and the Classical Inheritance*, Cambridge, Mass., 1992, 119–24.

88.　The curtain design at right is derived from an Assyrian floor threshhold, such as BM, ANE 118910. The battle scene at far left is closely derived from BM, ANE 124536. The central frieze is closely derived from BM, ANE 118914, 118916. The disposition of the frieze – its coloration and use of the 'sacred tree' motif to take up the wall's edges – suggests the influence not only of the artifacts in the museum but also of Layard's reconstruction of an Assyrian throne room. Layard's design is reproduced in Esin Atil, Charles Newton and Sarah Searight, *Voyages and Visions: Nineteenth-Century European Images of the Middle East from the Victoria and Albert Museum*, Washington, D.C., 1995, 78–9.

89.　'The Royal Academy Exhibition', *Art-Journal*, n.s., 14 (1875): 250.

90.　Michael Baxandall, *Painting and Experience in Fifteenth Century Italy*, Oxford, 1972, 47, 65–6.

91.　'Art in May', *Blackwood's Edinburgh Magazine*, 17 (1875), 763.

92.　John Ruskin, 'Academy Notes', in *The Works of John Ruskin*, 39 vols, eds E. T. Cook and A. Wedderburn, London, 1903-12, 14.274-7 at 274.

93.　Ibid., 275.

94.　*Lloyd's Weekly Newspaper*, 15 June 1853, quoted in Inge Krengel-Strudthoff, 'Archäologie auf der Bühne – das wiedererstandene Ninive: Charles Keans Ausstattung zu *Sardanapalus* von Lord Byron', *Kleine Schriften der Gesellschaft für Theatergeschichte*, 31 (1981), 19.

III.

Building Shared Imaginaries/

Effacing Otherness

Introduction:
Building Shared Imaginaries/Effacing
Otherness

By the time a critique of discourse is no longer able to affect the premises or the functioning of that discourse, it seems safe to say the discourse in question has become dominant. Timothy J. Reiss, *The Discourse of Modernism* (1982)

The extent of our responsibilities as academics and intellectuals to link museology, history, theory, and criticism to contemporary social conditions is an urgent and painfully obvious issue. The articles presented below link abstract thinking to concrete social responsibility by disinterring the troubling historical role that race 'science' has played in the formation of modern museum practices. We focus on the single, unresolved issue of 'race' as one of paramount importance to scrutinize because it links museological practice to contemporary philosophical and political issues, broader than any single disciplinary objective, concerning the formation of the modern subject. In short, the modern public museum, like modern anthropology in Johannes Fabian's classic critique of his own discipline, constructs its beholders through exhibition strategies implying distance, difference, and opposition, thereby visualizing the cosmos in terms invented by modern Western society.[1]

But what constitutes 'Western' in the modern era of economic and cultural globalization? Today we associate racism with ignorance and untenable fundamentalist ideologies, but in the decades surrounding the beginning of the twentieth century, leading scientists, progressive academics, and other intellectuals promoted racial ideas as a means of educating the middle and working classes of the modern, secular nation-state. As Fabian argues, and the contributions to this chapter of *Grasping the World* attest, the use of maps, charts, and tables in the service of public education signaled convictions deeply ingrained in the European empirical scientific tradition, where such quantified, diagrammatic forms of representation have connoted 'objective' forms of knowledge – or rather, such scientific forms of representation have performed illusionistic feats of 'objectivism', a term that sociologist Pierre Bourdieu coined. Following Fabian and Bourdieu, we define 'objectivism' as a dominating social practice that constitutes the world 'as a spectacle presented to an observer who takes up a "point of view" on the action [and] stands back to observe it', conceiving that this 'object is a thing intended for his cognition alone'.[2]

Exhibiting, collecting, browsing, artmaking, manufacturing, shopping, taste, and art historicizing are, moreover, historically interwoven practices that make ample use of such modern forms of representation. None of these practices can be adequately or critically understood apart from the others – as our choice of studies dealing with trade fairs, science museums, and art museums in Europe, the US, and Asia is intended to suggest. The role of museums in the amalgam within which we live has been 'to support the fantasy of origins we need to anchor us as we drift amongst the multiple choices of the intensely commodified present', as Neil Cummings and Marysia Lewandowska so aptly put it in their recent book *The Value of Things* (from which we include an excerpt in Chapter 5), a comparative history of two institutions, the British Museum and Selfridges Department Store.

For museology is by nature not simply complicit with modern social practices: it is constitutive of it. Carol Duncan's essay – a milestone in the critical history of museum scholarship when it was published in its initial form in 1980 – turns our attention to the Louvre once more, asking how subsequent public art museums perpetuated and transformed the functions previously associated with dazzling royal art collections meant to legitimate rulership. The larger question, Duncan writes, is what made museums so politically attractive and different from older displays of art: what kind of ritual does the public art museum state, and what is its ideological usefulness to modern states?

As Donna Haraway argues the case, 'social relations of domination are frozen into the hardware and logic' of the visual technology we know as museums. Educators who were worried about social disorders such as class war and social decadence pinned their hopes on positive science to envision peace and progress in the industrialized nation-state. Trustees and officers of museums – like H. S. Osborn of the American Museum of Natural History that is the subject of her case study – were charged with the task of promoting public health. Osborn, a leader of the movement for eugenics, conservation, and the rational management of capitalist society, claimed that children who passed through the museum's halls would become better citizens if the moral lessons of racial hierarchy and progress were explicit in its dioramas and other exhibition displays.

The public museum, as Annie Coombes and Beverly Grindstaff elaborate, was promoted as a type of public entertainment that, beyond popular events like world trade fairs, had value if they 'communicated the truth' (in Haraway's words). In England, in 1902 an Education Act announced objectives similar to self-conscious contemporary agendas of multiculturalism, by making provision for school children accompanied by their teachers to count museum visits as an integral part of the curriculum. Museums could only signify the colonized subject, Coombes argues, but world fairs literally captured these subjects and presented them in mock 'villages' that were always favorites with fairgoers and the press. Such exhibits, though they were often peopled by troupes of professional performers posing as village natives, fostered illusions of geographical proximity while the calculated sense of spectacle preserved the cultural divide by providing vicarious forms of tourism without necessitating actual travel to exotic places.

In the same decades around the turn of the twentieth century, existing cabinets of curiosities and ethnographic collections were reshaped into vehicles for constructing nationalist ideologies by providing instruction and 'rational amusement among the mass of the people'. The notion of an educational practice based on careful observation and study of artifactual material came primarily from a left middle-class intelligentia who believed that it was essential for museums to be seen as addressing a broad public. The concept of a national culture was, in fact, a construct that public museums made possible. At the same time, these forms of vicarious tourism had the inverse effect of accentuating the distance between Europeans and their colonial counterparts, as Beverly Grindstaff's study of the 1904 World's Fair in St Louis makes indisputably clear. The St Louis Fair's most widely visited attraction was a 47-acre display consisting of 1200 Filipinos, which attracted 18.5 million people during its seven-month run. These living displays, Grindstaff argues, operated as literal demonstrations of colonial precepts – lending racism a spatial dimension facilitated by academics such as Dean Conant Worchester, assistant professor of Zoology at the University of Michigan, who served as consultants and producers of literature for both specialist audiences and the general public.

In public museums and trade fairs alike, observed differences were presented as scientific indices of the comparative anatomy of races and peoples. The phrasing of civilization as a biological accomplishment, Grindstaff concludes, allowed racial hierarchies to be presented as self-evident. Moreover, in the case of the St Louis Fair, held shortly after the US purchased the Philippines from Spain, the 'twinned mechanisms' of race 'science' and classification deflected Philippine claims to self-rule – and this racialized discourse pervaded the political arena until 1935, when self-government was finally granted to the Philippines.

The displays of peoples at trade fairs and the educational practices of public museums of the late nineteenth and early twentieth centuries are both profoundly indebted to centuries-old debates over intellectual differences among human beings distinguished on the basis of visible characteristics. Racial qualities, like national characteristics, were considered to be in some sense innate, inherited, and distinguishing features of family groups. Since the 1790s, the word 'race', signifying permanent hereditary differences between family groups, was considered an important factor in determining peculiar cultural characteristics. The fundamental issue at stake was whether racial differences in mental ability existed – and if so, how were they inherited: could cultural acquisitions be passed on from one generation to the next? The anatomist Georges Cuvier, who claimed that negroes were stupid because they lacked civilization, was an early and influential proponent of the idea that permanent differences in mental capability were inherited 'racial' characteristics.[3] Cuvier ranked the '*human* races' according to their design, even devising a scale of intelligence on this visual basis, that gave 30 per cent to apes, 70 per cent to Negroes, 80 per cent to Europeans, *90 per cent to ancient Greek sculptures of men, and 100 per cent to sculptures of divinities.*[4] On the other hand, the Chevalier de Lamarck, a well-known early nineteenth-century biologist, assumed that genetic characteristics are culturally acquired.[5] Lamarckians were, for this reason, racial formalists who believe that genetic improvements in 'races' would result from providing individuals with a better social environment.[6]

Anthropological discussions, extending beyond scientific debates to the popular press and mass entertainment, emphasized that aesthetic capability manifested in artistic productions helped to define degrees of cultural progress, and hence degrees of humanness. Darwin's *Descent of Man* (1871) suggests how evolutionary theory was applied *in its crudest form* to the study of culture. Darwin placed savages at a point intermediary between man and animals – and even lower than some animals: 'Judging from the hideous ornaments and the equally hideous music admired by most savages, it might be argued that their aesthetic faculty was not so highly developed as in certain animals, for instance in birds.'[7]

In this chapter of *Grasping the World*, Sandra Esslinger studies the museum organized by the German Third Reich according to the tenets of Nazi *Volk* ideology. It should be recognized, Esslinger writes, 'that the Temple of German Art was the progeny of Enlightenment thinking', modeled directly on Winckelmann's ideas. No matter how misguided its mode of privileging reason through the application of 'scientific laws' appears to most people now, at the time of its conception, it had much in common with progressive eugenicist ideas for educating the public. Nazi art historians promoted the notion of classic or Hellenic beauty, considering any deviation degenerate. The predominant concern of the curators of the Temple of German Art was, moreover, to 'civilize' the public through an aesthetic education, as was that of the progressive advocates of early twentieth-century museums studied in this chapter by Coombes and Grindstaff. Using pre-existing social activities and familiar symbols, providing for the comfort of visitors in an architectural setting made expressly for the purpose of constructing *Volk* identity and behavior, the Nazis intended to ease people comfortably into their racist propaganda schemes.[8]

Recognizing 'race' in current museum practices

The classifactory schemes and display methods of contemporary museums belie any obvious debts to such problematic ideas and practices of moral education. Yet, as Homi Bhabha argues in an exhibition review of 1992 included below, making global art more readily available to the embrace of multicultural aesthetics or meticulous archival studies does not change 'the angle of visibility within the museum'. Cultural identity in contemporary museology – one says 'contemporary' but the point of the seven case studies in this chapter is that it has been there all along–is represented as an egalitarianism of authenticity. Yet the foundational assumption of this purported authenticity must be properly understood as a segregationist essentialism, along what Bhabha calls an aesthetic axis of 'equal distance equal[ling] equal difference'.

We have included Shelly Errington's study of 'cosmic theme parks' in the modern Republic of Indonesia, which argues that the contemporary corporatist performance of collective identity is not limited to nation-states with a predominantly European cultural heritage. She builds on anthropologist Clifford Geertz's claim that nation-building involves constructing a collective subject ('an experiential "we" from whose will the activities of the government seem spontaneously to flow'), and historian Benedict Anderson's character-ization of modern nation-states as 'imagined communities' that distinguish themselves from one another by their different visual symbols and 'semiotic technologies'. Errington argues that the distinctive spatial and temporal ordering of Balinese and Javanese representations derives from their 'concentric' cosmologies. She analyzes the state-sponsored national theme park of 'Taman Mini' and the international section of the Hatta-Sukarno airport outside the nation's capital of Jakarta. In both cases, iconic references to cosmology, in the form of architecture and spatial layout, are pressed into the service of 'an internal colonial power' with Java at the center of control.

This framing of the nation through amusements that informally educate the public by presenting ideology in the form of ordered public spaces is strongly reminiscent of the world trade fairs studied by Coombes and Grindstaff and of Esslinger's study of Nazi art museums. What is most oppressive about the appropriations in all cases is the manner in which visual symbols (such as parks configured as maps of the nation-state) appear to give equal time to different ethnic groups while simultaneously preserving the centrality of the ruling elite. The theme park of Taman Mini, Errington writes, 'is a fantasized community which is not a community at all, since no one lives there, but the fantasized image of a fantasy polity, an imaginary Indonesia mapped as a conflict-free, cleaned up version of the nation state'.

Museums defined as a set of social practices have been and remain a key instrument in the production and perpetuation of an imperialistic modernity practiced on a global scale. It is supremely disingenuous to proclaim that radical changes in scenography – whether under the rubric of a 'new' museology or not – constitute effective social critique. A major problem with such evaluations is that as long as the aesthetic ideology of 'originality' determines the 'value' of social critique, the critique itself operates at a symbolic level, displaced from the actual social conditions that the critique aims to reform.

Our modernities and their museologies are bound up with the circumstance of living on an event-horizon that never arrives, and that is pursued by bootstrapping ourselves step by step along a trail of 'afters' or 'posts' that seem to be headed to where we might wish ourselves to be found. This is commonly conceived as an imaginary fulfilment of some essential nature we would wish ourselves to be descended from but which is now obscured, lost, or stolen: a past to which we will always have a relationship simultaneously centrifugal and centripetal. Social existence in the modern nation-state, and even more so in its contemporary transnational corporatist permutations, involves an inherently unstable and fragile *triangulation* between the present moment, its past, and its future.

In turning to the articles gathered under the rubric of 'building shared imaginaries and effacing otherness', consider Gayatri Chakravorti Spivak's wideranging (self-)critique of postcolonial theory, in a book tellingly subtitled 'Toward a History of the Vanishing Present'. She writes from the (im)possible position of the native informant whose identity has not been shaped by the European heritage of philosophical aesthetics, not even its contemporary critique:

The possibility of the native informant is, as I have already indicated, inscribed as evidence in the production of the scientific or disciplinary European knowledge of the culture of others: from field-work through ethnography into anthropology. That apparently benign subordination of 'timing' (the lived) into 'Time' (the graph of the Law) cannot of course be re-traced to a restorable origin, if origin there is to be found. But the resistant reader and teacher can at least (and persistently) attempt to undo that continuing subordination by the figuration of the name – 'the native informant' – into a reader's perspective. Are we still condemned to circle around 'Idea, Logos, and Form' or can the (ex)orbitant at least be invoked?[9]

It is now a full decade since the National Gallery of Art in Washington mounted that remarkable exhibition entitled 'Circa 1492: Art in the Age of Exploration', which was the occasion for Bhabha's incisive critique. Bhabha articulated concrete ways in which this museological fabrication of a 'culture of Discovery' became a palimpsest of the colonial destruction of cultures. He suggested that the 'parallelisms' and cultural coevalities projected by the exhibition only wound up supporting the centrality of Western ideologies of time, progress, and social and cultural evolution. Getting beyond this is what is most urgently needed in contemporary museology no less than in art history, theory, and criticism. Yet unless our academic endeavors are linked explicitly to the oldest and most fundamental questions of how our societies should be run, they will remain facets of the corporatized aestheticism of identity politics and of the infotainment and edutainment industries that constitute cultural practice in the epoch called globalization.

A critique of the 'new museology' as a set of practices to make diverse populations governable is developed in Chapters 4, 5, and 6. Critical assessment of the ways in which the building of homogeneous shared imaginaries effaces otherness has, however, only barely begun. The major work of the socially responsible critical historian lies ahead. But we should heed the sobering lessons learned from our predecessors who embraced eugenics in the name of educating the masses. For no matter how strongly anyone insists that things 'represent' who and what we imagine ourselves truly to be, something will always be missing. Given what is available now about the lingering, largely unacknowledged debts of contemporary museums and academic endeavor to racial 'science', it is from the position of what is missing that an ethical critique of society must *now* originate.

NOTES

1. Johannes Fabian, *Time and the Other*, New York: Columbia University, 1983, p. 111.

2. Bourdieu, cited by Fabian, in *Time and the Other*, p. 139.

3. Cited by Nancy Stepan, *The Idea of Race in Science: Great Britain, 1800–1960*, Hamden, Conn.: Archon Books, 1982, 14. Anthony Pagden, *European Encounters with the New World: From Renaissance to Romanticism*, New Haven: Yale University Press, 1993, p. 11, cites sixteenth-century precedents of the idea of polygenism, early challenges to the Graeco-Christian notion of the integrity of the human race.

4. Cited by Stepan, *The Idea of Race in Science*, 14, citing Sir William Lawrence, *Lectures on Physiology, Zoology, and the Natural History of Man, delivered at the Royal College of Surgeons*, London: Callow, 1819, 335.

5. See further George W. Stocking, *Race, Culture, and Evolution: Essays in the History of Anthropology*, New York: Free Press, 1968, 234–69; Carl N. Degler, *In Search of Human Nature: The Decline and Revival of Darwinism in American Social Thought*, New York: Oxford University Press, 1991, 85–6. Theories of culturally acquired genetic characteristics were discredited in the late nineteenth century (replaced by race theory based on absolute genetic differences). Riegl's reference to Goethe may refer to Goethe's close association with Lavater, who encouraged theories of genetic inheritance based on *visual* characteristics (*Essai sur la Physiognomie*, 1781). On Goethe's racist image in the nineteenth-century popular press, see George L. Mosse, *Toward the Final Solution: a History of European Racism*, London: Dent, 1978, 26.

6. Most Lamarckians opposed miscegenation for this reason; see Stocking, *Race, Culture, and Evolution*. Stocking shows that many writers at the end of the nineteenth century combined elements of Lamarckian, pre-Darwinian thinking with some of Darwin's ideas. The following synopsis of anthropological issues is based substantially on Stocking.

7. Darwin, *The Descent of Man and Selection in Relation to Sex*, I, 64, as cited by Stepan, in *The Idea of Race in Science*, 54.

8. Sandra Lotte Esslinger, 'Art in the Third Reich: The Fabrication of National Cultural Identity', unpublished Ph.D. thesis, University of California at Los Angeles, 2001, 56, citing Mosse.

9. See Gayatri Chakravorti Spivak, *A Critique of Postcolonial Reason*, Cambridge, Mass. and London: Harvard University Press, 1999, Chapter 1: 'Philosophy', pp. 66–7, in the course of critiquing Kristeva's 'bewilderingly Eurocentric account of feminist critique'.

1.

Double Visions

Homi K. Bhabha

As you enter the first gallery of 'Circa 1492: Art in the Age of Exploration', your Acoustiguide – J. Carter Brown himself, the director of the National Gallery – leads you to a cabinet of late-medieval treasures: an ostrich egg. brought to Europe from North Africa in classical antiquity, and turned into a gold jug sometime in the 14th century: a rock-crystal elephant, carved in India in the 15th century, caparisoned with gold and enamel mounts somewhere in Europe during the 16th century, and made up as a salt cellar. In these exotic transformations, wide geographical distances conjure cunningly with historical circumstance. The creation of a global culture circa 1492, as it emerges in the 'sciences' of mapping and measurement and in the fantasy of cultural expansion, is a major narrative of this exhibit.

Immediately after these gilded Oriental treasures, your Acoustiguide draws you to the dark testimony of Hieronymus Bosch's *Temptation of St. Anthony*, 1500–1505. Bosch's 'absurdist' images play out the drama of evil, which they set in a theater of the dream symbol. In testing the limits of the *sensus communis* and of its pictorial conventions, they explore the problematic projection of the 'human' as it struggles, at the very threshold of early modernity, to become the representative figure in the arts. This is the other central focus of the show.

'Circa 1492' is an exhibit with a double vision: the eye expanding to hold the world in one space: the eye averted, awry, attenuated, trying to see the uniqueness of each specific cultural tradition and production. The show is crafted from a creative tension deep within the early modern moment. On the one hand, art is Map, striving to calculate the world picture on one continuous surface in two dimensions. On the other, Man conjures restlessly to break up that surface, to deepen it with dark dimensions, to personify it with perspective. The exhibition's unique message in 'this year of Discovery-Pride', as Daniel J. Boorstin writes in the catalogue's framing essay, 'is to become aware of the limits of the kinds of fulfillment that dominate our consciousness in an age of science'.

The Culture of Discovery, an invisible community forged in the spirit of quest, focused on ... an earth to be mastered and mapped ... But the Culture of Creation was a host of countless independents. Their only limits were their inherited styles and materials ... Their heterogeneous and chaotic worlds, instead of nourishing our pride in a generalized mankind, inspire our awe in the infinite capacities of atomic individuals ... We must be struck by the diffuseness and the disconnectedness of man's efforts in different places ... In the Culture of Creation there is no correct or incorrect, and the long run no progress. Works of art reveal no linear direction but experiments radiating in all directions. While the post-Columbian maps of the world make their predecessors obsolete, works of art are always additive.[1]

This dynamic of Discovery and Creation certainly goes a way toward questioning the idea of progress as a universal ethic of cultural development. There is an attempt here to revise the linear perspective upon which the West makes its claims to cultural supremacy, claims that it roots in a narrative which establishes Renaissance perspective as the natural one for the arts. The structuring principle of 'Circa 1492', as curator Jay A. Levenson informs us, is the 'horizontal survey'. Yet the show aims at a unified effect: from the effort 'to present each civilization on its own terms, not as it might have appeared to visiting Europeans of the period', a marvelous parallelism is to emerge.[2]

This is certainly controversial. Is it possible to 'present each civilization on its own terms' once the avowed purpose is to produce a global show of marvelous parallels? This parallelism itself, as an exhibition strategy, must be a critical interpretation of the skeined, cross-cultural history of the infiltration and conquest that followed from exploration, and that interpretation must come from somewhere. Yet for Michael Kimmelman of the *New York Times*, the terms of the exhibit are a 'conceptual hodgepodge', particularly in the later Asian and American sections, where 'whether Western formalism is the most revealing way to examine non-Western cultures is one more question that "Circa 1492" leaves open'.[3] He is right to point out that the appraisal of non-Western cultures is largely technical and esthetic, but why does a more pliant and useful critical or curatorial response to cultural difference fail to develop?

The answer lies in the parallelism that 'Circa 1492' promotes both as a cultural paradigm and, more significantly, as a form of spectatorship. Despite the show's three sections ('Europe and the Mediterranean World', 'Toward Cathay', and 'The Americas'), which attempt to provide local cultural contexts, the terms of the show are substantially set toward the end of the first part, in the subsection on the Renaissance titled 'The Mean and Measure of All Things'. In Europe, this is the moment of the emergence of the human figure as the 'universal' measure of culture; it is the moment of perspective; of the birth of the 'artist'; of Leonardo and Dürer; above all, for this exhibit, it is the moment that brings forth the show's most celebrated icon, Leonardo's *Portrait of a Lady with an Ermine*, c. 1490, his picture of Cecilia Gallerani, an accomplished and adventurous Milanese.

We arrive in her presence after encountering maps and astrolabes, trophies of Portuguese and Spanish discovery. Islamic treasures, anatomical and architectural drawings, and that arresting queen mother's head from Benin, which exhibits a formal quality 'without any uncertainty, to whose perfection any indication of humanity has yielded'.[4] With Cecilia Gallerani it is different: it is precisely her uncertainty, her enigmatic look away from the frame, that conveys 'il concetto dell'anima (the intentions of the subject's mind)'.[5] Cecilia's subtle glance away establishes or is emblematic of a whole tradition of looking at art and culture. And it is, ironically, through her distracted gaze that the spectator of 'Circa 1492' is first inscribed and then held to the ideology and iconography of 'humanness' that lies behind the attempt to present cultural difference in marvelous parallels.

For Cecilia's distraction displays that very quality of creative 'heterogeneity' that Boorstin recommends as the unique vision of 'Circa 1492'. It is a concept of heterogeneity precisely restricted to the 'atomic individual' – the authentic artist and the unique artwork. This is a concept that cannot be generalized into forms of cultural difference generated in and through the interaction and articulation of cultural systems. At the individual level, heterogeneity can only be expressive of preexisting 'differences'. But a theory of cultural difference must be able to explain those transformations in esthetic value and cultural practice that are produced through histories and broader patterns of cultural conflict, appropriation, and resistance to domination. The predominant perspective of 'Circa 1492' is to allow cultural heterogeneity at the individual level so long as the homogeneity of the (Western) notion of the human is left relatively uncomplicated within a universal esthetic realm. The parallel begins to look distinctly circular.

Let us imagine that as Cecilia looks away, her distracted gaze falls upon Dürer's portraits of a black man, from c. 1505–6 and of the enslaved woman Katherina, from 1521, to be found a few feet from the Leonardo. Suddenly I am caught between the master and the enslaved. The Acoustiguide tells me of Dürer's interest in the diversity of nature – 'in exotica imported from around the world'. Then I turn to the portraits, trying to decipher the 'intentions of the subject's mind': the black man dressed in what looks like a Venetian cape, the black woman who has had her hair 'confined within a European headdress'. In its spirit of parallelism, the catalogue suggests that Dürer goes beyond artistic and cultural stereotypes and shows himself 'sensitive to the personality as well as the exotic potential of his sitter'.[6] Can the two be compatible when exoticism erases rather than enhances personality? Since that is the case, can these portraits of Dürer's be more than naturalist studies? Can the 'mean and measure of all things' frame this radical heterogeneity of the human condition when the catalogue entry states that circa 1492 there were between 140,000 and 170,000 African slaves in Europe?

Where Cecilia's gaze and Katherina's downcast look cross, there is no parallelism, no equidistance. We are at the critical point of contesting histories and incommensurable subjects of humanity. Histories of the master come to be reinscribed in terms of, or in contention with, the enslaved or the colonized. Circa 1992, this will be the spectatorial position of the non-Europeans or half-Europeans, the African-Americans, the Chicanas and Chicanos, the Asian-Americans, the Latin Americans – to name only some of the hyphenated and hybridized peoples among other visiting Americans and Europeans – who now may visit the National Gallery, and who are now a significant part of the 'national' scene. These are, after all, the very peoples whose histories were most graphically and tragically made and unmade in the wake of the Age of Exploration, circa 1492. It is clearly in their direction that the organizers aim their laudable attempt to staunch the 'nationalist' sentiment of 'Discovery-Pride' and to complicate the Eurocentric celebration of Columbus. But the show is complicated by another kind of historical parallelism that is somewhat less marvelous, and much more melancholic.

Holbein's famous painting *The Ambassadors*, 1533, depicts the Nuremberg globe of c. 1526, which records the route of Magellan's voyage around the world, completed just a few years earlier. Amidst the display of the *vanitas* of Discovery – fur robes, scrolls, vainglory – there is that strange anamorphic disk in the foreground of the frame, which when viewed from an oblique angle reveals a skull. This skull is not simply the natural echo of death amidst the vanity of human wishes. Historically, it is the emblem of the death, disease, and destruction that constituted the 'desire' for the globe in the 15th and 16th centuries. 'The union of peoples, therefore, meant a union of germs, as death danced its macabre dance around the globe,' John Elliot writes in his brilliant catalogue essay, 'but death came in many forms, and not least by war ... It was to the sound of gunfire that European merchants fanned out across the world.'[7] Where does this history feature in Boorstin's dialectic of Discovery and Creativity? Or does it demand an angle of vision – a mode of address, a formation of spectatorship – that is at odds with the curatorial spirit of marvelous parallelism?

Holbein's anamorphic skull – the painting is not included in 'Circa 1492' – emerges as the emblem of the death and alienation at the very heart of Discovery Pride. It is not simply another historical theme or perspective that could be placed beside Boorstin's dialectic, within the same 'horizontal' survey. For the skull emerges only when the viewer declines from the horizontal plane of *The Ambassadors* and moves sideways, in a position no longer centered in the gaze of the picture. From this point of displacement, the skull turns uncannily into a cadaverous orb, contesting the authority and the iconography of that other glorious globe, the Nuremberg map above it. Of course, as Jacques Lacan points out, the viewer's eye is another sphere caught in this crossfire.[8] It is not that the viewer, seeing from the same space, has absorbed a different aspect of the work. The space of spectatorship itself has become transformative and contradictory. The work of art is caught in double historical frames with contending focal points. As the oblique angle of the skull displaces the right-angled view and horizontal axis of Holbein's central image of the Nuremberg globe, the culture of Discovery becomes a palimpsest of the colonial destruction of cultures.

This is not an academic art-historical issue. Circa 1992, the international or global art-show has become the prodigious exhibitionary mode of Western 'national' museums. Exhibiting art from the colonized or postcolonial world, displaying the work of the marginalized or the minority, disinterring forgotten, forlorn 'pasts' – such curatorial projects end up supporting the centrality of the Western museum. Parallelism suggests that there is an equidistant moment between cultures, and where better to stage it – who could better afford to stage it? – than the great metropolitan centers of the West. The promise of coevality with regard to space and presentation may well be kept; the choice of works of art from 'other' cultures may well be catholic and noncanonical. All this may make 'global' art more readily available to the embrace of multicultural esthetics or a meticulous archival study. But the angle of visibility within the museum will not change. What was once exotic or archaic, tribal or folkloristic, inspired by strange gods, is now given a secular national present, and an international future. Sites of cultural difference too easily become part of the post-Modern West's thirst for its own ethnicity; for citation and simulacral echoes from Elsewhere.

The global perspective in 1492 as in 1992 is the purview of power. The globe shrinks for those who own it; for the displaced or the dispossessed, the migrant or refugee, no distance is more awesome than the few feet across borders or frontiers. The parallelism of the modern museum, in its internationalist mode, turns on an esthetic axis of 'equal distance equal difference', but the history of culture has been neither so equitable nor so ecumenical. The postcolonial perspective suggests rather that in the presentation of cultures, Western and non-Western, we adopt the perspective of the 'parallax' (a word that enters the language circa 1594): 'The apparent displacement or difference in the apparent position of an object caused by actual change or difference of position of the point of observation.'[9] As the globe revolves, its other side uncannily discloses a skull.

As we enter the final phase of the exhibition, 'The Americas', the tragic history of globality circa 1492 becomes more apparent and the need for the parallax more pertinent. The great remains of the Inca or Aztec world are the debris of the Culture of Discovery. Their presence in the museum should reflect the devastation that has turned them from being signs in a powerful cultural system to becoming the symbols of a destroyed culture. There is no simple parallelism or equidistance between different historical pasts. A distinction must be maintained – in the very conventions of presentation – between works of art whose pasts have known the colonial violence of destruction and domination, and works that have evolved into an antiquity of a more continuous, consensual kind, moving from courts to collectors, from mansions to museums. Without making such a distinction we can only be connoisseurs of the survival of Art, at the cost of becoming conspirators in the death of History.

NOTES

1.   Daniel J. Boorstin, 'The Realms of Pride and Awe', in Jay A. Levenson, ed., *Circa 1492: Art in the Age of Exploration*, Washington, D.C.: National Gallery of Art, and New Haven: Yale University Press, 1991, p. 17.

2.   Levenson, 'Circa 1492: History and Art', in *Circa 1492*, p. 19.

3.   Michael Kimmelman, 'Circa 1492: An Enormous, Magnificent Muddle', *The New York Times*, 20 October 1991, p. II:37.

4.   See Ezio Bassani, 'Queen Mother Head', *Circa 1492*, p. 178.

5.   Martin Kemp, 'Portrait of a Lady with an Ermine (Cecilia Gallerani)', *Circa 1492*, p. 272.

6.   Jean Michel Massing, 'Portrait of a Black Man' and 'Portrait of Katherina', *Circa 1492*, pp. 288–9.

7.   John H. Elliot, 'A World United', *Circa 1492*, p. 648.

8.   See Jacques Lacan, 'Anamorphosis', *The Four Fundamental Concepts of Psycho-Analysis*, ed. Jacques-Alain Miller, trans. Alan Sheridan, New York and London: W.W. Norton & Company, 1981, pp. 79–91.

9.   *The Compact Edition of the Oxford English Dictionary*, 1971, s.v. 'parallax'.

2.

Teddy Bear Patriarchy:
Taxidermy in the Garden of Eden, New York City, 1908-1936

Donna Haraway

The American Museum of Natural History and the Social Construction of Scientific Knowledge: Institution

'Speak to the Earth and It Shall Teach Thee.'[1]

'Every specimen is a permanent fact.'[2]

From 1890 to 1930, the 'Nature Movement' was at its height in the United States. Ambivalence about 'civilization' is an old theme in US history, and this ambivalence was never higher than after the Civil War, and during the early decades of monopoly capital formation.[3] Civilization, obviously, refers to a complex pattern of domination of people and everybody (everything) else, often ascribed to technology – fantasized as 'the Machine'. Nature is such a potent symbol of innocence partly because 'she' is imagined to be without technology, to be the object of vision, and so a source of both health and purity. Man is not in nature partly because he is not seen, is not the spectacle. A constitutive meaning of masculine gender for us is to be the unseen, the eye (I), the author. Indeed that is part of the structure of experience in the museum, one of the reasons one has, willy nilly, the moral status of a young boy undergoing initiation through visual experience. Is anyone surprised that psychologists find 20th-century US boys excel in dissecting visual fields? The museum is a visual technology. It works through desire for communion, not separation, and one of its products is gender. Who needs infancy in the nuclear family when we have rebirth in the ritual spaces of Teddy Bear Patriarchy?

Obviously, this essay is premised on the inversion of a causal relation of technology to the social relations of domination: the social relations of domination, I am arguing, are frozen into the hardware and logics of technology. Nature is, in 'fact', constructed as a technology through social praxis. And dioramas are meaning-machines. Machines are time slices into the social organisms that made them. Machines are maps of power, arrested moments of social relations that in turn threaten to govern the living. The owners of the great machines of monopoly capital – the so-called means of production – were, with excellent reason, at the forefront of nature work – because it was one of the means of production of race, gender and class. For them, 'naked eye science' could give direct vision of social peace and progress despite the appearances of class war and decadence. They required a science 'instaurating' jungle peace, with its promise of restored manhood, complete with a transcendent ethic of hunting; and so they bought it.

This scientific discourse on origins was not cheap; and the servants of science, human and animal, were not tame. The relations of knowledge and power at the American Museum of Natural History are not caught by telling a tale of the great capitalists in the sky conspiring to obscure the truth. Quite the opposite, the tale must be of committed Progressives struggling to dispel darkness through research, education and reform. The great capitalists were not in the sky; they were in the field, armed with the *Gospel of Wealth*.[4] They were also often armed with an elephant gun and an Akeley camera.[5] This entire essay [of which an excerpt is reproduced here] has been about the 'social construction of knowledge'. There is no boundary between the 'inside' and 'outside' of science, such that in one universe social relations appear, but in the other the history of ideas proceeds. Sciences are woven of social relations throughout their tissues. The concept of social relations must include the entire complex of interactions among people, as individuals and in groups of various sizes; objects, including books, buildings, and rocks; and animals, including apes and elephants.[6]

But in this section of Teddy Bear Patriarchy, I want to explore one band in the spectrum of social relations – the philanthropic activities of men in the American Museum of Natural History which fostered exhibition (including public education and scientific collecting), conservation, and eugenics. These activities are the optic tectum of naked eye science, i.e., the neural organs of integration and interpretation. This essay has moved from the immediacy of experience, through the mediations of biography and story telling [note that this an excerpt]; we now must look at a synthesis of social construction.[7]

But first a word on decadence, the threat against which exhibition, conservation, and eugenics were all directed as coordinated medical interventions, as prophylaxis for an endangered body politic. The museum was a medical technology, a hygienic intervention, and the pathology was a potentially fatal organic sickness of the individual and collective body. Decadence was a venereal disease proper to the organs of social and personal reproduction: sex, race, and class. From the point of view of Teddy Bear Patriarchy, race suicide was a clinical manifestation whose mechanism was the differential reproductive rates of anglo-saxon v. 'non-white' immigrant women. Class war, a pathological antagonism of functionally related groups in society, seemed imminent. A burning question in the last decades of the

19th century concerned the energetic economy of middle class women undertaking higher education: was their health, reproductive capacity and nutritive function, imperiled; were they unsexed by diverting the limited store of organic energy to their heads at crucial organic moments? Nature was threatened by the machine in the garden; the proper interface of the Age of Man and the Age of Mammals could perhaps preserve the potency of the vision of nature and so restore the energy of man. These are strange concerns for the cyborgs of the late 20th century, whose preoccupation with stress and its baroque technicist, code-implicated pathologies makes decadence seem quaint. Infection and decay have been incorporated into coding errors signified by acronyms – AIDS. But for white, middle class Americans before World War II decadence mattered. Lung disease (remember Teddy Roosevelt's asthma and alcoholic brother, not to mention America's version of *Magic Mountain*), sexual disease (what was not a sexual disease, when leprosy, masturbation, and Charlotte Perkins Gilman's need to write all qualified?), and social disease (like strikes and feminism) all disclosed ontologically and epistemologically similar disorders of the relations of nature and culture. Decadence threatened in two interconnected ways, both related to functioning energy-limited productive systems. The machine (remember the iconic power of the railroad) and its fierce artificiality threatened to consume and exhaust man. And the sexual economy of man seemed vulnerable on the one hand to exhaustion and on the other to submergence in unruly and primitive excess. The trustees and officers of the museum were charged with the task of promoting public health in these circumstances.

EXHIBITION

The American Museum of Natural History was (and is) a 'private' institution, as private could only be defined in the US. In Europe the natural history museums were organs of the state, intimately connected to the fates of national politics.[8] Kennedy's history of the American Museum stresses how intimately connected the development of all the US natural history museums was with the origins of the great class of capitalists after the Civil War. The social fate of that class was also the fate of the museum; its rearrangements and weaknesses in the 1930s were reproduced in crises in the museum, ideologically and organizationally. Philanthropy from the hands of the Rockefellers was mediated by a very complex machinery for the allocation of funds and determination of worthy recipients. The American Museum was not buffered in that way from intimate reliance on the personal beneficence of a few wealthy men. The American Museum is a particularly transparent window for spying on the wealthy in their ideal incarnation, for they made dioramas of themselves.

The great scientific collecting expeditions from the American Museum began in 1888 and stretched to the 1930s. By 1910, they had resulted in gaining for the museum a major scientific reputation in selected fields, especially paleontology, ornithology, and mammalogy. The museum in 1910 boasted nine scientific departments and twenty-five scientists. Anthropology also benefited, and the largest collecting expedition ever mounted by the museum was the 1890s Jesup North Pacific Expedition so important to Franz Boas's career.[9] The sponsors of the museum liked a science that stored facts safely; they liked the public popularity of the new exhibitions. Many people among the white, protestant middle and upper classes in the United States were committed to nature, camping, and the outdoor life; Teddy Roosevelt embodied their politics and their ethos. Theodore Roosevelt's father was one of the incorporators of the museum in 1868. His son, Kermit, was a trustee during the building of African Hall. Others in that cohort of trustees were J. P. Morgan, William K. Vanderbilt, Henry W. Sage, H. F. Osborn, Daniel Pomeroy, E. Roland Harriman, Childs Frick, John D. Rockefeller III, and Madison Grant. These are leaders of movements for eugenics, conservation, and the rational management of capitalist society. They are patrons of science.

The first Great Hall of dioramas was Frank Chapman's Hall of North American Birds, opened in 1903. [Explorer and taxidermist Carl E.] Akeley was hired to enhance the museum's ability to prepare the fascinating African game, especially elephants; and he conceived the African Hall idea on his first collecting trip for the American Museum. Osborn hoped for – and got – a North American and Asian Mammal Hall after the African one. The younger trustees in the 1920s formed an African Big Game Club that invited wealthy sportsmen to join in contributing specimens and money to the African Hall. The 1920s were prosperous for these men, and they gave generously. Thirty to forty expeditions in some years were mounted in the 1920s to get the unknown facts of nature. There were over one hundred expeditions in the field for the American Museum in that decade.[10]

There was also a significant expansion of the museum's educational endeavors. Over one million children per year in New York were looking at 'nature cabinets' put together by the museum. Radio talks, magazine articles, and books covered the museum's popular activities, which appeared in many ways to be a science for the people, like that of the *National Geographic*, which taught republican Americans their responsibilities in empire after 1898. Significantly, both *Natural History*, the museum's publication, and *National Geographic* relied heavily on photographs.[11] There was a big building program from 1909 to 1929; and the Annual Report of the Museum for 1921 quoted the estimate by its director that 2,452,662 (any significant decimal places?!) people were reached by the museum and its education extension program, including the nature cabinets and food exhibits circulating through the city public health department.

Osborn summarized the fond hopes of educators like himself in his claim that children who pass through the museum's halls 'become more reverent, more truthful, and more interested in the simple and natural laws of their being and better citizens of the future through each visit'. He maintained also that the book of nature, written only in facts, was proof against the failing of other books: 'The French and Russian anarchies were based in books and in oratory in defiance of every law of nature.'[12] Osborn went beyond pious hopes and constructed a Hall of the Age of Man to make the moral lessons of racial hierarchy and progress explicit, lest they be missed in gazing at elephants.[13] He countered those who criticized the Halls and educational work as too expensive, requiring too much time that would be better spent on science itself. 'The exhibits in these Halls have been criticized only by those who speak without knowledge. They all tend to demonstrate the slow upward ascent and struggle of man from the lower to the higher stages, physically, morally, intellectually, and spiritually. Reverently and carefully examined, they put man upwards towards a higher and better future and away from the purely animal stage of life.'[14] This is the Gospel of Wealth, reverently examined.

PROPHYLAXIS

Two other undertakings in this period at the American Museum require comment: eugenics and conservation. They were closely linked in philosophy and in personnel at the museum, and they tied in closely with exhibition and research. For example, the notorious author of *The Passing of the Great Race*, Madision Grant, was a successful corporation lawyer, a trustee of the American Museum, an organizer of support for the North American Hall, a co-founder of the California Save-the-Redwoods League, activist for making Mt McKinley and adjacent lands a national park, and the powerful secretary of the New York Zoological Society. His preservation of nature and germ plasm all seemed the same sort of work. Grant was not a quack or an extremist. He represented a band of Progressive opinion, one terrified of the consequences of unregulated monopoly capitalism, including failure to regulate the importation of non-white (which included Jewish and southern European) working classes who invariably had more prolific women than the 'old American stock'. The role of the museum in establishing Parc Albert in the Belgian Congo has already been noted. Powerful men in the American scientific establishment were involved in that significant venture in international scientific cooperation: John C. Merriam of the Carnegie Institution of Washington, George Vincent of the Rockefeller Foundation, Osborn at the American Museum. The first significant user of the sanctuary would be sent by the founder of primatology in America, Robert Yerkes, for a study of the psychobiology of wild gorillas. Yerkes was a leader in the movements for social hygiene, the category in which eugenics and conservation also fit. It was all in the service of science.

The Second International Congress of Eugenics was held at the American Museum of Natural History in 1921 while Akeley was in the field collecting gorillas and initiating plans for Parc Albert. Osborn, an ardent eugenicist, believed that it was '[p]erhaps the most important scientific meeting ever held in the Museum'. All the leading US universities and state institutions sent representatives, and there were many eminent foreign delegates. The proceedings were collected in a volume plainly titled 'Eugenics in Family, Race, and State'. The Congress had a special fruit savored by Osborn. 'The section of the exhibit bearing on immigration was then sent to Washington by the Committee on Immigration of the Congress, members of which made several visits to the Museum to study the exhibit. The press was at first inclined to treat the work of the Congress lightly ... but as the sound and patriotic series of addresses and papers on heredity, the Family, the Race and the State succeeded one another, the influence of the Congress grew and found its way into news and editorial columns of the entire press of the United States.' Immigration restriction laws, to protect the Race, the only race needing a capital letter, from 'submergence by the influx of other races',[15] were passed by the United States Congress in 1923.

The 1930s were a hiatus for the Museum. Not only did the Depression lead to reduced contributions, but basic ideologies and politics shifted, making the formations discussed in this essay less relevant to the American ruling classes, although the Museum remained popular with New York's people way beyond the 1930s and eugenics sterilization laws have remained on the books into the late 20th century. The changes were not abrupt; but even the racial doctrines so openly championed by the Museum were publicly criticized in the 1940s, though not until then. Conservation was pursued with different political and spiritual justifications. A different biology was being born, more in the hands of the Rockefeller Foundation and in a different social womb. The issue would be molecular biology and other forms of post-organismic cyborg biology. The threat of decadence gave way to the catastrophes of the obsolescence of man (and of all organic nature) and the disease of stress, realities announced vigorously after World War II. Different forms of capitalist patriarchy and racism would emerge, embodied as always in a retooled nature. Decadence is a disease of organisms; obsolescence and stress are conditions of technological systems. Hygiene would give way to systems engineering as the basis of medical, religious, political, and scientific story telling practices.

To summarize the themes of Teddy Bear Patriarchy, let us compare the three public activities of the Museum, all dedicated to preserving a threatened manhood. They were exhibition, eugenics, and conservation. Exhibition has been described here at greatest length; it was a practice to produce permanence, to arrest decay. Eugenics was a movement to preserve hereditary stock, to assure racial purity, to prevent race suicide. Conservation was a policy to preserve resources, not only for industry, but also for moral formation, for the achievement of manhood. All three activities were a prescription to cure or prevent decadence, the dread disease of imperialist, capitalist, and white culture. All three activities were considered forms of education and forms of science; they were also very close to religious practice and certainly shared qualities, as well as professional interest, of medical practice. These three activities were all about preservation, purity, social order, health, and the transcendence of death, personal and collective. They attempted to insure preservation without fixation and paralysis, in the face of extraordinary change in the relations of sex, race, and class.

The leaders of the American Museum of Natural History would insist that they were trying to know and to save nature, reality. And the real was one. The explicit ontology was holism, organicism. There was also an aesthetic appropriate to exhibition, conservation, and eugenics from 1890 to 1930: realism. But in the 1920s the surrealists knew that behind the day lay the night of sexual terror, disembodiment, failure of order; in short, castration and impotence of the seminal body which had spoken all the important words for centuries, the great white father, the white hunter in the heart of Africa.[16] And the strongest evidence presented in this essay for the correctness of their judgment has been a literal reading of the realist, organicist artefacts and practices of the American Museum of Natural History. Their practice and mine have been literal, dead literal.

NOTES

1. *Job* 12:8, engraved on a plaque at the entrance to the Earth History Hall, American Museum of Natural History (hereafter AMNH).

2. H. F. Osborn, 54th Annual Report to the Trustees, p. 2, AMNH archives.

3. Leo Marx, *The Machine in the Garden* (London, Oxford, NY: Oxford UP, 1964); Roderick Nash, *Wilderness and the American Mind*, 3rd rev. edn (New Haven: Yale UP, 1982); Roderick Nash, 'The Exporting and Importing of Nature: Nature-Appreciation as a Commodity 1850–1980', *Perspectives in American History* XII (1979): 517–60.

4. Andrew Carnegie, 'The Gospel of Wealth', *North American Review*, 1889; G. William Domhoff, *Who Rules America?* (NJ: Prentice-Hall, 1967); Waldemar A. Nielson, *The Big Foundations* (NY: Columbia UP, 1972); Gabriel Kolko, *The Triumph of Conservatism* (NY: Free Press, 1977); James Weinstein, *The Corporate Ideal in the Liberal State, 1900–18* (Boston: Beacon, 1969); Robert Wiebe, *The Search for Order, 1877–1920* (NY: Hill and Wang, 1966); Richard Hofstadter, *Age of Reform* (NY: Knopf, 1955); E. Richard Brown, *Rockefeller Medicine Men* (Berkeley: U. Calif. Press, 1978); Paul Starr, *The Social Transformation of American Medicine*, esp. Chpts 3–6 (NY: Basic, 1982); Alexandra Oleson and John Voss, eds, *The Organization of Knowledge in Modern America, 1860–1920* (Baltimore: Johns Hopkins UP, 1979).

5. One capitalist in the field with Akeley was George Eastman, an object lesson in the monopoly capitalist's greater fear of decadence than of death. I am claiming that realism is an aesthetics

proper to anxiety about decadence, but what kind of realism is celebrated in a literature describing a septuagenarian Eastman getting a close-up photograph at 20 feet of a charging rhino, directing his white hunter when to shoot the gun, while his personal physician looks on? 'With this adventure Mr. Eastman began to enjoy Africa thoroughly ...', WLA, 270.

6. Bruno Latour, *Les microbes. Guerre et paix suivi de irreductions* (Paris: Metailie, 1984), pp. 171–265; Bruno Latour and Steve Woolgar, *Laboratory Life: The Social Construction of Scientific Facts* (Beverly Hills and London: Sage, 1979), esp. on inscription devices and 'phenomenotechnique'; Karin Knorr-Cetina and Michael Mulkay, eds, *Science Observed* (Beverly Hills, London, New Delhi: Sage, 1983).

7. In addition to material already cited (esp. John Michael Kennedy, *Philanthropy and Science in New York City: The American Museum of Natural History, 1868–1968*, Yale University Ph.D., 1968, Univ. Micro-films Inc., 69–13, 347 [hereafter Kennedy] and AMNH archives), major sources for this section include: 1) On decadence and the crisis of white manhood: F. Scott Fitzgerald, *The Great Gatsby* (1925); Henry Adams, *The Education of Henry Adams* (privately printed 1907); Ernest Hemingway, *Green Hills of Africa* (1935). 2) On the history of conservation: Roderick Nash, ed., *Environment and the Americans: Problems and Priorities* (Melbourne, Florida: Kreiger, 1979) and *American Environment: Readings in the History of Conservation*, 2nd ed. (Reading, Mass.: Addison-Wesley, 1976); Samuel Hays, *Conservation and the Gospel of Efficiency: The Progressive Conservation Movement, 1890–1920* (Cambridge: Harvard UP, 1959). 3) On eugenics, race doctrines, and immigration: John Higham, *Send These to Me: Jews and other Immigrants in Urban America* (NY: Atheneum, 1975); John Haller, *Outcasts from Evolution* (Urbana: Illinois UP, 1971); Allan Chase, *Legacy of Malthus* (NY: Knopf, 1977); Kenneth Ludmerer, *Genetics and American Society* (Baltimore: Johns Hopkins UP, 1972); Donald Pickens, *Eugenics and the Progressives* (Nashville: Vanderbilt UP, 1968); S. J. Gould, *The Mismeasure of Man* (NY: Norton, 1981); Stephan L. Chorover, *From Genesis to Genocide* (Cambridge: MIT Press, 1979); Hamilton Cravens, *Triumph of Evolution: American Scientists and the Heredity-Environment Controversy, 1900–41* (Philadelphia: Univ. of Pennsylvania Press, 1978). Complex concerns about sex, sexuality, hygiene, decadence, birth control are crucial to the production of sex research in the early decades of the 20th century in life and social sciences. Women scientists played a key role in generating this research. Rosalind Rosenberg, *Beyond Separate Spheres: Intellectual Roots of Modern Feminism* (New Haven: Yale UP, 1982). The incitement to discourse has been instrumental, to say the least, in the construction of 'self consciousness' and self description of women as a social group. See Catharine A. MacKinnon, 'Feminism, Marxism, Method, and the State: An Agenda for Theory', *Signs* 7, no. 3 (1982). The issue is closely connected to the 'being' of woman as spectacle and the need for a feminist theory of experience. Small wonder that film theory is becoming one of the richest sites of feminist theory. Teresa de Lauretis, *Alice Doesn't: Feminism, Semiotics, and Cinema* (Bloomington: Indiana UP, 1984) and Annette Kuhn, *Women's Pictures: Feminism and Cinema* (London, Boston, Melbourne, Henley: Routledge & Kegan Paul, 1982).

8. Camille Limoges and his collaborators at L'Institut d'histoire et de sociopolitique des sciences, Université de Montréal, provide the most complete analysis of the Paris natural history museums from the early 19th century. Gerald Holton and William A. Blanpied, eds, *Science and Its Public: The Changing Relation* (Dordrecht: Reidel, 1976).

9. Kennedy, 141ff. Osborn presided over considerable disbursements to the Department of Anthropology, despite his own opinion that anthropology was largely 'the gossip of natives'. Osborn was more inclined to favor the skeletons of dinosaurs and mammals, and he is responsible for building one of the world's finest paleontology collections. H. F. Osborn, *Fifty-two Years of Research, Observation, and Publication* (NY: AMNH, 1930).

10. Kennedy, 192.

11. Philip Pauly, *American Quarterly*, 1982.

12. Osborn, 'The American Museum and Citizenship', 53rd Annual Report, 1922, p. 2, AMNH archives.

13. Osborn, *The Hall of the Age of Man*, AMNH Guide Leaflet Series, no. 52.

14. Osborn, 'Citizenship', 54th Annual Report, p. 2.

15. Osborn, 53rd Annual Report, 1921, pp. 31–2. Ethel Tobach of the AMNH helped me interpret and find material on social networks, eugenics, racism, and sexism at the Museum. The organizing meetings for the Galton Society were held in Osborn's home.

16. Joseph Conrad, esp. *Heart of Darkness*, is crucial to this aspect of my story, especially for exploring complexities of language and desire. See also Fredric Jameson, 'Romance and Reification: Plot Construction and Ideological Closure in Joseph Conrad', *The Political Unconscious* (Ithaca: Cornell UP, 1981).

3.

From the Princely Gallery to the Public Art Museum: The Louvre Museum and the National Gallery, London

Carol Duncan

The Louvre was the prototypical public art museum. It first offered the civic ritual that other nations would emulate.[1] It was also with the Louvre that public art museums became signs of politically virtuous states. By the end of the nineteenth century, every Western nation would boast at least one important public art museum. In the twentieth century, their popularity would spread even to the Third World, where traditional monarchs and military despots create Western-style art museums to demonstrate their respect for Western values, and – consequently – their worthiness as recipients of Western military and economic aid.[2] Meanwhile in the West, museum fever continues unabated. Clearly, from the start, having a public art museum brought with it political advantages.

This [essay] will look at two of the most important public art museums in Europe, the Louvre Museum in Paris and the National Gallery in London. However different their histories and collections, both of these institutions stand as monuments to the new bourgeois state as it was emerging in the age of democratic revolutions. If the Louvre, whose very establishment was a revolutionary act, states the central theme of public art museums, the story of the National Gallery in London elaborates its ideological meanings. Its details were spelled out in the political discourse that surrounded its founding and early years, a discourse in which bourgeois and aristocratic modes of culture, including the new art-historical culture, were clearly pitted against each other. The larger question here is what made the Louvre and the other museums it inspired so politically attractive, and how did they differ from older displays of art? Or, to rephrase the question in terms of the theme of this book, what kind of ritual does the public art museum stage, and what was (and is) its ideological usefulness to modern states?

I

Ceremonial displays of accumulated treasure go back to the most ancient of times. Indeed, it is tempting to extend our notion of 'the museum' backwards into earlier eras and discover museum-like functions in the treasuries of ancient temples or medieval cathedrals or in the family chapels of Italian Baroque churches. Some of these older types of display come surprisingly close to modern museum situations.[3] Yet, however they may resemble today's public art museums, historically, the modern institution of the museum grew most directly out of sixteenth-, seventeenth-, and eighteenth-century princely collections. These collections, which were often displayed in impressive halls or galleries built especially for them, set certain precedents for later museums.[4]

Typically, princely galleries functioned as reception rooms, providing sumptuous settings for official ceremonies and framing the figure of the prince. By the eighteenth century, it was standard practice everywhere in Europe for princes to install their collections in lavishly decorated galleries and halls, often fitting individual works into elaborate wall schemes of carved and gilt panelling. The point of such show was to dazzle and overwhelm both foreign visitors and local dignitaries with the magnificence, luxury, and might of the sovereign, and, often – through special iconographies – the rightness or legitimacy of his rule. Palace rooms and galleries might also be decorated with iconographic programs that drew flattering analogies to the ruler – galleries of portrait busts of legendary emperors or depictions of the deeds of great monarchs of the past. A ruler might also surround himself with sculptures, paintings, and tapestries of a favorite classical god to add luster to his image – Louis XIV's appropriation of the sun-god Apollo is the most famous; in Madrid it was Hercules, celebrated in a series of paintings by Rubens, whose exploits were linked to the throne. In one way or another, these various displays of objects and paintings demonstrated something about the prince – his splendor, his legitimacy, or the wisdom of his rule.[5] As we shall see, public art museums both perpetuated and transformed the function of these princely reception halls wherein the state idealized and presented itself to the public.

The Louvre was not the first royal collection to be turned into a public art museum, but its transformation was the most politically significant and influential. In 1793 the French revolutionary government, seizing an opportunity to dramatize the creation of the new Republican state, nationalized the king's art collection and declared the Louvre a public institution.[6] The Louvre, once the palace of kings, was now reorganized as a museum for the people, to be open to everyone free of charge. It thus became a lucid symbol of the fall of the Old Regime and the rise of a new order. The new meaning that the Revolution gave to the old palace was literally inscribed in the heart of the seventeenth-century palace, the Apollo Gallery, built by Louis XIV as a princely gallery and reception hall. Over its entrance is the revolutionary decree that called into existence the Museum of the French Republic and ordered its opening on 10 August, to commemorate 'the anniversary of the fall of tyranny' (Figure 3.3.1). Inside the gallery, a case holds crowns from the royal and imperial past, now displayed as public property.[7]

The new museum proved to be a producer of potent symbolic meanings. The transformation of the palace into a public space accessible to everyone made the museum an especially pointed demonstration of the state's commitment to the principle of equality. As a public space, the museum also made manifest the public it claimed to serve: it could produce it as a visible entity by literally providing it with a defining frame and giving it something to do. In the museum, even the rights of citizenship could be discerned as art appreciation and spiritual enrichment. To be sure, equality of access to the museum in no way gave everyone the relevant education to understand the works of art inside, let alone equal political rights and privileges; in fact, only propertied males were full citizens. But in the museum, everyone was equal in principle, and if the uneducated could not use the cultural goods the museum proffered, they could (and still can) be awed by the sheer magnitude of the treasure.

As a new kind of public ceremonial space, the Louvre not only redefined the political identity of its visitors, it also assigned new meanings to the objects it displayed, and qualified, obscured, or distorted old ones. Now presented as public property, they became the means through which a new relationship between the individual as citizen and the state as benefactor could be symbolically enacted. But to accomplish their new task, they had to be presented in a new way. In a relatively short time, the Louvre's directors (drawing partly on German and Italian precedents) worked out a whole set of practices that came to characterize art museums everywhere. In short, the museum organized its collections into art-historical schools and installed them so as to make visible the development and achievement of each school. Certainly, it did not effect this change overnight. It first had to sort out the various, and in some ways, contradictory, installation models available at the time, and the different notions of artistic 'schools' that each entailed.[8]

Probably the most fashionable way of hanging a collection in the later eighteenth century was what might be called the connoisseur's or gentlemanly hang. This installation model was practiced internationally and corresponded rather precisely to the art education of European aristocrats. In the eighteenth and early nineteenth centuries, there was widespread agreement among cultivated men (and those few women who could claim such knowledge) that, aside from the sculpture of classical antiquity, the masters most worth collecting were sixteenth- and seventeenth-century Italian, Flemish, Dutch, and French. Men of taste and breeding, whatever their nationality, were

Figure 3.3.1   Louvre Museum, Paris, entrance to the Apollo Gallery. Photograph by Carol Duncan

expected to have learned key critical terms and concepts that distinguished the particular artistic virtues of the most popular masters. Indeed, such knowledge was taken as a sign of aristocratic breeding, and in the course of the eighteenth century it became the fashion to hang collections, including royal collections, in a way that highlighted the formal qualities of the various masters – that is, in a way that displayed one's knowledge of current critical fashions. A gentlemanly hang, be it in England, Italy, or France, might group together on one wall contrasting examples from opposing schools. For example, an Italian *Venus* or martyrdom on the right might be balanced by a Flemish *Venus* or martyrdom on the left, the better to show off their particular qualities of drawing, color, and composition; alternatively, works by various masters from the same school might be grouped together to complement each other.[9]

In the later eighteenth century, this gentlemanly type of installation was given increasing competition by newer, art-historical arrangements, versions of which were being introduced into certain private and princely collections.[10] In these new arrangements, more was made of the progress demonstrated by each school and its principal masters. By and large, this progress was measured in terms of a single, universal ideal of beauty, an ideal toward which all societies presumably evolved, but one that, according to experts, ancient sculpture and Italian High Renaissance painting most fully realized. As the administrators of the Louvre Museum put it in 1794, the new museum's goal was to show visitors 'the progress of art and the degrees of perfection to which it was brought by all those peoples who have successively cultivated it'.[11] And when, some years later, the noted German art expert Gustav Waagen toured English art collections, he could, in the same spirit, pronounce the National Gallery's *Resurrection of Lazarus* by Sebastiano del Piombo the star of the collection and indeed of all English collections combined, since, in his eyes, it was the one work that most embodied the genius of the Italian High Renaissance and therefore most achieved the universal ideal.[12]

These kinds of judgments concerned more than the merits of individual artists. Progress in art could be taken as an indicator of how far a people or an epoch evolved toward civilization in general. That is, the art-historical approach gave works of art a new cultural-historical importance and a new cognitive value. As such, they required new, more appropriate kinds of settings. Whereas older displays, princely and gentlemanly alike, commonly subordinated individual works to larger decorative schemes, often surrounding them with luxurious furnishings and ornaments, the new approach called for settings that would not compete with the art. At the same time, new wall arrangements were evolved so that viewers could literally retrace, work by work, the historical lines of development of both individual artists and their schools. In the course of the nineteenth century, the conviction that art must be valued and ranked according to a single ideal of beauty would be gradually modified; educated opinion would appreciate an ever greater range of schools – especially fifteenth-century Italian art – each for its own unique qualities, and would increasingly demand their representation in public collections.[13] In all of this, the concept of high art was being rethought. Rather than a rare attainment, it was coming to be seen as a necessary component of every society, an organic expression of one or another particular national spirit.[14] However, the language associated with the evolutionary approach and the habit of extolling ancient sculpture and High Renaissance art above all else, would hang on for a long time. Malraux noted how long this change took in the museum market: only late in the nineteenth century would different schools be treated fully as equals, and only toward the end of the century could a Piero della Francesca be rated as equal or superior to Raphael.[15]

Historians of museums often see the new art-historical hang as the triumph of an advanced, Enlightenment thinking that sought to replace earlier systems of classification with a more rational one. To be sure, the new construct was more in keeping with Enlightenment rationality. But more significant to the concerns of this study was its ideological usefulness to emerging bourgeois states, all of which, in the course of the nineteenth century, adopted it for their public art museums. Although still pitched to an educated elite and still built on a universal and international standard, the new system, by giving special emphasis to the 'genius' of national schools, could both acknowledge and promote the growth of state power and national identity.

The differences in these models of display amount to very different ritual structures. Just as the public art museum redefined the content of its displays, so it reconceptualized the identity of its visitors and their business in the museum. That is, as a new kind of dramatic field, the art museum prompted its visitors to assume a new ritual identity and perform a new ritual role. The earlier, aristocratic installation addressed the visitor as a gentleman and reinforced this identity by enabling him to engage in and re-enact the kind of discerning judgments that gentlemanly culture called 'good taste'. By asking him to recognize – without the help of labels – the identities and distinctive artistic qualities of canonized masters – Guido Reni, Claude, Murillo, and other favorites – the visitor-cum-connoisseur could experience himself as possessing a culture that was both exclusive and international, a culture that marked its possessor as a member of the elite.[16] In contrast, the public art museum addressed its visitor as a bourgeois citizen who enters the museum in search of enlightenment and rationally understood pleasures. In the museum, this citizen finds a culture that unites him with other French citizens regardless of their individual social position. He also encounters there the state itself, embodied in the very form of the museum. Acting on behalf of the public, it stands revealed as keeper of the nation's spiritual life and guardian of the most evolved and civilized culture of which the human spirit is capable. All this it presents to every citizen, rationally organized and clearly labeled. Thus does the art museum enable the citizen–state relationship to appear as realized in all its potential.

Almost from the beginning, the Louvre's directors began organizing its galleries by national school.[17] Admittedly, some very early displays presented works of art as confiscated treasure or spoils of a victorious army (this was the era in which French armies systematically packed up art treasures from churches and palaces all over Europe and sent them to the Louvre[18]). But by its 1810 reopening as the Musée Napoléon, the museum, now under the direction of Vivant Denon, was completely organized by school, and within the schools, works of important masters were grouped together. The conversion of the old palace into a public art museum had taken some doing architecturally, but in certain ways the old building was well equipped for its new symbolic assignment. It was, after all, already full of sixteenth- and seventeenth-century spaces originally designed to accommodate public ritual and ceremonial display (Figure 3.3.2). Its halls and galleries tended to develop along marked axes so that (especially in the rooms occupied by the early museum) visitors were naturally drawn from room to room or down long vistas. The setting was well suited to the kind of narrative iconographic program it now contained.

Thus ordered, the treasures, trophies, and icons of the past became objects of art history, embodiments of a new form of cultural-historical wealth. The museum environment was structured precisely to bring out this new meaning and suppress or downplay old ones. In this sense, the museum was a powerful transformer, able to convert signs of luxury, status, or splendor into repositories of spiritual treasure – the heritage and pride of the whole nation. Organized chronologically and in national categories along the museum's corridors, works of art now became witnesses to the presence of 'genius', cultural products marking the course of civilization in nations and individuals.[19] The ritual task of the Louvre visitor was to re-enact that history of genius, re-live its progress step by step and, thus enlightened, know himself as a citizen of history's most civilized and advanced nation-state.

Throughout the nineteenth century, the Louvre explained its ritual program in its ceiling decorations. An instance of this is still visible in what was originally the vestibule of the Musée Napoléon (the Rotunda of Mars), dedicated in 1810. Four medallions in the ceiling represent the principal art-historical schools, each personified by a female figure who holds a famous example of its sculpture: Egypt a cult statue, Greece the *Apollo Belvedere*, Italy Michelangelo's *Moses*, and France Puget's *Milo of Crotona*. The message reads clearly: France is the fourth and final term in a narrative sequence that comprises the greatest moments of art history. Simultaneously, the history of

Figure 3.3.2   The Old Louvre Palace, a former royal apartment converted to museum use in the nineteenth century. Photograph by Carol Duncan

Figure 3.3.3   Creating a genius ceiling in the central dome of the Louvre Museum, Daru taircase (mosaic decorations later removed). From *L'illustration*, 27 August, 1887. Photograph by Carol Duncan

art has become no less than the history of Western civilization itself: its origins in Egypt and Greece, its reawakening in the Renaissance, and its present flowering in modern France. The same program was elaborated later in the century in mosaic decorations for the five domed spaces above the Daru Stairway (Figure 3.3.3) (subsequently removed).

Other ceilings further expound the symbolic meanings of the museum's program. Throughout the nineteenth century, museum authorities used the ceilings to spell them out, lecturing visitors from above. They especially hammered home the idea of the state as protector of the arts. Often resorting to traditional princely iconography, images and insignia repeatedly identified this or that government or monarch as the nation's cultural benefactor. One ceiling, for example, decorating the museum's 1812 grand stairway (the stair is gone but the ceiling remains), represents *France in the Guise of Minerva Protecting the Arts* (by Maynier, 1819). The napoleonic insignia that originally surrounded it were later removed. Successive regimes, monarchical or republican, often removed the insignia of their predecessors in order to inscribe their own on the museum's walls and ceilings.

Increasingly the iconography of the museum centered on artists. For example, in the Musée Charles X (the series of rooms opened to the public in the 1820s), ceilings still celebrate great patron-princes of the past; but artists

Figure 3.3.4   The Louvre Museum, the newly decorated Salle des Etats in 1886. From *L'Illustration*, 30 October 1886. Photograph by Carol Duncan

are also abundantly present. As in later decorations, sequences of their names or portraits, arranged into national schools, grace the entablatures. Indeed, ever greater expanses of overhead space would be devoted to them as the century wore on. If anything, the nineteenth century was a great age of genius iconography,[20] and nowhere are genius ceilings more ostentatious than in the Louvre (Figure 3.3.4). Predictably, after every coup or revolution, new governments would vote funds for at least one such ceiling, prominently inscribing its own insignia among the names or profiles of the great artists so honored. Thus in 1848, the newly constituted Second Republic renovated and decorated the Salon Carré and the nearby Hall of Seven Chimneys, devoting the first to masters of the foreign schools, and the second to French geniuses, profiles of whom were alphabetically arranged in the frieze (Figure 3.3.5). It is relevant to recall that from the early nineteenth century on, most artists were very aware of themselves as candidates for the category of great artist so lavishly celebrated on the ceiling and plotted their artistic strategies accordingly.

It should be obvious that the demand for great artists, once the type was developed as an historical category, was enormous – they were, after all, the means by which, on the one hand, the state could demonstrate the highest kind of civic virtue, and on the other, citizens could know themselves to be

Figure 3.3.5   The Louvre Museum, detail of a genius ceiling in the Hall of Seven Chimneys, commissioned in 1848 by the French Republic. Photograph by Carol Duncan

civilized. Not surprisingly, quantities of great artists were now duly discovered and, in time, furnished with properly archetypal biographies by the burgeoning discipline of art history.[21] These conditions are perpetuated today in the institution of the giant retrospective. A voracious demand for great artists, living or dead, is obligingly supplied by legions of art historians and curators trained for just this task. Inevitably some of the great artists inducted into this role fill it out with less success than others. Even so, a fair or just good great artist is still a serviceable item in today's museum business.

The importance of the Louvre Museum as a model for other national galleries and as an international training ground for the first community of professional museum men is everywhere recognized. After the example of the Louvre, there was a flurry of national gallery founding throughout Europe, whose heads of state often simply designated an existing royal or imperial collection as a public art museum. Conversions of this kind had been made before the Revolution, in Dresden and Vienna, for example, but would continue now with greater speed. Under Napoleon's occupying armies, numerous public art museums were created in, among other places, Madrid, Naples, Milan, and Amsterdam. Of course, some of the new 'national galleries' were more like traditional princely reception halls than modern public spaces – more out to dazzle than enlighten – and one usually entered them as a privilege rather than by right.[22] Whatever form they took, by 1825, almost every Western capital, monarchical or Republican, had one.

The influence of the Louvre continued in the later nineteenth and twentieth centuries in the many public art museums founded in European provincial cities[23] and in other places under the sway of European culture. In New York, Boston, Chicago, Cleveland, and other American cities, museums were carefully laid out around the Louvre's organizing theme of the great civilizations, with Egypt, Greece, and Rome leading to a centrally placed Renaissance. When no Greek or Roman originals were on hand, as they were not in many American cities, the idea was conveyed by plaster casts of classical sculpture or Greek-looking architecture, the latter often embellished with the names or profiles of great artists from Phidias on; such façades are familiar sights everywhere.

As for the Louvre itself, despite a long history of expansions, reorganizations, and reinstallations, the museum maintained until very recently its nineteenth-century bias for the great epochs of civilization. Classical and Italian Renaissance art always occupied its most monumental, centrally located spaces and made the museum's opening statements.[24] In the course of the nineteenth century, it expanded its history of civilization to include the art of ancient Egypt, the Near East, Asia, and other designated culture areas. Just as these episodes could be added, so others could be subtracted without damaging the museum's central program: in the years after the Second World War, Impressionist painting and Far Eastern art were moved out of the Louvre altogether, the one to the Jeu de Paume, the other to the Musée Guimet. In terms of the museum's traditional program, neither collection – however valued as a collection – was essential, and, as one museum official affirmed, their subtraction actually clarified the museum's primary program:

It may be said that the Louvre collections form today a coherent whole, grouping around our western civilization all those which, directly or indirectly, had a share in its birth. ... At the threshold of history there stand the mother civilizations: Egyptian, Sumerian, Aegean. Then, coming down through Athens, Rome, Byzantium, towards the first centuries of our Christian era, there are the full blossomings of Medieval, Renaissance and Modern art. At the Louvre, then, we are on our own home territory, the other inhabited parts of the earth being dealt with elsewhere.[25]

The museum's commitment to lead visitors through the course of Western civilization continues to this day, even though a new entrance, new access routes and a major reinstallation allow visitors to map their own paths through a somewhat revised history of art. As I write this (in 1993), the museum is getting ready to unveil its latest expansion, the newly installed Richelieu Wing, in which, for the first time, northern European art will be given the kind of grand ceremonial spaces that, up until now, were usually reserved for French and Italian art. It appears that, in today's Louvre, French civilization will look more broadly European in its sources than before, more like a leading European Community state. Whatever the political implications of the new arrangement, the Louvre continues its existence as a public state ritual.

But 1993 is a long way from 1793. Of the legions of people who daily stream through the Louvre, most, whether French or foreign, are tourists. Which is to say that, as a prime tourist attraction, the museum is crucial to the city's economy. If it still constructs its visitors as enlightenment-seeking citizens, it must also cater to crowds of hungry, credit-card-bearing consumers in search of souvenirs and gifts. Besides a revised art-historical tour, therefore, the Louvre of 1993 also includes spacious new restaurants and a monumental shopping mall.[26] Such developments, however, belong to the Louvre's later years. We have still to consider more of the public art museum's significance in the nineteenth and early twentieth centuries, first in Britain.

[...]

II

Let us turn now to the National Gallery in London. If the Louvre is the prototype of the public art museum – and that is its status in the literature[27] – how are we to understand the National Gallery? The dramatic and revolutionary origins of the French museum, including its very site in what was once the royal palace, is unparalleled in the British example, whose founding, next to the Louvre's, seems sorely lacking in political and historical fullness. The decisive events and powerful symbolic ingredients that made the French example so much the archetype of the European public art museum are simply not present.

The first missing ingredient is a significant royal art collection of the kind that seventeenth- and eighteenth-century monarchs had often assembled and which then became the core of a national gallery. Certainly, England had once known such royal treasure: Charles I's famous and much admired collection of paintings. Broken up when Charles fell, the story of this collection – its destruction as much as its creation – must figure as the beginning of the story of public art museums in England.

Charles came to the English throne in 1625, bringing with him ideas about monarchy that were shaped by continental models and continental theories of the divine right of kings. Especially impressed by the haughty formality and splendor of the Spanish court, he sought to create on English soil similar spectacles of radiant but aloof power. Accordingly, he commissioned Inigo Jones to design a properly regal palace complete with a great hall decorated by Rubens (in 1635). A show of power in the seventeenth century also demanded a magnificent picture collection; elsewhere in Europe, church and state princes – Cardinal Mazarin and the Archduke Leopold William are outstanding examples – paid fortunes for the requisite Titians, Correggios, and other favorites of the day. Charles understood fully the meaning of such ceremonial display. So did his Puritan executioners, who pointedly auctioned off a large part of the king's collection. Not only did they feel a Puritan discomfort with such sensually pleasing objects; they also wished to dismantle a quintessential sign of regal absolutism.[28] The absence of a significant royal collection in England is as much a monument, albeit a negative one, to the end of English absolutism as the Louvre Museum is to the end of French absolutism.

This is only to say that the process of British state building was English, not French, as was the development of the symbols and public spaces which culturally articulated that process. In the England after Charles I, monarchs might collect art, but political realities discouraged them from displaying it in ways that recalled too much the regal shows and absolutist ambitions of the past. In fact, after Charles and a very few other grand seventeenth-century art collectors – in particular the Earl of Arundel and the Duke of Buckingham – there would be no significant English collections for several decades.[29] It was only after the Restoration that large-scale English picture-collecting would be resumed, most notably by the powerful aristocratic oligarchs to whom state power now passed. Meanwhile, British monarchs kept rather low public profiles as art collectors and art patrons.

Kensington Palace is a telling reminder of the modesty in which monarchy was expected to live, at least in the later seventeenth century. The residence of King William III and Queen Mary (installed on the throne in 1689), the building began as an unpretentious dwelling, certainly comfortable and dignified enough for its noble occupants – as seen in its two 'long galleries' filled with art objects – but not in any way palatial. It lacked the ceremonial spaces of an empowered royalty, spaces that would appear only later under Kings George I and II. William's picture gallery held a fine collection, but it remained a source of private pleasure, not regal display. In fact, various royal residences would end up with considerable holdings, but these were never institutionalized as 'the British Royal Collection'. Even now, they remain largely private; indeed, when displayed in the new Sainsbury Wing of the National Gallery in 1991–2, they attracted attention precisely because so much of the collection has been unfamiliar to the art-viewing public.[30]

Besides the want of a royal collection properly deployed as such, British eighteenth-century history lacks a potent political event that could have dramatically turned that collection into public property – in short, an eighteenth- or nineteenth-century type of democratic revolution. Of course, another way to get a public art museum (short of being occupied by a French army) was through the liberalizing monarchical gesture as seen on the continent, in which a royal collection was opened up as a public space in symbolic (if not direct political) recognition of the bourgeois presence. The French crown had been planning just such a move at the time of the Revolution. The Revolution took over that museum project but also redefined it, making what would have been a privileged and restricted space into something truly open and public. The revolutionary state thus appropriated the legacy of absolutist symbols and ceremonies and put them to new ideological use, making them stand for the Republic and its ideal of equality. The English ruling class, on the other hand, had rejected the use of a royal art collection as a national symbol just as deliberately as it had blocked the development of an absolutist monarchy. There was political room neither for the kind of art collection that the people could meaningfully nationalize nor for the kind of monarch who could meaningfully nationalize it himself.

By the late eighteenth century, however, the absence of a ceremonially important royal collection was more than made up for by those of the aristocracy. In fact, the British art market actually became the most active in the eighteenth-century Europe as both the landed aristocracy and a newly arrived commercial class sought the distinctive signs of gentlemanly status. Whether defending older class boundaries or attempting to breach them, men of wealth deemed it socially expedient to collect and display art, especially paintings. Italian, Flemish, and other old-master works of the kind prescribed by the current canons of good taste poured into their collections. As Iain Pears has argued, art collecting, by providing a unifying cultural field, helped the upper ranks of English society form a common class identity:

They increasingly saw themselves as the cultural, social and political core of the nation, 'citizens' in the Greek sense with the other ranks of society scarcely figuring in their understanding of the 'nation'.[31]

In short, here were the social elements of the 'civil society' of seventeenth- and eighteenth-century political philosophy, that community of propertied citizens whose interests and education made them, in their view, most fit to rule.[32]

To modern eyes, the social and political space of an eighteenth-century English art collection falls somewhere between the public and private realms. Our notion of the 'public' dates from a later time, when, almost everywhere in the West, the advent of bourgeois democracy opened up the category of citizenship to ever broader segments of the population and redefined the realm of the public as ever more accessible and inclusive. What today looks like a private, socially exclusive space could have seemed in the eighteenth century much more open. Indeed, an eighteenth-century picture collection (and an occasional sculpture collection) was contiguous with a series of like spaces (including, not incidentally, the newly founded British Museum[33]) that together mapped out the social circuit of a class. Certainly access to these collections was difficult if one did not belong to the elite.[34] But from the point of view of their owners, these spaces were accessible to everyone who counted, the:

finite group of personal friends, rivals, acquaintances and enemies who made up the comparatively small informal aristocracy of landed gentlemen, peers or commoners, in whom the chains of patronage, 'friendship' or connection converged.[35]

Displayed in galleries or reception rooms of town or country houses, picture collections were seen by numerous visitors, who often toured the countryside expressly to visit the big landowners' showy houses and landscape gardens.[36] Art galleries were thus 'public' spaces in that they could unequivocally frame the only 'public' that was admissible: well-born, educated men of taste, and, more marginally (if at all), well-born women.

Art galleries signified social distinction precisely because they were seen as more than simple signs of wealth and power. Art was understood to be a source of valuable moral and spiritual experience. In this sense, it was cultural property, something to be shared by a whole community. Eighteenth-century Englishmen as well as Frenchmen had the idea that an art collection could belong to a nation, however they understood that term. The French pamphleteers who called for the nationalization of the royal collection and the creation of a national art museum had British counterparts who criticized rich collectors for excluding from their galleries a large public, especially artists and writers.

Joshua Reynolds, Benjamin West, and Thomas Lawrence, the first three presidents of the Royal Academy, were among those who called for the creation of a national gallery or, at least, the opening up of private collections. Even before the creation of the Louvre, in 1777, the radical politician John Wilkes proposed that Parliament purchase the fabulous collection of Sir Robert Walpole and make it the beginning of a national gallery. The proposal was not taken up and the collection was sold to Catherine the Great. A few years later, the creation of the Louvre Museum intensified the wish for an English national collection, at least among some. Thus in 1799, the art dealer Noel Joseph Desenfans offered the state a brilliant, ready-made national collection of old masters, assembled for King Stanislas Augustus of Poland just before he abdicated. Desenfans, determined to keep the collection intact and in England, offered it to the state on the condition that a proper building be provided for it. According to the German art expert J. D. Passavant, the offer 'was coolly received and ultimately rejected'. Desenfans's collection was finally bequeathed to Dulwich College [...] and was, for another decade or so, the only public picture collection in the vicinity of London.

Why was Parliament so resistant to establishing a national gallery? In the years between the founding of the Louvre in 1793 and the fall of Napoleon in 1815, almost every leading European state acquired a national art museum, if not by an act of the reigning monarch then through the efforts of French occupiers, who began museum building on the Louvre model in several places. Why did the ruling oligarchs of Great Britain resist what was so alluring in Berlin, Madrid, and Amsterdam? The answer to this question, I believe, lies in the meaning of the art gallery within the context of eighteenth-century patrician culture.

Eighteenth-century Britain was ruled by an oligarchy of great landowners who presided over a highly ranked and strictly hierarchical society. Landed property, mainly in the form of rents, was the basic source of wealth and the key to political power and social prestige. Although landowners also engaged in commercial and industrial capitalist ventures, profits were normally turned into more land or land improvement, since that form of property was considered the only gentlemanly source of wealth. Living off rents was taken to be the only appropriate way of achieving the leisure and freedom necessary to cultivate one's higher moral and intellectual capacities. Apologists for the landowners argued that ownership of land was a precondition for developing the wisdom, independence, and civic-mindedness necessary for the responsible exercise of political power. They maintained that holdings in land rooted one in the larger community and made one's private interests identical with the general interest and well-being of the whole of society. Landowners, both old and newly arrived, thereby justified their monopoly of political rights on the basis of their land holdings.

In fact – and contrary to the claims of their apologists – the great landowners exercised power according to narrow self-interest. The business of government was largely a matter of buying and selling influence and positioning oneself for important government appointments, lucrative sinecures, and advantageous marriages for one's children. The more land one owned, the more patronage, influence, and wealth one was likely to command and the better one's chances to buy, bribe, and negotiate one's way to yet more wealth and social luster.[37] To be even a small player in this system required a great show of wealth, mediated, of course, by current codes of good taste and breeding. A properly appointed country house with a fashionably landscaped garden was a minimum requirement. If few landowners could compete with Sir Robert Walpole's Houghton, the Duke of Marlborough's Blenheim, or the Duke of Bedford's Woburn Abbey, they could nevertheless assemble the essentials of the spectacle. As Mark Girouard has described it,

Trophies in the hall, coats of arms over the chimney-pieces, books in the library and temples in the park could suggest that one was discriminating, intelligent, bred to rule and brave.[38]

Art collections, too, betokened gentlemanly attainments, and marked their owners as veterans of the grand tour (mandatory for any gentleman). Whether installed in purpose-built galleries or in other kinds of rooms they provided a display of wealth and breeding that helped give point and meaning to the receptions and entertainments they adorned. Compared to today's academic discourse, the critical vocabulary one needed to master was decidedly brief and the number of canonized old masters few: the Carracci, Guido Reni, Van Dyck, and Claude were among those most admired.[39] However shallow one's understanding of them, to display them in one's house and produce before them the right clichés served as proof that one was cultivated and discerning and fit to hold power. Whatever else they might have been, art collections were prominent artifacts in a ritual that marked the boundary between polite and vulgar society, which is to say, the boundary of legitimated power.[40]

Given the structure of the British oligarchy, the notorious self-interest of its ranking magnates, and the social uses of art displays, the unwillingness to create a national gallery until 1824 is not surprising.[41] Absorbed in a closed circle of power, patronage, and display, the ruling oligarchy had no compelling reason to form a national collection. Indeed, at this historical moment – an era of democratic revolutions – it had been good reason *not* to want one, since national galleries tended either to signal the advent of Republicanism or to give a liberalized face to surviving monarchies attempting to renew their waning prestige.⁴² The men who dominated Parliament had no reason to send either of these signals. Their existing practices of collection and display already marked out boundaries of viable power and reinforced the authority of state offices.⁴³

Parliament's claim to represent the interest of the whole society, when in fact self-enrichment had become the central operating principle of its members, was a contradiction that became ever more glaring and ever less tolerable to growing segments of the population. Over the first few decades of the nineteenth century, groups of industrialists, merchants, professionals, disgruntled gentry locked out of power, and religious dissenters mounted well-organized attacks on both the structure and policies of the government. They not only pressed the question of what class should rule, they also challenged aristocratic culture, contested its authority, and discredited some of its more prestigious symbols. Their most scathing and effective attacks on the culture of privilege would come in the 1820s and 1830s, when radicals and reformers, the Benthamites prominent among them, gave voice to widely felt resentments.⁴⁴ (The Benthamites were followers of the social reformer and utilitarian philosopher Jeremy Bentham, 1748–1832.) From those decades date proposals for public art galleries and campaigns to increase access to existing public museums and monuments. In the context of early nineteenth-century Britain, these efforts were highly political in nature and directly furthered a larger project to expand the conventional boundaries of citizenship. The cultural strategy involved opening up traditionally restricted ritual spaces and redefining their content – this as a means of advancing the claims of 'the nation'. The effort to define and control these spaces would build as the nineteenth century wore on.

This concern to defend and advance the rights of the political nation easily shaded into feelings of a broader nationalism, appearing elsewhere in western Europe in the early nineteenth century, as well as patriotic sentiments, which the wars with France intensified. The creation of the Louvre Museum and its spectacular expansion under Napoleon sharpened these feelings of English–French rivalry and gave them a cultural focus. The marvels of the Louvre caused acute museum envy not only among English artists and writers like Hazlitt, Lawrence, and West, but also among some of the gentleman collectors who sat in Parliament and felt the lack of a public art collection as an insult to British national pride. Both during and after the wars, however, the state was diffident about projects that might have fostered national pride. As the historian Linda Colley has argued, in late eighteenth- and early nineteenth-century England, to encourage nationalism was to encourage an inclusive principle of identity that could too easily become the basis of a political demand to broaden the franchise. It is thus no surprise that the expression of nationalist feeling came from outside the circles of official power. Typically, it took the form of proposals for cultural and patriotic monuments, as well as charitable institutions and philanthropic gestures.[45]

In 1802 the wealthy and self-made John Julius Angerstein, the creator of Lloyds of London, set up a patriotic fund for dependants of British war dead and contributed to it handsomely. He also published the names of everyone who contributed and exactly what each gave. The tactic exposed the landed aristocracy as selfish – their donations were generally meager – while publicizing commercial City men like Angerstein as patriotic, generous, and more responsive to the true needs of the nation. Angerstein clearly saw himself as the equal if not the better of any lord of the realm, and he lived accordingly. With his immense fortune and help of artist friends like Thomas Lawrence, he amassed a princely art collection of outstanding quality, installed it in magnificently decorated rooms in his house in Pall Mall, and – in pointed contrast to many aristocratic collectors – opened his doors wide to interested artists and writers. But not all doors were open to Angerstein. As a Russian-born Jew who lacked formal education – and was reputedly illegitimate to boot – he was never allowed to shake the appellation 'vulgar' and could never fully enter the highest ranks of society.

Nevertheless, after his death in 1823, Angerstein's art collection became the nucleus of the British National Gallery. With the help of Lawrence, the state was allowed to purchase the best of his collection – thirty-eight paintings – at a cost below their market value.[46] By now, sentiment in Parliament had shifted in favor of such a gallery; both Lord Liverpool, the Prime Minister, and his Home Secretary Sir Robert Peel backed the move. However, while the motion passed with relative ease, working out just where it would be and who would oversee it occasioned considerable political skirmishing. The trustees of the British Museum clearly expected to take it in hand, but had to give up that idea in the face of fierce parliamentary opposition. The problem was solved when the government was allowed to buy the remainder of the lease on Angerstein's house in Pall Mall, and the new National Gallery opened there in May, 1824. Thus, intentionally or not, Angerstein posthumously provided both the substance and site for a prestigious new symbol of the nation. There is every indication that he would have heartily approved and supported this transformation of his property. Both his son and executors thought so.[47] Indeed Angerstein's son believed that had it been proposed to his father that he contribute to a National Gallery, 'he might have given a part or the whole [of his collection] for such a purpose'.[48]

Which brings me back to the larger, historical issue with which I began this section. Although the story of the founding of the National Gallery lacks a clear-cut revolutionary moment, it nevertheless points to a growing acceptance of a new concept of the nation in Britain. Because the issue of nationalism looms so large in today's political news, and because the terms nation and nationalism are now so much in currency, we must take care not to read modern meanings into early nineteenth-century political discourse when it speaks of 'the nation'. In the eighteenth and early nineteenth centuries, one spoke of patriotism, not nationalism. Later ideas of the nation as a people defined and unified by unique spiritual yearnings or 'racial' characteristics, are foreign to the early nineteenth-century political discourse I am describing. Although there was great concern and interest in the uniqueness of national cultures, nations were generally understood and described in social, political, and economic terms, and the term 'nation' was normally used as a universal category designating 'society'. The word 'nation' was often used in the context of a middle-class campaign to dispute the claim of the privileged few to be the whole of the polity. In British political discourse, the nation could even be a code word for the middle class itself, one that highlighted the fact that British society consisted of more people than those presently enfranchised.[49] The founding of the National Gallery did not change the distribution of real political power – it did not give more people the vote – but it did remove a portion of prestigious symbolism from the exclusive control of the elite class and gave it to the nation as a whole. An impressive art gallery, a type of ceremonial space deeply associated with social privilege and exclusivity, became national property and was opened to all. The transference of the property as well as the shift in its symbolic meaning came about through the mediation of bourgeois wealth and enterprise and was legitimated by a state that had begun to recognize the advantages of such symbolic space.

The story, far from ending, was only at its beginning when the National Gallery opened in 1824. The struggle between the 'nation' and its ruling class was still heating up politically. Years of resentment against the aristocracy, long held in by the wars, had already erupted in the five years following the Battle of Waterloo (1815). If the violence had subsided, the political pressures had not. Throughout the 1820s, a strong opposition, often Benthamite in tone and backed by a vigorous press, demanded middle-class access to political power and the creation of new cultural and educational institutions. This opposition ferociously attacked hereditary privilege, protesting the incompetency of the aristocratic mind to grasp the needs of the nation, including its cultural and educational needs, and the absurdity of a system that gave aristocrats the exclusive right to dominate the whole. After the passage of the Reform Bill in 1832, elections sent a number of radicals to Parliament, where, among other things, they soon took on the cause of the National Gallery.

Debate was immediately occasioned by the urgent need to find a new space for the collection, since the lease on Angerstein's old house in Pall Mall would soon end and the building was slated for demolition. In April,

1832, Sir Robert Peel proposed to the House of Commons that the problem be solved by the erection of a new building on Trafalgar Square. He had in mind a dignified, monumental structure ('ornamental' was the term he used), designed expressly for viewing pictures. The proposal passed easily, but not before it sparked a lively discussion, with many members suggesting alternatives to it. A few members even toyed with the possibility of a British Louvre: instead of spending public money on a new building, they argued, why not put the collection in one of those royal buildings already maintained at public expense? Indeed, as one speaker noted, Buckingham Palace would make a splendid art gallery – it already had suitable space and, as a public art museum, it would be bigger and better than the Louvre! It was Joseph Hume who took the idea to its logical and radical conclusion. Since the nation needed a new art gallery, and since the government spent huge sums to maintain royal palaces which royalty rarely or never occupied, why not pull down a palace and build an art gallery in its place? In Hume's view, Hampton Court, Kensington Palace, or Windsor Castle would all make fine sites for a new public space.[50] Hume's proposal could hardly have been serious. But it does expose, if only for an instant, an impulse in the very heart of Parliament to dramatically displace vulnerable symbols of British royalty and claim their sites for the public.

As the new building on Trafalgar Square progressed, radical and reforming members of Parliament again concerned themselves with the National Gallery. In 1835, they created a select committee of the House of Commons and charged it to study the government's involvement with art education and its management of public collections.[51] The committee was full of well-known radicals and reformers, including William Ewart, Thomas Wyse, and John Bowring, long an editor of the influential Benthamite organ, the *Westminster Review*. The committee's immediate purpose was to discover ways to improve the taste of English artisans and designers and thereby improve the design and competitiveness of British manufactured goods. Its members, however, were equally intent on uncovering the ineptitude of the privileged gentlemen to whom the nation's cultural institutions were entrusted.

To the committee, the management of the National Gallery was a matter of significant political import. Most of its members were convinced that art galleries, museums, and art schools, if properly organized, could be instruments of social change capable of strengthening the social order. The numerous experts called in to testify to this truth repeatedly confirmed the committee's already unshakable belief that the very sight of art could improve the morals and deportment of even the lowest social ranks. Not surprisingly, the committee found the nation's improving monuments to be seriously mismanaged by their inept aristocratic overseers, who allowed entry fees and other obstacles to keep out most of the people. These issues were aired not only in the Select Committee *Report* of 1836 and its published proceedings, but also in subsequent parliamentary proceedings, in other public meetings, and in the press at large.

Reforming politicians were not only concerned with the utilitarian benefits of art. They also believed that culture and the fine arts could improve and enrich the quality of national life. To foster and promote a love of art in the nation at large was political work of the highest order. Thomas Wyse, a member of the Select Committee of 1836 and well known as an Irish reformer, addressed these concerns at some length in his public speeches. In 1837, he spoke at a gathering called for the purpose of promoting free admission to all places in which the public could see works of artistic and historical importance. The real issue in the question of free admission, argued Wyse, was the conflict between the needs of the nation and the interests of a single class. The outcome was important because art, far from being a mere luxury, is essential for a civilized life. Art is 'a language as universal as it is powerful', said Wyse; through it, artists leave 'an immediate and direct transcript' of moral and intellectual experience that embodies the full nature of man. The broad benefits of art therefore belong by natural right to everyone – the nation as a whole – and not just to the privileged few.[52] As Wyse argued elsewhere, however great English commercial achievements, no nation is whole without the arts:

Rich we may be, strong we may be; but without our share in the literary and artistic as well as scientific progress of the age, our civilization is incomplete.[53]

For Wyse, as for many other reformers of his day, progress toward this goal could be brought about only by removing from power a selfish and dull-witted aristocracy and replacing it with enlightened middle-class leadership. These ideas run through the Select Committee hearings of 1835 and its *Report* of the following year. Radical committee members pounced on anything that could demonstrate the ill effects of oligarchic rule, anything that, as one member put it, showed the 'spirit of exclusion in this country', a spirit that had allowed art-collecting gentlemen to monopolize the enriching products of moral and intellectual life.[54]

It was just now that the National Gallery, having lost its house in Pall Mall, was on the point of moving into its new building on Trafalgar Square.[55] The coming move provided an excellent opportunity to ask whether or not the National Gallery could be called a truly *national* institution. Here, certainly, was an entity purporting to serve the cultural needs of the nation. But did its planners and managers understand those needs? Alas, as so many testified, prompted and prodded by Ewart and the others, the National Gallery was a sorry thing compared to the Louvre, to Berlin's Royal Gallery, and to Munich's Pinakothek, the new picture gallery built as a complement to the Glyptothek.

As the eminent picture dealer Samuel Woodburn said, 'from the limited number of pictures we at present possess, I can hardly call ours a national gallery'.[56] But it was not merely the size of the collection that was wrong. As the Select Committee made plain, it was not enough to take a gentleman's collection and simply open it up to the public. In order to serve the nation, a public collection had to be formed on principles different from a gentleman's collection. It had to be selected and hung in a different way. And that was the crux of the problem. So testified Edward Solly, a former timber merchant whose famous picture collection, recently sold to Berlin's Royal Gallery, had been formed around advanced art-historical principles. Solly noted that whereas other nations gave purchasing decisions to qualified experts, in England the 'gentlemen of taste' who made them – creatures of fashion with no deep knowledge of art – were hardly up to the serious mental task of planning an acquisition program for a national collection worthy of the name. Solly's opinion was inadvertently backed by the testimony of William Seguier, the first keeper of the National Gallery.[57] Grilled at length, his ignorance of current museological practices was of great political value to the Committee. No, admitted Seguier, there was no plan for the historical arrangement of pictures according to schools. No, nothing was labeled (although he agreed it was a good idea), and no, he had never visited Italy, even though, as everyone now knew, Italy was the supreme source for a proper, publicly minded art collection. Nor was there any rationalized acquisitions policy, so that, as keeper, Seguier had been helpless to watch the build-up of Murillos and other things inappropriate to a national collection while nothing whatsoever by Raphael was acquired.

And what should a national collection look like? The Committee was well informed about continental museums and frequently cited the Louvre as a model of museum arrangement and management.[58] Although no one from the Louvre testified at the hearings, the Committee did have two renowned museum experts on hand. One was Baron von Klenze, director of Munich's new museum. His descriptions of its art-historical arrangements and labeling, not to mention its fire-proofing, air-heating, scientifically researched lighting and color schemes, inspired much admiration and envy. The other star witness was Dr Gustav Friedrich Waagen, a leading art-historical authority and director of the Royal Gallery at Berlin. He told the Committee that a public collection had to be historically arranged so that visitors could follow 'the spirit of the times and the genius of the artists'. Only then would they experience art's harmonious influence upon the mind. Dr Waagen also insisted that early Renaissance art was necessary to a good collection, as were representative works from even earlier times. The point to be made (and the Committee made it repeatedly) was that the traditional favorites among gentleman collectors, what still passed among them as 'good taste', would no longer do. The Committee therefore recommended that the National Gallery change its course and focus its efforts on building up the collection around works from the era of Raphael and his predecessors, 'such works being of purer and more elevated style than the eminent works of the Carracci'.[59] A taste for the Carracci was now disparaged as evidence of class misrule.

The Committee published its report in 1836, but the objectives for which it struggled were far from won. It would in fact require decades of political pressuring and Select Committee probings before the National Gallery would conform to the type developed on the continent. Although it would always be a picture gallery (and never a universal survey museum like the Louvre), it would eventually become one of Europe's outstanding public art museums, complete with elaborate genius ceilings and sumptuous galleries in which the history of art unfolds with the greatest possible quality and abundance. It is significant, however, that it would become a fully realized civic ritual only in the third quarter of the nineteenth century, the same era that brought universal male suffrage to much, if not all, of Britain. That is to say, the National Gallery came to rival the Louvre only when political developments forced the British state to recognize the advantages of a prestigious monument that could symbolize a nation united under presumably universal values. As the historian E. P. Thompson has noted, it is a peculiarity of British history that the formation of the bourgeois state – and of its supporting culture – evolved slowly and organically out of a complex of older forms.[60] So, too, the evolution of its National Gallery. However protracted, piecemeal and partial the process, eventually, in Britain as in France, the princely gallery gave way to the public art museum.

NOTES

For a fully annotated version of this essay see the original publication; omissions indicated here by bracketed ellipses.

1. Much of what follows draws from Carol Duncan and Alan Wallach, 'The Universal Survey Museum', *Art History* 3 (December 1980): 447–69.

2. For example, in 1975, Imelda Marcos, wife of the Philippine dictator, put together a museum of modern art in a matter of weeks. The rush was occasioned by the meeting in Manila of the International Monetary Fund. The new Metropolitan Museum of Manila, specializing in American and European art, was clearly meant to impress the conference's many illustrious visitors, who included some of the world's most powerful bankers. Not surprisingly, the new museum re-enacted on a cultural level the same relations that bound the Philippines to the United States economically and militarily. It opened with dozens of loans from the Brooklyn Museum, the Los Angeles County Museum of Art and the private collections of Armand Hammer and Nathan Cummings. Given Washington's massive contribution to the Philippine military, it is fair to assume that the museum building itself, a hastily converted unused army building, was virtually an American donation. (See 'How to put together a museum in 29 days', *ArtNews*, December 1976: 19–22).

    The Shah of Iran also needed Western-style museums to complete the façade of modernity he constructed for Western eyes. The Museum of Contemporary Art in Teheran opened in 1977 shortly before the regime's fall. Costing over $7 million, the multi-leveled modernist structure was filled with mostly American post-Second World War art – reputedly $30 million worth – and staffed by mostly American or American-trained museum personnel. According to Robert Hobbs, who was the museum's chief curator, the royal family viewed the museum and its collection as simply one of many instruments of political propaganda. See Sarah McFadden, 'Teheran report', and Robert Hobbs, 'Museum under siege', *Art in America* (October 1981): 9–16 and 17–25.

3. For ancient ceremonial display, see Joseph Alsop, *The Rare Art Traditions* (New York: Harper and Row, 1982), p. 197 (on temple treasures); Ranuccio B. Bandinelli, *Rome: The Center of Power, 500 BC to AD 200*, trans. P. Green (New York: Braziller, 1970), pp. 38, 43, 100 (on museum-like displays in temples, houses, and palaces); [...] Germain Bazin, *The Museum Age*, trans. J. van Nuis Cahill (New York: Universe Books, 1967), Ch. 1 (on the ancient world); and Francis Haskell, *Patrons and Painters: Art and Society in Baroque Italy* (New York and London: Harper and Row, 1971), Ch. 3 and *passim* (for displays in Italian Baroque churches and seventeenth-century palaces).

4. The princely gallery I am discussing is less the 'cabinet of curiosities', which mixed together found objects, like shells and minerals, with man-made things, and more the large, ceremonial reception hall, like the Louvre's Apollo Gallery. For a discussion of the differences, see Bazin, op. cit. (note 3), pp. 129–36; and Giuseppe Olmi, 'Science-honour-metaphor: Italian cabinets of the sixteenth and seventeenth centuries', in O. Impey and A. MacGregor (eds), *The Origins of Museums: The Cabinet of Curiosities in Sixteenth- and Seventeenth-Century Europe* (Oxford: Clarendon Press, 1985), pp. 10–11. [...]

5. For princely galleries see Bazin, op. cit. (note 3), pp. 129–39; Niels von Holst, *Creators, Collectors and Connoisseurs*, trans. B. Battershaw (London: G. P. Putnam's Sons, 1967), pp. 95–139 and *passim*.
    [...]

6. More exactly, it established an art museum in a section of the old Louvre palace. In the two hundred years since the museum opened, the building itself has been greatly expanded, especially in the 1850s, when Louis-Napoléon added a series of new pavilions. Until recently, the museum shared the building with government offices, the last of which moved out in 1993, finally leaving the entire building to the museum.

7. For Louvre Museum history, see Andrew McClellan, *Inventing the Louvre: Art, Politics, and the Origins of the Modern Museum in Eighteenth-century Paris* (Cambridge: Cambridge University Press, 1994). [...]

8. McClellan, op. cit. (previous note), gives a full account of the ideas that guided the installation of the very early Louvre Museum and of the difference between it and earlier installation models.

9. For some detailed descriptions of gentlemanly hangs, see ibid., pp. 30–9. [...]

10. For example, in the Uffizi in Florence, the Museum at Naples and in Vienna in the Schloss Belvedere, the latter installed chronologically and by school by Christian von Mechel (von Holst, op. cit. [note 5], pp. 206–8; and Bazin, op. cit. [note 3], pp. 159–63). See [...] André Malraux's *Museum without Walls*, trans. S. Gilbert and F. Price (Garden City, NY: Doubleday, 1967), for an extensive treatment of the museum as an art-historical construct.

11. Quoted in Yveline Cantarel-Besson (ed.), *La Naissance du Musée du Louvre*, vol. 1 (Paris: Ministry of Culture, Editions de la Réunion des Musées Nationaux, 1981), p. xxv.

12. Gustav Friedrich Waagen, *Treasures of Art in Great Britain (1838)*, trans. Lady Eastlake (London: 1854–7), vol. 1, p. 320.

13. For a good example of this, see William Dyce, *The National Gallery, Its Formation and Management, Considered in a Letter to Prince Albert* (London: 1853).

14. Raymond Williams, in *Culture and Society, 1780–1950* (New York: Harper & Row, 1966), Part I; and *Keywords* (New York: Oxford University Press, 1976), pp. 48–50 and 76–82, treats the changing meaning of such key critical terms as 'art' and 'culture'.

15. Malraux, op. cit. (note 10), gives an overview of this development in art-historical thinking.

16. See Iain Pears, *The Discovery of Painting: The Growth of Interest in the Arts in England, 1680–1768* (New Haven, CT and London: Yale University Press, 1988), for an excellent treatment of this.

17. For Louvre installations, see McClellan, op. cit. (note 7).

18. For accounts of this looting, see McClellan, op. cit. (note 7).

19. Genius is another of those terms that, by the early nineteenth century, already had a complex history and would continue to evolve. See Williams, *Culture and Society*, pp. xiv and 30–48, or

Malraux, op. cit. (note 10), pp. 26–7 and *passim*, for some of the changing and complex meanings of the term. At this point, genius was most likely to be associated with the capacity to realize a lasting ideal of beauty. But, new definitions were also in use or in formation – for example, the notion that genius does not imitate (and cannot be imitated), but rather expresses the unique spirit of its time and place (seen, for example, in statements by Fuseli, Runge, and Goya).

20. See Francis Haskell, *Rediscoveries in Art: Some Aspects of Taste, Fashion and Collecting in England and France* (Ithaca, NY: Cornell University Press, 1976), pp. 8–19.
    [...]

21. See Nicholas Green, 'Dealing in temperaments: economic transformation of the artistic field in France during the second half of the nineteenth century', *Art History* 10 (March 1987): 59–78, for an early phase of the literature of art-historical genius.

22. See von Holst, op. cit. (note 5), pp. 169–71, 204–5, 228–9; and Brazin, op. cit. (note 3), p. 214. The ornately decorated Hermitage Museum in St Petersburg was probably the most princely of these nineteenth-century creations in both its traditional installations and its visiting policy. Until 1866, full dress was required of all its visitors. Entrance to the Altes Museum in Berlin, the national gallery of the Prussian state, was also restricted, although in form it was a model of the new art-historical gallery. [...]

23. See Daniel J. Sherman, *Worthy Monuments: Art Museums and the Politics of Culture in Nineteenth-Century France* (Cambridge, MA and London: Harvard University Press, 1989).

24. See Duncan and Wallach, op. cit. (note 1), for a tour of the Louvre as it existed in 1978.

25. Georges Salles, director of the Museums of France in 'The Museums of France', *Museum* 1–2 (1948–9): 92.

26. For the new Louvre, see Emile Biasini, Jean Lebrat, Dominique Bezombes, and Jean-Michel Vincent, *Le Grand Louvre: A Museum Transfigured, 1981–1993* (Milan and Paris: Electra France, 1989).

27. See, for example, Nathanial Burt, *Palaces for the People: A Social History of the American Art Museum* (Boston and Toronto: Little Brown, 1977), p. 23; Alma Wittlin, *The Museum: Its History and Its Tasks in Education* (London: Routledge & Kegan Paul, 1949), pp. 132–4; and Francis H. Taylor, *Babel's Tower: The Dilemma of the Modern Museum* (New York: Columbia University Press, 1945), p. 17. I cite here only three of the many writers who have understood public art museums in terms of the Louvre.

28. Peter W. Thomas, 'Charles I of England: a tragedy of absolutism', in *The Courts of Europe: Politics, Patronage and Royalty, 1400–1800*, ed. A. G. Dickens (London: Thames & Hudson, 1977), pp. 191–201; Francis Haskell, *Patrons and Painters: Art and Society in Baroque Italy* (New York and London: Harper & Row, 1971), p. 175; and Pears, op. cit. (note 16), pp. 134–6. [...]

29. Pears, op. cit. (note 16), pp. 106 and 133–6; and Janet Minihan, *The Nationalization of Culture* (New York: New York University Press, 1977), p. 10. [...]

30. As Tim Hilton wrote of this exhibition in the *Guardian* (2 October 1991), p. 36, 'something seems not to be right' when people must pay £4 to view works that 'seem to be national rather than private treasures' and 'seem so obviously to belong ... in the permanent and free collections of the National Gallery upstairs'. As Hilton noted, the Queen's Gallery, a small, recently established exhibition space next to Buckingham Palace, has made selected portions of this collection available to the public; it does not, however, change the status of the collection as private property.

31. Pears, op. cit. (note 16), p. 3.

32. See J. G. A. Pocock, *Politics, Language and Time: Essays on Political Thought and History* (London: Methuen, 1972), especially Ch. 3, 'Civic humanism and its role in Anglo-American thought'.

33. The British Museum, founded in 1753 by Sir Hans Sloane, president of the Royal Society, is sometimes described as the nation's first public museum (see, for example, Margorie Caygill, *The Story of the British Museum* [London: British Museum Publications, 1981], p. 4). However, it began its life as a highly restricted gentlemanly space and was democratized only gradually in the course of the nineteenth century. The state did not appropriate public funds for its purchase, but rather allowed a lottery to be held for that purpose. Nor was it conceived as an art collection. Although today it contains several aesthetically installed galleries of objects now classified as 'art' (including the famed Elgin Marbles), it originated as an Enlightenment cabinet of curiosities – the museological category from which both science and history museums descend. See Caygill, ibid., and David M. Wilson, *The British Museum: Purpose and Politics* (London: British Museum Publications, 1989).

34. Pears, op. cit. (note 16), pp. 176–8; and Peter Fullerton, 'Patronage and pedagogy: the British Institution in the early nineteenth century', *Art History* 5(1) (1982): 60.

35. Harold James Perkin, *The Origins of Modern English Society, 1780–1880* (London: Routledge & Kegan Paul, 1969), p. 51.

36. Mark Girouard, *Life in the English Country House: A Social and Architectural History* (New Haven, CT and London: Yale University Press, 1978), p. 191.

37. For the social and political workings of eighteenth-century society, I consulted Asa Briggs, *The Making of Modern England, 1783–1867: The Age of Improvement* (New York: Harper & Row, 1965); Perkin, op. cit. (note 35); Philip Corrigan and Derek Sayer, *The Great Arch: English State Formation as Cultural Revolution* (Oxford and New York: Basil Blackwell, 1985); Edward P. Thompson, 'The peculiarities of the English', in *The Poverty of Theory and Other Essays* (New York and London: Monthly Review Press, 1978), pp. 245–301; and Raymond Williams, *The Country and the City* (New York: Oxford University Press, 1973).

38. Girouard, op. cit. (note 36), p. 3.

39. John Rigby Hale, *England and the Italian Renaissance: The Growth of Interest in Its History and Art* (London: Arrow Books, 1963), pp. 68–82.

40. Pears, op. cit. (note 16), explores this meaning of eighteenth-century collections in depth, especially in Chs 1 and 2. See also Corrigan and Sayer, op. cit. (note 37), Ch. 5.

41. For Parliament's neglect of the National Gallery after 1824, see Minihan, op. cit. (note 29), pp. 19–25.

42. For a good example of the latter see Steven Moyano's study of the founding of the Altes Museum in Berlin, 'Quality vs. history. Schinkel's Altes Museum and Prussian arts policy', *Arts Bulletin* 72 (1990): 585–608.

43. In any case, there was nothing in the eighteenth-century British concept of the state that would call for spending public money on art galleries (see John S. Harris, *Government Patronage of the Arts in Great Britain*, Chicago and London: University of Chicago Press, 1970, pp. 13–14). [...]

44. George L. Nesbitt, *Benthamite Reviewing: The First Twelve Years of the Westminster Review, 1824–1836* (New York: Columbia University Press, 1934); Briggs, op. cit. (note 37), Chs 4 and 5; and Perkin, op. cit. (note 35), pp. 287–91, 302.

45. Linda Colley, 'Whose nation? Class and national consciousness in Britain, 1750–1830', *Past and Present* (November 1986): 97–117.

46. The Prince of Orange had been willing to pay more, and the fear of losing the collection to a foreigner was a factor in prompting Parliament's approval of the purchase. At the same time, Sir George Beaumont, a prominent amateur and patron of the arts, made known his intention to give the nation paintings from his collection, on condition that the state provide suitable housing for them. Beaumont's offer, combined with the prestige of the Angerstein Collection, tilted the balance in favor of a national collection. For a blow-by-blow account of the legal and legislative history of the founding of the National Gallery, see Gregory Martin, 'The National Gallery in London', *Connoisseur* 185 (April 1974): 280–7; (May 1974): 24–31; and 187 (June 1974): 124–8. See also William T. Whitley, *Art in England, 1821–1837* (Cambridge: Cambridge University Press, 1930), pp. 64–74. [...]

47. As the latter wrote to a representative of the government: 'Well knowing the great satisfaction it would have given our late Friend that the Collection should form part of a National Gallery, we shall feel much gratified by His Majesty's Government becoming the purchasers of the whole for such a purpose.' Christopher Lloyd, 'John Julius Angerstein, 1732–1823', *History Today* 16 (June 1966): 373–9.

48. Ibid., p. 68.

49. See Benedict Anderson, *Imagined Communities: Reflections on the Origin and Spread of Nationalism* (London and New York: Verso, 1991), p. 4; and Eric J. Hobsbawm, *Nations and Nationalism* (Cambridge and New York: Cambridge University Press, 1990), Ch. 1, especially p. 18. [...]

50. *Parliamentary Debates (Commons)*, 13 April 1832, new ser., vol. 12, pp. 467–70; and 23 July 1832, new ser., vol. 14, pp. 643–5.

51. The committee was to discover 'the best means of extending a knowledge of the Arts and of the Principles of Design among the People ... (and) also to inquire into the Constitution, Management, and Effects of Institutions connected with the Arts' (*Report from the Select Committee on Arts, and Their Connection with Manufacturers*, in House of Commons, *Reports*, 1836, vol. IX. 1, p. iii).

52. In George Foggo, *Report of the Proceedings at a Public Meeting Held at the Freemason's Hall on the 29th of May, 1837* (London: 1837), pp. 20–3. [...]

53. In a speech delivered at the Freemason's Tavern on 17 December 1842, reproduced in John Pye, *Patronage of British Art* (London: 1845), pp. 176–85.

54. William Ewart, in House of Commons, op. cit. (note 51), p. 108.

55. Paid for by the government, the building would have to be shared with the Royal Academy, a situation, in the opinion of the Committee, that amounted to government support for a body that was the very soul of oligarchic patronage and actually retarded the cultivation of the arts in England. Much of its proceedings were devoted to an investigation of the R.A.

56. Ibid., p. 138.

57. Seguier was a successful art expert and restorer who had guided several high-ranking gentlemen in the formation of conventional aristocratic collections. Both George IV and Sir Robert Peel had availed themselves of his services (*Dictionary of National Biography*).

58. House of Commons, op. cit. (note 51), p. 137.

59. ibid., p. x.

60. Thompson, op. cit. (note 37), *passim*.

4.

Museums and the Formation of National and Cultural Identities

Annie E. Coombes

And so it is interesting to remember that when Mahatma Gandhi … came to England and was asked what he thought of English civilization, he replied, 'I think it would be a good idea.'[1]

Multi-culturalism has become, albeit belatedly in England, one of the buzzwords of the educational establishment. Exactly three years on from the Swann committee report, optimistically entitled *Education for All*, and in the wake of the ensuing debates on the relative merits of an initiative that may be 'multi-cultural' but is not necessarily always actively 'anti-racist', the controversy continues.[2] By April 1986, multi-culturalism was also on the agenda of the museum ethnographic establishment, at the annual conference of the Museum Ethnographers Group. In addition, specific proposals were advanced that a policy decision be made by the Group concerning dealings with the apartheid régime in South Africa.[3]

This essay is written then, in the context of what might be interpreted as the moment of a more self-consciously political conception of the roles available to museums in general. It also comes at a moment of renewed interest in the ethnographic collection as a possible site for academic anthropology's engagement with the multicultural initiative inspired by documents like the Swann Report. Moreover, such an involvement has the potential, acknowledged by both the anthropological establishment and its critics, of redeeming the discipline's tarnished reputation as a product and perpetrator of the colonial process.[4]

In order to understand some of the difficulties and contradictions arising from implementing a multi-cultural initiative in the display of material culture already designated 'ethnographic', I want to elaborate a case study situated at a comparable historical conjuncture in 1902, when the Education Act of that year announced the same objective of 'Education for All'. More specifically, the 1902 Act also made provision for school children accompanied by their teachers to count visits to museums as an integral part of their curriculum; an early indication of government recognition of the educational potential of such institutions.[5] Another effect of this Act was to generate a series of debates within a professional body which is still the official organ of the museums establishment today: the Museums Association.[6] The focus of these discussions was threefold: concern with the problem of attracting a larger and more diverse public, proving the museums' capacity as a serious educational resource and, in the case of the ethnographic collections, as a serious 'scientific' resource. While the existence of such debates cannot be taken as a measure of the efficacy of any resultant policies, it does give a clear sense of the self-appointed role of museums within the State's educational programme at this moment.

1902 was a significant year in other respects since it marked the renewal of concerted strategies by both contending parliamentary parties to promote the concept of a homogeneous national identity and unity within Britain. Imperialism was one of the dominant ideologies mobilised to this end. The Empire was to provide the panacea for all ills, the answer to unemployment with better living conditions for the working classes and an expanded overseas market for surplus goods. Through the policy of what was euphemistically referred to as 'social imperialism', all classes could be comfortably incorporated into a programme of expansionist economic policy in the colonies coupled with the promise of social reforms at home. It was in this context that museums and in particular the ethnographic sections, attempted to negotiate a position of relative autonomy, guided by a code of professional and supposedly disinterested ethics, while at the same time proposing themselves as useful tools in the service of the colonial administration.

The degree to which the museum as a site of the production of scientific knowledge and as the custodian of cultural property can claim a position of relative autonomy from the vagaries of party politics and State intervention, is an issue central to an understanding of the ethnographic collection's actual and possible role today.

I

The specific roles assigned to ethnographic collections in the discourses on museums and education produced from within the more catholic membership of the Museums Association needs to be seen in relation to another site producing knowledge of the colonial subject. Between 1900 and 1910 Britain hosted a number of National and International, Trade and Colonial exhibitions. Designated as both 'scientific demonstration' and 'popular entertainment', these 'spectacles' were the physical embodiment of different and sometimes conflicting imperial ideologies.[7]

Particularly relevant here is the fact that these extremely popular and well-attended events, held on massive purpose-built exhibition sites, nationwide, often mobilised the same heady rhetoric of education and national coherence which was to become the hallmark of the museum's appeal to the public at this time. While it is beyond the scope of this article to deal in detail with these events, they are an important element in gauging and comprehending the terms on which the ethnographic curators sought to define their domain and to establish their distinctive contribution to the national education programme after the 1902 initiative. In the face of the much greater popularity of the International and Colonial Exhibition, such a differentiation was only expedient.[8]

The obstacles that faced museum ethnographic curators in their efforts to acquire the same mass audience as the Exhibitions without relinquishing any academic credibility, are exemplified through contemporary debates concerning the problems posed by the museum building. Through the internal organisation and classification, in conjunction with the inevitable restrictions imposed by the architecture itself, the museum guided its public through its collections in a specific though not always linear narrative, encouraging implicit, if not explicit, associations. In view of ethnographic curators' claims to the popular (albeit 'scientific') accessibility of the presentation inside the building, it is significant that the external 'shell' – in the case of the larger municipal and national collections – was the 'temple' type. The imposing and distancing connotations of this type of public building were fully appreciated by many contemporary curators and resulted in a series of novel architectural schemes which were designed to overcome this obstacle.[9]

The Colonial exhibitions were notable for precisely the absence of such a monolithic structure and an apparent lack of rigorously imposed control over the viewing space. This semblance of endless choice and unrestricted freedom was an important factor in the effectiveness of these exhibitions in obtaining a broad basis of consent for the imperial project. Through the rhetoric of 'learning through pleasure', the exhibitions achieved the sort of popular appeal that the museums could only dream of. Far more successfully than the museum, whose exhibits could only signify the colonised subject, the exhibitions literally captured these potentially dangerous subjects and reproduced them in a 'safe', contained and yet accessible and supposedly open environment.

This usually meant constructing mock 'villages' stocked with items that were purportedly characteristic and representative of a particular culture. Often peopled by troupes of professional performers from different African societies, Ceylon or other participants from Ireland and Scotland, these 'villages' were always favourites for press attention. Railway and other transport networks within the exhibition grounds had the effect, reinforced by the text in the guidebooks, of allowing the visitor to travel metaphorically from one country to another without ever having to leave the site.[10] Consequently, they cultivated at one and the same time, both a sense of the availability *and* the containability of those societies represented. The 'villages' successfully fostered a feeling of geographical proximity, while the sense of 'spectacle' was calculated to preserve the cultural divide.[11] The possibility of possession as well as a sense of being an active participant at an 'event' rather than simply a passive observer were other aspects of the Exhibition that were lacking in the museum experience. The vicarious tourism on offer was available to all who passed the turnstile at the entrance to the exhibition site, providing they had the sixpenny fee that allowed them access to the so-called 'villages'.

The ensuing competition for the same broad public necessitated the implementation of certain policies in order for the ethnographic curators, in their capacity as museum administrators, to distinguish their appeal from that of the Exhibition. Such strategies served not only to differentiate the two institutions but, more importantly, to legitimise the museum as the domain of the 'authentic' educational experience in the face of the 1902 initiative.

The debate around the use of 'curio' and 'curiosity' as generic terms for ethnographic material is a case in point. Throughout the first decade of the twentieth century these terms were a bone of contention amongst museum officials and early acknowledged by them as one of the major hindrances to any effective educational use of ethnographic material. As evidence of the severity of the problem, the journal of the Museums Association published the following comments by an early visitor to the Liverpool County Museum's ethnographic rooms.[12] The visitor contended that one of the main troubles lay in the unfortunate fact that the public '... regard it as a storehouse of curiosities arranged to please and amuse. Certainly there are curiosities in every museum ... though the fact may be insisted that their original and foremost purpose is to educate'.[13] The solution advised by the influential body of the League of Empire in 1904 was the 'orderly arrangement and the transformation of mere curios into objects of scientific interest by appropriate classification'.[14]

An early guide from the Horniman Museum in London provides a colourful illustration of the eclectic display policy that the Association was up against. Prior to the Museum's transference into the hands of the London County Council in 1901, descriptions of the Ethnographic Gallery focused on the slave trade or social groups like the Dahomeyans or the Zulu, both of whom were identified in the popular consciousness as aggressive African fighters with a penchant for human sacrifice and gratuitous violence.[15] Prior to entering the 'African and Japanese Room' the visitor would have passed through the Annexe where a collection of 'deities' from China, India, Scandinavia and Peru were on offer, together with a Bhuddist shrine and 'a Chinese banner fixed on the wall, as also a 'skeleton in the cupboard, the bones and ligatures all shown and named; it is labelled: – "the framework on which beauty is founded"'.[16] Glass table cases in one room contained Swiss, African, Eskimaux (sic) Indian, Japanese and Chinese ivory carvings and a collection of Meerschaum pipes, while on top of such cases, 'are ranged glass Jars, containing Snakes, Lizards, Chameleons and a strange looking spiny lizard from Australia, together with a chicken with four legs and four wings but only one head, hatched at Surrey Mount' (the Museum's earlier name).[17] The visit culminated with a walk through the 'Zoological Saloon' and a meeting with the much publicised Russian bears, Jumbo and Alice, and the Sal monkey, Nellie!

II

The debates in the Museums Association over the classification of ethnographic material were considerably more complex and comprehensive than the resultant displays. The proposals revolved around the choice between a geographical or a typological organisation and the relevance of either for different types of anthropological museum. The general consensus delegated the former as the responsibility of the national collections and the latter as that of the local museums. The material at hand was broadly recognised as falling into the two categories of a biological unit and a cultural unit. Ideally, since 'Man's physical evolution and anatomical structure related directly with all his activities', race and culture were assumed to be 'intimately connected'. The objective for the curator was to demonstrate the relationship between the two.[18]

Sub-divisions according to tribe and nation, however, provoked discussion that provides us with a particular insight into the function of ethnographic collections in Britain. In this case, colonies as a category acquired the status of a homogeneous 'nation', as part of the British Empire. Evidently, by this definition 'nation' was too large a grouping to be practically implemented in

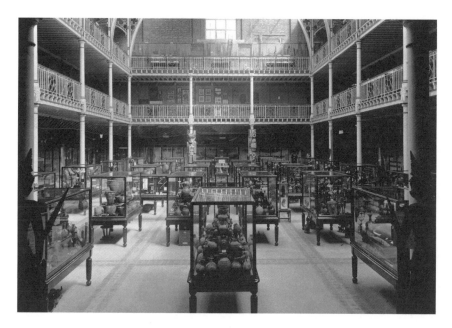

Figure 3.4.1   Pitt Rivers Museum, Oxford: general view of the collection, *c.* 1904

a museum! Nevertheless, the fact that a territorial possession of the British Empire had no recognised status as a nation outside of the Empire as a whole, had particular ramifications for any colony represented in the displays. Clearly, material culture from these countries functioned primarily as signifiers of British sovereignty. Above all, in this search for the perfect classification system, there was the certainty that somewhere there existed a 'natural' grouping. Since culture was seen to vary according to geographical and regional factors and since environmental factors created regional affinities within the same groups, the 'natural' choice was thought to rest with a geographical classification. This was the arrangement selected by most large British collections.

The other system advocated for smaller local collections was morphological or typological; the most exemplary, then as now, being the Pitt Rivers Museum in Oxford. The theoretical premise that the past could be found in the present was explicitly laid out here by inclusion of archaeological exhibits (mainly weapons and implements) from the Stone, Bronze and Early Iron Ages, alongside typological 'series' of material culture from various colonies. It was this type of organisation that was thought to illustrate more specifically the evolutionary nature of man. It concentrated on series of objects from all over the world, grouped according to function and divided into small exhibition groups with the aim of suggesting an evolutionary progression, by placing those forms classified as more 'natural' and organic at the beginning of the series culminating in more 'complex' and specialised forms. A feature of Pitt Rivers' collection which set it apart from others originally the property of one collector (such as Frederick J. Horniman), was that it was widely acknowledged as being 'no mere miscellaneous jumble of curiosities, but an orderly illustration of human history; and its contents have not been picked up haphazard from dealers' shops, but carefully selected at first hand with rare industry and judgement'.[19] The classification system employed was the touchstone of the collection, and it was this aspect that recommended it as a model for so many other museums.

This comparative and evolutionary system of classification, which placed the value of anthropology as 'tracing the gradual growth of our complex systems and customs from the primitive ways of our progenitors' through the use of material culture from extant peoples (all of whom were colonised), was the chosen taxonomy throughout this period.[20] Despite academic anthropology's increasing disenchantment with evolutionary theory at this time, it remained the most prevalent means of displaying ethnographic material. Even where this was not necessarily the case in museums, it is clear that this principle had acquired a considerable currency amongst many members of the museum public. In 1902 for example, the British Museum erected an exhibition in the pre-historic room to demonstrate the use of tools and weapons prior to the use of metals. A review of the exhibition in *The Standard*, drew the readers' attention to the ethnographic galleries, 'which should be visited, in order to study perishable objects still in use among races in a stage of culture corresponding more or less closely to that of the prehistoric races by whom the objects in this (the prehistoric room) were made'.[21] It is important to recognise that, whether intended by the British Museum or not, it is symptomatic of the conjuncture that existed in the 'public' consciousness that the reviewer was able to make such a comparison between the two rooms.

III

Moreover, there is also evidence that the evolutionary paradigm served as a direct means of promoting support for that concept of class unity which was so essential to the ideology of social imperialism. Although the primary objective of the Oxford museum was to facilitate academic research, Pitt Rivers was no newcomer to the conception of the museum as an institution with a broad educational role, appealing to a diverse public. Indeed he actually saw himself as one of the main progenitors of this initiative. The early history of the collection included a short sojourn in 1897 at the Bethnal

Green Museum in London's East End. It is not insignificant that it was located in an area of social deprivation and class conflict. In line with other similar institutions during the 1870s, the exhibits were used as an aid in the task of 'improving the masses'. Pitt Rivers' own intentions towards the working classes were quite explicitly set out in relation to the use of his collection. His lecture to the Society of Arts in 1891 makes it clear that not only was it important that the schema of the display conform to a 'scientific' classification, but that it was designed to educate 'the masses' to accept the existing social order:[22]

The masses are ignorant ... the knowledge they lack is the knowledge of history. This lays them open to the designs of demagogues and agitators, who strive to make them break with the past ... in drastic changes that have not the sanction of experience.[23]

In the light of this statement, the persistent preoccupation with evolutionary theory takes on new and more explicitly political overtones. Through its tangible exposition in the physical arrangement of ethnographic collections, it was a paradigm which emphasised the inevitability and indispensability of the existing social order and its attendant inequalities, while also stressing the need for a *slow* move towards technological advancement.[24]

Where Pitt Rivers is explicit in his political affiliations in relation to class interests (while still maintaining that science was essentially 'objective' and non-partisan), later uses of evolutionary theory were less overtly concerned with social control. Nevertheless, it was one of the most long-lived paradigms for the organisation of displays of material culture from non-Western societies and there are certain features of later applications which reproduce the political assumptions of this earlier model. In both typological and geographical arrangement, for example, cultural elements characterised in the museums literature as 'the intrusive, generalised elements of civilisation' of the non-European cultures, were deliberately eliminated. The curator was well aware that 'modern civilisation, has broken over all natural limits and by means of railroads and ships carries its generalised culture to the ends of the earth'.[25] But the resultant transformations brought about by this contact was not the designated domain of the ethnographic curator.[26] For the material in these displays, then, and by implication the cultures they represented, time stood still.

As a means of validating the expansion of ethnographic collections, the rhetoric often employed was one of the necessity of conservation and preservation in the face of the inevitable extinction of the producers of the material culture in their custody.[27] Paradoxically, of course, anthropology's desire for government funding in the museum context as in the academic sphere, necessitated its aiding and abetting this extinction by proposing itself as the active agent of the colonial government. By speeding the

Figure 3.4.2   Henry Balfour in the gallery showing the Eypological classification, Pitt Rivers Museum, Oxford

inevitability of such destruction, anthropologists encouraged the expansion of the market in ethnographia and boosted the already multiple values assigned to the discipline's objects of study thus enhancing the status of anthropological 'knowledge', while simultaneously ensuring that those societies who produced such material culture maintained their position at the lower end of the evolutionary scale, since they were destined not to survive.

Since, unlike the International and Colonial Exhibition, the colonised subject was not available in the 'flesh', their presence had to be signified by some other means. By 1902, the principle that physiognomic characteristics were accurate indicators of intellect and morality (early ingested as a tenet of certain anthropological theses) acquired new potency through its association with the eugenics movement, now marshalled more deliberately to the aid of the state. If evolutionism had ever looked like wavering, it was now here to stay. Consequently, in museum displays of material culture from the colonies, it was common practice to include photographs, casts of the face or of the figure, or even skeletons and skulls. These were supposed to demonstrate more nearly the relationship between the inherited and cultural features of any race since:

The man himself as he appears in his everyday life, is the best illustration of his own place in history, for his physical aspect, the expression of his face, the care of his person, his clothes, his occupations ... tell the story with much clearness.[28]

In 1903, the Physical Deterioration Commitee had recommended the setting up of an Imperial Bureau of Anthropology, whose anthropometry section was to be responsible for the collating of data on the physical measurements of those races coming under the jurisdiction of the British Empire.[29] Despite the fact that by 1908 the Royal Anthropological Institute was still fighting for some government support for the scheme, anthropometry had already been put to considerable use by anthropologists working within the British Isles.[30] The Physical Deterioration Committee, under whose aegis anthropometry came into its own in the following years, had originally been set up in response to medical reports on the poor state of health of the working class.[31] While this generated concern about the social circumstances of the mass of the population, the ensuing debate around the issues of deterioration versus degeneration was fuelled by the eugenists, who were still mostly convinced of the biological and inherited, rather than environmental, determinants of such a deterioration. If this complex 'scientific' philosophy had ambiguous implications for the working classes, its implications for colonised peoples are as insidious.[32]

The ethnographic curators' insistence that a person's physiognomy and the expression of the face could designate their position in history takes on particular significance in the context of this preoccupation with and popular visibility of the 'science' of anthropometry. The emphasis on the body as a feature of museum display would have made it difficult to avoid an association with the work of Francis Galton or Karl Pearson, especially at a time of increasing government advocation of eugenics (often in conjunction with 'anthropological' investigations) as a means of strengthening the national stock. Evidently, the Museums Association were fully aware of eugenics policies and the means by which the ideology of selective breeding was implemented as part of a policy of national regeneration. That the 1907 Presidential Address of the Association reads like a eugenics tract, therefore, comes as no surprise. At this meeting, a proposal was put forward for an Institute of Museums where once again the emphasis was educational, but where, significantly,

of equal importance would be a regard for heredity teaching, seeing that the teaching of evolution must be based upon it. Here the endeavour would be to instruct the public in the part that inherited traits, character, virtues, vices, capabilities, temper, diseases, play in the destinies of men ... and to popularise such branches of the subject of heredity as selection, variation and immunity.[33]

The fact that this practice of scrutiny so close to the prevalent eugenic ideology is present to such a degree in the discourse of the Museums Association, is another indication of the museums' willingness to participate in the state's concern for national regeneration, and points to a further complex of meanings inscribed in the objects in their collections that was far closer to home.

IV

One means of gauging the potential of the ethnographic collections, both as vehicles for a nationalist ideology *and* as sites for the proliferation of contradictory and therefore productive knowledges concerning the colonial subject, is through an examination of the discourses around education in the literature of the Museums Association for the period 1902–1910. It is through these discourses that museums constituted their 'ideal' publics and consequently the 'ideal' function of the collections in their custody.

Much of the discussion was formulated as a result of renewed interest in a concept known as the 'New Museum Idea'. The primary objective of this 'idea' was to 'afford the diffusion of instruction and rational amusement among the mass of the people' and only secondly 'to afford the scientific student every possible means of examining and studying the specimens of which the museum consists'.[34] The museum was thus designated as provider of both 'rational amusement' and 'scientific study' for two distinct publics while prioritising one. What is particularly interesting here is that the 'New Museum Idea' was anything but new by 1902. Between 1902 and 1910, however, the need to attract what was loosely referred to as 'the mass of the people', is revived as one of the central concerns for museum curators. How then was this purportedly liberal extension of the democratic principle of 'education for all' transformed through the institution of the museum, into a discourse inextricably implicated in imperial ideologies?

The notion of an educational practice based on the careful observation and study of museum collections had already been integral to both the Victoria and Albert Museum and the National Gallery from their inauguration in the 1850s. And here also it was designed to attract a certain sector of the working class. Although this early initiative came primarily from a left middle-class intelligentsia, demands from within the working classes for effective educational provision were later met by workers themselves through the Social Democratic Federation and other socialist organisations.[35] The fact that 'rational amusement for the mass of the people' was re-introduced as a focus of debate within the museums establishment in 1902, by which time the composition and strength of the working class had altered considerably, indicates a new function for this concept. With the rise of socialism and the subsequent organisation of a large proportion of the working class, it presented enough of a constituency to be a major target in the electoral campaigns of both the Liberals and the Conservatives throughout the period under discussion. If the museums wanted to carve out a role for themselves compatible with either party's campaign, it was essential that they were seen to address a broad public.

By 1902 it is possible to determine more precisely the publics that were sought by museums in Britain. The Education Act of that year had made provision for time spent in museums by children accompanied by their teachers to count as time spent in school. The *Museums Journal* of the same year expressed the hope that museums could occupy a territory 'neutral' enough to provide a common meeting ground for children from 'different class backgrounds' in so far as those from private, board and voluntary schools were seen to benefit from the Act in this respect. Furthermore, in conjunction with such adjectives as 'neutral' and 'objective', the museum was proclaimed as:

the most democratic and socialistic possession of the people. All have equal access to them, peer and peasant receive the same priviledges and treatment, each one contributes in direct proportion to his means to their maintenance and each has a feeling of individual proprietorship.[36]

The notion of the museum as an institution that transcended class barriers is particularly significant, not only in the light of the persistent claims for class unity made by organisations dedicated to juvenile education reform, but also in view of the constancy with which this rhetoric was applied in organisations dedicated to the 'ideal' of Empire, who also mobilised the pedagogic apparatus. The Primrose League, for example, was a society that specialised in popularising Empire through lectures in rural districts and was founded in 1883 with the aim of 'joining all classes together for political objects ... to form a new political society which should embrace all classes and all creeds except atheists and enemies of the British Empire'.[37] By 1900 the League claimed to include in its membership one and a half million workers and agricultural labourers. The special role of the museum for that sector of society described as having no life 'but this life of making money so that they can live', was 'to elevate [them] above their ordinary matter-of-fact lives'.[38]

By 1904 both the Horniman and the Manchester Museum were making claims for the conspicuous presence of both school groups and working-class participation. An exchange in the *Museums Journal* of the same year indicates the degree to which this was now a sensitive issue, in this instance, in the case of ethnographic collections. Free public lectures by A. C. Haddon, the Cambridge anthropologist, now advisory curator of the Horniman, had come in for sharp criticism since, 'The time for delivery … is 11.30 a.m. which showed that they were not altogether intended for the labouring classes.'[39] The Horniman felt this rebuff keenly enough to respond that despite this unfortunate time schedule 'large parties of workmen from various institutions … visited the museum'.[40]

Obviously one should not take the intention as a measure of its effectiveness, but it is important to point out here that the fact that both museums and other public displays of material culture from the colonies felt in some way obliged to define their publics as having a large working-class component, and in terms of an educational priority, is significant in itself, whether or not it was successfully implemented. The emphasis on this priority is more easily understandable in the context of social imperialism, whereby the working classes were wooed by both Liberals and Conservatives on two fronts: imperialism and social reform. As a principle, this policy was designed to unite all classes in the defence of nation and empire by focusing its campaign on convincing the working classes that their interests were best served by the development and expansion of Empire.[41] And it is evident as early as 1902 that museums' concern with constructing their image as an organ for popular education was, indeed, specifically calculated to ensure that they had a recognised part to play in what was acknowledged at the Museums Association annual conference that year, as the 'one great national work, the building up of the Empire through the elevation of the communities and the individual'.[42]

In 1903 this declared allegiance was compounded by the formation of the League of Empire, founded with the aim of bringing children from different parts of the Empire into contact with one another, and 'getting them acquainted' with parts of it other than those in which they lived, through correspondence, lectures and exchanges. The museums played a crucial role in this organisation and one which was clearly signalled by the distinguished line-up of museum directors and officials heading a sub-committee entitled 'School Museum Committee'. By 1907 the Museums Association was congratulating itself on the rather ambitious and dubious achievement of 'splendid success in educating and refining the masses of the population'.[43]

Museums' assumed role as specifically 'popular' educators concerned with encouraging working-class participation, received a further fillip of approval through a symposium organised under the aegis of the Empire League Educational Committee. This eight day conference, held in London in 1907, had a special interest for those involved in museum work. A section was inaugurated specifically to deal with museums and education. Even outside of the parameters of its own professional caucus, the museum was clearly recognised as an important element in furthering the objectives of the Empire. Any interpretation of this educative principle advocated by both

Leagues as simply a benevolent paternalism making use of Empire as a potential 'living geography lesson', should be dismissed after 1908. By this time it had been transformed into a more specific call for the recognition of the superiority of the European races:

The progress of colonisation and commerce makes it every year increasingly evident that European races and especially those of our own islands, are destined to assume a position in part, one of authority, in part, one of light and leading, in all regions of the world.[44]

Consequently since the British assumed the position of the world's teachers, it was essential that they were themselves well taught.

As late as 1909, the relevance of education, especially through the use of ethnographic collections, was as persistent a theme in general museums discourse as it was in the discourse of the professional body of academic anthropology, the Royal Anthropological Institute:

Heaven-born Cadets are not the only Englishmen who are placed in authority over native races ... There are Engine Drivers, Inspectors of Police ... Civil Engineers of various denominations ... to mention only a few whose sole opportunity of imbibing scientific knowledge is from the local museum of the town or city in which they have been brought up.[45]

Clearly, certain class sectors were seen as an indispensable means of promoting an image of the museum as the site of the consummation of a seamless and unproblematic national unity. Furthermore, the fact that the terms of this address are borrowed in no small measure from a 1907 speech by that ardent exponent of social imperialism, the Liberal MP Viscount Haldane, places it firmly within this political discourse.[46]

V

Part and parcel of this ideology of national unity was the constitution of the concept of a National Culture, and here too the ethnographic curator played a particular role. As early as 1904, Henry Balfour, Curator of the Pitt Rivers Museum in Oxford and President of the Anthropological Institute, laid plans for what he called a museum of national culture. Balfour went as far as specifying that this museum would denote 'British' in nature rather than possession, which was rather the function of material culture from the colonies as well as that in the larger survey museums. 'We want a National Museum,' he said, 'National in the sense that it deals with the people of the British Isles, their arts, their industries, customs and beliefs, local differences in physical and cultural characteristics, the development of appliances, the survival of primitive forms in certain districts and so forth.'[47] Although this objective was not realised in the museum context until much later, the proposal for a national, or, more accurately, 'folk' museum, is a persistent element in museums' discourse, throughout the years 1902–1912.[48]

Paradoxically, the same rhetoric of extinction and preservation, once applied by academic anthropologists to specifically colonised races as a means of validating anthropology's expansion, was now systematically applied to certain communities within the British Isles. The conception promoted by this rhetoric of a national British culture as a resilient 'folk' culture, surviving in rural communities, was a popular fantasy shared by those at both ends of the political spectrum, and it was assumed by certain members of the middle-class intelligentsia to be their responsibility to bring it to light in the common cause of national unity.[49] Since 1905 supposed 'folk' culture had already been officially mobilised in the sphere of juvenile education to instill a correct patriotic spirit. By October 1907, Cecil Sharp, that untiring middle-class campaigner for the revival of 'folksong', had published his collection of what he defined as 'authentic' folk music since it was

not the composition of an individual and as such, limited in outlook and appeal, but a communal and racial product, the expression, in musical idiom, of aims and ideals that are primarily national in character.[50]

While the effects of this discourse were visible through anthropological practice by those working within the discipline, it was not incorporated into museum practice. Its visibility in the public domain lies rather in the sphere of the 'amusement' section of the International and Colonial Exhibition. Here, Irish and Scottish Villages were reconstructed together with Dahomeyan, Somali, and Senegalese Villages. Without exception these are all produced through the official guidebooks as quaint 'survivals' in the anthropological sense. But while both European and African villages were produced as 'primitive', it was a 'primitiveness' that had already been clearly qualified in both cases, in terms that would have been familiar to a large proportion of the exhibition public through the discourse on national tradition constructed through the renewed interest in folklore. Consequently the proximity of these villages on site had the inverse effect of accentuating the distance between the European 'primitive' and their colonial counterpart. This was further reinforced by the suggestion in the guidebooks that, even in these supposedly simple European communities, there was evidence of an inherent superiority in relation to the colonised races represented. The predominance of adjectives such as 'healthy', 'beautiful' and 'industrious' together with descriptions of the Irish and Scottish living quarters as 'spacious', compare favourably with the constantly repeated assurances that the Africans are in fact much cleaner than they look.[51] Similarly, while the guidebooks are full of references to the ancient traditions of the Irish and the Scots, the Africans are accredited with no such history or tradition.[52]

Thus, what at first appears to constitute an irreconcilable contradiction – the construction of certain 'British' communities as themselves essentially 'primitive' – must be understood as a means by which both museums and exhibitions established the notion of an intrinsically national culture through the discourse of organisation. In addition, by emphasising the relative 'difference' of the black colonised subject, both the museum ethnographic collection and those 'villages' in the International and Colonial Exhibitions representing these peoples reinforced the illusion of a homogeneous British culture.

Because the educational policies adopted by the museums over the period 1902–1910 could be appropriated by either the more conservative ideology of national efficiency or the more liberal ideology of social reform, the ethnographic collections were able to negotiate a particular space for themselves. In an educational capacity they operated in the conjuncture between popular and scientific theories of race and culture, and thus acted as an agency for different imperial ideologies. There was, however, an ambivalence underpinning the relationship of the ethnographic curators to the colonial government. By declaring that their aim was to provide 'objective' education on 'neutral' territory, those anthropologists working within the museums establishment claimed a degree of independence from specific government policies. The emphasis on the 'scientific' nature of the knowledge produced through the classification and organisation of their collections on the other hand, was calculated to reinforce their role as purveyors of 'objective truth'. At the same time, as a deliberate strategy of survival, the new academic discipline of anthropology relied on the argument that anthropological knowledge as produced through museum collections, was an essential training for the colonial civil servant and an indispensible facilitator in the subjugation of the colonies. Furthermore, the focus on evolutionary paradigms as a means of representing material culture from the colonies to British publics reinforced some of the worst aspects of those racial stereotypes disseminated through the more propagandist International and Colonial Exhibitions.

VI

Now, nearly a century later, we find ourselves on the threshold of another educational initiative, equally optimistically referred to as 'Education for All' under the rubric of multi-culturalism.[53] It is a moment when debates on the restitution of cultural property take up prime time in the media. It is also a time dominated by the euphemism of 'rationalisation' for the Arts, Humanities and Education and by a government characterised by the outright hostility to ethnic minorities of Margaret Thatcher's infamous aliens speech and by the jingoism of her Falklands victory speech on the 2nd of July 1982:

We have learned something about ourselves, a lesson which we desperately needed to learn. When we started out, there were the waverers, and the fainthearts … There were those who would not admit it … but – in their heart of hearts – they too had their secret fears that it was true: that Britain was no longer the nation that had built an Empire and ruled a quarter of the world. Well, they were wrong.

How does a museum displaying the material culture of other nations negotiate a position of relative autonomy from the rabid xenophobia characterised by Thatcher's speech, while at the same time justifying its expansion and maintenance?

The controversy generated over an exhibition at the Museum of Mankind, 'The Hidden Peoples of the Amazon', is a useful marker of the problems involved in working towards any self-critical representation of other cultures within a museum context. It also demonstrates how difficult it is to escape the legacy left by the historical formation of the institution itself.

On the 8th August 1985, the Museum was picketed by representatives from Survival International and two Indian representatives from different Indian rights organisations. The demonstration concerned the absence in the display of any evidence of the ongoing struggle between the Indians and the Brazilian government or indeed of any resistance or self-determination by Indian groups such as themselves. According to Richard Bourne (Chairman of SI), one of the objections against incorporating evidence of such resistance into the exhibition was that it would have disrupted what was an essentially *'objective'* account.[54] It is also true to say that without the goodwill of the Brazilian Government it would have been extremely difficult to have carried out the extensive fieldwork necessary for the exhibition.

Evidently today, more than ever, the public ethnographic museum is caught between two stools. On the one hand, the museum still perceives itself as both purveyor of 'objective' scientific knowledge and as a potential resource centre for a broad-based multicultural education. On the other hand, it is clearly hostage to and sometimes beneficiary of the vagaries of different state policies and political régimes, and aware of the necessity of being seen to perform some vital and visible public function to justify its maintenance, while fighting to preserve a measure of autonomy.

A surprising degree of correspondence still evidently exists between the International and Colonial Exhibitions of old and certain contemporary ethnographic display practices. Now that both scientific exegesis and popular entertainment are contained within the same edifice, the invitation to partake of a vicarious tourism is as strong as ever an incentive to visit the Museum.

Furthermore, despite any criticism levelled at the museum as an institution, its authority speaks louder than the voices of those represented within its walls, as this passage from a recent *Arts Review* testifies:

During a week in or around the Amazon, I found it difficult to escape from the other tourists and enjoy even a semblance of the jungle ... This was all white man's territory and for a truer description of life with the Hidden Peoples of the Amazon I would recommend both this exhibition and the fascinating book that accompanies it.[55]

NOTES

This is a revised version of a paper given at the London Conference of the Association of Art Historians in March 1987. My thanks to Susan Hiller, Fred Orton, Michael Orwicz and Alex Potts for their critical comments on earlier stages of this essay and to John Mack at the Museum of Mankind for his valued support and criticism throughout the longer project which formed the context for this work.

1.   Salman Rushdie, 'The New Empire Within Britain', *New Society*, vol. 62, no. 1047, 1982, p. 417.

2.   *Education For All: the Report of the Committee of Inquiry into the Education of Children from Ethnic Minority Groups*, HMSO, March 1985. The Committee was initially chaired by Anthony Rampton until 1981 when Lord Swann took over. A. Sivanandan's comments on the distinction between a multi-culturalist education initiative and one that is actively anti-racist, are worth citing in full here:
  'Now there is nothing wrong with multiracial or multicultural education as such, it is good to learn about other races, about other people's cultures. It may even help to modify individual attitudes, correct personal biases. But that ... is merely to tinker with educational methods and techniques and leave unaltered the whole racist structure of the educational system. And education itself comes to be seen as an adjustment process within a racist society and not as a force for changing the values that make that society racist. "Ethnic minorities" do not suffer "disabilities" because of "ethnic differences" ... but because such differences are given a differential weightage in a racist hierarchy. Our concern ... was not with multi-cultural, multi-ethnic education but with anti-racist education. Just to learn about other people's cultures is not to learn about the racism of one's own.' A. Sivanandan, 'Challenging Racism: Strategies for the 80's', *Race and Class*, vol. xxv, no. 2, Autumn 1983, p. 5.
  For an excellent analysis of the multicultural experiment in one case study see also, Sneja Gunew, 'Australia 1984: A Moment in the Archaeology of Multiculturalism', in *Europe and its Others*, eds F. Barker et al., vol. 1, University of Essex, 1985, pp. 178–93.

3.   *Agenda of the Annual Conference of the Museum Ethnographers Group* (a Sub-Committee of the Museums Association), held on 25 April 1986, at the Bristol Museum and Art Gallery. Item 9.2 reports a discussion on the 'new' (my emphasis) importance of multicultural education and a request from some members that the MEG form a policy regarding dealings with the apartheid régime in South Africa.

4.   See, for example, the recent debates in one of the two journals of the Royal Anthropological Institute (*Anthropology Today*); Jean la Fontaine (President of the Institute), 'Countering Racial Prejudice: a Better Starting Point', vol. 2, no. 6, 1986, pp. 1–2: Mary Searle-Chatterjee, 'The Anthropologist Exposed: Anthropologists in Multi-Cultural and Anti-Racist Work', vol. 3, no. 4, 1987, pp. 16–18; Stephen Feuchtwang. 'The Anti-Racist Challenge to the U.K.', vol. 3, no. 5, 1987, pp. 7–8; Brian V. Street, 'Anti-Racist Education and Anthropology', vol. 3, no. 6, 1987, pp. 13–15.

5.   For a detailed analysis of the 1902 Education Act, see G. R. Searle, *The Quest For National Efficiency* (Berkeley and Los Angeles, 1971), pp. 201–16; E. Halevy, *History of the English People (Epilogue: 1895–1905. Book 2)* (Harmondsworth, 1939), pp. 114–129; B. Simon, *Education and the Labour Movement 1870–1920* (London, 1965), pp. 208–46.

6.   The Museums Association was founded in York in 1888 at the initiation of the York Philosophical Society as the professional body of museum curators and administrators. *The Museums Journal*, founded in 1901, was to represent the interests of all types of museums within Britain mainly, but also the Empire and later the Commonwealth and Dominions. The aim of the monthly publication was inter-communication between the museums in the association.

7.   One of the largest purpose-built exhibition sites in England was London's 'White City' built in 1907 by Imre Kiralfy and so called because it covered approximately 140 acres. For more details

concerning these exhibitions in Britain see Annie E. Coombes, '"For God and For England": Contributions to an Image of Africa in the First Decade of the Twentieth Century', *Art History*, vol. 8, no. 4, 1985, pp. 453–66 and 'The Franco-British Exhibition: Packaging Empire in Edwardian England', *The Edwardian Era* (Oxford, 1987), eds J. Beckett and D. Cherry, pp. 152–66; Paul Greenhalgh, 'Art, Politics and Society at the Franco-British Exhibition of 1908', *Art History*, vol. 8, no. 4, 1985, pp. 434–52; John M. MacKenzie, *Propaganda and Empire* (Manchester, 1984), pp. 96–121.

8.   The distinction was implicit rather than explicit and is demonstrated through the absence of almost any discussion or mention of exhibitions in the pages of the *Museums Journal* despite the active participation by members of the Museums Association and in particular by anthropologists. Such silence is stranger in view of the fact that many museums including the Horniman, Liverpool County Museum and the Pitt Rivers Museum acquired ethnographic material from such sources.

9.   See, for example, B. I. Gilman, *Museum Ideals of Purpose and Method* (Boston, 1923), pp. 435–42.

10.   See, for example, *The Imperial International Exhibition, Official Guide* (London, 1909), p. 43. Describing the 'amusement' entitled the 'Dahomey Village', the writer says, 'Entering the Gateway here, we are at once transported to Western Africa.' The entry for the 'Kalmuck Camp' in the same guide (p. 45) began, 'Entering their camp, we first detect them coming down the distant steep mountains with their camels and horses.'

11.   This division was clearly not maintained as rigorously as the authorities would have wished. See Ben Shephard, 'Showbiz Imperialism: The Case of Peter Lobengula', in *Imperialism and Popular Culture*, ed. John M. MacKenzie (Manchester, 1986), pp. 94–112. This examines an instance of marriage between an African 'performer' and a white woman and the ensuing furore over miscegenation in the press.

12.   *The Museums Journal* contained regular comments from visitors to the various collections.

13.   *Museums Journal*, vol. 2, March 1903, p. 269.

14.   Ibid., vol. 2, Sept 1904, p. 101.

15.   *First Guide to the Surrey House Museum*, n.d. (pre 1901), p. 9.

16.   Ibid.

17.   Ibid., p. 19.

18.   W. H. Holmes, 'Classification and Arrangement of the Exhibits of an Anthropological Museum', *Journal of the Anthropological Institute*, vol. xxxiii, 1902, pp. 353–72, p. 353; Christine Bolt, *Victorian Attitudes to Race* (London, 1971), p. 9.

19.   *University Gazette*, January 1883, p. 4.

20.   William H. Flower, 'Inaugural Address to the British Association for the Advancement of Science', *Nature*, vol. 40, Sept 1889, p. 465.

21.   *The Standard*, 3 March 1902.

22.   Lieutenant General Pitt Rivers, 'Typological Museums as Exemplified by the Pitt Rivers Museum at Oxford, and His Provincial Museum at Farnham, Dorset', *Journal of the Society of Arts*, vol. XL, 18 Dec 1891, pp. 115–122. This was also the theme of an address to the British Association For the Advancement of Science at Bath, 1888. For a history of the Pitt Rivers collection up to 1900 see William Ryan Chapman, *Ethnology in the Museum: A.H.L.F. Pitt Rivers (1827–1900) and the Institutional Foundation of British Anthropology*, 2 vols (unpublished D.Phil. dissertation, University of Oxford), 1981.

23.   Lieutenant General Pitt Rivers, *op. cit.*, p. 116.

24.   See Lieutenant General Pitt Rivers, *op. cit.*, p. 119. Evolutionary theory as applied in Pitt Rivers' collection clearly also had implications for the 'new woman'. In this passage Pitt Rivers describes a series of crates shown carried by women from various countries. According to him these were 'collected expressly to show the women of my district how little they resemble the beasts of burden they might have been if they had been bred elsewhere'.

25.   Holmes, *op. cit.*, p. 355.

26.   Ibid.

27.   See for example, *Annual Report of the Committee of the Public Libraries, Museums and Art Galleries of the City of Liverpool* (Liverpool, 1894), p. 15; *Museums Journal*, vol. 10, Nov. 1910, p. 155.

28.   Holmes, *op. cit.*, p. 356.

29. See *Man*, vol. 11, 1911, p. 157; A. Watt Smyth, *Physical Deterioration: Its Causes and the Cure* (London, 1904), pp. 13–14.

30. *Journal of the Royal Anthropological Institute*, vol. xxxviii, 1908, pp. 489–92; *Man*, no. 9, 1909, p. 128 describes the 'science' as demonstrating 'how measurement of physical and mental characteristics are a reliable test of physical deterioration and progress'.

31. See Watt Smyth, *op. cit.*

32. G. R. Searle, *Eugenics and Politics in Britain 1900–1914* (Leyden, 1976); G. R. Searle, 'Eugenics and Class', in *Biology, Medicine and Society 1840–1940*, ed. Charles Webster (Cambridge, 1981), pp. 217–43; David Green, 'Veins of Resemblance: Francis Galton, Photography and Eugenics', *Oxford Art Journal*, vol. 7, no. 2, 1984, pp. 3–16, provides a useful documentation of the interrelation between photographic techniques of recording social 'deviancy' and the classification deployed by some eugenists; Anna Davin, 'Imperialism and Motherhood', *History Workshop Journal*, 5, 1978, pp. 9–65, gives an excellent analysis of the contradictory implications of eugenic theory for British women. See also Jeffrey Weeks, *Sex, Politics and Society: the Regulation of Sexuality since 1800* (London, 1981); Frank Mort, *Dangerous Sexualities, Medico-Moral Politics in England Since 1830* (London, 1987).

33. *Museums Journal*, vol. 7, Dec 1907, p. 203.

34. William H. Flower, Presidential Address to the Museums Association, London, 1893. Reprinted in W. H. Flower, *Essays on Museums and Other Subjects Connected with Natural History* (London, 1898), p. 36.

35. For a detailed analysis of educational initiatives from within the working class see Brian Simon, *op. cit.*

36. *Museums Journal*, vol. 2, Sept 1902, p. 75.

37. See J. H. Robb, *The Primrose League, 1883–1906* (London, 1942), p. 148.

38. *Museums Journal*, vol. 2, July 1902, p. 11.

39. *Museums Journal*, vol. 3, Feb 1904, p. 266.

40. *Museums Journal*, vol. 4, Jan 1905, p. 235.

41. For a fuller discussion of the policy of social imperialism see Bernard Semmel, *Imperialism and Social Reform* (London, 1960), and G. R. Searle, *op. cit.*, 1971.

42. *Museums Journal*, vol. 2, July 1902, p. 13.

43. *Museums Journal*, vol. 7, July 1907, p. 8.

44. *Museums Journal*, vol. 8, July 1908, p. 12.

45. *Museums Journal*, vol. 9, Nov 1909, p. 202.

46. Viscount Haldane, *Universities and National Life* (London, 1912), p. 69 (given as a Rectoral Address in 1907). See also Viscount Haldane, *Education and Empire* (London, 1902); Brian Simon, *op. cit.*, Ch. 5, 'Imperialism and Attitudes to Education'.

47. Henry Balfour, 'Presidential Address', *Journal of the Anthropological Institute*, vol. xxxv, 1904, p. 16.

48. See, for example *Museums Journal*, vol. 3, June 1904, p. 403; *Museums Journal*, vol. 1, 1901–2, p. 173; *Museums Journal*, vol. 9, July 1909, pp. 5–18.

49. D. Harker, 'May Cecil Sharp Be Praised?', *History Workshop Journal*, vol. 14, Autumn 1982, p. 54.

50. C. Sharp, *English Folk Song: Some Conclusions*, Privately printed, 1907, p. x, quoted in D. Harker, *op. cit.*, p. 55.

51. See, for example, *Franco-British Exhibition Official Guide to the Senegalese Village*, London, 1908, p. 8.

52. See, for example, *The Franco-British Exhibition Official Guide*, London, 1908, p. 53. This lists no less than five 'realistic reproductions' of 'ancient monuments' included in the 'Irish Village' of Ballymaclinton.

53. See note 2.

54. R. Bourne, 'Are Amazon Indians Museum Pieces?', *New Society*, 29 Nov 1985 (my emphasis).

55. B. Beaumont-Nesbitt, 'The Hidden Peoples of the Amazon', *Arts Review*, 24 May 1985, p. 253.

5.

Creating Identity: Exhibiting the Philippines at the 1904 Louisiana Purchase Exposition

Beverly K. Grindstaff

Abstract

The Philippines Reservation at the 1904 World's Fair was a living display of nearly 1200 Philippine people. This exhibit presented a fused Philippine/Filipino identity through a series of strategies which first naturalised, then normalised, United States policy surrounding the Constitutionally illegal but de facto colonisation of the Philippines; impending Congressional assessment of Philippine competency for self-rule; and incarceration of Filipinos in American-administered prisons and reconcentration camps. The exhibit radically disavowed claims of a unified Philippine national identity through extensive, racialised display of disparate Filipino 'tribes', effectively shifting the grounds of identity from the political discourse of nation to the scientific discourse of the anthropological object.

Introduction: 'Exchanging living objects for text-books'

The Louisiana Purchase Exposition, 'The Greatest Exposition the World has Ever Seen', was held from 30 April to 1 December 1904 to commemorate the centennial of the Louisiana Purchase. It was by far the largest international exposition yet held, notable for its cost ($20 million, five million more than was paid for the Louisiana Territory itself) and its huge size (at 1240 acres it nearly doubled the previous largest fair, with over 200 acres of this being exhibition space).[1] Emerging in the mid-19th century, the World's Fairs were government-sponsored international showplaces for nations to present and hence compare their cultural, industrial and technological accomplishments and innovations. Along with similar international trade shows, congresses and small-scale fairs, World Fairs provided arenas in which to promote a cohesive image of nation predicated on and derived from the cumulative effect of its display. In effect, each nation presented its preferred identity relative to its peers.[2] Within the conditions of this general program, the St Louis event presented a thematic celebration of the once-controversial Louisiana Territory Purchase, and its massive scale glorified US expansionism in terms of realised economic gain. In its desired role as mass educational

ANTAERO, THE IGORROT, AT HOME.—"Mr. Roosevelt, I will return to the Philippines, and whip all your enemies;" these are the words that Antaero, the Igorrot (interpreted Antonio, the Chief), as saying, on their visit to the White House. On this occasion, out of honor to their host they wore suits of white duck. But no sooner did they return to their village than the white duck disappeared into suit cases, and they came out wearing strings of beads, breech clouts, and satisfied smiles. Antaero sits at the right in the picture, gazing at the camera with a face that is "childlike and bland." Most of the Igorrots are afraid of the kodak, and visitors are warned that if they take snap shots it is at their own risk. Antaero is proud of being able to sing, slowly, to be sure, "My Country, 'Tis of Thee." The thatched huts are fac similes of what we see in the islands. After a short occupancy, the Igorrot people made their surroundings quite homelike.

Figure 3.5.1   Antaero, The Igorrot, at Home, in *The Universal Exposition, a Portfolio of Official Photographic Views of the Louisiana Purchase Exposition, St Louis, 1904* (St Louis: Portfolio Publishing Co., 1904), n.p.

tool, the 1904 World's Fair in St Louis relied on visual images and displays to convey particular forms of knowledge; it sought to 'exchange pictures and living objects for text-books, and to make these ... the means whereby instruction is given and individual development [is] obtained'.[3]

The Fair's 'instruction' also encompassed contemporary political issues. The pressing American political issue of 1904 was the newly-purchased Philippine archipelago, with concerns centred on Philippine assertions for independence, the so-called 'Philippines Problem', and the impending 1905 Congressional assessment of Filipino competence for self-rule.[4] It is in this context one must consider the Fair's most prominent and widely visited attraction, the Philippines Reservation, a 47-acre display featuring nearly 1200 Filipinos exhibited from June through December 1904 (Figure 3.5.1). As Exposition President David R. Francis 'observed at the official dedication of the million-dollar exhibit in mid-June, the display from the Philippines alone justified the expense and labour that went into the entire fair'; an extremely popular attraction, it was ultimately visited by '99 out of a 100 fairgoers', or roughly 18.5 million people.[5]

The living display of 'native peoples' was not a new concept in 1904; indeed, small-scale 'Philippine villages' had appeared in the midway areas of the 1898 Trans-Mississippi and International Exposition in Omaha and the 1901 Pan-American Exposition in Buffalo.[6] Ample American precursors existed, with waxwork displays of the races of man established by Charles Willson Peale in 1797 and the living exhibit itself tracing back at least to the 1816 establishment of William Clarke's Western Museum.[7] Commercial versions of the living display included travelling ventures such as P. T. Barnum's Ethnological Congress of 1884–85, which promised to 'place upon exhibition the various types of humanity from all sections of the earth', and Buffalo Bill's Wild West Show; the latter ran for 6 months near the 1893 Columbian Exposition, attracting 4 million viewers to see, among other things, 'two hundred Indians, of various tribes'.[8]

Nor was the St Louis emphasis on racialised display of the living subject without precedent in illustrating and figuring political agendas. One prototype was the British ethnological congress of 'all the races of India', an adjunct display to the proposed General Industrial Exhibition of 1869–70 explicitly charged with addressing 'questions of miscegenation or separation'.[9] Imperialism informed popular European ethnography and anthropology exhibits such as the 'Briton, Boer and Black in Savage Africa' programme of the 1899–1900 winter season at Olympia in London, productions which played a significant 'role in the construction of the colonies to the British exhibition public'.[10] Living displays operated as literal demonstrations of colonial precepts, with race the driving mechanism. David Theo Goldberg notes the entry of race – and the coterminous emergence of the concept of nation – into European consciousness with the late-15th century voyages of discovery, expansion, and domination, and posits that the 'basic human condition – and so economic, political, scientific, and cultural positions – was taken naturally to be race determined'.

Defining race as 'the various designations of group differentiation invoked in the name of race', Goldberg writes that:

race undertakes at once to furnish specific identity to otherwise abstract and alienated subjectivities. Sufficiently broad, indeed, almost conceptually empty, race offers itself as a category capable of providing a semblance of social cohesion, of historical particularity, of *given* meanings and motivations to agents otherwise mechanically conceived as conduits for market forces and moral laws. It is an identity that can be stretched across time and space, that itself assumes transforming specificity and legitimacy by taking on as its own the connotations of prevailing scientific and social discourses.[11] (emphasis in original)

The World's Fairs and related expositions provided ideal venues for displaying visual evidences and giving meaning to the racialised subject, and all colonial powers ultimately exhibited their subjects in at least one exposition.[12] At the St Louis Exposition, the Philippine Reservation was presented in immediate parallel to the Fair's overall presentation of the Louisiana Territory and its indigenous peoples, an advantage as the Reservation sought to justify the Philippines expenditure and subsequent American government and military activities. Reliance on the racialised subject allowed the exhibit to give visible form to political metaphor, a form which effectively collapsed proto-nationalist Philippine claims to self-rule into issues of biological race. What was at stake was the crafting of Philippine identity relative to the United States, and here the Exhibit presented a Philippines which centred on a scientifically racialised construal of the indigenous and manifestly 'uncivilised' Igorot native.

The 'Philippines Problem'

Invested with issues of national identity and additionally overlaid with an explicit glorification of American expansionism, the 1904 World's Fair presented a particularly apt venue for satisfying American curiosity surrounding the new insular possession and, as this article will argue, for resolving the 'Philippine Problem'. The Philippines had largely entered American consciousness with the first major American victory of the Spanish–American War in Manila Bay in May 1898. Filipinos under Emilio Aguinaldo had allied with America, and soon after gained control of most of the Philippines following a revolution against Spain. The Filipinos subsequently proclaimed their intent towards independence. Rather than supporting their erstwhile allies in this claim, however, America instead purchased the Philippines from Spain under the 1898 Treaty of Paris at the end of the Spanish–American War, adding nearly 116 000 square miles to US possessions and effectively replacing the Spanish colonial presence with that of the US. This intensified pre-existing Filipino assertions to self-rule and spurred a greater political organisation. Strong anti-imperialist forces within the United States also opposed America's new position as a *de facto* colonial power in the Philippine annexation, and so divided the Senate that the treaty was ratified by a single vote on 6 February 1899. Other American opposition centred on the related likelihood of additional military action, a fear realised by the Philippine–American War of 1899–1902. Preliminary positioning of the purchase as an American business opportunity also threatened economic competition from Philippine labour and products.[13]

Standard World's Fair formulae positioned St Louis to function as a source of expedient information about the new possession, and in August 1901 the World's Fair Committee on State and Territorial Exhibits established that a Philippines exhibit would be included towards the specific end of making:

the exhibits of our insular possessions one of the most important and interesting features of the Fair. The people of America are anxious to know just what we have acquired, and, so far as it is possible, we propose to show them without making necessary a trip to the islands in the Pacific.[14]

By the time of this announcement extensive anthropological planning was well under way and the proposed Philippines exhibit already occupied a central place in the Fair's merging of human evolution and technological development.

The stated intention of the Philippines Reservation was to provide a 'scientific demonstration' of the possession's resources, geography and inhabitants in order to assuage American trepidations over the value and role of American involvement in the Philippines. But the final exhibit's emphasis was squarely placed on the Philippines' indigenous peoples, however, and presented a narrow vision built from the seeming-objectivity of science, architectural gesture, and the language of popular press accounts, racial slurs and political metaphor. Positioned literally and conceptually at the margins of the Fair's twinning of human accomplishment and biological development was the Philippines Reservation. Unlike countries participating in the Fair proper, the Philippines was not presented through its contemporary industrial products and cultural accomplishments as these were viewed as being European or American in origin. Representation was instead accomplished through ethnographic objects such as Igorot headhunter axes which, while technically accurate to a specific population, presented within the context of evolution and human progress an archaicising if not a prehistoric view of the Philippines. These objects were held exactly commensurate with their makers, and critically supported the mechanism by which the Reservation's 47 acres built an image of the Philippines upon its living people. Thus the Philippines was made synonymous with Filipino, and 'Filipino' was first fragmented into President Theodore Roosevelt's dismissive description of the Philippines as a 'jumble of savage tribes', a destabilising act which obviated Philippine nationalists' claims of political cohesion, then collapsed into the Fair's singular and sensationalised image of the 'uncivilised' – although civilisable – Igorot native: breechclouted, dog-eating, tightly enclosed and closely guarded, nominally human.

The classification of progress

The daunting task of spatially arranging and visually expressing the St Louis Exposition's 'process of development' fell to Frederick J. V. Skiff, Director of Exhibits, and former executive director of the Chicago Field Museum and former Colorado commissioner of immigration and statistics with 15 years of acclaimed experience organising international expositions.[15] The scientific and intellectual vitae of Skiff and his Exhibitions Advisory Board was a crucial legitimising factor which allowed the Philippines Exhibit to logically expand from a modest display of anthropological artefacts to an exhibit to illustrate the benefits of American attentions, and to finally open as a giant enclave filled with 75 000 anthropological objects and populated by 1102 people (gradually increased to almost 1200), funded by over a million dollars received directly from the United States Government with additional funds for 'postal, telegraphic and transportation facilities supplied by the Insular [American] government'.[16]

Skiff understood his task at St Louis as the ordering of a massive encyclopaedia possessing 'complete and authentic data on all subjects, ... prepared and classified so as to be effectively presented and of easy access'.[17] He devised a rigorous system which thematically overlaid the Fair site and its displays with a steady upward progression, conceptually splitting the Fair into 16 Departments corresponding to the developmental stages of man. Skiff accordingly divided the site's 1240 acres into '16 departments, 144 groups, and 807 classes' following 'the *process of the development* of the various arts, industries and sciences; their evolution from small and insignificant beginnings'.[18] In effect, the Fairgoer constantly followed an intricate map of evolutionary development arising from 'small and insignificant beginnings': Manufacturers and their raw materials; the great displays of the Electricity and Machinery Buildings juxtaposed to 'primitive' tools; American and European cultural exhibits housed in the Main Picture's Neoclassical opulence at farthest remove from the near-naked inhabitants of the thatched Igorot display.

'Showing the wild tribes in the Philippines under natural conditions'

'Now, for a moment,' a typical Skiff speech of late 1902 began, 'may I speak of a few of the features which the Exposition of 1904 anticipates in its great plan of life and motion?' The markers of civilisation privileged by Skiff included landscaping, physical culture,[19] 'special instruction classes illustrating the education of the Indian, the deaf and dumb, and the blind', the Fair's main power plant and 'modern garbage destroying plant', and the Philippines exhibit:

Families, groups and tribes of living people, an exhibition of the representatives of peculiar faraway aborigines, possibly fifteen different villages, designed for the scientific demonstration and conducted under the personal supervision of one of the well-known ethnological scientists of the United States. In this distinguishing contribution to life and motion of the Exposition the participation of the government of the Philippines Islands [as outlined previously by Civil Governor Taft] will provide a most attractive and instructive exhibit.[20]

Race critically underlies the machinations of Skiff's 'most attractive' design, with the Philippine body politic replaced by the Filipino body, and 'tribes' effectively shifting the grounds of identity from the political discourse of nation to the scientific discourse of the anthropological object. This action was already tautological.

In October 1898 Dean Conant Worcester, then an assistant zoology professor at the University of Michigan, published a popular press article, 'Knotty Problems of the Philippines', in conjunction with the third printing of his larger work *Philippine Islands and Their People*. Equal parts travelogue, naturalist account and political treatise, Worcester noted that Filipinos' 'utter unfitness for self-government at the present time is self-evident'. On the basis of the popularity and scientific authority of his works, Worcester was invited to the White House in December 1898 by President McKinley, where he communicated 'certain facts relative to the Philippine situation'. By the end of this visit the young zoologist had become McKinley's personal representative in the Philippines, where he served as commissioner and secretary of the interior from 1900 to 1913, conducting census surveys, compiling photo-documentation and writing additional works on the Philippines.[21] Worcester also drafted 'the scientific portion' of the 1899 investigative report of the Schurman Commission, a report undertaken to 'facilitate the most humane, pacific, and effective extension of authority throughout these islands' and to 'study the existing social and political state of the various populations'.[22]

Worcester's contribution to the Schurman Report was the biological fragmentation of the Philippine population into 84 distinct units, which he designated tribes. Utilising a racial taxonomy informed by his studies in botany and zoology, Worcester charted peoples according to primary criteria of skin colour, physical stature and intelligence (as determined by him), and then by acquired traits such as literacy and religion. This information was tabulated into three 'sharply distinct' biological races (Negrito, Malayan, and Indonesian), with each of these three columns further divided into rowed categories based on the remaining criteria (21, 47, and 16 per column, respectively). In short, Worcester provided a visual map that evolved from his darkest, denigrated Negrito ('little, woolly headed, black, dwarf savages') and culminated with the 'civilised tribes' of the Europeanised Indonesian ('physically superior [and] the colour of their skin is quite light. Many of them are very clever and intelligent').[23] Worcester's table lends racism a spatial dimension.

While Worcester does not appear in the Fair documentation by name, he belonged to the supporting Philippine Commission, and methods detailed in his academic and government texts, reports, and especially photographs and census work undertaken in his official capacity, inform Fair planning and its categories of civilisation:

Classed in terms of blood, the peoples of the world may be grouped in several races; classed in terms of what they do rather than what they merely are, they are conveniently grouped in the four culture grades of savagery, barbarism, civilization, and enlightenment.[24]

The first three 'culture grades' correspond to Worcester's racial division of Negrito, Malayan, and Indonesian; the fourth designation of enlightenment is the domain of the European races. Once divided into races, classes and grades, distinctions could be investigated, quantified and displayed.[25] In addition to 'these customary measures', photographs, casts and mouldings, and athletic tests of strength and endurance 'were introduced, in order that the results might indicate – so far as measurements may – the relative physical value of the different races of people'.[26]

Ethnography and the mechanisms of classification constitute only one portion of the organising committee discourse, and political expediency is never far from these scientific gestures. Skiff grasped the essential sameness of charting the natural and the social world, and his translation of the full blossoming of human civilisation and its predicted move into the future efficiently overlaid this biological organisation upon the spatial organisation of the Fair. But his plan's 16 Departments were allotted only 15 buildings, whose instantly legible structures corresponded to their display contents and whose rectilinear forms adhered to the civilised grid. There were no satisfactory structural prototypes for the final, absent Department that was to house the living anthropological display of the Philippines Reservation. Displaying a uniform conception of civilisation and progress, as well the specific appropriateness of historicist architecture, Skiff ultimately situated the exhibit in the ungridded siteless-ness of uncivilised, nomad space.[27]

Earlier displays of the sort noted previously normalised and even fed expectations for the live ethnographic object. They also carried a potent economic rationale, and St Louis financial planners were acutely aware that the 1900 Paris Exposition's 'marvellous collection of villages' had played a key role in its unprecedented $2 million profit margin.[28] Yet the populist informality of midway attractions lacked a critical legitimacy and 'colonial villages' were inseparable from colonial policy, a correlation St Louis planners sought to avoid in representing the Philippines. Bemoaning the lack of a 'scientific, or even an intelligent standpoint' in living displays, the Fair pursued a policy of authenticity which held faithful reproduction sufficient to visually convey all that needed to be known of an object, a way of life, a people. F. W. Putnam proposed the template of the realised Philippine Reservation, a plan which was to prompt later extremes such as the importation of a Moro chieftain's house to serve as the touchstone of legitimacy for dwellings constructed on the exhibit site. Putnam proposed that a

thorough exhibit of all types of peoples of the Philippines ... would be a grand display, if the native houses, utensils, weapons, manufactures, etc., were brought with the people and no makeshift imitation allowed, as was the case on the midway of Chicago ... If carried out in the proper scientific spirit, with strict adherence to truthful representation, and no humbuggery allowed from the very start, even in the slightest modification of exact conditions, such an exhibit would not only give a distinctive character to the exposition, but would also be one that could never be repeated.[29]

What elevated this proposal above its precursors and resolved the Fair planners' dilemma is what Annie E. Coombes terms the 'scientific' paradigm, by which 'authenticity' produces the human object: '[The] colonised races taking part in these enactments, ... [were both] ethnographical specimens and representatives of the "race" ... They simultaneously fulfilled the role of "curiosity" and "specimen", as both objects of amusement and scientific scrutiny.'[30] Insistence on 'truthful representation' thus allowed the Philippine Reservation to shift from stock midway attraction to become instead the flagship exhibit of the Fair's Department of Anthropology. 'Authenticity' allowed Skiff to incorporate the Reservation's objectified inhabitants into his overarching design of evolution and progress, necessitating in turn a didactic layout to facilitate the Fair's scientific and rhetorical mapping of the Filipino body. Two plans for the exhibit appear in the formal, published account of the Fair's planning; Charles E. Cutter, member of the St Louis Associated Press Office, filed the exhibit's preliminary design in January 1901.[31]

While ultimately not chosen, Cutter's rudimentary plan remains important as the conceptual blueprint of the realised Exhibit. It featured inhabited villages representing former US territories and present insular possessions, presenting a clear correspondence between the Louisiana Territory and the new Philippine acquisition, and its form consisted of concentric displays arranged about an elliptical lake designed for boat races and demonstrations. Spectators were to be seated in an elaborate amphitheatre (tellingly called the coliseum), where they would take in 'games, dances, modes of warfare, etc., of the various tribes of the possessions' staged on demonstration grounds directly encircling the lake. This performance area was bound by a ring of restaurants; curiosity shops hawking display memorabilia and 'native' craft; and small museums displaying tools, weapons, hunting equipment, and other items of archaeological, anthropological and historical interest. The outer wall delineating Cutter's planned exhibit effectively sealed the exhibit, with the ambulatory inside itself a continuous ethnographic display where the flowing progress of the Fairgoer is contrasted with the unchanging, stationary world of the subject, their representative dwellings, and 'their manner of living, dress, customs, etc.'. This spectrum of 'civilisation' terminates back in the group of viewing Fairgoers, who provide the display's anthropological fourth category of 'enlightened' people, and their exiting re-emphasises the implied need for containment. This sense of contained danger resonates with the Fair's anxiety over the critical divide between man and animal, a trepidation whose concern with documenting the 'thumbprints on the records of civilization' informs Cutter's plan.[32]

Inside the Philippines Reservation

The realised form of the Philippine exhibit represented a masterwork of politicised space, and to have simply walked the long mile to it from the hyperbolic grandeur of the central Fairground's 'Main Picture' would have served to distance oneself from all acknowledged markers of civilisation. Located at the farthest margin of the Fair's layout, one undid Skiff's carefully mediated journey through progress and moved back down the evolutionary tree to the final, symbolic remnant of the primordial world. The Philippine Reservation was located literally on the other side of the tracks, bound by lake and timber, and regardless of how one approached the complex was accessible only through the vast natural resources displays and increasing amounts of original landscape, both signalling a move back into the uncivilised world. In simple terms the Philippines Reservation was a partially moated, walled enclosure accessed by bridge, with a gridded central plaza which rapidly devolved into randomly sweeping walkways and more or less virgin forest. Nearly 100 buildings were included in its grounds, ranging from houses of simple nipa construction erected inside chain-link enclosures to the palatial Spanish administration building. Fair materials note that while:

all of the seventy or more groups of people in the archipelago could not be represented we had the least civilized in the Negritos and Igorots, the semi-civilized in the Bagabos [sic] and the Moros and the civilized and cultured in the Visayans, as well as in the constabulary and scout organizations. In all respects, commercially, industrially and socially, the exhibit was a faithful portrayal.[33]

The vestigial outline of Cutter's physical plan appears in the curved outline of the realised exhibit and its booths, demonstration grounds, and emphases on representative types and dwellings, information kiosks and small museums, with the external boundary of the exhibit partially supplanted by a heavy-walled replication of Intramuros, the 16th-century Spanish fortification surrounding Manila. A curved inner pathway functions much as the original ambulatory, with the living displays placed at intervals along it, and the central pool has been replaced in the final exhibit by the V-shaped natural lake at its perimeter. Middle areas of the final Exhibit housed Ethnology, Forestry and Horticulture displays specific to the Philippines, and a miniature Manila 'with streets and parks and complete sewerage, water and electric light and fire alarm systems' formed the centrepiece of the Exhibit; the sides of this Spanish colonial-style quadrangle were edged by a cathedral which doubled as a school, a 'typical Manila house', and a building each for commerce and government. The largest difference between the two plans is the final exhibit's sole concentration on the Philippines; the other insular possession and Native American segments were dispersed throughout the Fair, though largely to the entertainment strips of The Pike. Parallels to America's territorial past were primarily made through sculptural representations of defeated 'noble savages' prominently featured and scattered throughout the Fairgrounds.[34]

Fairgoers would have had ample opportunity to form a picture of the Philippines before setting foot in the Philippines Reservation. Early travel brochures advertising Manila as 'The Pearl of the Orient' and the 'Venice of Asia' highlighted the city's Spanish architecture and picturesque canals, and popular journals frequently featured illustrated articles on Philippine life and customs. Picture postcards provided another rich source of visual information. These items reflected a wide range of subjects viewed as exotic by American collectors. What began as a representation of the beauty and richness of traditional, indigenous Filipino culture typically appeared as sensationalised 'pictures of carabao, coconut trees, native "savages", and ... bare breasted Ifugao girls or datus with their several wives'.[35] Expectations engendered by these images would have been further tempered by journalism accounts and political metaphors which frequently characterised Filipinos as children, 'savages' and sub-humans.[36] These preconceptions inform the Philippines Reservation.

Imagine, then, the effect of entering the St Louis realisation of the Philippines. After viewing the latest in 20th-century technology, one undertook a backwards step in time to a massive 16th-century fortification temporally located at the dawn of modern time. 'After crossing a reproduction of the bridge of Spain which spans the Pasig River at Manila, the visitors entered the Philippine reservation' through the entree provided by the Europeanising influence of Spain's 1565 occupation. Immediately inside was Intramuros, and this ancient Manila fixed an image of a Spanish Philippines, rich in the tokens of civilisation. This initial portion presented a 'very satisfactory imitation' of a glorious, albeit lost, Spanish past on par with the magnificent buildings of the Main Fairground, and one could pace atop its solid masonry fortification while surveying the 'Philippine enclosure'. Upon stepping from this Walled City into the Exhibit proper one was, 'as if by magic, transported from the sixteenth century to the twentieth'.[37]

The first of the Exhibit's lessons began. The temporal overlap of ancient and modern Manila was mediated by the insertion of a giant relief map of the Philippines, 110 feet long and 75 feet wide, which established a geographical continuity between the two and fused over 350 years of Spanish influence to Philippine land. Located on the path directly outside the Walled City, this map detailed the over 3000 constituent islands of the Philippines to present the country as fundamentally fragmented, and provided a visual image that reinforced critical contemporary notions of geography as the determinant of a race's character. This map functioned as a symbol of the Philippines; it concretised and gave spatial reality to an abstract image of the Philippines, enabling classification and permitting a geography of dominion to be imagined.[38]

Geographically orienting Manila both past and present also situated key contemporary debates over America's legal role in the Philippines, for the city figured large in contemporary military and political actions. The successful 15 August 1898 siege of Spanish Manila by the combined American and Aguinaldo-led Filipino army was followed by the total exclusion of Filipinos from the city on the grounds of potential conflict with Spanish forces; a peace protocol with Spain signed that same day granted the United States control of 'the city, bay, and harbour of Manila pending the conclusion of a treaty of peace which shall determine the control, disposition, and government of the Philippines'.[39] Debate centred on whether 'Manila' defined just the walled portions of the city or the entire surrounding area, a debate perfunctorily settled in December 1898 when control was 'extended with all possible dispatch to the whole of the ceded territory'.[40] As noted above, this effectively replaced Spanish dominion of the Philippines with that of the United States, spawning open hostilities which culminated in the Filipino–American War. These debates were summarily figured – and resolved – in the exhibit's blithe representation of a multiple Manila, and the Exhibit foregrounded that portion of the Philippines most thoroughly European, hence civilised, and most unquestionably American.

The central plaza, as indicated, offered a fully operative vision of 1904 Manila arrayed in four precise grids of civilised space in the exact centre of the exhibit, and thus far the visiting Fairgoer would have had a rather benign introduction to the key city of the Philippines. Spinning off the four corners of the plaza, however, were irregularly drawn pathways that linked into a looping trail. This trail was studded with information pavilions, and to its 'south side were the quarters, camps and parade grounds of the Philippine constabulary and the Philippine scouts'. It was in this remnant of the Cutter ambulatory's break from the civilised grid that the real attraction of the Philippine Reservation began. The key spatial move from grid to the leisurely curves of pleasure ground and nomad space was accompanied by a corresponding shift in architecture, the rigid blocks of the walled entrance gradually giving way to the indolent grace of Spanish colonial facades, then into buildings of increasing hybridity which merged Western and indigenous styles and materials. The farther one moved from the representation of European-influenced Manila, the more 'primitive' were the buildings encountered, a double play on the Fair's theme of evolution and emphatically asserted geography as the exhibit incrementally 'went native'. The final buildings were those displaying the Negrito and Igorot, and vast amounts of imported nipa and bamboo were used in constructing these '[v]illages typical of the Philippine life from the lowest grade'.[41] Fair materials note that 'along the outskirts of this reservation are grouped the different tribes, whose sole claim to attention lies in their spectacular habit and mode of living'.[42]

Here the St Louis Exposition's meticulous language of progress and scientific nicety quickly dissipated amid the sensationalism of displaying the 'least civilized' Filipinos in the form of 41 Negritos and 114 Igorots, leaving only the supportive structures of architecture and material display to educate and indoctrinate Fairgoers. The Negrito functioned to anchor the Exhibit much as they did Worcester's official reports; as figures of intense curiosity, they 'are among the smallest people of the world, and their intellectual development is of the lowest order', and faced with exposure to the rigours of the civilised world 'it is believed that they will eventually become extinct'.[43] They were construed as less uncivilised than pre-civilisation, pre-dating architecture, tools, agriculture, ultimately humanity altogether; in the Fair's link between architectural form and human evolution, the Negrito's 'home is where he crouches at the foot of some sheltering tree to protect himself from the terrific bursts of tropical storms'.[44] The anxiety intimated by Cutter's plan was expressed in full in the 1904 Exhibit, and a Negrito man designated the 'Missing Link' stood as the formal starting point of the Fair's upward evolution.

The Igorot received the Exhibit's greater attention in part because they were believed biologically capable of progress, and hence better fit the Fair's emphasis on education and the government sponsor's self-described campaign toward 'bringing Filipinos to improve their condition'. Fair materials noted that American schools had accomplished more in three years than the Spanish had in 400,[45] and presented gradations of redeemable Filipinos in the form of inherently uncivilised Negritos ('little Negroes' destined for extinction) and civilisable Igorots, presented as both savage and salvageable. This also preserved the Fair's correlation between Native Americans and Filipinos, especially in regard to education, as in an opening day speech which noted that within the exhibit and beyond the shores of Arrowhead Lake 'will stand the Filipino, even as against the Red Man on the continent, just beyond the Pacific, ... and it is the aim of the Model Indian School to extend in influence across both intervening waters to the benefit of both races'.[46] This paraphrased Taft's goal of 'bringing Filipinos to improve their condition' and, in direct adherence to the Fair's thematic twinning, the Igorot were to benefit as Native Americans 'amenable to schooling and training already had': These Indians 'bore no [more] resemblance to their forebears than a dark complexion and racial characteristics', but were:

well-dressed, active, alert, ... [with a] mobility of countenance and an interested expression. ... Moreover, ... physical beauty is a common thing among Indians who have accepted the white man's ways. Education has, therefore, modified the physical, as it has changed the moral and mental character of the Indian, imparting gracefulness to features that were formerly irregular and unintellectual.[47]

The Igorot thus represented both the unimproved Filipino and the raw material of a future American-Filipino, ready to be altered to their very biology by the 'missionaries of civilisation' and superior to the Spanish-Filipino existing at the 1904 apex of Philippine civilisation.

Let us proceed to the Igorot display, 'the most interesting of the group to visitors if gate receipts were an indication', the dominant feature of the Philippine Reservation and, in most accounts, of the Fair itself. 'The whole represented an exact imitation of the surroundings in the home life ... [and in] this exhibit the people lived just as they do at home', and herein the visitor was presented with the 'daily program in this village', a roster that began at 9:30 am and continued until 5:00 pm and which consisted of staged marriage celebrations, annual memorials for deceased relatives, elections of village chiefs, arrow-shooting events, general dances and musical events, and demonstration of skills such as fire-making, harvesting and planting, weaving, and food preparation.[48] The Igorot village consisted of several acres 'enclosed by a high stockade, within which rough shacks were built of boards', and photographic evidences of this exacting copy of domestic life are punctuated by numbered placards indicating items of interest. House interiors are open, for Igorots 'do not erect partitions, but little fence-like enclosures instead; so that a visitor can look from one "room" into another'. This fortuitously normalised 'fence' and 'enclosure' architecturally permitted, even demanded, voyeuristic exploration of the temporary homes amid viewing of the scheduled events of daily Igorot life (see Figure 3.5.1). In practice, however, the Igorot display conformed to the expectations expressed without irony by the Fair's First Vice-President: 'Take the rope-making of Manila and the Philippines. Who cares about the rope?'[49] Here the Fairgoer was met with an astonishment of spectacle that beggared science to present a vast array of exuberant dances, the violent splash of dog slaughter, and nearly-naked bodies. It is difficult to determine from the records which of these activities most titillated the Fairgoers, though certainly no one left with any vivid impression of the Filipino as a viable player in global politics.

The Exhibit Igorot was the inhabitant of a display Philippines, exempt from any reality save that scientifically crafted for it – and that reality catered to vestigial midway sensibilities. Chief among the Igorot display's featured exploitations were the fascinations of nakedness and the near-fetishization of dog-eating, categories made possible by but conspicuously absent from the sterility of J. V. Skiff's classification. Coy photograph captions obsess with the lack of 'evening dress', and an account of the White House visit of Igorots Antaero and Antonio is subsumed in descriptions of their rapid switch from the temporary civilisation of white suits (pointedly worn in honour of their host) back to the uniform of 'beads, breech clouts, and satisfied smiles'. The anthropological object presented as men and women in diminutive loin-cloths was not readily mediated by science, and concern over reception of the 'wild tribes' centred equally on issues of modesty, authenticity, fear of parody, and political backlash. Immediately after the exhibit opened (two months after the Fair itself), Taft cabled Fair officials anxious to avoid 'any possible impression that the Philippine Government is seeking to make prominent the savageness and barbarism of the wild tribes either for show purposes or to deprecate the popular estimate of the general civilization of the islands', requesting in a later telegram a measure of actions taken as the 'President wishes to know'. Roosevelt himself intervened to rule against imposing a pants dresscode for men in favour of larger breechclouts, though women were to appear in skirts and chemises; Rydell notes that the 'nationwide awareness of the Igorot Village was assured by the massive publicity campaign undertaken by the exposition's and by the reservation's Department of Exploitation'.[50]

Concurrently, the racial pejorative 'dog-eater' was expanded into a massively documented and interactive literalisation. Fair publications such as *The Complete Portfolio of Photographs* and *The Universal Exposition, a Portfolio of Official Photographic Views* prominently feature photos that frequently duplicate among titles to track a St Louis man's sale of his dogs through the various actions involved in their slaughter, dressing and cooking. These photographs document the moments 'when most of the spectators got on their shocked expressions' as civilised housepets transformed into savage meals, and for $10 Fairgoers could participate in the 'dog feast'. While absent from most photograph captions, written information accompanying the displays differentiated between the 'three tribes' of Igorots presented at the Fair, and noted that of these, the 'Bontoc are the fighters and headhunters, [and] the dog-eaters of whom so much has appeared in the papers';[51] this conflation links all as particularly savage acts of aggression, a point that will be discussed later. Lifted from cultural context and foregrounded as a daily domestic occurrence, the vividness of the Bontoc ritual feast joined with Igorot nakedness to become the hallmark and colour popular reception of the Philippine Reservation and the Filipino.

In keeping with the Fair's insistence on education and scientific purpose, our imagined Fairgoer would necessarily encounter the myriad Department of Anthropology pavilions established within the exhibit to ensure that the visual lesson of the 'exhibit was moreover an honest one'.[52] These pavilions arranged 'books, manuscripts, albums and photographs of man from the earliest time to the present period' into a formal museum format (a 'place for learned occupation') in exact correlation to the living exhibits just beyond. Differences to be observed by the Fairgoing lay scientist were presented first here as scientific indices of the 'comparative and special anatomy of races and peoples', and included 'measurements, charts, and diagrams, to show the methods and results of comparative studies in the physical structures of living races. Also [included are] instruments and appliances used in anthropometric investigations'.[53]

The conclusions gained through these measures were the biases of Worcester, a premeditated discovery to be made anew by each Fairgoer. The filtering mechanism of this mediating somatology introduced the Philippine people solely as scientific objects, items to be measured, quantified and compared to the normative body of the Fairgoer (a norm which was, if nothing else, white; reports of Filipinos escorted through the Fairgrounds being struck and taunted as 'niggers' speak more to the Fair's internal policing of race than to specifically anti-Filipino tensions,[54] and non-whites appear almost exclusively at the Fair as adjuncts to international or midway displays). The 'story of man is to be told by specimens, casts, measurements, and photographs representing typical and comparative characteristics', and the solid facts of progress celebrated in the Fair's civilised sectors were here replaced by calculations of its possibility. This shift away from a distinctive, civilised humanity to an as-yet undistinguished entry from the originary tale of mankind fostered the full play of racial and cultural stereotypes and encouraged Fairgoers' dehumanising reception of the Exhibit's subjects.

The biases of the exhibited object can be more easily read than those of the display in its entirety, and one such example can serve to illuminate the whole. Within the Reservation was a display which consisted of '1024 photographs and 128 casts ... which are later to be placed in the National or other museums'. A selection of 160 of these photos was compiled into the *Album of Philippine Types: Christians and Moros*, a Fair publication claiming to represent 43 provincial tribes. Each category is depicted through two photographs of a single individual, with an information block on the opposite page providing vital statistics rendered to the third decimal; these include standing height, 'cephalic index', and height and breadth of nose for the individual portrayed. Averages of these statistics for ... 20 members of each biological group are also supplied.[55] The text's introduction orients readers with methods used in selecting, plotting and charting these types, and painstakingly delineates the subtle but critical variations of skin colour, relative facial projection, and head formation. The text asserts its value by insisting on its reasonableness: 'The result seems unquestionable' surfaces amid listings of head measurements; an equally random statement says, 'One of the results of the anthropometrical work done in Bilibid would seem to be a demonstration of the need of this classification.'

What remains foregrounded yet curiously absent in these materials is that all types were selected from Bilibid Prison, and all photographs appear in the twinned display of the mug shot. While consistent with Lombroso's inverse correlation of 'civilisation' and criminality,[56] in 1904 Bilibid prison occupied a certain notoriety in American public knowledge. On the Fourth of July in 1902 President Roosevelt had issued a proclamation declaring the Filipino–American War at an end and granting 'amnesty and pardon to political prisoners whose offenses were not complicated with murder, rape, arson or robbery, and who should consent to take the oath of allegiance to the United States'.[57] What was thus anthropologically presented in the 1904 Exhibit to introduce the indigenous Philippine population offered instead the sensationalist thrill of a rogues' gallery, and under the heading of '43 Provincial Types' Fairgoers encountered over a 1000 photographs documenting a Philippines populated by murderers, rapists and 'robbers', felons further tainted by their refusal to 'take the oath of allegiance to the United States', an encoded reference to Philippine nationalists.

These photographs intensified the Philippines Reservation's anthropology pavilions' emphasis on Negrito blow guns, Igorot headhunter axes, and gunpowder 'made by the insurgent army from charcoal, saltpeter and heads of safety matches'. Presented in conjunction with the display of 'war-like representative[s] of a Filipino tribe ... of such violent temper that it is impossible to peacefully assimilate them', it posited a biological basis linking head-hunting, dog-eating, and innate temperament, a link which made Filipino insurgency both natural and inevitable and American measures to squelch it necessary. This contributed to the seeming necessity of Igorot containment imparted by Reservation reiterations of fortifications, enclosures and fences, and forced translation of 400 constabulary and 391 scouts from civilised representatives of the Philippines into a necessary internal police force.

The most insidious, perhaps most important, comparison to be made by the Philippine Reservation does not appear in Fair documentation. While possible that American reception of the Igorots' native dress had not been anticipated, planning officials could not have missed the broad correlation between displaying Filipinos behind fences in St Louis and confining Filipino citizens behind fences in Philippine reconcentration camps. Surrounding village inhabitants with a representative Filipino regulatory force and limiting them to one hour per day away from their displays under the scientific premise of cultural preservation, all the while emphasising the exhibit's authenticity, would have figured and normalised the Philippine camps for curious spectators. Relocation efforts into the camps between 1902 and 1904 were taken under authorisation of the 1 June 1903 Philippines Commission Act No. 781, Section 6, which claimed to offer protection to 'lives and property of residents' from 'ladrones or outlaws'. These latter terms were applied to revolutionary figures who opposed American rule through guerrilla warfare and who largely received the support of those communities confined; 'these outlaws, or "ladrones" as they are locally termed, constitute the main reason for the existence for the constabulary, and [expeditions against outlaws is] the chief occupation of the force'.[58] By the time of the St Louis Fair, reconcentration efforts had affected 451 000 Filipinos, or one out of nine persons. These people encountered immediate problems with housing, food and over-crowding, all of which contributed to the camps' high mortality rates; they also suffered disastrous long-term impacts resulting from loss of crops and fixed capital stemming from widespread destruction of homes, property and animals adjudged necessary in the United States' curtailing of ladrone activity. A 1902 *Army and Navy Journal* account of the infamous Catbalogan camp recorded the 'pinched, hungry look [and] more or less cowed appearance' of camp inmates, the majority of whom 'were in rags', and it proffered a description of morale both contemptuous and indicative of racial hatred as official policy: 'They are a miserable-looking lot of little brown rats, and were utterly spiritless ... Nothing seems to break their apathy. One to whom I spoke kindly and questioned as to his treatment changed for a moment into a gleam of intelligence, but quickly resumed his original stare.'[59]

Accounts such as this were widely carried in the American press, but this pointedly was not the image nor the experience of viewing enclosed Filipinos at the 1904 St Louis Fair. Displaying Filipinos within multiple barricades to demonstrate their potential for civilisation demonstrated instead American policy's fundamental need for the scientific legitimisation of Skiff and Worcester et al. The interlocking networks of an organicised progress and the phrasing of civilisation as a biological accomplishment allowed racial hierarchies to be presented as self-evident, and lent a legitimacy to actions otherwise entirely lacking. This same science allowed Worcester to note camps such as Catbalogan as a favourable measure in the move towards a civilised Philippines: 'Many of the occupants of [General J. F. Bell's] reconcentration camps received their first lessons in hygienic living. Many of them were reluctant to leave the camps and return to their homes when normal conditions prevailed.'[60]

In presenting the Philippines to American audiences, the Philippine Reservation gave form to the twinned mechanisms of race science and classification utilised in governing the country and deflecting its claims to self-rule. Ultimately within this system political statements resist political language in favour of racialised discourse, as in this US intelligence assessment of Emilio Aguinaldo, President of the Republic: 'It is known that the family from which Aguinaldo came had for many years dominated the town of Cavite Viejo ... It is known that later there came an infusion of Chinese blood, which gave to Aguinaldo the subtlety and perseverance of that race. Such was probably the stock from which sprang this Malay chieftain,' notes US Army intelligence officer Captain R. M. Taylor in the official five-volume report, *The Philippine Insurrection against the United States of America*, an effort six years in the making.[61]

Conclusion

Turn-of-the-century science provided the Philippine Reservation with a seemingly logical armature for displaying racial stereotypes and cultural misconstruals. Events of daily and ritual life taken out of context and placed before the over 18 million Fairgoers who attended the exhibit took on cartoonish, even grotesque, dimensions. Nuanced and vital political discourse was superseded by the immediacy of spectacle as an alternate identity of the Philippines was given form at the Louisiana Purchase Exposition. Racial classifications privileging white skin were plotted onto spatial frameworks which accommodated race, geography, evolution, culture and 'civilisation' with equal ease – and to equivalent ends. In the end, the 'money, effort and thought devoted to the plan' yielded an expedient Philippines that conformed to and supported prevailing American policy regarding the Philippines, and a figuring of the Filipino body which seemingly justified the fostering intervention of the US in Philippine statecraft.

NOTES

1.   Walter B. Stevens, Secretary, Louisiana Purchase Exposition, 'Introduction', in J. W. Buel (ed), *Louisiana and the Fair: An Exposition of the World and its People and Their Achievements*, vol. I (St Louis: World's Progress Publishing Co., 1904), p. 8. Figures differ from those cited in Robert W. Rydell, *All the World's a Fair: Visions of Empire at American International Expositions, 1876–1916* (Chicago: University of Chicago Press, 1984).

2.   For a general overview of the World's Fairs, see Paul Greenhalgh, *Ephemeral Vistas: The Expositions Universelles, Great Exhibitions and World's Fairs, 1851–1939* (Manchester: Manchester University Press, 1988).

3. 'Educational Value of the World's Fair', *Literary Digest*, vol. 29 (13 August 1904), p. 192. Quote is from William F. Slocum, president of Colorado College, cited in Rydell, *All the World's a Fair*, p. 155.

4. Self-rule was the overriding issue of the 'Philippines Problem' in 1904, and was not to be resolved until the Philippines became a self-governed commonwealth in 1935 under the Tydings-McDuffie Act. For an indepth, contemporary account of this issue, see Henry Parker Willis, *Our Philippine Problem: A Study of American Colonial Policy* (New York: Henry Holt and Company, 1905).

5. David R. Francis, quoted in Rydell, *All the World's a Fair*, p. 170; fn. 33; citing 'Teaching English to Sixty Nine Different Tribes', *Portland Oregonian*, 17 September 1905, p. 44.

6. See Rydell, *All the World's a Fair*, pp. 120–5; 136–44. The term 'midway' originates with the Chicago Midway Plaisance of 1893, and designates the area of commercialised concessions, entertainments and 'ethnographic villages' markedly distinct from the Fair proper. 'The Midway, with its half-naked 'savages' and hootchy-kootchy dancers, provided white Americans with a grand opportunity for a subliminal journey into the recesses of their own repressed desires.'

7. Ellen Sacco, 'Racial Theory, Museum Practice: The Coloured World of Charles Willson Peale', *Museum Anthropology*, 20/2, Fall 1996; and Bill Brown, 'The Prosthetics of Empire', in Amy Kaplan and Donald E. Pease (eds), *Cultures of United States Imperialism* (Durham: Duke University Press, 1993), p. 141.

8. Bluford Adams, '"A Stupendous Mirror of Departed Empires": The Barnum Hippodromes and Circuses, 1874–1891', *American Literary History*, 8/1, Spring 1996, pp. 34–56, 45; Paul A. Tencotte, 'Kaleidoscopes of the World: International Exhibitions and the Concept of the Culture-Place, 1851–1915', *American Studies*, 28/1, Spring 1987, pp. 5–29, 18–19; Figure 7. Barnum's exhibits incorporated various broad, contemporary conceptions of race 'into the titles of the exhibit, which included the "Ethnological Congress of Heathens and Barbarians" and the "Ethnological Congress of Strange and Heathen Types of Human Beings"'. (Adams, 45)

9. Gyan Prakash, 'Science 'Gone Native' in Colonial India', *Representations*, 40, Fall 1992, p. 158; citing George Campbell, *Proceedings of the Asiatic Society, 1866*, p. 91. '[I]n the end, due to the lack of funds, such an exhibition was held in the Central Provinces only.'

10. Annie E. Coombes, *Reinventing Africa: Museums, Material Culture and Popular Imagination in Late Victorian and Edwardian England* (New Haven: Yale University Press, 1994), p. 87. See entire chapter, 'The Spectacle of Empire II: Exhibitionary Narratives', pp. 84–108.

11. David Theo Goldberg, *Racist Culture: Philosophy and the Politics of Meaning* (Cambridge, Mass.: Blackwell Publishers Inc., 1993), pp. 63; 6; 4. See also 'Introduction', pp. 1–13.

12. Benedict Burton, *The Anthropology of World's Fairs: San Francisco's Panama Pacific International Exposition of 1915* (Berkeley: The Lowie Museum of Anthropology, 1983), p. 46. See also, 'The Display of People', pp. 43–52.

13. The issue of Philippine self-rule and unified political voice is problematic, and not addressed in this paper's radical truncation of Philippine events, personages and political parties. While, e.g., analyses of the 1896 Revolution against Spain and the conflicts between Emilio Aguinaldo and Andres Bonifacio are important in understanding the terms of a Philippine national identity, it is the American construal of Philippine/Filipino identity and its display at the 1904 St Louis Exposition that is explored in this paper. Asserting an American-mediated Filipino 'identity', however, necessarily prompts discussion of this display's function within the Philippines. Of critical interest for future study are internal factors including conservative support of Spain by the *ilustrados*, and hierarchical privileging of Tagalogs and domestic construal of the Igorot and Negrito within the Philippines during this time. Other critical information as yet unavailable includes the circumstances surrounding the recruitment of the Filipinos present – and presented as anthropological objects – at the Fair; an account noting that the Igorots 'saved money, from one to five hundred dollars each' indicates that some form of pay was involved. [David Rowland Francis, *The Universal Exposition of 1904*, vol. 1 (St Louis: Louisiana Purchase Exposition Company, 1913), p. 570].

14. C. H. Huttig, Chairman of the World's Fair Committee on State and Territorial Exhibits, 'Mr. Cutter's Plan: Suggestions for An Ethnographical and Anthropological Display', *World's Fair Bulletin*, 2/10, August 1901 (St Louis: World's Fair Publishing Co.), p. 25.

15. Francis, *The Universal Exposition of 1904*, vol. 1, p. 56. 'In recognition of his services at Paris, [Skiff] was decorated by the French Government as an officer of the Legion of Honor; at the Columbian Exposition he received a bronze medal from France and a gold medal from

Germany. He is a member of the American Institute of Mining Engineers, the International Museums Association of England, the National Geographic Society, and the American Association for the Advancement of Science.'

16. Francis, *The Universal Exposition of 1904*, vol. 1, p. 564.

17. Frederick J. V. Skiff, Director of Exhibits, St Louis Exposition, 'Introduction', Buel, *Louisiana and the Fair*, vol. IX, p. iii. Compare this in kind and intent to Foucault: 'To observe, then, is to be content with seeing – with seeing a few things systematically. With seeing what, in the rather confused wealth of representation, can be analysed, recognized by all, and thus given a name that everyone will be able to understand (…)'. [Michel Foucault, *The Order of Things: An Archaeology of the Human Sciences* (New York: Vintage Books, 1966, 1994), pp. 134–5.]

18. 'A Good Feature. The Process of Manufactures to be Shown in Exhibits', *World's Fair Bulletin*, 2/9, July 1901, p. 8.

19. North America's first Olympic Games was transferred from Chicago to St Louis in conjunction with the Fair, with an 'anthropology meet' featuring 'the primitive tribes' also planned. See Rydell, *All the World's a Fair*, pp. 166–167, fn. 24.

20. 'Chicago and the World's Fair. Exposition Officials the Guests of the Chicago Commercial Club', *World's Fair Bulletin*, 4/4, February 1903, p. 27. Frederick J. V. Skiff address of 26 December 1902.

21. Richard Drinnon, *Facing West: The Metaphysics of Indian-Hating and Empire-Building* (Minneapolis: University of Minnesota Press, 1980), pp. 280–1; citing Dean Worcester, *The Philippines, Past and Present* (New York: 1914, 1921), p. 87; Worcester, 'Knotty Problems of the Philippines', *Century Magazine*, October 1898, pp. 873–9. See also *Philippine Islands and Their People: A Record of Personal Observation and Experience* (New York: Macmillan, 1898, 1899).

22. Willis, *Our Philippine Problem*, p. 18.

23. Drinnon, *Facing West*, pp. 292–294; citing the Schurman Commission Report, Part II (1899), 'The Native Peoples of the Philippines'.

24. W. J. McGee, Director of the Anthropology Exhibit, 'Trend of Human Progress', *American Anthropologist* 1 (July 1899), p. 413. Cited in Rydell, *All the World's a Fair*, p. 161; fn. 11.

25. Contemporary opponents of this racial division noted its deleterious effect on social practice in the Philippines, stating that it fostered 'race hatred of an extreme type'. See, Willis, *Our Philippine Problem*, pp. 250–1.

26. Marshall Everett [pseud.], *The Book of the Fair: The Greatest Exposition the World has Ever Seen. Photographed and Explained. A Panorama of the St. Louis Exposition* (Philadelphia: P. W. Ziegler, 1904), p. 276.

27. Anthony Vidler, *The Architectural Uncanny: Essays in the Modern Unhomely* (Cambridge, Mass.: The MIT Press, 1992), p. 214. Following Vidler, we 'might refer to the distinction, drawn by Deleuze and Guattari in their *Traité de nomadologie: La machine de guerre*, between "state" space and "nomad" space. A sedentary space that is consciously parcelled out, closed and divided by the institutions of power would then be contrasted to the smooth, flowing, unbounded space of nomadism; in western contexts, the former has always attempted to bring the latter under control.'

28. Everett, *The Book of the Fair*, pp. 73–74. See entire Chapter II, 'Previous International Expositions', pp. 59–74 for breakout of individual exhibit attendance and profit/loss statements of preceding expositions. Ethnographic villages feature prominently among World's Fair profit leaders.

29. 'Ethnological Department. Realistic Exhibits of Race – Life and Movement for the World's Fair', *World's Fair Bulletin*, 2/12, October 1901, p. 5. Letter from F. W. Putnam, Professor of Botany at Harvard University, former Chief of the Chicago Columbian Exposition Department of Ethnology in charge of living display of Native Americans.

30. Coombes, *Reinventing Africa*, p. 87.

31. 'Mr. Cutter's Plan', *World's Fair Bulletin*, 2/10, August 1901, p. 25. Plan reproduced in text of [original] article.

32. The metaphorical image of the thumb, distinguishing dichotic feature of man, figures large in the Fair's literature as the ethnologist searches out the tell-tale 'dusky thumbprint' on the historical record of mankind's progress; it also works as a ready pejorative, as here where the re-enactment of the Boer War is performed by 'descendants of races which have at least left thumbprints on the records of civilization'. ('Truly Biggest Show That Ever Came over the Pike', *Post Dispatch*, 1 May 1904, p. 3; as cited in Rydell, *All the World's a Fair*, p. 179, fn. 47) See also Coombes, *Reinventing Africa*, pp. 101–2, on animality and containment.

33. Francis, *The Universal Exposition of 1904*, vol. 1, pp. 564–565.

34. See, e.g. 'Protest of the Sioux', 'Cherokee Chief', and Solon H. Burglum's monumental Grand Basin installation depicting his 'conception of frontier life', in *The Complete Portfolio of Photographs of the World's Fair, St. Louis, 1904* (Chicago: The Educational Company, 1904), n.p.

35. Jonathan Best, *Philippine Picture Postcards 1900–1920* (Manila: Bookmark, Inc., 1994), pp. 2; 5–6; 11. Best's text documents images of the Philippines produced during this 'Golden Age of Picture Postcards', which he dates from 1898 to 1914.

36. See Christopher Vaughan, 'The 'Discovery' of the Philippines by the U.S. Press, 1889–1902', *The Historian*, 57/2, winter 1995, pp. 303–14. An emerging force at the turn of the century, 'there was a remarkable degree of thematic similarity in the press' discussion of the Philippines and its people (...). Filipinos were seldom allowed to speak for themselves in the US Press ...' (304). See also Figure 3.5.1 caption noting the 'childlike and bland' face of Antaero.

37. Photograph caption, 'The Walled City', *The Universal Exposition, a Portfolio of Official Photographic Views of the Louisiana Purchase Exposition, St. Louis, 1904*, intro. Frank Tyrrell (St Louis: Portfolio Publishing Co., 1904), n.p. 'When Americans arrived in Manila in 1898 they found a city renowned for its beauty and centuries old [sic] charm. In 1904, when the architect Daniel Burnham was sent by US President William Howard Taft to do the city planning for the modern American administration, he observed that the old walled city of Intramuros at the mouth of the Pasig River, was one of the best preserved medieval cities anywhere in the world (...)' (Best, *Philippine Picture Postcards 1900–1920*, p. 11).

38. Francis, *The Universal Exposition of 1904*, p. 567; Buel, *Louisiana and the Fair*, vol. 8, p. 3114. This map was surrounded by a circular plank walk and represented boundaries determined by the Treaty of Paris, and was displayed in conjunction with eight relief maps each 8 by 17 feet detailing encyclopaedic features such as religion and agriculture, and three more of key Philippine cities. See also Benedict Anderson, *Imagined Communities: Reflections on the Origin and Spread of Nationalism*, rev. ed. (London: Verso, 1994), esp. 'Census, Map, Museum', pp. 163–85.

39. Willis, *Our Philippine Problem*, p. 8.

40. President McKinley announcement of 21 December 1898, in *Correspondence Relating to the War with Spain*, vol. 2 (Washington, 1902), pp. 858–9. Cited in Willis, *Our Philippine Problem*, p. 12, fn. 1.

41. Francis, *The Universal Exposition of 1904*, vol. 1, p. 565.

42. Buel, *Louisiana and the Fair*, vol. 4, p. 1533.

43. Photograph caption to 'The Homeless Negritos', *The Universal Exposition*, n.p.; see related image in Rydell, *All the World's a Fair*, p. 175, Fig. 56.

44. Buel, *Louisiana and the Fair*, vol. 4, p. 1533.

45. Ibid., p. 1536.

46. Rydell, *All the World's a Fair*, p. 167, fn. 25; citing W. J. McGee, 'Anthropology', *Louisiana Purchase Centennial Dedication Ceremonies*, 43–4.

47. Buel, *Louisiana and the Fair*, vol. 8, p. 3070. See also Breitbart, *A World on Display: photographs from the St. Louis World's Fair 1904* (Albuqueque: University of New Mexico Press, 1997), Figures 23–5, 'Evolution of a Bontoc Igorot Man' (National Archives #350 BB 2–12, 2–13, 2–14. Photographer unknown, 1904), p. 26; photographs illustrate the process of 'improvement'.

48. Francis, *The Universal Exposition of 1904*, vol. 1, pp. 571; 572; 570. See Chapter XX, 'The Philippine Exposition', pp. 564–72 for a summary of the Exhibit.

49. 'Exposition of Processes. How the Louisiana Purchase Exposition Will Differ From Other World's Fairs', *World's Fair Bulletin*, 2/10, August 1901, p. 17. St Louis Exposition First Vice-President Corwin H. Spencer 'in a recently published interview'.

50. See Rydell, *All the World's a Fair*, pp. 172–4; fns. 38–40. Rydell locates the controversy within a volatile 'mixture of white supremacist sexual stereotypes and voyeurism'.

51. Buel, *Louisiana and the Fair*, vol. 4, p. 1543. See also Greenhalgh, *Ephemeral Vistas*, pp. 101–2.

52. Francis, *The Universal Exposition of 1904*, vol. 1, p. 565.

53. 'Anthropology. Historical Study of Man', *World's Fair Bulletin*, 4/7, May 1903, p. 32.

54. Rydell, *All the World's a Fair*, pp. 176–7, fn. 42; citing 'Filipinos Become a Fad to Foolish Young Girls', *Post-Dispatch*, 3 July 1904; 'Scouts Lose First Battle with Marines', *Post-Dispatch*, 7 July 1904.

55. *Daniel Folkmar, Album of Philippine Types (Found in Bilibid Prison in 1903): Christians and Moros (Including a Few Non-Christians)* (Manila: Bureau of Public Printing, 1904), Introduction, pp. 1–5. All references this section from Folkmar. Prof. Michael Salman of the UCLA History Department provided this resource; see also, Salman, '"Nothing Without Labor": Penology, Discipline, and Independence in the Philippines Under United States Colonial Rule, 1898–1914', in Vicente L. Rafael (ed.), *Discrepant Histories: Translocal Essays on Filipino Cultures* (Philadelphia: Temple University Press, 1995), pp. 113–29. For critical discussion of photography at and of the Exhibit, see Enrique B. de la Cruz and Pearlie Rose S. Baluyut (eds), *Confrontations, Crossings, and Convergence: Photographs of the Philippines and the United States, 1898–1998* (Los Angeles: the UCLA Asian American Studies Center and the UCLA Southeast Asia Program, 1998).

56. See Eric Breitbart, *A World on Display*, pp. 25–7. The photographs' format of front- and side-view close-ups (the 'mug shot') comes from the 19th-century French photographer Alphonse Bertillon, who 'developed what he called the "portrait parlé" – the "spoken image" – a technique that would enable criminologists to use photographs and a complex classification system as a means of identifying criminals ... Bertillon's idea [resembled] the theories of his contemporary, the Italian doctor Cesare Lombroso, regarding the possibility of identifying criminal traits as well as criminal physiognomy' (25).

57. This pardon is complicated in that the charge against political prisoners was largely redefined as 'brigandage' and equated with robbery, hence an imprisonable offence. See Willis, *Our Philippine Problem*, p. 135. The issue of 'brigandage' is pursued in Willis' 1905 commentary, pp. 130–6.

58. Willis, *Our Philippine Problem*, pp. 130–131; 126. See also, 'The Constabulary', pp. 120–49.

59. Drinnon, *Facing West*, p. 326; citing Moorfield Storey and Julian Codman, *'Marked Severities' in Philippine Warfare* (Boston: Geo. H. Ellis, 1902), pp. 90–91. Description is from 26 January 1902 interview with member of General Chaffee's party of visitors to Catbalogan.

60. Drinnon, *Facing West*, p. 291; citing Worcester, *Philippines Past and Present*, pp. 224–5.

61. William Henry Scott, *'Amor Patrio in the Philippine Insurgent Records'*, *Cracks in the Parchment Curtain and Other Essays in Philippine History*, foreword by Renato Constantino, 2nd ed. (Quezon City: New Day Publishers, 1985, c. 1982), p. 236. Taylor worked from nearly three tons of documents seized by the United States during the destruction of the first Philippine Republic. 'American President William Howard Taft, however, disapproved the publication of the book for reasons of political expediency', and it was first published by the Eugenio Lopez Foundation in 1971. Scott notes that the records 'constitute one of the most concentrated displays of *amor patrio* – love of country – in the world today ... Their content testifies to an ability to conceive and construct a constitutional republic, and their mere existence to a willingness to wage a war – and die – to defend it' (pp. 234–5). In other words, assertion of national identity by the Philippine body.

6.

Performing Identity:
The Museal Framing of Nazi Ideology

Sandra Esslinger

National-socialism desires that the art play a befitting part in the life of the German people again, that the people come into close contact with the art. May the House of German Art serve always and in loyalty this high and ideal task.
Catalogue to the Great German Art Exhibit, 1937.[1]

Figure 3.6.1   *Im Haus der Deutschen Kunst*, from the *Völkischer Beobachter*, July 14
1937, p. 5, Munich

The first monumental structure planned under the Nazi Regime was the
Temple of German Art (see Figures 3.6.1 and 3.6.2).[2] This was no small
undertaking – the Temple of German Art, a national museum, was to
present the 'true German art' to the German public. Because this museum
displayed artwork that was not *avant-garde* art and was considered by the
Nazis as exemplary of German artistic achievement, the artwork and the
museum are often omitted in the discourse of art history. If we omit this
moment in museum history, the historical lesson regarding a state's strategic
use of the museum to wield its power is lost. In Nazi Germany, the museum
acted as a frame wherein a prescribed process of forming the ideal citizen,
a subscriber to the Aryan spirituality, the *Volk*, was catalyzed. Thus, when
addressing a national museum, the Nazi Temple of German Art is the
quintessential exemplum of a ritual space that used ingrained culturally
defined practices – religious, democratic and museal – to contribute to the
molding of the ideal *Volk* citizen and to the proliferation of a national
ideology.

   The Nazi Museum is frequently ignored by art historians who contend it
displayed propaganda, not art. I believe this dismissal needs to be re-
considered, since the Temple of German Art, now known as the House of Art
(*Haus der Kunst*), had its most successful exhibits during Nazi Germany

Figure 3.6.2   Paul Ludwig Troost with Gerdy Troost and Leonhard Gall, *Temple of German Art*, 1937, Munich. Published in Sabine Brantl, *Haus der Kunst 1937–1997: Eine Historische Dokumentation* (Munich: Haus der Kunst, 1997), 2

when showing this 'propaganda'. Clearly this was a very popular venue for viewing what was called 'art'. The Nazi museum was a site where knowledge and power came together and were created anew and then disseminated. It was a space where criticism was prohibited, while information was offered and absorbed. The utilization of religious practices as well as the religiously oriented ideology of the Nazi museum further limited one's ability to question, resulting in the strengthening of the univocal statement of the Nazis.

The importance of art to the Third Reich cannot be overestimated. The intended use of art in the Third Reich was expressed in Hitler's speech at the Nuremberg Rally (August 1933) shortly after his appointment as Chancellor: 'We call upon our artists to wield the noblest weapon in the defense of the German people – German Art!'[3] The high value on visual culture assigned by Hitler was further demonstrated by the building of the 'New Glass Palace', the Temple of German Art in 1934 in Munich, only one year after Hitler's appointment as Chancellor,[4] and the use of pageantry, flags and a mass gathering, which he believed necessary for public enlightenment.[5] Furthermore, through the extraordinary dedication of the *Temple*, a public museum was given to the people by their 'Kaiser'. He 'returned' to the public their 'right' to their culture – a culture grown 'naturally' and 'organically'. It was a culture whose nucleus was a *Volk* community and a *Volk* culture promoted by public gatherings and pageantry. This was not new, however, to the Germans since visual culture, pageantry and the regalia of mass meetings are also tied to the Bavarian cultural practices of Catholicism so familiar to Hitler and his followers.[6]

Religious practices

The Catholic practices as models for framing the first annual *Great German Art Exhibition* (*GGAE*) in Munich in 1937 can be seen in the dedication and opening of the museum that was accompanied by the *Days of German Art*. The *Days of German Art* involved several days of ceremony that included parades, highlighting local costume and dance and a *tableaux vivant* of 'German History' – pageantry also associated with the practice of Catholicism in southern Germany.[7] In fact, Hitler readily acknowledged the Catholic Church as having mastered the use of the mass movement.[8] Leni Riefenstahl relates that 'He [Hitler] thought religion was necessary … [that] the Catholic Church was a lot more successful than the Protestant, which he considered too somber. The Catholic emphasis on ritual and ceremony … was more effective than Protestant austerity.'[9] This reveals the basis of Hitler's interest in emphasizing mass meetings and parades orchestrated by the party and the incorporation of visual culture and display, modeled after Catholic tradition.

However, the connection to religion does not end with analogous practices between the Nazi party and the Catholic Church. The *Temple* of German Art was an interesting choice in terminology, since the National Socialists proposed to develop a religion that was an interwoven part of the *Volk* culture. The religion was to be based on the reawakening of the *Volk* soul from pre-Christian times and incorporation of those elements of Christianity that were not Judeo. The religion was to 'evolve' from the *Volk* and for the *Volk* – a religion unique to this *Volk* alone, with a 'Nordic Christ'.[10] In the proposed national religion, the fascist transformed the Semitic religious themes of life-rejection, escapist/ascetic, priestly/clerical, scriptural, history/linear, salvation, and the cross of suffering into the fascist-identified Aryan themes of life-affirmation, worldly, heroic, ritual/festival, myth/cyclic, rebirth, and the evergreen tree.[11] The traditional church would be rendered unnecessary, and a new church would be designed 'to educate Nordic man to liberate his racial self ... [and] where man could be freed from the limitations of time and space while uniting with the Godhead'.[12] The church would take form in public places such as museums. Thus, the museum became a part of the community's cultural as well as spiritual education. Rosenberg claimed that the duty of the artist was, in part, to give the community an ideal image of itself. The 'Nordic' viewer was to lose track of time, place and distance. The viewer was put to rest so that (s)he would be able to contemplate the greater meaning of the artistic message.[13]

The Temple of German Art became such a theological space. This theological space when used in conjunction with the exhibition strategies of the modern museum became a powerful alliance to discipline the behaviour of exhibit audiences. Hitler, in his speech dedicating the House of German Art, stated that 'When the Cornerstone was laid for this building it signaled the beginning of the construction of a *temple* for art; not for a so-called modern art, but for an eternal German art ...'.[14] Thus, the Nazi museum can be viewed as a place where German artists displayed their art and provided a quiet contemplative environment wherein the religion could not only take form but it would be a process promoted by the relationship of German artists, their respective art works and the German public.

Simultaneously, the *Degenerate Art Show*, an afterthought to the *Great German Art Exhibition*, was thrown together and exhibited across the park. The *Degenerate Art Show* has had much recent attention, primarily since it displayed what we consider 'German' or 'avant-garde' art today. However, the museum practices of the Nazis, even in the setting of the *Degenerate Art Show*, have been paid little attention by art historians.[15] The *Degenerate Art Show* displayed the opposite of the *Great German Art Exhibition*. The *Degenerate* was an example of the 'degenerate' (non-)citizen, while the *German* exhibit displayed the 'ideal' German citizen.

The official Nazi 'ideal' art was a strange combination of nineteenth-century Biedermeier and Romantic dominated by Classical styles – it was an art that was easily legible to 'the masses'. It was an accepted visual vocabulary that evolved in Munich during the early twentieth century. This legible art was presented to the public in combination with a national museum – a site that framed the new German identity – a singular identity that previously had not existed. The citizens were provided an example of what they ought to be. They were offered legible art works in a seductive environment and provided with rituals in which to participate that would mold them into perfect Nazi citizens.

Democratic strategies

Within the Temple of German Art, the visitors, the virtual 'ideal' citizens, were enticed by democratic notions of ownership and of public right to 'their' art. The Nazis utilized democratic or public museological strategies in order to create and reform a citizenry into a resource for the government's aims; and, in fact, their use of the strategies was not uncommon to many governments. Democracy promises power to its citizens and sets up a desire to be one of its citizens. It provides a fiction of a unified singular citizenry – a useful manipulation not only to create a notion of the 'virtuous citizen' but also in the making of one.

The idea of the transformation of the people by the public museum reached its constructive end in Nazi museums by creating and defining what was meant by *Volk*. The Nazis took most of their actions in the name of the (re)emerging German *Volk* – a fictional singular entity, created for their propagandistic purposes. The construction of the *Volk* provided a malleable unified whole and a sense of community, unity and purpose for the previously multicultural body known as the *Volk*. Historically, the *Volk* was seen as the fragmented middle classes, who had suffered hardships due to defeat in World War I, to the Great Depression and to several recessions. This 'positive' construction of the *Volk* fantasy was an important subject position developed through 'democratic' museological strategies.

In the early twentieth-century modern art world of pre-war Germany, the popular classes were external to the world of modern/expressionist art. The art world remained composed of the 'elite', while the general public remained bystanders. The democratic post-revolutionary period promised to make accessible to the populace those things that hitherto were accessible only to the elite. The *Great German Art Exhibition* was an attempt to return to all classes their 'right' to participate in the art world. By constructing an 'inclusive' frame in which the citizenry of the Third Reich could participate, the Nazis attempted to combat the prevailing alienation of the middle classes – the *Volk*. The construction of this 'inclusive' frame strongly resembles the framing of public spaces and institutions in a modern democracy.

'Space' included the general architectural environment, the ways in which the objects were hung, ordered and labeled, and the social events, souvenirs and media which surrounded the exhibits. The latter extended the museum space outside – to the lives of the people – providing sites for socially and politically elicited behaviors and an epistemology. The museum was the context that constructed the objects/*Volk* as 'art'; the museum attempted to direct the appropriate behaviors of the viewers, reifying the status of the objects/*Volk* as 'art' works. These associated valuations and meanings not only provided a signifying structure that corresponded to the works of art but was also transposed onto a different signified, the actual groups or individuals that correlated to the works of art. The display was a narcissistic presentation of the visitor, that is, only the 'attractive' elements of the Nazi *Volk* ideology were represented within the frame of the museum. Thus, a semiological system was constructed within the space of the Temple of German Art that created a myth of the 'True German Identity', a type of mirror for the viewer and an ideal of the 'virtuous German citizen'.

The *GGAE* provided an arena wherein the audience could (per)form an identity of the citizenry in a national museum. The performance relied heavily upon pre-existing protocol and signifying systems, tropes, that were in place prior to the exhibition. The exhibition served the purpose of manipulating ideas already familiar and acceptable to the audience. Carol Duncan relates this manipulative and 'constructive' power of the museum:

To control a museum means precisely to control the representation of a community and some of its highest, most authoritative truths. It also means the power to define and rank people, to declare some as having a greater share than others in the community's common heritage – in its very identity. Those who are in the greatest accord with the museum's version of what is beautiful and good may partake of this greater identity.[16]

This process becomes clearer when a more detailed examination and description are undertaken of the environment of the Temple of German Art through two lenses: (1) modernist museum practices in the *GGAE*, and (2) the museum tour booklet and catalogue as frameworks for the viewers to follow.

Modernist museum practices

It should be recognized that the *House of German Art* was not only a kind of spiritual sanctuary but also was a modern museum; hence, the overall environment was in accord with associated museum practices. A desire to be a member of the *Volk* was promoted by approaching the rational, the scientific and the natural – all modernist museum practices. Modernism may be seen as a progeny of the Enlightenment in that it shares the leitmotivs of the privileging of reason, the assumption that the natural world is governed by rational scientific laws which are accessible through the scientific method of experiment, empirical observation and progress/evolution. The Enlightenment provided the epistemology, which has become naturalized in the modern/modernist world and has become the subject of postmodern critical evaluation. The major strategy arising out of this Enlightenment/modernist mode of thinking is the idea of a unitary end of history and of the subject, a master-narrative that tells the universally 'true' story and legitimizes this 'truth' through the consensus of authorities in their respective fields. This is a gross simplification of modernism; however, it provides a basis for discussion of modernist museum practices.

The ultimate realization of Enlightenment ideals has been seen in the revolutionary fervor which swept through America, France and England in the last quarter of the eighteenth century when the modern nation-state came into being. At that time, there was a series of legitimizing 'myths' or 'cultural fictions' that rose to the service of the modern nation-state. The two main 'cultural fictions' were the novel and the museum.[17] The museum and its sister institution, art history, were cultural fictions formed as part of the nation-state's need to create and maintain power. As a result of serving the needs of the nation-state, there were modernist forces and powers at play that were part of the covert existence of these two institutions. It is these covert forces and aims, residing in the very heart of modernist practices, that were exemplified in the general practice of art history and museology in the Third Reich and that were present in the Nazi art exhibit, the *Great German Art Exhibition* of Munich in 1937.

The policies which governed art in the Third Reich were strictly based on racism. However, that racism was a product of 'scientifically' legitimated thought. The discourse was based on modernist ideas such as genetics and natural and progressive evolution. Of course, this line of thinking was not exclusive to the Nazis but also took place in many other Western contexts where the Enlightenment and modernism had taken hold.[18] The following quote from *Mein Kampf* should illustrate the use of this modernist discourse and vocabulary within the context of Nazi thought:

Every animal mates only with a member of the same species ... Any crossing of two beings not at exactly the same level produces a medium between the level of the two parents. This means: the offspring will probably stand higher than the racially lower parent, but not as high as the higher one ... No more than Nature desires the mating of weaker with strong individuals, even less does she desire the blending of a higher with a lower race, since, if she did, her whole work of higher breeding, over perhaps hundreds of thousands of years, might be ruined with one blow ... It shows with terrifying clarity that in every mingling of Aryan blood with that of lower peoples the result was the end of the cultured people ...[19]

The progressive leitmotiv of modernism considered the evolution of humanity to move from 'rude' simplicity to 'civilized' complexity. In fact, many Enlightenment thinkers (Smith, Ferguson, Miller, and Kames) believed that there were four stages of human progress – hunting, pasturage, agricultural and commercial. Thus, the ultimate aim of evolution was that all the peoples of the planet would eventually catch up with the white European. It seems that one difference between the Enlightenment thought about human evolution and Hitler's version is that Hitler dared to overtly pronounce the pinnacle of evolution in his own time and in his own culture/race rather than 'politely' imply it.

The National Socialist movement set out to redefine the *Volk* as a *totality*: a race, a government, a set of customs and traditions and a religion based on mythological origins and uniqueness and predispositions of the Aryan race and soul.[20] Modernism was the frame for the Nazi myth, asserting that there was a unitary end of history and of the subject as well as a master-narrative, describing the totalized and true story of the totalitarian state. The art of the Third Reich was employed in a modernist fashion in order to foster the Nazi racial myth. Both Dr Schultze-Naumburg and Dr Hans Günther, Nazi art historians, promoted the notion that classic or Hellenic beauty was Nordic and any deviation was degenerate. They believed that works of art reflected the artist, specifically his or her race. If an artist was of inferior racial strain or one with mental or physical illness, the art work would have identifiable 'degenerate' features. People of a 'pure' blood line would produce classical beauty, a reflection of themselves.[21] Dr Walter Darre, a colleague of Dr Schultze-Naumburg, furthered this doctrine of racial art by fostering the idea that art should serve eugenic racial selection and promotion of the birth rate. All of this was solidified and made party doctrine with the publication of Rosenberg's *Myth of the Twentieth Century* in 1930. Thus, a work of true German art became a form of evidence or 'scientific proof' of the genetic make-up of the artist and demonstrated that which is beautiful and desirable as an 'ideal-I' or depicted the proper Aryan mate for propagation of the Nazi race. Thus, by utilizing the modernist myth of proof and evidence, relating to the 'scientific' foundations of genetics and evolution, the Nazi myth was not only legitimated but also procreated.

The uses of art within the institution of the museum acted as an educational instrument of modernist 'totalizing' and homogenizing in the Third *Reich*. This was further articulated by the appointed Nazi director of German art education, Robert Böttcher,[22] who promoted the ideas that art was the 'social cement' of society and that art should reflect the collective mentality of the people. He viewed art as important in the promotion of patriotism through an appreciation of German history, beauty and myth and in combating social unrest by providing enjoyment to Germans through exhibitions and museum tours.

The idea of art and the museum as educational tools or institutions is not an uncommon modernist notion. In fact, the following quote is a description of the British Museum of the eighteenth century: 'the Museum was endeavoring to educate all classes. A predominant concern of those interested in the education and the "civilizing" of the public was the use of the Museum as a means for providing an aesthetic education.'[23] The prime example of the use of Nazi art as 'education' of the people is seen in the 1937 *Great German Art Exhibition*. It was the beginning of the artistic legitimization of the new *Reich*, which required building of a cultural myth and legitimizing the Nazis as cultural benefactors and leaders of the new state by demonstrating what it meant to be German through art.

Preziosi views modern '[m]useums … [as] perform[ing] the basic historical gesture of *separating out of the present* a certain specific "past" so as to collect and recompose (to *re*-member) its displaced and dismembered relics as elements in a *genealogy* of and for the present'.[24] This was evidenced clearly in the opening of the *GGAE*. In Hitler's dedication speech, he referred to the museum as a 'Temple', – 'a House of Art for the German People', housing an art that corresponded 'to the ever-increasing homogeneity of our racial composition, and that would then in itself present the characteristics of unity and homogeneity … what it means to be German …'.[25]

It has been further suggested that the museum teaches us how to solve things, how to think and how to piece the world together in a coherent, rational and orderly manner – the natural – and that the present job of the museum seems to be to tie identity and cultural patrimony to a historical or mythical past. In short, the museum evokes and enacts 'a desire for panoptic or panoramic points of view from which it may be seen that all things may indeed fit together in a true, natural, real or proper order … convincing us that each of us could "really" occupy privileged synoptic positions … through the use of prefabricated materials and vocabularies … demonstration and proof, and techniques of stagecraft and dramaturgy';[26] and this is exactly what occurred in the lavish historical parade offered during the *Days of German Art*. To be extended a role in history or myth gave individuals the illusion that they occupied a panoptic position. What was meant by 'to be German' was offered in the events surrounding the opening of the exhibit as well as in the exhibit itself.

For the Nazis, the *GGAE* was the elixir that was going to heal a great society gone astray. It was a demonstration of what was beautiful and what it meant to be a subject in Nazi society. Major representative categories of the German exhibition of 1937 were Hitler and his leaders, womanhood, manhood and rural landscapes. Landscapes were used to represent an idealized rural Germany, while womanhood and manhood displayed idealized Aryans and Nazis divided along gender lines. Men held public offices and military positions and were breadwinners. In short, men dominated the public sphere, and the art works depicted men in such activities. Women dominated the private sphere. They were mothers, farmers' wives and housewives. The German Madonna and Child, or mothers happily nurturing their children, were the most frequently seen female images. The woman's role was in the household or as an allegory. Reproduction was the ultimate function of the woman. The woman held the 'natural' or 'biological' position in society. Farmers and landscapes were representations naturalizing the Aryan subject, while (re)presentations of Hitler and the leaders not only acted as venerable icons but also possessed a surveying panoptic gaze. Such categorization typifies the exhibits of modernist museums – 'for every race, there may be projected a legitimate "art" with its own unique spirit and soul; its own history and prehistory; its own future potential; its own respectability; and its own style of representational adequacy'.[27]

With this view of the modern museum, society can be united under aesthetic preferences and education that are administered by the state. In the case of the Nazis, the art was overtly used in order to control and direct 'desire' for an ego ideal as well as of the mate one desires. The ego ideal was comprised of gender identity and all of the *accoutrement* required of that subject position. The controlling and directing of taste also affected how one might have chosen a mate, for the mate must be aesthetically pleasing in order to be desired. The notion of beauty in the Third Reich was primarily physical, for beauty was the result of purity of the race. This beauty directly correlated to reproduction practices in Nazi society, which had as their ultimate goal the production of a pure Aryan race.

To promote this education and these aesthetic preferences, the modernist museum offered each object as a trap for the gaze. The art work was to speak directly to the viewer with a minimum of interference and distraction. In the *GGAE* museum space, the pieces were hung at eye-level with limited commentary. This, accompanied by the clear representational form of the sculpture or the painting, framed the work in a context of clear legibility. The frame of the entire exhibit and surrounding events disallowed any free play of meaning.

Furthermore, the intense interaction between the art works and the individual viewer provided the ultimate opportunity to 'personalize' the education. There were varied representations in the exhibit, catering to individual differences and diverse stations in society. Diversity is a strange term to use for the representations of the Aryan race; however, some diversity within the race was recognized – diversity in careers, age, and geographical locations. Thus, any Aryan was sure to find a painting which communicated to her/him and presumably offered an ego ideal or a desirable ideal mate. The masses could be tamed and educated in a museum space, which trapped and spoke directly to the viewers in personal terms. In sum, the *GGAE* offered, through a modernist environment, an 'enlightened' synoptic view of what was meant in being German and what it meant to be a German man or woman, stereotypical gender roles.

The Museum's guidebook and catalogue

The publications surrounding the *GGAE* played a major role in guiding and directing the visitors' views, experiences and interpretations of the works of art. The two major publications associated with the Temple of German Art were the 1934 publication of *Temple of German Art* and the 1937 catalogue of the exhibit, *Die Grosse Deutsche Kunst Ausstellung 1937*. There is redundancy within and between the two publications. The points, contexts and subject positions were overdetermined, even before one visited the exhibit.

The 1934 publication was written for English-speaking tourists by Karl Drechsel, in order to introduce the Temple of German Art and to justify its construction, location and historical significance. In no uncertain terms, the Nazi artistic program was set out in this 24-page booklet. It begins by stating the importance of art and art museums to the national identity:

Works of art are not a dispensable luxury for any nation … as the art activity of a country unveils a people's common soul, thus this artistic utterance reflects upon the view of life of all those who open their hearts and minds to its influence. Thus, the furtherance of a genuine, unadulterated German art must be and is one of the principal tasks of the national state, of the whole German people.[28]

The text reveals the art that is to be valued by the 'German people' and introduces the polarization of 'Degenerate art' versus 'German art', without using the term 'degenerate'. Art as a 'reflector' of the people is taken into a logical circularity in which 'the art productions of a people are the criterion according to which the vitality of a people can be judged, the instrument by means of which its vigor can be tested: art is the "breath of a nation's nostrils"'.[29] Thus, Nazi art is a reflection of the people; and the people are a reflection of their art.

According to the guidebook, the pre-Nazi post-World War I period is discussed as one wherein a false art was created, while the assumption of the power of the Nazis, 1933–1934, led to a time of recovery and renaissance of the 'German Spirit', a period which overcame decline. This was effected through 'political reunion':[30]

The 'Temple of German Art' now to be erected in place of the old 'Glass Palace' which was destroyed by a fearful conflagration [the 'Glass Palace' was a small-scale imitation of London's 'Crystal Palace' of 1851] will not merely signify the outer symbol of this indomitable will of the new government and the German people to rejuvenate that veritable German Art, but is, in the first place, to be its lasting domicile, its permanent home, by its works ever proclaiming at home and abroad the innermost substance of the German soul.[31]

The temple, the place wherein the 'true German soul' was to be embodied for eternity, was a symbolic limestone domicile. But why should Munich be the chosen city for the 'Temple'? The booklet tells us the art-historical mythology of the location: 'The race, populating the south-German towns and villages, so deeply rooted in its ancient, purely German traditions, so warm-hearted and hospitable, so fervent and nature-loving and genuine, has ever singly influenced art, has always occupied itself with its promotion and has at all times considered art as the reflector of its racial soul.'[32] In the midst of the post-World War I period Munich, with its Christian culture, was said to have protected the sanctuary of art from the destructive forces that contemporaneously reigned. Thus, Munich became the hallowed ground for the, great German temple, the *Temple of Art*. It was to represent the 'united German states and classes' along with the 'German will to cultural advancement'.[33] Munich was to be the art center of the world – a place of pilgrimage for not only Germans but tourists from everywhere. The guidebook provided a justification for the Nazi art program. It proposed a program that grew from the 'pure', 'original' German soul in a location where the 'original' traditions were left untouched. The lore of Munich's history provided a location ideal for the 'rebirth' of the mythological Aryan soul.

The official publication for the *Great German Art Exhibition* was the exhibition catalogue, the *Grosse Deutsche Kunstausstellung 1937: Im Haus der Deutschen Kunst zu München*.[34] There is minimal text in this publication. It is primarily a list of art works and artists and includes a section of reproductions of some of the choice pieces in the exhibit. The text is found under the subsections 'Foreword', 'Comments', and 'The Temple of German Art in Munich' and conspicuously avoids any discussion of specific art works or artists.

In this catalogue, the first large German exhibition since the destruction of the old 'Glass Palace' is presented to the 'German' and 'World' public. It becomes clear in the 'Foreword' that 'World' public does not mean the entire world but rather 'All of the German race, in Germany or in foreign countries …'.[35] In its inclusive language, exclusion is the operative subtext. The subject is the constructed Aryan.

The catalogue further sets the stage with regard to how this art came to be exhibited. The selection of the paintings was done in the academic tradition. According to the catalogue, a request was made public for German artists from everywhere in the world to submit paintings for 'examination'. Twenty-five thousand pieces were submitted; 15,000 were sent on to Munich; and 900 were exhibited – an almost 'democratic' process. The criteria for exhibition were as follows: 'It is clear that only the most complete, finished and best can be shown of what German art is able to achieve in this unique United German Art exhibition … Problematic and incomplete art will not now or ever have a chance of acceptance in the House of German Art.'[36] These criteria are to be met out of 'the obligation which lies in the architecture of the Temple of German Art! It is a building of the most perfect National Socialistic architecture'.[37] The building was presented as a gift from the *Führer* and Paul Ludwig Troost, the architect, to the German artists and people and the culture of the (Aryan) world. Again, this is a process of exclusion, laying claim to Aryan representative art. It sets up a power structure, which puts the Nazis in a position of judgment and recognition. They demonstrate by example 'good taste' and 'virtuous citizenship'.

The 'Foreword' concludes with a powerful statement of an exclusive, unified German identity, that shares a common history or deep history of the German past:

In the *Führer*'s words which stand above the entrance of the House of German Art, 'Art is an obligating mission of fanaticism, superior to one's fate.' May this sentence always stay in sight of the German artistic genius in all their works; that it [art] may be the fanatic fulfillment of their [the artists'] superior mission – from these highest artistic achievements, which are worthy of the great artistic German past and which are incomparable, a newly arisen highest expression of the greatness of [German] blood and earth, of the National Socialist position and of a world perception, a new German era is born.[38]

Thus, good taste, which is a trait held by the most exemplary of citizens, is institutionalized in the *GGAE*. If one desires to be part of the 'virtuous citizenry' and partake in the 'community's common heritage … in its very identity', one must accept the 'highest and most authoritative [Aryan] truths', consecrated (constructed/mythologized) within the walls of the Nazi (Fascist/ Aryan) museum/temple.

One of the most overlooked sections of the museum catalogue is that of the 'Comments'. It sets the visiting times and acts as a sort of legend for the symbols within the texts throughout the catalogue. However, the part of this section which relates to the sale of the art works is of theoretical interest. In a traditional museum setting, rarely does one find the works of art for sale. In this sense, the Temple of German Art operated like a gallery, offering contemporary art for sale. All sales and related transactions had to be handled through the museum, requiring a 20% down-payment. The works were released to the new owners after the exhibition closed and the balances had been paid. The ability to purchase identified 'cultural treasures' for one's own home offered the viewers an odd sense of availability. Interestingly, in the history of the Temple of German Art, the greatest number of attendees were present during the days of the *Great German Art Exhibitions*. The 1937 exhibition had 554,759 visitors.[39] Perhaps, the reason why this exhibition was so well attended was the construction of a specific desire – a desire for identity which could be attained in a material sense (as well as a psychological one). To put it simply, one could purchase one's 'Lacanian mirror', one's ideal.

The catalogue section on 'The Temple of German Art in Munich' delves deeper into the architecture of the building than the booklet, *The Temple of German Art*. The building was to be seen as a testament to the high priority art was given in the *Reich*. In importance, it was likened to the *Führer*'s speech at the 1933 Nuremberg Rally that, according to the catalogue, was 'the most important politico-cultural document of the newer history' in which 'the fundamentals [of the Thousand Year *Reich*] were laid out with the utmost clarity'.[40] The building was also an acknowledgment of the importance of Munich, where the 'balance and harmonious foundations in a century-long, unbroken development … arose organically'.[41] In the spirit of Hegel, the art works and the museum were intended to be an 'expression of the noblest and heroic desire of the Volk'.[42]

The concept of the museum as a frame is taken even further in the catalogue when the walls were used as the boundary or mold for the construction of a concept, that of Nazi art.[43] Nazi-endorsed German art was characterized as a 'survivor', which battled the Marxists and anarchists in order to stay true to its Germanness. Hitler was seen as the savior of art, who built a safe domicile with policed boundaries to protect against bastardization or contamination of the 'real' German art – 'the unremoveable border is visible again today [1937], between that which is art and that which is not art'.[44]

The catalogue's description of the museum also offers a mold or boundary where aspects of the 'modern' were absorbed or exiled. The text elaborately describes the museum's appearance – colonnades, stairways and materials – attempting to illustrate the enormous, yet simple, construction. It begins with a visitor crossing the street and walking up the front steps to the entry hall, detailing the minimal architectural embellishments – limestone, marble and mosaics (Figures 3.6.1 and 3.6.2). One is given the sense of an austere classical building, grandeur being expressed in the materials, space and light.[45] The plain, austerely geometric architectural elements gave one the impression that the Nazis had not escaped modernism. What was avoided was any display of technology.

For the Nazis, there was a conflict between using current technologies and being modern. From this perspective, the strengths, weaknesses and constructive power of the frame become apparent. The concept of the *Volk* was constructed/defined/described within the walls of the museum. The concept of the *Volk* was defined through a disparity in that those things which were seen as not part of the concept were exiled to the outside, that is, othered. The 'modern' was seen as anarchistic, Marxist, Jewish and degenerate. Yet the Nazis were not able to exile all the constitutive elements of 'modern'. The Nazis attempted to construct the 'modern' as 'other', equated with technological advance and the rise of metropolitanism. However, they also wanted to be seen as progressive and superior to their 'modernist other'. This conflict forced them to negotiate their position, however awkwardly. The negotiation was present in the architecture of the museum, which looked to antiquity for its design and materials and to modernity for its displays.

Technology and modernism were embraced through the lighting in the museum. The description in the catalogue gave lighting great importance by highlighting the care given to the tone and tint of the glass glazing. The light in the major exhibition rooms was provided mainly by great skylights, resulting in subdued natural light. In addition, special lighting fixtures were set behind the skylights for use in the evening or during poor weather. Despite the importance of the innovative lighting system, the matte glass and huge metal frames where these plates were suspended were not visible from the outside of the building, since the architrave was designed to obscure their view.

'Important and modern, in the best sense, are the extraordinarily clearly ordered rooms that benefit the visitor and make it impossible to get lost and tired'.[46] Overtly, this statement demonstrates how the modern was carefully inserted into the texts. Nazi progress was also affirmed through the description of the technology housed in the basement, that of climate controls and a bomb shelter. 'It may be said that the technical installations are among the most modern; however, the technical aspects are not visible from the outside.'[47]

Thus, the exhibition catalogue's description of the museum's architecture acted as a frame in which the objects were to be experienced by the viewers. The museum frame embraced the 'traditional', looking back to the Greeks and Romans. It embraced the eternal in its use of 'permanent' materials such as marble and limestone. It embraced the notion of progress in its 'modern only in the best sense'. It rejected 'modern in its worst sense' – anarchy, Marxism, Judaism and degeneracy. By virtue of the catalogue, the mold or frame was, in part, provided by the architecture of the museum for the construction of Aryan/*Volk* mythology/identity.

The catalogue directly acknowledged the visitors within the frame of the museum. The rooms were said to be organized so that fatigue and confusion were impossible. The comfort of the visitor was emphasized, providing an accessible environment. A mention of the 'elegant' restaurant and the 'cozy' basement *Bierstuber* informed the visitor that these facilities were open to the general public. The 'elegant' restaurant was 'for everybody – [and was] accessible outside of exhibition hours ... they [the visitors] should arise from the spirit of the Temple, an exemplary place of *groomed cultural expression*'.[48] In a surprisingly overt manner, the museum guide tells its visitors what should be their appropriate 'cultural expression', behavior and comportment. The 'spirit of the Temple' in its 'inclusive' language – 'for everybody' – applies to a very specific group of people, those who are *claimants* to the Aryan/*Volk* mythology/identity.[49]

The end of the text reiterates that the museum is a reflection of the art and the art is a reflection of the German soul and the museum. It states that:

National-Socialism is not a revolution. An immense German national feeling is being awakened. The overcoming of class distinctions and the joyful subordination of individuality under the singular German idea is constructive and not revolutionary. Only the clearing of the materialistic-Marxist rubble is revolutionary ... the actual nature of National-Socialism is consciousness of the deepest German values – a reorganization of the German soul and its goal as an organic growth of the German culture.[50]

This 'constructive' German idea was seen as a natural occurrence. Its growth, development and existence was 'organic'. There was no reason to question the German ideal since, as natural, it was as God intended. It implied that the German ideal followed 'natural laws' without question. Everything that fell outside this natural category was unnatural – aberrant, that is, the punishment for not complying.

In sum, the museum's publications not only provided an architectural frame for the construction of the *Volk* mythology/identity, but also described the atmosphere and appropriate behaviors for a Temple of Art. The texts themselves utilize language which placed limits on the audience or defined the appropriate subject (visitor). The texts 'historically documented' that the German/Aryan subjects have fought for their rights to exist – the polarization of 'us/Aryan/German' and 'them/other/degenerate' was definitively constructed. The Temple of German Art and its contents/contexts were solely intended for the 'us' to the exclusion of the 'them'. The text spoke to this Aryan audience; therefore, the voice spoke of an 'us'. It spoke of a common desire for Aryan/German/'our' representation.

Conclusion

The Temple of German Art provided a frame that not only promoted a desire to identify with the Thousand Year *Reich* but actually began molding the *Volk*. Nazi museum practices surrounding art and art policies were primarily modernist and democratic. The art served the purposes of Enlightenment, of evidence for racial and genetic purity and of evidence for a totalizing history of common origins, in other words, the construction of the 'German soul'.

The democratic notions of ownership and of public right to 'their' art were choreographed in such a way that the virtual 'citizenry' could perform their identities until they were (re)formed into a resource for the state. With the 'democratic' museological rhetoric came the empty promise of power, further enticing individuals to perform their identity as citizens. The state provided examples of what was 'true' and naturalized, all of this within the frame of the *Days of German Art* and the *Great German Art Exhibition*, wherein the regional religious and cultural practices were utilized. The Nazis not only adopted the Catholic emphasis on ritual, ceremony and visual culture, but also wanted to foster their own religion. Both Bavarian culture and the associated Catholic non-secular culture was also steeped in visual orientations. The Temple was framed to include all that would fit the ideal(ogical) citizenry of the Third Reich.

Perhaps the most powerful of the German modernist museum practices were exclusion and labeling. Those excluded from the exhibit were all those in the heterogeneous German society of the 1930s, who did not fit into the homogeneity of the 'German ideal' of 1937 – the Jew, the Bolshevik, the physically or mentally disabled, the homosexual and the *avant-garde*. Anyone who was not Aryan was 'degenerate;' and this complied with 'the will of nature', since evolution and mother nature wanted to produce only the most 'highly evolved human beings'. Thus, the frame not only provided the containment of the ideal citizen but policed the boundaries that prevented the 'other' from entering.

The museum began its construction of the ideal citizen, the *Volk*, with the museum catalogue and guidebook, which provided the historical myth behind the location and construction of the museum. The art works were accessible not only within the walls of the museum but available for purchase by the visitor. The dichotomy of the *Volk*/'us' and the 'Degenerate'/'them' was set up with regard to artistic practice. Hence, a written foundation for the dialogue between two simultaneous art exhibits was established. The *Volk*/'us' was constructed in the *Great German Art Exhibition*, while the 'Degenerate'/'them' was constructed in the *Degenerate Art Exhibition*. The dialogue provided the foundation for a narrative of progress that established the 'Degenerate Art Exhibition' as an undesirable 'deviation' or 'regression' from the 'acceptable' path of 'evolution' of the German race exemplified in the *Great German Art Exhibition*.

Democratic strategies were instrumental in constructing the ideal national and community citizen. Illusions of empowerment and the importance of the citizen were articulated within the frame of the museum space. The *Great German Art Exhibition* was given to the people as an accessible, non-elite, egalitarian space, while the 'elitist' art of the *Degenerate Art Exhibition* was an example of non-democratic space. This democratic public space was constructed as proper and incontestable, but the foreclosure of debate and questioning was what defined this space as totalitarian.

The processes associated with the museum defined, constructed, destructed, reflected, reified, included and excluded. In short, the function of the museum, the Temple of German Art, was to (re)construct – to mold – the world into its own image. A ritualized transformation took place, in which the world was given structure and meaning. The museum functioned as an institution that seemed inclusive through its mastery of illusionary techniques but that was ultimately exclusive. The symbolic exclusion within the museum space of 1937 Germany extended into the city spaces; and the labeling extended beyond city, state and country boarders. The scaffolding was erected to take the political and spiritual message to its ultimate realization of supporting the 'master race' by eliminating the gene pools that could 'prevent' them from attaining their goals. The museum was a powerful epistemological and metaphysical weapon, wherein the excluded and included experienced knowing a different type of world. The Nazi museum framed 'the ideal citizen' and the desire to become one by providing a stage for one to perform an identity as a disciple of the Thousand Year *Reich* and to become what he or she desired to be – a member of the mythological *Volk*.

NOTES

1. *Grosse Deutsche Kunstausstellung 1937: Im Haus der Deutschen Kunst zu München.* (Munich: Verlag Knorr & Hirth G.m.b.H., 1937), 25 (cited as *GDK* hereafter; all translations from this are by the author)

2. This translation of the *'Haus der Deutschen Kunst'* comes directly from the title of a guidebook published by the Third Reich for English-speaking visitors; see Karl Drechsel, M.A., *The Temple of German Art Munich* (Munich: F. Bruckmann A.G., Publishers, 1934). The literal translation is 'House of German Art'.

3. See the orientation to the Munich Art Museum 1937 in *Temple of German Art* (Munich: Haus der Deutschen Kunst, 1937), 1.

4. Berthold Hinz, *Art in the Third Reich* (New York: Pantheon Books, 1979), 6.

5. Adolph Hitler, *Mein Kampf* (Boston: Houghton Mifflin Company, 1971), 126, 259, 263, 477–9, 492–7 (originally published in 1927).

6. For further discussion see Sandra Esslinger, 'Art in the Third Reich: The Fabrication of National Cultural Identity', unpublished PhD dissertation, University California at Los Angeles, 2001 (Michigan: UMI, 2001) 9–81.

7. Esslinger, *Art in the Third Reich*, 44–56.

8. Hitler, *Mein Kampf*, diffused throughout.

9. Leni Riefenstahl, *Leni Riefenstahl: A Memoir* (New York: St Martin's Press, 1993), 210–11.

10. See Alfred Rosenberg, *Myth of the Twentieth Century* (Torrance, CA: Noontide Press, 1982), diffused throughout.

11. Stefan Arvidsson, 'Aryan Mythology as Science and Ideology', *Journal of the American Academy of Religion*, 67/2, June 1999.

12. James Whisker, *Social, Political and Religious Thought of Alfred Rosenberg* (Washington: University Press of America, 1982), 110.

13. Ibid., 120–2.

14. Benjamin Sax and Dieter Kuntz, *Inside Hitler's Germany: A Documentary History of Life in the Third Reich* (Lexington, Mass.: D. C. Heath and Company, 1992), 227.

15. See Sandra Esslinger, 'The Museum as a Political Media: A Semiological Assault', in *Semiotics of the Media: State of the Art, Projects, and Perspectives,* ed. Winfried Nöth (Berlin and New York: Mouton de Gruyter, 1997).

16. Carol Duncan, 'Art Museums and the Ritual of Citizenship', in *Exhibiting Cultures*, eds Ivan Karp and Steven Lavine (Washington and London: Smithsonian Institution Press, 1991), 101.

17. Donald Preziosi, *The Art of Art History: A Critical Anthology* (Oxford and New York: Oxford University Press, 1998), 508.

18. See Sander L. Gilman, *Difference and Pathology: Stereotypes of Sexuality, Race and Madness* (Ithaca and London: Cornell University Press, 1985).

19. Hitler, *Mein Kampf.*

20. Rosenberg, *Myth*, 428–43.

21. Hans F. K. Günther, *Rassenkunde des deutschen Volkes* (Munich: J. F. Lehmanns Verlag, 1923) and *Rasse und Stil* (Munich, 1926); Paul Schultze-Naumburg, *Gestaltung der Landshaft durch den Mänschen*, (Munich: J. F. Lehmanns Verlag, 1928).

22. He published *Kunst und Kunsterzeihung in dritten Reich* in 1933.

23. Inderpal Grewal, 'The Guide Book and the Museum: Aesthetics, Education and Nationalism in the British Museum' (unpublished, 1989), 2.

24. *The Art of Art History*, 511.

25. 'Hitler's Speech Dedicating the House of German Art', *Volkischer Beobachter*, July 19, 1937 from *Inside Hitler's Germany: A Documentary History of Life in the Third Reich*, eds Benjamin Sax and Dieter Kuntz (Lexington, Mass.: D. C. Heath and Company, 1992).

26. Preziosi, *The Art of Art History*, 511–12.

27. Ibid., 513.

28. Drechsel, *Temple*, 5.

29. Ibid., 6.

30. Ibid., 7–9.

31. Ibid., 10.

32. Ibid., 13–14.

33. Ibid., 18.

34. See note 1, above.

35. *GDK*, 5.

36. Ibid.

37. Ibid.

38. *GDK*, 6.

39. Sabine Brantl, *Haus der Kunst 1937–1997: Eine Historische Dokumentation* (Munich: Haus der Kunst, 1997), 86.

40. *GDK*, 17–18.

41. *GDK*, 18.

42. Ibid.

43. This comment is in reference to Gilles Deleuze's notion of individuation, which is found in his *Difference and Repetition*, trans. Paul Patton, New York: Columbia University Press, 1994. A clear discussion of Deleuze's ideas of individuation can be found in Ronald Bogue, *Deleuze and Guattari* (London and New York: Routledge, 1989), 60–1.

44. *GDK*, 19.

45. Duncan discusses the connection of the museum with the Greek and Roman temple architecture, which was adopted as fitting for the museum. It marks off the museum space as secular and ritualized, wherein a culture's identity is performed ('Art Museums', 91–2).

46. *GDK*, 22.

47. *GDK*, 24.

48. *GDK*, 22–3, italics mine.

49. This refers to Deleuze's definition of grounding in which he states: 'The operation of grounding renders the claimant *similar* to the ground, endowing it with resemblance from within and thereby allowing it to participate in the quality or the object which it claims. As similar to the same, the claimant is said to *resemble* – this, however, is not an external resemblance to the object but an internal resemblance to the ground itself'; Paul Patton, trans., *Difference and Repetition* by Gilles Deleuze (New York: Columbia University Press, 1994), 272.

50. *GDK*, 25.

7.

The Cosmic Theme Park of the Javanese

Shelly Errington

All polities are 'imagined', Benedict Anderson claimed in his influential book on nationalism (1991).[1] That does not mean, he asserts, that political communities are imaginary or that their self-imaginings are to be distinguished as 'genuine' or 'false'; but they are to be distinguished by their different 'styles' of imagining themselves. He contrasts two major styles of imagining a political community: the nation-state, on the one hand, and 'the great classical communities' such as the Ummah Islam, Christendom, and the Buddhist world, on the other. Each type of polity imagines the shape of its sovereignty differently. Anderson devotes the book to explicating the nation-state, and he uses the 'great classical communities' only as a foil, for the sake of contrast. Yet the contrast he sketches is striking.

The nation-state's sovereignty, he writes, 'is imagined as fully, flatly, and evenly operative over each square centimetre of a legally demarcated territory';[2] consequently, the *map* with its bounded, flat, and clear shape becomes a characteristic emblem of the nation-state. The shape of the sovereignty of 'great classical communities', by contrast, was circular and hierarchical. 'All the great classical communities conceived of themselves as cosmically central,' he writes, and their 'fundamental conceptions about "social groups" were centripetal and hierarchical, rather than boundary-oriented and horizontal'.[3]

The classical communities that existed prior to the nation-state (both colonial and independent) in Southeast Asia were the so-called 'Indic states' – the great Buddhist polities in what are now Myanmar (Burma) and Thailand,

and the Hindu-Buddhist polities of the islands of Bali and Java, which are now within the territorial borders of the Republic of Indonesia. Their self-imagining conformed nicely to Anderson's characterization of classical communities.

The Indic states of Southeast Asia imagined themselves as circular spaces, modeled on the realm of the Buddha. At the center of the realm of the Buddha is the Lord Buddha himself in his palace. The Buddhist universe surrounds him equally on all sides. Bodhisattvas and beings who have attained enlightenment sit closest to him. Less and less enlightened creatures exist at further and further distances from the center. On the extreme periphery lie animals, hungry ghosts, and demons. Humans are in between. Those humans who seek to follow the path of the Buddha to enlightenment must dissociate themselves from the world of violence and desire that ordinary humans live in. The path they must follow leads them symbolically from the periphery toward the center.

Translated into political imaginings, the center of a Southeast Asian Indic state was the kingdom. The surrounding peoples and territories were less and less central: the further from the center of power and prestige an individual, social stratum, or tributary state was located in space or social relations, the less important and more peripheral, literally or figuratively, it was. Consequently, the symbolic dimensions of 'inner' and 'outer' feature prominently in the state symbolism of these historical polities.

The Buddhist universe is always represented as radially symmetrical, a squared circle, a circular square. The name for this radial configuration is 'mandala'. In Buddhist iconography, the mandala is represented as a series of concentric circles or squares, or both, which are symbolically equivalent. (In some Buddhist representational traditions, squares represent earth; circles, heaven.)

Southeast Asian Indic states represented themselves to themselves with circular, radial, and conical images, like the royal umbrella and the banyan tree, which symbolically shade, protect, and encompass the underlings gathered beneath them. And these polities often likened themselves to mountains (such as Mount Meru in Java or Bali's sacred mountain, Gunung Agung), symbols suggesting a polity immobile in space and unchanging in time.

We can imagine these two ideal types of polities (the modern nation-state and the Southeast Asian kingdom) as constituting different spatial orderings of political meanings. One is flat, both territorially and socially (in the sense that its public consists of equal citizens), as well as spatially and legally homogeneous (Oregon is as fully a legal part of the United States as is New Jersey). The other ideal type is mountain-shaped and spatially and socially differentiated, with the most important political and social density at the center; its symbolic geography consists of concentric circles that gradually melt into each other at their invisible borders, spreading infinitely outward.

The contrast between these two spatial orderings is also temporal. The nineteenth-century European nation-state increasingly linked itself with the idea of human progress, a notion of history predicated on the assumption of unidirectional and open-ended change. The Southeast Asian Indic state (its court/center, to be sure) imagined itself as existing within an unchanging cosmic order. In the worst of times (rebellion, war, invasion, famine), it could become de-centered – obscured, or unfocused, or replaced by a rival center. These misfortunes would mean that this particular 'exemplary center' had become less exemplary than before; but the mandala-structure of the universe, kingdoms included, did not change.[4] In imagining themselves, different types of polities use different symbols and different semiotic technologies in order to represent themselves to themselves, and, by representing, try to produce and reproduce themselves as they believe themselves to be. The map, the census, and the museum, Benedict Anderson claims, are characteristic representations of nation-states' styles of self-imagining. As the Republic of Indonesia moves into advanced nation-building and self-construction, it, like other nation-states, models itself partly on European conceptions of nation-states (bureaucratic procedures and categories it learned from the colonial power that ruled it) and uses the emblems of self-imagining characteristic of nation-states. But it imagines itself also as the heir of its glorious past, whose expanding political destiny was interrupted by the hiatus of colonial oppression but whose current government seeks to restore the glory of empire.

Hybrid fantasy architecture

Far more than its neighbors Malaysia and the Philippines, Indonesia is engaged in a project of national self-imagining displayed in what I call 'hybrid fantasy architecture'. My aim in naming this type of building is not for the sake of creating a taxonomy: hybrid fantasy architecture of the type I want to point out here may indeed overlap with other genres. Nonetheless, it does seem to me that the hybrid architectural fantasy is an emerging genre in the world now, suitable especially for airports, hotels, and perhaps national and cultural theme parks. This style has three salient characteristics: (1) it exists on a grandiose scale, (2) it is made possible by heavy capital or state power, and sometimes a combination of both, and (3) it refers iconically to other architectures but serves functions different from the originals.[5] In the United States, the paradigmatic exemplars of hybrid fantasy architecture are the themed hotels and gambling casinos of Las Vegas – the Luxor is a fine example. It is truly gigantic (far larger than an Egyptian pyramid, its ads tell us), it cost millions of dollars to build and maintain, and it looks something like an Egyptian pyramid but is in fact a hotel and casino.

For the sake of clarifying and refining this style, I want to distinguish it from kitsch, fascist, and postmodern architecture. An example of pure kitsch is the 'Big-Duck' type of structure (Figure 3.7.1) decried by Robert Venturi, Denise Scott Brown, and Steven Izenour.[6] Big-Duck architecture substitutes 'for the innocent and inexpensive practice of applied decoration on a conventional shed the rather cynical and expensive distortion of program and structure to promote a duck'.[7] If architecture must be placed into only one of two categories, the decorated shed (consisting of ornament placed upon a conventional building) and the Big Duck (consisting of a building in the shape of something else), what I call hybrid fantasy architecture is obviously a type of duck: it is itself ornament, rather than a shed with cunning decor. It deviates from the ideal Venturi-defined Big-Duckness in two respects: its programs refer only to other architectures (not to ducks, etc. – not that it, any more than the Big Duck, would ever be mistaken for the original); and it exists on a huge scale made possible by heavy capital or state power or a combination thereof.

In these respects, it is reminiscent of fascist structures built in Nazi Germany: the Zeppelinfeld Stadion designed by Albert Speer was gigantic; embracing and reflecting Hitler's interest in Roman imperial architecture, it refers visually, if loosely, to it. The Great Altar of Pergamum inspired it, according to its designer, but it was a sports stadium, not a temple (see Scobie 1990: 87 and Watkin and Mellinghoff 1987).[8] Both fascist and hybrid fantasy architecture are gigantic, measured on a human scale; thus they bespeak power, even when (like the Las Vegas Luxor) they are sometimes ostensibly humorous or playful. What distinguishes hybrid fantasy from fascist architecture – although this is only a matter of degree – is first that hybrid fantasy structures quote the original more directly than fascist ones do (indeed, Nazi fascist architecture was more like a decorated giant shed than a giant duck). Second, hybrid fantasies may be intentionally or unintentionally somewhat comic, linking them to a kitsch sensibility, whereas fascist architecture is merely chilling.

Finally, whereas postmodern architecture in the manner of Charles Moore [(1925–1993), American architect who developed a humanistic approach that engages users within a clearly defined spatial monument; he felt that architecture should include a symbolic reference to the site] also refers to other architectures, and may be large and expensive, and may even be quite light-hearted, its quotes often combine to form a pastiche rather than a coherent programmatic whole. The state-sponsored and capital-intensive hybrid fantasies I am pointing to here are much closer in sensibility to kitsch and to fascism, which have often been partners, than to postmodern architecture's intelligence and playfulness.

73. "Long Island Duckling" from *God's Own Junkyard*

Figure 3.7.1   An example of 'Big-Duck' architecture in Long Island (*top*) and sketches (*bottom*) from *Learning from Las Vegas*, illustrating the difference between two basic types of architecture

In this chapter [of *The Death of Authentic Primitive Art and Other Tales of Progress*] I examine two examples of Indonesia's state-sponsored fantasy architecture – the national theme park 'Taman Mini' and the international section of the Hatta-Sukarno Airport at Chengkareng, both just outside the nation's capital, Jakarta. The architectures they refer to iconically are Indonesia's 'traditional' structures. This fantasy architecture is an expression of the hybrid visual discourse produced by a national impulse to construct nationhood from the remains of imagined and sometimes imaginary empires, supported by international capital in the service of local military power.

Taman Mini: Beautiful Indonesia-in-Miniature Park

My first case in point is Taman Mini Indonesia Indah – 'Beautiful Indonesia-in-Miniature Park'. Opened to the public in 1977, Taman Mini is a national cultural theme park lying on the outskirts of Jakarta.

When I first heard the name 'Taman Mini' but before I visited it, I assumed that it meant 'Miniature Village', and I expected slightly reduced models of houses, rather like those at Disneyland. In fact, the houses are approximately life-size in the section of the park where the cultures of Indonesia's provinces are represented. The 'mini' part of Taman Mini is not so much its individual elements but rather the fact that the whole of Indonesia has been shrunk to a government-controlled park, in which the unruly elements of yesteryear are shown in their cleaned-up versions, nicely arranged into government-designated provinces, each 'ethnic group' depicted by its 'typical' house – the whole of it framed by giant signifies of 'Bali' and 'Java'. In Taman Mini, not Indonesia but 'Indonesia' is made visible and available to both domestic and foreign tourists, who may traverse the miniature and fantasized nation-state of 'Indonesia' without leaving the environs of the capital of Indonesia.

Approaching it, the visitor first passes under giant arches in 'Balinese' style then comes to an enormous plaza (see Figure 3.7.2), the Alun-alun Pancasila (the Plaza of the Five National Principles), on whose other side (and framed by the Plaza) is the gigantic Audience Hall 'dubbed', as John Pemberton points out, 'in *Javanese* rather than Indonesian, the Grand-Place-of-Importance Audience Hall (Pendopo Agung Sasono Utomo)'.[9] The Audience Hall evokes a Javanese noble's house due to the shape of its roof, known as a *joglo*, although this particular joglo is grotesquely oversized.

Moving on, the visitor passes through a section of food-stalls and by the huge movie theater and arrives at the ethnic-groups section of the park. An artificial lake with islands in the shape of the Indonesian archipelago lies at its center, forming a map of the nation-state (see Figure 3.7.3). Indonesia's stunning cultural diversity is represented in the surrounding plots, one for

Figure 3.7.2   The gigantic Grand-Place-of-Importance Audience Hall at the entrance of Taman Mini with its oversize Javanese-style roof

each of the administrative provinces, each with a house or houses 'typical' of the 'ethnic groups' of each province.

If the map, the census, and the museum, as Benedict Anderson claims, are characteristic representations in nation-states' styles of self-imagining, then Taman Mini gives visible form to the Indonesian nation-state's self-imagining as tidily as if it had been designed by following a set of general rules.

The national *map* lies at Taman Mini's center. Maps emblematize and naturalize the boundaries of the nation-state. To illustrate the concept of a nation-state as a bounded entity, Ernest Gellner asks us to picture an ethnographic map before and after the age of nationalism, likening the first to a painting by Kokoschka, 'a riot of diverse points of colour … such that no clear pattern can be discerned in any detail', whereas a political map of nation-states more resembles a Modigliani: 'There is very little shading: neat flat surfaces are clearly separated from each other, it is generally plain where one begins and another ends, and there is little if any ambiguity or overlap.'[10]

Like nation-states, the ethnic groups within the state have clear boundaries. Bounded ethnic identities, like bounded and clearly demarcated territorial borders, are the creation of the nation-state. One of the impulses that produced taxonomies of ethnicities was the colonial nation-state's practice of making a

Figure 3.7.3   At the center of Taman Mini is an artificial lake with islands in the shape of the Indonesian archipelago. Around it lie miniature provinces, each containing 'typical' houses

census for categorization and control of the populace. Writing about the British in India during the nineteenth century, Bernard Cohn[11] has outlined the process by which the colonial power in effect invented taxonomies of bounded ethnicities and racial/cultural types by classifying the peoples it governed by location, language, physical type, and custom; such representations of typical specimens then entered into ethnographic atlases, and, eventually, ethnographic museums and world's fairs. By these means, categories of tribe and ethnicity became reified as objective knowledge, taken for granted as naturally occurring. By the mid-twentieth century, when most nation-states of Africa and Asia came into being, 'ethnic' difference had been totally naturalized and appeared to be part of the very structure of the world. Benedict Anderson points out that the newly independent nation-states of Asia and Africa that threw off their colonial oppressors in the mid-twentieth century nonetheless often adopted intact the colonial bureaucratic taxonomy of ethnic identity as well as the regional governing divisions whose rationale was often based upon them.

The parade of typical houses of the ethnic groups that compose the national park-museum of Taman Mini's 'Indonesia', then, reflects the *census* sensibility – for it requires a decision as to where cultural boundaries lie between adjacent ethnic groups and which ones are important enough to be represented in the park.

Taman Mini is a form of the *museum*, a variation on the open-air historical museum. The first of these, Skansen, was invented at the end of the nineteenth century in Sweden in order to preserve that nation's architectural heritage, which was fast disappearing as the country became more urban and industrial. As a type, the open-air museum merges with the cultural or historical park, which contains structures that exemplify and emblematize different cultures, historical periods, and even scenes (for example, the 'Main Street, U.S.A'. display at Disneyland). In Taman Mini, houses emblematize the typical, generic, and timeless architecture of Indonesia's constituent ethnic groups, rather than display historical periods or particular structures from different regions.

A note on miniature worlds

Inspired by the example of Sweden's Skansen, the first open-air national historical park (founded in the early 1890s), European nation-states built nations-in-miniature during the subsequent decades as ways to 'materialize the nation', to use Orvar Löfgren's phrase.[12] The open-air cultural theme park and historical re-creation are common forms of the museum, a type of didactic entertainment. Some are built with official state monies and purposes; some are simply money-making and advertisement ventures. Such open-air museums and their variants use different architectural styles to represent different, bounded cultures and historical periods. Whether they are literally miniature or not, many cultural and historical parks could be categorized as 'miniature worlds', since they try to re-create the experience – or merely the look – of a world of the past or in a distant place; and many are intended to preserve at least the image of a traditional world that is imagined to be disappearing, featuring architecture to emblematize either historical periods, nation-states, or ethnic groups.

While the genre of the miniature village looks surprisingly uniform in its conventions, this overt similarity masks many covert dissimilarities. The theories of display, representation, and layout obviously differ among miniature worlds depending on their purposes. Some are advertisements, in effect, for products (like Lego-Land in Denmark); they may be privately owned or foundation-owned attractions whose stated purpose is to educate, as well as to make enough money to maintain themselves (like Colonial Williamsburg); others are state-owned and state-maintained enterprises with an explicit connection to the promotion of national virtues or identities. Taman Mini fits into the last of these categories.

One issue for representational strategy is what, if any, period of time is represented. At Skansen houses from different historical periods, from the fourteenth century onward, were physically transported and placed next to each other in a park in Stockholm. A stroll through Skansen is a stroll through Swedish history – but not linearly, and various low-key amusements supplement the history lesson. Hawaii's Polynesian Cultural Center, owned and run by Brigham Young University, features different Polynesian island cultures (now most are nation-states, although that is underplayed in the park); they are represented by their 'typical' houses, which are built to scale by Polynesians. The time period featured appears to be the mid-1800s, when missionaries had spread across the Pacific and female Polynesians were consequently wearing muumuus rather than exposing their breasts and had learned the craft of quilting. (I infer this from the sale of quilting kits and muumuus at the park's shops.) At EPCOT Center's World Showcase in Florida, temporal periods are inconsistently represented in the display of eleven nation-states ringing an artificial lake. Each country is emblematized architecturally by a distinctive, usually grand, structure, scaled to conform to the others – thus, Japan is represented by a pagoda, Mexico by a pyramid. Temporality is inconsistent in this display because it is irrelevant: the point is not to show historical periods but to portray the generalized essence of the nation-state in its full eternal typicality. The alternative, then, to representing a particular historical era is to represent the eternal essences of the 'typical', whether country or culture, a plan also pursued at Taman Mini.

Sometimes the structures of the open-air museum are original buildings brought together and juxtaposed, as in Skansen; from this perspective, historic districts preserved intact, at least in their facades, are a form of the open-air museum. Sometimes the buildings are reconstructed to be completely accurate materially, like Williamsburg Colonial Village in Virginia; sometimes they are simulations that look very similar to the originals but differ in materials – like Disneyland's 'New Orleans Square' or the Field Museum's reconstruction of the market-place of Bora-Bora in its installation called 'Traveling the Pacific'.

A building's size has a semiotic dimension, because the scale of buildings in relation to the human body implicates phenomenological meaning. We tend to perceive smaller structures as toys or for children; they at least present themselves as unthreatening. Examples are Madurodam of the Netherlands, where the visitor wanders like a giant among knee- to waist-high representations, and Disneyland's five-eighths scale, whose rationale is said to be to make children feel comfortable. Full-scale meticulous reproductions (in both scale and other respects), like Williamsburg or the Polynesian Cultural Center, tend implicitly to claim historical or cultural accuracy and therefore educational value. Larger than full-scale buildings are, at the least, impressive. No consistently oversize themed cultural or historical park comes to mind as an example, probably because hugely oversize buildings tend to signify power, often the power of the state or the power of capital (as in fascist architecture and in Las Vegas). Miniature worlds may also be inconsistently scaled, but large enough to be impressive, like most of the emblematic buildings in the World Showcase section of Disney World's EPCOT Center.

At Taman Mini, scale representation is inconsistent. In the main section of twenty-seven provinces with their ethnic groups' house styles surrounding the lake, it is fairly consistent and fairly life-size. But gigantism is in evidence at the entrance, with its huge plaza and gigantic Audience Hall, featuring a rather distorted but fully recognizable Javanese-style roof. And miniaturization is in evidence at Taman Mini in the replica of Borobudur and in some of the Toraja houses and cliffs.

In spite of their differences, at a general level miniature worlds all seem to resemble each other loosely, and indeed, at a general level, they do. Yet to 'read' these parks as cultural artifacts, as signifiers of meanings, which are always partially local, requires us to unpack the local politics and epistemologies that produced them. The historical origins and current maintenance of national theme parks and state museums, for instance, are embedded in specific states' nation-building efforts: the ways the state chooses to materialize itself given its concepts of the nation-as-a-whole, the shape of the past, the place of the folk, modes of legitimizing power, and so on.

As in the cases just mentioned, Taman Mini's signifying medium consists of diverse architectural styles. Unlike these other cases, Taman Mini exists within the cultural and symbolic context of island Southeast Asia, where the house features large in the production and reproduction of 'traditional' cultural forms; and it exists within the political context of the Republic of Indonesia, where the military regime of General Suharto with his New Order politics drew heavily upon traditional architectural forms to project and construct national self-imaginings. Understanding how the house can be read in these other contexts will enable a deeper reading of Taman Mini as a political text of nationalist self-representation.

The house in Indonesia

Indonesia is a place not only of spectacular natural beauty but of spectacular built structures – think of the soaring rooftops of the clan houses of the Minangkabau of Sumatra, the temples of Bali, the royal courtyards of Central Java. Their extraordinary appearance is matched by their cosmic significance.[13] The term 'house' in many of the local languages signifies not just a physical structure but an extended social grouping, whose symbolic center has its physical locus in or at the structure, which provides a ritual site for its ceremony and self-imagining. It is not surprising that Claude

Lévi-Strauss calls the social formations of Indonesia 'sociétés à maisons' (house societies).[14]

Even ordinary-looking structures, like the rectangular houses on stilts of the Buginese of South Sulawesi, are built as microcosms of the universe, with three levels corresponding to the lower, middle, and upper worlds, as well as a navel post at the house's cosmic center where the house-spirit hovers.[15]

Among the more famous and striking examples of architectural cosmography are the *tongkonan* of the Toraja of South Sulawesi. Looming out, their roofs are supported by poles festooned with the horns of water buffalo slain at mortuary ceremonies, their meal long since divided in complex networks of debt and prestige. Granaries and house fronts are decorated with painted and incised signs signifying wealth, status, and fertility. These were usually 'clan houses', often rivaling each other in a ceremonial cycle. Although people slept in them, tongkonan were not primarily living spaces; they were places to store valuables, to place corpses prior to the mortuary ceremony (sometimes for many months), and to be visible emblems of the center of the clan.

The house, in sum, was and continues to be a densely meaningful sign – a palpable, indeed, a live-in and walk-through sign – that ties together cosmos, kinship, the relations between the sexes, hierarchy, and the inscription of directions on the body and in social geography (such as up/down, right/ left, and center/periphery).

THE HOUSE AS SIGN OF ETHNIC IDENTITY

Perhaps understandably, in modern Indonesia the 'typical' houses of different ethnic groups have come to signify that ethnicity. In cities, for instance, restaurants serving regional food often advertise themselves with a sign in the shape of the region's characteristic house shape. Probably hundreds of small restaurants throughout Indonesia call themselves 'Rumah Makan Padang' (*rumah makan* means restaurant; Padang is a city in Sumatra) and hang a cutout silhouette of a Minangkabau house over the door.

In the Toraja district, the house has also become a kind of floating sign whose signifying medium and social function vary but whose signified is always 'Toraja-ness' and 'typical'. The sign appears everywhere: as the shape of ceremonial pig-carriers, as grave-markers, as roadside neighborhood-watch shelters, as freestanding monuments, as emblems for government propaganda, as entrances to hotels and to churches, on T-shirts, on telephone books (Figure 3.7.4).

In a rhetorical move that Roland Barthes had already thought of, Toraja-style architectural elements are used to signify 'Toraja-style architecture'. In

Figure 3.7.4   In the Toraja district, the shape of the tongkonan clan-house appears everywhere

the hotel complex called 'Toraja Cottages', the hotel's two-storey buildings that contain the guest rooms (which are entirely European-style in other respects) are topped by enormous Toraja-style roofs, which necessitates, of course, distortion of the shape and size of the traditional roof.

The central government of Indonesia, likewise, uses bloated forms of local architecture for government buildings. The fundamental form of these buildings is of course derived from European models.[16] In Toraja-land, Toraja-style roofs, stretched and expanded in shape and size, top these typically enormous government buildings. Buildings like the Maranu Hotel, run by the government airline Garuda – a huge structure topped with a 'local' roof – clearly signify the central state in its local manifestation.

Toraja people are currently signifying themselves as 'Toraja' as well by making architectural references to tongkonan in the houses they build as their own dwellings. Traditional tongkonan, as I mentioned, were not really living spaces. With development has come electricity and indoor plumbing, as well as notions that interior architectural spaces can be lived in. Now Toraja are beginning to build the larger rectangular houses in the lowland Bugis style (without their cosmic significance, one presumes), adding elements to those houses derived from tongkonan architectural forms. The inventiveness is stunning. Toraja-style roof-shapes loom out from ordinary rectangular houses; or people may put Toraja-style granaries, real or miniature, in front of their rectangular houses; or they create whole entrances and doorways that evoke the front of a tongkonan but lead to an ordinary building. My favorite Toraja house is a magnificent structure built by a Toraja who made his fortune logging the tropical forests of Central Sulawesi. He has built more or less what William Randolph Hearst would have built, if Hearst had been a Toraja.

THE HOUSE AS A SIGN OF THE NATION

'What is the difference between a language and a dialect?' goes the joke. Answer: 'A language *is* a dialect ... with an army and a navy.' The standard high-status house form of Central Java might also have become a signifier of ethnicity if history had been different from what it was. But history was not different from what it was, and the Central Javanese *pendopo* (audience hall or ceremonial pavilion) with its distinctive roof-form called the *joglo* is increasingly becoming the language of the nation-state rather than the dialect of ethnicity.

Timothy Lindsey, drawing upon Prijotomo's comprehensive study of Javanese architecture,[17] calls it 'that quintessentially Javanese architectural motif, the seemingly endlessly mutating pendopo (pillared pavilion)', which in its simplest form is 'a foursided pyramidical roof supported by central columns and with additional support provided by further, smaller columns around the perimeter. From this simple model, endless variants have been developed.'[18] Standing to the front of the living quarters, the pendopo was the space where people of status and influence received petitioners and visitors, and where performances of music and dance could be held. It is shaded but open and protecting, the architectural equivalent of other signs of Indic kingship and high status, such as the banyan tree, the royal umbrella, and the sacred mountain. These are all radially symmetrical spaces with high centers that symbolize the encompassment of lesser, dependent beings by and under the high-status being at the center of the space.

As Suharto's New Order government embarked on its hybrid fantasy architecture project in the early 1970s, it looked 'back' in time for its iconography to the region's Indic states. In principle and in theory, any of several might have been chosen. The grandest of recent Indic states in the geographical region that was to become the nation-state of Indonesia were Yogyakarta and Surakarta in Central Java, Cirebon on the northern coast of Java, and Klungkung or several other kingdoms in Bali. Central Java had emerged as the definitive center of Javanese culture during the nineteenth century as a result of a mutual construction by the ruling aristocrats of the cities of Yogyakarta and Surakarta, and Dutch Java-centered rule of the East Indies.[19] The nineteenth-century elevation of Central Java (rather than some other former Indic state) as the preeminent spiritual and cultural center of what became the Republic of Indonesia has been embraced and maintained for reasons that are overdetermined. Most recently, under Suharto's New Order, it was promoted as the country's symbolic spiritual center. Not insignificantly, the icon chosen by Suharto's political party, Golkar, was the spreading banyan tree, an image of kingship in Southeast Asia's historical polities.

The pendopo with its distinctive roof shape, the joglo, also signifies the Indic mandala, the symbol of expansive power of centered kingship. This type of expansive center countenances no equals: it must be in conflict with them until one is defeated and absorbs the other as a deferential subordinate. But it is not exclusionary: it gladly incorporates diversity as inferiority and dependence upon itself. The pendopo with its joglo covering is the opposite of a clan house, tied to other and potentially equal rival clans, or houses, in a perpetual cycle of competitive ceremonies, exchanges, and marriages. Perhaps in part because of the centrist and encompassing ambitions of the kingship it represents – to be above rivals and encompassing them – the joglo is used increasingly in Indonesia to signify the general and unmarked rather than the particular, the ethnic, and the partial.

Near the pool at the Toraja Cottages hotel complex, for instance, is a bar shaded by a joglo roof. The hotel's dining room, likewise, is topped by a joglo, and its interior ceiling imitates the look of being under a joglo – complete with Central Javanese colonial Dutch-style lamps.

By the same token, the joglo may be emerging simply as the unmarked category of roofs that indicate national Indonesianness. Especially in Java, there is a tendency now to use the joglo as the roof of choice to indicate any government space or property, such as the kiosks in a market put up and owned by the government. The seismograph I came upon while wandering on the restored Borobudur monument in Central Java is topped with a joglo, clearly signifying that it is state property and should not be tampered with.

Taman Mini as Indic cosmograph

Back at Taman Mini, the wild semiosis of the provinces is tamed and controlled by the domesticating and nationalizing techniques of the map, the census, and the museum, the three characteristic representations of nation-states' styles of self-imagining; these characteristics make it obvious that Taman Mini was imagined by and for a nation-state. Yet some of Taman Mini's other aspects evoke the Indic classical communities that imagined themselves as cosmically central. If one were looking for an analogous set of three self-representations characteristic of the Southeast Asian Indic state, I would suggest the *genealogy*, the *state procession*, and the *cosmograph* – all of which Taman Mini also displays.

Southeast Asian rulers and nobles claimed legitimacy for their high status and inherent spiritual potency as due to their divine origins, expressed and tracked by their *genealogies*. Yet individuals could sometimes be blessed directly with divine energy and political potency, an overwhelmingly grand gift called *wahyu*. Thus in times of political unrest, leaders emerged whose earthly origins were humble but who clearly were blessed directly from the sources of cosmic energy and political potency. In those cases, this divine blessing bypassed inheritance. (The possibility of *wahyu* falling directly from the source of energy and good fortune explains, in contemporary Indonesia, the fact that some highly unlikely people have attained great status, wealth, and power.)

The factual and historical origins of Taman Mini strike most Western observers as distinctly uninspired. First, it is loosely modeled on Disneyland. (Mrs Suharto, whose idea it was to create Taman Mini, claimed direct inspiration from Disneyland.) Second, building the cultural park required that a space of about 100 hectares in the densely populated outskirts of Jakarta be cleared of hundreds of inhabitants; they were compensated inadequately, in their view, for their land, and sought legal help and publicity; anti-Mini protests spread across Indonesia in the early 1970s. The protests were to no avail, since military power backed the 'private' foundation run by Mrs Suharto. Thus Taman Mini's rather pedestrian historical origins *could* be told as a tale of state violence against its citizens in order to build a local version of an international corporation's theme park.

Countering these facts about Taman Mini's secular genealogy, the Suhartos have asserted the park's spiritual origins and authenticity as a sacred site with two rhetorical political countermoves that strive to bypass the historical facts and to sacralize the site as though it were a direct gift from above. One is Mrs Suharto's divine inspiration in creating the park, noted in Pemberton's account of Taman Mini:

In late August [1971], Mrs. Soeharto published an official rationale for the cultural park's proposed design and purpose. Opening with the patriotic salutation 'Freedom!' the First Lady described a sudden inspiration she had during her recent visit to Disneyland, 'I was inspired to build a Project of that sort in Indonesia, only more complete (*lengkap*) and more perfect, adapted to fit the situation and developments in Indonesia, both "materially" (*materiil*) and "spiritually" (*spirituil*)'.[20]

Pemberton notes that 'Mrs. Soeharto's account of how she was "inspired" (*diilhami*) with the "Beautiful Indonesia" Project concept appeals to a sense of divine inspiration and blessed mission.'

A second and more sustained rhetorical countermove has been the Suharto regime's effort to sacralize Taman Mini's Central Javanese-style buildings by transferring the *kramat* qualities (the sacred and potent energies) from the originals in Central Java (the royal palaces of Surakarta and Yogyakarta) to the structures at Taman Mini. Again, John Pemberton's account of Taman Mini – indeed of the idea of 'Java' itself in the imagination of Jakarta's Javanese elite – offers a stunning and persuasive account of the temporal and spatial displacements made to *kramat*-ize and authenticate this and other national projects. His account of Taman Mini gives special attention in this respect to the huge Audience Hall with its joglo-style roof at the entrance plaza, the Yogyakarta palace in the Javanese province section of the park, and the Indonesia Museum (added to the park and dedicated in 1980). Efforts were made to turn *these* structures, rather than the palaces and temples they were modeled on, into the 'originals'. Pemberton comments, 'With its exaggerated roof and durability of design, the Audience Hall would, perhaps, escape the quotation marks around "Beautiful Indonesia" by establishing itself as an original source, a cultural center of reference for future generations, the new locus of cultural inheritance.'

The *kramat*-izing of these structures took place through *processions* and ceremonies of various sorts. For example, the dedication of the Audience Hall in 1975 took the form of a royal procession:

Moving toward the Audience Hall one confronts the Indonesia Portal (Gapura Indonesia), an entrance normally kept locked, as the guidebook explains, yet opening for grand rituals (*upacara-upacara kebesaran*). Such was the case during the 1975 dedication of Mini when guests paraded through the Indonesia Portal on their way to the Audience Hall and observed mass folk dances on the frontal plaza. ... Lest the resonances of royal aspirations be lost on those attending Beautiful Indonesia's dedication, an offering was made on ritual behalf of the Audience Hall with Imelda Marcos planting a banyan tree – *the* emblem for Javanese royalty as well as the logo for the New Order's dominant political organization Golkar – in Mrs. Soeharto's orchid garden at Mini.[21]

On a similar note, when I visited the Indonesia Museum at Taman Mini, the grand entrance portal to the building was ostentatiously locked with a large chain and lock – it is used only for ceremonies, said a nearby guard – making it necessary to stoop down to enter through a small, low door to the side of the main entrance. This entrance device converts ordinary visitors into humble penitents, by obliging them to bow toward the structure upon the act of entering. In contrast to the large locked entrance portal, this diminutive doorway is, in effect, the servants' entrance to the sacred space.

Finally, Taman Mini's arrangement, as I show below, forms a *cosmograph*, an image that is structured like the cosmos and should therefore be read as a microcosm of it. Southeast Asian Indic cosmographs depicted the structure of the cosmos, ultimately based on the Buddhist universe, which was always a centered, radially symmetrical, and hierarchical space. Like the Buddha in his realm, the ruler sat in the sociopolitical hierarchy at the center and peak of his human realm, with lesser beings ranged around him in graded concentric tiers. City layouts and temples were constructed to replicate and therefore teach and constitute this centered political and social arrangement – structures like Angkor Wat in what is now Cambodia, and Borobudur in Java. These cosmographs were the icons and emblems by which the courts of Southeast Asian Indic states gave palpable form to themselves as centered, unmovable, hierarchical – encompassing lesser, tributary entities.

The prime feature to note about the Indic cosmograph in its transformation to a nationalist layout in Taman Mini is that it is a centered space, surrounded by a compliant, orderly, and lower-status periphery. I describe Taman Mini as a cosmograph by beginning with the periphery, that is to say, the ethnic groups that compose the nation, which are given visible form in the numerous house types displayed in the park. I then point out that the arrangement of the cultural park, with its central axis ringed by a supporting and orderly periphery and Taman Mini's architectural framing (which features signifiers of 'Java' and 'Bali'), assert the centrality of Javanese overlordship within the national cosmograph design.

THE ORDERLY PERIPHERY

When European states transformed themselves into *nation*-states during the course of the nineteenth century, they discovered/invented 'the folk'. The notions of the folk and of popular culture born in Europe in the late eighteenth and early nineteenth centuries contributed to the ideological basis of the romantic nationalism of the then-emerging continental European nation-states. It was at that time, writes Peter Burke, 'when traditional popular culture was just beginning to disappear, that the "people" or the "folk" became a subject of interest to European intellectuals'.[22] The earliest well-known enthusiasts of the folk, Herder and the Grimm brothers, were Europeanists rather than nationalists, Burke tells us; but he goes on to say that the more general impulse to explore folk songs, folk costume, and folktales was closely associated with nationalism, as European linguistic and political communities struggled to imagine themselves in the course of the nineteenth century as national entities that could become national states as well. The notion that the nation-state should be a unified community with a single language and a shared 'racial' and 'cultural' heritage dates from this period.

Orvar Löfgren points out that as nation-states made efforts to 'materialize' and make themselves visible to their own populace and to the other nation-states, certain cultural forms became standard, were seen as especially national, and therefore had to be found in all nation-states; a prime example is the production of national folk cultures.

The dress of the peasantry was synthesized into national costume and displayed at folk dance performances, which became an important way to stage national distinctiveness and cohesion. This symbol danced everywhere – at school speech days, in patriotic parades, at international exhibitions, and during state visits. It became especially important in Communist Eastern Europe, not least after Joseph Stalin's declaration that folk dance performances were important tools in the display of official national socialism. Throughout Eastern Europe and the Third World, this manifestation of distinctive national character and pride was created on the Soviet pattern. Every factory, school, or local council was supposed to have its own folklore ensemble.[23]

If, as Benedict Anderson suggests,[24] the nation-state became a 'module' with certain characteristics that had to be imitated by aspiring states or nations that wished to become nation-states, a nationalist version of the folk was clearly a component of the module.

What place, then, do the folk or their analogue have in Indonesia's national self-imagining, whose public expressions are controlled by Jakarta? The analogue of the folk in this instance consists not just of peasants but of the 'ethnic groups' of the nation-state. We will look in vain for romantic nationalism of the nineteenth-century European sort in Indonesia. For one thing, finding unity at the level of language or culture is prima facie impossible there. It is a country of great heterogeneity in almost any terms: religion, indigenous political forms, natural resources, ecological habitat, and local languages; therefore no simple appeals to unity on the grounds of uniformity will do.

State ideology, then, has tried to make a virtue of necessity: the country's motto is 'Unity in Diversity'. The strategy that emerged during the reign of General Suharto, especially visible in the state system of provincial and subprovincial museums that have been planned and built since the 1970s, was to assert (visually, in exhibits, and in other ways) that each ethnic group and province is distinctive and unique, yet each is equivalent and equal to other ethnic groups and provinces.

Provincial museums, for instance, usually have a mandatory 'Nusantara Room' featuring 'comparisons' with other provinces, often revealed in the form of bride-and-groom dolls dressed in wedding clothes. (The word *nusantara* means 'archipelago' and is often used as a poetic term for the nation-state of Indonesia, which consists of thousands of islands.) At Taman Mini some of the ethnic houses are open to the public. In them are displayed articles of costume and culture typical of that ethnic group. An almost universal feature of these displays is a pair of dolls wearing 'typical, traditional' wedding clothes. These exhibits seem to argue that custom is costume, that differences are superficial, and that, in the end, there is 'unity in diversity'. Paul Taylor has called this exhibition strategy of asserting equivalence in visual form the 'Nusantara concept of culture'.[25] The intended message of these 'comparisons', he writes, is to assert: 'We are distinctive as a province, but we are one with the rest of the archipelago.'[26]

NOTES

1. *Imagined Communities: Reflections on the Origin and Spread of Nationalism*, rev. and extended edn, London: Verso, 1991.

2. Ibid. p. 26.

3. Ibid., pp. 20, 22.

4. The term 'exemplary center' is Clifford Geertz's; see especially his *Negara: The Theatre State in Nineteenth-Century Bali*, Princeton: Princeton University Press, 1980.

5. Benedict Anderson's 'Cartoons and Monuments: The Evolution of Political Communication under the New Order', in *Language and Power: Exploring Political Cultures in Indonesia*, 94–120, Ithaca, N.Y.: Cornell University Press, 1990, inspired reflection on the relations between monuments, ideas about history, kitsch, and Suharto's New Order in several Indonesianists. One such is Timothy Lindsey's 'Concrete Ideology: Taste, Tradition, and the Javanese Past in New Order Public Space, in *Culture and Society in New Order Indonesia*, ed. Virginia Matheson-Hooker, 166–82, Kuala Lumpur and New York: Oxford University Press, 1993. Both Anderson and Lindsey are clearly referring to the kind of architecture I call 'Hybrid fantasy', with its shorthand references, but they use somewhat different for it and trace its genealogy and associations differently.

6. *Learning from Las Vegas*, Cambridge, Mass.: MIT Press.

7. Ibid., p. 163; see also pp. 87–103.

8. See Alexander Scobie, *Hitler's State Architecture: The Impact of Classical Antiquity*, University Park: Published for the College Art Association of America by the Pennsylvania State University Press, 1990, p. 87, and David Watkin and Tilman Mellinghoff, *German Architecture and the Classical Ideal*, Cambridge, Mass.: MIT Press, 1987.

9. 'Recollections from "Beautiful Indonesia": Somewhere Beyond the Postmodern', *Public Culture* 6(2), 1994, p. 249.

10. *Nations and Nationalism*, Oxford: Basil Blackwell, 1983, pp. 139–40.

11. 'The Census, Social Structure, and Objectification in South Asia', in *An Anthropologist among the Historians and Other Essays*, New York: Oxford University Press, 1987.

12. See Orvar Löfgren, 'Materializing the Nation in Sweden and America', *Ethnos* (2–4), 1993, pp. 161–96, and Tamas Hofer, 'Construction of "Folk Cultural Heritage"', *Ethnologia Europaica* 21(2), 1991, pp. 145–70.

13. The most comprehensible and readable summary and analysis of the symbols of traditional houses is Roxana Waterson's *The Living House: An Anthropology of Architecture in South-East Asia*,

Singapore: Oxford University Press, 1990; it draws on and cites the many classic articles on the topic, which is well studied in Southeast Asia.

14. *The Way of the Masks*, trans. Sylvia Modelski, Seattle: University of Washington Press, 1982.

15. Shelly Errington, 'The Cosmic House of the Buginese', *Asia* 1(5), 1979, pp. 8–14.

16. As, in theory in least, is the structure of the bureaucracy; but see Paul Taylor, 'The Nusantara Concept of Culture: Local Traditions and National Identity as Expressed in Indonesia's Museums', in *Fragile Traditions: Indonesian Art in Jeopardy*, ed. Paul Taylor, Honolulu: University of Hawaii Press, 1994, pp. 71–90.

17. J. Prijotomo, *Ideas and Forms of Javanese Architecture*, Yogyakarta: Gadjah Mada University Press, 1984.

18. 'Concrete Ideology: Taste, Tradition and the Javanese Past in New Order Public Space', in *Culture and Society in New Order Indonesia*, ed. Virginia Matheson Hooker, Kuala Lumpure and New York: Oxford University Press, 1993, p. 167.

19. See John Pemberton, *On the Subject of 'Java'*, Ithaca, N.Y.: Cornell University Press, 1994.

20. Ibid., p. 152.

21. Ibid., p. 160.

22. Peter Burke, *Popular Culture in Early Modern Europe*, New York: Harper Torchbooks, 1978, p. 3.

23. Löfgren, 'Materializing the Nation', p. 163.

24. In *Imagined Communities*.

25. In 'The Nusantara Concept of Culture'.

26. Ibid., p. 81.

IV.

Observing Subjects/Disciplining Practice

Introduction:
Observing Subjects/Disciplining Practice

> In the same process that constructs the world as view, man is constructed as
> subject.   Martin Heidegger, *The Age of the World Picture*

The question of 'who gets to represent what to who', as Craig Clunas puts it
in his essay 'China in Britain: the Imperial Collections' (included here),
constitutes the framework of the present chapter as well as of Chapter 6.
While such a question may have become particularly acute recently in a
number of countries as public governmental support of museums has given
way to the implicit and explicit constraints and demands of private and
corporate sponsorship, it has nonetheless underlain the entire history of
modern museological theory and practice, not to speak of that of the art
world as a whole, including art history and criticism. This has been both
explicit and implicit in the texts and commentaries of the four previous
chapters as well.

The essays collected in the present chapter address a number of fundamental aspects of modern museological stagecraft – the ways in which the
world came to be envisioned and *grasped*: the methods of exhibition, display,
and spectatorship alternatively referred to as an exhibitionary 'complex'
(Bennett), an exhibitionary 'order' (Mitchell), or as a facet of the 'constructed
space' of modern subjects (Hirst), these 'heterotopic' or 'other' spaces
(Foucault) having as their *raison d'être* the 'management of consciousness'
(Haacke). In a complementary manner, the essays in the final (sixth) chapter
below address evolving modes of inclusion and exclusion in museological
practices as well as changing attitudes toward the possibilities and impossibilities of representation itself.

In the essay included below, Craig Clunas observes that

'art' is not a category in the sense of a pre-existent container filled with different
contents as history progresses. Rather it is a way of categorising, a manner of
making knowledge which has been applied to a wider and wider set of
manifestations of material culture, paralleling the constant expansion of an 'art
market' applied to a wider and wider range of commodities.

As the essays and commentaries in the previous chapters have demonstrated
and argued, the art of art history and criticism is simultaneously a taxonomic
construct and a method or epistemological technology for producing knowledge
about peoples, places, and historical periods, and in particular the mentalities

and values taken to be characteristic of these. As Hans Haacke puts it with exemplary lucidity in the text included here ('Museums: Managers of Consciousness'), 'The art world as a whole, and museums in particular, belong to what has aptly been called "the consciousness industry".' As he has argued both in this and other texts no less than in his artistic, exhibitionary, and site-specific critical practices, museums today are above all in the business of molding and channeling consciousness as well as of creating and fostering a climate supporting prevailing distributions of power and capital, persuading the populace that 'the status quo is the natural and best order of things'.

Every museum, he argues, 'is perforce a political institution, no matter whether it is privately run or maintained and supervised by governmental agencies', and of course political considerations play important roles in the hiring and firing of curators, directors, and other personnel by boards of trustees made up almost invariably of corporate business executives for whom, as Haacke puts it, 'the term "culture" camouflages the social and political consequences resulting from the industrial distribution of consciousness'. He also argues that museological claims to canons of impartial scholarship suffer from idealist delusions about the 'nonpartisan' or non-socially-constructed character of consciousness.

Haacke's insights about the 'industrial character' of the modern manufacture of consciousness echo a long tradition of social critique accompanying the rise of modernity and the disciplinary institutions of the nation-state, as so powerfully addressed in the work of Michel Foucault. The latter's 1967 lecture, published in 1984 ('Of Other Spaces'), itself central to the work of Tony Bennett (whose essay 'The Exhibitionary Complex' is included below), puts forward the notion of the 'heterotopia' which may allow us to consider the space of the museum as occupying a complex, ambivalent space – a 'placeless place' that is neither utopian nor real but (to use a more contemporary term) virtual.

A museum, if one follows Foucault's argument, might be understood as a mirror-like entity which is simultaneously real and unreal, 'exert[ing] a sort of counteraction on the position that I occupy', galvanizing the processes of identification and subjectivity through inversion, contradiction, and implication. As he puts it in speaking of the mirror as heterotopia, 'from the standpoint of the mirror I discover my absence from the place where I am since I see myself over there ... [The mirror] makes this place that I occupy at the moment when I look at myself in the glass at once absolutely real, connected with all the space that surrounds it, and absolutely unreal, since in order to be perceived it has to pass through this virtual point which is over there.'

In a similar sense, the unreality or virtual reality of museological space can be said to support the 'real' space of daily life as its foundation and underpinning – a space of otherness that constitutes the delimitation of identity, as may also be familiar in the Lacanian psychoanalytic concept of the 'mirror phase' in the formation of selfhood, where (and when) the child first comes to 'envision' itself as an organic whole through its reflection in a mirror or in other things. One's authenticity is grounded in the artifice of what we construe as its 'reflection'.

For Foucault, heterotopias come into their fullest development when a society begins to articulate its break with traditional time, and they constitute powerful technological instruments for bridging that chasm. Whereas until the end of the seventeenth century museums and libraries were the expressions of individual taste and choice, Foucault argues, a different regime is proper to Western culture by the nineteenth century. Museums and libraries have become 'heterotopias' in which time never stops building up and topping its own summit. 'Belonging to our modernity' was:

the idea of accumulating everything, of establishing a sort of general archive, the will to enclose in one place all times, all epochs, all forms, all tastes, the idea of constituting a place of all times that is itself outside of time and inaccessible to its ravages, the project of organizing in this way a sort of perpetual and indefinite accumulation of time in an immobile place …

Perhaps one of the most important aspects of Foucault's notion of the heterotopia was the way in which it made it possible to critically juxtapose as complementarily heterotopic spaces, places and practices of apparently starkly differing things – trains, vacation villages, brothels, cemeteries, honeymoon motels, places reserved in certain traditional societies for menstruation, theme parks, college campuses, prisons, gardens, ships, retirement communities, colonies, museums …

In all of the essays in this chapter, the 'conditions of viewing' objects are construed as constitutive of those objects in much more than incidental or accidental ways, and these conditions form part of a web of complex structures of what Paul Hirst, following Foucault, calls discursive formations, that is, practices in which objects, entities, and activities are defined and constructed. Hirst's text included here, 'Power/Knowledge – Constructed Space and the Subject', is a lucid introduction to some basic Foucauldian concepts, illuminated by two examples of what he calls 'the ways in which social agents are constituted as persons with certain definite attributes and capacities within certain forms of building/institution'.

His two examples of subjectification, the centrally planned church in Renaissance Italy and the modern penitentiary prison, are taken from the context of Foucault's works, especially *The Order of Things*, *The Archaeology of Knowledge*, *Discipline and Punish*, and Volume 1 of *The History of Sexuality*. Hirst argues that the architecture of churches and of penitentiaries is a practice that is not merely of building but one of *transformation* – the transformation and 'construction' of human subjects, in a manner we would argue parallels museological practice and the stagecraft and dramaturgy of museums. The essay is situated here after Foucault's text on heterotopias and may serve to introduce some of the conceptual backgrounds against which the subsequent essays in this chapter may be read.

Appearing in the same year as Foucault's essay, the strong reputation of André Malraux's largely celebratory book *Museum without Walls* was created by hindsight as it came to be cited by art historians in the early years of critical writing about museums and museology. Malraux's virtual museum – what he called the 'imaginary' museum, made up of the sum of countless reproductions circulated in modern societies – contrasted with the limited resources of 'real' museums. As he put it, 'A museum without walls has been opened to us, and it will carry infinitely farther that limited revelation of the world of art which the real museums offer us within their walls.' It may be useful to compare Malraux's 'museum without walls' to Quatremère de Quincy's views of the city of Rome as the 'ultimate series of all series' of works of art of all times and places, discussed above in Chapter 1.

Tony Bennett's widely influential essay 'The Exhibitionary Complex' is deeply indebted to Foucauldian perspectives in a variety of ways, and indeed his 1995 book *The Birth of the Museum* begins with Foucault's definition of heterotopias and the paragraph just quoted above. For Bennett, that work provided an important way of clarifying the terms of the modernist opposition between transitory and fleeting social spaces such as fairs and amusement parks and more permanent and officially sanctioned museum institutions, an opposition that formed the major thrust of his book, whose second chapter reprinted the essay included here.

Bennett's text clarifies the fundamental problem to which the 'swarming of [modern] disciplinary mechanisms' (including here the museum) responded – namely, that of making large and diverse populations governable. He argues that 'the development of bourgeois democratic polities required not merely that the populace be governable but that it assent to its governance'. Museums evolved in modern nation-states as institutions whose hold over their publics depended upon their voluntary participation. This reiterates issues we have seen above in Chapter 1, in connection with the founding of the Louvre and the need to have the newly minted citizens of the Republic clearly understand the 'liberatory' character of the museum. Bennett connects the work of the museum to that of the ambitions of world exhibitions in the nineteenth century, which worked to 'render the whole world, as represented in assemblages of commodities [and in some instances of actual peoples in fairground 'native villages', as Bennett discusses], subordinate to the controlling vision of the spectator.' This 'specular dominance', was exquisitely crystallized by the Eiffel Tower, built for the 1889 Paris Exposition, which afforded 'an elevated vantage point over a micro-world which claimed to be representative of a larger totality'. The Tower's technology of vision was remarked upon by Roland Barthes in his collection of essays *The Eiffel Tower and Other Mythologies* (1979), most poignantly in a passage cited by Bennett:

An object when we look at it, becomes a lookout in its turn when we visit it, and now constitutes as an object, simultaneously extended and collected beneath it, that Paris which just now was looking at it.

Which we might associate both with the contents of any museum and with the museum itself as a modern institution.

The situation of *seeing and being seen* plays a prominent role in the next essay, by Timothy Mitchell, 'Orientalism and the Exhibitionary Order', which situates orientalism as 'a densely imbricated arrangement of imagery and expertise that organizes and produces the Orient as a political reality'. He sees orientalism not simply as a movement of one culture portraying another nor simply as an aspect of colonial domination, but as 'part of a method of order and truth essential to the peculiar nature of the modern world' – that is, as constitutive of the (Western) world which produced the Orient as an *effect*.

In his discussion of nineteenth-century Parisian exhibitions and the astonished reactions to them by Egyptians and other non-European visitors, Mitchell highlights the specificities of the modern European penchant for transforming the world into a representation or exhibition. The obsession with 'the organization of the view' entailed understanding the world as a system of objects whose very organization evoked some larger or deeper meaning or reality (the Spirit or Soul of a People or of a time and place, for example). That world demanded to be understood in terms of palpable distinctions between objects 'in themselves' and their 'meanings', a view compatible with an ethical view of the individual as represented in, as, and by his or her works. To inhabit such a world would be to live one's life as a tourist, *flâneur*, shopper, or anthropologist, in a dualistic universe characterized by distinctions between objects and meanings: 'representations' and the (perpetually elusive) 'realities' they portray or embody.

Mitchell's discussion of the establishment of the objectness of the (Islamic) Orient is complemented by Craig Clunas's presentation of the institutional framing of the (East Asian) Orient in the creation of the category of 'Chinese art' in British museums and academic institutions. He describes the gradual migration of Chinese objects from ethnographic collections to art museums and the gradual raising of the aesthetic and economic status of Chinese ceramics and other luxury commodities, and he describes the orientalist concentration on 'essences' which has pervaded the discourse on Chinese culture both in the West and elsewhere, where the art is taken as 'a reflection of essential and largely historically invariant characteristics of the "Chinese race"'. Clunas's essay considers the conditions of viewing objects as expressive of discourses of national and imperial identity.

The essays juxtaposed in this chapter link to those included both above and below both in terms of conceptual issues and the material and historical content discussed. In this regard, the present chapter recapitulates and places in the context of the modern nexus of power and knowledge many of the questions discussed earlier, and lays a groundwork for the case studies on the possibilities and impossibilities of museological representation contained in the final chapter.

1.

Introduction to Museum without Walls

André Malraux

A Romanesque crucifix was not regarded by its contemporaries as a work of sculpture; nor Cimabue's *Madonna* as a picture. Even Phidias' *Pallas Athene* was not, primarily, a statue.

So vital is the part played by the art museum in our approach to works of art today that we find it difficult to realize that no museums exist, none has ever existed, in lands where the civilization of modern Europe is, or was, unknown: and that, even in the Western world, they have existed for barely two hundred years. They were so important to the artistic life of the nineteenth century and are so much a part of our lives today that we forget they have imposed on the spectator a wholly new attitude toward the work of art. They have tended to estrange the works they bring together from their original functions and to transform even portraits into 'pictures'. Though a bust of Caesar or an equestrian statue of Charles V may remain for us Caesar and the Emperor Charles, *Count-Duke Olivares* has become pure Velazquez. What do we care who the *Man with the Helmet* or the *Man with the Glove* may have been in real life? For us, their names are Rembrandt and Titian. The portrait has ceased to be primarily a likeness of an individual. Until the nineteenth century a work of art was essentially a representation of something, real or imaginary. Only in the artist's eyes was painting specifically painting; and often, even to him, it was also a form of poetry. The effect of the museum is to suppress the model in almost every portrait (even that of a dream figure) and to divest works of art of their functions. It does away with the significance of Palladium, of saint and Savior; rules out associations of sanctity, qualities of adornment and possession, of likeness or imagination; and presents the viewer with images of things, differing from the things themselves, and drawing their *raison d'être* from this very difference. It is a confrontation of metamorphoses.

The reason the art museum made its appearance in Asia so belatedly (and, even then, only under European influence and patronage) is that, for an Asiatic, and especially the man of the Far East, artistic contemplation and the picture gallery are incompatible. In China, the full enjoyment of works of art necessarily involved ownership, except where religious art was concerned; above all it demanded their isolation. A painting was not exhibited, but unfurled before an art lover in a fitting state of grace; its function was to deepen and enhance his communion with the universe. The practice of confronting works of art with other works of art is an intellectual activity, and diametrically opposed to the mood of relaxation which alone makes contemplation possible. In Asiatic eyes, the museum may be a place of learning and teaching, but considered as anything else it is no more than an absurd concert in which contradictory themes are mingled and confused in an endless succession.

For over a century our approach to art has been growing more and more intellectualized. The museum invites comparison of each of the expressions of the world it brings together, and forces us to question what it is that brings them together. The sequence of seemingly antagonistic schools has added to the simple 'delight of the eye' an awareness of art's impassioned quest, of a re-creation of the universe, confronting the Creation. After all, a museum is one of the places that show man at his noblest. But our knowledge covers a wider field than our museums. The visitor to the Louvre knows that it contains no significant representation of either Goya or of the great English artists, of Piero della Francesca or of Grünewald, of the paintings of Michelangelo or even those of Vermeer. In a place where the work of art no longer has any function other than that of being a work of art, and at a time when the artistic exploration of the world is in active progress, the assemblage of so many masterpieces – from which, nevertheless, so many are missing – conjures up in the mind's eye *all* of the world's masterpieces. How indeed could this mutilated possible fail to evoke the whole gamut of the possible?

Of what is it necessarily deprived? Until the present, at least, of such things as stained glass and frescoes, which form part of a whole; of objects, such as sets of tapestries, which are difficult to display; of everything that cannot be moved or cannot be acquired. Even when the greatest zeal and enormous resources have gone into its making, a museum owes much to opportunities that chance has thrown its way. Napoleon's victories did not enable him to bring the Sistine to the Louvre, and no art patron, however wealthy, will take to the Metropolitan Museum the Royal Portal of Chartres or the Arezzo frescoes. From the eighteenth to the twentieth century what migrated was the portable, with the result that far more Rembrandt paintings than Giotto frescoes have been offered for sale. Thus the art museum, born when the easel picture was the one living form of art, came to be a museum not of color but of paintings; not of sculpture but of statues.

In the nineteenth century the 'grand tour' filled in the gaps left by the museums. But how many artists of the time were familiar with all of Europe's masterpieces? Gautier saw Italy (without seeing Rome) when he was thirty-nine; Edmond de Goncourt when he was thirty-three; Hugo as a child; Baudelaire and Verlaine, never. And yet Italy was the traditional heart of the 'tour'. They might have seen portions of Spain and Germany, and perhaps Holland; Flanders was relatively well known. The eager crowds that thronged the salons – composed largely of real connoisseurs – owed their art education to the Louvre. Baudelaire never set eyes on the masterpieces of El Greco, Michelangelo, Masaccio, Piero della Francesca, or Grünewald, Titian, or of Hals – or of Goya, though he had easy access to the Galerie d'Orléans. His *Phares* begins with the sixteenth century.

What had he seen? What, until 1900, had been seen by all those whose views on art still impress us as revealing and important; whom we take to be speaking of the same works, referring to the same sources, as those we know ourselves? Two or three of the great museums, and photographs, engravings, or copies of a handful of the masterpieces of European art. Most of their readers had seen even less. In the art knowledge of those days there existed an area of ambiguity: comparison of a picture in the Louvre with another in Madrid, in Florence, or in Rome was comparison of a present vision with a memory. Visual memory is not infallible, and successive periods of study were often separated by weeks of travel. From the seventeenth to the nineteenth century, pictures, interpreted by engraving, had *become* engravings; they had retained their drawing (at least relatively) but lost their colors, which were replaced by an interpretation in black and white; also, while losing their dimensions, they acquired margins. The nineteenth-century photograph was merely a more faithful print. The art lover of the time knew pictures in the same manner as we knew mosaics and stained-glass windows in the years preceding World War II.

Today, an art student can examine color reproductions of most of the world's great paintings and discover for himself a host of secondary works, as well as the archaic arts, the great epochs of Indian, Chinese, Japanese, and pre-Columbian sculpture, some Byzantine art, Romanesque frescoes, and primitive and 'folk' art. How many statues could be seen in reproduction in 1850? Since sculpture can be reproduced in black and white more faithfully than painting, our contemporary art books have found in it a realm in which they are eminently successful. At one time, the student visited the Louvre and some subsidiary galleries and memorized what he saw as best he could. We, however, have far more great works available to refresh our memories than even the greatest of museums could bring together.

A museum without walls has been opened to us, and it will carry infinitely farther that limited revelation of the world of art which the real museums offer us within their walls: in answer to their appeal, the plastic arts have produced their printing press.

2.

Texts/Contexts: Of Other Spaces

Michel Foucault

The great obsession of the nineteenth century was, as we know, history with its themes of development and of suspension, of crisis and cycle, themes of the ever-accumulating past, with its great preponderance of dead men and the menacing glaciation of the world. The nineteenth century found its essential mythological resources in the second principle of thermodynamics. The present epoch will perhaps be above all the epoch of space. We are in the epoch of simultaneity: we are in the epoch of juxtaposition, the epoch of the near and far, of the side-by-side, of the dispersed. We are at a moment, I believe, when our experience of the world is less that of a long life developing through time than that of a network that connects points and intersects with its own skein. One could perhaps say that certain ideological conflicts animating present-day polemics oppose the pious descendents of time and the determined inhabitants of space. Structuralism, or at least that which is grouped under this slightly too general name, is the effort to establish, between elements that could have been connected on a temporal axis, an ensemble of relations that makes them appear as juxtaposed, set off against one another, implicated by each other – that makes them appear, in short, as a sort of configuration. Actually, structuralism does not entail a denial of time; it does involve a certain manner of dealing with what we call time and what we call history.

Yet it is necessary to notice that the space which today appears to form the horizon of our concerns, our theory, our systems, is not an innovation; space itself has a history in Western experience and it is not possible to disregard the fatal intersection of time with space. One could say, by way of retracing this history of space very roughly, that in the Middle Ages there was a hierarchic ensemble of places: sacred places and profane places; protected places and open, exposed places; urban places and rural places (all these concern the real life of men). In cosmological theory, there were the supercelestial places, as opposed to the celestial, and the celestial place was in its turn opposed to the terrestrial place. There were places where things had been put because they had been violently displaced, and then on the contrary places where things found their natural ground and stability. It was this complete hierarchy, this opposition, this intersection of places that constituted what could very roughly be called medieval space: the space of emplacement.

This space of emplacement was opened up by Galileo. For the real scandal of Galileo's work lay not so much in his discovery, or rediscovery, that the earth revolved around the sun, but in his constitution of an infinite, and infinitely open space. In such a space the place of the Middle Ages turned out to be dissolved, as it were; a thing's place was no longer anything but a point in its movement, just as the stability of a thing was only its movement indefinitely slowed down. In other words, starting with Galileo and the seventeenth century, extension was substituted for localization.

Today the site has been substituted for extension which itself had replaced emplacement. The site is defined by relations of proximity between points or elements; formally, we can describe these relations as series, trees, or grids. Moreover, the importance of the site as a problem in contemporary technical work is well known: the storage of data or of the intermediate results of a calculation in the memory of a machine; the circulation of discrete elements with a random output (automobile traffic is a simple case, or indeed the sounds on a telephone line); the identification of marked or coded elements inside a set that may be randomly distributed, or may be arranged according to single or to multiple classifications.

In a still more concrete manner, the problem of siting or placement arises for mankind in terms of demography. This problem of the human site or living space is not simply that of knowing whether there will be enough space for men in the world – a problem that is certainly quite important – but also that of knowing what relations of propinquity, what type of storage, circulation, marking, and classification of human elements should be adopted in a given situation in order to achieve a given end. Our epoch is one in which space takes for us the form of relations among sites.

In any case I believe that the anxiety of our era has to do fundamentally with space, no doubt a great deal more than with time. Time probably appears to us only as one of the various distributive operations that are possible for the elements that are spread out in space.

Now, despite all the techniques for appropriating space, despite the whole network of knowledge that enables us to delimit or to formalize it, contemporary space is perhaps still not entirely desanctified (apparently unlike time, it would seem, which was detached from the sacred in the nineteenth century). To be sure a certain theoretical desanctification of space (the one signaled by Galileo's work) has occurred, but we may still not have reached the point of a practical desanctification of space. And perhaps our life is still governed by a certain number of oppositions that remain inviolable, that our institutions and practices have not yet dared to break down. These are oppositions that we regard as simple givens: for example between private space and public space, between family space and social space, between cultural space and useful space, between the space of leisure and that of work. All these are still nurtured by the hidden presence of the sacred.

Bachelard's monumental work and the descriptions of phenomenologists have taught us that we do not live in a homogeneous and empty space, but on the contrary in a space thoroughly imbued with quantities and perhaps thoroughly fantasmatic as well. The space of our primary perception, the space of our dreams and that of our passions hold within themselves qualities that seem intrinsic: there is a light, ethereal, transparent space, or again a dark, rough, encumbered space; a space from above, of summits, or on the contrary a space from below, of mud; or again a space that can be flowing like sparkling water, or a space that is fixed, congealed, like stone or crystal. Yet these analyses, while fundamental for reflection in our time, primarily concern internal space. I should like to speak now of external space.

The space in which we live, which draws us out of ourselves, in which the erosion of our lives, our time and our history occurs, the space that claws and gnaws at us, is also, in itself, a heterogeneous space. In other words, we do not live in a kind of void, inside of which we could place individuals and things. We do not live inside a void that could be colored with diverse shades of light, we live inside a set of relations that delineates sites which are irreducible to one another and absolutely not superimposable on one another.

Of course one might attempt to describe these different sites by looking for the set of relations by which a given site can be defined. For example, describing the set of relations that define the sites of transportation, streets, trains (a train is an extraordinary bundle of relations because it is something through which one goes, it is also something by means of which one can go from one point to another, and then it is also something that goes by). One could describe, via the cluster of relations that allows them to be defined, the sites of temporary relaxation – cafes, cinemas, beaches. Likewise one could describe, via its network of relations, the closed or semi-closed sites of rest – the house, the bedroom, the bed, etcetera. But among all these sites, I am interested in certain ones that have the curious property of being in relation with all the other sites, but in such a way as to suspect, neutralize, or invert the set of relations that they happen to designate, mirror, or reflect. These spaces, as it were, which are linked with all the others, which however contradict all the other sites, are of two main types.

First there are the utopias. Utopias are sites with no real place. They are sites that have a general relation of direct or inverted analogy with the real space of Society. They present society itself in a perfected form, or else society turned upside down, but in any case these utopias are fundamentally unreal spaces.

There are also, probably in every culture, in every civilization, real places – places that do exist and that are formed in the very founding of society – which are something like counter-sites, a kind of effectively enacted utopia in which the real sites, all the other real sites that can be found within the culture, are simultaneously represented, contested, and inverted. Places of this kind are outside of all places, even though it may be possible to indicate their location in reality. Because these places are absolutely different from all the sites that they reflect and speak about, I shall call them, by way of contrast to utopias, heterotopias. I believe that between utopias and these quite other sites, these heterotopias, there might be a sort of mixed, joint experience, which would be the mirror. The mirror is, after all, a utopia, since it is a placeless place. In the mirror, I see myself there where I am not, in an unreal, virtual space that opens up behind the surface; I am over there, there where I am not, a sort of shadow that gives my own visibility to myself, that enables me to see myself there where I am absent: such is the utopia of the mirror. But it is also a heterotopia in so far as the mirror does exist in reality, where it exerts a sort of counteraction on the position that I occupy. From the standpoint of the mirror I discover my absence from the place where I am since I see myself over there. Starting from this gaze that is, as it were, directed toward me, from the ground of this virtual space that is on the other side of the glass, I come back toward myself; I begin again to direct my eyes toward myself and to reconstitute myself there where I am. The mirror functions as a heterotopia in this respect: it makes this place that I occupy at the moment when I look at myself in the glass at once absolutely real, connected with all the space that surrounds it, and absolutely unreal, since in order to be perceived it has to pass through this virtual point which is over there.

As for the heterotopias as such, how can they be described, what meaning do they have? We might imagine a sort of systematic description – I do not say a science because the term is too galvanized now – that would, in a given society, take as its object the study, analysis, description, and 'reading' (as some like to say nowadays) of these different spaces, of these other places. As a sort of simultaneously mythic and real contestation of the space in which we live, this description could be called heterotopology. Its *first principle* is that there is probably not a single culture in the world that fails to constitute heterotopias. That is a constant of every human group. But the heterotopias obviously take quite varied forms, and perhaps no one absolutely universal form of heterotopia would be found. We can however classify them in two main categories.

In the so-called primitive societies, there is a certain form of heterotopia that I would call crisis heterotopias, i.e., there are privileged or sacred or forbidden places, reserved for individuals who are, in relation to society and to the human environment in which they live, in a state of crisis: adolescents, menstruating women, pregnant women, the elderly, etc. In our society, these crisis heterotopias are persistently disappearing, though a few remnants can still be found. For example, the boarding school, in its nineteenth-century form, or military service for young men, have certainly played such a role, as the first manifestations of sexual virility were in fact supposed to take place 'elsewhere' than at home. For girls, there was, until the middle of the twentieth century, a tradition called the 'honeymoon trip' which was an ancestral theme. The young woman's deflowering could take place 'nowhere' and, at the moment of its occurrence the train or honeymoon hotel was indeed the place of this nowhere, this heterotopia without geographical markers.

But these heterotopias of crisis are disappearing today and are being replaced, I believe, by what we might call heterotopias of deviation: those in which individuals whose behavior is deviant in relation to the required mean or norm are placed. Cases of this are rest homes and psychiatric hospitals, and of course prisons; and one should perhaps add retirement homes that are, as it were, on the borderline between the heterotopia of crisis and the heterotopia of deviation since, after all, old age is a crisis, but is also a deviation since, in our society where leisure is the rule, idleness is a sort of deviation.

The *second principle* of this description of heterotopias is that a society, as its history unfolds, can make an existing heterotopia function in a very different fashion; for each heterotopia has a precise and determined function within a society and the same heterotopia can, according to the synchrony of the culture in which it occurs, have one function or another.

As an example I shall take the strange heterotopia of the cemetery. The cemetery is certainly a place unlike ordinary cultural spaces. It is a space that is however connected with all the sites of the citystate or society or village, etc., since each individual, each family has relatives in the cemetery. In Western culture the cemetery has practically always existed. But it has undergone important changes. Until the end of the eighteenth century, the cemetery was placed at the heart of the city, next to the church. In it there was a hierarchy of possible tombs. There was the charnel house in which bodies lost the last traces of individuality, there were a few individual tombs and then there were the tombs inside the church. These latter tombs were themselves of two types, either simply tombstones with an inscription, or mausoleums with statues. This cemetery housed inside the sacred space of the church has taken on a quite different cast in modern civilizations, and curiously, it is in a time when civilization has become 'atheistic', as one says very crudely, that Western culture has established what is termed the cult of the dead.

Basically it was quite natural that, in a time of real belief in the resurrection of bodies and the immortality of the soul, overriding importance was not accorded to the body's remains. On the contrary, from the moment when people are no longer sure that they have a soul or that the body will regain life, it is perhaps necessary to give much more attention to the dead body, which is ultimately the only trace of our existence in the world and in language. In any case, it is from the beginning of the nineteenth century that everyone has a right to her or his own little box for her or his own little personal decay; but on the other hand, it is only from that start of the nineteenth century that cemeteries began to be located at the outside border of cities. In correlation with the individualization of death and the bourgeois appropriation of the cemetery, there arises an obsession with death as an 'illness'. The dead, it is supposed, bring illnesses to the living, and it is the presence and proximity of the dead right beside the houses, next to the church, almost in the middle of the street, it is this proximity that propagates death itself. This major theme of illness spread by the contagion in the cemeteries persisted until the end of the eighteenth century, until, during the nineteenth century, the shift of cemeteries toward the suburbs was initiated. The cemeteries then came to constitute, no longer the sacred and immortal heart of the city, but 'the other city', where each family possesses its dark resting place.

Third principle. The heterotopia is capable of juxtaposing in a single real place several spaces, several sites that are in themselves incompatible. Thus it is that the theater brings onto the rectangle of the stage, one after the other, a whole series of places that are foreign to one another; thus it is that the cinema is a very odd rectangular room, at the end of which, on a two-dimensional screen, one sees the projection of a three-dimensional space; but perhaps the oldest example of these heterotopias that take the form of contradictory sites is the garden. We must not forget that in the Orient the garden, an astonishing creation that is now a thousand years old, had very deep and seemingly superimposed meanings. The traditional garden of the Persians was a sacred space that was supposed to bring together inside its rectangle four parts representing the four parts of the world, with a space still more sacred than the others that were like an umbilicus, the navel of the world at its center (the basin and water fountain were there); and all the vegetation of the garden was supposed to come together in this space, in this sort of microcosm. As for carpets, they were originally reproductions of gardens (the garden is a rug onto which the whole world comes to enact its symbolic perfection, and the rug is a sort of garden that can move across space). The garden is the smallest parcel of the world and then it is the totality of the world. The garden has been a sort of happy, universalizing heterotopia since the beginnings of antiquity (our modern zoological gardens spring from that source).

Fourth principle. Heterotopias are most often linked to slices in time – which is to say that they open onto what might be termed, for the sake of symmetry, heterochronies. The heterotopia begins to function at full capacity when men arrive at a sort of absolute break with their traditional time. This situation shows us that the cemetery is indeed a highly heterotopic place since, for the individual, the cemetery begins with this strange heterochrony, the loss of life, and with this quasi-eternity in which her permanent lot is dissolution and disappearance.

From a general standpoint, in a society like ours heterotopias and heterochronies are structured and distributed in a relatively complex fashion. First of all, there are heterotopias of indefinitely accumulating time, for example museums and libraries. Museums and libraries have become heterotopias in which time never stops building up and topping its own summit, whereas in the seventeenth century, even at the end of the century, museums and libraries were the expression of an individual choice. By contrast, the idea of accumulating everything, of establishing a sort of general archive, the will to enclose in one place all times, all epochs, all forms, all tastes, the idea of constituting a place of all times that is itself outside of time and inaccessible to its ravages, the project of organizing in this way a sort of perpetual and indefinite accumulation of time in an immobile place, this whole idea belongs to our modernity. The museum and the library are heterotopias that are proper to Western culture of the nineteenth century.

Opposite these heterotopias that are linked to the accumulation of time, there are those linked, on the contrary, to time in its most fleeting, transitory, precarious aspect, to time in the mode of the festival. These heterotopias are not oriented toward the eternal, they are rather absolutely temporal [*chroniques*]. Such, for example, are the fairgrounds, these marvelous empty sites on the outskirts of cities that teem once or twice a year with stands, displays, heteroclite objects, wrestlers, snakewomen, fortune-tellers, and so forth. Quite recently, a new kind of temporal heterotopia has been invented: vacation villages, such as those Polynesian villages that offer a compact three weeks of primitive and eternal nudity to the inhabitants of the cities.

You see, moreover, that through the two forms of heterotopias that come together here, the heterotopia of the festival and that of the eternity of accumulating time, the huts of Djerba are in a sense relatives of libraries and museums. For the rediscovery of Polynesian life abolishes time; yet the experience is just as much the rediscovery of time, it is as if the entire history of humanity reaching back to its origin were accessible in a sort of immediate knowledge.

Fifth principle. Heterotopias always presuppose a system of opening and closing that both isolates them and makes them penetrable. In general, the heterotopic site is not freely accessible like a public place. Either the entry is compulsory, as in the case of entering a barracks or a prison, or else the individual has to submit to rites and purifications. To get in one must have a certain permission and make certain gestures. Moreover, there are even heterotopias that are entirely consecrated to these activities of purification–purification that is partly religious and partly hygienic, such as the hamman of the Moslems, or else purification that appears to be purely hygienic, as in Scandinavian saunas.

There are others, on the contrary, that seem to be pure and simple openings, but that generally hide curious exclusions. Everyone can enter into these heterotopic sites, but in fact that is only an illusion: we think we enter where we are, by the very fact that we enter, excluded. I am thinking, for example, of the famous bedrooms that existed on the great farms of Brazil and elsewhere in South America. The entry door did not lead into the central room where the family lived, and every individual or traveler who came by had the right to open this door, to enter into the bedroom and to sleep there for a night. Now these bedrooms were such that the individual who went into them never had access to the family's quarters; the visitor was absolutely the guest in transit, was not really the invited guest. This type of heterotopia, which has practically disappeared from our civilizations, could perhaps be found in the famous American motel rooms where a man goes with his car and his mistress and where illicit sex is both absolutely sheltered and absolutely hidden, kept isolated without however being allowed out in the open.

The last trait of heterotopias is that they have a function in relation to all the space that remains. This function unfolds between two extreme poles. Either their role is to create a space of illusion that exposes every real space, all the sites inside of which human life is partitioned, as still more illusory (perhaps that is the role that was played by those famous brothels of which we are now deprived). Or else, on the contrary, their role is to create a space that is other, another real space, as perfect, as meticulous, as well arranged as ours is messy, ill constructed, and jumbled. This latter type would be the heterotopia, not of illusion, but of compensation, and I wonder if certain colonies have not functioned somewhat in this manner. In certain cases, they have played, on the level of the general organization of terrestrial space, the role of heterotopias. I am thinking, for example, of the first wave of colonization in the seventeenth century, of the Puritan societies that the English had founded in America and that were absolutely perfect other places. I am also thinking of those extraordinary Jesuit colonies that were founded in South America: marvelous, absolutely regulated colonies in which human perfection was effectively achieved. The Jesuits of Paraguay established colonies in which existence was regulated at every turn. The village was laid out according to a rigorous plan around a rectangular place at the foot of which was the church; on one side, there was the school; on the other, the cemetery; and then, in front of the church, an avenue set out that another crossed at right angles; each family had its little cabin along these two axes and thus the sign of Christ was exactly reproduced. Christianity marked the space and geography of the American world with its fundamental sign. The daily life of individuals was regulated, not by the whistle, but by the bell. Everyone was awakened at the same time, everyone began work at the same time; meals were at noon and five o'clock; then came bedtime, and at midnight came what was called the marital wake-up, that is, at the chime of the churchbell, each person carried out her/his duty.

Brothels and colonies are two extreme types of heterotopia, and if we think after all, that the boat is a floating piece of space, a place without a place, that exists by itself, that is closed in on itself and at the same time is given over to the infinity of the sea and that, from port to port, from tack to tack, from brothel to brothel, it goes as far as the colonies in search of the most precious treasures they conceal in their gardens, you will understand why the boat has not only been for our civilization, from the sixteenth century until the present, the great instrument of economic development (I have not been speaking of that today), but has been simultaneously the greatest reserve of the imagination. The ship is the heterotopia *par excellence*. In civilizations without boats, dreams dry up, espionage takes the place of adventure, and the police take the place of pirates.

Translated from the French by Jay Miskowiec

3.

Power/Knowledge – Constructed Space and the Subject

Paul Q. Hirst

Spatial relations and their significance have long been of interest to anthropologists. At least since Durkheim and Mauss' *Primitive Classification* spatial relations and the distribution of constructions have been examined as embodying patterns of belief in respect of the social and natural worlds. A large literature exists on the layout and style of domestic housing, of which *Architecture Comparée* (1982) is a notable example. Architecture in Western societies presents a more challenging problem, for since the Renaissance it has presented itself as a rationalised and technical practice with its own history of developing solutions to technical, constructional and stylistic problems. Western architecture is part of the intellectual and cultural history of 'modernity', it separates itself from popular belief and vernacular practice in creating its own distinct structures as answers to problems within its own discourse and in relation to the increasingly differentiated demands of a technically sophisticated and market-oriented society. Nobody would consider either architectural theory or constructional practice as merely a branch of applied science, but in so far as we introduce cultural and stylistic consider-ations they too appear to be part of a distinct and continuous history quite different from the traditional beliefs of non-Western peoples. This history is properly considered the province of a distinct academic specialism, the history of ideas, rather than of anthropology. Urban sociology and the economics of built environments offer means of analysis within the social sciences of important aspects of the constructed spaces of capitalism and industrialism. Likewise a large literature exists on the social and psychological consequences of building types. But 'style' remains the province of aesthetics and the history of ideas.

The answer to this situation does not lie in a rigid separation of 'primitivism' and 'modernity' – accepting the architect as an 'engineer' and leaving to the anthropologist the edifices of the 'bricoleur' – nor can it consist in examining modern architecture as embodying 'beliefs' on the model of Durkheim, for it is the nature of the beliefs of the architect which are in question. I want to argue that the work of Michel Foucault offers an approach to the analysis of architecture as constructed space which breaks up the division of analysis into that appropriate to the history of ideas, the evolution of styles and constructional techniques, and that appropriate to the social sciences. This is because Foucault's work offers both a challenge to the conventional modes of analysis of the history of ideas and a means of treating architecture as at once an intellectual discourse and a social practice.[1] Further, it is of value to the social sciences because it offers an analysis of the forms of subjectification involved in modern constructed spaces – the ways in which social agents are constituted as persons with certain definite attributes and capacities within certain forms of building/ institution.

I will use two examples of such forms of subjectification – that proposed in the centrally planned church in the Italian Renaissance and that proposed for the modern penitentiary prison. These examples are not arbitrary. They are drawn from the context of Foucault's works. The former from his earlier analyses in *The Order of Things* and *The Archaeology of Knowledge* and the latter from his later works, *Discipline and Punish* and *The History of Sexuality, Vol. I*. The earlier works show us how his analysis of 'discursive formations' enables us to overcome the limitations of the history of ideas and examine in a new way the relationship between discourse, buildings and their social relations. The later works explicitly consider the prison as the exemplar of a new relationship between power and knowledge which develops at the beginning of the industrial era. The concept of power/knowledge enables us to pose the social consequences of architectural discourse and practice in a new way. These examples are also strategic in that they link crucial phases in the history of architecture as an autonomous discipline in the West, the rise of an 'intellectual' architecture in the Renaissance, in large measure confined within 'high culture', and the development of practices of construction attuned to the increasingly differentiated institutional spaces and purposes of industrial society.

A.   The statement and constructed space

The Archaeology of Knowledge is of interest in the analysis of the significance and social relations of constructed space because it broadens and transforms the concept of 'discourse'. *The Archaeology of Knowledge* occupies a similar theoretical space to the traditional history of ideas, but transforms it and goes beyond it. It offers the prospect of a less 'intellectualist' mode of analysis of broader application to social relations and products of a wide range of practices. 'Discursive formations' are patterns of order in statements quite distinct from the familiar unities of the history of ideas, authors, books, schools, etc. Foucault's vocabulary and method disposes of much of the supposed intellectual apparatus of the history of ideas. First and foremost it challenges the concept of 'idea' itself and its location in the 'mind' of a subject. Further it challenges the notion of 'influences' whereby ideas pass from subject to subject and undergo subtle transformations in new minds. 'Discursive formations' extend analysis beyond that product of the age of humanism, the 'author', and beyond the provinces of 'humane' learning.

Central to Foucault's category of 'discourse' is the concept of 'statement' – discourse is conceived as forms of order and inclusion/exclusion of statements. He defines the statement in a way that separates it very clearly from either a sentence or a proposition. Statements are not 'discursive' in the narrow sense of being linguistic or found merely in books. To give an example, consider the tabular form of presentation. A table as a statement can be more than a convenient visual device illustrating an otherwise 'discursive' text. Indeed, the 'table' can be a crucial and constitutive form of order in a discursive formation itself. Consider, for example, physiocratic economics. Quesnay's *Le Tableau Economique* constructs the economy as a totality of interrelated transactions between agriculture and the other non-productive sectors. A totality which is conceived and presented spatially. Such forms are no relic of the eighteenth century but can be encountered in transformed and highly mathematicised types of analysis such as Leontief's input-output matrix. Again we encounter in the eighteenth century other distinctly 'tabular' discourses, such as the classificatory natural history of Buffon and Linnaeus. Here the whole of living nature is regarded as a series of places, an order – conventional or natural – into which all living beings can be situated, as part of one exhaustive description/classification. This discursive order exists beyond books, in the systematic layout of museums and collections, in the practices of observing and classifying living beings themselves. In like manner, buildings or groups of structures can be regarded as 'statements', and their relations to discourses specified.

Foucault is concerned to remove the concepts of 'statement' and 'discourse' from the ghetto of 'ideas', to demonstrate that discursive formations may be regarded as complex structures of discourse-practice, in which objects, entities and activities are defined and constructed within the domain of a discursive formation. Thus we can regard practices of observing and recording observations as part of the order of statements, observing, drawing, presenting become discursive activities.

In his book *The Birth of the Clinic*, Foucault is concerned with the development of an observational-clinical medicine at the end of the eighteenth century. Foucault's crucial categories here are the 'body' and the 'clinical gaze'. The 'body' is a *discursive* object for Foucault, not a *natural* object, but the abstraction of the structures and processes enclosed by the skin as a distinct domain, separated from climate, diet, regimen and mode of social life. Previous medical systems had considered man in a space of humours and harmonies; they located and dispersed disease and the body in the environment and mode of life. Clinical medicine isolates and observes bodily states and processes. Its observational 'gaze' is the product of discursive and institutional conditions, it is part of an order of statements which works from observations in a clinical context to establish disease entities and aetiologies. But it is a 'gaze' nonetheless; observation produces results which are irreducible to their discursive conditions and which lead on to new 'statements', systematic classifications of what is 'seen'.

It should be clear that in Foucault's analysis statements are not regarded as the free products of the 'mind', rather statements have what he calls 'surfaces of emergence', that is, particular institutional-organisational conditions of knowledge under which it is possible for statements to appear. 'Statements' are not the products of human subjects in general, rather the statements which are part of definitive discursive formations emerge from what he calls 'enunciative modalities'. That is, definitely constructed subjects specific to the discursive formation, and qualified/constrained to 'speak' in definite ways. As we shall see, 'speaking' can be extended to practices such as building. Further, the subjects implicated in such forms of constructed statement are not merely those of the source of enunciation, definite forms of 'subjectification' are implied in constructions for the subjects who enter and inhabit them.

Foucault moves from author-as-subject toward a view of the subject as an agent/effect of a discursive formation. 'Enunciative modalities' means that only certain subjects are qualified and able to speak in particular ways, that certain statements cannot be made by everybody and anybody. Thus in *Madness and Civilisation* and *The Birth of the Clinic*, for example, judgements of insanity or clinical observations become the functions of particular statuses, those of psychiatrist and doctor. The determination of insanity becomes the function of the asylum. The clinical observation of the body develops within and requires the institutional construction of the teaching hospital. So knowledges and the subjects who produce them are connected with particular institutional conditions and forms of power. Foucault's earlier works thus anticipate in important ways the conception of power-knowledge developed in *Discipline and Punish* and his later works. Foucault differs most dramatically from the history of ideas as conventionally conceived not merely in his attention to fields beyond the province of 'humane' learning, for of course there are histories of medicine and of natural history and of economics. Where he differs most is in the way he links discourse to what must otherwise be regarded as the 'extra-discursive', the domain of the object. For what he does is to integrate investigative practices, observation *and* the products of observation within the discursive field. When things stop being words, conventionally they stop being treated as statements and become 'objects' rather than a part of discourse. Foucault, on the contrary, links in his concept of statement investigative practices or transformational activities and their constructed objects.

In this we can see his importance for the analysis of constructed space. Because, following Foucault, we can treat the statement as something that is not merely written down in words but which nevertheless can be part of a discourse. We can consider constructed objects as components of a discursive formation, and relate the practice of the construction, inclusion and exclusion of objects to the rules and patterns of such formations. In this way we can bridge the gap between theory in architecture and spatial constructs, not merely by treating constructs as examples of a theory, but examining how discourses enter into construction and how in consequence buildings or planned environments become *statements*. Hence we are offered the possibility of a link between a discursive formation, the institutional conditions in which it becomes a practice and the products of that practice, on the model of *The Birth of the Clinic*.

B. Neo-Platonism and the subject of the temple

In order to exemplify this I will consider the question of the 'influence' of Neo-Platonic theories on Renaissance architecture, using Rudolf Wittkower's *Architectural Principles of Humanism in the Renaissance*. In particular, we will consider the special place accorded to the centrally planned church.

In *The Order of Things* Foucault contrasts the *episteme* which governs certain key Renaissance discourses, and in which the organising forms of knowledge are a set of categories constituting forms of resemblance, with the subsequent and very different *episteme* which replaces it in the seventeenth century, and in which the dominant organising forms of knowledge are based on the concept of representation. What Foucault is concerned to examine in *The Order of Things* are successive *epistemes* which provide a matrix in which configurations of distinct knowledges share common methods and conceptions of objects. He is concerned with the dominant overall organisation of discourse which makes certain forms of existence of objects and ways of speaking about them possible. He prefaces the text with a quotation from the Argentinian writer Borges in which the latter refers to a classification of animals in a Chinese encyclopaedia. In this, animals are classified in diverse and bizarre ways, for example, as being innumerable, as being stuffed, as appearing as small as flies, and finally as being included in the present classification. Now to us such a form of putting animals together is incomprehensible because they appear to belong to wholly distinct and incompatible orders, there is no single frame for us in which these animals can be placed on the same plane of existence. That is because this classificatory scheme has quite different presuppositions from our own about what objects can exist and in what relation. Foucault goes on to cap this by citing the Renaissance naturalist Aldrovandi's *Treatise on the Serpent* which does something analogous to the encyclopaedia, treating of snakes along with griffins, dragons and all sorts of mythological beasts as if they were in the same register. Foucault's point is that it is not because Aldrovandi is ignorant, or stupid, or fails to observe that he does this, but because he has a quite different conception than our own of the order of knowledge, of the beings which are possible and of the status of knowledge of Ancient and Medieval texts in which such mythical creatures are referred to and described. It is in this spirit that Foucault goes on to reconstruct the dominant Renaissance *episteme*.

Foucault's conception is central to an understanding of the intellectual role of Neo-Platonism in certain key Renaissance discourses, such as architecture and the very particular relationship it establishes between subjects and certain spaces. Central to Neo-Platonic thought is the absence of a modern concept of the 'sign', in which words denote things by 'representing' or standing for them, and in which the sign and its referent are distinct registers. This enables us to comprehend the centrality and intellectual seriousness of the central Neo-Platonic doctrine of the interpenetration and respective mirroring of microcosm and macrocosm, a doctrine 'influential' beyond identifiably 'Neo-Platonic' thinkers. In this *episteme* the entire world from its smallest to its greatest part, from the humblest animal to God, consists of a series of resemblances, similarities and sympathies. We have here no concept of an arbitrary relation in which one thing, a 'sign', stands for, represents, another, rather all relations are *real* relations and connections between aspects of existence reflect their respective natures and their universal interpenetrations. Hence relations both have significance and are real relations, connections in nature. The entire universe is a set of resemblances and sympathies, with no space for the 'classical' gap between signs and existence. Renaissance thought is hyper-realist and makes symbolic or significatory connections/affirmations of common relations of form or nature. Hence we have a world presented to knowledge which consists of a series of emblems, traces, signatures, or resemblances which are the marks of that network of spiritual-real interconnections whereby the whole tissue of existence is held together. From this follows the Neo-Platonic linking of ideas and experience and the doctrine of the Book of the World, whereby the world itself is conceived as a language, as intelligible in itself. Such views are not confined to those who can, unjustly, be dismissed as devotees of magic and cabbalism such as Cornelius Aggrippa or as misguided mystics like Paracelsus, rather they are subscribed to by the leading 'conventional' intellectuals of the Italian Renaissance such as Marsilio Ficino or Pico della Mirandola, and in architecture men like Alberti.

There are in this *episteme* no 'gaps' between thought and signs and signs and objects as there are in Descartes and Locke. Now of course, with these later thinkers we have the rise of something which is still identifiable as the modern concept of the sign, which still has traces in Saussure. For Locke, for example, a sensation is the 'idea', the mental register, of a thing observed. The sign stands for an idea, it is a concept in the mind which represents by convention other concepts in the mind which are perceptions or sensations. Signs thus have a doubly complex relation to things, they 'represent' ideas, which in turn are the mental registers of sensations of things. Hence knowledge consists in what is perceived of the world of things by human sensations, themselves sensory-mental events, and signs order and stand for such sensations. Knowledge is thereby conditional on what is perceived and signs are referential but arbitrary in the selection of the signifiers which are to 'stand for' things. In this double gap arises the 'problem' of knowledge, that is the problem of the adequacy of the relation between ideas/sensations and the things thus perceived, and secondly, the adequacy of the relation between word and idea. But this 'problem' does not exist in the Renaissance *episteme* or in Neo-Platonic theory. All relations are *real* relations – we have a world of visible or intelligible traces of harmony, which give access to the cosmic order. There is no general problem of knowledge, only a problem of the proper *use* of the faculty of intellect and the sensitivity to experience – and this may require *spiritual* preparation which makes us fit to uncover and understand the harmonies and relations of the world-order. Instead of a problem of the adequacy of knowledge we have a need to sensitise the subject to knowledge, to create paths for the connection between spirit, intellect and experience.

A central question therefore in Renaissance thought is how to *present* those traces of harmony and cosmic order, not to 'represent' them but to make them *present* to human subjects. Geometry has a privileged position here. Geometry is the fundamental mirroring of the natural order, since it is both an elaborated science of ordered forms and is also the manifest and present form of the order of the world. The figures of geometry correspond to the constitutive proportions of the world, and the two fundamental proportional relations accessible to experience are those of the human body and those of the harmonic scale. Such 'devices' provide traces and resemblances whereby man can be put into immediate contact with the divine. Hence the familiar Vitruvian figure of an ideally proportioned human being within the space of a square superimposed on a circle has a philosophical significance which belies the fact that it is a commonplace.

But, of course, for the Neo-Platonic architectural theorist, the order of the world could best be revealed through conscious purpose, through the rationally planned design of the architect-adept which systematises experience and puts it at the service of intellect and its superior perception of cosmic order. Hence the philosophical and practical significance of an architecture which links science, art and spiritual concerns. Proportions in structures are therefore the visible and present resemblances of the order of man and the universe. Geometrically planned and appropriately proportioned buildings, in particular centrally planned churches, have an expressive significance and practical consequence which transcend those of mere form. A centrally planned church may be defined as a structure based on a geometrical figure such as a circle, an octagon or a circle overlaying a square, in which the construction is symmetrical and radiates from a single point. An early example of such a Renaissance building is Brunelleschi's S. Maria degli Angeli (begun 1434) in Florence (see Pevsner, 1963, p. 181 for an illustration). They are not to be conceived as a stylistic device, not merely the execution of an aesthetic idea in brick and stone, but rather the manifest presence and physical existence of cosmic order. This cosmic order divined and devised through intellect is in the physical presence of a building accessible to experience, and this experience in turn produces knowledge. In the Neo-Platonic theory a definite connection is established between intellect and experience. Thus forms are perceived in the intellect, although hinted at in experience, and by making the intellect's grasp of form present and intelligible to experience through rationalised structures so another route is provided whereby the mass of common men may directly experience the immanent order of the world, which is God. The true architect should therefore be a theorist and adept in order to construct buildings and specifically churches, which produce certain direct effects on the human subjects who approach and enter into them.

Philosophy is integral to this conception of architectural practice. The value of the philosophically adept and geometrically knowledgeable architect, intellectually and spiritually prepared for his task, is thus quite distinct from the craftsman-builder or the follower of formulas. The object of theoretical training is thus no simple claim to social status and professional superiority, it is the spiritual-intellectual preparation for an eminently practical function, not merely of constructing spaces but spaces which have expressive-experiential effects on the subject.

To turn to Wittkower, we can see that he identifies the ways in which the theoretical concepts of resemblance or sympathy are active in the architectural treatises of the period. Andrea Palladio in his *Quattro libri* says: 'We cannot doubt that the little temple we make ought to resemble this very great one, which by His immense goodness, was perfectly completed with one word of His' (*Preface*, Book IV, cited by Wittkower, p. 23). Again in summing up the central role of geometry and proportion in these discourses Wittkower remarks that: 'Renaissance artists firmly adhered to the Pythagorian concept "All is number" and, guided by Plato and the Neo-Platonists and supported by a long chain of theologians from Augustine onwards, they were convinced of the mathematical and harmonic structure of the universe and all creation' (Wittkower, p. 27). Such Neo-Platonic and allied discourses share three decisive characteristics, common rules of formation of statements:

i.   concepts of resemblance, harmony, sympathy, etc., which postulate analogous modes of existence of objects and of the relation between knowledge and the world;
ii.   a common relation to Antiquity, as the authentic source and the prefiguration of knowledge, knowledge thus proceeds by *recovery*;
iii.   that knowledge generates practices of transformation, practices which are not 'technologies' in the modern sense, but involve a distinct relation between subject and the world, a relation in which the world as spirit-existence and the subject as spirit-intellect are brought into harmony.

Thus something very specific is entailed in the notion of 'humanism' in these discourses, something quite different from the modern humanities. 'Humanism' involves subjective and spiritual transformation, and human learning is predicated on the discovery of the relations of resemblance between man, the order of the universe and God.

Hence we can see the highly particular 'practice' involved in such architecture; it is not merely the activity of construction, rather its aim is the transformation of human subjects. The essence of this transformation is spiritual and involves a privileged place for church architecture. Now, of course, medieval constructions seek to establish relations between man and God, insofar as we can interpret them, but the relation posited in the geometrically planned church is distinct, and is mediated through the experience of harmony.

Structures therefore provide a means of knowledge through experience. The structure is an experience-effect. Churches with certain forms and features can produce effects of piety, the recognition of God through the sympathies present in His temples and the correct rendering through experience of God's plan. In this conception we do not merely have an experience of space, but rather a set of effects which go beyond the building to the world and its Creator. So we can see Leone Battista Alberti means something highly specific by the statement: 'Without such sympathy between the microcosm of men and the macrocosm of God, prayer cannot be effective' (cited in Wittkower, p. 27). For it means we are dealing with the Church as a statement and as a transformatory practice. We are not merely concerned with a 'statement' in an architectural theory, but a concrete discourse-practice in architecture. Certain forms such as the circle are regarded as inherently symbolic and spiritually consequential; they are privileged not merely in an aesthetics of 'impressions', but in a doctrine that links experience, knowledge and religion.

This account gives the centrally planned church a definite religious and philosophical function. It is not the only possible account, and would be hotly disputed in certain quarters. The architectural historian Sir Nicholas Pevsner is a good example of an alternative view. Pevsner is aware there is a radical difference between the centrally planned churches of the Renaissance and Medieval churches, but he sees this as a consequence of the rise of an essentially secular humanism:

> For a central plan is not an other-worldly, but a this-worldly conception. The prime function of the medieval church had been to lead the faithful to the altar. In a completely centralised building no such movement is possible. The building has its full effect only when it is looked at from one focal point. There the spectator must stand and by standing there, he becomes himself 'the measure of all things'. Thus the religious meaning of the Church is replaced by a human one. Man is in the Church no longer pressing forward to reach a transcendental goal, but enjoying the beauty that surrounds him and the glorious sensation of being the centre of this beauty. *Outline of European Architecture*, p. 182

I hope the foregoing account will make clear how misguided this conception is. Man is indeed 'the measure of all things' but only because all things are mirrored in man, man is modelled on the Divinity and the order of the Cosmos. The opposition this-worldly/other-worldly is refused by Neo-Platonic doctrine, it has a religious seriousness of its own predicated on such a refusal. The subject of the temple is not an idle spectator, the experience of proportioned space is participation in the world-order. It is a rite-in-experience, which neither detracts from nor replaces but supplements and confirms the rites at the altars within.

The effects proposed for centrally planned churches in the treatises of Alberti and others remain 'intellectualist' ones, in that they depend entirely on the validity of the connections proposed in Neo-Platonic theory between proportion and experience. No additional mechanisms or techniques other than constructed space itself are introduced to ensure the production of the effects of subjectification proposed. Later discourses and practices have a quite different character, for there intervenes that peculiar relation between power and knowledge characteristic of the modern age. There is in these later edifices no such simple and elegant connection between space and its effects, buildings sustain particular patterns of *use*, techniques of power for which the structure offers a site. At first sight the example of Bentham we will consider in a moment appears to contradict this. Bentham appears to propose the penitentiary Panopticon as a simple 'idea in architecture' efficacious because of its unique spatial properties. But this is deceptive. Bentham is a pioneer of the reform of *administration*, what is crucial is not merely a certain constructed space but the regime of administration it permits and facilitates. As we shall see, this regime did not depend on exactly the spatial properties of panopticism. What Bentham introduces, however, is a definite functional relation between constructed space and power/knowledge, the prison is the site of an institution with a specific purpose and a distinct practice.

C.   Power-knowledge and the prison

Let us move to Foucault's later works, *Discipline and Punish* and *The History of Sexuality*, and consider his treatment of the relation between a new form of power and a new class of specialist structures which both develop toward the end of the eighteenth century. In these later works the key theoretical innovation is the systematic linking of the categories of power and knowledge to form a hybrid 'power-knowledge'. This Foucault regards as the consequence and the condition of the rise of forms of 'disciplinary power' from the eighteenth century onwards and which he considers the distinctive feature of modern forms of control of and transformation of subjects. Foucault's book *Discipline and Punish* is focused around an account of the development of the modern prison, and is concerned to challenge a pervasive Enlightenment view of truth and power as inherently opposed forces. Foucault considers this opposition to depend on what he calls the 'juridico-discursive' concept of power. In this conception power is regarded as a possession, it is something that the sovereign subject possesses and others do not have. The essence of this power consists in prohibition; it is essentially the power to say no, to forbid, to suppress. Power is thus conceived of as fundamentally negative, a punitive relation between dominant and subordinate subject. Power is possessed exclusively by dominant subjects and is a means of holding down and repressing subordinate subjects. We can see why in this juridico-discursive conception power and truth are perceived as in inevitable opposition. Truth must be considered as a means of critique of power and must at all costs avoid the corruption of power, because power is negative and is the exclusive property of subjects who hold others in suppression. Truth allied to power becomes corrupted by it, by the demands of limits to knowledge which follow from property and repression. So in the Enlightenment critique of this conception of power, held to be characteristic of Absolutism, power is held to deny, to suppress truth, and to work in darkness and through secrecy. Truth on the other hand is universal and should be the property of all men; it should bring enlightenment and promise emancipation and concord.

A very good example of this Enlightenment critique is the Italian penal reformer Cesare Beccaria's *Of Crimes and Punishments*, a point I will return to later. It attacks the tortures and arbitrary and excessive punishments held to be characteristic of Absolutism in the interests of a penal regime based on knowledge and law, in which punishments are certain and calculable, and in which law is a guide to action which can be known by all men and to which all men are subject.

In contradistinction to this essentially negative and sovereign-centred view of power Foucault argues that in the modern era power and knowledge cannot be separated and counterposed in this way because knowledge is productive of power. This involves a new view of power and new types of power, of which the most important is 'disciplinary power'. Power is transformative of those subject to it and uses knowledge as a resource in doing so. Far from being merely prohibitive, its controls are *productive*. Power does not merely draw on existing social resources in the form of a levy, but acts to create and multiply resources. Knowledge is a necessary resource of power, power needs definite knowledges in order to be productive. And, vice versa, power is a crucial resource of certain knowledges, this is because power constructs the 'surfaces of emergence' which makes discourses and knowledges able to function as such. Knowledge is thus implicated in institutions and definite power relations. A good example is clinical medicine which is tied directly to the health care for, and regulation of, the poor. Clinical-observational medicine depends on large numbers of cases being brought into the hospital, on the separation and classification of cases and on the controls and forms of institutional order which makes this possible. Clinical medicine uses the bodies of the poor as a resource of knowledge, to be dissected for research and teaching. As a result of a large number of cases gathered together the clinical observation of disease entities and the examination of the organic structures of cadavers make new knowledge possible. The hospital is not merely a site of care, but a machine of observation – a central institutional condition for the clinical 'gaze'. The new 'surfaces of emergence' in clinical medicine thus depend on definite institutions, and on their social and organisational and not merely their discursive conditions of existence.

In summing up his view of power-knowledge Foucault remarks:

> If power were never anything but repressive, if it never did anything but say no, do you really think one could be brought to obey it? What makes power hold good, what makes it accepted, is simply the fact that it doesn't only weigh on us as a force that says no, but that it traverses and produces things; it induces pleasure, forms knowledge, produces discourse. It needs to be considered as a productive network which runs through the whole social body, much more than as a negative instance whose function is repression.
>
> (*Power/Knowledge*, p. 119)

Thus Foucault does not merely link knowledge and power, whilst leaving the traditional repressive and sovereign-centred notion of power untouched.

Power is not simply a global relation between the sovereign, who is the source of prohibitive power, and the subjects who are subordinate to this power. Power does not proceed downwards from a single centre. Rather the power relation Foucault is concerned with has no simple centre but is diffused throughout the whole social body in complex networks and diverse relations. He refers to the need for a 'micro-physics of power', considering all the sites of its exercise and functioning and not merely the gross repressive forms associated with the state. Sites like hospitals, insane asylums, schools, etc., are considered as centres of power-knowledge. In order to consider such forms Foucault introduces the concept of 'disciplinary power'. The essence of such power is not repressive force but 'surveillance'. The 'surveillance' of subjects is a crucial mode in which they are transformed. Surveillance requires both knowledges and institutions ordered by knowledges for its functioning. It depends on the isolation and specification of individuals such that its controls can be brought to bear and can effect the work of the transformation/construction of subjects. Individuals are isolated from social collectivities and one another. Their conduct is brought under continuous inspection and subjected to norms of performance, a process Foucault calls 'normatising individuation'. Subjects are constructed in institutions in such a way that they too become a resource of power; workers in factories, children in the schools of the bourgeoisie, etc. Subjects are transformed into beings of a particular type, whose conduct is patterned and governed, and who are endowed with definite attributes and abilities. Such forms of power do not merely act upon workers or the poor, but also on the bourgeoisie themselves through education and the transformation of the home.

The model of this form of power based on surveillance, which individuates and transforms, is the penitentiary prison. And the archetypal form of such a prison as a system of power based on surveillance, where individuals are brought under what Foucault calls the 'eye' of power, is to be found in the English social reformer Jeremy Bentham's proposal for a panoptical prison. The Panopticon is a prison in which the conduct of all the inmates and all of its internal space is subject to inspection by the directive staff. The Panopticon is a circular structure whose floors are divided into series of cells around the circumference which isolate the inmates and at the centre of the structure is an inspection tower from which each of the cells on each of the floors can be observed. The principle is that light comes in through the windows or slits on the circumference of the structure such that each of the cells is back-lit. This makes it possible for the observer in the tower to see without being seen, for to the inmate the inspection tower is darkened and he or she cannot see through the slits on the tower into the centre. The prisoner, or a worker in a factory or the pupil in a school based on this model, does not know whether he is being observed or not. At any given moment the prisoner must presume himself to be under observation, with the consequence that conduct is governed by surveillance twenty-four hours a day. And so one person moving up from the inspector's lodge and walking round in the inspection tower can see each of the galleries in the structure. (For illustrations of the Panopticon see Foucault, 1977, plates 3 and 4.)

Bentham called the Panopticon an 'idea in architecture'. Its principle is that the many can be governed by the few and its object is in Bentham's pithy phrase 'to grind rogues honest'. This 'grinding' takes place through the uninterrupted surveillance of conduct. It should be said that when Bentham refers to an 'idea' here, he means the concept of a structure. The idea is a construction, a space which makes possible both a certain discourse and certain power relations. The Panopticon is both a construction and a 'statement' in construction. It is the space and site of a certain form of productive power. The 'gaze' of the inspector in the tower is a simple form of power-knowledge, it is productive both of controls over subjects and the remodelling of their conduct, just as the 'gaze' of the clinician in the hospital is productive of observational knowledges.

Bentham's 'idea' obviously did not spring from his own head alone. Foucault treats his model of such a construction as an example of a supra-individual 'strategy'. A 'strategy' is a definite pattern of means and objectives which can be discovered operating across a number of sites. The prison – of which the Panopticon is a model – is one of a series of structures embodying the surveillance principle. Bentham drew his initial conception of the inspection principle from his brother's visit to the Military School of Paris, built in 1751. In this school the dormitories were so constructed that each pupil was assigned a glassed-in cell and thus completely isolated from direct contact with his fellows he could be observed by the supervising master. This made it possible to regulate the extra-curricular conduct of the pupils and to prevent unacceptable sexual practices. This example of the inspection principle was by no means isolated. Diverse structures were being constructed in the mid-eighteenth century with the object of isolating and controlling individuals. Barracks and military hospitals are an example. Separation and inspection had both the objective of maintaining discipline and promoting hygiene – preventing the fevers which led to such high mortality in places where military personnel were crowded together. Great attention was paid not merely to separation of individuals and supervision, but also to promoting the flow of air and the drainage of waste. Hence both internal arrangements and structures as a whole were being transformed with regard to the 'strategy' of inspection and separation.[2] Bentham's Panopticon is distinct in that it is an elegant example of rationalising the whole structure such that it corres-ponds to certain demands of use, the whole construction is built around the strategy of inspection. In this it differs from merely setting up devices *within* an otherwise conventional structure as in the Military School or the systems of wards or pavillions in the military hospitals which were not wholly subordinated to the inspection principle. In this sense it is a systematically *functional* architecture, a space organised by certain demands of utilisation and worked out rigorously to facilitate them. A specific architecture is linked to the demands of administration and regime. The Panopticon is in many ways too simple, it appears to rely too directly on simple visibility to effect surveillance. Indeed, the most radical panoptical forms were never successful precisely because they ignored other demands such as circulation and services. But Bentham's conception is not merely to be found in the drawing, it depends also on his account of the mode of administration. Foucault uses it as an ideal-typical or radically simplified model of the form of power which is based on surveillance and normatising individuation. We must understand Bentham's plan as a structure *plus* the power relations necessary to accomplish its programme of subjectification.

We can contrast this functionalism with other structures planned according to a schema. In the centrally planned churches of Alberti and others in the Renaissance, the rationalisation of the structure is governed by the very different demands of its effects on subjects. The structure reflects a geometrical order and it is this order which has direct experience-effects on subjects. Space is governed by expressive relations and it is these relations which impinge on subjects rather than any distinct practice which utilises the space. Whilst the structure sustains and validates practices such as prayer, it is not a 'prayer-machine'. This is one example of a very different way in which a discourse and certain demands following from it are inscribed in a structure. Another one would be artillery fortification. Here again space is governed by geometrical considerations but those are not primarily expressive. Rather, in this case, the geometrical plan is subject to the demands of creating interlocking fields of fire and the dominant consideration in the rationalisation of the ground plan is that there be no dead ground which cannot be observed and swept with fire. Given the central role of the geometrical rationalisation of space it is not surprising that it was Italian Renaissance architects who developed the bastioned trace, and it is possible that some of the architects involved in the central innovations may have subscribed to Neo-Platonic theories – which may have facilitated the break with previous practice and the models offered by Antiquity. But geometricisation serves another function in the fortress from that in the church – one which certainly does not exclude expressive relations but which must accommodate them in the course of meeting military demands. In the centrally planned church the relation of the subject to God is very different from Bentham's inmate to the inspector in the Panopticon, the space of the church does not facilitate God's inspection of the subject, rather the relation is the other way round – it is the lesser subject perceiving in the spatial order of the church the eternal and unchanging nature of the greater subject, God. Transformation is not effected by power relations. Similarly, the spatial formula of the fortress is primarily directed outwards. Observation and inspection are primarily directed outwards towards the surrounding ground to be controlled by fire. Fortresses and citadels obviously did serve to overawe the towns they enclosed or adjoined, for example, Antwerp, street plans sometimes did reflect the demands of the assembly of troops and the limitation of damage from bombardment, but there was no simple and direct relation between the bastioned trace and the town plan or its social relations within. A perfect bastioned trace like Naarden in Holland could thus enclose a free citizenry.[3] These examples – the centrally planned church, the bastioned fortress and the penitentiary prison – show that discourses concerned with the rationalisation of space can lead to quite different forms of 'statement-structure' and involve quite different functional principles in rationalising space.

Clearly, prisons existed long before Bentham and long before the reform measures which led to the large-scale construction of penitentiary prisons in Europe and America from the late eighteenth century onwards. But the prison is transformed into the 'penitentiary', and this change of function involves a change in structure and the considerations acting on it. The first consideration is the spatial demand of facilitating the inspection principle, which leads to as radical a relation between structure and fields of vision as an artillery fortress although for very different functional demands. The second consideration is that the prison sustain a rigid timetable which effects every aspect of the life of inmates and that it facilitates the segregation of individuals and classes of offender. The 'strategy' embodied in the new type of prison is that it transform the conduct of its inmates through governing their behaviour. It is a 'penitentiary', the aim of which is to reform criminals and to bring them to full cognizance of their guilt. Previous prison structures were sites of incarceration or detention, for those awaiting execution or trial, or as a pressure to redeem a debt. I shall give two examples of prison structures here to contrast with the new penitentiary regime whose model is the Panopticon. One is George Dance the Younger's design for the New Newgate prison, and the other is the imaginary prisons in Giovanni Piranesi's *Carceri*. In Piranesi's case his prisons are what I shall call an imaginary architecture of 'supplice'.

'Supplice' is the form of exemplary punishment meted out by the monarch under the Ancien Regime to a regicide, parricide, traitor or other serious malefactor. Such crime is regarded as *lèse-majesté* – it is an affront to the power of the sovereign and is countered by a demonstration of the sovereign's dominion in the systematic destruction of the body of the offender in torture and execution. 'Supplice' thus fits directly with a conception of power as repression and a capacity exclusively possessed by the sovereign. Foucault's

Discipline and Punish opens with a contrast between the spectacle of the execution of a regicide in 1757 and a prison timetable for a juvenile reformatory eighty years later. These contrasting examples show two quite distinct regimes of punishment. The *Carceri* are an imaginary architecture which fits exactly with this exemplary and savage punishment as much as Bentham's Panopticon is an imaginary figuration of the new penitentiary prisons.

In several of the *Carceri* [for example, plate 3, 1st state, and plate 7, 2nd state] one can see wretched individuals groaning under instruments of torture, and tiny figures lost amidst the amazing lattice work of bridges, the immense machines and the vast decorative features. The prison is a vast theatre of torture, an imaginary structure which intimidates subjects by its bulk and monumental brutality. As such these prisons have no rationalised or evident plan. Rather they serve to make arbitrary power expressive and visible through the sheer mass of the structure which dwarfs the inmates and at the same time the darkness which pervades all despite the immensity of the internal space. Such prisons are sites for torture, incarceration and exemplary punishment, and their form is correspondingly monumental and expressive. They are quite different from the ordered cells pervaded by light of the Panopticon.

When I call the *Carceri* an 'imaginary architecture of supplice' it is true that this extends the meaning of 'supplice', for the closed space of the prison is not the public exemplary space of the scaffold. But the analogy holds because the *Carceri* are a massification of the dungeons and torture chambers of the Inquisition and the feudal order. The vast internal spaces of Piranesi's prisons turn them into a theatre equivalent to the publicity of the scaffold. They are at once a closed and dark space and at the same time an immense planless space open to the gaze of the spectator and expressive of an awesome arbitrary power. They are both darkness massified and darkness visible. They both enclose the victims, forever isolating them in the grip of repressive power, and admit the spectator as a voyeur. They combine as images the dungeon and the scaffold, the secret places of incarceration of the Ancien Régime and the public brutalities of exemplary punishment. They both horrify the spectator and make him party to a guilty secret.

To turn from Piranesi's imaginings to the practical demands of construction. The traditional function of the prison was to detain but its internal spaces were not rationalised according to any functional scheme of use because there was no conception of a 'regime' such as we find in the notion of a 'timetable' and in the surveillance necessary to make prisoners conform to it. In the purely custodial prison, prisoners were neither isolated from one another nor from outside, commonly they could purchase food and receive visitors. Privileged noble and bourgeois prisoners were permitted to recreate their domestic arrangements within the prison, at a price. Insofar as this type of building's function concerns its form, it relates primarily to the facade rather than to the organisation of its internal spaces. The custodial prison was often monumental, symbolising its strength and solidity, but its plan was *not* subject to the demands of inspection. George Dance the Younger's design for Newgate Prison (1770) illustrates this well (see Stroud, 1971, plate 29(c) for an illustration). It was immediately prior to Bentham's proposal for a Panopticon but it embodied a completely different 'idea in architecture'. It was dominated by a massive facade, visible from the street but not to the inmates, and specifically designed to impress passers-by. Within the facade, it was divided into three quadrangles. It was characterised by numerous dead angles of vision and had no principle of circulation such as would minimise the demands of inspection. Its internal arrangements did not permit easy isolation and classification of inmates. As such, it was an 'unpoliceable' building. But it was not designed systematically to regulate conduct, merely to contain prisoners. Its exterior symbolised its functions, to detain for debt or before execution (it was a preliminary symbolism to the scaffold), and to intimidate.[4]

Foucault's concept of 'disciplinarity' thus enables us to comprehend important differences in a certain class of structures. It enables us to see the Panopticon in terms of an architecture immersed in discourses and pursuant of strategy, as a form of power, rather than in terms of style. Newgate can be viewed in terms of conventional considerations of style and also found wanting as a device for a strategy, the one possibility is closely connected with the other. Conventional considerations of style and the demand for intimidating facade can happily co-exist. Inspection implies a new organisation of space, one in which style is secondary. A Panopticon could be built like a large shed. Foucault's concepts enable us fully to appreciate the difference between these two 'ideas'; it links architecture to the functioning of institutions, of power / knowledge and, thereby, provides us with another measure of structures than styles or technical solutions to constructional problems.

Bentham's Panopticon was never built but it is not an irrelevancy, a mere 'idea', for all that. For many prison structures did systematically pursue the demands of the inspection principle and of 'regime'. Radial and star plans, rows of cells in galleries, inspection towers are all testimonies to the relevance of Foucault's emphasis on Bentham. Prison regimes attempted to isolate and transform, as in the case of the American Auburn and Philadelphia systems. The Auburn Prison, in New York, was based on the system of solitary confinement and isolated work. Prison regimes have never worked as the reformers hoped and the prison has never 'succeeded' in its apparent task, reform. Again, these 'failures' do not undermine the centrality of the prison as a means of comprehending disciplinarity.[5]

Quite different constructional schemes are also attempts to pursue a 'disciplinary strategy'. For example, the Retreat at York constructed by William Tuke was purpose-built as an insane asylum. Its disciplinary mode is quite different from Bentham's inspection principle, but also embodies the strategy of 'normatising individuation'. The Retreat was constructed to sustain an architecture of impressions but one very different from Alberti's churches or Newgate gaol. For the impressions created by architecture are at the service of a transformative regime which is disciplinary. The Retreat combined the necessity of detaining the insane with a 'domestic atmosphere'. The patients were deceived by bars concealed as ordinary domestic sash windows and by walls which were hidden by the landscaping of the grounds. Discipline proceeded not through inspection by means of the functional organisation of visibility, but surveillance through domesticity. The restraint of the mad was to be achieved through the patterning of conduct on the domestic normality of 'family life'. Deviation becomes visible by its gross departure from ordered gentility. Surveillance works through a different mode and architecture is subordinate to the demands of the domestic management of the insane.

I could go on to multiply these examples in relation to the architecture of hospitals, schools, factories and so on, but space prohibits this. I have confined myself to the architectural consequences of the inspection principle, but Foucault's concepts offer the means to re-assess and analyse the vast mass of new 'special purpose' structures created from the nineteenth century onwards. Likewise, I could introduce Foucault's analysis of power-knowledge in relation to domestic housing, in particular the need to construct spaces for the formation of 'family life' among workers and the regulation of the sexuality of family members. Many interesting insights are to be found in this regard in Foucault's *History of Sexuality, Vol. 1* and in his co-worker Jacques Donzelot's *The Policing of Families*. This would entail another paper.

I have tried to show how Foucault's concepts can bridge a significant gap between the analysis of the constructed spaces of post-Renaissance Western societies in terms of either the history of ideas or the more conventional social scientific approaches to architecture and urban space. I have concentrated on the resources Foucault provides for the analysis of discourses which concern themselves with constructed space and for the analysis of such space as a discourse. Central in relation to this latter aspect are the connections between theories and practices of construction, modes of administrative regime in such constructions, and forms of constitution of distinct 'subjectivities'. Such an analysis is not the only one possible but it has a distinctive contribution to make. It enables us to analyse constructions which are neither vernacular nor objectifications of popular belief systems without lapsing either into intellectualism or technicism. It offers an approach which makes possible a different way of taking up some of the questions and concerns about the significance of constructed spaces in relation to non-Western societies posed by anthropologists in the very different intellectual, institutional and technical context of Western civilisation.

NOTES

1. See for example an architect's response to Foucault: M. Cacciari, F. Rella, M. Tafuri and G. Teyssot, *Il Dispositivo Foucault* (1977) – see also a revised translated version of Teyssot's article and the comments by the translator, David Stewart, in *Architecture & Urbanism*, Oct. 1980.

2. See Foucault (1976).

3. On fortress architecture, see Hale (1977) & Hughes (1974).

4. Interestingly enough there is considerable debate on the influence of the *Carceri* on Dance's design. Sir John Summerson in *Georgian London* notes such an influence. He also comments that Dance's plan was soon rendered obsolete by prison reform but does not dwell on why. He says: 'This composition is doubly remarkable. First, because of its Piranesian sense of the drama of restriction, and the deft accentuation of mass by recession at certain points. And second because of its vivid articulation ... Here was no mere "centre and wings" Academy picture, but a forceful expression of purpose, cruelly eloquent in all its parts' (Summerson, p, 148).
    Dorothy Stroud in her work on Dance comments on this frequent comparison but argues that the Newgate design owes little to Piranesi. Accepting Dance's familiarity with Piranesi's work she points to a Palladian influence (Stroud, p. 98). Wilton-Ely on balance accepts the primacy of a Piranesian influence: he is specially interesting on theatre sets for imaginary prisons in early eighteenth-century Italy and on post-Piranesian projects for monumental prisons, see 1978, ch. v.
    It is also only fair to mention here that monumental-expressive stylistic features continued to appear in prison designs and buildings throughout the nineteenth century – in gatehouses, crenellated walls, castle turrets, etc. However, in general, the design of cell blocks and their relation one to another did pay regard to the demands of inspection and circulation in a way earlier prisons did not.

5. There is now an extensive literature on the new prisons, on mental hospitals, etc., and their development from the late eighteenth century onwards. Perhaps the best book on the American systems mentioned above and on the chronology of prison construction is Rothman; on American and Italian prisons see Melossi and Pavarini, on English prisons Ignatieff and on asylums Doerner, and Scull. Donnelly Ch. 3 'The Architecture of Confinement' discusses very fully the architectural origins of eighteenth century prisons and lunatic asylums.

REFERENCES

Architecture Comparée 1982. les cahiers de l'a.d.r.i.l., Paris.

Beccaria, Cesare 1964. *Of Crimes and Punishments*, published with A. Manzoni, *The Column of Infamy*, OUP.

Cacciari, M., Rella, F., Tafuri, M., Teyssot, G. 1977. *Il Dispositivo Foucault*, Cluva Libreria, Venice.

Doerner, Klaus 1981. *Madmen and the Bourgeoisie*, Oxford, Blackwell.

Donnelly, Michael 1983. *Managing the Mind*, London, Tavistock.

Donzelot, Jacques 1980. *The Policing of Families*, London, Hutchinson.

Foucault, Michel 1970. *Madness and Civilisation*, London, Tavistock.

Foucault, Michel 1972. *The Order of Things*, London, Tavistock.

Foucault, Michel 1972. *The Archaeology of Knowledge*, London, Tavistock.

Foucault, Michel 1973. *The Birth of the Clinic*, London, Tavistock.

Foucault, Michel 1976. 'La Politique de la santé au XVIIIe siècle' in *Les Machines à guérir*, Paris, Institut de l'Environnement.

Foucault, Michel 1978. *Discipline & Punish*, London, Allen Lane.

Coucault, Michel 1978. *History of Sexuality*, Vol. 1, New York, Pantheon.

Foucault, Michel 1980. *Power/Knowledge*, ed. Colin Gordon, New York, Pantheon.

Hale, John 1977. *Renaissance Fortification, Art or Engineering?'*, London, Thames & Hudson.

Hughes, Quentin 1974. *Military Architecture*, London, Hugh Evelyn.

Ignatieff, Michel 1978. *A Just Measure of Pain*, London, Macmillan.

Melossi, Dario and Pavarini, Massimo 1981. *The Prison and the Factory*, London, Macmillan.

Palladio, Andrea n.d. *The Four Books of Architecture*, New York, Dover.

Pevsner, Nikolaus 1963. *An Outline of European Architecture*, Harmondsworth, Penguin.

Piranesi, Giovanni Batista 1973. *Le Carceri*, New York, Dover.

Rothman, D. J. 1971. *The Discovery of the Asylum*, Boston, Little Brown.

Scull, Andrew 1979. *Museums of Madness*, London, Allen Lane.

Skultans, Vieda 1979. *English Madness – Ideas on Insantiy 1580–1890*, London, Routledge.

Stroud, Dorothy 1971. *George Dance, Architext 1741–1825*, London, Faber.

Summerson, John 1978. *Georgian London*, Harmondsworth, Penguin.

Teyssot, G. 1980. 'Heterotopias and the History of Spaces', *Architecture & Urbanism*, Tokyo, October, No. 121, pp. 79–100.

Wilton-Ely, John 1978. *The Mind and Art of Giovanni Piranesi*, London, Thames & Hudson.

Wittkower, Rudolf 1973. *Architectural Principles in the Age of Humanism*, London, Academy Editions.

4.

Museums:

Managers of Consciousness

Hans Haacke

The art world as a whole, and museums in particular, belong to what has aptly been called 'the consciousness industry'. More than twenty years ago, the German writer Hans Magnus Enzensberger gave us some insight into the nature of this industry in an article which used that phrase as its title. Although he did not specifically elaborate on the art world, his article did refer to it in passing. It seems worthwhile here to extrapolate from and to expand upon Enzensberger's thoughts for a discussion of the role museums and other art-exhibiting institutions play.

Like Enzensberger I believe the use of the term 'industry' for the entire range of activities of those who are employed or working on a free-lance basis in the art field has a salutary effect. With one stroke that term cuts through the romantic clouds that envelop the often misleading and mythical notions widely held about the production, distribution and consumption of art. Artists as much as their galleries, museums and journalists, not excluding art historians, hesitate to discuss the industrial aspect of their activities. An unequivocal acknowledgment might endanger the cherished romantic ideas with which most entered the field, and which still sustain them emotionally today. Supplanting the traditional bohemian image of the art world with that of a business operation could also negatively affect the marketability of art-world products and interfere with fund-raising efforts. Those who in fact plan and execute industrial strategies tend, whether by inclination or need, to mystify art and conceal its industrial aspect and often fall for their own propaganda. Given the prevalent marketability of myths, it may sound almost sacrilegious to insist on using the term 'industry'.

On the other hand, a new breed has recently appeared on the industrial landscape; the arts managers. Trained by prestigious business schools, they are convinced that art can and should be managed like the production and marketing of other goods. They make no apologies and have few romantic hang-ups. They do not blush in assessing the receptivity and potential development of an audience for their product. As a natural part of their education they are conversant with budgeting, investment and price-setting strategies. They have studied organizational goals, managerial structures and the peculiar social and political environment of their organization. Even the intricacies of labor relations and the ways in which interpersonal issues might affect the organization are part of their curriculum.

Of course, all these and other skills have been employed for decades by art-world denizens of the old school. Instead of enrolling in arts administration courses taught according to the Harvard Business School's case method, they have learned their skills on the job. Following their instincts they have often been more successful managers than the new graduates promise to be, since the latter are mainly taught by professors with little or no direct knowledge of the peculiarities of the art world. Traditionally, however, the old-timers are shy in admitting to themselves and others the industrial character of their activities and most still do not view themselves as managers. It is to be expected that the lack of delusions and aspirations among the new art administrators will have a noticeable impact on the state of the industry. Being trained primarily as technocrats they are less likely to have an emotional attachment to the peculiar nature of the product they are promoting. And this attitude, in turn, will have an effect on the type of products we will soon begin to see.

My insistence on the term 'industry' is not motivated by sympathy for the new technocrats. As a matter of fact, I have serious reservations about their training, the mentality it fosters, and the consequences it will have. What the emergence of arts administration departments in business schools demonstrates, however, is the fact that in spite of the mystique surrounding the production and distribution of art, we are now and indeed have been all along dealing with social organizations that follow industrial modes of operation, and that range in size from the cottage industry to national and multinational conglomerates. Supervisory boards are becoming aware of this fact. Given current financial problems, they try to streamline their operations. Consequently, the present director of the Museum of Modern Art in New York has a management background, and the boards of trustees of other US museums have or are planning to split the position of director into that of a business manager and an artistic director. The Metropolitan Museum in New York is one case where this split has already occurred. The debate often rages only over which of the two executives should and will in fact have the last word.

Traditionally the boards of trustees of US museums are dominated by members who come from the world of business and high finance. The board is legally responsible for the institution and consequently the trustees are the ultimate authority. Thus the business mentality has always been conspicuously strong at the decision-making level of private museums in the United States. However, the state of affairs is not essentially different in public museums in other parts of the world. Whether the directors have an art-historical background or not, they perform, in fact, the tasks of the chief executive officer of a business organization. Like their peers in other industries they prepare budgets and development plans and present them for approval to their respective public supervising bodies and funding agencies. The staging of an international exhibition such as a Biennale or a Documenta presents a major managerial challenge with repercussions not only for what is being managed, but also for the future career of the executive in charge.

Responding to a realistic appraisal of their lot, even artists are now acquiring managerial training in workshops funded by public agencies in the United States. Such sessions are usually well attended, as artists recognize that the managerial skills for running a small business could have a bearing on their own survival. Some of the more successful artists employ their own business managers. As for art dealers, it goes without saying that they are engaged in running business. The success of their enterprises and the future of the artists in their stables obviously depend a great deal on their managerial skills. They are assisted by paid advisors, accountants, lawyers and public relations agents. Furthermore, collectors too often do their collecting with the assistance of a paid staff.

At least in passing, I should mention that numerous other industries depend on the economic vitality of the art branch of the consciousness industry. Arts administrators do not exaggerate when they defend their claims for public support by pointing to the number of jobs that are affected not only in their own institutions but also in the communications and particularly in the hotel and restaurant industry. The Tut show of the Metropolitan Museum is estimated to have generated $111 million for the economy of New York City. In New York and possibly elsewhere real-estate speculators follow with great interest the move of artists into low-rent commercial and residential areas. From experience they know that artists unwittingly open these areas for gentrification and lucrative development. New York's Soho district is a striking example. Mayor Koch, always a friend of the relators who stuff his campaign chest, tried recently to plant artists into particular streets on the Lower East Side to accomplish what is euphemistically called 'rehabilitation' of a neighborhood, but what in fact means squeezing out an indigenous poor population in order to attract developers of high-rent housing. The recent 'Terminal Show' was a brain-child of the city's Public Development Corporation. It was meant to draw attention to the industrial potential of the former Brooklyn Army Terminal building. And the Museum of Modern Art, having erected a luxury apartment tower over its own building, is also now actively involved in real estate.[1]

Elsewhere city governments have recognized the importance of the art industry. The city of Hannover in West Germany, for example, sponsored widely publicized art events in order to improve its dull image. As large corporations point to the cultural life of their location in order to attract sophisticated personnel, so Hannover speculated that the outlay for art would be amortized many times by the attraction the city would gain for businesses seeking sites for relocation. It is well documented that Documenta is held in an out-of-the-way place like Kassel and given economic support by the city, state and federal government because it was assumed that Kassel would be put on the map by an international art exhibition. It was hoped that the event would revitalize the economically depressed region close to the German border and that it would prop up the local tourist industry.

Another German example of the way in which direct industrial benefits flow from investment in art may be seen in the activities of the collector Peter Ludwig. It is widely believed that the motive behind his buying a large chunk of government-sanctioned Soviet art and displaying it in 'his' museums was to open the Soviet market for his chocolate company. Ludwig may have risked his reputation as a connoisseur of art, but by buying into the Soviet consciousness industry he proved his taste for sweet deals. More recently he recapitalized his company by selling a collection of medieval manuscripts to the Getty Museum for an estimated price of $40 to $60 million (see *A.i.A.* [*Art in America*], Summer '83). As a shrewd businessman, Ludwig used the money to establish a foundation that owns shares in his company. Thus the income from this capital remains untaxed and, in effect, the ordinary taxpayer winds up subsidizing Ludwig's power ambitions in the art world.[2]

Aside from the reasons already mentioned, the discomfort in applying industrial nomenclature to works of art may also have to do with the fact that these products are not entirely physical in nature. Although transmitted in one material form or another, they are developed in and by consciousness and have meaning only for another consciousness. In addition, it is possible to argue over the extent to which the physical object determines the manner in which the receiver decodes it. Such interpretive work is in turn a product of consciousness, performed gratis by each viewer but potentially salable if undertaken by curators, historians, critics, appraisers, teachers, etc. The hesitancy to use industrial concepts and language can probably also be attributed to our lingering idealist tradition, which associates such work with the 'spirit', a term with religious overtones and one that indicates the avoidance of mundane considerations.

The tax authorities, however, have no compunction in assessing the income derived from the 'spiritual' activities. Conversely the taxpayers so affected do not shy away from deducting relevant business expenses. They normally protest against tax rulings which declare their work to be nothing but a hobby, or to put it in Kantian terms, the pursuit of 'disinterested pleasure'. Economists consider the consciousness industry as part of the ever-growing service sector and include it as a matter of course in the computation of the gross national product.

The product of the consciousness industry, however, is not only elusive because of its seemingly nonsecular nature and its aspects of intangibility. More disconcerting, perhaps, is the fact that we do not even totally command our individual consciousness. As Karl Marx observed in the *German Ideology*, consciousness is a social product. It is, in fact, not our private property, homegrown and a home to retire to. It is the result of a collective historical endeavor, embedded in and reflecting particular value systems, aspirations and goals. And these do not by any means represent the interests of everybody. Nor are we dealing with a universally accepted body of knowledge or beliefs. Word has gotten around that material conditions and the ideological context in which an individual grows up and lives determine to a considerable extent his or her consciousness. As has been pointed out, and not only by Marxist social scientists and psychologists, consciousness is not a pure, independent, value-free entity, evolving according to internal, self-sufficient and universal rules. It is contingent, an open system, responsive to the crosscurrents of the environment. It is, in fact, a battleground of conflicting interests. Correspondingly, the products of consciousness represent interests and interpretations of the world that are potentially at odds with each other. The products of the means of production, like those means themselves, are not neutral. As they were shaped by their respective environments and social relations so do they in turn influence our view of the human condition.

Currently we are witnessing a great retreat to the private cocoon. We see a lot of noncommittal, sometimes cynical playing on naively perceived social forces, along with other forms of contemporary dandyism and updated versions of art for art's sake. Some artists and promoters may reject any commitment, and refuse to accept the notion that their work presents a point of view beyond itself or that it fosters certain attitudes; nevertheless, as soon as work enjoys larger exposure it inevitably participates in public discourse, advances particular systems of belief, and has reverberations in the social arena. At that point, art works are no longer a private affair. The producer and the distributor must then weigh the impact.

But it is important to recognize that the codes employed by artists are often not as clear and unambiguous as those in other fields of communication. Controlled ambiguity may, in fact, be one of the characteristics of much Western art since the Renaissance. It is not uncommon that messages are received in a garbled, distorted form and that they possibly even relay the opposite of what was intended – not to speak of the kinds of creative confusion and muddle-headedness that can accompany the art work's production. To compound these problems, there are the historical contingencies of the codes and the unavoidable biases of those who decipher them. With so many variables, there is ample room for exegesis and a livelihood is thus guaranteed for many workers in the consciousness industry.

Although the product under discussion appears to be quite slippery, it is by no means inconsequential, as cultural functionaries from Moscow to Washington make clear every day. It is recognized in both capitals that not only the mass media deserve monitoring, but also those activities which are normally relegated to special sections in the backs of newspapers. *The New York Times* calls its weekend section 'Arts and Leisure' and covers under this heading theater, dance, movies, art, numismatics, gardening and other ostensibly harmless activities. Other papers carry these items under equally innocuous titles such as 'culture', 'entertainment', or 'life style'. Why should governments, and for that matter corporations which are not themselves in the communications industry, pay attention to such seeming trivia? I think they do so for good reason. They have understood, sometimes better than the people who work in the leisure-suits of culture, that the term 'culture' camouflages the social and political consequences resulting from the industrial distribution of consciousness.

The channeling of consciousness is pervasive not only under dictatorships but also in liberal societies. To make such an assertion may sound outrageous because according to popular myth liberal regimes do not behave this way. Such an assertion could also be misunderstood as an attempt to downplay the brutality with which mainstream conduct is enforced in totalitarian regimes or as a claim that coercion of the same viciousness is practiced elsewhere, too. In nondictatorial societies, the induction into and the maintenance of a particular way of thinking and seeing must be performed with subtlety in order to succeed. Staying within the acceptable range of divergent views must be perceived as the natural thing to do.

Within the art world, museums and other institutions that stage exhibitions play an important role in the inculcation of opinions and attitudes. Indeed, they usually present themselves as educational organizations and consider education as one of their primary responsibilities. Naturally, museums work in the vineyards of consciousness. To state that obvious fact, however, is not an accusation of devious conduct. An institution's intellectual and moral position becomes tenuous only if it claims to be free of ideological bias. And such an institution should be challenged if it refuses to acknowledge that it operates under constraints deriving from its sources of funding and from the authority to which it reports.

It is perhaps not surprising that many museums indignantly reject the notion that they provide a blased view of the works in their custody. Indeed, museums usually claim to subscribe to the canons of impartial scholarship. As honorable as such an endeavor is – and it is still a valid goal to strive after – it suffers from idealist delusions about the nonpartisan character of consciousness. A theoretical prop for this worthy but untenable position is the 19th-century doctrine of art for art's sake. That doctrine has an avant-garde historical veneer and in its time did indeed perform a liberating role. Even today, in countries where artists are openly compelled to serve prescribed policies, it still has an emancipatory ring. The gospel of art for art's sake isolates art and postulates its self-sufficiency, as if art had or followed rules which are impervious to the social environment. Adherents of the doctrine believe that art does not and should not reflect the squabbles of the day. Obviously they are mistaken in their assumption that products of consciousness can be created in isolation. Their stance and what is crafted under its auspices has not only theoretical but also definite social implications. American formalism updated the doctrine and associated it with the political concepts of the 'free world' and individualism. Under Clement Greenberg's tutelage, everything that made worldly references was simply excommunicated from art so as to shield the grail of taste from contamination. What started out as a liberating drive turned into its opposite. The doctrine now provides museums with an alibi for ignoring the ideological aspects of art works and the equally ideological implications of the way those works are presented to the public. Whether such neutralizing is performed with deliberation or merely out of habit or lack of resources is irrelevant: practiced over many years it constitutes a powerful form of indoctrination.

Every museum is perforce a political institution, no matter whether it is privately run or maintained and supervised by governmental agencies. Those who hold the purse strings and have the authority over hiring and firing are, in effect, in charge of every element of the organization, if they choose to use their powers. While the rule of the boards of trustees of museums in the United States is generally uncontested, the supervisory bodies of public institutions elsewhere have to contend much more with public opinion and the prevailing political climate. It follows that political considerations play a role in the appointment of museum directors. Once they are in office and have civil service status with tenure, such officials often enjoy more independence than their colleagues in the United States, who can be dismissed from one day to the next, as occurred with Bates Lowry and John Hightower at the Museum of Modern Art within a few years' time. But it is advisable, of course, to be a political animal in both settings. Funding as much as one's prospect for promotion to more prestigious posts depend on how well one can play the game.

Directors in private US museums need to be tuned primarily to the frame of mind represented by the *Wall Street Journal*, the daily source of edification of their board members. They are affected less by who happens to be the occupant of the White House or the mayor's office, although this is not totally irrelevant for the success of applications for public grants. In other countries the outcome of elections can have a direct bearing on museum policies. Agility in dealing with political parties, possibly even membership in a party, can be an asset. The arrival of Margaret Thatcher in Downing Street and of François Mitterand at the Élysée noticeably affected the art institutions in their respective countries. Whether in private or in public museums, disregard of political realities, among them the political need of the supervising bodies and the ideological complexion of their members, is a guarantee for managerial failure.

It is usually required that, at least to the public, institutions appear nonpartisan. This does not exclude the sub rosa promotion of the interests of the ultimate boss. As in other walks of life, the consciousness industry also knows the hidden agenda which is more likely to succeed if it is not perceived as such. It would be wrong, however, to assume that the objectives and the mentality of every art executive are or should be at odds with those on whose support his organization depends. There are natural and honorable allegiances as much as there are forced marriages and marriages of convenience. All players, though, usually see to it that the serene facade of the art temple is preserved.

During the past twenty years the power relations between art institutions and their sources of funding have become more complex. Museums used to be maintained either by public agencies – the tradition in Europe – or through donations from private individuals and philanthropic organizations, as has been the pattern in the United States. When Congress established the National Endowment for the Arts in 1965, US museums gained an additional source of funding. In accepting public grants, however, they became accountable, even if in practice only to a limited degree, to government agencies.

Some public museums in Europe went the road of mixed support, too, although in the opposite direction. Private donors came on board with attractive collections. As has been customary in US museums, however, some of these donors demanded a part in policy making. One of the most spectacular recent examples has been the de facto takeover of museums (among others, museums in Cologne, Vienna and Aachen) that received or believed they would receive gifts from the German collector Peter Ludwig.[3] As is well known in the Rhineland, Count Panza di Blumo's attempt to get his way in the new museum of Mönchengladbach, down the Rhine from Ludwig's headquarters, was successfully rebuffed by the director, Johannes Cladders, who is both resolute and a good poker player in his own right.[4] How far the Saatchis in London will get in dominating the Tate Gallery's Patrons of New Art – and thereby the museum's policies for contemporary art – is currently watched with the same fascination and nervousness as developments in the Kremlin. A recent, much-noticed instance of Saatchi influence was the Tate's 1982 Schnabel show, which consisted almost entirely of works from the Saatchis' collection. In addition to his position on the steering committee of the Tate's Patrons of New Art, Charles Saatchi is also a trustee of the Whitechapel Gallery.[5] Furthermore, the Saatchis' advertising agency has just begun handling publicity for the Victoria and Albert, the Royal Academy, the National Portrait Gallery, the Serpentine Gallery and the British Crafts Council. Certainly the election victory of Mrs. Thatcher, in which the Saatchis played a part as the advertising agency of the Conservative Party, did not weaken their position (and may in turn have provided the Conservatives with a powerful agent within the hallowed halls of the Tate).

If such collectors seem to be acting primarily in their own self-interest and to be building pyramids to themselves when they attempt to impose their will on 'chosen' institutions, their moves are in fact less troublesome in the long run than the disconcerting arrival on the scene of corporate funding for the arts – even though the latter at first appears to be more innocuous.[6] Starting on a large scale towards the end of the sixties in the United States and expanding rapidly ever since, corporate funding has spread during the last five years to Britain and the Continent. Ambitious exhibition programs that could not be financed through traditional sources led museums to turn to corporations for support. The larger, more lavishly appointed these shows and their catalogues became, however, the more glamour the audiences began to expect. In an ever-advancing spiral the public was made to believe that only Hollywood-style extravaganzas are worth seeing and give an accurate sense of the world of art. The resulting box-office pressure made the museums still more dependent on corporate funding. Then came the recession of the seventies and eighties. Many individual donors could no longer contribute at the accustomed rate, and inflation eroded the purchasing power of funds. To compound the financial problems, many governments, facing huge deficits, often due to sizable expansions of military budgets, cut their support for social services as well as their arts funding. Again museums felt they had no choice but to turn to corporations for a bail-out. Following their own ideological inclinations and making them national policy, President Reagan and Mrs Thatcher encouraged the so-called private sector to pick up the slack in financial support.

Why have business executives been receptive to the museums' pleas for money? During the restive sixties the more astute ones began to understand that corporate involvement in the arts is too important to be left to the chairman's wife. Irrespective of their own love for or indifference towards art they recognized that a company's association with art could yield benefits far out of proportion to a specific financial investment. Not only could such a policy attract sophisticated personnel, but it also projected an image of the company as a good corporate citizen and advertised its products – all things which impress investors. Executives with a longer vision also saw that the association of their company, and by implication of business in general, with the high prestige of art was a subtle but effective means for lobbying in the corridors of government. It could open doors, facilitate passage of favorable legislation and serve as a shield against scrutiny and criticism of corporate conduct.

Museums, of course, are not blind to the attractions for business of lobbying through art. For example, in a pamphlet with the telling title 'The Business Behind Art Knows the Art of Good Business', the Metropolitan Museum in New York woos prospective corporate sponsors by assuring them: 'Many public relations opportunities are available through the sponsorship of programs, special exhibitions and services. These can often provide a creative and cost-effective answer to a specific marketing objective, particularly where international, governmental or consumer relations may be a fundamental concern'.[7]

A public relations executive of Mobil in New York aptly called the company's arts support a 'goodwill umbrella', and his colleague from Exxon referred to it as a 'social lubricant'.[8] It is liberals in particular who need to be greased because they are the most likely and sophisticated critics of corporations, and they are often in positions of influence. They also happen to be more interested in culture than other groups on the political spectrum. Luke Ritter, who as outgoing director of the British Association of Business Sponsorship of the Arts should know, recently explained: 'A few years ago companies thought sponsoring the arts was charitable. Now they realize there is also another aspect; it is a tool they can use for corporate promotion in one form or another.' Ritter, obviously in tune with his Prime Minister, was appointed as the new Secretary General on the British Arts Council.

Corporate public relations officers know that the greatest publicity benefits can be derived from high-visibility events, shows that draw crowds and are covered extensively by the popular media; these are shows that are based on and create myths – in short, blockbusters. As long as an institution is not squeamish about company involvement in press releases, posters, advertisements and its exhibition catalogue, its grant proposal for such an extravaganza is likely to be examined with sympathy. Some companies are happy to underwrite publicity for the event (which usually includes the company logo) at a rate almost matching the funds they make available for the exhibition itself. Generally, such companies look for events that are 'exciting', a word that pops up in museum press releases and catalogue prefaces more often than any other. Museum managers have learned, of course, what kind of shows are likely to attract corporate funding. And they also know that they have to keep their institutions in the limelight. Most shows in large New York museums are now sponsored by corporations. Institutions in London will soon be catching up with them. The Whitney Museum has even gone one step further. It has established branches – almost literally a merger – on the premises of two companies.[9] It is fair to assume that exhibition proposals that do not fulfil the necessary criteria for corporate sponsorship risk not being considered, and we never hear about them. Certainly, shows that could promote critical awareness, present products of consciousness dialectically and in relation to the social world, or question relations of power have a slim chance of being approved – not only because they are unlikely to attract corporate funding, but also because they could sour relations with potential sponsors for other shows. Consequently, self-censorship is having a boom.[10] Without exerting any direct pressure, corporations have effectively gained a veto in museums, even though their financial contribution often covers only a fraction of the costs of an exhibition. Depending on circumstances, these contributions are tax-deductible as a business expense or a charitable contribution. Ordinary taxpayers are thus footing part of the bill. In effect, they are unwitting sponsors of corporate policies, which, in many cases, are detrimental to their health and safety, the general welfare and in conflict with their personal ethics.

Since the corporate blanket is so warm, glaring examples of direct interference rare[11] and the increasing dominance of the museums' development offices hard to trace, the change of climate is hardly perceived, nor is it taken as a threat. To say that this change might have consequences beyond the confines of the institution and that it affects the type of art that is and will be produced therefore can sound like over-dramatization. Through naïveté, need or addiction to corporate financing, museums are now on the slippery road to becoming public relations agents for the interests of big business and its ideological allies. The adjustments that museums make in the selection and promotion of works for exhibition and in the way they present them create a climate that supports prevailing distributions of power and capital and persuades the populace that the status quo is the natural and best order of things. Rather than sponsoring intelligent, critical awareness, museums thus tend to foster appeasement.

Those engaged in collaboration with the public relations officers of companies rarely see themselves as promoters of acquiescence. On the contrary, they are usually convinced that their activities are in the best interests of art. Such a well-intentioned delusion can survive only as long as art is perceived as a mythical entity above mundane interests and ideological conflict. And it is, of course, this misunderstanding of the role that products of the consciousness industry play which constitutes the indispensable base for all corporate strategies of persuasion.

Whether museums contend with governments, power-trips of individuals or the corporate steamroller, they are in the business of molding and channeling consciousness. Even though they may not agree with the system of beliefs dominant at the time, their options not to subscribe to them and instead to promote an alternative consciousness are limited. The survival of the institution and personal careers are often at stake. But in nondictatorial societies the means for the production of consciousness are not all in one hand. The sophistication required to promote a particular interpretation of the world is potentially also available to question that interpretation and to offer other versions. As the need to spend enormous sums for public relations and government propaganda indicates, things are not frozen. Political constellations shift and unincorporated zones exist in sufficient numbers to disturb the mainstream.

It was never easy for museums to preserve or regain a degree of maneuverability and intellectual integrity. It takes stealth, intelligence, determination – and some luck. But a democratic society demands nothing less than that.[12]

NOTES

1. The Equitable Life Assurance Society bought and commissioned art works worth seven million dollars US for its new headquarters on New York's 7th Avenue. It also made space available for a branch of the Whitney Museum. Explaining this investment in art, Benjamin D. Holloway, the Chairman of Equitable's Real Estate Group, declared: 'We are doing these things because we think it will attract and hold tenants and that they will pay us rents we are looking for.' Quoted in *The New Yorker*, April 14, 1986.

2. This infusion of capital was insufficient to stem the decline of Mr. Ludwig's chocolate empire. In 1986, he was forced to sell his license to produce and market *Lindt* chocolate in Germany and the Netherlands. Even more trenchant was the take-over of all of his non-German production facilities (St-Hyaclnthe, Québec; St Albans, Vermont; Herentals, Belgium) including the van Houten label and distribution network by the Swiss Jacob Suchard AG. From first place, Mr Ludwig's chocolate company dropped to fourth among German chocolate manufacturers.

3. In September 1986, the new building of the Ludwig Museum was opened in Cologne. At the occasion, Mr Ludwig presented to the public busts of himself and his wife, Irene, which he had commissioned from Arnold Breker. Breker was the most celebrated artist of the Nazi regime. In interviews, Ludwig praised Breker and proposed that paintings and sculptures made under Hitler should be included in German museums.

4. Dr Cladders, who for several years was in charge of the German Pavilion at the Venice Biennale, has since retired from the directorship of the Museum in Mönchengladbach, and Count Panza di Blumo has sold a major portion of his collection to the Museum of Contemporary Art in Los Angeles.

5. During an exhibition of my works at the Tate Gallery in 1984, Charles Saatchi resigned from the Patrons of New Art committee of the Tate as well as from the Board of Trustees of the Whitechapel Gallery. Max Gordon, a friend of the Saatchis and the architect of the new Saatchi Museum in London, is still a member of the Whitechapel Gallery where a retrospective of Julian Schnabel was mounted in 1986.

6. The influence of the Saatchis has since grown considerably through a spectacular series of murders. They have become the largest advertising empire of the world, with sizeable off-shoots in public relations, lobbying and management consulting. As experienced toilers in those branches of the consciousness industry, the Saatchis now seem to have an impact on the artworld that matches or even exceeds that of other corporate art sponsors, particularly in regard to contemporary art. Carl Spielvogel, the head of one of the Saatchi & Saatchi subsidiaries in New York, is now the Chairman of the Metropolitan Museum's Business Committee, and Charles Saatchi is a Vice-Chairman of the Museum's International Business Committee.

7. Already in 1971, C. Douglas Dillon, the recently retired Chairman of the Metropolitan's Board of Trustees, wrote in the *Columbia Journal of World Business* (Sept./Oct. 1971): 'Perhaps the most important single reason for the increased interest of international corporations in the arts is the almost limitless diversity of projects which are possible. The projects can be tailored to a company's specific business goals and can return dividends far out of proportion to the actual investment required'.

8. In an op-ed page advertisement in the *New York Times* on October 10, 1985, Mobil explained under the headline: 'Art, for the Sake of Business', the rationale behind its involvement in the arts in these words: 'What's in it for us – or for *your* company? Improving – and insuring – the business climate'. More extensive reasoning is given by Mobil Director and Vice-President of Public Affairs, Herb Schmertz, in the chapter 'Affinity-of-Purpose Marketing: the Case of *Masterpiece Theatre*' in his book *Goodbye to the Low Profile: The Art of Creative Confrontation* (Boston: Little, Brown & Co., 1986).

9. The headquarters of Philip Morris in New York and the headquarters of the Champion International Corporation in Stanford, Conn. An additional branch has since been opened at the new headquarters of the Equitable Life Assurance Society in New York. Benjamin D. Holloway, Chairman and Chief Executive Officer of the Equitable Real Estate Group, a subsidiary of the insurance company, has joined the Whitney Museum Board of Trustees. When he was queried about his relationship through the exhibition program of the Museum at the Equitable Center by Michael Brenson of the *New York Times* (Feb. 23, 1986), he answered: 'I would be the last person in the world to censor them, but I'm responsible for what I do and they are responsible for what they do and if they do something irresponsible, they have to take the consequences.'

10. Philippe de Montebello, Director of the Metropolitan Museum, is quoted in *Newsweek* (Nov. 25,

1985): 'It's an inherent insidious hidden form of censorship … But corporations aren't censoring us – we are censoring ourselves.'

11. In 1984, Mobil threatened the Tate Gallery and the Stedelijk van Abbemuseum in Eindhoven with a law-suit. The oil giant objected to the reproduction of several works I had made on the activities of Mobil in the catalogue, which was co-published by the two institutions at the occasion of a one-man show at the Tate Gallery. As a precautionary legal measure, the two museums suspended the distribution of the catalogue. They resumed distribution to the public after about a year.

12. This is a slightly altered version of an essay that was originally delivered as a talk at the Annual Meeting of the Art Museum Association of Australia in Canberra, August 30, 1983, and published in *Art in America* in 1984. The photographs of volcanos erupting and surfers surfing were taken from slides bought by Haacke in Hawaii en route to his lecture in Canberra; these slides were projected during the talk [photographs not reproduced here].

5.

The Exhibitionary Complex

Tony Bennett

In reviewing Foucault on the asylum, the clinic, and the prison as institutional articulations of power and knowledge relations, Douglas Crimp suggests that there 'is another such institution of confinement ripe for analysis in Foucault's terms – the museum – and another discipline – art history'.[1] Crimp is no doubt right, although the terms of his proposal are misleadingly restrictive. For the emergence of the art museum was closely related to that of a wider range of institutions – history and natural-science museums, dioramas and panoramas, national and, later, international exhibitions, arcades and department stores – which served as linked sites for the development and circulation of new disciplines (history, biology, art history, anthropology) and their discursive formations (the past, evolution, aesthetics, Man) as well as for the development of new technologies of vision. Furthermore, while these comprised an intersecting set of institutional and disciplinary relations which might be productively analysed as particular articulations of power and knowledge, the suggestion that they should be construed as institutions of confinement is curious. It seems to imply that works of art had previously wandered through the streets of Europe like the Ships of Fools in Foucault's *Madness and Civilisation*; or that geological and natural-history specimens had been displayed before the world, like the condemned on the scaffold, rather than being withheld from public gaze, secreted in the *studiolo* of princes, or made accessible only to the limited gaze of high society in the *cabinets des curieux* of the aristocracy. Museums may have enclosed objects within walls, but the nineteenth century saw their doors opened to the general public – witnesses whose presence was just as essential to a display of power as had been that of the people before the spectacle of punishment in the eighteenth century.

Institutions, then, not of confinement but of exhibition, forming a complex of disciplinary and power relations whose development might more fruitfully be juxtaposed to, rather than aligned with, the formation of Foucault's 'carceral archipelago'. For the movement Foucault traces in *Discipline and Punish* is one in which objects and bodies – the scaffold and the body of the condemned – which had previously formed a part of the public display of power were withdrawn from the public gaze as punishment increasingly took the form of incarceration. No longer inscribed within a public dramaturgy of power, the body of the condemned comes to be caught up within an inward-looking web of power relations. Subjected to omnipresent forms of surveillance through which the message of power was carried directly to it so as to render it docile, the body no longer served as the surface on which, through the system of retaliatory marks inflicted on it in the name of the sovereign, the lessons of power were written for others to read:

The scaffold, where the body of the tortured criminal had been exposed to the ritually manifest force of the sovereign, the punitive theatre in which the representation of punishment was permanently available to the social body, was replaced by a great enclosed, complex and hierarchised structure that was integrated into the very body of the state apparatus.[2]

The institutions comprising 'the exhibitionary complex', by contrast, were involved in the transfer of objects and bodies from the enclosed and private domains in which they had previously been displayed (but to a restricted public) into progressively more open and public arenas where, through the representations to which they were subjected, they formed vehicles for inscribing and broadcasting the messages of power (but of a different type) throughout society.

Two different sets of institutions and their accompanying knowledge/power relations, then, whose histories, in these respects, run in opposing directions. Yet they are also parallel histories. The exhibitionary complex and the carceral archipelago develop over roughly the same period – the late eighteenth to the mid-nineteenth centuries – and achieve developed articulations of the new principles they embodied within a decade or so of one another. Foucault regards the opening of the new prison at Mettray in 1840 as a key moment in the development of the carceral system. Why Mettray? Because, Foucault argues, 'it is the disciplinary form at its most extreme, the model in which are concentrated all the coercive technologies of behaviour previously found in the cloister, prison, school or regiment and which, in being brought together in one place, served as a guide for the future development of carceral institutions'

(p. 293). In Britain, the opening of Pentonville Model Prison in 1842 is often viewed in a similar light. Less than a decade later the Great Exhibition of 1851 brought together an ensemble of disciplines and techniques of display that had been developed within the previous histories of museums, panoramas, Mechanics Institute exhibitions, art galleries, and arcades. In doing so, it translated these into exhibitionary forms which, in simultaneously ordering objects for public inspection and ordering the public that inspected, were to have a profound and lasting influence on the subsequent development of museums, art galleries, expositions, and department stores.

Nor are these entirely separate histories. At certain points they overlap, often with a transfer of meanings and effects between them. To understand their interrelations, however, it will be necessary, in borrowing from Foucault, to qualify the terms he proposes for investigating the development of power/ knowledge relations during the formation of the modern period. For the set of such relations associated with the development of the exhibitionary complex serves as a check to the generalizing conclusions Foucault derives from his examination of the carceral system. In particular, it calls into question his suggestion that the penitentiary merely perfected the individualizing and normalizing technologies associated with a veritable swarming of forms of surveillance and disciplinary mechanisms which came to suffuse society with a new – and all-pervasive – political economy of power. This is not to suggest that technologies of surveillance had no place in the exhibitionary complex but rather that their intrication with new forms of spectacle produced a more complex and nuanced set of relations through which power was exercised and relayed to – and, in part, through and by – the populace than the Foucauldian account allows.

Foucault's primary concern, of course, is with the problem of order. He conceives the development of new forms of discipline and surveillance, as Jeffrey Minson puts it, as an 'attempt to reduce an ungovernable *populace* to a multiply differentiated *population*', parts of 'an historical movement aimed at transforming highly disruptive economic conflicts and political forms of disorder into quasi-technical or moral problems for social administration'. These mechanisms assumed, Minson continues, 'that the key to the populace's social and political unruliness and also the means of combating it lies in the "opacity" of the populace to the forces of order'.[3] The exhibitionary complex was also a response to the problem of order, but one which worked differently in seeking to transform that problem into one of culture – a question of winning hearts and minds as well as the disciplining and training of bodies. As such, its constituent institutions reversed the orientations of the disciplinary apparatuses in seeking to render the forces and principles of order visible to the populace – transformed, here, into a people, a citizenry – rather than vice versa. They sought not to map the social body in order to know the populace by rendering it visible to power. Instead, through the provision of object lessons in power – the power to command and arrange things and bodies for public display – they sought to allow the people, and *en masse* rather than individually, to know rather than be known, to become the subjects rather than the objects of knowledge. Yet, ideally, they sought also to allow the people to know and thence to regulate themselves; to become, in seeing themselves from the side of power, both the subjects and the objects of knowledge, knowing power and what power knows, and knowing themselves as (ideally) known by power, interiorizing its gaze as a principle of self-surveillance and, hence, self-regulation.

It is, then, as a set of cultural technologies concerned to organize a voluntarily self-regulating citizenry that I propose to examine the formation of the exhibitionary complex. In doing so, I shall draw on the Gramscian perspective of the ethical and educative function of the modern state to account for the relations of this complex to the development of the bourgeois democratic polity. Yet, while wishing to resist a tendency in Foucault towards misplaced generalizations, it is to Foucault's work that I shall look to unravel the relations between knowledge and power effected by the technologies of vision embodied in the architectural forms of the exhibitionary complex.

Discipline, surveillance, spectacle

In discussing the proposals of late-eighteenth-century penal reformers, Foucault remarks that punishment, while remaining a 'legible lesson' organized in relation to the body of the offended, was envisioned as 'a school rather than a festival; an ever-open book rather than a ceremony' (p. 111). Hence, in schemes to use convict labour in public contexts, it was envisaged that the convict would repay society twice: once by the labour he provided, and a second time by the signs he produced, a focus of both profit and signification in serving as an ever present reminder of the connection between crime and punishment:

Children should be allowed to come to the places where the penalty is being carried out; there they will attend their classes in civics. And grown men will periodically relearn the laws. Let us conceive of places of punishment as a Garden of the Laws that families would visit on Sundays.

(p. 111)

In the event, punishment took a different path with the development of the carceral system. Under both the *ancien régime* and the projects of the late-eighteenth-century reformers, punishment had formed part of a public system of representation. Both regimes obeyed a logic according to which 'secret punishment is a punishment half-wasted' (p. 111). With the development of the carceral system, by contrast, punishment was removed from the public gaze in being enacted behind the closed walls of the penitentiary, and had in view not the production of signs for society but the correction of the offender. No longer an art of public effects, punishment aimed at a calculated transformation in the behaviour of the convicted. The body of the offender, no longer a medium for the relay of signs of power, was zoned as the target for disciplinary technologies which sought to modify behaviour through repetition:

> The body and the soul, as principles of behaviour, form the element that is now proposed for punitive intervention. Rather than on an art of representation, this punitive intervention must rest on a studied manipulation of the individual … As for the instruments used, these are no longer complexes of representation, reinforced and circulated, but forms of coercion, schemata of restraint, applied and repeated. Exercises, not signs …
>
> (p. 128)

It is not this account itself that is in question here but some of the more general claims Foucault elaborates on its basis. In his discussion of 'the swarming of disciplinary mechanisms', Foucault argues that the disciplinary technologies and forms of observation developed in the carceral system – and especially the principle of panopticism, rendering everything visible to the eye of power – display a tendency 'to become 'de-institutionalised', to emerge from the closed fortresses in which they once functioned and to circulate in a 'free' state' (p. 211). These new systems of surveillance, mapping the social body so as to render it knowable and amenable to social regulation, mean, Foucault argues, that 'one can speak of the formation of a disciplinary society … that stretches from the enclosed disciplines, a sort of social "quarantine", to an indefinitely generalisable mechanism of "panopticism"' (p. 216). A society, according to Foucault in his approving quotation of Julius, that 'is one not of spectacle, but of surveillance':

> Antiquity had been a civilisation of spectacle. 'To render accessible to a multitude of men the inspection of a small number of objects': this was the problem to which the architecture of temples, theatres and circuses responded … In a society in which the principal elements are no longer the community and public life, but, on the one hand, private individuals and, on the other, the state, relations can be regulated only in a form that is the exact reverse of the spectacle. It was to the modern age, to the ever-growing influence of the state, to its ever more profound intervention in all the details and all the relations of social life, that was reserved the task of increasing and perfecting its guarantees, by using and directing towards that great aim the building and distribution of buildings intended to observe a great multitude of men at the same time.
>
> (pp. 216–17)

A disciplinary society: this general characterization of the modality of power in modern societies has proved one of the more influential aspects of

Foucault's work. Yet it is an incautious generalization and one produced by a peculiar kind of misattention. For it by no means follows from the fact that punishment had ceased to be a spectacle that the function of displaying power – of making it visible for all to see – had itself fallen into abeyance.[4] Indeed, as Graeme Davison suggests, the Crystal Palace might serve as the emblem of an architectural series which could be ranged against that of the asylum, school, and prison in its continuing concern with the display of objects to a great multitude:

The Crystal Palace reversed the panoptical principle by fixing the eyes of the multitude upon an assemblage of glamorous commodities. The Panopticon was designed so that everyone could be seen; the Crystal Palace was designed so that everyone could see.[5]

This opposition is a little overstated in that one of the architectural innovations of the Crystal Palace consisted in the arrangement of relations between the public and exhibits so that, while everyone could see, there were also vantage points from which everyone could be seen, thus combining the functions of spectacle and surveillance. None the less, the shift of emphasis is worth preserving for the moment, particularly as its force is by no means limited to the Great Exhibition. Even a cursory glance through Richard Altick's *The Shows of London* convinces that the nineteenth century was quite unprecedented in the social effort it devoted to the organization of spectacles arranged for increasingly large and undifferentiated publics.[6] Several aspects of these developments merit a preliminary consideration.

First: the tendency for society itself – in its constituent parts and as a whole – to be rendered as a spectacle. This was especially clear in attempts to render the city visible, and hence knowable, as a totality. While the depths of city life were penetrated by developing networks of surveillance, cities increasingly opened up their processes to public inspection, laying their secrets open not merely to the gaze of power but, in principle, to that of everyone; indeed, making the specular dominance of the eye of power available to all. By the turn of the century, Dean MacCannell notes, sightseers in Paris 'were given tours of the sewers, the morgue, a slaughterhouse, a tobacco factory, the government printing office, a tapestry works, the mint, the stock exchange and the supreme court in session'.[7] No doubt such tours conferred only an imaginary dominance over the city, an illusory rather than substantive controlling vision, as Dana Brand suggests was the case with earlier panoramas.[8] Yet the principle they embodied was real enough and, in seeking to render cities knowable in exhibiting the workings of their organizing institutions, they are without parallel in the spectacles of earlier regimes where the view of power was always 'from below'. This ambition towards a specular dominance over a totality was even more evident in the conception of international exhibitions which, in their heyday, sought to make the whole world, past and present, metonymically available in the assemblages of objects and peoples they brought together and, from their powers, to lay it before a controlling vision.

Second: the increasing involvement of the state in the provision of such spectacles. In the British case, and even more so the American, such involvement was typically indirect.[9] Nicholas Pearson notes that while the sphere of culture fell increasingly under governmental regulation in the second half of the nineteenth century, the preferred form of administration for museums, art galleries, and exhibitions was (and remains) via boards of trustees. Through these, the state could retain effective direction over policy by virtue of its control over appointments but without involving itself in the day-to-day conduct of affairs and so, seemingly, violating the Kantian imperative in subordinating culture to practical requirements.[10] Although the state was initially prodded only reluctantly into this sphere of activity, there should be no doubt of the importance it eventually assumed. Museums, galleries, and, more intermittently, exhibitions played a pivotal role in the formation of the modern state and are fundamental to its conception as, among other things, a set of educative and civilizing agencies. Since the nineteenth century, they have been ranked highly in the funding priorities of all developed nation-states and have proved remarkably influential cultural technologies in the degree to which they have recruited the interest and participation of their citizenries.

Finally: the exhibitionary complex provided a context for the *permanent* display of power/knowledge. In his discussion of the display of power in the *ancien régime*, Foucault stresses its episodic quality. The spectacle of the scaffold formed part of a system of power which 'in the absence of continual supervision, sought a renewal of its effect in the spectacle of its individual manifestations; of a power that was recharged in the ritual display of its reality as "super-power"' (p. 57). It is not that the nineteenth century dispensed entirely with the need for the periodic magnification of power through its excessive display, for the expositions played this role. They did so, however, in relation to a network of institutions which provided mechanisms for the permanent display of power. And for a power which was not reduced to periodic effects but which, to the contrary, manifested itself precisely in continually displaying its ability to command, order, and control objects and bodies, living or dead.

There is, then, another series from the one Foucault examines in tracing the shift from the ceremony of the scaffold to the disciplinary rigours of the penitentiary. Yet it is a series which has its echo and, in some respects, model in another section of the socio-juridical apparatus: the trial. The scene of the trial and that of punishment traversed one another as they moved in opposite directions during the early modern period. As punishment was withdrawn from the public gaze and transferred to the enclosed space of the penitentiary, so the procedures of trial and sentencing – which, except for England, had hitherto been mostly conducted in secret, 'opaque not only to the public but also to the accused himself' (p. 35) – were made public as part of a new system of judicial truth which, in order to function as truth, needed to be made known to all. If the asymmetry of these movements is compelling, it is no more so than the symmetry of the movement traced by the trial and the museum in the transition they make from closed and restricted to open and public contexts. And, as a part of a profound transformation in their social functioning, it was ultimately to these institutions – and not by witnessing punishment enacted in the streets nor, as Bentham had envisaged, by making the penitentiaries open to public inspection – that children, and their parents, were invited to attend their lessons in civics.

Moreover, such lessons consisted not in a display of power which, in seeking to terrorize, positioned the people on the other side of power as its potential recipients but sought rather to place the people – conceived as a nationalized citizenry – on this side of power, both its subject and its beneficiary. To identify with power, to see it as, if not directly theirs, then indirectly so, a force regulated and channelled by society's ruling groups but for the good of all; this was the rhetoric of power embodied in the exhibitionary complex – a power made manifest not in its ability to inflict pain but by its ability to organize and co-ordinate an order of things and to produce a place for the people in relation to that order. Detailed studies of nineteenth-century expositions thus consistently highlight the ideological economy of their organizing principles, transforming displays of machinery and industrial processes, of finished products and *objets d'art*, into material signifiers of progress – but of progress as a collective national achievement with capital as the great co-ordinator.[11] This power thus subjugated by flattery, placing itself on the side of the people by affording them a place within its workings; a power which placed the people behind it, inveigled into complicity with it rather than cowed into submission before it. And this power marked out the distinction between the subjects and the objects of power not within the national body but, as organized by the many rhetorics of imperialism, between that body and other, 'non-civilized' peoples upon whose bodies the effects of power were unleashed with as much force and theatricality as had been manifest on the scaffold. This was, in other words, a power which aimed at a rhetorical effect through its representation of otherness rather than at any disciplinary effects.

Yet it is not merely in terms of its ideological economy that the exhibitionary complex must be assessed. While museums and expositions may have set out to win the hearts and minds of their visitors, these also brought their bodies with them creating architectural problems as vexed as any posed by the development of the carceral archipelago. The birth of the latter, Foucault argues, required a new architectural problematic:

that of an architecture that is no longer built simply to be seen (as with the ostentation of palaces), or to observe the external space (cf. the geometry of fortresses), but to permit an internal, articulated and detailed control – to render visible those who are inside it; in more general terms, an architecture that would operate to transform individuals: to act on those it shelters, to provide a hold on their conduct, to carry the effects of power right to them, to make it possible to know them, to alter them.

(p. 172)

As Davison notes, the development of the exhibitionary complex also posed a new demand: that everyone should see, and not just the ostentation of imposing façades but their contents too. This, too, created a series of architectural problems which were ultimately resolved only through a 'political economy of detail' similar to that applied to the regulation of the relations among bodies, space, and time within the penitentiary. In Britain, France, and Germany, the late eighteenth and early nineteenth centuries witnessed a spate of state-sponsored architectural competitions for the design of museums in which the emphasis shifted progressively away from organizing spaces of display for the private pleasure of the prince or aristocrat and towards an organization of space and vision that would enable museums to function as organs of public instruction.[12] Yet, as I have already suggested, it is misleading to view the architectural problematics of the exhibitionary complex as simply reversing the principles of panopticism. The effect of these principles, Foucault argues, was to abolish the crowd conceived as 'a compact mass, a locus of multiple exchanges, individualities merging together, a collective effect' and to replace it with 'a collection of separated individualities' (p. 201). However, as John MacArthur notes, the Panopticon is simply a technique, not itself a disciplinary regime or essentially a part of one, and like all techniques, its potential effects are not exhausted by its deployment within any of the regimes in which it happens to be used.[13] The peculiarity of the exhibitionary complex is not to be found in its reversal of the principles of the Panopticon. Rather, it consists in its incorporation of aspects of those principles together with those of the panorama, forming a technology of vision which served not to atomize and disperse the crowd but to regulate it, and to do so by rendering it visible to itself, by making the crowd itself the ultimate spectacle.

An instruction from a 'Short Sermon to Sightseers' at the 1901 Pan-American Exposition enjoined: 'Please remember when you get inside the gates you are part of the show.'[14] This was also true of museums and department stores which, like many of the main exhibition halls of expositions, frequently contained galleries affording a superior vantage point from which the layout of the whole and the activities of other visitors could also be observed.[15] It was, however, the expositions which developed this characteristic furthest in constructing viewing positions from which they could be surveyed as totalities: the function of the Eiffel Tower at the 1889 Paris Exposition, for example. To see and be seen, to survey yet always be under surveillance, the object of an unknown but controlling look: in these ways, as micro-worlds rendered constantly visible to themselves, expositions realized some of the ideals of panopticism in transforming the crowd into a constantly surveyed, self-watching, self-regulating, and as the historical record suggests, consistently orderly public – a society watching over itself.

Within the hierarchically organized systems of looks of the penitentiary in which each level of looking is monitored by a higher one, the inmate constitutes the point at which all these looks culminate but he is unable to return a look of his own or move to a higher level of vision. The exhibitionary complex, by contrast, perfected a self-monitoring system of looks in which the subject and object positions can be exchanged, in which the crowd comes to commune with and regulate itself through interiorizing the ideal and ordered view of itself as seen from the controlling vision of power – a site of sight accessible to all. It was in thus democratizing the eye of power that the expositions realized Bentham's aspiration for a system of looks within which the central position would be available to the public at all times, a model lesson in civics in which a society regulated itself through self-observation. But, of course, of self-observation from a certain perspective. As Manfredo Tafuri puts it:

The arcades and the department stores of Paris, like the great expositions, were certainly the places in which the crowd, itself become a spectacle, found the spatial and visual means for a self-education from the point of view of capital.[16]

However, this was not an achievement of architecture alone. Account must also be taken of the forces which, in shaping the exhibitionary complex, formed both its public and its rhetorics.

Seeing things

It seems unlikely, come the revolution, that it will occur to anyone to storm the British Museum. Perhaps it always was so. Yet, in the early days of its history, the fear that it might incite the vengeance of the mob was real enough. In 1780, in the midst of the Gordon Riots, troops were housed in the gardens and building and, in 1848, when the Chartists marched to present the People's Charter to parliament, the authorities prepared to defend the museum as vigilantly as if it had been a penitentiary. The museum staff were sworn in as special constables; fortifications were constructed around the perimeter; a garrison of museum staff, regular troops, and Chelsea pensioners, armed with muskets, pikes, and cutlasses, and with provisions for a three-day siege, occupied the buildings; stones were carried to the roof to be hurled down on the Chartists should they succeed in breaching the outer defences.[17]

This fear of the crowd haunted debates on the museum's policy for over a century. Acknowledged as one of the first public museums, its conception of the public was a limited one. Visitors were admitted only in groups of fifteen and were obliged to submit their credentials for inspection prior to admission which was granted only if they were found to be 'not exceptionable'.[18] When changes to this policy were proposed, they were resisted by both the museum's trustees and its curators, apprehensive that the unruliness of the mob would mar the ordered display of culture and knowledge. When, shortly after the museum's establishment, it was proposed that there be public days on which unrestricted access would be allowed, the proposal was scuttled on the grounds, as one trustee put it, that some of the visitors from the streets would inevitably be 'in liquor' and 'will never be kept in order'. And if public days should be allowed, Dr Ward continued:

then it will be necessary for the Trustees to have a presence of a Committee of themselves attending, with at least two Justices of the Peace and the constables of the division of Bloomsbury ... supported by a guard such as one as usually attends at the Play-House, and even after all this, Accidents must and will happen.[19]

Similar objections were raised when, in 1835, a select committee was appointed to inquire into the management of the museum and suggested that it might be opened over Easter to facilitate attendance by the labouring classes. A few decades later, however, the issue had been finally resolved in favour of the reformers. The most significant shift in the state's attitude towards museums was marked by the opening of the South Kensington Museum in 1857. [See Fig. 4.5.1] Administered, eventually, under the auspices of the Board of Education, the museum was officially dedicated to the service of an extended and undifferentiated public with opening hours and an admissions policy designed to maximize its accessibility to the working classes. It proved remarkably successful, too, attracting over 15 million visits between 1857 and 1883, over 6.5 million of which were recorded in the evenings, the most popular time for working-class visitors who, it seems, remained largely sober. Henry Cole, the first director of the museum and an ardent advocate of the role museums should play in the formation of a rational public culture, pointedly rebutted the conceptions of the unruly mob which had informed earlier objections to open admissions policies. Informing a House of Commons committee in 1860 that only one person had had to be excluded for not being able to walk steadily, he went on to note

Figure 4.5.1   The South Kensington Museum (later the Victoria and Albert Museum): interior of the South Court, eastern portion, from the south, c. 1876 (drawing by John Watkins). Reproduced by courtesy of the Board of Trustees of the Victoria and Albert Museum, London

that the sale of alcohol in the refreshment rooms had averaged out, as Altick summarizes it, at 'two and a half drops of wine, fourteen-fifteenths of a drop of brandy, and ten and half drops of bottled ale per capita'.[20] As the evidence of the orderliness of the newly extended museum public mounted, even the British Museum relented and, in 1883, embarked on a programme of electrification to permit evening opening.

The South Kensington Museum thus marked a significant turning point in the development of British museum policy in clearly enunciating the principles of the modern museum conceived as an instrument of public education. It provided the axis around which London's museum complex was to develop throughout the rest of the century and exerted a strong influence on the development of museums in the provincial cities and towns. These now rapidly took advantage of the Museum Bill of 1845 (hitherto used relatively sparingly) which empowered local authorities to establish museums and art galleries: the number of public museums in Britain increased from 50 in 1860 to 200 in 1900.[21] In its turn, however, the South Kensington Museum had derived its primary impetus from the Great Exhibition which, in developing a new pedagogic relation between state and people, had also subdued the spectre of the crowd. This spectre had been raised again in the debates set in motion by the proposal that admission to the exhibition should be free. It could only be expected, one correspondent to *The Times* argued, that both the rules of decorum and the rights of property would be violated if entry were made free to 'his majesty the mob'. These fears were exacerbated by the revolutionary upheavals of 1848, occasioning several European monarchs to petition that the public be banned from the opening ceremony (planned for May Day) for fear that this might spark off an insurrection which, in turn, might give rise to a general European conflagration.[22] And then there was the fear of social contagion should the labouring classes be allowed to rub shoulders with the upper classes.

In the event, the Great Exhibition proved a transitional form. While open to all, it also stratified its public in providing different days for different classes of visitors regulated by varying prices of admission. In spite of this limitation, the exhibition proved a major spur to the development of open-door policies. Attracting over 6 million visitors itself, it also vastly stimulated the attendance at London's main historic sites and museums: visits to the British Museum, for example, increased from 720,643 in 1850 to 2,230,242 in 1851.[23] Perhaps more important, though, was the orderliness of the public which in spite of the thousand extra constables and ten thousand troops kept on stand-by, proved duly appreciative, decorous in its bearing and entirely apolitical. More than that, the exhibition transformed the many-headed mob into an ordered crowd, a part of the spectacle and a sight of pleasure in itself. Victoria, in recording her impressions of the opening ceremony, dwelt particularly on her pleasure in seeing so large, so orderly, and so peaceable a crowd assembled in one place:

The Green Park and Hyde Park were one mass of densely crowded human beings, in the highest good humour and most enthusiastic. I never saw Hyde Park look as it did, being filled with crowds as far as the eye could see.[24]

Nor was this entirely unprepared for. The working-class public the exhibition attracted was one whose conduct had been regulated into appropriate forms in the earlier history of the Mechanics Institute exhibitions. Devoted largely to the display of industrial objects and processes, these exhibitions pioneered policies of low admission prices and late opening hours to encourage working-class attendance long before these were adopted within the official museum complex. In doing so, moreover, they sought to tutor their visitors on the modes of deportment required if they were to be admitted. Instruction booklets advised working-class visitors how to present themselves, placing particular stress on the need to change out of their working clothes – partly so as not to soil the exhibits, but also so as not to detract from the pleasure of the overall spectacle; indeed, to become parts of it:

426 Grasping the World

Here is a visitor of another sort; the mechanic has resolved to treat himself with a few hours holiday and recreation; he leaves the 'grimy shop', the dirty bench, and donning his Saturday night suit he appears before us – an honourable and worthy object.[25]

In brief, the Great Exhibition and, subsequently, the public museums developed in its wake found themselves heirs to a public which had already been formed by a set of pedagogic relations which, developed initially by voluntary organizations – in what Gramsci would call the realm of civil society – were henceforward to be more thoroughgoingly promoted within the social body in being subjected to the direction of the state.

Not, then, a history of confinement but one of the opening up of objects to more public contexts of inspection and visibility: this is the direction of movement embodied in the formation of the exhibitionary complex. A movement which simultaneously helped to form a new public and inscribe it in new relations of sight and vision. Of course, the precise trajectory of these developments in Britain was not followed elsewhere in Europe. None the less, the general direction of development was the same. While earlier collections (whether of scientific objects, curiosities, or works of art) had gone under a variety of names (museums, *studioli*, *cabinets des curieux*, *Wunderkammern*, *Kunstkammern*) and fulfilled a variety of functions (the storing and dissemination of knowledge, the display of princely and aristocratic power, the advancement of reputations and careers), they had mostly shared two principles: that of private ownership and that of restricted access.[26] The formation of the exhibitionary complex involved a break with both in effecting the transfer of significant quantities of cultural and scientific property from private into public ownership where they were housed within institutions administered by the state for the benefit of an extended general public.

The significance of the formation of the exhibitionary complex, viewed in this perspective, was that of providing new instruments for the moral and cultural regulation of the working classes. Museums and expositions, in drawing on the techniques and rhetorics of display and pedagogic relations developed in earlier nineteenth-century exhibitionary forms, provided a context in which the working- and middle-class publics could be brought together and the former – having been tutored into forms of behaviour to suit them for the occasion – could be exposed to the improving influence of the latter. A history, then, of the formation of a new public and its inscription in new relations of power and knowledge. But a history accompanied by a parallel one aimed at the destruction of earlier traditions of popular exhibition and the publics they implied and produced. In Britain, this took the form, *inter alia*, of a concerted attack on popular fairs owing to their association with riot, carnival, and, in their sideshows, the display of monstrosities and curiosities which, no longer enjoying elite patronage, were now perceived as impediments to the rationalizing influence of the restructured exhibitionary complex.

Yet, by the end of the century, fairs were to be actively promoted as an aid rather than a threat to public order. This was partly because the mechanization of fairs meant that their entertainments were increasingly brought into line with the values of industrial civilization, a testimony to the virtues of progress.[27] But it was also a consequence of changes in the conduct of fairgoers. By the end of the century, Hugh Cunningham argues, 'fairgoing had become a relatively routine ingredient in the accepted world of leisure' as 'fairs became tolerated, safe, and in due course a subject for nostalgia and revival'.[28] The primary site for this transformation of fairs and the conduct of their publics – although never quite so complete as Cunningham suggests – was supplied by the fair zones of the late-nineteenth-century expositions. It was here that two cultures abutted on to one another, the fair zones forming a kind of buffer region between the official and the popular culture with the former seeking to reach into the latter and moderate it. Initially, these fair zones established themselves independently of the official expositions and their organizing committees. The product of the initiative of popular showmen and private traders eager to exploit the market the expositions supplied, they consisted largely of an *ad hoc* melange of both new (mechanical rides) and traditional popular entertainments (freak shows, etc.) which frequently mocked the pretensions of the expositions they adjoined. Burton Benedict summarizes the relations between expositions and their amusement zones in late-nineteenth-century America as follows:

Many of the display techniques used in the amusement zone seemed to parody those of the main fair. Gigantism became enormous toys or grotesque monsters. Impressive high structures became collapsing or whirling amusement 'rides'. The solemn female allegorical figures that symbolised nations (Miss Liberty, Britannia) were replaced by comic male figures (Uncle Sam, John Bull). At the Chicago fair of 1893 the gilded female statue of the Republic on the Court of Honour contrasted with a large mechanical Uncle Sam on the Midway that delivered forty thousand speeches on the virtues of Hub Gore shoe elastics. Serious propagandists for manufacturers and governments in the main fair gave way to barkers and pitch men. The public no longer had to play the role of impressed spectators. They were invited to become frivolous participants. Order was replaced by jumble, and instruction by entertainment.[29]

As Benedict goes on to note, the resulting tension between unofficial fair and official exposition led to 'exposition organisers frequently attempting to turn the amusement zone into an educational enterprise or at least to regulate the type of exhibit shown'. In this, they were never entirely successful. Into the twentieth century, the amusement zones remained sites of illicit pleasures – of burlesque shows and prostitution – and of ones which the exposition themselves aimed to render archaic. Altick's 'monster-mongers and retailers of other strange sights' seem to have been as much in evidence at the Panama Pacific Exhibition of 1915 as they had been, a century earlier, at St Bartholomew's Fair, Wordsworth's Parliament of Monsters.[30] None the less, what was evident was a significant restructuring in the ideological economy of such amusement zones as a consequence of the degree to which, in subjecting them to more stringent forms of control and direction, exposition authorities were able to align their thematics to those of the official expositions themselves and, thence, to those of the rest of the exhibitionary complex. Museums, the evidence suggests, appealed largely to the middle classes and the skilled and respectable working classes and it seems likely that the same was true of expositions. The link between expositions and their adjoining fair zones, however, provided a route through which the exhibitionary complex and the disciplines and knowledges which shaped its rhetorics acquired a far wider and more extensive social influence.

The exhibitionary disciplines

The space of representation constituted by the exhibitionary complex was shaped by the relations between an array of new disciplines: history, art history, archaeology, geology, biology, and anthropology. Whereas the disciplines associated with the carceral archipelago were concerned to reduce aggregates to individualities, rendering the latter visible to power and so amenable to control, the orientation of these disciplines – as deployed in the exhibitionary complex – might best be summarized as that of 'show and tell'. They tended also to be generalizing in their focus. Each discipline, in its museological deployment, aimed at the representation of a type and its insertion in a developmental sequence for display to a public.

Such principles of classification and display were alien to the eighteenth century. Thus, in Sir John Soane's Museum, architectural styles are displayed in order to demonstrate their essential permanence rather than their change and development.[31] The emergence of a historicized framework for the display of human artefacts in early-nineteenth-century museums was thus a significant innovation. But not an isolated one. As Stephen Bann shows, the emergence of a 'historical frame' for the display of museum exhibits was concurrent with the development of an array of disciplinary and other practices which aimed at the lifelike reproduction of an authenticated past and its representation as a series of stages leading to the present – the new practices of history writing associated with the historical novel and the development of history as an empirical discipline, for example.[32] Between them, these constituted a new space of representation concerned to depict the development of peoples, states, and civilizations through time conceived as a progressive series of developmental stages.

The French Revolution, Germaine Bazin suggests, played a key role in opening up this space of representation by breaking the chain of dynastic succession that had previously vouchsafed a unity to the flow and organization of time.[33] Certainly, it was in France that historicized principles of museum display were first developed. Bazin stresses the formative influence of the Musée des monuments français (1795) in exhibiting works of art in galleries devoted to different periods, the visitor's route leading from earlier to later periods, with a view to demonstrating both the painterly conventions peculiar to each epoch and their historical development. He accords a similar significance to Alexandre du Sommerard's collection at the Hôtel de Cluny which, as Bann shows, aimed at 'an integrative construction of historical totalities', creating the impression of a historically authentic milieu by suggesting an essential and organic connection between artefacts displayed in rooms classified by period.[34]

Bann argues that these two principles – the *galleria progressiva* and the period room, sometimes employed singly, at others in combination – constitute the distinctive poetics of the modern historical museum. It is important to add, though, that this poetics displayed a marked tendency to be nationalized. If, as Bazin suggests, the museum became 'one of the fundamental institutions of the modern state',[35] that state was also increasingly a nation-state. The significance of this was manifested in the relations between two new historical times – national and universal – which resulted from an increase in the vertical depth of historical time as it was both pushed further and further back into the past and brought increasingly up to date. Under the impetus of the rivalry between France and Britain for dominion in the Middle East, museums, in close association with archaeological excavations of progressively deeper pasts, extended their time horizons beyond the medieval period and the classical antiquities of Greece and Rome to encompass the remnants of the Egyptian and Mesopotamian civilizations. At the same time, the recent past was historicized as the newly emerging nation-states sought to preserve and immemorialize their own formation as a part of that process of 'nationing' their populations that was essential to their further development. It was as a consequence of the first of these developments that the prospect of a universal history of civilization was opened up to thought and materialized in the archaeological collections of the great nineteenth-century museums. The second development, however, led to these universal histories being annexed to national histories as, within the rhetorics of each national museum complex, collections of national materials were represented as the outcome and culmination of the universal story of civilization's development.

Nor had displays of natural or geological specimens been organized historically in the various precursors of nineteenth-century public museums. Throughout the greater part of the eighteenth century, principles of scientific classification testified to a mixture of theocratic, rationalist, and proto-evolutionist systems of thought. Translated into principles of museological display, the result was the table, not the series, with species being arranged in terms of culturally codified similarities/dissimilarities in their external appearances rather than being ordered into temporally organized relations of precession/succession. The crucial challenges to such conceptions came from developments within geology and biology, particularly where their researchers overlapped in the stratigraphical study of fossil remains.[36] However, the details of these developments need not concern us here. So far as their implications for museums were concerned, their main significance was that of allowing for organic life to be conceived and represented as a temporally ordered succession of different forms of life where the transitions between them were accounted for not as a result of external shocks (as had been the case in the eighteenth century) but as the consequence of an inner momentum inscribed within the concept of life itself.[37]

If developments within history and archaeology thus allowed for the emergence of new forms of classification and display through which the stories of nations could be told and related to the longer story of Western civilization's development, the discursive formations of nineteenth-century geology and biology allowed these cultural series to be inserted within the longer developmental series of geological and natural time. Museums of science and technology, heirs to the rhetorics of progress developed in national and international exhibitions, completed the evolutionary picture in representing the history of industry and manufacture as a series of progressive innovations leading up to the contemporary triumphs of industrial capitalism.

Yet, in the context of late-nineteenth-century imperialism, it was arguably the employment of anthropology within the exhibitionary complex which proved most central to its ideological functioning. For it played the crucial role of connecting the histories of Western nations and civilizations to those of other peoples, but only by separating the two in providing for an interrupted continuity in the order of peoples and races – one in which 'primitive peoples' dropped out of history altogether in order to occupy a twilight zone between nature and culture. This function had been fulfilled earlier in the century by the museological display of anatomical peculiarities which seemed to confirm polygenetic conception of mankind's origins. The most celebrated instance was that of Saartjie Baartman, the 'Hottentot Venus', whose protruding buttocks – interpreted as a sign of separate development – occasioned a flurry of scientific speculation when she was displayed in Paris and London. On her death in 1815, an autopsy revealed alleged peculiarities in her genitalia which, likened to those of the orang-utan, were cited as proof positive of the claim that black peoples were the product of a separate – and, of course, inferior, more primitive, and bestial – line of descent. No less an authority than Cuvier lent his support to this conception in circulating a report of Baartman's autopsy and presenting her genital organs – 'prepared in a way so as to allow one to see the nature of the labia'[38] – to the French Academy which arranged for their display in the Musée d'ethnographie de Paris (now the Musée de l'homme).

Darwin's rebuttal of theories of polygenesis entailed that different means be found for establishing and representing the fractured unity of the human species. By and large, this was achieved by the representation of 'primitive peoples' as instances of arrested development, as examples of an earlier stage of species development which Western civilizations had long ago surpassed. Indeed, such peoples were typically represented as the still-living examples of *the* earliest stage in human development, the point of transition between nature and culture, between ape and man, the missing link necessary to account for the transition between animal and human history. Denied any history of their own, it was the fate of 'primitive peoples' to be dropped out of the bottom of human history in order that they might serve, representationally, as its support – underlining the rhetoric of progress by serving as its counterpoints, representing the point at which human history emerges from nature but has not yet properly begun its course.

So far as the museological display of artefacts from such cultures was concerned, this resulted in their arrangement and display – as at the Pitt-Rivers Museum – in accordance with the genetic or topological system which grouped together all objects of a similar nature, irrespective of their ethnographic groupings, in an evolutionary series leading from the simple to the complex.[39] However, it was with regard to the display of human remains that the consequences of these principles of classification were most dramatically manifested. In eighteenth-century museums, such displays had placed the accent on anatomical peculiarities, viewed primarily as a testimony to the rich diversity of the chain of universal being. By the late nineteenth century, however, human remains were most typically displayed as parts of evolutionary series with the remains of still extant peoples being allocated the earliest position within them. This was particularly true for the remains of Australian Aborigines. In the early years of Australian settlement, the colony's museums had displayed little or no interest in Aboriginal remains.[40] The triumph of evolutionary theory transformed this situation, leading to a systematic rape of Aboriginal sacred sites – by the representatives of British, European, and American, as well as Australian Museums – for materials to provide a representational foundation for the story of evolution within, tellingly enough, natural-history displays.[41]

The space of representation constituted in the relations between the disciplinary knowledges deployed within the exhibitionary complex thus permitted the construction of a temporally organized order of things and peoples. Moreover, that order was a totalizing one, metonymically encompassing all things and all peoples in their interactions through time. And an order which organized the implied public – the white citizenries of the imperialist powers – into a unity, representationally effacing divisions within the body politic in constructing a 'we' conceived as the realization, and therefore just beneficiaries, of the processes of evolution and identified as a unity in opposition to the primitive otherness of conquered peoples. This was not entirely new. As Peter Stallybrass and Allon White note, the popular fairs of the late-eighteenth and early-nineteenth centuries had exoticized the grotesque imagery of the carnival tradition by projecting it on to the representatives of alien cultures. In thus providing a normalizing function via the construction of a radically different Other, the exhibition of other people served as a vehicle for 'the edification of a national public and the confirmation of its imperial superiority'.[42] If, in its subsequent development, the exhibitionary complex latched on to this pre-existing representational space, what it added to it was a historical dimension.

The exhibitionary apparatuses

The space of representation constituted by the exhibitionary disciplines, while conferring a degree of unity on the exhibitionary complex, was also somewhat differently occupied – and to different effect – by the institutions comprising that complex. If museums gave this space a solidity and permanence, this was achieved at the price of a lack of ideological flexibility. Public museums instituted an order of things that was meant to last. In doing so, they provided the modern state with a deep and continuous ideological backdrop but one which, if it was to play this role, could not be adjusted to respond to shorter-term ideological requirements. Exhibitions met this need, injecting new life into the exhibitionary complex and rendering its ideological configurations more pliable in bending them to serve the conjuncturally specific hegemonic strategies of different national bourgeoisies. They made the order of things dynamic, mobilizing strategically in relation to the more immediate ideological and political exigencies of the particular moment.

This was partly an effect of the secondary discourses which accompanied exhibitions. Ranging from the state pageantry of their opening and closing ceremonies through newspaper reports to the veritable swarming of pedagogic initiatives organized by religious, philanthropic, and scientific associations to take advantage of the publics which exhibitions produced, these often forged very direct and specific connections between the exhibitionary rhetoric of progress and the claims to leadership of particular social and political forces. The distinctive influence of the exhibitions themselves, however, consisted in their articulation of the rhetoric of progress to the rhetorics of nationalism and imperialism and in producing, via their control over their adjoining popular fairs, an expanded cultural sphere for the deployment of the exhibitionary disciplines.

The basic signifying currency of the exhibitions, of course, consisted in their arrangement of displays of manufacturing processes and products. Prior to the Great Exhibition, the message of progress had been carried by the arrangement of exhibits in, as Davison puts it, 'a series of classes and sub-classes ascending from raw products of nature, through various manufactured goods and mechanical devices, to the "highest" forms of applied and fine art'.[43] As such, the class articulations of this rhetoric were subject to some variation. Mechanics Institutes' exhibitions placed considerable stress on the centrality of labour's contributions to the processes of production which, at times, allowed a radical appropriation of their message. 'The machinery of wealth, here displayed,' the *Leeds Times* noted in reporting an 1839 exhibition, 'has been created by the men of hammers and papercaps; more honourable than all the sceptres and coronets in the world.'.[44] The Great Exhibition introduced two changes which decisively influenced the future development of the form.

First, the stress was shifted from the *processes* to the *products* of production, divested of the marks of their making and ushered forth as signs of the productive and co-ordinating power of capital and the state. After 1851, world fairs were to function less as vehicles for the technical education of the working classes than as instruments for their stupefaction before the reified products of their own labour, 'places of pilgrimage', as Benjamin put it, 'to the fetish Commodity'.[45]

Second, while not entirely abandoned, the earlier progressive taxonomy based on stages of production was subordinated to the dominating influence of principles of classification based on nations and the supra-national constructs of empires and races. Embodied, at the Crystal Palace, in the form of national courts or display areas, this principle was subsequently developed into that of separate pavilions for each participating country. Moreover, following an innovation of the Centennial Exhibition held at Philadelphia in 1876, these pavilions were typically zoned into racial groups: the Latin, Teutonic, Anglo-Saxon, American, and Oriental being the most favoured classifications, with black peoples and the aboriginal populations of conquered territories, denied any space of their own, being represented as subordinate adjuncts to the imperial displays of the major powers. The effect of these developments was to transfer the rhetoric of progress from the relations between stages of production to the relations between races and nations by superimposing the associations of the former on to the latter. In the context of imperial displays, subject peoples were thus represented as occupying the lowest levels of manufacturing civilization. Reduced to displays of 'primitive' handicrafts and the like, they were represented as cultures without momentum except for that benignly bestowed on them from without through the improving mission of the imperialist powers. Oriental civilizations were allotted an intermediate position in being represented either as having at one time been subject to development but subsequently degenerating into stasis or as embodying achievements of civilization which, while developed by their own lights, were judged inferior to the standards set by Europe.[46] In brief, a progressivist taxonomy for the classification of goods and manufacturing processes was laminated on to a crudely racist teleological conception of the relations between peoples and races which culminated in the achievements of the metropolitan powers, invariably most impressively displayed in the pavilions of the host country.

Exhibitions thus located their preferred audiences at the very pinnacle of the exhibitionary order of things they constructed. They also installed them at the threshold of greater things to come. Here, too, the Great Exhibition led the way in sponsoring a display of architectural projects for the amelioration of working-class housing conditions. This principle was to be developed, in subsequent exhibitions, into displays of elaborate projects for the improvement of social conditions in the areas of health, sanitation, education, and welfare – promissory notes that the engines of progress would be harnessed for the general good. Indeed, exhibitions came to function as promissory notes in their totalities, embodying, if just for a season, utopian principles of social organization which, when the time came for the notes to be redeemed, would eventually be realized in perpetuity. As world fairs fell increasingly under the influence of modernism, the rhetoric of progress tended, as Rydell puts it, to be 'translated into a utopian statement about the future', promising the imminent dissipation of social tensions once progress had reached the point where its benefits might be generalized.[47]

Iain Chambers has argued that working- and middle-class cultures became sharply distinct in late-nineteenth-century Britain as an urban commercial popular culture developed beyond the reach of the moral economy of religion and respectability. As a consequence, he argues, 'official culture was publicly limited to the rhetoric of monuments in the centre of town: the university, the museum, the theatre, the concert hall; otherwise it was reserved for the 'private' space of the Victorian residence'.[48] While not disputing the general terms of this argument, it does omit any consideration of the role of exhibitions in providing official culture with powerful bridgeheads into the newly developing popular culture. Most obviously the official zones of exhibitions offered a context for the deployment of the exhibitionary disciplines which reached a more extended public than that ordinarily reached by the public museum system. The exchange of both staff and exhibits between museums and exhibitions was a regular and recurrent aspect of their relations, furnishing an institutional axis for the extended social deployment of a distinctively new ensemble of disciplines. Even within the official zones of exhibitions, the exhibitionary disciplines thus achieved an exposure to publics as large as any to which even the most commercialized forms of popular culture could lay claim: 32 million people attended the Paris Exposition of 1889; 27.5 million went to Chicago's Columbian Exposition in 1893 and nearly 49 million to Chicago's 1933/4 Century of Progress Exposition; the Glasgow Empire Exhibition of 1938 attracted 12 million visitors, and over 27 million attended the Empire Exhibition at Wembley in 1924/5.[49] However, the ideological reach of exhibitions often extended significantly further as they established their influence over the popular entertainment zones which, while initially deplored by exhibition authorities, were subsequently to be managed as planned adjuncts to the official exhibition zones and, sometimes, incorporated into the latter. It was through this network of relations that the official public culture of museums reached into the developing urban popular culture, shaping and directing its development in subjecting the ideological thematics of popular entertainments to the rhetoric of progress.

The most critical development in this respect consisted in the extension of anthropology's disciplinary ambit into the entertainment zones, for it was here that the crucial work of transforming non-white peoples themselves – and not just their remains or artefacts – into object lessons of evolutionary theory was accomplished. Paris led the way here in the colonial city it constructed as part of its 1889 Exposition. Populated by Asian and African peoples in simulated 'native' villages, the colonial city functioned as the showpiece of French anthropology and, through its influence on delegates to the tenth Congrèss internationale d'anthropologie et d'archéologie préhistorique held in association with the exposition, had a decisive bearing on the future modes of the discipline's social deployment. While this was true internationally, Rydell's study of American world fairs provides the most detailed demonstration of the active role played by museum anthropologists in transforming the Midways into living demonstrations of evolutionary theory by arranging non-white peoples into a 'sliding-scale of humanity', from the barbaric to the nearly civilized, thus underlining the exhibitionary rhetoric of progress by serving as visible counterpoints to its triumphal achievements. It was here that relations of knowledge and power continued to be invested in the public display of bodies, colonizing the space of earlier freak and monstrosity shows in order to personify the truths of a new regime of representation.

In their interrelations, then, the expositions and their fair zones constituted an order of things and of peoples which, reaching back into the depths of prehistoric time as well as encompassing all corners of the globe, rendered the whole world metonymically present, subordinated to the dominating gaze of the white, bourgeois, and (although this is another story) male eye of the metropolitan powers. But an eye of power which, through the development of the technology of vision associated with exposition towers and the positions for seeing these produced in relation to the miniature ideal cities of the expositions themselves, was democratized in being made available to all. Earlier attempts to establish a specular dominance over the city had, of course, been legion – the camera obscura, the panorama – and often fantastic in their technological imaginings. Moreover, the ambition to render the whole world, as represented in assemblages of commodities, subordinate to the controlling vision of the spectator, was present in world exhibitions from the outset. This was represented synecdochically at the Great Exhibition by Wylde's Great Globe, a brick rotunda which the visitor entered to see plaster casts of the world's continents and oceans. The principles embodied in the Eiffel Tower, built for the 1889 Paris Exposition and repeated in countless subsequent expositions, brought these two series together, rendering the project of specular dominance feasible in affording an elevated vantage point over a micro-world which claimed to be representative of a larger totality.

Barthes has aptly summarized the effects of the technology of vision embodied in the Eiffel Tower. Remarking that the tower overcomes 'the habitual divorce between *seeing* and *being seen*', Barthes argues that it acquires a distinctive power from its ability to circulate between these two functions of sight:

An object when we look at it, it becomes a lookout in its turn when we visit it, and now constitutes as an object, simultaneously extended and collected beneath it, that Paris which just now was looking at it.[50]

A sight itself, it becomes the site for a sight; a place both to see and be seen from, which allows the individual to circulate between the object and subject positions of the dominating vision it affords over the city and its inhabitants. In this, its distancing effect, Barthes argues, 'the Tower makes the city into a kind of nature; it constitutes the swarming of men into a landscape, it adds to the frequently grim urban myth a romantic dimension, a harmony, a mitigation', offering 'an immediate consumption of a humanity made natural by that glance which transforms it into space'.[51] It is because of the dominating vision it affords, Barthes continues, that, for the visitor, 'the Tower is the first obligatory monument; it is a Gateway, it marks the transition to a knowledge'.[52] And to the power associated with that knowledge: the power to order objects and persons into a world to be known and to lay it out before a vision capable of encompassing it as a totality.

In *The Prelude*, Wordsworth, seeking a vantage point from which to quell the tumultuousness of the city, invites his reader to ascend with him 'Above the press and danger of the crowd/Upon some showman's platform' (vii, 684–5) at St Bartholomew's Fair, likened to mobs, riotings, and executions as occasions when the passions of the city's populace break forth into unbridled expression. The vantage point, however, affords no control:

> All moveables of wonder, from all parts
> Are here – Albinos, painted Indians, Dwarfs,
> The Horse of knowledge, and the learned Pig,
> The Stone-eater, the man that swallows fire,
> Giants, Ventriloquists, the Invisible Girl,
> The Bust that speaks and moves its goggling eyes,
> The Wax-work, Clock-work, all the marvellous craft
> Of modern Merlins, Wild Beasts, Puppet-shows,
> All out-o'-the-way, far-fetched, perverted things,
> All freaks of nature, all Promethean thoughts
> Of man, his dullness, madness, and their feats
> All jumbled up together, to compose
> A Parliament of Monsters.

(vii, 706–18)

Stallybrass and White argue that this Wordsworthian perspective was typical of the early-nineteenth-century tendency for the educated public, in withdrawing from participation in popular fairs, also to distance itself from, and seek some ideological control over, the fair by the literary production of elevated vantage points from which it might be observed. By the end of the century, the imaginary dominance over the city afforded by the showman's platform had been transformed into a cast-iron reality while the fair, no longer a symbol of chaos, had become the ultimate spectacle of an ordered totality. And the substitution of observation for participation was a possibility open to all. The principle of spectacle – that, as Foucault summarizes it, of rendering a small number of objects accessible to the inspection of a multitude of men – did not fall into abeyance in the nineteenth century: it was surpassed through the development of technologies of vision which rendered the multitude accessible to its own inspection.

Conclusion

I have sought in this essay, to tread a delicate line between Foucault's and Gramsci's perspectives on the state, but without attempting to efface their differences so as to forge a synthesis between them. Nor is there a compelling

Figure 4.5.2   The Chicago Columbian Exposition, 1893: view from the roof of the Manufacturers and Liberal Arts Building. Photograph courtesy of the Chicago Historical Society, Chicago

need for such a synthesis. The concept of the state is merely a convenient shorthand for an array of governmental agencies which – as Gramsci was among the first to argue in distinguishing between the coercive apparatuses of the state and those engaged in the organization of consent – need not be conceived as unitary with regard to either their functioning or the modalities of power they embody.

That said, however, my argument has been mainly with (but not against) Foucault. In the study already referred to, Pearson distinguishes between the 'hard' and the 'soft' approaches to the nineteenth-century state's role in the promotion of art and culture. The former consisted of 'a systematic body of knowledge and skills promulgated in a systematic way to specified audiences'. Its field was comprised by those institutions of schooling which exercised a forcible hold or some measure of constraint over their members and to which the technologies of self-monitoring developed in the carceral system undoubtedly migrated. The 'soft' approach, by contrast, worked 'by example rather than by pedagogy; by entertainment rather than by disciplined schooling; and by subtlety and encouragement'.[53] Its field of application consisted of those institutions whose hold over their publics depended on their voluntary participation.

There seems no reason to deny the different sets of knowledge/power relations embodied in these contrasting approaches, or to seek their reconciliation in some common principle. For the needs to which they responded were different. The problem to which the 'swarming of disciplinary mechanisms' responded was that of making extended populations governable. However, the development of bourgeois democratic polities required not merely that the populace be governable but that it assent to its governance, thereby creating a need to enlist active popular support for the values and objectives enshrined in the state. Foucault knows well enough the symbolic power of the penitentiary:

> The high wall, no longer the wall that surrounds and protects, no longer the wall that stands for power and wealth, but the meticulously sealed wall, uncrossable in either direction, closed in upon the now mysterious work of punishment, will become, near at hand, sometimes even at the very centre of the cities of the nineteenth century, the monotonous figure, at once material and symbolic, of the power to punish.
>
> (p. 116)

Museums were also typically located at the centre of cities where they stood as embodiments, both material and symbolic, of a power to 'show and tell' which, in being deployed in a newly constituted open and public space, sought rhetorically to incorporate the people within the processes of the state. If the museum and the penitentiary thus represented the Janus face of power, there was none the less – at least symbolically – an economy of effort between them. For those who failed to adopt the tutelary relation to the self promoted by popular schooling or whose hearts and minds failed to be won in the new pedagogic relations between state and people symbolized by the open doors of the museum, the closed walls of the penitentiary threatened a sterner instruction in the lessons of power. Where instruction and rhetoric failed, punishment began.

NOTES

1. Douglas Crimp, 'On the museum's ruins', in Hal Foster, ed., *The Anti-Aesthetic: Essays on Postmodern Culture*, Washington, Bay Press, 1985, p. 45.

2. Michel Foucault, *Discipline and Punish: The Birth of the Prison*, trans. A. Sheridan, London, Allen Lane, 1977, pp. 115–16; further page references will be given in the text.

3. Jeffrey Minson, *Genealogies of Morals: Nietzsche, Foucault, Donzelot and the Eccentricity of Ethics*, London, Macmillan, 1985, p. 24.

4. This point is well made by MacArthur who sees this aspect of Foucault's argument as inimical to the overall spirit of his work in suggesting a 'historical division which places theatre and spectacle as past'. John MacArthur, 'Foucault, Tafuri, Utopia: essays in the history and theory of architecture', unpublished M.Phil. thesis, University of Queensland, 1983, p. 192.

5. Graeme Davison, 'Exhibitions', *Australian Cultural History*, 2 (1982/3), Canberra, Australian Academy of the Humanities and the History of Ideas Unit, ANU, p. 7.

6. See Richard D. Altick, *The Shows of London*, Cambridge, Mass. and London, The Belknap Press of Harvard University Press, 1978.

7. Dean MacCannell, *The Tourist: A New Theory of the Leisure Class*, New York, Schocken Books, 1976, p. 57.

8. See Dana Aron Brand, *The Spectator and the City: Fantasies of Urban Legibility in Nineteenth-Century England and America*, Ann Arbor, Mich., University Microfilms International, 1986.

9. For discussions of the role of the American state in relation to museums and expositions, see, respectively, K. E. Meyer, *The Art Museum: Power, Money, Ethics*, New York, William Morrow, 1979, and Badger Reid, *The Great American Fair: The World's Columbian Exposition and American Culture*, Chicago, Nelson Hall, 1979.

10. Nicholas Pearson, *The State and the Visual Arts: A Discussion of State Intervention in the Visual Arts in Britain, 1780–1981*, Milton Keynes, Open University Press, 1982, pp. 8–13, 46–7.

11. See Debora Silverman, 'The 1889 exhibition: the crisis of bourgeois individualism', *Oppositions: A Journal of Ideas and Criticism in Architecture*, Spring 1977, and Robert W. Rydell, *All the World's a Fair: Visions of Empire at American International Expositions, 1876–1916*, Chicago, University of Chicago Press, 1984.

12. See H. Seling, 'The genesis of the museum', *Architectural Review*, 131 (1967).

13. MacArthur, 'Foucault, Tafuri, Utopia', pp. 192–3.

14. Cited in Neil Harris, 'Museums, merchandising and popular taste: the struggle for influence', in I. M. G. Quimby, ed., *Material Culture and the Study of American Life*, New York, W. W. Norton, 1978, p. 144.

15. For details of the use of rotunda and galleries to this effect in department stores, see John William Ferry, *A History of the Department Store*, New York, Macmillan, 1960.

16. Manfredo Tafuri, *Architecture and Utopia: Design and Capitalist Development*, Cambridge, Mass., MIT Press, 1976, p. 83.

17. For further details, see Edward Millar, *That Noble Cabinet: A History of the British Museum*, Athens, Ohio, Ohio University Press, 1974.

18. A. S. Wittlin, *The Museum: Its History and Its Tasks in Education*, London, Routledge & Kegan Paul, 1949, p. 113.

19. Cited in Millar, *That Noble Cabinet*, p. 62.

20. Altick, *The Shows of London*, p. 500.

21. See David White, 'Is Britain becoming one big museum?', *New Society*, 20 Oct. 1983.

22. See Audrey Shorter, 'Workers under glass in 1851', *Victorian Studies*, 10: 2 (1966).

23. See Altick, *The Shows of London*, p. 467.

24. Cited in C. H. Gibbs-Smith, *The Great Exhibition of 1851*, London, HMSO, 1981, p. 18.

25. Cited in Toshio Kusamitsu, 'Great exhibitions before 1851', *History Workshop*, 9 (1980), 77.

26. A comprehensive introduction to these earlier forms is offered by Olive Imply and Arthur MacGregor, eds, *The Origins of Museums: The Cabinet of Curiosities in Sixteenth- and Seventeenth-Century Europe*, Oxford, Clarendon Press, 1985. See also Bazin, below, note 33.

27. I have touched on these matters elsewhere. See Tony Bennett, 'A thousand and one troubles: Blackpool Pleasure Beach', *Formations of Pleasure*, London, Routledge & Kegan Paul, 1983, and 'Hegemony, ideology, pleasure: Blackpool', in Tony Bennett, Colin Mercer, and Janet Woollacott, eds, *Popular Culture and Social Relations*, Milton Keynes, Open University Press, 1986.

28. Hugh Cunningham, *Leisure in the Industrial Revolution*, London, Croom Helm, 1980, as excerpted in Bernard Waltes, Tony Bennett, and Graham Martin, eds, *Popular Culture: Past and Present*, London, Croom Helm, 1982, p. 163.

29. Burton Benedict, 'The anthropology of world's fairs', in Burton Benedict, ed., *The Anthropology of World's Fairs: San Francisco's Panama Pacific Exposition of 1915*, New York, Scolar Press, 1983, pp. 53–4.

30. For details, see McCullough, *World's Fair Midways: An Affectionate Account of American Amusement Areas*, New York, Exposition Press, 1966, p. 76.

31. See Colin Davies, 'Architecture and remembrance', *Architectural Review* (Feb. 1984), p. 54.

32. See Stephen Bann, *The Clothing of Cllo: A Study of the Representation of History in Nineteenth-Century Britain and France*, Cambridge, Cambridge University Press, 1984.

33. G. Bazin, *The Museum Age*, New York, Universal Press, 1967, p. 218.

34. Bann, *The Clothing of Clio*, p. 85.

35. Bazin, *The Museum Age*, p. 169.

36. For details of these interactions, see Martin J. S. Rudwick, *The Meaning of Fossils: Episodes in the History of Paleontology*, Chicago, University of Chicago Press, 1985.

37. I draw here on Michel Foucault, *The Order of Things: An Archaeology of the Human Sciences*, London, Tavistock, 1970.

38. Cuvier, cited in Sander L. Gilman, 'Black bodies, white bodies: toward an iconography of female sexuality in late nineteenth-century art, medicine and literature', *Critical Inquiry*, 21: 1 (Autumn 1985), pp. 214–15.

39. See David K. van Keuren, 'Museums and ideology: Augustus Pitt-Rivers, anthropological museums, and social change in later Victorian Britain', *Victorian Studies*, 28: 1 (Autumn 1984).

40. See S. G. Kohlstedt, 'Australian museums of natural history: public practices and scientific initiatives in the 19th century', *Historical Records of Australian Science*, 5 (1983).

41. For the most thorough account, see D. J. Mulvaney, 'The Australian Aborigine 1606–1929: opinion and fieldwork', *Historical Studies*, 8 (1958), pp. 30–1.

42. Peter Stallybrass and Allon White, *The Politics and Poetics of Transgression*, London, Methuen, 1986, p. 42.

43. Davison, 'Exhibitions', p. 8.

44. Cited in Kusemitsu, 'Great exhibitions before 1851', p. 79.

45. Walter Benjamin, *Charles Baudelaire: A Lyric Poet in the Era of High Capitalism*, London, New Left Books, 1973, p. 165.

46. See Neil Harris, 'All the world a melting pot? Japan at American fairs, 1876–1904', in Ireye Akira, ed., *Mutual Images: Essays in American–Japanese Relations*, Cambridge, Mass., Harvard University Press, 1975.

47. Rydell, *All the World's a Fair*, p. 4.

48. Iain Chambers, 'The obscured metropolis', *Australian Journal of Cultural Studies* (Dec. 1985), p. 9.

49. John M. MacKenzie, *Propaganda and Empire: The Manipulation of British Public Opinion, 1880–1960*, Manchester, Manchester University Press, 1984, p. 101.

50. Roland Barthes, *The Eiffel Tower, and Other Mythologies*, New York, Hill & Wang, 1979, p. 4.

51. Ibid., p. 8.

52. Ibid., p. 14.

53. Pearson, *The State and the Visual Arts*, p. 35.

6.

Orientalism and the Exhibitionary Order

Timothy Mitchell

It is no longer unusual to suggest that the construction of the colonial order is related to the elaboration of modern forms of representation and knowledge. The relationship has been most closely examined in the critique of Orientalism. The Western artistic and scholarly portrayal of the non-West, in Edward Said's analysis, is not merely an ideological distortion convenient to an emergent global political order but a densely imbricated arrangement of imagery and expertise that organizes and produces the Orient as a political reality.[1] Three features define this Orientalist reality: it is understood as the product of unchanging racial or cultural essences; these essential characteristics are in each case the polar opposite of the West (passive rather than active, static rather than mobile, emotional rather than rational, chaotic rather than ordered); and the Oriental opposite or Other is, therefore, marked by a series of fundamental absences (of movement, reason, order, meaning, and so on). In terms of these three features – essentialism, otherness, and absence – the colonial world can be mastered, and colonial mastery will, in turn, reinscribe and reinforce these defining features.

Orientalism, however, has always been part of something larger. The nineteenth-century image of the Orient was constructed not just in Oriental studies, romantic novels, and colonial administrations, but in all the new procedures with which Europeans began to organize the representation of the world, from museums and world exhibitions to architecture, schooling, tourism, the fashion industry, and the commodification of everyday life. In 1889, to give an indication of the scale of these processes, 32 million people visited the Exposition Universelle, built that year in Paris to commemorate the centenary of the Revolution and to demonstrate French commercial and imperial power.[2] The consolidation of the global hegemony of the West, economically and politically, can be connected not just to the imagery of Orientalism but to all the new machinery for rendering up and laying out the meaning of the world, so characteristic of the imperial age.

The new apparatus of representation, particularly the world exhibitions, gave a central place to the representation of the non-Western world, and several studies have pointed out the importance of this construction of otherness to the manufacture of national identity and imperial purpose.[3] But is there, perhaps, some more integral relationship between representation, as a modern technique of meaning and order, and the construction of otherness so important to the colonial project? One perspective from which to explore this question is provided by the accounts of non-Western visitors to nineteenth-century Europe. An Egyptian delegation to the Eighth International Congress of Orientalists, for example, held in Stockholm in the summer of 1889, traveled to Sweden via Paris and paused there to visit the Exposition Universelle, leaving us a detailed description of their encounter with the representation of their own otherness. Beginning with this and other accounts written by visitors from the Middle East, I examine the distinctiveness of the modern representational order exemplified by the world exhibition. What Arab writers found in the West, I will argue, were not just exhibitions and representations of the world, but the world itself being ordered up as an endless exhibition. This world-as-exhibition was a place where the artificial, the model, and the plan were employed to generate an unprecedented effect of order and certainty. It is not the artificiality of the exhibitionary order that matters, however, so much as the contrasting effect of an external reality that the artificial and the model create – a reality characterized, like Orientalism's Orient, by essentialism, otherness, and absence. In the second half of the article, I examine this connection between the world-as-exhibition and Orientalism, through a rereading of European travel accounts of the nineteenth-century Middle East. The features of the kind of Orient these writings construct – above all its characteristic absences – are not merely motifs convenient to colonial mastery, I argue, but necessary elements of the order of representation itself.

La rue du Caire

The four members of the Egyptian delegation to the Stockholm Orientalist conference spent several days in Paris, climbing twice the height (as they were told) of the Great Pyramid in Alexandre Eiffel's new tower, and exploring the city and exhibition laid out beneath. Only one thing disturbed them. The Egyptian exhibit had been built by the French to represent a street in medieval Cairo, made of houses with overhanging upper stories and a mosque like that of Qaitbay. 'It was intended,' one of the Egyptians wrote, 'to resemble the old aspect of Cairo.' So carefully was this done, he noted, that 'even the paint on the buildings was made dirty'.[4] The exhibit had also been made carefully chaotic. In contrast to the geometric layout of the rest of the exhibition, the imitation street was arranged in the haphazard manner of the bazaar. The way was crowded with shops and stalls, where Frenchmen, dressed as Orientals, sold perfumes, pastries, and tarbushes. To complete the effect of the Orient, the French organizers had imported from Cairo fifty Egyptian donkeys, together with their drivers and the requisite number of grooms, farriers, and saddlers. The donkeys gave rides (for the price of one franc) up and down the street, resulting in a clamor and confusion so lifelike, the director of the exhibition was obliged to issue an order restricting the donkeys to a certain number at each hour of the day. The Egyptian visitors were disgusted by all this and stayed away. Their final embarrassment had been to enter the door of the mosque and discover that, like the rest of the street, it had been erected as what the Europeans called a facade. 'Its external form was all that there was of the mosque. As for the interior, it had been set up as a coffee house, where Egyptian girls performed dances with young males, and dervishes whirled.'[5]

After eighteen days in Paris, the Egyptian delegation traveled on to Stockholm to attend the Congress of Orientalists. Together with other non-European delegates, the Egyptians were received with hospitality – and a great curiosity. As though they were still in Paris, they found themselves something of an exhibit. '*Bona fide* Orientals,' wrote a European participant in the Congress, 'were stared at as in a Barnum's all-world show: the good Scandinavian people seemed to think that it was a collection of *Orientals*, not of *Orientalists*.'[6] Some of the Orientalists themselves seemed to delight in the role of showmen. At an earlier congress, in Berlin, we are told that 'the grotesque idea was started of producing natives of Oriental countries as illustrations of a paper: thus the Boden Professor of Sanskrit at Oxford produced a real live Indian Pandit, and made him go through the ritual of Brahmanical prayer and worship before a hilarious assembly. ... Professor Max Müller of Oxford produced two rival Japanese priests, who exhibited their gifts; it had the appearance of two showmen exhibiting their monkeys.'[7] At the Stockholm Congress, the Egyptians were invited to participate as scholars, but when they used their own language to do so they again found themselves treated as exhibits. 'I have heard nothing so unworthy of a sensible man,' complained an Oxford scholar, 'as ... the whistling howls emitted by an Arabic student of El-Azhar of Cairo. Such exhibitions at Congresses are mischievous and degrading.'[8]

The exhibition and the congress were not the only examples of this European mischief. As Europe consolidated its colonial power, non-European visitors found themselves continually being placed on exhibit or made the careful object of European curiosity. The degradation they were made to suffer seemed as necessary to these spectacles as the scaffolded facades or the curious crowds of onlookers. The facades, the onlookers, and the degradation seemed all to belong to the organizing of an exhibit, to a particularly European concern with rendering the world up to be viewed. Of what, exactly, did this exhibitionary process consist?

An object-world

To begin with, Middle Eastern visitors found Europeans a curious people, with an uncontainable eagerness to stand and stare. 'One of the characteristics of the French is to stare and get excited at everything new,' wrote an Egyptian scholar who spent five years in Paris in the 1820s, in the first description of nineteenth-century Europe to be published in Arabic.[9] The 'curiosity' of the European is encountered in almost every subsequent Middle Eastern account. Toward the end of the nineteenth century, when one or two Egyptian writers adopted the realistic style of the novel and made the journey to Europe their first topic, their stories would often evoke the peculiar experience of the West by describing an individual surrounded and stared at, like an object on exhibit. 'Whenever he paused outside a shop or showroom,' the protagonist in one such story found on his first day in Paris, 'a large number of people would surround him, both men and women, staring at his dress and appearance.'[10]

In the second place, this curious attitude that is described in Arabic accounts was connected with what one might call a corresponding *objectness*. The curiosity of the observing subject was something demanded by a diversity of mechanisms for rendering things up as its object – beginning with the Middle Eastern visitor himself. The members of an Egyptian student mission sent to Paris in the 1820s were confined to the college where they lived and allowed out only to visit museums and the theater – where they found themselves parodied in vaudeville as objects of entertainment for the French public.[11] 'They construct the stage as the play demands,' explained one of the students. 'For example, if they want to imitate a sultan and the things that happen to him, they set up the stage in the form of a palace and portray him in person. If for instance they want to play the Shah of Persia, they dress someone in the clothes of the Persian monarch and then put him there and sit him on a throne.'[12] Even Middle Eastern monarchs who came in person to Europe were liable to be incorporated into its theatrical machinery. When the Khedive of Egypt visited Paris to attend the Exposition Universelle of 1867, he found that the Egyptian exhibit had been built to simulate medieval Cairo in the form of a royal palace. The Khedive stayed in the imitation palace during his visit and became a part of the exhibition, receiving visitors with medieval hospitality.[13]

Visitors to Europe found not only themselves rendered up as objects to be viewed. The Arabic account of the student mission to Paris devoted several pages to the Parisian phenomenon of *'le spectacle'*, a word for which its author knew of no Arabic equivalent. Besides the Opéra and the Opéra-Comique, among the different kinds of spectacle he described were 'places in which they represent for the person the view of a town or a country or the like', such as 'the Panorama, the Cosmorama, the Diorama, the Europorama and the Uranorama'. In a panorama of Cairo, he explained in illustration, 'it is as though you were looking from on top of the minaret of Sultan Hasan, for example, with al-Rumaila and the rest of the city beneath you'.[14]

The effect of such spectacles was to set the world up as a picture. They ordered it up as an object on display to be investigated and experienced by the dominating European gaze. An Orientalist of the same period, the great French scholar Sylvestre de Sacy, wanted the scholarly picturing of the Orient to make available to European inspection a similar kind of object-world. He had planned to establish a museum, which was to be:

a vast depot of objects of all kinds, of drawings, of original books, maps, accounts of voyages, all offered to those who wish to give themselves to the study of [the Orient]; in such a way that each of these students would be able to feel himself transported as if by enchantment into the midst of, say, a Mongolian tribe or of the Chinese race, whichever he might have made the object of his studies.[15]

As part of a more ambitious plan in England for 'the education of the people', a proposal was made to set up 'an ethnological institution, with very extensive grounds' where 'within the same enclosure' were to be kept 'specimens in pairs of the various races'. The natives on exhibit, it was said,

should construct their own dwellings according to the architectural ideas of their several countries; their … mode of life should be their own. The forms of industry prevalent in their nation or tribe they should be required to practise; and their ideas, opinions, habits, and superstitions should be permitted to perpetuate themselves. … To go from one division of this establishment to another would be like travelling into a new country.[16]

The world exhibitions of the second half of the century offered the visitor exactly this educational encounter, with natives and their artifacts arranged to provide the direct experience of a colonized object-world. In planning the layout of the 1889 Paris Exhibition, it was decided that the visitor 'before entering the temple of modern life' should pass through an exhibit of all human history, 'as a gateway to the exposition and a noble preface'. Entitled 'Histoire du Travail', or, more fully, 'Exposition retrospective du travail et des sciences anthropologiques', the display would demonstrate the history of human labor by means of 'objects and things themselves'. It would have 'nothing vague about it', it was said, 'because it will consist of an *object lesson*'.[17]

Arabic accounts of the modern West became accounts of these curious object-worlds. By the last decade of the nineteenth century, more than half the descriptions of journeys to Europe published in Cairo were written to describe visits to a world exhibition or an international congress of Orientalists.[18] Such accounts devote hundreds of pages to describing the peculiar order and technique of these events – the curious crowds of spectators, the organization of panoramas and perspectives, the arrangement of natives in mock colonial villages, the display of new inventions and commodities, the architecture of iron and glass, the systems of classification, the calculations of statistics, the lectures, the plans, and the guide books – in short, the entire method of organization that we think of as representation.

The world-as-exhibition

In the third place, then, the effect of objectness was a matter not just of visual arrangement around a curious spectator, but of representation. What reduced the world to a system of objects was the way their careful organization enabled them to evoke some larger meaning, such as History or Empire or Progress. This machinery of representation was not confined to the exhibition and the congress. Almost everywhere that Middle Eastern visitors went they seemed to encounter the arrangement of things to stand for something larger. They visited the new museums, and saw the cultures of the world portrayed in the form of objects arranged under glass, in the order of their evolution. They were taken to the theater, a place where Europeans represented to themselves their history, as several Egyptian writers explained. They spent afternoons in the public gardens, carefully organized 'to bring together the trees and plants of every part of the world', as another Arab writer put it. And, inevitably, they took trips to the zoo, a product of nineteenth-century colonial penetration of the Orient, as Theodor Adorno wrote, that 'paid symbolic tribute in the form of animals'.[19]

The Europe one reads about in Arabic accounts was a place of spectacle and visual arrangement, of the organization of everything and everything organized to represent, to recall, like the exhibition, a larger meaning. Characteristic of the way Europeans seemed to live was their preoccupation with what an Egyptian author described as *'intizam almanzar'*, the organization of the view.[20] Beyond the exhibition and the congress, beyond the museum and the zoo, everywhere that non-European visitors went – the streets of the modern city with their meaningful facades, the countryside encountered typically in the form of a model farm exhibiting new machinery and cultivation methods, even the Alps once the funicular was built – they found the technique and sensation to be the same.[21] Everything seemed to be set up before one as though it were the model or the picture of something. Everything was arranged before an observing subject into a system of signification, declaring itself to be a mere object, a mere 'signifier of' something further.

The exhibition, therefore, could be read in such accounts as epitomizing the strange character of the West, a place where one was continually pressed into service as a spectator by a world ordered so as to represent. In exhibitions, the traveler from the Middle East could describe the curious way of addressing the world increasingly encountered in modern Europe, a particular relationship between the individual and a world of 'objects' that Europeans seemed to take as the experience of the real. This reality effect was a world increasingly rendered up to the individual according to the way in which, and to the extent to which, it could be made to stand before him or her as an exhibit. Non-Europeans encountered in Europe what one might call, echoing a phrase from Heidegger, the age of the world exhibition, or rather, the age of the world-as-exhibition.[22] The world-as-exhibition means not an exhibition of the world but the world organized and grasped as though it were an exhibition.

The certainty of representation

'England is at present the greatest Oriental Empire which the world has ever known,' proclaimed the president of the 1892 Orientalist Congress at its opening session. His words reflected the political certainty of the imperial age. 'She knows not only how to conquer, but how to rule.'[23] The endless spectacles of the world-as-exhibition were not just reflections of this certainty but the means of its production, by their technique of rendering imperial truth and cultural difference in 'objective' form.

Three aspects of this kind of certainty can be illustrated from the accounts of the world exhibition. First there was the apparent realism of the representation. The model or display always seemed to stand in perfect correspondence to the external world, a correspondence that was frequently noted in Middle Eastern accounts. As the Egyptian visitor had remarked, 'Even the paint on the buildings was made dirty.' One of the most impressive exhibits at the 1889 exhibition in Paris was a panorama of the city. As described by an Arab visitor, this consisted of a viewing platform on which one stood, encircled by images of the city. The images were mounted and illuminated in such a way that the observer felt himself standing at the center of the city itself, which seemed to materialize around him as a single, solid object 'not differing from reality in any way'.[24]

In the second place, the model, however realistic, always remained distinguishable from the reality it claimed to represent. Even though the paint was made dirty and the donkeys were brought from Cairo, the medieval Egyptian street at the Paris exhibition remained only a Parisian copy of the Oriental original. The certainty of representation depended on this deliberate difference in time and displacement in space that separated the representation from the real thing. It also depended on the position of the visitor – the tourist in the imitation street or the figure on the viewing platform. The representation of reality was always an exhibit set up for an observer in its midst, an observing European gaze surrounded by and yet excluded from the exhibition's careful order. The more the exhibit drew in and encircled the visitor, the more the gaze was set apart from it, as the mind (in our Cartesian imagery) is said to be set apart from the material world it observes. The separation is suggested in a description of the Egyptian exhibit at the Paris Exhibition of 1867:

A museum inside a pharaonic temple represented Antiquity, a palace richly decorated in the Arab style represented the Middle Ages, a caravanserai of merchants and performers portrayed in real life the customs of today. Weapons from the Sudan, the skins of wild monsters, perfumes, poisons and medicinal plants transport us directly to the tropics. Pottery from Assiut and Aswan, filigree and cloth of silk and gold invite us to touch with our fingers a strange civilization. All the races subject to the Vice-Roy were personified by individuals selected with care. We rubbed shoulders with the fellah, we made way before the Bedouin of the Libyan desert on their beautiful white dromedaries. This sumptuous display spoke to the mind as to the eyes; it expressed a political idea.[25]

The remarkable realism of such displays made the Orient into an object the visitor could almost touch. Yet to the observing eye, surrounded by the display but excluded from it by the status of visitor, it remained a mere representation, the picture of some further reality. Thus, two parallel pairs of distinctions were maintained, between the visitor and the exhibit and between the exhibit and what it expressed. The representation seemed set apart from the political reality it claimed to portray as the observing mind seems set apart from what it observes.

Third, the distinction between the system of exhibits or representations and the exterior meaning they portrayed was imitated, within the exhibition, by distinguishing between the exhibits themselves and the plan of the exhibition. The visitor would encounter, set apart from the objects on display, an abundance of catalogs, plans, sign posts, programs, guidebooks, instructions, educational talks, and compilations of statistics. The Egyptian exhibit at the 1867 Exhibition, for example, was accompanied by a guidebook containing an outline of the country's history – divided, like the exhibit to which it referred, into the ancient, medieval, and modern – together with a 'notice statistique sur le territoire, la population, les forces productives, le commerce, l'effective militaire et naval, l'organisation financière, l'instruction publique, etc. de l'Egypte' compiled by the Commission Impériale in Paris.[26] To provide such outlines, guides, tables, and plans, which were essential to the educational aspect of the exhibition, involved processes of representation that are no different from those at work in the construction of the exhibits themselves. But the practical distinction that was maintained between the exhibit and the plan, between the objects and their catalog, reinforced the effect of two distinct orders of being – the order of things and the order of their meaning, of representation and reality.

Despite the careful ways in which it was constructed, however, there was something paradoxical about this distinction between the simulated and the real, and about the certainty that depends on it. In Paris, it was not always easy to tell where the exhibition ended and the world itself began. The boundaries of the exhibition were clearly marked, of course, with high perimeter walls and monumental gates. But, as Middle Eastern visitors had continually discovered, there was much about the organization of the 'real world' outside, with its museums and department stores, its street facades and Alpine scenes, that resembled the world exhibition. Despite the determined efforts to isolate the exhibition as merely an artificial representation of a reality outside, the real world beyond the gates turned out to be more and more like an extension of the exhibition. Yet this extended exhibition continued to present itself as a series of mere representations, representing a reality beyond. We should think of it, therefore, not so much as an exhibition but as a kind of labyrinth, the labyrinth that, as Derrida says, includes in itself its own exits.[27] But then, maybe the exhibitions whose exits led only to further exhibitions were becoming at once so realistic and so extensive that no one ever realized that the real world they promised was not there.

The labyrinth without exits

To see the uncertainty of what seemed, at first, the clear distinction between the simulated and the real, one can begin again inside the world exhibition, back at the Egyptian bazaar. Part of the shock of the Egyptians came from just how real the street claimed to be: not simply that the paint was made dirty, that the donkeys were from Cairo, and that the Egyptian pastries on sale were said to taste like the real thing, but that one paid for them with what we call '*real* money'. The commercialism of the donkey rides, the bazaar stalls, and the dancing girls seemed no different from the commercialism of the world outside. With so disorienting an experience as entering the facade of a mosque to find oneself inside an Oriental cafe that served real customers what seemed to be real coffee, where, exactly, lay the line between the artificial and the real, the representation and the reality?

Exhibitions were coming to resemble the commercial machinery of the rest of the city. This machinery, in turn, was rapidly changing in places such as London and Paris, to imitate the architecture and technique of the exhibition. Small, individually owned shops, often based on local crafts, were giving way to the larger apparatus of shopping arcades and department stores. According to the *Illustrated Guide to Paris* (a book supplying, like an exhibition program, the plan and meaning of the place), each of these new establishments formed 'a city, indeed a world in miniature'.[28] The Egyptian accounts of Europe contain several descriptions of these commercial worlds-in-miniature, where the real world, as at the exhibition, was something organized by the representation of its commodities. The department stores were described as 'large and well organized', with their merchandise 'arranged in perfect order, set in rows on shelves with everything symmetrical and precisely positioned'. Non-European visitors would remark especially on the panes of glass, inside the stores and along the gas-lit arcades. 'The merchandise is all arranged behind sheets of clear glass, in the most remarkable order. … Its dazzling appearance draws thousands of onlookers.'[29] The glass panels inserted themselves between the visitors and the goods on display, setting up the former as mere onlookers and endowing the goods with the distance that is the source, one might say, of their objectness. Just as exhibitions had become commercialized, the machinery of commerce was becoming a further means of engineering the real, indistinguishable from that of the exhibition.

Something of the experience of the strangely ordered world of modern commerce and consumers is indicated in the first fictional account of Europe to be published in Arabic. Appearing in 1882, it tells the story of two Egyptians who travel to France and England in the company of an English Orientalist. On their first day in Paris, the two Egyptians wander accidentally into the vast, gas-lit premises of a wholesale supplier. Inside the building they find long corridors, each leading into another. They walk from one corridor to the next, and after a while begin to search for the way out. Turning a corner they see what looks like an exit, with people approaching from the other side. But it turns out to be a mirror, which covers the entire width and height of the wall, and the people approaching are merely their own reflections. They turn down another passage and then another, but each one ends only in a mirror. As they make their way through the corridors of the building, they pass groups of people at work. 'The people were busy setting out merchandise, sorting it and putting it into boxes and cases. They stared at the two of them in silence as they passed, standing quite still, not leaving their places or interrupting their work.' After wandering silently for some time through the building, the two Egyptians realize they have lost their way completely and begin going from room to room looking for an exit. 'But no one interfered with them,' we are told, 'or came up to them to ask if they were lost.' Eventually they are rescued by the manager of the store, who proceeds to explain to them how it is organized, pointing out that, in the objects being sorted and packed, the produce of every country in the world is represented.[30] The West, it appears, is a place organized as a system of commodities, values, meanings, and representations, forming signs that reflect one another in a labyrinth without exits.

The effect of the real

The conventional critique of this world of representation and commodification stresses its artificiality. We imagine ourselves caught up in a hall of mirrors from which we cannot find a way out. We cannot find the door that leads back to the real world outside; we have lost touch with reality. This kind of critique remains complicitous with the world-as-exhibition, which is built to persuade us that such a simple door exists. The exhibition does not cut us off from reality. It persuades us that the world is divided neatly into two realms, the exhibition and the real world, thereby creating the effect of a reality from which we now feel cut off. It is not the artificiality of the world-as-exhibition that should concern us, but the contrasting effect of a lost reality to which such supposed artificiality gives rise. This reality, which we take to be something obvious and natural, is in fact something novel and unusual. It appears as a place completely external to the exhibition: that is, a pristine realm existing prior to all representation, which means prior to all intervention by the self, to all construction, mixing, or intermediation, to all the forms of imitation, displacement, and difference that give rise to meaning.

This external reality, it can be noted, bears a peculiar relationship to the Orientalist portrayal of the Orient. Like the Orient, it appears that it simply 'is'. It is a place of mere being, where essences are untouched by history, by intervention, by difference. Such an essentialized world lacks, by definition, what the exhibition supplies – the dimension of meaning. It lacks the plan or program that supplies reality with its historical and cultural order. The techniques of the world exhibition build into an exterior world this supposed lack, this original meaninglessness and disorder, just as colonialism introduces it to the Orient. The Orient, it could be said, is the pure form of the novel kind of external reality to which the world-as-exhibition gives rise.

Before further examining this connection between the features of Orientalism and the kind of external reality produced by the world-as-exhibition, it is worth recalling that world exhibitions and the new large-scale commercial life of European cities were aspects of a political and economic transformation that was not limited to Europe itself. The new department stores were the first establishments to keep large quantities of merchandise in stock, in the form of standardized textiles and clothing. The stockpiling, together with the introduction of advertising (the word was coined at the time of the great exhibitions, Walter Benjamin reminds us) and the new European industry of 'fashion' (on which several Middle Eastern writers commented) were all connected with the boom in textile production.[31] The textile boom was an aspect of other changes, such as new ways of harvesting and treating cotton, new machinery for the manufacture of textiles, the resulting increase in profits, and the reinvestment of profit abroad in further cotton production.

At the other end from the exhibition and the department store, these wider changes extended to include places such as the southern United States, India, and the Nile valley.

Since the latter part of the eighteenth century, the Nile valley had been undergoing a transformation associated principally with the European textile industry.[32] From a country that formed one of the hubs in the commerce of the Ottoman world and beyond and that produced and exported its own food and its own textiles, Egypt was turning into a country whose economy was dominated by the production of a single commodity, raw cotton, for the global textile industry of Europe.[33] The changes associated with this growth and concentration in exports included an enormous growth in imports, principally of textile products and food, the extension throughout the country of a network of roads, telegraphs, police stations, railways, ports, and permanent irrigation canals, a new relationship to the land (which became a privately owned commodity concentrated in the hands of a small, powerful, and increasingly wealthy social class), the influx of Europeans (seeking to make fortunes, transform agricultural production or make the country a model of colonial order), the building and rebuilding of towns and cities as centers of the new European-dominated commercial life, and the migration to these urban centers of tens of thousands of the increasingly impoverished rural poor. In the nineteenth century, no other place in the world was transformed on a greater scale to serve the production of a single commodity.

Elsewhere I have examined in detail how the modern means of colonizing a country that this transformation required – new military methods, the reordering of agricultural production, systems of organized schooling, the rebuilding of cities, new forms of communication, the transformation of writing, and so on – all represented the techniques of ordering up an object-world to create the novel effect of a world divided in two: on the one hand a material dimension of things themselves, and on the other a seemingly separate dimension of their order or meaning.[34] Thus it can be shown, I think, that the strange, binary order of the world-as-exhibition was already being extended through a variety of techniques to places like the Middle East. If, as I have been suggesting, this binary division was, in fact, uncertain and it was hard to tell on close inspection where the exhibition ended and reality began, then this uncertainty extended well beyond the supposed limits of the West. Yet at the same time as these paradoxical but enormously powerful methods of the exhibition were spreading across the southern and eastern shores of the Mediterranean, the world exhibitions began to portray, outside the world-as-exhibition and lacking by definition the meaning and order that exhibitions supply, an essentialized and exotic Orient.

There are three features of this binary world that I have tried to outline in the preceding pages. First, there is its remarkable claim to certainty or truth:

the apparent certainty with which everything seems ordered and represented, calculated and rendered unambiguous – ultimately, what seems its political decidedness. Second, there is the paradoxical nature of this decidedness: the certainty exists as the seemingly determined correspondence between mere representations and reality; yet the real world, like the world outside the exhibition, despite everything the exhibition promises, turns out to consist only of further representations of this 'reality'. Third, there is its colonial nature: the age of the exhibition was necessarily the colonial age, the age of world economy and global power in which we live, since what was to be made available as exhibit was reality, the world itself.

To draw out the colonial nature of these methods of order and truth and thus their relationship to Orientalism, I am now going to move on to the Middle East. The Orient, as I have suggested, was the great 'external reality' of modern Europe – the most common object of its exhibitions, the great signified. By the 1860s, Thomas Cook, who had launched the modern tourist industry by organizing excursion trains (with the Midland Railway Company) to visit the first of the great exhibitions, at the Crystal Palace in 1851, was offering excursions to visit not exhibits of the East, but the 'East itself'. If Europe was becoming the world-as-exhibition, what happened to Europeans who went abroad – to visit places whose images invariably they had already encountered in books, spectacles, and exhibitions? How did they experience the so-called real world such images had depicted, when the reality was a place whose life was not lived, or at least not yet, as if the world were an exhibition?

The East itself

'So here we are in Egypt,' wrote Gustave Flaubert, in a letter from Cairo in January, 1850:

What can I say about it all? What can I write you? As yet I am scarcely over the initial bedazzlement ... each detail reaches out to grip you; it pinches you; and the more you concentrate on it the less you grasp the whole. Then gradually all this becomes harmonious and the pieces fall into place of themselves, in accordance with the laws of perspective. But the first days, by God, it is such a bewildering chaos of colours ... [35]

Flaubert experiences Cairo as a visual turmoil. What can he write about the place? That it is a chaos of color and detail that refuses to compose itself as a picture. The disorienting experience of a Cairo street, in other words, with its arguments in unknown languages, strangers who brush past in strange clothes, unusual colors, and unfamiliar sounds and smells, is expressed as an absence of pictorial order. There is no distance, this means, between oneself and the view, and the eyes are reduced to organs of touch: 'Each detail reaches out to grip you.' Without a separation of the self from a picture, moreover, what becomes impossible is to grasp 'the whole'. The experience of the world as a picture set up before a subject is linked to the unusual conception of the world as an enframed totality, something that forms a structure or system. Subsequently, coming to terms with this disorientation and recovering one's self-possession is expressed again in pictorial terms. The world arranges itself into a picture and achieves a visual order, 'in accordance with the laws of perspective'.

Flaubert's experience suggests a paradoxical answer to my question concerning what happened to Europeans who 'left' the exhibition. Although they thought of themselves as moving from the pictures or exhibits to the real thing, they went on trying – like Flaubert – to grasp the real thing as a picture. How could they do otherwise, since they took reality itself to be picturelike? The real is that which is grasped in terms of a distinction between a picture and what it represents, so nothing else would have been, quite literally, thinkable.

Among European writers who traveled to the Middle East in the middle and latter part of the nineteenth century, one very frequently finds the experience of its strangeness expressed in terms of the problem of forming a picture. It was as though to make sense of it meant to stand back and make a drawing or take a photograph of it; which for many of them actually it did. 'Every year that passes,' an Egyptian wrote, 'you see thousands of Europeans traveling all over the world, and everything they come across they make a picture of.'[36] Flaubert traveled in Egypt on a photographic mission with Maxime du Camp, the results of which were expected to be 'quite special in character' it was remarked at the Institut de France, 'thanks to the aid of this modern traveling companion, efficient, rapid, and always scrupulously exact'.[37] The chemically etched correspondence between photographic image and reality would provide a new, almost mechanical kind of certainty.

Like the photographer, the writer wanted to reproduce a picture of things 'exactly as they are', of 'the East itself in its vital actual reality'.[38] Flaubert was preceded in Egypt by Edward Lane, whose innovative *Account of the Manners and Customs of the Modern Egyptians*, published in 1835, was a product of the same search for a pictorial certainty of representation. The book's 'singular power of description and minute accuracy' made it, in the words of his nephew, Orientalist Stanley Poole, 'the most perfect picture of a people's life that has ever been written'.[39] 'Very few men,' added his grandnephew, the Orientalist Stanley Lane-Poole, 'have possessed in equal degree the power of minutely describing a scene or a monument, so that the pencil might almost restore it without a fault after the lapse of years. ... The objects stand before you as you read, and this not by the use of imaginative language, but by the plain simple description.'[40]

Lane, in fact, did not begin as a writer but as a professional artist and engraver, and had first traveled to Egypt in 1825 with a new apparatus called the camera lucida, a drawing device with a prism that projected an exact image of the object on to paper. He had planned to publish the drawings he made and the accompanying descriptions in an eight-volume work entitled 'An Exhaustive Description of Egypt', but had been unable to find a publisher whose printing techniques could reproduce the minute and mechanical accuracy of the illustrations. Subsequently he published the part dealing with contemporary Egypt, rewritten as the famous ethnographic description of the modern Egyptians.[41]

The problem for the photographer or writer visiting the Middle East, however, was not just to make an accurate picture of the East but to set up the East as a picture. One can copy or represent only what appears already to exist representationally – as a picture. The problem, in other words, was to create a distance between oneself and the world and thus constitute it as something picturelike – as an object on exhibit. This required what was now called a 'point of view', a position set apart and outside. While in Cairo, Edward Lane lived near one of the city's gates, outside which there was a large hill with a tower and military telegraph on top. This elevated position commanded 'a most magnificent view of the city and suburbs and the citadel', Lane wrote. 'Soon after my arrival I made a very elaborate drawing of the scene, with the camera lucida. From no other spot can so good a view of the metropolis ... be obtained.'[42]

These spots were difficult to find in a world where, unlike the West, such 'objectivity' was not yet built in. Besides the military observation tower used by Lane, visitors to the Middle East would appropriate whatever buildings and monuments were available in order to obtain the necessary viewpoint. The Great Pyramid at Giza had now become a viewing platform. Teams of Bedouin were organized to heave and push the writer or tourist – guidebook in hand – to the top, where two more Bedouin would carry the European on their shoulders to all four corners, to observe the view. At the end of the century, an Egyptian novel satirized the westernizing pretensions among members of the Egyptian upper middle class, by having one such character spend a day climbing the pyramids at Giza to see the view.[43] The minaret presented itself similarly to even the most respectable European as a viewing tower, from which to sneak a panoptic gaze over a Muslim town. 'The mobbing I got at *Shoomlo*,' complained Jeremy Bentham on his visit to the Middle East, 'only for taking a peep at the town from a thing they call a *minaret* ... has canceled any claims they might have had upon me for the dinner they gave me at the *divan*, had it been better than it was.'[44]

Bentham can remind us of one more similarity between writer and camera, and of what it meant, therefore, to grasp the world as though it were a picture or exhibition. The point of view was not just a place set apart, outside the world or above it. Ideally, it was a position from where, like the authorities in Bentham's panopticon, one could see and yet not be seen. The photographer, invisible beneath his black cloth as he eyed the world through his camera's gaze, in this respect typified the kind of presence desired by the European in the Middle East, whether as tourist, writer, or, indeed, colonial power.[45] The ordinary European tourist, dressed (according to the advice in *Murray's Handbook for Travellers in Lower and Upper Egypt*, already in its seventh edition by 1888) in either 'a common felt helmet or wide-awake, with a turban of white muslin wound around it' or alternatively a pith helmet, together with a blue or green veil and 'coloured-glass spectacles with gauze sides', possessed the same invisible gaze.[46] The ability to see without being seen confirmed one's separation from the world, and constituted at the same time a position of power.

The writer, too, wished to see without being seen. The representation of the Orient, in its attempt to be detached and objective, would seek to eliminate from the picture the presence of the European observer. Indeed, to represent something as Oriental, as Edward Said has argued, one sought to excise the European presence altogether.[47] 'Many thanks for the local details you sent me,' wrote Théophile Gautier to Gérard de Nerval in Cairo, who was supplying him with firsthand material for his Oriental scenarios at the Paris Opéra. 'But how the devil was I to have included among the walk-ons of the Opéra these Englishmen dressed in raincoats, with their quilted cotton hats and their green veils to protect themselves against ophthalmia?' Representation was not to represent the voyeur, the seeing eye that made representation possible.[48] To establish the objectness of the Orient, as a picture-reality containing no sign of the increasingly pervasive European presence, required that the presence itself, ideally, become invisible.

Participant observation

Yet this was where the paradox began. At the same time as the European wished to elide himself in order to constitute the world as something not-himself, something other and objectlike, he also wanted to experience it as though it were the real thing. Like visitors to an exhibition or scholars in Sacy's Orientalist museum, travelers wanted to feel themselves 'transported … into the very midst' of their Oriental object-world, and to 'touch with their fingers a strange civilization'. In his journal, Edward Lane wrote of wanting 'to throw myself entirely among strangers … to adopt their language, their customs, and their dress'.[49] This kind of immersion was to make possible the profusion of ethnographic detail in writers such as Lane, and produce in their work the effect of a direct and immediate experience of the Orient. In Lane, and even more so in writers such as Flaubert and Nerval, the desire for this immediacy of the real became a desire for direct and physical contact with the exotic, the bizarre, and the erotic.

There was a contradiction, therefore, between the need to separate oneself from the world and render it up as an object of representation, and the desire to lose oneself within this object-world and experience it directly; a contradiction that world exhibitions, with their profusion of exotic detail and yet their clear distinction between visitor and exhibit, were built to accommodate and overcome. In fact, 'experience', in this sense, depends upon the structure of the exhibition. The problem in a place such as Cairo, which had not been built to provide the experience of an exhibition, was to fulfill such a double desire. On his first day in Cairo, Gérard de Nerval met a French 'painter' equipped with a daguerreotype, who 'suggested that I come with him to choose a point of view'. Agreeing to accompany him, Nerval decided 'to have myself taken to the most labyrinthine point of the city, abandon the painter to his tasks, and then wander off haphazardly, without interpreter or companion'. But within the labyrinth of the city, where Nerval hoped to immerse himself in the exotic and finally experience 'without interpreter' the real Orient, they were unable to find any point from which to take the picture. They followed one crowded, twisting street after another, looking without success for a suitable viewpoint, until eventually the profusion of noises and people subsided and the streets became 'more silent, more dusty, more deserted, the mosques fallen in decay and here and there a building in collapse'. In the end they found themselves outside the city, 'somewhere in the suburbs, on the other side of the canal from the main sections of the town'. Here at last, amid the silence and the ruins, the photographer was able to set up his device and portray the Oriental city.[50] [...]

In claiming that the 'East itself' is not a place, I am not saying simply that Western representations created a distorted image of the real Orient; nor am I saying that the 'real Orient' does not exist, and that there are no realities but only images and representations. Either statement would take for granted the strange way the West had come to live, as though the world were divided in this way into two: into a realm of 'mere' representations opposed to an essentialized realm of 'the real'; into exhibitions opposed to an external reality; into an order of models, descriptions, texts, and meanings opposed to an order of originals, of things in themselves.[51] What we already suspected in the streets of Paris, concerning this division, is confirmed by the journey to the Orient: what seems excluded from the exhibition as the real or the outside turns out to be only that which can be represented, that which occurs in exhibitionlike form – in other words, a further extension of that labyrinth that we call an exhibition. What matters about this labyrinth is not that we never reach the real, never find the promised exit, but that such a notion of the real, such a system of truth, continues to convince us.

The case of Orientalism shows us, moreover, how this supposed distinction between a realm of representation and an external reality corresponds to another apparent division of the world, into the West and the non-West. In the binary terms of the world-as-exhibition, reality is the effect of an external realm of pure existence, untouched by the self and by the processes that construct meaning and order. The Orient is a similar effect. It appears as an essentialized realm originally outside and untouched by the West, lacking the meaning and order that only colonialism can bring. Orientalism, it follows, is not just a nineteenth-century instance of some general historical problem of how one culture portrays another, nor just an aspect of colonial domination, but part of a method of order and truth essential to the peculiar nature of the modern world.

NOTES

1. Edward Said, *Orientalism* (New York, 1978).

2. Tony Bennett, 'The Exhibitionary Complex', *New Formations*, 4 (Spring, 1988), 96. Unfortunately, this insightful article came to my attention only as I was completing the revisions to this article.

3. See esp. Robert W. Rydell, *All the World's a Fair: Visions of Empire at American International Expositions, 1876–1916* (Chicago, 1984); see also Bennett, 'Exhibitionary Complex'.

4. Muhammad Amin Fikri, *Irshad al-alibbd ila mahasin Urubba* (Cairo, 1892), 128.

5. Fikri, *Irshad*, 128–9, 136.

6. R. N. Crust, 'The International Congresses of Orientalists', *Hellas*, 6 (1897), 359.

7. Ibid. 351.

8. Ibid. 359.

9. Rifa'a al-Tahtawi, *al-A'mal al-kamila* (Beirut: al-Mu'assasa al-Arabiyya li-l-Dirasat wa-l-Nashr, 1973), 2: 76.

10. Ali Mubarak, *Alam al-din* (Alexandria, 1882), 816. The 'curiosity' of the European is something of a theme for Orientalist writers, who contrast it with the 'general lack of curiosity' of non-Europeans. Such curiosity is assumed to be the natural, unfettered relation of a person to the world, emerging in Europe once the loosening of 'theological bonds' had brought about 'the freeing of human minds' (Bernard Lewis, *The Muslim Discovery of Europe*, London, 1982, 299). See Mitchell, *Colonising Egypt* [Cambridge and New York: Cambridge University Press, 1988], 4–5, for a critique of this sort of argument and its own 'theological' assumptions.

11. Alain Silvera, 'The First Egyptian Student Mission to France under Muhammad Ali', in Elie Kedourie and Sylvia G. Haim (eds), *Modern Egypt: Studies in Politics and Society* (London, 1980), 13.

12. Tahtawi, *al-A'mal*, 2: 177, 199–20.

13. Georges Douin, *Histoire du règne du Khédive Ismail* (Rome, 1934), 2: 4–5.

14. Tahtawi, *al-A'mal*, 2: 121.

15. Quoted in Said, *Orientalism*, 165.

16. James Augustus St John, *The Education of the People* (London, 1858), 82–3.

17. 'Les origines et le plan de l'exposition', in *L'Exposition de Paris de 1889*, 3 (15 December 1889), 18.

18. On Egyptian writing about Europe in the 19th c. see Ibrahim Abu-Lughod, *Arab Rediscovery of Europe* (Princeton, 1963); Anouar Louca, *Voyageurs et écrivains égyptiens en France au XIXe siècle* (Paris, 1970); Mitchell, *Colonising Egypt*, 7–13, 180 n. 14.

19. Theodor Adorno, *Minima Moralia: Reflections from a Damaged Life* (London, 1978), 116: on the theater, see e.g. Muhammad al-Muwaylihi, *Hadith Isa ibn Hisham, aw fatra min al-zaman*, 2ND edn. (Cairo, 1911), 434, and Tahtawi, *al-A'mal*, 2: 119–20; on the public garden and the zoo, Muhammad al-Sanusi al-Tunisi, *al-Istitla'at al-barisiya fi ma rad sanat 1889* (Tunis, 1891), 37.

20. Mubarak, *Alam al-din*, 817.

21. The model farm outside Paris is described in Mubarak, *Alam al-din*, 1008–42; the visual effect of the street in Mubarak, *Alam al-din*, 964, and Idwar Ilyas, *Mashabid Uruba wa-Amirka* (Cairo, 1900), 268; the new funicular at Lucerne and the European passion for panoramas in Fikri, *Irshad*, 98.

22. Martin Heidegger, 'The Age of the World Picture', in *The Question Concerning Technology and Other Essays* (New York, 1977).

23. International Congress of Orientalists, *Transactions of the Ninth Congress, 1892* (London, 1893), 1: 35.

24. Al-Sanusi, *al-Istitla'at*, 242.

25. Edmond About, *Le Fellah: souvenirs d'Egypte* (Paris, 1869), 47–8.

26. Charles Edmond, *L'Egypte à l'exposition universelle de 1867* (Paris, 1867).

27. Jacques Derrida, *Speech and Phenomena and Other Essays on Husserl's Theory of Signs* (Evanston, Ill., 1973), 104. All of his subsequent writings, Derrida once remarked, 'are only a commentary on the sentence about a labyrinth' ('Implications: Interview with Henri Ronse', in *Positions* (Chicago, 1981), 5). My article, too, should be read as a commentary on that sentence.

28. Quoted in Walter Benjamin, 'Paris, Capital of the Nineteenth Century', in *Reflections: Essays, Aphorisms, Autobiographical Writings* (New York, 1978), 146–7.

29. Mubark, *Alam al-din*, 818; Ilyas, *Mashabid Uruba*, 268.

30. Mubarak, *Alam al-din*, 829–30.

31. Benjamin, 'Paris', 146, 152; Tahtawi, *al-A'mal*, 2: 76.

32. See André Raymond, *Artisans et commerçants au Caire au XVIIIe siècle* (Damascus, 1973), 1: 173–202; Roger Owen, *The Middle East in the World Economy 1800–1914* (London, 1981).

33. By the eve of World War I, cotton accounted for more than 92 per cent of the total value of Egypt's exports (Roger Owen, *Cotton and the Egyptian Economy*, Oxford, 1969, 307).

34. See Mitchell, *Colonising Egypt*.

35. Gustave Flaubert, *Flaubert in Egypt: A Sensibility on Tour*, trans. Francis Steegmuller (London, 1983), 79.

36. Mubarak, *Alam al-din*, 308.

37. Flaubert, *Flaubert in Egypt*, 23.

38. Eliot Warburton, author of *The Crescent and the Cross: or Romance and Realities of Eastern Travel* (1845), describing Alexander Kinglake's *Eothen, or Traces of Travel Brought Home from the East* (London, 1844; reprint edn, 1908); cited in *The Oxford Companion to English Literature*, 5th edn, (Oxford, 1985), s.v. 'Kinglake'.

39. Edward Lane, *An Account of the Manners and Customs of the Modern Egyptians*, reprint edn (London, 1908), pp. vii, xvii.

40. Stanley Lane-Poole, 'Memoir', in Edward Lane, *An Arabic–English Lexicon*, reprint edn (Beirut, 1980), vol. V, p. xii.

41. Leila Ahmed, *Edward W. Lane: A Study of His Life and Work* (London, 1978); John D. Wortham, *The Genesis of British Egyptology, 1549–1906* (Norman, Okla., 1971), 65.

42. Quoted in Ahmed, *Edward Lane*, 26.

43. MuhmanmadMuwaylihi, *A Study of Had-ith 'Is-a ibn Hish-am, Muhammad al-Muwaylihi's View of Egyptian Society during the British Occupation*, 3rd edn, trans. Roger M. A. Allen (Albany: State University of New York Press, 1974), 405–17.

44. Jeremy Bentham, *The Complete Works*, ed. John Bowring (Edinburgh, 1838–43), 4: 65–6.

45. Cf. Malek Alloula, *The Colonial Harem* (Minneapolis, 1986).

46. *Murray's Handbook for Travellers in Lower and Upper Egypt* (London, 1888).

47. Said, *Orientalism*, 160–1, 168, 239. My subsequent analysis is much indebted to Said's work.

48. J. M. Carré, *Voyageurs et écrivains français en Egypte*, 2nd edn (Cairo, 1956), 2: 191.

49. Quoted in Lane, *Arabic–English Lexicon*, 5: vii.

50. Gérard de Nerval, *Oeuvres*, ed. Albert Béguin and Jean Richer, i: *Voyage en Orient* (1851), ed. Michel Jeanneret (Paris, 1952), 172–4.

51. Cf. Jacques Derrida, 'The Double Session', in *Dissemination* (Chicago, 1981), 191–2, *Speech and Phenomena*, and 'Implications'.

7.

China in Britain:
The Imperial Collections

Craig Clunas

When I was fourteen I went to London with my father. We were on the way to Cambridge, where I was to investigate the possibility of studying Chinese. I visited the Victoria and Albert Museum for the first time, and there in a large room titled 'Far Eastern Art' I was enthralled to see a great carved lacquer seat, labelled 'Throne of the Emperor Ch'ien-lung' (Figure 4.7.1). While the uniformed warder looked away (or pretended to), I knelt down and put my forehead to the black linoleum in homage.

These are not the tales curators tell. Their role in maintaining objects (in both senses of the word) demands that they suppress such embarrassing personal engagements and secret fetishisms, which threaten to reopen the space between the viewer and the artefact. The throne was there, and the Emperor of China sat on it. Now it is here, and you the visitor view it. Do not ask how it got here, or where it was from 1770 to now; that does not matter. You are here to engage with 'China', not with 'Britain', so do not ask what the presence of the throne of the emperor of China might tell you about 'Britain', and its narratives about 'China' over the two centuries since the thing was made. Admission of this bit of adolescent theatricality may undermine my professional identification as a member of the staff of that same museum, entrusted by the British state with the power to place that same 'throne', write about it and display it. However, failure to admit to it, to accept the object's presence in South Kensington as being an untroubling and natural occurrence, which need not touch anyone's fantasy life today, can only in the end reproduce a stifling identity of self-regard. What follows is a step towards the compilation of the inventory which Gramsci saw as

Figure 4.7.1   Throne, carved lacquer on a wood core, c. 1775–80. Taken from the Nan Yuan hunting park in 1901. Reproduced by courtesy of the Board of Trustees of the Victoria and Albert Museum, London

necessary, if a consciousness of myself and my colleagues as a product of the historical process to date is to be produced. The dates, deeds and institutional affiliations of past scholars which I write down here are presented not simply as 'what happened', but rather as an essential part of any critical elaboration of present practice in the production of 'Chinese Art' in Britain, in a context where the displays of the major public museums are the principal visible constructions from which a discourse of 'Chinese culture' can be derived.

Possessions/identities

C. B. Macpherson's work[1] on the political theory of possessive individualism in eighteenth-century England has made familiar the notion that possessions are seen as constitutive of identity within the dominant discourses of political and moral economy in Britain. More recently, the work of Susan Stewart[2] and James Clifford[3] has extended this notion to the position that possessing is also central to the generation and sustaining of the identities of collectivities. This is particularly so in the case of the imagined community of the nation state. The National Museum acts as a key site of promotion of the existence and validity of the state formation. It does so with particular force in that the discursive practices at the heart of the museum lay claim to scientific objectivity, to a transcendental mimesis of what is 'out there'. It thus can act with particular force to validate the claims to sovereignty and independence by proving through displays of archaeology and ethnography the inevitability of the existence of the actually contingent conditions which give it its very existence.

The 'British Museum' could never be restricted to British things, for to do so would set a limit to the reach of British power, as well as to the gaze of the all-comprehending and autonomous subject. The British colonial presence in China differed from that in India in duration and intensity, but many of the same practices in the field of culture can be observed, practices constitutive of a 'British' identity differentiated not only from the other of Asia but from more immediate colonial rivals such as France and latterly the United States. In what follows I want to look at some changes in the presentation of material from China in the British Museum and the Victoria and Albert Museum in London, two institutions directly patronised and supported by the British state, conscious that the framing of Chinese objects in these institutions conditions their viewing as expressive of discourses of national and imperial identity. The interplay of private and public possession, between individual collectors and public museums which they patronised and supported, and which ultimately came to possess the objects they had amassed, is of particular importance in forming the collections of material out of which representations of 'China' and 'Chinese art' were manufactured in Britain. I write with intentional ambiguity about Britain's possession of the 'throne' of China, to which I bowed as a teenager.

The institutional framing of 'Chinese art' in Britain

It is impossible to discuss the creation of the broader category 'Chinese art' in Europe and America over the past hundred years without first accepting the existence of a discourse (and a gendered discourse) of China which has its primary locus in the context of domestic consumption, since it is against, or by contrast with, what is done in the home that so much of what happens in the institutional context of museums and of the academy is defined. This is particularly striking in the case of objects of luxury consumption for the Chinese domestic market redirected by the museum, and put under the category 'decorative arts': chairs, items of clothing, ceramic wine jars, personal religious images, to take a few random examples. Chinese elite categorisations of art, as expressed in texts as well as in the practices of the art and craft markets excluded much of the Chinese material subsequently displayed in the museum context in Britain.

Indeed 'art' is not a category in the sense of a pre-existent container filled with different contents as history progresses. Rather it is a way of categorising, a manner of making knowledge which has been applied to a wider and wider set of manifestations of material culture, paralleling the constant expansion of an 'art market' applied to a wider and wider range of commodities. It remains a site of conflicting interpretations, fissured on class and gender lines, among others, and the right to define something as 'art' is typically seen as an important attribute of those dominant in society at a given moment. Crucial to this way of categorising in European museum and academic practice is the strategy whereby notions of function must largely be removed from the objects of the exercise. In order to be an object of 'decorative art' a cup must no longer be drunk from, and questions of how it would be drunk from have to be occluded. Thrones must no longer be bowed down to. Objects transferred from the domain of 'ethnography' to that of 'art' typically find diachronic links privileged at the expense of connections with others which have failed to make the transition.[4]

But narrative art history is only one interpretative framework into which the things made in China have been construed in Europe and America. Despite its role as the dominant paradigm in the United States today, it is arguable whether it has ever actually taken root in Britain at all. Another framework of representation has historically flourished here, one with an equal power of generating discourse, though this time originating in the study of the natural world: the framework of taxonomy. This in the later nineteenth century, and most particularly in Britain, exercised a powerful hegemony over the ordering of man-made products as well as over those of nature.[5] It is the programme of a universal taxonomy of 'the industrial arts' which formed the explicit project of the South Kensington Museum, known after 1899 as the Victoria and Albert Museum. In 1863 (immediately after the Second Opium War against China) the Lords of the Committee of the Council on Education had stated 'that the aim of the Museum is to make the historical and geographical series of all decorative art complete, and fully to illustrate human taste and ingenuity'.[6]

The aim of completeness was qualified by the exclusion from the South Kensington collections of the material culture of those peoples, dubbed 'primitive', who had neither art nor history. They were consigned to the historic present of ethnography collections, represented in 1863 primarily by the British Museum but later in the century by collections such as those of the Horniman Museum in London and the Pitt Rivers Museum in Oxford.[7]

It is very hard to research the history of a museum. The point of a museum is that it has no history, but represents the objects it contains transparently, in an unmediated form. It is even harder to create a history of the display of Chinese material in British museums, since very little descriptive or pictorial information exists as to what was shown where when, what juxtapositions (almost the most powerful creators of meaning in display) were made, which objects were privileged by particularly prominent positioning, and what was said about them on labels. This is more than an accident, or a piece of forgetfulness on the part of my predecessors. The museum cannot allow itself to document its own frequently changing display arrangements, since then it will have a history, and if it becomes a historical object in its own right then it can investigated, challenged, opposed or contradicted.[8]

There have in fact been many changes in the contexts and categories into which Chinese artefacts have been inserted in Britain. Only some of these contexts have involved a deployment of the notion of 'Chinese art', but all have operated with the notion of an integral 'Chinese culture', for which certain types of luxury artefact, mediated through the international art market and categorised by British individual and institutional collectors, was a satisfactory synecdoche.

Chinese objects came to the British Museum in the founding bequest of Sir Hans Sloane in 1753, and appear at first to have been included under the rubric of 'Ethnography'. That this was felt to be in some sense inadequate by the mid-nineteenth century is shown by the complaint in David Masson's *The British Museum, Historical and Descriptive* (1850) that works of China and Japan were crammed into 'five paltry cases' among a 'collection of articles illustrative of the manners and customs of nations lying at a distance from our own, as well as of rude ancient races'.[9] Masson argued that there should be distinct rooms for the antiquities of China, India and Japan, which should be separated from those of more primitive peoples.

There was clear privileging of Chinese and Japanese pictorial works throughout the nineteenth century, though this owed more to Western notions of the hierarchy of the arts than it did to any recognition of their equal prominence in any scheme of things to be found in China. The fact that they were a 'higher' art form is shown by their inclusion in the collections of the Department of Prints and Drawings (formed out of the Department of

Antiquities as far back as 1836), where they were collected and curated on a par with European material.

This is a significant point. At a time when Chinese ceramics were still, at least administratively, the same thing as canoes and weapons, a Hiroshige print was the same as a Rembrandt print. A picture could not, by definition, be simply an 'antiquity', a piece of historical evidence, but was of necessity part of the realm of (fine) art. A Chinese picture could be bad art, failed art, but it could not cease to be art at this point. Note, however, that there was no question of including Chinese painting with Western painting in the National Gallery, and it remained alongside items (prints) which occupied a subsidiary, if still honoured, ranking in the Western canon.

London's other major institutional collection, the South Kensington Museum, has also included Chinese material since its inception in the Museum attached to the central design school of the Department of Practical Art in the decades immediately prior to the Great Exhibition of 1851.[10] The initial aim of the collection was stringently didactic, aimed at improving the quality of British manufactured goods in a situation of intense commercial rivalry, above all with the French. Consequently the South Kensington Museum aimed to concentrate on 'Ornamental Art', which meant excluding pictures and sculpture (though this programme was modified shortly after its inception, and a considerable quantity of Chinese pictures acquired).

In the historicist climate of the time China was a perfectly acceptable source of design solutions, though one held in lower esteem by many. In *The Grammar of Ornament*, first published in 1856, the designer and theorist Owen Jones (someone closely associated with the whole South Kensington project) could write that Chinese art was totally familiar, through the medium of imported goods, and could condemn it thus: 'The Chinese are totally unimaginative, and all their works are accordingly wanting in the highest grace of art – the ideal.'[11] The complaint is really one about 'the Chinese mind', to which an assemblage of designed objects will provide an infallible key. Nevertheless large quantities of objects in a variety of media were accumulated at South Kensington, in an institution which became increasingly confused as the nineteenth century wore on as to whether it was there to educate British craftsmen by exposing them to a broad range of often contemporary practice, or there to assemble a great historical corpus of material in which connoisseurly criteria of quality would be the deciding factor.

Ceramics as the flowering of Chinese art

In the inter-war years and after the Department of Ceramics was broadly responsible for the sustenance and construction of 'Chinese Art' within the

Victoria and Albert Museum. With what were, both numerically and in terms of prominence in display, the most important Chinese collections, and with internationally renowned scholars such as William Bowyer Honey (1891–1956) and Bernard Rackham (1877–1964) on its staff, the Department exercised an unofficial hegemony, as guardian of the master narrative in which 'Chinese ceramics' and 'Chinese art' were collapsed into each other.

However, during the inter-war period, the British Museum's sub-department of Oriental Prints and Drawings (established in 1913) employed the young Arthur Waley (1889–1968), nowadays better remembered as a translator of Chinese and Japanese literature.[12] Waley had been employed by Laurence Binyon (1899–1943), author in 1908 of *The Painting of the Far East*.[13] Both Waley and Binyon enjoyed wide literary reputations which gave them an authority not essentially derived from their museum offices. Although his championing of painting might make him seem a more faithful transmitter of 'traditional' Chinese connoisseurly criteria, Binyon's views are those of the classic orientalist position as defined by Said, where 'the East' cannot represent itself, but must be revealed to itself by the Western expert, who has penetrated its essential and unchanging characteristics. They are summed up in a series of lectures delivered at Harvard in 1933–4, and dedicated to his great American contemporary Langdon Warner, Director of the Freer Gallery.[14] These construct 'Chinese art' as a reflection of essential and largely historically invariant characteristics of 'the Chinese race', and are full of typically reductive aphorisms – 'The Chinese have kept their eyes fresh', 'This race has always had a turn to the fabulous … It [Chinese art] has its roots deep in the earth.' Binyon certainly shared the view described above that it was the early achievements of Chinese culture that were the touchstone of quality, and that these were in some sense unknown to the Chinese themselves; 'for it is only in the present century that the real achievements of Chinese art have been revealed'.[15] He also provided a theoretical underpinning for the prominent role given to ceramics in museum collections, in his typically florid panegyric in Bergsonian vein to a Tang dynasty ceramic jar.

No less than a great picture or statue, this vase typifies what art is and art does: how it has its being in the world of the senses yet communicates through the senses so much more than we can express in words. You cannot tell the body from the spirit, the thing expressed from its expression. The complete work is filled with a mysterious life like a human personality.[16]

The anonymity of potters saved the connoisseur from even having to consider any named, individuated Chinese maker as a conscious social or political actor. No actual person had made the pot, it had been made by 'the race'.

Chinese art and imperial decline

The years after the First World War saw a major shift in the valuation of Chinese art in Britain, with a collapse in the status of the types of Qing (1644–1911) porcelain which had been the focus of interest for an early generation of collectors (like Stephen Bushell[17] and those advised by him), and a new engagement with the art of early China. It has been traditional to view this in rather mechanistic terms, as the simple reaction to the increased opportunity to see early Chinese things concomitant with the progress of excavation, legal and illegal, in China. Clearly there was a connection between railway building and the flood of tomb ceramics on to the market. But it is also the case that changed attitudes made for a greater receptivity to early Chinese artefacts. (After all, plenty of bronzes were available above ground in the Qing period, but there is no evidence that they moved Whistler or Oscar Wilde in the same way as Kangxi blue-and-white ceramics.) Rachel Gotlieb's description of a tired Europe refreshing itself from the vital springs of more primitive cultures is clearly part of the larger picture of appropriation of the other seen in the art of the Cubists and Surrealists.[18] In the particular case of China, the otherness is seen as distance in time, not space. Chinese culture has a glorious past, a decayed and exhausted present and no future.

Running parallel to this development, expressed above all in critical writing like that of Roger Fry, was a deepening fetishisation by the Victoria and Albert Museum of objects manufactured at what was deemed to be both the apogee and the end of 'traditional China', the eighteenth century. The reign of the Qianlong emperor (1736–95) was held to mark the last era of artistic excellence before the catastrophic nineteenth-century 'decline' (the causes of which, if they are discussed at all in artistic literature, are usually put down to something like 'exhaustion' on the part of the 'tradition'). The role of imperialism in China's 'decline' is not commented on. The Qing empire disappeared in 1911, closely followed by the emperors of Russia, Germany and Austria. By 1920 only the emperors of Abyssinia, Japan and the King-Emperor George V kept their thrones. The latter ruled over territories which were expanded after the First World War, reaching a physical extent from which they were so swiftly to shrink. It is in the light of this that we must examine the fascination with the Chinese imperial court which was to permeate writing about, collecting and displaying Chinese artefacts in an institution like the Victoria and Albert Museum. The signs of rulership (crowns, thrones and other regalia) had been prominent in the Indian courts of the Great Exhibition of 1851, the event from which the Victoria and Albert Museum rhetorically derived (and continues to derive) legitimacy.[19] The fascination with the imperial provenance of the loot from the 1862 sacking of the Summer Palace was reflected in the museum's collecting in the decades after the event, but the supply of objects of high enough status and sufficient aesthetic quality was seen as necessarily limited before the ending of Qing rule.

In 1922 the museum was given what has remained one of its most famous and most reproduced treasures. It is a late-eighteenth-century throne-chair, looted from an imperial hunting park to the south of Peking in the 1901 multi-national invasion of China, and sold on the London art market by Mikail Girs, a White Russian *émigré* who had been Tsarist ambassador there at that time. It cost £2,250, and earned the donor of those funds the thanks of Queen Mary, who was known to have 'expressed a hope that, by some means, it might find a place' in the museum which bore her husband's grandparents' names. The throne has remained on display ever since, labelled until recently, 'The [note the definite article] throne of the Emperor Ch'ien-lung'.[20]

The screen with which it once formed a pair remains unpublished in the Museum of Ethnography in Vienna, but then possession of the screen of China is not the same thing as possession of the throne of China. (It would of course be recognised that Qing political discourse made no room for a 'throne of China', no ruler's seat which is symbolically equated with right of rule. The object's meaning is entirely a product of its context of display.) In Susan Stewart's terms, the throne is more of a souvenir than an item in a collection:

we need and desire souvenirs of events that are reportable, events whose materiality has escaped us, events that thereby exist only through the invention of narrative. Through narrative the souvenir substitutes a context of perpetual consumption for its context of origin. It represents not the lived experience of its maker but the 'secondhand' experience of its possessor/owner. Like the collection it always displays the romance of contraband, for its scandal is its removal from its 'natural' location. Yet it is only by means of its material relation to that location that it acquires its value.[21]

As the British Empire became more and more remote, souvenirs of the emperor such as the 'throne of China' played a greater and greater role in the national imaginary, as nostalgia for one empire slid across into nostalgia for all, and souvenirs of empire became fetishes of consolation. British colonial power in China was less effective in 1922 than it had been two decades earlier, at the point of the looting of the 'throne', and was to decline significantly over the next two decades leading to its collapse under Japanese assault. The throne thus comes to signify not the empire from which it was taken, but the equally vanished empire which took it.

Chinese art in the academy

Percival David (1892–1964), while also building up a major private collection of Chinese ceramics, provided in 1930 the funds for an experimental lectureship in Chinese Art and Archaeology, to be tenable at the School of Oriental and African Studies (SOAS), London University.[22] This lectureship, the first formal teaching to be made available in Britain in the field, was first given to Walter Perceval Yetts (1878–1957), who had no academic background in Chinese art history. In 1932 the post was made into a Chair attached to the Courtauld Institute of Art, and funded by the Universities China Committee in London, a grant-giving body funded by the monies extorted from the Chinese government by Britain as part of the 'Boxer indemnity' after 1901.

Yetts was succeeded as a teacher of Chinese Art and Archaeology at London University by S. Howard Hansford (1899–1973), who initially also had no formal background in art history or academic sinology, having worked rather until his mid-thirties with the family firm of Wright and Hansford, China and Japan Merchants. Hansford's SOAS lectureship was made up to a Chair in 1956, and he held the post till 1966, when he was succeeded by William Watson. In Hansford's inaugural lecture he took the opportunity to review the study of the subject in Britain, but first of all to stress the long history of 'archaeoloatry – the worship of antiquity' in China. In a further statement, very much in the manner of the orientalist concentration on 'essences' he argues that 'all Chinese' are conscious of the antiquity and unity of their civilisation, and adds: 'The Chinese, like the British, are quite sure that they are the salt of the earth, and do not feel the need of proving it by tedious argument.'[23]

His definition of the field is one which begins with bronzes, then Buddhist sculpture, then 'glyptics' i.e. the jade carving which was his own special field. For the study of these subjects London, with its three major museum collections, its private collections, and above all its thriving art market, 'offers conditions as near ideal as possible', and in particular better than those of China. He accepts that the torch of scholarship in this field has passed to Americans and Germans, while the major collections are all in Japan or the USA. He never mentions China, and we are left with the clear impression that Oriental Art is too important a subject to be left to Orientals.

The end of empire and the art of empire

Hansford's 1956 inaugural lecture was delivered in a context in which the study of Chinese art in Britain seemed to him indeed to be flourishing. What was happening in London at this period was the emergence of a more distinctive profile for 'Chinese art'. Distinguished now from 'ethnography' at the British Museum (in 1946) and recognised at the Victoria and Albert Museum as a distinct phenomenon by the creation of the 'Primary Gallery' (1952), above all enshrined in the prestigious Percival David Foundation of Chinese Art (1952), as well as supported by a flourishing art market and the collectors grouped around an expanded Oriental Ceramic Society, the subject seemed to enjoy a new degree of discursive coherence, but one still centred on museums rather than on academic teaching. The Percival David Foundation remains at the time of writing the only teaching institution in Chinese art, and from 1966 to the present its Head has been a scholar whose career began in a museum (William Watson, 1966–83; Roderick Whitfield, 1983–).

This discursive coherence nevertheless operated in a political climate of massively reduced British colonial power in Asia. After the end of the Malaysian 'emergency' (fought as Britain's contribution to the global containment of communism in Asia) such power was now focused almost solely on China, through the retention of Hong Kong. Yet throughout this period, and down to the present, colonialism was displaced into culture. Hong Kong remained invisible to the public culture represented in museums like the Victoria & Albert Museum and the British Museum, and 'China' remained, the two colliding only in the last decade with the reinstallation of the galleries at both the Victoria and Albert and British Museums using funds donated by individuals from the Hong Kong business community.[24] As government restrictions on museums' budgets mirror national economic decline, and as the private sector of corporate and personal sponsorship becomes the major support for once-imperial institutions, the question of who gets to represent what to who comes to the fore. To a sector of the museum's visitors, the loot of empire is what they expect to see, a literal 'empire of things'. In this world of insecure meanings and private fetishisms, the continued presence of major displays of Chinese art in the national museums, paid for with money from Hong Kong, come to seem in their entirety like souvenirs of that empire which is fast vanishing into the imaginary consolations of the costume drama.

NOTES

1. *The Political Theory of Possessive Individualism: Hobbes to Locke*, Oxford: Oxford University Press, 1962.

2. *On Longing: Narratives of the Miniature, the Gigantic, the Souvenir, the Collection*, Durham, N.C.: Duke University Press, 1993.

3. *The Predicament of Culture: Twentieth-Century Ethnography, Literature and Art*, Cambridge, Mass.: Harvard University Press, 1988.

4. Ibid., pp. 224–5.

5. R. A. Stafford, 'Annexing the landscapes of the past: British imperial geology in the nineteenth

century', in J. Mackenzie, *Imperialism and the Natural World*, Manchester: Manchester University Press, 1990, pp. 67–89.

6.   J. Earle, 'The taxonomic obsession: British collectors and Japanese objects, 1852–1986', *Burlington Magazine*, vol. 128 (1986), p. 866.

7.   A. E. Coombes, 'Museums and the formation of natural and cultural identities', *Oxford Art Journal*, 11 (1988), pp. 57–68.

8.   R. Lumley, *The Museum Time Machine: Putting Cultures on Display*, London: Routledge, 1988; P. Vergo (ed.), *The New Museology*, London: Reaktion, 1989.

9.   E. Miller, *That Noble Cabinet: A History of the British Museum*, London: Deutsch, 1973, p. 222.

10.   A. Burton, 'The Image of the Curator', *Victoria and Albert Museum*, 4 (1985), pp. 373–87.

11.   E. Gombrich, *The Sense of Order*, London: Phaidon, 1979, p. 56.

12.   Waley worked for the British museum from 1913 to 1930 and produced a catalogue of the Dunhuang paintings in 1931, which is still reckoned of some value today. Waley represented the exceptional figure of the self-taught genius and remarked quite correctly in 1923 that it was simply impossible to learn in London the kind of Chinese needed to equip one for a study of Chinese painting (though the idea of going to China to learn it was equally rejected) (T. H. Barrett, *Singular Listlessness: A Short History of Chinese Books and British Scholars*, London: Wellsweep Press, 1989, p. 47).

13.   Laurence Binyon was very much the *fin-de-siècle* aesthete in his views, a man for whom his work on *The Painting of the Far East* was but one strand in a career equally devoted to Western art, poetry, and historical drama.

14.   C. H. Binyon, *The Spirit of Man in Asian Art*, Cambridge, Mass.: Dover, 1936, p. 16.

15.   Ibid., p. 7.

16.   Ibid., p. 21.

17.   Prior to 1939, only one attempt had been made at South Kensington to address the entire field of 'Chinese art', and to improve the scholarly treatment of the Chinese collections in line with the European holdings, but this had been done right at the beginning of the century by recourse to knowledge held by a private collector, in this case Stephen Wooton Bushell (d. 1908). The South Kensington Museum commissioned his *Chinese Art* (originally of 1904, but with numerous reprints), using the museum's pieces as illustrations almost exclusively.

18.   R. Gottlieb, '"Vitality" in British art pottery and studio pottery', *Apollo* 127 (1988), pp. 163–7.

19.   C. Breckenridge, 'The politics of colonial collecting: India at the World's Fairs', *Comparative Studies in Society and History*, 31 (1989), pp. 203–4.

20.   *Nominal File: J P Swift*, Victoria and Albert Museum Registry.

21.   *One Longing*, p. 135.

22.   S. H. Hansford, *The Study of Chinese Antiquities*, London: School of Orientalism and African Studies, 1956, p. 3.

23.   Ibid., p. 4.

24.   The T. T. Tsui Gallery of Chinese Art opened at the Victoria and Albert Museum in 1991, and the Joseph Hotung Gallery of Oriental Antiquities opened at the British Museum in 1992.

V.

Secularizing Rituals

Introduction:
Secularizing Rituals

> Only retrospectively, though a narrative manipulation of the sequence of events, can the accidental of the first object *become* the beginning of a collection. In the plot it is pre-historic, in the story it intervenes *in medias res*. The beginning, instead, is a meaning, not an act.
>
> Mieke Bal, 'Telling Objects: a Narrative Perspective on Collecting' (1994)

In 1978 Carol Duncan and Alan Wallach published a scathing review of the Museum of Modern Art in New York; it is reprinted below as the opening article of this chapter. The essay appeared first in the centrist journal *Studio International* and soon thereafter in the radical leftist review *Marxist Perspectives*. Emphatically rejected by most of the museum establishment, their controversial thesis that the museum presented viewers with an architectural 'script' that bore 'striking resemblance' to 'ritual' in 'traditional societies' galvanized oppositional camps and inaugurated a new contentious era in the field of museum studies. The core of the authors' critique is that the modern art museum translates the 'ideology of late capitalism' into an apparent but disingenuous monument to the freedom of the human spirit that actually reinforces and glamorizes 'precisely the values and experiences it apparently rejects' by elevating competitive individualism and alienated human relations to a 'universal and timeless realm'. The authors compared MOMA's floorplan to a labyrinth, a pan-cultural symbol of regeneration, but insisted that the building and its collection offered only a delusory 'hall of mirrors'.

At roughly the same moment that Duncan and Wallach presented their politically charged argument that museums are effective ideological instruments intrinsic to the debased modern condition, historians of art studying the pre-modern world began to publish on the contexts in which museums and princely collections functioned in dynastic state formations before the creation of nation-states beginning with the French Revolution. Critical museum studies have grown out of diverse political sympathies employing a variety of methodologies, as the literature collected in *Grasping the World* only begins to suggest.

The most significant and, indeed, surprising, conclusion to be drawn *now* after a generation of intensive critical-historical inquiry is that the activities associated with collecting and display, while they may have historical roots in Christian liturgy and collections of relics and religious paraphernalia, rarely invoked religious ceremony directly. Public and private museums, and cultural activities associated with them since early humanism, primarily involved scientific investigation and secular forms of political domination. The ancient past, not Christian doctrine, typically gave authority to practices associated with collecting – even in the case of ecclesiastical collections like those Paula Findlen discusses in Chapter 2 of *Grasping the World* – and no doubt contributed to the flexibility and longevity of the idea of the museum.

In her study of the earliest activities of collecting and display included in this chapter, Claudia Lazzaro characterizes the princely custom of keeping menageries of large and wild animals as a sign of power that sixteenth-century European heads of state revived, on the basis of ancient Roman tributes and gift-exchanges with one another and with Byzantine, West Asian, and North African rulers. Exotic animals and representations of them, along with other imported precious objects, including specimens from the 'New World', were all made familiar by their assimilation to the classical tradition. The Graeco-Roman heritage provided the conceptual framework for the cultural construction of wild nature in contrast to human civilization, a contrast performed in lavish and often violent public festivals staged to commemorate state events. Gifts were a double-edged commodity in a system of diplomacy through exchange: triumphal imagery explicitly invoked ancient forms of tribute, while simultaneously representing foreign 'worlds' in a role of subservience.

How do such historical practices, once central to the idea of princely collecting, bear on the contemporary critique of museums? First and foremost, the evidence suggests that the passage from religious to secular 'rituals' is inappropriately imposed on historical data, resulting in an unacknowledged narrative of cultural evolutionism. Duncan and Wallach cite a 1768 description by Goethe of the newly created Dresden Gallery as a sanctuary set up for the sacred purposes of art – and many other similar examples of period testimony could be given. Nonetheless, the narrative structure of positing the 'end' of a religious world view and the 'beginning' of a secular world that masks the survival of theological practices in modern society is not simply or even accurately an artifact of bourgeois thought inherited from Enlightenment thinkers.

It appears that we have inadvertently accepted at face value a position framed by Enlightenment philosophers that masks an older and more insidious hierarchy. The ceremonies and other activities associated with museums and princely collections were always 'secular' in both the pre-modern sense of worldly and the modern sense (acquired only in the nineteenth century) of non-religious. The humanist revival of classical antiquity, beginning in the fourteenth century on the Italic peninsula, spreading to the rest of Europe and its colonies over the next four centuries, gathered advocates as well as producing local variants (such as French or Finnish neoclassicism) and eliciting direct inversions (such as English nationalist sentiment or German romanticism).

Appeals to the authority of European civilization, past and present, retain one overarching feature: they grant superiority to 'us' over 'others'. The presently widespread notion that museums present the public with the secular equivalent of religious 'ritual' needs to be re-thought in light of *historical* attitudes towards ritual in these circumstances. Is it possible that the anthropological model of 'ritual' in its application to museum activities reinscribes a Protestant criticism of Catholic ceremony already previously inscribed in the writings of certain Enlightenment writers? Such an investigation is beyond the scope of this volume, but well worth consideration.

Duncan and Wallach and others blame the 'ideology of late capitalism' for transforming communal activities into subjective experiences that deny individuals any real community or spiritual transcendence. Recent investigations of collecting and display bring to light long-term continuities that point away from religion as the simple cause and towards deeper-seated relationships between material display of status in general ('symbolic capital', to use another term introduced by Bourdieu) and profiteering. Lazzaro's study deals with gift-exchange in a barter economy. The remaining case studies in this chapter foreground the formation and maintenance of collective identity in the emerging era of an international monetary economy – European states ran on 'capital' before the era of industrialized capitalism. Luxury goods or 'surplus accumulation' presents its own, as yet under-studied, dynamics. The idea of the museum foregrounds these complex social processes.

In a short article included below, contemporary with Duncan and Wallach's critique of MOMA, Thomas DaCosta Kaufmann presented in 1978 the first results of his extensive study of the court of Rudolf II of Prague, Holy Roman Emperor and first among European collectors as well. Rudolf II's collection functioned partly as a form of public display to express his imperial magnificence directly and to reinforce his claims to power symbolically. Much like the animals (actual and imitated by artistic means) that Duke Cosimo II and other rulers flaunted less than a century earlier, Rudolf's *Kunstkammer* was regularly used for formal diplomatic functions. To make this princely form of self-representation intelligible, Rudolf II also built and decorated rooms on his Prague estate for displaying his collection on the classicizing model of the Italian *tribuna*, originally a type of room with niches for the display of sculpture. The arrangement of rooms built around 1590 to house Rudolf's collections attests to the systematic organization and programmatic arrangement of materials, grouped under the ubiquitous Aristotelian categories of *naturalia* and *artificialia* then in use throughout

Europe, as contributions by Giuseppe Olmi and others in Chapter 2 of this volume describe. Kaufmann concludes that Rudolf's collection signified the ruler's mastery of nature – his actual possession of the universe in microcosm was an expression of his symbolic mastery of the greater world.

A similar iconography is the subject of the next essay: Hans-Olof Boström's study of a diplomat and private dealer who assembled portable 'curiosity cabinets' or *Kunstschranken* foregrounds the theme of profit that threads through all the articles in this chapter. In this seventeenth-century continuation of gift-exchange as an enterprise run by private individuals for profit, Philip Hainhofer, a silk merchant from an Augsburg mercantile family ennobled by the same Rudolf II for successfully interceding between Catholic and Lutheran factions, assembled luxury articles on speculation for sale to wealthy patrons. Boström describes Hainhofer's miniature *Kunstkammers* as collections of objects once made for utilitarian purposes re-utilized for their symbolic value relative to the subject who owned them, conferring a personalized identity much like the collections assembled by Rudolf II and other rulers and members of the intelligentsia, except that Hainhofer's material identities were 'ready-mades'.

Class differences were fluid throughout the early modern history of this collecting tradition, as burghers emulated the self-fashioning strategies of the aristocracy. Hainhofer's greatest masterpiece ended up with a king, Gustavus Adolphus II of Sweden, but only because the Town Councillors of Augsburg purchased it as a gift for the king to avert a Swedish invasion in 1632. *Kunstschranken*, like their more magnificent relatives on a larger scale, functioned as models of the cosmos, containing mobile objects grouped in a gradual transition from Nature to Art. They served as interactive memory theatres for diversion and amusement – Boström describes them as shorthand versions of the macrocosm that mirrored the 'ungraspable world though an intelligible, unchangeable, and easily memorized order'.

Hainhofer assembled his collections for profit, providing an interesting case study of the important role that capitalism played in the gradual transition to a consumer society during the roughly two centuries pre-dating the Industrial Revolution. Francis Haskell and Nicholas Penny likewise studied the twinned mechanisms of profit-making and surplus accumulation necessary for fashioning a personal identity and attaining social status. Their essay, excerpted here from *Taste and the Antique* (1981), shows that the modern idea of the museum is inextricably linked with the history of accelerating consumerism in the mid-eighteenth century, the formative period of nation-building. The seemingly insatiable desire of an educated bourgeoisie for certain luxury goods – ancient sculpture is the focus of this study of eighteenth-century Rome – emulates longstanding aristocratic forms of displaying power (and displacing it to a symbolic level). Royalty, however, derived their power directly from inherited forms of property-ownership – not indirectly from the ownership of objects that conferred social status symbolically, and was attained sheerly by economic means.

The common denominator throughout the upper and middle classes is the symbolic value attached to classical antiquity to provide patrimony. Haskell and Penny emphasize a social network involving natives and foreigners. They document the activities of significantly placed individuals such as Cardinal Alessandro Albani, whose entrepreneurial ambitions to the point of ruthlessness resulted in the sale of heavily restored and even illicitly obtained antiquities to foreign collectors. Under the licensing system in force during the mid-eighteenth century, popes such as Clement XII, who founded a new museum in his own name to house recent discoveries in this era of burgeoning excavation, could technically prevent the export of particular objects if they were considered to be of great importance. Yet this right was evaded by dealers in antiquities like Albani who managed to manipulate the restriction to turn even greater profits.

In this cultural milieu, the recognition of any given sculpture as an ancient masterpiece depended heavily on modern technologies of reproduction, namely engravings, published catalogues, rhapsodic descriptions by travelers, plaster and stone copies. The thriving enterprise that supported collecting also enabled an increasingly wide social sector to participate, on a sliding economic scale, in this revivalism of and identification with ancient civilization. Even the brisk business of restoring ancient fragments to imaginatively conceptualized wholes contributed to the widespread popularity of classical antiquity as something that could be individually 'owned'.

The driving force of capitalism is more apparent when collecting is studied as an intergenerational social phenomenon. The escalating, international story of consumerism and status-seeking continues in the essay contributed by Magnus Olausson and Solfrid Söderlind, commissioned for this volume, which is written from the perspective of the same foreign collectors of Roman antiquities with whom Albani and his peers did business. Gustavus III, the Swedish king who succeeded the recipient of Hainhofer's greatest master-piece, assembled a collection of ancient sculpture that became the basis of the Swedish national museum, inaugurated in 1792, the very year that the king was assassinated. Although Olausson and Söderlind do not discuss the matter, the king's art advisor Carl Fredrik Fredenheim was supported by nobility who play a crucial role in both sets of events. Here is a case in which art was directly involved in the transition from a feudal to a modern state organization.

From the Swedish perspective, the legitimacy of transition from a dynastic form of government to a modern nation-state was problematic in an additional respect that bears on the history of museums, collective identity-formation, and capitalistic enterprise, in that the king and therefore the entire Swedish nation descended geographically and genetically outside the Roman *limes*. Questions of authenticity and legitimacy shaped the national cultural patrimony in late eighteenth-century Sweden in terms that were, on the one hand, particular to its geopolitical position with regard to the legacy of classical antiquity and the socio-cultural status that this legacy conferred. The exhibition displays planned and executed by Fredenheim used antiquities shipped from Rome to evoke the living drama of an imaginary Antiquity filtered through the suggestive lens of Winckelmann and his immediate legacy. A hall lined with over-life-size statues of the Muses (their identities manufactured during the process of restoring sculptural fragments) featured *Athena/Minerva* at one end and an eroticized sleeping *Endymion* on axis at the other end of a space that, lit by torchlight and moonlight, was used to initiate elite members in private nocturnal ceremonies with Masonic overtones (see the frontispiece to this volume). Although more studies would be welcome, it seems the Masonic Order played an important role in the transition from dynastic collections to public museums throughout Europe.[1]

Sweden's position as 'outsider' to the direct line of classical antiquity potentially aligned it with other nation-states that could not claim classical antiquity as their own heritage. In a future study, it would be worth comparing the formation of cultural identities in nation-states whose advocates came from diverse subject positions, ranging from sympathies similar to that of Fredenheim, who identified with the ruling class's love of classical antiquity but opposed its hegemonic politics out of his own, different class interests. Sweden's own assimilationist behavior was gradually replaced by modernist notions of nationalist cultural identity enacted, as Söderlind notes in another study, in a German art historical display opening at the Nationalmuseum in 1866.[2]

The last two articles in this chapter continue to address historical and contemporary interconnections between national identity and consumerism. As we have already seen in Sandra Esslinger's essay included in Chapter 3, the Nazis' express purpose in creating the German Temple of Art was to provide a sense of community and historical identity. The Nazis' imitation of religious ceremony was an intentional adaptation, never mentioned directly by Duncan and Wallach, though their language alludes to it, unintentionally or not. Self-interest at the expense of public good is also the subject of the final essay in this chapter, to which Esslinger's study provides a chilling comparison. Rosalind Krauss's 'The Cultural Logic of the Late Capitalist Museum' is a sustained analysis of the museum's aesthetic environment in complicity with corporate capitalism, as Duncan and Wallach introduced the topic a decade earlier. Krauss argues that a profound shift is currently taking place in the context in which museums operate, due to the changing profile of their boards of trustees who have abandoned the notion of the museum as a guardian of the public patrimony in favor of conceiving of it as a corporate entity with a 'highly marketable inventory and desire for growth'. 'Late capitalism' constitutes 'a generalized universal industrialization' that now penetrates into all sectors of social life. The separation of curatorial from managerial skills is 'wildly skewing the museum's judgment in the favor of those who stand to profit'. The present-day organization of museums into specializations has much in common with other 'industrialized areas of leisure', Krauss argues, drawing on Marxist economist Edward Mandel's analysis that 'noninvested surplus capital' – terms which also describe the holdings of museums – set the dynamics of late capitalism in motion by producing a 'falling rate of profit' which in turn 'accelerates the process of transition to monopoly capitalism'.

The commitment of some artists – minimalists in her argument, the twentieth-century avant-garde in Duncan and Wallach's analysis – to relinquish the conception of unique original art has resulted in an internal contradiction. How is it possible, Krauss asks, that an artistic movement that wished to attack commodification and technologization somehow carries the codes of those very conditions in its art? This paradox, Krauss offers, is inherent in modernist art's relation to capital: the artist produces an alternative to capitalist production that can also be read as a function of it. Minimalism, for example, philosophically committed to the primacy of lived bodily experience, strove to provide the viewing subject with work contingent on the changing conditions of the spatial field. Yet, in its use of industrial materials and shapes, and its adoption of seriality (i.e., reproducibility), this art partakes of the same formal conditions that structure consumer capitalism: and it is in this same world of commodities that minimalist art's structure of experience is consumed by a technologized subject who experiences its fragmentation as euphoria, unballasted by past knowledge, awash in a maze of signs and simulacra.

As compelling as this analytical framework is in some respects, it is less than convincing in its blanket devaluation of all art and aesthetic experience: is there no way out of the hall of mirrors? The final selection in this chapter is an excerpt from a book published by London-based artists Neil Cummings and Marysia Lewandowska, who examine the social role of art and other objects in the definition and fabrication of cultural values. *The Value of Things* combines economic terminology (the title references Marx's classic dyad of exchange value v. use value) with a semiotic analysis of social organization. Cummings and Lewandowska compare art and money as two symbolic systems, their central thesis being that the mechanisms for ascribing value to art objects and those governing exchange value in (other) commodity exchanges are fundamentally indistinguishable. Museums, they argue, hold sequences of redundant historical artifacts, held in conserved perfection 'to support the fantasy of origins we need to anchor us as we drift amongst the multiple choices of an intensely commodified present'.

'Collision' portrays the long history of convergence between the museum and the department store as a paradigmatic chapter in the modern dissolution of previously clear (or clearly imagined) demarcations between the cultural and economic. The historical situation out of which contemporary middle-class citizens emerged justifies the authors' 'twinned histories', as they put it, of the two quintessentially modern institutions that occupy 'privileged sites' within the social organization of contemporary society. Each in its own way renders the fundamental similarities and redundancies with the other invisible. The authors' interventionist project breeches the subdisciplinary boundaries – still in place but increasingly porous – between museology, advertising theory, the heritage industries, and philosophical aesthetics, to name just a few. By virtualizing the exchange value of art objects, and by problematizing the idea of art as a kind of thing rather than as a way of using things under certain conditions (the 'when' rather than the 'what' of art), they respond to current criticism that the majority of artistic practices operate in a reductive denial of actual social realities. The authors accept the circumstance that corporate capitalism is neither late nor wilted but really is here for the duration. Artists and academics have no power to halt or even deter the grinding mechanisms of profit-production. What they can do effectively is to offer consciousness-raising alternatives to the mindless, spectatorial participation in the game-playing, mind-deadening social order we all unavoidably occupy. To read Cummings and Lewandowska, and indeed to read all the articles in 'Secularizing Rituals' attentively, is to become deeply aware that all of us are complicit in our current situation, and none of us is immune from the immanent critique.

NOTES

1. The relationships between European and American Freemasonry and the foundation and organization of new civic museums in the late eighteenth and early nineteenth centuries is a complex and as yet poorly investigated phenomenon. The bibliography on early Freemasonry is Europe, particularly in Britain, France, Germany, Austria, Italy etc., is quite enormous. With regard to Sweden at the time of Gustavus Adolphus III, see (in Swedish) Roger de Robelin, 'Reuterholm och Tempelcreutz', in Solfrid Söderlind, ed., *En Hovmans Fåfänga. Gustaf Adolf Reuterholm och den Gustavianska Porträttkonsten*, Gripsholms Slott, 1991, pp. 47–61, with a useful bibliography on the 250-year history of Freemasonry in Sweden. See also with regard to Britain (and in particular the house-museum of master-mason Sir John Soane), Donald Preziosi, 'The Astrolabe of the Enlightenment', Chapter 5 of D. Preziosi, *Brain of the Earth's Body: Art, Museums, and the Phantasms of Modernity, the 2001 Slade Lectures in the Fine Arts at Oxford*, Minneapolis and London, Minneapolis: University of Minnesota Press, 2003, pp. 95–132.
2. 'Från ädel antik till gammalt gods', in *Gips: Tradition i konstens form*, Stockholm, 1999.

1.

The Museum of Modern Art as Late Capitalist Ritual: An Iconographic Analysis

Carol Duncan and Alan Wallach

In recent years art historians have become increasingly interested in understanding works of art in relation to their original physical settings – the churches, palace rooms, or temples for which they were made. These efforts reveal how a context can endow its objects with meaning, and, reciprocally, how the objects contribute to the larger meaning of the space they decorate. In our society the museum is the characteristic place for seeing art in the original. Like the church or temple of the past, the museum plays a unique ideological role. By means of its objects and all that surrounds them, the museum transforms ideology in the abstract into living belief.[1]

Museums, as modern ceremonial monuments, belong to the same architectural class as temples, churches, shrines, and certain kinds of palaces. Although all architecture has an ideological aspect, only ceremonial monuments are dedicated exclusively to ideology. Their social importance is underscored by the enormous resources lavished on their construction and decoration. Absorbing more manual and imaginative labor than any other type of architecture, these buildings affirm the power and social authority of a patron class.[2] But ceremonial monuments convey more than class domination. They impress upon those who see or use them a society's most revered values and beliefs.

The museum, like other ceremonial monuments, is a complex architectural phenomenon that selects and arranges works of art within a sequence of spaces. This totality of art and architectural form organizes the visitor's experience as a script organizes a performance. Individuals respond in different ways according to their education, culture, class. But the architecture is a given and imposes the same underlying structure on everyone. By following the architectural script, the visitor engages in an activity most accurately described as a ritual. Indeed, the museum experience bears a striking resemblance to religious rituals in both form and content.[3]

In the museum, painting and sculpture play the same role as in other types of ritual architecture. In a church or palace, walls function primarily to mark out and shape a space appropriate to specific rites or ceremonies. The paintings, statues, and reliefs affixed to or embedded in the walls constitute an integral part of the monument – in a sense its voice. These decorations articulate and enlarge the meaning of the activities on the site. In most traditional monumental architecture the various decorative elements, taken together, form a coherent whole – what art historians call an iconographic program. These programs usually rest upon authoritative literary sources – written or orally transmitted myths, litanies, sacred texts, epics. Monumental iconographic programs frequently evoke a mythic or historical past that informs and justifies the values celebrated in the ceremonial space. As visual commentaries they elucidate the purpose of the consecrated ground.[4]

Thus, the images of John the Baptist that often decorated the walls of baptistries gave meaning to the ritual of baptism. Monastery dining halls frequently incorporated images of the Last Supper so that the monks could associate their own mealtime gatherings with Christ's sacrifice. Similarly, medieval choir screens – partitions separating the church choir from the surrounding ambulatory – sometimes displayed reliefs that illustrated the principal moments of the Crucifixion. Obviously, neither the church, nor the ambulatory, nor the choir screen was built solely to provide space or a wall support for the reliefs. Rather, the reliefs were intended to give meaning to the pilgrim's walk around the choir.

The museum serves as a ceremonial monument; its space and collection present an ensemble of art objects that functions as an iconographic program.[5] Historians of premodern and nonwestern art usually acknowledge ritual contexts,[6] but conventional art historians ignore the meanings works of art acquire in the museum and insist that the viewer's experience of art is – or should be – shaped by the artist's intention as embodied in the object.[7] Museums almost everywhere sanction the idea that works of art should, above all, be viewed one-by-one in an apparently ahistorical environment. They define the museum's primary function as housing objects in a neutral space within which they may be contemplated. According to prevailing beliefs, the museum space itself, apart from the objects it shelters, is empty. A structured ritual space – an ideologically active environment – usually remains invisible, experienced only as a transparent medium through which art can be viewed objectively and without distraction.

Museums, like medieval abbey churches, town cathedrals, and palace chapels, tend to conform to one of a few well-established types, the two most important in the West today being such traditional state or municipal museums as the Metropolitan Museum of New York and such modern art museums, as New York's Museum of Modern Art.[8] Generally, each corresponds to a different moment in the evolution of bourgeois ideology and has its own iconographic tradition. Indeed, the iconographic program of any particular museum is almost as predictable as that of a medieval church and is equally dependent on authoritative doctrine. The conventional art history found in the encyclopedic textbooks of Gardner, Janson, Arnason, and others[10] supplies the doctrines that make these modern ceremonies coherent.

The Museum of Modern Art in New York City (MOMA) in its way represents the Chartres of mid-twentieth-century modern art museums. As Chartres provided the prototype for the High Gothic cathedral, so MOMA provides the prototype for the modern art museum. Representing a new and foreign taste when built in the 1930s, it quickly became a model not only for every American city with aspirations to high culture but for all the capitals of the West.[11] More than any other museum, MOMA developed the ritual forms that translated the ideology of late capitalism into immediate and vivid artistic terms – a monument to individualism, understood as subjective freedom.

A visit to MOMA begins with the façade. To appreciate fully its original effect, the visitor must imagine away all the post-World War II construction in the neighborhood. When planned in the 1930s, the neighborhood, although rapidly changing, still consisted mainly of elegant residences that dated from the late nineteenth and early twentieth century. When new, the clean, purified forms of MOMA's gleaming steel and glass façade announced the coming of a new aesthetic – a future of efficiency and rationality.[12] Since World War II the area around the Museum has become crowded with high-rise corporate headquarters, almost all built in the International Style MOMA pioneered. MOMA is now overwhelmed by its megalithic neighbors. But, originally, it offered an outpost of modernity, and its crisp, unsentimental lines strikingly contrasted with the Victorian rhetoric of its neighbors.

MOMA presents a cool face to the outside world: impersonal and silent – a wall of glass. An older ceremonial structure, like the gothic revival church of St Thomas next door to the Museum, addressed the world around it through its architectural language, implying the existence of an ideal community the values and beliefs of which it celebrated. The church's elaborate portals and sculptural decorations proclaimed the ritual meaning of the space inside. MOMA belongs to the age of corporate capitalism. It addresses us not as a community of citizens but as private individuals who value only experience that can be understood in subjective terms. MOMA has no message for a 'public' world. The individual will find meaning only in the building's interior. The blankness of the translucent exterior wall suggests the separation of public and private, external and internal.

By employing the conventional rhetoric of public buildings, such traditional museums as the Metropolitan Museum of New York or the National Gallery of London dramatize the moment of passage from exterior to interior – from the everyday world to a space dedicated to the contemplation of higher values. Here, too, the architecture asserts the existence of a community. The entrance invites a first step in a communal rite, the different moments of which the architecture marks. At MOMA the script also begins at the entrance. But the terms of entry differ as much as the architecture. Only a glass membrane, stretching from pavement to overhang, stands between the street and the interior. No steps mark the passage. Even while still part of the flow of the street, you are visually drawn into the interior. Suddenly detached from the stream of pedestrian traffic, you pass through the revolving doors and move into the low but expanding space of the ground floor.[13] There is no one conscious moment of passage. Separated from the movement of the street, you are released into the space of the interior like a molecule into a gas.

The ground floor is an open, light-filled space. You feel as if you can go wherever you wish. There are no architectural imperatives like those of the Metropolitan, with its grand stairway and succession of great halls. On MOMA's ground floor you experience a heightened sense of individual free choice – a major theme of the building as a whole.

Now you choose where to go. A museum, like a church or temple, serves different people in different ways.[14] If you are a regular and informed visitor, you probably came to see a specific exhibition or film. If not, your unfamiliarity with the building may result in a sense of spatial disorientation. The space of MOMA's ground floor creates a tension that later stages of the architectural script will eventually resolve. At this moment the problem is to find your way.

Ahead is the garden – obviously a resting place not yet earned by the newcomer. To the left and right are temporary exhibition spaces. (See Figure 5.1.1.) The large spaces house major exhibitions and retrospectives, while the smaller, located near the cafeteria, accommodate recent trends. These first floor galleries normally increase the newcomer's sense of bewilderment. The experienced visitor already knows that you cannot comprehend them until you have traveled the main ceremonial route – the permanent collection located on the second and third floors.[15]

The aura surrounding MOMA's permanent collection is unmatched by any other collection of modern art. Educated opinion literally identifies MOMA's collection with the mainstream of modern art history. Visitors come to MOMA convinced that they will find not simply masterpieces but works that stand as the turning points in that history: *Starry Night, Les Demoiselles d'Avignon, Ma Jolie, The Red Studio, Broadway Boogie-Woogie, Guernica*. From the time of its founding, MOMA's trustees, led by the Rockefellers, promoted an image of glamorous modernity and liberalism that contrasted sharply with older types of museums and their nineteenth-century ideologies.[16] No other collection of modern art received such generous support and publicity for acquisitions, exhibitions, publications, and public relations. Increasingly, after World War II MOMA's view of modern art achieved institutional hegemony in academic art history, art education, and the higher reaches of the gallery world and the art

1st floor

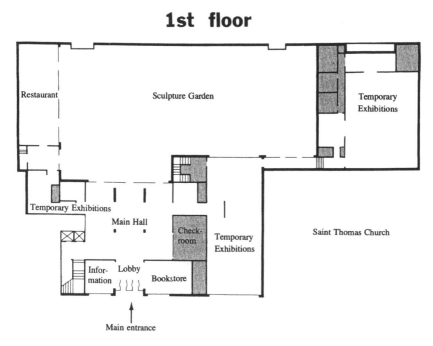

Figure 5.1.1   Plan of first floor showing only ceremonial spaces (in white)

press.[17] The image of the collection as the unique embodiment of modern art history remains established – that is, institutionally enforced. As the Museum recently said in its *Members Calendar* of June 1977:

> The Museum of Modern Art's collection of modern painting, sculpture, drawing, prints, architecture, design, photography and film are the greatest in the world. A selection from the collections, on view in the Museum's galleries, offers an unrivaled review of the modern masters and movements that have made the period from about 1885 to the present one of the most varied and revolutionary in the entire history of art.[18]

The professionals who built the Museum's collection during the 1920s and 1930s held definite views about modern art and its historical development and sought out works accordingly. Alfred Barr, the Museum's first curator of painting and sculpture, regarded French painting, in particular Picasso and Cubism, as more significant than American art or other currents of European vanguardism. He and his colleagues insisted that they chose works on the basis of artistic quality. Reference to artistic quality or aesthetics can, however, obscure the role of ideology in selection. The works MOMA acquired express with extraordinary fullness and imagination a system of values, above all a belief in a certain kind of individualism. Trustees John Hay Whitney and

Nelson A. Rockefeller emphasized this in *Masters of Modern Art*, a sumptuously produced guide to the collection:

We believe that the collection of the Museum of Modern Art and this publication represent our respect for the individual and for his ability to contribute to society as a whole through free use of his individual gifts in his individual manner.[19]

Nineteenth-century art contained individualism within the representational conventions of naturalism. However individualistic the content of the work, it addressed the viewer in a conventional – socially shared – visual language that represented a 'real' and 'objective' external world. Modern high art expresses individualism largely through the use of unconventional visual languages: Each artist strives to invent a distinctive one, implicitly denying the possibility of a shared world of experience. Increasingly, beginning with Cézanne and late Impressionism, Van Gogh and Expressionism, Gauguin and Symbolism, inner experience emerges as the more real and significant part of existence. The more subjective and abstract the visual language, the more unique and individualized the artist's consciousness.[20]

As you walk through MOMA's permanent collection, you are aware of seeing a succession of works by artists whose uniqueness has been established in the authoritative literature and whose distinctive stylistic traits are easily recognizable. These works, although presented as emblems of individualism, conform to the Museum's well-defined art-historical scheme. Individual artists acquire significance – art-historical importance – according to how much they contributed to the evolution of the total scheme. The installation makes this evident. As in all museums, the visitor perceives works of art as so many moments in a historical scheme. Michael Compton, Keeper of the Tate Gallery, speaking at a symposium of museum curators, rightly observed:

What we do is ... present art in such a way that, you'll notice if you watch people going around the museum, they will look at each painting for an average of 1.6 seconds. I think when they see a painting, they can hardly be thinking anything but ah, that's an example of Cubism; an example of Pre-Raphaelitism; what a nice Mondrian; and so on. They never actually confront the individual painting.[21]

At MOMA the rooms that contain the permanent collection are linked to each other as in a chain, so that the visitor must follow a prescribed route. Off this main route are several cul-de-sacs and secondary routes, the content of which the Museum thereby designates as subsidiary to its central history of modern art. These detours and dead ends include the history of photography, modern sculpture, decorative arts, and prints.

As you advance along the prescribed route, the iconographic program emphasizes the principal moments and turning points of this history. Works given special weight are framed by doorways and are often visible from several rooms away. Works deemed less important hang in corner spaces,

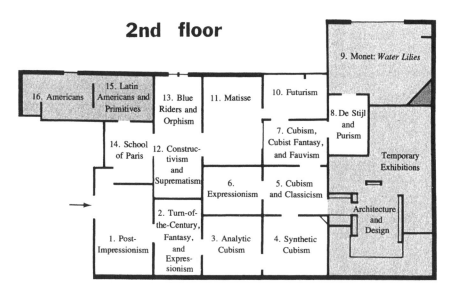

Figure 5.1.2 Plan of second floor galleries. The main route is white; secondary routes are shaded

tiers, or off the main route. Certain works are to be experienced as signposts – as culminating moments in the authorized history – while others are secondary manifestations or, in the galleries off the main route, completely outside the mainstream of modern art history: Orozco, Siqueiros, Hopper, Shahn.[22]

In brief, that history records the increasing dematerialization and transcendence of mundane experience. The highlights of the route, which frame and define the history of modern art, are Cubism, Surrealism, and Abstract Expressionism. Everything else – German Expressionism, Matisse, Dada – acquires significance in relation to these three central movements. Thus, according to MOMA, the history of modern art begins with Cézanne, who confronts you at the entrance to the permanent collection. The arrangement makes his meaning obvious. He foreshadows Picasso and Cubism – that is, the decisive breakdown of tangible form. From Picasso and Cubism issue almost everything else: Léger, the Futurists, the Constructivists. Once the supremacy of Cubism has been established, you encounter other tendencies that appear derivative or subordinate: Matisse, die Brücke, Blue Riders. Before you leave the second floor, the history of modern art has already been detached from the material world – Kandinsky, Malevich – a moment of enlightenment marked by the first and only window on the main route. On the third floor the mainstream of modern art recommences with *Guernica*, which in this context represents not so much the horror of the Spanish Civil War as an inevitable

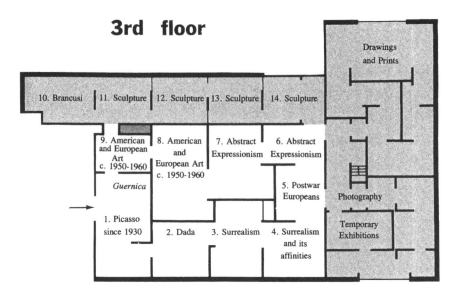

3rd floor

Drawings
and Prints

| 10. Brancusi | 11. Sculpture | 12. Sculpture | 13. Sculpture | 14. Sculpture |

| 9. American and European Art c. 1950-1960 | 8. American and European Art c. 1950-1960 | 7. Abstract Expressionism | 6. Abstract Expressionism |

Guernica

→

1. Picasso since 1930

2. Dada   3. Surrealism   4. Surrealism and its affinities

5. Postwar Europeans   Photography

Temporary Exhibitions

Figure 5.1.3   Plan of third floor galleries. The main route is white; secondary routes are shaded

development from Cubism to Surrealism. Here, after Picasso, Miró is presented as the prototypical Surrealist. With him modern abstraction reaches new heights of individualism and subjectivity. Up to this point the installation preserves the art-historical program MOMA's curators developed in the Museum's early years and have since extended to include American Abstract Expressionism. Indeed, in the Museum Abstract Expressionism appears as the logical fulfillment of the original historical scheme.[23]

A succession of small rooms displays the permanent collection. There are no straight vistas, no large spaces, no organizing hallways. The route twists and turns. It is difficult to maintain a clear sense of direction. Of the twenty rooms along the main route, only one has windows despite the building's glass façades. To walk through the permanent collection is to walk through a labyrinth.[24] We intend more than a spatial analogy. The structure of MOMA's ritual conforms to the archetypal labyrinth experience.

The labyrinth, a basic image in world cultures, appears in literature and drama as well as in ceremonial architecture and other ritual settings. Whatever its cultural context, the image contains certain core elements:

It always has to do with death and re-birth relating either to a life after death or to the mysteries of initiation ... the presiding personage, either mythical or actual, is always a woman ... [and] the labyrinth itself is walked through, or the labyrinth design walked over, by men.[25]

Figure 5.1.4   Entrance to the Permanent Collection. Photographic by Carol Duncan and Alan Wallach © Carol Duncan and Alan Wallach, 1978 and 2002

Figure 5.1.5   Permanent Collection with Boccioni's *The City Rises* and Matisse's *The Music Lesson*. Photograph by Carol Duncan and Alan Wallach © Carol Duncan and Wallach, 1978 and 2002

Passage through the labyrinth is an ordeal that ends in triumph – a passage from darkness to light and thus a metaphor for spiritual enlightenment, integration, rebirth. The ancient labyrinthine structures in palaces and temples, as well as those described in primitive myths, were associated with the earth and the Great Mother Goddess and were often located underground.[26]

MOMA's labyrinth, however, lies above the earth. Seen from the outside, the blue translucent glass of its exterior wall hints at the realm of transcendence to which the labyrinth will lead. From the outside, the glass wall is a mysterious curtain that reflects the sky. It is impossible to guess what lies behind it. MOMA's Bauhaus-inspired design signaled progress, science, and rationality. But, in effect, it is a rational cover wrapped around an irrational core, and, as one critic observed, even the rational-looking exterior does not correspond to the division of space inside.[27] We do not suggest that MOMA's architects consciously thought of a labyrinth when they designed the Museum, nor that MOMA's curators thought of a labyrinth when they installed the collection. We do suggest that the labyrinth form organizes ritual activity.[28]

In MOMA you wind through a series of narrow, silent, windowless white spaces. These rooms have a peculiar effect. They inhibit speech: If you speak at all, you speak in low tones and only to those who have come with you.

This is an intensely private place. You move silently over carpeted floors and between featureless, luminous walls, insubstantial by comparison with the works of art they support. You are in a 'nowhere', a pristine blankness, a sunless white womb/tomb, seemingly outside time and history.[29] Here, as in most labyrinths, the substance of the ritual is an internal drama.

As you pass through MOMA's white, dream-like labyrinth night, the gaze of the Great Mother finds you again and again. Often she confronts you head-on, her two eyes round and bulging, the petrifying stare and the devouring mouth of the Gorgon Medusa now before you as the awesome and grotesque goddess-whores of Picasso, Kirchner, De Kooning. In the passage through Surrealism she is often a beast – a giant praying mantis. Everywhere she poses the threat of domination. Sometimes, as in Munch's man-killing vampire, her beauty is a snare. In Léger's sphinxes her look is frozen, her body a great steel machine. The entire labyrinth is her realm, but she is most present when you approach the threshold of a higher spiritual level – that is, at moments of art-historical 'breakthroughs'. Even before you enter the first cubist room, her eyes are on you (*Les Demoiselles*). She intercepts you (Picasso's *Girl Before the Mirror* and *Seated Bather*) just before you reach Miró's surrealist *Creation of the World*. You risk her gaze (De Kooning's *Woman*) as you advance towards Jackson Pollock. She personifies the dangers of the route first run by the artists themselves.[30]

The labyrinth emphasizes the terrible aspects of the goddess, her power to engulf, ensnare, petrify, castrate. But in the garden outside, amidst trees, waters, animals, and earth, her power will be celebrated as a positive force, expressed by the swelling volumes of her massive body. Bronze statues of her are everywhere, standing high and triumphant on platforms and pedestals (Lachaise) or crouching low near the water where she washes clothes or plays (Renoir, Maillol; Fig. 5.1.5). Nearby, MOMA's cafeteria patrons enjoy her bounty on warm summer days. Outside, she can appear in all her creative power because only there, in the realm of nature, can female creative power be acknowledged as fertility and procreativity. But even there she does not dominate. Near the garden's center, on the highest pedestal of all, stands Rodin's *Balzac* exalting male procreativity as artistic potency.[31]

Inside the labyrinth the principle of creativity is defined and celebrated as a male spiritual endeavor in which consciousness finds its identity by transcending the material, biological world and its Mother Goddess. Salvation, understood as a male norm, is alienation from the Mother and her realm. It is integration with spirit, light, intellect. The garden contains reminders of the Terrible Mother of the labyrinth (e.g., Lipschitz's *Figure*), just as images of the labyrinth occasionally echo the traits of the garden Goddesses (Matisse). In fact, both Goddess and Mother are different aspects of the Great Mother, who, in the labyrinth, emerges as dangerous. It is she who must be overcome. The way to do so is made clear by the iconography.

Figure 5.1.6   The garden with Maillol. Photograph by Carol Duncan and Alan Wallach © Carol Duncan and Wallach, 1978 and 2002

In the labyrinth the pictures lead you along a spiritual path that rises to ever higher levels of transcendence. They do so not only through their increasingly abstract formal language but also through their themes and subjects. On the second floor the iconography celebrates the victory of thought over matter and weight (Cubism, Purism, de Stijl), the supremacy of light, movement, and air (Futurism, Orphism), and the first triumphs of mysticism (Suprematism and Blue Riders). Your experience on the third floor becomes increasingly mystical, unnamable, sublime. Here spirit eclipses reason entirely. You begin with Surrealism, which unseated the last vestiges of reason and history and their hold on vanguard language, and you end in the Abstract Expressionist realm of myth as a substitute for history (Gorky, Pollock, Gottlieb, Motherwell) and mystical faith in which abstract form signifies the Absolute (Rothko, Newman, Reinhardt). The increasingly dematerialized and abstract forms as well as the emphasis on such themes as light and air proclaim the superiority of the spiritual and transcendent while negating the world of human emotions and needs. Images of labor are, for the most part, absent. When they do appear, as in Boccioni's *City Rises*, they are treated in mythic terms. Love as a reciprocal human relationship does not exist, while the need for love appears only in distorted, nightmare images of women – paralyzing Gorgons and devouring females. MOMA's ritual walk is a walk through an irrational world in which everyday experience looms as monstrous and unreal compared with the higher realm of dematerialized spirit. In effect, MOMA treats the content of everyday life as irrelevant – an obstacle to be overcome on the path to spiritual enlightenment. These 'mundane' and 'vulgar' aspects of existence must be suppressed. This suppression – a virtue according to the labyrinth script – leads to 'aesthetic detachment'. In the words of Mark Rothko:

Freed from a false sense of security and community, the artist can abandon his plastic bank-book, just as he abandoned other forms of security. Both the sense of community and of security depend on the familiar. Free of them, transcendental experiences become possible.[32]

Enlightenment in the labyrinth means detachment from the world of common experience and material need. As the ritual unfolds, greater sacrifices are required. On the third floor history and then even myth are renounced. To quote Barnett Newman:

We are freeing ourselves of the impediments of memory, association, nostalgia, legend, myth, or what have you, that have been the devices of Western European painting … The image we produce is the self-evident one of revelation, real and concrete, that can be understood by anyone who will look at it without the nostalgic glasses of history.[33]

Without history or myth there remains only an underlying human condition. Rothko wrote:

I am interested only in expressing the basic human emotions – tragedy, ecstasy, doom, and so on – and the fact that lots of people break down and cry when confronted with my pictures shows that I *communicate* with those basic human emotions. These people who weep before my pictures are having the same religious experience I had when I painted them.[34]

But the logic of renunciation is relentless. It leads to the final revelation: The ultimate value is nothingness – the transcendent void. As Reinhardt described it:

No lines or imaginings, no shapes or composings or representings, no visions or sensations or impulses, no symbols or signs or impastos, no decoratings or colorings or picturings, no pleasure or pains, no accidents or readymades, no things, no ideas, no relations, no attributes, no qualities – nothing that is not of the essence.[35]

The triumph of Abstract Expressionism, then, is the triumph of spirit. Now, at the end of the labyrinthine route, spirit and only spirit is visible, and only the visible can be 'real'. With Abstract Expressionism the ritual is complete. Through the ritual the visitor lives an experience the structure of which follows a traditional pattern of Western religious thought that portrays human life as a struggle between the material and the spiritual – between the demands of corporeal existence and the longing for unity with the Divine.

Traditional religious thought describes the triumph of spirit over matter as a necessary 'alienation', which frees consciousness from the demands of everyday existence.[36] The alienation of traditional theologies is in many ways equivalent to the concept of freedom as it appears in late bourgeois ideology. In the ideology of modernist art, as embodied in MOMA, it takes the form of aesthetic detachment – the ultimate value in artistic experience. A characteristic moment of both religious and aesthetic alienation is ecstasy – an overpowering sense of liberation and elevation. Abstract Expressionism produced similar feelings. Clyfford Still wrote:

> By 1941, space and the figure in my canvases had been resolved into a total psychic entity, freeing me from the limitations of each, yet fusing into an instrument bounded only by the limits of my energy and intuition. My feeling of freedom was now absolute and infinitely exhilarating.[37]

And Richard Pousette-Dart:

> Art for me is the heavens forever opening up, like asymmetrical, unpredictable, spontaneous Kaleidoscopes. It is magic, it is Joy, it is gardens of surprise and miracle. It is energy, impulse. It is total in its spirit.[38]

The everyday world, ostensibly banished from consciousness, nevertheless haunts the labyrinthine way. The labyrinth is, in fact, not a realm of transcendence but of inversions in which the repressed realities of the mundane world return, as it were, disguised as monstrous, overwhelming forces. Irrational powers that seem beyond comprehension own and rule both worlds. Anxiety and self-doubt characterize both worlds: The struggle for existence that pervades everyday life outside is reflected inside in the lonely, fearful, upward-striving of the individual. The labyrinth ritual glamorizes the competitive individualism and alienated human relations that characterize contemporary social experience. It reconciles the visitor to pure subjectivity by equating it with 'the human condition'. And in the garden, as in the outside world, that which satisfies material needs appears not as the result of labor but as if by magic – gifts of a great nature goddess.[39]

As an institution MOMA appears to be a refuge from a materialist society: a cultural haven, an ideal world apart. Yet, it exalts precisely the values and experiences it apparently rejects by elevating them to the universal and timeless realm of spirit. MOMA's ritual is a walk through a hall of mirrors in which isolation, fear, and numbness appear as exciting and desirable states of being. Thus MOMA would reconcile you to the world, as it is, outside.

NOTES

An earlier version of this essay appeared in *Studio International* No. 1 (London, 1978). We are grateful to George Collins, Tom Lyman, and Ted Solotaroff for their critical readings of our manuscript and numerous helpful suggestions. We also wish to thank Elizabeth Fox-Genovese for all her patient work.

1. It has been frequently observed that museums produce ideology. However, critiques usually focus on the management of museums in the interests of an elite. Our concern is with the museum experience itself – with the way museums and museum art realize ideology.

2. Giulio C. Argan, discussing the Renaissance origins of modern urban monuments and the architectural tradition to which the public museum belongs, argues that these Renaissance buildings functioned ideologically as visible symbols of State authority. See *The Renaissance City* (New York, 1969), 22–29. Museums communicate authority not only to the affluent and 'cultivated' museum user. For those who never venture inside, the visible – and usually prominent – fact of the museum may reinforce a sense of social exclusion. By contrast, the more the visitor knows the uses of the museum the more he or she is likely to identify with the social authority underlying high culture. For a critical sociological study of the museum public, see Pierre Bourdieu and Alain Darbel, *L'Amour de l'art: Les musées d'art européens et leur public* (Paris, 1969). Bourdieu and Darbel found that 'Museums betray in the smallest details of their morphology their real function which is to reinforce among some people the feeling of belonging and among others the feeling of exclusion' (p. 165).

3. Victor Turner, in 'Frame, Flow and Reflection: Ritual and Drama in Public Liminality', in Michael Benamou and Charles Caramello, eds, *Performance in Post-Modern Culture* (Milwaukee, 1977), 33–55, compares the products of modern high culture to rituals. According to Turner, such forms as the theatre, novels, and art exhibitions provide scripts or 'doing codes' performed by individuals. He compares their structure to those of rituals in simpler and traditional societies. Turner's *The Ritual Process* (Ithaca, N.Y., 1977), 94 ff., and Arnold van Gennep's *The Rites of Passage* (1908), trans. Monika B. Vizedom and Gabrielle L. Caffee (Chicago, 1960), explore in detail features common to certain kinds of rituals. The notion of architecture as ritual form is brilliantly developed in Frank E. Brown's *Roman Architecture* (New York, 1961). Brown argues that Roman architecture not only originated in ritual activity, but that 'it required it, prompted it, enforced it' (p. 10).

   That a museum visit is a ritual may at first appear to be stretching a metaphor. We live in a secular age. Museums, although often compared to temples or shrines, are deemed secular institutions. But the separation between the secular and the religious is itself a part of bourgeois thought and has effectively masked the survival in our own society of older religious practices, and beliefs. From the beginning bourgeois society appropriated religious symbols and traditions to its own ends. The legacy of religious patterns of thought and feeling especially shaped the experience of art. While Winckelmann and other eighteenth-century thinkers were discovering in art all the characteristics of the sacred, a new kind of cultural institution, the public art museum – Temples of Art, as the age styled them – was evolving a corresponding ritual. In 1768 Goethe described this new kind of art space – the Dresden Gallery – as a 'sanctuary', the splendor and richness of which 'imparted a feeling of solemnity ... which so much more resembled the sensation with which one treads a church', but here 'set up only for the sacred purposes of art'. *The Autobiography of Johann Wolfgang von Goethe*, trans. John Oxenford (New York, 1969), 346–347. Germain Bazin, noting this new religious attitude toward art, writes, 'No longer existing solely for the delectation of refined amateurs, the museum, as it evolved into a public institution, simultaneously metamorphosed into a temple to human genius.' *The Museum Age*, trans. Jane van Nuis Cahil (New York, 1967), 160.

4. Established art history generally studies iconography only in relation to literary sources, pictorial traditions, or religious beliefs. For us, iconography includes more than the correlation of images with texts or other images. We aim to understand the role iconography plays in mediating between ideology in the abstract and specific, subjective experience.

5. Most museum art was produced before museums existed and was usually intended for some other ceremonial setting. But the original purpose for which a work was made has never prevented its being put to a new use. Art history furnishes numerous precedents in which objects made for one context were transported to another and integrated into an entirely different iconographic program. Kurt W. Forster has studied an outstanding example in 'Giulio Romano's "Museum" of Sculpture in the Palazzo Ducale at Mantua', paper delivered at the Annual Meeting of the College Art Association of America, 1978, New York City.

6. For examples, see Thomas W. Lyman, 'Theophanic Iconography and the Easter Liturgy: The Romanesque Painted Program at Saint-Sernin in Toulouse', in Lucius Grisebach and Konrad Renger, eds, *Festschrift für Otto von Simpson zum 65. Geburtstag* (Frankfurt, 1977), 72–93; O. K. Werckmeister, 'The Lintel Fragment Representing Eve from Saint-Lazare, Autun', *Journal of the Warburg and Courtauld Institutes*, XXXV (1972), 1–30, and Andree Hayum, 'The Meaning and Function of the Isenheim Altarpiece: The Hospital Context Revisited', *Art Bulletin*, LIX (1977), 501–517.

7. The original intentions of artists are not immediately relevant to this study since our concern is

not the production of art but its reception – the way art institutions structure and mediate the experience of art today.

8. Less important types include museums that specialize in ethnic or regional art as well as the robber-baron mansion. A large traditional museum may swallow whole one or more of the less important types in such special sections as the Met's Lehman rooms or the modern American wing.

9. For medieval iconography, see Emile Mâle, *The Gothic Image*, trans. Dora Nussey (New York, 1958).

10. Helen Gardner, *Art Through the Ages* (New York, 1926, and numerous subsequent editions); H. W. Janson, *History of Art*, 2nd edn (New York, 1977); and H. H. Arnason, *History of Modern Art*, 2nd edn (New York, 1977).

11. Terry Smith, the Australian art historian, analyzing the effects of American high-cultural imperialism, points out that 'many American cultural institutions have international programs. The Museum of Modern Art is perhaps the most active – in the past twelve months it has toured exhibitions throughout Europe, South America, Australia and elsewhere. Such exhibitions may not be intended as tools of cultural imperialism, but it would be naive to believe that they do not have precisely this effect'. 'The Provincialism Problem', *Artforum* (Sept. 1974), 59.

12. Long before MOMA moved into its new quarters, it had promoted the International Style – the steel and glass architecture of Gropius and the Bauhaus – as the true style of the twentieth century, the only style to embody the rational, scientific spirit of modern mass society. The Museum energetically advocated this line in a series of exhibitions beginning with the 1932 show, *Modern Architecture*. In the Catalogue (New York, 1932), 180, Louis Mumford called for a new architecture based on the values of the future: 'science, disciplined thinking, coherent organization, collective enterprise and that happy impersonality which is one of the highest fruits of personal development'. When the Museum's own Bauhaus-inspired building was completed, the press greeted its glass curtain walls and steel frame as 'the last word in functional architecture' and 'a definite object lesson in those kinds of beauty which are distinctively our own because they are obtainable only by means of twentieth-century materials and building methods'. See 'Modern Museum Moves into its New Home', *Art Digest* (May 15, 1939), 8; and Talbot F. Hamlin, 'Modern Display for Works of Art', *Pencil Points* (Sept. 1939), 618. Since the 1960s scholars have increasingly pointed to the ease with which corporate capitalism appropriated the machine-made look the Bauhaus glamorized. See, for example, Joseph Masheck, 'Embalmed Objects: Design at the Modern', *Artforum* (Feb. 1975), 49–55.

13. The original design of the ground floor level has been altered, but the effect of the exterior remains substantially unchanged. See Hamlin, *Pencil Points* (Sept. 1939), 616. For plans, elevations, and other details of the original building, see Philip S. Goodwin and Edward D. Stone (the original architects), 'The Museum of Modern Art, New York', *Architectural Review* (Sept. 1939), 121–124.

14. Bourdieu and Darbel, *L'Amour de l'art*, passim.

15. Yet Richard Oldenburg, MOMA's Director, argues (to no avail, as he himself acknowledges) that what happens in the first floor minor galleries has nothing to do with the permanent collection upstairs. Speaking at a symposium on modern art museums, he said: 'You get a confusion in people's minds between the enshrined art and the art you're trying to present for interest and edification'. Oldenburg also referred to the 'awful assumption that too large a part of our public makes, that anything that is enshrined in the museum, even if just in a brief show of modest proportions, has some kind of direct relationship to the fact that on the second and third floors we have a permanent collection with acknowledged masterpieces'. 'Validating Modern Art', *Artforum* (Jan. 1977), 52. For an analysis of how special exhibitions and their installations reinforce MOMA's art-historical mainstream, see Alan Wallach, 'Trouble in Paradise', *Artforum* (Jan. 1977), 28–35.

16. This image was well established in the press before the Museum moved to 53rd Street in 1939. The new glass building confirmed MOMA's image as a new museum type. 'Not a trace of the conventional, musty museum remains', wrote one critic. 'A Lesson in Museum Architecture', *The Studio* (Jan. 1940), 21. Henry Russell Hitchcock, the architectural historian, also praised the new building as an embodiment of a new museum concept. Institutions such as MOMA, he wrote, 'function in a way which is different if not impossible for institutions which conceive their essential duty as being the preservation of the old values rather than the discovering of new ones'. 'Museum in the Modern World', *Architectural Review* (Oct. 1939), 147–8. For a history of MOMA, see Russell Lynes, *Good Old Modern* (New York, 1973).

17. William Rubin, present Director of Painting and Sculpture at MOMA, remarked in an interview:

'Modern art education during and just after World War II was, in the first instance, very much a question of this museum and its publications. I was Meyer Schapiro's student for many years. But even *his* sense of modern art was conditioned by what was to be seen in this museum.' See 'Talking with William Rubin: "Like Folding Out a Hand of Cards"', *Artforum* (Nov. 1974), 47. Interviewing Rubin were Lawrence Alloway and John Coplans.

18.   MOMA often informs the press that its new acquisitions are of the highest art-historical importance. See, for example, 'Picasso Gives Work to Museum Here', *New York Times*, Feb. 11, 1971.

19.   *Masters of Modern Art* (New York, 1958), 7.

20.   Eli Zaretsky analyzes the modern conditions in which this new realm of subjectivity develops. See *Capitalism, The Family, and Personal Life* (New York, 1976).

21.   *Artforum* (Jan. 1977), 38.

22.   William Rubin talked at length about his installation of the permanent collection in the *Artforum* interview (supra, n. 17). His aim, he says, is to place 'large key pictures' on 'the axes of the viewer's passage' (through doorways) in order to make visible certain art-historical relationships.

23.   MOMA orthodoxy has led to an art-historical bind. Abstract Expressionism perfectly completed the inner logic of its doctrines. Although MOMA has collected post-Abstract Expressionist art, it is not integrated into the Museum's permanent iconographic program. Art of the 1960s and 1970s appears in temporary installations, usually on the first floor. Since MOMA orthodoxy is so deeply rooted in the art ideology of the 1950s, during the last decade or so the Museum has lost much of the influence it once had in the art world. Lawrence Alloway and John Coplans question William Rubin about this development in an interview in 1974. See 'Talking With William Rubin: "The Museum Concept is Not Infinitely Expandable"', *Artforum* (Oct. 1974), 51–7. In another interview (*Artforum*, Nov. 1974, 46–53), Alloway and Coplans ask Rubins about the Museum's presentation of early twentieth-century art. These critics clearly think that the collection and its installation present a biased view of art history: 'You wanted to bring in Cubism good and early to show a nice, secure basis for a constructive Cubist line, which is sympathetic to you. …'. Rubin defends the 'art historical judgement' that determines the installation. He also discusses MOMA's acquisition policies of the past, largely the work of Alfred Barr. Rubin admits 'lacunae' in Barr's selection, but says, 'I find that my own views about the collection and about the exhibiting of it are very much like Alfred's. That's partly because I was brought up on Alfred's museum and on the collection as he built it.'

24.   When the building first opened, Talbot Hamlin complained about the 'disquieting feeling as of being in a labyrinth' produced by the division of the interior space into 'a large number of small rooms, one entered from the other' and 'the circulation from one to the other so irrevocably fixed'. *Pencil Points* (Sept. 1939), 618.

25.   John Layard, *Stone Men of Malekula, Vao* (London, 1942), 652. Layard drew from his own field work in Malekula and elsewhere as well as from the work of others. According to C. N. Deeds, who studied ancient Egyptian, Cretan, and Greek labyrinths, the labyrinth was originally a tomb structure and later evolved into a temple. Its architectural form was determined by the ritual activity – dances and dramas – it contained. The myths thus dramatized involved the annual death and resurrection of a king god, often symbolized by a sacrificial bull. See Deeds, 'The Labyrinth', in Samuel H. Hooke, ed., *The Labyrinth: Further Studies in the Relation between Myth and Ritual in the Ancient World* (London, 1935), 1–42.

26.   Erich Neumann, *The Great Mother* (New York, 1963), 76; Vincent Scully, *The Earth, The Temple and The Gods* (New York, 1969), Ch. 2; and Deeds, 'The Labyrinth', 26.

27.   Talbot Hamlin observed that 'a glance at the interior shows that the great thermolux window has little relation to what exists behind it – two stories of gallery and one of offices. It is not logical …' *Pencil Points* (Sept. 1939), 615.

28.   In fact, the preoccupation of the Surrealists and Abstract Expressionists with myth and ritual – nourished by the writings of Freud and Jung – is well known. Labyrinth imagery (bulls, minotaurs) frequently appears in their work, e.g., Picasso's cover design for the Surrealist journal *Minotaure* which hangs in MOMA. Pollock's *Pasiphae*, 1943 (Lee Krasner Collection, New York), and De Kooning's *Labyrinth*, 1946 (Allan Stone Gallery, New York), also refer directly to the labyrinth myth; and Motherwell's numerous *Elegies to the Spanish Republic*, one of which hangs in MOMA, suggest, as one critic put it, 'the phallus and "cojones" of the sacrificial bull' (Eugene Goosen, cited in Irving Sandler, *The Triumph of American Painting*, New York, 1970, 207).

29. 'The experience of the labyrinth, whether as a pictorial design, a dance, a garden path, or a system of corridors in a temple, always has the same psychological effect. It temporarily disturbs rational conscious orientation to the point that … the initiate is "confused" and symbolically "loses his way". Yet in this descent to chaos the inner mind is opened to the awareness of a new cosmic dimension of a transcendent nature.' Joseph L. Henderson and Maud Oakes, *The Wisdom of the Serpent: The Myths of Death, Rebirth and Resurrection* (New York, 1963), 46.

30. A. Bernard Deacon, the anthropologist, recorded a Melanesian myth with a labyrinth that has exactly the structure we are describing here: a devouring female guarding the threshold to a realm of spiritual transcendence. 'Geometrical Drawings from Malekula and Other Islands of the New Hebrides', *Journal of the Royal Anthropological Society of Great Britain and Ireland*, LXIV (1934), 129–30. See also John Layard, 'Maze-Dances and the Ritual of the Labyrinth in Malekula', *Folklore*, XL VII (1936), 123–70.

31. In the *Balzac*, Rodin consciously equated virility with creativity and thought of Balzac's grasping his erect penis under his robe as the preliminary nude studies show explicitly. See Albert E. Elsen, *Rodin* (New York, 1963), 88–105.

32. Rothko, in Herschel B. Chipp, ed., *Theories of Modern Art* (Berkeley, 1970), 548.

33. Newman, in ibid., 553.

34. Rothko, in Robert Rosenblum, *Modern Painting and the Northern Romantic Tradition* (New York, 1975), 215.

35. Reinhardt, 'Art-as-Art', *Art International* (Dec. 1962), 37.

36. Trent Schroyer, *The Critique of Domination* (Boston, 1975), 47.

37. Still, in Maurice Tuchman, ed., *New York School* (exhibition catalogue, Los Angeles County Museum of Art, 1965), 32.

38. Pousette-Dart, in ibid., 26.

39. For an analysis of the specific conditions of production and consumption that MOMA's iconography celebrates, see Zaretsky, *Capitalism, The Family, and Personal Life*, esp. 56–77.

2.

Animals as Cultural Signs: Collecting Animals in Sixteenth-Century Medici Florence

Claudia Lazzaro

In the Renaissance animals were understood in a variety of ways, but above all in terms of contemporary conceptualizations of nature, which ranged from a domesticated nature, altered or tamed by humans, to wild nature, an uncontrollable force in opposition to civilization. In this sense, animals are cultural signs, embodying a complex of ideas about nature that also define and sustain contemporary notions of civilization and culture. In this society, the paradigms of nature and culture, wild and civilized, were both in opposition and interlocked. The wildness of animals contrasted with human culture, but appropriating that wildness was also a demonstration of human power and magnificence. Such assumptions about animals and their relationship to humans inform visual representations, collections of both living animals and images of them, spectacles, and rituals – from public animal fights to diplomatic gift-giving. Classical antiquity played a profound role in this, providing models for the paradigms of nature and culture as well as the specific representations of them, from works of sculpture to the spectacles of animal slaughter.

Animals were generally conceived of not independently of humans, but in complex relationships with them. Animals provided food, clothing, and medicine, but equally, they reflected human values, virtues, and conduct in heraldry, symbols, emblems, and many other ways.[1] The enthusiasm for animals in the Renaissance was not disinterested. Animals were understood within a system of associations: they were significant to contemporaries because they embodied multiple associations (from literature, history, mythology, and so on) and symbolic meanings on many different levels. This way of thinking derived from classical antiquity, but it was vastly extended by the end of the sixteenth century. The study of animals increased dramatically as well, following the precedents of classical texts and accompanied by a new empirical observation. In the sixteenth century, the different ways of knowing animals, from ancient authority, direct experience, symbolic meanings, and multiple associations, co-existed, even if in direct conflict.

A great impetus to the study of animals was the variety of unfamiliar ones that entered Europe through the encounters with other continents from the late fifteenth century. Since the ancients had already known Asia and Africa, the exploration of these two continents was framed as one of rediscovery of classical antiquity. As antiquity provided the framework for understanding animals in general, so it also gave a means for comprehending the new animals to appear in Europe. This was one of the strategies of assimilation and domestication through which the strange was made familiar.[2] The newly known animals were also assimilated into existing ideas of wild, savage, and barbarian, as were the continents that they signified.[3] In the ensuing hierarchical conceptualization of the world, by the end of the sixteenth century the spectrum from civilized to wild came to characterize the relationship of Europe with the other known continents and cultures.

I

The point of departure for my investigation of these issues and the principal vehicle for presenting them here is an artificial grotto in a sixteenth-century Medici garden filled with sculpted animals, both native species and those from Asia and Africa. The garden at Castello, on the outskirts of Florence,

Figure 5.2.1   Central niche of the grotto, Villa Medici, Castello, 1565–72.
Photograph by Claudia Lazzaro

was begun about 1537 for Duke Cosimo de' Medici, but the existing interior decoration – the surface of rough calcified concretions or stalactites and the carved animals – belongs to a second project, from 1565 to 1572.[4] Inside the spacious grotto there are three niches, each with a great tub above which stand over 36 large-scale sculptures of animals (see Figures 5.2.1, 5.2.2, and 5.2.3) carved out of colored hard stone. Distributed among the three groups are native species, both domestic and wild – a goat, lamb, and wolf, a horse, three different European deer, a bear, bull, the auroch or wild ox of Europe, and various others. There are also one or two prominent non-European animals from Asia and Africa in each niche: in the center niche (Figure 5.2.1) an Indian elephant as well as the familiar lion; a North African camel in the right (Figure 5.2.2); and in the left a giraffe and an Indian rhinoceros (Figure 5.2.3). These are joined by smaller non-native species, a gazelle in the center niche, a leopard, Indian goat, and monkey in the right one and another monkey in the left one. Although the grotto displays a great variety of fauna, the animals do not represent an encyclopedic collection of known species in the late sixteenth century. Rather the assortment presents specific messages about the power and magnificence of the Medici, conveyed through general concepts of nature and culture, wild nature and civilization.

Figure 5.2.2   Right niche of the grotto, Villa Medici, 1565–72. Photograph by
Claudia Lazzaro

II

Modern studies of the grotto have examined it in the context of Medici
imagery and the themes in the rest of the garden. Most posit an allegorical
meaning for the whole, with reference to a literary text or mythological
figure.[5] Implicit in these interpretations are various assumptions of the
discipline of art history and about the Italian Renaissance. The traditional art
historical approach is to ask the meaning of the specific animals in this

Figure 5.2.3   Left niche of the grotto, Villa Medici, 1565–72. Photograph by Claudia Lazzaro

particular context and to seek a literary text that the collection in some way illustrates. My approach includes the iconographic, but also goes considerably beyond it. Some of the animals do have specific symbolism and they may correspond with a text, but they do so because the symbols and stories, like the animals generally, draw on contemporary constructs of nature and culture and conventional ways of representing them in images, texts, and social practices. To understand how contemporaries could have apprehended the messages in the grotto, it is necessary to look at both the specific meaning of individual animals for the Medici and the larger meanings for this culture of animals in general as well as particular configurations of them. Since the concern here is with visual representations, it is also necessary to examine the pictorial conventions, cultural assumptions, and intellectual expectations that mediate between the animals and their representation. In the grotto the most familiar animals, the domestic and native ones, are generally the most naturalistic. The strange could no more be 'truthfully' reproduced in images than put into words. Visual representations can domesticate and assimilate the wild and strange as well as convey associations, symbolic meanings, and cultural constructs. These approaches to the animals in the grotto are essential to its interpretation since there are no human figures or narrative references, only the animals themselves and their rustic setting.

In the sixteenth century, sculpted animals were an appropriate decoration for such a grotto, since it was a commonplace that animals lived in caves, mountainous areas, and forests. In the playful reiteration of nature in Renaissance gardens, representations of animals, whether made of topiary, paint, or stone, were accordingly located in grottoes, the *bosco* or wood, and parks.[6] The grotto at Castello was the admitted inspiration for an imaginary grotto in a text from the end of the sixteenth century by Agostino del Riccio, which contained 29 different animals. In his account, reasoning visitors puzzle out the identity of each species.[7] In contrast to human reason, the animals signify nature in at least two of the ways it was construed in the Renaissance. The domesticated sheep, goats, and ram suggest the pastoral view of nature, in harmony with humans, which was celebrated in the popular literary genre. The wild animals, including the non-European examples, and the rocky cliffs, caves, and forests where they roam, refer to a nature that is *not* domesticated, that is wild or savage, *selvaggio* in Italian. The grotto at Castello domesticates wild nature through imitation and also through the reuse of natural materials in a patently artificial setting. The representations of animals (with real horns and tusks) similarly domesticate the force of nature.

III

In the city, actual living animals – indeed wild animals – were kept in captivity. There the force of nature was not domesticated, only restrained, dominated by a captor who thereby appropriated its power.[8] In Florence wild animals were a conspicuous presence from at least the thirteenth century, particularly lions, the official animal of Florence, which were kept in stables near Palazzo Vecchio, and from 1550 near San Marco.[9] The Marzocco, the emblematic representation of the Florentine lion, and the living examples that it signified were conflated in the caged lions and the public rituals in which they participated. Other animals were also kept, some of them acquired through gifts, in a long and widespread tradition of collecting wild animals, and over time increasingly exotic ones, as signifiers of power and magnificence. These animals conferred prestige on the government or ruler who possessed them by their rarity, grandeur, and fierceness, but also by their captivity.

The animals in the Florentine menagerie acquired their various meanings for contemporaries through the social practices in which they were involved. Not merely kept, but explicitly displayed, they impressed, entertained, and epitomized the wild and strange against which culture and the familiar could be defined. In their location at San Marco, the animals could be observed by passers-by on the street and from a viewing area in the adjacent amphitheater.[10] The Frenchman Montaigne's journal of his visit to Florence in 1580 considered the animals worthy of enumeration. In addition to the stable of horses, he saw a camel, some lions and bears, and two animals that were unfamiliar to him: 'a sheep of a very strange shape' and a tiger ('an animal the size of a very big mastiff and the shape of a cat, all marked in black and white'). Typically, the strange was described in terms of the familiar. Some visitors were privileged to view the animals in the company of their ultimate masters: the keeper told Montaigne that Grand Duke Ferdinando and Duchess Christina came with 'gentlemen' to watch the animals.[11]

The caged animals also appeared in public spectacles, which were controlled displays of wildness, staged for Florentines and foreign visitors alike. These included horse races and jousts, animal fights on a small scale in the viewing amphitheater, and, above all, the spectacular fights or *caccie*, literally 'hunts', in the great piazzas. In the *caccie* mostly wild animals, but also some domestic ones, were pitted against each other and incited to violence. In the fifteenth century two such animal fights were held in Florence in honor of visiting foreign dignitaries and there were many more in the sixteenth century. In the great spectacle in 1459 for the visit of Count Galeazzo Maria Sforza, son of the Milanese duke, together with Pope Pius II (as in later ones), the Piazza della Signoria was blocked off and bleachers were set up within it. Wild boars, wolves, bulls, wild horses, dogs, and other animals were let into the square, then lions were introduced in anticipation of a bloody battle.[12] Lions – kings of the beasts, symbols of pride, and emblems of Florence – were pitted against other wild animals with a hoped-for show of force in entertainment meant to be read on multiple levels, all of which together would impress foreign visitors with the prowess of their hosts. A contemporary poem characteristically interweaves different readings of the events, effortlessly comprehending the lions as multivalent signs. The poem explains how the lions walked around the piazza with a proud spirit, while the other animals trembled. The lion attacking a horse is referred to as a Marzocco (the emblem of Florence), showing itself to be the ruler of the beasts.[13] On the other hand, when the lions did not fight after this show of force, their pacific behavior was interpreted as an indication of the friendship between the Sforza count and the Commune of Florence.[14]

Both symbolism and violence increased in the much more prevalent *caccie* of the sixteenth century within the altered political climate of the Medici dukes and grand dukes. In one such animal fight in 1514 (the year of the election of Pope Leo X, the first Medici pope), according to a contemporary, two lions, bears, leopards, bulls, buffaloes, stags, and many other beasts of various kinds participated, along with horses and dogs. Since the lions were unwilling to fight, apparently intimidated by the tumult of the crowd, the human participants provoked them.[15] In this spectacle the lions assumed an additional association with the newly elected Medici pope, who, in choosing the name Leo (Leone, or lion, in Italian), identified himself and the papacy with Florence. The lions, however, remained reluctant to act out either the political message encoded in the fight or the contemporary concept of wild animals, which is that they demonstrate their wildness by fighting.

Despite the passive animals, that day's events brought home the relationship of the animals in captivity and on public display to the forces of nature that they epitomized. The city square was transformed into a natural setting, with a large fountain and a mock wood around. The crowd in the piazza was composed of Florentines, including women and children, Romans, and other foreigners. As they all watched, stallions and a mare in heat were introduced, which this time did the expected.[16] If the topiary and sculpted animals in gardens domesticated and tamed wild nature, this recreation of a natural setting in the circumscribed area of the piazza represented the opposite: thoroughly undomesticated wild nature urged to manifest its wildness in the civilized city.

Under the Medici dukes, the *caccie* became more frequent and more violent, and featured the wholesale slaughter of animals. In one of these in Piazza Santa Croce during the carnival of 1545, on three successive days there was a slaughter of bulls, along with a battle of lions, bears, a wild boar, stag, and other animals.[17] Some of the most extreme examples occurred during the lavish festivities to celebrate the wedding of Grand Duke Francesco I and Joanna of Austria in 1565. Bulls were slaughtered in all the piazzas, and so too were a stream of animals (rabbits, hares, roebucks, foxes, porcupines, and badgers, then stags, boars, and bears, and finally some wild horses) in another spectacle. The obvious parallel with the imperial Romans was explicitly noted by a contemporary: the chase was seen as 'again renewing the ancient pomp of the Roman hunts'.[18] Once again, however, the animals in captivity would not respond as their counterparts in the wild, or rather, in accordance with contemporary notions of the behavior of wild animals, which the fights and hunts attempted to recreate artificially in both the city and the countryside. As was common practice, the animals were not left to their instincts: a great tortoise filled with men was introduced into the arena to excite a 'most fierce' lion so that it would fight with a 'valiant' bull.[19] As a demonstration of Medici power and magnificence following ancient precedent, humans appropriated the wildness of animals and did violence to them, first by provoking, then by killing them.

IV

There was a reciprocal relationship between the representations of the animal kingdom in the city square and those in art, both of which did not represent natural animal behavior so much as the cultural construction of wild nature, with which human civilization could be contrasted. The lion fights in the piazza actualized images in art from antiquity to the Renaissance, at the same time that the fights themselves must have inspired their visual representation. Images of animals became a distinct genre from the fifteenth century and fighting animals comprised a significant number of them in both paintings and prints. Among several engravings and drawings of animals fighting is a Florentine engraving of about 1460 (Figure 5.2.4), which depicts wild animals – lions and leopards – attacking horses and oxen, in this instance perhaps directly inspired by events of the previous year in the piazza.[20] In the Palazzo Medici there were numerous paintings featuring animals or animals fighting beginning in the fifteenth century, from panels by Paolo Uccello and Pesellino to Piero di Cosimo's animal sketchbook and Cosimo I's study, painted like a garden bower with a great variety of birds.[21] Animals and animal fights may have been popular subjects for interior decoration, but in the Medici residences they also reinforced the association of wild nature with the power of the ruler, while the preponderance of lions made unmistakeable the identification of Florence with its Medici rulers.

As the number and violence of the animal fights in the piazzas increased in the sixteenth century, evoking ancient Roman precedents more explicitly, so too did contemporary artistic representations of them more obviously evoke ancient models. Late in the sixteenth century the ancient colossal group of a lion attacking a horse inspired a bronze statuette by Giambologna. Its companion piece, a lion attacking a bull, also followed ancient precedents.[22] As we have seen, the literal animal combats in the piazzas of Florence acted out a concept about animals, which is that they demonstrate their wildness by fighting, and also another concept, that the harnessing of this wildness in

Figure 5.2.4   Anonymous, Florentine, *Wild animals attacking horses and oxen*, engraving, c. 1460. Courtesy of the Louvre, Collection Rothschild © Réunion des Musées Nationaux

a staged fight is a demonstration of power. Encapsulating and enshrining the fights in dramatic visual representations is a parallel expression of power – witness the giving of Giambologna's statuettes as diplomatic gifts.[23] Antiquity profoundly influenced all this, and much else of the way of construing the world and representing it in rituals in the fifteenth and sixteenth centuries.

V

Animals do fight, but not always; 'fighting animals' is instead a cultural construct, which can be seen again in another of its manifestations, the paradigm of paired enemies. Animals were understood as having innate antipathies, some observed in nature, others known from the lore of classical antiquity and medieval bestiaries.[24] Common pairs include the cat and mouse and wolf and lamb, but equally legendary was the innate hatred of camels for horses, noted in antiquity by Pliny the Elder in his *Natural History* and repeated in a late sixteenth-century treatise on domestic animals.[25] The rhinoceros was known as the adversary of the bear, since an epigram by Martial contained the trope of a rhinoceros tossing a bear, an image that came to characterize their enmity.[26] Another famous enmity was that between rhinoceros and elephant, which was described by Pliny and widely disseminated in the Middle Ages. The paradigm of paired enemies also determined how contemporaries dealt with Asian and African animals, known to antiquity but later only through lore, when the actual animals appeared in Europe. In 1515 in Lisbon, where both a rhinoceros and an elephant had just arrived from India as diplomatic gifts, a fight was staged between them.[27] Again, however, the animals defied what was expected of them: the young elephant took flight at the first sight of his opponent.

Several of these legendary enemies inhabit the grotto at Castello, but the consequent displays of wildness are strikingly absent. The camel and horse both occupy the right niche, oblivious to each other (see Figure 5.2.2). The left niche (see Figure 5.2.3) contains a bear and a rhinoceros, equally unconcerned with each other's presence. There is some conflict, but only among a few much smaller animals. In the left niche the dog appears to glare at the jumping cat on the other side of the greyhound and a lamb lies beneath the wolf. In the right niche a dog is overturned at the feet of a boar; and beneath the prancing horse another unidentifiable animal lies supine. These illustrate the fighting behavior of animals, but it is far outweighed by the general remarkable lack of violence. The animals for the most part stand in static poses, or in active ones, but without any interaction. Even the overturned animals seem calculated in their placement. The aim of this collection of animals is something other than a demonstration of their wildness.

As fighting animals were a cultural construct, so too are animals that are *not* fighting, particularly the coexistence of wild and domestic animals. The *topos* derives from classical antiquity, in texts such as Virgil's *Eclogues*, in which this peaceful coexistence is a metaphor for the harmony of the golden age.[28] So too in the grotto at Castello, the overall absence of fighting between wild and domestic animals and among the large, wild ones signifies harmony. Harmony in nature is also associated with the idea of nourishment, keyed by the presence of the unicorn in the central niche (see Figure 5.2.1), the only mythical animal in the grotto. The existence of unicorns was much debated in the sixteenth century; nevertheless, in 1569 Cosimo de' Medici spent a considerable sum for the horn of one, whose power as an antidote to poison was well known.[29] Unicorns were believed to purify water with their horns, while other animals wait patiently and harmoniously by the water source, and thus in garden fountains they denote spring water.[30] In the grotto it was appropriately spring water that formerly spurted from mouths, horns, and ears of the animals, and seeped from the stalactites on the walls. Since building aqueducts to bring spring water to Florence was one of Duke Cosimo's accomplishments, the animals in the grotto suggest a further political reading: the spring water brought by Cosimo tames the wild beasts and creates harmony, as his good rule does to his state. Since the central niche carries the most overt Medici symbolism, it is not surprising that all examples of conflict are relegated to the side niches.

VI

Classical antiquity provided precedents for animal hunts, artistic models for fighting animals, accounts of animal antipathies, and much more – the conceptual framework for the understanding and study of animals. Renaissance natural history was based on the writings of Aristotle, Pliny the Elder, and other ancient authors, made possible through the translation and publication of ancient texts (after the invention of the printing press in the fifteenth century).[31] In the fifteenth and sixteenth centuries Asian and African animals were similarly known via the ancients, since many had been familiar to them. Elephants, camels, giraffes, and many others were described in Pliny's *Natural History*, Ptolemy's *Geography*, and Strabo's *Geography*. The Latin translation of Ptolemy's *Geography*, made early in the fifteenth century, was a best-seller by mid-century, even before it was printed in 1475. Ptolemy's Latin text was the source for most of the parts on Asia in Sebastian Münster's *Cosmographia* of 1544.[32]

In the extensive literature commemorating the first encounters of Europeans with America, one of the persistent themes is the way that the New World was understood through the framework of the old, particularly Christianity and classical culture.[33] This is especially the case for the exploration of the new worlds of Asia and Africa, which was framed as a rediscovery of classical antiquity. As a result, through the sixteenth century, the animals discussed in ancient texts were privileged. That the animals at Castello are only from worlds known to the ancients and do not include any American examples, except the turkey, reflects a broader situation,[34] although there are also more particular reasons for the selection in the grotto.

The relationship between the discovery of non-European worlds and the rediscovery of classical antiquity is particularly apparent in the decoration of the Vatican Loggetta of Cardinal Bibbiena, painted about 1516 by Giovanni da Udine. The decorative scheme was directly inspired by the recently discovered frescoes in the Domus Aurea, the Golden House of Emperor Nero. Giorgio Vasari relates that the painted rooms stupefied Raphael and Giovanni da Udine, who were among the first to see them. Giovanni da Udine's Loggetta in the Vatican is uncannily similar to its Roman model. In the vault, climbing plants delineate compartments, as in the ancient frescoes, and painted inside each is one of the exotic animals in Pope Leo's menagerie. Among them are several of the same animals as in the Castello grotto – a camel, boar, giraffe, and elephant. Vasari also saw there a chameleon, civet cats, apes, parrots, lions, baboons, and mandrills.[35]

The nearly contemporaneous rediscoveries of ancient decorative schemes and of the animals of Asia and Africa were associated in the minds of contemporaries. The exotic animals were made familiar by their assimilation into the classical tradition, as Michael Ryan has argued in a broader context.[36] The term used for them was 'strange' – different from the known, but not 'exotic', an expression not in currency until the eighteenth century and one that suggests a fuller sense of both what constitutes the identity of the familiar and what must be its opposite in the other.[37]

VII

In the sixteenth century both a reliance on ancient authority and empirical observation characterized the flourishing activity of naturalists. The geographical range and number of species studied expanded greatly and the 1550s saw several important publications by Guillaume Rondelet, Pierre Belon, and Konrad Gesner. Almost fifty years later the Bolognese naturalist Ulisse Aldrovandi began publication of a twelve-volume *Natural History*, published from 1599 to 1648.[38] The texts of Gesner (*Historiae animalium*, published 1550–1558) and Aldrovandi followed the model of Pliny's *Natural History* in not only describing the animals, but also cataloguing their history, habitat, legends, and symbolism. Gesner added to this basic information all known associations, etymology, practical and medicinal uses to mankind, and symbolism derived from the animal's actions, character, and appearance. These last were formulated in proverbs, hieroglyphs, and emblems. The concern of Gesner's and Aldrovandi's texts was not only the animals themselves, but their significance to humans, much of which was derived from sources in classical antiquity. Gesner presented the animals as they were understood by contemporaries – in a complex system of similitudes, which Foucault has called the *episteme* of the sixteenth century. In the particular context of natural history, William Ashworth has termed this an emblematic world view, for both the system of associations and the myriad hidden meanings of everything in the cosmos.[39] The ways in which animals were meaningful also increased enormously over the second half of the sixteenth century. This is apparent in works on hieroglyphics and emblematics, among them Piero Valeriano's *Hieroglyphica* (Basel, 1556), concerning the allegorical significance of animals, and Joachim Camerarius' monumental

Symbolorum et emblematum (1593–1604), a book of 400 emblems involving plants and animals. Among them is an emblem of a rhinoceros tossing a bear, along with a giraffe, camel, elephant, and other Asian and African animals.

Exotic animals were easily assimilated into this emblematic world view since many of those newly known in the sixteenth century had an established cultural history from antiquity. For animals from America and others unknown to the ancients, meanings and emblems might be invented anew,[40] but others received only brief accounts without the traditional list of associations. The understanding of animals began to change only in the seventeenth century, and then only through texts devoted exclusively to the animals of the New World, for which there were no known similitudes or hidden meanings.[41]

The numerous publications in natural history in the sixteenth century were guided, in varying measures, by ancient authority, the growing system of similitudes, and also a new empirical observation, aided by the representational skills developed by artists from the fifteenth century.[42] If observation conflicted with the first two, it did not cancel them out. Empirical observation was a significant aspect of fifteenth-, and especially sixteenth-, century representations of animals, but it did not displace other ways of knowing the world. The function of images, even in many of the natural history texts, was not exclusively the production of scientific knowledge, understood in modern terms, but rather the illustration of the subject in its cultural matrix: not the actual animal, but the contemporary understanding of it, which required instead a normative image.

Some of the normative images represent the animal sitting, standing, and acting out characteristic gestures and actions. For example, at Castello the mountain goat in the left niche (Figure 5.2.3) is represented in a typical pose of grazing among the rocks. A number of these images were derived from the great repertoire of animals in ancient sculpture, such as Giambologna's colossal group of a lion fighting a horse. As in the natural history texts, many sixteenth-century images follow models from antiquity, which were modified by observation. The bull at Castello (see Figure 5.2.1) repeats a common ancient type with its turned head, folds of skin on the neck, prancing pose, and tail swung back over its torso. The static quality of the grouping in the grotto derives in part from the use of such models and types; even when active or looking out, they are not interactive with the surrounding space or a posited viewer. Repetition of a model was also a means of making associations or hidden meanings evident. The wild boar, or *cinghiale*, in the right niche (see Figure 5.2.2) is a close copy of a specific ancient sculpture, one highly esteemed in the sixteenth century, which was given by Pope Pius IV to Cosimo de' Medici in 1560.[43] The sculpture thus sets up a series of associations between the wild animal, ancient sculpture, the papacy, and the ruler of Florence. Other models came from pattern books, such as the seated leopard in the right niche of the grotto, with its characteristic and aristocratic pose (see Figure 5.2.2).

Representations of animals had a long history, some despite inaccuracies and unchecked by further observation from nature. Just as the sources of knowledge about animals were interlocked, so too were those for their illustration, again because animals were not so much important in their own right as in a grid of associations. Illustrations to natural history texts were no different in reusing earlier images, particularly, but by no means exclusively, when the actual animal was not available for observation.[44] In the collection in the grotto at Castello, the images derive from ancient sculpture, pattern books, long medieval tradition, and treatises on natural history (such as the greyhound from Gesner in the left niche), as well as travel literature, emblem books, and other sources. In some component, empirical observation was also incorporated into the representations, just as the horns and tusks are real, not sculpted.

VIII

The strange animals from Asia and Africa were likewise assimilated into existing visual traditions, which reinforced associations in an increasingly complex web of meaning. The Indian single-horned rhinoceros, for example, was rare in Europe, but the image of the animal was quite common. The rhinoceros that was supposed to fight the elephant in Lisbon in 1515 was the first seen in Europe since the third century. A sketch of it found its way into the hands of Albrecht Dürer, whose famous woodcut (see Figure 5.2.5) remained the almost universally accepted image of the animal for almost three centuries, in spite of its glaring inaccuracies and the existence of a more correct representation. The plated animal in the grotto at Castello, with its fictitious dorsal spiral horn, is also based on Dürer's. The inscription on most editions of the woodcut is from Pliny, who told of its fight to the death with the elephant.[45] It has been suggested that Dürer's woodcut, with its double horn and plates reminiscent of contemporary armor, illustrates the idea of the animal better than a more accurate image might.[46]

The giraffe, like the rhinoceros, was practically unknown in Europe before the fifteenth century and was not common until the nineteenth century. The normative image in the Renaissance was also based ultimately on the first encounter with the actual animal in the fifteenth century and it persisted because of a particular cultural resonance. On his voyage to Egypt in about 1443, Cyriacus of Ancona saw a giraffe and made a drawing of it in a letter,

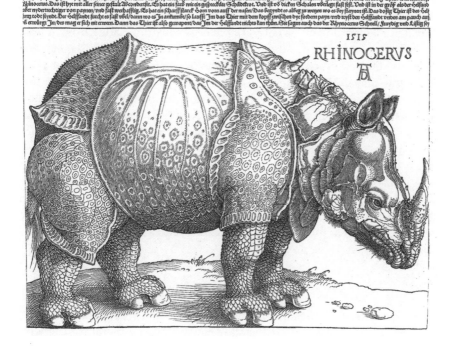

Figure 5.2.5   Albrecht Dürer, *Rhinoceros*, woodcut, 1515, the Metropolitan Museum of Art, New York, Gift of Junius Morgan, 1919 (19.73.159). Courtesy of the Metropolitan Museum of Art, New York

which inspired many later versions.[47] A Florentine engraving, apparently based on this drawing but reinforced by the living animal, was used to illustrate a description of a giraffe's arrival in Florence in 1487 as a diplomatic gift.[48] This in turn was the model for the sculpted animal at Castello. The steeply sloping rear body with short hind legs, long thin neck and large head may be influenced by the imperfect knowledge that the ancients had of the animal. Called a *camelopardalis*, it was understood as a hybrid of more familiar creatures: a camel for its great size, a leopard for the spots, and a lion in the hind quarters and flanks.[49] The ancient Greek author Strabo, who wrote the first account of the giraffe, believed it to be a domestic animal, which allowed it to function, along with a camel, another non-European, 'strange', but also domestic animal, as a signifier of the early stages of civilization.

The fixed representation of the camel was crystallized in the travel journal of the explorer to the Middle East, André Thevet, whose *Cosmographie de Levant* was first published in 1554. Thevet described several exotic animals including a giraffe, hippopotamus, crocodile, elephant, camel, lion, and wild ass, which he illustrated with woodcuts.[50] The figure of the camel suggests that some features were observed from life, but the combination of a camel with a monkey riding on its back is a pictorial construct dating from at least the late fifteenth century and repeated in the grotto at Castello. The monkey illustrates the domesticity of the camel, standing in for its human counterpart and at the same time relegating the animal to the earlier stages of civilization. In Thevet's woodcut, the fruit-eating monkey astride the camel itself dates from late antiquity. In the grotto this monkey type is also present, but in another niche. In contrast to its exotic companions at Castello – the rhinoceros and giraffe – the apple-eating monkey as well as the leg-scratching one riding the camel were familiar in Western art from manuscript borders and other sources.[51] Living specimens of the exotic animals were also known, although they remained thoroughly foreign, probably through the eighteenth century. Representations of them, however, made the strange animals familiar, domesticating them through their assimilation into a long visual tradition.

IX

Collections of non-European animals, as well as their representations, were popular among rulers and aristocrats. They indicated a literal contact with the enlarged world and implied a metaphorical possession of it. Keeping menageries of large and wild animals as a sign of power was also an old custom, as we have seen with those of the Florentine Republic, the Medici Duchy, and Pope Leo X in Rome. Cosimo de' Medici's second son, Cardinal Ferdinando, likewise spent a large sum on animals. He kept bears, lions, ostriches, and other wild animals at his villa in Rome and moved them with him to Florence in 1588 when he returned to assume the position of grand duke.[52] Giving such animals as gifts was also a common practice among the most distinguished rulers of Europe. Like the animal fights in the piazzas, this was another ritual of power inspired by ancient Roman tributes and those of Byzantine, Near Eastern, and North African rulers.[53] In 1542 the Viceroy of Naples sent two tigers to Duke Cosimo in Florence.[54] Grand Duke Francesco de' Medici in 1572 sent to Albrecht V of Bavaria a miscellany of exotica, including parrots, Indian sheep, and crocodiles.[55] Francesco received in turn three elks in 1587, sent from Sweden by a merchant from Lucca, which were the first of this northern European animal to be seen in Florence.[56] These gifts are witness to international relations in the sixteenth century, as well as to the continuation of a long tradition of viewing rare animals, preferably also both very large and wild, as diplomatic currency.

Among such gifts were major ones to members of the Medici family, which were recorded in artistic representations, poems, and other contemporary accounts and which became part of the family lore. The gifts were also an early and significant means of contact between Florence and the worlds beyond Europe. In 1487 the Sultan of Egypt, seeking diplomatic aid, sent an embassy to Lorenzo the Magnificent bearing precious objects and exotic animals, among them a giraffe, camels, monkeys, a lion, and Indian goats, all of which are represented in the grotto at Castello. The giraffe, which caused a great stir, was the first ever seen in Florence and only the second in Italy – the first was in Rome in 46 BC when Julius Caesar returned in triumph from Africa.[57] This extraordinary animal, little known even in antiquity, signified to contemporaries Lorenzo's foreign standing.[58] The distinct tradition of Florentine representations served to identify the animal with the place that was so honored by its presence.

In the system of exchange and language of diplomacy of the Renaissance, gifts were a two-sided commodity.[59] On the election of a new pope, foreign sovereigns were expected to send a gift of obedience. In 1514 King Manuel I of Portugal, who wanted favors and concessions from Leo X, gave him a spectacular gift, which both highlighted his own magnificence and bestowed it upon the recipient. Along with spices, gold, gems, rare plants, parakeets, Indian fowl and dogs, a cheetah, and a Persian horse, his ambassador presented an Indian elephant to Pope Leo.[60] The gifts acknowledged Portugal's mastery over lands in Asia, Africa, and America, while also implying that the newly conquered realms submitted to papal authority.

The elephant made an enormous impression, and before its death in 1516 was paraded in Roman festivals and drawn by Raphael.[61] Another drawing from the circle of Giulio Romano preserves a livelier, if more fantastic, elephant type than Raphael's.[62] This image, with a furled trunk and the small ears of the Indian elephant, was the model for the Elephant Fountain made by Giovanni da Udine in 1526 for the Villa Madama in Rome of Cardinal Giulio de' Medici (later Pope Clement V). By following the same type as both drawing and fountain, the representation of the elephant in the central niche at Castello alludes to both the recipient, Pope Leo X, and to Pope Clement V. In the sixteenth-century *episteme* of similitudes, analogies were inferred from visual resemblance. With its appearance in the grotto of Cosimo I, this particular representation of the elephant, through its accumulated associations, could signify the power of the Medici dynasty, epitomized in the elephant gift. The same was true of the rhinoceros. Since the elephant gift was such a success, in the following year King Manuel shipped off to the pope a yet more rare specimen, the rhinoceros that he had just received from India, although the animal perished during its journey from Lisbon. The sculpted rhinoceros in the grotto recalls the great gift to Pope Leo. It resembles Dürer's woodcut (see Figure 5.2.5), which also inspired an emblem of Alessandro de' Medici which emphasized the indomitable will of both animal and duke.[63] The rhinoceros, like the elephant and giraffe, was incorporated into a Medici myth; the representations of these animals, through the repetition of visual signs that carried multiple associations, was similarly ideological.

X

Animals and other precious objects presented among contemporaries as diplomatic gifts evoked ancient tributes, an association that was made explicit through images. One of these is in the early sixteenth-century decoration of the grand *salone* of the Medici villa of Poggio a Caiano, a villa associated with both Lorenzo the Magnificent, who built it in the fifteenth century, and Pope Leo X, who commissioned the later decoration. In the scene of the *Tribute to Caesar in Egypt*, painted by Andrea del Sarto in 1521 (and expanded by Alessandro Allori in 1582), the diplomatic gifts to Lorenzo are conflated with an ancient tribute to Caesar.[64] While the subject purports to be from ancient history, the giraffe in the distance and the Indian goats, lion, and parrots in the left foreground were gifts not to the Roman emperor, but emphatically to Lorenzo from the Sultan of Egypt.[65] The association would have been clear since this was the only giraffe known to contemporaries, and later the reference was made explicit by Raffaello Borghini in his discussion of the *salone* in *Il Riposo*, dialogues on art published in 1584.[66]

The form of the visual representation of the *Tribute to Caesar* also underlines the conflation of ancient and fifteenth-century tributes. The giraffe with its long, graceful neck and curiously proportioned body was familiar from other Florentine images. In addition to the telling giraffe, the other animals painted in the scene, including the monkeys, civet cat, and chameleon, along with the New World turkey and horses added by Allori, reinforce the idea of homage from all parts of the known world.[67] The setting of this tribute is presumably Egypt (recalling the Sultan of Egypt), which is interpreted as a classical city with a circular temple, round arch, and statuary.[68] The silhouette of the giraffe, framed by the distant mountain, is juxtaposed with the statue on a pedestal, the visual relationship between classical artifact and exotic natural creature suggesting again the parallel between rediscovery and discovery. The ancient past was used typically to give authority to the present and also to represent the non-European worlds in a role of subservience. The tributes that signified these worlds implied that they were submissive to the dominant authority of the classical ruler, be he Caesar or Lorenzo.

A significant aspect of the political propaganda of the later Medici beginning with Cosimo I was the emphasis on continuity in the Medici family, merging the two branches to create a family dynasty and blurring the distinction between republic and principate.[69] The grotto at Castello continues this program of propaganda, since individual animals were associated with more than one member of the Medici family. The predominant non-European animals were received in one or another of the tributes, to Lorenzo or to Leo. It was not necessary to include a recipient of the gifts as well, since the central animals (see Figure 5.2.1) stand in for both Florence and her succession of Medici rulers. The lion, proud king of the beasts, alludes simultaneously to the Florentine Marzocco, Pope Leo X, and Grand Duke Cosimo. The goat at its side resembles Cosimo's astrological sign, the Capricorn. The four-horned ram nestled beneath the lion is the device of Cosimo's son, Francesco, who was made regent in 1564.[70] Without ambassadors or recipients, the grotto carries associations of tribute, dynasty, and the power of the Medici, along with the civilizing of wild nature and the harmony of good rule.

XI

In the grotto at Castello, Medici power is defined in terms of the greatly increased knowledge of the world and the concomitant interest in defining differences, both within Europe, which was emerging as a concept, and between Europe and the other continents. This is evident in a number of publications, some that we have seen: in the fifteenth century Ptolemy's and Strabo's geographies and the *Descriptio Asiae et Europae* of Aeneas Sylvius Piccolomini, and in the sixteenth, Leandro Alberti's *Descrittione di tutta Italia* (1550), the cosmographies of Sebastian Münster and André Thevet, accounts of voyages, several collected in G. B. Ramusio's *Delle navigationi et viaggi* (1554), and the travel journals that led to the guidebooks of the next century.[71]

The four continents also became familiar through personifications, which appeared by the end of the sixteenth century, as in the early example of them in Cesare Ripa's *Iconologia* of 1603.[72] In the personifications, the continents are characterized by the relationship of nature and culture, on a spectrum from civilized, the standard for which was set by Europe, to barbarian, embodying qualities of wild nature. This hierarchy of civilization is conveyed through dress, attributes, and animals. Ripa's illustration of Europe (see Figure 5.2.6) follows the text, which describes 'the first and principal part of the world', as crowned and dressed in regal garments. Behind her in the illustration is a horse, the quintessential embodiment of European aristocratic and classically based culture. At the feet of Europe are emblems of the Christian religion, an owl, book, musical instruments, and other attributes of the liberal arts, denoting, Ripa explains, Europe's superiority in all these endeavors.

None of the other continents is accompanied by indications of cultural accomplishments: they are defined only by flora, fauna, and geography in a descending scale of civilization. Asia, in rich garments, is represented with

DI CESARE RIPA.   333
E V R O P A.

di frutti, perciòche come dimoſtra Straboneᐧnel luoco citato di ſopra, e
queſta parte ſopra tutte l'altre ſeconda, & abondante di tutti quei beni,
che la natura ha ſaputo produrre,come ſi potrà vedere da alcune ſue par-
ti da noi deſcritte.

Si rappreſenta che tenghi con la deſtra mano il tempio, per dinotare,
ch'in lei al preſente ci è la perfetta, & veriſſima Religione, & ſuperiore
à tutte l'altre.

Moſtra con il dito indice della ſiniſtra mano Regni, Corone, Scet-
tri, Ghirlande, & altre ſimili coſe, eſſendo che nell' Europa vi ſonno i
maggiori, e più potenti Principi del Mondo; come la Maeſtà Ceſarea,
& il Sommo Pontefice Romano, la cui auttorità ſi ſtende per tutto,
doue hà luocho la Santiſsima, & Cattholica Fede Chriſtiana, la
                                                                  quale

Figure 5.2.6   *Europe*, engraving by Cesare Ripa, *Iconologia*, 1603. Photograph by
Claudia Lazzaro

fruit, flowers, an incense burner denoting its spices, and a camel. Africa, nearly nude in the text although not in Ripa's illustration, wears an elephant headdress, holds a scorpion and cornucopia, and is accompanied by a lion, poisonous snakes, and vipers, all suggesting a wild and uncivilized continent. Finally, America, with only her shameful parts covered, as Ripa explains, wears a feathered headdress and holds a bow and arrow. One foot rests on a head pierced with an arrow, demonstrating the barbarity of her people. Beside her is a reptile, a ferocious animal that devours not only other animals but also humans.[73] The animals were selected not only because they are native to the respective regions, but, equally importantly, as signifiers of the cultural paradigms that informed the personifications.

Animals were part of a construct of nature; wild animals spoke to assumptions about the force of nature. The public animal hunts and visual representations of fighting animals were demonstrations of this wildness, but also of the power of the individual or state that harnesses the wildness. Exotic animals indicated the magnificence of their owners, because of their rarity and expense, but also because they signified less civilized, more wild, or barbarian parts of the world. In the animal tributes the appropriation of the force of nature that the exotic animals signified is also a demonstration of the domination of a superior civilization, be it Florence, the Catholic Church, or Europe. Classical antiquity is a key element in the assumptions and paradigms behind this set of associations. It provided the foundation for natural science and the familiarity with Asia and Africa that made their fauna and flora accessible to study. The tenacious imitation of the ancients was also an obstacle to their study.[74] Models from classical antiquity served as well to legitimate Europe's claims of superiority and authority. For much of the next two centuries classical forms and paradigms continued to dominate and define Western, and especially Italian, culture. The cultural biases embedded in Ripa's personifications of the continents were also a long-enduring legacy of the Renaissance.

NOTES

This is an abridged version of my 'Animals as Cultural Signs: A Medici Menagerie in the Grotto at Castello', in *Reframing the Renaissance: Visual Culture in Europe and Latin America 1450–1650*, ed. Claire Farago (New Haven and London, 1995), pp. 197–227, 331–5, 367–73.

1. Keith Thomas, *Man and the Natural World: A History of the Modern Sensibility* (New York: Pantheon, 1983), for the understanding of nature in relationship to humans. For other aspects of the interaction of nature and culture, see my *The Italian Renaissance Garden: from the Conventions of Planting, Design, and Ornament to the Grand Gardens of Sixteenth-Century Central Italy* (New Haven and London: Yale University Press, 1990), especially Chapter 1.

2. Much of the recent scholarship on cultural encounters, especially with America, examines the various strategies of assimilation. I have benefited in particular from J. H. Elliott, *The Old World and the New 1492–1650* (Cambridge: Cambridge University Press, 1970); Anthony Grafton, with April Shelford and Nancy Siraisi, *New Worlds, Ancient Texts: The Power of Tradition and the Shock of Discovery* (Cambridge, MA and London: Belknap Press, 1992); Peter Mason, *Deconstructing*

America: Representations of the Other (London and New York: Routledge, 1990); Anthony Pagden, *The Fall of Natural Man. The American Indian and the Origins of Comparative Ethnology* (Cambridge: Cambridge University Press, 1986); and Michael T. Ryan, 'Assimilating New Worlds in the Sixteenth and Seventeenth Centuries', *Comparative Studies in Society and History* 23 (1981), pp. 519–38.

3. For concepts of wildness, see Hayden White, 'The Forms of Wildness: Archaeology of an Idea', *Tropics of Discourse: Essays in Cultural Criticism* (Baltimore: The Johns Hopkins University Press, 1978), especially pp. 150–7.

4. Giorgio Vasari presumably designed the grotto, and the sculptor of the animals may have been the little-known Antonio di Gino Lorenzi. The present neo-classical exterior of the grotto dates from the eighteenth century. For the dating and history of the grotto, see David R. Wright, 'The Medici Villa at Olmo a Castello: Its History and Iconography', Ph.D. dissertation, Princeton University, 1976), pp. 202–7. For a discussion of the grotto and its garden context, see my *Renaissance Garden*, and Christian Acidini Luchinat in Acidini Luchinat and Giorgio Galletti, *Le ville e I giardini di Castello e Petraia a Firenze* (Florence: Pacini Editore, 1992), pp. 108–23. Charles Avery, *Giambologna: The Complete Sculpture* (Mt. Kisco, N.Y.: Moyer Bell, 1987), p. 151, attributes the animals to Cosimo Fancelli in the 1550s.

5. Liliane Châtelet-Lange, 'The Grotto of the Unicorn and the Garden of the Villa di Castello', *Art Bulletin* 50 (1968), 51–8, concludes that the grotto illustrates the Greek *Physiologus* and must have allegorical significance. Wright, 'Castello', pp. 298–300, determines that the grotto represents Orpheus taming the beasts with his lyre (based on one early seventeenth-century account which noted a statue of Orpheus there, although no earlier visitors mention it), which has an allegorical significance for the contemporary situation of Cosimo de' Medici in Florence. Claudia Conforti, 'La grotta "degli animali" o "del diluvio" nel giardino di Villa Medici a Castello', *Quaderni di Palazzo Te* 6 (1987), pp. 71–80, discusses the grotto in terms of Cosimo de' Medici's identification with Orpheus, replacing an earlier program that played on the identification of Cosimo with Neptune and Pan. E. Mourlot, '"Artifice naturel" ou "nature artificielle": les grottes Médicéennes dans la Florence du XVIè siècle', in *Ville et campagne dans la littérature italienne de la Renaissance*, 2 vols (Paris: Université de la Sorbonne Nouvelle, 1976–77), vol. 2: p. 340, discusses the grotto only briefly and generally as a glorification of Cosimo. My discussion in *Renaissance Garden*, pp. 178–81, emphasizes the Medici references of individual animals.

6. See my *Renaissance Garden*, pp. 137–40, 200, 202–6, 266–67, and 311, n. 58.

7. Detlef Heikamp, 'Agostino del Riccio, "Del giardino di un re"', in *Il giardino storico italiano*, ed. G. Ragionieri (Florence: Leo S. Olschki, 1981), pp. 80–9.

8. Yi-Fu Tuan, *Dominance and Affection: The Making of Pets* (New Haven and London: Yale University Press, 1984), pp. 70–8.

9. Guglielmo Volpi, *Le feste di Firenze del 1459: notizia di un poemetto del sec. XV* (Pistoia: Libreria Pagnini, 1902), pp. 18–19, n. 2, who notes that the street, Via dei Leoni, still records their presence. Joan Barclay Lloyd, *African Animals in Renaissance Literature and Art* (Oxford: Clarendon Press, 1971), 40; and Simari in *Natura viva in Casa Medici* (Flroence: Centro Di, 1985), p. 27.

10. Simari in *Natura viva*, pp. 27–8.

11. *Montaigne's Travel Journal* trans. D. M. Frame (San Francisco: North Point Press, 1983), 65; Avery, *Giambologna*, p. 147.

12. Richard C. Trexler, *Public Life in Renaissance Florence*, 2nd ed. (Ithaca: Cornell University Press, 1991), p. 263, n. 158; and Rab Hatfield, 'Some Unknown Descriptions of the Medici Palace in 1459', *Art Bulletin* 52 (1970), pp. 232–7. Volpi, *Feste di Firenze*, pp. 16–20; Luca Landucci, *Diario fiorentino dal 1450 al 1516*, ed. I. Del Badia (Florence: G. C. Sansoni, 1883), p. 347; and Lloyd, *African Animals*, p. 39.

13. Volpi, *Feste di Firenze*, 19. 'I gran leoni andavan passeggiando/Per la gran piazza coll'animo fero:/Tutti gli altri animali si stan tremando./ Con un gran salto altissimo e leggero/Sopr'un cavallo un marzocco avventossi, /Mostrando delle besite esser l'impero ...'.

14. Volpi, *Feste di Firenze*, 20. According to two contemporary observers (Volpi, 17), the animals were spurred on by a Trojan horse-like giraffe, filled with 'brave men' (although another identified it as a *palla* or ball).

15. Landucci, *Diario fiorentino*, pp. 345–7; and Lloyd, *African Animals*, pp. 39–40.

16. Landucci, *Diario fiorentino*, 346, and Bartolomeo Masi, *Ricordanze di Bartolomeo Masi, Calderaio Fiorentino dal 1478 al 1526*, ed. G. Corazzini (Florence: Sansoni, 1906), pp. 143–4, who both note

that many foreigners, including Romans and four cardinals in disguise, attended. Trexler, *Public Life*, pp. 508–9, interprets the events in the piazza as a representation of the violence and biological forces, no different from those of animals, that were part of Florentine history.

17. Michel Plaisance, 'La Politique culturelle de Côme Ier et les fêtes annuelles à Florence de 1541 à 1550', *Les Fêtes de la Renaissance*, ed. Jean Jacquor and Elie Konigson, 3 vols (Paris: Éditions du Centre National de la Recherche Scientifique, 1975), vol. 3: p. 136.

18. Giorgio Vasari, *Le vite de 'più eccelenti pittori scultori ed architetti*, ed. G. Milanesi, 8 vols (Florence: G. C. Sansoni, 1906), vol. 7, p. 580.

19. Vasari, *Vite*, vol. 8, pp. 580–1.

20. The engraving of wild animals attacking horses and oxen is catalogued in Arthur M. Hind, *Early Italian Engraving*, 7 vols (London: B. Quaritch for Knoedler, 1938–48), vol. 1, p. 62, no. A.II.3. Dogs attacking a bear is in *The Illustrated Bartsch* vol. 24. *Early Italian Masters* ed. Mark Qucker (New Ork: Abaris, 1980), p. 211, no. 8(145); Lucantonio's engraving is in Hind, vol. 1, p. 214, no. D.III.4.

21. Vasari, *Vite*, vol. 2, p. 208, vol. 3, p. 37, vol. 4, p. 138, and 6:455. For the study, painted by Bachiacca some time before 1547, see also Scott J. Schaefer, 'The Studiolo of Francesco I de' Medici in the Palazzo Vecchio in Florence', 2 vols, Ph.D. Dissertation, Bryn Mawr College, 1976, p. 137.

22. *Giambologna 1529–1608: Sculptor to the Medici*, eds Charles Avery and Anthony Radcliffe, (London: Arts Council of Great Britain, 1978), pp. 186–8, cats. 170, 171, and also cats. 166, 172, 173, and 174; Avery, *Giambologna*, pp. 59–60 and cats. 139–41.

23. Avery, *Giambologna*, p. 235, and see note above.

24. Bestiaries ultimately derived from a second century Greek text, called *Physiologus*. On the history and content of medieval bestiaries, see Florence McCulloch, *Medieval Latin and French Bestiaries*, rev. edn (Chapel Hill: The University of North Carolina Press, 1962); and Wilma George and Brunsdon Yapp, *The Naming of the Beasts: Natural History in the Medieval Bestiary* (London: Duckworth, 1991).

25. Pliny, *Natural History*, 8.26.68; Giovanvettorio Soderini, *Il trattato degli animali domestici*, ed. A. Bacchi della Lega (Bologna: Romagnoli dall'acqua, 1907), p. 185.

26. F. J. Cole, 'The History of Albrecht Dürer's Rhinoceros in Zoological Literature', in *Science, Medicine and History. Essays in Honour of Charles Singer*, ed. E. A. Underwood, 2 vols (London: Oxford University Press, 1953), vol. 1, pp. 241 and 341. Martial (*Spect.* 22) wrote that the rhinoceros 'tossed a heavy bear with his double horn'. The image was repeated in Piero Valeriano's *Hieroglyphica* (Basel, 1556) and Joachim Camerarius' *Symbolorum et emblematum* (1593–1604).

27. Cole, 'Dürer's Rhinoceros', vol. 1, p. 337; Donald F. Lach, *Asiain the Making of Europe*, 2 vols (Chicago: The University of Chicago Press, 1970), vol. 2, pt. 1:159 and pp. 161–2; and T. H. Clarke, *The Rhinoceros from Dürer to Stubbs), 1515–1799* (London: Wotheby's Publications, 1986), pp. 155–62.

28. Virgil, Eclogue 4.22, 'cattle will not fear the lion's might', in *The Eclogues*, trans. Guy Lee (New York: Penguin Books, 1984), 57. The literary *topos* of harmony between wild and domestic animals deriving from Virgil is noted by J. M. C. Toynbee, *Animals in Roman Life and Art* (Ithaca: Cornell University Press, 1973), p. 21. A similar image is in the prophecy of Isaiah (11.6), in which the wolf dwells with the lamb, the leopard with the kid.

29. Lucia Tongiorgi Tomasi in *Livorno e Pisa: due città e un territorio nella politica dei Medici*, exhib. cat. (Pisa: Nistri-Lischi e Pacini Editori, 1980), 545. The existence of the unicorn is debated in Andrea Bacci, *L'alicorno* (Florence: Giorgio Marescotti, 1573).

30. Châtelet-Lange, 'Grotto of the Unicorn', 52–6, discusses the source of this *topos* from the Greek *Physiologus* and gives relevant examples, both literary and artistic, from Lorenzo de' Medici's *Selve d'amore* of the last quarter of the fifteenth century, to a painting by Filippino Lippi of the end of the century, and an engraving by Jean Duvet of about 1540 with exotic and European animals facing each other on either side of a stream. I disagree with her thesis, however, that the grotto illustrates this account. For garden fountains, see my *Renaissance Garden*, 135

31. *The Age of the Marvellous*, ed. Joy Kenseth, exh. cat. (Hanover: Hood Museum of Art, Dartmouth College, 1991), pp. 219–20; and Lloyd, *African Animals*, p. 23.

32. Ruthardt Oehme, introduction to the expanded 1550 edition of Sebastian Münster, *Cosmographei*, 1550, facs. edn (Amsterdam: Theatrum Orbis Terrarum, 1968); and *Age of the Marvelous*, pp. 302–3.

33. See note 2.

34. Stephen Olaf Turk Christensen, 'The Image of Europe in Anglo-German Travel Literature', in *Voyager à la Renaissance. Actes du Colloque de Tours, 1983*, ed. Jean Céard and Jean-Claude Margolin (Paris: Maisonneuve et Larose, 1987), pp. 257–8, makes this point on a larger scale.

35. Vasari, *Vite*, vol. 6, pp. 551–5, and vol. 4, p. 362. Nicole Dacos and Caterina Furlan, *Giovanni da Udine 1487–1561* (Udine: Casamassima, 1987), pp. 23–4 and 44–5.

36. Ryan, 'Assimilating New Worlds'.

37. Vasari refers to non-European animals as 'animali strani', 'bizzarri animali', and 'altri animali più strani'. The first use of 'esotico', denoting flora, fauna, etc., from other continents, is in 1736; the word is more common in the second half of the eighteenth century. *Vocabolario degli Accademici della Crusca*, 12 vols (Florence: Galileiana di M. Cellini & C., 1886), vol. 5, p. 307.

38. F. David Hoeniger, 'How Plants and Animals Were Studied in the Mid-Sixteenth Century', in *Science and the Arts in the Renaissance*, ed. J. W. Shirley and F. D. Hoeniger (Washington, London and Toronto: Associated University Presses, 1985), pp. 130–48; Willly Ley, *Dawn of Zoology* (Englewood Cliffs, N.J.: Prentice-Hall, 1968), pp. 126–34 and 154–5; and Lloyd, *African Animals*, pp. 34–6 and 78–94.

39. Michel Foucault, *The Order of Things: An Archaeology of the Human Sciences* (New York: Pantheon Books, 1970), pp. 17–45; and William B. Ashworth, Jr, 'Natural History and the Emblematic World View', in *Reappraisals of the Scientific Revolution*, ed. David C. Lindberg and Robert S. Westman (Cambridge: Cambridge University Press, 1990), pp. 303–32. My discussion owes much to Ashworth, and also to Wolfgang Harms, 'On Natural History and Emblematics in the 16th Century', in *The Natural Sciences and the Arts: Aspects of Interaction from the Renaissance to the 20th Century*, ed. Allan Ellenius (Stockholm: Almqvist & Wiksell, 1985), pp. 67–83.

40. Harms, 'Natural History and Emblematics', 67–9, with the example of new emblems for the bird of paradise.

41. Ashworth, 'Emblematic World View', pp. 318–19.

42. James S. Ackerman, 'Early Renaissance "Naturalism" and Scientific Illustration', in *Natural Sciences and the Arts*, and Ackerman, 'The Involvement of Artists in Renasisance Science', in *Natural Sciences and the Arts*, pp. 94–129, deals with some of the issues discussed here in the fifteenth century through the 1540s.

43. Francis Haskell and Nicholas Penny, *Taste and the Antique* (New Haven and London: Yale University Press, 1981), pp. 161–3, cat. 13. It was reportedly excavated together with other figures in a hunting scene and was displayed in the Uffizi (where it remains) by 1591 with two dogs and a man. For the date of the gift (1560) and of its arrival in Florence (1567–68), see Margaret Daly Davis, 'La galleria di sculture antiche di Cosimo I a Palazzo Pitti', in *Le arti del principato mediceo* (Florence: SPES, 1980), pp. 33 and 43, n. 56. Acidini Luchinat, *Castello*, 117, states that the existing boar in the grotto was executed in 1791–92 by Innocenzo Spinazzi, although without an archival reference or documentation. If this is true, the question remains whether the replacement is a copy of the original, which seems the most likely hypothesis. (The garden at that time was in the possession of the Lorenese ruler of Tuscany, Ferdinand III.)

44. Ashworth, 'The Persistent Beast: Recurring Images in Early Zoological Illustration', in *Natural Sciences and the Arts*, pp. 46–66, and Ashworth, 'Marcus Gheeraerts and the Aesopic Connection in Seventeenth-Century Scientific Illustration', *Art Journal* 44 (1984), pp. 132–8. Ackerman, in '"Naturalism" and Scientific Illustration', and 'Artists in Renaissance Science', makes a similar point.

45. The above account is derived from Clarke, *Rhinoceros*, pp. 9, 16–27, 109, and 155–62; Cole, 'Dürer's Rhinoceros', vol. 1, pp. 337–56; and Lach, *Asia*, vol. 2,pt. 1, pp. 158–71. Clarke, p. 109 and fig. 79, also notes an engraving after Dürer's woodcut by the Florentine Enea Vico of 1548.

46. David Knight, *Zoological Illustration*, (Folkstone, England: Dawson, 1977), pp. 15–16. Clarke, *Rhinoceros*, pp. 20–2, notes the similarity of the animal's plates to the armor in one of Dürer's drawings.

47. Phyllis Williams Lehmann, *Cyriacus of Ancona's Egyptian Visit and its Reflections in Gentile Bellini and Hieronymus Bosch* (Locust Valley, N.Y.: J. J. Augustin, 1977), p. 10, and fig. 33 illustrates the manuscript in the Biblioteca Medicea-Laurenziana.

48. Lamberto Donati, 'La Giraffa', *Maso Finiguerra* 3 (1938), pp. 147–68; and Lloyd, *African Animals*, p. 51 and fig. 33, for the engraving in Sigismondo Tizio's 'Historiae Senenses', Bibl. Vaticana, Ms. Chigi. G.11.36. For the engraving, see also Hind, *Early Italian Engraving*, vol. 5, p. 307 and vol. 7, pl. 911. Masi, *Ricordanze*, 18, tells of its death soon after.

49. Lloyd, *African Animals*, p. 96; Charles D. Cuttler, 'Exotics in Post-Medieval European Art: Giraffes and Centaurs', *Artibus et Historiae* 23 (1991), pp. 161–79; and Christianne L. Joost-Gaugier, 'Lorenzo the Magnificent and the Giraffe as a Symbol of Power', *Artibus et Historiae* 16 (1987), pp. 91–4.

50. Lach, *Asia*, p. 2, pt. 1:88, notes that André Thevet collected and made drawings, from which woodcuts were made by Jean Cousin and his shop.

51. Horst W. Janson, *Apes and Ape Lore in the Middle Ages and the Renaissance* (London: The Warburg Institute, University of London, 1952), pp. 15–16 and 43–4; and see the one illustrated in Lloyd, *African Animals*, p. 15, fig. 9. Janson, pp. 110–11 and Plate XIa, notes an ape in a mid-thirteenth-century English manuscript border eating a fruit with one hand and scratching his leg with another, which must have been a more common motif than his single example suggests.

52. Glenn M. Andres, *The Villa Medici in Rome*, 2 vols (New York and London: Garland, 1976) vol. 1, pp. 176 and 306, and vol. 2, p. 125, n. 354.

53. Cuttler, 'Exotics', p. 165, gives a number of examples.

54. Landucci, *Diario fiorentino*, 377; and Agostino Lapini, *Diario fiorentino dal 1252 al 1596*, ed. Giuseppe Odoardo Corazzini (Florence: G. C. Sansoni, 1900), p. 103

55. Schaefer, 'Studiolo of Francesco', pp. 101–2.

56. Lappini, *Diario fiorentino*, p. 258.

57. Landucci, *Diario fiorentino*, pp. 52–3; Vasari, *Vite*, vol. 8, p. 114; Donati, 'Giraffa', pp. 247–68; Lloyd, *African Animals*, pp. 49–52; Julian-Matthias Kliemann, *Politische und humanistische Ideen der Medici in der Villa Poggio a Caiano: Untersuchungen zu den Fresken der Sala Grande* (Bamberg: Bamberger Fotodruck Schadel & Wehle, 1976), pp. 15–17 and 19–20; and Joost-Gaugier, 'Lorenzo and the Giraffe', pp. 94–5.

58. Trexler, *Public Life*, p. 460.

59. On diplomatic gifts, see Trexler, *Public Life*, pp. 323–6.

60. Lach, *Asia*, 2, pt. vol. 1, pp. 136–9; and Silvio A. Bedini, 'The Papal Pachyderms', *Proceedings of the American Philosophical Society* 125 (1981), pp. 75–90.

61. Lach, *Asia*, 2, pt. 1:135–149; and Matthias Winner, 'Raffael malt einem Elefanten', *Mitteilungen des Kunsthistorischen Institutes in Florenz* 11 (1964), pp. 71–109.

62. Winner, 'Raffael', pp. 104–5.

63. Paolo Giovio, *Ragionamenti sopra I motti, et disegni d'arme, et d'amore* (Venice: Giordano Ziletti, 1556), pp. 37–9; Karla Langedijk, *Portraits of the Medici, 15th to 18th Centuries*, 3 vols (Florence: Studio per Edizioni Scelte, 1981–87), vol. 1, p. 238, no. 1.38r.

64. John Shearman, *Andrea del Sarto*, 2 vols (Oxford: Clarendon Press, 1965) vol. 1, pp. 78–9 and 85, and vol. 2, p. 246, no. 57; Kliemann, *Poggio a Caiano*, pp. 15–22; and Janet Cox-Rearick, *Dynasty and Destiny in Medici Art: Pontormo, Leo X, and the Two Cosimos* (Princeton: Princeton University Press, 1984), pp. 107–10, and 87–116 for the *salone*. This is one of four historical allegories decorating the *salone*. Andrea del Sarto's *Tribute to Caesar* was one of two historical allegories planned by Paolo Giovio; the other two belong to a later program by Vincenzo Borghini. Questions have been raised about which Caesar (Caesar Augustus or Julius Caesar) and which tribute, since Vasari, *Vite*, vol. 5, p. 36, identified it only as a tribute of animals to Caesar, and Raffaele Borghini later specified the tribute to Caesar in Egypt (Kliemann, p. 22; and Cox-Rearick, pp. 108–10), but the fresco is not an accurate representation of an historical scene and does not appear to correspond with a specific event.

65. Landucci, *Diario fiorentino*, pp. 52–3, lists the giraffe, goats, wethers, and a large lion; Vasari, *Vite*, vol. 8, p. 114, notes parrots, monkeys, camels, and the giraffe. Others, in Kliemann, *Poggio a Caiano*, pp. 16 and 173, add the brown race-horse. Cox-Rearick, *Dynasty and Destiny*, p. 107, argues that the scene alludes to Pope Leo X primarily and Lorenzo only secondarily, while Kliemann, p. 19, believes the opposite.

66. Raffaele Borghini, *Il Riposo* (Florence: Giorgio Marescotti, 1584), p. 626, explained that it referred to when Lorenzo was presented with foreign animals.

67. Vasari, *Vite*, vol. 5, p. 36, in the life of Andrea del Sarto, identifies the animals as 'pappagalli ... che sono cosa rarissima; ... capre indiane, leoni, giraffi, leonze, lupi cervieri, scimie ...'. Kliemann, *Poggio a Caiano*, p. 18, identifies the animal facing the dog as a civet cat, which is likely given the resemblance to the figure in Pierre Belon's *Observations*, illustrated in Lloyd,

African Animals, fig. 71, who notes, p. 97, that the Florentine consul in Alexandria owned one. For Allori's additions, see Silvestro Bardazzi and Eugenio Castellani, *La Villa Medici di Poggio a Caiano*, 2 vols (Parma: Edizioni del Palazzo, 1981), vol. 2, p. 513.

68.   On the comparison of ancients and exotics, see Ryan, 'Assimilating New Worlds', pp. 527–9 and *passim*.

69.   Samuel Berner, 'Florentine Society in the Late Sixteenth and Early Seventeenth Centuries', *Studies in the Renaissance* 18 (1971), pp. 179–86. This is one of the themes of Cox-Rearick, *Dynasty and Destiny*.

70.   Valeriano's first book of the *Hieroglyphia*, on the lion, was dedicated to Cosimo. Langedijk, *Portraits*, vol. 2, p. 889, no. 42.89r, for Francesco's device. The ram also referred to Francesco's astrological sign, Aries. Also in the niche is a bull, which may allude to Cosimo as well, since a charging bull is on one of his medals. Langedijk, 1:491, no. 27.149r.a.

71.   Denys Hay, *Europe: the Emergence of an Idea* (Edinburgh: Edinburgh University Press, 1968), pp. 99–106; and Christensen, 'Image of Europe', pp. 257–80. For Leandro Alberti, see Hay, 'The Italian View of Renaissance Italy', *Renaissance Essays* (London and Ronceverte: The Hambeldon Press, 1988), pp. 381–8.

72.   Cesare Ripa, *Iconologia*, 1603, facs. edn (Hildesheim: Georg Olms Verlag, 1984), pp. 332–9. The personifications are not in Ripa's first unillustrated edition of 1593. For sixteenth-century personifications of the four continents, see *America: Bride of the Sun* (Ghent: Imschoot, 1992), pp. 301–4; Hugh Honour, *The New Golden Land: European Images of America from the Discoeries to the Present Time* (New York: Pantheon Books), pp. 84–9; Honour, *The European Vision of America* (Cleveland: The Cleveland Museum of Art, 1975), pp. 112–19; and Claire Le Corbeiller, 'Miss America and Her Sisters: Personifications of the Four Parts of the World', *The Metropolitan Museum of Art Bulletin* 19 (1961): pp. 207–23. Hay, *Europe*, pp. 104–5, discusses the significance of Ripa's images.

73.   For the superiority of Western culture, in addition to the sources noted above, see Richard G. Cole, 'Sixteenth-Century Travel Books as a Source of European Attitudes toward Non-White and Non-Western Culture', *Proceedings of the American Philosophical Society* 116 (1972): pp. 59–67.

74.   This has been suggested in a larger context by Elliott, *Old World and the New*, pp. 15–16, and 32; and by Grafton, *New Worlds, Ancient Texts*, p. 6.

3.

Remarks on the Collections of Rudolf II: The *Kunstkammer* as a Form of *Representatio*

Thomas DaCosta Kaufmann

A series of recent discoveries calls for the reinterpretation of the fabled and long misunderstood collections of the Emperor Rudolf II of Habsburg (reigned 1576–1612). Since Julius von Schlosser's treatment of the late Renaissance *Kunst- und Wunderkammer*, Rudolf's collections have until recently been regarded as a kind of circus sideshow lacking any organizing principle or orderly display. Unicorn horns and magic stones are said to have been heaped up alongside great paintings by Dürer and Brueghel throughout the rooms of the imperial castle in Prague. The Emperor is supposed to have grown increasingly mad as he spent his days contemplating his strange, secret treasure instead of tending to affairs of state.[1]

I would like to sketch in brief outline a different picture, in the hope of stimulating further discussion. I believe that we can now see Rudolf II's collections not only as a refuge for contemplation, but also as an expression of his imperial magnificence and a symbol of his claims to power. Information about visits to his *Kunstkammer*, its disposition and display, a contemporary inventory, and the imagery of key objects made for it suggests that the imperial collections had an orderly arrangement, a symbolism of their own, and a role in contemporary diplomacy. Rudolf II's *Kunstkammer*, like much of the art and public ceremony of his reign, was a form of *representatio*, of imperial self-representation.

First of all Rudolf's collections were by no means kept secret from outsiders. While, like other princely collections of the time, Rudolf's was not normally accessible to commoners – although several saw it – it was regularly used for formal diplomatic functions. The Savoyard envoy to the imperial court, Carlo Francesco Manfredi di Luserna, reports that ambassadors were customarily shown the collections before their departure from Prague.[2] Ambassadors were also taken to the *Kunstkammer* when the Emperor wanted to give a sign of his favor in order to make a specific political point. For example, when in September, 1601, the Venetian ambassador Piero Duodo congratulated Rudolf on military successes against the Turks, the Emperor rewarded Duodo with a visit to the *Kunstkammer*.[3] Dignitaries on state visits to Prague were also usually taken to see the Emperor's collections. Cardinal Alessandro D'Este, Archduke Maximilian III, Grand Master of the Teutonic Knights and Regent of the Tyrol, the Elector Duke Christian II of Saxony, and Duke Maximilian I of Bavaria are known to have seen it. It is significant that on Christian II's visit to Prague in 1607 the only private audience he had with the Emperor was spent visiting the collections.[4] Rudolf II seems to have spoken in and through his *Kunstkammer*.

Other avid collectors like Christian II or Maximilian of Bavaria, with whom Rudolf carried on a lively exchange of gifts, would no doubt have understood one of the messages of the Emperor's *Kunstkammer*. This message, as suggested in contemporary writing, was that a prince expresses his *virtus*, his worth, in his collections. And so just as Rudolf II demonstrated one of the imperial virtues, his magnanimity, in the gifts he sent to other courts, he may be said to have exhibited his magnificence in his collections.[5] One perceptive observer who would have been familiar with collections, since his own family had a very important one in Italy, explicitly recognized this. Cardinal d'Este wrote that on his visit to Prague Rudolf took him to see 'his most recondite and valuable things, and particularly his paintings, marvelous for their quantity and quality. Besides them vases of precious stones of various kinds, statues, and clocks ... a treasure worthy of him who possesses it (*tesoro degno di chi il possede*).'[6] Thus it may have been something more than a sense of quality alone that drove Rudolf to possess masterpieces by Dürer, Brueghel, Raphael, Correggio, and Titian, *commessi in pietre dure*, fine sculpture by Adriaen De Vries and Giambologna, and clocks in abundance. He may have had something else in mind when he amassed what, in comparison with other courts north of the Alps, was the biggest and best collection of its time. In an age of princely collectors, Rudolf had a *Kunstkammer* that was worthy of his rank as Holy Roman Emperor, as first among European rulers: he was first among collectors.[7]

Rudolf's collections consequently received a disposition that emphasized their role as a form of imperial display. Rudolf transformed the Prague castle to include special housing for his *Kunstkammer*; in reality he acted very differently from the traditional portrayal of him as uninterested in architecture and the orderly exhibition of his collections. From about 1590 a group of artists and artisans, mainly of Italian origin, under the direction of Martino Gambarini and Giovanni Maria Filippi, built and decorated rooms for the collections in the first and second floors above the stables in what is now the second courtyard of the Prague castle. One of the rooms Rudolf had constructed was the famed 'Spanish Room' (*Spanischer Saal*) – a picture gallery. Next to it was the so-called 'New Room' (*Neuer* or *Neu Saal*), a hall for the display of sculpture, articulated by niches in which were placed stucco and bronze statues by the imperial sculptor Adriaen De Vries. Both the Spanish and New Rooms had ceilings with illusionistic paintings by Pauwel and Jan Vredeman de Vries. In a series of smaller vaulted rooms in the adjoining wing were placed objets d'art, small sculptures, jewels, books, and natural objects. Alongside these rooms ran a corridor in which paintings were hung; additional paintings were to be found in galleries on the second floor of this wing.[8]

I believe we can now identify a drawing in Munich, formerly thought to be a plan for the Antiquarium there, as a preliminary design for the New Room in Prague[9] [not reproduced here]. The style of the figures and decorative details is that of Rudolf's court painter, Bartholomäus Spranger. In comparison with a drawing signed by Spranger of slightly later date [not reproduced here], the Munich drawing not only reveals the same ductus of line, handling of wash, type and stance of figure, and fleeting characterization of facial features, with eyes and noses indicated by open loops, but also treats details like the mascarones and the profile of the socle of the figure in the right-hand niche similarly. We know that Spranger was involved with decorative projects both in Italy and in palaces in Vienna and Prague, where one of his frescoes has been rediscovered.[10] Rudolf was thus using some of his most experienced, as well as best, talents to design the space for his collections.

The drawing shows niches for the display of sculpture like those in the New Room, which later engravings also represent with rectangular panels similar to those shown here. Though the sculpture is not drawn to scale, several pieces can be identified with works that were probably in the Emperor's collection. For example, the group of Nessus and Deianeira resembles bronzes by De Vries and Giambologna that probably belonged to Rudolf.[11] The copy of the Torso Belvedere perched on a socle must also have been in Prague, because a contemporary portrait of the court artist Hans von Aachen shows it in a similar place, posed on a pediment. Spranger's drawing again emphasizes the formal character of rooms for Rudolf's collection, and at the same time points to parallels with the Italian *tribuna*, a type of room with niches for the display of sculpture exemplified by the *Antisala* of the Marciana Library in Venice.[12]

The disposition of rooms in the palace to house the collections further corresponds to the systematic organization and programmatic arrangement revealed in a recently published inventory of the *Kunstkammer* from the years 1607–11. The inventory deals with objets d'art, small sculpture, scientific instruments, books, and naturalia. These are just the objects kept in a separate wing of the palace adjoining the Spanish Room, and the fact that they are cataloged according to type suggests that they may have constituted a distinct part of the collection. One may perhaps assume that paintings and sculpture had their own inventories. At any rate the listing of objects in the 1607–11 inventory proceeds logically according to material and then according to size. The entire collection is cataloged rationally; it may be grouped under the general categories of *artificialia* and *naturalia*.[13]

The inventory thus demonstrates that the collection not only had its own system of classification similar to that of other contemporary collections, but also that, like them, it was encyclopedic in scope. Like the *Studiolo* of Francesco I de'Medici in Florence or the *Kunstkammer* of Archduke Ferdinand of the Tyrol in Ambras, but on an even larger scale, Rudolf's *Kunstkammer* contained choice examples of all that was to be found in nature or made by man.[14] It thus embodied a conception of the Renaissance world view in which the world of man, the microcosm, may be seen to parallel the greater world, or macrocosm. By having specimens of all parts of creation, Rudolf II's *Kunstkammer* represented the universe in microcosm. In the words of a Renaissance topos applied by Samuel a Quiccheberg in a book of 1565 to the *Kunstkammer*, Rudolf's collection, like others of the time, was a theater of the world.[15]

With Rudolf II it is difficult to know, however, how much the notion of a *Kunstkammer* as a theater of the world is metaphor and how much magic. For Quiccheberg's conception is drawn specifically from a book by Giulio Camillo on the memory theater. In Camillo's system there are not only correspondences but also magical links between the microcosm and the macrocosm. Man may form a magic memory through which he grasps the world, reflecting the macrocosm of the universe in the microcosm of his mind. Through the mediation of the imperial *antiquarius* Jacopo Strada, Quiccheberg's conceptions were no doubt known in Prague, and where Quiccheberg had used Camillo's system for its organizing principles, Rudolf may have grasped at the esoteric significance implicit in the comparison of *Kunstkammer* to memory theater.[16] Did the Emperor, who is otherwise known to have been fascinated with what we might call occult thinking, also view the objects in his *Kunstkammer* as talismans which would strengthen his power? Did he think of his *Kunstkammer* as a magical memory theater through which he could grasp and control the greater world?[17]

However we interpret Rudolf's own point of view, the notion of a theater of the world, to be organized and perhaps controlled by man, guides us into the realm of thinking in which originated the symbolism of key objects made especially for the *Kunstkammer,* and through them toward an understanding of the principle of the collection as a whole. For much of the iconography of the Rudolfine *Kunstkammer* pieces portrays the world as a microcosm controlled by the Emperor. Take for example the fountain by Wenzel Jamnitzer, presented to the Emperor, of which four figures from the base still survive in Vienna (see Figure 5.3.1). From a seventeenth-century description[18] we know that the fountain once stood ten feet high and when assembled must thus have been a central object in the *Kunstkammer*. It represented the cosmos in the form of an imperial crown standing on a base; to give an idea of the shape of its upper part, the crown made for Rudolf II (Figure 5.3.5) is illustrated here. Four gods representing the four seasons made up the base. Above them came gods and creatures symbolizing the four elements. Above them in the heavenly sphere were four winds and four archangels. Then came four eagles said to stand for the House of Austria. In the place of the topmost diadem sat Jupiter astride an eagle, symbolizing the Emperor. This was a common enough association in Rudolfine, and indeed imperial, iconography, as in an allegory by von Aachen in the Harrach Collection. Jupiter sits astride an eagle, with Bellona beside him holding an imperial crown, and casts down thunderbolts against the Emperor's enemies, the Turks. On what would correspond to the outer bands of a crown the fountain further displayed symbols of the body politic of the earthly empire, including finally, on the lower circumference, arms of the Habsburgs' lands.

Similar imagery symbolizing the Emperor's control of the world characterizes other works contained in Rudolf's collections, including pictures by the imperial painter Giuseppe Arcimboldo (see Figure 5.3.3). Arcimboldo's paintings of the *Seasons* and the *Elements* have been associated with the *Kunstkammer* ever since Schlosser first published his thesis that these images

Figure 5.3.1   Wenzel Jamnitzer and Johann Gregor von Schardt, *Spring*, from fountain, Vienna, Kunsthistorisches Museum

Figure 5.3.2   Crown of Rudolf II, 1602, Vienna, Weltliche Schatzkammer

were jokes expressing the disorder of Rudolf's mind and the unseriousness of his collections.[19] And indeed in another sense we can make a connection between them, for like the *Kunstkammer*, Arcimboldo's work is based on the system of correspondences of microcosm to macrocosm and in turn to the body politic.[20] We can however no longer accept the traditional notion that Arcimboldo's pictures are simply jokes. Poems presented with his paintings when they were given to the Emperor reveal instead that they are allegories of imperial power. Arcimboldo's images of the *Seasons* and *Elements* were meant to suggest that as the objects exist together in harmony in the individual

Figure 5.3.3   Giuseppe Arcimboldo, *Fire*, 1566, Vienna, Kunsthistoriches Museum

heads – the cannon and wicks in *Fire* (Figure 5.3.3) for instance – and as
harmony also exists between the individual heads representing the elements
and seasons, so does the world exist in harmony under the beneficent rule of
the Emperor. As the Emperor rules over the world of states, the body politic,
so he may be seen to rule over the seasons and elements, which consequently

are adorned with Habsburg emblems. *Fire*, for example, wears the Golden Fleece and the coat of arms of the House of Austria, and *Winter* wears another Habsburg device, the striking iron from the chain of the Fleece, and the letter M for Emperor Maximilian II, for whom this particular image was made. Arcimboldo's portrait of Rudolf II as Vertumnus is the culmination of this sort of imagery, depicting him directly as god of the seasons and implicitly as god of the elements, and, with its combination of fruits and flowers from all seasons, suggesting the return of a golden age with his reign.[21]

The imagery of Jamnitzer's fountain and Arcimboldo's painting is in turn directly related to the decoration of the Prague castle under Rudolf II. Another illusionistic ceiling by Pauwel Vredeman de Vries is described by Karel Van Mander as a depiction of Jupiter in the midst of the four elements, and the parts of the year, the twelve months.[22] The imagery of this ceiling seems furthermore to parallel the message expressed in the rooms containing Rudolf's collection below. As Zeus above rules the elements and parts of the year, so Rudolf rules the microcosm below, his *Kunstkammer*.

This symbolism seems further to support a new interpretation of Rudolf II's collections. Rudolf's *Kunstkammer* had a role in diplomacy that was stressed by its stately setting. It had a carefully organized content based on the system of correspondences. It is clear that it had at least one convincing message, since perceptive observers like Cardinal d'Este could see it as worthy of the Emperor. I believe that we may also consider Rudolf's possession of the world in microcosm in his *Kunstkammer* an expression of his symbolic mastery of the greater world.

NOTES

This article is a revised version of a paper read at the 65th annual meeting of the College Art Association of America in Los Angeles in February, 1977, which was in turn based on material in a chapter of my dissertation. 'Variations on the Imperial Theme: Studies in Ceremonial, Art, and Collecting in the Age of Maximilian II and Rudolf II'. Harvard University, 1977, published as *Variations on the Imperial Theme in the Age of Maximilian II and Rudolf II*, New York and London, 1978.

1. Schlosser's interpretation is presented in his *Die Kunst- und Wunderkammern der Spatrenaissance*, Leipzig, 1908, pp. 76–82, following in part that of Josef Svatek, 'Die Rudolfinische Kunstkammer in Prag', in *Culturhistorische Bilder aus Bohmen*, Vienna, 1879, pp. 227ff. In her recently published introduction 'Die Kunstkammer Kaiser Rudolfs II. in Prag, ein inventar aus den Jahren 1607–1611', in 'Das Kunstkammerinventar Kaiser Rudolfs II. 1607–1611', *Jahrbuch der Kunsthistorischen Sammlungen in Wien*, vol. 72, 1976 (published in January 1977), pp. xii–xvi, Rotraud Bauer reviews and criticizes the previous interpretation of Rudolf II's collections. Her introduction now provides the most convenient and complete bibliography on the collections. R. J. W. Evans, *Rudolf II and his World: A Study in Intellectual History*, Oxford, 1973, p. 178 n. still argues, however, that Rudolf used his collection for 'private contemplation' and that he was 'very secretive about its contents'.

2. The commoners Ulrich Krafft, Jacques Esprinchard, and Melchior Goldast all saw the collection: for convenient references to their visits see Evans, *Rudolf II and his World*, p. 178 n. Di Luserna's remarks were occasioned by a visit to Rudolf's *Kunstkammer* in 1604; Vincenzo Promis, ed., 'Ambasciata di Carlo Francesco Manfredi di Luserna a Praga nel 1604', *Miscellanea di Storia Italiana edita per cura della Regla deputazione di storia patria*, vol. 16, ser. 2, 3, 1877, pp. 583, 594, and

Adolfo Venturi, 'Zur Geschichte der Kunstsammlungen Kaiser Rudolfs II.', *Repertorium für Kunstwissenschaft*, vol. 7, 1885, p. 15.

3. Vienna, Haus-, Hof-, und Staatsarchiv, Dispacci di Germania (hereafter HHStA), Secreta 31, September 10, 1601, cited in part in H. von Voltelini, 'Urkunden und Regesten aus dem K.u.K. Haus-, Hof-, und Staatsarchiv in Wien', *Jahrbuch der Kunsthistorischen Sammlungen des Allerhöchsten Kaiserhauses*, vol. 19, 1898, reg. no. 16257.

4. Cardinal d'Este's visit is reported in a letter of August 23, 1604, Archivio Storico Estense, Modena, Carteggio Ambasciatori Estensi, Busta 183, quoted in part in German translation in Venturi, 'Zur Geschichte', p. 15. Archduke Maximilian III's visit is mentioned in another letter of August 23, 1604, by Girolamo Manzuolo, Archivio Storico Estense, Modena, Carteggio Ambasciatori Estensi, Busta 69. Sources for Duke Christian II's visit are Felix Stieve, ed., *Die Politik Baierns 1591–1607*, part 2 (*Briefe und Akten zur Geschichte des dreissigjährigen Krieges*, vol. 5), Munich, 1883, reg. no. 898–900; an account of Federigo Soranzo, HHStA, Secreta 37, July 8 and 16, 1607; and that of the papal nuncio Antonio Caetani, M. Linhartova, ed., *Antonii Caetani Nuntii Apostolici apud Imperatorem Epistulae et Acta 1607–1611*, vol. 1, Prague, 1932, p. 148. For Duke Maximilian I's visit see Stieve, *Die Politik Baierns*, part 1, Munich, 1879, p. 1, and Helmut Dotterweich, *Der Junge Maximilian*, Munich, 1962, p. 127.

5. See, for example, the discussion of the ideological basis of the Bavarian collections in Renate von Busch, *Studien zur Sud-deutschen Antiken-sammlungen des 16. Jahrhunderts*, dissertation, Tübingen, 1973, pp. 102ff., 110f., 160ff. The founding documents of the Munich *Schatzkammer* state that it was meant to express and increase the reputation of the Wittelsbachs: H. Brunner, ed., *Schatzkammer der Residenz*, Munich, 1970, pp. 7ff. For the concept of magnificence see, for example, A. D. Fraser Jenkins, 'Cosimo de' Medici's Patronage', *Journal of the Warburg and Courtauld Institutes*, vol. 33, 1870, pp. 162–70.

6. I am quoting from the Italian text of Cardinal D'Este's letter in Modena, *loc. cit.*, which in the version printed in Venturi, 'Zur Geschichte', p. 15, has had a fateful effect on the interpretation of the collections (for which see Bauer, 'Die Kunstkammer Kaiser Rudolfs', p. xii).

7. Evans, *Rudolf II and his World*, p. 178, calls Rudolf *'primus inter pares'* among collectors. See also the remarks in H. Trevor-Roper, *The Plunder of the Arts in the Seventeenth Century*, London, 1971. Rudolf's efforts to obtain and preserve the Ambras *Kunstkammer* and his interest in the establishment of a dynastic collection may also be a reflection of the idea of a collection as a representative form of the rank and glory of the House of Austria; see A. Lhotsky, 'Die Geschichte der Sammlungen', *Festschrift des Kunsthistorischen Museums in Wien*, part 2, vol. 1, Vienna, 1941/1945, pp. 240, 289. In an essay published subsequent to the completion of this paper Peter Thomas succinctly states 'The *Kunstkabinett* itself was a form of propaganda ...'; 'Charles I of England: The Tragedy of Absolutism', in A. G. Dickens, ed., *The Courts of Europe*, London, 1977, p. 201.

8. This paragraph summarizes the important article by Jarmila Krčálová, 'Poznámky k rudolfinské architektuře', *Umění*, vol. 23, no. 6, 1975, pp. 479–525.

9. Erich Hubala, 'Ein Entwurf für das Antiquarium der Münchener Residenz 1568', *Münchener Jahrbuch der bildenden Kunst*, vol. 9–10, 1958–59, pp. 141–2, fig. 6. Both the lack of resemblance to other designs for or the actual appearance of the Antiquarium and the presence of what seems to be post-antique sculpture (e.g., the Nessus and Deianeira group) in the drawing militate against Hubala's attribution, however, Konrad Oberhuber first suggested (orally) that the drawing was by Spranger. Differences of ink and style in the drawing suggest that it may in fact be by two hands: the figures and details by Spranger, and the elevation without shading by an architectural draftsman, probably one of the court *Baumeister* with whom Spranger presumably cooperated.

10. For Spranger's work as a decorator see Konrad Oberhuber, 'Die stilistische Entwicklung im Werk Bartholomäus Sprangers', unpublished dissertation. Vienna, 1958, pp. 74ff, and Jaroír Neumann, 'Kleine Beiträge zur rudolfinischen Kunst und ihre Auswirkungen', *Umení*, vol. 18, no. 3, 1970, pp. 142–50.

11. Although no Nessus and Deianeira group is mentioned in the 1607–11 inventory of Rudolf's collection, an inventory of 1619 describes such a sculpture, possibly identifiable with a work by de Vries: see Lars Olaf Larsson, *Adrian de Vries*, Vienna and Munich, 1967, pp. 53f. The provenance of similar groups by Giambologna, which the sculpture depicted in the drawing resembles even more closely, is discussed in Elizabeth Dhanens, *Jean Boulogne, Giovanni Bologna Fiammingo*, Brussels, 1956, pp. 200ff. As the 1607–11 inventory does not mention Rudolf II's large-scale sculpture and antiquities, both of which were housed in the New Room, it of course stands to reason that objects shown in the drawing would not be found in this inventory.

12. Karel Van Mander, *Het Schilderboek* ..., Haarlem, 1604, fol. 291r, mentions that von Aachen had sent Pieter Isaacsz. several drawings including a self-portrait, which must have served as the source of the image illustrated here as Fig. 4 [not reproduced here; it was Jan Pietersz. Saenredam after Peter Isaacz, *Portrait of Hans von Aachen*, engraving, 1601 (Munich, Staatliche Graphische Sammlung)]. A preparatory drawing for the print by Isaacsz. is in the Kunsthalle, Hamburg, inventory no. 22066. For the *tribuna* type see Marilyn Perry, 'The Statuario public of the Venetian Republic', *Saggi e Memoria di storia dell'arte*, vol. 8, 1972, pp. 75–150, which also cites further literature on the *Antisala*; Detlef Heikamp, 'Zur Geschichte der Uffizien-Tribuna und der Kunstschränke in Florenz und Deutschland', *Zeitschrift für Kunstgeschichte*, vol. 26, no. 3/4, 1963, pp. 193–268; and Jeffrey M. Muller, 'Rubens's Museum of Antique Sculpture: An Introduction', *The Art Bulletin*, vol. 59, no. 4, pp. 571–82. The New Room in Prague is not of course specifically patterned on the Pantheon, whose use as a model is discussed by Perry and Muller. The model for Prague, as for the Munich *Antiquarium*, may rather have been Giulio Romano's design for the palace in Mantua, discussed most recently by Kurt Forster, 'Giulio Romano's "Museum" of Sculpture in the Palazzo Ducale at Mantua', lecture delivered at the 66th annual meeting of the College Art Association of America in New York, January, 1978. Giulio's designs were recorded in drawings made for Jacopo Strada, and perhaps owned by his son Ottavio; both Jacopo and Ottavio served in the role of imperial *antiquarius*.

13. For the interpretation of the organization of Rudolf's collections see Erwin Neumann, 'Das Inventar der rudolfinischen Kunstkammer von 1607–11', *Analecta Reginensia I, Queen Christina of Sweden, Documents and Studies*, Stockholm, 1966, pp. 262–5, and Bauer, 'Die Kunstkammer Kaiser Rudolfs'. Neumann's interesting suggestion of a category of *scientifica* seems to me rather to be subsumed under *artificialia*.

14. See Luigi Salerno, 'Arte, Scienza e collezioni nel Manierismo', *Scritti in Onore di Mario Salmi*, vol. 3, n.p., 1963, pp. 198ff; Luciano Berti, *Il Principe dello Studiolo*, Florence, 1967; Helkamp, 'Geschichte der Uffizien-Tribuna', pp. 208f.; Niels von Holst, *Creators, Collectors, and Connoisseurs*, London, 1967, p. 103; and Elisabeth Scheicher, 'Kunstkammer', in *Die Kunstkammer, Sammlungen Schloss Ambras*, Innsbruck, 1977, p. 15.

15. Samuel a Quiccheberg, *Inscriptiones vel tituli Theatri Amplissimi* ..., Munich, 1565. For an important early discussion on the relation of Quiccheberg's ideas to collecting – a subject which has by now gained a fairly extensive bibliography – see Rudolf Berliner, 'Zur älteren Geschichte der allgemeinen Museumslehre in Deutschland', *Münchener Jahrbuch der bildenden Kunst*, vol. 5, 1928, pp. 324–52. For the topos of the theater of the world see R. Bernheimer, 'Theatrum Mundi', *The Art Bulletin*, vol. 38, no. 4, 1956, pp. 225–47.

16. Quiccheberg, *op. cit.*, fol. 14v, explicitly states that he is not using the world *theatrum* metaphorically, as other writers have done, but has taken it from Camillo. For a brilliant explication of Camillo's thought see Frances A. Yates, *The Art of Memory*, Harmondsworth, 1966, pp. 173ff. Although she does not refer to Quiccheberg or Strada, Dame Frances has also suggested that Rudolf II's *Kunstkammer* may have been planned along the lines of a memory system, in *The Rosicrucian Enlightenment*, London, 1972, p. 68. Jacopo Strada had also been active in the formation of the Munich collections, to which Quiccheberg's book is immediately related: see Bauer, 'Die Kunstkammer Kaiser Rudolfs', p. xxxvii.

17. For Rudolf and the 'occult arts' see Evans, *Rudolf II and his World*, pp. 196ff. It is possible that Rudolf's collections may have in turn inspired an occult system. Dame Frances Yates has suggested to me that the organization of Giordano Bruno's *De Imaginum Signorum ... compositione* (*Opera Latina Conscripta*, Florence, 1889, pp. 87ff.) with its symbolism and complex images was inspired by Rudolf's *Kunstkammer*, which Bruno may have seen while on his visit to Prague.

18. This description is based on a report printed in Hans Boesch, 'Urkunden und Auszüge aus dem Archiv und der Bibliothek des Germanischen Museums in Nürnberg', *Jahrbuch der Kunsthistorischen Sammlungen des Allerhöchsten Kaiserhauses*, vol. 7, 1889, reg. no. 4732.

19. Schlosser, *Die Kunst- und Wunderkammern*, p. 88.

20. Salerno, 'Arte, Scienza e collezioni', and Sven Alfons, *Giuseppe Arcimboldo, Tidskrift för Konstvetenskap*, vol. 31, 1957, pp. 151ff. also relate the microcosm-macrocosm analogy expressed in Arcimboldo's painting to the *Kunstkammer*.

21. Thomas DaCosta Kaufmann, 'Arcimboldo's Imperial Allegories', *Zeitschrift für Kunstgeschichte*, vol. 39, no. 4, 1976, pp. 275–96.

22. Van Mander, *Het Schilderboek*, fol. 276v. Another description contained in an evaluation of De Vries' paintings by the Elders of the Prague Painters' Guild describes the room with the ceiling as located between the palace (*palacz*) and the 'Summer House' (*weystupek anebo zumrhauz*) of

Rudolf II; Prague, Statní Ustrŭdni Archiv, Stará Manipulace, F 73/3, February 13, 1599, cited by Karl Köpl, 'Urkunden und Regesten aus dem K. K. Statthalterei Archiv in Prag', *Jahrbuch der Kunsthistorischen Sammlungen des Allerhöchsten Kaiserhauses*, vol. 12, 1891, reg. no. 8320. According to a reconstruction of the Prague castle in the 17th century by Jan Morávek ('Giuseppe Mattei a "Nova Staveni" pražského hradu 1638–1644', *Uměni*, vol. 5, 1957, p. 342) the 'Summer House' of Rudolf II adjoined the wing containing Rudolf's collections, and specifically the gallery with Rudolf's paintings. Thus a room connecting the 'Summer House' to the palace would in fact lead directly to the imperial collection. Could the decoration of the ceiling have been chosen deliberately as an iconographic prelude to the *Kunstkammer*?

4.

Philipp Hainhofer and Gustavus Adolphus's Kunstschrank

Hans-Olof Boström

In a letter of July 1607, Duke Wilhelm V of Bavaria informed his son, the reigning Duke Maximilian I, of a 'citizen of Augsburg, whom, apart from his religion, I hold to be an honourable and intelligent young man, who is learned as well as being a merchant and in whose house I saw all kinds of foreign and strange things as well as almost an entire *Kunstkammer*'.[1]

The man described thus was the merchant Philipp Hainhofer, twenty-nine years old at the time.[2] The Duke had made his acquaintance a year before when visiting the *Kunstkammer* which he mentions.[3] Hainhofer had laid its foundations in 1604 and it was soon to become one of the objects of interest in Augsburg which no distinguished traveller neglected to visit.

Hainhofer was already a prominent man in his home town when Duke Wilhelm met him. He belonged to an old merchant family which had been ennobled by Emperor Rudolf II and which had married into the so-called *Mehrergesellschaft* in Augsburg, a political group uniting the patricians on the one hand and the merchants' guild on the other.[4] In 1605 he had been elected to the city's Greater Council and in 1607 he succeeded his uncle, Hieronymus Hörmann, as political agent to Henry IV of France. This signalled the beginning of his diplomatic career. Soon he was agent to several German princes, conveying political and cultural information from France and Italy in particular and representing his patrons at princely ceremonies (baptisms, marriages, funerals) as well as at political gatherings.

Hainhofer was well suited to such missions. During his years of study in Italy and, later, in Cologne and Holland, he had acquired an extensive knowledge of languages and a profound humanist education. His chief subject of study was law, but throughout his life he also took a lively interest in theology. A convinced Lutheran (hence Duke Wilhelm's only reservation), he displayed great tolerance of religious opponents; this was, in any case, a condition of his successful business with Catholic princes. For example, he did not hesitate to procure relics from North-German princes for the fervent Catholic Wilhelm V.[5]

To begin with, Hainhofer's trade was mainly in Italian silk, but it soon came to include objects of art and luxury articles of all kinds. Increased dealings with princely patrons expanded his field of enterprise still further. He might be commissioned to obtain Netherlandish tapestries or English sheep for Duke Maximilian I of Bavaria,[6] a stallion or pet dog for Archduke Leopold V of Austria,[7] horses, dogs, musicians, domestic servants, spices, provisions, clocks and, above all, books for Duke Augustus the younger of Brunswick-Lüneburg, the foremost German book-collector of his time[8] – in fact, anything suitable for the court of a prince.

His *Kunstkammer*, too, played a part in his commercial activities. Its exhibits might be exchanged or sold and hence it was in a continual state of flux and expansion. Unfortunately, we possess no inventory of the collection: it is only from Hainhofer's letters that we can gain a rough idea of its contents.[9] At first, it seems to have consisted mainly of *conchylia* and *etnographica*, objects which Hainhofer bought for the most part from Dutch merchants on his regular visits to the Lent and Autumn fairs at Frankfurt.[10] The *Kunstkammer* rapidly expanded to include a large number of coins and medals as well as antiquities. Hainhofer maintained a network of what he calls 'representatives and friends' in several European cities.[11] They provided him with the articles necessary for his trade as well as with pieces for his collection and supplied him with the information he communicated to his patrons. The widespread Italian Lumaga family occupied an important place in Hainhofer's commercial activities: it had branches in Nürnberg, Paris, Lyon, Genoa and Turin.[12] In Florence, his brother Christoph was his most important business contact until the latter's death in 1616. It is likely that Hainhofer also utilized the services of the great commercial firms of his native city. The Fugger company, for instance, had branches throughout Europe, that in Lisbon probably providing Hainhofer with the South American items in his collection. Furthermore, he was, of course, visited by the many foreign merchants who passed through Augsburg.

Hainhofer was very proud of his *Kunstkammer*, especially its shells. Once he tells us that 'no one here has such fine shells as I'[13] and, after seeing the 'shells and sea fauna' in the ducal *Kunstkammer* in Munich, he says, 'I should not wish to exchange mine for these'.[14] How dear to his heart his collection was is demonstrated by the statement that 'when someone presents me with a foreign object for my *Kunstkammer*, whether it be of *rebus naturalibus* or *artificialibus*, I experience more pleasure than if he had given me cash'.[15]

Hainhofer was naturally eager to see other *Kunstkammern* and visited several of the great princely collections of the age: the *Kunstkammer* at Munich in 1603 and 1611, the Duke of Württemberg's at Stuttgart in 1616, that of the Saxon Elector at Dresden in 1617 and 1629 and Archduke Ferdinand II's at Ambras in 1628.[16] The most famous one – the Emperor Rudolf II's – he never saw but was well informed about it from his correspondence with artists and friends in Prague, among them his cousin Melchior Hainhofer, who in 1610 was appointed as Imperial Court Councillor.[17]

In his travel-reports Hainhofer often gives expression to his enthusiasm for what he has seen. On being allowed to visit the *Kunstkammer* in Stuttgart, he exclaims: 'I hold this to be a greater act of grace than any that has ever been accorded me and the news has given me more pleasure than anything else I can imagine.'[18] During his stay in Munich in 1611, he visited the *Kunstkammer* three times, but believed that 'to see everything properly not even two or three days are sufficient, rather as many months or more'.[19] And at Ambras in 1628, he complained when dinner was to be served: 'I should much rather have visited the *Kunstkammer* than eat the finest meal.'[20]

In his *curriculum vitae* Hainhofer lists the distinguished visitors to his own *Kunstkammer*. They include, besides a large number of German princes, Archduke Leopold V of Austria, King Gustavus Adolphus of Sweden and the unfortunate Elector Palatine Frederic V, the former *Winterkönig* (all three shortly before their deaths in 1632), some Medici and Orsini princes and several travelling English aristocrats.[21] Among the latter was the most distinguished English collector of the time, Thomas Howard, second Earl of Arundel. On his diplomatic mission to Emperor Ferdinand II in 1636, Lord Arundel spent a week in Augsburg towards the end of July. In the diary kept by William Crowne during the mission no mention is made of a visit to Hainhofer, but Hainhofer himself proudly records that the earl 'came to see my curiosities'.[22] As early as 1626 Hainhofer had asked the German poet Georg Rudolph Weckherlin, at that time Under-Secretary of State to Charles I, to 'bring me into contact with that lover of painting the Earl of Arundel'.[23]

Many of Hainhofer's social equals – patricians, merchants, scholars – had *Kunstkammern* of their own: his truly original achievement lies in his multi-purpose furniture pieces, especially his great *Kunstschränke*. These *Mehrzweckmöbel*, manufactured under his supervision by dozens of artists and craftsmen from various guilds, are, or were at least intended to be, miniature *Kunstkammern*. This is true of the cabinets now in Uppsala and Florence as well as the remains of a *Mehrzweckmöbel* in Vienna. The case of the Pomeranian *Kunstschrank* in Berlin, destroyed in the Second World War, is somewhat different. Unlike the other cabinets I have mentioned, it did not contain collections of *naturalia* and *artificialia*, but instead included a set of instruments for virtually every human occupation. This difference is mainly due to the fact that the cabinet was meant to form only a part of the *Kunstkammer* in the ducal castle at Stettin, for which Hainhofer delivered a plan in 1615.[24]

The Pomeranian *Kunstschrank* was begun first (in 1610), but constant expansion of the not particularly extensive original project delayed its completion until 1617.[25] In the meantime, another cabinet, smaller but otherwise closely related to the Pomeranian one, had been delivered to the Grand Duchess Maria Magdalena of Tuscany in 1613.[26] It is not known to have survived.

These cabinets were made to commission. The other three which I have mentioned were manufactured at Hainhofer's own risk and expense. His untiring efforts to sell them make for amusing reading in John Böttiger's monograph on the *Kunstschrank* given to Gustavus Adolphus. He dispatched letters to princes all over Europe, enclosing descriptions of the cabinets in Latin, English, French, Italian or German. Among those approached – usually via business contacts – were the kings of Denmark, Poland, Spain, England and France, the Queen of France, the Duke of Orléans, Emperor Ferdinand II, Empress Maria Anna and the *Signoria* of Genoa.[27]

In December 1632 Hainhofer wrote to Georg Rudolph Weckherlin in London asking him to find some nobleman, or perhaps the king or queen, to buy 'a fine table' (the piece of furniture now in Vienna), the drawers of which contained 'medicinal and toilet articles, all kinds of playthings, a musical instrument and many other fine objects'.[28] Hainhofer probably met Weckherlin in 1616 in the latter's home town of Stuttgart, while both were taking part in the splendid ceremonies surrounding the princely baptism in March of that year.[29] This is just one of many examples of Hainhofer's ability to use casual acquaintances to promote his affairs.

The *Kunstschrank* in Florence – or *stipo tedesco* as it is usually called – was made between 1619 and 1626, and by 1628 Hainhofer had already succeeded in selling it to Archduke Leopold V of Austria, who in turn presented it to his wife's nephew, Grand Duke Ferdinand II of Tuscany.[30] It now has its place in the Museo degli Argenti in the Pitti Palace.

Before concentrating on Gustavus Adolphus's *Kunstschrank*, I will dwell upon two further, less well-known cabinets. The first, a small one now belonging to the Rijksmuseum in Amsterdam, was made at the end of the 1620s. On his own initiative Hainhofer sent it in 1631 to Duke Augustus of Brunswick-Lüneburg, advising him that it would make a suitable gift for 'the King of Sweden's wife', Queen Maria Eleonora. The Duke, however, was not interested in acquiring it but promised to try to find a buyer.[31] It was probably purchased by a member of the Orange dynasty and reached Holland

Figure 5.4.1   The Pomeranian *Kunstschrank*, formerly Berlin, destroyed in the Second World War

in this way. According to Hainhofer the greater part of its contents was lost during transportation to Duke Augustus.

A small *Kunstschrank*, mentioned above, in Vienna, has a certain similarity to the Amsterdam cabinet, while its crest of minerals and shells finds its counterpart in the 'mountain' at the top of the Uppsala *Kunstschrank*. It was made between 1631 and 1634 and was bought by Duke Augustus, but not

Figure 5.4.2   The *Kunstschrank* bought by Duke Augustus as a gift for Count Carl Gustaf Wrangel. Kunsthistoriches Museum, Vienna

until 1647, immediately before Hainhofer's death. Its history thus far could be traced in documents by Detlef Heikamp, and Arne Losman succeeded in pursuing its story a little further.[32] Immediately after the purchase, the Duke presented it to the Field Marshal Count Carl Gustaf Wrangel, supreme commander of the Swedish army in Germany at the time. The purpose of the gift was to help to obtain of Swedish subsidies to the Lutheran duchy Braunschweig-Wolfenbüttel. It was a valuable gift: the Duke was ready to pay 6,000 thalers for it, equivalent to the price of 230 ordinary saddle-horses (though Hainhofer's heirs had great difficulties in getting the money).[33]

This *Kunstschrank* was considered lost until a few years ago, when I was able to show that it is identical with a piece of furniture in the Kunsthistorisches Museum in Vienna, known under the erroneous name of Emperor Rudolf II's cabinet.[34] Hainhofer's own detailed description of it, now in the Herzog August Bibliothek in Wolfenbüttel, corresponds entirely with the preserved *Kunstschrank*.[35] The main reason why the cabinet in Vienna had not earlier been identified with the *Kunstschrank* bought by Duke Augustus might be that originally it was only part of a larger piece of furniture, which also contained a now lost large table, with several drawers and compartments under the top. It was brought to Sweden, where in 1776 it got a new stand in the shape of a cupboard – still preserved in Vienna –

signed by the Swedish cabinet-maker Georg Haupt. In the beginning of the nineteenth century it was bought at a sale in Stockholm by the Austrian envoy Count Franz von und zu Lodron-Laderano and soon afterwards was added to the imperial collections in Vienna.

The *Kunstschrank* of Gustavus Adolphus was manufactured between 1625 and 1631.[36] The name of the cabinet-maker who made the joinery of the Pomeranian cabinet, the *stipo tedesco* and the Vienna cabinet is known through documents: Ulrich Baumgartner. The similarities, even in details, between Gustavus Adolphus's *Kunstschrank* and the Florence and Vienna cabinets points to him as the maker of the Uppsala cabinet as well. It remained in Hainhofer's house until the Swedish king's troops entered Augsburg in April 1632. The Lutheran councillors, who were reinstated by Gustavus Adolphus, wished to welcome the king with a magnificent gift, so the council bought the cabinet from Hainhofer for 6,500 thalers (though he received only 6,000 gulden). The presentation ceremony took place in the Fugger palace, with Hainhofer demonstrating it for the king, whom he describes as 'versed in all sciences and a master of all arts'.[37]

Hainhofer had tried to play a role as mediator between Catholics and Lutherans prior to the surrender of Augsburg; as a reward for this and other services, his was one among the eighteen Lutheran families elevated to the rank of patrician (the so-called *Schwedengeschlechter*).[38] He was also appointed one of the council's three building inspectors (*Bauherren*), supervising public building in Augsburg and being responsible for all municipal expenses. Furthermore, he was even granted some Swabian villages, which, however, he was politically shrewd enough not to accept.[39] Following the conquest of Augsburg by imperial troops in 1635, Hainhofer lost both his patrician status and his seat on the council.

Little more than six months after receiving the *Kunstschrank* Gustavus Adolphus was killed, and not until the following year was it transported to Sweden.[40] First it was placed in the royal castle of Svartsjö, but was later transferred to that at Uppsala. In 1694 Carl XI donated it to Uppsala University; today it is the *pièce de résistance* of the University Museum, *Museum Gustavianum*.

The *Kunstschrank* was at an early date deprived of its huge collection of coins and medals, which became part of the university's numismatic museum. In the course of the eighteenth century its minerals were also removed and transferred to the Department of Chemistry. With these exceptions the contents of the cabinet have survived almost intact. Unfortunately, the description that went with it, as with the other *Kunstschränke*, is lost. Thus it is difficult to comprehend fully the system behind the collection of objects. However, considerable help is provided by the inventory of contents intended to accompany the *stipo tedesco* but never delivered with it.[41] This exhibits

Figure 5.4.3   Gustavus Adolphus's *Kunstschrank*, detail

similarities with the contents of the Uppsala cabinet; indeed, many items are identical.⁴² It is certain that Hainhofer's own *Kunstkammer* provided the greater part of the hundreds of objects in the *Kunstschrank* in Uppsala. Of the planned content of the Florentine cabinet, he says that it was 'brought together over a period of twenty years'.⁴³

Hainhofer calls the *stipo tedesco* 'a small *Kunstkammer*' and both the composition of the contents listed in the inventory and the items in the Uppsala cabinet do in fact represent small-scale versions of princely *Kunstkammern*.⁴⁴ The inventory divides the objects into two main categories: *naturalia* and *artificialia*. Natural products worked by human hand are classed among the *naturalia* – for instance, carved precious stones, rosaries, a knife, fork and spoon of amber, and bowls of *terra sigillata* or serpentine. This system of classification has its counterpart in princely *Kunstkammern* and certainly derives from the arrangement of the elder Pliny's *Historian naturalis*. Within these two main sections the objects are grouped according to material and function, geographical and chronological criteria being of secondary importance. This, too, accords with the *Kunstkammern*. Like many of them, Hainhofer's *Kunstschränke* give expression to the desire for an all-embracing documentation of the world and of human activities. In the Uppsala cabinet the animal, plant and mineral kingdoms are represented, the four continents known at that time and every historical period from antiquity till Hainhofer's own day. Tools and instruments fulfilling the needs of everyday life, of work and study, stand side by side with those supplying pastimes and aesthetic pleasure. As with the *Kunstkammern*, this quest for universality is modified by a focus on the rare, the peculiar, the precious and, in the case of artefacts, on objects characterized by artistic refinement, a high level of craftsmanship and the surmounting of technical difficulties.

The cabinet contains, further, a large number of objects supposedly possessing prophylactic or medicinal properties or considered effective as aphrodisiacs: bezoars, a *pomambra*, a musk pouch, cups of *lignum Guaiacum*, a bowl and a mug of *terra sigillata*, and so on. The minerals originally belonging to the cabinet were also, perhaps, selected with regard to the magical properties attributed to the various stones.

Hainhofer often states that his *Kunstschränke* also had to satisfy the demand for *Kurzweil* (i.e. for pastimes or diversions).⁴⁵ To this category of objects in the Uppsala cabinet belongs the chess set and other parlour games, as well as sets of playing cards, on the back of which the tunes of thirteen popular love songs are noted. Several objects in the cabinet aim at surprise effects, especially those intended 'for vexation'.⁴⁶ There are vexing mirrors distorting the reflected image, vexing spectacles breaking up reality into facets, artificial eggs, fruit and bread cheating those who take hold of them, halves of nuts with illusionistic wire insects, wooden spoons with two handles or bowls, a mug one cannot drink from and, finally, two pairs of vexing gloves one cannot put on since they are sewn together. Such practical jokes were immensely popular in the Mannerist and Baroque periods – one thinks, for example, of the Archduke Ferdinand II's iron chair at Ambras which held anyone captive who sat down in it or of the surprise jets of water which soaked strollers in the palace parks of the time.

The cabinet's anamorphoses may also be placed in this 'amusement' category. They surprise the beholder in a way similar to the objects already mentioned, giving him an 'Aha!' experience as the distorted picture regains its correct proportions. Two of them are so-called perspective anamorphoses, the third a mirror anamorphosis with a painting on copper of an elegant gentleman. The mirror anamorphosis can be perceived correctly only with the aid of a cylindrical or conical mirror and it was at the time Hainhofer included one in his *Kunstschrank* a recent invention.[47]

Beneath the 'mountain' is a virginal, which may be played in a number of ways. Firstly, a drawer can be taken out of the cabinet's pedestal and, by a simple manipulation, converted into steps granting access to the keyboard. Conversely, the virginal can be taken out of the cabinet and placed on the folding table likewise to be found in the pedestal. Finally the virginal is equipped with a mechanism which allows three compositions to be played automatically. Originally the virginal was linked mechanically to a clock hidden in the 'mountain', thus making it possible to set it off automatically at a predetermined moment in time. Correctly adjusted, it also played automatically when the doors were opened.

It is evident from Hainhofer's letters to his patrons that the *Kunstschränke* also were intended to fulfil practical functions. The later Hainhofer cabinets were delivered – or so was the intention – stuffed with objects, but potentially they were pieces of storage furniture, where 'a potentate should put beautiful jewels, splendid relics or records and writings', as Hainhofer puts it with reference to the *stipo tedesco*.[48] About the same cabinet he writes that it should be for 'use and service', and the Vienna cabinet should be 'for service and use as well as for recreation and parade'.[49] A 'childbed-chest' for Sophia Elisabeth of Mecklenburg, third spouse of Duke Augustus of Brunswick-Lüneburg, is according to Hainhofer 'intended for daily necessary use, comprehensive and convenient' and several times he calls his cabinets 'household utensils'.[50]

Most scholars of the present generation have, however, been inclined either to ascribe to the artifacts in the collections of the cabinets nothing but luxury purpose or to see them as carriers of symbolic meaning, as Tjark Hausmann has maintained about the Pomeranian *Kunstschrank*. He admits that the tools in the cabinet 'have serviceable form and are functioning without objection' but he considers them as miniatures which were not aimed for practical use but are 'multileveled, ambiguous, pointing in several directions'.[51] There are several miniatures in Gustavus Adolphus's *Kunstschrank*, but the toilet-requisites, the surgical instruments, the writing implements and the mathematical instruments are no more miniatures than the eating-implements or the weapons (with the exception of a couple of miniature pistols, which, however, function perfectly). Not even the instruments in the Pomeranian cabinet, which Hausmann is referring to, are really miniatures.

Hausmann's statement is, however, at the same time wrong *and* right. The artifacts were *potentially* functioning; they had a *latent* working capacity. But the symbolic function *was* more important; as soon as the instruments had been 'decontextualized' and brought into the new context of the *Kunstschrank*, they acquired a new dimension, and became what Krzyszt of Pomian has called 'semiophores', i.e. carriers of sign or carriers of meaning, whose characteristics have been filtered through 'the social place', the proximity to other things, the verbal or verbalizeable context, the composition and character of the consumer and so on.[52] One could also refer to the concept of the 'symbolic *milieu*', introduced by the Swedish art historian Gregor Paulsson in connection to Ernst Cassirer's concept 'symbolic form'.[53] Paulsson's concept denotes the 'social' context which decides where on the scale between 'pure utility' and 'pure symbol' an artifact should be placed.

Compare also Jean Baudrillard's comments on collections in his book *Le Système des objets*:

Possession cannot apply to an implement, since the object I utilize always directs me back to the world. Rather it applies to that object once it is *divested of its function and made relative to a subject*. In this sense, all objects that are possessed submit to the same *abstractive operation* and participate in a mutual relationship in so far as they each refer back to the subject. They thereby constitute themselves as a *system*, on the basis of which the subject seeks to piece together his world, his personal microcosm. Thus any given object can have two functions: it can be utilized, or it can be possessed. […] the object pure and simple, divested of its function, abstracted from any practical context, takes on a strictly subjective status. Now its destiny is to be collected.[54]

The same encyclopaedic intention as regarding the contents finds expression in the pictorial programme of the *Kunstschrank* in Uppsala, consisting for the main part of oil miniatures on different sorts of semi-precious stones. It is more extensive than in Hainhofer's other cabinets and may in part be understood as a combination of those of the Pomeranian and Florentine *Kunstschränke*. If the iconographical content of the former may be summarized as the triumph of Art and Science – of civilization – over Nature, then that of the latter is, in Hainhofer's own words, 'a compendium of all Holy Scripture'.[55]

The biblical component in the iconography of Gustavus Adolphus's cabinet is represented by hundreds of pictures, ranging from Genesis to Revelation. The four sides of the large double doors of the front side have Old Testament subjects which are subsumed into the four elements, one on each side. As examples can be mentioned some of the motifs of the outside of the left door: Moses and the burning bush; Elijah taken up to heaven in a chariot of fire; fire from the presence of the Lord consumes Nadab and Abihu, the sons of Aaron; the Lord rains down burning sulphur on Sodom and Gomorrha; Elijah calls down fire from heaven, which consumes the king of Samaria's captain and his fifty men; the Lord descending on Mount Sinai in fire; the fire of the Lord falls and burns up the sacrifice of Elijah.

Every fire depicted is fire from Heaven. Perhaps Hainhofer in his unconventional use of the elements as ordering principle for these passages from the Bible is influenced by the Lutheran author Johann Arndt. In his widespread *Four Books on True Christianity*, Arndt identified the fourth element, Fire, with Heaven, in accordance with Paracelsus, one of the sources of inspiration to his mystically flavoured piety.[56] Hainhofer was a fervent admirer of Arndt; in a letter to Duke Augustus of Brunswick-Lüneburg he wrote: 'My appetite for his *True Christianity* is unquenchable.'[57]

The insides of the double doors of the opposite side of the cabinet have scenes of Old Testament miracles or of Christ and his disciples miraculously healing the sick and raising the dead. This is in accordance with the function of this side of the *Kunstschrank*: behind the doors pharmaceutical instruments have their place.

Also present in the pictorial programme are the traditional allegories of the four elements, of the five senses, of the virtues and of time and place. One feature does not appear to the same degree in Hainhofer's other cabinets: the large number of allegories of love, some of them with very uncommon subjects, mostly taken from the poetry or history of classical antiquity. The prelude to this part of the iconography is to be seen in the magnificent crowning wine ewer consisting of half of a Seychelles nut mounted in silver to represent the ship of Venus. Note that a couple of coral twigs on the 'mountain', put together of minerals and *conchylia* and upon which the ewer stands are carved in the shape of a hand in the so-called *fica* gesture; with the thumb between the index finger and the next, this gesture was thought to avert all kinds of evil.[58] And the Seychelles nut was thought to be an exceptionally effective antidote to poison.[59]

Hidden among depictions of the glory and richness of life on earth there are also some *vanitas* pictures, reminding the beholder of Death's presence and the transitoriness of all things. There are so-called *Verkehrbilder*, two of which represent the beautiful faces of a man and woman respectively which, when turned upside down, change into grinning skulls. Another depicts a landscape

Figure 5.4.4   Ewer of Seychelles nut crowning the *Kunstschrank* of Gustavus Adolphus

which, when rotated ninety degrees, becomes a man's head in profile. Similar to these are four allegories of the seasons represented in the manner of Arcimboldo, i.e. as heads comprised of flowers, fruits, leafless branches, and so on. Finally, in the central section, wooden intarsias depict Augsburg at the

Figure 5.4.5 *The Israelites crossing the Red Sea,* oil painting on alabaster by Johann König in Gustavus Adolphus's *Kunstschrank*

outbreak of the Thirty Years War with the newly erected town hall and arsenal by Elias Holl and with an interior of a cabinet-maker's workshop.

Only one of the paintings on the exterior or in the interior of the *Kunstschrank* is signed: a large alabaster slab painted by Johann König with depictions of the Israelites Crossing the Red Sea on one side and the Last Judgement on the other. The artist has been very skilful in using the texture of the stone to give the illusion of clouds, rocks and mighty cascades. In works of art of this kind one may perceive how, as Hainhofer describes it, 'Art and Nature play with one another.'[60] He often expressed his enthusiasm for things exhibiting a gradual transition from Nature to Art, objects in which Nature seems to work like an artist and the artist in the manner of Nature. In particular he admired 'ruin marble' or 'landscape stone' with, as he puts it, 'self-made landscapes and buildings'.[61] He imported slabs of this stone from Florence, either already decorated or, more frequently, unpainted stones which 'with paint can be helped a little to represent something'.[62] Landscape stones are often used in the Uppsala *Kunstschrank*, above all in its folding table and writing-desk.

Johann König was the author also of a couple of other paintings in the Uppsala *Kunstschrank*. But who was the diligent master behind all the other paintings? Comparative stylistic studies point unequivocally towards the Augsburg painter Anton Mozart, who had earlier collaborated with Hainhofer on the Pomeranian cabinet.[63] But there is one problem with that attribution: Mozart died in May 1625, the same year in which the joinery work on the cabinet seems to have begun.[64] One of the intarsias in the central section of the front side is, however, dated that year through an inscription, so the main part of the cabinet might have been completed that same year. Mozart was known as a quick painter and could perhaps have made the paintings during the few months before his death. Of course, Hainhofer could also have ordered the paintings in advance, in the autumn of 1624 or even earlier. Hainhofer had a deep distrust of unreliable and boozing artists and artisans and might have wished to be safe rather than sorry.

Also these paintings, on agate, jasper, lapis lazuli and other semi-precious stones, display the same interaction of Art and Nature as the paintings on alabaster and landscape stone. The Mannerist *topos* of Art and Nature as working side by side in similar ways or in symbiosis with each other was by no means new to Hainhofer. He had had opportunities to see comparable works of art on his youthful journeys of study – for example, during a three-week stay in Florence. Francesco I's *studiolo* in the Palazzo Vecchio, the grotto in the Boboli gardens and the grottoes and fountains in the park of the Medici villa at Pratolino (which Hainhofer describes in his diary) betray the same attitude towards Art and Nature.[65] He surely also visited the *Opificio delle pietre dure*, founded some ten years previously, where he could see how slabs of landscape stone were 'helped a little' to become works of art and how *pietre dure* were put together to form still lifes of birds and flowers.[66] From the same workshop he later imported the *pietra dura* and some of the ruin marble which adorn the cabinet in Uppsala.[67]

But comparable objects were to be found nearer Augsburg than that: the grotto in the Munich *Residenz*, for example, or the writing utensils and

Figure 5.4.6   Writing desk in Gustavus Adolphus's *Kunstschrank*

caskets by the Nürnberg silversmith Wenzel Jamnitzer with their animals and plants cast from nature and their crowning configurations of sand and stone, objects summed up in the term *stil rustique* introduced by Ernst Kris.[68] In fact, Jamnitzer's caskets are probably the prototypes of the 'mountains' in Hainhofer's *Kunstschränke* in Uppsala and Vienna.[69] Of course, Hainhofer could also have studied many phenomena exhibiting a symbiotic relationship between Art and Nature in the great *Kunstkammer* at Ambras, which, however, he did not visit until 1628.[70]

On the writing-desk belonging to the Uppsala *Kunstschrank* there is a picture, unsigned but certainly by Johann König, depicting Hercules shooting at Nessus, who has seized and carried off his wife Deianeira. This motif can be interpreted as an allegory of Virtue triumphing over raw Nature, thus liberating Man. The painting is among the items originally intended for the *stipo tedesco*.[71] Surrounding the painting are silver inlays depicting the traditional *quadrivium* of the *artes liberales* but also some *artes mechanicae*: tailoring, minting, printing, goldsmithing, watchmaking, painting and the art of perspective, that is forms of art and handicraft practised in Augsburg. A comparison with similar silver inlays in the writing-desk of the Pomeranian *Kunstschrank* is instructive. They depict study, printing, painting and mathematics. These are occupations connected in one way or another with the actual function of the desk, and are thus quite different from the fusion of the conventional seven *artes liberales* with *artes mechanicae* in the desk of the Uppsala cabinet.

Among the *Artes Liberaliores* in the widespread occultist work *Utriusque cosmi historia* by the Oxford doctor Robert Fludd a similar extension of the traditional liberal arts is to be found.[72] It is not unlikely that Hainhofer had studied Fludd's work, of which the first volume was published in Oppenheim in 1617, between the completion of the Pomeranian cabinet and the beginning of work on the Uppsala *Kunstschrank*. He was by no means uninterested in occult sciences of the type practised by Fludd. This is evident among other testimonies from the book *Cabala, Spiegel der Kunst und Natur: in Alchymia*, which was published in Augsburg in 1615 by the Lutheran publisher Stephan Michelspacher, several of whose publications Hainhofer seems to have sponsored. In the preface to the *Cabala*, Michelspacher mentions him as 'the distinguished *liebhaber* and *aestimator* of such artifices'.[73] Later Hainhofer became a friend of the Lutheran theologian Johann Valentin Andreae, another admirer of Johann Arndt and, in his youth, one of the founding fathers of the Rosicrucian movement.[74] This movement had been defended by Fludd, but he never seems to have come into personal contact with Andreae who, for theological reasons, soon renounced all connections with the Rosicrucians.[75]

The model of the cosmos in the first part of Fludd's work does in fact show similarities also with the organization of both *Kunstkammern* and *Kunstschränke*, even if it is difficult to prove any direct connection. In the plate depicting the model of the universe at the beginning of the first volume, an ape appears as a symbol of the arts, held in chain by Nature who in turn is guided by God.[76] This is an illustration of the old doctrine of painting as *simia della natura*, Art as the ape of Nature, which Hainhofer apparently subscribed to, although he hardly possessed a logically thought-out conception of art. For example, in Dresden in 1629 he fell to admiring a tombstone on which the figures are represented so illusionistically that they seem 'to stand there in person', and on another occasion he refers to the anecdote about Apelles and the horse of Alexander the Great.[77]

Anyone who has read *The Art of Memory* and other publications by Frances Yates knows what an important role that concept plays in Robert Fludd's *Utriusque cosmi historia*.[78] Arne Losman has suggested that Hainhofer's *Kunstschränke* may be interpreted as *theatri memoriae*.[79] The research on memory theatres and *ars memoriae* has become somewhat of a fad in the last few decades, and one could suspect that Losman's idea was a whim produced by the *Zeitgeist*, if it were not for the fact that there is documentary evidence for Hainhofer's profound interest in the art of memory. One instance is that one of the authorities on that subject, the Dutch Lambert Schenkel, seems to have been his preceptor during his studies in Holland and that Hainhofer in 1614 together with a few other interested citizens heard him lecture on *ars memoriae* during a visit to Augsburg. This information can be found in the foreword to an edition of Schenkel's *Exemplum speciminis artis memoriae* published in Augsburg in the same year.[80] Francis Yates states that Schenkel died around 1603, a statement that since then has been repeated in the literature, but Ludwig Volkmann's estimation from 1929 that Schenkel lived until about 1620 must be more accurate.[81]

That a *Kunstschrank* could serve as a memory theatre is in accordance with an old *topos*: as early as the fourteenth century memory was compared to a cupboard, an *armarium scripturarum*, where the *loci* correspond to the drawers, and we encounter the same metaphor in Lodovico Dolce's dialogue on memory from 1575.[82] Also the title of the 1610 edition of Lambert Schenkel's tract on the art of memory, *Gazophylacium artis memoriae* ('The Treasury Safe of the Art of Memory'), makes evident that the comparison of the art of memory to a piece of furniture was a common metaphor.[83]

In addition Hainhofer's friendship with Johann Valentine Andreae might give some support to the interpretation of the *Kunstschränke* as memory theatres. Andreae's Utopian city *Christianopolis* has been characterized as an 'immense mnemotechnical picture theatre'.[84] The *Kunstschränke* with their collections and series of allegorical images of the elements, of the dimensions of time and space and of the place of man in the cosmos constitute a 'shorthand' version of macrocosm. In this way, the *Kunstkammern* as well as the *Kunstschränke* mirrored or represented the multifarious, chaotic and ungraspable world through an intelligible, unchangeable and easily memorized order. They are late manifestations of the sixteenth-century episteme Michel Foucalt writes about in *The Order of Things*: 'the sixteenth century superimposed hermeneutics and semiology in the form of similitude. To search for a meaning is to bring to light a resemblance. To search for the law governing signs is to discover the things that are alike'.[85]

Gustavus Adolphus's *Kunstschrank* was granted an interesting survival after it was donated to Uppsala University by King Carl XI, thereby to some extent getting a new function besides those I have outlined. As early as 1701 the authorities of the university exhorted the public to increase the numismatic collections of the cabinet with gifts.[86] Already in the same year the eminent numismatist Elias Brenner donated a collection of old Swedish coins, and this gift was followed by many others; John Böttiger lists 100 donations – many of them containing several items – during the eighteenth and the early nineteenth centuries.[87] The donors were aristocrats, officers, aldermen, professors, vicars, doctors, apothecaries, and accountants. Most of the gifts were closely suited to the original contents of the *Kunstschrank*: exotic or otherwise remarkable *naturalia*, artifacts from the Near East or China but also from Africa and even North America. Further relics were earth and a piece of wood from the Holy Sepulchre, as well as a model of the Holy Sepulchre.[88] There are what is said to be Achilles' ashes and fragments of brick from Virgil's house at Baiae.[89] But a new vein manifests itself in a bias towards Swedish history and the glorious deeds of the nation's past. There are axes, daggers and buckles from prehistoric times, a medal of the sixteenth-century kings Gustavus I and Erik XIV, a drawing depicting the latter, and a series of boxwood medals of Swedish kings, explorers, scientists and writers.[90] There are more curious relics such as an ivory death's head, said to have been carved by Gustavus I, stones from the castle where the same king was thought to have been born, a piece of velvet from the sarcophagus of Erik XIV, a stone from the battlefield of Lützen where Gustavus Adolphus fell in 1632, a button taken from a coat owned by Carl XII, a piece of the garter Queen Louisa Ulrica wore at her wedding to King Adolph Fredric in 1744, a ball of yarn spun by Louisa Ulrica, and samples of the silver brocade from the coronation robes of Gustavus III and his consort Sophia Magdalena from 1771.[91]

Together these things form a sanctuary of national relics, a memorial to the nation's great past. In a way, the *Kunstschrank* was made into a national museum *en miniature* long before any public museums were opened in Sweden.

NOTES

1. B. Volk-Knüttel, 'Maximilian I. von Bayern als Sammler und Auftraggeber. Seine Korrespondenz mit Philipp Hainhofer 1611–1615', *Quellen und Studien zur Kunstpolitik der Wittelsbacher vom 16. bis zum 18. Jarhundert* (Mitteilungen des Hauses der Bayerischen Geschichte 1), Munich and Zürich, 1980, pp. 84, 121, n. 21.

2. For the biography of Hainhofer, see H.-O.Boström, 'Hainhofer, Philipp', in *Dictionary of Art*, ed. Jane Turner, vol. 14, London and New York, 1996, pp. 51–2 (with bibliography). See also J. Lüdtke, *Die Lautenbücher Philipp Hainhofers (1578–1647)* (with bibliography), Göttingen, 1999, and H.-O.Boström, *Det underbara skåpet, Philipp Hainhofer och Gustav II Adolfs konstskåp* (Acta Universitatis Upsaliensis, ser. C 70), Uppsala, 2001, pp. 53–93.

3. 'Philipp Hainhofers Reise-Tagebuch, enthaltend Schilderungen aus Franken, Sachsen, der Mark Brandenburg und Pommern im Jahr 1617', *Baltische Studien*, 2:2, Stettin, 1834, p. xxii.

4. Cf. A. Rieber, 'Das Patriziat von Ulm, Augsburg, Ravensburg, Memmingen, Bibrach', *Deutsches Patriziat 1430–1740* (Büdinger Vorträge 1965), Limburg an der Lahn, 1968, p. 309; I. Bátori, *Die Reichsstadt Augsburg im 18. Jahrhundert: Verfassung, Finanzen und Reformversuche* (Veröffentlichungen des Max-Planck-Instituts für Geschichte 22), Göttingen, 1969, pp. 21–2.

5. C. Haeutle, 'Die Reisen des Augsburgers Philipp Hainhofer nach Eichstädt, München und Regensburg in den Jahren 1611, 1612 und 1613', *Zeitschrift des Historischen Vereins für Schwaben und Neuburg*, 8, 1881, pp. 143–4; J. Böttiger, *Philipp Hainhofer und der Kunstschrank Gustav Adolfs in Upsala*, vols 1–4, Stockholm, 1909–10, vol. 1, p. 15; J. Böttiger, 'Försök till en konturteekning av Philipp Hainhofers personlighet', *Tillägg till Philipp Hainhofer und der Kunstschrank Gustav Adolfs in Upsala*, Stockholm 1923, pp. 6–7.

6. Volk-Knüttel, *op. cit.*, pp. 84, 121, n. 11.

7. Böttiger, *op. cit.* 1909–10, vol. 1, pp. 19, 60; Böttiger, *op. cit.* 1923, p. 6.

8. *Sammler, Fürst, Gelehrter: Herzog August zu Braunschweig und Lüneburg 1579–1666*, Ausstellung der Herzog August Bibliothek in Wolfenbüttel, Wolfenbüttel 1979, pp. 79, 80, 163, 173, 315–19; A. Fink, 'Das Augsburger Kunsthandwerk und der dreissigjährige Krieg', in H. Rinn (ed.), *Augusta 955–1955, Forschungen und Studien zur Kultur- und Wirtschaftsgeschichte Augsburgs*, Augsburg, 1955, pp. 323–4; *Der Briefwechsel zwischen Philipp Hainhofer und Herzog August d.J. von Braunschweig-Lüneburg*, ed. by R. Gobiet, Munich, 1984, *passim*.

9. O. Doering, 'Des Augsburger Patriciers Philipp Hainhofer Reisen nach Innsbruck und Dresden', *Quellenschriften für Kunstgeschichte und Kunsttechnik des Mittelalters und der Neuzeit*, new ser. 10, Vienna, 1901, pp. 251–89.

10. Böttiger, *op. cit.* 1909–10, vol. 1, pp. 3, 5, 38.

11. '[…] factorn vnd amicis'. O. Doering, 'Des Augsburger Patriciers Philipp Hainhofer Beziehungen zum Herzog Philipp II von Pommern-Stettin, Correspondenzen aus den Jahren 1610–1619', *Quellenschriften für Kunstgeschichte und Kunsttechnik des Mittelalters und der Neuzeit*, new ser. 6, Vienna, 1894, p. 9.

12. For correspondence with members of the Lumaga family, see Herzog August Bibliothek, Wolfenbüttel, Cod. Guelf. 17.27 Aug. 4°, *passim*.

13. Doering, *op. cit.* 1894, p. 93.

14. Haeutle, *op. cit.*, p. 96.

15. Doering, *op. cit.* 1901, p. 252.

16. O. Hartig, 'Unbekannte Reisen des jungen Hainhofer nach München und Stuttgart 1603–1607', *Der Sammler, Unterhaltungs- und Literaturbeilage der München-Augsburger Abendzeitung* 118, 1924; A. Langenkamp, *Philipp Hainhofers Münchner Reisebeschreibungen, Eine Kritische Ausgabe* (diss.) 1–2, Berlin 1990; Haeutle, *op. cit.*, pp. 55–148; A. von Occhclhäuser, 'Philipp Hainhofers Bericht über die Stuttgarter Kindtaufe im Jahre 1616', *Neue Heidelberger Jahrbücher*, 1, 1891, pp. 254–335; 'Philipp Hainhofers Reise-Tagebuch', *op. cit.*, pp. 134–5; Doering, *op. cit.* 1901, pp. 84–8, 157–79.

17. Staats- und Stadtbibliothek, Augsburg, Cim. 66, fol. 58r. Letters from Philipp Hainhofer to his cousin Melchior Hainhofer are to be found in Herzog August Bibliothek, Wolfenbüttel, Cod. Guelf. 17.23 Aug. 4°, fols. 22^r–22^v, 26^v–30^v, 111^r–112^r; Cod. Guelf. 17.24 Aug. 4°, fols. 4^v–5^v, 91^v–93^r, 124^v–126^r, 153^v–154^v. Cf. Cod. Guelf. 17.23 Aug. 4°, fol. 264^r.

18. Oechelhäuser, *op. cit.*, p. 306.

19. Haeutle, *op. cit.*, p. 105.

20. Doering, *op. cit.* 1901, p. 88.

21. Staats- und Stadtbibliothek, Augsburg, Cim. 66, fol. 62^v, 63^r, 89^v; Herzog August Bibliothek Wolfenbüttel, Cod. Guelf. 60.9 Aug. 2°, fols 3^v, 7^v, 8^r, 10^r, 11^v, 13^r, 13^v, 14^r, 14^v, 15^r; 'Philipp Hainhofers Reise-Tagebuch', *op. cit.*, pp. xxii, xxv, xxvi, xxviii, xxix, xxx.

22. Staats- und Stadtbibliothek, Augsburg, Cim. 66, fol. 87^r; Herzog August Bibliothek, Wolfenbüttel, Cod. Guelf. 60.9 Aug. 2°, fol. 13^r; *Baltische Studien, op. cit.*, p. xxix. Cf. F. C. Springell, *Connoisseur and Diplomat, The Earl of Arundel's Embassy to Germany in 1636 as recounted in William Crowne's Diary, the Earl's letters and other contemporary sources with a catalogue of the topographical drawings made on the journey by Wenceslaus Hollar*, London, 1963, pp. 77–8, 125, nn. 165–6.

23. Herzog August Bibliothek, Wolfenbüttel, Cod. Guelf. 17.27 Aug. 4°, fol. 78^v.

24. Doering, *op. cit.*, 1894, pp. 272–6; J. Lessing and A. Brüning, *Der Pommersche Kunstschrank*, Berlin, 1905, p. 8.

25. Lessing and Brüning, *op. cit.*; T. Hausmann, 'Der Pommersche Kunstschrank, Das Problem seines inneren Aufbaus', *Zeitschrift für Kunstgeschichte*, 22, 1959, pp. 337–52; D. Alfter, *Die Geschichte des Augsburger Kabinettschranks*, Augsburg, 1986, pp. 42–6; Boström, *op. cit.* 2001, pp. 112–18.

26. Volk-Knüttel, *op. cit.*, pp. 88–9; Boström, *op. cit.* 2001, pp. 118–19. Cf. G. Himmelheber, 'Ulrich und Melchior Baumgartner', *Pantheon*, 33, 1975, p. 114.

27. Böttiger, *op. cit.* 1909–10, vol. 1, pp. 49, 51, 57–60, 62–4.

28. Herzog August Bibliothek, Wolfenbüttel, Cod. Guelf. 17.27 Aug. 4°, fols. 383^r–384^r. Cf. L. W. Forster, Weckherlin und Hainhofer, *Respublica Guelpherbytana, Wolfenbütteler Beiträge zur Renaissance- und Barockforschung*, Festschrift für Paul Raabe, Amsterdam 1987, pp. 425, 430–1. See also J. Bepler, 'Augsburg – England – Wolfenbüttel, Die Karriere des Reisehofmeisters Hieronymus Hainhofer', *Augsburg in der Frühen Neuzeit, Beiträge zu einem Forschungsprogramm* (Colloquia Augustana 1), ed. by J. Brüning and F. Niewöhner, Berlin, 1995, p. 123.

29. Oechelhäuser, *op. cit.*; L. W. Forster, *Georg Rudolf Weckherlin, Zur Kenntnis seines Lebens in England* (Basler Studien zur deutschen Sprache und Literatur 2), Basel, 1944, pp. 27–31, 60.

30. D. Heikamp, 'Zur Geschichte der Uffizien-Tribuna und der Kunstschränke in Florenz und Deutschland', *Zeitschrift für Kunstgeschichte*, 26, 1963, pp. 193–268; C. Piacenti Aschengreen, *Il Museo degli Argenti a Firenze*, Milan, 1968, pp. 19, 174; Alfter, *op. cit.*, pp. 50–3; Boström, *op. cit.* 2001, pp. 120–7.

31. *Welt im Umbruch, Augsburg zwischen Renaissance und Barock*, exh. cat., Augsburg, 1980, 2, p. 473; Alfter, *op. cit.* 1986, pp. 50–3; R. Baarsen, *Duitse meubelen/German furniture*, Rijksmuseum,

Amsterdam, 1998, nr 6; R. Baarsen, 'Een Augsburgs pronkkabinet', *Bulletin van het Rijksmuseum* 28:1–2, Amsterdam, 2000, pp. 11–15; Boström, *op. cit.* 2001, pp. 127–30.

32. Heikamp, *op. cit.* 1963, pp. 233–4; A. Losman, *Carl Gustaf Wrangel och Europa, Studier i kulturförbindelser kring en 1600-talsmagnat*, Stockholm, 1980, pp. 64–71.

33. Losman, *op. cit.*, p. 66.

34. H.-O.Boström, 'Ein wiederentdeckter Hainhoferschrank', *Kunst und Antiquitäten*, 4, 1993, pp. 32–6; H.-O.Boström, 'Ein wiederentdeckter Hainhoferschrank', *Konsthistorisk tidskrift*, 64, 1995, pp. 129–46; Boström, *op. cit.* 2001, pp. 130–7. Cf. G. Bach, 'Philipp Hainhofer und ein Kabinettschrank des Kunsthistorischen Museums in Wien', *Jahrbuch der kunsthistorischen Sammlungen in Wien*, 91, 1995, Vienna, 1996, pp. 111–51.

35. *Der Briefwechsel, op. cit.*, pp. 836–61.

36. Böttiger, *op. cit.*, 1909–10; Alfter, *op. cit.* 1986, pp. 53–7; Boström, *op. cit.* 2001.

37. Böttiger, *op. cit.* 1909–10, vol. 1, p. 69.

38. 'Philipp Hainhofers Reise-Tagebuch', *op. cit.*, p. xxviii; *Die Chronik des Jakob Wagner über die Zeit der schwedischen Okkupation in Augsburg von 20. April 1632 bis 28. März 1635*, ed. by W. Roos, Augsburg, 1902, pp. 15–16. Cf. *Der Briefwechsel, op. cit.*, p. 586.

39. Herzog August Bibliothek, Wolfenbüttel, Cod. Guelf., 60.9 Aug. 2°, fols. 12^r–12^v.

40. Böttiger, *op. cit.* 1909–10, vol. 1, p. 71–4.

41. Doering, *op. cit.* 1901, pp. 131–8.

42. Böttiger, *op. cit.* 1909–10, vol. 1, p. 65; Boström, *op. cit.* 2001, pp. 253–7.

43. Böttiger, *op. cit.* 1909–10, vol. 1, p. 59.

44. Ibid. Cf. Heikamp, *op. cit.*, pp. 234, 256.

45. E.g. Doering, *op. cit.* 1901, p. 22. Cf. Boström, *op. cit.* 2001, p. 267.

46. Böttiger, *op. cit.* 1909–10, vol. 1, pp. 31–3; vol. 2, pp. 59–60; vol. 3, pp. 17–18, 34, 70, 88.

47. J. Baltrusaitis, *Anamorphoses ou magie artificielle des effets merveilleux*, Paris, 1969, pp. 135–7, 151; F. Leeman, J. Elffers, and M. Schuyt, *Anamorphosen, Ein Spiel mit der Wahrnehmung, dem Schein und der Wirklichkeit*, Cologne, 1975, pp. 133.

48. Böttiger, *op. cit.* 1909–10, vol. 1, p. 59.

49. Doering, *op. cit.* 1901, p. 131; Heikamp, *op. cit.*, p. 265.

50. *Der Briefwechsel, op. cit.*, p. 828; Heikamp, *op. cit.*, p. 256.

51. Hausmann, *op. cit.*, pp. 348, 350.

52. K. Pomian, *Der Ursprung des Museums, Vom Sammeln*, Berlin 1993, pp. 84–6, 88. Cf. A. Schnapp, *The Discovery of the Past: The Origins of Archaeology*, London, 1996, pp. 167–77.

53. G. Paulsson, *Die soziale Dimension der Kunst*, Bern, 1955.

54. Quoted from J. Baudrillard, The system of collecting, in *The Cultures of Collecting*, ed. J. Elsner and R. Cardinal, London, 1994, p. 7.

55. Böttiger, *op. cit.* 1909–10, vol. 1, p. 41.

56. Arndt, J.: *Vier Bücher vom wahren Christentums*, Amsterdam, 1664 (1st ed. 1606–09), p. 872. Cf. Boström, *op. cit.* 2001, p. 163.

57. *Der Briefwechsel, op. cit.*, p. 362.

58. Kriss-Rettenbeck, L.: *Feige: Wort-Gebärde-Amulett, Ein volkskundlicher Beitrag zur Amulettforschung*, Munich, 1955; L. Hansmann and L. Kriss-Rettenbeck, *Amulett und Talisman, Erscheinungsform und Geschichte*, Munich, 1977, pp. 258–9, 320–2.

59. E. Kris, *Goldschmiedearbeiten des Mittelalters, der Renaissance und des Barock, Beschreibender Katalog* (Publikationen aus den Kunsthistorischen Sammlungen in Wien 5), Vienna 1932, pp. 49–51; J. McCurrach, *Palms of the World*, New York, 1960, pp. 124–7; E. von Philippovich, *Kuriositäten, Antiquitäten*, Braunschweig, 1966, pp. 499–502; R. Fritz, *Die Gefässe aus Kokosnuss in Mitteleuropa 1250–1800*, Mainz, 1983, pp. 63–6.

60. Doering, *op. cit.* 1901, p. 117.

61. Ibid., p. 44.

62. Volk-Knüttel, *op. cit.* 1980, p. 107.

63. Boström, *op. cit.* 2001, pp. 222–6.

64. Böttiger, *op. cit.* 1909–10, vol. 1, p. 62.

65. Herzog August Bibliothek, Wolfenbüttel, Cod. Guelf., 60.22 Aug. 4°, pp. 231–2. For Pratolino, see L. Zangheri, *Pratolino, il giardino delle meraviglie*, vol. I: *Testi e documenti* (Documenti inediti di cultura toscana 2), Florence, 1979.

66. Herzog August Bibliothek, Wolfenbüttel, Cod. Guelf., 60.22 Aug. 4°, p. 231. Cf. F. Rossi, *Malerei in Stein, Mosaiken und Intarsien*, Stuttgart, Berlin, Cologne and Mainz, 1969, p. 130; A. M.Giusti, P. Mazzoni and A. Pampaloni Martelli, *Il museo dell'opificio delle pietre dure a Firenze*, Milan, 1978; A. M.Giusti, *Pietre Dure: Hardstone in Furniture and Decorations*, London, 1992, pp. 35–79.

67. The slab with a representation of a naval battle with Jonah and the whale on the writing-desk of the Uppsala cabinet is very similar to a painting on landscape stone in the Museo dell'opificio delle pietre dure in Florence, which is attributed to the circle of Filippo Napoletano (another similar painting belongs to the *Kunstschrank* in Vienna). Also other representations on the Uppsala desk are very close to paintings from the Napoletano circle. Cf. Boström, *op. cit.* 2001, pp. 135–6, 192–4.

68. E. Kris, 'Der Stil "Rustique", Die Verwendung des Naturabgusses bei Wenzel Jamnitzer und Bernard Palissy', *Jahrbuch der Kunsthistorischen Sammlungen in Wien*, new ser. 1, 1926, pp. 137–208.

69. Cf. *Wenzel Jamnitzer und die Nürnberger Goldschmiedekunst 1500–1700*, exh. cat., Germanisches Nationalmuseum, Nürnberg, 1985, pp. 226–7, 411–12.

70. Doering, *op. cit.* 1901, pp. 84–8. Cf. E. Scheicher, *Die Kunst- und Wunderkammern der Habsburger*, Vienna, Munich and Zürich, 1979, pp. 73–136.

71. Cf. Doering, *op. cit.* 1901, p. 136.

72. R. Fludd, *Utriusque cosmi maioris scilicet minoris, metaphysica, physica atque technica historia*, vol. I:1:i, Oppenheim, 1617, p. 17.

73. Michelspacher, S.: *Cabala, Spiegel der Kunst vnd Natur: in Alchymia*, Augsburg, 1615, preface unpaginated: '[…] solcher Artificien sonderlicher liebhaber vnnd aestimator'. Cf. H. Gier, 'Augsburger Buchwesen und Kunst der Druckgraphik im zweiten Jahrzehnt des 17. Jahrhunderts, Der Verlag von Stephan Michelspacher, sein Gönner Philipp Hainhofer und der Kupferstecher Lucas Kilian', *Augsburg, die Bilderfabrik Europas, Essays zur Augsburger Druckgrafik der frühen Neuzeit*, ed. by J. R. Paas, Augsburg, 2001, pp. 55–70.

74. Cf. J. V. Andreae, *Christianopolis 1619*, Originaltext und Übertragung nach D. S. Georgi 1741, ed by R. van Dülmen, Stuttgart, 1972; R. van Dülmen, *Die Utopie einer christlichen Gesellschaft, Johann Valentin Andreae (1586–1654)*, vol. 1, Stuttgart, 1978; J. W. Montgomery, *Cross and Crucible, Johann Valentin Andreae (1586–1654), Phoenix of the theologians*, vol. 1, The Hague 1973; *Cimelia Rhodostaurotica, Die Rosenkreuzer im Spiegel der zwischen 1610 und 1660 entstandenen Handschriften und Drucke*, exh. cat., Amsterdam and Wolfenbüttel, 1995, *passim*; U. Eco, *Serendipities, Language and Lunacy*, London, 1999, pp. 10–17.

75. *Robert Fludd and his Philosophicall Key*, being a transcription of the manuscript at Trinity College, Cambridge, with an introduction by A. G. Debus, pp. 2, 29; W. H.Huffman, *Robert Fludd and the End of the Renaissance*, London and New York, 1988, p. 142; *Cimelia Rhodostaurotica, op. cit.*, pp. 121.

76. Fludd, *op. cit.* 1617, pp. 4–5. Cf. H. W. Janson, *Apes and Ape Lore* (Studies of the Warburg Institute 20), London, 1952, pp. 301–4.

77. Doering, *op. cit.* 1901, p. 229.

78. F. A. Yates, *The Art of Memory*, Harmondsworth, 1978 (1st edn 1966), pp. 310–29.

79. A.Losman, 'Minnets teater', *En värld i miniatyr, Kring en samling från Gustav II Adolfs tidevarv* (Skrifter från Kungl. Husgerådskammaren 2), Stockholm, 1982, pp. 5–12.

80. L.Schenckelius, *Exemplvm speciminis artis memoriae*, Augsburg, 1614, p. 2.

81. Yates, *op. cit.* 1978, p. 291; L. Volkmann, 'Ars memorativa', *Jahrbuch der Kunsthistorischen Sammlungen in Wien*, new ser. 3, 1929, p. 177.

82. L. Bolzoni, 'Das Sammeln und die ars memoriae', *Macrocosmos in microcosmo, Die Welt in der Stube, Zur Geschichte des Sammelns 1450 bis 1800* (Berliner Schriften zur Museumskunde 10), ed. A. Grote, Opladen, 1994, pp. 136, 139.

83. Ibid., p. 139.

84. W. Braungart, *Die Kunst der Utopie, Vom Späthumanismus zur frühen Aufklärung*, Stuttgart, 1989, p. 78.

85. M. Foucault, *The Order of Things: An Archaeology of the Human Sciences*, New York, 1973 (1st ed. 1966), p. 29. Cf. P.Findlen, *Possessing Nature: Museums, Collecting, and Scientific Culture in early modern Italy*, Berkeley, Los Angeles and London, 1994, pp. 393–407.

86. J.Böttiger, *Gustaf II Adolfs konstskåps öden i Upsala* (Uppsala universitets årsskrift 1913: program 2), Uppsala, 1913, p. 11.

87. Ibid., pp. 12, 14, 49–75.

88. Ibid., pp. 53, 72–3.

89. Ibid., p. 73.

90. Ibid., pp. 49, 55–8, 65–6.

91. Ibid., pp. 69, 71–3.

5.

Museums in Eighteenth-Century Rome

Francis Haskell and Nicholas Penny

On 10 December 1728 Nicolas Wleughels, director of the French Academy in Rome, wrote to the Duc d'Antin, Surintendant des Bâtiments du Roi, in Paris: 'The King of Poland has sent someone here who has bought all the antique statues that belonged to Prince Chigi and a large proportion of the collection formed by Cardinal Alessandro Albani. Some time ago the King of Spain removed the collections of Don Livio Odescalchi, which were considerable. So it is that, bit by bit, this unfortunate country is being stripped.'[1] In some ways the situation was even bleaker than Wleughels indicated: he could, for instance, also have mentioned that when in Rome in 1716–17 an Englishman, Mr Thomas Coke of Holkham in Norfolk, had been able to acquire at least two statues of importance – a 'Lucius Antonius' and a Diana. The heads of both these statues were admitted to be additions – the former, improbably, ascribed to Bernini, the latter, plausibly, to Rusconi – and in any case the statues were not equivalent to the *Farnese Hercules* and *Venus de' Medici*, which may just be discerned behind Coke in the portrait which Trevisani painted of him when in Rome, but they had been illustrated only a dozen years previously in the anthology published by de Rossi of the finest sculptures in the city.[2] Against such depredations the popes put up a tough, but not always successful, resistance. Rumour had it that Mr Coke had been arrested for a time;[3] Pope Clement XI was said to be adamant, in the face of extreme pressure, in withholding an export licence from the Duc d'Orléans who had hoped to remove the Odescalchi sculptures (which had formerly belonged to Queen Christina of Sweden) as well as the Old Master paintings:[4] and his successor's acquiescence, when pressed by the King of Spain, must certainly have been motivated by the desire to ease some exceptionally troublesome negotiations in which he was currently engaged.[5] And so the *Faun with Kid* and the *Castor and Pollux*, of which the Richardsons had said that 'there are no Finer Statues in Rome', left the city for ever, as the *Germanicus* and the *Cincinnatus* had done forty years earlier, and – so it seemed – as many more masterpieces might well be doing in the next few years.

One palliative to this state of affairs lay in the hands of Wleughels himself. In 1725 the Academy, over which he presided, took an eight-year lease on the palace of the Marchese Mancini in the Corso opposite the Palazzo Doria, and in this large, handsome building (which was purchased twelve years later) the casts after the antique, on which so much store had been set by successive directors, could at last be properly installed.[6] As the visitor climbed up the staircase to the first floor, he saw the *Farnese Hercules* in a well-lit niche on his left; a little further up, along rather a dark corridor, was the *Farnese Flora*; flanking the door in the first room were the *Lion* and the *Boar*; beyond, could be seen *Paetus and Arria*, and next to them Niobe clutching her young daughter from the *Niobe Group*. And so the visit continued: in one large room were the *Dancing Faun*, the *Commodus as Hercules*, the *Antinous*, the *Germanicus*, the *Cincinnatus*, the children of *Niobe*; elsewhere were portraits of the King and Queen of France, copies of Raphael's frescoes in the Vatican, splendid tapestries and painted columns – and everywhere, elegantly placed, were plaster versions of those statues whose proportions had been measured and whose features had been analysed by artists and scholars from all over Europe: the *Laocoon*, the *Dying Gladiator*, the *Spinario*, the *Hermaphrodite*. ... As statues were uncovered in fresh excavations, so casts were added, even though in Paris the authorities were no longer interested in buying marble copies for the royal household.[7] Only in the Palazzo Mancini could the full range of the most famous antique statues be examined at leisure and in comfort, and it was to this collection that foreign connoisseurs were often forced to resort for advice and sometimes to have copies (at one remove from the originals) made for themselves.[8]

Among the visitors to the Academy was Cardinal Alessandro Albani, the most enthusiastic and spendthrift of eighteenth-century Roman art patrons, who particularly pressed the director to include casts of the principal antiquities to be found in France, 'for in some way or another it is essential to bring back to Rome what has been removed from the city'.[9] Cardinal Albani had good reason to urge such a policy. Having already sold many of his own antiquities to Augustus the Strong of Poland, he was soon trying to dispose of the remainder. Although the French were not interested in 'curiosities of this kind',[10] it must have seemed inevitable that most of the several hundred 'statues, busts, heads, bas-reliefs, herms, urns with bas-reliefs, Egyptian antiquities, decorated vases, lions and columns'[11] assembled by the Cardinal would go abroad – probably to England where Albani was advised to sell them.[12] And then, in 1733, Pope Clement XII made a move which changed the nature of Roman sculpture collections more than anything that had been done since Julius II had established the Belvedere statue court in the first years of the sixteenth century. He bought all the Albani antiquities and made them the nucleus of a new museum on the Capitol.[13]

We have already pointed out that the first sculptures to be seen on the Capitol since antiquity had been donated by Pope Sixtus IV in 1471. During the early sixteenth century important additions were made to these, culminating in the installation of the *Marcus Aurelius* in 1538, which was followed by some purchases and private gifts, and above all by the transference to the Conservators of large numbers of statues from the Vatican in 1566 and the next few years. In the middle of the seventeenth century Michelangelo's project of a twin palace on the other side of the piazza from that of the Conservators was completed and a certain number of statues were placed in it. In 1720 Pope Clement XI bought from the Cesi family a group of well-known statues – the Rome seated above the *Weeping Dacia* with the two Barbarian Captives – and these were placed in the courtyard of the palace of the Conservators. But it was only with the purchase of Cardinal Albani's sculptures that the Capitoline collections were radically transformed.

Albani had managed to acquire from various sources a few sculptures which had once been very famous (above all the *Della Valle Satyrs* and the *Cesi Juno*), though they had been a little neglected in more recent years. The real attraction of his collection, however, consisted of a statue of *Antinous*, excavated at Hadrian's Villa, and a very large group of ambitiously identified portrait busts. Although there can be no doubt that these Philosophers and Emperors, placed in rooms named after them, were enthusiastically inspected by foreign visitors to Rome, they are not included in our catalogue, for – as has already been mentioned [earlier in *Taste and the Antique*] – the interest they aroused depended more on their historical than their aesthetic distinction, as is made clear in a rapturous letter from the Abbé Barthélemy to the Comte de Caylus:

The first time that I went into the Capitoline Museum I felt a shock of electricity. I do not know how to describe to you the impression made on me by the bringing together of so much richness. This is no longer just a collection: it is the dwelling place of the gods of ancient Rome; the school of the philosophers; a senate composed of the kings of the East. What can I tell you of it? A whole population of statues inhabits the Capitol; it is the great book of antiquarians.[14]

The Albani sculptures had hardly been installed before new demands began to be made on the available space, for it was now that a barely explored treasure trove began to be extensively exploited, and, as a result, the next few years recalled the time a century earlier when the great Roman families had vied with each other in adding to the patrimony of recognised masterpieces.

The ruins of the villa which the Emperor Hadrian had built for himself about twenty miles from Rome had been known and discussed ever since the fifteenth century.[15] Occasional excavations brought statues to light, but it was not until 1550 that Cardinal Ippolito II d'Este, governor of the adjoining town of Tivoli, began to pursue these with some vigour in order to decorate his beautiful Villa d'Este, while Pirro Ligorio, his antiquarian and part-time architect,[16] wrote various treatises about Hadrian's Villa which gave it real fame among scholars.[17] However, of the many statues which were excavated at this time none acquired true celebrity. During the seventeenth century excavations continued sporadically, but as the property was divided among some forty-five separate owners little could be done on a systematic scale. In 1724, however, an elusive collector and amateur dealer, Count Fede, began buying up as much of the estate as he could; when he had accumulated a substantial portion he beautified it by planting the great cypresses which are still such a feature of the Villa[18] and undertook more thorough investigations than had yet been possible, and in this he was followed by the other principal landowners on the site – the Jesuits, and the Bulgarini family who, however, rather rashly sold their rights to the ambitious and erudite Monsignor Furietti.

A series of spectacular discoveries followed in quick succession. Among the earliest must have been the full-length *Antinous* which Cardinal Albani sold to the Pope in 1733; some two years after this transaction had been completed the Cardinal got hold of a bas-relief of Hadrian's favourite – both these representations of Antinous were quickly ranked with the most famous works to have survived from antiquity; in 1736 the *Faun in Rosso Antico* was dug up, and in the same year Furietti excavated the two *Centaurs* and, shortly after, a mosaic which aroused great interest; in 1744 the *Flora* came to light. All these were much publicised and engraved after only a short delay, and thus, in little more than a decade, about half a dozen statues of world-wide fame (but, for the most part, notably different in character from the ones to be seen in the Borghese and Ludovisi Villas) had been added to the stock of those which had been attracting universal attention for more than a century.

It is hard to determine to what degree such a very distinguished provenance must be held responsible for the great celebrity of these works. Hadrian was well known as an art lover, and to some extent his villa could be thought of as the Belvedere statue court of ancient Rome – and thus as a guarantee of quality. Though scholarly opinion was sometimes critical of what had been found there (the *Furietti Centaurs*, for instance), public enthusiasm, and hence the repeated copies which were so essential for establishing the fame of a work, must have been fired by the reflection that these sculptures had belonged to the Emperor himself; and indeed from the 1730s onwards the lure of Hadrian's Villa was to be a potent one for art lovers and speculators of all kinds.

No one played a greater part in exploiting its resources than Cardinal Albani (1692–1779), whose name has already been frequently mentioned in this chapter and who for more than half a century dominated the international world of collectors and scholars who flocked to Rome. But though his informed love of art was never in doubt and though the beautiful villa– museum built for him by Carlo Marchionni on the Via Salaria attracted great enthusiasm not only through its huge collection of antique (including Egyptian) sculpture but also through its ceiling fresco of Parnassus by Anton Rafael Mengs, Albani's direct influence on the theme of our book [*Taste and the Antique*] was limited by doubts about his personal integrity. Like many people who traffic in works of art he was suspected of being 'tant soit peu fripon',[19] of charging extortionate prices,[20] and of giving his enthusiastic endorsement to evident duds.[21] And the fact that, unlike the great collecting cardinals of the seventeenth century, he was as much concerned with selling as with buying helped to bring an element of notoriety to two related practices which had hitherto been accepted virtually without question: the automatic 'baptism' of anonymous portraits and figures, and their drastic restoration. As early as 1728, when the first of Albani's collections was on the market, Montesquieu was told that 'in Rome, when they see a serious-looking man without a beard, he is a consul; with a long beard, a philosopher; and a young boy, an Antinous'.[22] Later travellers repeated again and again the opinion that 'Cardinal Albani is in our days the restorer-in-chief of Antiquity. The most mutilated, disfigured, incurable pieces are, through him, given back the flower of youth, *nova facit omnia*; the fragment of a bust which, even if it were whole, would have been *una testa incognitissima* to all the antiquarians receives from him both a new life and a name which indelibly settles its destiny.'[23] And it is notable that such mocking charges were launched well before the overriding impact made on current ideas of nomenclature and restoration [...] by the man whose support by Albani has given the Cardinal his greatest fame in the eyes of posterity: his librarian Johann Joachim Winckelmann.

Following the purchase of Albani's first set of marbles, successive popes bought regularly for the Capitoline Museum both from old collections and from new excavations – in 1752, for instance, Benedict XIV acquired from the Stazi family, which had owned it for nearly a century, a *Venus* soon to become one of the most admired sculptures in Rome; and his successor Clement XIII was able to buy the already famous *Centaurs* from the heirs of Cardinal Furietti. Nevertheless, the threat of outside competition grew ever more dangerous. Charles Bourbon, King of newly independent Naples, needed classical statuary to decorate the palaces he was having built, and, as nothing unearthed at Herculaneum could begin to rival in prestige the famous sculptures to be seen in Rome, he toyed with the idea both of having copies made of many of the heads in the Capitoline Museum and also of purchasing some of the well-known collections which were rumoured to be unofficially on the market – those of the Este, for instance, and of the Mattei. But there was a far more ominous threat: as early as 1755, Luigi Vanvitelli, the architect Charles had invited from Rome to design his palace at Caserta, dropped a clear hint that, just as the King had taken the Farnese pictures from Parma to Naples, so too he could do the same with the Farnese sculptures which he had also inherited.[24]

More immediately pressing was the menace of the English. In 1749 Matthew Brettingham the Younger was in Rome to buy more sculptures – with the active encouragement of Cardinal Albani who used his influence to annul inconvenient export regulations[25] – for the same Mr. Coke (by now Earl of Leicester) who, nearly forty years earlier, had taken back to England the Diana and other distinguished pieces;[26] and it was not long before two Englishmen, Thomas Jenkins and Gavin Hamilton, were shipping home large quantities of antique sculpture, much of it from Hadrian's Villa. Under the licensing system then in force, the popes were entitled to one-third of any excavation carried out within their dominions and could also prevent the export of any other specific pieces which were considered to be of great importance.[27] This right was frequently exerted – but also frequently evaded, the more easily so as Cardinal Albani was only one among many highly placed individuals keen to make a profit from the fabulously rich English.[28]

The legendary fame (or notoriety) enjoyed by these English collectors in the second half of the eighteenth century and the extraordinary number of sculptures imported by them and their agents into England[29] makes it particularly necessary to estimate with some care the importance of their activities in the context of our book [*Taste and the Antique*], which is concerned with the creation, the diffusion and the eventual dissolution of a 'canon' of universally admired antique statues. When we do this we realise that the part played by the English in this process was a comparatively small one. Despite what appeared to be unlimited wealth, no English collector was able to buy any of the really celebrated antiquities in Rome. Sculptures were acquired from almost every established collection – but they were not the most famous pieces: it is in fact impossible to trace to an English collection any piece of antique sculpture which had previously been illustrated in an

Italian anthology of the most famous and beautiful statues with the exception of Mr Coke's *Diana* and '*Lucius Antonius*'. Nor were the English any more successful in acquiring really well-known sculptures which had recently been excavated. Huge sums, for instance, were said to have been offered for the *Furietti Centaurs* – but in vain. Only in the last third of the eighteenth century when English dealers (such as Gavin Hamilton) were themselves conducting excavations at Hadrian's Villa and elsewhere in the papal territories did it become possible to remove sculptures acknowledged to be of the highest quality, among them the colossal marble vase discovered in 1771. This was purchased by Sir William Hamilton and sold after restoration to the Earl of Warwick, who for a long time forbade casts to be made of it (although he did encourage Lord Lonsdale to make a full-scale replica in solid silver); but bronze and cast-iron replicas of the Warwick Vase (which is now in the Glasgow Museum) were eventually made, and it was copied on a reduced scale in silver, bronze, marble, porcelain and terracotta by artists using the prints made by Gavin Hamilton's business associate Piranesi – and these helped to establish it as perhaps the most famous antique marble vase after those in the Borghese and Medici collections and the first item, it was reported, on Napoleon's list of the works of art to be expropriated after the conquest of Great Britain.[30]

The two most highly esteemed statues to be exported from the papal states to England were versions of works which had long been among the most famous in Europe: the *Cincinnatus* (by then known as *Jason*) and the *Belvedere Antinous* (by then known as *Meleager*). Both were excavated by Gavin Hamilton, the former at Hadrian's Villa in 1769 and the latter at Tor Colombaro two years later; after the Pope had declined to purchase the Cincinnatus because it was too expensive and the Antinous because he already owned the one in the Vatican, both were sent to join Lord Shelburne's collection in London.[31] Even though Canova is said to have supported the view expressed in Rome at the time of its export that the new *Antinous* (now in the Ludington collection, Santa Barbara) was superior to the old, and even though modern scholars have often agreed with Gavin Hamilton that the same could be said of the new *Jason* (now in the Ny Carlsberg Glyptothek, Copenhagen, as *Hermes*), neither statue had a chance in the late eighteenth and early nineteenth centuries of competing with rivals in the public collections of Rome and Paris. A group of casts of notable works which had been exported from Rome was displayed in the Accademia di S. Luca and elsewhere, but these were not sufficient to keep the memory of the statues themselves alive among men of taste.[32]

Sculptures in the British Museum clearly stood a better chance of achieving international celebrity than those in private houses whether in London or the country – a fate so obscure, according to a German visitor to Italy, that they might as well never have been excavated.[33] There was great enthusiasm among English connoisseurs for a Venus which came to the Museum with the Townley collection in 1805 and this might have been more widespread if the statue had been at all noted in Rome before its export, but its discovery by Gavin Hamilton at Ostia in 1775 had been deliberately concealed and it had been shipped to England as two separate fragments.[34] Even more popular was a female bust also from Charles Townley's collection which, under the name of Clytie,[35] was extensively reproduced in marble, plaster and parian ware. Goethe owned two casts of this,[36] but in general its fame does not seem to have spread much beyond England.

No European man of taste keen to study the most beautiful and famous antique statues would, before 1800, have thought of crossing the Channel to visit England, but the scholar scanning the index of Carlo Fea's Italian edition of Winckelmann's *History of Ancient Art* would have noted how many more works were mentioned in English than in French, Spanish or German collections, and might well have feared in 1768 when the Barberini sold to Charles Townley the 'Youths quarrelling over a Game of Knuckle-Bone' (a much noted group which some had even connected with Polyclitus)[37] that other even more valued treasures would be disposed of – the Barberini Vase, for instance, which did in fact go to England, and the *Barberini Faun*. Indeed it was in 1768 that Bartolommeo Cavaceppi, the Pope's chief restorer, published a large illustrated volume of antique statues that had been repaired in his studio. Of the sixty plates, thirty-four reproduced works already belonging to Englishmen, while seventeen showed others in German collections. The remainder were divided between Cardinals Albani and Furietti and Count Fede.[38] A year later Cavaceppi published a second volume. This time all sixty works illustrated were for sale. The message was clear enough. The popes might intervene, of course, but with the Capitoline Museum already full, where would they be able to place all the statues that might at any time come on the market from half the collections in Rome, let alone those that were being dug up every day?

Meanwhile once again the situation within Italy became desperate. In about 1769 Pietro Leopoldo, the Lorenese Grand Duke of Tuscany, inaugurated a long campaign to rationalise the Medici collections which had been left to Florence, and during the course of this he decided – on the advice of Anton Rafael Mengs[39] – to establish a cast gallery for the Accademia delle Belle Arti and to bring to the city the most famous works of art that were scattered throughout Tuscany and elsewhere – actions which, it was hoped, would help to revive the arts and give birth to 'nuovi Bonarroti'.[40] Among these works of art were the antiquities that still remained in the Villa Medici, some of which (the *Niobe Group*, the *Apollino*, and even the *Lion*) were among the principal sights of Rome. Pope Clement XIV protested vigorously, but there was nothing he could do. By June 1770 the *Niobe Group* was already in Florence, to be installed some ten years later in a specially built room in the Uffizi. Soon after, the other antiquities from Rome were displayed in Florence.

The Pope's impotence did not pass unnoticed in Naples, where the King's chief minister, the Marchese Tanucci, was engaged in bitter controversy with the Papacy over the political and ecclesiastical independence of the kingdom.[41] 'Doubtless so as to make these negotiations easier and to put the Pope in a better mood', as Cardinal de Bernis commented sarcastically,[42] Tanucci brought up once again the possibility of removing the Farnese antiquities – the most celebrated private collection in Europe. In fact the threat did not materialise for another fifteen years or so, when the terms of Cardinal Farnese's will of 1587 that the collections should remain for ever in Rome were finally set aside, and the *Hercules*, the *Flora*, the *Bull*, the *Callipygian Venus* and many more were removed from the family's palaces in the city. Already, however, there seemed a strong possibility that the collections of Florence (which had been an outstanding centre for visitors ever since the first removals from the Villa Medici nearly a century earlier) and of Naples (where the excavations at Herculaneum and Pompeii had begun to attract very great interest) would soon rival, if not actually surpass, those of Rome – at the very time when enthusiasm for antiquity was everywhere rising to a peak.

It was in these circumstances that Pope Clement XIV, who had been enthroned in 1769, decided on drastic action. Almost simultaneously he began to buy whatever became available – the *Meleager*, for instance, was acquired in August 1770 – and to build a new museum behind the Vatican palace to house the acquisitions he was already making and planning to extend on an ever increasing scale.[43]

Little of real importance had been done to the Vatican collections since the reign of Pius V, though a huge porphyry vase had been added to the statue court[44] and parts of the Library had been used to accommodate various private gifts, bequests and purchases which had been split up into a 'Museo Cristiano' and a 'Museo Profano'. Clement XIV's project envisaged two major steps: the ground floor of the medieval villa of Innocent VIII, which remained intact and more or less deserted behind the statue court, was to be refurbished as a museum, and the dignity of the statue court itself was to be enhanced by the building of a handsome octagonal loggia so devised as to provide a series of frames for the most famous sculptures. These arrangements and the extensive campaign of restoration and of purchases (which required the cooperation of every dealer in Rome) were in the hands of the antiquarian Giambattista Visconti and his brilliant son Ennio Quirino, whose catalogue of the new museum, published over a period of many years, made an impact on eighteenth-century archaeological studies second only to that of Winckelmann.

It is not, however, our intention to discuss here what soon became the most famous museum in the world except in so far as it impinged on the most celebrated sculptures displayed in it and the responses aroused by them. Such issues are not easy to assess, for Clement XIV's museum only survived for a short time before it was drastically altered and extended by his successor Pius VI, and at no period did Visconti reveal very much about his principles of display. Moreover, the guidebooks and travellers of the period veer between copying and contradicting each other, often so blatantly that it is tempting to deduce that during these years frequent changes were made in 'grading' some of the sculptures in the statue court. Certain features emerge clearly: the *Nile* and the *Tiber*, which had reclined in the centre of the court since the early sixteenth century, were now removed from it and separated.[45] This did not imply any doubts about their quality, for each was given a small room of its own fashioned out of the loggia of Innocent VIII's villa. The principal figures – the *Apollo*, the *Laocoon*, the *Antinous*, the *Commodus as Hercules* and the *Venus Felix* – were left in the monumentalised court, but the *Standing Venus* and the *Tigris* were taken out of it. On the other hand, the *Seated Paris*, a statue recently acquired from the Altemps family, in whose palace it had been much admired throughout the eighteenth century, was given a niche of its own in the court[46] – a momentary glory, for this arrangement was soon to be changed.

Clement XIV died in 1774, much derided (like the Renaissance popes) for his supposed attachment to paganism[47] – not surprisingly, perhaps, for he had done more for the public appreciation of antique sculptures than any of his predecessors for two and a half centuries. His successor Gianangelo Braschi, who took the name of Pius VI, had as treasurer always been the moving force behind the new museum. Once in power he extended it with lavish and ruthless efficiency, pulling down Innocent VIII's little chapel (with its frescoes by Mantegna) which had been carefully preserved under Clement. Once again, however, our only interest here is in the fate of those sculptures with which we have been concerned in this book. The basic structure of the statue court remained unchanged, but it seems that Pius VI found it as difficult as his predecessor to decide which figures, apart from the five which had survived the previous alterations, were worthy of special prominence. The Altemps *Paris* was removed, and the scanty evidence at our disposal suggests that two other recently acquired statues were successively put in its place: first, standing *Lucius Verus*,[48] and then a *Genius of Augustus*.[49] In the event the new arrangement lasted for not much longer than the previous one, for the French armies saw to it that the most important statues were all taken to Paris; but, confused as it is, this episode of the reappraisal of the statue court is of notable interest, demonstrating as it does some of the practical consequences for a great museum director of those changes in taste which […] he himself had helped to bring about.

Yet such moving around of sculptures constituted only a small aspect of the reorganisation of the collections. Each one of the great standing statues, hitherto solitary in a garden setting, was now surrounded by herms and sarcophagi, bas-reliefs and columns, often let into the imposing new walls and always arranged for decorative effect – it being sometimes acknowledged that they were of little aesthetic merit.[50] The reclining *Nile* and *Tiber* now presided over rooms teeming with sculptures of the most varied kinds from the venerated *Meleager* to dogs recently dug up from Hadrian's Villa. Some visitors deplored this dilution of quality;[51] others were enthusiastic about:

the most magnificent and grand combination that perhaps has ever been beheld or can almost be imagined. Never were the divinities of Greece and Rome honoured with nobler temples; never did they stand on richer pedestals; never were more glorious domes spread over their heads; or brighter pavements extended at their feet. Seated each in a shrine of bronze or marble, they seemed to look down on a crowd of votaries and once more to challenge the homage of mankind; while kings and emperors, heroes and philosophers, drawn up in ranks before or around them, increased their state and formed a majestic and becoming retinue.[52]

Yet, in many ways, little enough had changed. Not one antique statue gained lasting additional fame in the new museum. Visitors still hurried, as they had been doing for so long, to enthuse over the *Apollo*, the *Antinous* and the *Laocoon* and in so doing scarcely paused to comment on the vast wealth of freshly acquired statuary. And the impulse felt by so many of them to express in print their very conventional feelings about masterpieces that had already been described countless times before clearly enhanced the prestige of old favourites rather than drew attention to new discoveries. Familiarity bred not contempt but an irresistible urge to rhapsodise, and never were the disclaimers (which had become conventional as early as the beginning of the seventeenth century) about the need for yet another account of the most famous antique statues so frequently repeated and so little heeded as they were by the end of the eighteenth century. By then there can have been few people in the Western world with even moderate claims to taste still unaware that, in the words of an earlier writer,

there are some statues which the connoisseurs have established as examples and rules, each of its own kind: the Venus de' Medici, the Dancing Faun [le petit Faune], the Arrotino [le paysan qui écoute] and the Wrestlers (these four pieces are in the palace of the Grand Duke of Florence), and (in Rome) the Apollo Belvedere, the Farnese Hercules, the Laocoon. And these statues cannot be sufficiently looked at, for it is from them that the Moderns have built up their system of proportions, and it is they which have virtually given us the arts.[53]

This consciousness was heightened by the reproductions of these works that were by now to be found all over Europe and were beginning to spread to the United States.

NOTES

1. Anatole de Montaiglon (ed.), *Correspondance des directeurs de l'Académie de France à Rome avec les Surintendants des Bâtiments*, 18 vols, Paris 1887–1912, VII, p. 480.

2. Paolo Alessandro Maffei, *Raccolta di statue antiche e moderne, data in luce … da Domenico de Rossi*, Rome 1704, plates CXLV, CXLVII; Adolf Michaelis, *Ancient Marbles in Great Britain*, Cambridge 1882, pp. 59, 308–9, 313–14.

3. Matthew Brettingham, *The Plans, Elevations and Sections of Holkham in Norfolk … also a descriptive account of the Statues, Pictures and Drawings; not in the former edition*, London, 1773, p. 4.

4. Montaiglon, *Correspondence*, V, pp. 368–91 (many references).

5. Ludwig Pastor, *The History of the Popes from the close of the Middle Ages*, 40 vols, London 1894–1953, XXXIV, pp. 35–7.

6. Montaiglon, *Correspondance*, VII, pp. 333–7.

7. Ibid., IX, p. 489.

8. Ibid., X, p. 434 (Filiippo Farsetti, 1753).

9. Ibid., VII, p. 381.

10. Ibid., VIII, p. 258.

11. H. Stuart Jones (ed.), *A Catalogue of the Ancient Sculptures preserved in the Municipal Collections of Rome: The sculptures of the Museo Capitolino*, Oxford 1912, pp. 385–98.

12. Lesley Lewis, *Connoisseurs and Secret Agents in Eighteenth Century Rome*, London 1961, p. 92.

13. Stuart Jones, pp. 385–98.

14. Abbé [Jean Jacques] Barthélemy, *Voyage en Italie … imprimé sur ses lettres originales écrites au Comte de Caylus*, Paris 1801, p. 95 (10 February 1756).

15. Herman Winnefeld, *Die Villa des Hadrian bei Tivoli*, Berling 1895, pp. 4–5.

16. David R. Coffin, *The Villa d'Este at Tivoli*, Princeton 1960.

17. Erna Mandowsky and Charles Mitchell, *Pirro Ligorio's Roman Antiquities*, London 1963.

18. Salvatore Aurigemma, *Villa Adriani*, Rome 1961, p. 28.

19. Paolo Maria Paciaudi, *Lettres de Paciaudi au Comte de Caylus*, edited by A. Sérieys, Paris An XI [1802], p. 318.

20. Montaiglon, *Correspondance*, VIII, p. 396.

21. Luigi Vanvitelli, *Le lettere*, edited by Franco Strazzullo ?, 3 vols, Galatina 1976–7, I, pp. 583, 590, 592ff., 601.

22. Montesquieu, *Oeuvres complètes*, edited by André Masson, 3 vols, Paris 1950–5, II, p. 1317 (*Voyages d'Italie*).

23. [Pierre Jean Grosley], *Observations sur l'Italie et sur les Italiens données en 1764, sous le nom de deux gentilhommes suédois*, new edition, 4 vols, London 1770, II, pp. 294–5; see also [Abbé de Guasco], *De l'usage des statues chez les anciens*, Brussels 1768, p. xxiii; Justi, 1866–72, II, p. 305.

24. Vanvitelli, I, pp. 115, 440, 446, 505, 516; II, p. 176, 300, 366.

25. Lewis, pp. 151–4.

26. Matthew Bettingham, 'Accounts of Works of Art Bought in Rome', Holkham MS. 744; Michaelis, p. 71.

27. Carlo Pietrangeli, 'Il Museo Clementino Vaticano', *Atti della Pontificia Accademia Romana di Archeologia* (Rendiconti), 1951–2, XXVII, pp. 89–90.

28. Lewis, pp. 154ff.; Justi, 1866–72, III, pp. 32–8.

29. Michaelis, pp. 55–128.

30. James Dallaway, *Of Statuary and Sculpture*, London, 1816, p. 186; David Udy, 'Piranesi's "Vasi": The English Silversmith and his Patrons', *Burlington Magazine*, 1978, p. 141; *Burlington Magazine*, 1979, p. 141.

31. Michaelis, pp. 454–5, 466.

32. Johan Wolfgang von Goethe, *Werke*, Abteilung I (published works), 63 vols, Weimar 1887–1918, XXXII, p. 323 (*Italienische Reise*); Giovanni Winckelmann, *Storia delle arti del disegno presse gli antichi*, edited by Carlo Fea, 3 vols, Rome 1783–4, II, p. 199; Ennio Quirino Visconti, uniform edition Milan 1818–1837, *Museo Pio-Clementino*, II, plate XLIII; August von Kotzebue, *Erinnerungen von einer Reise aus Liefland nach Rom und Neapel*, 3 vols, Berlin 1805, III, p. 23.

33. Kotzebue, IIIm, p. 23.

34. [Richard Payne Knight], *Specimens of Antient Sculpture*, I, London 1809, plate XLI.

35. A. H. Smith, *A Catalogue of the Sculpture in the Department of Greek and Roman Antiquities, British Museum*, 3 vols, London 1892–1904, III, pp. 28, 147–9.

36. Willi Ehrlich, *Goethes Wohnhaus um Frauenplan in Weimar*, Weimar 1978, pp. 16, 20.

37. Abbé Richard, *Description historique et critique de l'Italie*, 6 vols, Dijon and Paris 1766, p. 73; Winckelmann, II, p. 196; Dallaway, pp. 311–12; Michaelis, p. 97.

38. Another two belonged to the Capitoline Museum and the Bailli de Breteuil.

39. Tommaso Puccini, *Dello stato delle Belli Arti in Toscana: Lettera … al signore Prince Hoare*, [Pistoia] 1807, pp. 20–1.

40. Angelo Fabroni, *Dissertazione sulle statue appartenenti alla favola di Niobe*, Florence 1779, p. 21.

41. Pastor, XXXVIII, p. 162.

42. Montaiglon, *Correspondance*, XII, p. 318.

43. Pietrangeli; Seymour Howard, 'An Antiquarian Handlist and the Beginnings of the Pio-Clementino', *Eighteenth Century Studies*, 1973, VII, no. 1.

44. Michaelis, p. 54.

45. Pietro Rossini, *Il Mercurio errante delle grandezze di Roma*, 10th edition, enlarged, 2 vols, Rome 1776, I, pp. 275–7.

46. Ibid.

47. Pastor, XXVIII, p. 543.

48. See the plan at the beginning of Vol. I (1782) of the folio edition of Visconti's *Pio-Clementino*; [Mary] Berry, *Extracts of the Journals and Correspondence of Miss Berry from the year 1783 to 1852*, edited by Lady Theresa Lewis, 3 vols, London 1865, I, pp. 111–12 (22 April 1784).

49. Marien Vasi, *Description du Musée Pio-Clementino et de la galerie des tableaux du Palais Vatican*, Rome 1792, p. 9; Pasquale Massi, *Indicazione antiquaria del pontificio museo Pio-Clementino in Vaticano*, Rome 1792, p. 25. The *Lucius Versus* was presumably Visconti (*Pio-Clementino*), I, plate IX, and the *Genius of Auguste*, ibid., III, plate II.

50. Vasi, p. 9.

51. M. de Lalande, *Voyage en Italie*, second edition, enlarged, 7 vols, Yverdon 1787–8, p. 197.

52. Rev. John Chetwode Eustace, *A Classical Tour through Italy*, second edition, revised, London 1814, p. 291.

53. Montesquieu, I, p. 1318 (*Voyage d'Italie*).

6.

The Genesis and Early Development of the Royal Museum in Stockholm: A Claim for Authenticity and Legitimacy

Magnus Olausson and Solfrid Söderlind

At the end of May 1775, a young Swedish artist visited the Parc Monceau in Paris, the picturesque garden that was being laid out by playwright Louis Carrogis de Carmontelle for the then Duc de Chartres. His observations well reflect the ambiguity of the concept of a museum: 'This small Garden is a representation of Rome in miniature with its Antiquities, Colonnades, Obelisques and diverse ancient remnants, of them the greater part in Marble. This has cost the Prince a considerable sum of money; notwithstanding he ceaselessly perseveres in augmenting this Museum.'[1] The notion of a museum (like that of a theater) had a very broad meaning in those days, and one might well ask whether the two concepts were actually closely related. There is undoubtedly a theatrical quality in the Duc's open-air museum. Its creator, Carmontelle, was of the opinion that: 'On ne s'amuse que d'illusions transportons, dans nos Jardins, les changements de scène des Opéras; faisons-y voir, en réalité, ce que les plus habiles Peintres pourroient y offrir en décorations, tous les temps & tous les lieux.'[2]

The most famous construction in Parc Monceau, the *naumachie* which with its colonnade was probably intended to resemble an equivalent feature in the Villa Adriana at Tivoli (i.e. Hadrian's villa at Tibur), consisted of parts from the sepulchral monument of Catherine de'Medici in St-Denis.[3] For Carmontelle, it sufficed to create an illusion of bygone times, but other contemporaries demanded historic authenticity. The German garden theorist C. C. L. Hirschfeld was of the opinion that doubt would soon make itself felt if one were to come across Greek ruins in an English park situated in some place other than the region of the Mediterranean. He concluded his criticism of the architectural falsifications of the day, by exclaiming: '... quelle contradiction entre l'object & son site!'[4] Beside the demand for historic credibility, there was also an ethical aspect. His contemporary William Gilpin considered that 'a ruin is a sacred thing'.[5] It was not something you could manipulate or move.

A similar line of reasoning could just as readily have been applied to collections of antiquities which had at some time in the same way been part of another context. Was it reasonable to move antiquities from their authentic environment, the sites where they had been found, such as Rome? This had long been a sensitive question. When one of the foremost representatives of Italian art, Gian Lorenzo Bernini, visited Paris in 1665, he explained to his hosts, according to the cicerone Chantelou, that the masterpieces (implying the antiques) should remain in Rome; this was because they in their turn were the well from which new generations of painters and sculptors were to fetch sustenance. Bernini considered that it was only through an untiring study of antiques that one could acquire absolute mastery.[6]

Bernini's view of the matter was clear and unequivocal. Notwithstanding, Paris was still on the right side of the historical border, the Roman *limes*. It became directly more complicated with places situated north of this, in *ultima Thule*. The requirement as to historic authenticity did not allow for antique sculptures to be moved to a more northern latitude. For a long time this was also made impossible by virtue of the actual lack of antiques. The Pope's export controls were rigorous, and made it difficult even for the most prominent crowned heads of Europe, such as Charles I of England and Louis XIV of France, to acquire coveted works of art in marble and bronze.[7] During the reign of Queen Kristina, some antiques did indeed find their way to such distant places as Stockholm, but it is symptomatic that this was as a part of the great war booty that the Swedes brought back from, among other places, Prague, in the final phases of the Thirty Years' War.[8]

Queen Kristina's collection of antiquities, however, was but an episode. The part that the Queen chose not to take with her to Rome after her abdication in 1654 was destroyed in the great fire which consumed the palace in Stockholm in 1697. It was not until Gustav III that Sweden again found itself with a collector on the throne with the ambition to acquire antiquities. The King's attitude did not differ particularly from that of other contemporary princes. For reasons of prestige, Gustav III – like his cousin Catherine II, Empress of Russia – preferred to purchase antique works in marble and bronze. Admiral Carl August Ehrensvärd, philosopher of art, made fruitless attempts to engage the King's interest in plaster casts instead of what were, in his eyes, mediocre antique marble originals.[9]

Gustav III's purchases and the issue of legitimacy

During Gustav III's Italian journey of 1783–84, several art dealers vied with each other for the Swedish monarch's favour. For the King's official art agent in Rome, Francesco Piranesi, the disappointment was of course considerable when his competitor Giovanni Volpato was the first to sell a collection of antiques to the eminent tourist from Sweden. What caught Gustav's interest was a suite of sculptures portraying Apollo playing a cithara and the nine Muses. After his return from Naples and further visits to Volpato's studio,

Figure 5.6.1   View of the Greater Stone Gallery of the Royal Museum with *Apollo and the Nine Muses* together with *Endymion*, Pehr Hilleström, oil on canvas, Rbg 40. Photo: Nationalmuseum, Stockholm

the King purchased these Muses.[10] There is cause to suspect that Volpato's old friend the sculptor Johan Tobias Sergel was actively involved in this acquisition. According to Piranesi, no other member of the royal suite had appreciated Volpato's antiques.

It was not a case of an authentic suite of Muses from Roman antiquity, but a conglomerate of converted marble fragments. It should, however, be emphasized that the separate parts all had an interesting provenance. Together, they formed a superposition of various collections in which the names of most of the great connoisseurs and dealers of the day appear, such as Gavin Hamilton, Henry Tresham, Bartolomeo Cavaceppi and finally Giovanni Volpato.[11] The theme itself was of course prestigious, and the ensemble that Volpato and the others succeeded in putting together naturally alluded to the illustrious group of Nine Muses and Apollo in the Vatican. It was therefore hardly surprising that Gustav III should succumb to the temptation to buy Volpato's *Muses*. The Swedish King would have been hard pressed to find a better trophy from his Roman visit.

Piranesi naturally did all he could to belittle the value of the sculptures, but in a letter to one of the King's advisors, Royal Secretary Carl Fredrik

Fredenheim, he also gives some interesting information as to how Gustav III intended to arrange his newly acquired antiques: 'His Majesty saw them and thought that they would well suit the purpose he had in mind. I believe it was a question of situating them in gardens or a summer pavilion.'[12] By good fortune, a plan has survived; penned by Gustav III's own hand, this has to be seen in the context of Piranesi's remark. The King himself has phrased the heading: 'Project pour faire du Rocher qui termine le Jardin de Drottningholm. Le Parnasse avec Apollon & les neuf muses'.[13]

How had Gustav III intended to arrange Volpato's *Muses* and the *Apollo*? Muncken Rise at the far end of the French garden seemed to offer the best solution for a Parnassus in a Swedish setting. The King evidently planned to place the statues on a stony slope in the rustic style, where a highly situated formation of stone blocks was to provide the main accent. From this summit, the King had projected a cascade of water which would pour down the slope, a copy of the fountain of Castalia. In the immediate vicinity of the mouth of the cascade, there would be a sculpture of Pegasus, and below this the King had thought to situate the nine *Muses* on either side of the *Apollo playing a Cithara*. The whole arrangement was to be framed by dense foliage.

Gustav III's choice of Muncken Rise, in the background of the garden, was not only a result of the natural possibilities offered by the topography. The placing of the Muses would present a direct contrast to the Parnassus from the 1670s in Tessin's stairwell at the Palace. If the King's plans had been realized, in the spirit of the eighteenth century he would have had the Parnassus 'moved out' to a more 'realistic' setting.

Beside the traditional form of the motif, Gustav III had, however, made an addition. Below the sphere of the Muses, the King had chosen to place their terrestrial spokesmen, and to do this by contrasting what he called 'les poètes anciens' with 'les poètes modernes'. Gustav III grouped them together so that one pair consisted of the antique tragedians Sophocles, Aeschylus and Euripedes together with their later colleagues Racine, Corneille and Voltaire. The next row gathered together the great epic poets: Homer, Vergil and Ovid and their equivalents from a later age, Tasso, Ariosto and Dante. In between these two groups, the King placed Molière, Aristophanes, Terence and Plautus, all of them representing the genre of comedy.

Antique sculptures were much appreciated features in gardens during the Renaissance.[14] But sculpture in such a setting was not just a heritage with its roots in antiquity. Many of the gardens of the Roman villas, for instance, were places where antique works had been found. Diaries and newspaper items reveal that Gustav III was a frequent visitor to many of the gardens in Rome, and he had many opportunities to study a variety of arrangements which included antique sculptures. A particularly common theme was Apollo and the Muses together with Pegasus and Parnassus. This motif could be

Figure 5.6.2   Gustav III's project for a sculptural display in the garden of
Drottningholm called *Projet pour faire du Rocher qui termine le Jardin de Drottningholm,
le Parnasse avec Appollon & les neuf muses*, pen and ink. Photo: National Archives,
Stockholm

seen in, for instance, the Villa Madama, Giardino de Bufalo, Pius IV's Casino,
the Villa d'Este, the Villa Lante in Bagnaia, the Villa Mattei and so on. The
literary character that Gustav had intended to give to his Drottningholm

Parnassus could be found in the Villa Aldobrandini and elsewhere. The King was of course thoroughly familiar with the most famous pictorial expression of this theme, Raphael's *Il Parnasso*. It is easy to understand that the Scandinavian climate made it impossible to realize Gustav III's plans for a Parnassus in the park at Drottningholm. Sergel had been emphatic in advising against such a method of display. Instead, the King chose a more conventional solution: a museum gallery.

There was, however, a long delay before the King could enjoy his new acquisitions. *Apollo* and the *Muses* had been crated ready for despatch by July 1784, but an export licence was required, besides which the matter of the Piranesi collection had not yet been finalized. In the course of Gustav III's visit, Piranesi had in vain tried to interest the King in purchasing these works; according to Piranesi himself, this failure was primarily due to the machinations of the King's advisor on artistic matters, the sculptor Sergel.[15] It is a fact that Sergel, like the other courtiers in the King's suite, was decidedly antipathetic towards the ingratiating Roman art agent.

In desperation, Piranesi now turned to Carl Fredrik Fredenheim who had previously – against the wishes of Sergel – succeeded in influencing the King's choice of an art agent in Rome.[16] Fredenheim now embarked upon a counter-offensive in favour of Piranesi, and seems in part to have been successful.[17] When the art agent was being appointed, Fredenheim had already emphasized the importance of Piranesi's many artistic contacts and, not least, the fact of his being related to the Pope's valet. This connection directly into the Papal bedchamber would, in Fredenheim's opinion, considerably facilitate all applications for export licences made on behalf of the Swedish King. During the autumn of 1784, Fredenheim's continued efforts resulted in Gustav III finally acquiring the Piranesi collection of antiques in exchange for an annual pension for life.

The relatively strict regulations of the Vatican State restricting the export of antiques were a visible reminder of the great ethical issue of whether it was historically correct to remove the masterpieces of antiquity from their original setting. Neither Gustav III nor the members of his suite can have been unaware of this problem. In the seventeenth century, Swedes had pointed out that Rome had already been plundered by the Visigoths, but now there was a need for a considerably more subtle argument: the comparison between the corrupt Papal power and what was called *la décadence des Beaux-Arts en Italie*. Before Gustav III arrived in Rome on his travels, he had already written to his brother Karl (later King Karl XIII) in December 1783:

In the modern era, apart from the ravages of time, Italy, the cradle of the arts and sciences, seems about to return to that barbarous state out of which it had once dragged the rest of Europe. The arts are no longer what they were and, in the whole of Italy, there is but a single famous painter, Pompeo Batoni. Italy cannot even bring forth a sculptor worthy of comparison with Sergel. And, with respect to the architects, the modern buildings I have seen are more suited to the Germans than to the land of Vitruvius and Palladio.[18]

Gustaf III did not change his opinion when he finally came to Rome. In the Swedish court, this pronounced standpoint gave rise to some surprise.[19] The King was, however, supported by his former tutor, Councillor of the Realm Nils-Adam Bielke, who saw the decline of morals as the main cause.[20] Gustav III, for his part, found that the crisis in the contemporary arts was not just a phenomenon of decadence in general, but was political in its essence. He predicted that Papal power would soon collapse.[21] This was a view evidently shared by most people close to the King. His secretary in 'the travelling chancellery', Gudmund Göran Adlerbeth, also predicted Rome's future fate in similar terms: 'The Pope will no doubt be returned to his former calling of bishop, and Rome shall fall into ruins for a second time.'[22] Adlerbeth even made the same connection between the paralysis of the Roman city apparatus and cultural stagnation. Nor could he see any blame in Rome's artistic treasures being removed. 'Paintings, statues and monuments must with time become scattered abroad and moved to those places whither riches and taste call them.'[23] One may assume that Adlerbeth in this way wished to give legitimacy to his King's ambition to take antique sculptures to Stockholm. It had become all the more pressing to find suitable arguments since Adlerbeth, during his visit to Rome, had been harassed by treacherous questions from the learned Frenchman d'Agrincourt wondering whether the Swedes were not indeed the present-day descendants of those Goths who once had ravished Rome. Adlerbeth of course denied this, and, on another occasion, succeeded in turning the same statement to Gustav III's favour.[24]

The Roman antiques and the Haga Palace

Following Sergel's advice, the King had abandoned the idea of a Parnassus at Drottningholm, and, during his continued sojourn in Rome, worked on an alternative solution. He now intended to place *Apollo* and the nine *Muses* in a gallery which was to be one of the major rooms in a new palatial residence at Haga.[25] The King, admittedly, already had the architect Fredrik Magnus Piper at work on the plans for this so-called casino, but the acquisition of the Muses changed the circumstances. Nonetheless, the King's idea of uniting a residential suite with a museum building remained. When Piper's plans finally reached Rome in the summer of 1784, Piranesi immediately handed them over to the French architect Léon Dufourny as a basis for further work.

This was the real beginning of Gustav III's idea of giving his collection a more magnificent architectonic frame. Dufourny had promised to submit

Figure 5.6.3   Cross-section of the Temple of Amor at Haga, engraved by Henrik Beskow after the design of Louis Jean Desprez, 1788, etching, NMH G A 139/1975. Photo: Nationalmuseum, Stockholm

plans within four months, but in fact it took all of four years. On behalf of the King, Piranesi reminded the architect on repeated occasions, but to no avail. Dufourny had, for his part, blamed the delay on the fact that the circumstances of the project were continually being changed. In November 1785 the King purchased the Brahelund property which was adjacent to the Haga estate, and this meant that the new palace was now to be built on a different site. Dufourny was also forced to compete with architects in Sweden, first Olof Tempelman and later Louis Jean Desprez. The uncertainty of the situation meant that Dufourny hesitated, despite having completed the drawings by May of 1787. Later that year, Dufourny did nevertheless send the measurements of a number of antique columns that had been found in Ostia during the summer, and which he now proposed incorporating into a special temple building intended for Sergel's sculpture group *Amor and Psyche*.

Dufourny's suggestion would no doubt have pleased Gustav III. The inclusion of antique spoils in the architectural setting at Haga would naturally have added to the degree of authenticity, a fact which the King must have seen as extremely tempting. The rival architect Desprez was thus not slow to pirate Dufourny's suggestion; Desprez now re-worked his own proposal for a temple of Amor on the basis of Dufourny's measurements of the columns.

Additionally, Desprez made sure that his own version was publicized by having his pupil Beskow engrave the design for the Temple of Amor.

It thus seemed as if Dufourny had definitely lost when eventually he submitted his Haga plans to Stockholm early in 1788. But although the construction of the great palace had already been under way for two years, Gustav III still showed a considerable degree of interest in Dufourny's project. Perhaps the King was fascinated by the various theatrical arrangements: the plans included a theatre in the middle of the palace that within two hours could be transformed into a hall for a banquet or a concert, and in front of the palace there was a large area suited for festivities that was to be laid out in the form of an antique arena with a *spina* in the centre and with stands that would accommodate 10,000 spectators. In his prospectus, Dufourny promised that the same feature could be converted into a *naumachia* if water was channelled in from Lake Brunnsviken.

Apart from these fantasies, Dufourny does seem to have remained loyal to the requirements that Gustav III had once stipulated in Rome pertaining to a combined royal residence and private museum. One of the most important elements in Dufourny's proposal for a palace building, what he termed the *Pavillon des Muses*, was the sculpture gallery for the nine *Muses* and *Apollo*. The relatively simple plans could not have given a complete picture of the way in which Dufourny intended to solve the difficult problem of lighting in a massive building lacking light wells, but the accompanying written commentary reveals that the architect conceived of windows set high to provide light from above.

A cross-section drawing by Dufourny of the Muses' gallery has been preserved in the Nationalmuseum in Stockholm. This drawing, which once belonged to Sergel, shows that the architect intended placing the antique sculptures on a high podium where they would be outlined against drapery painted behind them. The walls would be crowned by a continuous frieze. Finally, the ceiling consisted of a coffered tunnel vault, rhythmically divided by sectioned transverse arches, decorated with festoons of laurel leaves.

Gustav III's positive reception of Dufourny's proposals, combined with his reluctance to let Desprez look at them, made Desprez nervous. But his apprehension turned out to be unfounded and, in fact, his only real fears were that the building funds might run out or the King might die. The construction of the palace continued and was not particularly affected by the war against Russia. In the autumn of 1787, Desprez had replaced Tempelman as the senior architect and, under his guidance, the palace was extended to include two enormous side wings as well as a monumental staircase. While the residential rooms retained something of a private character in Dufourny's concept, these were now turned into state rooms. In Desprez's palace, the nine *Muses* and the *Apollo* were to be placed in an

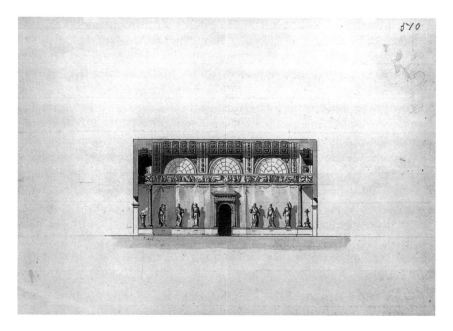

Figure 5.6.4 Cross-section of the Muses' gallery designed by Louis Dufourny, 1788, NMH 686/1890. Photo: Nationalmuseum, Stockholm

even more prominent position – in niches in the domed rotunda in the heart of the building. However, the assassination of Gustav III put a stop to these glorious plans.

From a private to a public museum

At the time of Gustav III's death on 29 March 1792, the nine *Muses* and the *Apollo playing a Cithara* were situated in the King's private suite at the Royal Palace in Stockholm. This had been a provisional arrangement when the pieces arrived on the frigate *Gripen* in September 1785. The *Endymion* [see the Frontispiece to this volume], which was regarded at the time as the best piece in the King's collection, did not reach Stockholm until 1786. This sculpture, which was said to have been found at the Villa Adriana, was sited together with the *Muses* in the most prestigious part of Gustav III's private museum, known as the Little Gallery. The other parts of the collection – primarily Piranesi's collection of antiquities, which differed considerably from the others on account of its Baroque/decorative character[26] – were kept in four adjoining side rooms. These five rooms in the royal suite were to form the nucleus of the Royal Museum, founded on 28 June 1792, almost exactly three months after Gustav III's death, as 'a publick memorium' to the patronage of the fine arts by the King during his lifetime.[27]

One cannot but be surprised by the speed with which the new institution came into being. Perhaps this, too, is the reason for the widespread understanding that it was Gustav III's own ideas that formed the basis for the new public museum facility.[28] The historical reality is a great deal more complicated; indeed, there is no simple answer, because Gustav III's intentions were never actually recorded.

Two special circumstances must be considered in this context: the prevailing view concerning royal and state property, and the concept of the public right of access. In the first case, one can observe the fact that the Royal Museum was founded six months before the estate inventory proceedings of the late Gustav III were formally completed on 2 December. During these proceedings, the issue of the dividing line between a King's personal property and that of the state was raised by Gustav III's former Chancellor of the Realm, Erik Ruuth, as indicated in the records:

A King who has had the Command and Order of the Monies of the Resources of the State, for whatsoever noble Purposes he has seen requisite, cannot thereby be said to have acquired a Property to be inherited by Law. Should a King have such a Right he would then freely be able to extend his Wealth in such a Manner as he saw fit to his Heirs' Profit and Benefit, while bringing to the State only Disadvantage and Loss.[29]

Ruuth's standpoint is of fundamental interest because it shows that at the time there did not seem to be a real consensus on the principles regarding what should be considered the King's private property and that of the State. Ruuth, however, was entirely logical in his manner of reasoning. He maintained that property acquired with funds from the public purse should remain public property.[30] The issue was solved once and for all on 4 December by a royal document which decreed that all the art collections of the deceased King were now the property of the state.[31]

Nevertheless, the museum continued to have strong personal links to the monarch. Carl Fredrik Fredenheim, who was appointed head of the new institution, spoke at this time of the museum as 'King Gustav the 4th Adolph's art collection'.[32] A few years later, when Fredenheim made the first inventory of the collection, he used the term 'the King's Museum'.[33] In this context, it is relevant to note that the Royal Museum was not only situated in the Palace, it was also formally a part of the royal household.

The very notion of a public right of access was in itself rather unclear and ambiguous. The degree of public accessibility was dependent upon one's social status, rank and dignity. In 1763, the Governor of Stockholm issued a decree 'for those who wish to walk in His Majesty's garden beside the Church of St Jacob and in the other garden called by the name of the hop yard'.[34] These gardens, once exclusively reserved for royalty, now became open to the public, but this public access was not unrestricted. What were termed 'the lower people', referring to lackeys, labourers, and maid-servants, were prohibited from entering. Even when they were following their masters to the royal gardens, they were obliged to wait outside the iron gates.

Another instance concerns admission to the royal palaces. Francisco de Miranda, who later became a South American revolutionary hero, describes how he and his servant were let into Drottningholm Palace and left to wander around fairly freely in the royal apartments. Miranda noted that the King had left his writing desk in considerable disorder with books and documents all over the place. Suddenly finding himself face-to-face with Gustav III, Miranda saw how His Majesty became irritated and asked his page who the unknown visitor was. 'He [the page] answered that he only knew that I was a noble foreigner, who wished to see the interesting things in the palace. The King said that this was fine, and let him see what you know of.'[35]

Miranda would no doubt have been granted similar access to Haga, had that palace been completed. But this does not necessarily mean that the royal premises were open to a wider public except on special occasions, at events such as the carrousel tournaments. In 1785, due to a period of continuous heavy rain, it had been necessary to arrange an ingenious system of signals in order to inform the population of the capital when the festivities were to begin. Word was thus spread among the public that five cannon shots from the salute battery in Stockholm meant that they should immediately set out for Drottningholm.[36] Similar assumptions were certainly behind Dufourny's proposal, mentioned above, to arrange a large arena close to the Haga Palace. But apart from festivities of this nature, Gustav III demanded complete privacy when he was at Haga. The immediate vicinity was roped off, information as to which was conveyed to the public on notices put up on the order of the Governor.[37]

Seen against this background, it is uncertain whether Gustav III really intended to turn his private collection into a museum which would be open to the public, as has been claimed in earlier studies. The report is apocryphal, but it probably has its origins in the period immediately after the death of Gustav III. The source could well be Carl Fredrik Fredenheim. No one else close to the King had been more familiar with his intentions than Fredenheim. But what purpose could he have had in ascribing to the King the ambition to establish a public art museum, if this information lacked substance in actual fact? One explanation may be sought in his personal ambition and striving.

The role of Fredenheim

Fredenheim's position as advisor to Gustav III on matters of art and collecting was the fruit of a purposeful career. At first, his chances of becoming a confidant of the King were poor, considering the importance placed on birth in those times. Carl Fredrik Fredenheim, born as Mennander, had admittedly a maternal grandmother who belonged to the gentry, but he himself had only recently been raised to the nobility and thus was considered an upstart.[38] He developed an interest in history at an early age, collecting manuscripts as well as old portraits. Fredenheim's gift – a portrait of the Swedish statesman Axel Oxenstierna – to Gustav III when the King visited Ekolsund in 1775, was no doubt an attempt to court royal favour.[39] Not without pride, he tells of how the King on the same occasion had listened to his translation of Tacitus' description of the reign of Galba.[40] At this early stage, Fredenheim was at pains to establish his reputation as an *antiquarius*.

By virtue of his position as secretary of the Cabinet for Foreign Correspondence, Fredenheim was responsible for matters concerning Pomerania, which meant he had regular contact with the Swedish Governor, Prince Fredrik Wilhelm von Hessenstein. As a result of von Hessenstein's journey to Rome in 1781–82, which was for the purpose of formalizing relations with the Pope, Fredenheim came to be involved with various matters concerning Italy.[41] His expectations of being able to accompany Gustav III on an Italian journey, however, were dashed at this time.[42] On the other hand, the appointment of Francesco Piranesi as Gustav III's art agent was a success for Fredenheim, and gradually helped strengthen his position. The fact that he alone had the honour of helping the King unpack and arrange the newly arrived antiques in September 1785 was a further recognition of the sovereign's favour. This led Fredenheim, during his sojourn in Rome in 1789, to propose to Gustav III that he be appointed curator of the King's art collection. He even asked Cardinal de Bernis to pen a letter of recommendation to the King.[43] At the time, however, Gustav III had other things on his mind due to the war against Russia (1788–90).

Fredenheim did not see his wish fulfilled until some months after the death of Gustav III. When the Royal Museum was founded as a public memorial to the late King in June 1792, Fredenheim was also appointed as the first director. This was of course a perfectly logical consequence, as the new museum would not have seen the light of day so soon after the death of Gustav III, had it not been for Fredenheim's energetic efforts to influence those who had acquired power.

The actual establishment of the museum did not, however, mean that the question of the premises was also settled. It was not until 12 February 1793 that it was decided to use the ground floor of the library wing for the new institution.[44] Even after he had managed to start fitting out the museum, Fredenheim still felt that people were seeking to thwart his work, and on more than one occasion he met with the same unsympathetic attitude: 'À quoi sert cela?' (What is the purpose of it all?). Fredenheim cared little for the opinion of his critics: 'I hope that we shall never degenerate into such barbarians that it shall be necessary to reply to such a question. Otherwise, foreigners will come to answer instead of us.'[45]

Fredenheim confided these thoughts to Chancellor of the Realm, Fredrik Sparre, Count Carl Gustav Tessin's nephew and heir, who, for several years, provided the museum director with direct access to the Guardian Regent, Duke Karl. In an undated memorandum addressed to Sparre, and probably penned in the spring of 1793, Fredenheim deals with the matter of the name and thereby the very genesis of the Royal Museum:

Nothing could be more appropriate than that King Gustaf IVth Adolph's art collections should bear the name of their Founder King Gustaf the IIIrd, and of the Realm which they shall come to adorn. Thus, above the portal to the upper room of the Museum it should be announced: MUSEUM SVECO-GUSTAVIANUM. and in the great gallery and arcade of the museum, above the apollo, shall be the following inscription: GUSTAVUS_III_INSTITUIT_CAROLUS_DUX _SUDERMANIAE_INSTRUXIT_SUB_ AUSPICIIS_GUSTAVI_IV_ ADOLPHI_MDCCLXXXXIII.[46]

Fredenheim commented upon both the choice of words and their meaning: 'No other language could express so much: *institutit* and *instruxit*, both honouring in equal manner, seem to stand in the correct place and, apart from the sense of found, *instituere* can also imply the sense of conceive'. Gustav III is here thus ascribed the role of inspirer as well as founder of the new museum. In many ways, this was a brilliant move by Fredenheim. His claim could not be challenged by anybody, but neither could it be verified. When Fredenheim was attacked by critics for wasting state funds on something that was 'not of use', he could simply refer to the late King. Fredenheim then remarked on the role of the Guardian Regent, Duke Karl, and the young boy-King: '*Instruere* is to build as well as to give shape and life. *Auspicia* is an expression of protection, the start of a new epoch, as well as a wish for success.' Fredenheim summed up the various roles of those involved in the creation of the Royal Museum: 'founded by Gustav III, established by Karl and protected by Gustaf IV Adolph'.

Fredenheim ends his letter by revealing that he hoped it would be possible to set up the inscribed tablet during 1793. This was not to happen. The museum was ready the following year. The tablet was not, however, put up until 1796.[47] The wording was different too:

ANTIQVITATUM_ET_ARTIUM_CULTIORUM_REGIA_CIMELIA _A_GUSTAVO_III_MAXIMAE_ LOCUPLETATA_GUSTAVUS_IV _ADOLPHUS_CAROLO_DUCE_SUDERMANIAE_TUTELAM_

GERENTE_ UT_COMMODO_AC_DECORO_PUBLICO_REDACTA _ET_ORDINATA_
INSERVIANT_PROVIDIT_HOC_ INSTITUENS_ MUSEUM_MDCCXCIV.[48]

The new text was formally approved by Gustav IV Adolf on 16 October
1794.[49] Fredenheim had been so thorough that he had asked Marini, head of
the Vatican archives, to first read and approve the inscription before it was
carved on the tablet in Rome. In order to achieve the desired degree of
authenticity, the inscription was carved in the same style of letters used on
Canova's monument to Pope Clement XIV.[50]

The most remarkable factor, however, was the new content of the
instruction. The short and concise original wording was now quite long.
This meant that the seemingly obvious distribution of roles was also lost.
Gustav III was no longer the founder, but had become the collector. The boy-
King was instead accredited with having founded the museum under the
supervision of the Guardian Regent, Duke Karl. But there was an addition,
too. In his first suggestion, Fredenheim had been content to praise the
'immortality of the founders'.[51] In the final version of the text, the phrasing
had been considerably expanded. The museum was no longer just a memorial,
a thing of beauty. According to the inscription, it should also 'serve the
public good'.

It is perfectly clear that something had happened in 1793–94. In a poor
country like Sweden, it was without doubt difficult to justify the spending of
a considerable sum of money on a memorial. In order to meet his detractors,
Fredenheim had come upon the idea that the Royal Museum should also be
of service to the public:

Should one object that the country is poor, it must be observed that the objects [the
sculptures] are already purchased and that it is precisely in a poor country (where
the inhabitants love all manner of luxury other than that which comes from genius
and good taste) that it is indeed appropriate for the monarch to concern himself
with the arts and one should thus be grateful towards a King who arranges so that
the citizens shall always have the pleasure of this.[52]

Taking into account Fredenheim's skill at finding such effective arguments
in an awkward situation, and also the efficient manner in which he
subsequently managed the new institution, it does not seem too bold to
assume that it was not Gustav III's ideas but rather those of Fredenheim
which formed the basis of the establishment of the Royal Museum as a
cultural institution open to the general public.

The Royal Museum: the first ten years

The museum was dominated by the two sculpture galleries situated in the
library wing of the Palace.[53] The Volpato and Piranesi collections were

displayed so that they were clearly distinguishable: the Volpato pieces in the outer, large gallery, and Piranesi's collection in the inner gallery. The *Apollo* and the nine *Muses* were positioned along the inner long wall of the large gallery. A number of other larger items could also be displayed there, particularly the *Endymion* and the *Priestess* as well as Piranesi's *pièces entassées*. Piranesi's collection was arranged in the inner gallery in a manner tending towards a Baroque atmosphere, as opposed to the larger gallery's modern, Neoclassical character.[54]

The larger sculpture gallery with its coffered supporting arches had the more extravagant interior, and this matched the importance of the exhibited works too. The *Endymion* was placed at the far end on the centre line, in front of Piranesi's decorative 'composite' pieces, and was regarded as an object for contemplation, a masterpiece fully comparable to the best that had been preserved in Rome.[55] The high prestige that was accorded the *Endymion* was further enhanced by the fact that the suite with the *Apollo and the Muses* was presented as the only such suite outside the Museo Pio-Clementino in the Vatican. Fredenheim's 1794 publication *Ex Museo Regis Sveciae antiquarum e marmore statuarum/Apollinis Musagetae Minervae Paciferae ac Novum Musarum series integra post Vaticanam unica cum aliis selectis Priscae Artis Monimentis* emphasized this as a special quality already in the title, an opinion that most probably was derived from Volpato's persuasive arguments.

The museum also comprised the earlier royal collections of paintings, drawings and engravings as well as coins, but these were exhibited on another floor of the palace. The museum's rationale as well as its appearance were thus dominated by the sculpture galleries. Access to the museum could be gained from the Logården, which was open to the public for walking. Artist Pehr Hilleström's idealized illustrations of the galleries and the Logården stress both the view from outdoors and the fact that the visitors belong to the upper social classes.[56] They also highlight the importance of the sculptures for the concept of the museum. From the exterior, the museum clearly gave the impression of being an exhibition of antiquities, a fact that was obvious to visitors during the first decade, although it actually also comprised other noteworthy collections.

After Fredenheim – political conditions on the European continent

Fredenheim's personal qualities and network had been of considerable, not to say vital, importance for the genesis of the Royal Museum, and this could be seen also after his death in 1803. For it seems as if the ideological continuity was then broken, despite the fact that that there were still several participants in Swedish cultural life who themselves had had direct contact with Gustav

III and had taken part in his journey to Italy, or had been involved in its consequences back home in Sweden. This, of course, most particularly affected the Royal Museum, and its curatorial plans and exhibition activities seem to have faded away.

But Fredenheim's death does not entirely explain the museum vacuum in Sweden during the first fifteen years of the nineteenth century. Notably, political changes of a revolutionary, not to say horrifying, nature took place within the country. These, in turn, were bound up with events on the continent.

The Napoleonic wars had drastically affected art collections throughout Europe. In the familiar tradition of war, single pieces and larger collections were transported to France in the late 1790s. Napoleon was himself strongly influenced by contemporary notions about historical rulers, in particular Alexander the Great, which meant that his art policy too was governed by such magnificent visions. In accordance with this attitude, France sought to place itself beyond comparison as regards prestige and outward appearance. From such a perspective, every argument for authenticity and legitimacy paled.

Antique sculptures acquired a central role in Napoleon's dramaturgy when two of the most renowned antiques were brought to Paris in a triumphal procession in July 1798. These were the *Apollo Belvedere* and the *Capitoline Venus*, which, along with other items of art booty, were placed in the Musée Napoléon in the Palais du Louvre (1803–15),[57] established in 1803 as an extension of, and successor to, the Musée Central des Arts that had been opened in the Louvre in 1793.[58] There, the most famous works could be compared without the observer having to take the roundabout route of plaster casts and engravings.

The symbolic value of the Musée Napoléon in Paris cannot be under-estimated, and should not be forgotten when examining museum organization in other parts of Europe at the time. The new museum in Paris gave rise to a systematic cataloguing which can be seen as the start of the inventory and catalogue work of art museums which was to continue for the whole of the nineteenth century.

The movement of works of art during the Napoleonic wars also led to a certain confusion throughout Europe. It was not easy to keep track of the whereabouts of the great masterpieces. The plaster-cast collection at the Academy of Fine Arts in Stockholm published a catalogue in 1806, when the Musée Napoléon was still intact. In most cases, it recorded both where the original was held *before* the wars as well as its present location in Paris. It sometimes seems as if the author of the catalogue had been uncertain as to where an original sculpture was actually kept at the time, because the location details are often incomplete.[59]

This confusion did not last long, however. In the same way that the realm of Alexander the Great collapsed after his early death, Napoleon's rearrangement of Europe lasted no longer than his own immediate power. After his fall, Europe would be recreated, and thereby also the context in which the pieces had previously belonged. This was regulated during the Congress of Vienna in 1814–15. Wilhelm von Humboldt was one of Prussia's two delegates at the Congress of Vienna and was among those who investigated how art booty should be dealt with. Humboldt had lived in Paris 1797–1801, during which time he witnessed the arrival of the looted Italian works of art. He was also the German ambassador in Rome in 1802–09, at which time he himself acquired plaster casts as well as some antique fragments and reliefs in marble. As a private collector, he had some knowledge of the field and he worked effectively for the return of Napoleon's art booty to its former owners.

Humboldt indirectly supported the view of the *limes* that previous generations had espoused, namely that antique works of art should remain in their original sites and within the borders of the ancient Roman empire when it was at its greatest. But the situation was complex, and the Congress of Vienna was only authorized to deal with the art that had been moved during the Napoleonic wars, and not before. The issue thus had more of a legal character. The situation that applied at the time to Gustav III's acquisitions in Italy was another matter, although the questions surrounding the removal of original works from any country were just as topical.

The arguments about authenticity and legitimacy had to be modified for the circumstances of each new acquisition. Nevertheless, the same arguments tended to recur, such as the notion of a general 'decline' of the Mediterranean area, which could appear to be supported by the politically unstable situation in Greece as well as the weakened position of the Pope as a temporal prince in Rome. This could then be contrasted with grandiose plans for the construction and extension of major cultural centres in central Europe. The idea of Munich as 'The New Athens of Europe' could itself appear to give legitimacy to moving antique sculpture to Bavaria, a region which admittedly had the same advantage as Paris and London of being situated within the ancient Roman *limes*. If it had instead been a matter of the brilliantly classical centre that was built in Helsinki, the new capital of the Grand Duchy of Finland, at the time, arguments would have had to be adjusted to suit the ambitions and the possibilities of acquiring works. But the planners had neither the ambition nor the opportunity.

Humboldt was also of the opinion that good copies of the originals not only worked well in spreading the right education in areas which were beyond the boundaries of the historical Graeco-Roman sphere, but they could also be considered to be fully acceptable representatives for sculpture as idea and form. Consequently, in the 1820s, he established a sculpture gallery in his own home outside Berlin, Schloss Tegel, whose collection primarily consisted of plaster copies of the most sought-after antique masterpieces, including several from the inaccessible collection of Prince Luigi Boncompagni Ludovisi in Rome. Only one contemporary work of sculpture, namely Bertel Thorvaldsen's *Mercury*,[60] was placed beside the antique copies. This idealistic view of copies of antique remains, which had gained acceptance among intellectual circles particularly in the German states, came to be of decisive importance for a change in the concept of the museum from the 1820s and thereafter.

Political conditions in Sweden

The Napoleonic empire had a lasting effect on political legitimacy as such: the old Swedish royal house, for example, did not regain its status after the restoration. The struggles for royal power within Sweden were intimately connected with the upheaval on the continent, and the Napoleonic Marshal who was called to the Swedish throne remained there even after the Congress of Vienna.

Sweden, which prior to the Napoleonic wars had comprised a relatively large but sparsely populated territory on the periphery of Europe, was still, in the late eighteenth century, involved in the game of the major powers, and it had been party to various political alliances according to how the balance of power swung to one side or otherwise changed. The monarch had also been the protector of Lutheran believers in northern Europe since the days of Gustav II Adolf. Territorially, Finland was still a part of the Swedish realm, as was some of Pomerania on the north German Baltic coast.

Gustav IV Adolf was the Swedish monarch who lost control of the intricate net of political connections with other European states. His situation became untenable during the years when Napoleon's empire was at its most expansive. Finland was lost to Russia and relations with Napoleon and his opponents were dangerously unstable. Gustav IV Adolf was forced to abdicate in the spring of 1809 and was exiled abroad for all time, together with his family, which also meant the young Crown Prince Gustaf. The deposed King's uncle, the former Guardian Regent Duke Karl, was now chosen as the new king.

After a short interlude, during which a Danish prince was named heir to the Swedish throne (soon thereafter to die after falling off his horse), Napoleon's marshal Jean-Baptiste Bernadotte was chosen to be the new Swedish Crown Prince in the late summer of 1810. The election admittedly took place in the *Riksdag*, but it was preceded by secret negotiations in Paris without a mandate from the government of the realm. Bernadotte came to

Sweden where he was met with admiration and high expectations, and in reality soon took over the duties of the monarch from his adoptive father. As Crown Prince, Bernadotte was given the name Karl Johan, and after he ascended the throne in 1818 the ordinal number XIV. Within a couple of years of his arrival in Sweden, Karl Johan had compensated the Swedish realm for the loss of Finland by bringing Norway into a union with Sweden, with himself as ruler of the new unified state.

The strong links with France that had characterized the nobility during the time of Gustav III thus received a new impetus but under totally different conditions. Karl Johan never learnt the language of his new country; instead, the administrative apparatus surrounding him became bilingual. This presupposed that the ministers and court functionaries were thoroughly familiar with the French language. Such a French-oriented cell at the heart of the Swedish state could also have been culturally active, as had been the case with Gustav III and his court. But although Karl Johan might well have been aware of the politically symbolic value of cultural manifestations, no research has yet been able to prove that a well-thought-out plan stood behind his achievements. However, it is clear that they reflected his experiences with French politics and his various postings in the Italian and German regions.

Instead, state-sponsored cultural life is usually described as neglected, unorganized and confused during his reign, due to the lack of a culturally minded prince (meaning Gustav III). A long research tradition has led to that opinion becoming so deep-rooted that, until recently, it has been difficult to determine how cultural life was organized and which initiatives of importance nevertheless were taken by both Karl Johan and particular individuals. A common understanding has been that Swedish cultural life at the time was isolated from the larger world, but in fact detailed examination of the surviving material shows that instead there continued to be a strong reliance upon a handful of individuals whose international orientation was considerable and, above all, of a classical character. While these individuals were physically present in *ultima Thule*, their souls were in Rome. Had this not been the case, the Royal Museum would undoubtedly have come to nothing as an official institution during the political crisis.

Museum plans

During the last ten years, there have been a number of discoveries in the archives which show that there were several plans for museum buildings on a grand scale and that these were put forward before, as well as after, Karl Johan's reign. They concern the organization and display of existing art collections in suitable premises, in accordance with concepts of the museum at the time, and this included a limited degree of accessibility.

At the very beginning of the nineteenth century, besides the Royal Museum there was a collection of sculptures at the Academy of Fine Arts, only a few hundred metres distant.[61] The greater part of both collections consisted of antique sculptures, but they were very different. The collection in the library wing of the palace was, as indicated above, compiled and restored in accordance with the eighteenth century's understanding of antiquity. Educated members of the public had access to the collection two days a week, and pupils from the Academy could study there under the guidance of a *conducteur*.

Since 1780, the Art Academy had been housed in a separate building, the Meyer mansion. The antique collection at the Art Academy consisted of plaster casts, primarily of what were then the most highly regarded antiques. The so-called Tessin collection from the late 1690s formed the core, and it was added to on several occasions with donations and purchases from private individuals. As was the case with many other academy collections throughout Europe, this was above all intended for drawing studies from the model, and it was rather inaccessible due to a shortage of space. The Meyer mansion did not include any galleries as such, which meant that the collections were spread over a large number of rooms in the building.

In 1780, the architect Carl Fredrik Adelcrantz had already designed an extension which would house a gallery for these plaster casts, and Fredenheim, who from 1796 was also President of the Academy, brought up the matter again after Adelcrantz's death.[62] Some years later, after Fredenheim died, the plan was forgotten.

If the plan for the plaster-cast museum at the Art Academy had been realized, both of the public collections of antiquities in Stockholm would have complemented each other in terms both of architecture and content. The canon of sculpture could have been compared with the marble collections that had been brought to Sweden from Rome, and two museums with a classical stamp, arranged by the same curator, would have been within walking distance of each other. Despite the fact that none of this came about, Fredenheim's work did however bear fruit, to the extent that the academy's plaster casts were restored by the *garde de marbres* of the Royal Museum, Carl Magnus Hägerflycht, and arranged and catalogued by the academy's teachers.[63] But they were never put on display in a museum context.

In 1799, Fredenheim tried to do something about the museum premises at the palace. At the time, with the help of his Italian contacts, he had accomplished the purchase of a large collection of paintings for the Royal Museum. Known as the Martelli collection, it consisted of several hundred

Italian paintings that had been acquired to complete the museum's collection of paintings, previously dominated by Netherlandish and French works.[64] Such a significant expansion of the museum would have necessitated a re-organization of its premises at the palace, and a memorandum, probably written by Fredenheim himself, describes the plan as follows:

It is thus time that Your Majesty should be graciously pleased to instruct where such a quantity of art objects shall be kept in a manner well and fitting so that above all they should not be disturbed by being often moved. Since Your Majesty has given these collections a sanctuary, in honour of the memory of Your Majesty's Father, then might not Your Majesty extend that same noble consideration to those persons charged with carrying out Your Majesty's benign patronage of the Arts? A room sufficiently large, such as these paintings require, is now said only to be found on the ground floor of the Southern Wing of the Palace beside the Logården yard, which matches the Museum's Marble Galleries, and nothing could be more becoming and suitable than that paintings be kept on the one side and marbles and diverse objects on the other side of a Terrace, a site worthy to unite the beauties of Art and Nature.[65]

There is, however, no further mention of this proposal in the annals until 1816, despite the fact that the Martelli collection arrived at the Palace in 1803. The Museum's secretary, Olof Sundell, carried out an inventory of the museum's pieces in 1816 at which time he found almost 1,200 paintings spread throughout the various rooms of the Stockholm Palace. He suggested the following solution:

Should the southern wing be utilized in its entirety, in such a manner that both storeys were converted into one room by which the same good lighting could be effected for all Paintings through a split-level window upon the roof, and by this means all the Paintings could be united, and should the basement also be fitted as the Marble Gallery, this would then give access to another rich collection, of another type, which for the present time is so spread out that it can hardly be known.[66]

Sundell's proposal was based on the same idea as Fredenheim's, and was probably derived from it. By dividing off the Royal Palace's northern and southern wings facing the Strömmen waterway, the art museum could be gathered together, united by an English garden in what was known as the Logården. This, in turn, would mean that the existing Palace building would be used to create a separate museum unit with its own entrance from the Skeppsbron quayside. This was indeed a grandiose proposal because it implied not only that the King and the court would make room for the state-owned art museum, but also that the centuries-old palace building could be adapted to fulfil the museum's needs for both light and space. Conceptually, such a museum would have cloven the Palace into two parts. Visually, the most accessible part of the compact building would have been transformed into an institution open to the public with a flower garden in which they could freely walk.

Figure 5.6.5   View from outdoors of the Royal Museum and the gardens of Logården, Royal Palace, Pehr Hilleström, oil on canvas, RBG 42. Photo: Nationalmuseum, Stockholm

But none of all this was to come about. The only successful museum project that was actually carried out in this period was the actual establishment of the Royal Museum in 1792–94. That is where Fredenheim's influence and approach are most visible. Seen from a pragmatic, administrative perspective, the 1799 plan can be called a smart move. By first establishing galleries with antique sculpture and then pushing through the purchase of a large collection of paintings *en gros* from war-torn Italy, there was now a weighty argument for expanding the museum with specially fitted premises for the collection of paintings. Because this was never realized, it is difficult to comment with any accuracy upon the principles that Fredenheim had intended to apply when arranging and hanging the paintings. However, his work can be described as systematic and governed by an idea of a large, state-owned museum, with public access, situated in the Stockholm Palace.

Fredenheim's inheritance

We can to some extent discuss these unrealized museum plans by taking in account Fredenheim's own ideas and those of the museum administration, which was working to systematize the collection from about 1815. Fredenheim's successor was very much caught up in a great deal of dreary practical problems. The Martelli collection, for example, arrived in Stockholm in May 1803, two months after Fredenheim's death, and was found to be of surprisingly uneven quality – this opinion of the time was also shared by later researchers – in contrast to its reputation prior to delivery. Weaker pieces had to be culled from the collection, and the widespread disappointment with the collection did not help in securing funds to fit out the southern wing of the Palace. These were also politically troubled times, a fact which also precluded better funding for museum activities. Paintings had to be squeezed in wherever room could be made.

With its extended premises, the museum was a problem even for those funding it, and the first sign of this was in 1816, the same year that Sundell carried out his inventory of the paintings, and when the second proposal for re-fitting the southern wing was also put forward. The sculpture galleries were then provided with extra funding, in part to arrange items from Sergel's estate, which had been purchased the year before, but including an annual sum to cover modest running expenses.[67]

The monies that were allocated meant in practice that some of Fredenheim's organization of the museum could be resumed. On the instructions of the Chamberlain, the museum was to be kept open four days a week between 10 a.m. and 1 p.m., as well as on Wednesdays and Saturdays for those who so wished. The state-employed conservators who had started work in 1793 – a *garde des tableaux* for painting, a *garde des marbres* for sculpture and a *garde des médailles* – had all long since disappeared but could now be replaced with hired-in services, an arrangement that was to last into the twentieth century.

The conservation programme and the inventories were practical measures which allowed the museum's managers to acquaint themselves with the collections, but the public had no equivalent possibilities. The need was felt for printed catalogues, but this required resources in excess of the existing funds. The only earlier publication was Fredenheim's work *Ex Museo Regis Sveciae* ... of 1794, which contained engravings after Volpato's series with the *Muses* and *Apollo* as well as some pieces from the Piranesi collection. The prints had been made by engravers in Rome and Stockholm and, of necessity, this limited the size of the edition, which is why such an expensive project would hardly have been able to continue. This was solved by having the newspaper publisher and lithographer Fredrik Boye (Boije), in cooperation with artist Alexander Clemens Wetterling, present a selection of paintings, each in turn described with one page of text and a contour-drawn lithograph. This work was given the title *Kongl. Svenska Museum* and was published in instalments between 1821 and 1823.[68] The publishers had specially indicated their ambitions in the preface by stating that 'The edition exhibits insignificant typographical beauty, experience having shown that it is only such works that can be sold in Sweden, without loss to the Publisher. This work is better than *Le Manuel du Muséum francais* and worse than *Landon's Annales du Musée*, but costs only half the price of the first-named.'[69]

The Boye and Wetterling edition meant that the attention of the public was drawn to the painting collection, which previously had been neglected. But only a few years later, the collections were augmented by two important private donations of Roman and Egyptian antiquities. The latter came from Anastasy, an art dealer from Alexandria who had also been the Swedish Consul in Egypt. At the same time, the first in a series of new colossal statues was completed; Karl XIV Johan had been persuaded to commission these from two Swedish sculptors in Rome, Johan Niklas Byström and Bengt Erland Fogelberg.

About twelve years after the Boye and Wetterling publication, the museum expanded considerably, but with such different types of objects that its original presentation was broken up. A previously unused room had already been prepared for Sergel's sculptures in 1815, but there was no space for further pieces. Two smaller rooms, situated at either short end of the inner gallery, were fitted out by curator Lars Jacob von Röök; one, arranged in the form of an Egyptian burial chamber, was completed in 1833, and the other was prepared for the display of majolica and Greek vases. But the painting collection had not yet not been housed in special premises, and was in urgent need of attention.[70]

In this pressing situation, the original sculpture galleries could no longer be left untouched. Paintings were hung in the smaller gallery and modern sculpture was moved to the large gallery. From the 1830s to the 1860s the various collections became all the more mixed, until it was no longer possible to discern the original idea of the museum. Photographs from the 1860s show a museum whose interior had been changed beyond recognition, and which was also difficult to appreciate visually. The observer was now expected to study the objects one by one, separate from the room as a whole, which no longer had any connection with the arrangement. The Classical ideal was certainly still strong, but modern sculpture was now guaranteed a place where it could be compared with antique models, and the models were not the antique sculptures in the museum but casts of the famous antiquities in Rome, Paris, Munich and so on.

Idealist conceptions of sculpture demanded that only the best antique pieces should be exhibited. Because it was both economically and legally impossible to acquire some (or even just one) of the admired statues that were being dug up in Greece and Italy at the time, good plaster casts had to be obtained instead. These copies were thought to be much more important than authentic but lower-rated antique marble sculptures. The Royal Museum began to acquire plaster casts (starting with a Niobid group) in 1836, these acquisitions reaching a peak in the mid-1860s, when the new Nationalmuseum building was completed.[71]

But Fredenheim's museum of antiquities did not split at its seams without causing pain to those who cared for the Royal Museum. What really concerned its supporters was not the loss of the Neoclassicist arrangement and the fact that the antique sculpture had been ousted. What was really intolerable was the way everything was crowded together, along with the obvious need for exhibition space for the other groups of objects. The museum was no longer seen as a place for aesthetic and didactic contemplation as a whole; instead it had become a large and splintered collection of objects in urgent need of larger premises and a systematic art-historical treatment.

In fact, the situation was regarded as untenable as early as 1828, when the first proposal for a separate national museum was discussed (but not approved) by the Riksdag. In the minds of the parliamentarians and of the museum's curator, von Röök, this new museum was something totally different from the institution that Fredenheim had created. It would embrace all the antiquarian treasures of the realm – its historical monuments, literary works and aesthetic values, all presented in accordance with a system directly modelled upon those of the rapidly expanding German museum world. In this new museum, sculpture would have its fair share, but it would no longer dominate the visual arts. Museum directors were both pragmatically and idealistically motivated in their purchases of plaster casts of the most highly valued antique sculptures, and less interested in the exhibition of the kinds of marble compilations that had enchanted Fredenheim and his contemporaries to the very limits of ecstasy. Authenticity was no longer of interest, and the question of legitimacy was now obsolete.

Translation from the Swedish by Rod Bradbury

NOTES

1. Royal Library, Stockholm, Ms M 238, 'Carl Gustaf Fehrmans resejournal 1774–78', p. 16.

2. L. Carrogis, called Carmontelle, *Jardin de Monceau, près de Paris, appartenant à S.A.S. Mgr le duc de Chartres*, Paris 1779, p. 4.

3. *Grands et petits heures du Parc Monceau*, exh. cat. Musée Cernuschi, Paris 1981, p. 36.

4. C. C. L. Hirschfeld, *Théorie de l'art des jardins*, Leipzig 1781, vol. III, p. 129.

5. W. Gilpin, *Observation ... on Cumberland and Westmoreland*, London 1786, vol. II, p. 186.

6. P. Fréart de Chantelou, *Journal de voyage du Cavalier de Bernin en France*, Clamecy 1981, p. 182.

7. See F. Haskell and N. Penny, *Taste and the Antique*, New Haven and London 1982, p. 38 passim. [See the extract from this work in this volume.]

8. A.-M. Leander Touati and M. Olausson, *Ancient Sculptures in the Royal Museum*, vol. I, Stockholm 1998, p. 23–25.

9. Ibid., p. 40.

10. Ibid., p. 43.

11. Ibid., pp. 111–117.

12. Royal Library, Stockholm, Ms Ep F 7:4:1, fol. 139, F. Piranesi to C. F. Fredenheim, 14 May 1784.

13. National Archives, Rostein Papers, Ms E 5190. See M. Olausson, 'Gustav III:s Drottningholmsparnass. Ett okänt projekt för de nio muserna', *Konsthistorisk Tidskrift* 53, 1984, pp. 115–120.

14. See E. Blair MacDougall, 'Imitation and Invention: Language and Decoration in the Roman Renaissance Garden', *Journal of Garden History* 5:2, 1985, pp. 119–134.

15. Royal Library, Stockholm, Ms Ep F 7:4:1, fol. 91, F. Piranesi to C. F. Fredenheim, 29 November 1783: 'Mons. Sergel, celui est l'auteur assuré de mon malheur'. Cf ibid., fol 94: Piranesi to Fredenheim, 6 December 1783.

16. Ibid., fol. 119: F. Piranesi to C. F. Fredenheim, 9 April 1784.

17. National Archives, Stockholm, Börstorps Papers, Ms E 2949, undated promemoria from C. F. Fredenheim to F. Sparre. See also ibid., Ms E 3061, F. Sparre to C. Sparre, 26 March 1784.

18. National Archives, Stockholm, K 368, Gustav III to Hertig Karl (XIII), 13 December 1783.

19. Uppsala University Library, Ms F 515, Carl Fredrik Scheffer to Gustav III, 26 December 1783: 'Elle /S.M. le Roy/ ne puisse s'ennuyer au milieu des chefs d'oeuvre qu'ont produits les âges les plus renommés par la perfection dans tous les Genres.'

20. National Archives, Stockholm, Bielke Papers, Ms E 2424, N. A. Bielke to Gustav III, 9 March 1784: 'Ce que V. M. me fait la grace de me dire, sur la décadence des Beaux Arts en Italie, me paroit un effet naturel de l'Epidemie du Siècle; l'Inapplication et la Suffisance.' Cf. Gustav III to N. A. Bielke, 24 January 1784, Archives of Christineholm.

21. Gustav III to Elis Schröderheim, 28 January 1784, published in *Elis Schröderheims skrifter till Konung Gustaf III:s historia*, ed. E. Tegnér, Lund 1892, p. 210.

22. G. G. Adlerbeth, *Gustav III:s resa till Italien*, ed. H. Schück (Sv. *Memoarer och Bref*, vol. V), Stockholm 1902, p. 191.

23. Ibid., p. 192.

24. Ibid., p. 163.

25. For a thorough study on the Haga project, see Olausson 1984. Cf. M. Olausson, 'Léon Dufourny and the Muse Gallery of King Gustavus III', *Nationalmuseum Bulletin* 12:2, 1988, p. 103 passim.

26. Leander Touati and Olausson 1998, p. 79.

27. National Archives, Stockholm, *Inrikes civilexpedition, registratur* fol. 413, Royal decree of 28 June 1792.

28. Cf. *Antik konst*, ed. O. Antonsson, Stockholm 1958, p. 7.

29. Quoted from C. A. Hessler, *Staten och konsten i Sverige*, Stockholm 1942, p. 14.

30. Ibid. Obviously Ruuth was thinking about the acquisition of Drottningholm Palace on 3 March 1777.

31. O. Granberg, *Svenska konstsamlingarnas historia*, vol. III, Stockholm 1931, p. 12.

32. National Archives, Stockholm, *Kabinettet för utrikes brevväxling*, vol. 31, C. F. Fredenheim to F. Sparre, undated (spring 1793).

33. Nationalmuseum, the Archives, D III a:1, fol. 1, Inventory of 1793 drawn up by Fredenheim.

34. N. G. Wollin, 'Kungsträdgården i Stockholm. II', *S:t Eriks årsbok*, 1924, p. 106 passim.

35. F. de Miranda, *Vjajes, Diarios 1787–1788* (= *Archivio del general Miranda 3*), Caracas 1929, p. 29 passim (7 October 1787).

36. F. A. von Fersen, *Historiska skrifter*, vol. VI, Stockholm 1870, p. 41.

37. Public announcement (undated, 1789) stating that there was no access for the public, Palace Archives, Drottningholm, в II a:5.

38. See B. Hildebrand, 'Fredenheim', *Svenskt Biografiskt Lexikon*, vol. 78, Stockholm 1965, pp. 446–9.

39. Royal Library, Stockholm, Ms I. f. 18, fol. 43–4, 'C. F. Fredenheims Lefverne 1748–49'.

40. Royal Library, Stockholm, Ms I. f. 19:1, fol. 45, 'Concept-Biographie til år 1796'.

41. For an account of Prince von Hessenstein's mission to Rome, see A. Palmqvist, *Die römisch-katolische Kirche in Sweden nach 1781* dissertation, Uppsala 1954. Historians are still in the dark concerning the details of the Prince's journey. It is known that he arrived in Rome at the end of February 1781. After a long sojourn in Naples, he returned to Rome in March 1782, only to leave for Sweden the following month. (Cf. letter from C. A. Ehrensvärd to Catharina Elisabeth Ehrensvärd, 26 February 1781, quoted from G. Bergh, *C. A. Ehrensvärds brev*, vol. I, Stockholm 1916, p. 16). See also letters from Fredenheim to Prince von Hessenstein 1781–82, Royal Library, Stockholm, Ms Ep F 7:1. The secretary of the Prince, Magnus Retzius, who joined his master on the journey, served as an intermediary between Fredenheim and F. Piranesi (see Royal Library, Stockholm, Ms I. f. 19:1, fol. 78, 'Concept-Biographie til år 1796').

42. National Archives, Stockholm, Börstorp Papers, E 2949, C. F. Fredenheim to F. Sparre, 18 October 1782.

43. Uppsala University Library, Ms F 501, Cardinal de Bernis to Gustav III, 14 January 1789. Cf. Royal Library, Stockholm, Ms I. f. 19:1, fol. 121, 'Concept-Biographie til år 1796'.

44. National Archives, Stockholm, *Inrikes civilexpedition, registratur*, fol. 233, Royal decree, 12 February 1793. See also *Stockholms Slotts historia*, vol. III, ed. Martin Olsson, Stockholm 1941, p. 159.

45. National Archives, Stockholm, Börstorp Papers, E 2949, C. F. Fredenheim to F. Sparre, 22 August 1794: 'j'éspère que nous ne serons jamais assez barbares pour qu'on aura besoin d'y repondre: ou les étrangers y repondront pour nous'.

46. English translation of Latin inscription: 'Founded by Gustav III, arranged by Karl, Duke of Södermanland, under the auspices of Gustav IV Adolf in the year 1793', National Archives, Stockholm, *Kabinettet för utrikes brevväxling*, vol. 31, C. F. Fredenheim to F. Sparre, undated letter (spring 1793).

47. According to the letter to F. Sparre (see n. 46), it had been Fredenheim's intention to have the inscription carved in marble by the Royal Mason, Johan Adolph Göthe. However, Fredenheim changed his mind. After having composed the new version of the inscription, Fredenheim ordered the tablet in Rome, in 1795, and had it 'carved similarly to Canova's Monument to Clemens XIV. Arrived here by frigate in 1796' (Royal Library, Stockholm, Ms I. f. 19:1, fol. 163, 'Concept-Biographie til år 1796').

48. The new wording may be translated thus: 'For the antiquities and liberal arts in the Royal treasure so richly increased by Gustav III, Gustav IV Adolf, when Karl, Duke of Södermanland ruled as regent, established this museum in 1794, so that the collected and arranged items may be of general use and adornment.'

49. Palace Archives, Stockholm, *Slottsbyggnadsdirektion, inkommande handlingar*, 16 October 1794.

50. See above, n. 47.

51. See above, n. 45.

52. National Archives, Stockholm, Börstorp Papers, C. F. Fredenheim to F. Sparre, 22 August 1794: 'Si on objecte la pauvreté, les choses y sont, et c'est précisément dans un pays pauvre (ou les particuliers aiment tout autre luxe que celui du génie et le grand goût dans les arts) que le Souverain fait bien de s'en charger et ou on doit savoir gré à un Roi qui presen/t/ les plaisirs permanents aux citoyens ...'. The principle of unrestricted access for the general public was not yet self-evident. This is seen clearly from the discussion which took place about 1800 in the Academy of Fine Arts concerning the annual Salon. Prior to that date, exhibitions had always been free of charge. In an attempt to make them less accessible for the general public, it was suggested that there should be an admission fee. Although this suggestion was rejected, it was adopted seven years later. (See L. Looström, *Den svenska konstakademien under första århundradet of hennes tillvaro 1735–1835*, Stockholm 1887, p. 397.)

53. Leander Touati and Olausson 1998, pp. 64–72.

54. Cf. ibid., n. 26.

55. F. de Miranda (cf. above, n. 35) compared *Endymion* to the most highly estimeed sculptures in the Belvedere, after his first visit to the Royal Palace in Stockholm, 23 September 1787.

56. Hilleström's paintings are described in Leander Touati and Olausson 1998, pp. 68–70, and in S. Söderlind and U. Johnsson, 'Hilleström och verkligheten', *Kongl. Museum: Rum för ideal och bildning*, ed. S. Söderlind, Stockholm 1993, pp. 65–70.

57. See Haskell and Penny 1982, pp. 148 and 318; for the Musée Napoléon in general, see J. Châtelain, *Dominique Vivant Denon et le Louvre de Napoléon*, Paris 1973, and P. Wescher, *Kunstraub unter Napoleon*, Berlin 1976.

58. See A. McClellan, *Inventing the Louvre: Art, Politics and the Origins of the Modern Museum in Eighteenth-century Paris*, Cambridge 1994, and A. McClellan, 'The Musée du Louvre as Revolutionary Metaphor during the Terror', *Art Bulletin* 1988, pp. 300–13.

59. *Förteckning på kgl. Målare- och Bildhuggareakademiens samlingar af böcker, estamper, statyer, buster, bas-reliefter m.m.*, Stockholm 1806.

60. This sculpture is still displayed as part of a composition with plaster casts of antique sculpture in the round in the Schloss Tegel Antikensaal, as are the *Papirius* group and *Paettus and Arria*, both from the Ludovisi collection. See Haskell and Penny 1982, pp. 284, 290.

61. The plaster-cast collection of the Art Academy is only described in various works in Swedish, most recently in the articles 'Tessins gipser' (by Johan Cederlund) and 'Från ädel antik till gammalt gods' (by Solfrid Söderlind) in S. Söderlind, ed., *Gips: Tradition i konstens form*, Stockholm 1999, pp. 93–113 and 115–55. Tessin's plaster collection is also briefly mentioned in Haskell and Penny 1982, p. 79.

62. Söderlind 1999, p. 117.

63. Ibid.

64. Per Bjurström, *Nationalmuseum 1792–1992*, Stockholm-Wiken 1992, p. 80.

65. Nationalmuseum, the Archives, KM *Koncept 1798–1859, Utkast till Underdånight Memorial*, 16 November 1799.

66. Nationalmuseum, the Archives, KM *Koncept 1798–1859, odaterad och oavslutad PM*, c. 1816.

67. Nationalmuseum, the Archives, KM *Kungl. brev*, 6 juli 1815; KM *Kungl. brev*, 24 April 1816; KM *Koncept 1798–1859, Ödmjukt Memorial till statskontoret*, 7 March 1817.

68. *Kongl. Svenska museum. Samling of Contur-teckningar, med en analytisk och critisk beskrifning öfver hvarje ämne*, Stockholm 1821–23.

69. Ibid., 'Företal'.

70. The course of events is summarized in Bjurström 1992, pp. 86–103, and Söderlind 1993, pp. 98–109.

71. Söderlind 1999, p. 119 passim.

7.

The Cultural Logic of the Late Capitalist Museum

Rosalind Krauss

May 1, 1983: I remember the drizzle and cold of that spring morning, as the feminist section of the May Day parade formed up at République. Once we started moving out, carrying our banners for the march towards the Place de la Bastille, we began our chant. 'Qui paie ses dettes s'enrichit,' it went, 'qui paie ses dettes s'enrichit,' in a reminder to Mitterand's newly appointed Minister of Women's Affairs that the Socialists' campaign promises were still deeply in arrears. Looking back at that cry now, from a perspective firmly situated at the end of the '80s, sometimes referred to as 'the roaring '80s', the idea that paying your debts makes you rich seems pathetically naive. What make you rich, we have been taught by a decade of casino capitalism, is precisely the opposite. What makes you rich, fabulously rich, beyond your wildest dreams, is leveraging.

July 17, 1990: Coolly insulated from the heat wave outside, Suzanne Pagé and I are walking through her exhibition of works from the Panza Collection, an installation that, except for three or four small galleries, entirely fills the Musée d'Art Moderne de la Ville de Paris. At first I am extremely happy to encounter these objects – many of them old friends I have not seen since their early days of exhibition in the 1960s – as they triumphantly fill vast suites of galleries, having muscled everything else off the walls to create that experience of articulated spatial presence specific to Minimalism. The importance of this space as a vehicle for the works is something Suzanne Pagé is conscious of as she describes the desperate effort of remodeling vast tracts of the museum to give it the burnished neutrality necessary to function as background to these Flavins and Andres and Morrises. Indeed, it is her focus on the space – as a kind of reified and abstracted entity – that I finally find most arresting. This climaxes at the point when she positions me at the spot within the exhibition that she describes as being, for her, somehow the most riveting. It is in one of the newly stripped and smoothed and neutralized galleries, made whitely luminous by the serial progression of a recent work by Flavin. But we are not actually looking at the Flavin. At her direction we are scanning the two ends of the gallery through the large doorways of which we can see the disembodied glow produced by two other Flavins, each in an adjoining room: one of these an intense apple green light; the other an unearthly, chalky blue radiance. Both announce a kind of space-beyond which we are not yet in, but for which the light functions as the intelligible sign. And from our point of view both these aureoles can be seen to frame – like strangely industrialized haloes – the way the gallery's own starkly cylindrical, International Style columns enter our point of view. We are having this experience, then, not in front of what could be called the art, but in the midst of an oddly emptied yet grandiloquent space of which the museum itself – as a building – is somehow the object.

Within this experience, it is the museum that emerges as powerful presence and yet as properly empty, the museum as a space from which the collection has withdrawn. For indeed, the effect of this experience is to render it impossible to look at the paintings hanging in those few galleries still displaying the permanent collection. Compared to the scale of the Minimalist works, the earlier paintings and sculpture look impossibly tiny and inconsequential, like postcards, and the galleries take on a fussy, crowded, culturally irrelevant look, like so many curio shops.

These are two scenes that nag at me as I think about the 'cultural logic of the late capitalist museum', because somehow it seems to me that if I can close the gap between their seeming disparateness, I can demonstrate the logic of what we see happening, now, in museums of modern art.[1] Here are two possible bridges, flimsy perhaps, because fortuitous, but nonetheless suggestive.

1. In the July 1990 *Art in America* there occurs the unanalyzed but telling juxtaposition of two articles. One is the essay called 'Selling the Collection', which describes the massive change in attitude now in place according to which the objects in a museum's keeping can now be coolly referred to, by its director as well as its trustees, as 'assets'.[2] This bizarre Gestalt-switch from regarding the collection as a form of cultural patrimony or as specific and irreplaceable embodiments of cultural knowledge to one of eying the collection's contents as so much capital – as stocks or assets whose value is one of pure exchange and thus only truly realized when they are put in circulation – seems to be the invention not merely of dire financial necessity: a result, that is, of the American tax law of 1986 eliminating the deductibility of the market value of donated art objects. Rather, it appears the function of a more profound shift in the very context in which the museum operates – a context whose corporate nature is made specific not only by the major sources of funding for museum activities but also, closer to home, by the makeup of its boards of trustees. Thus the writer of 'Selling the Collection' can say: 'To a great extent the museum community's crisis results from the free-market spirit of the 1980s. The notion of the museum as a guardian of the public patrimony has given way to the notion of a museum as a corporate entity with a highly marketable inventory and the desire for growth.'

Over most of the course of the article, the market understood to be putting pressure on the museum is the art market. This is, for example, what Evan Maurer of the Minneapolis Institute of Art seems to be referring to when he says that in recent years museums have had to deal with a 'market-driven operation' or what George Goldner of the Getty means when he says that 'there will be some people who will want to turn the museum into a dealership'. It is only at the end of the essay, when dealing with the Guggenheim Museum's recent sales, that some larger context than the art market's buying and selling is broached as the field within which deaccessioning might be discussed, although the writer does not really enter this context.

But 'Selling the Collection' comes back-to-back with quite another article, which, called 'Remaking Art History', raises the problems that have been spawned within the art market itself by one particular art movement, namely Minimalism.[3] For Minimalism almost from the very beginning located itself, as one of its radical acts, within the technology of industrial production. That objects were fabricated from plans meant that these plans came to have a conceptual status within Minimalism allowing for the possibility of replication of a given work that could cross the boundaries of what had always been considered the unreproducibility of the aesthetic original. In some cases these plans were sold to collectors along with or even in place of an original object, and from these plans the collector did indeed have certain pieces refabricated. In other cases it has been the artist himself or herself who has done the refabrication, either issuing various versions of a given object – multiple originals, so to speak – as is the case with the many Morris glass cubes, or replacing a deteriorated original with a contemporary remake as in the case of Alan Saret. This break with the aesthetic of the original is, the writer of this essay argues, part and parcel with Minimalism itself, and so she writes: 'If, as viewers of contemporary art, we are unwilling to relinquish the conception of the unique original art object, if we insist that all refabrications are fraudulent, then we misunderstand the nature of many of the key works of the '60s and '70s. ... If the original object can be replaced without compromising the original meaning, refabrication should raise no controversy.'

However, as we know, it is not exactly viewers who are raising controversy in this matter, but artists themselves, as Donald Judd and Carl Andre have protested Count Panza's various decisions to act on the basis of the certificates they sold him and make duplicate versions of their works.[4] And indeed the fact that the group countenancing these refabrications is made up of the works' owners (both private collectors and museums) – that is, the group normally thought to have most interest in specifically protecting the status of their property *as* original – indicates how inverted this situation is. The writer of this essay also speaks of the market as playing some role in the story she has to tell. 'As the public's interest in the art of this period grows,' she says, 'and the market pressures increase, the issues that arise when works are refabricated will no doubt gain prominence as well.' But what the nature of either 'the issues' or the 'market pressures' might really be, she leaves it to the future to decide.

In the bridge I am setting up here, then, we watch the activity of markets restructuring the aesthetic original, either to change it into an 'asset', as in the case outlined by the first article, or to normalize a once-radical practice of challenging the very idea of the original through a recourse to the technology of mass production. That this normalization exploits a possibility *already* inscribed in the specific procedures of Minimalism will be important to the rest of my argument. But for now I simply point to the juxtaposition of a description of the financial crisis of the modern museum with an account of a shift in the nature of the original that is a function of one particular artistic movement, to wit, Minimalism.

2. The second bridge can be constructed more quickly. It consists merely of a peculiar rhyming between a famous remark of Tony Smith's from the opening phase of Minimalism and one by the Guggenheim's Director, Tom Krens, made last spring. Tony Smith is describing a ride he took in the early 1950s on the New Jersey Turnpike when it was still unfinished. He is speaking of the endlessness of the expanse, of its sense of being cultural but totally off the scale of culture. It was an experience, he said, that could not be framed, and thus, breaking through the very notion of frame, it was one that revealed to him the insignificance and 'pictorialism' of all painting. 'The experience on the road,' he says, 'was something mapped out but not socially recognized. I thought to myself, it ought to be clear that's the end of art.' And what we now know with hindsight on this statement is that Tony Smith's 'end of art' coincided with – indeed, conceptually undergirded – the beginning of Minimalism.

The second remark, the one by Tom Krens, was made to me in an interview and also involves a revelation on a turnpike, the Autobahn just outside of Cologne.[5] It was a November day in 1985, and having just seen a spectacular gallery made from a converted factory building, he was driving by large numbers of other factories. Suddenly, he said, he thought of the huge abandoned factories in his own neighborhood of North Adams, and he had the revelation of MASS MoCA.[6] Significantly, he described this revelation as transcending anything like the mere availability of real estate. Rather, he said, it announced an entire change in – to use a word he seems extremely fond of – *discourse*. A profound and sweeping change, that is, within the very conditions within which art itself is understood. Thus, what was revealed to him was not only the tininess and inadequacy of most museums, but that the encyclopedic nature of the museum was 'over'. What museums must now do, he said he realized, was to select a very few artists from the vast array of modernist aesthetic production and to collect and show these few in depth over the full amount of space it might take to really experience the cumulative impact of a given oeuvre. The discursive change he was imagining is, we might say, one that switches from diachrony to synchrony. The encyclopedic museum is intent on telling a story, by arraying before its visitor a particular version of the history of art. The synchronic museum – if we can call it that – would forego history in the name of a kind of intensity of experience, an aesthetic charge that is not so much temporal (historical) as it is now radically spatial, the model for which, in Krens's own account, was, in fact, Minimalism. It is Minimalism, Krens says in relation to his revelation, that has reshaped the way we, as late twentieth-century viewers, look at art: the demands we now put on it; our need to experience it along with its interaction with the space in which it exists; our need to have a cumulative, serial, crescendo towards the intensity of this experience; our need to have more and at a larger scale. It was Minimalism, then, that was part of the revelation that only at the scale of something like MASS MoCA could this radical revision of the very nature of the museum take place.

Within the logic of this second bridge, there is something that connects Minimalism – and at a very deep level – to a certain kind of analysis of the modern museum, one that announces its radical revision.

Now even from the few things I've sketched about Minimalism, there emerges an internal contradiction. For on the one hand there is Krens's acknowledgement of what could be called the phenomenological ambitions of Minimalism; and on the other, underscored by the dilemma of contemporary refabrication, Minimalism's participation in a culture of seriality, of multiples without originals – a culture, that is, of commodity production.

That first side, it could be argued, is the aesthetic base of Minimalism, its conceptual bedrock, what the writer of the *Art in America* article called its 'original meaning'. This is the side of Minimalism that denies that the work of art is an encounter between two previously fixed and complete entities: on the one hand, the work as a repository of known forms – the cube or prism, for example, as a kind of geometric a priori, the embodiment of a Platonic solid; and on the other, the viewer as an integral, biographically elaborated subject, a subject who cognitively grasps these forms because he or she knows them in advance. Far from being a cube, Richard Serra's *House of Cards* is a shape in the process of forming against the resistance, but also with the help of the ongoing conditions of gravity; far from being a simple prism, Robert Morris's *L-Beams* are three different insertions within the viewer's perceptual field such that each new disposition of the form, sets up an encounter between the viewer and the object which redefines the shape. As Morris himself wrote in his 'Notes on Sculpture', Minimalism's ambition was to leave the domain of what he called 'relational aesthetics' and to 'take relationships out of the work and make them a function of space, light, and the viewer's field of vision'.[7]

To make the work happen, then, on this very perceptual knife-edge – the interface between the work and its beholder – is on the one hand to withdraw privilege both from the formal wholeness of the object prior to this encounter and from the artist as a kind of authorial absolute who has set the terms for the nature of the encounter, in advance. Indeed, the turn towards industrial fabrication of the works was consciously connected to this part of Minimalism's logic, namely, the desire to erode the old idealist notions about creative authority. But on the other hand, it is to restructure the very notion of the viewing subject.

It is possible to misread a description of Minimalism's drive to produce a kind of 'death of the author' as one of creating a now all-powerful reader/ interpreter, as when Morris writes: 'The object is but one of the terms of the newer aesthetic. … One is more aware than before that he himself is establishing relationships as he apprehends the object from various positions and under varying conditions of light and spatial context.' But, in fact, the nature of this 'he himself [who] is establishing relationships' is also what Minimalism works to put in suspension. Neither the old Cartesian subject nor the traditional biographical subject, the Minimalist subject – this 'he himself establishing relationships' – is a subject radically contingent on the conditions of the spatial field, a subject who coheres, but only provisionally and moment-by-moment, in the act of perception. It is the subject that, for instance, Maurice Merleau-Ponty describes when he writes: 'But the system of experience is not arrayed before me as if I were God, it is lived by me from a certain point of view; I am not the spectator, I am involved, and it is my involvement in a point of view which makes possible both the finiteness of my perception and its opening out upon the complete world as a horizon of every perception.'[8]

In Merleau-Ponty's conception of this radically contingent subject, caught up within the horizon of every perception, there is, as we know, an important further condition. For Merleau-Ponty is not merely directing us towards what could be called a 'lived perspective'; he is calling on us to acknowledge the primacy of the 'lived *bodily* perspective'. For it is the immersion of the body in the world, the fact that it has a front and a back, a left and a right side, that establishes at what Merleau-Ponty calls a level of 'preobjective experience' a kind of internal horizon which serves as the precondition of the meaningfulness of the perceptual world. It is thus the body as the preobjective ground of all experience of the relatedness of objects that was the primary 'world' explored by the *Phenomenology of Perception*.

Minimalism was indeed committed to this notion of 'lived *bodily* perspective', this idea of a perception that would break with what it saw as the decorporealized and therefore bloodless, algebraicized condition of abstract painting in which a visuality cut loose from the rest of the bodily sensorium and now remade in the model of modernism's drive towards absolute autonomy had become the very picture of an entirely rationalized, instrumentalized, serialized subject. Its insistence on the immediacy of the experience, understood as a bodily immediacy, was intended as a kind of release from the forward march of modernist painting towards an increasingly positivist abstraction.

In this sense, Minimalism's reformulation of the subject as radically contingent is, even though it attacks older idealist notions of the subject, a kind of Utopian gesture. This is because the Minimalist subject is in this very displacement returned to its body, regrounded in a kind of richer, denser subsoil of experience than the paper-thin layer of an autonomous visuality that had been the goal of optical painting. And thus this move is, we could say, compensatory, an act of reparations to a subject whose everyday experience is one of increasing isolation, reification, specialization, a subject who lives under the conditions of advanced industrial culture as an increasingly instrumentalized being. It is to this subject that Minimalism, in an act of resistance to the serializing, stereotyping, and banalizing of commodity production, holds out a promise of some instant of bodily plenitude in a gesture of compensation that we recognize as deeply aesthetic.

But even if Minimalism seems to have been conceived in *specific* resistance to the fallen world of mass culture – with its disembodied media images – and of consumer culture – with its banalized, commodified objects – in an attempt to restore the immediacy of experience, the door it opened onto 'refabrication' nonetheless was one that had the potential to let that whole world of late capitalist production right back in.[9] Not only was the factory fabrication of the objects from plans a switch from artisanal to industrial technology, but the very choice of materials and of shapes rang with the overtones of industry. No matter that Plexiglass and aluminum and Styrofoam were meant to destroy the inferiority signalled by the old materials of sculpture like wood or stone. These were nonetheless the signifiers of late 20th-century commodity production, cheap and expendable. No matter that the simple geometries were meant to serve as the vehicles of perceptual immediacy. These were as well the operators of those rationalized forms susceptible to mass production and the generalized ones adaptable as corporate logos.[10] And most crucially, the Minimalist resistance to traditional composition which meant the adoption of a repetitive, additive aggregation of form – Donald Judd's 'one thing after another' – partakes very deeply of that formal condition that can be seen to structure consumer capitalism: the condition, that is, of seriality. For the serial principle seals the object away from any condition that could possibly be thought to be original and consigns it to a world of simulacra, of multiples without originals, just as the serial form also structures the object within a system in which it makes sense only in relation to other objects, objects which are themselves structured by relations of artificially produced difference. Indeed, in the world of commodities it is this difference that is consumed.[11]

Now how, we might ask, is it possible that a movement that wished to attack commodification and technologization somehow always already carried the codes of those very conditions? How is it that immediacy was always potentially undermined – infected, we could say – with its opposite? For it is this always already that is being tapped in the current controversy about refabrication. So, we could ask, how is it that an art that insisted so hard on specificity could have already programmed within it the logic of its violation?

But this kind of paradox is not only common in the history of modernism, which is to say the history of art in the era of capital; it could be said to be of the very nature of modernist art's relation to capital, a relation in which, in its very resistance to a particular manifestation of capital – to technology, say, or commodification, or the reification of the subject of mass production – the artist produces an alternative to that phenomenon which can also be read as a function of it, another version, although possibly more ideated or rarified, of the very thing against which he or she was reacting. Fredric Jameson, who is intent on tracing this capital-logic as it works itself out in modernist art, describes it, for example, in Van Gogh's clothing of the drab peasant world around him in an hallucinatory surface of color. This violent transformation, he says, 'is to be seen as a Utopian gesture: as an act of compensation which ends up producing a whole new Utopian realm of the senses, or at least of that supreme sense – sight, the visual, the eye – which it now reconstitutes for us as a semi-autonomous space in its own right'.[12] But even as it does this, it in fact imitates the very division of labor that is performed in the body of capital, thereby 'becoming some new fragmentation of the emergent sensorium which replicates the specializations and divisions of capitalist life at the same time that it seeks in precisely such fragmentation a desperate Utopian compensation for them'.[13]

What is exposed in this analysis is then the logic of what could be called cultural reprogramming or what Jameson himself calls 'cultural revolution' And this is to say that while the artist might be creating a Utopian alternative to, or compensation for, a certain nightmare induced by industrialization or commodification, he is at the very same time projecting an imaginary space which, if it is shaped somehow by the structural features of that same nightmare, works to produce the possibility for its receiver fictively to occupy the territory of what will be a next, more advanced level of capital. Indeed, it is the theory of cultural revolution that the imaginary space projected by the artist will not only emerge from the formal conditions of the contradictions of a given moment of capital, but will prepare its subjects – its readers or viewers – to occupy a future real world which the work of art has already brought them to imagine, a world restructured not through the present but through the next moment in the history of capital.

An example of this, we could say, would be the great *unités d'habitation* of the International Style and Le Corbusier, which rose above an older, fallen city fabric to project a powerful, futuristic alternative to it, an alternative celebrating the potential creative energy stored within the individual designer. But insofar as those projects simultaneously destroyed the older urban network of neighborhoods with their heterogeneous cultural patterns, they prepared the ground precisely for that anonymous culture of suburban sprawl and shopping-center homogeneity that they were specifically working to counter.

So, with Minimalism, the potential was always there that not only would the *object* be caught up in the logic of commodity production, a logic that would overwhelm its specificity, but that the *subject* projected by Minimalism also would be reprogrammed. Which is to say that the Minimalist subject of 'lived bodily experience' – unballasted by past knowledge and coalescing in the very moment of its encounter with the object – could, if pushed just a little farther, break up entirely into the utterly fragmented, postmodern subject of contemporary mass culture. It could even be suggested that by prizing loose the old ego-centered subject of traditional art, Minimalism unintentionally – albeit logically – prepares for that fragmentation.

And it was that fragmented subject, I would submit, that lay in wait for the viewer to the Panza Exhibition in Paris – not the subject of lived bodily immediacy of 1960s Minimalism, but the dispersed subject awash in a maze of signs and simulacra of late 1980s postmodernism. This was not just a function of the way the objects tended to be eclipsed by the emanations from themselves that seemed to stand apart from their corporeal beings like so many blinking signs – the shimmering waves of the floor pieces punctuating the groundplan, the luminous exhalations of the light pieces washing the corners of rooms one had not yet entered. It was also a function of the new centrality given to James Turrell, an extremely minor figure for Minimalism in the late 1960s and early 1970s, but one who plays an important role in the reprogrammation of Minimalism for the late 1980s. The Turrell piece, itself an exercise in sensory reprogramming, is a function of the way a barely perceptible luminous field in front of one appears gradually to thicken and solidify, not by revealing or bringing into focus the surface which projects this color, a surface which we as viewers might be said to perceive, but rather by concealing the vehicle of the color and thereby producing the illusion that it is the field itself which is focusing, that it is the very object facing one that is doing the perceiving *for* one.

Now it is this derealized subject – a subject that no longer does its own perceiving but is involved in a dizzying effort to decode signs that emerge from within a no longer mappable or knowable depth – that has become the focus of many analyses of postmodernism. And this space, which is grandiloquent but somehow no longer masterable by the subject, seeming to surpass the reach of understanding like an inscrutable emblem of the multinational infrastructures of information technology or of capital transfer, is often referred to in such analyses as 'hyperspace'. It, in turn, is a space that supports an experience that Jameson calls 'the hysterical sublime'. Which is to say that precisely in relation to the suppression of the older subjectivity – in what could be called the waning of affect – there is 'a strange compensatory decorative exhilaration'.[14] In place of the older emotions there is now an experience that must properly be termed an 'intensity' – a free-floating and impersonal feeling dominated by a peculiar kind of euphoria.

The revision of Minimalism such that it addresses or even works to produce that new fragmented and technologized subject, such that it constructs not an experience of itself but some other euphorically dizzy sense of the museum as hyperspace, this revisionary construction of Minimalism exploits, as we have seen, what was always potential within Minimalism.[15] But it is a revision that is, as well, happening at a specific moment in history. It is happening in 1990 in tandem with powerful changes in how the museum itself is now being reprogrammed or reconceptualized.

The writer of 'Selling the Collection' acknowledged that the Guggenheim's deaccessioning was part of a larger strategy to reconceive the museum and that Krens himself has described this strategy as somehow motivated or justified by the way Minimalism restructures the aesthetic 'discourse'. What, we might now ask, is the nature of that larger strategy, and how is Minimalism being used to serve as its emblem?

One of the arguments made by analysts of postmodern culture is that in its switch from what could be called an era of industrial production to one of commodity production – an era, that is, of the consumer society, or the information society, or the media society – capital has not somehow been magically transcended. Which is to say, we are not in either a 'postindustrial society' or a 'postideological era'. Indeed, they would argue, we are in an even purer form of capital in which industrial modes can be seen to reach into spheres (such as leisure, sport, and art) previously somewhat separated from them. In the words of the Marxist economist Ernest Mandel: 'Far from representing a "post-industrial society" late capitalism thus constitutes *generalized universal industrialzation* for the first time in history. Mechanization, standardization, over-specialization and parcellization of labor, which in the past determined only the realm of commodity production in actual industry, now penetrate into all sectors of social life.'[16]

As just one example of this he gives the Green Revolution, or the massive industrialization of agriculture through the introduction of machines and chemicals. Just as in any other industrialization, the old productive units are broken up – the farm family no longer makes its own tools, food, and clothing – to be replaced by specialized labor in which each function is now independent and must be connected through the mediating link of trade. The infrastructure needed to support this connection will now be an international system both of trade and of credit. What makes this expanded industrialization possible, he adds, is the overcapitalization (or noninvested surplus capital) that is the hallmark of late capitalism. It is this surplus that is unlocked and set in motion by the falling rate of profit. And it in turn accelerates the process of transition to monopoly capitalism.

Now noninvested surplus capital is exactly one way of describing the holdings – both in land and in art – of museums. It is the way, as we have seen, that many museum figures (directors and trustees) are now, in fact, describing their collections. But the market they see themselves responding to is the art market and not the mass market; and the model of capitalization they have in mind is the 'dealership' and not industry.

Writers about the Guggenheim have already become suspicious that it is the one exception in all this – an exception, most would agree, that will be an extremely seductive pattern for others to follow once its logic becomes clear. The *New York Times Magazine* writer of the profile on MASS MoCA was, indeed, struck by the way Tom Krens constantly spoke not of the museum but of the 'museum industry', describing it as 'overcapitalized', in need of 'mergers and acquisitions' and of 'asset management'. And further, invoking the language of industry, he spoke of the museum's activities – its exhibitions and catalogues – as 'product'.

Now from what we know from other industrializations, we can say that to produce this 'product' efficiently will require not only the break-up of older productive units – as the curator no longer operates as combined researcher, writer, director, and producer of an exhibition but will be increasingly specialized into filling only one of these functions – but will entail the increased technologization (through computer-based data systems) and centralization of operations at every level. It will also demand the increased control of resources in the form of art objects that can be cheaply and efficiently entered into circulation. Further, in relation to the problem of the effective marketing of this product, there will be the requirement of a larger and larger surface over which to sell the product in order to increase what Krens himself speaks of as 'market share'. It takes no genius to realize that the three immediate requisites of this expansion are 1) larger inventory (the Guggenheim's acquisition of three hundred works from the Panza collection is a first step in this direction); 2) more physical outlets through which to sell the product (the Salzburg and Venice/Dogana projects are potential ways of realizing this, as would be MASS MoCA);[17] and 3) leveraging the collection (which in this case most specifically does not mean selling it, but rather moving it into the credit sector, or the circulation of capital;[18] the collection will thus be pressed to travel as one form of indebtedness; classically, mortgaging the collection would be the more direct form of leveraging).[19] And it also does not stretch the imagination too much to realize that this industrialized museum will have much more in common with other industrialized areas of leisure – Disneyland say – than it will with the older, preindustrial museum. Thus it will be dealing with mass markets, rather than art markets, and with simulacral experience rather than aesthetic immediacy.

Which brings us back to Minimalism and the way it is being used as the aesthetic rationale for the transformation I am describing. The industrialized museum has a need for the technologized subject, the subject in search not of affect but of intensities, the subject who experiences its fragmentation as euphoria, the subject whose field of experience is no longer history, but space itself: that hyperspace which a revisionist understanding of Minimalism will use it to unlock.

NOTES

1. Throughout, my debt to Fredric Jameson's 'Postmodernism, or The Cultural Logic of Late Capitalism', (*New Left Review*, no. 146 [July-August 1984], pp. 53–93) will be obvious.

2. Philip Weiss, 'Selling the Collection', *Art in America*, vol. 78 (July 1990), pp. 124–31.

3. Susan Hapgood, 'Remaking Art History', *Art in America*, vol. 78 (July 1990), pp. 114–23.

4. See *Art in America* (March and April 1990).

5. The interview took place May 7, 1990.

6. MASS MoCA (The Massachusetts Museum of Contemporary Art), a project to transform the 750,000 square feet of factory space formerly occupied by Sprague Technologies Inc. into a museum complex (that would not only consist of gargantuan exhibition galleries, but also a hotel and retail shops), proposed to the Massachusetts Legislature by Krens and granted funding in a special bill potentially underwriting half its costs with a $35 million bond issue, is now [as of the original publication of this article in 1990] nearing the end of a feasibility study, funded out of the same bill, and being conducted by a committee chaired by Krens. See Deborah Weisgall, 'A Megamuseum in a Mill Town. The Guggenheim in Massachusetts?', *New York Times Magazine* (3 March 1989).

7. Robert Morris, 'Notes on Sculpture', in G. Battcock, ed., *Minimal Art*, New York, Dutton, 1968.

8. Maurice Merleau-Ponty, *Phenomenology of Perception*, trans. Colin Smith, London, Routledge and Kegan Paul, 1962, p. 304.

9. This analysis of the contradictions internal to Minimalism has already been brilliantly argued by Hal Foster in his genealogical study of Minimalism. See Hal Foster, 'The Crux of Minimalism', in *Individuals, A Selected History of Contemporary Art: 1945–1986*, Los Angeles, The Museum of Contemporary Art, 1986. His argument there, that Minimalism simultaneously completes *and* breaks with modernism, announcing its end, and his discussion of the way much of postmodernism in both its critical modes (the critique of institutions, the critique of the representation of the subject) and its collaborative ones (the transavant-garde, simulation) is nascent within the Minimalist syntax, both spatial and productive, is a complex articulation of the logic of Minimalism and anticipates much of what I am saying about its history.

10. This argument was already suggested by Art & Language's critique of Minimalism. See Carl Beveridge and Ian Burn, 'Donald Judd May We Talk?', *The Fox*, no. 2 (1972). That Minimalism should have been welcomed into corporate collections came full circle in the 1980s when its forms served as the, perhaps unwilling, basis of much of postmodern architecture.

11. Foster, p. 180.

12. Jameson, p. 59.

13. Ibid.

14. Ibid., p. 61.

15. The various 1970s projects, organized by Heiner Friedrich and sponsored by the Dia Foundation,

which set up permanent installations – like de Maria's *Earth Room* or his *Broken Kilometer* – had the effect of reconsecrating certain urban spaces to a detached contemplation of their own 'empty' presence. Which is to say that in the relationship between the work and its context, these spaces themselves increasingly emerge as the focus of the experience, one of an inscrutable but suggestive sense of impersonal, corporatelike power to penetrate art-world locales and to rededicate them to another kind of nexus of control. Significantly, it was Friedrich who began, in the mid-1970s, to promote the work of James Turrell (he is also the manager, for the Dia Foundation, of Turrell's mammoth *Roden Crater*).

16. Ernest Mandel, *Late Capitalism*, London, Verso, 1978, p. 387, as cited in Foster, p. 179; and in Jameson, 'Periodizing the '60s', *The Ideologies of Theory*, Vol. II, Minneapolis, University of Minnesota Press, 1988, p. 207.

17. Projects at different stages of realization include a Salzburg Guggenheim, in which the Austrian Government would presumably pay for a new museum (designed by Hans Holein) and endow its operating expenses in return for a New York Guggenheim-managed program, part of which would entail the circulation of the Guggenheim collection into Salzburg. In addition, there are negotiations for a Venice Guggenheim in the quarters of the former Customs House (the Dogana).

18. That as part of its industrialization the Guggenheim is willing to deaccession not just minor objects but masterpieces is a point made by 'Selling the Collection', where Professor Gert Schiff is quoted as saying of the deaccessioned Kandinsky, 'It really was a centerpiece of the collection – they could have sold almost anything but not that', and former director, now trustee, Tom Messer, is described as 'uncomfortable with the transaction' (p. 130). Another detail in this report is the extraordinary spread between Sotheby's estimate on this Kandinsky ($10–15 million) and its actual sale price ($20.9 million). In fact, on the three works auctioned by the Guggenheim, Sotheby's underestimated the sales by more than 40 percent. This raises some questions about 'asset management' in a domain, like the Guggenheim's, of increasing specialization of professional roles. For it is clear that neither the museum's staff nor its director had a grip on the realities of the market, and relying on Sotheby's 'expertise' (not, of course disinterested), they probably deaccessioned one more work than they needed to in order to accomplish their target, which was the purchase of the Panza collection. It is also clear – not only from Schiff's comment but also from one by William Rubin to the effect that in thirty years of experience he had never seen a comparable Kandinsky for sale, and that chances are that in the next thirty years there will not be another – that the separation of curatorial from managerial skills is wildly skewing the museum's judgment in the favor of those who stand to profit – in the form of fees and percentages of sales – from any 'deal' that takes place: auctioneers, dealers, etc.

19. In August 1990, the Guggenheim Museum, through the agency of The Trust for Cultural Resources of the City of New York (about which more later), issued $55 million of tax-exempt bonds to J. P. Morgan Securities (who will presumably remarket them to the public). This money is to be used for the museum's physical expansion in New York City: the annex to the present building, the restoration and underground expansion of the present building, and the purchase of a warehouse in midtown Manhattan. Counting interest on these bonds, the museum will, in the course of fifteen years, have to pay out $115 million to service and retire this debt.
     The collateral for these bonds is curious, since the issuing document reads: 'None of the assets of the [Guggenheim] Foundation are pledged for payment of the Bonds.' It goes on to specify that the museum's endowment is legally unavailable to be used to meet the obligations of the debt and that 'certain works in the Foundation's collection are subject to express sale prohibitions or other restrictions pursuant to the applicable gift instruments or purchase contracts'. That such restrictions apply only to 'certain works' and not to all works is also something to which I will return.
     In light of the fact that no collateral is pledged in case of the museum's inability to meet its obligations on this debt, one might well wonder about the basis on which Morgan Securities (as well as its partner in this transaction, the Swiss Bank Corporation) agreed to purchase these bonds. This basis is clearly threefold. First, the Guggenheim is projecting its ability to raise the money it needs (roughly $7 million per year over and above its current [the date in the bond issuance document is for FY 1988] annual expenses of $11.5 million [on which it was running a deficit of about 9 percent, which is *extremely* high for this kind of institution]) through, on the one hand, a $30 million fund drive and, on the other, added revenue streams due to its expansion of plant, program, markets, etc. Since its obligation is $115 million, the fund drive, even if successful, will leave over $86 million to raise. Second, if the Guggenheim's plans for increasing revenue (added gate, retail sales, memberships, corporate funding, gifts, plus 'renting' its collection to its satellite museums, among others) by the above amount (or 70 percent above its current annual income) do not work out as projected, the next line of defense the bankers can fall back on will be the ability of members of the Guggenheim's board of

trustees to cover the debt. This would involve a personal willingness to pay that no trustee, individually, is legally required to do. Third, if the first two possibilities fail and default is threatened, the collection (minus, of course, 'certain works'), though it is not pledged, is clearly available as an 'asset' to be used for debt repayment.

In asking financial officers of various tax-exempt institutions to evaluate this undertaking, I have been advised that it is, indeed, a 'high-risk' venture. And I have also gleaned something of the role of The Trust for Cultural Resources of The City of New York.

Many states have agencies set up to lend money to tax-exempt institutions, or to serve as the medium through which monies from bond drives are delivered to such institutions, as is the case with The Trust for Cultural Resources. But unlike The Trust for Cultural Resources, these agencies are required to review the bond proposals in order to assess their viability. The review carried out by agency employees is clearly made by people not associated with the institutions themselves. The Trust for Cultural Resources, although it brokers the money at the behest of the government like the state agencies, has no staff to review proposals and therefore has no role in vetting the bond requests. What it seems to do instead is to give the proposal its bona fides. Given the fact that the members of the trust are also major figures of other cultural institutions (Donald Marron, for example, is president of the board of trustees of The Museum of Modern Art), the trust's own trustees are, in fact, potential borrowers.

8.

Collision

Neil Cummings and Marysia Lewandowska

In the present day, it is no longer possible to structure culture according to a reassuringly binary model. Just as ideologically, 'free' trade cannot be simply contrasted with the top-down command economies of 'welfare' states, so fine artefacts and antiquities cannot be opposed in kind to popular or domestic products.

Before the First World War, this kind of outmoded, oppositional model was perfectly embodied, and enthusiastically disseminated by the museum and the department store. The organisation of both institutions was built around static hierarchies of knowledge. Information passed slowly upward through their respective management structures, and decisions or reactions retraced its path downward and outward. Because of its inherent inflexibility, this 'top-down' system was only suited to the accumulation and classification of value through things as long as the nature of those things and the practices of shoppers/visitors remained fairly consistent.

After the onset of hostilities in 1914, these static principles began to dissolve, along with all the other comforting certainties of social and economic life. The patrician policies applied in the museum (defining and redefining its narratives for an educated élite, but with the expectation that wider society should also adhere to their definitions of taste) began to be superseded by a

Figure 5.8.1   One of a world-wide chain of 'Museum Stores' in Hampstead, London

new interpretation of what 'doing' culture should actually consist of. But by employing essentially nineteenth-century management ideologies coupled with lazy exhibitionary practices, neither the museum nor store was equipped to adjust to this or any of the other vast cultural shifts that would follow in the decades after the end of the war.

This lack of responsiveness seemed particularly acute during the upheaval of the 1960s, as the pace of material life accelerated and the networking of electronic communication systems irrevocably began to alter traditional mechanisms of social, economic, sexual and intellectual exchange. As these changes washed around them, the museum and store may have adjusted in scale (downsizing occasionally in response to economic pressure), but still retained markedly unreconstructed, bureaucratic cores. Despite this complacency, events outside their doors precipitated radical alterations in the nature of the institutions' respective constituencies. Both were having to face newly differentiated and multiple flows of shoppers, visitors and goods that produced fragmented and sometimes contradictory demands. The imagined mass of 'mass consumption' had fractured into lifestyle clusters, groups with requirements that could no longer be responded to with a rigid management hierarchy or single exhibition strategy.

[Marginal note: After the Second World War, economist John Maynard Keynes founded the Arts Council of Great Britain (the principal Government

Figure 5.8.2

funding agency for cultural production). Using as its model the British Broadcasting Corporation (BBC), the Council was consciously intended to work in opposition to mass popular culture; Government-funded through taxation, its purpose was to ensure Britain retained a cultural sphere protected from the vagaries of the marketplace.]

Even the stores, which had been born with and were central to a networked promotional industry, remained hampered by antiquated management policy and a reactionary vision both of their own potential and that of their audience. They proved to be a long way behind the cutting edge of the accelerating market, generally defaulting to complement ranges (selling muted tones and easy-fit to middle-aged suburbanites) by using merely the most convenient systems to acquire stock; buyers were sent abroad to sample passively the conservative wares of vast corporate trade fairs. It appeared that the store, like the museum, could be condemned to lie remaindered in a cultural backwater, permanently disengaged from the active interpretation of the past and present of things.

In 1980s Britain, during the course of a single decade (an era characterised by what is known, normally pejoratively, as 'Thatcherism') Government policy destroyed the link between the reliance of 'culture' and its institutions on funding from the state, and introduced the market as a new disciplinary force. Museums were forced to respond to management discourses that encouraged

Figure 5.8.3

strategies for mass participation, popular and entertaining exhibitions, 'blockbuster' displays and 'fun days out'. With a return to nineteenth-century museological policy and its focus on open access, State-supported cultural institutions faced greater pressure to produce what their audience appeared to want ('your visitors are your customers'), but without the imperative to educate, merely to entertain. Increasingly commercialised through entrance charges, branded exhibitions, and the necessity of wooing corporate sponsors, museums were forced to justify their funding through grants with direct reference to audience numbers and educational programmes: to become more 'rational' and accountable. They now marketed themselves as 'heritage' sites, as quasi-theme parks, full of 'interactive' push-button technologies. Much was made of museums' revenue-producing souvenir shops, relaxing cafés, corporate opportunities, promotional consultants, 'development teams' and retail tie-ins. At the British Museum, in popular tourist re-enactments of excursions to the Great Exhibition, thousands of 'customers' – many of them schoolchildren or overseas visitors – thronged the marble halls, or jammed the 'signature' architectural extension. But behind this popular gloss, academic and exhibitions policy still showed an unchanging arrogance. The culmination of decades of social change seems to have been that the museum has moved towards the store in its market-orientated funding policy: and that the store (itself under pressure from other more efficient and stripped-down retail operations) has reverted to the theatrical 'exhibition' style of its beginning, concentrating on displays of sequences of 'lifestyle choices' that dazzle with promise.

We now increasingly play out our lives through what we want and display; ethical, moral and ideological 'choices' accompany the more mundane decisions of trying things on to see if they fit, or wondering if an item is affordable. The political imperative – expressed by phrases such as 'Green shopping', 'fair trading' or 'made using sustainable resources' – has as a result of fashion now become just another routine encouragement to buy. Participation in all the glitter of the intensified aesthetic present becomes a complex 'cultural' practice performed amongst a range of possible alternatives. The long history of convergence between the museum and the store is just part of a dissolution of the previously clear demarcation between the cultural and the economic. Indeed, any notion of the two institutions being radically opposed can now only be supported as an ideological proposition, rather than by reality.

VI.

Inclusions and Exclusions:

Representing Adequately

Introduction:

Inclusions and Exclusions: Representing Adequately

> For at the intersection of psychic and capitalist fetishism, the narratives such analyses entail turn collecting into something else again: a tale of social struggle. This struggle over 'ameliorations' by means of an attack on someone else's property with the help of money; negotiation over prices; elimination of a rival; accomplishment of the task of developing 'taste'; expertise competing with that of others – all these plots engage subjects on both sides of the 'logic of narrative possibilities', and on both sides of gender, colonialist and capitalist splits ... Paradoxically, the narratives of collecting enable a clearer vision of this social meaning.
>
> Mieke Bal, 'Telling Objects: A Narrative Perspective on Collecting' (1994)

The collected texts and introductory essays in the first five chapters of this book should have made clear the following: that the nationalist paradigm adopted by the founders of the Louvre (and followed by many other new public museums in the nineteenth century) made different cultural formations apparently commensurable with one another in museological representation and display, while at the same time maintaining implicit hierarchies of aesthetic and ethical value and cognitive, cultural, and technological advancement. As the essays by Bohrer, Clunas, Mitchell, Bhabha, Coombes, Grindstaff, Appadurai and Breckenridge and others have argued, this paradoxical egalitarianism was performed over a (not entirely covert) substrate of racial theory. To leave Europe (and its colonial extensions) was to enter a past peopled by inferior races frozen in earlier stages of cultural and ethical development. And, as Errington demonstrated, the corporatist performance of collective identity is no longer limited to nation-states with a predominantly European heritage, but has been readily adapted by modern nations (such as, in her case, Indonesia) with their sponsorship of nationalistic theme parks portraying sanitized 'fantasy polities' of ethnic origins, historical continuity, and uniform, untroubled progress.

The essays in Chapters 4 and 5 have addressed the performative and dramaturgical dimensions of these modes of representation and knowledge-production; these methodologies of power/knowledge characteristic of earlier and more recent phases of modernity. The exhibitionary orders of museological practice, as various authors whose texts are collected here have argued, not only 'manage consciousness' but fabricate, maintain, and naturalize the individual and collective consciousness of modern subjects. The present chapter brings together texts which in varying ways attempt to address the problems and paradoxes encountered in contemporary museological practices which seek to loosen the Gordian Knot of identificatory ideologies and the optical illusion of their egalitarianism and commensurability. Some of these texts (Canclini, Simpson, Berlo and Phillips, Appadurai and Breckenridge) explicitly address the problems and contradictions inherent in multiculturalist and postcolonialist writings of the past two decades while seeking effective methods of portrayal and display adequate to the expectations, cultural traditions, and histories of the portrayed. In the course of these essays and excerpts it will become evident that adequate solutions to cultural and ethnic misrepresentation can no longer justifiably consist of 'equalizing' the quantity or quality of 'content' among peoples and cultures in museums but must substantively rethink the exhibitionary polity of museum practice as such.

The problem in other words is no longer simply one of 'adequate' representation, but of 'representation' itself imagined as being unproblematic. And the fundamental problem of museology in the most general and far-reaching sense is the seemingly inherent presumption that a museum is or can only be a *representational artifact* in the literal sense. Such an issue has been addressed on many fronts and from a variety of perspectives throughout this volume. The aforementioned authors share the view, as succinctly put by Susan Vogel in her essay below, that 'The museum must allow the public to know that it is not a broad frame through which the art and culture of the world can be inspected, but a tightly focused lens that shows the visitor a particular point of view.' This remark resonates with that of Craig Clunas cited above at the beginning of the Introduction to Chapter 4, there addressed to 'art' and art history, and, it might be added, may be extended to an understanding of 'history' as such, as we have seen in the essays by Hayden White and Michel de Certeau in Chapter 1.

The excerpt included below from James Clifford's widely celebrated book *The Predicament of Culture*, on 'Histories of the Tribal and the Modern', resonates powerfully with these earlier essays and provides a conceptual framework as well as a complementary case-study (of the notorious exhibit 'Primitivism in 20th Century Art' mounted by New York's MOMA in 1984–85) for appreciating the innovative insights of the other texts in this chapter. Clifford's critique may be juxtaposed with Homi Bhabha's review reprinted above in Chapter 3, which echoes some of the same themes.

Moira Simpson's essay provides a good summary of developments since the 1960s in trying to meet the challenges of cultural diversity by museums in various parts of the world, and she cites a number of significant changes in museological ideology and practice in recent years. The book to which the excerpt reprinted here served as an introduction (*Making Representations: Museums in the Postcolonial Era*, 1996) examines a series of innovative contemporary museological practices. Yet in the years since the appearance of that volume, some of these innovations have become standard practice in many places, and seem less and less convincing, given that without exception all accept the foundational assumption that museums are 'representational' artifacts. There may be no easy way out of this double bind.

Simpson's introductory essay, however, charts the connections between changes in museum policies and practices and the civil rights movement in the US in the late 1960s and early 1970s, recalling the fact that not a few changes in exhibitionary policies came about precisely because of quite explicit, widespread, and often vociferous protests against museums by citizens and artists of color. This situation led to increased community participation in exhibitions and educational programs that better reflected the complex composition of contemporary society. As the former director of a Maryland museum succinctly put it, 'the destiny of the museum is the destiny of the community; their relationship is both symbiotic and catalytic.'

In varying ways, the authors in this chapter are in agreement that the very first step in redressing the inadequacies – not to speak of the violence (for that is what in essence it is) of misrepresentation (but then what representation is not a mis-?) – should be the attempt to find ways to make explicitly visible the 'subject-position' of museum managers in regard to the processes of collection, selection, and display. Clifford's insights about the patent linkages of the racist policies of a contemporary museum of modern art with the marketplace in elitist commodities were central to the extraordinarily heated debates about the museum and its policies at the time of the civil rights movement – a point largely lost or patently ignored in the exponential acceleration of museological corporatizing.

The essay by artist Rasheed Araeen, 'From Primitivism to Ethnic Arts' (1991), originated as a lecture for the Slade School in London in 1985/6, and discusses the ways in which both the Hegelian metaphysics underpining Western art history and theory and Western myths of 'progress' and of the 'burden' of the West to raise the rest of the world to civilization (Gibbon; Gobineau and Le Bon, etc.) still deeply inform art historical, critical, and museological practices. Araeen also addresses the 'Primitivism' exhibit mounted by William Rubin at MOMA, and draws upon the work of Partha Mitter in his discussion of Hegel's *Philosophy of History*.

In his talk, the author very concretely foregrounds his own subject position as a politically active artist of color, whose previous invitation to do a series of art performances at the Slade was quietly shelved when authorities learned of the explicitly political nature of his work. He uses this story as an introduction to a discussion of the ways in which liberal scholarship has been intertwined historically with the discourse of colonialism, slavery, and the exploitation of subject populations and their resources. His lecture addresses the status and representation of non-European cultures in Western scholarship and popular knowledge since the eighteenth century, and it lucidly connects these issues with the rise of art history and notions of artistic and cultural progress.[1] The notion of the 'primitive', he argues, is never not absent in art historical and museological theory and practice.

This essay may be read in conjunction with the next selection, whose authors, Arjun Appadurai and Carol Breckenridge, claim that museums in India occupy what in Western eyes may seem to be an ambiguous place. The tensions they see between the dynamic contexts from which objects in Indian museums were originally derived and the 'stasis' such objects appear to succumb to in museums resonates with issues raised back in Chapter 1 in the text by Mieke Bal on fetishism and collecting, which focuses more generally upon the inherently re-contextualizing 'narrative' stagecraft of collections.

They discuss the contradictory pressures toward the stabilizing and fixing of cultural identity and patrimony and the destabilizing of identities achieved by different ways of displaying and viewing objects. The museological 'ambiguity' they consider has resulted from the existence of a still-vibrant and living past in the present, the lack of sharp separations of sacred objects and those of daily life, and the continuing lack of alienation of the population from its biological and cosmological environments. The authors develop several not unexpected hypotheses to account for the coexistence of different forms of cultural literacy, chief among them a deep interdependence of various sites and modes of seeing, from cinema, television, religious festivals, sport, tourism, and museums, with varying emphases on communal viewing and interpretative construal. A critical feature of the cultural field within which museum-viewing in India (and by implication other non-Euroamerican contexts) needs to be located, they argue, lies in the importance of 'interocular experiences' which reinforce and contextualize each other. Yet arguably, the 'coexistence' or 'hybridity' of these sites and modes of seeing is itself an artifact of already-instantiated 'authenticities' and homogeneities, an intensely ethnocentrist presumption: who, indeed, determines authenticity?

The latter question is at the heart of Nestór García-Canclini's essay ('Remaking Passports: Visual Thought in the Debate on Multiculturalism') which contributes to the contemporary discourse of multiculturalism in his discussion of contemporary artistic practices that, in contrast to the situations described by Appadurai and Breckenridge in India, are 'delocalized' and incapable of assimilation to the frameworks of nationalist/ethnocentrist art histories, resembling in effect the polyglot and 'migrant identities' of their artists. 'Who issues passports anyway?', Canclini asks. In so doing, he raises the issue of diaspora and transitional, transitory, and migratory identity as potentially *central* rather than marginal to the processes of identification in the contemporary world.

Janet Berlo and Ruth Phillips's 1995 essay ('Our [Museum] World Turned Upside Down: Re-presenting Native American Arts') addresses some of the implications of various Native American attitudes towards objects, museums, and display, calling attention to beliefs (among the Kwakwaka'wakw people, for example) regarding ownership as located primarily in the mental concept behind an object and in rights of reproduction, and only secondarily in an object itself. One consequence of this recognition of the different status and nature of objects may be seen in the Cape Mudge Museum on Vancouver Island, where objects are increasingly being re-circulated as objects of ceremonial use, and then returned to the collection. The authors note that

as the return of collections and individual objects proceeds, a different kind of access will become available. When art-historical researchers revisit objects in Native American communities, they will find them differently presented, embedded in different texts from which much can be learned. The community perspective may well be more continuous with the historical and cultural truths that originally shaped the objects.

In short, the 'subject–object' divide that has underlain many fundamental presumptions about museology and art history and that has been addressed from a variety of points of view throughout this volume is now itself being seen in its historicity and cultural specificities – marking what may prove to be the most radical, deeply rooted change in our understanding of the 'framing' of memory (always in a very real sense a frame-up) and in the very 'idea' of the museum (now more and more a retrospective narrative about presumed origins.

We include two texts which address issues of contemporary artistic practice in and in relationship to museums. The first illustrates the fact that in an increasingly corporatized and neo-feudalist (globalized) economy, 'marginalization' knows no bounds. In her 1994 essay 'The Museum of Contemporary Art, Los Angeles: An Account of Collaboration between Artists, Trustees, and an Architect', Jo-Anne Berelowitz recounts the history of exclusions and inclusions of various constituencies concerned with the development of the Los Angeles MOCA as a major national museum over nearly a decade of debate and discussion, planning and promotion. 'Collaboration', she demonstrates, has quite specific limits when financial considerations underwrite taste and philanthropic zeal.

She begins with the official commemorative plaque in the museum's entrance as providing a particular narrative myth of origins, and unfolds the complex history behind the official story of the institution's design and development. It becomes clear in her investigation that the opinions, attitudes, and expertise of various individuals and of diverse groups and communities came to be subsumed in and buried beneath the underlying politico-economic agenda of those instrumental in initiating the MOCA project. This was the desire to establish a 'world-class institution' staffed by the most prominent directors and curators on the (then-current) international scene, and containing a world-class collection of recent art drawn from bequests of major local, national, and international collectors, many of whom (five of eight) came unsurprisingly to serve on the institution's Board of Trustees. The museum collection was to be contained within a 'signature' building by an internationally-prominent architect (the one selected was the Japanese architect Arata Isozaki).

MOCA officially opened in 1986. What the official story occluded was the role of the very large, extremely diverse, and extremely vociferous Los Angeles artistic community in bringing the museum project to completion, the group increasingly marginalized and ultimately ousted from the planning processes. In 1983, a building that came to be called The Temporary Contemporary – more recently and more orthodoxly renamed after a wealthy local patron (Geffen) – was opened in a former warehouse in Little Tokyo, east of the MOCA site. The structure, whose interior was radically re-designed by Frank Gehry, constituted the kind of museum space the artistic community felt to be more appropriate as a venue for contemporary art; Isozaki in effect was seen as allying himself against the artistic community and with the powerful class of politicians and corporate donors.

The resultant situation has been a split museum institution – a signature art history museum on Bunker Hill, and a popular art museum in Little Tokyo. Berelowitz's extensive interviews with all of those involved in bringing MOCA to fruition included many members of the artistic community, one of whom expressed the situation this way:

The doors started to shut very clearly and definitely on the artists as soon as there was a board of trustees. Historically, patrons consider the artists at best second-class citizens. My contention has always been that if dealers and patrons could possibly get the art without having to deal with artists, that would be their ideal world.

A situation which is in no way unique or for that matter at all new. The next selection deals squarely with the technologies of 'framing memory', which, as will be evident, go to the heart of (retrospectively) engendering (in all senses of the word) the 'idea' of the museum and the artifice of its practice. Andrea Liss's essay, 'The Identity Card Project and the Tower of Faces at the United States Holocaust Memorial Museum', deals with the museum's project of including each visitor in the history of a particular individual who may or may not have lost his or her life in the Nazi concentration camps. Each visitor is issued an identity card bearing information about a person, in order, as the former director of the museum's permanent collection, Martin Smith, put it, 'The identity card project came out of our desire to establish an immediate bonding with a person and a place.' Such bondings are staged almost inevitably as disjunctive, given the random association between the visitor's gender, age, and status and that of the person depicted and discussed in the card. As Liss suggests,

Everywhere in the museum – from the vague memory of the disembodied city outside, which the museum's architecture tries to efface, to the intricate workings of the simulated environments it houses – the visitor is reminded that he or she is in a vast space of articulated re-creation. To thus create a fusion of identities without gaps between the museum visitor and the remembered Holocaust victims would verge on the dangerous as well as the inconceivable.

Liss describes the 'profound visibility and simultaneous elusiveness' of this process, and suggests that the truly impossible bonding of the identity card project was appropriately commensurate with the profoundly unbridgeable gap between the visitor and the victim: 'Indeed, the issuance of mock identity cards could turn out to be a mourning and a bearing witness turned inside out and strained at the seams. This strange fusion of selves represents a desire for urgency camouflaged as a transfixed form of displaced nostalgia.'

In one sense, the identity card project may be emblematic of much of what has been at stake in modern museology more broadly, precisely through occlusion and coy elision: namely, the bonding of subjects and objects, with the staging of objects in museums and exhibitions eliciting by materializing 'identity' for its subjects – who become subjects precisely through such encounters, whether in museums or elsewhere in modern life.

The last selection in this volume addresses the issue of subjecthood by reviewing three recent reinstallations of well-known African collections, at the British Museum, the Horniman Museum (London), and the National Museum of Natural History at the Smithsonian (Washington, DC). The new installations claim to replace representational conventions tied to primitivism and cultural evolutionism that 'implicitly deny the modernity of Africa and the authenticity of diasporic African culture', but their success varies, Ruth Phillips finds. The approach adopted by the British Museum is 'startlingly Eurocentric', making 'no reference to compelling recent art historical research on the objects' entanglement in histories of violence, colonial power, and racist discourses about art', in which the British Museum itself played a central role. The installations at the Horniman Museum and the Smithsonian, by contrast, are inspired by recent collaborative models that work with indigenous peoples to convey a 'contemporaneity and proximity' that collapses the distance between Europe and Africa, while intentionally problematizing politically sensitive issues of ownership. Yet even in these two cases, the thematic approach is inevitably reductive, and categories (such as 'Wealth') are still keyed to the dominant culture's point of view. Phillips holds out hope, however, that museums can serve as transformative spaces where 'outworn and dangerous stereotypes are countered by images and representations that make diverse cultural groups recognizable not only to others but also to themselves'.

Which returns us to where we began, with the problem of the nature of meaningful relationships (and non-relationships) between what the ideology crystallized in our etymologies distinguishes despite our best intentions as 'subjects' and 'objects', recalling the observation of Robert Harbison quoted at the beginning of this volume about art being 'troublesome not because it is not delightful but because [of] the failure [of things] to make our lives as paradisal as their prospects'. Thinking seriously with and about museums, as the readings in this book will have made clear, entails seriously addressing some of our most basic presumptions and expectations about ourselves, whether or not we imagine ourselves, however fleetingly or permanently, to be reflected or re-presented therein.

NOTE

1. See in this connection Donald Preziosi, 'The Art of Art History', in Preziosi, ed., *The Art of Art History*, Oxford: Oxford University Press, 1998, 507–25.

1.

Cultural Reflections[1]

Moira Simpson

> Society will no longer tolerate institutions that either in fact or in appearance
> serve a minority audience of the élite.   (D. F. Cameron[2])

The politics of change

Over the past forty years or so, there has been a tremendous blossoming of cultural expression amongst indigenous peoples and other ethnic minority groups, resulting from a growing awareness of the importance of cultural heritage and the desire for free expression and civil rights. The decades since the Second World War have been years of upheaval and change in the relationship between European nations and those that they had dominated and exploited during the colonial era. Some of the most dramatic and violent were the struggles undertaken by the former colonial nations in their fights for independence. Following the end of the conflict in Europe, attention turned to political issues in countries in Africa and Asia where peoples were fighting for political and cultural autonomy and demanding independence. The determination to end centuries of colonial rule and exploitation in these countries was echoed by the political awakening of indigenous peoples and cultural minority groups in western nations.

This trend was particularly significant in North America where groups which previously had felt unrecognised, undervalued, or disadvantaged as a result of ethnicity, age, gender or sexual preferences began vocalising their frustrations, promoting their strengths, and demanding their rights. The 1950s and 1960s witnessed civil rights disturbances across North America with demonstrations and rioting as suppressed minority groups fought against inequality and racism inherent in every sector of society. In the United States, this period saw the emergence of the black civil rights movement, led by Martin Luther King, and the establishment of more forceful militant 'black power' groups, such as the Black Panthers, determined to achieve improved social and political rights for African Americans. Other groups were also struggling to attain basic civil rights in the USA: Mexican Americans formed El Movimiento and took new pride in their culture, turning the previously derogatory term 'Chicano' into a description they now embrace with pride. American Indians were reclaiming their cultural heritage and fighting for their rights after centuries of confrontation and exploitation of their land and resources, and decades of pressure to assimilate into American and Canadian society while being treated as second-class citizens. They formed pan-Indian organisations such as the American Indian Civil Rights Council (1969) and the National Indian Brotherhood (1969) (renamed the Assembly of First Nations in 1982), the Native American Rights Fund (1970), and the militant American Indian Movement (1968), to fight for self-determination, tribal recognition, the resolution of land claims and broken treaty agreements, and other issues affecting American Indian communities. As with the black civil rights campaign, there was a move from rhetoric to action during the late 1960s and the 1970s.[3]

In November 1969, American Indians took over Alcatraz Island in San Francisco, maintaining control for eighteen months despite the telephones, electricity and water being cut off by the US authorities.[4] Their action was an ironic allusion to the landing of Columbus and his crew in the Americas in 1492, described by George P. Horse Capture as 'a grand culmination of the civil rights decade';[5] a catalyst for much of the change that has followed.

For the first time since the Little Bighorn, the Indian people, instead of passively withdrawing and accepting their fate, had stepped forward in the bright sunshine and let it be known that they were Indian and proud, and their present situation must and would change.[6]

Three years later, a group of Indians retraced the 'Trail of Tears' of the 1830s with their own 'Trail of Broken Treaties' which led to a seven-day occupation of the Bureau of Indian Affairs in Washington, DC, which they renamed the

'Native American Embassy'. In February 1973, members of the Oglala Sioux and the American Indian Movement returned to Wounded Knee, the site of the massacre of 300 Sioux by US troops in 1890, to draw attention to government violations of the 1868 Fort Laramie Treaty. There they were confronted by heavily armed government troops and a 71 day siege followed during which two Indians were killed.

This was a period of intense cultural activity, political fervour, and the emergence of an irrepressible determination to fight for political representation and the preservation of the identity of minority cultures as a distinct part of American society. Reflecting their desire to be American but also to acknowledge their distinct cultural background, there has developed a nomenclature of ethnic identity linked with American nationality resulting in terms such as Native American, African American, Italian American, Chicano, and so on. New federal legislation such as the Indian Self-Determination Act of 1972 and the Native American Religious Freedom Act of 1978 provided tribal groups with greater autonomy. During the 1970s black studies and Indian cultural studies programmes flourished in American colleges and schools. Such movements have brought an end to the concept of the melting pot of US culture and established the importance of maintaining cultural diversity within a national framework.

American museums and the civil rights movement of the 1960s

Museums were not immune from criticisms and militant actions. Critics expressed dissatisfaction with the activities of mainstream museums and art galleries, and the ways in which black and other minority cultures were represented and interpreted in exhibitions. These institutions were perceived by many to be unsatisfactory: serving a cultural élite, staffed primarily by whites, reflecting white values, and excluding from the interpretive process the very peoples whose cultures were represented in the collections. Ethnic minority groups were poorly represented on museum staffs, and so felt they had little or no power over the content of museum exhibitions – a situation which was particularly frustrating for those who continued to suffer the effects of widely held misconceptions, stereotyping and inaccurate representation. Many artists of minority cultural backgrounds felt marginalised by museums and art galleries which were perceived to represent only the dominant white culture, and failed to provide equality of opportunity to artists of non-European origin. Museums came under increasing criticism for their Eurocentric approach towards the representation of cultures. They were seen to hold little relevance to the majority of peoples' lives and to be failing to meet the needs of minority communities in particular. While most criticisms of museums have been confined to the pages of professional journals or voiced at conferences and symposia, museums have not entirely escaped the protests and activities of political activists and occasionally have attracted more vociferous debate and censure including demonstrations, often noisy and sometimes violent.

The Black Emergency Cultural Coalition was established in the autumn of 1968 and, over the next few months, launched a campaign against the Whitney Museum demanding greater black representation amongst works purchased, artists exhibited, membership of the selection and purchasing committees, and on the museum staff.[7] They began by picketing the museum but settled down to meaningful discussions which resulted in agreement over increasing representation of work by black artists.

In January 1969, a group calling itself the Art Workers' Coalition was established in New York and launched an attack on the policies of the Museum of Modern Art (MOMA).[8] The Coalition, whose membership was composed of artists, writers, film-makers, and critics, urged the MOMA to have 'more cultural relevance' for blacks and Puerto Ricans and submitted a thirteen-point proposal, the demands of which included 'the extension of MOMA activities into ghetto communities, the formation of an artists' committee to arrange shows at the museum, free admission at all times, and the opening of a gallery for black artists' work' (Glueck, 1969a).[9] They also spilled cans of blood in the galleries, and demanded that the MOMA close until the Vietnam War was over and sell $1 million worth of its collection, giving the proceeds to the poor.[10]

On the 18th of January in the same year, the exhibition *Harlem on My Mind* opened at the Metropolitan Museum of Art. The exhibition consisted of photos, slides, and videos of Harlem, the black neighbourhood in upper Manhattan. While the exhibition proved to be very popular in some quarters, it also attracted much criticism and anger leading to demonstrations and acts of vandalism. Anger was aroused amongst blacks by the fact that it did not contain works of art by black artists and therefore showed 'a white man's view of Harlem'. In January 1969, a group of demonstrators picketed a preview and a black-tie cocktail and dinner party at the museum. On the same day several paintings, including a Rembrandt, were slightly damaged by vandals who scratched an 'H' on them, referring to Hoving, the director.[11] Two weeks later, paintings were defaced, obscenities were scrawled on the wall of the museum, and a guard injured while attempting to stop further vandalism.[12]

African Americans and Puerto Ricans expressed their anger and frustration of white museums and other cultural institutions at a *Seminar for Neighborhood Museums* held at MUSE in Brooklyn in 1969. In the spring of 1971, American Association of Museums meetings in New York City were disrupted by protesters who presented a manifesto and fought for the microphone on the platform, calling for reform in museums and art galleries.[13]

The events of 1967–71 marked a climax to a period of social unrest and militant action which had addressed wide-ranging concerns from anti-war sentiment to the failure of US–Indian treaties, and from the unrecognised value of the elderly to the cultural inequities of the art world. The passions and resentments that such protests released, reflected frustration over decades of lack of self-determination, misinterpretation, marginalisation and exclusion, but served to draw attention to people's grievances and the need to address their differing cultural needs. In the United States, the civil disturbances and the cultural revival movement focused attention on the cultural needs of ethnic communities and disadvantaged inner city residents. Changing demographics, such as industrial and commercial growth or decline, population shifts from rural to urban areas and vice versa, changes in ethnic profile caused by immigration, and the growth of tourism bringing influxes of visitors, have caused communities to re-examine their past and present experiences.

In the late 1960s and early 1970s, museum curators in the United States gradually began to recognise that the needs of inner-city residents and minority groups were not being met and so began the growth of community museums and a rethinking of the traditional museum role. It was generally felt that museums were not relating to the urban poor; that many cultural programmes offered by museums were merely continuing the 'cultural colonialism' of the past and doing little to make museums more accessible or relevant to them: instead museums needed to play a more socially significant role and respond directly to issues of concern to the public.[14] In the face of the demonstrations which had so disrupted university and college campuses, Kenneth Hopkins recommended fifteen steps to deal with confrontation; recommendations which, unfortunately, remain as necessary today, demonstrating how much progress must still be made in democratising museums.[15] During the 1970s and 1980s, exhibitions which focused more closely upon social concerns began to be presented by a number of museums in the United States, particularly the newly developed community museums such as Anacostia, MUSE, and the Museum of the City of New York.[16]

In 1971 the Museum of the City of New York began to introduce a series of community orientated projects to serve the needs of the local population: primarily black and Puerto Rican groups living in Harlem. The Museum of the City of New York and Anacostia Neighborhood Museum presented exhibitions dealing with topics of social concern in urban residential areas such as drug addiction and the problem of rats.[17] Such issues, while not the typical subject matter of museums, were of great interest and concern to the residents of the inner-city neighbourhoods which these museums served. These new museums were recognised as being very effective in providing relevant exhibitions, events and educational activities. Furthermore, community involvement was increasingly seen as being crucial to the successful implementation of programmes of exhibitions and activities which better reflected the cultural composition of society and the issues of relevance to the communities in which the museums were situated. John Kinard,[18] the former director of Anacostia Museum, commented that 'the destiny of the museum is the destiny of the community; their relationship is both symbiotic and catalytic'.

Such political and cultural revival by peoples who had suffered years of oppression, subjugation and exploitation was not, of course, limited to the USA: it reflected a growing world-wide trend which saw indigenous and minority peoples in many parts of the world forming political organisations to fight for the settlement of old treaties, the resolution of land rights issues, and equality of opportunity in all spheres of social and political life. The developments in American museums had repercussions throughout the international museum community and were part of a widespread change in attitude towards the role of the museum in relation to the community. However, the museum profession has continued to be dominated by white staff, and the perennial problem of Western-trained anthropologists and historians studying and representing 'the Other' continues to be a major issue, attracting criticism from indigenous peoples and those from other ethnic groups who still feel isolated and excluded from the process of representation. An Aboriginal Australian member of the committee involved in the establishment of a community-based Aboriginal research unit at the University of Adelaide expressed this frustration saying: 'We are tired of being researched; we want to be in the research ourselves, to have a say in what needs to be studied'.[19] The involvement of members of ethnic groups, as partners in the planning process, as advisors, and as staff members, has come to be one of the major issues facing the museum profession in recent years.

Since the 1970s, issues of cultural diversity and related matters have featured prominently on the programmes of numerous regional, national and international conferences attesting to the growing professional concern. *The Role of Anthropological Museums in National and International Education* was a multinational seminar held in Denmark in 1974. *Preserving Indigenous Cultures: A New Role for Museums* was a regional seminar held in Adelaide, Australia, in September 1978 which presented a series of perspectives concerning the current and potential role of museums in assisting in the preservation of the material culture and cultural traditions of peoples across the Pacific region. Participants were drawn from many cultures throughout the region and represented museum staff as well as many other professions.

In 1986, the British Museum in London hosted an international conference entitled *Making Exhibitions of Ourselves: The Limits of Objectivity in Representations of Other Cultures*. The American Association of Museums and the Canadian Museums Association have addressed these issues as major themes of their annual conferences over a number of years. In 1990, sixteen museum curators from Europe and North America attended the *Taonga Maori* conference in Wellington, New Zealand. The conference was organised and funded by the New Zealand Government, but initiated by Maori elders following the successful US tour of the *Te Maori* exhibition in 1984. Invitations were issued to a number of curators in major overseas museums inviting them to participate in a discussion about Maori beliefs concerning *taonga* (treasures) in overseas museum collections. Lectures and comments by Maori speakers forcefully conveyed the strength of Maori feelings concerning the care, display and ownership of Maori *taonga* and had a profound impact upon several of the participants. Issues associated with the disposition of the dead were addressed by archaeologists at the *First Intercongress on Archaeological Ethics and the Treatment of the Dead* in Vermillion, South Dakota, USA, in 1989 and at the Fourth WAC Congress in Cape Town in 1999[20].

From these conferences and meetings have come a number of publications: edited collections of conference papers which document the discussions and concerns within the profession and the development of new approaches to museology, stimulating greater dialogue and fuelling the drive for change. Most notable amongst these have been the twin volumes *Exhibiting Cultures*[21] and *Museums and Communities*[22] arising out of two conferences held at the International Center of the Smithsonian Institution in Washington, DC: *The Poetic and Politics of Representation* in 1988 and *Museums and Communities* in 1990. The Association of Art Museum Directors (AAMD) has addressed similar issues in relation to American art museums in two symposia held in 1990 and 1991, the proceedings of which were published in *Different Voices*.[23] Dealing with related issues in the field of archaeology, a major series of publications entitled *One World Archaeology* arose out of the proceedings of the World Archaeological Congress in 1986 at the University of Southampton in England, and has since included over forty-four texts of papers drawn from subsequent meetings of the World Archaeological Congress.

Also emanating from the activities of the World Archaeological Congress were two documents which provided the most progressive examples of professional policy guidelines concerning the treatment of human remains and which have been influential in museological policy development in several countries. The Vermillion Accord, a paper drafted by Professor Michael Day, called for 'mutual respect for the beliefs of indigenous peoples as well as the importance of science and education' and received the full support of all the anthropologists and indigenous peoples represented at the Intercongress in 1989.[24] The following year, the World Archaeological Congress adopted the First Code of Ethics, listing the principles and rules which should guide professional practice when dealing with the archaeological material of indigenous peoples.[25]

Significant changes in ideology and practices have resulted from the social and political pressures of recent decades. Cultural diversity has come to be an issue of great professional concern and many curators have attempted to address criticisms and instigate new practices, involving communities much more closely in the research and interpretation process and addressing issues of concern to the communities themselves. In some instances this has involved trying quite radical or innovative interpretive approaches with varying degrees of success. Many others have been slow to adapt and have continued to use the culturally exclusive practices of conventional museology, and so have continued to alienate themselves from ethnic communities and attract criticism and sometimes vocal demonstrations of dissatisfaction amongst those represented.

NOTES

1. Reprinted from M. Simpson, *Making Representations: Museums in the Post-colonial Era*, London and New York: Routledge, 1996, 2001.

2. 'The Museum, a temple or the forum', in *Curator* 14(1), p. 23.

3. V. Deloria, *God is Red*, New York: Grosset and Dunlop, 1983.

4. R. DeLuca, '"We hold the rock?" The Indian attempt to reclaim Alcatraz Island', *California History*, 62(1) (1983), pp. 2–23; G. P. Horse Capture, 'An American Indian perspective', in H. J. Viola and C. Margolis (eds), *Seeds of Change: Five Hundred Years Since Columbus*, Washington, DC: Smithsonian Institution Press, 1991, pp. 186–207.

5. Horse Capture, 'An American Indian perspective', p. 86.

6. Ibid., p. 88.

7. G. Glueck, 'Into the mainstream, everybody', *New York Times*, 15 June 1969, p. 24.

8. G. Glueck, '"J'accuse, Baby" she cried', *New York Times*, Sunday 20 April 1969.

9. Ibid.

10. E. P. Alexander, *Museums in Motion: An Introduction to the History and Function of Museums*, Nashville: AASLH, 1979, p. 227.

11. M. Arnold, 'Paintings defaced at Metropolitan; one a Rembrandt', *New York Times*, Friday 17 January 1969, p. 1.

12. 'Metropolitan guard injured by vandal writing obscenity', *New York Times*, 2 February 1969, p. 74.

13. Cameron, 'The Museum', p. 18.

14. Cameron, 'The Museum"; J. V. Noble, 'Museum prophecy: the role of museums in the 1970s', *Curator* 14(1) (1971), pp. 69–74; M. W. Robbins, 'The neighbourhood and the museum', *Curator* 14(1) (1971), pp. 63–8; J. R. Kinard, 'Intermediaries between the museum and the community', in ICOM, *The Museum in the Service of Man Today and Tomorrow: The Museum's Educational and Cultural Role*, Ninth General Conference Papers, Paris: International Council of Museums, 1972.

15. K. R. Hopkins, 'Is confrontation in your future?', *Curator*, XIII/2 (1970), pp. 123–4.

16. J. R. Kinard, 'The neighbourhood museum as a catalyst for social change', *Museum*, 148, 37(4) (1985), pp. 217–23.

17. J. V. Noble, 'Drug scene in New York', *Museum News*, 50(3) (1971), pp. 10–15: J. R. Kinard and E. Nighbert, 'The Anocastia Neighbourhood Museum, Smithsonian Institutions, Washington DC', *Museum*, 24(2) (1972), pp. 102–9.

18. 'The neighbourhood museum', p. 220.

19. Cited in F. Gale, 'Community involvement and academic response: the University of Adelaide Aboriginal Research Centre', in *Aboriginal History*, 6(2) (1982), p. 130.

20. C. Fforde, J. Hubert and P. Turnbull, 'The Dead and Their Possession: Repatriation in Principle, Policy and Practice', *One World Archaeology*, 43, London: Routledge, 2002.

21.   I. Karp and S. Lavine (eds), *Exhibiting Cultures: The Poetics and Politics of Museum Display*, Washington DC and London: Smithsonian Institution Press, 1991.

22.   I. Karp, C. M. Kreamer, and S. Lavine (eds), *Museums and Communities: The Politics of Public Culture*, Washington DC and London: Smithsonian Institution Press, 1992.

23.   AAMD, 1992.

24.   M. Day, 'Archaeological ethics and the treatment of the dead', *Anthropology Today*, 6(1) (February 1990), pp. 15–16.

25.   'W.A.C. First Code of Ethics', *Anthropology Today*, 6(6) (1990), p. 24.

2.

Histories of the Tribal and the Modern

James Clifford

You do not stand in one place to watch a masquerade.   An Igbo saying

During the winter of 1984–85 one could encounter tribal objects in an unusual number of locations around New York City. This chapter surveys a half-dozen, focusing on the most controversial: the major exhibition held at the Museum of Modern Art (MOMA), '"Primitivism" in 20th Century Art: Affinity of the Tribal and the Modern'. The chapter's 'ethnographic present' is late December 1984.

The 'tribal' objects gathered on West Fifty-third Street have been around. They are travelers – some arriving from folklore and ethnographic museums in Europe, others from art galleries and private collections. They have traveled first class to the Museum of Modern Art, elaborately crated and insured for important sums. Previous accommodations have been less luxurious: some were stolen, others 'purchased' for a song by colonial administrators, travelers, anthropologists, missionaries, sailors in African ports. These non-Western objects have been by turns curiosities, ethnographic specimens, major art creations. After 1900 they began to turn up in European flea markets, thereafter moving between avant-garde studios and collectors' apartments. Some came to rest in the unheated basements or 'laboratories' of anthropology museums, surrounded by objects made in the same region of the world. Others encountered odd fellow travelers, lighted and labeled in strange display cases. Now on West Fifty-third Street they intermingle with works by European masters – Picasso, Giacometti, Brancusi, and others. A three-dimensional Eskimo mask with twelve arms and a number of holes hangs beside a canvas on which Joan Miró has painted colored shapes. The people in New York look at the two objects and see that they are alike.

Travelers tell different stories in different places, and on West Fifty-third Street an origin story of modernism is featured. Around 1910 Picasso and his cohort suddenly, intuitively recognize that 'primitive' objects are in fact powerful 'art.' They collect, imitate, and are affected by these objects. Their own work, even when not directly influenced, seems oddly reminiscent of non-Western forms. The modern and the primitive converse across the centuries and continents. At the Museum of Modern Art an exact history is told featuring individual artists and objects, their encounters in specific studios at precise moments. Photographs document the crucial influences of non-Western artifacts on the pioneer modernists. This focused story is surrounded and infused with another – a loose allegory of relationship centering on the word *affinity*. The word is a kinship term, suggesting a deeper or more natural relationship than mere resemblance or juxtaposition. It connotes a common quality or essence joining the tribal to the modern. A Family of Art is brought together, global, diverse, richly inventive, and miraculously unified, for every object displayed on West Fifty-third Street looks modern.

The exhibition at MOMA is historical and didactic. It is complemented by a comprehensive, scholarly catalogue, which includes divergent views of its topic and in which the show's organizers, William Rubin and Kirk Varnedoe, argue at length its underlying premises.[1] One of the virtues of an exhibition that blatantly makes a case or tells a story is that it encourages debate and makes possible the suggestion of other stories. Thus in what follows different histories of the tribal and the modern will be proposed in response to the sharply focused history on display at the Museum of Modern Art. But before that history can be seen for what it is, however – a specific story that excludes other stories – the universalizing allegory of affinity must be cleared away.

This allegory, the story of the Modernist Family of Art, is not rigorously argued at MOMA. (That would require some explicit form of either an archetypal or structural analysis.) The allegory is, rather, built into the exhibition's form, featured suggestively in its publicity, left uncontradicted, repetitiously asserted – 'Affinity of the Tribal and the Modern'. The allegory has a hero, whose virtuoso work, an exhibit caption tells us, contains more affinities with the tribal than that of any other pioneer modernist. These affinities 'measure the depth of Picasso's grasp of the informing principles of tribal sculpture, and reflect his profound identity of spirit with the tribal peoples'. Modernism is thus presented as a search for 'informing principles' that transcend culture, politics, and history. Beneath this generous umbrella the tribal is modern and the modern more richly, more diversely human.

The power of the affinity idea is such (it becomes almost self-evident in the MOMA juxtapositions) that it is worth reviewing the major objections to it. Anthropologists, long familiar with the issue of cultural diffusion versus independent invention, are not likely to find anything special in the similarities between selected tribal and modern objects. An established principle of anthropological comparative method asserts that the greater the range of cultures, the more likely one is to find similar traits. MOMA's sample is very large, embracing African, Oceanian, North American, and Arctic 'tribal' groups.[2] A second principle, that of the 'limitation of possibilities', recognizes that invention, while highly diverse, is not infinite. The human body, for example, with its two eyes, four limbs, bilateral arrangement of features, front and back, and so on, will be represented and stylized in a limited number of ways.[3] There is thus a priori no reason to claim evidence for affinity (rather than mere resemblance or coincidence) because an exhibition of tribal works that seem impressively 'modern' in style can be gathered. An equally striking collection could be made demonstrating sharp dissimilarities between tribal and modern objects.

The qualities most often said to link these objects are their 'conceptualism' and 'abstraction' (but a very long and ultimately incoherent list of shared traits, including 'magic', 'ritualism', 'environmentalism', use of 'natural' materials, and so on, can be derived from the show and especially from its catalogue). Actually the tribal and modern artifacts are similar only in that they do *not* feature the pictorial illusionism or sculptural naturalism that came to dominate Western European art after the Renaissance. Abstraction and conceptualism are, of course, pervasive in the arts of the non-Western World. To say that they share with modernism a rejection of certain naturalist projects is not to show anything like an affinity.[4] Indeed the 'tribalism' selected in the exhibition to resemble modernism is itself a construction designed to accomplish the task of resemblance. He and Benin sculptures, highly naturalistic in style, are excluded from the 'tribal' and placed in a somewhat arbitrary category of 'court' society (which does not, however, include large chieftanships). Moreover, pre-Columbian works, though they have a place in the catalogue, are largely omitted from the exhibition. One can question other selections and exclusions that result in a collection of only 'modern'-looking tribal objects. Why, for example, are there relatively few 'impure' objects constructed from the debris of colonial culture contacts? And is there not an overall bias toward clean, abstract forms as against rough or crude work?

The 'Affinities' room of the exhibition is an intriguing but entirely problematic exercise in formal mix-and-match. The short introductory text begins well: 'AFFINITIES presents a group of tribal objects notable for their appeal to modern taste.' Indeed this is all that can rigorously be said of the objects in this room. The text continues, however, 'Selected pairings of modern and tribal objects demonstrate common denominators of these arts that are independent of direct influence.' The phrase *common denominators* implies something more systematic than intriguing resemblance. What can it possibly mean? This introductory text, cited in its entirely, is emblematic of the MOMA undertaking as a whole. Statements carefully limiting its purview (specifying a concern only with modernist primitivism and not with tribal life) coexist with frequent implications of something more. The affinity idea itself is wide-ranging and promiscuous, as are allusions to universal human capacities retrieved in the encounter between modern and tribal or invocations of the expansive human mind – the healthy capacity of modernist consciousness to question its limits and engage otherness.[5]

Nowhere, however, does the exhibition or catalogue underline a more disquieting quality of modernism: its taste for appropriating or redeeming otherness, for constituting non-Western arts in its own image, for discovering universal, ahistorical 'human' capacities. The search for similarity itself requires justification, for even if one accepts the limited task of exploring 'modernist primitivism', why could one not learn as much about Picasso's or Ernst's creative processes by analyzing the *differences* separating their art from tribal models or by tracing the ways their art moved *away* from, gave new twists to, non-Western forms?[6] This side of the process is unexplored in the exhibition. The prevailing view-point is made all too clear in one of the 'affinities' featured on the catalogue's cover, a juxtaposition of Picasso's *Girl before a Mirror* (1932) with a Kwakiutl half-mask, a type quite rare among Northwest Coast creations. Its task here is simply to produce an effect of resemblance (an effect actually created by the camera angle). In this exhibition a universal message, 'Affinity of the Tribal and the Modern', is produced by careful selection and the maintenance of a specific angle of vision.

The notion of affinity, an allegory of kinship, has an expansive, celebratory task to perform. The affinities shown at MOMA are all on modernist terms. The great modernist 'pioneers' (and their museum) are shown promoting formerly despised tribal 'fetishes' or mere ethnographic 'specimens' to the status of high art and in the process discovering new dimensions of their ('our') creative potential. The capacity of art to transcend its cultural and historical context is asserted repeatedly.[7] In the catalogue Rubin tends to be more interested in a recovery of elemental expressive modes, whereas Varnedoe stresses the rational, forward-looking intellect (which he opposes to an unhealthy primitivism, irrational and escapist). Both celebrate the generous spirit of modernism, pitched now at a global scale but excluding – as we shall see – Third World modernisms.

At West Fifty-third Street modernist primitivism is a going Western concern. It is, Varnedoe tells us, summing up in the last sentence of the catalogue's second volume, 'a process of revolution that begins and ends in modern culture, and because of that – not in spite of it – can continually expand and deepen our contact with that which is remote and different from us, and continually threaten, challenge, and reform our sense of self'.[8] A skeptic may doubt the ability of the modernist primitivism exhibited at MOMA to threaten or challenge what is by now a thoroughly institutionalized system of aesthetic (and market) value; but it is appropriate, and in a sense rigorous, that this massive collection spanning the globe should end with the word *self*.

Indeed an unintended effect of the exhibition's comprehensive catalogue is to show once and for all the incoherence of the modern Rorschach of 'the primitive'. From Robert Goldwater's formalism to the transforming 'magic' of Picasso (according to Rubin); from Lévy-Bruhl's mystical *mentalité primitive* (influencing a generation of modern artists and writers) to Lévi-Strauss's *pensée sauvage* (resonating with 'systems art' and the cybernetic binarism of the minimalists); from Dubuffet's fascination with insanity and the childish to the enlightened rational sense of a Gauguin, the playful experimentalism of a Picasso or the new 'scientific' spirit of a James Turrell (the last three approved by Varnedoe but challenged by Rosalind Krauss, who is more attached to Bataille's decapitation, *bassesse*, and bodily deformations[9]); from fetish to icon and back again; from aboriginal bark paintings (Klee) to massive pre-Columbian monuments (Henry Moore); from weightless Eskimo masks to Stonehenge – the catalogue succeeds in demonstrating not any essential affinity between tribal and modern or even a coherent modernist attitude toward the primitive but rather the restless desire and power of the modern West to collect the world.

Setting aside the allegory of affinity, we are left with a 'factual', narrowly focused history – that of the 'discovery' of primitive art by Picasso and his generation. It is tempting to say that the 'History' section of the exhibition is, after all, the rigorous part and the rest merely suggestive association. Undeniably a great deal of scholarly research in the best *Kunstgeschichte* tradition has been brought to bear on this specific history. Numerous myths are usefully questioned; important facts are specified (what mask was in whose studio when); and the pervasiveness of tribal influences on early modernist art – European, English, and American – is shown more amply than ever before. The catalogue has the merit of including a number of articles that dampen the celebratory mood of the exhibition: notably the essay by Krauss and useful contributions by Christian Feest, Philippe Peltier, and Jean-Louis Paudrat detailing the arrival of non-Western artifacts in Europe. These historical articles illuminate the less edifying imperialist contexts that surrounded the 'discovery' of tribal objects by modernist artists at the moment of high colonialism.

If we ignore the 'Affinities' room at MOMA, however, and focus on the 'serious' historical part of the exhibition, new critical questions emerge. What is excluded by the specific focus of the history? Isn't this factual narration still infused with the affinity allegory, since it is cast as a story of creative genius recognizing the greatness of tribal works, discovering common artistic 'informing principles'? Could the story of this intercultural encounter be told differently? It is worth making the effort to extract another story from the materials in the exhibition – a history not of redemption or of discovery but of reclassification. This other history assumes that 'art' is not universal but is a changing Western cultural category. The fact that rather abruptly, in the space of a few decades, a large class of non-Western artifacts came to be redefined as art is a taxonomic shift that requires critical historical discussion, not celebration. That this construction of a generous category of art pitched at a global scale occurred just as the planet's tribal peoples came massively under European political, economic, and evangelical dominion cannot be irrelevant. But there is no room for such complexities at the MOMA show. Obviously the modernist appropriation of tribal productions as art is not simply imperialist. The project involves too many strong critiques of colonialist, evolutionist assumptions. As we shall see, though, the scope and underlying logic of the 'discovery' of tribal art reproduces hegemonic Western assumptions rooted in the colonial and neocolonial epoch.

Picasso, Léger, Apollinaire, and many others came to recognize the elemental, 'magical' power of African sculptures in a period of growing *négrophilie*, a context that would see the irruption onto the European scene of other evocative black figures: the jazzman, the boxer (Al Brown), the *sauvage* Josephine Baker. To tell the history of modernism's recognition of African 'art' in this broader context would raise ambiguous and disturbing questions about aesthetic appropriation of non-Western others, issues of race, gender, and power. This other story is largely invisible at MOMA, given the exhibition's narrow focus. It can be glimpsed only in the small section devoted to 'La création du monde', the African cosmogony staged in 1923 by Léger, Cendrars, and Milhaud, and in the broadly pitched if still largely uncritical catalogue article by Laura Rosenstock devoted to it. Overall one would be hard pressed to deduce from the exhibition that all the enthusiasm for things *nègre*, for the 'magic' of African art, had anything to do with race. Art in this focused history has no essential link with coded perceptions of black bodies – their vitalism, rhythm, magic, erotic power, etc. – as seen by whites. The modernism represented here is concerned only with artistic invention, a positive category separable from a negative primitivism of the irrational, the savage, the base, the flight from civilization.

A different historical focus might bring a photograph of Josephine Baker into the vicinity of the African statues that were exciting the Parisian avant-garde in the 1910s and 1920s; but such a juxtaposition would be unthinkable in the MOMA history, for it evokes different affinities from those contributing to the category of great art. The black body in Paris of the twenties was an ideological artifact. Archaic Africa (which came to Paris by way of the future – that is, America) was sexed, gendered, and invested with 'magic' in specific ways. Standard poses adopted by 'La Bakaire', like Léger's designs and costumes, evoked a recognizable 'Africanity' – the naked form emphasizing pelvis and buttocks, a segmented stylization suggesting a strangely mechanical vitality. The inclusion of so ideologically loaded a form as the body of Josephine Baker among the figures classified as art on West Fifty-third Street would suggest a different account of modernist primitivism, a different analysis of the category *nègre in l'art nègre*, and an exploration of the 'taste' that was something more than just a backdrop for the discovery of tribal art in the opening decades of this century.[10]

Such a focus would treat art as a category defined and redefined in specific historical contexts and relations of power. Seen from this angle and read somewhat against the grain, the MOMA exhibition documents a *taxonomic* moment: the status of non-Western objects and 'high' art are importantly redefined, but there is nothing permanent or transcendent about the categories at stake. The appreciation and interpretation of tribal objects takes place within a modern 'system of objects' which confers value on certain things and withholds it from others.[11] Modernist primitivism, with its claims to deeper humanist sympathies and a wider aesthetic sense, goes hand-in-hand with a developed market in tribal art and with definitions of artistic and cultural authenticity that are now widely contested.

Since 1900 non-Western objects have generally been classified as either primitive art *or* ethnographic specimens. Before the modernist revolution associated with Picasso and the simultaneous rise of cultural anthropology associated with Boas and Malinowski, these objects were differently sorted – as antiquities, exotic curiosities, orientalia, the remains of early man, and so on. With the emergence of twentieth-century modernism and anthropology figures formerly called 'fetishes' (to take just one class of object) became works either of 'sculpture' or of 'material culture'. The distinction between the aesthetic and the anthropological was soon institutionally reinforced. In art galleries non-Western objects were displayed for their formal and aesthetic qualities; in ethnographic museums they were represented in a 'cultural' context. In the latter an African statue was a ritual object belonging to a distinct group; it was displayed in ways that elucidated its use, symbolism, and function. The institutionalized distinction between aesthetic and anthropological discourses took form during the years documented at MOMA, years that saw the complementary discovery of primitive 'art' and of an anthropological concept of 'culture'.[12] Though there was from the start (and continues to be) a regular traffic between the two domains, this distinction is unchallenged in the exhibition. At MOMA treating tribal objects as art means excluding the original cultural context. Consideration of context, we are firmly told at the exhibition's entrance, is the business of anthropologists. Cultural background is not essential to correct aesthetic appreciation and analysis: good art, the masterpiece, is universally recognizable.[13] The pioneer modernists themselves knew little or nothing of these objects' ethnographic meaning. What was good enough for Picasso is good enough for MOMA. Indeed an ignorance of cultural context seems almost a precondition for artistic appreciation. In this object system a tribal piece is detached from one milieu in order to circulate freely in another, a world of art – of museums, markets, and connoisseurship.

Since the early years of modernism and cultural anthropology non-Western objects have found a 'home' either within the discourses and institutions of art or within those of anthropology. The two domains have excluded and confirmed each other, inventively disputing the right to contextualize, to represent these objects. As we shall see, the aesthetic-anthropological opposition is systematic, presupposing an underlying set of attitudes toward the 'tribal'. Both discourses assume a primitive world in need of preservation, redemption, and representation. The concrete, inventive existence of tribal cultures and artists is suppressed in the process of either constituting authentic, 'traditional' worlds or appreciating their products in the timeless category of 'art'.

Nothing on West Fifty-third Street suggests that good tribal art is being produced in the 1980s. The non-Western artifacts on display are located either in a vague past (reminiscent of the label 'nineteenth-twentieth century' that accompanies African and Oceanian pieces in the Metropolitan Museum's Rockefeller Wing) or in a purely conceptual space defined by 'primitive' qualities: magic, ritualism, closeness to nature, mythic or cosmological aims.[14] In this relegation of the tribal or primitive to either a vanishing past or an ahistorical, conceptual present, modernist appreciation reproduces common ethnographic categories.

The same structure can be seen in the Hall of Pacific Peoples, dedicated to Margaret Mead, at the American Museum of Natural History. This new permanent hall is a superbly refurbished anthropological stopping place for non-Western objects. In *Rotunda* (December 1984), the museum's publication, an article announcing the installation contains the following paragraph:

Margaret Mead once referred to the cultures of Pacific peoples as 'a world that once was and now is no more'. Prior to her death in 1978 she approved the basic plans for the new *Hall of Pacific Peoples*.[15]

We are offered treasures saved from a destructive history, relics of a vanishing world. Visitors to the installation (and especially members of *present* Pacific cultures) may find a 'world that is no more' more appropriately evoked in two charming display cases just outside the hall. It is the world of a dated anthropology. Here one finds a neatly typed page of notes from Mead's much-disputed Samoan research, a picture of the fieldworker interacting 'closely' with Melanesians (she is carrying a child on her back), a box of brightly colored discs and triangles once used for psychological testing, a copy of Mead's column in *Redbook*. In the Hall of Pacific Peoples artifacts suggesting change and syncretism are set apart in a small display entitled 'Culture Contact'. It is noted that Western influence and indigenous response have been active in the Pacific since the eighteenth century. Yet few signs of this involvement appear anywhere else in the large hall, despite the fact that many of the objects were made in the past 150 years in situations of contact, and despite the fact that the museum's ethnographic explanations reflect quite recent research on the cultures of the Pacific. The historical contacts and impurities that are part of ethnographic work – and that may signal the life, not the death, of societies – are systematically excluded.

The tenses of the hall's explanatory captions are revealing. A recent color photograph of a Samoan *kava* ceremony is accompanied by the words: 'STATUS and RANK were [sic] important features of Samoan society', a statement that will seem strange to anyone who knows how important they remain in Samoa today. Elsewhere in the hall a black-and-white photograph of an Australian Arunta woman and child, taken around 1900 by the pioneer ethnographers Spencer and Gillen, is captioned in the *present* tense. Aboriginals apparently must always inhabit a mythic time. Many other examples of temporal incoherence could be cited – old Sepik objects described in the present, recent Trobriand photos labeled in the past, and so forth.

The point is not simply that the image of Samoan *kava* drinking and status society presented here is a distortion or that in most of the Hall of Pacific Peoples history has been airbrushed out. (No Samoan men at the *kava* ceremony are wearing wristwatches; Trobriand face painting is shown without noting that it is worn at cricket matches.) Beyond such questions of accuracy is an issue of systematic ideological coding. To locate 'tribal' peoples in a nonhistorical time and ourselves in a different, historical time is clearly tendentious and no longer credible.[16] This recognition throws doubt on the perception of a vanishing tribal world, rescued, made valuable and meaningful, either as ethnographic 'culture' or as primitive/modern 'art'. For in this temporal ordering the real or genuine life of tribal works always precedes their collection, an act of salvage that repeats an all-too-familiar story of death and redemption. In this pervasive allegory the non-Western world is always vanishing and modernizing – as in Walter Benjamin's allegory of modernity, the tribal world is conceived as a ruin.[17] At the Hall of Pacific Peoples or the Rockefeller Wing the actual ongoing life and 'impure' inventions of tribal peoples are erased in the name of cultural or artistic 'authenticity'. Similarly at MOMA the production of tribal 'art' is entirely in the past. Turning up in the flea markets and museums of late nineteenth-century Europe, these objects are destined to be aesthetically redeemed, given new value in the object system of a generous modernism.

The story retold at MOMA, the struggle to gain recognition for tribal art, for its capacity 'like all great art … to show images of man that transcend the particular lives and times of their creators',[18] is taken for granted at another stopping place for tribal travelers in Manhattan, the Center for African Art on East Sixty-eighth Street. Susan Vogel, the executive director, proclaims in her introduction to the catalogue of its inaugural exhibition, 'African Masterpieces from the Musée de l'Homme', that the 'aesthetic-anthropological debate' has been resolved. It is now widely accepted that 'ethnographic specimens' can be distinguished from 'works of art' and that within the latter category a limited number of 'masterpieces' are to be found. Vogel correctly notes that the aesthetic recognition of tribal objects depends on changes in Western taste. For example it took the work of Francis Bacon, Lucas Samaras, and others to make it possible to exhibit as art 'rough and horrifying [African] works as well as refined and lyrical ones'.[19] Once recognized, though, art is apparently art. Thus the selection at the Center is made on aesthetic criteria alone. A prominent placard affirms that the ability of these objects 'to transcend the limitations of time and place, to speak to us across time and culture … places them among the highest points of human achievement. It is as works of art that we regard them here and as a testament to the greatness of their creators'.

There could be no clearer statement of one side of the aesthetic anthropological 'debate' (or better, *system*). On the other (anthropological) side, across town, the Hall of Pacific Peoples presents collective rather than individual productions – the work of 'cultures'. But within an institutionalized polarity interpenetration of discourses becomes possible. Science can be aestheticized, art made anthropological. At the American Museum of Natural History ethnographic exhibits have come increasingly to resemble art shows. Indeed the Hall of Pacific Peoples represents the latest in aestheticized scientism. Objects are displayed in ways that highlight their formal properties. They are suspended in light, held in space by the ingenious use of Plexiglas. (One is suddenly astonished by the sheer weirdness of a small Oceanic figurine perched atop a three-foot-tall transparent rod.) While these artistically displayed artifacts are scientifically explained, an older, functionalist attempt to present an integrated picture of specific societies or culture areas is no longer seriously pursued. There is an almost dadaist quality to the labels on eight cases devoted to Australian aboriginal society (I cite the complete series in order): 'CEREMONY, SPIRIT FIGURE, MAGICIANS AND SORCERERS, SACRED ART, SPEAR THROWERS, STONE AXES AND KNIVES, WOMEN, BOOMERANGS'. Elsewhere the hall's pieces of culture have been recontextualized within a new cybernetic, anthropological discourse. For instance flutes and stringed instruments are captioned: 'MUSIC is a system of organized sound in man's [sic] aural environment' or nearby: 'COMMUNICATION is an important function of organized sound.'

In the anthropological Hall of Pacific Peoples non-Western objects still have primarily scientific value. They are in addition beautiful.[20] Conversely, at the Center for African Art artifacts are essentially defined as 'masterpieces', their makers as great artists. The discourse of connoisseurship reigns. Yet once the story of art told at MOMA becomes dogma, it is possible to reintroduce and co-opt the discourse of ethnography. At the Center tribal contexts and functions are described along with individual histories of the objects on display. Now firmly classified as masterpieces, African objects escape the vague, ahistorical location of the 'tribal' or the 'primitive'. The catalogue, a sort of *catalogue raisonné*, discusses each work intensively. The category of the masterpiece individuates: the pieces on display are not typical; some are one of a kind. The famous Fon god of war or the Abomey shark-man lend themselves to precise histories of individual creation and appropriation in visible colonial situations. Captions specify *which* Griaule expedition to West Africa in the 1930s acquired each Dogon statue.[21] We learn in the catalogue that a superb Bamileke mother and child was carved by an artist named Kwayep, that the statue was bought by the colonial administrator and anthropologist Henri Labouret from King N'Jike. While tribal names predominate at MOMA, the Rockefeller Wing, and the American Museum of Natural History, here personal names make their appearance.

In the 'African Masterpieces' catalogue we learn of an ethnographer's excitement on finding a Dogon hermaphrodite figure that would later become famous. The letter recording this excitement, written by Denise Paulme in 1935, serves as evidence of the aesthetic concerns of many early ethnographic collectors.[22] These individuals, we are told, could intuitively distinguish masterpieces from mere art or ethnographic specimens. (Actually many of the individual ethnographers behind the Musée de l'Homme collection, such as Paulme, Michel Leiris, Marcel Griaule, and André Schaeffner, were friends and collaborators of the same 'pioneer modernist' artists who, in the story told at MOMA, constructed the category of primitive art. Thus the intuitive aesthetic sense in question is the product of a historically specific milieu. See Chapter 4 [in *The Predicament of Culture*].) The 'African Masterpieces' catalogue insists that the founders of the Musée de l'Homme were art connoisseurs, that this great anthropological museum never treated all its contents as 'ethnographic specimens'. The Musée de l'Homme was and is secretly an art museum.[23] The taxonomic split between art and artifact is thus healed, at least for self-evident 'masterpieces', entirely in terms of the aesthetic code. Art is art in any museum.

In this exhibition, as opposed to the others in New York, information can be provided about each individual masterpiece's history. We learn that a Kiwarani antelope mask studded with mirrors was acquired at a dance given for the colonial administration in Mali on Bastille Day 1931. A rabbit mask was purchased from Dogon dancers at a gala soirée in Paris during the Colonial Exhibition of the same year. These are no longer the dateless 'authentic' tribal forms seen at MOMA. At the Center for African Art a different history documents both the artwork's uniqueness and the achievement of the discerning collector. By featuring rarity, genius, and connoisseurship the Center confirms the existence of autonomous artworks able to circulate, to be bought and sold, in the same way as works by Picasso or Giacometti. The Center traces its lineage, appropriately, to the former Rockefeller Museum of Primitive Art, with its close ties to collectors and the art market.

In its inaugural exhibition the Center confirms the predominant aesthetic-ethnographic view of tribal art as something located in the past, good for being collected and given aesthetic value. Its second show (March 12–June 16, 1985) is devoted to 'Igbo Arts: Community and Cosmos'. It tells another story, locating art forms, ritual life, and cosmology in a specific, changing African society – a past and present heritage. Photographs show 'traditional' masks worn in danced masquerades around 1983. (These include satiric figures of white colonists.) A detailed history of cultural change, struggle, and revival is provided. In the catalogue Chike C. Aniakor, an Igbo scholar, writes along with co-editor Herbert M. Cole of 'the continually evolving Igbo aesthetic': 'It is illusory to think that which we comfortably label "traditional" art was in an earlier time immune to changes in style and form; it is thus unproductive to lament changes that reflect current realities. Continuity with earlier forms will always be found; the present-day persistence of family and community values ensures that the arts will thrive. And as always, the Igbo will create new art forms out of their inventive spirit, reflecting their dynamic interactions with the environment and their neighbors and expressing cultural ideals.'[24]

Cole and Aniakor provide a quite different history of 'the tribal' and 'the modern' from that told at the Museum of Modern Art – a story of invention, not of redemption. In his foreword to the catalogue Chinua Achebe offers a vision of culture and of objects that sharply challenges the ideology of the art collection and the masterpiece. Igbo, he tells us, do not like collections.

The purposeful neglect of the painstakingly and devoutly accomplished *mbari* houses with all the art objects in them as soon as the primary mandate of their creation has been served, provides a significant insight into the Igbo aesthetic value as *process* rather than *product*. Process is motion while product is rest. When the product is preserved or venerated, the impulse to repeat the process is compromised. Therefore the Igbo choose to eliminate the product and retain the process so that every occasion and every generation will receive its own impulse and experience of creation. Interestingly this aesthetic disposition receives powerful endorsement from the tropical climate which provides an abundance of materials for making art, such as wood, as well as formidable agencies of dissolution, such as humidity and the termite. Visitors to Igboland are shocked to see that artifacts are rarely accorded any particular value on the basis of age alone.[25]

Achebe's image of a 'ruin' suggests not the modernist allegory of redemption (a yearning to make things whole, to think archaeologically) but an acceptance of endless seriality, a desire to keep things apart, dynamic, and historical.

The aesthetic-anthropological object systems of the West are currently under challenge, and the politics of collecting and exhibiting occasionally become visible. Even at MOMA evidence of living tribal peoples has not been entirely excluded. One small text breaks the spell. A special label explains the absence of a Zuni war god figure currently housed in the Berlin Museum für Völkerunde. We learn that late in its preparations for the show MOMA 'was informed by knowledgeable authorities that Zuni people consider any public exhibition of their war gods to be sacrilegious'. Thus, the label continues, although such figures are routinely displayed elsewhere, the museum decided not to bring the war god (an influence on Paul Klee) from Berlin. The terse note raises more questions than it answers, but it does at least establish that the objects on display may in fact 'belong' somewhere other than in an art or an ethnographic museum. Living traditions have claims on them, contesting (with a distant but increasingly palpable power) their present home in the institutional systems of the modern West.[26]

Elsewhere in New York this power has been made even more visible. 'Te Maori', a show visiting the Metropolitan, clearly establishes that the 'art' on display is still sacred, on loan not merely from certain New Zealand museums but also from the Maori people. Indeed tribal art is political through and through. The Maori have allowed their tradition to be exploited as 'art' by major Western cultural institutions and their corporate sponsors in order to enhance their own international prestige and thus contribute to their current resurgence in New Zealand society.[27] Tribal authorities gave permission for the exhibition to travel, and they participated in its opening ceremonies in a visible, distinctive manner. So did Asante leaders at the exhibition of their art and culture at the Museum of Natural History (October 16, 1984–March 17, 1985). Although the Asante display centers on eighteenth- and nineteenth-century artifacts, evidence of the twentieth-century colonial suppression and recent renewal of Asante culture is included, along with color photos of modern ceremonies and newly made 'traditional' objects brought to New York as gifts for the museum. In this exhibition the *location* of the art on display – the sense of where, to whom, and in what time(s) it belongs – is quite different from the location of the African objects at MOMA or in the Rockefeller Wing. The tribal is fully historical.

Still another representation of tribal life and art can be encountered at the Northwest Coast collection at the IBM Gallery (October 10–December 29, 1984), whose objects have traveled downtown from the Museum of the American Indian. They are displayed in pools of intense light (the beautifying 'boutique' decor that seems to be modernism's gift to museum displays, both ethnographic and artistic). But this exhibition of traditional masterpieces ends with works by living Northwest Coast artists. Outside the gallery in the IBM atrium two large totem poles have been installed. One is a weathered specimen from the Museum of the American Indian, and the other has been carved for the show by the Kwakiutl Calvin Hunt. The artist put the finishing touches on his creation where it stands in the atrium; fresh wood chips are left scattered around the base. Nothing like this is possible or even thinkable at West Fifty-third Street.

The organizers of the MOMA exhibition have been clear about its limitations, and they have repeatedly specified what they do not claim to show. It is thus in a sense unfair to ask why they did not construct a differently focused history of relations between 'the tribal' and 'the modern'. Yet the exclusions built into any collection or narration are legitimate objects of critique, and the insistent, didactic tone of the MOMA show only makes its focus more debatable. If the non-Western objects on West Fifty-third Street never really question but continually confirm established aesthetic values, this raises questions about 'modernist primitivism's' purportedly revolutionary potential. The absence of any examples of Third World modernism or of recent tribal work reflects a pervasive 'self-evident' allegory of redemption.

The final room of the MOMA exhibition, 'Contemporary Explorations', which might have been used to refocus the historical story of modernism and the tribal, instead strains to find contemporary Western artists whose work has a 'primitive feel'.[28] Diverse criteria are asserted: a use of rough or 'natural' materials, a ritualistic attitude, ecological concern, archaeological inspiration, certain techniques of assemblage, a conception of the artist as shaman, or some familiarity with 'the mind of primitive man in his [sic] science and mythology' (derived perhaps from reading Lévi-Strauss). Such criteria, added to all the other 'primitivist' qualities invoked in the exhibition and its catalogue, unravel for good the category of the primitive, exposing it as an incoherent cluster of qualities that at different times have been used to construct a source, origin, or alter ego confirming some new 'discovery' within the territory of the Western self. The exhibition is at best a historical account of a certain moment in this relentless process. By the end the feeling created is one of claustrophobia.

The non-Western objects that excited Picasso, Derain, and Léger broke into the realm of official Western art from outside. They were quickly integrated, recognized as masterpieces, given homes within an anthropological-aesthetic object system. By now this process has been sufficiently celebrated. We need exhibitions that question the boundaries of art and of the art world, an influx of truly indigestible 'outside' artifacts. The relations of power whereby one portion of humanity can select, value, and collect the pure products of others need to be criticized and transformed. This is no small task. In the meantime one can at least imagine shows that feature the impure, 'inauthentic' productions of past and present tribal life; exhibitions radically heterogeneous in their global mix of styles; exhibitions that locate themselves in specific multicultural junctures; exhibitions in which nature remains 'unnatural'; exhibitions whose principles of incorporation are openly questionable. The following would be my contribution to a different show on 'affinities of the tribal and the postmodern'. I offer just the first paragraph from Barbara Tedlock's superb description of the Zuni Shalako ceremony, a festival that is only part of a complex, living tradition:[29]

Imagine a small western New Mexican village, its snow-lit streets lined with white Mercedes, quarter-ton pickups and Dodge vans. Villagers wrapped in black blankets and flowered shawls are standing next to visitors in blue velveteen blouses with rows of dime buttons and voluminous satin skirts. Their men are in black Stetson silverbanded hats, pressed jeans, Tony Lama boots and multicolored Pendleton blankets. Strangers dressed in dayglo orange, pink and green ski jackets, stocking caps, hiking boots and mittens. All crowded together they are looking into newly constructed houses illuminated by bare light bulbs dangling from raw rafters edged with Woolworth's red fabric and flowered blue print calico. Cinderblock and plasterboard white walls are layered with striped serapes, Chimayó blankets, Navajo rugs, flowered fringed embroidered shawls, black silk from Mexico and purple, red and blue rayon from Czechoslovakia. Rows of Hopi cotton dance kilts and rain sashes; Isleta woven red and green belts; Navajo and Zuni silver concha belts and black mantas covered with silver brooches set with carved lapidary, rainbow mosaic, channel inlay, turquoise needlepoint, pink agate, alabaster, black cannel coal and bakelite from old '78s, coral, abalone shell, mother-of-pearl and horned oyster hang from poles suspended from the ceiling. Mule and white-tailed deer trophy-heads wearing squash-blossom, coral and chunk-turquoise necklaces are hammered up around the room over rearing buckskins above Arabian tapestries of Martin Luther King and the Kennedy brothers, The Last Supper, a herd of sheep with a haloed herder, horses, peacocks.

NOTES

1. William Rubin, ed., *'Primitivism' in Modern Art: Affinity of the Tribal and the Modern*, 2 vols, New York: Museum of Modern Art, 1984.

2. The term *tribal* is used here with considerable reluctance. It denotes a kind of society (and art) that cannot be coherently specified. A catchall, the concept of tribe has its source in Western projection and administrative necessity rather than in any essential quality or group of traits. The term is now commonly used instead of *primitive* in phrases such as *tribal art*. The category thus denoted, as this essay argues, is a product of historically limited Western taxonomies. While the term was originally an imposition, however, certain non-Western groups have embraced it. Tribal status is in many cases a crucial strategic ground for identity. In this essay my use of *tribe* and *tribal* reflects common usage while suggesting ways in which the concept is systematically distorting. See Morton Fried, *The Notion of Tribe*, Menlo Park, Calif.: Cummings, 1975, and William Sturtevant, 'Tribe and State in the Sixteenth and Twentieth Centuries', in *The Development of Political Orgaization in Native North* America, ed. Elizabeth Tooker, Washington: The American Ethnological Society, 1983.

3. These points were made by William Sturtevant at the symposium of anthropologists and art historians held at the Museum of Modern Art in New York on November 3, 1984.

4. A more rigorous formulation than that of affinity is suggested in Michel Leiris, 'The African Negroes and the Arts of Carving and Sculpture', in *Interrelations of Cultures*, Westport, Conn.: UNESCO, 1953. How, Leiris asks, can we speak of African sculpture as a single category? He warns of 'a danger that we may underestimate the variety of African sculpture; as we are less able to appreciate the respects in which cultures or things unfamiliar to us differ from one another than the respects in which they differ from those to which we are used, we tend to see a certain resemblance between them, which lies, in point of fact, merely in their common differentness' (p. 35). Thus, to speak of African sculpture one inevitably shuts one's eyes 'to the rich diversity actually to be found in this sculpture in order to concentrate on the respects in which it is *not* what our own sculpture generally is'. The affinity of the tribal and the modern is, in this logic, an important optical illusion – the measure of a *common differentness* from artistic modes that dominated in the West from the Renaissance to the late nineteenth century.

5. See, for example, Rubin's discussion of the mythic universals shared by a Picasso painting and a Northwest Coast half-mask (Rubin, *'Primitivism'*, 328–30). See also Kirk Varnedoe's association of modernist primitivism with rational, scientific exploration (in Rubin, *'Primitivism'*, 201–3, 652–3).

6. This point was made by Clifford Geertz at the November 3, 1984, symposium at the Museum of Modern Art (see n. 2).

7. Rubin, *'Primitivism'*, pp. x, 73.

8. Ibid., p. 682.

9. The clash between Krauss's and Varnedoe's dark and light versions of primitivism is the most striking incongruity within the catalogue. For Krauss the crucial task is to shatter predominant European forms of power and subjectivity; for Varnedoe the task is to expand their purview, to question, and to innovate.

10. On *négrophilie* see Jean Laude, *La peinture française* (1905–1914) et 'l'art nègre', Paris: Maspéro, 1968; for parallel trends in literature see Jean-Claude Blachère, *Le modèle nègre: aspects littéraires du mythe primitiviste au XXe siècle chez Apollinaire, Cendrars, Tsara*, Dakar: Nouvelles Éditions Africains, 1981 and Gail Levin, '"Primitivism" in American Art: Some Literary Parallels of the 1910s and 1920s', *Arts*, Nov. 1984. The discovery of things 'nègre' by the European avant-garde was mediated by an imaginary America, a land of noble savages simultaneously standing for the past and future of humanity – a perfect affinity of primitive and modern. For example, jazz was associated with primal sources (wild, erotic passions) and with technology (the mechanical rhythm of brushed drums, the gleaming saxophone). Le Corbusier's reaction was characteristic: 'In a stupid variety show, Josephine Baker sang "Baby" with such an intense and dramatic sensibility that I was moved to tears. There is in this American Negro music a lyrical "contemporary" mass so invincible that I could see the foundation of a new sentiment of music capable of being the expression of the new epoch and also capable of classifying its European origins as stone age – just as has happened with the new architecture' (quoted in Charles Jencks, *Le Corbusier and the Tragic View of Architecture*, London: Penguin, 1973, p. 102). As a source of modernist inspiration for Le Corbusier, the figure of Josephine Baker was matched only by monumental, almost Egyptian, concrete grain elevators, rising from the American plains and built by nameless 'primitive' engineers (Rayner Banham, *A Concrete Atlantis: U.S. Industrial Building and European Modern Architecture*, Cambridge, Mass.: MIT Press, 1986, p. 16). The historical narrative implicit here has

been a feature of twentieth-century literary and artistic innovation, as a redemptive modernism persistently 'discovers' the primitive that can justify its own sense of emergence.

11. Jean Baudrillard, *Le système des objets*, Paris: Gallimard, 1968.

12. Raymond Williams, Culture and Society, 1780–1950, New York: Harper and Row, 1966. The twentieth-century developments traced here redeploy these ideas in an intercultural domain while preserving their older ethical and political charge.

13. On the recognition of masterpieces see Rubin's confident claims ('*Primitivism*', pp. 20–1). He is given to statements such as the following on tribal and modern art: 'The solutions of genius in the plastic arts are all essentially instinctual' (p. 78, n. 80). A stubborn rejection of the supposed views of anthropologists (who believe in the collective production of works of tribal art) characterizes Rubin's attempts to clear out an autonomous space for aesthetic judgment. Suggestions that he may be projecting Western aesthetic categories onto traditions with different definitions of art are made to seem simplistic (for example p. 28).

14. See Rubin, '*Primitivism*', pp. 10, 661–89.

15. P. 1.

16. Johannes Fabian, *Time and the Other: How Anthropology Makes its Object*, New York: Columbia University Press, 1983.

17. Walter Benjamin, *The Origin of German Tragic Drama*, London: New Left Books, 1977.

18. Rubin, '*Primitivism*', p. 73.

19. Susan Vogel, 'Introduction', in *African Masterpieces from the Musée de l'Homme*, New York: Harry Abrams, 1985, p. 11.

20. At the November 3, 1984, symposium (see n. 3) Christian Feest pointed out that the tendency to reclassify objects in ethnographic collections as 'art' is in part a response to the much greater amount of funding available for art (rather than anthropological) exhibitions.

21. See Michel Leiris, *L'Afrique fantôme*, 1934, reprinted with new introduction, Paris: Gallimard, 1950, and Chapter 2 [in *The Predicament of Culture*].

22. Susan Vogel and Francine N'Diaye, eds, *African Masterpieces from the Musée de l'Homme*, New York: Harry Abrams, 1985, p. 122.

23. Vogel, 'Introduction', p. 11.

24. Herbert Cole and Chike Aniakor, eds, *Igbo Arts: Community and Cosmos*, Los Angeles: Museum of Cultural History, UCLA, 1984, p. 14.

25. Chimia Achebe, 'Foreword' to Cole and Aniakor, *Igbo Arts*, p. ix.

26. The shifting balance of power is evident in the case of the Zuni war gods, or Ahauuta. Zuni vehemently object to the display of these figures (terrifying and of great sacred force) as 'art'. They are the only traditional objects singled out for this objection. After passage of the Native American Freedom of Religion Act of 1978 Zuni initiated three formal legal actions claiming return of the Ahauuta (which as communal property are, in Zuni eyes, by definition stolen goods). A sale at Sotheby Parke-Bernet in 1978 was interrupted, and the figure was eventually returned to the Zuni. The Denver Art Museum was forced to repatriate its Ahauutas in 1981. A claim against the Smithsonian remains unresolved as of this writing. Other pressures have been applied elsewhere in an ongoing campaign. In these new conditions Zuni Ahauuta can no longer be routinely displayed. Indeed the figure Paul Klee saw in Berlin would have run the risk of being seized as contraband had it been shipped to New York for the MOMA show. For general background see Steven Talbot, 'Desecration and American Indian Religious Freedom', *Journal of Ethnic Studies* 12(4) (1985).

27. Sidney Moda Mead, ed., *Te Maori: Maori Art from New Zealand Collections*, New York: Harry Abrams, 1984. An article on corporate funding of the arts in the *New York Times*, Feb. 5, 1985, p. 27, reported that Mobil Oil sponsored the Maori show in large part to please the New Zealand government, with which it was collaborating on the construction of a natural gas conversion plant.

28. In places the search becomes self-parodic, as in the caption for works by Jackie Winsor: 'Winsor's work has a primitivist feel, not only in the raw physical presence of her materials, but also in the way she fabricates. Her labor – driving nails, binding twine – moves beyond simple systematic repetition to take on the expressive character of ritualized action.'

29. 'The Beautiful and the Dangerous: Zuñi Ritual and Cosmology as an Aesthetic System', *Conjunctions*, 6 (1984), p. 246.

3.

Always True to the Object, in Our Fashion

Susan Vogel

Almost nothing displayed in museums was made to be seen in them. Museums provide an experience of most of the world's art and artifacts that does not bear even the remotest resemblance to what their makers intended. This evident fact lies at the very heart of museum work (which is a work of mediation) and should be a preoccupation of all museum professionals, though most museum visitors seem practically unaware of it. An art exhibition can be construed as an unwitting collaboration between a curator and the artist(s) represented, with the former having by far the most active and influential role. Ironically, the curator's name rarely even appears in the information available in an exhibition (except as the author of the catalogue), and the public is given the false impression of having come into contact with 'Goya', 'Warhol', or 'African art', for example. Museums, it seems to me, have an obligation to let the public know what part of any exhibition is the making of the artists[1] and what part is the curator's interpretation. Disentangling those two elements, however, may not be easy, since at least some of the curator's understanding of his or her material may rest on unquestioned and unexamined cultural – and other – assumptions.

Virtually the only art made to be exhibited in galleries (as opposed to perhaps serving as decoration in galleries) is the art of our own recent history, that is, Western art since the late eighteenth century. In some measure, we have attributed to the art or artifacts of all times the qualities of our own: that its purpose is to be contemplated, and that its main qualities can be apprehended visually. Egyptian tomb furnishings and Renaissance altars – to say nothing of African art – are routinely exhibited in art museums without a clear examination of even the most basic questions: Can they be regarded as art in our sense? Were they made by people who thought of themselves in terms that correspond to our definition of 'artist'? If not, how do we acknowledge that while displaying them in art museums?

African art provides a useful and particularly sharp instance of the distortion produced by exhibiting in museums objects made for quite different purposes. African art has not been included in art museums long enough for its presence to be accepted unthinkingly. If the audience knows one thing about African art, it knows these objects were never meant to be seen in museum buildings. This makes it a fruitful subject for exploring museum presentations, or dislocations – or, as we might most profitably consider it, the recontextualization of objects in museums.

I am a museum practitioner, not a theorist. I have spent most of my professional life creating exhibitions: one permanent installation and many temporary exhibitions. They have been art exhibitions created of material objects in concrete settings, addressed to specific audiences in specific cities at specific moments in time. Mine have all been exhibitions of African art – an art not automatically recognized as art, from a place not politically neutral. While working on them I have taken into account what the audience knew or believed about Africa and have developed strategies to deal with their expectations. Maybe the strategies have resulted in theories.

Western culture has appropriated African art and attributed to it meanings that are overwhelmingly Western. We are aware that the meanings we give to the objects visiting in our homes and museums are not those that inspired their creators. We may be less clear about what the original status (art? craft? sacra?) and meaning might have been.

Many Westerners feel too sharply their ignorance of the original contexts of African art and are too ready to let it blind them to the art's visible qualities. They are less daunted by the impossibility of seeing *any* work of art with the eyes of the original audience, much less those of the artist. The cultural context of much of the world's art, particularly that large segment which is religious in inspiration, is remote from the contemporary museum-going public. If nothing else, the aura of faith and reverence with which it was regarded by its intended audience is missing for most of us. We can be insiders only in our own culture and our own time.

That said, I have come to feel that the museum dealing with culture (and even more with non-Western art) cannot adopt the authoritative voice commonly heard in museums of Western art and science. We are too far from the voices of the original owners and makers, too locked into the perspectives of our own culture to presume to be faithful to the object in any exalted way. We can be faithful only in our fashion, which often means we are, like Cole Porter's heroine, only barely faithful, or not at all. And we can be faithful only in the fashion of our time.

Several recent Center for African Art exhibitions have attempted to be faithful in different ways. All renounced the authoritative voice; each represented a strategy for dealing with the drastic recontextualization of African art in Western museums. One that dealt overtly with the selection of exhibition objects, 'The Art of Collecting African Art',[2] showed not only the objects that were the pride of the collector, but the works that had been passed over as mediocre, altered, restored, or forged. The exhibition invited the viewer to look closely and form his or her own opinion before reading the label that revealed my opinion. Labels were personal, opinionated, and informal in tone rather than didactic.[3] This exhibition was intended to encourage careful looking and did not attempt to teach connoisseurship.[4]

Two other exhibitions sought to empower the visitor to look critically at works of African art and at the same time to heighten awareness of the degree to which what we see in African art is a reflection of ourselves. The first, 'Perspectives: Angles on African Art', considered the ways we in the West project our needs and our fantasies upon Africa; the second was 'Art/ artifact'. Both exhibitions examined Americans rather than Africans: the audience was the subject of the first exhibition, the museum the subject of the second.

'Perspectives: Angles on African Art'[5] explored the different things African art has come to represent by inviting ten individuals who seemed to hold different points of view to select objects and to discuss their selections and perspectives. The ten cocurators were Americans and Africans who had some connection to African art, though only two were academically trained as African-art specialists. The labels in the exhibition consisted of signed comments by the cocurators. Most were highly personal, arguable opinions that invited the visitor to agree or disagree. The spectrum of outlooks interpreted African art as a national patrimony; a personal heritage; objects in an art collection; part of the study of art history, or of anthropology; an influence on twentieth-century art; material for artists to draw upon in different ways; and the expression of living religious and political beliefs.[6]

Despite their individuality and their differences, the cocurators were all concerned with the dichotomy between appreciation and understanding, form and meaning; between what David Rockefeller calls the artistic sense, and the scholarly one. It was not a question we raised explicitly in the Perspectives interviews, though it was mentioned again and again. Ivan Karp, an anthropologist, put it most clearly: 'I'm really torn between the arguments that are made for universal aesthetic criteria and the idea that we can only truly appreciate something from the point of view of the people for whom it was originally made – that aesthetics are "culture bound".'[7] This question is fundamental to the consideration of all non-Western art: How do we legitimately understand or appreciate art from a culture we do not thoroughly know? I suspect most of our visitors are troubled by the issue in an inexplicit way.

The artist cocurators were the least preoccupied by the cultural context of the objects, which they confidently approached as pure sculptural form. Nancy Graves said, 'The art is here for us to appreciate intuitively. One may get more information about it which enhances it, but its strength is here for anyone to see.'[8] Iba N'Diaye makes no reference to meaning in his commentaries, and describes drawing objects as the way he learned to see them.[9] Romare Bearden feels that information can even inhibit perception: 'I had to put the books down and just look at how I felt about it. The books get in the way sometimes.'[10] For James Baldwin, the only way to understand is through direct experience. 'You want to find out?' he asks. 'Go and expose yourself. You can't find out through a middleman anyway.' He also says, 'There's this curious dichotomy in the West about form and content. The form *is* the content.'[11] In this he echoes the African sculptor and diviner, Lela Kouakou, who recognizes no distinction between the two.[12]

William Rubin argues that the distinction between form and content is theoretical, since neither an understanding of the cultural context nor a personal appreciation is possible as a pure experience. 'The choices are not between a total contextual reconstruction – which is a mythic pursuit – and a pure aesthetic response, whatever that is. We don't respond to art objects with one particular set of responses that are isolatable as aesthetic. We respond to them with our total humanity.'[13] Dr Ekpo Eyo, a Nigerian archaeologist, goes further, suggesting that an intermingling of scholarship and emotional aesthetic response leads to understanding. Speaking of his personal experience with archaeological objects, he says, 'The more I looked at them, the more I studied them, the more I appreciated their beauty over and above the information about their context. They were beautiful! The more I described them and handled them, the more emotionally attached to them I became. It's like having a baby: you look at the baby all the time, and you begin to discover many things about it which you could not see at first. My eyes opened.'[14]

In Perspectives we did not abdicate completely our role as providers of information. We produced a checklist that contained information on the use and meaning the objects had for the original African owners. While I feel the authoritative voice inhibits the visitor, I hardly recommend uninformed free association before African objects – or any other intellectually determined objects – as a particularly full way to experience them if other means are available. But Perspectives was not about African art. It was about approaches to African art.

The exhibition that focused on the museum was 'Art/artifact'.[15] Again, this exhibition was not about African art or Africa. It was not even entirely about art. It was an exhibition about perception and the museum experience, focusing on the ways Westerners have classified and exhibited African objects over the past century. With some objects considered art and others artifacts, our categories do not reflect African ones and have changed over time. The exhibition showed how we view African objects (both literally and figuratively), arguing that much of our vision of Africa and African art has been conditioned by our own culture. I felt that unless we acknowledge that African art as we see it has been shaped by us as much as by Africans, we cannot see it at all.

Figure 6.3.1   Mijikenda memorial posts displayed as sculptures. Posts from many graves have been assembled to create an aesthetic and spectral presence unlike anything ever seen by the Mijikenda. Such posts may or may not have been regarded as aesthetic objects by their makers and users. Installation view of 'Art/artifact' at the Center for African Art, New York, 1988. Photo courtesy of the Center for African Art.

The exhibition approached the question of perception through individual objects and through installation styles. Recognizing that the physical setting of an object is part of what makes it identifiable as art, the installation showed art objects and nonart objects in such a way as to raise the question in the viewer's mind and to make the trickery of the installation evident. A hunting net from Zaire was one nonaesthetic, nonsignifying object that bore a spurious resemblance to some contemporary artworks. It was reverently displayed in a pool of light on a low platform. (Ironically, an unanticipated response demon-strated the success of the trickery in some quarters; I and several African-art dealers received inquiries from art collectors about where they might acquire such a marvelous net.) The inverse of this was the display of some extraordinarily fine pieces of African figure sculpture, unemphatically shown in the style of natural-history museums in a case evenly filled with many objects of unequal aesthetic interest, quantities of text, and pictures, which created an all-over 'anthropological wallpaper' effect. The indiscrimin-ate assemblage made it hard to see the sculptures as great works of art, though they were perfectly visible.

Figure 6.3.2   Recreation of the Hampton Institute curiosity room with a Mijikenda post in the corner near a Cameroon drum. The unprotected, rather casual presentation of these objects suggests that they are not very valuable, and does not suggest that the visitor should regard them as works of art. Installation view of 'Art/artifact' at the Center for African Art, New York, 1988. Photo courtesy of the Center for African Art

The exhibition also considered the contexts in which Westerners have seen African art. It began with a clean white room in which African art and artifacts (such as the net) were displayed for their formal qualities only. No information was provided above the most minimal: 'Net, Zande people, Zaire'. The next area was small but important: it contained an unedited and untranslated videotape showing the installation of a Mijikenda memorial post, accompanied by a label stating that only the original audience could have the original experience – that all other settings were inauthentic and arbitrary to a greater or lesser degree (Figure 6.3.1). The third area reconstructed a 'curiosity room' from 1905 in which the mixture of manmade and zoological specimens and a lack of information implied that these were interesting but almost unknowable objects that demonstrated no aesthetic intent (Figure 6.3.2). The fourth area showed objects in a natural-history-museum style, including the case described above (Figure 6.3.3), and a full diorama showing three men at the installation of a Mijikenda post (Figure 6.3.4). The last area displayed objects as in an art

Figure 6.3.3   Display in the style of a natural-history museum. Objects are used to illustrate points about African culture (e.g. 'The Place of the Dead in the World of the Living'), not for their intrinsic qualities. The evenness of the display indicates that these objects are to be regarded equally, though some are in fact fine works of art and others are ordinary. In this context, the Mijikenda post takes on a banal appearance. Installation view of 'Art/artifact' at the Center for African Art, New York, 1988. Photo courtesy of the Center for African Art

museum, as valuable treasures protected by Plexiglas and haloed in sanctifying spotlights (Figure 6.3.5).

The exhibition was not meant to be chronological or arranged in ascending order of legitimacy. The labels pointed out that natural-history museums and dioramas are not out of date, and that a display very like the art-museum one was used by Alfred Steiglitz in 1914, about the time when African objects were beginning to be considered art. The exhibition stressed that these different styles reflected differences in attitude and interpretation, and that the viewer was manipulated by all of them.

As visitors left the exhibition to wander into other displays, I hoped they would be able to regard all museum activities with a wiser and more critical eye, eventually to become aware of the less publicly visible choices made by museums that influence what they see when they look through the Plexiglas at an object.

Figure 6.3.4   Diorama in the style of a natural-history museum, showing the installation of a Mijikenda post. The diorama allowed the museum to show many aspects of material culture, social interaction, and environment simultaneously. The presentation discourages the viewer from singling out the Mijikenda post for special attention, and makes its boundaries unclear – are the two smaller posts part of it? The cloths? The pot and gourds? Installation view of 'Art/artifact' at the Center for African Art, New York, 1988. Photo courtesy of the Center for African Art

Politically aware visitors often focus on the value and ownership of museum objects, on questions regarding how the works arrived in the museum, who paid for the exhibition, and who profits from it. But these are only the most obvious issues among many more subtle ones. The museum is teaching – expressly, as part of an education program and an articulated agenda, but also subtly, almost unconsciously – a system of highly political values expressed not only in the style of presentation but in myriad facets of its operation. The banners in front of the building tell the visitor what really matters before he or she has entered the display. The museum communicates values in the types of programs it chooses to present and in the audiences it addresses, in the size of staff departments and the emphasis they are given, in the selection of objects for acquisition, and more concretely in the location of displays in the building and the subtleties of lighting and label copy. None of these things is neutral. None is overt. All tell the audience what to think beyond what the museum ostensibly is teaching.

Figure 6.3.5 Presentation of African sculptures in the style of an art museum. Each piece is isolated to be contemplated as a work of art. The presentation under Plexiglas suggests that each work is uniquely valuable and must be protected. The Mijikenda posts again appear, here as abstracted figure sculpture. Installation view of 'Art/artifact' at the Center for African Art, New York, 1988. Photo courtesy of the Center for African Art

The radical dislocation of most objects in museums has become a firmly established tradition in the West. Many museum visitors expect to see in art museums practically everything from tombs and altars to shoes and clocks; the visitors' relative lack of experience of these artifacts in their original contexts makes them unaware of how much the museum itself influences what they see.

The fact that museums recontextualize and interpret objects is a given, requiring no apologies. They should, however, be self-aware and open about the degree of subjectivity that is also a given. Museum professionals must be conscious about what they do and why, and they should inform the public that what it sees is not material that 'speaks for itself' but material filtered through the tastes, interests, politics, and state of knowledge of particular presenters at a particular moment in time. The museum must allow the public to know that it is not a broad frame through which the art and culture of the world can be inspected, but a tightly focused lens that shows the visitor a particular point of view. It could hardly be otherwise.

NOTES

1. If indeed they are to be considered artists in the African case. This is an example of a fundamental and potentially distorting assumption that remains an unexamined – or at least unarticulated – foundation underlying many African-art exhibitions.

2. The catalogue by the same title (published in 1988 by the Center for African Art) contains texts on collecting and illustrations of the objects in collections, but none of the comparative objects.

3. A case full of Baule masks had a label stating: 'CAUTION: THERE ARE FAKES IN THIS CASE. Face masks; Baule, Ivory Coast; Wood, paint, metal, fiber. Such masks are worn in entertainment dances. Here are two blatant fakes, an honest reproduction, two extraordinary old masks, and two merely authentic masks.' Beyond the case was a second label identifying the specific masks: 'From left to right: 1. A forgery, betrayed by its excessive delicacy and insipid expression. Compare the timidity of the decoration around the chin, and the meager little bird, with the others. 2. A fake. The lusterless surface and rote carving are typical of recent fakes. 3. An authentic mask probably dating from the 1940s or 1950s. Though the carving is vital and vigorous (compare this lusty bird with the others), it is heavy and the face is expressionless. 4. A reproduction, carved with competence, even virtuosity, but without deep conviction. No attempt has been made to age the mask or falsify the surface; no holes for the attachment of a putative costume have been made around the perimeter. 5. A great masterpiece. This mask, published early, probably dates from the nineteenth century. Its deeply contemplative expression, and the inspired reduction of the birds to just heads, reveal the hand of a great artist. It has preserved its original surface with all the variations of color and texture normally found on an old mask.'

4. Some academics and those uninterested in the workings of taste and connoisseurship found this an unsatisfying exhibition, though it was popular with the public, who enjoyed testing their own judgment. If I were doing this show again I would include on the initial labels more information of the kind needed to judge the objects, or I would isolate and identify a good example for comparison.

5. Shown at the Center for African Art, New York; the Virginia Museum of Fine Arts; Richmond, the San Diego Museum of Art; and the Birmingham Museum of Art between February 1987 and March 1988. The catalogue by the same title was published in 1987 by the Center for African Art and Harry N. Abrams, Inc.

6. They were: Romare Bearden, Nancy Graves, and Iba N'Diaye, artists; Robert Farris Thompson, Africanist art historian; Ivan Karp, Africanist anthropologist; James Baldwin, writer; David Rockefeller, banker and collector; Ekpo Eyo, Africanist archaeologist; Lela Kouakou, Baule diviner and artist; William Rubin, modernist art historian.

7. *Perspectives: Angles on African Art*, 83.

8. Ibid., 99.

9. Ibid., 163.

10. Ibid., 67.

11. Ibid., 115.

12. Ibid., 148–59.

13. Ibid., 51.

14. Ibid., 35.

15. The catalogue of the same title was published in 1987 by the Center for African Art and Prestel Verlag. It contained contributions by Susan Vogel, Arthur Danto, R. M. Gramly, Jeanne Zeidler with Mary Lou Hultgren, Enid Schildkrout, Thomas McEviley, Kim Levin, and James Farris. 'Art/artifact' was seen at the Center for African Art, New York; the Buffalo Museum of Science; the Virginia Museum of Fine Arts, Richmond; the Dallas Museum of Art; the Henry Art Gallery, Seattle; the Carnegie Art Museum, Pittsburgh; the Denver Museum of Natural History; and the Wight Art Gallery, Los Angeles, between February 1988 and June 1990. The migration of the exhibition between art museums and science museums exactly reflects the issue it raises.

4.

From Primitivism to Ethnic Arts

Rasheed Araeen*

The subject of my talk is somehow unusual and it is also unusual for an institution like the Slade to open its doors to it and ask someone like me to come here and speak. It is unusual because the issue here is something which has always been considered outside the ethics or limits of art and art education by the bourgeois/liberal establishment. Only a few years ago I was invited here to do a series of art performances. But, when the nature of my work became known to the higher authorities, no other than those who teach humanities here, no other than those who talk about universal human values and are never tired of talking about the freedom of expression we have in this country, the invitation was shelved and it was shelved quietly and without an explanation, as if nothing had happened. After being fed up waiting for months, when I approached the individual who had invited me in the first place (and I believe he was serious in his invitation), I did not even receive an apology. I was not naive enough to be surprised by the action of the authorities, but one expects some kind of courtesy in such matters, particularly from those who claim to have a monopoly on civilized values.

I am therefore very pleased that I have been invited[1] to speak to you; not only to speak to you but to explore the question of racism that underlies primitivism and how this question is relevant to how we perceive the artistic function of non-European peoples and their cultures in our contemporary society today. I also hope that this invitation is not a freak incident but signifies a change taking place inside the art institutions to represent the aspirations of this society, which is no longer an exclusively white society as it was before the Second World War.

The above incident is not an isolated incident. It is the kind of thing that one faces all the time if one is not prepared to conform to the institutional constraints. The ideas of total freedom and freedom for every individual, irrespective of colour, creed, or race, in the Western societies is the kind of myth that begins to explode when one enters into the domain of ideology that underpins the institutions of these societies. Without necessarily going into an elaborate argument it can be said that the ideas and values that

* This ... was a paper delivered as part of the 'Primitivism' series of seminars organized by Susan Hiller at the Slade School of Art (University of London) in winter 1985–6, and was published initially in Third Text, no. 1, autumn 1987.

support these institutions are of a hierarchical nature, and this hierarchy is maintained through patriarchy as well as through a world-view that developed during the West's imperial domination of the world over the last few centuries. This domination continues today in the form which is described as neo-colonialism. What is not often recognized is the fact that neo-colonialism now exists within Western metropolises with large populations of non-European peoples from the ex-colonies of Asia, Africa, and the Caribbean, the purpose of which is to perpetuate their status of subservience to the dominant white society. The incoming African/Asian cultures have provided an opportunity for the development of a new primitivism that goes under the official title of Ethnic Arts.[2]

I'm not suggesting here that institutions like the Slade are directly responsible for the development of this new situation. On the contrary, these institutions are unaware of what has been happening outside their doors. In fact they often shut their doors on the assumption that what is happening outside has little to do with them. The intellectual complacency and smugness of these institutions have played a large part in not confronting this situation. It is time that they should wake up and face up to the reality of this society if they have any humanistic or educational function to perform.

The Slade is indeed a liberal institution, and I use the word 'liberal' in its generic and positive sense. It is governed and run by a set of rules, not always visible, and a general intellectual ethos which together emphasize its humanistic function and which thus exclude any activity that would cast a shadow on its presumed objectives. I am not being sarcastic now. I am only pointing out the functional boundaries of art and art-educational institutions, which may be questionable in the light of the new reality of this society today, but which nevertheless claim to have a deep concern for the promotion of knowledge, human achievements, enlightenment and welfare, irrespective of colour, creed, or race. Such aims and objectives are indeed laudable and I will not cast a shadow of doubt on their sincerity, neither would I think of suggesting any other function for these institutions.

However, it is also important that we do take note of the fact that the ethics which govern these institutions, and indeed their educational function, were formulated at a time in the nineteenth century when England was at the height of its colonial power, ruling and educating a large proportion of the world as its subject people. Liberal scholarship has thus been part of colonial discourse and even today this remains fundamental to these institutions, not only in Britain but in the whole Western world, as well as in that part of the post-colonial world which is still under Western influence or domination. And it seems that we really cannot deal with this subject outside this context.

These institutions in fact embody and represent specific ideas and values, a philosophy that is specific to the (Western) dominant culture, as a result of which there exists a view which separates Western people from the peoples of the rest of the world. This separation is rationalized by accentuating cultural differences between the west and others by the development of a philosophical discourse that gives Western man a historically advanced position, a position that justifies his messianic ambitions in the world. Equipped with the ideas of progress and World-Spirit (Hegel), he performs the task of providing both material and intellectual leadership to the world in its advance towards perfection and ultimate salvation. In his missionary vision to transform the world into his own image, the world becomes other than himself: a pagan or primitive entity that has been trapped in the irrationality of its past history, in its primeval or pre-rational existence. In fact this entity does not even possess consciousness of itself, its own past, present, and future. It is the victim of its own timelessness, a static condition characterized and contained by ethnic, tribal, communal, irrational, unconscious, traditional … modes of existence. The victim must therefore be rescued, not necessarily for its own sake, but for the sake of the advancement of humanity.

The 'primitive' can now be put on a pedestal of history (modernism) and *admired* for what is missing in Western culture, as long as the 'primitive' does not attempt to become an active subject to define or change the course of (modern) history.

What I am trying to establish here is that primitivism has little to do with the actual conditions of the peoples or cultures it refers to, but it is an idea in Western culture by which others are defined in various periods of its recent history. As a projection and representation of non-European peoples and their cultures in Western philosophy or discourse, it in turn justifies Western colonial expansion and domination. In other words, primitivism is a function of colonial discourse, and it is therefore imperative that we try to look at the nature and complexity of this discourse.

The imperative becomes clear when we realize that the task here is really to explore the relationship between primitivism, racism, and the idea of so-called 'Ethnic Arts' that has been recently introduced in Britain; and it seems to me that the question of racism is central here. This is an extremely difficult task, not because it has not been undertaken before in this context but the attractiveness of being drawn into the rhetoric of anti-racist slogans and denunciation is enormous, given the blessing it is receiving from some quarters that claim to be radical. The radicalism of these institutions of the left is as questionable as those institutions which appear to keep a distance from politics in this respect.

To deal with the history of the idea of primitivism in Western culture, as a function of colonial discourse which goes beyond the point in history when the 'artefacts' of African/Oceanic cultures were appropriated by modernism, would require volumes of books in order to do justice to its enormity and complexity. And yet I find it necessary at least to cast a glance at this history. The attempt to sift through only the relevant material in order to pick those components which are essential to our issue is in itself an enormous task, and it would be foolish on my part to think of doing all this, not only that we are restricted by the format of this presentation, but the expertise required for this purpose is not altogether at my disposal.

I must also take note of the fact that I am on difficult ground here. I am entering into the domain of others, the domain of the specialists: art historians, art critics, anthropologists, psychologists, etc. Not that the specialist knowledge worries me much (it can be useful as well as intimidating), but the reason why specialist knowledge builds barriers around itself to protect its so-called autonomy, is in fact to protect itself from an ideological scrutiny – thus keeping so-called political questions out of this domain; and I find this highly questionable. As Edward Said in his remarkable book *Orientalism* says: 'These are common ways by which contemporary scholarship keeps itself pure' so much so that 'philosophers will conduct their discussion of Locke, Hume, and empiricism without ever taking into account that there is an explicit connection in these classic writers between their "philosophical" doctrines and racial theory, justification of slavery, or arguments for colonial exploitation'.[3]

I have really a task ahead of me for which I am perhaps not well equipped, but that should not prevent me from putting forward my own understanding of the matter. These notes are in fact rough and rudimentary, but they are meant only to draw question marks around some ideas in Western culture which are related to our subject and also draw attention to the fact that we cannot continue to ignore these ideas while discussing contemporary reality no matter how unpleasant they might be. It is in fact my aim to establish somehow that these ideas are very much part of the contemporary reality, as it is represented by contemporary liberal institutions or/and scholarship and also as it exists on a more general level of 'collective consciousness' of this society today.

But before we go further I shall declare my own position, both my shortcomings and self-interest, from the outset. I am a practising artist within the context of modernism, and I shall speak to you *as an artist*. I have chosen verbal language to express myself, not because I enjoy writing or speaking (I would rather spend this time to make a work of art) but because the issue here is related to my own position, and if I do not deal with this issue nobody else will. We do not have any professional writer on art who fully recognizes this issue or understands the complexity of its influences on contemporary consciousness or perception.

I also believe that an artist is not a dumb maker of art objects. S/he has a rational mind, like anybody else, and there is no reason why this mind should not also be put to use in the verbal articulation of ideas.

Having said this, let me tell you briefly why I am here in this country. Not that I am particularly interested in telling you my life story, but the point I am making is relevant in relation to what we are considering. About thirty years ago in Karachi I was introduced to modern art, through the information we used to get in the magazines and books imported from the west, as well as through the activities of contemporary Pakistani artists. I became so fascinated by the 'progressive' aspect of modernism that I decided to devote my life to its pursuit. I decided to abandon the professional career of an engineer and came here to establish myself as an artist. Soon after my arrival I became active in the post-Caro period, and what I did then was the result of and belongs to that historical period. But by the early '70s I began to realize that whatever I did, my status as an artist was not determined by what I did or produced. Somehow I began to feel that the context or history of modernism was not available to me, as I was often reminded by other people of the relationship of my work to my own Islamic tradition. ... Now I am being told, both by the right and the left, that I belong to the 'Ethnic Minority' community and that my artistic responsibility lies within this categorization. It is my intention to show you later that this categorization is the function of a new primitivism in Britain. In other words, the issue is directly related to my position as an artist in this society. My position is therefore *within* the text, and if this text has any significance it is due to this position.

Trying to deal with the question of primitivism and racism, in its full complexity and objectivity, is therefore for me to be able to jump successfully over all the pitfalls of personal frustrations and anger of the last twenty or so years, and also not to be bogged down by what some of my white friends call my fantasy of seeing racists and imperialists everywhere. I do not wish to deny my paranoia, but I can assure you with all my rational abilities that I do not see racists and imperialists everywhere. If I did, the prospects for me would be too gruesome. As for the paranoia (or whatever) of my friends or others I cannot do much about it except humbly to advise them that they should at least try to see things beyond my supposed chip on the shoulder. On my part I shall try to be as objective as possible, given the circumstances, and my main attempt here would be to find a common ground for a dialogue, in order to understand the meaning of all this within the context of the contemporary world we *all* share and live in today.

Primitivism in western art did not start with Gauguin, as the Museum of Modern Art (MOMA), New York, would have us believe. What about Delacroix? What about orientalist paintings in nineteenth-century Europe? What about the images of Africans particularly in the work of Hogarth?[4] It is true that with Gauguin there started a historically different relationship between Western art and other cultures, a historical watershed that changed the direction of western art away from its ethnocentric Graeco-Roman tradition of classicism since the Renaissance. It is not the purpose of this paper to go into the nature of this specific relationship, in the sense of finding out who did what and why. I am more interested in the status of the cultures called 'primitive' within this relationship, and in turn the status of the peoples implicated in this relationship. Did the admiration and fascination of the modern artist for these cultures, which could be from any part of the non-European world, help improve the status of these cultures in Western consciousness? The answer appears to be No, as the MOMA exhibition[5] of 1984–5 showed. This can be explained by reference to the reality of non-European people who live in Western metropolises and whose status in society is characterized by both the bigotry of the extreme right and fascination of the white liberal/left with the exotic.

Before we go further, I would like to describe to you my visit to MOMA in New York in 1984, when the famous exhibition '"Primitivism" in 20th Century Art' was on. To tell you the truth I was overwhelmed by what I saw, not only by some extremely beautiful and powerful works of African sculpture that I had not seen before, and perhaps will not see again, but also by the works of some European artists. Picasso's *Les Demoiselles d'Avignon* had a magical presence and it was difficult not to feel that. The texts displayed around were sometimes interesting and informative but at other times also disturbing in the way they mediated between the work of the modern artist and the so-called 'primitive' art. I came out of the museum with a mixed feeling of exhilaration (just seeing all those works together) and also with some anger. I talked to some people about this later including some black artists, and the general feeling was lack of interest and cynicism. Some shrugged their shoulders, saying what else would one expect from MOMA, and others denounced the whole thing as another imperialist enterprise, with which I somehow agreed.

Back in London, and going through the texts in the massive glossy catalogue of about 700 pages, the denunciation of the exhibition as an imperialist enterprise (it could not be anything else) became more clear. It is not that there were no informative or interesting texts, but it seems that the purpose underlying all this scholarship was to perpetuate further the idea of primitivism, to remind the so-called 'primitives' how the West admires (and protects and gives values to) their cultures and at the same time tell the modern artist, who could only be the Western artist, the importance of this in his[6] continuing historical role as an advancing force.

It is not my aim here to denounce this exhibition as merely an imperialist enterprise or turn my back on it in favour of more contingent social and political issues in the Third World. We have a responsibility to look at such cultural manifestations critically, more importantly, with a perspective which is not Eurocentric, and at the same time it should be done within the framework of contemporary practices: art, art criticism, and art historical scholarship. The point is that those who have been seen as 'primitives' are in fact part of today's society, and to ignore their actual position in this respect is to indulge again in imperialist fantasies. I take issue here with those Marxists who say that the Museum of Modern Art in New York is a temple of imperialism, and the only way we can deal with it critically is within and in relation to its function in advanced capitalism. Any attack on this temple must be launched from a position of class struggle. It is not that I disagree with this view, but this view often ignores the issue of racism underlying contemporary cultural imperialism, both world-wide and within Western societies. It seems therefore that we cannot continue sweeping the issue of racism under the carpet of Marxism, and we really need to look specifically into all those ideas in Western culture to see how these ideas have under-pinned a world-view of which racism is an important part. We ought to pay more attention to the emerging Third World scholarship[7] in which it is reiterated that classical Marxism *alone* is inadequate in the understanding of the relationship between racism and imperialism both in its historical and contemporary sense.

However, I would now like to draw your attention to some of the beautiful African sculptures[8] I saw in the MOMA exhibition. I have chosen these works for their extraordinary formal qualities. I am aware that I might be accused of reducing these works to only aesthetic qualities and perhaps seeing them with the eyes of a Western observer. The reason for this limited treatment, is only to prove a point which is very relevant in our context.

I am aware that I am being very selective about these works, and I am also presenting these works out of their social contexts and without much historical information. By whom and for whom are these works produced and under what socio-economic conditions? I do believe that we cannot understand the full significance of art works without taking into account the socio-economic and political conditions under which they are produced. The difficulty here is that we do not have this information. (And even if we did have this information, it would not have been possible for me to go into a full analysis within the scope of this chapter.)

What I therefore propose, contingently, is that we should look at these works as we would do in the case of any other work in an exhibition or museum, and try to respond to them – ignoring their anthropological interpretations. The intricate and complex formal and spatial qualities of these works tell us that these works are the products of highly sophisticated and intellectually engaged minds. At this point, I have deliberately not concerned myself with their sensuous qualities in order to avoid the pitfalls of that discourse which attributes sensuousness to irrationality. However, these works debunk the Western myth about them, of being produced by an unconscious and irrational mind. They might have been produced for some ritual purposes. But so are many works in Western culture which are made for religious purposes. Do we reduce the works of Western culture only to religious meanings when we look at them or analyse them? Why do we have a different attitude towards the works of non-European cultures? Why do we not accept that African artists were able to transcend the imposed specific function (whatever that may be) of their roles as artists and were able to produce works which were multilayered in terms of concerns, functions, and meanings resulting from their own individual creative imaginations?

It is commonly believed that African peoples themselves were not aware of the aesthetic qualities of what they were producing and that it was the West which 'discovered' these qualities and gave the African 'objects' the status of art. It is true that Africans did not write books on aesthetics, plasticity, or formalism (or whatever relates to art), but to deduce from this that African artists were not aware of what they were doing is to indulge in the kind of stupidity which can only result from a mental blockage or an intellectual dishonesty. Even a cursory study of various world cultures shows us that ritual itself does not demand the kind of formal complexity and perfection we find in many African works. Let us here take the example of a Mumuye sculpture from Nigeria, illustrated on page 43 of MOMA's catalogue: the way the human body is transformed into small geometrical spaces, and then interrelated to form a whole does not display either an expressionistic *Angst* or a ritual concern. It is more likely to be the result of a fascination and highly concentrated engagement with *space*, to create a *sculptural* space which is formally independent of naturalistic human form and yet at the same time represents the human body. I have yet to come across such a spatial complexity in a figurative sculpture in the west, even in the twentieth century.

My above comments do not deny other aspects of African sculpture, which may be religious, ritualistic, ceremonial, or whatever. The point is that we cannot reduce it to one particular aspect and certainly not to those aspects which are attributed to primitivism. African sculpture is profoundly complex, which is the result of rational minds, and not to recognize its complexity would be not to understand its true achievement.

What I am trying to say here is not altogether new. Modern anthropology tells us that what we used to think of as simple phenomena or structures of so-called 'primitive' societies are in fact highly complex projections of rational minds in no way less developed than the contemporary/modern mind. However, the ideas of modern anthropology have made no impact on art historical scholarship, on art criticism, or on Western consciousness in general about the people who have been explicitly primitivized in the past. The ideas of nineteenth-century Europe are still with us today and they are being used to *define* and *fix* the positions of non-European peoples in such a way that they are deprived of their active and critical functions in contemporary cultural practices. This is particularly true in relation to the development of modern art in the twentieth century. If African/Asian cultures have not produced (or are not known to have produced) great artists in this century it is not because Afro/Asian peoples lack mental or intellectual ability or/and modern consciousness. The reasons are different and they are to do with the colonial primitivization of the non-European world, and this primitivization continues today in the form of ethnicization of non-European cultures globally as well as within Western societies.

Edward Said describes orientalism 'as a system of knowledge about the Orient, an accepted grid for filtering through the Orient into Western consciousness ... the idea of European identity as a superior one in comparison with all non-European peoples and cultures'.[9]

We can easily replace the word 'orientalism' with 'primitivism', particularly when we know that the word 'primitive' was in fact used frequently for *all* non-European cultures up to the end of the nineteenth century, notwithstanding that orientalism does have its own specific boundary in the same way as primitivism now exclusively refers to African/Oceanic cultures. William Rubin of MOMA refers to it as modern primitivism. Mr Rubin is perhaps right in also saying that 'Primitivism is ... an aspect of history of modern art', but then to imply that this does not mean to reflect upon the status of the cultures and peoples primitivism refers to is to add insult to injury. However, I shall leave this matter here as my real intention is to go beyond the context of the twentieth century and show that primitivism as an idea or perception was already there as part of Western consciousness before it entered into its modernist phase. I am therefore using the term 'primitivism' in a much broader and more general sense to reflect upon Europe's attitude towards all non-European cultures as part of the development of its art historical scholarship or discourse since the mid-nineteenth century.

However, I find it necessary again to reiterate that this paper does not concern itself much with the catalytic role African/Oceanic 'artefacts' played early this century in the development of modern art (cubism) or the role they have been playing since, as objects for appropriation by the Western artist. My main concern is with the question of the *status* and *representation* of non-European cultures in Western scholarship and popular knowledge since the eighteenth century, and, more importantly the implication today of this history *vis-à-vis* the *status* of non-European peoples in the modern world. The idea of the colonial Other as a group of racial stereotypes, with their equivalent cultural stereotypes, has played an important part in the development of primitivism in colonial discourse. And it seems that these stereotypes are still with us today and provide a source (though often unconsciously) for racist ideas both in popular consciousness, institutions, and scholarship.

What is interesting and central to Western scholarship since the Renaissance is the idea of progress, which in the eighteenth century began to be rationalized for universal enlightenment and advancement. The methodology used for this purpose was to do comparative studies and analyses of world cultures and to establish their interrelationships and their relative positions in the preconceived universal hierarchy. The adaptation of the Graeco-Roman tradition in post-Renaissance Europe is understandable, but the consequences of placing Greek art at the top of the hierarchy can only be grasped in relation to the function of colonial discourse. The concept of a universal history of art was developed in the eighteenth century, as part of colonial discourse, and since has been continually developing as a function of the idea of progress, constantly evaluating and appropriating world cultures within its own terms of reference.

The history of universal art was conceived as the history of human progress towards some kind of perfection, and modern art is seen to be the latest phase in its linear continuity. The concern for human progress towards betterment, towards some kind of perfection and salvation, is not a Western invention. But the theory of linear progress and freedom, based on an ideological framework in which all the different cultures and races of people are chained together in a hierarchical order, is specifically Western, based on the idea of progress in Western philosophy.

In general, we can say that some kind of idea of progress must exist in all peoples and in all cultures throughout history, even when the nature and manifestation of it might vary from people to people. If the human species has evolved from its primeval origin through a process of reflection and rationalization, then this process must belong to all peoples and cultures even if it does not give rise to ideas about linear progression. That there existed and exist complex social organizations in all cultures is not disputed. All cultures produce ideas, beliefs, values, and some kind of cultural artefacts – temporary or permanent – in their attempt at survival, subsistence, and improvement. The ability to move beyond one's own territory and relate to other people and establish a sophisticated system of interrelationships that goes beyond one's mere need or concern for subsistence, must also belong to all human beings irrespective of racial or ethnic differences. There is no scientific evidence to prove the contrary. Many civilizations and cultures throughout history had in themselves the idea of progress.

But the idea of progress under consideration here is different and is specific. It is specific only to Western civilization, particularly since the Renaissance.

What is singular about Western civilization[11] is its grotesque ambition to supersede every other culture or civilization in its schizophrenic desire to expand, dominate, control, and rule everything on earth. It is perhaps a paradox of history, given all the material and cultural resources at its disposal, that the West had to rationalize its idea of progress through constructing a philosophy of racial superiority. It can be argued that once the Augustinian idea of all human races originating from one source began to be questioned after the Reformation, giving rise to a conflict between monogenetic and polygenetic theories, this inevitably led to pseudo-secular liberal scholarship and to human classification based on the knowledge available then. What is important here is to recognize that this had no empirical basis. The hierarchical classification was constructed as a conceptual framework of an *a priori* idea of universal progress 'under the tutelage of the west', a phrase used by Edward Gibbon to stress the West's responsibility to educate and civilize 'savage nations' in order to safeguard Western civilization from its likely downfall.

In the following pages I shall discuss some of those ideas, which are applicable to the development of the discipline of art history in the West, which today is the main discipline that determines the nature and evaluation of contemporary art practices, and their place in the history of art. The general ideas related to the notion of progress are in fact an integral part of the development of the concept of art history; the concept of a universal art history being synonymous with the notion of universal progress – of course, determined and realized by the West. What is interesting is that within this concept of history there are peoples who are considered to be incapable of any *modern* progress by themselves, and this incapability is often attributed to racial differences.

Winckelmann is considered to be the first writer to write a universal history of art, published in 1764, in which he employed the prevailing doctrine in order to establish a hierarchical structure for world cultures. Winckelmann's formulation, which established the supremacy of Greek art over the arts of all other cultures only by using the argument of climatic determination that attributes backwardness to hot climate, was important for later historians, particularly Creuser and Hegel. Once the supremacy of Greek art was established, this 'led to the seizing upon the shapes of Greek and Roman bodies', as pointed out by Robert Nisbet in his book *History of the Ideas of Progress*,

as criteria for the biological best in the modern world; biological and also mental and cultural best! The fusion of the two Enlightenment obsessions – science and belief in Greco-Roman superiority – helped popularise the use of 'scientific' measurements and other tests for the determination of who among modern peoples were closest to the Greeks and Romans, and also who were farthest and therefore the most primitive and backward.[12]

Hegel is an extremely important figure in European thought, and his influence has been universal as one of the major philosophers of the idea of progress. What concerns me – and I am mainly paraphrasing Partha Mitter's ideas from his book *Much Maligned Monsters*[13] – is the way Hegel uses India as a model of a 'primitive' culture and then builds up the whole evolutionary continuum in which the west takes up the most advanced position. The result of this, by implication, is not only that non-European peoples are seen as belonging to the past, but that they also become fixed entities with historically exhausted physical and mental abilities.

One is amazed by the extent of the fascination with and admiration of the west for other cultures, and the amount of effort it puts into documenting, studying, contextualizing, and philosophizing world cultures, with an ambivalence that has been its constant hallmark. It first builds up a complex ideological framework to look at others and their cultures, and, by fixing them in past historical periods, rationalizes its own position as the final link in the chain of human evolution. Hegel's ideas provide an extremely important framework in this respect, especially those relating to the development of art history. I quote Partha Mitter here.

For Hegel, every nation had a preordained place in his 'ladder' of historical progress and reflected a unique 'national spirit'. Hegel also argued that each particular facet of nation or culture was interlined with the rest, for the national 'spirit' permeated all spheres of life. The conclusion was that if we were to judge a particular type or tradition of art we must first of all see what particular national spirit it represented and to what particular point in history that nation in turn belonged. ...
Paradoxically, his dynamic principle of history, the dialectics of change, only helped to establish a fundamentally static image of Indian art, its immemorial immutability, its unchanging irrationality, and its poetic fantasy, all predetermined by the peculiar Indian national spirit. It needs to be repeated here that Hegel's characterisation of the Indian 'spirit' was not based on empirical evidence but determined essentially by India's temporal position in Hegelian metaphysics. ... It was thus condemned to remain always outside history, static, immobile, and fixed for all eternity.[14]

While earlier philosophers of the idea of progress thought in terms of cultures and civilization arranged in linear order, rather than in terms of races, in the nineteenth century racist hypotheses – partly derived from Darwin's theory of evolution – became increasingly common as explanations of the vivid differences of cultures on earth. Gobineau's *Essay on the Inequality of Human Races* (1853–55) 'is the source of racist conceptions of human progress which, during the late nineteenth century, spread throughout Western civilisation',[15] but the idea of 'fixity' of certain peoples or races with their specific cultural achievements fixed in the past, is evident in most Western scholarship, such as in Hegel's *Philosophy of History* and *History of Art*, which have been highly influential in the development of modern art historical scholarship. It is, in fact, my contention that there is no essential or basic difference between liberal scholarship, such as represented by Hegel, and explicitly racialist theories. From Winckelmann to Creuser to Hegel to Ruskin to Fergusson, and in our present day Lord Clark and Professor Gombrich ... it is the same story. It is the same grand narrative, in which the detail and emphasis change from time to time but every chapter ends on the same note: the west's inherent superiority over all other peoples and cultures.

The ideas of 'racial romantics', such as Gustave Le Bon, for whom a style of art was determined from the start by the unique spirit of a race, and whose special talents could not be imitated by people belonging to a different race without exposing themselves to grave dangers, may not be very helpful in understanding institutional racism in Western societies today, because these institutions have now become highly sophisticated and bureaucratized and they do not express their attitudes openly and explicitly. The institutions are nevertheless heirs to the ideas of Western scholarship. Notwithstanding the fact that institutional policies often present a misunderstanding of these ideas, they are never explicitly rejected; instead there is often a 'silence', but when sometimes things do come out they echo the same ideas of nineteenth-century primitivism.

However, it is not necessary for these ideas to exist openly in their extreme forms, particularly when there is no essential or basic difference between the liberal and extreme positions: the former providing the latter with a respectable shield or mask to protect it from a radical attack. The most extreme ideas can either lie dormant under the carpet of liberalism (just ignore them!) or they will seep through and appear on its multicoloured surface, as has happened recently in Britain, in the form of a benevolent multiculturalism with all its fascination with and admiration for exotic cultures. What is not fully realized, by either white or black[16] people, is that the ideas which are essential to the kind of multiculturalism which is being promoted in Britain today, come from the racial theories of art discussed earlier.

Many of the ideas of the 'racial romantic' thinkers, such as Le Bon and Chamberlain, were in fact recognized as extreme by some of their contemporaries and by later historians. Yet they did re-emerge in Nazi Germany, which only shows that ideas do not die or disappear from institutions or common consciousness just because we can ignore their importance in normal circumstances.

It could be argued, though, that I am unnecessarily indulging in ideas which should be forgotten or considered 'archaic' since we are no longer living in the nineteenth century. Marxism, moreover, rejects the metaphysics of Hegelian dialectics, and on this basis we should safely ignore all those racially based ideas in Western discourse or philosophy. This argument betrays the complacency of those who have been impotent or reluctant to do anything about it in practice. The ideas of racial or ethnic determinism as part of 'Ethnic Arts' have now been with us officially for almost ten years, and what did the 'left' do about them? Nothing. It preferred to sit on the fence or/and give out its usual sermons; and in other cases actively supported what I call new primitivism. However, it needs to be recognized that Marxist scholarship is marginal to dominant bourgeois culture and, within it, cannot really change the basis of contemporary art practice, or make a direct intervention in institutional structures where the ideas of racial cultural stereotypes still prevail.

I would like to start this section by mentioning the name of John Ruskin, who is quite a darling of the British art establishment. He believed that there was 'no art in the whole of Africa, Asia or America', and he expressed such an attitude towards other cultures often, openly, and viciously. I cannot attribute such a viciousness to his likely spiritual protégé, Peter Fuller,[17] who believes that good painting or sculpture is not possible without good drawing. I am not disputing here the importance of basic drawing in art practice – although it is not always necessary, the emphasis somehow expresses the kind of attitude that went into teaching the 'primitives' in the colonies, how to draw, and how to draw from the plaster casts of classical sculptures.

The 'primitive' has now indeed learned how to draw, how to paint, and how to sculpt; also how to read and how to write and how to think consciously and rationally, and has in fact read all those magical texts that gave the white man the power to rule the world. The 'primitive' today has modern ambitions and enters into the Museum of Modern Art, with all the intellectual power of a modern genius, and tells William Rubin to fuck off with his primitivism: you can no longer define, sir, classify or categorize me. I'm no longer your bloody objects in the British Museum. I'm here right in front of you, in the flesh and blood of a modern artist. If you want to talk about me, let us talk. BUT NO MORE OF YOUR PRIMITIVIST RUBBISH.

I did promise you that I would not go into an angry rhetoric, and it is unfair also to pick on an individual, particularly William Rubin whom I have never met. He probably is a very nice guy; and I should perhaps apologize to him for my rudeness if I ever meet him. However, the institutional authority that he represents exists throughout the Western world, and I do not see why the *anger* of the 'primitive' against this authority has no legitimacy given the dialectics of what this authority has perpetuated all over the world.

The anger is not an inability to communicate on 'civilized' terms or within an intellectual framework of modern cultural practices. On the contrary, it is the inability of the institutions to recognize and respond to the modern aspirations of all peoples irrespective of race, colour, or creed that has created a confrontational situation. This may not be a very happy situation, but that is what is happening in our contemporary world. I do not want to take you around the world. This would complicate the matter. However, I will draw your attention to what is happening in Britain (in Bristol, Liverpool, Birmingham, Southall, Brixton, etc.)[18] which, in my view, is the failure of this society to come to terms with the aspirations and demands for equality for all people in this society. This failure is also noticeable in liberal scholarship and art institutions, not that similar consequences of street riots are being foreseen here. There is a general lack of will to face up to the reality of post-war Britain. There is a lack of will to listen to those who had no voice during the colonial era but who are now part of a 'free' and modern society and want to speak and establish a meaningful dialogue across racial and cultural boundaries. If you had read my correspondence in my book *Making Myself Visible*,[19] or/and elsewhere, you would know what I mean by all this. What one often faces is the brick wall of silence, arrogance, and self-righteousness.

I am not suggesting here that there has been no awareness of the problem, or that nothing whatsoever has changed. But what is being done generally and officially is highly objectionable. Right from the very day African/Asian peoples set their feet on this soil (my concern here is only with the post-war period), the whole official machinery was set in motion to deal with them. Since then special research units have been set up under various organizations for the sole purpose of studying their *traditional* customs, beliefs, behaviour, values, and what not, and also what are called ethnic cultural artefacts; all lumped together and labelled ethnographical material. I am not an anthropologist or a sociologist, but it is not difficult to see what this game is all about.

The establishment, if not this society in general, is surprised and amazed that these people, who have been given the *privilege* of coming to this country, should now demand more. The 'primitive' demanding equality and self-representation within a modern society is unthinkable. There must be something wrong with them. They don't know what they want. *We* know what they want.

The problem is that these people are uprooted – say the experts of the race relations industry – from their own cultures, from their own traditions, and as a result they are feeling alienated and frustrated in this highly complex technological society. We shall therefore provide them with all the facilities to bring here and practise their own traditional cultures; and let them enjoy themselves. After all they are no longer our colonial subjects.

The need for various peoples to have their own cultures, particularly when they find themselves in an alien and hostile environment, is not something we should dispute. But the way this is being approached and manipulated has taken us away from the basic question of equality for all peoples within a modern society. It would be foolish not to recognize the differences between European and non-European cultures, but it has been the function of modernism since early in this century to 'eliminate' the importance of these differences in its march towards an equal global society. Why are these differences so important now? Instead of seeing the presence of various cultures within our modern society as our common asset, why are they being used to fulfil the specific needs of specific people? Does this not somehow echo the philosophy of apartheid?

The answers to these questions are not easy, particularly when the 'difference' is now being internalized by many people in the black community, and is seen as essential to their cultural survival. My attempt, in the following pages, is to deal with some aspects of what is a difficult and complex situation.

The history of primitivism is full of humbug. Lies, distortions, ignorance, confusions, etc., are *rationalized* into 'truths' that give the system credibility and power. The discontent and resistance of the underprivileged are turned into issues of culture, a shift that is manageable within the prevailing ideology. And thus a new conceptual and administrative framework is set up to deal with the demands of what the establishment calls ethnic minorities. This seems to have all the hallmarks of neo-colonialism, with specific features specific to metropolitan conditions, rationalized by a body of scholarly work done under the race relations and ethnic studies within some British universities and polytechnics;[20] and it does not seem unreasonable to call this scholarship neo-colonial discourse.

Homi Bhabha, who has recently made an important contribution towards understanding the complexity and ambivalence of the colonial stereotype, has suggested that we should treat colonial discourse – i.e. liberal scholarship – as part of colonial power:

> It is an apparatus that turns on the recognition and disavowal of racial/cultural/historical differences. Its predominant strategic function is the creation of space for a 'subject people' through the production of knowledge in terms of which surveillance is exercised and a complex form of pleasure/unpleasure is incited. It seeks authorisation for its strategies by the production of knowledge of coloniser and colonised which are stereotypical but antithetically evaluated. The objective of colonial discourse is to construe the colonised as a population of degenerate type on the basis of racial origin, in order to justify conquest and to establish systems of administration and instruction.[21]

The 'degenerate' is no longer easily recognizable as it has become a cultural stereotype that attracts the tremendous admiration and fascination of the white society. The cultural traditions that colonialism once wanted to suppress and destroy are allowed to 're-emerge' for 'the creation of space' that is essential for the surveillance of neo-colonial relations. The idea of 'Ethnic Arts' is central to this development.

But, first, let us go back to colonial times. The idea of progress and freedom was also proclaimed in the colonies. In fact colonialism was often justified on the basis that it brought progress to the colonized people, and would ultimately also provide a framework for the freedom of all humankind. This was particularly incorporated in the colonial education system, the purpose of which was, of course, to create a Westernized elite for colonial administration.

One of the consequences of this education was that the educated elite in the colonies became uprooted from its own cultural traditions, and this was particularly the case *vis-à-vis* the visual arts. Even when the traditions were not forgotten or ignored altogether, they became marginal or were exoticized internally in relation to the production of contemporary art in the capital cities.

My account and analysis here are generalized and oversimplified. There were, of course, exceptions to the rule: there were constant oppositions to the colonial type of education. However, the influence of colonial education remained predominant. And, paradoxically, this education provided the leadership for anti-colonial struggles.

The models which were the basis of art education in the colonies were often outmoded, conservative, and backward. When European artists were revolting against and overthrowing the whole tradition of Graeco-Roman classicism early this century, as part of their search for new modes of expression that would represent the spirit of modern times, art students in the colonies were being taught how to draw faces from the Graeco-Roman casts imported from Europe. Modern art, therefore, also gave a basis to African and Asian artists to oppose the traditions of conservativism, European as well as indigenous. This opposition was often also part of the artists' participation in anti-colonial struggles.

As a matter of fact, many artists in the Indian subcontinent, including Sri Lanka, formed groups, often called 'progressive groups', to discuss, practise, and propagate the ideas of modernism; and I believe similar things happened in the rest of the colonies as well. The progressiveness of these groups was manifested in their support for freedom from colonialism, as they realized that without this freedom it would not be possible to fulfil their aspirations for their own modern societies based on science and technology.

Immediately after independence, art became a focus and expression of newly found, modern freedom. There was a frenzy of enthusiasm and search for the latest modes of modernist expressions and styles; but the artists, at the same time, found themselves in a difficult situation. There were no modern institutions to support and recognize them. This created a post-colonial dilemma among many Third World intellectuals, particularly visual artists, whether to stay in their own countries and fight for their place at whatever cost or to leave for the West which offered better prospects.

Some did leave, particularly the ambitious ones; and that is how we had the first generation of African/Asian artists in Britain immediately after the war.

It is important to mention that some of these artists, after initial difficulties and frustrations, did eventually receive some support and recognition in Britain. By the end of the 1950s they were well accepted by the establishment, but it so happened that their short-lived recognition and success were partly to do with the fact of their being 'different'. I am not suggesting that there was something wrong with their being different, and in no way am I implying that the support they received was based only on the cultural difference. There was a post-colonial euphoria among the liberal intelligentsia, and it is important to recognize that many British people genuinely looked forward to a new and equal relationship between the different peoples within the spirit of Commonwealth. Why then, did not this euphoria last beyond the early 1960s? This is an important and difficult question, and trying to deal fully with it would drag us into the politics of the post-war transatlantic relationship that developed in the 1960s. However, it seems that American domination of the British art scene, beginning in the 1960s, did play some role in this change.

However, Souza was admired for expressing the anguish of being a Christian from a predominantly Hindu country, that is, India. The funny thing is, that he began to paint such paintings only after he had stayed in Britain for some years. Both Shemza and Avinash who developed their specific styles after living in Britain for some time, were taken up for the exoticism of their respective cultures, rather than being understood in the context of their problematic relationship with modernism. The success of some black artists in Britain today is also due to the exoticism of their work, which has been legitimized in the context of neo-primitivism within the reactionary 'postmodernism' promoted by corporate interests.

My own work of the 1960s, i.e. minimal sculpture, also attracted some interest but in most cases it was seen as 'Islamic art'. The point is that this thing called 'Islamic art' never entered my head before I heard about it from others in connection with my work. As far as I am concerned, my work was the result of my fascination with and understanding of modernist sculpture in Britain in the early 1960s, particularly of Caro. My attempt was to go further than what my modern precursors were doing, and what I produced is similar to what is today internationally recognized as minimalism.

It is not my purpose to dwell on my own achievement. But what I am saying here clearly illustrates the prevalence of the ideas of primitivism and how they are used to exclude non-European artists from the history of modernism. The suggestion seems to be that I have been carrying my culture all the time in my unconscious, and that it found expression *naturally*. My consciousness of modern history and my intellectual efforts to produce something new within this context appears to have no significance.

I accept that my work has an affinity with Islamic geometric art, which may be the result of the influence of Islamic culture I come from. But the same is true in the case of the English artist Tess Jerry, who accepts the influence of Islamic art on her work, and also in the case of French artist François Morellet, whose work was inspired by his visit to Granada in Spain. We could say the same thing about some American minimalists who had great admiration for what they called 'oriental art'. Barnett Newman and Ad Reinhardt were particularly inspired by what they considered to be the aesthetics of meditation and contemplation as opposed to the expressionism of Western art of the time, and both are important figures in the history of minimalism (modernism). If Islamic art has in fact influenced modern art, particularly in recent times, what, then, is at issue here? In order to understand this complex issue, one has to understand the *difference* between the 'Orient' and the 'modern', the former being a category of primitivism which can enter the latter, but only if it is transformed through the consciousness which, according to Hegelian philosophy, is an attribute of European people only.

There is no contradiction here. The consistency of the Western/bourgeois world-view is the consistency of the philosophy of modernism. It appears to me that the terms of reference of modern art as a progressive force unfolding continually on the basis of Hegelian dialectics of *Thesis, Antithesis and Synthesis* is not available to the colonial Other. The *Thesis* represents an Authority, which is the authority of the west over the world; and it seems that this authority can only be challenged at a particular time in bourgeois history within its own terms of reference and through what Hegel calls 'World-Spirit'. It is therefore understandable why the access to modernism is blocked whenever the colonial Other appears in front of it, because the *difference* between the 'primitive' and the 'modern' is fundamental to this Western authority ...

The idea of this 'difference' is not only the prerogative of academic philosophical discourse, but it is part of the collective consciousness of Western societies. I am not suggesting here that this necessarily represents a pejorative attitude of the white society towards non-European people, or that it is exclusively part of it. Often this 'difference' is invoked in a 'positive' manner to appreciate something that is missing from the dehumanizing Western culture. It so happens that the ideological implications of this 'difference' are not often or commonly understood.

Before I go further I would like to give you another example of this 'difference' which I encountered personally. In 1980 I was invited by the Ikon Gallery in Birmingham to participate in a group show, and I was *persuaded* by its then director to do a particular work about which I was initially reluctant. But when the other participating artists came to know about my work, they strongly objected to my being in the show. I was eventually asked to withdraw. The interesting thing is the reason they gave for my exclusion: 'the show is to do with sources for work *deep within the imagination* and this source is profoundly *different* from yours – since the ritual is, as it were, a *normal occurrence* albeit in a particular milieu' (emphases added).[22] I wrote back arguing that 'all artistic activity is to do with imagination', and the response was a blunt refusal to enter into any kind of further argument.

The reason why this 'difference' is invoked again and again, and consistently, whenever a person of African/Asian origin appears on the scene, can also be understood in terms of what Martin Barker has argued in his book *The New Racism*, the emergence of a new racism in Britain today which is not based on the idea of white superiority but on the maintenance of a *separate status* for black people based on cultural differences:

It is called up by the stimulus of those who are genetically unrelated, whose cultures reveal their different origins, and specifically those who display their genetic difference on their skin. Of course, it is not claimed that these outsiders are degenerate, immoral, inferior; they are just different. ... It is all the more dangerous, if that is conceivable, than older forms, because it can ward off any spectres of Nazism; all the time such writers, politicians and activists will distance themselves from doctrines of superiority/inferiority because racism is not possible or needed in that form any longer. The unit has passed on, and now takes a new form: we have a 'natural' tendency to stay apart from culturally alien things; even if they are not inferior, they are culturally different.[23]

Although the above quote refers to the New Tory philosophy, it should not be, in my view, attributed exclusively to the right. The idea of 'difference' is fundamental to the idea of 'Ethnic Arts' which is being supported by both the right and the left. My argument is not against the presence and recognition of all the different cultures in Britain today. They can and should in fact play an extremely important critical role in the development of this society into an equal multiracial society. But the idea that the creative abilities of black people are 'fixed' or can only be realized, even today, *within* the limits of their own traditional cultures is based on the racist philosophy of 'ethnic determinism' in art developed during the late nineteenth century. What worries me most is the fact that even our socialists[24] do not seem to realize the implication of their support for separate 'Ethnic Arts'. They may be well-meaning in their expedient support for the cultural activities of black people, but that does not mean that we should ignore its harmful consequences.

The issue of multiculturalism is extremely complex, and it is not my purpose here to go into this complexity. However, the question of 'Ethnic Arts' is different and it should not be confused with the need for a multicultural society. The idea of 'Ethnic Arts' has not fallen from the sky, nor was it something that was demanded by black artists or cultural workers themselves. It is part of the emerging neo-colonialism within Britain, and it is sad that 'socialists' are also instrumental in its development.

The policy of 'Ethnic Arts' has been systematically and insidiously introduced into the system, through the cultural management of the desires, aspirations, and demands of black people for equal status in this society. The Establishment had realized from the beginning that these demands would be made, and it also knew that it would be impossible to meet them within the prevailing reality or ideology. It would be in fact detrimental to the political power of both the major parties: Labour and Tory. So, what was to be done? The demands could not be ignored indefinitely. The idea of a black functionary class, a buffer, is not a new thing in the colonial apparatus. *When chickens come home to roost, you don't let them inside the house.* The creation of black functionaries (well-versed in antiracist rhetorics, almost ignorant or mediocre in artistic matters, intellectually timid ...), who would speak on behalf of their respective African, Asian, or Caribbean communities, dealing only with their specific different needs, would do the job. This, in turn, would help disenfranchise black people in terms of their demands for equal power within the dominant culture or mainstream as they would be turned into *minority* cultural entities. And thus emerges a *new* 'primitive' within Western metropolises, no longer a Freudian unconscious, but physically present within the dominant culture as *an exotic*, with all the paraphernalia of grotesque sensuality, vulgar entertainments ...

A voice: your culture still has spirituality, why bother with our sick and material world?

Another voice: I would have thought that you would have preferred to be outside the history (of art).

The pyramid of Western civilization, built on top of all the cultures of the world, is thus yet again saved from the onslaught of the 'primitive' outsider. For centuries Western civilization not only occupied the summit, but also formed its own crust all around this pyramid; the rationality of the Enlightenment turning the whole thing into a white monolith. But as this rationality began to falter by the end of the nineteenth century and there appeared cracks on the surface of the monolith, it seems that other cultures poured out of its repressed interior, its unconscious. This indeed fascinated the Western artist, the avant-garde of the world, who is always present on such historic occasions. What poured out of the cracks, with all the exotic forms and colours, was something that had been deliberately kept hidden away from him all those years. Overwhelmed by his new 'discovery', he cursed all those who put him into the chains of rationality, deprived him of the sensuous pleasures of the unconscious, and thus prevented him from becoming a free and complete *man*. Dazzled as he was with his new insight into humanity, he began to play with his newly discovered material. His new-found creativity turned the material into patchwork that covered the whole pyramid. The history of these patchworks is the history of twentieth-century modern art with all its radicalism and internationalism. But under these patchworks, we see the same order, same hierarchy, same Eurocentric ideas, values, and attitudes. It is no wonder that the History of Modern Art remains an exclusive territory of the west, accessible only to the children of the Enlightenment. The Other remains perpetually outside history.

The great monolith is now covered with patchworks of every conceivable form and colour, shape and material, high technology intermingling with the material from so-called 'primitive' cultures, forming a great spectacle which is as fascinating to watch as *The Triumph of the West*.[25] Even before the final episode of this BBC film, its narrator has already said that we in the West have perhaps failed in the ideas of the Enlightenment and the real triumph will perhaps be in the East.[26] What he is suggesting is to me another slippery slope. The idea of building wedges into the cracks looks more interesting.

NOTES

1. I am indeed grateful to Susan Hiller for this invitation.

2. The idea of 'Ethnic Arts' was first suggested by Naseem Khan in her book (1976) *The Art Britain Ignores*, London: jointly sponsored by the Commission for Community Relations, the Gulbenkian Foundation, and the Arts Council of Great Britain.

3. Edward W. Said (1978) *Orientalism*, London: Routledge & Kegan Paul. Said here refers to the work of Harry Bracken (Winter 1973) 'Essence, accident and race', *Hermathena* 116.

4. David Dabydeen has pointed to the ambivalence of black images in Hogarth's work in his book (1985) *Hogarth's Blacks: Images of Blacks in Eighteenth-Century English Art*, Denmark/England: Dangaroo Press.

5. '"Primitivism" in 20th Century Art', New York, Museum of Modern Art. A massive catalogue (two volumes) under the same title was published to accompany the exhibition (1984).

6. Masculine gender here is deliberately used to emphasize the (white) male domination of modernist discourse.

7. I have particularly in mind Frantz Fanon, Edward Said, Gayatri C. Spivak, and Homi Bhabha.

8. The sculptures are *Mumuye* from Nigeria, *Dogan* from Mali, *Boyo* from Zaire, *Luba* from Zaire, reproduced in the MOMA catalogue (n. 5) on pp. 43, 50, 56, and 161 respectively.

9. Said, op. cit.

10. I am thinking particularly of the achievements of Egyptian, Chinese, Indian, and Islamic civilizations.

11. I am not proposing an essentialist view. My remarks should be read in the context of modern capitalism.

12. Robert Nisbet (1980) *History of the Ideas of Progress*, London: Heinemann. Nisbet here refers to the work of George L. Mosse, *Towards the Final Solution: A History of European Racism*.

13. Partha Mitter (1977) *Much Maligned Monsters*, Oxford: Clarendon Press.

14. ibid.

15. Nisbet, op. cit.

16. The word 'black' is used throughout this chapter for people of both African and Asian origins, who live in the west and whose status is often determined by white racism.

17. Drawing as basic to good painting or sculpture is not Fuller's own original idea. It is an accepted fact in western art; and an emphasis on *freehand* drawing can also be found in the early writing of John Berger. However, what Peter Fuller is now proposing is for the development of nationalist British art which is grounded in the experience of English pastoral traditions and which is free from foreign influences, in total disregard of the reality of a multicultural British society. Fuller, in fact, represents a pathetic aspect of a common English phenomenon which begins its intellectual life with extreme left and ends with extreme right.

18. Some of the towns and cities where open confrontation between the police and black communities took place in recent years, resulting in street riots.

19. Rasheed Araeen (1984) *Making Myself Visible*, London: Kala Press.

20. See Jenny Bourne's essay (1984) 'Cheerleaders and ombudsman: the sociology of race relations in Britain', *Race & Class* XXI, 4.

21. Homi Bhabha (November/December 1983) 'The other question – the stereotype and colonial discourse', *Screen* 24.

22. Araeen, op. cit.

23. Martin Barker (1981) *The New Racism: Conservatives and the Ideology of the Tribe*, London: Junction Books.

24. Most art institutions and funding bodies now recognize and support the category of 'Ethnic Arts', but the GLC's initiative and support in this respect is worth special attention [editors' note: The Greater London Council was shortly afterwards disbanded by the Thatcher government]. A large amount of public money was dispensed by merely employing a staff of black functionaries (under the policy of positive discrimination) who had nothing to do with the arts; in fact, the money was wasted through gross ignorance, inefficiency, and nepotism, and in many cases preference was given in support of community projects which were meant to enhance the Labour Party's electoral position in the black community.

25. *The Triumph of the West*, a BBC film series written and narrated by the historian J. M. Roberts, which traced the history of Western civilization going back to the Greeks.

26. His reference here is to Japan's post-war economic success.

5.

Museums are Good to Think:
Heritage on View in India

Arjun Appadurai and Carol A. Breckenridge

One of the striking facts about complex societies such as India is that they have not surrendered learning principally to the formal institutions of schooling. In this type of complex society, urban groups tend to monopolize postsecondary schooling and the upper middle class tends to control the colleges and universities. In such societies, therefore, learning is more often tied to practical apprenticeship and informal socialization. Also, and not coincidentally, these are societies in which history and heritage are not yet parts of a bygone past that is institutionalized in history books and museums. Rather, heritage is a live component of the human environment and thus a critical part of the learning process. These observations are particularly worth noting since societies such as India are often criticized for having created educational institutions where learning does not thrive and where credential-ism has become a mechanical mode for selection in an extremely difficult economic context. Informal means of learning in societies such as India are not, therefore, mere ethnographic curiosities. They are real cultural resources that (properly understood and used) may well relieve the many artificial pressures placed upon the formal educational structure. Museums are an emergent component of this world of informal education, and what we learn about museums in India will tell us much of value about learning, seeing, and objects, which in turn should encourage creative and critical approaches to museums (and informal learning arrangements in general) elsewhere.

Museums in India look simultaneously in two directions. They are a part of a transnational order of cultural forms that has emerged in the last two centuries and now unites much of the world, especially its urban areas.[1] Museums also belong to the alternative forms of modern life and thought that are emerging in nations and societies throughout the world. These alternative forms tend to be associated with media, leisure, and spectacle, are often associated with self-conscious national approaches to heritage, and are tied up with transnational ideologies of development, citizenship, and cosmopolitanism. Conducting an investigation of museums, therefore, entails being sensitive to a shared transnational idiom for the handling of heritage while simultaneously being aware that this heritage can take very different national forms.

Museums and heritage

Although there is a growing literature (largely by scholars outside the museum world) that concentrates on museums, collecting, objects, and heritage, these discussions do not generally extend to museums in India. Our concern is to build on a few recent efforts in this direction as well as some earlier ones,[2] so that comparative evidence from non-Western, post-colonial societies can be brought into the mainstream of theory and method in this area.

In anthropology, there is a renewed interest in objects, consumption, and collection more generally.[3] What emerges from the literature on this topic is that objects in collections create a complex dialogue between the classificatory concerns of connoisseurs and the self-reflective politics of communities; that the presence of objects in museums represents one stage in the objects' cultural biographies;[4] and that such classified objects can be critical parts of the 'marketing of heritage'.[5] Here we are reminded that objects' meanings have always reflected a negotiated settlement between long-standing cultural significations and more volatile group interests and objectives.

A related set of discussions explicitly links museums to material culture in a consciously historical way.[6] We are reminded that archaeological and ethnographical collections emerged out of a specific set of political and pedagogical aims in the history of anthropology;[7] that collections and exhibitions cannot be divorced from the larger cultural contexts of philanthropy and ethnic or national identity formation; that anthropologists and 'natives' are increasingly engaged in a dialogue out of which cultural identity emerges; and that museums contribute to the larger process by which popular culture is formed. As far as India is concerned, museums seem less a product of philanthropy and more a product of the conscious agenda of India's British rulers, which led them to excavate, classify, catalogue, and display India's artifactual past to itself. This difference affects the ethos of Indian museums today, and also affects the cultural dynamics of viewing and learning.

Another relevant body of literature emphasizes the relationship between museums and their publics as well as their educational mission.[8] For the most part, these studies lack a sense of the historical and cultural specificity of the different publics that museums serve. While the public sphere has been most richly discussed in terms of the last three hundred years in Europe,[9] there are now a host of non-Western nations that are elaborating their public spheres – not necessarily ones that emerge in relation to civil society, but often ones that are the result of state policies in tandem with consumerist interests. Thus, there is a tendency in these discussions for the idea of 'the public' to become tacitly universalized (through some of these studies are concerned with sociological variations within visitor populations). What is needed is the identification of a specific historical and cultural public, one which does not so much *respond* to museums but is rather *created*, in part, through museums and other related institutions. In India, museums need not worry so much about finding their publics as about making them.

There is, of course, a vast body of literature that is about art in relation to museums. This literature is not very relevant to the Indian situation because, except for a small minority in India and for a very short period of its history, and in very few museums there, art in the current Western sense is not a meaningful category. Art continues to struggle to find a (bourgeois) landscape it can be comfortable in.[10] In place of art, other categories for objects dominate, such as handicraft, technology, history, and heritage. Of these, the one on which we focus is the category of heritage.

History becomes heritage in various ways.[11] Artifacts become appropriated by particular historical agendas, by particular ideologies of preservation, by specific versions of public history, and by particular values about exhibition, design and display. Tony Bennett's concept of 'the exhibitionary complex'[12] and Donna Haraway's argument that natural history has the effect of naturalizing particular histories[13] both remind us that museums are deeply located *in* cultural history, on the one hand, and are therefore also critical places for the politics *of* history, on the other. Ideologies of preservation might frequently conceal implications for transformation.[14] For example, the effort to present vignettes of life from other societies often involves the decontextualization of objects from their everyday contexts, with the unintended result of creating aesthetic and stylistic effects that do not fit the original context. In other cases, objects that were parts of living dramas of warfare, exchange, or marriage become mechanical indicators of culture or custom. In yet other cases, the politics of cultural patrimony and political conquest are concealed in the technical language of ethnographic signage. All of these examples reveal a tension between the dynamic contexts from which objects were originally derived and the static tendencies inherent to museum environments. This is a valuable tension to bear in mind as we explore the context of museums in India, where the politics of heritage is often intense, even violent.

Among anthropologists, folklorists, and historians, there has recently been a spate of writing about the politics of heritage.[15] Much of this work suggests (in some cases using non-Euro-American examples) that the appropriation of the past by actors in the present is subject to a variety of dynamics. These range from the problems associated with ethnicity and social identity, nostalgia, and the search for 'museumized' authenticity, to the tension between the interests states have in fixing local identities and the pressures localities exert in seeking to transform such identities. The result is a number of contradictory pressures, some toward fixing and stabilizing group identities through museums (and the potential of their artifacts to be used to emblematize existing or emergent group identities), and others that attempt to free and destabilize these identities through different ways of displaying and viewing objects.

This body of literature is a reminder that heritage is increasingly a profoundly political issue and one in which localities and states are often at odds, and that museums and their collections are in the midst of this particular storm. Focusing on the politics of heritage in India brings out the place of Indian museums in these politics, and problematizes the cultural modes of viewing, traveling, experiencing, and learning in which heritage is negotiated.

The cultural and conceptual background

The public sphere in contemporary India, as in the rest of the world, has emerged as part of the political, intellectual, and commercial interests of its middle classes. In India in the last century, this public sphere has involved new forms of democratic politics, new modes of communication and transport, and new ways in which class, caste, and livelihood are articulated. We are concerned with one dimension of this evolving public sphere, which we call public culture. By public culture we mean a new cosmopolitan arena that is a 'zone of contestation',[16] and different classes and groups formulate, represent, and debate what culture is (and should be). Public culture is articulated and revealed in an interactive set of cosmopolitan experiences and structures, of which museums and exhibitions are a crucial part.

On the surface, museums as modern institutions have only a short history and appear to emerge largely out of the colonial period:

The museums started under British rule had been intended mainly for the preservation of the vestiges of a dying past, and only subsidiarily as a preparation for the future. Museums were the last haven of refuge for interesting architectual fragments, sculptures and inscriptions which saved them from the hands of an ignorant and indifferent public or from unscrupulous contractors who would have burned them to lime, sunk them into foundations or melted them down. Into the museums the products of the declining indigenous industries were accumulated, in the vain hope that they might serve as models for the inspiration of artisans and the public. Mineralogical, botanical, zoological and ethnological collections were likewise started, though rarely developed systematically: often they did not grow beyond sets of hunting trophies.[17]

As a consequence, until recently most museums in India have been moribund and have not been a vibrant part of the public cultural life of its people. One early analysis of this 'failure' of museums in India comes from Hermann Goetz. The factors he identifies as reasons for this failure include the fragmentary nature of many collections, the failure of industrial art to inspire capitalist production, and the lack of response to natural-history collections by a public 'still living in the world of myths'.[18]

The ambiguous place of museums in India is partly a result of long-standing cultural and historical factors: first, India still has a living past found especially in its sacred places and spaces, so there is little need for 'artificial' conservation of the Indian heritage; second, the separation of sacred objects (whether of art, history, or religion) from the objects of everyday life had not really occurred; and third, the separation of human beings from the overall biological, zoological, and cosmological environment in which they lead their ordinary lives had barely begun.

More recently, museums have begun to play a more vigorous role in Indian public life. In part this is because of a renewed concern with education as one element of social and economic development; in part because private commercial enterprises have begun to use an exhibition format for displaying their wares; and in part because museums have become plugged into a circuit of travel, tourism, pilgrimage, and leisure that has its own distinctive history and value in Indian society.

Here it may be useful to make a historical contrast. Museums in Europe and the United States have been linked to department stores through a common genealogy in the great nineteenth-century world's fairs. But in the last century, a separation of art and science and of festivity and commerce has taken place in these societies, with the objects and activities in each category fairly sharply distinguished in terms of audience, curatorial expertise, and visual ideology. In India, such a specialization and separation are not a part of either the past or the present.

This is not to say that there are not department and chain stores in contemporary India. There are, and they are clearly distinguishable from public festivities as well as from permanent exhibits in museums. Rather, there is a gray zone where display, retailing, and festivity shade into one another. It is precisely because of this gray zone that museums have taken on fresh life; objects in India seem to flow constantly through the membranes that separate commerce, pageantry, and display. The two major forms that characterize the public world of special objects in contemporary India are the exhibition-cum-sale and the ethnic-national festival. The exhibition-cum-sale is a major mode of retailing textiles, ready-to-wear clothing, books, and home appliances. These merchandizing spectacles (which recall the fairs of medieval Europe) are transient, low-overhead, mobile modes for transporting, displaying, and selling a variety of goods. In them, in contrast to department stores, ordinary consumers have a chance to combine gazing, longing, and buying. This combination of activities, which is at the core of the informal schooling of the modern Indian consumer, is bracketed between two other, more permanent poles. One pole is the modern museum – whether of art, craft, science, or archaeology – in which the Indian viewer's visual literacy is harnessed to explicitly cultural and nationalist purposes. The other pole is the newly emergent, Western-style department store, where gazing and viewing also go on but buying is the normative goal. In our usage, *gazing* implies an open-ended visual and sensory engagement tired up with fantasy and desire for the objects on display, while *viewing* implies a more narrowly framed, signage-guided visual orientation.

Framing these three display forms and contributing most actively to the regeneration of the museum experience is the festival form, especially as it has been harnessed by the Indian state in its effort to define national, regional, and ethnic identity. Such festivals are on the increase throughout the world[19] and everywhere represent ongoing debates concerning emergent group identities and group artifacts.

In India, the museum-oriented Festival of India, first constructed in 1985 as a vehicle for the cultural display of India in foreign nations and cities, quickly became indigenized into a massive internal festival called Apna Utsav (Our Festival), which began in 1986 and now has an elaborate national and regional administrative structure. Part of a vast state-sponsored network for local and interregional displays of art, craft, folklore, and clothing, these spectacles of ethnicity are also influencing the cultural literacy and visual curiosity of ordinary Indians in a manner that gives further support to the reinvigoration of museums, on the one hand, and the vitality of exhibition-cum-sales, on the other. What is thus emerging in India, and seems to be a relatively specialized cultural complex, is a world of objects and experiences that ties together visual pleasure, ethnic and national display, and consumer appetite. Museums, marginal in the eyes of the wider Indian public in the last century, have taken on a new role in the last decade as part of this emergent constellation of phenomena.

This constellation, which may be called the 'exhibition complex' (museum-festival-sale), is further energized by new technologies of leisure, information, and movement in contemporary India. Cinema and television (and the landscapes and stars that they display), packaged pilgrimages and tours (which take thousands of ordinary Indians outside their normal locales as part of 'vacation' experiences), and the growing spectacularization of political and sports events (especially through television), all conduce to a new cosmopolitan receptivity to the museum, which would otherwise have become a dusty relic of colonial rule. It is these new contexts of public culture that are now transforming the Indian museum experience.

The photographs in this essay constitute a narrative parallel to the text. They provide a representative visual sample of the archive of visual experiences that Indian visitors bring to museums. They are meant to convey the points of contact between different segments of Indian visual reality, which range from film and television images to mythic and political scenarios, and constitute the 'interocular field' within which the museum experience operates and to which we refer in the conclusion.

Museums in India have to be seen in tandem with exhibitions of several sorts, and as parts of a larger cosmopolitan world of leisure, recreation, and self-education for wide sectors of the Indian population. Nothing of this emergent cosmopolitanism can be grasped without also understanding the impact that modern modes of communication have had on Indian public life. Print media, especially newspapers and magazines, have a history going back over a century in India (as in the West) but the last decade has seen an explosion of magazines and newspapers (both in English and in the vernacular languages), which suggests both a quantum leap in Indian readers' thirst for news, views, and opinion and the eagerness of cultural producers to satisfy this thirst profitably. Film (both documentary and commercial) has a history in India that clearly parallels its history in the West, and remains today the dominant medium through which large numbers of Indians expend time and money allotted to entertainment. Television and its sister technology, video recordings, have entered India in a big way and constitute a new threat to the cultural hegemony of cinema, while at the same time they extend the reach of cinematic forms to the smaller towns and poorer citizens of India.

Though Indian television programming is controlled by the state (just as radio programming is), it already has a very large component of privately produced soap operas, docudramas, and other forms of televised entertainment. This is, of course, in addition to a fairly large amount of state-sponsored and state-controlled programming, which ranges from news programs (which are still largely state-controlled) to live sports programs, 'cultural performances', and informational programs on everything from birth control to new farming techniques. In general, though a number of the most popular serials on Indian television are variations of the Hindi film formula, many television programs have a historical, cultural, or documentary dimension. In television above all, it is the Indian heritage that is turned into spectacle. The most striking examples of this process are the three most popular trials and tribulations of the partition of India as experienced by a large Punjabi extended family, and the television serializations of the two great Indian epics, the *Ramayana* and the *Mahabharata*, for the weekly broadcast of which the whole television-watching audience of India apparently dropped everything. Thus, museums are part of a generalized, mass-media-provoked preoccupation with heritage and with a richly visual approach to spectacles.

Museums and public culture

In countries such as India, the challenge of training skilled teachers, the rudimentary resources available for primary and secondary education, and the bureaucratization and politicization of higher education, all mean that education outside formal settings has continued to be crucial to the formation of the modern citizen. Such education – which involves learning the habits, values, and skills of the contemporary world – happens through a variety of processes and frameworks, including those of the family, the workplace, friendship networks, leisure activities, and media exposure. Museums and the exhibition complex in general form an increasingly important part of this non-formal educational process, the logic of which has been insufficiently studied, especially outside the West.

Museums are also a very complex part of the story of Western expansion since the sixteenth century, although they are now part of the cultural apparatus of most emergent nations. Museums have complex roots in such phenomena as cabinets of curiosities, collections of regalia, and dioramas of public spectacle.[20] Today, museums reflect complex mixtures of state and private motivation and patronage, and tricky transnational problems of ownership, identity, and the politics of heritage. Thus museums, which frequently represent national identities both at home and abroad, are also nodes of transnational representation and repositories for subnational flows of objects and images. Museums, in concert with media and travel, serve as ways in which national and international publics learn about themselves and others.

Museums provide an interesting contrast with travel, for in museums people travel short distances in order to experience cultural, geographical, and temporal distance, whereas contemporary tourists often travel great distances in short spaces of time to experience 'otherness' in a more intense and dramatic manner. But both are organized ways to explore the worlds and things of the 'other'. In the public cultures of nations such as India, both museums and tourism have an important domestic dimension, since they provide ways in which national populations can conceptualize their own diversity and reflect (in an objectified way) on their diverse cultural practices and histories. Such reflexivity, of course, has its roots in the colonial experience, during which Indians were subject to a thoroughgoing classification, museumification, and aestheticization in the museums, fairs, and exhibitions of the nineteenth and early twentieth centuries.[21] Finally, both museums and travel in India today would be hard to imagine apart from a fairly elaborate media infrastructure, as has been suggested already.

The media are relevant to museums and exhibitions in specific ways. For example, verbal literacy affects the ways in which people who come to museums and exhibitions are able to understand the objects (and signage) that are at the center of them. Thus, the issue of the ability to read is critical. Media are also important in the form of advertising, particularly through billboards, newspaper advertisements, and television coverage, which in many cases inform people about exhibitions (especially those associated with national and regional cultural representations). Literacy (both verbal and visual) is also relevant to the ways in which pamphlets, photographs, and posters associated with museums are read by various publics as they travel through different regions, visit various sites, and purchase inexpensive printed publicity materials associated with museums, monuments, and religious centers. Exposure to the media affects as well the ways in which particular groups and individuals frame their readings of particular sites and objects, since media exposure often provides the master narratives within which the mini-narratives of particular exhibitions and museums are interpreted. Thus, for example, the National Museum in Delhi and its various counterparts in the other major cities of India offer specific narratives of the colonial, precolonial, and postcolonial periods (for example, the classification of the tribal as 'primitive').

Viewers do not come to these museums as cultural blanks. They come as persons who have seen movies with nationalist themes, television serials with nationalist and mythological narratives and images, and newspapers and magazines that also construct and visualize the heroes and grand events of Indian history and mythology.

In addition, it is important to reiterate that the museum experience is part and parcel of learning to be cosmopolitan and 'modern'. This learning process has a consumption (as well as a media) dimension. Whether for city dwellers or for villagers, the experience of visiting museums is always implicitly connected to the consumption of leisure and pleasure. As regimented as many groups visiting Indian museums may seem, visits to museums and exhibitions are part of the pleasures of seeing, and visual pleasure has a very deep and special logic in the Indian context. In the annual traveling commercial exhibition known as the Ideal Home Exhibition, for example, the mastery of modern modes of domestic technology and lifestyle is the key to the exhibition experience, even for those who do not actually buy anything.

There is a complex dialectic among the experiences that Indians have in the ethnic-national museums (that is, museums where national heritage and ethnic identity are key concerns), in art museums, and in commercial exhibitions. In each case, they are being educated in different forms of cultural literacy: in the first case, they are being educated in the objectified narratives of nationality and ethnicity; in the second case, in the experience of cosmopolitan aesthetics; and in the third case, in the habits and values of the modern, high-tech householder. These three forms of cultural literacy play a central role in the construction of the modern Indian, who is drawn into the visual and auditory narratives of modern citizenship by his or her experiences in museums and exhibitions. The outstanding question is, how does the museum and exhibition experience help create such cultural literacy?

A major theoretical cue comes from what has been called 'reception theory',[22] a body of ideas developed largely out of postwar German neo-Marxism, but now modified by interaction with reader-response theory and associated approaches to problems of audience analysis in mass-media studies. From this rather diffuse and developing body of theory, four hypotheses can be suggested as especially relevant to those postcolonial societies outside the Euro-American axis, such as India, in which nationalism, consumerism, and leisure have become simultaneous features of contemporary life for important segments of the population. We see these hypotheses as particularly applicable to societies such as India, since in them the connoisseurship of 'art' as a distinct category is relatively undeveloped, the visiting of museums is not sharply separated from other forms of leisure and learning, and the idea of expert documentation and credentials in the interpretation of objects has not displaced the sense that viewer groups are entitled to formulate their own interpretations.

The first hypothesis is that sacralized objects and spaces generate specialized modes of viewing and interaction, which are likely to be rooted in historically deeper modalities of seeing as a cultural practice. In the Indian case, there is a considerable literature showing that the mutual gaze (*darsan*) of sacred persons or objects and their audiences creates bonds of intimacy and allegiance that transcend the specifics of what is displayed or narrativized in any given context.[23] The faculty of sight creates special bonds between seer and seen. Museum-viewing may be expected, therefore, to display some transformation of this long-standing cultural convention.

The second is that the reception of specialized sites and spaces is a profoundly communal experience, and the objects and landscapes of museums are viewed by 'communities of interpretation'[24] in which the isolated viewer or connoisseur is a virtually absent type. Thus, in any museum or exhibition in India (with the possible exception of certain museums devoted to 'modern' art) the lonely and private gaze that we can often observe at places such as the Museum of Modern Art in New York is absent. Viewing and interpretation are profoundly communal acts.

The third hypothesis is that viewers are not likely to be passive and empty receivers of the cultural information contained in exhibitions and museums. Rather, as in all societies, they come with complex ideas of what is likely to be seen, and share this knowledge in highly interactive ways among themselves and with those few 'experts' who are cast in the role of explainers. Thus museums and exhibitions are frequently characterized not by silent observation and internal reflection, but by a good deal of dialogue and interaction among the viewers, as well as between them and whoever is playing the role of guide. Here the museum experience is not only visual and interactional, it is also profoundly dialogic; that is to say, it is an experience in which cultural literacy emerges out of dialogues in which knowledge, taste, and response are publicly negotiated among persons with very diverse backgrounds and expertise. In many cases, the near-absence in Indian museums of docents and the underdevelopment of the idea that exhibited objects need to be explained (either by signage or by guides or docents) create a much wider space for discourse and negotiation among viewers: viewers are left free to assimilate new objects and arrangements into their own prior repertoires of knowledge, taste, and fantasy. Such freedom characterizes a great many Indian museums, even those in which there is a strong effort to determine viewer interpretations, but is true only of smaller, less intensively curated, less well-funded museums in the contemporary United States and Europe. There is thus a profound tension between the museum or exhibition as a site of defamiliarization, where things are made to look strange, and the viewer-dominated process of dialogue and interpretation, which familiarizes cosmopolitan forms and narratives into larger master narratives from other arenas of public life, such as travel, sport, and cinema. Thus, the museum experience has to be understood as a dialogue moment in a larger process of creating cultural literacy, in which other media-influenced narratives play a massive role.

Fourth, the responses of viewers, gazers, and buyers vary significantly, along at least two axes: (1) the type of exhibition or museum to which they are exposed; and (2) personal characteristics, such as the class, ethnic group, and age group to which they belong. These differences create significant variations within a larger common structure that is predictable from the previous three theoretical assumptions. Since the study of reception is in a general way not highly developed and is especially poorly developed for the study of readerships outside Europe and the United States (and even less so for reception in contexts such as museums), further examination of the exhibition complex could make a significant contribution to more general methodological debates.

Much of the structure, organization, taxonomy, and signage strategy of Indian museums is colonial in origin. Thus while the *contexts* of current museum-viewing may require new applications of reception theory, the *texts* contained in many museums (that is, the collections and their associated signage) require the analysis of colonial modes of knowledge and classification.

Conclusions

Like many other phenomena of the contemporary world, museums in contemporary India have both internal and external logics. As far as the rest of the world is concerned, there is no denying that museums constitute part of an 'exhibitionary complex'[25] in which spectacle, discipline, and state power become interlinked with questions of entertainment, education, and control. It is also true that museums everywhere seem to be increasingly caught up with mass-media experiences.[26] Finally, museums everywhere seem to be booming as the 'heritage industry'[27] takes off.

In India, each of these global impulses has crosscut a particular colonial and postcolonial trajectory in which new visual formations link heritage politics to spectacle, tourism, and entertainment. In making this link, it seems that older Indian modes of seeing and viewing are being gradually transformed and spectacularized. While the investigation of the museum experience in India is only in its infancy, we would like to suggest that it will need to focus especially on the deep interdependence of various sites and modes of seeing, including those involved in television, cinema, sport, and tourism. Each of these sites and modes offers new settings for the development of a contemporary public gaze in Indian life. The gaze of Indian viewers in museums is certainly caught up in what we would call this interocular field (the allusion here, of course, is to intertextuality, as the concept is used by the Russian literary theorist Mikhail Bakhtin). This interocular field is structured so that each site or setting for the disciplining of the public gaze is to some degree affected by viewers' experiences of the other sites. This interweaving of ocular experiences, which also subsumes the substantive transfer of meanings, scripts, and symbols from one site to another in surprising ways, is the critical feature of the cultural field within which museum-viewing in contemporary India needs to be located. Our effort in this paper has been to argue for the importance of such an interocular approach to museums in India, and perhaps everywhere else in the contemporary world where museums are enjoying a fresh, postcolonial revival.

NOTES

1. See, for example, Arjun Appadurai, 'The global ethnoscape: notes and queries for a transnational anthropology', in R. G. Fox (ed.), *Recapturing Anthropology: Working in the Present* (Santa Fe, NM: School of American Research, 1991).

2. For a more recent work, see Carol A. Breckenridge, 'The aesthetics and politics of colonial collecting: India at world fairs', *Comparative Studies in Society and History* 31(2) (1989): 195–216. Earlier efforts include Ray Desmond, *The India Museum, 1801–1809* (London: Her Majesty's Stationery Office, 1982); Hermann Goetz, 'The Baroda Museum and Picture Gallery', *Museum* 7(1) (1954): 15–19; and Grace Morley, 'Museums in India', *Museum* 18(4) (1965): 220–60.

3. Arjun Appadurai (ed.), *The Social Life of Things: Commodities in Cultural Perspective* (Cambridge: Cambridge University Press, 1986); Burton Benedict (ed.), *The Anthropology of World's Fairs: San Francisco's Panama Pacific International Exposition of 1915* (Berkeley: Scolar, 1983); James Clifford, *The Predicament of Culture: Twentieth-Century Ethnography, Literature, and Art* (Cambridge, MA: Harvard University Press, 1988); Virginia R. Dominguez, 'The marketing of heritage', *American Ethnologist* 13(3) (1986); 546–66; Nelson H. H. Graburn, (ed.), *Ethnic and Tourist Arts: Cultural Expressions from the Fourth World* (Berkeley: University of California Press, 1976).

4. Igor Kopytoff, 'The cultural biography of things: commoditization as process', in Arjun Appadurai (ed.), *The Social Life of Things: Commodities in Cultural Perspective* (Cambridge: Cambridge University Press, 1986).

5. Dominguez, 'The marketing of heritage', *American Ethnologist* 13(3) (1986): 54–66.

6. Michael Ames, *Museums, the Public, and Anthropology: A Study in the Anthropology of Anthropology* (Vancouver: University of British Columbia Press, 1986); Douglas Cole, *Captured Heritage: The Scramble for Northwest Coast Artifacts* (Vancouver: Douglas & McIntyre, 1985); Neil Harris, 'Museums, merchandising, and popular taste: the struggle for influence', in Ian M. G. Quimby (ed.), *Material Culture and the Study of American Life* (New York: Norton, 1978); Masatoshi Konishi, 'The museum and Japanese studies', *Current Anthropology* 28(4) (1987): S96–S101; Mark P. Leone, Parker B. Potter, Jr, and Paul A. Shackel, 'Toward a Critical Archaeology', *Current Anthropology* 28(3) (1987): 283–302; Ian M. G. Quimby (ed.), *Material Culture and the Study of*

American Life (New York: Norton, 1978); George W. Stocking, Jr, *Objects and Others: Essays on Museums and Material Culture*, History of Anthropology, Vol. 3 (Madison: University of Wisconsin Press, 1985).

7. Leone, Potter, and Shackel, 'Toward a Critical Archaeology', *Current Anthropology* 28(3) (1987): 283–302.

8. W. S. Hendon, F. Costa, and R. A. Rosenberg, 'The general public and the art museum: case studies of visitors to several institutions identify characteristics of their publics', *American Journal of Economics and Sociology* 48(2) (1989): 231–43; Kenneth Hudson, *Museums of Influence* (Cambridge: Cambridge University Press, 1987); Leone, Potter, and Shackel, 'Toward a critical archaeology'; Michael H. Frisch and Dwight Pithcaithley, 'Audience expectations as resource and challenge: Ellis Island as case study', in Jo Blatti (ed.), *Past Meets Present: Essays about Historic Interpretation and Public Audiences* (Washington, DC: Smithsonian Institution Press, 1987); Elliot W. Eisner and Stephen M. Dobbs, 'Museum education in twenty American art museums', *Museum News* 64(2) (1986): 42–9; Danielle Rice, 'On the ethics of Museum education', *Museum News* 65(5) (1987): 13–19; Sheldon Annis, 'The museum as staging ground for symbolic action', *Museum* 38(3) (1986): 168–71.

9. Jürgen Habermas, *The Structural Transformation of the Public Sphere: An Inquiry into a Category of Bourgeois Society*, trans. Thomas Burger with the assistance of Frederick Lawrence (Cambridge, MA: MIT Press, 1989).

10. Cf. Pierre Bourdieu, *Distinction: A Social Critique of the Judgement of Taste*, trans. Richard Nice (Cambridge, MA: Harvard University Press, 1984).

11. Robert Lumley (ed.), *The Museum Time-Machine: Putting Cultures on Display* (New York: Routledge, 1988); Jo Blatti (ed.), *Past Meets Present: Essays about Historic Interpretation and Public Audiences* (Washington, DC: Smithsonian Institution Press, 1987); Robert Hewison, *The Heritage Industry: Britain in a Climate of Decline* (London: Methuen, 1987); Donald Horne, *The Great Museum: The Re-Presentation of History* (London: Pluto, 1984).

12. Tony Bennett, 'The exhibitionary complex', *New Formations* 4 (1988) [reproduced in this volume]: 73–102.

13. Donna Haraway, 'Teddy bear patriarchy: taxidermy in the Garden of Eden, 1908–1936', *Social Text* 11 (Winter 1984–5) [an excerpt from which is reproduced in this volume]: 20–64.

14. See Blatti, *Past Meets Present*, especially the following essays therein: Michael J. Ettema, 'History museums and the culture of materialism'; Jane Greengold, 'What might have been and what has been – fictional public art about the real past'; and Michael Wallace, 'The politics of public history'.

15. Shelly Errington, 'Fragile traditions and contested meaning', *Public Culture* 1(2) (1989): 49–59; Richard Handler, *Nationalism and the Politics of Culture in Quebec* (Madison: University of Wisconsin Press, 1988); Michael Herzfeld, *Ours Once More: Folklore, Ideology, and the Making of Modern Greece* (Austin: University of Texas Press, 1982); Eric Hobsbawm and Terence Ranger (eds), *The Invention of Tradition* (Cambridge: Cambridge University Press, 1983); Richard Johnson et al. (eds), *Making Histories: Studies in History-Writing and Politics* (London: Hutchinson, 1982); William W. Kelly, 'Rationalization and nostalgia: cultural dynamics of new middle class Japan', *American Ethnologist* 13(4) (1986): 603–18; Jocelyn S. Linnekin, 'Defining tradition: variations on the Hawaiian identity', *American Ethnologist* 10(2) (1983): 241–52; David Whisnant, *All That Is Native & Fine: The Politics of Culture in an American Region* (Chapel Hill: University of North Carolina Press, 1983).

16. Arjun Appadurai and Carol A. Breckenridge, 'Why public culture?', *Public Culture* 1(1) (1988): 5–9.

17. Hermann Goetz, 'The Baroda Museum and Picture Gallery', *Museum* 7(1) (1954): 15.

18. ibid.

19. For example, see Richard Handler, *Nationalism and the Politics of Culture in Quebec* (Madison: University of Wisconsin Press, 1988).

20. See Richard Altick, *The Shows of London* (Cambridge, MA: Harvard University Press, 1978) for descriptions of these dioramas in the development of museums in England.

21. C. A. Breckenridge, 'The aesthetics and politics of colonial collecting'.

22. For example, Jane Feuer, 'Reading *Dynasty*: television and reception theory', *South Atlantic Quarterly* 88(2) (1989): 443–60.

23. For example, Diana L. Eck, *Darshan: Seeing the Divine Image in India*, 2nd edn (Chambersburg, PA: Anima, 1985); J. Gonda, *Eye and Gaze in the Veda* (Amsterdam: North Holland, 1969).

24. Stanley Fish, *Is There a Text in This Class? The Authority of Interpretive Communities* (Cambridge, MA: Harvard University Press, 1980).

25. Bennett, 'The exhibitionary complex'.

26. Lumley, *The Museum Time-Machine*.

27. Hewison, *The Heritage Industry*.

6.

Remaking Passports:
Visual Thought in the Debate on
Multiculturalism

Néstor García Canclini

How do we interpret the changes in contemporary visual thought? One of the greatest difficulties rests in the fact that tendencies do not develop from one paradigm to the next. We are not displacing ourselves from one type of rationality and visuality to another as in the Renaissance or in the transition from classicism to romanticism, nor as in the substitution that happened amongst the avant-gardes throughout the 20th century. A real reorganisation has emerged from the intersection of multiple, simultaneous processes. Rather than changing, art appears to be vacillating. I am going to linger over one of those fluctuations which I consider to be crucial in the debate on identities: I am referring to the oscillation between a national visuality and the deterritorialised and transcultural forms of art and communication. Concerning the basis of this analysis, we might ask ourselves what type of visual thinking can speak today significantly in the discordant dialogue between fundamentalism and globalisation.

How are artists thinking?

This is difficult to answer if we consider that the polemic at the core of the modern aesthetic, that opposition between romanticism and classicism, persists even into postmodernity. For the romantics, art is a production of the intuitive and solitary genius; in the same way, reception is defined as an act of unconditional contemplation, the empathy of an individual sensitive disposition which allows itself to be penetrated by the mysterious eloquence of the work. Classical thought, by contrast, always works to subordinate sensibility and intuition to the order of reason: artistic production should be a way of presenting multiple meanings and expand the world in relation to its forms; we the spectators see those images in diverse ways – from the different codes imprinted in us by our social and educational structures – searching for the geometry of the real or expressionistically lamenting its loss.

The history of modern art, written as the history of avant-gardes, has contributed to the maintenance of this disjunction: on one hand, Surrealism, Pop Art and 'Bad Painting', for example; and on the other, constructivism, the Bauhaus, geometricism and all the self-reflexive artists from Marcel Duchamp to the conceptualists, for whom art is a mental activity. The disillusioned farewell to the avant-gardes did not end this dichotomy; some postmoderns nostalgically pursue the order of Hellenic or Renaissance symmetry (even if it is under the sceptical-ironic form of the ruin), others place their irrationalist vocation in the enigmatic exuberance of rituals and tribal objects. In the former case, the artist as archaeologist or restorer of classical harmony; in the second, as a 'magician of the earth'. Such work, part of the hypothesis of contemporary epistemology, at least since Gaston Bachelard and Claude Lévi-Strauss, argues that the theory of art stems from the dilemma between rationalism and irrationalism. I agree with Michel Serres when he said that Bachelard is the last romantic (his cultural psychoanalysis adopted a non-positivist polysemy of meaning) and the first neo-classicist (because he reunited 'the clarity of form for freedom and the density of content for understanding').[1] His new scientific spirit coincides, up to a point, with that of Lévi-Strauss when he demonstrated that the difference between science and magic, or between science and art, is not the distance between the rational and the pre-rational, but between two types of thought, one expressed in concepts and the other submerged in images. Magic and art are not weak or babbling forms of science, but – together with it – strategic and distinct levels in which nature and society allow themselves to be attacked by questions of knowledge.[2]

The second hypothesis is that a theory of art capable of transcending the antagonism between thought and intuition could contribute to a re-elaboration of the dilemmas of the end of the century, when all the socio-cultural structures are destabilised and we ask ourselves if it is possible to construct imaginaries that do not empty into irrational arguments. We need to discover if the actual organisation of the aesthetic field (producers, museums, galleries, historians, critics and the public) contributes, and in what way, to the elaboration of shared imaginaries. It is not only the wit of a picture or the will of the artist that is inserted in or isolated from social history; it is also the interaction between the diverse members of the field (as both cultural system and market) which situates the significance of art in the vacillating meaning of the world.[3] In posing the problem in this way it is possible to include in the question something about how art thinks today, even its innovative gestures: what capacity to think about a world orphaned of paradigms do transgressive or deconstructive works possess that are submitted to the order of the museums and the market?

Our third hypothesis is that this contribution of art is enabled by tendencies which are not only dedicated to thinking about the national but also to multiculturalism and globalisation. It seems unattractive to elaborate this theme from the perspective of Latin American art, because many artists are moving in that direction; but the strategies of the market, of international exhibitions and of the critics almost always banish it to the margins as the magic realism of local colour. Even when our people migrate extensively and a large part of our art work and literature is dedicated to *thinking* about the multicultural, Latin America continues to be interesting only as a continent of a violent nature, of an archaicism irreducible to modern nationality, an earth fertilised by an art conceived as tribal or national dreaming and not as thinking about the global and the complex.

How is the nation thinking, how is the market thinking?

Are the artists thinking the nation or thinking for it? When one observes, for example, the stylistic uniformity of French Baroque, Mexican muralism or American pop, one might ask if the artists of those currents thought the nation in their work or if they left the pre-existing cultural structure to shape the configuration. Individual differences in creative gestures are undeniable, but in the larger trajectory of these movements there has prevailed the enunciation of an 'ideology of images', a national community, that has proclaimed the heroism of the citizen, from David and Duplessis in pre-Revolutionary France,[4] across the reiterations of Diego Rivera, Siqueiros and their innumerable followers in Mexican legends, and through the work of Jasper Johns, Claes Oldenburg, Rauschenberg and others in the imaginary of the American consumer.

It is not possible to enter here into a debate on how far the possessions or patrimony of a nation condition fine art discourses and to what degree personal innovations evade such conditioning.[5] Rather, I am interested in emphasising that the modern history of art has been practised and written, to a great extent, as a history of the art of nations. This way of suppressing the object of study was mostly a fiction, but it possessed a verisimilitude over several centuries because the nations appeared to be the 'logical' mode of organisation of culture and the arts. Even the vanguards that meant to distance themselves from the sociocultural codes are identified with certain countries, as if these national profiles would help to define their renovative projects: thus, one talks about Italian futurism, Russian Constructivism and the Mexican Muralist School.

A large amount of actual artistic production is made as an expression of national iconographic traditions and circulates only in its own country. In this way fine art remains one of the nuclei of the national imaginary, scenarios of the dedication and communication of signs of regional identities. But a sector, increasingly more extensive in the creation, the diffusion and the reception of art, is happening today in a deterritorialised manner. Many painters whom critical favour and cultural diplomacy promote as the 'big national artists', for example Tamayo and Botero, manifest a sense of the cosmopolitan in their work, which partly contributes to their international resonance. Even those chosen as the voices of more narrowly defined countries – Tepito or the Bronx, the myths of the Zapotecos or the Chicano Frontier – become significant in the market and in the exhibitions of American art insofar as their work is a 'transcultural quotation'.[6]

It is not strange that time and again international exhibitions subsume the particularities of each country under conceptual transnational networks. The shows in the Georges Pompidou Centre, 'Paris-Berlin' and 'Paris-New York', for example, purported to look at the history of contemporary art not suppressing national patrimonies but distinguishing axes that run through frontiers. But it is above all the art market that declassifies national artists, or at least subordinates the local connotations of the work, converting them into secondary folkloric references of an international, homogenised discourse. The internal differences of the world market point less to national characteristics than to the aesthetic currents monopolised by the leading galleries, whose headquarters in New York, London, Paris, Milan and Tokyo circulate work in a deterritorialised form and encourage the artists to adapt to different 'global' publics. The art fairs and the biennials also contribute to this multicultural game, as one could see in the last Venice Biennale, where the majority of the 56 countries represented did not have their own pavilion: most of the Latin Americans (Bolivia, Chile, Colombia, Costa Rica, Cuba, Ecuador, El Salvador. Mexico, Panama, Paraguay and Peru) exhibited in the Italian section, but that mattered little in a show dedicated, under the title 'Puntos cardinales del arte/ Cardinal Points of Art', to exhibiting what today is constituted as 'cultural nomadism'.[7]

As these international events and the art magazines, the museums and the metropolitan critics manage aesthetic criteria homologous to the criteria of the market, so the artists who insist on national particularity rarely get recognition. The incorporation for short periods of some territorial movements into the mainstream, as happened with Land Art, or recently, with marginal positions, such as the Chicanos and Neomexicanists, does not negate the above analysis. The short-term speculations of the art market and their 'innovative and perpetual turbulence'[8] is as harmful in the long run to national cultures as to the personal and lengthy productions of artists; only a few can be adopted for a while to renovate the attraction of the proposition. It is in this sense that thinking today for much visual art means to be thought by the market.

From cosmopolitanism to globalisation

References to foreign art accompany the whole history of Latin American art. Appropriating the aesthetic innovations of the metropolises was a means for much art to rethink its own cultural heritage: from Diego Rivera to Antonio Berni, innumerable painters fed on Cubism, Surrealism and other Parisian vanguards to elaborate national discourses. Anita Malfatti found in New York expressionism and Berlin Fauvism the tools to reconceptualise Brazilian identity, analogous to the way Oswald de Andrade utilised the Futurist Manifesto to re-establish links between tradition and modernity in São Paulo.

This cosmopolitanism of Latin American artists resulted, in most cases, in the affirmation of the self. A national consciousness has existed, torn by doubts about our capacity to be moderns, but capable of integrating into the construction of repertoires of images the journeys, the itinerant glances, which would differentiate each people. The foreign 'influences' were translated and relocated in national matrices, in projects which united the liberal, rationalist aspiration for modernity with a nationalism stamped with the romantic, by which the identity of each people could be one, distinctive and homogeneous.

The pretension of constructing national cultures and representing them by specific iconographies is challenged in our time by the processes of an economic and symbolic transnationalisation. Arjun Appadurai groups these processes into five tendencies: a. the population movements of emigrants, tourists, refugees, exiles and foreign workers; b. the flows produced by technologies and transnational corporations; c. the exchanges of multinational financiers; d. the repertoires of images and information distributed throughout the planet by newspapers, magazines and television channels; e. the ideological models representative of what one might call western modernity: concepts of democracy, liberty, wellbeing and human rights, which transcend the definitions of particular identities.[9]

Taking into account the magnitude of this change, the deterritorialisation of art appears only partly the product of the market. Strictly speaking, a part is formed by a greater process of globalisation of the economy, communications and cultures. Identities are constituted now not only in relation to unique territories, but in the multicultural intersection of objects, messages and people coming from diverse directions.

Many Latin American artists are participating in the elaboration of a new visual thought which corresponds to this situation. There is no single pathway for this search. One is amazed that the preoccupation with decentring the artistic discourse from national niches crosses as much through the express-ionistic romantics as those who cultivate rationalism in conceptual practices and installations.

I agree with Luis Felipe Noé and his defence of an aesthetic that 'doesn't need a passport'. We cannot, he says, interrogate identity as a simple reaction against cultural dependency: to pose it in that way is like proposing 'to reply to a policemen who requires documents of identity or like a functionary who asks for a birth certificate'. For this reason, he affirms that the question whether there exists a Latin American art is one that is 'absurdly totalitarian'.[10]

Rather than devote ourselves to the nostalgic 'search for a non-existent tradition', he proposes we take on the diverse Baroque nature of our history, reproduced in many contemporary painters by 'an incapacity to make a synthesis faced with the excess of objects'. He pleads for an expressionistic painting, like that of his own work: trying to feel oneself primitive in the face of the world, but transcended not so much by nature as by the multiplicity and dispersion of cultures. In this way, his paintings escape from the frame, reach from ceiling to floor, in tempestuous lands that 'rediscover' the Amazons, historical battles, the glance of the first conquistador.[11]

In another way, of a conceptual character, Alfredo Jaar realises an analogical search. He invented a Chilean passport, in which only the covers replicated the official document. Inside, each double page opened to show the barbed wire of a concentration camp which receded towards an infinity uninterrupted by the mountains. The scene could be in his native Chile or in Hong Kong – where he made a documentary for the Vietnamese exiles – or in any of those countries where people speak seven languages and which repeat the phrase 'opening new doors', written in the sky of this closed horizontal: English, Cantonese, French, Italian, Spanish, German and Japanese. They correspond to certain nations with harder migration problems and with a more restrictive politics of migration. As the document of identification, at the same time national and individual, the passport is made to locate the origin of the traveller. It enables the passage from one country to another, but also stamps people by their place of birth and at time impedes them from change. The passport, as a synthesis of access entrapment, serves as a metaphor to men and women of a multicultural age, and amongst them to artists for whom 'their place is not within any particular culture, but in the interstices between them, in transit'.[12]

How can we study this delocalised art? By contrast to those explanations referring to a geographic milieu or a social unity, many actual artistic works need to be seen 'as something transported'. Guy Brett used this formula for the 'airmail' paintings of Eugenio Dittborn, those 'fold-up and compartmented rafts' that one receives in order to return: they are for 'seeing between two journeys'.[13] They are supported by a poetic of the transitory, in which their own peripheric nation – in this case Chile, the same as Jaar – can be the point of departure, but not the destination. Neither is any metropolis, as believed by some cosmopolitan Latin Americans, because the 'airmail' paintings, said Roberto Merino, also change metropolises into places of transit. Without centre, without hierarchical trajectories, these works, like those of Felipe Ehrenberg, Leon Ferrari, and many others who make postal art, speak about Chile, Mexico or Argentina but overflow their own territories, because the works' journeys make its external resonance a component of the message.

Dittborn used to include little houses in his paintings. The same tension between the journey and the period of residence is encountered in the maps and beds of Guillermo Kuitca. His images name at the same time the relation between particular territories and deterritorialisation. On one hand, street maps like that of Bogotá, whose streets are not drawn in lines but in syringes, or the maps of apartments made with bones, reflectors which illuminate uninhabited beds, the recording machines and the microphones without personages which allude to the terror in Argentina. 'During the time of the Malvinas I started to paint little beds ... it was a period of depression and what I wanted to transmit in the work was that I was staying quiet with the paint-brush in my hand, and, to produce the painting, what was moving was the bed.'[14]

The quietude of the brush while the context was transformed, while people travel. In painting over the mattress maps of Latin America and Europe, Kuitca reconfigures the tensions of many exiles: from Europe to America, from one America to another, from America again to Europe. Is it for this reason that the 'beds are without homes'?[15] To organise the world, Kuitca poses it at the same time as travel and rest: the maps of cities on the mattresses seem intended to disrupt rest. He wants to reconcile the romantic sense, uncertain or simply a painful journey with the organised space of a regular mattress, or conversely, exasperate the rigorous geometry of the maps, superimposing them over the territory of dreams. The map as a ghost, or the bed as a root: bedmaps, in this way migrates the person who looks for roots.

706 Grasping the World

Who gives passports?

These works do not allow us to interrogate them for social identities and the identity of art. But they attempt to be an art that recognises the exhaustion of ethnic or national mono-identities, which thinks to represent very little but talks about local and non-temporal essences. The material that creates their icons are not uniquely persistent objects, the monuments and rituals that gave stability and distinction to the culture are also related to passports, the beds with maps, the vibrant images of the media. Like today's identities, their works are polyglot and migrant, they can function in diverse and multiple contexts and permit divergent readings from their hybrid constitution.

But these multicultural reformulations of visual thinking are in conflict with at least three tendencies in the artistic camp/context. In the first place, in front of the inertia of the artist, intermediaries and public that continue to demand from art that it is representative of a pre-nationalised globalised identity. In the second place, the artist who relativises national traditions has difficulty being accommodated by state promotion which expects work from its creators that has the capacity to show to the metropolis the splendour of many centuries of national history.

Finally, the Latin American artists who work with globalisation and multiculturalism interact with the strategy of museums, galleries and critics of the metropolis who prefer to keep them as representatives of exotic cultures, of ethnic alterity and Latin otherness, that is, in the margins. In the US, George Yúdice observes, the multicultural politic of the museums and universities has been useful more to the recognition of difference than as an interlocutor in a dialogue of equality, to situate them as a subaltern corner of the *American way of life*. 'If before, they asked Latin Americans to illustrate pure surrealism, as in the case of Alejo Carpentier, with his "marvellous realism" or his *santeria*, now today they are asking that Latin Americans become something like "Chicano" or "Latino".'[16] Also, in Europe, the mechanisms of determination of artistic value hope that Latin Americans act and illustrate their difference: in a recent multicultural exhibition that took place in Holland, *Het Klimaat* (The Climate), the catalogue maintained that 'for the non-western artist or intellectual it is above all essential to create and recreate the historical and ideological conditions that more or less provide the possibility to exist'. The Argentinean artist Sebastián López challenged this 'condescending point of view' which relegates foreign artists to exhibiting their work in the alternative circuits: 'While the European artist is allowed to investigate other cultures and enrich their own work and perspective, it is expected that the artist from another culture only works in the background and with the artistic traditions connected to his or her place of origin (even though many Dutch managers of cultural politics, curators, dealers were ignorant of these traditions and their contemporary manifestations). If the foreign artist does not conform to this separation, he is considered inauthentic, westernised, and an imitator copyist of "what we do". The universal is "ours, the local is yours".'[17]

Thinking today is, as always, thinking difference. In this time of globalisation this means that visual thinking transcends as much the romantic conceit of nationalism as the geometric orders of a homogenous transnationalism. We need images of transits, of crossings and interchanges, not only visual discourses but also open, flexible reflections, which find a way between these two intense activities: the nationalist fundamentalism which seeks to conjure magically the uncertainties of multiculturalism, and on the other, the globalising abstractions of the market and the mega exhibitions, where one loses the will and desire for re-formulating the manner in which we are thought.

Translated from the Spanish by E. P. Quesada

NOTES

This paper was first presented at the 17th Symposium of Art History, hosted by the Instituto de Investigaciones Estéticas de la UNAM and the Comité Internacional de Historia del Arte, in Zacatecas, 23–28 September, 1993.

1. Michel Serres, 'Análisis simbólico y método estructural', in Andrea Bonomi and others, *Estructuralisme y filosofía*, Nueva Vision, Buenos Aires, 1969, p. 32.

2. Claude Lévi-Strauss, *El pensamiento salvaje*, FCE, México, 1964, pp 30–3.

3. For this form of enquiry we should not forget the founding work of Rudolf Arnheim, *El pensamiento visual*, Eudeba, Buenos Aires, 1971, which connects well with the contributions of Howard S Becker, Pierre Bourdieu and Fredric Jameson, whose possible complement I discussed in *Culturas hibridas, Estrategias para entrar y salir de la modernidad*, Grijalbo-CNCA, México, 1990, Chs 1 and 2.

4. As expressed by Nicos Hadjinicolau (*Historia del arte y lucha de clases*, 5th edition, Siglo Veintuno, México, 1976, Ch. 5), but this author relates 'ideology in the image' to social class and dismisses the nationalist differences that also have an effect on styles. Although I do not have space here to develop this critique, I want to at least say that a non-reductionist sociological reading, besides social class, ought to take into account other groups that organise social relations: nation, ethnicity, generation, etc.

5. I analysed this theme in 'Memory and Innovation in the Theory of Art', in *South Atlantic Quarterly*, Duke University Press, vol. 92, No. 3, 1993.

6. See *Art from Latin America: The Transcultural Meeting*, exhibition catalogue; exhibition curated by Nellie Richard, The Museum of Contemporary Art, Sydney, 10 March–13 June, 1993.

7. The formula belongs to the curator of the Biennale, Achille Bonito Oliva, quoted by Lilia Driben, 'La XLV Bienal de Venecia, los puntos cardinales del arte nómada de 56 paises', *La Jornada*, 23 August 1993, p 23.

8. See the illuminating chapter on this theme, 'Le marché et le musée' in Raymonde Moulin, *L'Artiste, l'institution et le marché*, Flammarion, Paris, 1992.

9. Arjun Appadurai, 'Disjuncture and Difference in the Global Cultural Economy', in *Global Culture, Nationalism, Globalization and Modernity*, (ed) Mike Featherstone, Sage Publications, London, Newburg Park-New Delhi, 1990.

10. Luis Felipe Noé, 'Does art from Latin America need a passport?' in *Being America, Essays on art, literature and identity from Latin America*, (eds) Rachel Weiss and Alan West, White Pine Press, New York, 1991.

11. Luis Felipe Noé, 'La nostalgia de la historia en el proceso de imaginación plástica de América

Latina', in *Encuentro artes visuales e identidad en América Latina*, Foro de Arte Contemporáneo, México, 1982, pp 46–51.

12.   Adriana Valdés, 'Alfredo Jaar: imágenes entre culturas', *Arte en Colombia International*, 42, December 1989, p 47.

13.   Guy Brett and Sean Cubitt, *Camino Way. Las pinturas aeropostales de Eugenio Dittborn*, Santiago de Chile, 1991.

14.   Martin Rejtman, 'Guillermo Kuitca. Mirada interior', *Claudia*, Buenos Aires, November 1992, No. 3, p 68. Reproduced by Marcelo B Pacheco in 'Guillermo Kuitca: inventario de un pintor', *Un libro sobre Guillermo Kuitca*, IVAM Centre del Carme, Valencia, 1993, p 123.

15.   The phrase is from Jerry Saltz, 'El toque humano de Guillermo Kuitca', in *Un libro sobre Guillermo Kuitca*, op cit.

16.   George Yúdice, 'Globalización y nuevas formas de intermediación cultural', paper presented at the conference 'Identidades, políticas e integración regional', Montevideo, 22–23 July, 1993.

17.   Sebastián López, 'Identity: Reality or Fiction', *Third Text*, 18, 1992, pp 32–4, cited by Yúdice, op cit. See also the issue of *Les Cahiers du Musée National d'Art Moderne* dedicated to the exhibition 'Les magiciens de la terre', No. 28, 1989, especially the articles by James Clifford and Lucy Lippard.

7.

Our (Museum) World Turned Upside Down: Re-presenting Native American Arts

Janet Catherine Berlo and Ruth B. Phillips

> Our aim is the complete *u'mista* or repatriation of everything we lost when our world was turned upside down.   Gloria Cranmer Webster[1]

The vast majority of Native American objects in private and public collections are the legacy of the high period of colonialism that lasted from about 1830 to 1930.[2] In the subfield of art history devoted to the arts of Native North America, the most urgent issues surrounding the collecting and display of these objects arise directly from the imperialist histories of their formation. Prodded by Native American activists and academic theorists, historians and curators of Native American art are today rethinking the most funda-mental questions: Who has the right to control American Indian objects, many of which are thought by their makers not to be art objects but instruments of power? Who has access to knowledge (even simply the knowledge gained from gazing upon an object of power), only those who have been initiated, or all who pass through the doors of a cultural institution? Who has the right to say what the objects mean, and whether and how they are displayed? And how will Native Americans, as they assume increasingly authoritative roles in museum representation, remake the museum as an institution?

Native American arts are still radically underrepresented in arts institutions, both academic and museological,[3] perhaps because they are less easily aligned with Western fine-art media and genres than African, Oceanic, or Pre-Columbian objects. Even more than other 'tribal' objects, Native American arts have largely fallen within the domain of anthropology. The manner in which we have framed the preceding statements, however, indicates key discursive conventions that need to be interrogated at the start of this discussion. The paradigms of art and artifact, spawned respectively by art history and anthropology, have structured most past discussions of collecting and display. They have been constructed as a binary pair of opposites comprising a closed system. Discussions of their problematics have tended to begin and end with the evaluation of their respective merits as representation.[4]

The tendency of poststructuralist and postcolonial critiques of the museum (a notable feature of which has been a focus on the representation of non-Western cultures) has been to flatten out the distinction between art and artifact. Recent critiques privilege the importance of the systemic and intertextual relationships between ethnography and art history, *both* of which were engaged by the imperialist project of inscribing relationships of power.[5] The 'relic room' of the amateur collector of Native American archaeology, with its quiltlike arrangements of 'frames' of arrowheads, the spacious, evenly lit installation of the art gallery, the exhibition hall of a world's fair, and anthropology halls of the early twentieth century are increasingly seen as intersecting spaces for the display of objects. All invoke formal, aesthetic, and intellectual templates that are equally arbitrary in relation to other cultural systems of priority and prerogative: all privilege the sense of sight over other modes of knowing: all make captured objects available to our surveillance.[6]

To a postcolonial sensibility, the difference between the jeweler's case and the specimen case seems, ultimately, of less significance than the wholesale historical appropriations of patrimonies and of voice that have led to the presence of these objects in Western collections. Both art-historical and anthropological practices of collecting and display have proceeded from the same tragically misconceived set of assumptions about the nature of progress and the inevitability of assimilation. They have both been forms of mortuary practice, laying out the corp(u)ses of the Vanishing American for post-mortem dissection in the laboratory, for burial in the storage room, and for commemoration in the exhibition.

On collecting

> Dollar bills cause the memory to vanish, and even fear can be cushioned by the
> application of government cash. I closed my eyes ... and I saw this: leaves
> covering the place where I buried Pillagers, mosses softening the boards of their
> grave houses, once so gently weeded and tended. ... I saw the clan markers
> [Fleur] had oiled with the sweat of her hands, blown over by wind, curiosities
> now, a white child's toys.   Louise Erdrich, *Tracks*

During the century from about 1830 to 1930, an extraordinary quantity of
objects became 'toys of the white child', to be rearranged according to the
taxonomies of science, or admired as objects of the aestheticizing gaze.[7] One
explorer, reporting in 1880 to the Department of the Interior about a Yup'ik
Eskimo graveyard in southwest Alaska, announced that he had found 'a
remarkable collection of grotesquely carved monuments and mortuary posts
[which] would afford a rich harvest of specimens to any museum'.[8]

A few figures, chosen almost at random, indicate the astonishing scale and
rapidity of this 'harvest', as it occurred inexorably across the continent.
Between 1879 and 1885 the Smithsonian collected over 6,500 pottery vessels
made by Pueblo women from Acoma and Zuni, villages of just a few hundred
inhabitants.[9] Between 1888 and 1893 George Emmons sold over 4,000 pieces
of Tlingit art to the American Museum of Natural History, including
'hundreds of supernaturally potent artworks' belonging to Tlingit shamans.[10]
The numbers grew more staggering and more wildly disproportionate in
relation to the demography of Native American communities. By 1911 Stuart
Culin returned from his collecting expeditions to the West with over 9,000
artifacts for the Brooklyn Museum, including Zuni kachina masks and War
God figures from sacred shrines.[11]

The vacuum sweep of Native American objects into public and private
collections was prosecuted with a systematic thoroughness that routinized
what amounted to the rape of entire cultural patrimonies. In sheer volume,
the greatest collector of all was George Heye, founder of the Museum of the
American Indian, the largest single repository of aboriginal objects from the
Americas, with holdings numbering over a million items.[12] A journalist,
describing Heye's mode of collecting, reported (only slightly tongue in cheek)
that 'what George enjoyed most on his automobile trips was hunting up
Indian reservations'. He was so obsessive that 'he felt that he couldn't
conscientiously leave a reservation until its entire population was practically
naked'.[13]

Great violence has been done to Native American communities in the
names of salvage anthropology and, since the early twentieth century,
primitivist art collecting. During campaigns against Plains Indians in the
second half of the nineteenth century, military officers had their Indian

scouts strip the corpses of the men, women, and children they had just killed. Moccasins, drawings, and weapons became personal trophies, some of which were later sent to the Smithsonian Institution and other museums.[14] In an (in)famous incident in British Columbia in 1922, Kwakwaka'wakw (Kwakiutl) participants in a banned potlatch were blackmailed with the threat of imprisonment into surrendering most of their ceremonial regalia to government officials.[15]

Although the history of Native American art collecting is marked by many such episodes of plunder and seizure, cash transactions were most common. They cloaked the process of appropriation in a normalizing fiction.[16] Acts of purchase not only ensured peaceful surrenders; they also reassured buyers of the progress Native Americans were making toward assimilation through their participation in the rituals of commodity exchange.

In the late twentieth century an official ethos of multiculturalism and pluralism has replaced assimilationism. It is cultural evolutionist ideology, not Native Americans, that has vanished. We are left, however, with vast hoards of objects acquired under what can be considered, at best, mistaken assumptions and, at worst, outright coercion. The consequences of the wholesale removal of objects have been particularly serious in North America. The totalizing construct of 'primitive art' obscures differences among colonized peoples that are worth remembering. The demographic and political imbalances affecting internally colonized minorities such as Native Americans allow the institutions of the dominant culture to exert even more effective hegemonic control than is the case in 'third-world' countries of Africa and other regions. Extensive missionization, the residential schooling system, and the pervasive reach of the media of mass communication inscribed stereotypes of 'Indianness' and led many aboriginal people to accept the myth that their very existence constituted an anachronism.

Many individual Native people were led by this process to collaborate in the process of collecting, believing that the museum was the only place in which a record of aboriginal cultures would eventually be preserved. Yet, as Edward Said has pointed out, in the imperial encounter, 'there was *always* some form of active resistance, and in the overwhelming majority of cases, the resistance finally won out'.[17] Although the collaborations of Native Americans facilitated anthropological collecting projects, they can also be considered a form of resistance to the nihilism that threatened. There were more overt acts of resistance as well. During Culin's 1902 trip to Zuni, for example, a village crier circulated through the town, warning people, upon pain of death, not to sell sacred objects to him.[18]

On display

> The hand that collects the basket, displays the cloth and photographs the
> weapon is removed from the hand that wove the basket, wore the cloth or
> wielded the weapon.   Loretta Todd[19]

The interventions of art history and art criticism in the representation of
Native American objects occurred several decades later than those of
anthropology, and their impact has been more evident in practices of display
than in those of collecting.[20] The paradigm of 'primitive art', no less than
that of the scientific specimen, trains the gaze on the object: the museum, as
Svetlana Alpers has argued, is first and foremost a way of seeing.[21] Yet
pluralism invokes emic (indigenous) perspectives on objects. For many
aboriginal peoples the most important thing about an object may be the way
in which it restricts the gaze. The vision-inspired paintings on Plains shields,
among the most visually attractive and tautly designed examples of Plains
graphic art, were sacred to their owners; though displayed on stands, they
were normally hidden by a painted cover. Many Pueblo figural paintings
and sculptures were sequestered in the semisubterranean kiva, a space often
restricted to initiated males.

   Part of the postcolonial Native American agenda has been the outright
removal of certain classes of objects from the kind of democratic exposure
enjoined by the art gallery or museum. The most well-known case is the
repatriation of Zuni *Ahayu:da* (war-god images). These simple, abstract male
figures have a visual eloquence that has appealed to many twentieth-century
artists;[22] more important, they are among the most sacred of Zuni religious
icons, and their place is in remote open-air hillside shrines where they are
supposed to weather and return to the elements. (There, the Zuni say, their
power works for all humankind.)[23] Since the historic moment in 1978 when
the Zuni Tribal Council prevented Sotheby Parke Bernet from auctioning one
of these sacred figures, more than fifty *Ahayu:da* have been repatriated to the
Zuni people from collections as diverse as the Denver Art Museum, the
Smithsonian, the University of Maine, some private collections, and the
Brooklyn Museum.[24] The idea of the removal of significant art objects from
museums, where they have resided for perhaps a century, strikes terror into
the hearts of some curators and art historians. Yet, as Zuni councilman Barton
Martza has observed, 'white society must learn that some of our traditional
culture is for Zunis only'.[25] Although this is perhaps the hardest lesson for the
dominant culture to accept, it is by no means an isolated example. The same
message emerges from the interventions of a number of Iroquois faith keepers
and political leaders in relation to *Hadui* (False Face) masks worn by traditional
Iroquois healers. These masks, regarded as the most important sculptural

products of Iroquois carvers, have long been identified by scholars as canonical objects of Iroquois 'art'.[26] Many contemporary Iroquois object strenuously to their presence in public museum displays and have successfully called for their removal to restricted storage areas.[27]

On addressing the problematics

> But they can't fool me. In those basement rooms without windows or in spacious labs with bright lights, when no one is looking, they throw their heads back, eyes close and fingers touch; fragile threads, polished stone and massive masks. For a moment their hands – the collector, the cataloger, the curator, the anthropologist – have become the hands before, the hands that shaped and prayed.
> Loretta Todd[28]

Michael Baxandall has described the museum exhibition as a field in which at least three agents are independently in play – makers of objects, exhibitors of made objects, and viewers of exhibited made objects. He observes that each of the three agents is playing a different game in the field.[29] Yet the observant ethnographer of Native American art history and museology today, trying to track the rules of representation as we move toward the end of the century, would certainly discover that there are, in fact, many more players than this, and the number of rule books has proliferated well beyond Baxandall's estimate. In Native American art-historical practice, the makers of objects and the exhibitors of objects increasingly will find themselves at odds if long-term and meaningful collaboration on every level of the curatorial process does not take place, and if they cannot redefine their legitimate common interest in objects. This has been occurring in many places with results that may disturb the comfortable routines of the museum but that will ultimately offer new and stimulating perspectives on objects that museums hold.[30]

The history of violence done to Native American communities by the collecting projects of our forebears, whether in the name of science, art, or sentimental commemoration, informs almost the entire corpus of Native American objects on which art-historical study has depended. Far-reaching new policies and legislative acts that regulate museum practice and allow Native Americans to reclaim or otherwise gain access to much that was removed from their communities are now in force in the United States and Canada.[31] At this moment it is urgent that we consider the benefits of empowerment and of collaboration as much as the difficulties, for this historical unfolding, unless scholars can address it honestly and constructively, has the potential to silence art-historical work. We have to accept, first of all, that scholars and aboriginal people will not always agree in their readings of objects, that different forms of authority will be recognized, and different facts privileged. Access to objects will also change, not always in conformity with late twentieth-century Western standards of equity.[32] But, as the return of collections and individual objects proceeds, a different kind of access will become available. When art-historical researchers revisit objects in Native American communities, they will find them differently presented, embedded in different texts from which much can be learned. The community perspective may well be more continuous with the historical and cultural truths that originally shaped the objects.[33]

Objects matter in cultural process, especially among peoples who have not relied on written texts for the recording of knowledge. Stripped bare of their traditional objects of use, beauty, and power, Native American communities have suffered interruptions of historical memory, paralysing failures in the generational transfer of political and sacred power, and the cessation of organic growth in many ancient stylistic and iconographic traditions.[34] Gloria Cranmer Webster's words, with which we opened this essay, link the past with the future:

We do not have a word for repatriation in the Kwak'wala language. The closest we come to it is the word *u'mista*, which describes the return of people taken captive in raids. It also means the return of something important. We are working towards the *u'mista* of much that was almost lost to us. The return of the potlatch collection is one *u'mista*. The renewed interest among younger people in learning about their cultural history is a kind of *u'mista*. The creation of new ceremonial gear to replace that held by museums is yet another *u'mista*. We are taking back, from many sources, information about our culture and our history, to help us rebuild our world which was almost shattered during the bad times. Our aim is the complete *u'mista* or repatriation of everything we lost when our world was turned upside down, as our old people say.[35]

The *u'mista* of confiscated Kwakwaka'wakw art remains one of the most important contemporary examples of the re-emplacement in a Native American community of objects displaced earlier in the century. In their new locations at the U'mista Centre at Alert Bay, British Columbia, and at the Cape Mudge Museum on nearby Vancouver Island, they are presented in ways that differ not only from standard, non-Native museums but also from the way they would have been seen in these communities in the 1920s.[36] (In other words, today aboriginal people often 'museumize' their objects too.) At the Cape Mudge Museum, masks and other objects are periodically removed and refurbished so that they can be worn in potlatches. The incremental changing of the objects that occurs as a result of use – anathema to Western conservation practices – are acceptable because Kwakwaka'wakw beliefs locate ownership primarily in the mental concept behind the object and in rights of reproduction, and only secondarily in the object itself. Nevertheless, the repatriation of historical objects has been an essential step in permitting the rearticulation of such principles of indigenous knowledge, many of which are in danger of being forgotten. It has also set in motion a new cycle of artistic production and reproduction.[37] The insights gained from this process, both by Native and non-Native parties to it, have already resulted in the re-presentation of Kwakwaka'wakw objects in urban museums serving largely non-Native audiences that more accurately reflect the ways in which contemporary Native Americans understand their own heritage.[38] The dismantling of the imperialist legacy of collecting and display has only just begun, but it is already clear that the old illusion of ideal panoptical vision has been shattered. The partial views that replace it offer insights into the meanings of objects that more accurately reflect the multiple ways of knowing that are emerging in the late twentieth century.

NOTES

1. G. C. Webster, 'From Colonization to Repatriation', in G. McMaster and L. Martin, eds, *Indigena: Contemporary Native Perspectives*, exh. cat., Canadian Museum of Civilization, Hull, Que., 1992, 37.

2. These dates not only encompass the most intensive period of collecting, but also correspond to two significant events in official US policy toward Native Americans, underlining the connection between the official adoption of assimilationist policies and the process of collecting. The year 1830 marks the date of the American Indian Removals Act, whose intent was to remove all Native Americans from the eastern half of the continent. In 1933, John Collier was appointed Commissioner of Indian Affairs, and began to reverse many key elements of assimilationist policy, including proscriptions on the observance of Native religions which require the use of objects. W. Sturtevant ('Does Anthropology Need Museums?', *Proceedings of the Biological Society*, LXXXII, 1969, 619–50) has termed the period 1840–1940 'The Museum Age'.

3. Native American art is included in only a small number of university art-history curricula, despite the fact that it is the indigenous cultural patrimony of our continent. It is also less often included, or included in much smaller numbers, in North American art museums than other 'tribal' arts.

4. See R. B. Phillips, 'Fielding Culture: Dialogues between Art History and Anthropology', *Museum Anthropology*, XVIII, no. 1, 1994, 39–46; and idem, 'How Museums Marginalise: Naming Domains of Inclusion and Exclusion', *Cambridge Review*, CXIV, no. 2320, 1993, 6–10. The bibliographies of the two articles include many of the recent commentaries on these issues.

5. James Clifford models the systemic nature of object circulation in 'On Collecting Art and Culture'. *The Predicament of Culture*, Cambridge, 1988, Chap. 10. See also G. Stocking, ed., *Objects and Others: Essays on Museums and Material Culture*, Madison, Wisc., 1985; Susan M. Pearce, *Museums, Objects and Collections: A Cultural Study*, Washington, D.C., 1992; and I. Karp and S. D. Lavine, eds, *Exhibiting Cultures: The Poetics and Politics of Museum Display*, Washington, D.C., 1991.

6. See S. Alpers, 'The Museum as a Way of Seeing', in Karp and Lavine, eds (as in n. 5), 25–32.

7. See Sturtevant (as in n. 2).

8. I. Petroff, *Report on the Population, Industries, and Resources of Alaska*, US Department of the Interior, Tenth Census (1880), Washington, D.C., 1884, 133.

9. J. Batkin, *Pottery of the Pueblos of New Mexico, 1700–1940*, exh. cat., Taylor Museum of the Colorado Fine Arts Center, Colorado Springs, 1987, 16.

10. A. Jonaitis, *From the Land of the Totem Poles: The Northwest Coast Indian Art Collection at the American Museum of Natural History*, exh. cat., New York Seattle, 1988, 87, 97. See also D. Cole. *Captured Heritage: The Scramble for Northwest Coast Artifacts*, Seattle, 1985.

11. D. Fane, I. Jackins, and L. Breen, *Objects of Myth and Memory: American Indian Art at the Brooklyn Museum*, exh. cat., Seattle, 1991, 23.

12. The Museum of the American Indian became part of the Smithsonian in 1989, and was renamed the National Museum of the American Indian. It is now directed by a Native American staff and is formulating policy on repatriation, and new approaches to research and display. For a brief statement of such policies, see W. R. West, Jr, 'Research and Scholarship at the National Museum of the American Indian: The New Inclusiveness', *Museum Anthropology*, XVII, no. 1, 1993, 5–8; and idem, 'Cultural Resources Center to House Collections *Native Peoples*, VII, no. 3, Spring 1994, 66.

13. R. Wallace, 'A Reporter at Large: Slim-Shin's Monument', *New Yorker*, Nov. 19, 1960, 106. The lines cited are voiced by an unnamed 'eminent professor of anthropology, once associated with the Heye Foundation'.

14. This traffic in personal items was not entirely one-way, however. To cite just one example of the multiple exchanges of objects between cultures: a small notebook kept by a member of the 7th Cavalry in the 1870s was captured by a Cheyenne warrior named High Bull who pulled it from its owner's dead body at the Battle of Little Big Horn in 1876. High Bull turned it into a drawing book. A few months later, High Bull was killed in battle by US soldiers, who reclaimed the notebook. It came to rest in George Heye's collection, which eventually became a national museum run by Native Americans. See P. Powell, 'High Bull's Victory Roster', *Montana: The Magazine of Western History*, XXV, no. 1, 1975, 14–21.

15. Kwakwaka'wakw anthropologist Gloria Cranmer Webster ([as in n. 1], 35) daughter of one of the chiefs involved, writes: 'Those who were charged under the potlatch law did not have to serve their gaol sentences if their entire villages agreed to give up their ceremonial gear, including masks, rattles, whistles, and coppers. The federal government paid the owners a total of $1,450.50 for several hundred objects, which were crated and shipped to Ottawa. There, what came to be known as the Potlatch Collection, was divided between the Victoria Memorial Museum (later the National Museum of Man and now the Canadian Museum of Civilization) and the Royal Ontario Museum. Thirty-three artifacts were purchased by George Heye'.

16. Native American artists were also engaged in the large-scale production of objects for sale to outsiders. These objects have often been regarded as 'inauthentic' by both art and anthropology collectors. See R. B. Phillips, 'Why Not Tourist Art?: Significant Silences in Native American Museum Collections', in G. Prakash, ed., *After Colonialism: Imperial Histories and Post-Colonial Displacements*, Princeton, N.J., 1994, 98–125. Market production of Native American art is a complex topic that raises different issues in relation to museum representation, ownership, and repatriation, a full discussion of which is beyond the scope of this paper.

17. E. Said, *Culture and Imperialism*, New York, 1993, xii.

18. Fane, Jacknis, and Breen (as in n. 11), 60. The more recent and highly successful campaign of Zuni activists to reclaim the sacred objects that collectors like Culin succeeded in acquiring (discussed below), or the recent return of wampum belts from the National Museum of the American Indian to the Six Nations Iroquois, or reclamations of numerous medicine bundles by members of many Plains Indian communities can be regarded as examples of the eventual winning out of individual and collective memory. For a discussion of the wampum-belt incident, see W. Fenton, 'Return of Eleven Wampum Belts to the Six Nations Iroquois Confederacy on Grand River, Canada', *Ethno-history*, xxxvi, 1989, 392–410.

19. L. Todd, 'Three Moments after "Savage Graces"', *Harbour*, III, no. 1, 1993, 57–62.

20. See J. C. Berlo, 'Introduction: The Formative Years of Native American Art History', in J. C. Berlo, ed., *The Early Years of Native American Art History*, Seattle, 1992, 1–21; and W. J. Rushing, 'Marketing the Affinity of the Primitive and the Modern: René d'Harnoncourt and "Indian Art of the United States"', in ibid., 191–236. Native American objects were 'discovered' after those of Africa and Oceania, in part because works executed in the fine-art formats of painting and monumental sculpture are relatively less common in Native American traditions. See W. Rubin, ed., *'Primitivism' in Twentieth Century Art: Affinity of the Tribal and the Modern*, exh. cat., Museum of Modern Art. New York, 1985; and W. J. Rushing, *Native American Art and Culture and the New York Avant-Garde, 1910–1950*, Austin, Tex., 1995.

21. Alpers (as in n. 6).

22. See Rubin, ed. (as in n. 20), 29–32.

23. T. J. Ferguson and B. Martza, 'The Repatriation of Zuni *Ahayu:da*', *Museum Anthropology*, XIV, no. 2, 1990, 7–15. See also W. L. Merrill, E. J. Ladd, and T. J. Ferguson, 'The Return of the *Ahayu:da*: Lessons for Repatriation from Zuni Pueblo and the Smithsonian Institution', *Current Anthropology*, xxxiv, no. 5, 1993, 523–67.

24. It is noteworthy that the process of collaboration with Zuni tribal elders during the preparation

for the 1991 Brooklyn show 'Objects of Myth and Memory' laid the groundwork for the repatriation of Brooklyn's war-god statuary. Stuart Culin's own fieldnotes from 1902 and 1903 supported the Zunis' legal claim that these thirteen sacred figures (more than existed in any other institution) had been removed from religious shrines for purchase by Culin (Diana Fane, curator, Brooklyn Museum, personal communication, Nov. 1991).

25. Ferguson and Martza (as in n. 23), 11.

26. The primacy of the mask in tribal art has, undoubtedly, much to do both with the primitivist delight in African masks and the ease with which such carvings can be hung on the wall.

27. Iroquois have employed a number of strategies to control the display of False Face masks over the years. Initially, arrangements were made for proper ritual care of masks held in storage, but objections to the display of the masks steadily grew. During the Calgary showing of 'The Spirit Sings: Artistic Traditions of Canada's First Peoples', an Iroquois group brought a lawsuit against the Glenbow Museum to force it to remove a False Face mask from the exhibition. Although the court rejected the request, the mask was voluntarily removed at the exhibition's second venue. The museum at the Woodlands Cultural Centre at the Six Nations reserve at Brantford. Ontario, displays a mask still attached to the tree trunk from which it was being carved – the reasoning being that, frozen in the process of carving, it has not yet become an autonomous power object.

28. Todd (as in n. 19), 57.

29. M. Baxandall, 'Exhibiting Intention: Some Preconditions of the Visual Display of Culturally Purposeful Objects', in Karp and Lavine, eds (as in n. 5) 13–41.

30. Recent major exhibitions which have involved collaboration between museum curators and Native scholars and artists include 'Chiefly Feasts: The Enduring Kwakiutl Potlatch', curated by Aldoma Jonaitis for the American Museum of Natural History, New York (1991), with the section on the modern potlatch curated by G. C. Webster, 'Art of the American Indian Frontier', curated by David Penney for the National Gallery of Art, Washington, D.C. (1992), in consultation with George P. Horse Capture; 'Visions of the People: A Pictorial History of Plains Indian Life', curated by Evan M. Maurer for the Minneapolis Institute of Arts (1992), in consultation with George P. Horse Capture; and 'A Time of Gathering: Native Heritage in Washington State', curated by Robin Wright for the Burke Museum, University of Washington, Seattle (1989), in conjunction with co-curator Roberta Haines, as well as Vi Hilbert and a host of Native advisers; and 'Reflections of the Weaver's World' curated by Ann Lane Hedlund for the Denver Art Museum (1992), in consultation with Navajo weavers.

31. In the US, the Native American Graves and Repatriation Act (NAGRA), passed by Congress in 1990 as Public Law 101–601, provides for the carrying out of inventories, the disclosure of holdings to the descendants of the makers of Native American objects, the return of all human skeletal remains, and the repatriation of objects of a sacred or mortuary nature. Debates on the ramifications of this law appear in *Museum Anthropology*, xv, 1991, passim.
      In Canada, a policy rather than a law has been formulated, by the Task Force on Museums and First Peoples, appointed by the Canadian Museums Association and the Assembly of First Nations in 1989. Its report, *Turning the Page: Forging New Partnerships between Museums and First Peoples*, Ottawa, 1992, was ratified by both organizations. It establishes a model of partnership between aboriginal people and museums, and makes recommendations in three major areas, repatriation, access and interpretation, and implementation. See T. Nicks, 'Partnerships in Developing Cultural Resources: Lessons from the Task Force on Museums and First Peoples', *Culture*, xii, no. 1, 1992, 87–94.

32. At the Makah-run museum built to house the important finds from Ozette, a Northwest Coast site destroyed by a mudslide in the 16th century, access to certain objects is barred to women, in accordance with Makah custom. Plains Indians visiting the Canadian Museum of Civilization have requested that menstruating women not come into contact with certain medicine objects, a requirement virtually impossible to meet under the contemporary guidelines of gender equity and protection of privacy.

33. See J. Clifford, 'Four Northwest Coast Museums: Travel Reflections', in Karp and Lavine, eds (as in n. 5), 212–54. For a recent, penetrating analysis of the complexities of the history of Native-made objects in museum collections and their relationships to contemporary Native peoples, see A. Jonaitis and R. Inglis, 'Power, History, and Authenticity: The Mowachat Whalers' Washing Shrine', in M. Torgovnick, ed., *Eloquent Obsessions: Writing Cultural Criticism*, Winston-Salem, N.C., 1994, 157–84.

34. Nevertheless, the past thirty years have witnessed a stunning resurgence of artistic creativity, expressed both in the revival of nearly lost art forms and the employment of hybrid fine-art styles that are a sophisticated mix of Euro-American and indigenous American forms and

genres. Discussion of this is beyond the scope of this brief essay. See McMaster and Martin, eds (as in n. 1), and the works cited in their bibliography.

35. Webster (as in n. 1), 37.

36. For example, they are not in glass cases, and they are grouped according to the order in which they appear in a potlatch, rather than according to Western taxonomies.

37. J. Ostrowitz's dissertation in progress, 'Privileging the Past: Art, History, and Historicism on the Northwest Coast', Columbia University, addresses this rich and subtle cycle of the use and reuse of objects and ideas in Kwakiutl culture. See also idem, 'Trailblazers and Ancestral Heroes: Collaboration in the Representation of a Native Past', *Curator*, xxxvi, no. 1, 1993, 50–65.

38. See A. Jonaitis, ed., *Chiefly Feasts: The Enduring Kwakiutl Potlatch*, exh. cat., American Museum of Natural History, New York, New York/Seattle, 1991, esp. Chaps 1, 5. Not only did Gloria Cranmer Webster curate the section of the potlatch show that was concerned with the 20th century (see n. 30), she was also adviser to the Canadian Museum of Civilization's Grand Hall, so that her vision of a Kwakiutl community house and its potlatch furnishings is presented there as well.

8.

The Museum of Contemporary Art, Los Angeles:
An Account of Collaboration between Artists, Trustees and an Architect

Jo-Anne Berelowitz

Set into the wall in the lobby of the Museum of Contemporary Art is a large stone tablet commemorating the institution's origin and history. Etched into its surface is the museum's official story. It relates that:

The Museum of Contemporary Art was conceived in Los Angeles in 1979. A group of citizens shared their visions with Mayor Tom Bradley who appointed a Museum Advisory Committee with William A. Norris, Chairman and Marcia Weisman, Vice Chairwoman. The Advisory Committee and the Community Redevelopment Agency subsequently came together to provide for the museum. The site would be provided by the Community Redevelopment Agency, construction funds by Bunker Hill Associates, and qualifying endowment funds by the museum's Charter Founders.

Leading players who guided the institution through its birth and formative years are honoured and acknowledged by name: founding chairman of the Board, Eli Broad; founding president, William A. Norris; inaugural chairman, William F. Kieschnick; inaugural vice chairman and chairman of the Building Committee, Frederick M. Nicholas; inaugural president, Lenore S. Greenberg;

director, Richard Koshalek. The professional staff, the trustees and the supportive community are acknowledged more generally as collective bodies. Their contributions, we are told in the concluding lines, 'brought world attention to this young institution'.

By mapping a sequence of events from point of origin to dénouement (the transformation of a vision into a world-famous museum) the tablet's narrative effects a tidy coherence. But the representation, like all narratives, is a construction, an ordering of meaning, and its neat closure comes at the expense of what it excludes. Certain key players were excluded from this account, most notably a core group of local artists who worked with passionate dedication for two years to bring to reality their dream of a Los Angeles museum of contemporary art. The following pages present their engagement with and subsequent peripheralisation from this project.

Los Angeles' lack of a museum of contemporary art was long felt to be a major lacuna in the city's cultural life. The city had, once, fleetingly during the 1960s, been host to a contemporary art museum. Or rather, the contiguous city of Pasadena had once had a museum that showed new and exciting American art. But its board of trustees embarked on an ambitious building campaign that bankrupted the institution, and in 1973 it was sold to Norton Simon, who turned it into a repository for his collection of Impressionist masters. Its demise left only the Los Angeles County Museum to showcase contemporary art; but the County is a general purpose 'universal' museum, and its department of contemporary art represents only a minor part of its overall operations. Thus, effectively from 1973 Los Angeles had no art museum that focused on contemporary issues, a situation that the local art community experienced as a severe lack in the city's cultural life and in the development of the careers of its members. Over the years a number of proposals had been made to rectify the situation, but they had come to nothing. Los Angeles seemed doomed to its characterisation as a 'cultural wasteland' whose only culture, as critics loved to point out, was in its yogurt. However, in 1979 a unique confluence of events reopened the possibility of a museum of contemporary art, and when local artists were alerted to them, they marshalled their energies to ensure that the possibility would become fact.

The reinvigoration of the idea of a museum came from prominent supporters of long-time city mayor Tom Bradley. In 1979 Marcia Weisman, a wealthy art collector, and William Norris, lawyer, political savant and recent art collector, independently suggested to Bradley that Los Angeles needed a museum of contemporary art. The suggestion resonated with Bradley whose political machine was then ambitiously transforming Los Angeles into a 'world city' that would assume authority as America's capital of the Pacific Rim. Recognising that 'world cities' offer culture as well as international trade and that a museum would further his internationalist ambitions, Bradley appointed a Museum Advisory Committee with Norris as chairman to look into museum possibilities and to investigate possible sites.

Offer of a site came from the city's Community Redevelopment Agency (or CRA as it is more generally known). Established in 1948 as a public body, empowered with the right of eminent domain (the allocation of land resources by a government agency for ostensibly public purposes), the CRA had a mandate to implement urban renewal in Los Angeles. Gaining power under the Bradley regime, fuelled by the growth agenda of Bradley's power machine, the Agency interpreted its mandate to mean the transformation of a derelict downtown into the highrise-spiked megalopolis of Bradley's desire. In 1979 when the idea of a contemporary museum was resuscitated, the Agency was considering the disposition of 11.2 acres on Bunker Hill, prime real estate in the heart of the financial and legal centre of the city and adjacent to the Music Center, downtown's principal cultural facility. CRA consensus was that the land should be offered to a single developer as an integrated mixed-use project consisting of office towers, condominiums, a hotel, a cinema complex, restaurants, shops and a cultural element. Preliminary plans had been drawn, mapping out the disposition of the various components. At this point the cultural element had been conceived merely as a large box labelled CULTURE. As the largest redevelopment package ever offered to a developer, this was certainly the largest project ever undertaken in the twenty-one-year history of the twenty-five-square block downtown renewal area. Thus far, renewal had proceeded piecemeal, additively. There was nothing to pull the pieces together and the city still lacked a heart. A project of this magnitude could, if carefully orchestrated, supply downtown with its desired centrepiece.

In conformity with Agency stipulations, one and a half per cent of the total capital investment (a billion dollars) would have to be spent on fine art. When the Agency learned of the quest for a museum site, the dynamics of their project shifted and clarified: instead of spending the money on discrete art objects dispersed over the development's area, they would fund a museum. A major art museum in downtown Los Angeles would help solve the dilemma of how to transmogrify an agglomeration of highrises into a city with a meaningful core. The CULTURE box could now be assigned a *high* cultural function.

The Museum Advisory Committee met with the CRA and agreement was reached that the city would provide land and a building for the museum. The project developer (yet to be selected) would provide money to build a museum of approximately one hundred thousand square feet of interior space at an estimated amount of $16 million.[1] However, there would be no municipal funds for the museum's operating expenses. These would have to come from the private sector and would have to be raised by the museum advocates. Norris's task, now that he had a site and a building, would be to form a board of trustees who would raise a permanent endowment of at least $10 million, an amount adequate to generate 35–40 per cent of operating expenses.[2]

The first three million came in quickly. The first million was donated by Eli Broad, a multinational property developer who was then beginning to collect contemporary art. In return for his largesse, he was made founding chairman of the Board. The second million was donated by Max Palevsky, philanthropist, film producer and founder of a software empire. For his million dollars he would become chairman of the Architecture Committee, overseeing all matters pertaining to the museum's architecture. In a letter of 3 April 1980, he made his position quite clear to the museum's board of trustees: 'If, at some future time, the architectural decision is made on other grounds by other people … [he would] feel no obligation to the Museum.'[3] This contractual condition would reverberate at a later stage in the museum's history when Palevsky's control over architectural matters was, indeed, revoked. The third million was donated by a multinational oil conglomerate, the Atlantic Richfield Corporation. One of their highest ranking officers, William F. Kieschnick, soon to be their chief executive officer, joined MOCA's board of trustees and was later to be the museum's inaugural chairman.

By this stage the local artists had been drawn into the project. In late August they convened a meeting at movie producer Tony Bill's screening room in Venice Beach. About one hundred and fifty artists showed up and Mayor Bradley put in a brief appearance, asking the artists for their support and input. The room held Los Angeles's most prominent, successful and emerging artists including Sam Francis, Ed Moses, Tony Berlant, DeWain Valentine, Robert Graham, Chuck Arnoldi and Alexis Smith. Discussion was heated, and almost as many ideas were generated as there were artists to generate them. Eventually when they disbanded, agreement had been reached on only one point: that they would meet again. A second meeting was held a week later, in early September, with the participants now reduced to half their former number. But there was one notable new addition: light-and-space artist Robert Irwin, whose charismatic leadership would exercise a formative influence on the nascent museum.

The meeting factionalised into two groups: those who viewed the project as an opportunity to design a spectacular building that would bear their signature and in which they would showcase their work, and those who saw it as an opportunity to provide Los Angeles with what it had for so long lacked: a forum for the exchange and generation of artistic ideas, a venue hospitable to the diversity of its artistic citizenry. Los Angeles had long been home to the second largest artistic community in the world, but, unlike New York, it was a community dispersed over a wide geographic area, without a central focus to give it coherence and without a major facility to service it. In the conflict that now arose between personal ambition and enlightened awareness of a benefit for the greater whole, it was the latter constituency that prevailed, but not without a struggle. A temporary truce was established when a core group of about twenty artists from both sides of the dispute banded together to form the Artists Advisory Council, with the agenda of establishing the artists' goals and ideas for the new museum. It became apparent that the faction focusing on a museum that would itself be a work of art was outnumbered. Angered at their loss of control, they stormed out of the meeting, which then collapsed. At that point it seemed unlikely that any agreements would be reached.

It was then that Irwin began to exercise the leadership role that he would sustain over the next three years. That evening he called every member of the Council, cautioning them that their effectiveness as a body was dependent on their maintenance of a united front. Most of the dissidents never returned, but the core group that did buried their differences and worked together for three years, meeting every Monday night from seven to midnight, debating ideas on what a contemporary museum should be, from curatorial policy to directorships, architecture, fundraising, trustees, representation, social and political implications. Their discussions had wide-ranging effects on the eventual museum for they alone of the various constituencies engaged in the project understood the architectonics of museum design.[4] Local architect Coy Howard joined the artists as a consultant to provide professional expertise and to advise on issues pertaining to city planning.

By this time the CRA had begun to solicit proposals for the project from various developers. Competition for the project narrowed down to five developers: Bunker Hill Associates, a Los Angeles-based team that included Canadian firm Cadillac Fairview in a consortium with Los Angeles firms; Boston firm Cabot and Forbes; local investment builder Maguire Partners; Chicago-based Metropolitan Structures Inc.; and Olympia and York/Trizec of Canada and Los Angeles. As representatives of the Artists Advisory Council, Howard and Irwin attended various CRA meetings to familiarize themselves with the five developers, to examine their plans and understand their attitudes towards the projected museum.

It very quickly became clear to them that the CRA had only the vaguest notions about museum design. In contrast, the Artists Advisory Council held very clear ideas. Over a long series of intensive planning sessions, they had set down requirements for floor loads, heights of ceilings, loading docks, lighting. Cognisant of their expertise, Norris invited them to participate in a workshop to evaluate the five proposals. Carefully scrutinising all five plans, they recommended Maguire's as the most interesting and most favourable to the museum.[5] Ranked lowest on their list was Cadillac Fairview, seemingly not at all interested in the museum, for their design team, headed by Canadian architect Arthur Erickson, had relegated it to the entertainment function of an Angeleno curiosity. Erikson had designed a structure cantered over the street, its angled walls transparent to passing motorists who would thus be able to view the art as they drove by, the world's first drive-by museum, uniquely adapted to the vehicular mode of the Los Angeles lifestyle! The artists hated it, but the CRA, driven by different considerations, thought otherwise. Impressed by Cadillac Fairview's claim to be able to pay for the entire project in cash, the CRA held a public meeting on 14 July 1980, to announce Cadillac Fairview as the winning developer.[6]

The awarding of the contract to Cadillac Fairview was a tremendous blow to the artists, the first major hurdle they encountered in the attainment of their goals, for they all felt that a museum designed by Erickson would be a disaster, resulting in a building that would in no way be sympathetic to their needs. Their needs were threefold: the first was that the museum be actively engaged with the larger art community, as opposed to being a static repository of collections of already renowned, perhaps defunct, artists. For a long time the artists were filled with trepidation as to whether they would attain this goal, for it ran counter to a course on which the trustees seemed determined to steer the museum. Many of the trustees, themselves collectors, or aspiring collectors, conceived museums to be mirror versions of their own art-engagement, albeit on a grander scale. This difference in focus between the artists and the trustees can be understood in terms of a differential reading of the sign 'museum'. The artists wanted the institution to serve as an active forum for the exchange of artistic ideas; the trustees wanted it to signify 'collection'. Initially it seemed as if the will of the trustees would prevail, for they named the museum-to-be 'The Los Angeles Museum of Modern Art'. Since the period of historical modernism ended in the 1960s, that designation would have meant that the museum would show only dead or late-career artists; no emerging or mid-career artists would get in, nor active exchange of ideas take place. Choosing an appropriate name for the museum was thus a major issue. Robert Irwin and Sam Francis were able to convince the trustees to make the focus contemporary rather than modern, and so it was named the Museum of Contemporary Art.[7]

Their second goal tied in with their first, for the artists wanted a grass-roots director who would be actively engaged with the art community and share their values. However, they recognised that a grass-roots director would be unlikely to carry weight in the international arena and, since Los Angeles had been marginalised for so long, they were eager for their museum to achieve international prominence. For this they would need a director of international renown. Since no one could be both a grass-roots person and an art-world celebrity, they conceived the idea of a dual directorship. As Irwin expressed it:

There was no single person who was Mr. Magic, who could do everything we wanted them to. We needed a young grass roots person and we needed a real superstar, someone with charisma and focus to draw people into [the project]. Sam Francis was a good friend of Pontus Hulten and I of Richard Koshalek. Best young museum person in the country, untried and untested. Couldn't have raised ten cents on his name! Hulten was an international star who had to report only to the President of France. A different ball game! Royalty! Sam felt Pontus would be interested. Big question: could they or would they work together? Sam went and visited Pontus; I went and visited Richard. Richard was willing to take the secondary role. So basically Pontus became the front man and Richard came in as his executive. It worked. It knocked the art world on its arse, gave the whole thing a sense of scale. Dynamic![8]

Indeed it was. Pontus Hulten was then the most widely known museum director in the world, for since 1973 he had served as the founding director of the Beaubourg, the most talked-of museum in the world, where he had put together controversial, enormously popular shows that drew more than a million people apiece, many of whom had never attended art museums before. Prior to that he had been responsible, since 1953, for the planning and development of Stockholm's Moderna Museet, becoming its director in 1959, an institution known throughout the museum community for its lively and innovative programming. The fifty-five-year-old Hulten was impressive not only for his curatorial and directorial skills but also as a personality. A huge man, barrel-chested, athletic-looking, with shaven head, he possessed great charm, was renowned for his humour, had a reputation for being an artists' museum man, and was known and respected by collectors the world over.

The thirty-eight-year-old Koshalek's background was more modest. He had served as director of the Hudson River Museum in Yonkers for four years, during which he had managed to salvage the institution from a dire financial situation and turn it into a major local attraction whose programmes even New Yorkers deemed worth the visit. His first job had been at the Walker Art Center in Minneapolis where he had served under Martin Friedman, subsequently becoming curator. For much of his tenure there, the Walker was under construction, and Koshalek had learned to operate what he called 'a guerilla museum', engineering exhibitions without a building by staging them in unexpected sites such as department stores and vacant lots. The fact that MOCA did not yet have a building would in no way discourage him. After the Walker he had served as assistant director of the Visual Arts Programme for the National Endowment for the Arts, and then as director of the Fort Worth Art Museum where he had commissioned works and curated shows by contemporary painters and performance artists, as well as organising programmes on film and music. He was well known to contemporary artists, scholars and critics and had a reputation for being on the cutting edge of current art issues.

Again, the trustees adopted the artists' suggestions, and in August 1980 a public announcement was issued naming Pontus Hulten director of the new museum and Richard Koshalek deputy director. Irwin had been right, for the dual directorship did, indeed stun the art world, and the international art presses excitedly proclaimed the news. The appointments had enormous strategic resonances, for until this point the museum's reality had existed primarily on paper as a negotiated agreement between the CRA, a developer, and a handful of people who were committed to making it happen. It still had no building and no collection. But now it had the most famous museum administrator in the world as its director. Suddenly Los Angeles no longer seemed the cultural wasteland that critics had loved to deride. Rather, it seemed poised as the new cultural capital of the West Coast, a construal that began with the appointment of Hulten and became more prevalent as the 1980s wore on. Of course, both construals – that Los Angeles was a cultural wasteland and that it was becoming the cultural capital of the west – are myths. But as Irwin astutely noted:

Myths figure very big in these things. In fact, I felt that was one of the main strategies that we had. And that was the other thing the artists talked about and I tried to talk to the board about: that what we had going for us was a myth: this myth of the West Coast, true or untrue, the myth that the world was moving west, that the east was getting old. It had moved from Europe to the East Coast and now it was going to the West Coast and then off to the Pacific. I love the idea! The thing with MOCA was: we had a myth on our hands. First, we had no collection, no building. We had nothing! But once we got Pontus, we had this thing rolling and it was this great myth. It catalysed everything! When you think about it, for the first six, seven years there was literally nothing there [on the site that MOCA was to occupy]. No substance whatsoever. Which, by the way, is an advantage, because when you're building a myth, the minute you have to reveal the thing, it's not as good, because it never is. We rolled the dice at it. Artists should know about myth-building, because we're in the myth-building business. That's not *what* we do, but it's certainly an extension of what we do; because when you speak about changing the nature of perception, changing the nature of reality, you're playing with people's myths …[9]

And that is precisely what they did. MOCA's history has always been more than the sum of a piece of real estate added to a deal between the CRA and a developer, added to a building with collections and a curatorial agenda. Rather, it has been about dreams, visions, ambitions. Clearly, the artists understood this very well in terms of establishing their own goals. Mayor Bradley, city planners, developers and boosters (promoters of urban development projects) have understood it very well in terms of theirs. Viewed from a panoptic perspective, MOCA was always a project designed to change the nature of perception about Los Angeles, a device for the re-visioning of the city. But not all of the dreams could come true, for artists, trustees and city boosters dream very differently. MOCA would thus become a site and cause of struggle, as rival dreamers battled over whose vision would prevail.

Initially, however, the different interest groups worked together and the trustees were amenable to the artists's suggestions. After recruiting Pontus Hulten and achieving the dual directorship, the artists felt that the museum's stature would be further served by internationalising the board of trustees, and again the board adopted their suggestion. And so a select cadre of superstar collectors was solicited: Dominique de Menil, Count Guiseppe Panza di Buomo, Peter Ludwig and Seji Tsutsumi. All had had considerable experience serving as officers of major museums scattered across the globe. Their recruitment was another brilliant strategic move that kept the museum in the heat of the international spotlight. Both Hulten's appointment and the election of an international board of trustees were very effective in catalysing fund-raising, for MOCA was now the hottest club in town, and everyone wanted to join. In the words of one participant:

At a certain point it became an unbelievable thing. I mean people were driving up in wheelbarrows giving money. You couldn't even stop them from giving. Everyone wanted to be on the initial patrons' list. The dump truck kept coming. It became the thing that everyone did. There was a whole series of parties and dances. People became involved. Once they were involved, they wanted to be more involved because it seemed like a fun thing to be involved with.[10]

The PR was brilliant and the community responded. The artists were as involved in fund-raising as the trustees, hosting dozens of fund-raiser parties. By the end of 1980 the endowment campaign was within a couple of million of attaining its goal. The next big challenge would be the architecture; and it was here, more than with any other issue pertaining to the museum, that the artists felt that a great deal was at stake. Their paramount goal was to design a building that met their needs. It was, unquestionably, the most difficult goal to attain.

The history of MOCA's building, or, more accurately, buildings, is a complex one. At around the time of the selection of a developer, an Architecture Committee was formed. Headed by Max Palevsky (who had stipulated control of the design as the condition of his million-dollar donation), its other members were artist-representatives Robert Irwin, Sam Francis and Coy Howard. Later they were joined by Pontus Hulten. The artists were able to convince Palevsky and the CRA that any design by Erickson would foredoom the museum to failure. They wanted to select their own architect, someone of international renown willing and able to work with the artists as members of a design team. The architect's personality thus became an issue, for they needed someone who could set aside ego and 'signature' in favour of teamwork, who was open to discussion about the appropriate relationship between art and architecture in a museum building. The artists knew that they would have to make their participatory goals very clear, establishing an architect's acceptance of them as a primary condition of employment. After some deliberation they narrowed their choice to six internationally-renowned architects: Sir James Stirling, Kevin Roche, Frank Gehry, Arata Isozaki, Richard Meier and Edward Barnes. In the autumn of 1980 the Architecture Committee set off on a series of international travels to interview the architects and to inspect museums and other facilities designed by them.

Their choice fell upon Japanese architect Arata Isozaki, a close friend of committee member Sam Francis. Isozaki's résumé included the design of two major museum buildings: the Kitakyushu City Museum of Modern Art and the Gunma Prefectural Museum, both in his typical signature style that combined an aggressive sculptural quality with a repetitive expression of square modules. It was not, however, his museums that appealed to the Architecture Committee, but his factories, which had a bare-bones kind of beauty, very straightforward, with minimal detail, precisely what the artists had in mind. They felt that Isozaki understood their sensibility and that they would be able to work together. In January 1981 Isozaki was named the architect of the Museum of Contemporary Art.

However, the committee soon became unhappy with Isozaki: he did not conform to specified deadlines, attend scheduled meetings or visit Los Angeles when his contract stipulated. More seriously, the committee began to question his basic ability to do the job. As a result of the many meetings of the Artists' Advisory Council, the Architecture Committee had a very clear understanding of how they wanted the new museum to be, and Isozaki seemed not at all interested in their specifications. They found his interior plans unworkable, for his galleries related awkwardly, little consideration had been given to the movement of people through them, columns blocked viewing lines, doors interrupted primary exhibition halls, loading-docks were too small to accommodate artworks and skylights were inadequate. More serious yet was a fundamental difference of approach: the committee's principal focus at this stage was on the *internal* spaces of the museum; they wanted to design it from the inside out, to produce an interior plan that would work effectively as a museum, and then, after that task was accomplished, to make it look like a great building on the outside. Isozaki wanted to begin with the façade, to design it in his own personal style or 'signature'. His priorities, in other words, ran directly counter to those of the committee.

In the spring of 1982 the situation hit crisis point when Isozaki presented yet another model that the committee found unacceptable and that ignored their guidelines. Once again, they felt that the architect had focused his energies on the façade at the expense of the functional organisation of internal spaces. The façade was, indeed, distinctive: Isozaki had dressed the buildings in Indian red sandstone, and had angled and elevated the structure that housed the library and board room, so that it served as a gateway. In conformity with his love of geometric volumes, he raised the pyramidal skylights above the southernmost galleries, so that the façade read as a dialogue between geometric forms. While the committee found little to like, the developer and CRA were delighted with the model, for they felt that its signature style would benefit the overall project and turn it into a landmark, enhancing all of downtown by its distinctiveness. But the committee, more intent on creating a venue for art than a monument for downtown, sent Isozaki away to redraft the design, imposing on him the condition that unless he followed their recommendations, they would fire him.

In late March he returned with a design that adopted the artists' blueprint and that basically followed their guidelines: clearly articulated, austere, functional spaces with high ceilings and plain floors; a disposition of galleries that could host two concurrent but unrelated exhibitions, each with its own entrance; loading docks that could easily accommodate outsize contemporary artworks; skylights that maximised the natural light. The exterior was now a plain warehouse-like façade that faced across a sunken plaza to another equally plain structure that had been stripped bare of its pyramids. The low, box-like buildings resembled the industrial warehouses that house so many artists' lofts and in which so much contemporary art gets made. It conveyed the message that the art inside would be art-in-process. It was, in short, the ideal, quintessential, contemporary artist space. There was no longer any trace of the architect's forceful signature style.

The committee was at last satisfied. In celebration, the museum's board of trustees invited the press and their founding members (who now numbered in the several hundreds) to a balloon-lined reception on Grand Avenue (the future site of the museum) to eat fruit off the asphalt and to view the architectural models. It was to be another fun-filled MOCA affair, but one of the guests was not in a party mood: Isozaki. Profoundly unhappy with the model he had felt constrained to produce, he drew the press aside to tell them how little he liked it, how disappointed he was at its selection, how much he preferred his earlier, rejected January model. He told them that he had been forced to adhere to the committee's guidelines 'or be fired'.[11]

The press now leapt into the fray and attacked the Architecture Committee for imposing restraints on an architect of such international renown, framing the issue in terms of an architect's right to artistic autonomy. MOCA, so long the darling of the press, now received its first negative publicity. The Architecture Committee, now under attack, decided to discharge Isozaki from his primary role as architect, retaining him as design adviser only.

Accordingly, Palevsky wrote to the architect informing him of his dismissal. This action served only to fuel the press, and the Board of Trustees, anxious to avoid additional fallout, moved quickly to contain the crisis. On 3 May 1982, they held a meeting to discuss the issue. Of all the principals involved, Isozaki commanded the most international stature, with the possible exception of Sam Francis, who was, in any event, aligned with Isozaki. A majority of the members felt that public support for Isozaki, both local and international, was now so strong that to fire him would alienate potential donors, and since the museum was in the midst of a major endowment campaign, it could ill afford to ignore public opinion. The board decided to retain Isozaki, granting him licence to design his own façade. Their action effectively absolved Isozaki of blame which was, instead, levelled at the Architecture Committee which they disbanded, replacing it by a Building Committee without artist representation. The artists thus lost the ability to further affect the physical form of the space that had once held their hopes and aspirations. They were now effectively out of the design process.

Palevsky too, became marginalised. Since he had lost control of the architectural process, he felt that the board of trustees had contravened the contractual agreement he had spelled out when he had pegged his million-dollar donation to his continued authority over architectural decisions. He felt that he was now freed from any further financial obligation to the museum and that moneys already contributed should be returned to him. In 1984 he filed suit against the museum. Once again, MOCA was the subject of negative publicity.

Although the Isozaki-designed building was not to open until December 1986, MOCA began hosting exhibitions and functioning as a museum in November 1983. Original plans had been for Isozaki's building to open in time for the 1984 Olympic Games (which Los Angeles hosted), but it rapidly became evident that this deadline would not be met. The Artists' Advisory Council was keenly aware that the public's support of the museum could not be sustained over a protracted gestation, and so they persuaded the board to establish an interim facility in which the museum could begin its operations. In addition to sustaining the interest of patrons, the establishment of a temporary space had other advantages: it would carry none of the strictures on decorum that a $16 million edifice would be bound to impose; it could be experimental and lively, for the trustees, fixated on the monument on Bunker Hill, would cast a more lenient eye on the affairs of a temporary venue.

An abandoned warehouse in Little Tokyo was selected as the temporary facility. Local architect Frank O. Gehry was entrusted with its renovation, budgeted to cost one and a half million dollars. Sensitive both to the needs of the artists and to the inherent qualities of the raw space, Gehry kept his

Figure 6.8.1   MOCA at The Geffen Contemporary, 152 North Central Avenue, Los Angeles, California 90013. Architect: Frank Gehry (Photo: Squidds and Nunns)

interventions to a minimum. 'My job,' as he put it, 'was not to screw it up.'[12] What he did was clean it up: he steam-cleaned the redwood ceiling and perforated it with skylights and a clerestory; put in huge plate window-and-door entrances; enlivened it with ramps and concrete stairs; brought the electricity, plumbing and accessibility to current standards; painted the concrete floors and wall partitions silvery grey, and added movable white backdrops to accommodate artworks. Leaving the façade unaltered except for the new entrance doors, he erected a canopy of steel and chain to create a pedestrian plaza. The result was stunning: 45,000 square feet of exhibition space,[13] copious and flexible enough to accommodate almost any artwork, it looked like an expanded version of an artist's studio loft and was, indeed, exactly the sort of facility that the artists were trying to convince Isozaki to create (see Figure 6.8.1).

The Temporary Contemporary (or TC as it is more commonly known) opened to the public on 23 November 1983, and was a huge and instant success. It was every artist's dream of how a contemporary art museum should look, and it so enthralled the public that questions were raised as to whether a second facility on Bunker Hill was now rendered superfluous.[14] Perhaps it was, but so much money had already been invested in the project on the hill that no one meant seriously to repudiate it. Critics who raised the question immediately answered it by acknowledging that the two buildings could serve very different functions. Such, indeed, was the hope of the artists, for it was now evident that they would have little further input on the design of the building on Bunker Hill. The Temporary Contemporary could answer to their needs, while the building on the hill would satisfy the trustees' and developer's conception of a downtown museum in a major metropolitan area.

The opening exhibition in the temporary facility met the artists' highest hopes: it involved no collection, was ephemeral, experimental, site-specific, multi-disciplinary and commissioned works from active, mid-career artists. Entitled 'Available light', it was a collaborative performance piece by New York choreographer Lucinda Childs, Los Angeles architect Frank Gehry and San Francisco composer-in-residence John Adams. Gehry constructed the seating arrangements and the stage across which Ms Childs's dancers performed their stripped-down ballet to John Adams's music for synthesiser. In spite of their disappointments with the design process on Bunker Hill, the artists felt that their dream might still come true, for the show seemed to augur an institution whose spirit was of the laboratory, not the embalmer. MOCA would be a space for lively interaction between engaged artists, not a mausoleum in which to worship the canonised.

But 'Available light' was followed by 'The first show'. Featuring the treasures of eight prominent collectors, it was a showcase of modernist masterpieces, a celebration of acquisition, of traditional museological activity. Five of the eight collectors – de Menil, Ludwig, Panza, Rowan and Weisman – were MOCA trustees, and the exhibition honoured them and, by implication, all who collected on such a scale. The exhibition's very title, 'The first show', negated its more experimental predecessor, 'Available light', while its theme placed a premium on collecting and collectors. If one of its curatorial premises was to woo trustee-collectors into donating their work to the new institution, then it was an undisputed success, for Taft and Rita Schrieber (among the eight collectors honoured by the show) later bequeathed their collection to MOCA, which also acquired Panza's extraordinary ensemble of abstract expressionist and pop art for the bargain price of $11 million. Acquisition of this prized collection focused MOCA's Janus-faced ambivalence more firmly in the direction favoured by the trustees, making it less a forum for the exchange of artistic ideas than a repository for acknowledged great works.

In November 1986 the Isozaki-designed building was officially opened, first to a selected cadre of invited guests, then to the general public (see Figure 6.8.2). The press and museum professionals immediately proclaimed

Figure 6.8.2   MOCA at California Plaza, 250 South Grand Avenue, Los Angeles, California 90012. Architect: Arata Isozaki (Photo: Michael Moran)

it as a masterpiece. It was, indeed, a signature building, bearing the unmistakable stamp of Isozaki. The internal spaces, however, carried the stamp of the artists' recommendations; once they had been ousted from the process, Isozaki had adopted their blueprint. The large stone tablet recounting the museum's history was cemented prominantly into the lobby wall for all to read, foregrounding the trustees, eliding the artists who were not only not acknowledged for their contributions but who had watched their dreams and hopes for a different kind of museum slip away. Their comments on the experience serve as coda to this narrative.[15]

Of course, the big battles came with the architect. We wanted a building that was like the Temporary Contemporary ... We were really scared and scornful of the edifice complex. The building there on Grand Avenue is fine, but my heart as well as that of most of the artists in this town is with the Temporary Contemporary space. I don't know, I don't know what to think of the experience.

Isozaki, that building that he did. I mean, it was a political building. It was purely a product of politics. He came in here, and I remember, we had meetings with him when he was in the process of designing the building, and he didn't give a shit about our ideas, Well, I don't blame him, because he envisioned himself as being an

Figure 6.8.3   MOCA at California Plaza, 250 South Grand Avenue, Los Angeles, California 90012. Image of Monroe curve in Broad Lobby entrance. Architect: Arata Isozaki (Photo: Tim Street-Porter)

artist, which he is. I don't want other people telling me how to paint a painting, so he doesn't want other people telling him how to build a building. The difference is: he accepted as a premise that there would be a dialogue with the artists. Then he said: Piss off. I think he just allied himself politically with those who had power to support his position, and then just basically pushed everybody aside.

Once the principals, the board of trustees, came into play, it was obvious that we weren't going to do anything, because they were going to run it the way they wanted to run it, and they weren't interested in asking us or involving us in any way. There was no recognition of our involvement. None. Personally, I have very negative feelings about the place, because of that. Basically, this is a place that's used as a tool to further the careers of whoever's involved with it.

We wanted this to be an institution for artists, and whoever worked on it would work with us, and it was not going to be dominated by boards of trustees and by the architectural edifice complex and the inflexibility of the art market and international mandates ... Basically, we wanted power! God! Artists don't ever have any power in something like this because you have to have funds and you have to have money and you have to have support from the community and a lot of artists on the committee were people like me, who are social outsiders.

We wanted it to be much more fluid. I think Irwin's fantasy – and I think maybe it was shared subliminally by a lot of us – was, we sort of pictured this *bubble* that would kind of bulge one way when we wanted it to, and bulge another way when we wanted that. That it would be this real *fluid* kind of thing in which artists could come and go and do their thing, and it wouldn't just fossilise itself as museums do.

It really got disappointing to me when I realized it was going to be a big fancy building.

I think there was a certain point that we all bit the bullet and understood that in any public facility the developers, oddly enough, were the ones in power. To swallow all of that is real painful when you're an idealist. I think Los Angeles is a very hard city to be an idealist in. It has such movie star tendencies to look at things as glamorous. I don't know how we would ever be able to overcome that image in this culture

The doors started to shut very clearly and definitely on the artists as soon as there was a board of trustees. Historically, patrons consider the artists at best second-class citizens. My contention has always been that if dealers and patrons could possibly get the art without having to deal with artists, that would be their ideal world.

NOTES

1. This amount, calculated in 1979/80 dollars, was indexed to inflation, so that the final dollar amount was calculated to be $22 million.
2. The remaining balance would come from memberships, admissions, grants and other sources.
3. Letter from Palevsky to Broad, dated 3 April 1980.
4. Key members included Robert Irwin, Sam Francis, Alexis Smith, Karen Carson, Tom Wudl, Peter Alexander, DeWain Valentine, Vija Celmins, Lita Albuquerque, Melinda Wyatt, Gary Lloyd, Peter Lodato, Fred Eversly, Robert Heinecken, Joe Fay, Roland Reiss and Guy Dill.

5. The Maguire Thomas proposal was also ranked first by local architectural critics.

6. Irwin tells how, at a pivotal meeting, the Cadillac Fairview representative 'whacked his hip pocket with the flat of his hand and exclaimed: 'I can pay for this project out of my hip pocket.' Norris describes the same event as 'the deep pocket strategy of Cadillac Fairview'. Cadillac Fairview was the dominant partnership in an association known as Bunker Hill Associates. They subsequently went bankrupt and their role in the consortium was assumed by Metropolitan Structures Inc.

7. The name was changed on 11 July 1980.

8. Robert Irwin, interviewed 16 June 1990.

9. Irwin, interview.

10. This interviewee has requested anonymity.

11. Reported by Joseph Giovannini, *Herald Examiner* architecture critic, 'Dispute over design for the Museum of Contemporary Art', *Los Angeles Herald Examiner*, 29 March 1982.

12. Quoted in Pilar Vilades, 'The undecorated shed', *Progressive Architecture*, March 1984.

13. About 9,000 more than the permanent facility.

14. For example, William Wilson, art critic for the *Los Angeles Times*, wrote: 'No sooner was the place launched … than the voice of the people spake unto the fates, saying "This is terrific. Who needs a fancy new museum building up on Bunker Hill, even by so distinguished an architect as Arata Isozaki, when we have this urban miracle"', 8 December 1984.

15. These statements were made by artists who served on the Artists' Advisory Council. The interviews occurred from June 1990 to October 1990. For obvious reasons I have not revealed their identities.

9.

The Identity Card Project and the Tower of Faces at the United States Holocaust Memorial Museum

Andrea Liss

> In the work of mourning, it is not grief that works; grief keeps watch.
> Maurice Blanchot, *The Writing of the Disaster*

Upon entrance to the United States Holocaust Memorial Museum in Washington, D.C., the visitor is 'invited to register' for an identity card.[1] The visitor is directed to a computer-processing area in the foyer of the frighteningly vast and hollow space of the Hall of Witness. Here preprinted cards await the visitor (see Figure 6.9.1). The cards are printed with a photograph and a brief text about the Holocaust victims and survivors they represent. The information is gleaned from much longer histories that the survivors or the families of those who perished have offered to the museum

Figure 6.9.1   Identity cards at the United States Holocaust Memorial Museum.
Courtesy of the United States Holocaust Memorial Museum Photo Archives

for public use. The cards are organized by these persons' ages and genders. The museum visitor is directed to choose from among these cards to select an identity card representing a Holocaust victim whose bare traces of identity are approximately matched to the visitor's random and impersonal statistics. The initial concept for the identity card project would have had the visitor record his or her age and gender directly into the computer. He or she would then have been 'matched' by the computer with a compatible 'companion' and then issued a corresponding card.

The cover of the identity card bears the logo and the organizing authoritative logic of the museum's symbolic imprint. In this guise, the name of the museum appears in full below the eagle crowned with the logo 'For the dead *and* the living we must bear witness'.[2] Each identity card is also marked with a four-digit number, computer printed as if it were freshly stamped. Opening the identity card and reading the inside front page reveal the vital statistics of the person who experienced the Holocaust: name, date of birth, place of birth, and place of residence. Printed directly above these data looms a close-up black-and-white pre-Holocaust photograph of the person/subject in question. The visitor journeys through the permanent exhibition with this eerie conflation of passport and death sentence in hand. As the project was initially devised, the visitor would again be invited to enter the identity card into a computer at the end of each floor of the permanent exhibition to obtain further information about his or her extended double. The documentation added at each computer station would correlate with the years that the exhibition chronicles. When the museum first opened, the computer stations positioned at each floor were still in operation; however, like those at the entrance, these have also been deinstalled. The museum's project director, Michael Berenbaum, stated that the computers at the end of each floor were developed to handle one million cards. The planners never anticipated the enormous number of visitors, and after three months, as Berenbaum puts it, the computers were 'used up'.[3] Until the museum can reinstate the computers, visitors now receive the full text about their identity card companion before entering the narrative sections of the permanent exhibition. The permanent exhibition is divided up into chronological sections: making up the fourth floor, where the exhibition begins, is 'The Assault 1933–1939'; on the third floor is 'The Holocaust 1940–1944'; and the second floor lays claim to 'Bearing Witness 1945–'. The identity card's unfolding biographical narrative was designed to both parallel and intervene in the larger historical narrative being produced in the massive 40,000-square-foot permanent exhibition. Thus by the time the visitor had descended the exhibition's floors, his or her card would be filled with a condensed text revealing whether or not their ghost guide survived the atrocities. As the identity card now [1988] functions – or malfunctions – the visitor enters the museum and chooses from among piles of cards that are placed, almost carelessly, in two boxes marked solely by gender.

It is more than coincidence that this punctuated facsimile marking the bare minimum of a Holocaust victim's pre-Holocaust life and the unfolding ruin of his or her existence afterward echo the horror of the Nazis' actual marking of bodies. The metaphors to the brutal labeling are hardly masked. Indeed, the philosophy driving the strategies of the museum's permanent exhibition program is based on bringing the horrors close to the surface, refusing to 'sanitize' them. The museum's guiding approach was largely formulated by Martin Smith, former director of the museum's permanent exhibition program. Significant to the profile of the United States Holocaust Memorial Museum is that Smith is not a museum professional. He was chosen to formulate the museum's theoretical underpinnings and their exposition in the permanent exhibition precisely because of his experience as an independent documentary filmmaker.[4] Given the first museum director Jeshajahu Weinberg's hopes for the museum to 'introduce a three-dimensional multi-media approach' that he wanted to differentiate from the more traditional ways of telling Holocaust history, Smith's past work with photographs and film footage as documents and storytelling devices harmonized well with the museum's goals.[5] Before the actual exhibitions were installed, Smith reflected on his working philosophy as it guided the difficult and daunting task toward formulating the permanent exhibition at the United States Holocaust Memorial Museum:

That any individual who wasn't part of the event can comprehend the event seems to me beyond the realm of reason. Even the survivors themselves cannot comprehend the event. They can perhaps occasionally comprehend the part and parcel of it. My own response in terms of looking at the exhibition has been affected by questions bearing on to what extent are we pushing or should we push the barriers of respectability, acceptability, horror – which has recently come up with the NEA [National Endowment for the Arts] thing about claiming you shouldn't have photographs of the Holocaust placed in front of people. If you are going to stop that sort of funding and you really believe that the arts should not engage in images of social distress, you should go around removing the crucifix in front of every Roman Catholic church in the land.

I think we cannot avoid looking at some of the worst of the material. But what is the worst anyway? I find just looking at people's heads and feet when they are deceased as distasteful as anything else, like pubic hair and everything else that has caused me any number of worries. My belief is that if you do not put them on display, then you are diminishing the extent of the horror and what the experience actually meant. But I would be absolutely opposed to sanitizing it. When I first came in, they asked me what my approach would be and I said that the job was impossible, but I'm not in favor of sanitizing it: I'm sure that whatever we do is going to be offensive to very many people. I don't think that is the fault of the institution – it is the fault of the subject matter.

The irony is that I don't trust the medium of documentary photography at all, and I don't even trust historical records. They are all coming through the filter system of human memory, and all memory is written to advance a particular point of view. I do, however, think that the only way to handle the event is via a documentary approach. But I don't believe either documentary films or photographs alone can do it. It was important to establish the physical reality of the Holocaust ... which is why we've got a barracks from Auschwitz-Birkenau, which is why we've got a railcar, which is why we have a rescue boat, which is why we've got the uniforms. ... The exhibition will be a mixture of photographs, films, documents, and artifacts. I think increasingly with time people will be more and more skeptical about visual imagery and about film, and rightly so. ... The difference between our museum and most museums is that the photograph as object is of very little interest to us as far as the permanent exhibit is concerned. We are using photographs as evidentiary and storytelling vehicles.[6]

Note that Smith referred to his difficult task to restage the museum visitor's approach to the Holocaust as 'impossible'. Caught between displaying the horror of the experiences and guarding against 'the worst of the material', Smith's thoughts resonate with the paradoxes implied by Berenbaum when he stated that 'we wanted to come as close as possible to desecration without redesecrating'.[7]

The museum's unflinching approach is even more literally tangible from the first steps the visitor takes into this mammoth edifice of simulated memory. With his or her identity card companion in hand, the visitor enters the museum's permanent exhibition via one of three thin gray elevators whose eerie steel and industrial feel evoke a claustrophobic finality. Once the elevator doors shut, the lights dim and narrated film footage enacting the US liberation of the camps begins to play on two screens positioned above the doors.[8] After viewing burned landscapes and devastated bodies, the viewer as victim and witness hears these last words pronounced before the elevator arrives at its destination: 'You can't imagine. Things like that don't happen.' After this approximately twenty-second journey – the footage is timed to end at the moment the elevator arrives at the fourth floor – the doors open onto a view that frames a large black-and-white photographic blowup of US soldiers standing before a pile containing calcinated corpses at the Ohrdruf concentration camp at the time of liberation. A video monitor set into the wall immediately follows this enlargement. It plays film footage taken by George Stevens (who later directed *The Anne Frank Story* [1959]) of American soldiers arriving at a camp. Both of the photographs are from the National Archives in Washington, D.C., and like the film, were taken by the US military during the liberation of the camps.[9] A smaller color photograph picturing a man who survived Buchenwald follows this monitor.

It can be argued that these photographic and filmic images, as the first artifactual evidence the viewer faces, lay the foundation for the Americans as the saviors and the silent narrators/witnesses to the viewer's experience within his or her journey through the United States Holocaust Memorial Museum. This institution's nationalistic framing of memory is hardly hidden. The multiple ways in which the museum frames the visitor as Jew, as victim, as transformed witness, and as a reborn American citizen are not accidental.[10] Yet I focus here less on a critique based on the museum's transparent subtext in order to consider more deeply its complex approaches to photographic representation. These three introductory documents make the visitor's entrance into the permanent exhibition difficult and complicated. The photographic blowup presents a wide, horizontal expanse to the horrific scene whose format suggests an environmental tableau that one could walk into – but it is an impossible invitation. In the film footage, listless bodies with graven faces wander aimlessly across the viewer's numbed lens. 'Liberation' is hardly played on a triumphant note. The color photograph employed as the last image in the museum's introductory wall creates an important and unusual disruption from the black-and-white documentary rhetoric of the past brought into the viewer's present.[11] These three images function more like a punctuated epilogue transposed to the beginning of the story, especially since the 'real' beginning of the museum's chronological story opens just after this wall with a sketching out of the presence of diverse minority populations throughout Europe before Hitler's rise to power.

The vital question thus brings its own pressure to bear on what remains to be told, toward what can be told. What forms of photographic nomenclature can be presented in the name of acknowledging the impossible? The Lyotardian echo reverberates 'to bear witness to differends by finding idioms for them'.[12] The most troubling issues for Smith at the United States Holocaust Memorial Museum were precisely those that confuse the fine line between the near-impossibility of confronting Holocaust memory and history as palimpsest, the responsibility of 'telling the story', and the difficult indispensability of employing documentary photographs. One might hear echoing in Smith's concerns Theodor W. Adorno's now well-known warning from the immediate postwar years of the dangers of aestheticizing the events. In explaining his initial and often misinterpreted phrase about the inability of art to represent the Holocaust, 'To write poetry after Auschwitz is barbaric,' Adorno later wrote, 'Through the aesthetic principle of stylization, an unimaginable fate still seems as if it had some meaning; it becomes transfigured, with something of the horror removed.'[13] Note the similarities between what came to be mistaken as Adorno's taboo on Holocaust representation and some of the reasons that fuel contemporary unease with documentary's presumptions. Both arguments are profoundly concerned that the viewer is brought into the scene under false pretenses. Furthermore, Smith's decision not to 'sanitize' the events is akin to Adorno's guarding against displacing their horror. Given such warnings, to assume to represent the enormity and incommensurability of the Shoah will always be a horrible if not disrespectful reduction of the realities. What, then, are the museum's divided strategies for addressing the paradoxes of telling this history and the modes of address it constructs between the visitor and the difficult material through the identity card project?

Held carefully in the visitor's hand or nestled nonchalantly in a coat pocket, the identity card might hold out the possibility of working across the relentlessly graphic, massive, and chronological view of history projected throughout the elaborately storied exhibition. Indeed, the exhibition team devised the identity card project as a way to break down the history of the Holocaust into what they refer to as human terms, 'to educate visitors by personalizing the experience'. The museum's press release, issued before the museum opened in April 1993, further projected that 'visitors will be encouraged to keep their identity cards when they leave the Museum as tangible remembrances of their visit'. Speaking about the majority of photographic images picturing people as ghost facades of their former selves, such as those that arrest the visitor upon his or her entrance into the permanent exhibition, Smith rhetorically asked, 'Why would a robust, McDonald's-fed, eighteen-year-old American *boy* have any connection to these emaciated figures? The identity card project came out of our desire to establish an immediate bonding with a person and a place.'[14]

The notion of bonding is indeed key to the tantalizing concept underlying the identity card project. At stake is precisely how the texture of this bonding between the contemporary museum viewer and his or her extended double from the past will be staged. Also crucially at issue is how the photographic and textual markers that represent the Holocaust victim will formulate the proximities and the distances between that absent person and the variable identities of the museum visitor(s). In other words, how will normative positions of objectivity (in this case, the museum visitor's) and subjectivity (the person to be remembered, or in this case, the 'subject' viewed) be maintained, refracted, or abridged? If it is the museum's goal that the visitor arrive at some form of empathy toward the human specter that has guided her through and across the permanent exhibition, it relies heavily on the possibility of imaginative projection. First, to write the shadow of a Holocaust victim's experiences through the inscription of a single photograph and an attenuated text calls forth its very (im)possibility. Further, to attempt to reach across the chasm of unimaginable realities and incommensurable events and to bring in the visitor's ability to imagine, to be open to the Holocaust other, are necessary presumptions. The identity card project tantalizes precisely because it acknowledges the presence of a viewer who receives information on cognitive and emotional registers. Through its anticipation of the viewer's projection of her own subjectivity into the participatory process, the identity card project provokes the possibility of intervening in traditional documentary presentations that presume that looking is based on purely objective dynamics.

Despite the museum's rhetoric that it will 'tell the full story',[15] the actual thinking toward the identity card is more closely aligned with Elie Wiesel's notion of a metaphorical and literal gate or barrier to full knowledge. Irving Howe has also written against the possibility of full disclosure and has called for representations that work in 'tentative and modest solidarity with those who fell'.[16] The refusal, or the inability, to grant full disclosure to the representation of historical events correlates with the identity card's appropriate inability to create smooth mergings between the museum spectator and images of Holocaust victims. In fact, it is the identity card project's very reliance on the museum visitor's subjectivity and self-investment – the skeletal allowance of his or her own biographical data driving the issuance of the card – that mimics the notion of a perfect mirror staging. An extreme and yet probable case of a shattering of rather than a conflation with one's doubled persona could occur if the visitor refuses affinity with his or her issued ghost. Smith has given thought to the possibility of such built-in confrontations:

Somebody may be offended by having their personal identity card represent a homosexual, to which my response is, if a Fundamentalist Christian comes in, would he be satisfied being coupled with a Jew? So if you don't issue a Jew, where do you go? Are we going to allow a Jew to say, 'No, I don't want to hear about some dissenting Christian?'[17]

Although such surface disjunctures are built into the maneuverings of the identity card, the project is more conceptually driven by attempts to formulate imaginative projection tending toward empathy. What, then, are its safeguards, its soft barriers that warn against facile bonds of sameness between the museum visitor and the persons pictured and described on the cards? This crucial question might itself assume too much, might retrospectively be in vain, because a marking of differences is always already in place in the strange and unpredictable commingling of identities that the identity card attenuates. No matter what is announced about the project's ability to pair and to compare, the workings of the identity card could never occur through seamless identifications. Everywhere in the museum – from the vague memory of the disembodied city outside, which the museum's architecture tries to efface, to the intricate workings of the simulated environments it houses – the visitor is reminded that he or she is in a vast space of articulated re-creation. To thus create a fusion of identities without gaps between the museum visitor and the remembered Holocaust victims would verge on the dangerous as well as the inconceivable.

It is the photographed face of the Holocaust victim that paradoxically promises to ward off slipping into false realisms and facile mimetic mergings endemic to the estranged documentary tradition. The photograph of the face on the identity card functions as an arbiter or a boundary zone between the interchangeable subjective and objective identities of the viewer and the memorialized other. It also creates a stopgap between the disputed terrain of the remembered and recountable historicized past of the individual to be thus commemorated and the private space of his or her unknowable and unrecountable life. In its profound visibility and simultaneous elusiveness, the hovering small-scale photographic face is a trace that obliquely excludes parts of a map to a larger history. The intangibility of the face and the photograph as both presence and absence mirrors the tensions in the photographic representation of intractable events. The employment of the face on the identity cards suggests a point of arrest bridging the utter horror depicted through the mass of Holocaust-related documentary photographs and the sheer refusal to depict the atrocities. It serves as a vital buffer zone across the unpresentable and a tentative temptation to represent. It is both perverse and appropriate that the image of the face returns in an orchestrated maneuver meant to counteract the Nazis' mass-scale elimination and extermination of bodies, faces, and identities. The photographic act of giving back identities and names takes place here through dialectic means. The identity card conflates and restages the Nazis' perverse criminalizing of innocent persons while it seeks to enact recuperative acts of commemoration. Yet the identity card's attempt to restore the personhood of the individuals who perished or who suffered immeasurably is only provisionally accomplished by the degree to which the unknown museum visitor can or will take in these memorized histories.

The uneasy point of intersection between the past and the present in the identity card's construction of historical memory is further played out through the confusion of verb tenses written into its condensed biographical sketches. For example, the identity card documenting the unfolding of Haskel Kernweis's fatal entanglement with the Nazis moves between the present and past tenses. The text that introduces Haskel with his photograph and bare data of existence reads:

Haskel comes from a small village in Galicia. His family is very religious. His mother raises geese, chickens, and vegetables for the family to eat. Haskel walks 5 miles to public school in the morning, and goes to religious school in the afternoon.

Having established a trace of Haskel's pre-Holocaust existence, the text is brought consecutively into focus as the visitor moves through the floors of the exhibition space:

1933–1939: Haskel now calls himself 'Charley', for his passion is no longer religion but English. He spends much of his time learning English from a torn, old grammar book. He writes to Eleanor Roosevelt telling her that he loves English and wants to speak it in America one day. She responds enthusiastically. The German police order Charley to work for them.

1940–1944: Charley is told by the Germans to dismantle the ghetto in Kolbushova, then hears that he is to be killed upon completion of the job. He escapes into the woods with a group of Jewish men.

The present tense is unfortunate here for it works too hard and in vain to force the reality of Haskel into *our* present. The entire machinery of memory that is being so carefully constructed at the United States Holocaust Memorial Museum is being performed so that the memory of the past will be reformulated in the present. Indeed, the references to Eleanor Roosevelt and to America as a monumentalized haven are a bit too fitting, if not self-serving, to the museum's purpose. To pretend that the brutal and complete past can be written in the form of an innocent, innocuous, and intimate present verges on the absurd, without pushing it far enough for us to pause on the incongruity of the task. It is hardly fitting to the memory of the person Haskel, whom we will never know.

The past tense enters this historical-diaristic narrative indicator at the terse point where the text intimates Haskel's death, in the middle of the 1940–1944 section: 'One day, Charley went into a town to buy bread. Waiting for him were a group of Polish peasants.' And it then continues, more aligned to the narrative and more in justice to Haskel's memory, in the simple past: 'His friends found him – dead, a pitchfork stuck into his chest. 1945 –

Charley's entire family was gassed at Belzec. Only one of the Jewish fighters who went to the woods with him survived the war.'

The identity card project entices the viewer because it brings photographically and textually into view realities that will always be out of reach. The presumptuous contention at work is that the identity card's strategy of bonding can, indeed, write across chasms of the unknowable to arrive at some point of provisional fusion. The identity card experiment suggests one way to approach the inevitable dilemma of representing the unrepresentable, but in its move toward feigned intimacy it more deeply reinforces the abyss of distance it so emphatically seeks to shore up. This reaching across to the unknowable represents a desire to render present that which can never be completely absent. This poignant and haunting desire to seek idioms for the horrible sublime that gives life to the identity card project bears in it the oscillating drives animating the dynamics of mourning itself.

Sigmund Freud characterized mourning as an act that can be accomplished through the 'economic' incorporation of the lost other into the self, but not without the expenditure of much psychic energy. Freud's theory of mourning was developed through his study and treatment of individual psychoses and was not conceived to embrace the extraordinary phenomena of historical trauma and genocide. The Freudian model of 'successful' mourning lays potent ground for theorizing the intersubjective relationships between the self and the departed other in relatively normative situations of loss or actual death. Yet if the ability to distance oneself from the lost other and to recover from the loss is gained through deep internal psychic struggle, accomplished mourning provocatively suggests that traumatic loss of incommensurable proportion – both individually and historically – would create an ongoing if not thwarted process of mourning. Mourning and melancholy might need to be considered as intertwining psychic states in which the mourner cannot completely let go of the other. The memory of the other must hover impalpably between the self and the other.

Working from Freud in his crucial text on mourning, friendship, and unreadability, *Mémoires for Paul de Man*, Jacques Derrida weaves a discussion of a transfigured narcissism in which the self comes to understand its imprecise proximities with the grieved other through the simultaneous process of possible and impossible mourning:

Memory and interiorization: since Freud, this is how the 'normal' 'work of mourning' is often described. It entails a movement in which an interiorizing idealization takes in itself or upon itself the body and voice of the other, the other's visage and person, ideally and quasi-literally devouring them. This mimetic interiorization is not fictive; it is the origin of fiction, of apocryphal figuration. It takes place in a body. Or rather, it makes a place for a body, a voice, and a soul which, although 'ours', did not exist and had no meaning *before* this possibility that one *must* always begin by remembering, and whose trace must be followed. *Il faut,* one *must*: it is the law, that law of the (necessary) relation of Being to law. We can only live this experience in the form of an aporia: the aporia of mourning and of prosopopeia, where the possible remains impossible. Where *success fails*. And where faithful interiorization bears the other and constitutes him in me (in us), at once living and dead. It makes the other a *part* of us, between us – and then the other no longer quite seems to be the other, because we grieve for him and bear him *in us*, like an unborn child, like a future. And inversely, the *failure succeeds*: an aborted interiorization is at the same time a respect for the other as other, a sort of tender rejection, a movement of renunciation which leaves the other alone, outside, over there, in his death, outside of us.[18]

This eloquent articulation figures possible mourning as Freud's clinical description of incorporation; impossible mourning would be the refusal to take the grieved other within oneself so completely, so definitively. Derrida's plea for tender rejection counters the self's almost obscene desire to overwhelm the other, 'over there, in his [or her] death'. In his earlier text, 'Fors', the foreword to Nicolas Abraham and Maria Torok's study *The Wolf Man's Magic Word: A Cryptonymy*, Derrida calls attention to Torok's distinctions between incorporation and introjection:

The question could of course be raised as to whether or not 'normal' mourning preserves the object *as other* (a living person dead) inside me. This question – of the general appropriation and safekeeping of the other *as other* – does it not at the same time blur the very line it draws between introjection and incorporation, through an essential and irreducible ambiguity? Let us give this question a chance to be reposed. For Maria Torok, 'incorporation, properly speaking', in its 'rightful semantic specificity', intervenes at the limits of introjection itself, when introjection, for some reason, fails. Faced with the impotence of the process of introjection (gradual, slow, laborious, mediated, effective), incorporation is the only choice: fantasmatic, unmediated, instantaneous, magical, sometimes hallucinatory.[19]

The instantaneous and fantasmatic longing that enacts the mourning of incorporation takes us back to the United States Holocaust Memorial Museum and Martin Smith's desires for the identity card project: 'to establish an immediate bonding with a person and a place'. Given that the museum opted for the abbreviated version of mourning, the one that Derrida ironically yet gravely noted that Maria Torok described as 'the only choice', the museum has no other choice in hoping that casual visitors – tourists, that is – would quickly come to some point of empathy with their Holocaust doubles. The notion of mourning as a process of incorporation is closely enmeshed with the longing toward figurative bonding that Smith and his colleagues hoped the identity card would attain. Incorporation and the identity card project conjoin specifically in the dilemma of the place of the other. Where is the place of the departed other, and where is he or she simultaneously displaced through the processes of incorporation set into motion through the identity card? The identity card pleads for instantaneous, immediate, and yet impossible bonding. It bears in it the haunted oscillations between loving proximity and irrevocable distance toward the other. As Maria Torok aptly phrased it, 'The more the self keeps the foreign element as a foreigner inside itself, the more it excludes it. The self *mimes* introjection.'[20] The question arises as to whether the imaginative projection of living in the name and in the place of the Holocaust other allows for a respectful taking in or incorporation of his or her memory without the concurrent process of introjection. In the enmeshed workings of incorporation and introjection, or possible and impossible mourning, the safekeeping of the other must always simultaneously participate in its veiled exclusion, its tender rejection.

The identity card calls the viewer to take in memories through the abbreviated processes of self-investment and self-effacement. The museum visitor cloaks him- or herself in the identity of the departed or brutalized other. But the level of intake may not be sustained enough to prepare for the profitable return of introjection, for the ability to find a space of appropriate distance leading to respectful and inevitable otherness. Under cover in the identity card project rests a curious inversion of investments. One particular twist to these ploys of identification, as Jonathan Rosen noted, is that 'there is a reverse principle at work here, as if everyone were expected to enter the museum an American and leave, in some fashion, a Jew'.[21] And as James E. Young has elucidated this mismatching, 'Imagining oneself as a past victim is not the same as imagining oneself – or another person – as a potential victim, the kind of leap necessary to prevent other "holocausts".'[22] So much is at stake in the museum visitor's investment to take in the Holocaust other as victim that the identity and personhood of the memorialized other risk being lost in the process. Indeed, the issuance of mock identity cards could turn out to be a mourning and a bearing witness turned inside out and strained at the seams (see Figure 6.9.2). This strange fusion of selves represents a desire for urgency camouflaged as a transfixed form of displaced nostalgia. The United States Holocaust Memorial Museum's attempt at empathy might better function as a reminder that the few circulating photographs documenting the Nazi ruin of the lives of the people pictured on the identity cards did little to alert the Allies or to bring them to action. Especially given the identity card's simulacrum of a US passport, we might then ask how the documentary photographs featuring American soldiers liberating the camps on display in the permanent exhibition can pretend to function as warning signals on the level of lucid historical objectivity. As Rosen and Liliane Weissberg have noted, the identity card's smug assurance of safe harboring in the name of Americanism takes no account of the thousands of deliberately falsified passports and other documents of feigned identity sought after by those who attempted refuge.[23] The current manipulation and presence of these images both reanimate and haunt the past lives of the people pictured. The photographs and the identity cards unintentionally yet translucently

Figure 6.9.2   Identity card stations at the United States Holocaust Memorial Museum. Courtesy of Michael Dawson.

perform that lack of response as mute and potent witnesses. Thus in their tantalizing (im)possibility, the identity cards tear at the photographic wound that would make of memory a souvenir.

While the museum travelers literally traverse and descend the three floors of the permanent exhibition with their expendable identity cards in hand, a different construction of photographic memory-work is being tried in an adjoining section of the exhibition space. Set off from the main arenas of chronological articulation are four tower alcoves that are filled with intimate possessions that belonged to those who perished. These objects are also presented alongside the instruments responsible for their owners' deaths. The Tower of Faces promises to be the most effective and expansive of these metaexhibitions.[24] The Tower of Faces is a space covered from top to bottom with 1,032 photographs of former residents of the small shtetl town of Ejszyszki taken between 1890 and 1941 (see Figure 6.9.3). Eishyshok, the town's name in Yiddish, is located near Vilna in what is now Lithuania. The Jewish community in Ejszyszki, whose population was about 3,500 by 1939, had lived there for almost nine hundred years. The community was known for its Talmudic academy and rich cultural life. The Tower of Faces is a 54-

Figure 6.9.3   Tower of Faces. Courtesy of the Yaffa Eliach Shtetl Collection and the
United States Holocaust Museum Photo Archives

foot-high, 16-foot-by-28-foot skylit tower space designed to stage a very specific approach between the museum visitor and the photographs of Ejszyszkians pictured in a variety of secular activities. Rather than having visitors enter the alcove as if it were an easily accessible and perusable room, the exhibit designers chose to have the fifth floor of the museum removed at the point where it would connect with the tower's interior space. The visitor's journey through the Tower of Faces is thus possible only by crossing over a translucent glass bridge at the third and fourth floors. The photographs of the former townspeople of Ejszyszki are laminated over aluminum sheets and mounted on a lattice frame angling inward as it rises from its base on the third floor to its fifth-floor ceiling. As the museum's newsletter describes the effect, 'Visitors will be able to peer over the side of the bridge and view the photographs from Ejszyszki seemingly floating above and cascading below them.'[25] This expansive sensation also gives rise to the numbing realization that the tower also resembles a chimney.

Unlike the identity card's mode of address based on insistent self-identifications, the Tower of Faces stages the presence of the spectator in a space distinct from the sphere occupied by the Ejszyszkians. We are allowed to pass through the photographically haunting identities of the Jews from Ejszyszki; no forced attempt is made to psychically bond him or her with us as their pre-Holocaust likenesses bring us near. Absent, too, from this more gentle memory-trial are the strained anticipation and parceled telling of the brutalities at work in the identity card project. The events that occurred at Ejszyszki are recounted after the visitor passes through the photographic chamber via the glass bridge for the first time. The text panel recounts how, during the period of the Jewish high holidays in 1941, from 25 to 26 September, the Nazi mobile killing squads or *Einsatzgruppen* rounded up people from the synagogues, took them to the marketplace and then to the fields outside the town. Throughout Europe and with the help of non-German collaborators, the *Einsatzgruppen* mass-murdered more than two million Jews and still-unmeasured numbers of Gypsies, Byelorussians, and Russians before the organized plan of the concentration and exterminations camps was in place. The visitor's second encounter with the vivid photographic ghosts of the slaughtered Ejszyszkians, those few who survived, and their ancestors occurs on the third floor of the museum, at which point the visitor crosses the glass bridge yet another time.

Within the complex of displays of dehumanization that the museum inevitably stages, the Tower of Faces is remarkable because it is the only space in the museum that implicitly rather than explicitly addresses the genocide. It pictures people fully integrated into the activities of a community run by consensus rather than the most violent of force, where the said and not-said of the everyday of peoples' lives address the viewer rather than a confrontation with images that strip away any possibility of identification between the photographed and the viewer.

Interestingly, the Tower of Faces is preceded by two corridor exhibition spaces that emphasize the failure of what the Tower of Faces was precisely set up to elicit: the ability to partially identify with and respond to the personhood of the people pictured. The first of the two spaces is devoted to narrating what the US public knew about Hitler's Final Solution and about American immigration policies.[26] The narrator's voice recounts that 97 percent of the US population disapproved of Hitler's actions but that at least 77 percent did not support providing refuge. This audio and videotape section ends by inferring that these statistics were the result of perceptions in the United States that European Jews were unsophisticated rural people who could not possibly integrate into this country's modern urban texture.

Ironically, what is presented as perception and not fact in the first space is unwittingly offered as justification in the next area. On the walls of this room hang glass-framed photographs by Roman Vishniac, photographs that picture rural and urban religious European Jews in isolated, darkened, and mystical environments that emphasize otherworldliness as well as the real material world of anti-Semitism in the 1930s. These images seem light-years away from the 'progress' and familiarity of American cities and, for that matter, from the modernity of Jewish homes in European cities and towns – scenes of which are pictured within the Tower of Faces. It is patently odd that Vishniac's remarkable photographs – whose specificity about particular religious communities on the verge of danger is often unfortunately misinterpreted as nostalgic generalizations about piousness and antiquity – could paradoxically justify the interpretive strand about American indifference that flows from the audiovideo room into this space. The room in which the Vishniac photographs dwell is further displaced within the flow of the storied units because of its physical appearance: it is fully carpeted in pastel blue, appointed with comfortable sitting chairs, and affixed to its entryway is a large mezuzah. Here is an opulent space that mimics domesticity without irony. Furthermore, its walls are lined with Vishniac's photographs framed and presented more as fine art pictures than as proof, or as Martin Smith phrased it, as 'evidentiary or storytelling devices'. The poshness and eerie calm of this room are a strange antecedent to the staging involved in entering the Tower of Faces, a space in which the very accoutrements of domesticity and daily life are put into question rather than simulated. Perhaps the uncanniness of this room and the way it punctures and belies the smooth flow of the narrative point out that the museum's only recourse to presenting history is as a staging. Here the staging has come loose from its own frame.

The Tower of Faces and the identity card project are both photographic strategies animated by ambivalent desires to intervene in the museum's predominantly massive, depersonalized, and chronological telling of the events of the Holocaust. The unraveling or, more precisely, the filling up of information on the identity card progresses on a path parallel to the larger narrative. Because of the identity card's plea for assimilation of the Holocaust victim's history into the museum visitor's supposedly singular identity, the articulation of the past into the present remains a story of easily separable spaces of time and memory. The visitor never returns to the same place and time again; history is told in a logically sequential framework. The histories and identities of the town and the people of Ejszyszki circulate on a different register in the Tower of Faces. They are provocatively staged through repetitions of almost identical spaces that do not follow one after the other. The first tenuous crossing of the glass bridge is repeated on the next lower floor only after the museum visitor has undergone the full onslaught of the fourth- and third-floor exhibitions. The second entrance into the photographic tower creates an echoed experience that functions more in harmony with the layered way in which memories overlap and intrude on the mental time zones of the past and the present, especially involving circumstances of extreme traumatic dislocation. Chronological time stands still in trauma; furthermore, it is sealed away into a space where psychic time takes over.[27] In her book *A Scrap of Time*, Polish Holocaust survivor Ida Fink writes about her own tenuous return to the remembrance of the unarticulated and immeasurable past:

I want to talk about a certain time not measured in months and years. For so long I have wanted to talk about this time. ... I wanted to, but I couldn't; I didn't know how. I was afraid, too, that this second time, which is measured in months and years, had buried the other time under a layer of years, that this second time had crushed the first and destroyed it within me. But no. Today, digging around in the ruins of memory, I found it fresh and untouched by forgetfulness.[28]

The dilemmas and the interweavings between chronologically measurable calendar time and the cyclical structure of time in nature and memory – a time, however, that never returns as the same – are constant themes of tension, rebirth, and joy in Jewish tradition. The ability of the Tower of Faces to both evoke the 'ruins of memory', as Ida Fink described her own internal journey, and to provoke historical memory so vividly through the resilient re-visioned faces attests to a specific tradition of Holocaust remembrance related to the larger Jewish tradition that overlaps chronological time and cyclical space. *Yisker biher*, literally 'tombstones of paper', refers to the religious and historical obligation to remember annihilated communities as well as the collective and individual memorial books themselves spontaneously produced by survivors who perform this commemorative work. After the first contemporary *yisker biher* were produced following the pogroms in Central and Eastern Europe after World War I, these memorial books proliferated after the genocides of

World War II. The aftermath of the Nazi mass murders and the disappearance of entire communities profoundly redefined the purpose of the *yisker biher*. Their task became ever more doubled: to chronicle the events of destruction and to simultaneously attest to the memory and vibrancy of what was. In his essay 'Remember and Never forget', Nathan Wachtel describes the traditional format of the memorial books as including an introductory historical section on the cultural life of the community in question, followed by individual and group accounts, with photographs if they survived, of the times before World War I, the period between the two wars, and then the genocide.[29] Wachtel reminds us that the time periods composing these histories often overlap and their recounting is overlaid with the survivor-writers' own diverse and spontaneous memories. Bleeding beyond the historical edges of the *yisker biher* are the grassroots acts by survivors to enliven and reenact the spirit of the lives that made up their communities.

The Tower of Faces partakes of the *yisker biher* memorial tradition in its overlapping structure of historical and memorial narratives so that the exuberance of peoples' lives is conveyed as vividly as their destruction. Where the memorial books accomplish these doubled deeds primarily with words and memoirs, the Tower of Faces insists on the prewar vitality of Ejszyszki through its overwhelming photographic assemblage of community activity. That the archive composing these photographs was painstakingly reassembled by a survivor of Ejszyszki reaffirms the Tower of Faces' affinity with the production of the *yisker biher* books. Yaffa Eliach, now Breuklundian Professor of Judaic Studies at Brooklyn College, was a young girl when the *Einsatzgruppen* murders occurred. Her parents managed to escape from the synagogue, fled, and were reunited with Yaffa three weeks later in another town. After the liberation of the town by Russian troops, she returned to Ejszyszki with her family. On 20 October 1944, the local Polish population staged a pogrom against the surviving twenty-nine Jews, killing Yaffa's mother and younger brother. In the face of this double dying her father paid the Polish residents of the town, who had taken over the formerly Jewish-owned homes, for the few remaining photographs still housed in these occupied spaces.[30] Over the years, Eliach procured still more photographs by contacting fellow townspeople who emigrated before the Holocaust and by tracking the records of the Ejszyszki Society in Chicago. The majority of the five thousand photographs in her archive, however, were reassembled by tracing relatives and friends to whom Ejszyszkians may have sent copies of photographs before 1941. The grave irony of Eliach's re-collection process is that her grandmother and grandfather, Alte and Yitzhak Uri Katz, were the prominent town photographers before the *Einsatzgruppen* murders of 1941 occurred.[31] Their practice was then taken over by her non-Jewish competitor. None of the negatives from Eliach's grandmother's practice survived.

Returning to Derrida's reading of Maria Torok's description of the processes of introjective mourning as 'gradual, slow, laborious, mediated, effective', we see how deeply at variance are the workings of the identity card project from those animating the Tower of Faces. The Tower of Faces as an effective act of remembrance is doubly maintained by Eliach's arduous task of re-collection and the deed of love underlying it. Indeed, the laborious and resilient archival work that has taken place, and which is visible only through explication, is evoked through the tempered labyrinthian passageway through which the spectator is led. The recurring glass bridge allowing entrance into the broken prism of lives and destruction suggests a slow unfolding and a tender yet unswerving approach to the events. If the small photographic semblances of persons on the identity cards buffer the museum visitor from the horrific while they also allow the accompanying text to do its narrative work, the photographs measuring one to three feet in height that line the Tower of Faces not only become performative bridges to representation but also pervade the hauntingly articulated space. While the faces on the identity cards are staged to plead for the assimilation of their identities with the visitors', the tower's accumulative photographic likenesses perform otherness not through a forced notion of sameness, but through a startling revelation of difference. That is, the faces can be construed as giving something to the viewer rather than asking the viewer to efface the subject to be mourned by abridging the acts of mourning. The towering faces mime solace and offer provocative sites of repose. Walter Benjamin's dialectic discussion of the portrait in relationship to the 'cult of remembrance' touches on this double-edged dilemma of the power of the photographic face. Writing in 1936 not without some trace of regret, he was thinking about the technical reproduction of the human countenance as the last retrenchment of photography's cult value:

It is no accident that the portrait was the focal point of early photography. The cult of remembrance of loved ones, absent or dead, offers a last refuge for the cult value of the picture. For the last time the aura emanates from the early photographs in the fleeting expression of a human face. This is what constitutes their melancholy, incomparable beauty.[32]

The vibrant images in the Tower of Faces do not fulfill the cult of remembrance through facile refuge. These are not just any anonymous mementos commemorating a life's passing through natural or even fore-shortened death. They are passing figures to the cult of remembrance and even more impressive signals of the severe rupture in the notion of a natural death. Their gentle weight cuts between solace and warning (see Figure 6.9.4). As Eliach has written:

Because of the events that were soon to transpire, these 'survivor photos' take on a new dimension in the post-Holocaust era. To look at them now is to know that behind each peaceful image lurks a tragic tale of death and destruction. Intended

Figure 6.9.4   Family photograph in the Tower of Faces. The wedding of Sarah
Plotnik and Pessah Avrahami, one of the last weddings in Eishyshok on the eve of
the storm. Sitting at the table (right to left): Mr Hamarski, his daughter, Dvorah,
Benyamin Kabacznik, wife Liebke, son Yudaleh, Reb Arie-Leib Kudlanski, Reb
Dovid Moszczenik, and Eliyahu Plotnik, father of the bride. Second row (right to
left): Mrs Hamarski, five family members, twin sisters of the bride, Mikhle and
Braine, the bride, Sarah, the groom, Pessah, Zipporah, mother of the bride, and two
relatives. Third row: the family youngsters. Only the bride and groom who made
aliyah to Eretz-Israel survived. Dovid died a natural death: Benyamin, Liebke, and
Yudaleh were murdered by the Armia Krajowa (the Polish home army); and the
majority of the other people were killed in the September 1941 massacre. A few were
killed in Ghetto Radun and Lida. Courtesy of the Yaffa Eliach Shtetl Collection and
the United States Holocaust Memorial Museum Photo Archives

simply as mementos of happy times and family occasions, the 'survivor photos' now
have the much weightier task of restoring identity and individuality to the
otherwise anonymous victims of the Nazis. ... the photographs 'rescue' these
victims posthumously, redeem them from the conflagration that left behind mere
ashes and smoke in their wake. The photographs have become the only 'grave' these
children shall ever have, the only record of their existence, and for many survivors,
the only tangible remnants of their past.[33]

   As the Tower of Faces installation insinuates, the task of mourning is
compounded immeasurably when the deaths and the losses surpass the
normal paradigm of a life that ended naturally. In 'Mourning and Melancholia'
from 1917, Freud discusses the work the ego undertakes to be 'set free' from
the lost one in order for 'the loss of the object' to be 'surmounted'.[34] While
the workings of both the identity card and the Tower of Faces involuntarily

defy Freud's notion of mastery over the lost one, they do so in very different ways. The identity card acknowledges that it can never simulate the long and arduous processes of introjective mourning. Rather than giving up the lost loved one or the 'object', as Freud's model for less severe or natural cases of loss suggests, the identity card project seeks its mock adoption. The Tower of Faces, however, sets up a soft barrier between the taking in of an analogized self and keeps its distance from the trespass of sites of deaths and identities that never had the luxury of being fixed. Strategically placed out of the visitor's reach, the photographs gather around them spaces of mourning without conclusion. Indeed, many survivors are still searching for conclusive links between the people they mourn and the actual circumstances of their murders – knowing names, dates, and death sites would make the indeterminate less unsettling.

Unlike the identity card project, which gets caught between performing as a pastiche history lesson and as a device for mourning, the similarly doubled obligation of the Tower of Faces acknowledges the riddled (im)possibility of mourning itself. Rather than miming the dual processes of mourning and drawing the viewer in through crucial yet overtly artificial identifications with the lost or traumatized Holocaust other as in the identity card project, in the Tower of Faces the dynamics between museum visitor and the mourned other are at once more modest and far-reaching. The hovering photographs in the Tower of Faces challenge the viewer's sense of precarious involvement in the terror and stage the entire apparatus to perform more as a fluctuating memorial rather than as a stable and self-assured monument. The piercing portraits bring into focus philosopher Emmanuel Lévinas's difficult formulations of facing, otherness, and alterity:

This incommensurability with consciousness, which becomes a trace of the one who knows where, is not the inoffensive relationship of a knowledge in which everything is equalised, not the indifference of spatial contiguity; it is an assimilation of me by another, a responsibility with regard to men we do not even know. The relationship of proximity cannot be reduced to any modality of distance or geometrical contiguity, not to the simple 'representation' of a neighbour; it is already an assignation – an obligation, anachronistically prior to any commitment.[35]

NOTES

1. The following discussion on the identity card project and the Tower of Faces is based in part on the museum's publicity as well as interviews I conducted with key planning members of the permanent exhibition team in Washington, D.C., in August 1990, March 1992, and April 1993; the last visit took place at the time the museum opened to the public (26 April). The United States Holocaust Memorial Museum is the nation's first officially sanctioned and federally mandated (but privately funded) institution in this country dedicated to the memory of and continued education about the Holocaust. The concept for the museum was instituted by an act of Congress on 7 October 1980, under the auspices of President Jimmy Carter. It is located adjacent to the Mall, between 14th Street and Raoul Wallenberg Place (formerly 15th Street), east of Independence Avenue and within view of the Washington Monument and the Jefferson Memorial.

2. Similar assumptions about ownership of a historical event also occur when the name of the museum appears abbreviated, in its perhaps unconscious act of conforming to the bureaucratized economies of Washington, D.C. The museum's use of the acronym USHMM serves to neutralize the frenetic dynamics that the institution houses and animates. The presumptions of abbreviating only underline the authoritative and definitive name that inaugurates this institution. For a countermeasure in a very different genre, a literary act that names and safeguards reference to Holocaust memory without laying authoritative claim to it, see Jacques Derrida, *Feu la cendre* (Paris: Des Femmes, 1987). This book has been translated into English by Ned Lukacher as *Cinders* (Lincoln: University of Nebraska Press, 1991).

3. Berenbaum made these comments in his keynote address at the conference 'Articulations of History'.

4. Smith is known for his work with historical subjects and what he himself refers to as 'difficult' material. His *The World at War* television special about World War II aired on US television. His work at the museum was produced in tandem with exhibition designer Halph Appelbaum. Ralph Appelbaum Associates, a New York City firm, specializes in the planning and design of natural, cultural, and social history museums. The firm designed the permanent exhibition at the newly renovated Jewish Museum in New York on four thousand years of Jewish culture and identity. Another of the firm's commissions is *A Vision of the Americas*, a new installation for the Smithsonian Institution, which the firm said will 'challenge misconceptions about Native Americans'. Some of their past projects include the permanent installation *Native Peoples of the Southwest* at the Heard Museum, Phoenix, Arizona (1984), and the traveling exhibition *Jackie Robinson: An American Journey* (1987) for the New York Historical Society.

5. Weinberg's comments were reported by Judith Weinraub, 'Passing On the Memory of the Holocaust', *Washington Post*, 2 February 1990, c4.

6. From my interview with Martin Smith at the temporary offices of the United States Holocaust Memorial Museum in Washington, D.C., 22 August 1990.

7. Berenbaum made this statement in his keynote address at the Boston conference.

8. My thanks go to Raye Farr, who replaced Martin Smith as director of the permanent exhibition program, for giving me a tour of the museum model in early March 1992. Farr is currently director of the museum's film programs.

9. See Robert H. Abzug's compelling study *Inside the Vicious Heart: Americans and the Liberation of Nazi Concentration Camps* (New York and Oxford: Oxford University Press, 1985).

10. For a lucid and focused essay on the museum's attempt to transform the visitor's psychic identity and to stage the experience as a lesson in democracy, see especially Greig Crysler and Abidin Kusno. 'Angels in the Temple: The Aesthetic Construction of Citizenship at the United States Holocaust Memorial Museum', *Art Journal*, special issue on Aesthetics and the Body Politic, ed. Grant Kester 56:1 (Spring 1997), 52–64. For more sympathetic readings of the museum's strategies, see Edward Linenthal's study *Preserving Memory: The Struggle to Create America's Holocaust Museum* (New York: Penguin, 1995). See also Harold Kaplan, *Conscience and Memory: Meditations in a Museum of the Holocaust* (Chicago and London: University of Chicago Press, 1994), which muses on the museum in Washington, D.C., as the backdrop to his contention that the museum will have a 'civilizing' effect on its viewers and will achieve a kind of mourning and healing through its 'democratic' principles. The museum has also published its own history of itself. See Michael Berenbaum, *The World Must Know: The History of the Holocaust as Told in the United States Holocaust Memorial Museum* (Boston: Little, Brown, 1993).
    See also the chapters 'The Plural Faces of Holocaust Memory in America' and 'Memory and the Politics of Identity: Boston and Washington, D.C.', in James E. Young, *The Texture of Memory: Holocaust Memorials and Meaning* (New Haven, Conn., and London: Yale University Press, 1993); and Peter Novick, 'Holocaust Memory in America', in *The Art of Memory: Holocaust Memorials in History*, ed. James E. Young (Munich and New York: Prestel-Verlag and The Jewish Museum, 1994). The exhibition of the same name, curated by Young, was open at the Jewish Museum in New York from 13 March to 31 July 1994 and traveled to the Deutsches Historisches Museum, Berlin from 8 September to 13 November 1994, and to the Münchner Stadtmuseum, Munich from 9 December 1994 to 5 March 1995.

11. For a study attentive to the different ways that color photography creates meaning in American documentary conventions, see Sally Stein's forthcoming book *The Colorful and the Colorless: American Photography and Material Culture between the Wars* (Washington, D.C.: Smithsonian Institution Press).

12. Jean-François Lyotard, *Differend: Phrases in Dispute*, trans. Georges Van Den Abbeele, Minneapolis: University of Minnesota Press, 13.

13. Adorno's phrase appears in Theodor W. Adorno, 'Cultural Criticism and Society', in his *Prisms*, trans. Samuel and Shierry Weber, Cambridge, Mass.: MIT Press, 1981, 34; his later explanation appeared in Adorno, 'Engagement', in *Noten zur Literature III* (Frankfurt am Main: Suhrkamp Verlag, 1965), 125–27.

14. Interview with Martin Smith (emphasis is mine) (see note 6).

15. From a statement included in the museum's publicity packet.

16. Irving Howe, preface to Janet Blatter and Sybil Milton, *Art of the Holocaust*, intro. Henry Friedlander, pref. Irving Hower, New York: Rutledge Press, 1981, 11.

17. Interview with Martin Smith.

18. Jacques Derrida, *Mémoires for Paul de Man*, trans. Cecile Lindsay, Jonathan Culler, Eduardo Cadava, and Peggy Kamuf (New York: Columbia University Press, 1986), 34–5. I am moved by Derrida's reconfigured ideas on mourning in this text. I pointedly do not address the complex issue of Paul de Man and the politics of collaboration during World War II. In his study *Stranded Objects: Mourning, Memory, and Film in Postwar Germany* (Ithaca, N.Y., and London: Cornell University Press, 1990), Eric L. Saniner employs de Man's ideas on mourning and language as he excuses himself from dealing with the political ramifications of what he characterizes as de Man's contribution to 'the cause of collaboration'. He writes: 'What interests me in the present context is the relation between a past scarred by these words, as few as they may be, and the subsequent writings of de Man which are informed by an uncompromising rigor' (15). In Shoshana Felman's writing, especially the essay 'After the Apocalypse: Paul de Man and the Fall to Silence', in Felman and Dori Laub's *Testimony: Crises of Witnessing in Literature, Psychoanalysis, and History* (New York and London: Routledge, 1992), she continuously repeats the action of defending and justifying de Man. See Dominick LaCapra's astute essay 'The Personal, the Political and the Textual: Paul de Man as Object of Transference', *History and Memory* 4:1 (Spring/Summer 1991), in which, as the title of his piece suggests, he addresses the issue of de Man's early writings compared to those of the later de Man in terms of how they 'involve an exchange between past and present that is best approached through the problem of transference and the manner in which one negotiates it. This transferential dimension has, I think, been largely ignored, denied, repressed or acted out rather than thematized in the attempt to work it through' (5).

19. Derrida, 'Fors', foreword to Nicolas Abraham and Maria Torok, *The Wolf Man's Magic Word: A Cryptonomy*, trans. Nicholas Rand (Minneapolis: University of Minnesota Press, 1986), xvii.

20. Quoted in ibid.

21. Jonathan Rosen, 'America's Holocaust', *Forward*, 12 April 1991.

22. James E. Young, *The Texture of Memory*, 344.

23. This observation about the blind spots in the mechanisms of the identity card have been most lucidly noted by Jonathan Rosen in 'America's Holocaust', and by Liliane Weissberg in her essay 'Memory Confined', *Documents* 4/5 (Spring 1994).

24. Articles on the Tower of Faces have appeared in both the popular press as well as in more specialized art, architecture, and cultural journals. Among these, see Andrea Liss, 'Contours of Naming: The Identity Card Project and the Tower of Faces at the United States Halocaust Memorial Museum', *Public* 8 (1993), 108–34; Ziva Freiman, 'Memory Too Politic', *Progressive Architecture* (October 1995), 62–9; and for essays that discuss the tower in relation to other contemporary art and installation projects, see Ken Johnson, 'Art and Memory', *Art in America* (November 1993), 90–9; Lenore D. Miller, 'Manipulated Environments: Photomontage into Sculpture', *Camerawork* 21:1 (Spring/Summer 1994), 22–7. For a range of the articles that appeared in the popular press, see the report in *Life* (April 1993); and Michael Kernan, 'A New Monument to Remembering – with a Mission', *Smithsonian* 24:1 (April 1993), 50–60.

25. 'A Tower of Faces, a Tower of Life', *The United States Holocaust Memorial Museum Newsletter* (March 1991), 5.

26. For studies on this issue, see Deborah Lipstadt, *Beyond Belief: The American Press and the Coming of the Holocaust* (New York: Free Press, 1986); David S. Wyman, *The Abandonment of the Jews: America and the Holocaust, 1941–1945* (New York: Pantheon, 1984); and Henry L. Feingold, *The Politics of Rescue: The Roosevelt Administration and the Holocaust, 1938–1945* (New Brunswick, N.J.: Rutgers University Press, 1970).

27. I deal in more length with the crucial theme of trauma and its relation to representation in later chapters, especially in Chapter 4 [of *Trespassing through Shadows*].

28. Ida Fink, *A Scrap of Time*, trans. Madeline Levine and Francine Prose (New York: Pantheon Books, 1987), 3.

29. Nathan Wachtel, 'Remember and Never Forget', *History and Anthropology* (1986): 307–35.

30. From my interview with Yaffa Eliach in Brooklyn, 4 May 1993.

31. Eliach's grandmother took over the business after her husband passed away. Their assistants B. Szrejder and R. Lejbowicz also took photographs that were selected for the Tower of Faces from the Yaffa Eliach Shtetl Collection.

32. Walter Benjamin, 'The Work of Art in the Age of Mechanical Reproduction', in *Illuminations*, ed. Hannah Arendt, trans. Harry Zohn, New York: Schocken Books, 1973, 226.

33. This text is part of Eliach's foreword to the book that accompanied an exhibition of photographs on the fate of children in Europe just before, during, and after the Holocaust, *We Were Children Just Like You* (Brooklyn, N.Y.: Center for Holocaust Studies, Documentation and Research, 1990), 6–7. The exhibition opened at the Milton Weill Art Gallery of the 92nd Street Y in New York City. Photographic collections included various files from Eliach's archives, including the Ejszyszki Shtetl Collection, as well as the collections from Beth Hatefutsoth, Hadassah Archives, HIAS, Yad Vashem, and YIVO, among them.

34. Sigmund Freud, 'Mourning and Melancolia', in *General Psychological Theory: Papers on Metapsychology*, ed. Philip Rieff (New York: Macmillan, 1963), 164–79.

35. Emmanuel Lévinas, *Otherwise Than Being or beyond Essence*, trans. Alphonso Lingis (The Hague: M. Nihoff, 1981), 100–1.

10.

Where Is 'Africa'? Re-Viewing Art and Artifact in the Age of Globalization

Ruth B. Phillips

The Sainsbury African Galleries. The British Museum, London. Long-term exhibition, opened March 2001.

African Worlds. The Horniman Museum and Gardens, London. Long-term exhibition, opened April 1999.

African Voices. National Museum of Natural History, Smithsonian Institution, Washington, D.C. Long-term exhibition, opened December 1999.

'Africa, whatever it is, is everywhere,' Holland Cotter recently wrote in the Sunday *New York Times*.[1] 'It's far more than just a continent. It's a global diaspora, an international culture and a metaphor with fantastical associations for the West: gold, savages, "darkest", "deepest", liberation, devastation' (2002: AR1). Cotter was reviewing a temporary exhibition of contemporary

African art, the genre that has most favored the re-presentation of Africa in terms of new and newly understood realities of globalization and trans-nationalism. In this essay, I look at three recent exhibitions that, because they are permanent reinstallations of well-known African collections, present a tougher test of the responsiveness of museums to these late-20th-century coordinates for the relocation of 'Africa'.[2] The exhibitions are *African Worlds* at London's Horniman Museum, *African Voices* at the Smithsonian's National Museum of Natural History, which both opened in 1999, and the Sainsbury African Galleries at the British Museum, which opened in 2001.

To varying degrees, the installations they replace represented Africa as distant from and prior to the space and time of Western modernity. In both the Horniman's universal survey exhibition of world ethnology and the Smithsonian's 1960s Hall of African Peoples the geographical space of 'Africa' was confined to regions south of the Sahara and, disproportionately, to West and Central Africa, while the time of Africa was confined to the fictive ethnographic present (Fabian 1983). As numerous analyses have demons-trated, these representational conventions are tied to primitivism and cultural evolutionism (Clifford 1988; Errington 1998; Hiller 1991; Price 1989; Stocking 1985; Vogel et al. 1988). They inscribe essentialized notions of race and implicitly deny the modernity of Africa and the authenticity of diasporic African cultures. The exhibitions of the British Museum's African collections that immediately preceded the new installations in the Sainsbury Galleries were a series of rotating, temporary, special topic exhibits staged at the Museum's off-site ethnographic branch, the Museum of Mankind in London's Burlington Gardens. While these exhibits contextualized objects more fully than had the main building's typological displays, overall they continued to represent Africa as a set of distanced, localized cultures.

The British Museum's Sainsbury Galleries of African Art

Few would have predicted the dramatic change in installation approach that has occurred in the new Sainsbury Galleries. Funded by a gift from renowned collectors Robert and Lisa Sainsbury, the galleries are dedicated to Henry Moore. A lengthy text panel just outside the entrance includes Sir Robert's statement that, 'What I am is someone who liked artists who liked primitive and were influenced by primitive. ... I liked Henry Moore's carving – Henry Moore liked primitive.' Although the anonymous curatorial voice hastily intervenes to explain that, 'Primitive in this context is shorthand. As Moore himself remarked, "primitive" is misleading if it is taken to imply crudeness or incompetence', the notion of the primitive is imprinted on the visitor through these multiple repetitions and frames the value of the African objects on exhibition in terms of the 'wealth of experience and inspiration' (to further quote the text panel) they have provided for modern Western artists.

The introductory space presents large and dramatic examples of contemporary African art by artists from Egypt and North, South, East and West Africa. Their prominence strongly signals the exhibition's acceptance both of the revisionist 'whole Africa' approach and of the authenticity of contemporary modernist African art. The 600-plus objects displayed in the four large rooms that lead off this space are grouped into seven categories based on media, technology, and function. As the text panels in the exhibition announce, these categories are Woodcarving, Pottery, Forged Metal, Masquerade, Brasscasting, Personal Adornment, and Textiles (Figure 6.10.1).

The curators, Christopher Spring, Nigel Barley, and Julie Hudson, have written that this rather startlingly Eurocentric and old-fashioned material culture classification 'is less arbitrary than it might at first seem, as a whole philosophy often underlies each different material and technology, and this can be used as a means of shedding light on African history and social life' (2001:21). In this context, they argue, Benin brass casting can, for example, 'be seen to be about the strength and durability of kingship' (2001:21). However, the main text panel for the Benin section – the first of two genres of African art I will use to sample each of the exhibitions discussed in this essay[3] – reveals the problematic politics of this imposed, etic, thematic structure and the objective curatorial voice through which the public is addressed. It reads:

In 1897, following an attack on a British consular mission, a British punitive expedition took Benin City and sent the King, Oba Oronramwen into exile. Many of the brass objects from Benin City fell to the troops and others were sold abroad to defray the costs of the expedition and compensate the victims. Benin brasswork was totally unknown in the West as it had been confined almost entirely to the royal palace and it so confounded current ideas about Africa that some refused to believe that it could be of exclusively Benin origin.

In this narrative, the 'victims' are white, the soldiers are guiltless, the Victorian rationale for the sale and dispersal of the kingdom's treasures is repeated uncritically, and the tropes of wonder and curiosity are exploited. Although the panel concludes with a statement about modern Benin and the restoration of court ritual, it makes no reference to compelling recent art historical research on the objects' entanglement in histories of violence, colonial power, and racist discourses about art – or the British Museum's own central role in these histories (Coombes 1994). The curators stress their new installation's re-creation of the original sight lines for the mounted plaques, but the highly decorative and aestheticized installations overwhelm this worthy achievement, and act,

Figure 6.10.1   Installation of Benin brass plaques in the Brasscasting section,
Sainsbury Galleries of African Art, British Museum. Photo: Ruth B. Phillips

rather, to anesthetize and efface the other history of imperialism and
appropriation (Figure 6.10.2).

The curators have evocatively described the Sainsbury Galleries as 'highly
aesthetic – white walls, open displays, enormous but very light cases, a clear
plastic cliff of throwing knives frozen in mid-flight, a steel tree of pots that
spirals up from floor to ceiling, and a whole wall of Benin plaques floating

Figure 6.10.2   The Mende mask (bottom centre), Masquerade section, Sainsbury Galleries of African Art, British Museum. Photo: Ruth B. Phillips

on slim poles' (Spring et al. 2001:37). The new 'house style', they explain, results from the 'move from a simply ethnographic museum to a more catholic institution', and from the fact that 'curators and [the] public are nowadays much more aware of the peculiarities of the museum gallery as a particular kind of space' (Spring et al. 2001:37) (Figures 6.10.1 and 6.10.3). The Mende Sande Society mask on display tests this proposition. It is displayed in the Masquerade section amidst numerous other examples of canonical mask genres. The overall curatorial intent is to provide a level of ethnographic context within the aesthetic envelope and to amplify the basic information provided by the individual object labels, through strategic juxtapositions with videos and contemporary works, and with more spacious and striking 'open', or out of case, installations of selected objects in the same category (Spring et al. 2001:34). In the present case, while proximity to the Sokari Douglas Camp figure of a Kalabari masquerader at the far end of the room might possibly 'lead [the visitor] to question what a mask might be' (Spring et al. 2001:24), it cannot provide understandings culturally specific to the Mende. The brief text, furthermore, not only contains factual errors, but ignores a substantial body of recent feminist scholarship on Sande (Boone 1986; MacCormack 1980; Phillips 1995). The curators' use of the ethnographic present is particularly problematic given the horrific violence Mende people were suffering in Sierra Leone even as the following label was being written: 'The Mende have one of the few African masking traditions where masks are worn and performed by women, as events of the Sande Society. It may be that this is because male and female initiation groups here operate in parallel'. The art installation paradigm, which implies dominant processes of connoisseurship, is also curiously at odds with the unexceptional quality of the example chosen from the British Museum's fine collection of Mende masks, and with the difficulty of seeing the individual pieces clearly. As elsewhere in the Sainsbury Galleries, the elegance of the exhibit design recalls the glossy displays of a superior department store, privileging the impression of quantity and variety over both ethnographic specificity and aesthetic singularity.

'African Worlds' at the Horniman Museum

The Horniman Museum's 'African Worlds' is also an object-centered exhibition that borrows aspects of its installation approach from the art museum, and, like the Sainsbury Galleries, it too introduced a radical shift in design (Figures 6.10.4 and 6.10.5). However, while the British Museum's curators had to fit into a predetermined institutional style, Anthony Shelton, who was then the Horniman's chief curator, worked with hand-picked designer Michael

Figure 6.10.3   Partial view of installation of Benin brass plaques, 'African Worlds'
exhibition, Horniman Museum. The combination of object labels and booklets is
used throughout the exhibition to provide four levels of textual interpretation.
Photo: Ruth B. Phillips

Figure 6.10.4   The Mende masks in the Horniman Museum's 'African Worlds'
exhibition. A photograph of Mrs Beatrice Wusi is visible in the text panel (lower
right) adjacent to her commentary on the masks. Photo: Ruth B. Phillips

Cameron to create a 'new visual language' that would express the specific
concepts that inform 'African Worlds' (2000:5). This takes the form of a
modernist installation designed to sit uneasily within the classical vaulted
space of the gallery. The materials are aggressively industrial and the cases
incorporate asymmetrical, cubist, jarring, and disruptive elements. 'It was …
considered essential,' Shelton has written, 'to convey a sense of alienation in
the gallery: alienation in the sense that these objects were displaced, far removed
from the conditions of their usage and original signification' (2000:13).

Figure 6.10.5   Introductory text to the Wealth section, 'African Worlds', United States National Museum of Natural History, Smithsonian Institute. Photo: Ruth B. Phillips

Shelton's curatorial approach also presents a sharp contrast to that of the British Museum team. Inspired by recent collaborative models developed by North American museums working with indigenous peoples, he created a curatorial committee of African and British professionals. They identified eight themes that reflect both European and African social, political, and cognitive categories: 'Patronage; Different Natures; Men/Women; Ancestors and Morality; Royalty and Power; Text, Image, History; Cycles of Life; and Parody and Humour' (Shelton 2000:11) (see Figure 6.10.6). Similarly, Shelton collected interpretive statements from people of African and Carribbean descent living in London. These are given pride of place on the object labels – even though some criticize or express sadness about museum treatment and ownership of African objects.

The postcolonial historical sensibility and poststructuralist multivocality of 'African Worlds' is evident in its approach to the display of Benin brasses. These are installed in cases that suggest open wall safes, designed to maintain clear visibility while conveying both notions of value and ambivalence about the presence of these objects in contemporary Britain. The main text panel gives a detailed history of the kingdom of Benin from CE 900 and the destruction wrought by the British expedition in 1897. It explicitly problematizes the issue of ownership, highlighting the two prominent Nigerian cocurators, Joseph Eboreime and Emmanuel Arinze, who developed the historical interpretation that is presented and who, as it states, have also appealed 'to the conscience of the world for a meaningful dialogue for a peaceful resolution of this shame of history'.

A local, diasporic reality informs the presentation of the Horniman's Mende masks in 'African Worlds'. They are interpreted by Mrs. Beatrice Wusi, a Mende wife and community worker living in London. Wusi's commentary breaks down the exoticism of African female initiation through its presentation of the mask as the embodiment of an aesthetic and moral ideal, and of Sande as an institution of contemporary validity invested with important social responsibility. She states of the Sande masker, or *sowei*, 'It's supposed to be a mythical being that comes and teaches the children, the initiates, how to behave, how to sit properly.' 'She teaches them how to dance. You see how they do her hair, her neck. Everything that we consider beauty ... it's in there. It is something that personifies excellence. Anything that is good is in this. Really beautiful. You can see the culture in it. It's the leader, it's the mistress. That's what sowie [*sic*] is' (Figure 6.10.7). Because the expert speaking voice belongs to a woman living in London, the label, like the others in 'African Worlds', conveys contemporaneity and proximity that works to collapse the distance between Europe and Africa.

Figure 6.10.6   The Mende mask installation in 'African Worlds', United States
National Museum of Natural History, Smithsonian Institution. The field photograph
and label text contextualize the mask within Sierra Leonean women's initiation and
concepts of wealth. Photo: Ruth B. Phillips

'African Worlds' at the Smithsonian's National Museum of Natural History

The Smithsonian's decision to reinstall its African exhibits was stimulated directly by complaints from Africans and African Americans about racist and offensive aspects of the old 1960s displays. The curators, Mary Jo Arnoldi, Christine Kreamer, and Michael Mason, thus had a clear mandate to respond to contemporary critiques and new historical constructs of Africa and the diaspora (2001:17–19). As in the Horniman exhibit, the curators of 'African Worlds' collaborated closely with Africans both in Africa and in Washington. The exhibition is organized along a central historical timeline punctuated by openings that lead into exhibits addressing contemporary African life and cultures. Grouped under three broad themes, these sections are entitled 'Living in Africa', 'Working in Africa', and 'Wealth in Africa', each interpreted by means of large photo murals, interactive modules, and a mixture of historic and contemporary artifacts. The curators' desire 'to increase understanding of the continent's modernity and its contemporary relevance' (Arnoldi et al. 2001:24) is manifested in the fact that nearly 70 percent of the objects they chose or acquired specifically for the new exhibit were made after 1960.

The curators finalized their exhibition design only after testing a prototype exhibit module on typical Washington visitors. As a result, they abandoned an initial 'poetic' relationship of text and object for a more unambiguous and didactic approach (Arnoldi et al. 2001:24) – rejecting, that is, the kind of reliance on the visitor's ability to infer meaning that is characteristic of art museums and that was utilized both in the Sainsbury Galleries and, to some extent, in the Horniman. The Benin display, which is part of the 'Living in Africa' section, exemplifies the exhibition's twin emphases on history and on contemporaneity, and its privileging of the voices of Africans. The main case features a poster created by Benin authorities for the centenary of the Punitive Expedition. It gives a detailed account of the 1897 invasion, reproduces a famous photo of the British soldiers surrounded by their loot, and includes a statement from the current Oba honoring 'all our gallant heroes who fell during the British invasion'. The installation thus foregrounds an artifact that is itself a historical/commemorative representation generated by contemporary Africans, causing the Benin brass in the display case to lose its meaning as art object and to become an illustrative adjunct to the poster.

The Mende mask in 'African Worlds' is subordinated to a thematic message that is cultural rather than historical (Figure 6.10.8). It appears in the Wealth in Africa section, where it is juxtaposed with a modern Luba king's staff, an Ethiopian graduation robe and diploma, and a fantasy coffin from Ghana. This eclectic assemblage is intended to challenge Western understandings of 'wealth' with the notion that, as the text panel states, in Africa, 'wealth takes various forms: money, knowledge, and connections between people'. The installation of the Mende sowei mask under this rubric illustrates the limitations and reductionism that characterize all thematic exhibition structures to a greater or lesser degree. The complex iconographic meanings of the sowei mask and its references to female enculturation and the initiation cycle to which its performances are integral makes all the more evident the arbitrariness of attaching so complex a set of meanings to the singular notion of 'wealth'. The visual impact of the mask is also reduced by the crowding and bad lighting that characterize the exhibit (which should have been given a larger space by the Smithsonian). As elsewhere in 'African Worlds', the objects, whether art or artifact, are grouped under the thematic of 'Wealth' and tend to become unidimensional props or illustrations for an abstract concept. In the specific case of the Mende mask, the sense of bustling, contemporary vitality projected by the installation also elides any apprehension of the war, anarchy, and tragedy experienced by the Mende during the 1990s. This was a conscious design on the part of the curators, who wanted 'African Worlds' to counter 'media coverage that tends to emphasize Africa's problems' (Arnoldi et al. 2001:20).

Museums and/as 'Modernity at Large'

In a lecture delivered at New York City's Museum of Primitive Art in 1959, Robert Redfield provided a classic statement of the spatial and temporal distance that the high modernist discourses of both art criticism and anthropology constructed between Africa, presented as a series of bounded and local cultures, and the West, represented as mobile and cosmopolitan. 'There is no one in any better position to attempt to find reasons for the artistic success of the primitive artist', he wrote,

than we modern Western outsiders for the reason that no one else has as much experience with many kinds of art ... The great civilizations of wide influence represent a coming together of various traditions. They are a mixing, a stimulating, a comparing of one traditional way with another ... Western civilization is such a civilization. It is here in the West that some people have gone farthest in developing an interest in and appreciation of art derived from some knowledge of the arts of many traditions. [1959:34]

These remarks occur in the course of a searching comparison of the kinds of understandings produced in viewers by the two installation paradigms of art and artifact. In arguing that they are not antithetical, but rather complementary and parallel paths to understanding, Redfield also reveals the art and artifact approaches to museum display to be typical of a range of objectifying modernist technologies that reify a Eurocentric orientation to geographic space and an evolutionary structuring of universal time. For the purposes of this discussion, Redfield's essay serves as a benchmark that allows us to assess the changes that have occurred between his mid-20th-century moment of high modernism and our present moment of global/post/modernism. Powerful evidence of a new consensus is evidenced by the fact that, despite their differences, all three of the exhibitions I have briefly discussed refute Redfield's dichotomies and assert the equivalent cosmopolitanism of an Africa constructed as inclusive of the diaspora, and just as mixed, hybrid, and contemporary as the West.

This discussion has, however, also revealed the continuing deployment of the modernist display paradigms of art and artifact, which seem to have only gained in rhetorical strength now that they are no longer so strictly tied to the discipline-specific museums that bred them. A question that logically follows is, Why, in the light of three decades of poststructuralist and postcolonial critique, do these object-centered and objectifying modes of installation continue to retain their exclusive holds on museum display? The answer, I think, is both simple and complicated. It has to do, on the one hand, with a profound desire that remains deeply rooted in Western cultures for the experiences of 'resonance and wonder' that are produced by the presentation of objects as artifact and art (Greenblatt 1991). The modern museum is a physical and spatial environment purpose-built to be a container for objects thus displayed. The 'museum effect' is a function of the Western tradition of ocularcentrism (Alpers 1991). It creates material objects as signs for knowledge and cognition and/or as points of access to spiritual and aesthetic experience. What has happened in at least two of the recent exhibits is not the rejection of this basic proposition, but rather a loosening of fixed relationships between certain signifiers and signifieds that had been established under modernist ideologies of progress and linked constructs of time and space. Benin brasses are no longer only curiosity or 'loot', the African mask is no longer only 'primitive' or 'art'. As multivocal curatorial processes do their work, these objects are being tied to new and different meanings attributed to them by people who have long lived within Western nations or who are now more closely connected through travel, media, and capital flows, but whose understandings of these objects have not before been reflected by the museums that own them.

As Arjun Appadurai has phrased it, globalization *is* 'modernity at large' (1996). Under colonialism, and even more after its formal ending, the West has been exporting museums and their technologies of representation as integral parts of modernity's archiving, memorializing, and nation building practices (Anderson 1991; Dominguez 1992; Kirshenblatt-Gimblett 1998). What these three exhibitions show, then, is how successfully museological conventions have been exported and, to some extent, translated, so that now, in the era of globalization, museum savvy can be reimported to the 'mother countries' through collaborative curatorial processes. As illustrated by both 'African Worlds' and 'African Voices', such processes typically engage Western-trained African museum professionals and non-professional community members who are mentored into the conventions of Western museological practice – and often come to constitute a cadre of regular museum collaborators adept at manipulating its conventions and characteristic technologies. Just as modernist ceramics by Magdalene Odundo, sculptures of masquerade figures by Sokari Douglas Camp, or Somali and Egyptian ethnographic artifacts have become part of the new, revised museum canon of African art and artifact, so has collaborative curation become the new museum practice that expresses contemporary pluralist ideology.[4] Yet, despite the continuing allegiance of Western museums and their audiences to modernist installation paradigms and their increasing dissemination beyond Europe and North America, the new orientations displayed by these new exhibitions are highly significant. When we compare them to those they replaced, there can be no doubt that the impacts of globalization on Western museums are no less important for the circular path traveled by the vectors of revisionism. To the degree that new exhibitions about Africa, or any other region of the world, engage with postcolonial critiques of the museum, they will serve as transformative spaces where outworn and dangerous stereotypes are countered by images and representations that make diverse cultural groups recognizable not only to others but also to themselves.

REFERENCES CITED

Alpers, Svetlana 1991 'The Museum as a Way of Seeing'. In *Exhibiting Cultures: The Poetics and Politics of Museum Display*. Ivan Karp and Steven D. Lavine, eds, pp. 25–32. Washington, DC: Smithsonian Institution Press.

Ames, Michael M. 1992 *Cannibal Tours and Glass Boxes: The Anthropology of Museums*. Vancouver: University of British Columbia Press.

Anderson, Benedict 1991 *Imagined Communities: Reflections on the Origin and Spread of Nationalism*. London: Verso.

Appadurai, Arjun 1996 *Modernity at Large: Cultural Dimensions of Globalization*. Minneapolis: University of Minnesota Press.

Arnoldi, Mary Jo, Christine Mullen Kreamer, and Michael Atwood Mason 2001 'Reflections on "African Voices" at the Smithsonian's National Museum of Natural History'. *African Arts* 34(2): 16–35, 94.

Boone, Sylvia Ardyn 1986 *Radiance from the Waters: Ideals of Feminine Beauty in Mende Art*. New Haven, CT: Yale University Press.

Clifford, James 1988 'Histories of the Tribal and the Modern'. In *The Predicament of Culture: Twentieth-Century Ethnography, Literature, and Art*, pp. 189–214. Cambridge, MA: Harvard University Press.

1997 *Routes: Travel and Translation in the Late Twentieth Century*. Cambridge, MA: Harvard University Press.

Coombes, Annie 1994 *Reinventing Africa: Museums, Material Culture and Popular Imagination*. New Haven, CT: Yale University Press.

Cotter, Holland 2002 'From the Ferment of Liberation Comes a Revolution in African Art'. *New York Times*, February 17:2(1):AR1, 40–42.

Court, Elsbeth 1999 'Africa on Display: Exhibiting Art by Africans'. In *Contemporary Cultures of Display*. Emma Barker, ed., pp. 147–173. New Haven, CT: Yale University Press.

Dominguez, Virginia 1992 'Invoking Culture: The Messy Side of "Cultural Politics"'. *South Atlantic Quarterly* 91(1):19–42.

Errington, Shelley 1998 *The Death of Authentic Primitive Art and Other Tales of Progress*. Berkeley: University of California Press.

Fabian, Johannes 1983 *Time and the Other*. New York: Columbia University Press.

Fisher, Jean, ed. 1994 *Global Visions: Towards a New Internationalism in the Visual Arts*. London: Kala Press.

Greenblatt, Stephen 1991 'Resonance and Wonder'. In *Exhibiting Cultures: The Poetics and Politics of Museum Display*. Ivan Karp and Steven D. Lavine, eds, pp. 42–56. Washington, DC: Smithsonian Institution Press.

Hiller, Susan, ed. 1991 *The Myth of Primitivism: Perspectives on Art*. New York: Routledge.

Kasfir, Sidney Littlefield 1995 'Field Notes: Reimagining Africa'. *Museum Anthropology* 12(1): 45–53.

Kirshenblatt-Gimblett, Barbara 1998 *Destination Culture: Tourism, Museums, and Heritage*. Berkeley: University of California Press.

MacCormack, Carol P. 1980 'Nature, Culture, and Gender, a Critique'. In *Nature, Culture and Gender*. Carol P. MacCormack and Marilyn Strathern, eds, pp. 1–24. Cambridge: Cambridge University Press.

Mirzoeff, Nicholas, ed. 2000 *Diaspora and Visual Culture: Representing Africans and Jews*. New York: Routledge.

Phillips, Ruth B. 1995 *Representing Woman: Sande Masquerades of the Mende of Sierra Leone*. Los Angeles: Fowler Museum of Cultural History.

Price, Sally 1989 *Primitive Art in Civilized Places*. Chicago: University of Chicago Press.

Redfield, Robert 1959 'Art and Icon'. In *Aspects of Primitive Art*. New York: Museum of Primitive Art.

Shelton, Anthony 2000 'Curating African Worlds'. *Journal of Museum Ethnography* 12:5–20.

Spring, Christopher, Nigel Barley, and Julie Hudson 2001 'The Sainsbury African Galleries at the British Museum'. *African Arts* 34(3):18–37, 93.

Stocking, George W., Jr, ed. 1985 *Objects and Others: Essays on Museums and Material Culture*. Madison: University of Wisconsin Press.

Vogel, Susan, ed. et al. 1988 *Art/Artifact: African Art in Anthropology Museums*. New York: The Center for African Acrylic.

NOTES

1. A version of this essay was presented at a panel on 'Museums and Globalization' organized by Ruth Iskin and Saloni Mathur at the College Art Association meeting in Philadelphia in February 2002.

2. On diaspora, pluralism, and their implications for curatorial work see Clifford 1997 (especially Chs 1, 7, and 10), as well as useful volumes edited by Fisher (1994) and Mirzoeff (2000).

3. For a number of reasons, I have chosen the installations of Benin objects and Mende masks as diagnostic genres. Both are 'canonical' genres, the brasses because of their historical importance and generally acknowledged qualities of craftsmanship and artistry, and the Mende Sande Society masks because they are regularly used by museums to illustrate the role of African art in initiation. In addition, the Benin material raises central issues around colonialism, appropriation, and power, while the Mende masks (which were the subject of my 1979 doctoral dissertation) have been the focus of feminist rereadings of African art.

4. For further examples and discussion of the new canon see Court 1999. For further discussion of collaborative models in general see Ames 1992, and for an earlier example of the model used in an African exhibition see Kasfir 1995.

Chronological Index of the Texts

The 41 essays collected in *Grasping the World* deal with historical material spanning over half a millennium, from the medieval and early modern periods to the beginning of the twenty-first century. As the anthology is organized thematically rather than strictly chronologically, the following is a chronological cross-index of essays and excerpts grouped by author and historical period(s) dealt with in each essay (rather than by date of publication), listed alphabetically by author, with a numerical reference to the chapter in which the essay appears and the number of the text in that chapter. While all the texts included have theoretical and historiographical import, some essays are of general interest for their more explicit theoretical argumentation; these are grouped together in a final section (G).

A. Regarding medieval and early modern issues:

Ashworth (2.3) William B. Ashworth Jr, 'Natural History and the Emblematic World View', in *Reappraisals of the Scientific Revolution*, eds David C. Lindberg and Robert S. Westman, Cambridge and New York: Cambridge University Press, 1990, pp. 312–25 (EXCERPT).

Boström (5.4) Hans-Olof Boström, 'Philipp Hainhofer and Gustavus Adolfus's *Kunstschrank* in Uppsala', in *The Origins of Museums*, eds Oliver Impey and Arthur MacGregor. Oxford: Clarendon Press, 1985, pp. 90–101 (REVISED).

Carruthers (2.1) Mary Carruthers, 'Collective Memory and *Memoria Rerum*: An Architecture for Thinking', *The Craft of Thought: Meditation, Rhetoric, and the Making of Images, 400–1200*, Cambridge: Cambridge University Press, 1998, pp. 7–21 (EXCERPT).

Findlen (2.4) Paula Findlen, 'The Museum: Its Classical Etymology and Renaissance Genealogy', *The Journal of the History of Collections*, 1/1 (1989), pp. 59–78.

Kaufmann (5.3) Thomas DaCosta Kaufmann, 'Remarks on the Collection of Rudolf II: The *Kunstkammer* as a Form of *Representatio*', *The Art Journal*, 38 (1978), 22–8.

Lazzaro (5.2) Claudia Lazzaro, 'Animals as Cultural Signs: Collecting Animals in Sixteenth-Century Medici Florence', from *Reframing the Renaissance: Visual Culture in Europe and Latin America 1450–1650*, ed. Claire Farago, London and New Haven: Yale University Press, 1995, pp. 197–228 (CONDENSED REVISION).

Olmi (2.2) Giuseppe Olmi, 'Science-Honor-Metaphor: Italian Cabinets of the Sixteenth and Seventeenth Centuries', in *The Origins of Museums*, eds Oliver Impey and Arthur MacGregor, Oxford: Clarendon Press, 1985, pp. 1–16.

B.   On post-Revolutionary Europe to the mid-nineteenth century:

Bann (1.4) Stephen Bann, 'Poetics of the Museum: Lenoir and Du Sommerard', in *The Clothing of Clio: A Study of the Representation of History in Nineteenth-Century Britain and France*, Cambridge and New York: Cambridge University Press, 1984, pp. 77–92.

Déotte (1.3) Jean-Louis Déotte, 'Rome, the Archetypal Museum, and the Louvre, the Negation of Division', in *Art in Museums*, ed. Susan Pearce; New Research in Museum Studies: An International Series, 5, London and Atlantic Highlands, N.J.: Athlone Press, 1995, pp. 215–32.

Duncan (3.3) Carol Duncan, 'From the Princely Gallery to the Public Art Museum: The Louvre Museum and the National Gallery, London', in *Representing the Nation: A Reader. Histories, Heritage and Museums*, eds David Boswell and Jessica Evans. London: Routledge, 1999, pp. 304–31.

Haskell and Penny (5.5) Francis Haskell and Nicholas Penny, 'Museums in Eighteenth-Century Rome', in their *Taste and the Antique: The Lure of Classical Sculpture 1500–1900*, New Haven: Yale University Press, 1981, pp. 62–73.

Olausson and Söderlind (5.6) Magnus Olausson and Solfrid Söderlind, 'The Genesis and Early Development of the Royal Museum in Stockholm – A Claim for Authenticity and Legitimacy', essay commissioned for this volume.

C.   On the late nineteenth and early twentieth centuries:

Bohrer (2.5) Frederick N. Bohrer, 'Inventing Assyria: Exoticism and Reception in Nineteenth-Century England and France', *The Art Bulletin*, 80/2 (June 1998), 336–56 (REVISED)

Clunas (4.7) Craig Clunas, 'China in Britain: The Imperial Collections', in *Colonialism and the Object: Empire, Material Culture, and the Museum*, ed. Tim Barringer and Tom Flynn, London and New York: Routledge, 1998, pp. 41–51.

Mitchell (4.6) Timothy Mitchell, 'Orientalism and the Exhibitionary Order', *Comparative Studies in Society and History*, 31 (1989), reprinted from *The Art of Art History: A Critical Anthology*, ed. Donald Preziosi, Oxford: Oxford University Press, 1998, pp. 455–72.

D.   Regarding the twentieth century (to World War II):

Coombes (3.4) Annie E. Coombes, 'Museums and the Formation of National and Cultural Identities', *Oxford Art Journal*, 11/2 (December 1988), pp. 57–68.

Esslinger (3.6) Sandra Esslinger, 'Performing Identity: The Museal Framing of Nazi Ideology', essay commissioned for this volume.

Grindstaff (3.5) Beverly K. Grindstaff, 'Creating Identity: Exhibiting the Philippines at the 1904 Louisiana Purchase Exposition', *National Identities*, 1/3 (1999), pp. 245–63.

Haraway (3.2) Donna Haraway, excerpt from 'Teddy Bear Patriarchy: Taxidermy in the Garden of Eden, New York City, 1908–1936', *Social Text*, 11 (Winter 1984/85), pp. 52–8. (EXCERPT)

E.   On issues and institutions since World War II:

Araeen (6.4) Rasheed Araeen, 'From Primitivism to Ethnic Arts', in *The Myth of Primitivism: Perspectives on Art*, ed. Susan Hiller, London and New York: Routledge, 1991, pp. 158–92.

Berlo and Phillips (6.7) Janet Catherine Berlo and Ruth B. Phillips, 'Our (Museum) World Turned Upside Down: Re-presenting Native American Arts', in 'The Problematics of Collecting and Display, Part I', *Art Bulletin*, 77/1 (March 1995), pp. 6–10.

Berelowitz (6.8) Jo-Anne Berelowitz, 'The Museum of Contemporary Art, Los Angeles: An Account of Collaboration between Artists, Trustees and an Architect', in *Art Apart: Art Institutions and Ideology across England and North America*, ed. Marcia Pointon, Manchester: Manchester University Press, 1994, pp. 267–84.

Bhabha (3.1) Homi Bhabha, 'Double Visions', *Artforum*, 30/5 (1992), pp. 85–9.

Canclini (6.6) Néstor García Canclini, 'Remaking Passports: Visual Thought in the Debate on Multiculturalism', *Third Text*, trans. E. P. Quesada (1994), pp. 139–46, reprinted from *The Art of Art History: A Critical Anthology*, ed. Donald Preziosi, Oxford: Oxford University Press, 1998, pp. 498–506.

Clifford (6.2) James Clifford, 'Histories of the Tribal and the Modern', in his *The Predicament of Culture*. Boston: Harvard University Press, 1988, pp. 189–214.

Duncan and Wallach (5.1) Carol Duncan and Alan Wallach, 'The Museum of Modern Art as Late Capitalist Ritual: An Iconographic Analysis', *Marxist Perspectives* (Winter 1978), pp. 28–51.

Krauss (5.7) Rosalind Krauss, 'The Cultural Logic of the Late Capitalist Museum', *October*, 54 (Fall 1990), pp. 3–17, reprinted in *October: The Second Decade, 1986–1996*, eds Rosalind Krauss et al.,pp. 427–41. Cambridge, Mass. and London: MIT Press, 1997.

Vogel (6.3) Susan Vogel, 'Always True to the Object, in Our Fashion', in *Exhibiting Cultures: The Poetics and Politics of Museum Display*, eds Ivan Karp and Steven D. Lavine, Washington and London: Smithsonian Institution Press, 1991, pp. 191–204.

F.   Texts since 1995 on Post-World-War II Topics:

Appadurai and Breckenridge (6.5) Arjun Appadurai and Carol A. Breckenridge, 'Museums are Good to Think: Heritage on View in India', in *Representing the Nation: A Reader. Histories, Heritage and Museums*, eds David Boswell and Jessica Evans, London: Routledge, 1999, pp. 404–20.

Cummings & Lewandowska (5.8) Neil Cummings and Marysia Lewandowska, 'Collision', in their *The Value of Things*, preface by Nick Barley and Stephen Coates, Basel, Boston, and Berlin: Birkhäuser and London: 2000, pp. 111–17.

Errington (3.7) Shelly Errington, 'The Cosmic Theme Park of the Javanese', in her *The Death of Authentic Primitive Art and Other Tales of Progress*, Berkeley and London: University of California Press, 1998, pp. 188–217.

Liss (6.9) Andrea Liss. 'The Identity Card Project and the Tower of Faces at the United States Holocaust Memorial Museum', in her *Trespassing through Shadows: Memory, Photography, and the Holocaust*, Minneapolis: University of Minnesota Press, 1998, pp. 13–37.

Phillips (6.10) Ruth B. Phillips, 'Where Is "Africa"? Re-Viewing Art and Artifact in the Age of Globalization', *American Anthropologist*, 104/3 (September 2002), 944–52.

Simpson (6.1) Moira Simpson, 'Cultural Reflections', in her *Making Representations: Museums in the Postcolonial Era*, London and New York: Routledge, 1996, pp. 7–13.

G.   Essays of general theoretical and historical interest:

Bal (1.5) Mieke Bal, 'Telling Objects: A Narrative Perspective on Collecting', in *The Cultures of Collecting*, eds John Elsner and Roger Cardinal, London: Reaktion Books and Cambridge, Mass.: Harvard University Press, 1994, pp. 97–115.

Bennett (4.5) Tony Bennett, 'The Exhibitionary Complex' (1988), reprinted in *Thinking about Exhibitions*, eds Reesa Greenberg, Bruce W. Ferguson, and Sandy Nairne, London: Routledge, 1996, pp. 81–112.

de Certeau (1.2) Michel de Certeau, 'Psychoanalysis and its History', in *Heterologies: Discourse on the Other*, trans. Brian Massumi, foreword Wlad Godzich; Theory and History of Literature, vol. 17, Minneapolis and London: University of Minnesota Press, 1986, pp. 3–16.

Foucault (4.2) Michel Foucault, 'Texts/Contexts: Of Other Spaces', *Diacritics*, 16/1 (Spring 1986), pp. 22–7.

Haacke (4.4) Hans Haacke, 'Museums: Managers of Consciousness', *Parachute*, 46 (March–May 1987), pp. 84–8.

Hirst (4.3) Paul Q. Hirst, 'Power/Knowledge – Constructed Space and the Suject', in *Power and Knowledge: Anthropological and Sociological Perspectives*, ed. R. Fardon, Edinburgh: Scottish Academic Press, 1985, pp. 171–89.

Malraux (4.1) André Malraux, 'Introduction', *Museum Without Walls*, trans. Stuart Gilbert and Francis Price, Garden City, New Jersey: Doubleday, 1967, 9–12.

White (1.1) Hayden White, 'The Fictions of Factual Representation', in *Tropics of Discourse*, Baltimore and London: Johns Hopkins University Press, 1978, pp. 121–34.